Automatic Pianos

A Collector's Guide to the Pianola, Barrel Piano, & Aeolian Orchestrelle

Arthur W. J. G. Ord-Hume

4880 Lower Valley Road, Atglen, PA 19310 USA

Published by Schiffer Publishing Ltd.
4880 Lower Valley Road
Atglen, PA 19310
Phone: (610) 593-1777; Fax: (610) 593-2002
E-mail: info@schifferbooks.com
For the largest selection of fine reference books on this and
related subjects, please visit our web site at
www.schifferbooks.com
We are always looking for people to write books on new and
related subjects. If you have an idea for a book, please
contact us at the above address.

This book may be purchased from the publisher.
Include $3.95 for shipping. Please try your bookstore first.
You may write for a free catalog.

In Europe, Schiffer books are distributed by
Bushwood Books
6 Marksbury Ave. Kew Gardens
Surrey TW9 4JF England
Phone: 44 (0)20 8392-8585; Fax: 44 (0)20 8392-9876
E-mail: info@bushwoodbooks.co.uk
Free postage in the UK. Europe: air mail at cost.
Please try your bookstore first.

Library of Congress Cataloging-in-Publication Data

Ord-Hume, Arthur W.J.G.
  Automatic pianos : a collector's guide to the pianola,
barrel piano, & Aeolian orchestrelle / by Arthur W.J.G.
Ord-Hume
     p. cm.
  Includes bibliographical references (
   ISBN 0-7643-2024-6 (hardcover)
1. Mechanical musical instruments. 2. Mechanical
pianos—Collectors and collecting. I. Title.
  ML1050.069 2004
   786.2—dc22

                    2004000002

Designed by Mark David Bowyer
Type set in Aldine 721 BT / Dutch 801 Rm BT

ISBN: 0-7643-2024-6
Printed in China

Contents

Acknowledgements

Many people have shared information with me over the past forty and more years and to them I express my gratitude. I have learned at the feet of men who were old when I was young and I have, I hope, been able to pass on all that I have learned to future generations. To avoid any potential implication of preference, I shall name my mentors and helpers alphabetically, with notes or observations to expand where necessary.

To begin with, then, my thanks go to the following: J C Allen of Steinway Pianos in London. D F Andrews of Boyd Pianos in London. W J Bassil of J & J Goddard in London. Broadwood Pianos Ltd and members of the Broadwood family. L K Busby of Blüthner Pianos in London. The late Tom Farrell, piano-action designer. H R Goodall of the Aeolian Corporation in New York. D R Heckscher of Heckscher & Company, London. M R Hecksher of Heckscher & Company, London. The late Gordon Iles of the Artona Music Roll Company. The late S J Murdoch, formerly of the Harrods Piano Department in London. Mr Phelps Jnr of Phelps Pianos in London. Reg Richings, professional restorer.

Individual collectors and enthusiasts who have helped me in one way or another include: The late Bruce Angrave, artist, humorist and lover of Aeolian Orchestrelles. Douglas Berryman, one-time owner of the West Cornwall Museum of Mechanical Music (now dispersed) and presently living in the United States. Q David Bowers, historian and writer from New Hampshire. Mary Belton, piano-restorer and formerly of the Original Pianola Shop in Brighton. Tony A G Bird of Reading, barrel-piano collector. Bill Edgerton, piano constructor and collector of Darien, Connecticut. The late Dr Howard and Helen Fitch of Summit, New Jersey. Joseph Fox of Black Mountain, North Carolina, collector and writer. Tony Morgan, one time of Harrods and Kemble pianos, now a professional restorer. The late Akio Morita, founder of Sony Corporation, lover of reproducing pianos and a much missed friend.

The late Dr Cyril de Vere Green, collector, lover of mechanical musical instruments, and founder of the Musical Box Society of Great Britain. The late Simon Haskel of Barnes, South West London, kindred spirit, friend and a man who appreciated fine instruments. Joseph Hutter of New York, Orchestrelle collector and restorer. Dr Jan Jaap Haspels, director and conservator at the Nationaal Museum van Speelklok tot Pierement, friend and collaborator for more than thirty years, and Astrid Daelmans at the same institution. Cees G Nijsen of Eindhoven. Roland Graus, secretary of the Nederlandse Pianola Vereniging. The famously eccentric late Frank Holland, OBE, founder of the British Piano Museum, and renowned player-piano collector and remembrancer.

Robert Hough of Devon, friend, collector and restorer who lives in a house aptly named Aeolian Court. Dr Antonio Latanza, director of the Museum of Musical Instruments in Rome, and a close colleague who has devoted much study to the Italian barrel piano and its evolution. Ian Marshall, trustee of the British Piano Museum and managing director of Ampico Ltd, today involved in building construction work. Gustave Mathot of Brussels, a man with a fine library and an outstanding collection of unusual instruments. Dick van Minnen, senior restorer at the Nationaal Museum van Speelklok tot Pierement and good friend. Dr Paul D Ottenheimer, collector of Philadelphia, who once shared his collection of US musical instrument promotional material.

The late Gerry Planus, musical-box dealer and Orchestrelle collector who lived happily in Blackheath, London, but much later died in distressing circumstances in the United States. The late Harvey Roehl of The Vestel Press, New York, close friend as well as an enthusiastic owner of many fine instruments and a specialist publisher of mechanical music material. Arthur A Reblitz, piano historian and technician. The late Hughes Ryder of Cranford, New Jersey, delver into American musical instrument history. Jere Ryder of Cranford, New Jersey, craftsman and friend. Steve Ryder of Cranford, New Jersey, mechanical music admirer and friend. The late David Snelling, collector and enthusiast. Gerald Stonehill, Duo-Art expert and researcher.

For allowing me into their homes to examine and photograph their instruments during my many visits to the United States, my thanks to James and Sherrie Krughoff, Tim Trager, Martin Persky, Dr Simon and Mabel Zivin, William and Dee Kavouras, Jack and Mildred Hardman – just to name a very few.

There are many others including Werner Baus, Dr Jürgen Hocker and Siegfried Wendel in Germany, the late Hon Murtogh Guinness of New York, Michael Woolf in New Zealand, Paul Ziff in Leeds, Keith Harding in Gloucestershire, Bill Lindwall in Stockholm, Sweden – and so on.

It is to be regretted that within these lists there are the names of so many who have passed on: that, however, is the way of life. All these have in one way or another helped me in my task by sharing information, allowing access to instruments for photography, or by providing ephemera. Without their help, this work would be that much poorer. To those whom I may have omitted from this list of credits, my apologies for the oversight. Some of the material used has also appeared in *The Music Box*, the Journal of the Musical Box Society of Great Britain, and also in *Music & Automata*, the historic magazine of mechanical music of which I was proud to be editor for eight years. Certain of the text here also expands greatly on material published in *The New Grove Dictionary of Music & Musicians* to which I was honoured to be a contributor.

Many National and Institutional Museums have been of assistance as have libraries, both of national standing and local public, as has the Public Records Office, Birmingham Museum, The British Library, the Patent Office Library, the Science Museum and the Victoria & Albert Museum, both of South Kensington, the Deutsches Museum, Munich, The Nationaal Museum van Speelklok tot Pierement, Utrecht, Prague National Museum, and the New York Public Library. Auction houses Christie's South Kensington and Sotheby's have been of great help in drawing my attention to rare pieces that have passed through their hands over the decades and in providing illustrations. The British Broadcasting Corporation should also be thanked for encouraging – and producing – my many radio programmes on mechanical music during the heydays of intelligent broadcasting.

Dr Robert Palmieri, who has so masterfully compiled and edited both editions of *The Encyclopedia of Keyboard Instruments* (to which I have been an honoured contributor), has been of great help to me by searching out dates of some of the lesser-known Aeolian recording artists. Thanks, too, to Steve Ryder (*nom.cit.*) for taking me to the old Aeolian factory and assisting in my research into New Jersey's 'Aeolian Township' which actually predated the setting up of the present-day township of Garwood within which the Aeolian factory remains still stand to this day. Garwood's centenary in 2003 consequently builds on the foundations laid by the Tremaines when the area was mostly open land.

To those collectors' and enthusiasts' societies across the world my thanks must also go. These comprise, again in alphabetical order, Robin Pratt, secretary of the American Musical Instrument Collectors Association (AMICA); Michel Gollet, secretary of the Association des amis des instruments et de la Musique Mécanique (AAIMM); Ian Savins, secretary of the Australian Collectors of Mechanical Musical Instruments (ACMMI); Ralf Smolne, secretary of the Gesellschaft für Selbstspielende Musikinstrumente e.V. (GSM); J van Oost, secretary of the Kring van Draaiorgelvrienden (KvD); The Administrator of the Musical Box Society International (MBSI); Alan Wyatt, secretary of The Musical Box Society of Great Britain (MBSOGB); Jo Jongen, secretary of the Nederlandse Pianola Vereniging; Lorraine Aressy, secretary of the Perforons la Musique; Tony Austin, secretary of The Player Piano Group (PPG).

Of course there are others – private collectors, friends who have send material to me as well as general correspondents. To these all my appreciation goes along with apologies for not being able to mention everybody by name.

A special word here regarding picture credits. We live in difficult times and increasingly collectors are becoming concerned regarding matters of security. So many private collectors have expressly entreated me not to publish their names with their photographs that I have concluded that the fairest procedure is to elide all such attributions except in one or two specific instances and in the case of Museums and Institutions that are less sensitive.

A special word of thanks to my publisher, Peter Schiffer, for still speaking to me after I defaulted on the delivery date of the manuscript to the extent of almost two years over the promised completion date. There were many reasons for this, the one I could not control being the floods that swept Britain two years back.

As I have written before, I do not mind anybody making use of any of my material in any way that they wish, with the sole proviso that they must always give credit to both source and author. This applies to material 'borrowed' for an exhibition, abstracted for educational study, or extracted and published in magazine or book form in any language. I regret having to mention this but to the annoyance of both my publishers and myself there have been too many instances of my material being used, especially by both non-British and even respected Museum sources, without any form of credit whatsoever. Unlike some particular pen-pushers who have an oft-inflated view of the value their own work and would willingly kill (metaphorically) for cash, use my material for free – but *please* say where you got it from!

Preface

It was back in 1967 that my then publishers, the old and respected London house of George Allen & Unwin Ltd (now long-since disappeared in one of those dreadful 1980s 'mergers' that has decimated the corpus of one-time serious London book publishers), suggested that I might write a book on player pianos as a companion to the small book I had just produced for them on musical boxes. The only justification I could think of for taking on such a task was that I owned seven of the things and had restored them to reasonable playing condition. Even so, I couldn't imagine how I could fill a whole book on such a topic but eventually I agreed. That first title, called simple *Player-Piano*, appeared three years later in 1970 with an American edition handled by A S Barnes. To the surprise of my publishers (and myself), it sold out very quickly. Clearly there were more people out there with player pianos than either my publisher or I knew about.

A decade passed during which my collection of player-pianos grew. Allen & Unwin then put forward the idea of a reprint of the old work. I suggested that a new and more up-to-date book was probably a better idea. However, for reasons that I shall draw a discreet veil over, I was unable to devote much time to its preparation as a result of which, at the behest of the publisher, great chunks of the first book were re-printed with the minimum of edit or update. It was a bad start but it was to get worse! It was decided that because the book now contained a great deal more historical detail than the first, it was going to be too big! Cutting out the entire section on restoration saved the day, but spoiled the book. These extra chapters on restoring the instrument then appeared as a separate title. Unfortunately, the two halves were published a year apart, one in 1983 and the other in 1984. Was it Occam's Razor or merely the Judgement of Solomon? Whatever it was it made for a bit of a hotchpotch.

Both these books, produced expensively in ridiculously small print-runs of but a few hundred, are long out of print. Today they fetch silly prices on the second-hand book market. Meanwhile the interest in player pianos has remained strong. Hardly a week goes by without somebody asking where to find a copy of one of these early books or, more commonly, considering my books to be like No.16 buses and asking how soon the next one will be coming along!

When I started out on my quest for information on self-acting pianos (and there's more about that term later on), it was an uphill struggle. Not many people appreciated them – and fewer actually went to the bother of collecting so obsolesce an object. But things began to change and societies for collectors were formed in Britain and America and, more recently, in Germany, France, Italy and Australia. Now many people around the world share my interest and finding information is not quite so hard as it once was. The freedom of access to archives in what used to be East Germany and the immense enthusiasm and research carried out by German collectors has helped to fill many of the gaps in our knowledge of the European side of the instrument.

There are some self-indulgent people who gain curious personal pleasure from the nefarious practice of comparing different editions of a book to see how much (or how little) new work the author has put into it. These literary anoraks will have a field-day here for they will be overjoyed to find that the historical facts and the general story of the self-acting piano both, curiously, remain the same as in my previous books. History and facts do not alter, merely refine and enlarge, as more minutiae are unearthed. Time often allows the discovery of fresh data, so history can expand and details may be more fulsome, but other than that, it's the same old facts although maybe retold afresh. Corrections and additions have been made where necessary. Other than that, this is a whole new book!

All this calls into question the fundamental purpose of a book of this type. Why a book on automatic pianos? Why *this* one? Most of my readers will be collectors and restorers and, like myself, questors for information. It is popular today to promote a book as being 'the entire history' or 'everything you ever wanted to know' on a subject. Books of this type that purport to offer such total satisfaction by its proclaimed exhaustive treatment of its subject are, as far as I am concerned, doomed to failure. They are deeply suspect for no such book exists in any subject and nor may any work of such unequivocal totality ever be produced. Consequently I make no such claims for this present book. No, the fact is that we are all learning. To my mind, a book such as the one you are holding exists to encourage and inspire further work, to stimulate you, the reader, into finding out more. It serves as a narrow but illuminated passageway that offers opportunities for further exploration.

In modern business parlance, it's time for the Mission Statement! What's this book for? My goal is to pass on experience and information. Information is the most important thing in life and you cannot have enough of it – even if you do not necessarily think you need it, or need it all at once. I want to encourage people to collect player-pianos and to be able to look after them. But I fight shy of boring the non-technical Pianola-lover with too much technical detail. I choose to tread that narrow and risky path between the incidental trivia of background detail that diminishes user-appeal (another 20th-century business term!), and an exhaustive and voluminous theoretical and engineering tome that few might read and most would disdain. Remember the shrewd words of Goethe: *wer vieles bringt, wird manchem etwas bringen.*[1]

For these reasons I shall tell you how the instrument came into being and I shall tell you how it works and how to look after it and keep it working well for you. But I am not going into extensive detail on specific types of instrument or action: for these I provide a detailed Bibliography and I shall direct you to other and specific books where necessary. Most people who own and operate a player-piano do not wish to be too technical, relying upon others to undertake overhaul work. Nevertheless, people who own players should know exactly how they work and ought to be able to make minor adjustments and repairs as they go. I give you some basic advice on this type of 'running repair'. I also offer some advice on the choice of materials to use, for there is a wide variety of confusing material (and opinion) regarding such matters.

I also give you fairly exhaustive detail on makers and brand-names because both these aspects form the greater percentage of queries from collectors. Furthermore there is no other single volume that provides this information.

I have only been involved with player pianos for fifty-one years (although I saw my first in 1934) and I know that there are others who may rightly claim more experience in some areas than myself, but as to the overall picture, I have spent most of those fifty-one years on historical digging. I was able to talk with craftsmen and inventors – people that are now no longer with us. I visited old player-piano factories, long since disappeared, and spoke with fascinating old men, now all dead, whose lives, in one way or another, were touched by the player. This book is thus a tribute to their memory.

It is inevitable that there is more to be learned in history of the self-acting piano just as there are fresh discoveries in every other aspect of history on an almost daily basis. In the past, some have not appreciated this and have unwisely demonstrated their own limitations by inopportune criticism of the shortcomings of others. Musicologists have always been highly suspicious of anything mechanical involved in making music, while those who avow the benefits of mechanical music quite often have no grounding whatsoever in the science and the art of music.

Over the years this has produced an amusing scenario where the player-piano protagonists have staunchly upheld their instrument as an acceptable replacement for a human player. At the same time, the accredited musical historian has ignored mechanical music and its instruments, considering them akin to the work of the devil. Some justification for this can be found in some really awful gramophone records that were produced of automatic pianos and these did the pneumatically-operated piano no favours at all. It also has to be said that some instruments that are demonstrated with great reverence to museum visitors today are in truly disgraceful playing condition and do infinitely more harm than good to the reputation of the instrument. I shall have more to say on this subject later on for it is one that I feel very strongly about. I *may* just choose to 'name and shame' some leading museums…

But to return to the juxtaposed points of view of the player-piano collector and the musicologist, it is hard to get them both to talk the same language. Expressed another way, there is one bunch of fanatics pedalling their way solemnly through rolls of Wagner and Stravinsky who talk in knowing tones about the sanctity of their instruments when all they mean is the adjustment of their valves, bleed holes and expression levers. And there's another bunch of high-brows that deny any merit in instruments that make music other than by hand on a 'real' instrument. These people are as fettered as the first group, the only difference being that they are probably better qualified to enter the realms of the bigot. Letters after the name, though, do not excuse failure to consider C P E Bach's music for the player-piano's distant cousin – the harp-clock (*harfenuhr* or dulcimer-playing clock) or, from the late 20th century, Conlon Nancarrow's *Pianola Music*.

No, I fear that both camps have to learn to live in harmony. While player-piano collectors in general know little about music, composition and performance (at least when they start collecting), and musicologists remain unfazed by talk of sixteen levels of expression by vacuum, it is time for both to get real and try to accept each other. Considered in its proper place, the player piano can offer a serious contribution to the world of music. This aspect will be developed at the proper time later on in this book.

Many years ago, I used to present radio broadcasts on mechanical music in the naive belief that I could convert some of the dye-hard musicologists of the value of mechanical instruments. The fact that my programmes, all on that once-dedicated serious music channel known then as the BBC's Third Programme, were transmitted so late at night that even I could not stay awake to hear them, did not help my cause. Over the years, the curiosity of a few people in middling positions resulted in a few engagements to deliver University lectures. These were presented to those who at least had enquiring minds.

Invited, incredibly, to address a major music conference on the mechanical interpretation of music, all went well – until somebody realised that I was not at that time a kosher musicologist but a mere interloper in the world of genuine music! My address completed, one person clapped – and then, finding he was alone, pretended he was swatting an incautious fly, looked embarrassed and sank back into his seat.

But I had sewn a disturbing seed. And when, soon afterwards, I gave a first-time-ever broadcast performance of a series of otherwise unknown compositions preserved only on mechanical instruments, the Big Door opened slightly. Hired to guest-edit a special edition of a respected music journal that was to be devoted to mechanical music, I knew that at last I had succeeded in my cause. I became welcomed in the academic corridors of music where my comparatively vast knowledge on a very tiny aspect of the music world proved sufficient to gain acceptance as a member of the musicologist's fraternity.

Mind you, Sir Thomas Beecham (the renowned orchestral conductor whom I was privileged to know through my father's own musical work) was probably correct when he famously proclaimed that 'a musicologist is a man who can read music but cannot hear it'. To this might be added that a player-piano player is a man who uses his mechanical skills to work a machine that makes music – and afterwards expects a round of applause for his efforts! After all, you don't thank the engine-driver for pulling your train along, however much skill he has applied to the reading of the signals of the Permanent Way.

As the years since those historic times have passed, attitudes towards mechanical music and mechanical interpretation have changed vastly. And when, in the fullness of time, the first-ever University degrees in mechanical music were awarded, I was proud to be associated in these momentous events in my professional capacity. It was hard to resist the release of a slight smirk at thoughts of the one-time renowned British professor of music who once famously said to me: '*Mechanical* music, indeed! *Toy* music, more like it!' – and strode off in a Grade A huff to immerse himself in a real chordal *zergliederung* to facilitate his *bogenstrichbezeichnungen*.

My own personal musical credentials preceded my later qualifications in engineering – and both preceded my much later aptitude and career as a professional historian. This means that I am able to see the problems of both camps and consider them from several very differing standpoints. I understand the pianolist who gains his satisfaction from playing music to the very best of his ability that he has gained and perfected by practice on his instrument that he has carefully adjusted. I also understand the musicologist and the professional pianist that has spent most of his life in keyboard practice to attain the peak of ability capable of giving a finely honed live performance.

There is a difference that it has taken me years to find. It's simple, really. The ordinary piano is a wicked and unforgiving task-mistress that rewards lack of practice very cruelly. The player piano, though, is a relaxing experience and what our American cousins term 'fun'. It doesn't call for much effort to give a passing performance from a music-roll. The concert pianist, on the other hand, must always drive himself to maintain his standard of ability. That's hard work: it's a career! And, although some would have us think otherwise, there's no such thing today as a professional pianola-player!

We British take our hobbies very seriously. It is a failing in British temperament that to us our spare-time activities often become a second vocation encouraging loss of serious blood, sweat, toil and tears. Both the French and the Americans, on the other hand, have a more sensible approach and see this sort of spare-time activity as mental relaxation and view it as fun. Only the Germans may rival the Brits in single-mindedness and take their pleasure with the seriousness of a ritualistic audience of Wagner's *Ring Cycle* – presented without intervals! But who is to say which of these approaches is right? So long as we are individually happy and gain satisfaction from our interests, then that, I'll wager, is reward enough!

There are, of course, personality problems. Collectors know everything and proclaim it loudly while suffering fools (defined as anybody outside their collecting circle) with structured – but nevertheless pseudo – condescension and superiority. The trouble is that most musicologists are exactly the same, only they are, in general, better at arguing their corner. Armed with musical jargon and a curious propensity for demonstrating every point using a chordal progression in measured sevenths, they are, like some collectors, poor guests at a barbecue party. And yes, over the years I have picked up a bit of raw, untreated psychology!

Player pianos are a bit like investing in stocks and shares – their value may go down as well as up. In fact over the past thirty years they have done just that. Several times actually. This is good for it means that people are not usually tempted to buy instruments as an investment. Were that to be the case, the investors would take out from the market fine examples thereby artificially increasing the value of the rest. It is bad in that if somebody cannot get a good price for his or her instrument, they may well scrap it and I have heard of too many fine instruments ending up on a bonfire.

No, pianos have not really appreciated much over the years, although the people who appreciate *them* are still on the increase both in Britain and in America. And for this reason it is still possible to pick up an instrument at a bargain price. Just while this book was in preparation, a big musical-instrument sale in the Midlands saw a Hupfeld Dea upright together with eighty 73-note piano rolls knocked down for £35 ($50). Why, the rolls alone were worth three or four times that amount! It's all a question of having the right person at the right place at the right time! Recently, three collectors attending a West Country sale took an ordinary player piano (estimated at £200 to £300) to over £800 [$1,280] (with auctioneers' commission) merely because all three of them wanted it!

Of course, there are some antique dealers the world over who believe that anything old, mechanical and musical must rival a Renoir in value: these people may once in a while be lucky and find a genuine mug, a novice from whom they may scoop a fortune, but more likely they will be left with their instrument unsold and have to face up to that antique-dealers' anathema – the cut price 'to clear'. At a recent and very prestigious London antiques fair – one of those where the exhibitors sport bow-ties with Pooh-bear waistcoats and perpetually have the pained expression of repressed acute flatulence upon their faces – an early reproducing grand piano was exhibited by a furniture dealer. The price tag was so high that, like an international 'phone number, it didn't register anything other than 'Wow!' and I promptly forgot the price, probably through shock. The worst part was that the piano looked rough and unrestored and probably sounded that way. That sort of thing does nobody any good, certainly not the player piano!

Again, piano rolls often turn up at one of the many weekend 'antique fairs' that have proliferated in recent years. Usually they are described as 'piano scrolls' and, with such clear links to the Dead Sea, are usually priced accordingly. Naturally that is neither the place nor the way to acquire your music library!

I can assure you that excellent, reasonably-priced instruments do turn up regularly. The player-piano was once (for a few short years) the most popular form of piano so there are still quite a few of them about. Like everything from old cars to Old Masters, it's a case of keeping your eyes open. I'll have more to say about finding and buying pianos at the proper time later on. What you will find, however, is that although these things were very expensive when new, their value in terms of today's cash, has fallen through the floor. This is because other forms of popular domestic entertainment (made possible by the availability of the motor-car, TV, computers, cheap and reliable birth-control, and pre-prepared snack meals) have all served to modify the manner in which we live out our lives. Player pianos are not essential: TV and computer games are...

So what have I learned in the thirty-five or so years since my first player-piano book? I think it's important that you should know because this is the whole reason why I should presume to be trying to tell you about the instrument. Well, I have as you might expect learned that there is always something new out there. And that the older one gets the more truth there is in the ancient adage that one never stops learning. When we are young and enthusiastic we believe we know it all and proclaim our pitifully inadequate knowledge with magisterial bearing. As we get older the one thing we all learn, to our cost and embarrassment, is how little we knew yesterday. This curbs our youthful urge to pontificate. The words 'may', 'might' and 'I may be wrong but...' increasingly replace the 'without doubt', 'it is certain' and 'I know because I am right' that we wrote in earlier times.

I have also learned to refine some of the repair processes that I described earlier and I have found improved methods and techniques for restoration. And, since there is no substitute for practice, I've seen and worked on a whole lot more pianos and other musical instruments of all types. Ideas on restoration materials have also changed: few can forget the fiasco of that awful plastic material that we all enthusiastically covered our bellows with in the 1960s, only to have to strip it all off within a year or two. The specialist detail restoration of players is the subject of another book to which I shall introduce you at the right time.

My full-time work as director and senior archivist in The Library of Mechanical Music & Horology affords me access to all manner of material from all over the world and this is an important part of my own learning-curve. I am often asked (usually by 50-year-old youngsters) when I am going to retire! The answer is simple – why should I since I am having such a good time!

I saw my very first player piano in the early 1930s when I was about six years old. It was alleged to be the very latest in player pianos and the owner, an old lady who's increasing arthritis denied her the chance to continue playing by hand, proudly showed it to my father and me. I still recall my reaction to seeing the keys moving up and down as if under the command of an invisible human pianist. The music was the least of my young concerns and I burst into tears and sought the comfort of my father's hand. It was, I was sure, a haunted piano! As a frequent visitor to that house, I was terrified of being alone near that awful instrument in case it started playing at me. I was literally scared out of my young wits!

Fear and curiosity both having roughly similar root emotions, I later recalled that piano and sought an explanation for its seemingly paranormal behaviour. The rest, so the familiar saying goes, is history. I still think that player pianos are rather magical only now instead of terror I marvel at the ingenuity of the craftsmen who made them. Finding out how they worked and then making them work again is in itself something magical.

Another roll-playing mechanism that is a sort of player-piano sister is the Aeolian Orchestrelle. Although not a stringed instrument, this renowned player reed-organ has a place in many collections on both sides of the Atlantic. Player-piano collectors are attracted by the similarity in operation. However, while one of my early books on mechanical organs dealt briefly with this mechanism, no detail instructions currently exist in print for the benefit of the collector and restorer. About 35 years ago I produced a duplicated 'service manual' for the instrument but since then there has been nothing available by way of printed literature for the owner of one of these fine machines. A large proportion of the people who write to me on restoration matters are concerned with servicing this once very popular and still very desirable instrument.

Since so many of the restoration techniques are similar to those of the player piano – and because the small remainder are very different – it strikes me as sensible to include a short chapter to take the reader beyond the player stringed instruments into the realms of the Aeolian Orchestrelle which, after all, was built by one of the greater player-piano makers in the world. I therefore describe how they work and what to do if they don't.

I hope, therefore, that the present volume will offer sufficient information to take you successfully through the greater majority of instruments that you will come across in your search for mechanical musical instruments of this type.

'He who brings much brings something for most.'
Johann Wolfgang von Goethe [1749-1832].]

Arthur W. J. G. Ord-Hume
Guildford, Surrey, England.
October, 2003

Introduction

Self-playing pianos. That's a curious expression and yet it is possibly the most accurate description of the instruments that I shall be describing. This is because the subject of this book includes mechanically-playing instruments, pneumatically-played ones, ones that are operated by foot-pedalling, others that are worked by electricity, some that are worked by discs that are pierced with holes or punched with projections, and ones that are worked by strips of wood with studs or lengths of cardboard with holes.

No one word is really right as a collective noun for all these variations. The world of mechanical music – an accepted generic term – is embellished with misnomers and misunderstandings. Some talk of 'automatic music', yet there is no such thing and this is perhaps the most heinous of the mistakes usually made by those who are bereft of knowledge. Automatic music, if there be such a thing, can surely be a term that must only apply to something quite random like an Aeolian harp. But our piano with its player mechanism is both musical and pre-programmable and is thus an instrument that brushes shoulders with the highest computer technology of the modern age for at its heart is a *pneumatic* computer!

What *shall* we call it? I think 'Automatic pianos' is the nearest, but there was an ancient term (current in use during the 18th and 19th century) which I believe is even better. It is one that also conveys something of the magic of the automatic musical instrument. It is 'self-acting' as in 'self-acting pianos'. There is a drawback, though, for it is a rather esoteric term. I have shunned using it for the title of this book for the simple reason that most wouldn't understand it. Its origins are too scholarly and this, after all, is a story for ordinary people like you and me. A book with a meaningless title is quickly passed over, however important or informative it might be. The fact remains that what we are talking about are pianos that, to a greater or lesser extent, go by themselves *because* they are self-acting.

There are two principal categories of self-acting piano that I shall be dealing with. The first is the mechanical action, the predominant form of which is found in the barrel piano. The second is the pneumatic action, which includes the player piano. Within both categories are numerous other forms of the instrument, generally by their very nature uncommon and some rare.

Each of these categories of mechanism requires its own individual style of musical programme. While the pneumatically-operated mechanisms make use of the 'paper-as-a-valve' principle as in the form of perforated paper or, occasionally, thin perforated card, the mechanical systems have by far the greater range of music-playing systems. These range from the pinned wooden barrel through punched card discs, pinned wooden boards, discs with projections and several other variations on these styles. The earliest were pure mechanical, the extensive middle-period of the instrument was pneumatic and the last electrical.

So let's summarise the self-playing piano so that we have a point of reference.

Before pneumatic actions, pianos were played using a pinned wooden barrel. Built as an extra feature of an ordinary keyboard instrument that could be played by hand, the normal piano was augmented by a pinned wooden cylinder placed inside the case under the keyboard. This barrel was provided with a mechanical keyframe and a series of linkages or stickers, which extend behind the soundboard to the top of the piano-forte and operate an additional set of hammers striking the strings through a gap in the soundboard. The barrel was set in motion by a clockwork motor.

These inchoate player-pianos were essentially indoor instruments for the drawing-room, and one style was made with no keyboard.

There were also spring-driven clockwork barrel pianos, also for drawing-room use and without manual keyboard. In other types of barrel piano, mechanical operation is by turning a hand-crank. While the domestic automatic piano dispensed with the cumbersome barrel in favour, first, of Debain's Antiphonel studded wooden strip piano-player, then the perforated roll of the piano-player and later player piano, the keyboardless hand-turned barrel piano enjoyed one-and-a-half centuries of popularity as a street instrument. The street barrel piano is thought to have emanated from Italy around 1800.

A faded image from the distant past. A small Pasquale street barrel piano mounted on a cart drawn by a patient donkey plies the streets of grand Victorian houses at Ryde on the Isle of Wight. The hopeful notice on the end of the piano reminds us that not everybody gave alms to the poor itinerant street musician. The picture dates from the 1920s.

The large street piano mounted on a handcart also came from Italy and migrant craftsmen took their skills all over Europe and North America. These open-air instruments, sometimes called 'cylinder piano', 'piano organ' or, often (incorrectly) 'barrel organ' or 'hurdy-gurdy', underwent a variety of improvements, models being made with mechanically-driven repeating actions and known as 'mandoline' pianos, while others included percussion in the shape of drum, triangle and xylophone or wood-block. Some were augmented by further mechanical means to show advertisements and featured a travelling picture display built into the vertical fall. Early in the 20th century, a new style of instrument was introduced having coin-freed spring-driven clockwork motors and these were widely used in public places particularly public bars. In France and Belgium these were developed into large and decorative barrel-playing cafe pianos often with decorative carved cases and embellished with mirrors.

As distinct from the barrel piano, a player piano is a pianoforte that has a self-playing mechanism capable of playing from perforated paper music-roll or piano-roll.

By 1890, the first pneumatically-controlled piano-players were being manufactured. Suction-operated, the piano-player, also called a cabinet or push-up player, was the forerunner of the player piano and was generally in the form of a self-contained device containing the pneumatic mechanism. When set in front of an ordinary piano, a row of felt-covered wooden fingers at the back rested on the keyboard to play it.

This device was then a logical step to the player-piano. Here, instead of calling for a large and separate cabinet with which to play the piano, the 'interior-player' action (having the player mechanism wholly contained within the body of the piano itself) made all earlier mechanical systems obsolete.

In the beginning, instruments that played on 58 of the keyboard's notes were common. Other models were produced which worked on 61, 65, 70, 73, 82, and 88 notes. The lack of standardisation was a major problem to the manufacturers of music-rolls. In 1910, player manufacturers agreed to standardise on 65 and 88 notes for all pianos.

Various pneumatic functions could be incorporated between the music roll and the piano hammer to regulate or vary the force applied to the hammer, and, in its developed form, this became, first, the expression piano and, subsequently, the reproducing piano.

The Reproducing Piano is a type of player piano which, when using specially-punched reproducing music rolls, might re-enact the original touch and expression of the recording pianist.

As early as 1895, both mechanical and pneumatic piano players were provided with a rudimentary means by which the treble notes could be played louder than those in the bass and vice-versa. It was this crude system which marked the quest not so much for the automation of the piano and its music, as for replication of the real performer's playing.

A significant development came when an employee of the Aeolian Company perfected the Themodist expression system, whereby individual notes could be made to sound out over or within an accompaniment (the Germans had actually got there earlier but not quite so neatly). Next it was found that by varying the vacuum tension between the separate halves of the valve chest and combining this with a Themodist-type accenter, and applying the same technique to both halves of the keyboard, a much more realistic performance could be produced.

Italian street musicians frequently performed amazing feats of strength and endurance with their instruments. It was not uncommon for them to push or pull their barrel pianos from Farringdon in East London four or five miles to Mayfair and Kensington in their quest for a living. Here museum owner Keith Harding attempts to get one moving up the street outside his Northleach premises.

Instruments having this type of artificially-enhanced music-roll performance were called 'expression pianos' and they were mainly produced in Germany and America for use in public places.

By 1904, Edwin Welte of Freiburg, followed the next year by Hupfeld of Leipzig, found a means of pneumatically controlling expression in several stages between bass and treble. This marked a significant step towards introducing an automatic degree of pianistic interpretation or expression and was achieved using specially-made music rolls which could control the operating vacuum pressure as well as the sustaining and soft pedals of the piano.

The first real reproducing piano was the Welte Mignon invented by Karl Bockisch and Edwin Welte in 1905. The Welte reproducing system, which produced the various shades of piano-playing by the careful adjustment of the suction levels in the piano's expression mechanism, was patented and formed the basis of all the reproducing pianos which were made subsequently.

Prof. Eugen d'Albert für »Welte-Mignon« spielend.

The first production reproducing piano was the Welte-Mignon and here is an archive picture showing Eugen d'Albert preparing to 'cut' rolls for the instrument. The men who perfected the Welte system were Karl Bockisch (seen left leaning on the recording machine) and Edwin Welte, on the right reading a score. The beautifully-panelled music-room of the famed Freiburg factory, together with the special Feurich recording piano fell victim to the Allied bombs of World War II which laid waste this famous centre for mechanical music.

Player pianos represented a significant major industry supported by all the infrastructure in the form of advertising, marketing, promotion and so on. It is, though, the advertising that demonstrates the development of the age and gives us a fascinating insight into not just the different styles of advertising used in Europe, Britain and America, but also the social expectations of the time. Put simply, these old adverts are snapshots of taste. This rich aspect is discussed and illustrated elsewhere.

The physical production of instruments called for special tools and techniques, for a whole new range of outworkers or external suppliers that specialised in player parts, and for skills that had to be added to those of the normal pianoforte construction. The manufacture of player-pianos became one of the major industries of the western world. The number of manufacturers throughout the world and in America in particular is almost impossible to assess accurately: many companies were insignificant or short-lived in their contribution to the 2.5 million instruments sold in the USA between 1900 and 1930. In London alone, a 1922 trade directory listed no fewer than 52 makers. In 1900 171,000 'ordinary' pianos were made and 6,000 self-acting. By 1925, the total of 136,000 ordinary pianos had been exceeded by no fewer than 169,000 self-acting player-pianos. The peak of the player-piano's vogue was in the mid-1920s. Every piano retailer sold players and their rolls. Many lending libraries were established where for a small sum, a number of rolls could be borrowed.

During the 1929-1931 Depression, the market collapsed and player sales dwindled virtually to nothing. Despite a concerted attempt to revive the player-piano market in London in the early 1930s the industry was finished long before the outbreak of World War II in September 1939.

The industry was also dependent on its repertoire of music-rolls and the artists that made these rolls. Leading concert pianists were sought out and persuaded not only to record special piano-rolls, but also to make comments on the instrument and its music. One feels that the more money offered for such words, the more fulsome the tribute!

The player-piano was killed off by a combination of changing social life. First was the availability of the cheap motor-car which enabled people to have greater than ever mobility. With less time to spend in the home, music for the masses became less important. The advance of radio and the gramophone tended to some extent to replace that which they had lost through diminishing participation. It was, though, war, particularly WWII, which changed forever the social dependence on mechanical music that had dominated the previous four hundred years.

From the early 1930s through the Second World War, the player-piano remained a symbol of another age that was rapidly being forgotten. It was possibly this bit about being rapidly forgotten that inspired inventors to revamp the player-piano concept and come up with a new generation of so-called 'key-top' players. Electrically-operated, these sat on top of the piano keyboard and all the mechanism was contained in the horizontal golf-bag sized case which played the piano from a familiar punched music roll.

Funnily enough, even this was not a new idea since the first mechanically-operated pneumatic key-top plays had appeared at the beginning of the 20th century. However, the key-top of the 1950s was something of a nine-day wonder and despite heavy promotion over a very few short years, the self-playing piano's brief revival turned out to be a last gasp before the coffin-lid was screwed down for good. And then along came computer technology!

As the 20th century entered its last quarter, so-called digital technology came along. Of course, one could say that digits have been involved in playing pianos since the very earliest days – but these were *electronic* digits, digits that formed codes of numbers. Instead of familiar foot-operated exhausters and levers, the new-age player piano had a disc-drive and a 'volume' control knob. And an 'on-off' switch.

New-age grand pianos for public places appeared. Restaurants, hotel foyers, office headquarters lobbies – all had pianos that quietly tinkled away playing the classics or popular melodies using floppy disks. Like most things electronic, though, the romance had gone from the machine. I mean it is hard to get excited about a solid-state circuit, for it is just that – sort of solid! No pulley-wheels, no provocatively pulsating leather-covered bellows, no pieces of live rubber tube and rubberised cloth-covered diaphragms – and no fascinating movements to watch. In short, no life!

It would be churlish not to bring the player-piano story up to date and to ignore the new-era self-acting pianoforte, but please don't expect me to warm to the things! I am personally more happy with the old systems for they are cheap, easy to repair – and you don't need to be a qualified electronics geek to sort out why they won't work.

Original player pianos are getting thin on the ground these days but they are still quite cheap and it is up to us (that's you and me) to keep them alive to pass on to future generations so that they may see how clever were out forefathers at making music out of air.

I thought it would also be a good idea to start the tale with a brief history of mechanical music and its instruments so that you may know what else is out there. As well as that, the pneumatic player piano has a first cousin – the player organ, usually a reed instrument, and occasionally a pipe-playing organ. I think these are greatly underrated instruments and, because I happen to like them, I have added as a bonus a couple of Chapters describing how they work and how to maintain and play them. After the player piano, they should present no great difficulties but I offer a few pointers to those aspects that are different and need careful attention.

Player pianos (and player organs) are examples of simple science. Let anybody turn up their noses at science and they are in for a nasty shock! Science is everywhere. Its framework guides us in virtually everything we do. While in real life one may search in vain for a triangle with a square on its hypotenuse, and I admit I have never seen an E that equalled MC squared, science – certainly at player piano level – is fun for it is all about moving columns of air and making them do things like play music!

There was always a certain cachet to owning a Steinway, especially in Britain. Here is that intrinsically British instrument, a pedal-electric Duo-Art which could be played in three ways: by hand, remotely by electricity using the built-in electric motor and pump, or by foot-pedals. This style of Pianola Duo-Art was quite unknown in the United States but was a feature of some Steinway and Weber installations for the UK market.

This volume is thus really a celebration of past technology, of the achievements of a past age. If you want something more modern, then start with a primer in electronics!

A word about the way this book is organised. It is arranged in four sections comprising three sets of chapters and a set of appendices. The first seven chapters describe the history and development of automatic stringed instruments – player pianos and barrel pianos – and outline the industry that produced them. The second group of chapters, totalling five, describes how these instruments actually work and describes the principles of mechanical playing from barrel through pneumatic actions and finally to the perforated paper music rolls that pneumatic pianos play. It concludes with an overview of modern technology and the record/playback piano. The third group of chapters, which totals six, describes to you the basics of care and maintenance leading up to restoration and how to keep these instruments into tip-top performing condition. It also describes player reed organs, the most popular being the Orchestrelle, and tells you how to look after it. This section includes instructions on the correct way to play pneumatic roll-playing instruments and concludes with some advice on on-going care and maintenance. Finally there are five appendices that offer reference information including a listing of manufacturers and principal agents, brand names, music-roll types, dating pianos and, lastly, a guide to valuation.

No modern home in Edwardian Britain was complete without its piano and the variety most coveted was the player-piano. In those days electricity was still a very new thing and many homes up and down the country were still illuminated by gas or oil. Not surprisingly, then, when in July 1912 Wolverhampton's West Park was the setting for a public exhibition to promote the concept of electricity in the home, the organisers sought to display as many electrical objects as possible. Star of this particular show-stand is the Hopkinson *Electrelle* electric player piano ('sole agents E A Walton, 16 Darlington Street'). It was a brave show but the makers of the 65-note *Electrelle* went into receivership exactly a year later through over-spending while attempting to perfect an 88-note version. The name 'Electrelle' was also used by an American maker around this time.

The question of prices, an essential part of the history of instruments, is a horny one because not only has the value of money changed enormously over the years, but so has the buying power of currency. As an example of this, a black-and-white television receiver in the 1950s was more expensive to buy than a family car, and a washing machine was about half that value. In the intervening years, these two products have altered out of all recognition. While washing machines have become 'automatic' and programmable, the TV is in colour and offers far more picture channels than the 1950s instrument. In Britain, for example, only one station was available and that only transmitted for around five hours a day! In the 1950s a colour TV receiver cost between £700 and £1,000 of 1950s-value earnings.

Today, with satellite and cable TV, Teletext services and video recorders, the average run-of-the-mill TV costs one-twentieth of the price of a family automobile. It is also about comparable in cost to a mid-range washing-machine! On top of this, the volume of production affects unit costs since mass-produced goods are inevitably cheaper than those produced in limited numbers by labour-intensive methods. And TV receivers were until twenty or so years ago hand-built by factories that were chock-a-block with dexterous-fingered young ladies. In just terms of numbers of pound notes or dollar bills, the TV of that time was at least twice as expensive as a receiver of today and performed but a fraction of the functions of its modern equivalent.

The real way to produce cost-comparisons, then, is ideally not in numbers of pounds Sterling or US dollars, but by the hours of work the wage-earner must put in so that he or she can afford a product. This opens up a fresh mare's-nest of problems. Average wages are just that – they have to account for the huge disparity between the lowest wage-earners and the highest company executive's take-home pay. Statistics tell us that the gap between these two ends of the earnings table is ever extending. In 1850 the manual worker's hourly wage was around one-fifteenth of the wages of what today would be called the executive class. In the year 2000, it was calculated to be approximately one-twentieth.

If you've followed this so far, then I am impressed! It just is not possible to find time (or space) to compute every value in true comparative terms. Nevertheless, some very basic comparison is, I feel, necessary. If we find that a particular instrument cost £150 or $300 in 1905, then it would be interesting for us to know what that would be worth today. Before British currency was revalued against the dollar at the time of World War II, a rough guide to the rates of exchange was four dollars to the pound or, in British currency of the time, a dollar was five shillings. Also at this time, many British manufacturers priced their goods in that special and rather elitist currency – the guinea. A term widely associated with the two extremes of horse-racing and the art world (Sotheby's and Christie's, for example, priced goods this way), the guinea was actually one pound and one shilling or, in today's currency, £1.05p.

By this time, heads are swelling and brains aching at attempting to de-confuse the confusion! Convinced that I had to produce a massive conversion table that could somehow allow for the variable dollar/pound exchange described above, I had already poured a large Malt whisky and loaded the shotgun when a solution occurred to me. Sure, it is hardly an elegant one, but it seems to be the least confusing. Here's what I have decided to do. When a value comes up in text either in English pounds or US dollars (the only two currencies that really concern us here), I immediately translate that value into its companion currency. And where I want you to know what that's worth right now, I then take both figures and translate them into today's values. What you will find, then, is a sequence like this: £1,250 [$5,980]: £69,669 [$111,490] which translates as that at the time in question, a quoted price of £1,250 (then equivalent to $5,980) would now be equal to £69,669 or $111,490.

This will always be related to a date, and each calculation and conversion is made using my own derived algorithm that is based on both historic and current exchange rates as accepted by the London *Financial Times* and the New York *Wall Street Journal*.

I do hope this is clear and that it will help you to appreciate the contemporary value of instruments (and others costs) in terms of the values of today. But be reminded that these figures are for information only and do not bear any relationship to the modern, present-day International Price Guide – the money you can expect to have to spend to buy an instrument today – which is to be found in Appendix 5.

Since player-pianos were devised, a significant part of the world has gone Metric. Although there's nothing very wrong in this, it makes translation of contemporary measurements a bit on the ludicrous side. While America, sensibly, still uses the basis of Imperial measurement, the British abandoned their birthright several years ago and chose to look to France for rather more than the cheese and wine that had hitherto willingly been imported from it.

This has created problems in that half of the British people don't understand Metric measurements and probably fewer Americans do. Converting every dimension into another system is cumbersome. It is therefore my decision that I quote dimensions and weights, where necessary, in their original form.

Anybody who can't (or won't) understand is advised to go out and buy one of those useful little books of conversion tables. Where I consider it important to understand something, I may choose to express it in both Imperial and Metric units – merely out of cussedness.

Events turn a full circle with the revival of interest in the reproducing piano that came about in post-War years. Here we see a unique concert given at London's Queen Elizabeth Hall and organised by The Player Piano Group. It is the autumn of 1972 and the music is Grieg's Piano Concerto played by soloist Percy Grainger who had died three years earlier. The secret lay with the Duo-Art reproducing rolls he had recorded fifty years earlier.

While ordinary people cherished uprights, those who had the space naturally preferred the 'grand'. Here the author gives a recital on a Blüthner Triphonola at the Nationaal Museum van Speelklok tot Pierement in Utrecht in 1972.

At a public exhibition staged at the Science Museum in London in the 1980s Richard Cole of The Player Piano Group demonstrates a Phonola push-up in conjunction with a modern Kemble baby grand. The visitors were presented with an insight into pre-First World War German technology in a performance given by a fully restored instrument in perfect condition by a performer who was skilled in understanding how to get the best out of a perforated piano-roll. Sadly most museums possess neither the instruments nor the ability to mount such a presentation.

The fine gilt decorated mahogany cabinet of a weight-driven clockwork barrel piano made in London by John Longman around 1790. *National Museum, Utrecht.*

Portable street piano with *tableau vivante* dating from the mid-19th century.

Debain *Piano Mécanique* combined mechanical and finger piano. The *planchette*-playing mechanical player is positioned on top of the piano and accessed by raising the lid.

The handsome case with stained-glass decoration housing a spring-wound clockwork 42-key unidentified Bohemian barrel-playing piano orchestrion.

Opening the case of the Bohemian piano orchestrion reveals bass drum, cymbal and wood blocks percussion. This unusual instrument had automatic damper and *piano-e-forte* control operated by special long bridges on the barrel. Although played from a pinned barrel, the action incorporates a kicking-shoe-type hammer accelerator to produce a loud tone when required.

**Paul Lochmann's Original Musikwerke of Leipzig designed and built many
automatic instruments. One was this decorative piano orchestrion** *Original
Concertino* **that plays using musical-box type punched metal discs almost 28-
inches (71 cm) in diameter. The case bears the name of a retailer on its
pediment.** *National Museum, Utrecht.*

Inside the *Original Concertino* can be seen in addition to a curious 36-note symmetrical piano, an octave of tubular bells, bass drum, side drum (with six beaters), and a crash cymbal. The whole instrument is powered by a 120-kg weight that has to be would up to the top of the case periodically. *National Museum, Utrecht.*

Pierre Paul Van Roy of Aalst in Belgium created this ornate clockwork-driven café piano around 1930. With its etched and polished mirror panels in the front, this would have formed a focal point in a public bar or restaurant. *National Museum, Utrecht.*

With a repertoire of popular dance music, Van Roy's spring-driven café piano features a large barrel that in addition to the diagonally-strung piano played a wood xylophone (bass end) and a metalophone (treble end). The piano has an iron frame. *National Museum, Utrecht.*

Detail of the Van Roy café piano. The coin-operated mechanism offers a choice of music that includes two foxtrots, two one-steps, a waltz, a tango, a java, a 'scottish' and a passo-doble. *National Museum, Utrecht.*

Close-up showing the barrel pins, the bass hammers and the xylophone. *National Museum, Utrecht.*

Racca *Piano Melodico* reiterating-action book-playing piano. This model, in the form of a grand piano, is the largest made with a fully chromatic compass of six octaves. The style of decoration is special to this example which was originally in the one-time West Cornwall Museum of Mechanical Music.

Racca of Bologna also made piano-players. Here is a picture of a rare survivor of this brand of push-up that bears the name of this important Italian maker.

Welte-Mignon reproducing piano playing 'red' rolls. This, one of the pioneering systems, employed what was called a 'floating expression' level and used pneumatic lock-and-cancel valves, seen in the frame to the left of the spool-box.

Simple controls for the Welte-Mignon placed at either end of the tracker bar. The white cylindrical object lower right of spoolbox is a mercury pot for the on-off switch – a point contact operated by a pneumatic motor.

Two generations of trefoil motor. Welte's characteristic three-lobe rotary roll-drive motor was very smooth and silent in operation, yet needed a small flywheel to ensure smoothness of running. In the upper illustration is seen the wind-motor as applied to a Welte-Mignon *vorsetzer* piano-player with flywheel on adjacent layshaft and linked by drive-belt. In the lower view is seen the developed version in the Welte-Mignon reproducing piano. This time the flywheel is incorporated on the single drive shaft. The brass eccentric that links the three motors by short wooden connecting rods is also clearly seen here. In both pictures the small pneumatic motor that operates the on-off switch is seen to the lower right. With its small pot of mercury, this was essential in times when the only electrical supply was Direct Current – but it still operates with Alternating Current. It is also a reminder that many German-made instruments of this time tended to spill mercury is handled carelessly.

Built by Aeolian to the special order of a New Bedford, Massachusetts, client, this walnut case houses a particularly rare type of Aeolian instrument – an electrically operated remote Duo-Art reproducing roll-playing console for an Aeolian fully-automatic organ. Built in the autumn of 1927, this cost $475 (£118) ex-factory (Garwood, New Jersey). The customer, who was president of Dartmouth Manufacturing Corporation, had spent $27,900 (£6,975) on what was clearly a very large Aeolian Pipe Organ – and even that total was discounted from Aeolian's ledger-price of $31,242.50 (£7,810 12s 6d).

Removing the cabinet panels shows the complex of electrical relays that are operated from the music roll which is placed under the top lid. This rare piece now belongs to Robert Hough of the Musical Box Society of Great Britain who acquired with it a file of correspondence revealing the problems Aeolian faced in keeping their client, W H Langshaw, happy. Aeolian's organ studios managing director Frank Taft seems to have been under great pressure and there are several references to his being 'away for a short rest'.

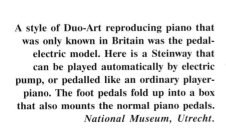

A style of Duo-Art reproducing piano that was only known in Britain was the pedal-electric model. Here is a Steinway that can be played automatically by electric pump, or pedalled like an ordinary player-piano. The foot pedals fold up into a box that also mounts the normal piano pedals.
National Museum, Utrecht.

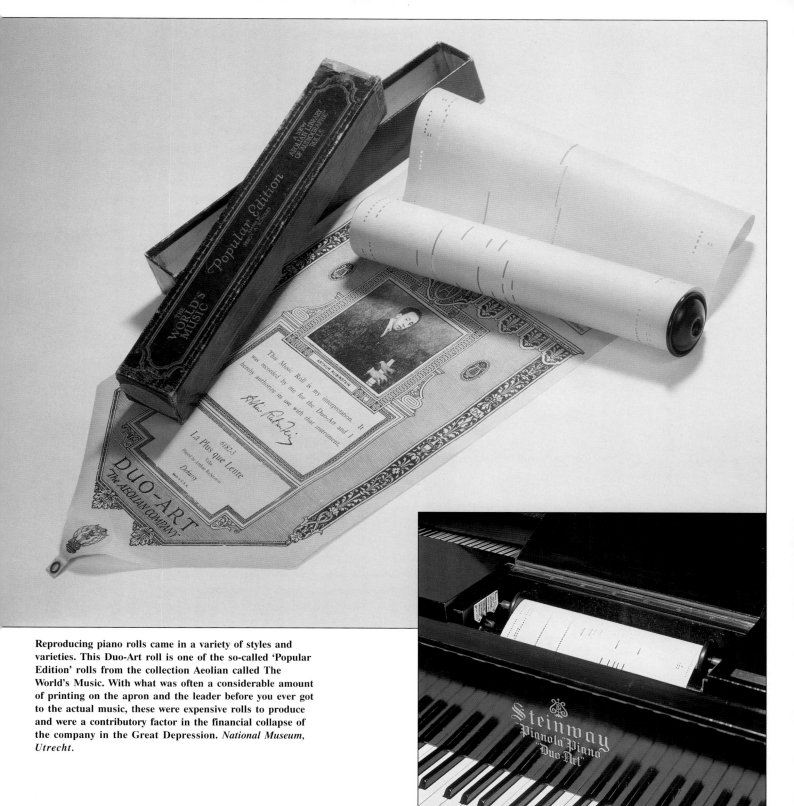

Reproducing piano rolls came in a variety of styles and varieties. This Duo-Art roll is one of the so-called 'Popular Edition' rolls from the collection Aeolian called The World's Music. With what was often a considerable amount of printing on the apron and the leader before you ever got to the actual music, these were expensive rolls to produce and were a contributory factor in the financial collapse of the company in the Great Depression. *National Museum, Utrecht.*

Every maker of a reproducing piano action sought to place their mechanisms in the most prestigious pianos of the age. The best courted Steinway and Aeolian followed Welte as being the action to promote the Steinway – or was it the other way round? In the end, Steinway demanded top rank in Aeolian's piano-brand pile and although the Weber and the Steck were pretty close to the Steinway in quality, their prices had to be artificially depressed to create what Steinway called for – a major price differential for their company name. *National Museum, Utrecht.*

Next to the Welte-Mignon, the most successful of the German reproducing pianos was the Leipzig-built Hupfeld Tri-Phonola introduced in 1918. This fine example dates from about 1925 and, like many Hupfeld instruments, uses a quality Rönisch piano. Interesting here is the use of the detached cabinet to house the electrically-driven suction pump and to double up as a storage cabinet for a few of the special music-rolls. *National Museum, Utrecht.*

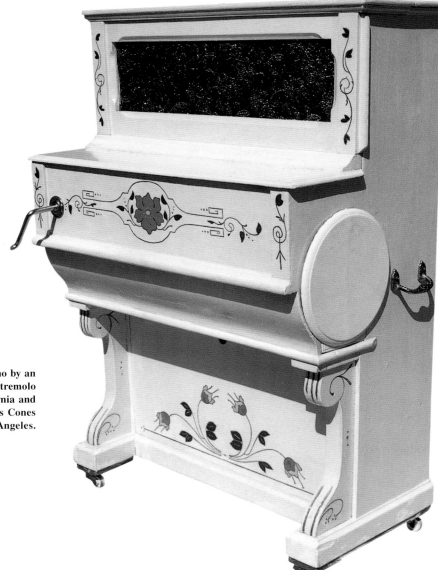

An unusually small street piano by an unidentified maker, this 30-note tremolo instrument was found in California and sympathetically restored by Charles Cones of Los Angeles.

The proportions of this small instrument are revealed by this internal view showing the 15-note reiterating mechanism with its hardwood hammer heads for the treble half. The layshaft and bevel gearing of the tremolo drive can be seen above the barrel drive worm. The bass notes have ten free-hanging weighted dampers.

The name of Vincente Llinares of Barcelona is associated with the manufacture of modern street pianos under the trade name Faventia. He was certainly in business in 1930 and his later instruments, obtainable new well into the 1970s, used moulded plastic parts. The instruments were always bright and well-made. Here is one from the collection of Charles Cones of Los Angeles which appears to date from the 1930-50 era.

Since the beginning of the piano, the variation in case styles has been a seemingly endless process with every taste and fashion catered for. Player pianos seemed to give impetus to this practice with anachronisms such as the Louis XVI styles of Aeolian, Romano-Greco styles from Welte, and *art nouveau* from Ampico and Bechstein. Allegedly humble uprights were their own harbingers of style and this 1920s player has one of the most attractive case designs. The property of an Ironbridge, Shropshire, collector, this fine piano is a Lipp with a Canadian Higel action.

Opened up and ready to pedal, the Higel Lipp is most attractively presented inside and out.

The fallboard bears the name of a South Coast factor, Ernest Watts & Son Ltd of 24 Queen's Road, Brighton, and 54 Church Road, Hove. The business was founded in 1895. At the back of the spoolbox is a shield-shaped metal label reading 'Patented September 25, 1909, 21946'.

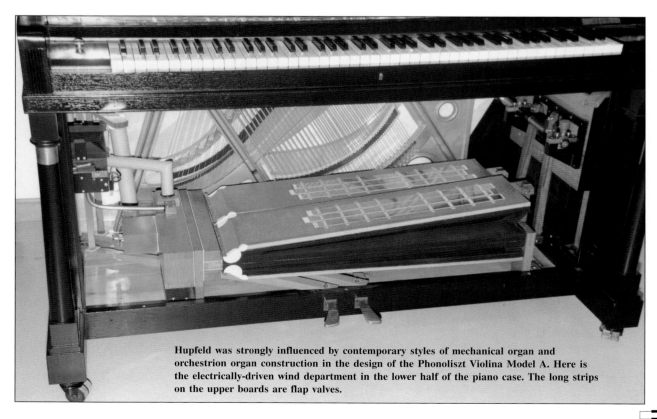

Hupfeld was strongly influenced by contemporary styles of mechanical organ and orchestrion organ construction in the design of the Phonoliszt Violina Model A. Here is the electrically-driven wind department in the lower half of the piano case. The long strips on the upper boards are flap valves.

One of the most ornately-cased Ampico reproducing pianos is this from a Musical Box Society International member who has been fortunate in securing not only a unique instrument but the matching duet piano-bench.

Hupfeld Phonoliszt violin-playing pianos are scarce today. Pneumatic instruments that demanded quality maintenance were virtually doomed to minimal survival in a past age when skills and experience were at their lowest ebb. Today these fine pieces can be restored to mint condition. This flat-fronted Phonoliszt Violina Model A is in a striking black and gold finish. Hupfeld used this style of casework for a number of its orchestrions with minor variations as needed.

Open for playing, the Model A Phonoliszt Violina reveals its three violins in the upper portion of the piano case. When first marketed in 1908 it created a sensation and later a noted violinist of the time described it as 'the eighth wonder and marvel of our time'.

Hupfeld violin players were all built around the foundation of an electrically-driven expression piano. The majority of instrument made to the Model A design played one roll. This specimen is thought to be a unique survivor of the twin-roll Model A. *National Museum, Utrecht.*

Three violins and two music rolls make this Model A Phonoliszt Violina a formidable entertainment instrument. *National Museum, Utrecht.*

The greater majority of surviving Hupfeld Phonoliszt Violina instruments is of the bow-fronted Model B style and this example is one of the finest examples. Like all these Leipzig-made orchestral pianos, the foundation is a Rönisch piano. *National Museum, Utrecht.*

Just before the outbreak of the First World War in 1914 Hupfeld announced its astounding double Phonoliszt-Violina that played no fewer than six violins. Styled after the Model B only with twin towers, this instrument became the 'Holy Grail' of collectors for many years. It is uncertain whether Hupfeld actually made any or, if they did, how many. Rumours abounded about instruments that may have existed, but nothing was certain. Museum owner and instrument restorer Siegfried Wendel in Germany decided it was time to find out what this wondrous creation sounded like. Using original Patent drawings and specifications and with the expertise that has led him to build and restore many other instruments of this era, Wendel went and built one from scratch. Here is that unique double Model B performing in the music room of a collector in America.

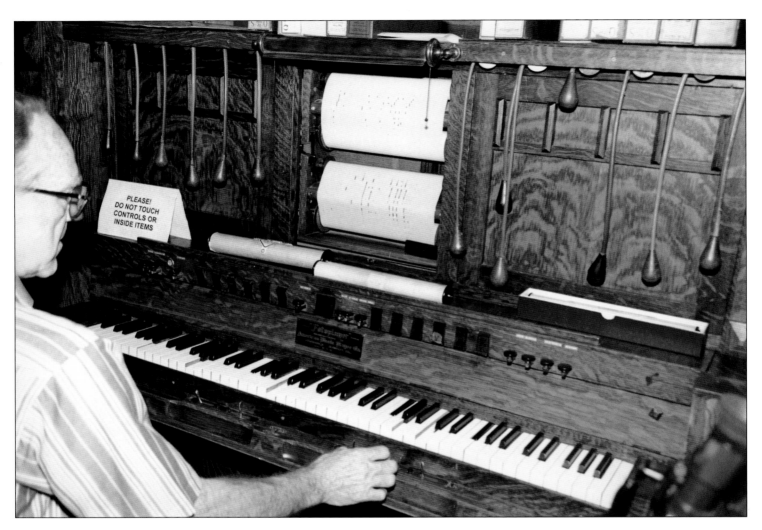

A short-lived era in the world of mechanical music was that of the theatre 'photoplayer' to accompany the silent movie. While the early bioscope presentations were initially sideshows at the fairground, by the years immediately preceding the outbreak of the 1914-18 War, both cinemas and their audiences were courting a different and more discerning class of customers. The films themselves were no longer presented as curiosities but had thematic content – what today would be described as a 'plot'. Pianists did their best to provide suitable background music but enterprising people saw the opportunity for this to develop in a proper accompaniment to the silver screen. So was born the 'photoplayer', a form of manually-controlled super orchestrion that could provide locomotive whistles, barking dogs, the clangour of the fire truck and the sound of a fusillade of bullets on demand. Here is one of these instruments made by the American Photo Player Company – its trademark Fotoplayer.

Mechanical stringed instruments came in all forms from the automatic banjo through to one of the nicest yet least popular coin-operated entertainment machines – the automatic harp built by J W Whitlock & Company of Rising Sun, Indiana. Patented in 1899, the Automatic Harp was marketed by Wurlitzer after 1905 but this delicate and fine-sounding electrically-driven machine that gently plucked its strings with a clever pneumatic mechanism was too quiet for the noisy saloons and restaurants. Today it is an instrument prized by collectors.

Best remembered for its fine disc-playing musical boxes, the Regina Company of Rahway, New Jersey, ventured into automatic pianos and the first Regina Sublima Piano instruments appeared in November 1904. Early instruments were clockwork spring driven but the majority were electrically powered. All, however, featured a mechanical action. The origins were German for the instrument was very similar to the Polyphon Orchestrion I which played a 73-note music roll or the 44-note Model III. These rolls were punched from thick green-coloured glazed manila paper needed to work the mechanical hammer keys. A reiterating mechanism produces a sound not unlike a balalaika.

The Berlin company Kuhl & Klatt made a large number of electric pianos and orchestrion pianos between 1900 and 1912, many of which could be driven by wet-cell electric accumulator. There is a strong similarity between these and the instruments built by August Eduard Dienst of Leipzig and there may have been a product tie-up. Here is a xylophone piano with a large-compass xylophone operated by the music roll and visible at the top of the case front.

A rarity in automatic pianos is the 39-note disc-playing Pianette produced in limited quantities in the very early 1900s by F G Otto & Sons of Jersey City, New Jersey. This 39-note piano was described by its makers as 'automatically adjusted' and unlikely to get out of order. Few were made and very few survived. The late Hughes Ryder of New Jersey had the good fortune to acquire all that was left some many years ago – a pile of derelict parts.

Inside the case of this magnificently-restored specimen can be seen the allegedly dust-proof box that covers the hammer mechanism. Power comes from a long-running clockwork motor claimed to run 25 minutes on one winding. Note the unusual division of the iron frame.

Removing the angled wooden dust-cover reveals a unique feature of the Otto Pianette which is the double set of hammers, the inset and shorter ones providing soft playing and controlled from their own disc projections. The discs are 21-inches in diameter and this instrument produces an automatic soft or loud effect according to which particular hammer is activated – the short and soft-toned, or the long and loud. Restored and photographed by Jere Ryder, the pictures are by courtesy of instrument owner Emery Prior.

Chapter 1
A Brief Introduction to Mechanical Musical Instruments

According to the dictionaries, mechanical instruments of music are those that produce their sounds automatically from a pre-determined, pre-programmed mechanical source and are operated either without human participation (by clockwork, water, wind or electricity), or with musically unskilled human aid, such as by turning a handle or pumping bellows to provide air at pressure or suction. Because the prime feature of the instrument is that it can produce musical sounds each time it is operated and since its music is provided from a precise and repeatable mechanical programme, each playing is an original performance. By definition, then, this category excludes machines such as gramophones, phonographs and Aeolian harps.

That's it in a nutshell, anything that goes by itself and makes music. Fine – but how did it all start? Mechanical music has its origins in the remote past. The first self-playing instruments, based on the flute, are thought to pre-date the Christian era. It is said that Apollonius of Perga (3rd century BC) devised automata, including singing birds, worked by a waterwheel that also pumped air into a whistle.

With the development of both music and technology the scene was set for the evolution of proper self-playing instruments. The ancient peoples of Asia and Egypt had 'automatic statues' which moved or spoke and this inspired Hero of Alexandria (1st century AD) to devise automaton temple doors and a mechanically played instrument.

Most early self-playing devices of this period seem to have been of the random form which, like the Aeolian harp, could not replicate any given theme. They lacked the vital component, which distinguishes the automatophon from such instruments – the repeatable element that comes from using a mechanical programme to render exact repetition possible.

Just when this was introduced is uncertain but the first written-down description of a mechanical instrument with such a programme source was that presented between 813 and 833 by three of the leading organisers of Arab science in Baghdad – the so-called Bānū Mūsā (Brothers Musa – Muhammad, Ahamad and Hasan). The mechanism described was a flute played from a rotating cylinder on the surface of which were projecting pegs to lift levers which uncovered the apertures in the body of the flute.

In Europe, Leo IV the Philosopher (865-911 AD) is reputed to have created automata for Theophilus Ikonomachus, Emperor of Byzantium, comprising mechanical birds that sang and fluttered in an artificial tree. Konrad von Würzburg (c.1250) mentioned an artificial tree upon which perched birds that moved their wings and sang. In the late 15th century, Leonardo da Vinci proposed a spinet accompanied by two drums apparently played from a cylinder.

Europe was an early breeding ground for the dance-band or orchestrion piano. Pierre Eich of Belgium made the *Solophone* in the early 1920s. Eich, who continued in business up to the outbreak of the Second World War, was one of the last remaining makers of mechanical instruments and piano orchestrions in the world.

The flourishing of mechanical music really began in the period from the 15th to the 17th century. But it was the early perfection of the mechanical organ and the self-playing carillon that represented the principal providers of mechanical music at this time. Stringed instruments were the next to arrive being introduced at the end of the 16th century.

This period was one of rich patronage in Central Europe and if the Low Countries became the focus of the relatively simple carillon, it was the capital city of the Holy Roman Empire, Augsburg, that became the focus of art and craft. Not surprisingly automata and mechanical music were part of that scene. The work of craftsmen such as the Bidermanns, father and son, who made mechanical organs and spinets, Achilles and Veit Langenbucher, also making clockwork spinets, Matthais Rungells, Hans Schlottheim and others marked a noble transition from the Middle Ages to the great era of self-playing musical instruments.

These artists gloried in exploring different ways to achieve their goal. Automaton scenes crafted in silver offered little space for conventional clockwork music mechanisms, yet they contrived to succeed by using, for example, concentric tracks on the face of a wheel as a musical programme, or projections on the narrow rim of a large wheel. Some of these pieces also marked the earliest use of the regal or reed-pipe in their tiny organs.

A brief description of how these things worked would not be amiss at this point. A mechanical instrument comprises four parts: *[1]* the musical element (pipes, strings, bells, tuned steel teeth); *[2]* the musical programme (barrel or cylinder, tune disc or perforated card, metal or paper); *[3]* a mechanical interface between *[1]* and *[2]*; a source of energy to set the instrument into play.

1. The musical element is normally familiar and, with the possible exception of the tuned steel tooth (*eg:* the musical-box comb), recognisable as similar to features of a non-mechanical instrument.

2. The musical programme in its most common form is a cylinder the surface of which is provided with projections representing the particular note-sequence of the music to be played. The oldest and most common form is a wooden barrel, the outer surface of which is made of a close-grained wood (traditionally poplar) into which are driven pins (short notes) and staples of various lengths (longer notes). Metal cylinders were used for the large church carillons and smaller musical clocks and, at the end of the eighteenth century, musical boxes. In general, punched discs with projections were used in disc-playing musical-boxes (end of the 19th century) and pierced metal, card or paper for organettes. Perforated paper is used for pneumatic actions used in player-pianos.

This *Solophone* plays music rolls 325mm wide and notice how they are arranged to roll 'inside out' across the tracker bar merely to ensure full contact between paper and bar. Requiring both a pressure and a suction wind department in the same way that early Welte pipe organs needed the two, the bellows incorporate feeders and exhausters in the form of inverted and superimposed see-saws. An extensive range of violin-toned organ pipes in addition to a large-compass xylophone combined to make this one of the more remarkable of the European piano-orchestrions.

3. The interface comprises a method of linking the programme source to the musical element. This is typically a keyframe (a row of mechanical levers) or tracker-bar (used in paper-roll controlled pneumatic actions).

4. Energy to set in motion the sequence of performance is provided from *[a]* a clockwork motor (which may be spring- or weight-driven); *[b]* hand-turned with a crank handle; *[c]* pneumatically driven by an air motor (as in a player piano), or *[d]* electrically driven (as in some piano-orchestrions, violin-players and coin-operated instruments).

The process of noting or transferring music onto the barrel is ancient but was first defined through the writings of Engramelle *[29]* and Dom Bedos *[3]*, both of whom devoted considerable effort into illustrating the form and system of barrel-pinning and the arrangement and ornamentation of music for mechanical performance.

During the early days of mechanical music, inventors believed that the wholly-automatic instrument was asking too much of the ordinary credible person's intellect and that it was necessary to create an apparent human performer to be seen to be 'playing' the instrument. This is a conviction that exists throughout Far Eastern culture where even into modern times automatic mechanisms have the figure of the *kara-ko* or 'false automaton' which appears to be turning the mechanism.

Lifesize figures apparently performing on instruments are an ancient concept. In more recent times the works of Jacques de Vaucanson (1709-1782), the Jaquet-Droz (father and son), Henri Maillardet, and Johann Gottfried Kaufmann have variously entertained and challenged: the automaton player of Prussian cavalry marches is once said to have stayed an enemy attack.

Vaucanson, during 1738-1744, exhibited his pieces across Europe. Among these he showed an 'Image playing on the German-Flute' and another 'no less wonderful than the first, playing on the Tabor and Pipe'.

These craftsmen were rare characters and, consequently few in number. Keenly recalled is the work of Pierre Jaquet-Droz (1721-1790), Henri Louis Jaquet-Droz (1752-1791), Henri Maillardet (1745-c.1815), and Frederick Kaufmann (1786-1866), son of J C Kaufmann, whose trumpet-playing android is to be seen today in the Deutches Museum, Munich. Re-discovered in the past decade is the android clarinettist made by Cornelis Jacobus van Oeckelen (1798-1865) of Breda in 1838.

Most of these automaton figures or androids do not actually perform on the instrument, but synthesize a performance from a mechanical contrivance within their bodies. Kaufmann's life-size trumpeter, for example, had a large barrel organ in his chest that played trumpet-like beating reeds to synthesize the sound of a real trumpet. As distinct from life-size performers, father and son Pierre and Henri Louis Jaquet-Droz also created at least three remarkable automata one of which was of a child playing a small pipe-organ by actually depressing the keys with her fingers under the control of a complex barrel mechanism and radial cams to control the position of the forearm.

One of the wonders of the early 20th century was the self-playing violin. Ludwig Hupfeld began experimenting in this direction as early as 1900 and production of his first model, called the *Phonoliszt-Violina*, followed around 1907. It entered the market the following year. Hupfeld's team of inventors comprised Robert Frömsdorf and Johann and Ludwig Bajde and one early device was a keyboard-operated violin. The production *Phonoliszt-Violina* was a fully-pneumatic instrument and had on display three violins mounted inside a cage containing a rotating bow wheel. Only one string on each violin was actually played. This early model is demonstrated daily in the Nationaal Museum van Speeldoos tot Pierement, Utrecht.

One or two automata, then, actually did play a normal musical instrument and these are numbered amongst the highest echelon of what is today a rare breed. An example of such a figure is that comprising *La Joueuse de tympanon*, today preserved (and fully restored) in the Conservatoire des arts et Metiers in Paris. This remarkable piece was built for Marie Antoinette by clock- and instrument-maker Peter Kintzing (1746-1816) and David Roentgen. In this an elegant young lady is seated before a dulcimer which she proceeds to play, her fingers depressing the actual instrument keys as a complex barrel-controlled mechanism operates her arms radially and her fingers up and down. The music played by this automaton includes an air from 'Armide' by Gluck.

Kintzing is best remembered for a style of compound musical clock that married a pipe-organ with a dulcimer. Marie Antoinette also owned one of these instruments which is now in the care of the Du Pont Foundation at Nemours Foundation, Wilmington, Delaware, and another is in the Conservatoire des Arts et Metiers in Paris. Both of these pieces also play music by Gluck. Kintzing was responsible for a school of clockmaking in Nieuweid that seems to have specialised in this style of compound clock with organ and dulcimer.

I made mention that behind the creators of these marvellous musical mechanisms lay the era of rich patronage in Central Europe. What is today southern Germany was the birthplace of practical clockwork music and Augsburg, the focus of the great arts and crafts, became the cradle of this particular metier. Here was crafted some of the most amazing musical automata that marked a noble transition from the Middle Ages to the great era of self-playing musical instruments.

Perhaps the best-known automatic violin besides the Hupfeld was the Mills *Violano-Virtuoso* made in Chicago. Designed by a Swedish émigré Henry Sandall, it bears a striking similarity to the ancient Swedish folk instrument called the *nyckelharpa* except that this one is a fully-engineered, electro-magnetically operated automat combining piano and violin worked by a perforated paper music-roll.

These artists gloried in exploring different ways to achieve their goal. Automaton scenes crafted in silver offered little space for conventional clockwork music mechanisms, yet they contrived to succeed by using, for example, concentric tracks on the face of a wheel as a musical programme, or projections on the narrow rim of a large wheel. Some of these pieces also marked the earliest use of the regal or reed-pipe in their tiny organs.

Much of this immensely fruitful development was halted by the onset of the Thirty Years War (1618-1648), an event that inspired Schiller to write that it 'put out the spark of culture in Germany'. Certainly it stifled artistic development for several generations. It was not until the beginning of the 18th century that mechanical music once more began to flourish and this heralded what was to be its richest epoch. Indeed, the period from 1720 through to 1820 may rightly be called 'the Golden Century' as mechanical instruments became true musical interpreters. This was the time of the musical clock in Vienna where a whole industry sprang up to vie in making the finest instruments which would perform, note perfect, all the popular music.

Musically speaking, this age was of immense importance for the programme barrels of these organs and spinets preserve for us today the exact style of ornamentation and performance which was expected of them when newly-built. It is only in very recent times that this stunningly obvious fact has become accepted and now these instruments are coming in for more study than ever before. They can provide real clues to some horny problems for us such as the correct speed of the minuet, the precise difference between Allegro and Adagio, and the culture of 17th-18th century ornamentation.

At the end of the 20th century the Phonogrammarchiv der Österreichischen Akademie der Wissenschaften in Vienna, under its enthusiastic director Dr Helmut Kowar, embarked on an ambitious programme of examining and recording all available Viennese musical clocks and analysing their repertoire.

During the two thousand and more years of mechanical instruments (with the principal developments having taken place, as we have seen, since the end of the 17th century), almost every instrument of music has been automated. From the church organ through to the harmonica or mouth organ, from flute to banjo and even the violin - all have been the subject of attention from resourceful inventors.

As the 1920s approached, instruments were expected to do more than merely sound like an automatic piano. As effects were added, so it became fashionable for these effects to be increasingly more visible. The German *Weber Grandezza*, an electrically-driven piano-jazz band, displayed its attributes for all to see.

Carillons first appeared in Europe in the 14th century. These could be played manually (by striking the 'keys' of a form of keyboard with the fist) or sounded automatically using a large drum or barrel, initially of iron, later of bronze, into the surface of which were screwed iron pegs. These pegs engaged a series of levers as the drum revolved so as to operate hammers to strike the bells.

Unlike common church bells that are 'rung' by swinging, those of the carillon remain stationary, it being the hammers that move in order to sound the bell.

Despite the attrition caused by two World Wars and the normal wear and tear on their mechanisms, there remain a large number of ancient carillons still playable in Holland and Belgium while several notable new ones have been created over the past forty years: in 1988 I was commissioned to design and build a large public one that today plays regularly in London's Leicester Square.

Attempts to replace the cumbersome carillon barrel began in the 1950s with perforated-card playing mechanisms (as installed, but no longer used, at Bourneville in England). Modern carillons, such as that in Leicester Square use solid-state electronics with EPROM-based tune libraries and electro-magnetic solenoid-driven bell-hammers.

The first mechanical organs predated the construction of the oldest surviving barrel organ (built 1502) which is in the walls of the Hohen Salzburg (restored to perfection in 2002). The barrel was also the programme source for the hydraulic organs (water organs) popular in Italian gardens in the 16th-18th centuries. In 1980, the lost technology of this most impressive of instruments was re-discovered (in my London workshop) and the ancient instrument in the Quirinal Palace, Rome, was rebuilt and brought back to playing condition.

By the end of the 17th century, the miniature barrel-organ or *serinette* was in use for encouraging caged birds to sing.

It was at the beginning of the 18th century that the church and chamber barrel organ began to establish a following in Great Britain. Automatic music for the home and also for the church as a welcome replacement for the often poor-quality church bands was possible at comparatively low cost and up until 1860 the market for barrel organs was rich enough to inspire a majority of organ-builders to offer these instruments.

While the majority of both church and secular instruments were hand-operated by means of a crank-handle, a few clockwork-powered examples also appeared. Of these, most were driven by the energy from a descending weight which was wound up to the top of the case to begin with. Spring-powered clockwork was less popular in Britain than in France and Austria.

There are two definitions of 'musical clock'. Generally, the German *Flötenuhr* means a clockwork-driven organ which may or may not be associated with a time-indicating clockwork. The great musical and automaton clock of Strasbourg (1574), the smaller indoor clocks of Isaac Habrecht (1544-1620) and the domestic table musical clock of Nicholas Vallin dated 1598 were the progenitors of a rich era of musical clocks which performed on a small carillon of bells, an equally small pipe-organ or a string instrument like a dulcimer. Many clockwork organs were made in Vienna during the 'golden century' (1720-1820) and they attained high musical quality. Composers who wrote music expressly for the instrument included Handel, Haydn, Mozart and Beethoven. By the early part of the 19th century, the instrument became to decline in popularity.

Small comb-playing musical-box movements were incorporated in Viennese mantel clocks: many of the early ones featured high-quality movements by the best local makers. By the end of the 19th century, disc-playing musical mechanisms were built into clocks including 'longcase' musical hall-clocks.

Built around a Gabriella upright piano, the French *Seybold Piano-Accordeon-Jazz* was another of these dancehall entertainers. Note the neat use of metal tubing and heavy-duty pump work in the lower case.

The musical box began as no more than a curious novelty adjunct to a utilitarian object. Seals, scent-bottles, snuff-boxes and watches were produced which played simple melodies on a compass of notes ranging from as few as five and seldom exceeding fourteen. By the second decade of the nineteenth century, however, the mechanism had been improved and enlarged to the point where the cylinder musical box could be launched as a stand-alone musical interpreter.

At the time of London's Great Exhibition of 1851, the predominantly Swiss makers were able to produce musical boxes that exhibited the highest possible musical quality. The high cost of manufacture and the limited repertoire of its cylinder meant that the musical box had a limited appeal. When the disc-playing musical box was invented in Germany in 1886 it offered cheap music from a very large inventory of titles. The effect on the Swiss industry was to remove both its virtual monopoly of the musical-box market and to hasten mass-production methods. The overall result was a significant reduction in quality and price.

But what was the reason behind this crafting of automatic musical instruments?

There is no doubt that mechanical instruments were first created as novelty items. Because the music which they played was in general in the contemporary idiom, they were not revered as musical interpreters although it seems to have been essential that they performed as well as, if not better than, a human performer.

As novelty items, however, they were nevertheless anything but toys. Only for the wealthy, they were high up among the objects considered suitable as gifts between monarchs, noblemen and diplomats. When Elizabeth I decided to give a present to the Sultan of Turkey in 1599, it was an enormous musical clock some 14 feet high containing a carillon, barrel organ and automaton birds which she chose. In Central Europe, gifts exchanged between rulers were richly-created mechanical instruments, frequently with clocks and automata.

The aristocracy, of which Central Europe suffered an abundance during this period, took an almost naive pleasure in in-

corporating music into the most unlikely objects to surprise and delight their guests. This created an environment for makers to be at their most innovative. At the time of Haydn, for example, small organs built into decorative urns, even a musical settee, were not exceptional. In the Royal Palace in Madrid is a chandelier with two separate barrel organ concealed in its lustres.

This rich sponsorship excluded the public at large for whom the only mechanical music they might hear came from a church carillon or, later, a barrel organ in church. In Vienna, centre of the musical-clock industry during the 'golden century' (1720-1820), all fashionable public places such as cafes and restaurants had musical clocks that played the best of popular music to their clientele.

While this still fell short of offering music for the masses, by 1834 it was possible to calculate that four-sevenths of the music actually heard by people in the majority of towns and cities came from mechanical instruments played in the streets by itinerant musicians. As that century drew to a close new statistics suggested that street barrel organs and pianos accounted for more than 85 percent of the music heard by the average town-dweller.

The era of the silent cinema created a demand for musical accompaniment and the earliest movie theatres employed a pianist who extemporised to the best of their ability as the film progressed. Some were very good, but by no means all. And an ordinary piano could not produce sound effects like horses galloping, gunshots, cow-bells and railroad whistles. Enter the special-effects cinema piano! These were built around a normal roll-playing instrument to which was added a variety of sound-effect devices. More complex ones had extension side cabinets containing further effects. This is a *Fotoplayer*, the trade name for the product of The American Photo Player Company, silent cinema orchestra. Capable of playing two special musical selection rolls and alternating between the two at the flick of a switch, side chests contain full percussion, chimes, bells, pipe organ and so on. The so-called 'cow-tails' hanging over the keyboard are pull-downs for operating additional sound effects such as rifle-shots, motor horns, fire sirens and more. This piece was the property of the late Harvey Roehl who was both a skilled keyboard pianist as well as a most adroit performer on it.

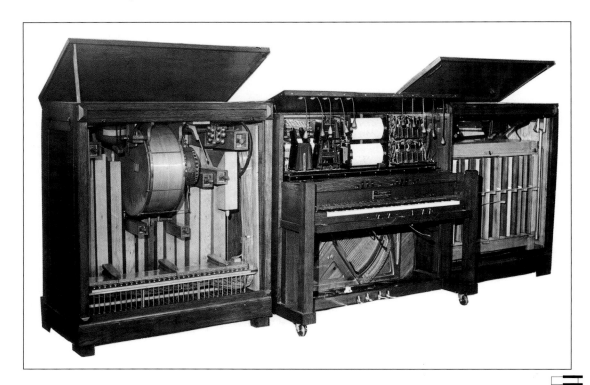

The increasing availability of the musical box during the 2nd half of the 19th century did bring music into the home. It was music that united families in life and worship and for this reason many musical boxes were provided with at least one hymn tune to which the family would sing on Sundays.

Concurrent with the goal of self-playing instruments has been the quest for methods of recording an extemporary keyboard performance. Called Melography [see 82], this was the first real method of 'recording' a live performance, its very need being superseded by the arrival of the first magnetic wire recorders at the end of the 19th century and the tape recorder in the second quarter of the 20th century.

Melography was inspired by the fine organists who had the ability to extemporise at the keyboard. Whereas their dexterity was of but fleeting existence, Melography could preserve it for a future occasion. Exactly the same need existed for the harpsichord and, even more so, the piano. The mechanism, exotic and expensive as well as cumbersome and difficult to present in a form that could be played back domestically, Melography died with the mid-Victorian era and remained dormant until the era of the pneumatically-played piano.

By the 1850s, ownership of the piano, admittedly usually the cheaper 'cabinet' piano, increased as the instrument assumed the role of a status symbol. As the 19th century approached its final quarter, the homes of the ordinary people were increasingly filled with music with the arrival first of the domestic reed organ, known generically as the American organ, but known in America as the 'parlor organ'.

While musical education was widespread and most women and many men experienced an education that embraced music, the exigencies of domestic life often meant that time for keyboard practice was insufficient to attain presentable levels of competence. It was this almost overlooked portion of the domestic keyboard market that embraced the self-playing piano with gusto. Now everybody and anybody could have the ability to play the classics, popular songs and the patriotic music of the age with a good degree of accomplishment.

As formal piano teaching declined in the aftermath of World War I, the player-piano brought music of an acceptable quality into homes everywhere. In 1920, 70 percent of the 364,000 pianos manufactured in the United States of America were player-pianos: by the year of the Depression - 1929 - of 120,000 pianos made in total, players still accounted for more than a third of production.

The player-piano was also responsible for educating the otherwise musically challenged masses about the corpus of music available to them. For many who could not master the keyboard, it allowed them access to the enjoyment of music through actual 'performance' and brought within the grasp of those with an enquiring, adventurous nature the works of composers which they might never otherwise have thought to hear.

From about 1880 onwards, and with the exception of those pieces made solely for domestic use, almost all American-made instruments were coin-operated.

The mechanical banjo was introduced in the United States in the 1890s. Played from a perforated paper roll, the Encore Automatic Banjo was electrically powered and was thus one of the earliest of American electric instruments. Its particular cleverness concerned the manner in which it plucked the strings.

An electrically-driven roll-playing mechanical harp was invented by Whitlock of Indiana in 1899. Manufactured by Wurlitzer, it enjoyed only short-lived popularity because it was too quiet for use in public places.

A very large number of makers produced electrically-operated pianos for use in bars and public places. A less-refined development of the piano-orchestrion, these pianos incorporated percussion effects, mandoline attachments (producing a sound from the piano action by interspersing a metal or leather device between hammer and spring), xylophone and, in many cases, wooden organ pipes. Some were made for mechanical playing only: others could also be played by hand. From this was developed the automatic theatre orchestra or 'photoplayer' intended for the silent cinema. This very large and complex type of instrument could be played by hand or from one, sometimes two, special piano rolls and included a variety of sound effects such as sleigh bells, locomotive whistles, pistol shots and horses' hooves in addition to full piano and pipe organ.

Virtually every manufacturer of church organs was able to provide an automatic player for the instrument when the regular human organist was indisposed or otherwise prevented from finger-playing. In the 19th century this was the so-called 'dumb organist' that sat upon the top of the keyboard and played faultless music from a pinned barrel inside a box, through to highly-developed automatic pneumatic player actions that were based on player-piano technology. These played either normal 58-65-88-note rolls or could play fully-interpreted music with automatic control of organ stops, the position of the swell-shutters, combinations and couplers all from a paper roll having no fewer than 176 rows of perforations in it.

The automatic player was popular in the case of residence organs as well and instruments by Schiedmeyer, Aeolian, Estey and Welte were installed in the homes of the rich. The greatest sophistication of these players came in the 1920s with Skinner (later to combine with Aeolian), Austin and Kimball while one of the more expansive systems was developed by Möller in Maryland with its Artiste player that could be used in church or the home. The majority of these were brought to a premature end with the Wall Street Crash and subsequent years of struggle.

Mechanical music was also combined with gambling or arcade machines combining a moving display (horse-race piano).

The arrival of the gramophone encouraged some makers to try to increase their market share by incorporating the new appliance into their instruments. Player pianos were built with gramophones built in to the upper part of the case, and the disc musical-box became the phonopectine by the addition of a device for playing both musical-box discs and record discs. In due course, pianos were even built that incorporated radio receivers in their cabinets!

Oh dear! Far from being a novelty, the mechanical musical instrument had come of age. It enjoyed the unique position of being whatever you wanted it to be – a no-skills fun instrument with which to entertain yourself and your friends, or an instrument capable of skilful use as a serious musical interpreter. And the player piano was the most marvellous device in the world for, in those days *before* wireless and the gramophone came along to despoil it, it could bring the music of your choice into your home. It was your instrument and the choice of music-rolls that it played was yours!

The 21st century with its slickness, speed and endless haste still allows you the thrill of playing your own choice of music on your very own piano. That stands for something!

Automatic pianos achieved the zenith of perfection with the development of the reproducing piano. One of the leading exponents was the Aeolian Company headquartered in New York with factories in New Jersey and, in Britain, at Hayes, Middlesex. For the American market, Aeolian developed a range of high-quality decorative styles. Here is one of the New York products for the early 1920s. Described as Design No.3010 'Spanish', the text accompanying this catalogue illustration reads: 'This case of Spanish design has as one of its beautiful features contrasting inlays of ebony and boxwood on the leghead, panels and music desk – a detail frequently found in Spanish work. The legs are twisted, with a heavy connecting stretcher that is rather close to the floor. This combination of inlays, carving, pilasters and panel is exceptionally effective, and great care has been taken to tone it to a soft antique finish'.

Chapter 2
The Earliest Automatic
String-playing Musical Instruments

Both the player-piano and the barrel piano are string-playing instruments. It stands to reason, then, that if we are going to understand how they developed we should look right back to the first automatic musical instruments that produced their music using tuned metal strings. While we are about it, we might well invest a few moments to look at the whole history of mechanical music. But rather like the condensed histories found in popular encyclopaedias, we will not be looking in depth at this history – the Bibliography at the end of this book will guide you to further study into this history if you so wish. No, our overview shall be merely sufficient to enable us to appreciate and understand the family of automatic string-players.

The history of automatic musical instruments is probably not much shorter than that of conventional musical instruments. All indications are that the two were developed more or less together and proceded along parallel paths into the first quarter of the last century. The ancient Egyptians knew the peculiar pleasures generated by musical sounds. Relics of the earliest civilisations present indications that music has been around for many thousands of years, whether it is from musical stones, tuned sticks or the whistle, both human (using lips and teeth) and artificial (causing wind to pass a free vibrating reed or across an opening as in a natural flute. Archaeologists have unearthed the evidence: we may only wonder at the achievements of past races that we have hitherto been content to dismiss as 'primitive'. The more we learn of these forgotten people the more we marvel at their arts and culture, skills and craftsmanship.

In the days when alchemy and perpetual motion were believed to be attainable goals, making a musical instrument that would play by itself was just an extension of an invention even if it was probably thought by some to touch on sorcery and witchcraft. Like many other clever men the inventor may well have had to run the gauntlet if he was to avoid a fiery end at the village stake.

But automatic instruments there were. Percussion instruments of bamboo and metal, still with us today in the form of the popular yet acutely annoying suburban garden wind-chimes, are of considerable antiquity while the principles of the Aeolian harp go back to ancient Egypt and Greece. The whistle and its larger brother the flute are equally old and it may come as a surprise to some to know that the Romans had pipe organs: popular as objects depicted in sculptures, the remains of at least two of these organs have been found – one so complete that (to the total dismay of true historians and preservationists) it was 'restored' to playing condition.

The first written-down description of a self-playing organ did not appear until the 7th century AD. While it is tempting to take the simplistic viewpoint and say that this marked the invention of the automatic organ, this is a wholly unrealistic approach. One has to remember how very few people in the world could read, let alone write. And the survival of what little was written is but a tiny percentage of the original works. Again, there was a natural reserve about writing down a description of something with which everybody was familiar. Writing materials were themselves rare as was, no doubt, the time and

facility for writing, so why waste resources writing down something everybody else knew. If the automatic organ were at that time fairly common, then understandable nobody would bother to sit down and write a description of it. Social standing was another governing factor. If something were associated with the lower orders of Man, then it would not be described. Were it to be associated with the upper stratum of human life, the potential writer might not have access to it. No, the chronicles written down during the first thousand years of our more recent history are few and far between and those who could write with a news-reporter's insight on a new invention were very seldom in at the birth.

The big problem that string-hitting instruments all suffered from was the need to compromise between the force needed to hit the string hard, and the resistance created by the pins lifting the hammer. We will come up against this time and time again with the early mechanical piano and find that the problem was unsolved until the advent of the 'kicking-shoe' action. But in the 18th century, when this fine clock was made, for the music to stand any chance of being heard, the strings had to be struck very hard with only the force available from the barrel pin. For this reason the hammer heads were made of brass and the shanks were extremely long. As the barrel pin engaged with the hammer tail, the hammer was drawn a comparatively long distance from the strings so that when released a relatively light spring could bring the hammer hard to the string.

The oldest surviving automatic musical instrument in the world is a barrel-operated pipe organ that is built into the high outer wall of Salzburg Castle. This is known as the Salzburg Stier. Mind you, it is, as you might expect, a bit like the hundred year old broom that's had ten new handles and fifteen new heads. It has been rebuilt and 'restored' over the centuries, the last revamp being completed in 2002 to mark its 500th anniversary. This one, though, was conducted by an international team devoted to reverting the instrument to its original specification or as close as possible can be.

Played using a wooden cylinder or barrel having projecting pins on its surface, the Salzburg Stier thus employed technology that was pretty old even at the start of the 16th century. By the end of that century, Augsburg had become the European centre of the curious craft of clockwork-driven stringed instruments. The pre-eminence of Augsburg at so early a date is not difficult to explain. The principal seat of commerce in southern Germany, it was a place where wealthy merchants and their masters met and could expand cultural ties between the states of Germany. It thus enjoyed a rich trade in artefacts such as watches, jewellery, instruments and musical automata.

Surviving pieces from these earliest times are rare indeed, yet in the literary archives there are to be found various references to the existence of musical automata providing music from either the pinned barrel or the pinned wheel.

There was nothing new about stringed instruments. Their origins go back into pre-history and the dulcimer was mentioned in literature as early as *circa* 1400 while the virginal was well established by the sixteenth century. The curiously-named 'couched harp' or spinet was developed in the seventeenth and eighteenth centuries. These early string instruments featured just one string to each note. The first application of the pinned barrel to their playing seems to have come at about the beginning of the seventeenth century. In the year 1636, the French mathematician and scholar Marin Mersenne (1588-1648) wrote:

> One can still recall in our time the invention of drums or barrels employed to play several pieces of music on spinets without the use of the hand, for the Germans are so ingenious that they make them play more than fifty different pieces by means of several springs which, when set in motion, ballets with several figures leap and move to the rhythm of the songs without any need to touch the instrument after having wound the spring.

It seems likely that Mersenne had seen and heard such instruments but had not entirely understood the operation or principle of pinning tunes on barrels. It is extremely unlikely that as many as fifty tunes were pinned at so early a time. And no subsequent mechanical instrument known to me offers so vast a repertoire of music. This total probably refers to the total repertoire of an individual tune-pinner than the number of melodies he could hammer into a small barrel.

Mersenne's reference is not the sole one to be found. About sixty years later, the German mathematician and philosopher Erhard Weigel (1625-1699) wrote about such instruments of automatic music: '... especially at Nahe-Kussen near Augsburg, desks, chests and all kinds of decorative cabinet-work are made and sent far and wide throughout the whole world.'

A handful of named craftsmen are known to us today through their skilful surviving works. Among these stand out the names of Samuel Bidermann, father and son, and Veit Langenbucher who made musical automata of a very high order. Samuel Bidermann the elder was born at Ulm in 1540 and

died in Augsburg in 1622. He was a renowned organ builder and maker of spinets known as *ottavinos* — clockwork-driven, self-playing barrel-programmed instruments. After his death his work was continued by his sons, Samuel the younger (1600 until at least 1653) and Daniel (1603-1663).

Several known items by the Bidermanns are preserved to this day, all being of a size that would sit comfortably on a table, generally incorporating a clock or time-piece and also moving tableaux or displays of figures acting out the allegory of a parade or historical/mythological event.

Dulcimer-playing clocks were very popular between the last quarter of the 18th and the first quarter of the 19th centuries. Mostly emanating from Europe and from Germany and Austria in particular, these clocks were often of prodigious height for the simple reason that the 'strung back' or wood-framed dulcimer was straight-strung with thin wire strings. With a modern piano, the low notes are represented by strings that are heavily wrapped in copper wire so that they do not have to be very long: in these clocks that pre-dated wire-wrapping, a strung-back well over eight feet long was not uncommon. Here is a Dutch-made example with a novel feature. The two matching side chests form a significant duty. The left-hand one opens up to reveal a large number of spare tune-barrels, while the right-hand one opens out into a transformational flight of steps. This gives the owner easy access to the clock for winding and for changing the barrel.

These pieces featured mechanical spinets usually in combination with a small organ that played on pipes or regals (a pipe that makes its sound through 'beating' reeds like a shawm or modern oboe). Several of these remarkable instruments have survived, one being sold in New York in 2002 for around half a million dollars. Although a stringed instrument, remember that the spinet is more like the harpsichord than the piano in that it sounds the strings not by striking them with a hammer but by plucking them with a jack as in the full-sized instrument.

As we have seen, Augsburg was home to several craftsmen who made this style of stringed instrument. There is evidence that the Augsburg makers collaborated with each other on making certain pieces – that is when they were not at loggerheads as to whom had the rights to making musical automata (see Groiss).

One of this clearly elite team of craftsman was Matthäus Runggel. Again a man who had no qualms about how his name was spelled (two final letters 'l' have been seen), Runggel is known for several pieces, perhaps the most interesting and complete of which is the automaton clock known as DerHottentottentanz (*Dance of the Hottentots*) which is in the Staatliche Mathematisches und Physics museum in Dresden. Described in *Barrel Organ [73]*, it is unusual in that it incorporates a clockwork-driven barrel organ as well as a spinet action, both having the same compass of 16 notes. This is pictured in Bassermann-Jordan *[2]*. A very similar instrument with the same characteristic of a coupled barrel organ and spinet, again of 16 notes, features in an unsigned Augsburg musical clock now in Switzerland and illustrated in Chapuis's *Le Monde des Automats [16]*.

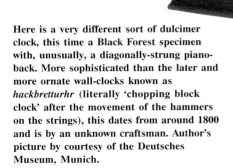

Here is a very different sort of dulcimer clock, this time a Black Forest specimen with, unusually, a diagonally-strung piano-back. More sophisticated than the later and more ornate wall-clocks known as *hackbretturhr* (literally 'chopping block clock' after the movement of the hammers on the strings), this dates from around 1800 and is by an unknown craftsman. Author's picture by courtesy of the Deutsches Museum, Munich.

This last-mentioned piece includes a rotating stage upon which a small display of automaton figures gyrate. Chapuis describes in detail the many features of this item, which include a most interesting and unusual method of moving the central figure on the principle, which later came to be known as the Roskopf watch barrel.

In 1979, a mechanism described as 'constructed by Rungel[*sic*] of Augsburg' was sold by auction in Geneva. This is described in the sale catalogue as combining spinet and organ mechanisms plus a clock, although the timepiece is not to be seen in the illustration. One of the two pictures illustrating this particular lot is taken from Chapuis and does not show the same instrument. Both mechanisms, though, share a strong family resemblance.

Similar in very many respects to these two pieces, both as regards the mechanism and the external appearance, is a small temple-like musical clock in the Nationaal Museum van Speelklok tot Pierement in Utrecht. This piece bears the monogram of Veit Langenbucher which is particularly interesting since the style and construction of the barrel and the shape of its pins are in accordance with those of Bidermann. Veit Langenbucher's monogram is a large letter V to the right-hand stroke of which is attached a slightly smaller letter B. The apex of the V is extended rightwards to underscore the letter B. Again this piece has 16 notes and plays three tunes on a small rectangular spinet. This is illustrated in *Music & Automata*, Spring 1983, p.13.

The late-lamented Time Museum in Rockford, Illinois, sold off many of its greatest treasures before the residue was installed as a Chicago city attraction. As mentioned briefly just now, in 2002, one of its most outstanding and important items, a Langenbucher clockwork spinet and organ automaton, was disposed of by public auction in New York. This was probably the finest of the Augsburg musical automata and had originally been acquired from a German family that might just have provided a link back to the piece's earliest days. In poor mechanical condition (I examined this while it was still in the possession of Time Museum founder Seth Attwood), it has nevertheless survived in perfect and largely unrestored condition, its major defect being the apparent transposition of wheels in its clockwork going train.

But it was a clockwork, barrel-playing spinet that is thought to have formed an item in the collection of musical instruments left by Henry VIII. In the catalogue prepared at the time of his death is a piece, mistakenly entered under the heading of 'virgynalles', described as being:

ITEM: An Instrumente that Goethe with a whele without playinge upon, of woode vernisshed yellowe and painted blewe with vi round plates of siluer pounced with anticke garnished with an edge of copper and guilte.

This was clearly a barrel-playing stringed instrument and although it subsequently 'disappeared', the description bears a striking similarity to several other clockwork table instruments known to have been built in the era before Henry's demise that survive to this day. In fact one of these pieces, in the Howard de Walden Collection at Dean Castle, Kilmarnock, may just be the one that Henry owned for, when it was restored to playing condition in 1957, it was found to match in almost every detail the description in the old catalogue – even down to the six silver medallions embossed and enriched with painted figures. One other clue to support a claim that this is indeed Henry's 'instrumente' is that the paintings, which appeared to have been added at some time in antiquity but after the original manufacture, depicted figures in Flemish-style costumes. While we always have to be very careful about circumstantial evidence, it is known that King Henry's Keeper of Musical Instruments was Flemish.

I believe there must have been a number of these instruments known at least amongst the well-to-do of the age for there is a curious allusion in an early performance of Shakespeare's *Cymbeline* that has survived. In Act IV, Scene 2 there is a cave scene in which the well-known dirge 'Fear no more the heat of the sun' appears. Now this must originally have been sung but, in the text as it has come down to us, we have Imogen's brother Arviragus commenting on himself and his brother Guiderius:

'And let us, Polydore, though now our voices have got the mannish crack, sing him to the ground'.

This suggests that their youthful voices have broken preventing them from singing. There is a chance that a mechanical instrument came to the rescue since, with the boy actors' voices disabled with the approach of manhood, the dirge had to be spoken to the accompaniment of mechanically-played music forming the solemn melody called for in the stage direction. Indeed, Belarius says:

'My ingenious instrument! Hark, Polydore, it sounds! But what occasion hath Cadwal now to give it motion? Hark!'

Good solid Shakespeare, but what were the chances of the Bard being aware of mechanical instruments of this kind? Well, he wrote *Cymbeline* in either 1609 or 1610 and its first performance was in 1611 (it was, though, not published until 1623). The bard seems to have mixed in fairly patrician circles and there is every possibility that he saw clockwork spinets and became intrigued enough to recall the event later. There is one more little piece of incidental evidence that I think is of curious importance. While so many of Shakespeare's dramatic comedies were written for the general public and the audiences of the Globe theatre in London, his final plays (including *Cymbeline*) were written for the more aristocratic and sophisticated audiences of the Blackfriars theatre – in other words people to whom clockwork spinets would not represent an unknown art or technology. It remains an open-ended case, though, because whatever we may suppose (or choose to believe) nobody can ever be certain now. Enough books and theses have been written on the bard without confusing the issue over 'an Instrumente that Goethe with a whele...'

There is no doubt, though, that these mechanical spinets were valuable and scarce items even at that time. Some indication of that value is gleaned from the fact that comparatively so many of them (possible half a dozen) have survived. In other words, they were taken care of. There is one in Nuremberg's Germanisches Nationalmuseum and this seems to be the work of Samuel Bidermann Jnr – which means it was after Shakespeare's era (he was born about 1564 and died in 1616) and dates from about 1640.

Other survivors include one at Donauwörth near Augsburg where, in the Fürstlich Oettingen-Wallenstein'sche Bibliothek und Kunstsammlungen at the Schloss Harburg near Donauworth itself near Augsburg is a piece dated 1606. This is signed on the jackrail *Johannes Bidermann MDCVI*. Another, this time in St Petersburg's Institute for Scientific Research on the Theatre & Music, is signed *Samuel Biderman*

Augusta, 1627. The Bidermann family spelled their name sometimes with one letter 'n', mainly with two, and Augusta was the Latin name for Augsburg, centre of the Holy Roman Empire and taking its name from the Roman Emperor Augustus. This particular example has a compass of three octaves F – f, and has a small keyboard of 37 manual keys. The same collection in the one-time Leningrad (so called from 1924 until 1991) holds a further example which, while undated, is larger with a compass spanning three octaves and a sixth – E – c, 45 keys.

Of the same number of keys, but of a somewhat different 'short-octave' C – c compass, is another clockwork spinet in the Schlesisches Museum in Breslau. Here the barrel plays six tunes the titles of which are written on a label. The first is a 'joyful procession announced by the blowing of the trumpeter' by Jr Kay and relating to the May procession held in Nuremberg. This suggests that the piece was made to mark the occasion of the reception of the Emperor Matthias by the City of Nuremberg in 1612. Whether made before or after the event is uncertain but it carries a label reading *Samuel Bidermann, Instrumentmacher in Augsburg* suggesting Samuel Bidermann the elder and can be no later than the year of inscription.

This second view, this time from the back looking forwards, shows how the automaton drive shaft is operated. In an age before bevel gearing, 'the miller's turn' was employed – a reference to the engineering of windmills where frequently a rotary drive was turned at right angles by the sideways meshing of long-toothed wheels.

Probably the work of his son yet bearing the identical label is a piece thought to date from 1625-30 and today in Vienna's Kunsthistorisches Museum. Believed slightly later in origin, a further undated specimen in the same museum has a C – c four-octave compass and plays six melodies. This instrument bears four identical labels each reading *Samuel Biderman, Instrumentmacher in Augsburg*.

Two final pieces are worth mentioning. The first, bearing the Latinised form of the address as *Samuel Biderman Augusta*, turned up in Paris. Associated with the former Old Savoye Collection there and later with the renowned Tagger collection, it is described (in Donald Boalch *Makers of the Harpsichord & Clavichord*, Oxford, 1974) as being of 'two-octaves and eight notes'. And finally we look to the Gustav Adolf collection in Uppsala where an unsigned and undated instrument survives. Acquired by the City Council of Augsburg in 1632 from Philip Hainhofer, musical automaton maker, it was presented to the King of Sweden.

Marks other than signed labels or inscriptions on these instruments link them directly with Augsburg. All workers who crafted such items were required to be members of the City guild and this allowed them to use the Augsburg hallmark which was a stylised pine-cone, usually stamped into the wood in several places. This appears almost like an egg in a shallow egg-cup, the 'egg' being cross-hatched. Another mark is a small rectangle containing the capital letters EBEN meaning 'ebony'.

Other characteristics of the Bidermann instruments include having the naturals of the keyboard overlaid with ivory, the sharps being of black-stained pear wood with ebony veneer. All three instruments have a wooden barrel for the automatic mechanism. These bear the characteristic ruling and dividing practised by the Bidermanns, the surface of the barrel being scored laterally and circumferentially to produce a grid of small squares. Each of these squares is divided between the six tunes of Items 1 and 2 and the four of Item 3. Vertical markings show the lengths of four crochets and the divisions numbered around the circumference in Indian ink. The pins of the quavers and the repeated crochets are of steel whilst those of the shorter notes are of brass, the longer values having brass pins bent over into a hooked shape like an inverted letter 'L'.

By removing the mechanism from the case one can see the extremely simple construction almost as fresh today as when it left its maker's workshop more than four and a half centuries ago. This view looks from front to back and shows details of the jack action. The long pivoted lifting pieces run along the bottom of the case while each jack is contained in a channelled box-like guide.

In all these clockwork instruments, a spring in a brass spring barrel drives the movement with winding by catgut fusee. The actual gear train differs between the instruments as might be expected with a complex piece that is hand-made meaning that every item is unique to that example.

Talking of Samuel Bidermann, earlier I mentioned Veit Langenbucher. The family Langenbucher was extensive and were specialists in the making of musical automata and musical instruments. Sorting out today who made what is very complex and rather uncertain – there was no hard and fast rule that said makers had to put their names on the items they made. What is known is that the brothers Samuel and Daniel Bidermann succeeded to their craft from Samuel Bidermann the elder who, presumably, was their father. As we have seen, they made clockwork spinets with barrel-playing mechanisms and, usually, keyboards for manual playing.

Achilles and Balthasar Langenbucher seem to have specialised in the making of the musical components of automata which, in the instruments that I have seen, comprises the spinets and the organs, possibly even the complete musical mechanism excluding the musically-pinned barrel.

What is known is that Veit Langenbucher, who was a prolific maker of these musical mechanisms, was a pupil of Achilles Langenbucher. The relationship between them, however, is quite unknown and it may have even been two distinct same-named families. Suffice it to say that Veit made and marked many instruments, his distinctive mark being a simple monogram of the two letters 'V' and 'L' represented as a broad letter 'V' having the horizontal line of the 'L' affixed to its point.

For the story of an unusual lawsuit over the making of musical automata and concerning the Bidermann and Langenbucher families, *see* Groiss *[40]* but be warned that the original German text also contains the Langenbucher family tree, stupidly elided from the English title. However, the complete article, in English and with the missing *Stammbaum*, is to be found in *Music & Automata*, Vol. 1, No. 1, *pp.*10 *et seq*: this also illustrates a Veit Langenbucher organ-spinet.

If these wonderful pieces playing their 16th century dance repertoire were the finest examples of Southern German cultural art and craft, their very fragility served to underscore the vitally important part that they played in the history of their times.

Their survival was not inevitable, and the 1939-45 War exacted a terrible cull on musical automata of this rich period. Far too numerous are the items that were lost, the greater majority of these being in German museums that were in the line of fire. One piece still talked of in museum circles was the marvellous automatic spinet that closely resembled Bidermann workmanship which existed in Salzburg's Carolina Augusteum Museum. Cruel though this, and many other losses were, even more regrettable was that before the war very few people appreciated just what they were and the immense value of the music that they preserved. Nobody thought to examine and study them. A few contemporary musicologists showed sufficient curiosity to look at one or two pieces, but they were the exceptions. How we revere today the studies of Albert Protz who photographed and drew just a few of these works of great craft and art. Thankfully, he also transcribed the music of some as well and published this information in his magnificent study *[88]* that appeared just after the war began. Cruelly his book was also a victim of the war and most of the copies were destroyed before proper publication could be achieved.

These clockwork spinets were made in three distinct varieties. First was the barrel-and-finger model that combined manual playing via a little keyboard with mechanical playing via a pinned wooden barrel. Then there was the wholly mechanical instrument in a cabinet with no keyboard. And finally there was the mechanically-operated instrument that was built into a clock so that it could be set to play by the clock mechanism itself (i.e. every three hours) in which case there was always provision for a 'manual override' to let the owner operate it at any time he chose.

All of the instruments I have so far described here pluck their strings with properly contrived plectra. Another form, nearer to the piano in playing system, is the dulcimer in which the strings are struck by hammers. Almost always associated with very grand clocks, the so-called dulcimer clock (in German *harfenuhr*, mistakenly but popularly translated as 'harp-playing clock') first appeared around the beginning of the 18th century. The wooden-framed and lightly-strung dulcimer was arranged vertically behind the clockwork and the hammer mechanism was directly comparable to that used in the carillon clock. The music was pinned on a barrel in the same way.

Because it produced a soft and delicate sound rather like the spinet, it led itself to the playing of high-class music. One Berlin maker, I C Kruger, produced several pieces that played music especially composed by C P E Bach. This is illustrated in Ord-Hume *Musical Clock [82]*.

Essentially an adjunct to a quality-made timepiece, and so far not found on its own as an automatic musical instrument, the harp or dulcimer clock was made in Germany and also in the Low Countries more or less contemporaneously with its more popular cousin, the flute-playing clock. Its period appears to have been from the first half of the eighteenth century through to the middle of the nineteenth century. Large numbers were built for the aristocracy and the common rich but even so, very few examples survive, no doubt because of the fact that they needed fairly constant retuning and thus were probably considered by their owners to be more trouble than they were worth. They also had the disadvantage that, as with the flute-playing clock, they were frequently very tall (sometimes in excess of 14 feet) and could only stand in a room with a high ceiling: no use in the modern home with its 8-foot-high plasterboard.

Thirty or so years ago, one of these dulcimer clocks appeared in England. It was derelict and, since the dulcimer soundboard was badly split and warped, not a note would sound. There was no indication as to what it might play. The musical compass was very large: no fewer than 49 notes comprising C, D, E, thence fully chromatic to d³. Because of the length of the open-stringed dulcimer (of 8ft pitch – the same as a normal piano's 'middle C') it was a very, very tall clock and stood well over 12 feet in height. Accompanying it were two matching chests having dummy drawer fronts. In one of these, a dozen spare pinned wooden music barrels (each playing two melodies) were stored and these were accessed by lifting the hinged top of the chest like a lid. The difficulty of changing the barrels at such a height was addressed by the other chest, for it opened out into a sort of 'library steps' staircase that allowed you to climb in safety to the giddy heights of the clock face.

When this wonderful clock was fully restored with a rebuilt and restrung dulcimer the first barrel turned out to play two of the pieces that CPE Bach composed specially for *harfenuhr*. This sort of find may be infrequent but when it comes it is a rare moment indeed!

While these dulcimer clocks were of the very highest quality and played equally fine music, there was a demand for a lower-cost, simpler string-playing musical clock. If Berlin was the centre of the elite *harfenuhr*, the Black Forest became the hub for the somewhat coarser *hackbrettuhr*. The name, mind you, was rather tongue-in-cheek because in German it translates as 'chopping-board clock', an allusion to the 'thrashing about' of the larger hammers on the strings rather like a butcher with his chopping block. With compasses seldom in excess of twenty-one notes and more usually 16 (the diatonic scale c¹ to c³ with an additional f#²), these were immensely popular and could indeed be very musical: remember that this simple scale was that selected by Joseph Haydn for his twelve simplest organ-clock compositions. For details of some of these clocks see Haspels *[45]* and for details of the Haydn musical clocks and their music see Ord-Hume *[76]*.

Looking down inside the open top of the Veit Langenbucher clockwork spinet seen in the previous illustration, one can see the 16-note spinet, soundboard (with delicate paper rosette) and 'straight' bridge. The row of jacks that pluck the strings is situated under the wide dark-wood cover at the left end. The floral painting on the soundboard is a unique feature. The small lever to the left of centre in the lid engages with the rotating arm that protrudes through the soundboard and is provided to operate the automaton display in the cupola on top of the ebony case.

It is known that the earliest automatic instrument to be perfected was the organ and this attained musical perfection at a very early age. To attain a similar level of perfection with a stringed instrument was much harder. To understand why we have to look at the musical programme that was common at the time – the pinned wooden barrel. Now compare the two musical mechanisms, that of the barrel organ with that of the barrel piano, and a fundamental difference appears. In the case of the organ, the projection in the surface of the barrel serves to raise a key that controls a pallet in a wind chest. In other words very little force need be applied to the key in order to perform a simple job – that of admitting wind in a controlled manner, in this case to the organ pipe.

The dulcimer, spinet or piano, however, must look for its operation to the barrel projection and a hammer connection that is so arranged that a blow of relatively considerable force can be applied, via the hammer, to the musical string. A minimum of three times the force is called for. The stringed instrument therefore has to be of much more robust a construction than the corresponding pipe organ. This means more driving power (a larger spring motor or a heavier weight to work the mechanism). Where one was operating a simple valve, the other was setting in motion a mechanism! From the mechanical aspect, the dulcimer mechanism had to be much more robust.

The engineering was thus involved and called for a thorough knowledge of the mechanics of levers in order to succeed. All this would lead, almost inevitably, to the first keyboard instrument that produced its sound by striking the strings with hammers.

Another maker of this type of instrument was Veit Langenbucher, also of Augsburg. This miniature temple contains a spinet and automaton display and dates from the early part of the 17th century. Here the Author (left) and Dr Jan Jaap Haspels, director/conservator of the Nationaal Museum van Speelklok tot Pierement in Utrecht, examine a particularly fine specimen.

As we have seen, long before the first pianoforte was made, the art of programming music for automatic playing was fairly well developed. I shall come back to that again in a moment.

Creating a mechanical orchestra seems to have been a recurring goal through the latter half of the 18th century and the 19th centuries. Developed from the barrel organ, one of the earliest was that created by the Black Forest émigré, Johann Georg Strasser who sold it in St. Petersburg for 10,000 roubles in 1801. The name 'orchestrion' was coined by the Abbé Georg

Joseph Vogler (b.1749; d. 1849) and given to a large organ with which he toured England and the Continent in 1789. During the 19th and early 20th centuries, the term 'orchestrion' was applied to any complex mechanical instrument played by pinned barrels, perforated cards or paper rolls.

The father of Pëtr Ilyich Tchaikovsky lived in a large house in St Petersburg where also resided a large orchestrion organ made by Strasser. The young Tchaikovsky, who was born in 1840, was brought up listening to the works of Mozart, Rossini and others performed on this instrument. And when fresh music was required, a local skilled clock-maker provided new pinned barrels.[1]

From Maelzel's Panharmonicon and Kaufmann's Chordaulodion to Winkel's Componium, orchestrions were capable of performing the popular classical repertoire to perfection and makers such as Welte and Imhof & Mukle excelled in this craft. From their origins as a development of the organ, the form evolved centred around the mechanical piano. These so-called piano-orchestrions included percussion effects and frequently a pipe organ.

Piano-orchestrions began as barrel-operated instruments and there were many makers in Bohemia and Prussia, France and the Low Countries. Soon the barrel was replaced by perforated paper music-rolls allowing more compact and musically variable instruments to be made. This industry reached its zenith in the United States of America during the period 1900-1925, but was gone by the early 1930s.

The pinned wooden barrel represented the highest development of the art and its use and capabilities were understood at least as early as the eighth century AD. And remember that the oldest surviving barrel organ is dated 1502. So it was that when Bartolomeo Cristofori, born in Padua in 1655, built his first arpicembalo chi fa il piano e il forte (a harpsichord that produces soft and loud) in about 1698 the technique for automatic playing was already in existence.

People have argued long and hard over whom it was that actually invented the piano. Historians generally accept that Cristofori was the father of the instrument and without doubt it was he who solved the two most vital problems over making a string-striking action – the free-moving hammer escapement and the hammer back-check. Others, of course, have claimed earlier inventors. A Dutch-made instrument constructed a century before that of the Italian had small hammers attached to the keys, but no dampers. This is claimed to have been made for a French nobleman and was probably no more than an isolated example of experimental work. And a rare manuscript in the Bibliothèque Nationale in Paris appears to describe an instrument of the pianoforte type, that is to say with hammers to strike the strings. This is dated 1430, an incredible three centuries before Christofori made his first instrument and became the accredited inventor.

There were others such as Frenchman Jean Marius who submitted four plans for clavecins à maillets (hammer harpsichords) for examination by the Academy of Sciences in Paris in 1716, the great German keyboard instrument maker Gottfried Silbermann of Freiburg, and finally Christoph Gottlieb Schröter from Saxony. None of these offers incontrovertible evidence of a challenge to the claim of Cristofori at the end of the 17th century. While the arguments rumble on still, even as early as this epoch positive if more primitive means of mechanical playing were understood. The piano thus grew up in an era when it was virtually inevitable that sooner or later it would receive the same treatment as the pipe organ and become capable of automatic playing.

We have been talking, perhaps glibly, about the pinned barrel without going into the musical aspects very deeply. It's time to get a few facts into our minds about music and pins. The translation of music into the pins on a barrel is an ancient art probably first described in print at the beginning of the 17th century. In 1615, French engineer Salomon de Caus published a book entitled *Les Raisons des Forces Mouvantes [15]* and illustrated this with a detailed drawing showing a cylinder pinned with the first six bars of a madrigal by Alessandro Striggio (1535-1590). This seminal work was followed, in 1618, by the English philosopher and physician Robert Fludd (1574-1637) who Latinised his name as de Fluctibus who described four different types of barrel or cylinder in his book *De Naturae Simia [31]*. The German Jesuit mathematician and writer on music Athanasius Kircher (1602-1680) followed in 1650 with his no less a learned treatise *Musurgia Universalis [52]*.

The art was expanded in 1775 by the French naturalist, mechanic and priest, Father Joseph Marie Engramelle (1727-1781) *[29]* and then taken to its most detailed conclusion in 1778 by another monk, Father François Bedos de Celles. Bedos showed by way of wonderful engravings precisely how to translate music into barrel pins and his work has inspired generations since. His extraordinary four-volume work, *L'Art de Facteur d'Orgues*, dealt extensively with every aspect of organ-building and has remained the principal text on the subject for the past two and a quarter centuries. The barrel-pinning aspect was featured in Ord-Hume *[72]* and is currently described, together with some pinning arrangements, [in *83*].

Since earliest times there had been felt a need for some means of recording musical performances. Before the development of reliable pneumatic and, later, electro-magnetic music-recording systems during the first quarter of the 20th century, music-lovers and musicians alike were aware that music, like speech, was a fleeting thing that could only vaguely be consigned to memory. The wish was two-fold. First to preserve the extempore renditions of composers and performers which, as history relates, were sometimes astonishing both in variety and in length not to mention creativity. And second was the need for some method of transferring music from the keyboard to the barrel without the lengthy process of 'marking out'.

An English cleric, The Rev John Creed, proposed a machine 'to write down extempore voluntaries as fast as any master shall be able to play them upon and Organ, Harpsichord, etc'. Unfortunately, news of this was not published until 1747, after the good clergyman had passed on.

Earlier, the Swiss mathematician and writer on music Leonard Euler (1707-1783) had come up with a design for a machine for doing just this. It was eventually built in Berlin by an engineer named Hohfeld in about 1752

Looking for all the world like a small portable writing desk, the Samuel Bidermann clockwork compound spinet is seen here complete and open ready for playing by hand. On the side of the case at the back can be seen the controls for starting and stopping the clockwork as well as changing the tune using a knife/bolt/lever system. On the lower rail near the centre can be seen the hole for the winding key.

and consisted of two revolving cylinders between which a long band of paper was passed. The positions and durations of notes played were marked by a series of pencils connected to the keyboard keys. This machine was preserved in the Berlin Academy of Arts & Sciences until the building was destroyed in a fire.

How reliable Euler's system was is impossible to judge at this point in time. However, the name that Euler proposed for his machine – the Melograph – remained and from it was named the process by which it noted down performed music – Melography.

Meanwhile a German inventor named Johann Friedrich Unger (1716-1781) of Einbeck challenged Euler's claim, saying he had invented a similar machine in 1745. His claim remains unsubstantiated. But there were others with the same intent such as a Frenchman named Carreyre who, in 1827, presented to the French Institute a 'melographic piano'. And then much later in 1881 Jules Carpentier exhibited at the Paris Exposition a 'repeating Melograph' attached to a small harmonium. This, said the inventor, would write down ordinary music played extemporaneously on the instrument *dans le langage*[sic] *de Jacquard* by electro-magnetically punching holes in paper to produce a 'note-sheet' which could then be played back on another instrument. I shall explain the reference to Jacquard in due course.

Rather more sophisticated is this compound barrel-and-finger clockwork spinet with regals which was made about 1575 by Samuel Bidermann of Augsburg. Now preserved in the Germanisches Nationalmuseum, Nuremberg, the piece is seen here in dismantled condition with the keyboard, fusee-wound iron clockwork motor and wooden barrel removed from beneath the organwork and the spinet which is seen standing at the back. Notice the curious long single-legged 'staples' on the barrel which produce the long organ notes.

This question of recording a musical performance remained a recurring theme throughout the 19th century and numerous inventors tackled it and a number of patents appeared in Europe and America. All were more or less made redundant when the first music-roll recording pianos appeared around the beginning of the 20th century.

Among the inventors, though, we find some interesting propositions, some verging on the preposterous, but all involving complicated machinery. What is probably the most detailed of these devices was that of a Liverpudlian man named Cantelo who was granted British Patent No.22,282 on November 16th 1895.

John Louis Cantelo lived at 154 Selborne Street, Liverpool, and described his profession as that of book-keeper. His invention, described as a 'useful attachment for pianofortes or other musical instruments having keyboards...', used bell-cranks that conveyed the movement of each keyboard key via a thin cord passing over pulley-wheels to a complex clockwork driven printing head that converted key depressions into dots and dashes on a travelling spool of paper.

One assumes that Mr Cantelo must have built one of his machines yet it is curious that nothing further was ever heard of this friction-rich proposal. Pneumatics were the first to dispense with mechanisms of this type, followed by electric solenoid-driven systems.

Reverting to the pinned barrel, the notation for arranging music on the surface of a barrel or cylinder has to be transcribed effectively at right-angles to the normal notation for printed music. The complete length of the music, as measured by the number of bars, now becomes the length of the piece of paper which in turn is equal to the circumference of the barrel. The bars are marked horizontally across the paper from side to side, and the various notes and their lengths are 'written' vertically.

In order to set a piece of music of, say, forty bars length on to a barrel, the circumference of the barrel is taken as the length of the music and also the paper pattern. This length is then ruled to produce forty horizontal spaces. The paper is then subdivided again, this time vertically and at a spacing equal to that of the fingers or keys of the playing mechanism. This grid is now marked out for the tune in accordance with the musical notation.

Now it is stuck onto the surface of the barrel and the pins or bridges (in the case of an organ) inserted. It is common to put more than one tune on each barrel, and therefore the paper is then marked over with different tunes, each one being displaced laterally a given distance equal to the lateral shift of the barrel needed to bring another set of tune pins under the keyframe.

Again, once the master strip of ruled paper has been created, this pattern may be used for marking similar pieces of paper, either by 'pricking' the location of each pin through the paper or by printing by lithography. It is only necessary to transfer the location of each musical note and the ground ruling or grid is of no importance.

Now this type of musical arrangement is known as 'metronomic' because every note is given its precise location and value. By comparison, when music is played by hand, it is much more free-flowing partly because the notes and phrasing is interpreted by a human brain rather than a precisely-set pin. One is reminded of the comment of Artur Schnabel to the *Chicago Times* when, in response to some question from the reporter, he replied: 'I play the notes the same as anyone else, but it is the silences between the notes where I put the expression.'

Mechanically there were considerable problems to face if any expression was to be put into a piano played by a barrel. The mechanical difficulties to be faced in reproducing in any way faithfully the tones and colours of stringed keyboard instruments by mechanical means were far greater than those needed to achieve the same ends for the mechanical organ. In fact comparison between piano and organ was a 'chalk and cheese' job. When, in 1817, organ-builders Flight & Robson of London completed their remarkable Apollonicon organ, they were confident in proclaiming that it could perform with a degree of perfection at least equal to that of an accomplished performer. Equipped with sets of three barrels, which between them played whole overtures and lengthy operatic selections, this instrument could interpret to a wondrous degree.

Many great organists of the time also performed on this manual and self-acting instrument, which had no fewer than five separate co-lateral keyboard consoles. Later rebuilt to an even larger design with six separate keyboard consoles, the Apollonicon always included in its performances a popular operatic overture performed from its three barrels. These were claimed by many to be note-perfect when compared with the orchestral scores.

A high degree of perfection from the barrel-programmed pipe organ was a practical reality by the time Queen Victoria came to the throne. By the time of the Great Exhibition in 1851, European makers such as Blessing, Welte, Kaufmann and others had taken the art to new peaks.

Yet still, at this time, the mechanical barrel piano was struggling hard, trying its best to offset its uncompromising tone and its inability to attain either perfection of interpretation or purity of tone. It could not be a pianoforte, merely a mechanical string-hammerer. Subtlety of expression was quite beyond it.

There were many inventions thought up to improve the quality of its performance. These, in being reliant on the state of the musical engineering of the time, tended to be of indifferent effect, some working to a greater or, more frequently, lesser extent. Most suffered the defects of incorrect theory and inherent impracticability. Even the drawing-room barrel-and-finger pianos of John Longman, about which more in a moment, were restricted to playing metronomically-pinned music either soft or loud.

If the barrel-organ was well established at the beginning of the 16th century, then the barrel-operated piano was, by comparison, a very late starter. It began uncompromisingly enough as a street instrument – a rather coarse machine, basic and without much in the way of refinement. It was a device to bring music to the public but, more to the point, it was the means for the mendicant to earn alms. Put simply, it was hired out to those who needed to go begging. It was an object of derision and, frequently, a public nuisance like the organ-grinders with which it associated.

The earliest automatic stringed instruments known to survive comprise a small clutch of spring-driven clockwork table spinets from the middle of the 16th century. Some of these are actually compound instruments that combine a spinet and an organ, usually provided with small harsh reed pipes that are known as regals. Pictured here is a strange 'octave spinet' which is believed to be the oldest surviving of such pieces. It comes from the collection formed by the late Lord Howard de Walden at Dean Castle, Kilmarnock in Scotland and the legend is that it was acquired from the estate of King Henry VIII after his death. Unfortunately this cannot be substantiated.

There is no certainty as to its date or place of invention but it seems to have emerged towards the latter part of the fourth quarter of the 18th century. Researches in Italy by Dr Antonio Latanza suggest that it was an Italian invention and that the mass exodus of Italian workers and craftsmen at the start of the 19th century resulted in the almost instantaneous spread of the style and technology across the northern hemisphere from Moscow, Berlin and London through to New York, Boston and Philadelphia.

Something of a sea-change was about to take place with the self-acting piano. While the Italians were championing the idea of the barrel piano as outdoor entertainment and popular music, there were those who saw the instrument as part of the domestic furniture in an environment where it might dispense genteel music suitable for the home. This gave us elegant indoor barrel pianos such as John Longman's tall cabinet piano driven by a weight, or Imhof's impressive clockwork sideboard piano. London makers gave us combined barrel and keyboard pianos that could carry on playing while the pianist went out for a break. The common barrel piano was now refined into the elegant piece of drawing-room furniture.

Nobody was to know that the greatest challenge for the domestic piano lay directly ahead. And nobody could imagine the enormous developments that were just around the corner.

Pinned barrels in barrel organs, musical clocks and cylinder musical boxes could only play music of a fixed length. This length had to be a multiple of the diameter of the cylinder. Where, for example, four or more tunes were played, each tune was the length of time needed for the cylinder to make one revolution. In practice it was a little bit shorter since the barrel had to have a clear, unpinned strip along its length at the point where the tunes could be changed by sliding the barrel sideways. This was to avoid likely damage to the tips of the movable keys and the barrel pins should the two collide sideways. If a tune was too long to conform to this requirement, then it had to be abbreviated: if it was too short, it was either left that way or it was 'padded out' to a degree and in a style that reflected the skill (or lack of skill) practised by the barrel arranger.

Some cylinders, instead of simply turning once to play a tune, could make a number of revolutions in order to play one long and continuous melody. A feature generally associated with high-quality musical clocks, this was achieved by moving the barrel sideways very slightly while it rotated, generally by using a cam (see Ord-Hume [81 and 82]). In practice, the length of tune, although extended considerably, was finally limited by the number of times the barrel could be shifted on its spiral or cam before the width between the keyframe keys was all used up. Normally, spiral barrels could move seven turns on a screw before a special 'stop' mechanism lifted the keyframe well clear of the barrel surface and allowed the barrel to move back to the beginning point again.

The skill of the music arranged was thus to ensure that the music was arranged to play at the right speed to fill the available playing time. Musically it was not a universally good system if a melody had to be played in a fixed duration. If the cylinder or barrel offered a small choice of lengths available, then those lengths were themselves too few and inflexible. What was needed was a musical programme that was not tied to the circumferential length of a barrel.

In 1846, this seemingly irreducible restrictive limitation to artistic expression was broken by a French inventor and piano-manufacturer named Alexandre Debain (1809-1877). His idea was to take the principle of the pinned barrel but instead of having a cylindrical pinned surface he 'flattened it out' to create a series of wooden boards that could be of different and differing lengths. Each board had a toothed steel rack along one edge so that it could be drawn through a type of keyframe. Debain called his mechanism the Antiphonal and it could be fitted to an ordinary piano keyboard or even that of an organ, and played by gently pumping a ratchet handle up and down. This was a wholly-mechanical player, the projections on the boards (which Debain called *planchettes*) depressing levers at the keyframe that pushed down the piano keys. This would be styled a key-top player.

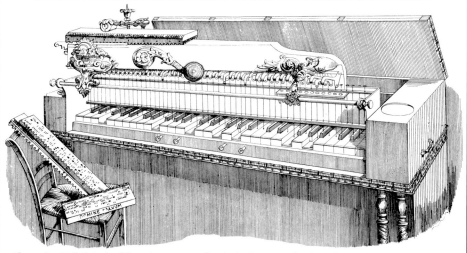

THE FIRST KEY-TOP MECHANICAL PIANO PLAYER
Add-on players for keyboard instruments started with barrels: Debain's revolutionary Antiphonel used pinned wooden boards

Alexander Debain's Antiphonel was a mechanical player mechanism that could be fitted to any keyboard instrument for automatic playing. It appeared in several forms and was later built into an upright case as a keyboardless piano, and with a keyboard as an automatic-and-finger piano. This drawing, reproduced from the original 1846 Patent application, shows the earliest key-top model of the Antiphonel with sections of the musical programme – the wooden planchettes – on a close-by chair

Each piece of music was represented by a stack of these planchettes. Numbers on their ends showed the playing order with the advantage that sections could be repeated as required simply by taking the required section of music and putting it through the playing mechanism a second (or more) time.

By the time of the Great Exhibition held in London in 1851, Debain had refined his system further and besides the key-top player introduced a dual mechanical and finger instrument that had the Antiphonel mechanism built into it. As well as this, he had a mechanical-only played Antiphonel piano that had no keyboard. The selling advantage of this instrument was clear. The planchettes were of varying lengths from 4-inches to 24-inches in length and a section eight inches long could contain as much music as was written on a page of manuscript. The limitation on length of music played no longer existed.

Debain's planchettes addressed one of the barrel-piano's problems – the limitation in tune-length – but not the other, that of bulk. A pile of planchettes needed to play music could be impressive if it was a long piece of music. To give the performer any chance of keeping them in the right order, they had to be kept in a wooden case, one for each tune. If length was solved, the bulkiness of the music was anything but cured.

It was another Frenchman who came up with an answer, although it has to be said that he probably had no idea what the problem was! This is because his invention was for a system with an application far and away from pianos. His name was mechanician and inventor Joseph Marie Jacquard (1752-1834). Now Jacquard was a silk-weaver who applied his creative mind to devising some sort of attachment to a loom that would enable patterns to be woven automatically. Between 1801 and 1808 he laboured to devise a system of punched cards which could be 'read' by the mechanism that controlled the needles. In other words, a card that was punched with a pattern of holes could be used to control a loom so that the pattern could be woven. In effect it was precursor to those punched-card computers that ruled our lives in the 1950s. These were the invention of the American inventor Herman Hollerith (1860-1929).

It is the burden of inventors to be misunderstood and poor old Jacquard was not spared from this. Because his modified loom dispensed with the skills of the operator's hands, his fellow silk weavers considered their livelihoods threatened and disrupted its introduction. After an uphill struggle to convince his critics of its benefits, it was accepted and by 1812, some 11,000 were in use in France. Jacquard's system revolutionised the weaving industry from that moment forwards and the descendents of his invention control looms the world over to this very day.

This inspired the French inventor Claude Félix Seytre to use perforated card to the playing of a musical féliment (the *autopanphone*) in 1842. The important part about this invention was that the cardboard was employed to perform a mechanical movement on levers. This meant that the cardboard, already very thick, was nevertheless not very durable. Seytre's idea was thus inspirational but his experimental autopanphone was not commercially viable because it was technically faulted.

Programming by punched card created the computer of the 19th century and eventually the system was applied to control the playing of fairground organ and then the mechanical piano. Working on the principle of the Ariston organette and the fairground pipe organ, a keyframe was used to play the action. Like Seytre's invention, it was neither practical nor durable. More development was needed and the idea of using air as a moderator and power unit gradually grew in the minds of engineers. The punched card could now serve merely as a sliding valve rather than a moving lever.

It took a while and it was not until 1884 that the first piano-player was seen in London. In that year a furniture exhibition was held at north London's Agricultural Hall, Islington. Here, surrounded by the normal trappings of a mid-Victorian furnishing show, was a Chickering grand piano – and in front of it stood a cabinet player called The Miranda Pianista. A contemporary report describes the thing in some detail:

> Projecting from one side of the 'Miranda' is a series of wooden levers or fingers exactly the width of the pianoforte keys to be operated upon. These levers are moved in accordance with

holes in perforated cards, as in the Jacquard loom, a series of small pneumatic valves (worked automatically by a reservoir bellows) producing the motive power. On placing the Miranda in position in front of the piano and turning a handle, the perforated cards are drawn through, and the mechanical fingers are moved with an exactness not always obtained even by expert pianoforte players. The matter of stronger or weaker touch is possible, to the extent desired by the performer. Further, the ordinary pedals of the pianoforte are extended and carried through to the front of the invention so as to be under the control of the performer.

This early punched-card piano was patented in all European countries and was handled in London by Ellis Parr whose business, The Automatic Musical Instrument Company of 27, Penton Street, London N, was one of the earliest trade houses to handle mechanical musical instruments in Britain. Parr already held the agencies for several German makers of ordinary pianofortes and was the co-patentee of the disc-playing musical box *[Ord-Hume, 81]*. After the showing at the Agricultural Hall, Parr laboured hard to set up his trade outlets for the Miranda and its manufacture. However, the whole enterprise was about to grind to an unexpected and no doubt expensive halt.

In January 1885, the musical industries trade paper *Musical Opinion* reported that Ellis Parr had been appointed the London agent for the instrument and that its manufacture was to be undertaken in Germany by the Hanover piano makers Karl Haake (established in 1836). This was, in fact, a logical choice since Parr already had the London agency for Haake pianos. The report went on to say that instruments would be placed 'very shortly' before the trade.

The following July, Parr published the first advertisement for the Miranda Pianista from his new address in London, 99 Oxford Street. It was now ready for delivery into the trade.

What happened next combined bombshell with farce for the following issue of the paper contained a prominent message directed to the trade from the Charterhouse Street, London, offices of the Paris-based musical-instrument firm of Jerome Thibouville-Lamy.

> I beg to state that I bought the patent of the instrument named the 'Pianista' in 1872. Since then I have improved the instrument in many ways: my last patent is dated 1883 . The Miranda Pianista is simply a variation of my old system. Yours very truly, J . Thibouville-Lamy (10 August 1885).

The effect of this on the trade reaction to the Miranda need only to be imagined. What happened regarding the Parr-Haake deal is unknown and it is worth noting that in April of that year Parr and his company had confidently anticipated a dividend of nearly 30 per cent on the projected first year of trading. And this had appeared in the press. Significantly no further reference to the Miranda appeared after this, Parr's company, Automatic Music Company of 3, Copthall Buildings, London, EC, quietly folded and within a year Parr had retired from business.

While all this was going on, the Thibouville-Lamy Pianista appeared playing books of perforated and folded cardboard music. This enjoyed a limited success, selling well in Europe. A curious feature was that if the operating handle was turned slowly, the music came out equally slow and quite soft. Turning the handle rapidly speeded up the music and made it louder! The basis, surely, of a rather rudimentary expression system!

Ellis Parr was only one of many who lost money and reputation in the music trade for various reasons. Like the Miranda Pianists, there were many inventions that were to contribute to the turbulent history of mechanical music. Piano players that were operated by perforated cardboard discs and owed much of their operating principles to the diminutive organette were just another dead end amidst many, for the real answer lay not in punched card but in perforated paper.

While claims as to who was the first to use paper as a travelling valve for a pneumatic system are legion, and many, justifiably, claimed by John McTammany [61], the perfection of a paper-operated piano-playing system came not from Britain or America but from Southern Germany. When in 1887, the Welte Company of Freiburg im Breisgau finally perfected and patented just such a system, the practical piano-player and, eventually, the player piano and all that followed was within sight. All that was needed was the ingenuity of various inventors to make a perfect production product. The might and wealth of American industry turned it all into mass reality.

From string-playing musical clock with its pinned wooden barrel, through (as we shall see in the next Chapter) a host of variations on the theme of the pinned wooden barrel, an automatic musical performer of rather variable quality flourished into an instrument of sufficient quality and perfection to be able to hold its own on the concert platform.

---

1. This was described in detail in a BBC TV historical documentary transmitted in 1999 and for which I was musicological consultant.

The instrument seen here is curious in that it bears an almost exact similarity to one described in the inventory of instruments held by Henry VIII at the time of his death in 1547. This catalogue refers to 'An Instruments that Goethe with a whele without playinge upon, or woode vernisshed yellowe and painted blewe with vi round plates of siluer pounced with anticke garnished with an edge of copper and guilte'. Unfortunately it cannot be proved beyond all reasonable doubt that this was King Henry's instrument but there is ample evidence to suggest it came from the hand of the same craftsman. It can only be played mechanically by its clockwork mechanism and it has no keyboard. The stop/start and change buttons are placed centrally on the front.

Alexander Debain's *Antiphonel* appeared in 1846 and was what would later be styled a key-top player. Designed to fit onto any keyboard – organ or piano – it not only converted an ordinary finger instrument into an automatic machine but it dispensed with the large and cumbersome pinned wooden barrel. It played music from pre-studded wooden boards called *planchettes*. This meant that the owner of such a device could acquire the music of his choice from a catalogue of music. Here is a rare example of one of those first players which was operated by an ingenious double-ratchet mechanism: all the performer had to do was to rhythmically move the ornate handle up and down with the right hand while feeding the series of numbered boards representing the music into the guide rail on the top using the left hand.

By the time of The Great Exhibition of 1851, Debain had improved his instrument further, building it into a special keyboardless piano to create a single instrument. The ratchet handle had now been replaced by a full circle handle that was wound by the performer. It was now called the *Piano Mécanique*.

Here the keyframe of the instrument is visible – and the studded *planchette* has been rested on top upside down to reveal the pins that played the music.

Simplicity is revealed by opening the lower doors of the piano case showing the straight-strung piano frame.

In its time, Debain's invention was so successful that soon there was a demand for a mechanical-and-finger version. This sired the last in the *Antiphonel* series of *Pianos Mécanique* and seen here closed up. There is now a keyboard while the *Antiphonel* mechanism is placed on top of the piano. Gone, though, was the simplicity of the early machine for this model had two complete piano actions – one to be played from the manual keyboard and one from the *planchette* action. Note the large lever just visible under the treble end of the keyboard. When this was pulled over to the left, the entire manual hammer action was swung forwards clear of the strings and a second set of hammers, these hanging downwards from the top, were brought in line with the strings.

The two hammer actions are seen here in this view. Note that those for the mechanical player are fewer in number than the full piano compass. Stacked on top of the *Piano Mécanique* are the studded boards that go to performing one tune.

A fine example of a piece of furniture that conceals a mechanical piano, this Imhof & Mukle 54-note barrel instrument was made in the Black Forest during the first half of the 19th century. There is a foot-operated sustaining pedal.

Inside the Imhof & Mukle domestic barrel piano we find one ten-tune barrel in play and another in store below. A feature of many instruments of this type is the gravity damper, a row of which can be seen extending almost half way through the compass from the bass end. These worked automatically and needed no additional connections to anything since they consisted of felt-faced wooden blocks pivoted from a wire so that they hung down over the strings. A lead weight in lower part ensured that the block touched the strings just sufficiently to damp out residual vibrations after striking. When the hammer struck the string, the damper would bounce clear long enough for the note to sound.

The domestic barrel piano developed along the lines of the conventional quality drawing-room piano gradually developing an almost conscious urge to disassociate itself from the raucous street version or the clockwork one in the public house. The instant pianos became possible without using the pinned barrel, everybody breathed a sigh of relief. Here is an example made by an unidentified Central European maker during the first half of the 19th century. Originally, the clear glass in the top fall would have been an opaque panel of pleated silk while the lower door would almost certainly have been of solid wood. The only clue to its mechanical capability would then have been its increased case depth – and the winding handle.

Opening the front of the piano reveals a fine early sticker-type action. The handle on the right side of the piano case is for operating the tune-change mechanism. Note the diagonal trap work for the pedals – a necessary resort in order to clear the barrel mechanism. The instrument is from the collection of Gustave Mathot in Belgium.

London-made this handsome
clockwork barrel piano is by John
Longman of Cheapside who claimed
a Patent on his mechanical action.
Some four or five example of
Longman's clockwork pianos survive
but this is by far the most richly
decorated. Formerly in the de Vere
Green collection in London it is now
in the Nationaal Museum van
Speelklok tot Pierement in Utrecht.

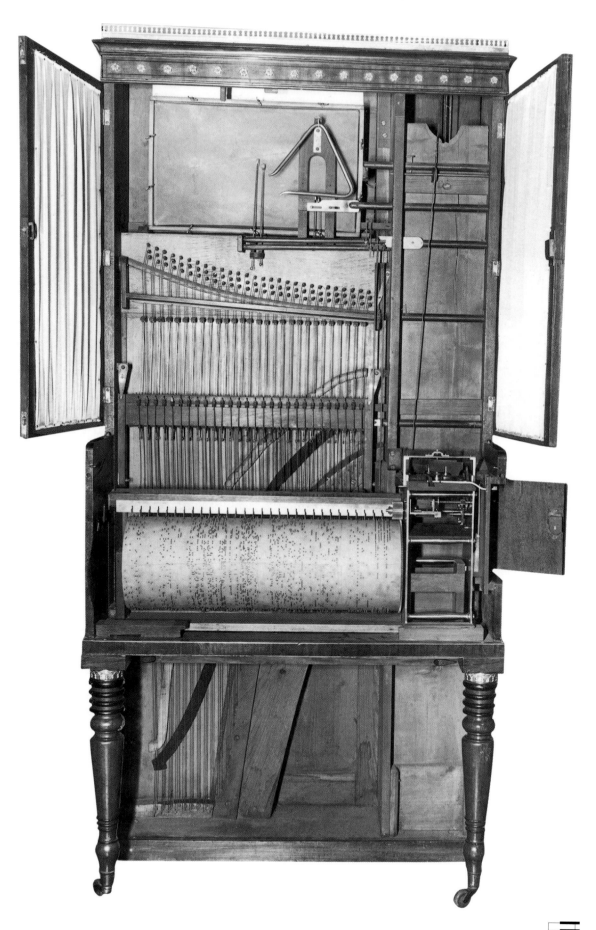

Removing the case panels and opening the doors reveals the simple majesty of this fine drawing-room piano. Five stop knobs protrude from the right-hand upper side and these control drum *piano* or *forte* (by moving the drum closer to the hammers), triangle on and off, sourdine (a felt strip mute interposed between hammers and strings), and primary *piano* or *forte* by adjusting the position of the keyframe. There are 28 notes represented as trichords (three strings to each note) and ten tunes on the single barrel.

Chapter 3
Barrel Pianos: Their History, Development and Manufacture

In the previous Chapter we saw how the first automatic musical instruments played their music from the pinned wooden or metal barrel or cylinder. From the Flanders carillon of the Low Countries, the sounds of which first rang out from their pinned bronze drums in the 14th century right up to modern times, the barrel was the one constant feature. It was cheap and easy to make, easy to pin and, unlike any other subsequent medium, if you got tired of the melodies that were pinned to its surface, you could pull out all the pins and start over again. It was this one feature that has kept the barrel piano on the streets for almost two centuries because it could always be adjusted to play the music of the time. It might forever produce 'modern' music – if desired. Other than the radio set and modern CD player, there is no other means of musical entertainment than may make that claim!

But we are ahead of the story and I want to talk about the beginnings of the barrel-operated piano and relate some of the history of the more unusual types of instrument.

In the previous Chapter I showed that the barrel-programmed automatic pianos were replaced first by mechanical actions such as Debain's *Antiphonel* that used short lengths of wooden board called *planchettes*, one surface of which was provided with metal projections representing the pinning pattern of the tune to be played. Next came the system of punched cards used by Jacquard in programming silk-weaving looms. This inspired Seytre to apply the principles of perforated card to the playing of a musical instrument in 1842. But it was to take until the 1880s before punched card might be successfully used in production piano-players. These were cabinets containing the mechanical mechanism that were positioned in front of an ordinary piano keyboard so that wooden fingers could act upon the keys.

What I believe is interesting is that although these devices seemed superior to the barrel and were thought certain to replace it, obsolescence for the barrel did not entirely happen. In fact, the *planchette*-playing piano, despite many variations and improvements, died out with its inventor. The cardboard-playing piano, a French invention and later, as we shall see in a moment, superbly developed and refined in Italy, was also something of a dead end. What actually happened was that one half of the automatic piano stayed in the popular and public domain (streets and public houses) with the pinned wooden barrel, while the other half became very refined and played perforated paper rolls faultlessly to people in, metaphorically speaking, their ballrooms.

The barrel piano owed its origins to the barrel organ, the earliest form of mechanical pipe organ that was virtually fully developed by the time the first barrel pianos came along. It used the same principles, even if they were applied in a somewhat different way. They derived as a progressive development from the mechanical spinets, described in the previous chapter, and the barrel organ of pre-Christian origin.

We have seen that stringed instruments struck by hammers go back at least as far as the sixteenth century. The incorporation of these mechanisms into long-case clocks that contained barrel mechanisms to play music on dulcimers was widespread in Germany *[82]* and these fascinating pieces were not uncommon in the eighteenth and early nineteenth centuries.

In 1793, a London by the name of Charles Clagget published a little booklet in which he described what he called his 'Aiuton or ever-tuned organ' which was a percussion instrument playing on a series of special tuning forks. Similar in principle to the Dulcitone invented by the Scotsman Thomas Machell and manufactured and sold by him in a number of styles between 1910 and 1936, Clagget's Aiuton was said also to be capable of being played using a pinned wooden barrel. Its inventor thought it might replace both the piano and the organ. Unfortunately it didn't and no example of this interesting instrument is known.[1]

One of the more memorable of early images of street music was this study captured by Victorian photographer O J Reijlander who portrayed a youthful street musician with his Hicks-style portable piano. He called it *Have a Tune Miss* recalling one of the more delicate approaches to receipt of alms from a public that was at best ambivalent to the music of he streets and at worst downright hostile. The picture, taken around 1872-4, depicts a style of piano already at that time almost 70 years old. The pleated silk front with its central pressed-brass Royal Coat of Arms confirms it as an original Hicks product. The heavy cloth over the top of the instrument was a necessary protection against rain. The poor lad, however, had merely a cap and a jacket to fend off the elements.

The earliest identifiable 'street piano' appears about the end of the 18th century and the opening of the 19th. Its popularity in Great Britain is attributable to a piano maker named Hicks in Bristol who, in the first few years of the nineteenth century, was a principal maker of small portable instruments.

While Bristol sounds an unlikely location for such an instrument, the roots are certainly Italian. Many Italians came to Britain through the ports of both London and Bristol and one might imagine that an alert and enterprising piano maker might have seen the familiar portable street organ and decided to try to make a small street piano along similar lines. Alternatively, he may have seen an early Italian instrument and copied it with a version of his own.

Although there has been considerable research into the origin of the street piano, most recently through the extensive work of Dr Antonio Latanza of Rome, the true answer may never be known. The extreme privations of the Italians over the period in question (*see* Forli, *Lacrime dell'emigrazione,* 1905) forced large numbers to emigrate Northwards to the rest of Europe and across the Atlantic to the United States taking with them the art and craft of the large street piano. These were transported around on hand-carts.

The transition from the cart-propelled piano to the small portable suggests that somebody conceived on the idea that if organ-grinders carried small pipe organs (occasionally reed organs) on their backs, then there was the potential to make and sell small pianos to introduce a fresh sound on the streets of our cities.

To translate the large barrel piano into the small and portable variant seems to have been if not exactly a stroke of genius, then a bold and useful step and the evidence implies that this transformation was English rather than Italian. Mention has already been made of the Hicks of Bristol involvement. The Hicks family were prolific workers and, from 1805 up to at least 1850, they produced many such instruments in Bristol and, later, in London as well. One of the members of the extended Hicks family was still pinning street organ and pi-

ano barrels well into the second half of the last century. At least one member of the family travelled to America and established a branch of his art and craft in New York.

But Hicks was not alone for a second name played a leading part in the small barrel piano. This was the Distin family. The Distins were to make a name for themselves in the field of military band wind instruments and many 19th century patents bear this name. What concerns us here, though, is that the Distins made barrel pianos in the Hicks style in both Bristol and London. These were technically and stylistically virtually identical. (*See* Appendix 2). The reason is not hard to identify, for we find that Henry Distin was Hick's apprentice.

There is also a very similar barrel piano in the Marino Marini collection in Italy said to date from around 1810 and to have been the work of Volontè Pietro of Como. This merely adds to the confusion as to whether Hicks invented the style or anglicised a product of Italian origin. While I am inclined to consider that the barrel piano was an Italian invention, lack of dated evidence makes it impossible to prove that Italian-made 'Hicks-style' pianos predated the work of the great Bristol family.

All things considered, then, Joseph Hicks appears to have been the inventor of the instrument which has subsequently come to be called variously cylinder piano, barrel organ (incorrect), street piano, piano-organ (travesty), hurdy-gurdy (incorrect), grinder organ (incorrect), mechanical dulcimer (perhaps the most apt). Even the word 'piano' must be adopted with reserve for certainly at the beginning, it was incapable of varying its sound output and was far more *forte* than *piano*. Although 'mechanical dulcimer' is thus nearer the truth terminologically speaking, cylinder piano or barrel piano may more readily be understood.

The style of piano identified with the Hicks family was curious in that precisely the same format was used for examples which quite clearly were not for outdoor use, but were articles of furniture. This fine specimen with its veneered cabinet and bun feet (which could be later additions) was never made for the street urchin, but is otherwise identical to its much-travelled sisters.

The date of invention is equally uncertain: it is claimed by Percy Scholes (*Oxford Companion to Music*, 8th ed. 1950) as 1805; John Clarke (*Musical Boxes*, 2nd ed, 1952) says 1810. We have already sees that the techniques and skills necessary to construct such an instrument were known well before that time and I feel inclined to suggest that the earlier date is more probably correct.

So what do we know about this man Hicks? Joseph Hicks was the son of a famed cabinet-maker named Peter Hicks, who was admitted a freeman of Bristol on 12 October 1812. The last entry in the Rates Books which Langwill [57] has traced for Joseph is 1847.

A specimen of this type of small street piano existed in the collection of the late George Brown of 'Harmony Hill', New Jersey, and bore the mark: 'George Hicks, Hand-Organs and Cylinder Pianos, Brooklyn, LI.' This instrument is identical to those made by Hicks in England and, in the absence of concrete evidence, it may be suggested that George was either the brother or the son of Joseph Hicks, emigrating to America probably about 1820.

One John Hicks of Clerkenwell, London, was building the same type of instrument *c.*1850 and it is more than likely that he too was related to Joseph. The name of Joseph Hicks crops up again on a much larger instrument in which the barrel paper watermark is 1846. The address given is Pentonville, London. Whether this implies that Joseph (of Bristol) died in 1847 and Joseph (of London) was a son, or whether Joseph left Bristol in 1847 and came to London, remains unresolved. There is a close similarity between all the instruments bearing the name Hicks and the trade of cabinet-maker is certainly evidenced in the good workmanship and appearance of their cases.

With the apparent exception of the large one by Joseph Hicks in London, referred to above, these early pianos were intended for use by street musicians. Street music is as much part of life as any other form of music and was particularly so at this time. Indeed, a study of this subject, its sociological influence and its general effect on the public at large would itself require a large monograph. The wandering musicians either played ordinary musical instruments (where they had the ability) or relied upon mechanical ones.

Its principal parts comprised a wooden barrel carrying metal pins and staples that corresponded to the music to be played, a piano frame or strong back, and a means of rotating the barrel, usually band crank, worm shaft and cog-wheel. Between barrel and piano strings was a set of very simple sprung hammers mounted transversely across the instrument in a keyframe. The back was a rigidly braced rectangle supporting a braced soundboard with bridge and strung with metal piano strings.

With the front and barrel falls removed this 22-note portable piano reveals its simple interior workings. Although there is no maker's name, it is typical of its genre. The front of the case bears a transfer or decal for Alfred Hayes of Cornhill, London who factored the instrument. The winding handle is a replacement. Note the presence of a damper or mute rail traversing the strings immediately above the hammers. The control knob for this protrudes from the left side. It intersperses a felt strip betwixt hammer and strings to produce a much softer sound.

The small barrel pianos, barrel pipe organs and the barrel harmoniums of later years were extremely popular – at least with their players. This enthusiasm was not always shared by those within earshot and the mass exposure of citizens in their homes to noisy musicians in the road outside, invariably playing the same tune over and over again, jarred nerves. It encouraged high blood pressure, fostered questions in Parliament, and engendered ineffectual by-laws. None served to stem the remorseless tide of mechanical music in the streets. The Victorian writer, John Leech, claimed he was sent to an early grave because he was being driven mad by the noise of 'organ grinders'.

The acerbic Professor Charles Babbage (1792-1871), thought by some to be the originator of the modern computer by virtue of his invention of the 'difference engine', was without doubt a mathematical visionary and inventor extraordinary. But he was nothing if not a cantankerous genius and he justly earned for himself the title of organ-grinder's Public Enemy Number One. Like his contemporary Thomas Carlyle, he claimed his concentration was extremely sensitive to distracting sounds and he reckoned that a quarter of his life's working power was destroyed by the audible nuisance of 'organ-grinders' and other street musicians performing outside his house in Dorset Street, London. Babbage took up petitions against them, complained to his Member of Parliament,

badgered the police to arrest them and, so it is related, once pursued a fleet-footed member of this maligned fraternity for a mile across London before finding a policeman who was willing to run him in.

Street musicians carried with them the stigma of being foreign, drunk, rough and dirty, although probably not necessarily in any particular order. Consequently they were not the sort of people good clean-living decent people would wish to associate with. The dangers of such generalisations were brought home many years later when, as a curious stunt, Viscount Hinton, son of William Henry Poulett, 6th Earl of Crewkerne & Droxford, Hampshire, hired himself a street piano and plied the cobbles of Mayfair to see if anybody recognised him.

To return to early 19th century London, the closing years of the reign of George III saw the resurgence of street music using mechanical barrel pianos. Pall Mall in London was the first street to be illuminated by gaslight in 1807, breaking for the first time the Stygian gloom that cloaked London's nightlife. While the underworld of pickpockets and prostitutes thought providing street lighting unsporting because it restricted their trade, the itinerant musicians benefited since they could now play after dark and gain revenue from the theatre-goers and promenaders.

Here we see the barrel removed from the case through the large circular opening on the right side. The barrel also shows its brass axis which, at the left end, contains ten parallel grooves into which the tune-change knife locates.

I have already said that after the death of Joseph Hicks, his teachings survived in the hands of his ex-apprentice, Henry Distin. Now Distin was to continue for many years producing instruments very similar to those of Hicks, playing eight or ten tunes on 23 notes. All these pianos had wooden frames; indeed, with the exception of the hammer shafts and the sundry brass springs and steel linkages, they were made entirely of wood. The barrel was made of poplar, the timber used for almost all organ and piano barrels on account of its even grain and consequent suitability for pinning. The tall, narrow piano back was heavily framed in pine to take the compressive loads caused by string tension: the iron frame for normal pianofortes, an American invention, did not come until 1825, so there was nothing unusual in this style of construction.

With the finger pianoforte, the total pull of all the strings on the wooden frame was often as much as 30 tons and thus it was not uncommon during the interval of a concert or piano recital for the tuner to come to the rostrum and retune the instrument. The much smaller street piano suffered, to a lesser extent, from the same problem and thus there was plenty of work to be had for the Distins and the Hicks's, maintaining their products in service. The fact that these street pianos went out of tune so quickly and also that their operators usually either couldn't care less or, quite probably, were not musical enough to notice only fanned the rising distaste of the public for this sort of music. Henry Distin later moved to Philadelphia, where he was still alive in 1898 – his eightieth year.[2]

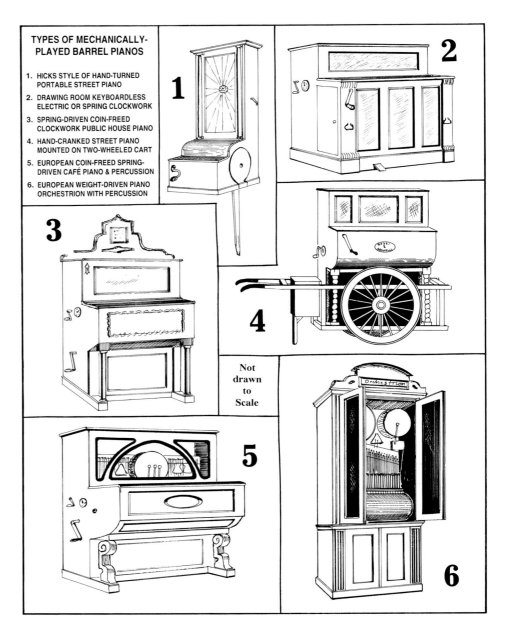

TYPES OF MECHANICALLY-PLAYED BARREL PIANOS

1. HICKS STYLE OF HAND-TURNED PORTABLE STREET PIANO
2. DRAWING ROOM KEYBOARDLESS ELECTRIC OR SPRING CLOCKWORK
3. SPRING-DRIVEN COIN-FREED CLOCKWORK PUBLIC HOUSE PIANO
4. HAND-CRANKED STREET PIANO MOUNTED ON TWO-WHEELED CART
5. EUROPEAN COIN-FREED SPRING-DRIVEN CAFÉ PIANO & PERCUSSION
6. EUROPEAN WEIGHT-DRIVEN PIANO ORCHESTRION WITH PERCUSSION

Not drawn to Scale

Neither Hicks nor Distin had the monopoly on this style of portable street piano and we find that there were other makers who produced them. These include Baylis, Sharp and Taylor. Since all these made virtually identical instruments, the only conclusion one may draw is that probably all of these men were at some time associated with Hicks, possibly, like Distin, as employees or apprentices.

Human nature being all that it is, street musicians treated the portable piano with ambivalence. It was lighter to carry than many of the larger pipe barrel organs[3] but it required much more frequent tuning. The piano was also cheaper to buy or hire, but its upkeep was more expensive.

Joseph W Walker was apprenticed to the London pipe-organ builder George Pike England. It was he who seems to have been the first to combine the visible advantages of both instruments and devise a portable street barrel organ that was virtually identical in appearance to the Hicks/Distin type of barrel piano. These are rare today and I know of only two, one of which I completely rebuilt back in 1958. While the average street barrel organ tended to be a smaller, more compact instrument, it still proved necessary to nest the wooden organ pipes by mitring them to compact shapes in order to get them to fit into the narrow case width.

Besides the street barrel piano, the instrument lent itself into adaptation for the Victorian parlour and mechanical pianos were built by several barrel-organ and piano makers. Among these should be singled out William Rolfe of Cheapside, London. He built both barrel organs and normal square pianos while his son, Thomas Hall Rolfe, concentrated more on the mechanical piano or, to be more precise, the barrel-and-finger piano. It was Thomas Hall who, in 1825, took out patents for improvements on the self-acting pianoforte that included a method of pinning the barrels to produce loud or soft notes by regulating the length of the pins. This was a method later to be perfected by Schmidt in Germany. Rolfe was not along in making these combination instruments, although his are the most sought after due to their quality.

That ancient and respected journal of the British music trade *Musical Opinion* published an interesting diary piece in its issue for September 1912 – around the peak of the player-piano market in the years that led up to the 1914-18 war. It was clearly a barrel-and-finger instrument of this type that inspired these words:

There is, indeed, nothing new under the sun. Attention has recently been called to the fact that even the automatic piano player is not such a novel invention as most people suppose it to be. *The Manchester Courier* for March 15th, 1828, has an advertisement headed 'Self-Performing Pianoforte'. It describes some of those beautiful and valuable instruments which, besides all the usual properties of a pianoforte, possesses the peculiar and pleasing addition of a mechanical arrangement by which several approved pieces of music are performed in the most brilliant style without the assistance of any performer, while at the same time it may be accompanied by the performer at the keys if desirable. The advertisement adds that 'for quadrille parties, assemblies or ball-rooms, and in all situations where a performer is not present it proves a valuable acquisition'. It would be interesting to know if a specimen of this 'self-performing pianoforte' is extant.

Even these were not the earliest. Again it was the London trade magazine that drew our attention to an event, then a century old, in its issue for April 1916 under the heading 'Early Mechanical Pianofortes'. This stated:

The following advertisement appeared in *The Times* a century since, — viz, Wednesday March 6th, 1816, '*A Newly Invented Musical Instrument.* — Two handsome cabinet pianofortes, that play themselves in a most brilliant and correct style all the fashionable country dances, waltzes, reels, etc., one of which will be parted with on reasonable terms. Would particularly suit a foreign market, as a great curiosity. Apply to A.B. 82 Newgate St.'

An early mechanical piano was that produced in about 1820-25 by Clementi, Collard & Company, the London music publishers and musical instrument makers. Muzio Clementi (1752-1832) was a man of many talents. Infant prodigy, keyboard virtuoso, composer of merit in many styles, he is remembered today merely for his sonatas for piano and harpsichord. He came to England at the age of fourteen and was a concert performer until he was almost sixty, at which point he abandoned public performances, joined the London firm of Longman & Broderip and took to the manufacture of musical instruments, among them some fine church and domestic barrel pipe organs. Upon the dissolution of that firm, he manufactured under his own name until he teamed up with Collard.

As well as making barrel pipe organs and ordinary pianofortes, he made the 'Self-Acting Pianoforte'. This was a combined manual and mechanical instrument so that, if desired, the two functions could be performed together, one played by hand and the other by a 'horizontal cylinder similar to that of a barrel organ and set in motion by a steel spring', which latter was capable of performing the 'most intricate and difficult compositions' and of playing for half an hour without rewinding. The self-acting mechanism acted upon only eighteen of the piano notes.

Describing this machine, Thomas Busby, in his *Concert Room Anecdotes* (1825), relates:

The time in which it executes any movement may be accelerated or retarded at pleasure; and while by the delicacy and perfection of the mechanism the *piano* and *forte* passages are given with correctness and effect, the *forzandi* and *diminuendi* are produced by the slightest motion of the hand applied to a sliding ball at the side of the instrument.

The portable existed in many varieties with from 16 notes upwards in compass. Here are two specimens that appeared in a London saleroom almost 30 years ago. That on the left has lost its original pleated silk front yet retains its central coat of arms. That on the right has had its front replaced with crudely-gathered cloth in a bolection-moulded frame. This one is also appreciable wider.

Another London maker of barrel organs of this era was John Courcell who came from France and settled here in 1847. Although he was later to become well known for his church organs, in his early days Courcell explored the possibilities of the mechanical piano building an instrument called the Cylindrichord in which the piano keys were depressed by a mechanical escapement set in motion by a pinned barrel and keyframe.

Thomas Busby classified the Cylindrichord as an 'admirable and efficient substitute for a first-rate performer on the pianoforte' and wrote of it:

> In small or family parties, where dancing to the music of the pianoforte is practised, a person totally unacquainted with music, a child or a servant, may perform, in the very best and most correct style, quadrilles, waltzes, minuets, country dances, marches, songs, overtures, sonatas, choruses, or indeed any piece of music, however difficult. This instrument is extremely simple and differs altogether from the barrel or self-playing pianoforte; it can be accommodated to the height or dimensions of any pianoforte, and when not in use for that purpose, forms a piece of elegant furniture.

How effective these instruments were we have only the eulogies of the perceptive Busby from which to judge. The fact is that it was not possible to make a mechanical piano that was a faithful interpreter. The direct linkage of a barrel to the mechanism of the piano was simply not good enough. The barrel pin even at its best was not up to providing the motive force on the hammer action of the period.

In 1832 a mechanical piano (and a 'grand' at that) was in use at the Grecian Hall (later the Royal Grecian Saloon), Eagle Tavern, City Road, London. The instrument was used to open the evening performances and, in the programme for 17 February 1832, we read that 'The Self-Acting Grand Piano Forte will commence every evening at 7.0 precisely'. An undated newspaper cutting in the Enthoven Collection (Victoria and Albert Museum) refers to the fact that the self-acting pianoforte 'has now been repaired and sounds very much better'. Was this one of Clementi's instruments? Can it be one about which Thomas Busby wrote so glowingly? Alas! history does not relate and, some time before 1836, the instrument had been replaced by a more conventional and probably more acceptable band of human instrumentalists.

Other than barrel-and-finger instruments, there were keyboardless barrel-only pianos made for the indoor market. During the 1850s, thoughts were turning towards larger barrel pianos and two other famous barrel organ manufacturers – Imhof & Mukle and T C Bates the organ-builders – directed their attentions to the making of fine instruments which would blend with the fashionable interior furnishing styles and decor of the period.

The Black Forest makers Imhof & Mukle, renowned for organ-playing musical clocks and 'cottage' barrel-playing pipe organs, produced some particularly attractive hand-wound and clockwork pianos in ornamental cases richly endowed with ormolu decoration. These had 54 notes and were provided with storage space for a second barrel in the bottom. Extra cylinders could be bought for £10 and many were pinned for dance and popular music of the time. One example I have seen plays selections from *The Bohemian Girl by* Balfe (1843). The tone of these Imhof instruments was comparable to that of the contemporary pianoforte.

The long-established firm of Theodore Charles Bates & Son of Ludgate Hill, London, produced a clockwork cylinder piano which stood 7 feet high, was 4 feet 7 inches wide and 2 feet 3 inches deep. A large instrument in all respects, it was also provided with a manual keyboard and the compass included what was contemporarily known as 'extra notes' to bring the number of notes to 85. It also featured a manual keyboard. The cylinder for mechanical playing was 3 feet 9 inches long and was placed in the bottom of the case along with the action which acted upon almost the entire compass of the pianoforte. Bates also built weight-driven pianos standing 4 feet 6 inches high and playing cylinders that were three feet long.

John Longman, another London barrel-organ maker, built an individualistic version of the keyboardless clockwork-driven upright piano. Provided with a range of 'stops' including drum, triangle, *unacorda*, mute, and forte, three instruments are in accessible ownership, the most ornate example, from the former Cyril de Vere Green Collection, being in the Nationaal Museum van Speelklok tot Pierement. A fine, but unadorned, example from the former Murtogh Guinness Collection can now be seen in The Morris Museum, New Jersey. The third example, which is not currently in playing condition, is in the charming and unusual National Trust property *A La Ronde* at Exmouth, Devon.

These mark the successful transition from chamber barrel-organ to domestic barrel-piano, but the path to music in the home was not straightforward as can be judged by the large number of people who invented systems that were either never produced or turned out to be marketing failures.

A recurring approach was the logical one of making something that would play a normal finger piano. William Youens built a mechanism patented in December 1859 that could be placed on the keyboard of a piano or harpsichord for mechanical playing. Unlike Alexandre Debain's Antiphonel playing mechanism of 1846, which used flat, studded wooden boards or 'planchettes' to produce movement via stickers to the keys, Youens used the barrel as the musical programme source.

This was located in a frame with a set of weighted levers, one for each piano key. Unlike conventional organ or piano barrels, the music was represented not by pins on the barrel surface but by holes or depressions. When the ends of the levers dropped into these openings in the barrel, their opposite ends contacted the keys. The force of contact, and thus the volume of sound produced, could be varied by the form and shape of the barrel note holes. This keyboard player was intended to be operated either by hand or by clockwork.

Two British piano-technicians, William Gillet and Charles Bland, improved on the Hicks system in 1869 when they devised a modification to the barrel piano so that it incorporated a reiterating action with continuously-beating hammers. The hammers were always in motion but allowed to contact the musical strings only when the correct key was lifted by a barrel pin. Their invention did not catch on, though, and in 1874 Daniel Imhof thought up a combined damping and sustained device for barrel pianos played with ordinary Hicks-type hammers.

Daniel Imhof had amassed a tremendous amount of experience using pinned barrels for the orchestrion organs which his firm, Imhof & Mukle, manufactured at Vöhrenbach in the Black Forest. He devised a number of improvements to the basic mechanism, particularly with regard to the tonality.

Two views of a curious 16-note instrument fitted with a fretted front. This reveals the box-lock hasp in the top lid which is the means of closing the piano from the front fall.

Instead of a crank handle, the manual and mechanical piano made by Jean Lacape & Cie in 1882 was operated by a foot treadle which turned the barrel for mechanical playing.

The development and refinement of the large hand-turned street piano was entirely due to the inventiveness of the Italians. It is a curious fact that, although the barrel-piano makers from that country travelled to almost every part of the Northern Hemisphere, it was in London that these men found the creative environment to invent features and take out by far the most Patents.

The departure of the Italian musicians and artisans from their native land began during the deprivations of second half of the nineteenth century. They settled in France, Germany, and Britain in their quest for livelihood. There are gruesome tales of men who actually walked from their homeland to Berlin, others to England, smuggling themselves onto steamers to cross the Channel. Some made it across the Atlantic to set up workshops in New York. All of these people had been driven from Italy by the privations and economic futility of the era. And all of them enriched their adopted home cities where they finally settled.

So-called Italian quarters sprang up and with them the pasta-houses and street-piano workshops. The history of these makers is sometimes hard to unravel for they set up partnerships and companies, frequently changing addresses, re-forming with compatriots from other firms and creating a web of sometimes short-lived businesses. In fact, examining business records and Post Office directories reveals that almost every one of the Italian makers in London worked at some time or another with his contemporaries. What remains of this period of flux is firm evidence of a continual striving for perfection and improvement.

Many names stand out from this rich era, one being that of Giuseppe Chiappa. He set up a street-organ and piano works in the Clerkenwell district of London in 1864 with fellow Italian, Giovanni Fersani. This particular quarter of London, the Farringdon Road area of the watch- and clock-making district of Clerkenwell, was to become the home of the street barrel-piano industry and practically all of the subsequent firms had their homes and their work premises either here or in near-by Warner Street and its environs. In the immediate vicinity were the lodging houses of Saffron Hill, Chiappa and Fersani made large barrel pianos that were transported on handcarts or donkey-carts. They may not have been the first but they were certainly among the earliest to enter this profession.

In 1878 they took out a patent for a combined street piano and organ played from one barrel. Half the instrument was a piano operated by pins on the wooden drum, and the other half played a 'cornet accompaniment' from pins and bridges set in the second half of the barrel. This combination instrument must have been hard work to play for the handle also had to pump wind for the organ component via reciprocators from a crankshaft that formed part of the barrel drive worm gear. This would have had to be pumped continually, even when the 'accompaniment' wasn't actually playing. None of these compound instruments has survived and the conclusion must be that they were unpopular with the hirers. There would also have been the problem of keeping the two instruments in good condition since changes in weather (temperature and humidity) would have played havoc with the tuning.

A Patent appeared in 1879 in the name of J Y Smith for a method of regulating the actions of the combined barrel organ and piano and then, the following year, the trio of Alexander Capra, J B Rissone and S Detoma jointly patented improvements to barrel piano action that established the form and style of all that followed.

Next to the cuckoo clock, the street piano was a very simple instrument comprising wood, iron wire, a large quantity of (usually) square-section iron pins, an a cast iron or brass worm shaft fitted with a cast winding handle. Sundry stock iron strip, a few stout steel-wire springs and a set of piano-strings completed the list of materials. It was this simplicity that allowed the makers to set up manufacture without too much investment in plant and machinery.

In detail, the piano consisted of a vertical wooden frame that formed the back of the piano. This was very solidly made with thick bracing timbers for its purpose was to resist the enormous tension of the strings. Attached to this frame was the soundboard, usually of spruce or ordinary clear pine. Fixed in a precise location across this was a trapezoidal-section curved hardwood strip to form the bridge over which the strings passed in such a way that they pressed down onto the bridge.

The wire strings were looped onto steel pegs (hitch pins) driven into the bottom of the frame and attached to screwed tensioning pins (wrest pins) at the top so that the tension of the strings could be adjusted for accurate tuning.

Across the width of the piano and pivotally attached to each side was a stout frame, usually reinforced with a bar of rectangular-section iron, into which were set on a continuous wire pivot the piano hammers and their action springs. This whole unit was called the key-frame.

In front of this was a large wooden barrel – more properly a hollow wooden cylinder – onto the surface of which was set the programme of tunes to be played. Normally a barrel would play between six and ten melodies, each melody being played by one rotation of the cylinder. To change the tune to play the next one, the whole barrel was shifted sideways by small increments, normally less than one-eighth of an inch and this was done using an iron wheel the face of which was arranged as a series of steps. This cam was linked to the hammer frame so that when the barrel was shifted the delicate hammer-tails were lifted clear of the barrel pins to prevent damage. Unlike the cylinder musical box, to which there was a mechanical family likeness, the tune could be changed at will, even in the middle of a performance, by indexing the cam with the handle provided. All these parts are shown in the accompanying illustration.

Each individual musical note in the scale was represented by wire strings as in the ordinary pianoforte. The base strings were copper-covered and usually the extreme two or three bass notes would be sounded by single strings. The remainder of the wrapped strings would be bichords – two strings tuned in unison. The central portion of the piano scale was strung in trichords – three strings in unison. Some larger pianos and most indoor or café pianos used four or even five strings in unison for the extreme treble register. The reason for this is that the higher up the scale the shorter the wire strings and therefore the less energy they could produce when struck by the piano hammer. This weakness could be overcome by increasing the number of strings for that note.

Earlier I mentioned Alexander Capra. It was he who built a barrel piano with 'mandolin harp' effect in 1890. Each string was plucked by a rotating cylinder holding three spring-wire plectra. The plectra throughout the piano compass were kept in rotation by a linkage from the crank handle and were brought into contact with the strings by the normal function of the barrel key and connecting levers.

Capra went on to think of a way of getting the best of both worlds from the ordinary pianoforte and in 1880 he was granted British Patent number 4725 for 'improvements to the piano action for playing either manually or from a pinned wooden barrel'. The outcome was the Per Omnes Pianoforte, advertised in 1881 by Capra, Rissone & Detoma. This was a somewhat bulbous-fronted piano with a keyboard, a barrel and a handle for turning. 'The Per Omnes arrangement', said the advertisements, 'can be attached to any piano at a small cost.' None is known to survive. The following year, 1882, Capra went one further and patented a piano player using a pinned barrel and stickers which would fit on an ordinary piano keyboard. Again this seems to have been a short-lived invention.

The partnership of Capra and Rissone now turned its attention towards the other possible markets for the barrel piano. Most public houses had pianos for people to play but, as can be imagined, they suffered a lot of hard use and after a few pints most bar-visiting pianists found their talent diminishing. Why not have an automatic piano for the bar! So appeared the first clockwork-driven automatic barrel piano. Unlike the domestic instruments mentioned earlier, these were robust direct descendents of the street piano and, in exchange for the insertion of one penny, they would give forth a tune. Power was provided by a heavy-duty spring motor. The first of many such clockwork pianos, termed 'automatics', this appeared in 1884 and proved an immediate success. Quickly other makers also made pianos of this kind.

Capra's mandolin piano of 1890 plucked its strings using a mechanism that was far from ideal. It could readily fall out of adjustment and was neither durable nor really loud enough for open-air use. The real answer had actually come twenty-one years earlier when two piano-makers named Gillett and Bland had invented the reiterating hammer action. This was a method for continuously and rapidly striking the piano strings without the need of special closely-set barrel pins. If the pins were set too close together on the barrel, there was a severe limitation on the speed of repetition since the hammer tail, in falling off the barrel pin after one strike, would hit the next pin too soon. This severely limited the speed of repetition. When the two inventors thought up their design for continuously-beating string hammers in 1869, they were on the threshold of perfecting what was later to be known as the 'mandolin' effect in which, when a note is sounded, the hammer strikes the strings several times in quick succession. With sustained notes, the effect is supposed to resemble the sound of a mandolin. To produce the necessary 'long' notes, the mandolin notes were not pinned in the usual piano way but their duration was marked by barrel-organ-type staples in the barrel surface which held the reiterating mechanism in play for the desired duration.

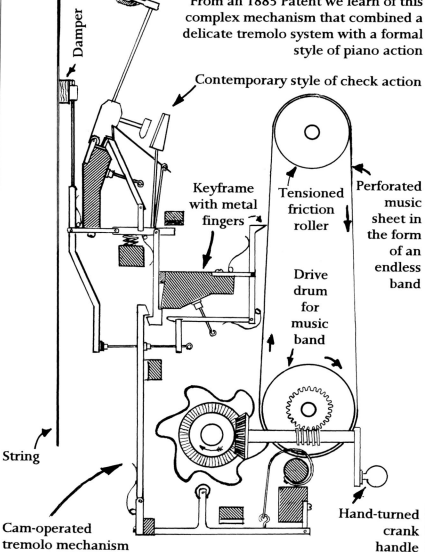

EHRLICH'S ENDLESS-BAND DESIGN FOR A TREMOLO-ACTION PIANO

Paul Ehrlich of Leipzig invented many mechanical instruments that played endless bands of perforated cardboard. From an 1885 Patent we learn of this complex mechanism that combined a delicate tremolo system with a formal style of piano action

Damper

Contemporary style of check action

Keyframe with metal fingers

Tensioned friction roller

Drive drum for music band

Perforated music sheet in the form of an endless band

String

Cam-operated tremolo mechanism

Hand-turned crank handle

This proposition would have been anything but durable with too many points of individual adjustment and regulation needed for correct playing. No examples of this mechanical piano are believed to have ever been built.

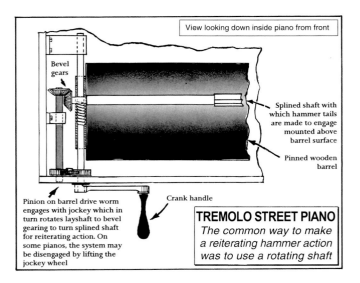

Bevel gears

Splined shaft with which hammer tails are made to engage mounted above barrel surface

Pinned wooden barrel

Crank handle

Pinion on barrel drive worm engages with jockey which in turn rotates layshaft to bevel gearing to turn splined shaft for reiterating action. On some pianos, the system may be disengaged by lifting the jockey wheel

TREMOLO STREET PIANO
The common way to make a reiterating hammer action was to use a rotating shaft

Joseph Piana Canova of Clerkenwell was another maker who thought up improvements to the beating-hammer tremolo or mandolin effect in 1902.

Forerunner of the great Hupfeld organisation, J M Grob & Company of Eutritzsch near Leipzig was the first to produce a practical mandolin effect from a street piano. A fluted steel shaft was arranged between specially shaped sprung hammers and the piano strings. The hammertails, which were not rigidly attached to the hammers themselves, were moved by long bridges on the barrel. The bridges raised the hammertails and held them for the appropriate length of musical time, drawing the actual hammer against the rotating shaft by means of a spring. The result was the staccato striking of the string.

Some two years later, in 1890, Capra improved on Grob's invention and so successful was this modification of the barrel piano that during the next twenty years almost every manufacturer of consequence perfected his own system of achieving this effect.

The clockwork piano with its ability to produce music – especially popular music – without effort, became popular not just with the more genteel middle classes, but in places of working-class entertainment and the seamier sides of life. If the Eagle Tavern's Grecian Hall piano played for the entertainment of those who journeyed out to the edge of London in the 1830s, by the time the century was closing places far less fashionable were keen customer for such instruments. One notorious place was the old Hotel de Provence on the corner of Cranbourn Street in Leicester Square. In the 1890s and the early 1900s it was a popular venue for night-time entertainment involved with meeting ladies of dubious repute. There was a downstairs cafe featuring a long bar and marble-topped tables. Upstairs there were what was politely described as 'rooms available'. All the waiters, somewhat surprisingly, were German and fights were commonplace. The police used to raid the establishment regularly and could reckon on six or so patrons being arrested nightly. A clockwork piano was one of the more moralistic attractions to the scene. The old building, changed and rendered respectable in the 1930s, survived until April 1941 when it met an untimely end in the blitz.

It was an age when invention and ingenuity went hand in hand and before long the idea of the automatic had sired the café piano, still clockwork-driven, but with ever-increasing complexity. In 1884 Ludwig Potthoff and Hilmar Golf of Berlin patented a most complicated barrel attachment to a keyboard piano. Here the barrel mechanism was mounted beneath the keyboard and, when played mechanically, the barrel pins operated a linkage of primary and secondary levers and cams, terminating in a secondary piano key which in turn set in motion the piano action in the same manner as the pianist's fingers.

It took another German to see that this degree of complexity was really unnecessary since all that had to be moved was the actual hammer, not the complete action. Johann Gerhard Gottfried Schmidt of Köpenick near Berlin, perfected

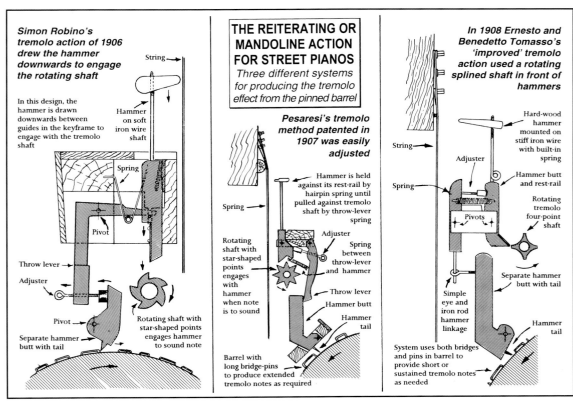

Simon Robino's tremolo action of 1906 drew the hammer downwards to engage the rotating shaft

String

In this design, the hammer is drawn downwards between guides in the keyframe to engage with the tremolo shaft

Hammer on soft iron wire shaft

Spring

Pivot

Throw lever

Adjuster

Pivot

Separate hammer butt with tail

Rotating shaft with star-shaped points engages hammer to sound note

THE REITERATING OR MANDOLINE ACTION FOR STREET PIANOS
Three different systems for producing the tremolo effect from the pinned barrel

Pesaresi's tremolo method patented in 1907 was easily adjusted

Spring

Rotating shaft with star-shaped points engages with hammer when note is to sound

Hammer is held against its rest-rail by hairpin spring until pulled against tremolo shaft by throw-lever spring

Adjuster

Spring between throw-lever and hammer

Throw lever

Hammer butt

Hammer tail

Barrel with long bridge-pins to produce extended tremolo notes as required

In 1908 Ernesto and Benedetto Tomasso's 'improved' tremolo action used a rotating splined shaft in front of hammers

String

Adjuster

Spring

Pivots

Simple eye and iron rod hammer linkage

System uses both bridges and pins in barrel to provide short or sustained tremolo notes as needed

Hard-wood hammer mounted on stiff iron wire with built-in spring

Hammer butt and rest-rail

Rotating tremolo four-point shaft

Separate hammer butt with tail

Hammer tail

a simple barrel mechanism, again under the piano keys, to do just that. He also patented the principle, first registered by Rolfe in 1825, that the volume of the note depended on the force exerted on the hammer-tail by the return spring and thus the loudness of a note could be varied by altering the distance which the pins protruded from the surface of the barrel.

In Bologna, Italy, Giovanni Racca and W Seward were making barrel pianos for use in indoor public places, and Francesco Getto of Ivrea made small portable street pianos similar to those of Hicks. Getto, however, succeeded in improving on the detail of Hicks's design in many ways, not the least of which was the use of thinner music strings on a somewhat larger soundboard to produce a brighter and more singing tone.

Clockwork barrel pianos, thought to have first been made either in London or Brussels, found a ready market not just in England but also throughout Europe and was now being produced by many makers for a market that was encouragingly receptive. It was in an endeavour to break fresh ground that in 1898 the firm of Gregori Pasquale & Company (Charles Romano and Pasquale Amato) placed the clockwork motor actually in the end of the wooden barrel. It was wound through a hole in the barrel access door. It was obviously necessary to let the spring motor right down before attempting to remove

the barrel for changing and it also required that each replacement barrel had a spring motor built into it.

A combination automatic piano – one that could be hand-turned or clockwork-driven – arrived on the scene in 1899 from the workshops of P Rossi, C Rossi and Loreto Spinelli. It included percussion effects by way of a set of tuned saucer bells and a drum. Once again, the spring motor was housed inside one end of the barrel.

Street pianos underwent a subtle revolution as the Victorian era came to a close. In 1903, Luigi Pesaresi coupled a fortune-telling device to a street piano. This comprised a wheel that could be set spinning behind a window set in the front fall of the piano case.

Another Clerkenwell maker, Luigi Villa of Granville Square, Farringdon Road, also thought about the additional commercial possibilities offered by the street piano as a result of which in April 1903 he took out a Patent for a method of displaying advertisements through a large window in the front fall. He used a system of levers and links, intermittently moved by pins in the end of the music barrel, to convert the continuous rotary motion of the barrel into an intermittent rotation of vertical rollers as each end of the case. These rollers carried a travelling blind upon which were mounted advertisements.

THE BARREL - AND - FINGER PIANO ATTRACTED INVENTORS WITH DESIGNS THAT EXTENDED FROM THE SIMPLE TO THE OVER-COMPLEX

Two different approaches from Patent Application drawings held in the archives of The Patent Office in London

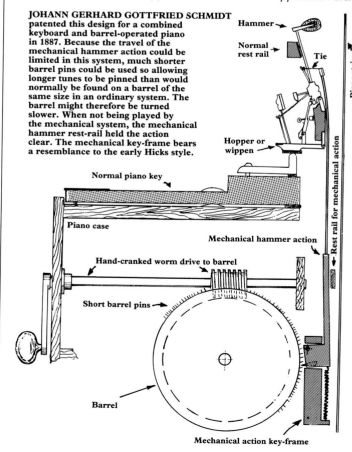

JOHANN GERHARD GOTTFRIED SCHMIDT patented this design for a combined keyboard and barrel-operated piano in 1887. Because the travel of the mechanical hammer action could be limited in this system, much shorter barrel pins could be used so allowing longer tunes to be pinned than would normally be found on a barrel of the same size in an ordinary system. The barrel might therefore be turned slower. When not being played by the mechanical system, the mechanical hammer rest-rail held the action clear. The mechanical key-frame bears a resemblance to the early Hicks style.

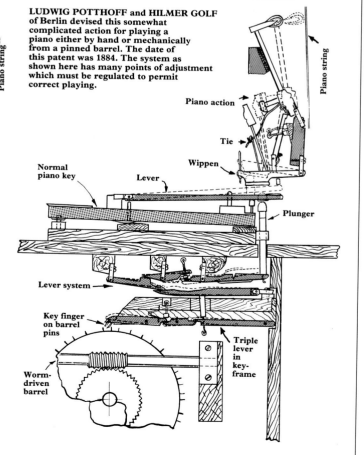

LUDWIG POTTHOFF and HILMER GOLF of Berlin devised this somewhat complicated action for playing a piano either by hand or mechanically from a pinned barrel. The date of this patent was 1884. The system as shown here has many points of adjustment which must be regulated to permit correct playing.

Villa's Patent was a variation on the moving picture fronts which appear to have dated from the end of the nineteenth century. Operation was from the same two vertical rollers, but in that instance they received a steady motion via bevel gearing on the end of the winding handle. The canvas blind portrayed a continuous scene either of country life or the bustling city (the former seems to have been the more popular) and these were almost always very finely painted. Their durability was poor, though, for the continual flexing of the fabric over the rollers ultimately cracked and flaked the oil painting.

The life of a street piano was arduous in the extreme. Most of the streets were cobbled which meant that the instrument was continually being jolted and shaken during transit from place to place. One musician is known to have had his 'pitch' in the wealthy quarter of Mayfair to which he pushed his piano from lodgings in Clerkenwell every morning and took it back again at night – a total distance of around five miles.

But it was not just the continual transit on iron-tyred cartwheels that wreaked the most havoc on these timber-framed pianos. It was climate and, more importantly, its rapid changes that was the piano's worst enemy. The effects of wind, rain, hot sun and rapid changes from one extreme to the other caused warping of the frames, separation of the glued joints and splitting of the timbers. Loose soundboard ribs were a frequent and quite objectionable problem for the instrument suddenly started to sound tinny and muted in one particular part of the compass and the loose pieces would make a buzzing sound like a wasp in a jam-jar.

There was, however, one lasting and all-too common problem associated with temperature and humidity. It was one that was so serious it could mean the end of an instrument – or at the very least a major rebuild. This was the tendency of the wooden wrest-plank or pin-block to split along its length and tip forward as a result of the string tension. Because the instruments were cheaply and quickly built, this sort of problem usually marked the end of the life of an instrument for it would seldom justify the labour and time for repair.

Even if it survived these problems, loosening of the tuning pins (wrest-pins) through expansion and contraction of the wood was an ever-present hazard. At its best, then, the street piano seldom remained in tune for long (which only added to its public unpopularity) and its life was short. Its days usually

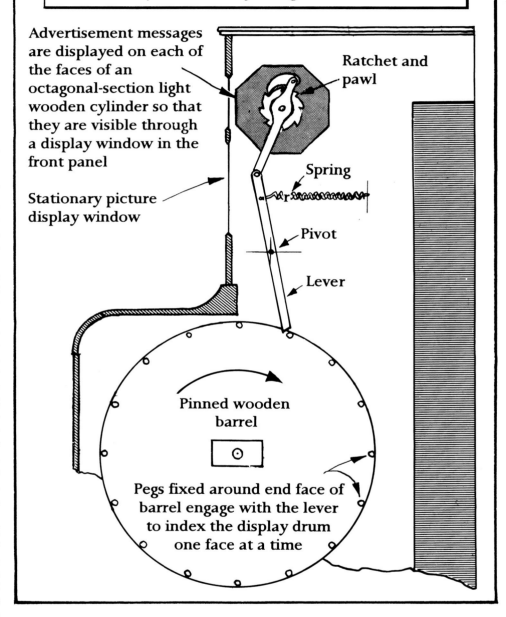

DISPLAYING ADVERTISEMENTS ON THE STREET PIANO

The first commercial use of the instrument was the showing of moving advertisements: it was patented by Luigi Villa in 1904

Advertisement messages are displayed on each of the faces of an octagonal-section light wooden cylinder so that they are visible through a display window in the front panel

Stationary picture display window

Ratchet and pawl

Spring

Pivot

Lever

Pinned wooden barrel

Pegs fixed around end face of barrel engage with the lever to index the display drum one face at a time

ended in a ritualistic chopping-up as winter approached so as to keep its owner and his stove warm in the wintertime.

If it was coping with the climate that was the street-piano owner's *bête noire*, a bold attempt to remedy this shortcoming was offered by Rossi and Spinelli. They built clockwork pianos having iron frames. Intended for indoor use, they were not a success because the tone suffered badly through poor design of the soundboard.

If ever there was an instrument that should have had an iron frame, then it was the street piano. As it was this never came about for the simple reason that the greater weight it would have entailed would have drastically reduced how far the old men of the streets could push them.

Weather-proofing was a tarpaulin sheet of oiled canvas that was normally tied onto the top lid of the piano. When it rained, undoing the straps would allow the cloth fall down over the front and back. Not that this usually stopped the performer from playing. He had paid his sixpence hiring charge for the day and had to get his money back with profit – and if you stayed silent you weren't earning! A tarpaulin sheet muted the sound of the music, so not surprisingly the earliest opportunity was taken to tie the sheet back up again – and let the piano get wet! On top of this, London was very frequently shrouded in thick fog and the density of moisture droplets in the air greatly reduced the distance a barrel-piano's sound might travel. Small wonder, then, that the canvas would be left tied up, the wet would get into the workings, the hammers would swell – and another piano would be destined for the stove.

The coin-freed piano was probably another London invention and possibly from the workshop of Gregori Pasquale who had set up his business in London in 1895 and remained working steadily until 1940. The coin-freed attachment to a clockwork barrel piano allowed a tune to be played by the insertion of a penny that tipped a balanced arm to let the clockwork motor run and allowing a tune to be played. Usually most makers organized it so that the tune would be played twice for one coin. It speaks well of the design and execution of these instruments that, although there was only the smallest gap in the pinning between the beginnings and ends of the tunes, the mechanism always stopped in the right place after its two revolutions. Chiappa made improvements to this mechanism in 1901 and became one of London's largest manufacturers of this type of instrument, probably ranking very close to that prolific maker Pasquale.

There were few technical limitations to the barrel piano regarding as to what it could and could not do. On the other hand, the clockwork piano did have a fairly serious drawback that was directly due to the way in which it worked. On a hand-turned instrument, it is second nature to the skilled operator to apply the correct force on the winding handle to keep the music playing steadily regardless of any fluctuating load on the handle. Say, for example, a massive chord of ten simultaneous notes was to be sounded. Instinctively, as the resistance to the turning of the barrel was felt, the player would increase force. The load on the winding handle was ever changing and only a human operator could make the necessary continuous adjustment to suit the demand.

By comparison, the clockwork-driven motor operated at constant speed and, naturally, produced a steady torque curve. It could not compensate for short and heavy loads. The upshot was that even the best of the automatics was unable to strike more than five strings at once without 'jumping'. Although the huge spring motors of the big café pianos minimized this, the defect always had to be concealed from the listener by distraction in the form of additional percussion effects.

The hand-wound piano, with its human player's natural sensitivity, could strike eight or more notes at a time without demur. This is why manufacturers were able so make the street piano into a more florid interpreter of music by employing many more barrel pins and exercising their often highly-developed barrel-notation skills to the full.

A plain piano case devoid of curves embellished with a gold tapestry-work silken front. Made in Denmark, this 26-note instrument has a curious feature. All the strings except the lowest three are trichords. Instead of using but a pair of wrapped wires for the bass, the lowest notes here are of plain wire – but in fours! The soundboard also has a fine central fretted rose suggesting that the unknown maker may have been more at home with domestic styles.

Naturally there was one way to minimize this effect and that was to fit over-large motors. This is what many makers did, especially in Belgium, where café piano motors are probably three to four times more powerful than needed. Well-geared and with a large centrifugal governor, these motors can cope with most of the needs for constant power. In the final analysis, though, it was up to the music-arranger and the barrel-pinner to ensure that the music did not overtax the power unit.

Several of the London makers saw the potential for opportunities in other towns across the country and opened up branches elsewhere. The two most popular towns were Manchester and Glasgow. As some time or another, many of the larger street piano and organ makers opened works in these places. Gavioli, for instance, was making organs for a while in the Great Ancoats Street area of Manchester.

Almost *jugendstil* or *arts and crafts* in decorative style, this unusual piano in a light-wood case has a looking-glass front.

One piano maker who remained in the Manchester area for life was D Antonelli, who specialised in clockwork barrel instruments. In November 1901 he patented a method of removing the barrel for changing without disturbing the rest of the mechanism. This was a very great step forward and the Antonelli improvements were to be felt throughout the entire industry in a short space of time. Hitherto, to change a barrel was a fairly lengthy business, demanding, for example, great care in realigning the new barrel. Antonelli retained his barrels in a fixed location in the piano case, pushing them into the right position with a leaf spring on the access door.

Developments in London may have been very numerous but, to a certain extent, it was the same everywhere that the Italians settled. In New York makers such as Maserati (operated by the one non-motor-car mad member of an otherwise famed racing-car family) served the American street musicians' needs.

The developments in England were rapidly expanded across Europe and by the early years of the twentieth century there was a thriving business in the manufacture of clockwork barrel pianos for use in cafés and other public places. Belgium, Holland and France became the European centres of mass production and very many makers were employed in supplying what today seems to have been an insatiable demand for these relatively low-cost instruments. In Belgium, the instruments were frequently built with street-organ-type proscenium fronts, richly carved and sometimes provided with mirrors. Some of these were of very large proportions and included an octave or more of nested hemispherical bells, wood-block percussion, drum and triangle, and occasionally xylophone.

The clockwork instrument also underwent a small revolution at the hands of Eugene deKleist of the North Tonawanda Barrel Organ Factory near New York. He was perfecting a barrel piano, later to be known as the 'Tonophone', for the Wurlitzer Company. DeKleist, who came from Düsseldorf in Germany, went back to Fourneaux system in that he used a barrel and key frame system combined with pneumatic action. The pins on the barrel lifted a key that was connected by a tracker to a wind chest, admitted air into a small pneumatic motor or bellows and thus allowed the string to be struck by a hammer connected to one of the bellows boards. Driven by an electric motor, deKleist's Tonophone was patented in July 1901.

Within a few years deKleist's Tonophone pneumatic barrel piano was selling well in America. It was being produced and sponsored by Wurlitzer. In time, the original mechanism was improved and in 1902 and 1903 deKleist took our further patents.

Barrel-playing pneumatic pianos, already experimented with since the time of Fourneaux, still appeared. Rose, Coop & Rissone of Regent Street, London, applied the coin-freed mechanism to one such piano-player which they made in 1903. This seems to have been their last fling in the world of barrel pianos for after that they seem to have discontinued barrel instruments. Pesaresi & Son concentrated mostly on 40- and 44-note automatic street instruments, usually fitted with tremolo or mandolin effect, but they were made only in small numbers - for some reason they were unpopular with users.

The clockwork barrel piano found a popular market in cafés, public houses, and other public places such as those that could not afford the far more costly showground organ. In the same way that the modern juke-box can be controlled remotely by customers seated at their tables in a café, so did Thomas Linforth Jones contrive to set clockwork pianos playing in 1905. He used 'electro-magnetism energization' by the insertion of a coin in a remotely mounted coin-slot box to free the detent on the piano's clockwork mechanism. Any number of such coin-slot boxes could be connected to the one instrument.

The era of the street piano in Britain was largely at an end by the outbreak of the 1914-18 war. Nevertheless it was to remain in production in Europe, particularly the southern part of France and also Belgium, well into the 1930s. This was surprising since by that time it might have been thought obsolete in the light of the electric pneumatic-action instruments that had infiltrated the mechanical musical instrument scene.

The so-called mandolin or tremolo effect on a street barrel piano seems to have retained popularity over a long time. The instrument was reasonably loud and its sound was sufficiently different to that made by an ordinary street piano that it would attract attention. Windows opened and maids and children looked out – and that was usually followed by a little money!

Every maker of consequence devoted efforts to devising his own system that might be sufficiently different from that of his rivals that he could not be accused of patent infringement. The general idea of the reiterating hammer remained virtually the same as that which appears first to have been used by Grob in Leipzig in 1818. In that original form, the hammer was made in two parts that were connected by a tension spring. Between the two parts rotated a splined shaft. A sustained note on the string was represented by a bridge or staple on the barrel, instead of the usual pin. This bridge held the lower part of the hammer in such a way that the hammer arm and head was placed in engagement, under the load of the spring, with the rotating shaft, thus imparting a staccato beating to the string.

A drawback to the rotating-shaft system for creating a mandolin effect was the appreciably greater wrist-power needed to play the instrument. Even when in good order, more than twice the force was required and one can imagine that after a few hours' playing the piano operator would be feeling in need of a beer and a rest. The disadvantages were thus significant as far as the musician was concerned.

Who first thought of adding a *tableau vivante* to a portable piano is uncertain but this type of addition appeared in London and Berlin while in the Black Forest portable street organs were made with the same type of moving scene. Ideal for the performer who did not have the adjunct of a monkey, this form of portable piano incorporated an animated display revealing dancers, conjurors and magicians all operated from special pins upon the barrel. This form of instrument was popular between 1800 and 1850 but because of the delicacy of the display – plus the fact that children would often damage them by trying to pull off the moving figures – means that their survival today is restricted.

In 1905 Julius Carl Hofmann of Vienna again modified the beating-hammer system and, in the same year, Spinelli built the first split-bridge mandolin piano. This had a soundboard with two treble bridges that effectively divided it so as to provide two sets of strings for the treble notes, allowing two hammers to be used to sound one note. By pinning the barrel to work each hammer alternately, a mandolin effect could be achieved without the complication of bevel gears and beating hammers.

Simon Robino, described as a musical instrument maker of Manchester, patented his own version of the beating-hammer tremolo in 1906 but his system involved a complex movement of the hammer as compared with other designs of the time. His hammers were drawn down by bell crank-shaped hammer-tails until they engaged in a starwheel that kicked them against a return spring.

Clerkenwell's Warner Street was, as we have seen, a haven for the barrel-piano makers and another maker there was Vincenzo Pozzouli. He dispensed with the complex trappings of the tremolo devices of his contemporaries and, in 1906, made a mandolin piano having four bridges — the first being a mandolin, the second a piano, the third a second mandolin, and the fourth a bass piano. He also used hardwood hammers. This must have produced a formidable sound.

Despite these improvements, they cannot have proved very successful, for still the rotating-shaft tremolo method was being improved upon by the larger makers and, in April 1907, Luigi Pesaresi registered another Patent for yet another different system.

One might have thought that there would have been a limit to the variations on the same theme but as it was to turn out the idea still had not yet run its course. In the following year Ernesto and Benedetto Tomasso, who made barrel pianos in Leeds, devised another such system. This one was different insomuch as the rotating shaft was in front of the hammers as distinct from being between hammers and strings.

A curious type of barrel piano introduced about 1910 was the 'zither-banjo', which produced a distinctive, clear sound not at all unlike that of a banjo. Its distinctive characteristic, however, was that it was very loud. Canon Wintle asserted 'that it could be heard a mile away'. The secret lay in the mandolin-like duplication of strings and a very thin sharply-bowed soundboard.

In the years leading up to the outbreak of war in 1914, the barrel piano was under pressure from what must at that time have seemed the revolutionary design of the book-music-playing piano which offered the advantages of being smaller and lighter for it did away entirely with the enormous pinned wooden barrel. It is thought that Chiappa was the first to change to this type of instrument back in the mid-1890s. Whilst the barrel continued to have its staunch followers, cardboard music had to be the way ahead. An extra bonus was that the music was readily available and could be carried or stored with ease. The heavy barrel together with its restricted repertoire represented in pins which were so liable to damage must disappear, thought the pundits.

They were to be proved wrong for the 'astonishing revelation' was that the cardboard-music street piano was not a success. It was instrumental in fostering its own individual shortcomings. The Italian musicians soon tired of the books of music which rapidly wore out, tore or got lost. Whilst book music was fine for an indoor piano or even a fair organ, the street piano was an instrument exposed to rough use, the exigencies of the weather and the wear of continual movement along cobbled streets. Damp weather meant that the cardboard also got damp, lost its strength and then tore. And that, usually, was the end of that book of music. Moreover, the barrel makers offered a very quick and cheap repinning service and could set new music on existing barrels with great finesse. One should therefore not be surprised that few, if any, of these cardboard-music instruments for street use have survived.

There is a rather curious barrel piano, at present unplayable, in the collection of Walt Bellm of Sarasota, Florida. In shape and proportions, the case is no different from that of a normal barrel piano. The normal type of circular barrel access door is to be found on the right side and a clockwork motor is in the conventional left-hand position inside. The piano back is straight-strung on an iron, unmarked frame.

Joseph Hicks worked in Pentonville, north London and no doubt realising that the portable piano's days were numbered as larger instruments appeared in increasing numbers he turned to domestic instruments on exactly the same principle. This elegant 41-note piano stands on a matching cabinet with hexagonal tapered legs.

In place of the wooden barrel, however, there is a cylinder of perforated metal. Both ends of this hollow cylinder are provided with square-shaped drive perforations which engage with drive cogs. The start/stop mechanism is operated from cutouts in the extreme outer edges of the metal, as also appear to be other features such as damper and mute. The keyframe is made of very heavy channel-section iron on the front edge of which are mounted the keys. These are of stamped punched steel with an escapement action. A damper for the lower half of the strings is operated by slots and, in places, large square holes pierced around the centre of the cylinder's length. A felt-covered mute is provided which can be swung up under the hammers by means of a knob in a slide hole on the right side of the case.

There is no indication as to the maker of this unusual piano although as it was bought in Copenhagen it was almost certainly European in origin. This mystery would have remained unsolved had not a piano orchestrion been identified in the collection of Stockholm collector Bill Lindwall which has precisely the same mechanism. It was then but a short dig amidst the patents to identify both instruments as coming from the factory of Lochmann in Leipzig.

Inside is Joseph Hicks' imprinted trademark on the soundboard. Note that all except the lowest three notes are trichords. This piano has a particularly fine if delicate tone.

Despite all the patents and design improvements undertaken in London, it has to be concluded that clockwork barrel pianos did not reach as high a state of perfection in England as in other parts of the world. Probably related to the different trends in popular entertainment in public places, they were to reach their zenith elsewhere in Europe as well as in America, where they proceeded onwards through the whole gamut of mechanical musical instrumentation.

The Wurlitzer company, which first commissioned deKleist's Tonophone pneumatic barrel piano, went on to make mechanical banjos, harps, zithers, guitars and even jazz bands. The call for musical entertainment has always been greatest in America and the later machines made to accompany silent films in picture theatres achieved a remarkable degree of perfection and flexibility. The Photoplayers of the 'twenties combined a wide range of effects in a basic roll-operated pneumatic piano mechanism and Wurlitzer constructed an incredible number of full-orchestra theatre organs, some of which crossed the Atlantic and were installed in British picture-palaces.

We have to conclude that the British clockwork barrel piano, other than for the entertainment of the British working classes as they drank, never ascended very far above its street hand-cranked brothers.

How different from things in Italy, Austria, Belgium, Holland and France where mechanical pianos with percussion accompaniment were popular in cafés and restaurants. Rossi made a number of these in Italy, as did makers such as Crubois in France during the second decade of the twentieth century. Crubois continued making these instruments at least until the late 1920s and they featured a partial iron frame, drum and triangle and castanets. These were all spectacularly-cased, coin-freed and driven by clockwork motors.

Just as the barrel-piano industry was established in Britain by Italian immigrants and flourished, so were similar industries established in other parts of Europe as more or less the same time. Spain in particular possessed a large and flourishing manufacturing industry.

An Italian named Apruzzese came to Salamanca, Spain, in 1883 and began making barrel pianos. The business he founded moved to Madrid in 1906 and, in the same year, the last owner, Antonio Apruzzese, was born. He was to be the last remaining member of the family to be engaged in piano work and also the last surviving barrel-piano restorer in Madrid.

Probably the best of the Spanish makes were the instruments built by Luis Casali, another Italian. He settled in Barcelona and began business early in the 1880s. The firm comprised three partners – Casali, Pombia (who was responsible for the actual construction), and Subirands, whose job it was to transcribe music for the wooden barrels. So successful were their instruments that the firm was awarded gold medals at the Brussels Exhibition of 1895, having earlier received a similar award in Spain in the year 1886.

A vital key to the success of the Italian emigrants was that wherever they settled they quickly assimilated the local musical idiom. They did not make the mistake of trying to impose Italian music to people to whom it was unfamiliar but instead knew that to get people to respond, to dance even – and to give alms – meant playing music they knew. For this reason you find London-made pianos playing the Cockney tunes and the patriotic songs of the time, French pianos playing French popular music, and New York pianos playing the latest American dance music.

It was this characteristic of adaptation which was the key to the success of the Italians. Nowhere is this more noticeable that with Spanish-made instruments where, so quickly, the Italians mastered the sometimes difficult, broken rhythms of the Spanish dances. These pianos included percussion effects such as the drum, bells and, most common of all, the castanet. Triangles were sometimes to be found as well. The musical programme would invariably include at least one *paso doble* in its programme and these and similar dances came over particularly well.

The Spanish barrel piano was built with 30, 35, 40, 45, 56 and 60 hammers and the larger models were made to be fitted into a donkey cart. Felt-covered hammers, then common to most other European makers, were dispensed with in favour of plain walnut hammers when it was discovered that the hard hammer-heads produced a brighter and louder sound. Wooden, unfelted hammers had, of course, been used by Hicks, Distin and others in England for tenor and treble notes and twentieth-century tremolo pianos were all to make use of uncovered wooden hammers.

If the barrel piano only appeared as an indoor instrument in a few isolated instances alongside its street variety, it was in Sweden that the instrument appeared solely as a domestic music machine. Sweden's contribution to the history of mechanical musical instruments is small but not insignificant since the pianos produced were radically different from those made anywhere else in the world. Johan Petter Nyström of Karlstad produced the Reform-Orgel in 1891. This was an unusual variant of the genus American organ (ie it sucked its reeds instead of blowing them as in she harmonium) that could also be played automatically by means of a perforated disc.

The other instrument to emerge from this part of Scandinavia was the Pianoharpa, which is said so have been the invention of I F Nilsson of Öster Korsberga, Lemnhult, Saxhult. Resembling a rather deep-topped table with a lift-up lid, this was no article of artistic furniture, but rather more a country-style and plain product. Musically, these were not particularly inspiring machines and not too many seem to have been built. However, on 13 August 1889 a Swedish patent number 2239 was issued in the names of Anders Gustaf Andersson

and his brother, Jones Wilhelm Andersson, for improvements in the Pianoharpa type of instrument.

As Bill Lindwall related in his scholarly article in 'The Music Box', (Vol 8 *pp*.2-6), the Andersson brothers lived in the tiny village of Näshult outside the small town of Vetlanda in the southern part of Sweden. They were carpenters with a workshop where domestic furniture and similar utilitarian articles were produced expressly for the home market. As this time, Sweden was still a somewhat impoverished nation with an economy centred on agriculture. So hard was the peasant style of life that many Swedes left to seek their livelihoods elsewhere. This was the time when the migration of Swedish people to America began. Most people lived poorly and under extreme circumstances (*see* 'Music & Automata', Vol 1, *pp*.134-40). It was into this tough environment that the Anderssons produced their Pianoharpa. The economic conditions that surrounded its creation justify its rather unprepossessing appearance and cheap construction. Pianoharpas had very small soundboards and the hammer action was rather primitive which is why they were tonally rather bland.

Even so, the instrument must have enjoyed some popularity because quite a number of Pianoharpas were produced. No patents were applied for regarding the instrument itself, only for two specific mechanical features that Andersson designed himself. One of these was for a rotatable bar which enabled the keys to be depressed slightly so as to increase the distance between the hammers and the strings. This served as an adjustable rest-rail, making it possible to moderate the volume of sound produced. The little Pianoharpa measured 76 cm high, 93 cm wide across the front, and 49cm deep from

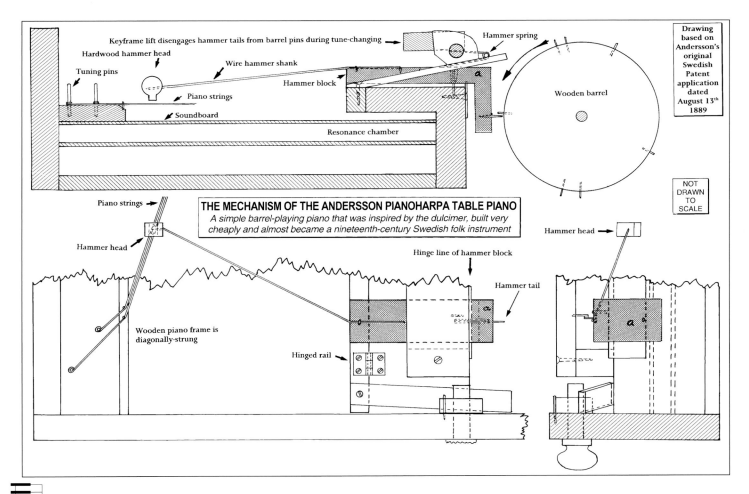

THE MECHANISM OF THE ANDERSSON PIANOHARPA TABLE PIANO
A simple barrel-playing piano that was inspired by the dulcimer, built very cheaply and almost became a nineteenth-century Swedish folk instrument

front to back. The crank handle at the front of the case turned the pinned 105cm-diameter wooden barrel which had a length of 64 cm. The barrel was moved laterally via a knife and bolt system as found in the early street piano or barrel organ so as to change the tunes, of which there were twelve to the barrel.

Most Pianoharpa barrels featured the popular Swedish music of the period but there were exceptions: for example there were barrels with only hymns or folk tunes. Interestingly enough, only ten programmes of music were ever provided for the Pianoharpa and an index of tunes shows the titles available.

At the time Lindwall was researching the history of this piece, he made contact with an aged collector (then in his seventies) who lived not far from Vetlanda. He knew a nephew of the Andersson brothers who himself was seventy years old and who died in the spring of 1978. This man had passed on some of the early history of the Pianoharpa and recalled that as a young boy he had helped to pin the barrels after finishing school for the day. He was certain that only ten barrels had ever been designed and said that when an instrument was sold it was accompanied by three barrels. Unfortunately the soft wood from which barrels were made was prone to infestation by wood worm and many instruments became so damaged from worm holes that they were thrown out. Only a few survive today.

While the Swedes were producing these rather primitive instruments, elsewhere in the Northern hemisphere the barrel piano had developed a stylised construction. Durable instruments for street use in all weather now replaced the exquisitely subtle tunes of the drawing-room instruments conceived much earlier in the century by British craftsmen such as Rolfe. And as the other end of the scale the new indoor instrument was the handsome example of cabinet-maker's skill housing the weight-driven iron-framed instrument often with a performance embellished with drum (sometimes bass and side-drum), triangle, xylophone and bells. This was the piano orchestrion, so called because the instrument included an automatic damper or long and short pins, so producing a true piano-e-forte effect.

In Germany and Central Europe as a whole, the piano orchestrion underwent considerable refinement and some magnificent instruments were produced which were barrel-operated and quite often had iron frames of superb quality. The early ones sometimes incorporated clocks: others were made for use in cafés and other public places. Ultimately, these were the progenitors of the pneumatically played piano orchestrions which approached complete orchestras in themselves.

Across in Bohemia and the Austro-Hungarian empire, the piano orchestrion reached its zenith of musical and mechanical perfection. Almost all of these instruments were weight-driven and incorporated a variety of effects such as xylophone, drum, cymbal and occasionally wood blocks or castanets. In their developed form, they achieved hitherto unheard goals in musical expression, producing piano and forte effects with panache from the special programme pins on the barrel.

The division of the barrel piano frame into two halves was an early improvement that enabled the uncluttered arrangement of percussion and effects controls, taking commands not only from each end of the barrel but also from the centre where special bridges, some of great length (arc of barrel circumference), controlled the operation of dampers and a simplified form of action rail. These very long bridges frequently wore thin in the middle and even although they were usually supported under the span of the bridge with single pins, worn pi-

anos with vague effects can usually be diagnosed as suffering from thin bridges, age having caused them to bend in the middle, so letting the key waver between 'on' and 'off'.

One of the most impressive developments achieved by these makers was the creation of the drumroll effect. Back in the days of the Black Forest-style of orchestrion organ it had been the practice with large instruments to have a special, separate drum motor with its own driving weight. A keyframe key freed the stop-start detent on this unit and the descending weight caused a multi-cammed shaft to rotate, a series of spring-loaded hammers sequentially striking the drum as the shaft turned to produce rapidly-repeating taps on the drum.

It was not without its problems, though, for this drum-roll clockwork would sometimes run down before the end of the music and necessitate rewinding. Later pneumatic versions used the forerunner of the pneumatic reiterating motor using a pair of balanced valves effectively linked by a coiled length of tubing with an expansion or buffer air reservoir in the middle. American makers were left to devise the neat repeating motor used on coin-freed pianos made by firms such as Link, Nelson-Wiggen and Wurlitzer.

The solution thought up by the Bohemain makers was elegantly simple. Most of these instruments used a steam-engine type flying-ball governor rather than the usual speed-regulating air-brake. On the very top of this governor was fitted a small brass wheel with an offset pivot hole to which was connected an eccentric link. This in turn was connected to a long link arm on a very thin, low-mass cross shaft extending the width of the instrument at a position above the strings but below the drum. The drum sticks were attached to this cross shaft using a leaf spring and the hammer was checked during the no-play part of the music by a simple escapement. When a drum roll was required, a barrel bridge would free the hammer that at once came under the influence of the very rapidly oscillating axis rod, its movement being imparted from the eccentric the governor. The result was a high-speed drum roll of great precision. So precise, in fact, that one single pin in the barrel was sufficient to produce a short, sharp, definable repetition.

Among the many makers who produced barrel piano orchestrions and clockwork barrel pianos in Bohemia was the Prague maker J Klepetář, who made a large number of fine and imposing instruments. One style featured a 34-note iron-framed piano, two drums, a triangle and a cymbal. Power was provided by a clockwork mechanism using an iron weight of about 60kg, which was wound up to top of the case back. As it slowly descended, it transmitted its kinetic energy to the driving train through pulleys and gears. All but the four lowest strings on this style featured trichords, the very lowest ones being bichords. Like most of these instruments, this one was coin-freed, playing twice or three times on one coin. This Klepetář piano played a barrel 9½ inches in diameter and 25½ inches long.

Other makers in Prague around the turn of the nineteenth century included men such as J Stychs, Wenzel Hrubés and Jan Rubes. Later, Diego Fuchs formed the 'Erste Prager Musikwerke- und Orchestrionfabrik' in the Wenzelplatz and became a prime maker, while Ignaz Klepetář became a main agent for many makers in Prague's Eisengasse. By this time, though, the barrel piano orchestrion was at last losing out to the new electric pianos.

Édouard Jacques Bourquin of Paris was to contribute the last significant improvement to the barrel piano in the sum mer of 1922 when he made use of the revolver-barrel mechanism first used by London barrel-organ maker James C Bishop, and later by Forster & Andrews and T C Bates on some of their church barrel organs. Bourquin mounted a number of tune barrels between the flanks of a pair of large wheels. Each barrel was indexed in turn against the piano-string hammer-tails and was played. The barrels turned on a spiral as they played, thus enabling quite lengthy tunes to be performed from one barrel. On the completion of a barrel, the mechanism would disengage, rotate one barrel out of the way and bring the next into place, and then play again.

Several times in this narrative I have mentioned Canon Wintle. This remarkable man played a major part in the history of the British street-piano business between the wars. There is not much doubt that without his contribution we would have far fewer instruments preserved today. His interest, though, was not so much the pianos as bringing some dignity to war veterans who faced being cast into the dole queues of the agricultural depression that followed the 1914-18 war.

Canon Algernon O Wintle was rector of Lawshall, a village near Bury St Edmunds in Suffolk. Seeing the increasing deprivation of ex-soldiers who could not find any work, he hit on the idea of employing them in the repairing and restoration of barrel pianos at the Old Rectory. Consequently he set up a workshop in the Rectory grounds and founded the East Anglian Automatic Piano Company.

To the surprise of some of his parishioners – and the chagrin of a few – the Church grounds now echoed to the strains of Edwardian popular songs emanating from the ever-increasing piles of rather tatty instruments that found their way into Lawshall. Wintle's business specialised in the restoration and tuning of old street instruments as well as the repinning of old and new barrels. No new pianos were made and the instruments which were rebuilt were either sold or hired out to charitable organisations.

Canon Wintle unquestionably gave a new lease of life to many instruments that might otherwise have fallen into decay and been destroyed. However, in so doing he almost always saw that the name of the original maker was obliterated and replaced by that of the EAAPC – usually in the form of an oval blue rubber stamp applied to the barrel paper prior to repinning. When Wintle died in 1959 the firm closed and most of the remaining stock of sundries was dispersed or destroyed. An auction of effects, miraculously captured on newsreel film, lasted two days but nothing fetched even realistic prices.

In the sale was also a large stock of mostly complete pianos. Some of these were extremely ornate and clearly were amongst the earliest surviving examples of the genre. On the passing of Canon Wintle, these pianos changed hands several times and ultimately ended up in store in a warehouse in Hull, Yorkshire. I was requested by a museum to examine and catalogue the pieces with a view so their acquisition and this I prepared to do. The sight in that warehouse was one very hard to describe. There were so many pianos, stacked three high and many rows deep, that is was not even possible to count them, let alone create a catalogue! Some had beautifully veneered and inlaid cases, others were black-painted pub-type pianos, a few were in original rather pretty pastel colours. The lot was finally sold and transported in several truck-loads down to Cornwall to await the lengthy job of restoration. It is a matter of great regret that having survived so long, a large number of pianos, barrels and parts of others were destroyed in store when fire broke out in an adjacent building. Enough remained to ensure that the work Wintle so enthusiastically started will, in part at least, now be completed.

Many people believe that the existence of a barrel piano today marks the survival of an instrument dating from the turn of the nineteenth century. In truth, this is probably far from the case since the life of these instruments was comparatively short in service. They were still being built in she 1930s and Canon Wintle extensively rebuilt many, many instruments up to the end of the 1950s.

As for barrel pianos in general, the majority of surviving examples date from the years between the wars and, with a few exceptions, earlier models just have not survived. The Italians who worked on these to keep them playing on the streets were under no delusions as to their worth. They were cheap to build and maintain but once they ceased to become an economic proposition they were burned. (For a description of the making and operation of street pianos, see 'The New Penny Magazine' for 12 January 1901, which contains an article entitled *All About Piano Organs*. This was reprinted in *Clockwork Music* [71], pp. 293-8).

Although this 40-note piano has an iron frame and is no longer really 'portable', it is instantly recognisable from its family likeness. Which is surprising since this one was made in Curaçao, Dutch Antilles, as recently as 1979. Known as a Ca'i-organ it was made by Rafaël Pieter and plays eight melodies. The first 16 notes are bichords, the lowest seven of which are copper-wrapped. Nine of these bass notes mount gravity dampers. The upper 24 notes are trichords. All of the hammers have hard leather faces to produce a loud tone. This is preserved in the Nationaal Museum van Speelklok tot Pierement, Utrecht.

As you will already have gathered, the close relationship of makers and the inevitable swapping of workers all engendered instruments of similar appearance and performance. Where no original name survives, or where it has been removed, it is almost impossible to discover the true maker and date. The tunes a barrel piano plays are also of no use as a clue to its date because barrels were continually being repinned or replaced.

The street piano's repertoire had to keep up with the times for then as now it was really only the current popular tune that would attract attention and induce listeners to part with their money. Canon Wintle (who, as a boy, used to spend much time with the 'organ-grinders' as well as Simon Robino, the Manchester manufacturer of street pianos) analysed their music. Of the ten tunes pinned to each barrel, he said, the first two were invariably waltzes, the third a quickstep in two-four time, then a jig, hornpipe or Scottish reel followed by a foxtrot in four-four time. The sixth would be a two-step in six-eight time whilst the seventh was usually reserved for a special tune to suit the customer. This might be a pop song or maybe something more exotic - Wintle once set Mozart's *Eine Kleine Nachtmusik* on one! The eighth tune on the barrel would be another waltz or perhaps a march whilst the ninth could again be a march or perhaps an aria from an opera. The tenth and last tune might again be from the opera, or it could be a hymn or a sentimental song. Musically speaking, the street piano catered for a wide variety of tastes and it was nothing uncommon to find so-called 'classical' music on the clockwork pianos used in public houses.

The art of barrel-pinning was jealously guarded amongst the various makers, 'the secret of the clock-face', as it was termed, being passed on only to their own children. While there is little doubt that the earlier barrel pianos were all pinned using the index and pointer method (this is described fully with examples in *The Mechanics of Mechanical Music [72]*), there is evidence that the marking out of barrels was also done on the drawing board. George Eves (in his article 'Toni Pins a Barrel' first published in The World's Fair and reprinted in The Music Box Vol 7 p.328) described the process as follows:

Now a piano barrel starts off as a slab of well-seasoned beech or birch. This first of all gets a steel spindle in its centre, and it is on the centres the ends are [fitted so] that the drum is turned to the length and diameter the particular instrument demanded. On to it then was glued a sheet of brown paper, which just met end to end, which carried the seven, nine or eleven tunes in the form of hundreds of little black dots.

Toni bought the sheet music of the tunes he wanted in the Charing Cross Road and posted it back to his native country, where the musical maestros translated crochets, quavers, semiquavers, etc, into myriads of black dots on the master copy. These were then printed off on a hand press and sent back in the form of copy. To look as these sheets and the faceless dots was to marvel at the ability of the man who could convert music to dots. The sheet glued on, it was rubbed down hard with a 'boner' and then a calico bandage four inches wide was wound tight over it all like a sleeve. This was then set aside for a week after which time the cocoon was removed.

Almost perfect in scale is this nine-tune miniature street piano built by an unknown maker in the early part of the last century.

The next job was to key on one side of the steel spindle the bronze gear wheel, which would, in due course, mate with the worm wheel on the turning handle spindle. Next the paper-covered drum was set up in a stand, which was nothing more than the innards of a discarded street instrument, and up to this the 'pinner' drew a high stool after providing himself with a box of pins, a special 2-oz hammer, a depth punch and a sharp bradawl. And there he was, all set for a week's or maybe two weeks' work driving in hundreds of cast steel pins.

On every dot the bradawl made a starting hole for the pin, which was then hammered in gently until it was in roughly far enough. Then the depth punch was set to get the pin down to its precise homing. This punch had a hole drilled in one end which accommodated the pin snugly and in depth it gauged the correct amount the pin should stand out from the drum.

This job would go on for days on end. Some 'pinners' worked in bands round the drum; the gearing answered to a couple of turns on the handle. Others worked in lines across the drum but whichever method, by the time all those hundreds of pins had been inserted, it reflected music. The whole art of this job was that the pins had to be dead upright, as a pin leaning either forward or backwards meant the note sounded either early or late; excruciating to the ears of these professionals.

New barrel pianos are being produced today in Spain and Greece and these are usually small instruments having 32 notes, two clappers and one triangle. Featuring nylon and plastics in their construction, they are pleasing little devices and are referred to as *pianos a manubrio*. They also appear in Greece where they go by the name *Laterna*.

In Britain the street piano has, to all intents and purposes, disappeared forever. They do occasionally turn up in the hands of collectors who bring them out for a charity event, but they are no longer the vital earning tools of the impoverished. I last saw one plying its trade in London's West End more than fifty years ago. Yes, the barrel piano has departed from the street scene forever and remains only as a vague association with memories of the hansoms, trams, fog and the 'twopence-a-pint' pubs of the early years of the last century.

_____

1. Only one copy of Clagget's booklet on his Aiuton and other of his instruments, published in 1793, is known to exist. Entitled *No. I. [sic] of MUSICAL PHÆNOMENA.* It was formerly in the Galpin collection and now in the British Museum. It was reproduced in facsimile in *The Music Box,* Volume 4, 1970, pp. 498-509.

2. The name Distin is famous in the banding world for Henry Distin's father, a solo bugler in the Grenadiers, was supposed to test all the musical instruments for the British bands. One day he chanced to try a bugle that had been sent down from the Tower of London. It had been badly driven through the body. Distin tried the instrument — only to discover that it played a new note (bugles at this time, in keeping with most horns, had pistons). Thus inspired, he bought an old bugle and bored extra hols in it unril he found which of them created the new notes that would be usable. As a result of this chance episode the keyed bugle was perfected.

3. The lightest instrument in the street-musician's quiver was the portable barrel-playing harmonium or reed organ while those that limited their performances to use of the domestic organette got away even lighter still.

The miniature piano has 27 notes, the first seven being bichords, the remainder trichords. The thirteen lowest notes are struck by large piano-felt hammers, the next eight by hardwood hammers with chrome leather faces, and the remainder with solid ebony hammers.

Another 40-note piano with indoor attributions is this unnamed example in a nicely proportioned rosewood case with a silk front with central rosette.

Away from the portable and portable-domestic instrument, the more rough-and-ready street piano was invariably mounted on a two-wheeled handcart. Those who hired out pianos always had more pianos than carts for the latter were more expensive. If a piano had to be repaired, or a new barrel pricked, pinned and installed, then it would be taken off its cart and another put in its place. The carts thus covered more mileage than the pianos!

A 48-note instrument, possibly by Pesaresi, suspended in a non-standard hand-cart. The piano wire used by the makers was often poor quality or, shall we just say not the best. In order to produce the volume of sound needed, strings were multiplied especially at the upper register which intrinsically sounded 'thin'. The top sixteen notes of this piano each comprise five strings, the lowest 32 are three strings and the remainder four each – all adding up to something of a tuner's nightmare!

A more conventional and better-balanced handcart but this time with an unusually proportioned piano on board. Note the very high relative position of the barrel and winding handle, characteristics of the large Spanish street piano. This one, made in Barcelona by Pombia, plays a rich programme of Spanish music.

Here is a typical street piano in the sort of condition in which they are frequently found – rather knocked about and generally tatty. The pictures in the upper front fall are recent additions. The clue to its provenance comes from the rather crudely scraped-off name cartouche on the front. This suggests that it has at one time passed through the hands of that uniquely unconventional cleric, Canon A O Wintle. His East Anglian Automatic Piano Company offered employment to discharged servicemen after the First World War. They built up and restored many instruments over the years, but always erased the name of the original maker.

Canon Algernon O Wintle, who died in 1959, was both unconventional and controversial. A great self-publicist, he had postcards printed with his portrait so that he could distribute them at fairs he attended. He was, nevertheless, a good if self-taught music arranger and barrel-pinner who should be remembered today as a person who probably saved more street-pianos from destruction than he destroyed by over-restoration.

WITH BEST WISHES
FROM

Lawshall Rectory,
Bury St. Edmunds.

P.T.O.

Made immediately before the 1939-45 War, this modern-day mini-barrel piano was the forerunner of an industrial revival in both Spain and Greece that sees these instruments still in production to this day.

Emile Tadini of Nice made clockwork café pianos of a somewhat idiosyncratic construction. From the outside all looks fairly conventional.

The back of Tadini's café piano reveals fanned posts to create a large and unencumbered space for the enormous clockwork motor with its speed-regulating governor and coin-drop mechanism.

A nice touch: Tadini's tune-list is contained in a gilded *art nouveau* frame.

'Pianos ELCÉ' was the trademark of C Luche of 70, rue des Tournelles in Paris. This is a typical French-style of clockwork café piano dating from around the late 1920s-early 1930s.

Clockwork-driven ten-tune café piano made by Keith Prowse & Company Ltd of London. One style of piano this firm introduced for use in public places was called the Pennyano.

By the immediate post-war years, café pianos in Britain were undergoing a period of minimum decoration. This one, by an unidentified maker, is typical of the style of the 1919-20 era.

Inside we find a clean and simple straight-strung wooden back, the clockwork motor immediately in line under the barrel, and a coin-box affixed to the floor of the piano.

Made in Lugano, Switzerland, and looking perhaps grotesque in floral sunglasses, this café piano with its case ears, drooping mouth and incised forehead is the work of Rossi, Peppena e Figlio and dates from the 1930s.

Café pianos had to be seen as well as heard. A Croubois of Granville did not go in for grotesque appearances, just noise and his huge 'automatic', pictured here, did just that. Date of manufacture is about 1923.

Inside the Croubois piano we find a 58-note keyframe played piano and a percussion accompaniment comprising a triangle, four-beater drum and two woodblocks.

Canon Wintle once claimed that, given a fair wind, a mandoline piano could be heard at a distance of more than a mile. Whether or not this is quite true is not for me to say, but these instruments could certainly be loud. Here is one of them showing the mechanism for the reiterating treble action. The normal barrel-turning worm shaft carries a pinion just inside the case front. This engages with a wheel that turns a layshaft extending to the back of the piano where a pair of bevel gears serves to turn a shaft placed behind the hammers and in front of the strings. This carries at its treble end a splined shaft that in turn makes the hardwood hammers repeatedly hit the strings. The pattern of barrel-pinning shows the dramatic change from normal pins for the conventional action in the left, bass end of the piano, to bridges in the right-hand treble half to generate the sustained notes.

In the mid-1880s a Swedish engineer named I F Nilsson of Lemnhult Saxhult invented a very cheap table piano that he called the *Pianoharpa*. Each barrel played 12 tunes.

After Nilsson's instrument appeared, two brothers from Vetlanda, Anders Gustaf and Jones Wilhelm Andersson designed an improved form of the instrument for which they were granted a Patent in 1889. Much shallower than the original, this was intended as a piece of furniture: it could be used as a table even when in use. Many styles were made, all cheaply and durably made and decorated merely by hand-painting in the Scandinavian style.

Chapter 4
Mechanical Player Actions
and the Birth of The Pneumatic Player

As the nineteenth century approached its conclusion, and with it the Victorian era waned, great changes were afoot. Musically speaking, the barrel piano was coming to the end of the road. While probably still acceptable for playing popular music and snatches from the opera in the street, the inherent limitations of the pinned barrel and associated mechanics were beginning to show through. For a start, the instrument did not sound much like the familiar drawing-room piano. In fact it sounded coarse, unrefined and, to some influential ears, common. Unlike the staid and stately barrel-and-finger parlour instrument of William Rolfe, or John Longman's soft-toned 'wall-climbing' automatic, the common barrel piano was, well – common.

One reason for this was that the street piano was built down to a weight that could be carried (in the instance of Hicks and Distin) or pushed (like a Pesaresi, Spinelli or a Tomasso). Lightweight pianos had light frames which meant low-tension stringing. And there lay the heart of the problem. Only in a 'real' piano of the drawing-room could heavier construction (and later iron frames) give the extra tension that was needed for the tone and sustaining power associated with the refined instrument.

For some while, as I explained in the previous Chapter, barrels had been fitted to domestic pianos, but here again there were restrictions on the length of music played and the mechanics of pinning. It was hard to be really expressive with a heavy mechanical hammer action. While the barrel organ, which had very low-mass lightweight parts to be moved in order to make its sound, had mastered complex music and very rapid ornamentation (*see* Ord-Hume *The Musical Clock* [82]), the piano was like a ham-fisted baboon when confronted by that sort of music.

The heavier-strung pianofortes with their iron frames were not suitable for simple hammer actions like a basic barrel piano. The escapement action, which is pretty much as old as the piano itself and existed as early as 1720, and proper dampers were imperative.

All this pointed clearly to just one thing. The next improvements in mechanising the piano could only come if one started from a 'real' pianoforte. Expressed another way, now was the time to take a conventional finger piano and try to work it artificially by making it into an automatic piano.

In the previous Chapter we took a fairly exhaustive look at the development of the barrel piano from both the street and the home using a barrel carrying on its surface a series of projections so arranged that as the barrel was rotated they operate hammers that strike musical strings. This was derived from the earliest mechanical instruments beginning with chimes and the carillon and through to the organ.

A refinement of the barrel was the pinned brass cylinder used in musical clocks from the 17th century onwards. Before this a miniature carillon barrel of iron or bronze was provided with pegs which, as in the case of musical clocks of the 17th and 18th century, could be repositioned to make different tunes play. The brass cylinder also became standardised in the popular musical box of the late 18th and nineteenth centuries.

Mechanical musical instruments had given rise to a whole variety of associated ideas and technologies in the form of those that played metal discs or perforated card strips. There was even a comb-playing musical box that was played by a perforated paper roll: neither durable nor very practical. The disc musical box was an undoubted success, offering changeability of music easily, quickly and for little cost. But even this important feature of the later musical box was diminished, as was the need for the musical box industry itself, when the phonograph was introduced. Musical boxes then degenerated into mere novelties – devices to produce soothing tinkling rather than to undertake the more serious business of interpreting music.

Practical automatic pianos and church and chamber organs, though, called for barrels of such large dimensions that they presented a serious disadvantage. One only has to look at the large barrel-playing orchestrion organs and military bands to see that the barrels reached such prodigious proportions that it required two men to change the music. And you needed a large amount of secure space in which to store the barrels when they were not in the instrument. There was a constant risk of damage to the relatively delicate pins. Damaged pins meant spoiled music.

There had to be some other form of music programme for such instruments which would be less cumbersome and less liable to damage through careless handling. It was not from the world of music that a solution first came but, as outlined in Chapter Two, from the heady world of the silk-weaver.

Joseph Marie Jacquard (1752-1834) of Lyon, France, was destined to become a highly respected weaver in silk, a position he earned by his efforts to improve the existing looms upon which patterned cloth was woven. The looms were made to weave different designs in different colours and the selection of the proper colour controls had to be executed deftly by highly trained personnel. Jacquard worked on the idea that *if* he could bring all his loom controls together as small spring-loaded keys on a control board then they could be selected in any prearranged order by passing across them a strip of cardboard, suitably punched with holes or slots. By feeding long strips of cardboard across these keys, intricate and varied patterns could be woven accurately by semi-skilled operators.

In Italy, Giovanni Racca devised what was to be Italy's most successful mechanical piano – after the barrel-operated instruments. The *Piano Melodico* played perforated cardboard book music and employed a most ingenious mandoline or reiterating action a feature of which was that the force of the blow on the strings was infinitely variable so as to produce a realistic soft-to-loud gradation. Racca's mechanism was a self-contained mechanical player that was built in a number of different sizes right up until the early years of the 20th century.

Jacquard's control system for looms required that the design of the patterned cloth to be woven was first set out on graph paper as a greatly magnified plan of the finished cloth, showing the weave interlacings in detail. The design was then transferred to cards into which holes and slots were punched on a machine known to this day as a 'piano machine' and worked by a foot treadle.

The complete bundle of cards was then laced together into an endless chain and fixed to a square drum on the Jacquard machine normally situated above the loom. As each card was presented to a matching set of tiny levers – they were known in the trade as 'needles' – the interlacing of one pick of weft was completed according to the instructions passed on by the perforations in the card.

It is said that Jacquard worked on his machine between the years of 1801 and 1808. He must have had a working model finished quite early on for he was awarded a medal at the Paris Exhibition of 1801, and, after interviews with Napoleon and Carnot, he got himself seconded to work at the Conservatoire des Arts a Métiers in Paris. Here he worked on his loom, incorporating ideas from a loom conceived in 1745 by Vaucanson (who is perhaps better known as a maker of spectacular automata). Messrs Bouchon and Falcon had done similar work in 1725 and 1728 respectively.

After perfecting and refining his special loom and its method of control, Jacquard returned to his native Lyons only to be given a hostile reception by the local silk-weavers. They feared redundancy should his machine be adopted. Just as

James Hargreaves had seen his spinning-jenny smashed up by those who gave vent to similar sentiments in England in 1764, Jacquard witnessed the burning of his loom by the angry mob. As with most revolutionary ideas and inventions back through history, the first reaction of the masses is often negative and groups of hot-headed pessimists rise up generating passions that can turn to vandalism. Today, labour forces go on strike as a rather more civilised method of objecting to things workers view as likely to upset the fine balance of industrial relations.

Using the Racca action, the cabinet-style *Piano Orchestrion* was a grand instrument in many ways. Still capable of being played by hand-turning the wheel, this example was truly self-playing being driven from a small hot-air engine contained in the lower cabinet.

Of course, the inevitable happened and after all the initial wrath was spent, the capabilities of Jacquard's loom and its long-term benefits to the trade were gradually recognised. Jacquard lived to see his looms in almost universal use generating prosperity for his native city. The new loom could weave delicate patterns in carpets and produce fine cloth quicker and cheaper than the old hand methods. The Emperor Napoleon, ever one to recognise technical genius that would boost the industrial reputation of his country, rewarded Jacquard with a pension of £60 [$250] and a royalty of £2 [$8.00] on each loom built. He also awarded him the Cross of the Legion of Honour. Jacquard died an industrial hero in 1834 and, six years later, a statue of him was erected in Lyons. Fittingly it stood on the spot where his first loom had been publicly burned.

What Jacquard had achieved was a means to apply a series of operations to a set of control keys using holes in cardboard. Axminster carpets, rugs, complicated stitches - all these patterns were being automated by cardboard strips which passed over the control keyboard of looms. The keys were held firmly down as the strip moved steadily along. When a hole or a slot came up to a key, the key would rise through the cardboard and some mechanical linkage at its opposite end would control a function of the loom. That it was possible for a spring-loaded key to rise and fall by the passage of a perforated card strip was the making of mechanical music to come. Whether the end of the key was connected to a loom shuttle control, or to an organ windchest, or to a pneumatic lever to work a mechanism to strike a musical string was of no consequence. The secret was in using punched cardboard to move the key.

Jacquard did not know that in the years that followed his demise his loom improvement would be applied to the playing of automatic musical instruments. The first to look specifically at punched holes for player actions was Alexander Bain of Hampton Wick, Middlesex, in England. In 1847, he was granted British Patent No 11,886 for an instrument controlled by a perforated paper roll in which the holes directly controlled the passage of air through reeds. Bain even suggested that his system could also be used with an electromagnetic device so that more than one instrument could be played simultaneously. However, his invention related solely to the control of musical production by a pattern of holes in paper which corresponded to a musical score: it did not specifically mention pianos, nor could his system of direct interaction be employed, as it stood, for operating a piano.

In the year following Bain's invention, Duncan Mackenzie was granted a British Patent No 12,229 in August 1848 for improvements to the Jacquard system whereby it might be employed for playing musical instruments. This was the first direct linking of the Jacquard system with playing musical instruments. Unfortunately, the British patent law requirements at this time did not call for proof of invention by way of any working models. This meant that Patents were granted on applications that offered the flimsiest of detail as to how the invention might work. There is thus no knowing if Mackenzie's mechanism was ever tried out and, if so, with what degree of success.

This anomaly in the otherwise strict patent laws is even more demonstrable in the case of the Patent that was granted to Charles Dawson of Islington (then in Middlesex, now North London). In his Patent (number 12,307 of 1848) he described his occupation as professor of music, and he then set about describing how to play instruments either mechanically or automatically. There is a flute, keyboard instruments and a mechanical organ. We do know that the mechanical organ was actually built and he exhibited it in the musical instrument section of the Great Exhibition of 1851. By that time he was describing himself as an organ builder with premises at 395 Strand.[1]

While it would be very hard to judge Dawson's mechanically-played organ as a resounding success (no others were built to that pattern after the Exhibition), it was, nevertheless, historically significant. The historian William Pole, who was responsible for producing the catalogue entitled *Musical Instruments in the Great Exhibition of 1851*, describes it in the following words:

> Mr Dawson exhibits a mechanical organ on a new construction which he calls an autophon, and for which he has a patent. This instrument has no wind chest, valves or keys, but the wind is conveyed directly from the bellows to the channels of the soundboard by a row of passages, which are cut through trans-

versely by a long horizontal slit, just large enough to admit a sheet of pasteboard. The pasteboard is pierced with a number of holes, corresponding to the given tune to be played, and is drawn through the slit by rollers, turned by a winch; when, therefore, the holes come opposite the passages in succession they admit wind to the soundboard and cause the corresponding notes to play. This instrument might be called a *jacquard* organ. It is simple, and does away with barrels, and many other expensive parts; but it has the disadvantage of admitting the wind gradually into the pipes, and cutting it off gradually from them; the effect of which is a disagreeable wavering at the commencement and termination of the note.

Dawson's wind control, rather than being governed by a quick-acting pallet, was turned on and off as if by a slow water tap. Musically it must have been a disaster which leaves one curious as to why a man who was, at different times, a self-proclaimed music professor and an organ-builder, could have exhibited an instrument that so clearly was short on refinement!

But while Dawson's device was a few tweaks short of a success, the problem seemed already to have been conquered by two American inventors, Adoniram F Hunt and James S Bradish of Warren, Ohio. They were granted an American Patent No 6006 on January 9th 1849 for a method of playing an octave on a piano keyboard using perforated cardboard strips that passed between rollers and over a keyframe. There was even a system for emphasising certain notes so that a theme or melody would stand out from the accompaniment. It is very unlikely that this went beyond the patent and model stage and no further information exists outside the patent specification. Nevertheless the Hunt and Bradish Patent is another important step in the journey to the player piano.

Most of these early Patents fall into a similar category – significant, yet not commercially viable. Take, for example, that awarded to Jean-Henri Pape of London. A Frenchman and a master piano builder, he was in business between 1844 and 1848 in New Bond Street and also for a time in Little Newport Street, Leicester Square. He applied for French Patent No 5923 of 1850 for an unusual mechanism at the centre of which was a barrel containing a large number of spring-loaded pins. This was rotated in conjunction with a perforated cardboard sheet. When a pin found a hole, it passed through and so could strike the keyboard keys of a piano or organ.

In a non-characteristic incomplete, inaccurate and unsympathetic brief section on the mechanical pianoforte in her book *The Piano Forte*, Rosamond F Harding (*p.*283) refers to Jean-Henri Pape's invention of 1851 and says:

> His mechanism was worked by means of a handle, weights and springs, but it is unnecessary to describe it, as Debains 'piano mécanique' was by far the most perfect mechanical contrivance for this purpose at that time.

By this curiously ill-informed statement the learned doctor on the one hand omits to note that Debains instrument had a compass of 61 notes and was provided with no facility for rapid repetition of notes, and on the other that the barrel as a means of programming music for the pipe organ and, indeed, the pianoforte had attained a high degree of perfection. Thomas Rolfe's instrument of 1824, for example, would play the whole compass of the piano. Harding, we find, was not sympathetic to mechanically-produced music in any form!

'Jacquard cards' now appear with increasing regularity, an early application being the 'self-acting piano or seraphone' pat-

ented in 1849 by William Martin. The inventions of Joseph Antoine Testé have over the years been held up as of being important in the development of the player, yet like others before and after they were merely inconsequential stepping stones. Testé proposed the Jacquard principle for the playing of mechanical organs in 1863, improving upon it during the next year and taking out several patents.

Electricity, another but recently discovered technology, was suggested by an inventor named J Amman two years later. His idea for electromagnetic piano-playing employed a Jacquard card that was moved between the two contacts of an early form of solenoid. In England, Alfred Barlow suggested using an endless band of paper which had holes punched in it in order to play a reed instrument. This was one of the forerunners of the reed instruments later to be known as organettes and the date was 1870. Another electromagnetic system was used in the following year by E Molyneux to open the pallets of his reed organ which was played using a perforated paper strip.

Sounding as if they were covering all eventualities (in case it didn't work), Charles Abdank de Laskarewski and Thomas Herbert Noyes specified in their patent specification the use of either a pinned barrel or a perforated card or paper strip on their mechanical musical instrument of 1873. This played on tuning-forks rather like Claggets Aiuton.

One of the most prolific inventors in the world of mechanical music was Paul Ehrlich of Leipzig. He patented a system of perforated tune sheets for organettes in the summer of 1876. These were intended for the mechanical playing of 'automatic organs, harmoniums &c' and had wedge-shaped holes so that the keys passed slowly through the slots and the opening of the pallet could be controlled to produce louder or softer notes. The method, Ehrlich claimed, could also be used for musical boxes and pianos.

Ehrlich later made a disc-playing piano-player using cardboard discs of exactly the same style and appearance as those used on his highly successful Ariston organette and Orpheus disc piano, only they were 16.11/16-inches (423 mm) in diameter. The Norwegian maker Johann Petter Nyström of Karlstad used Ehrlich's style of disc-driven mechanism for his novel 'Nyström's Reform-orgel' which was a reed organ in the 'parlor organ' style that could be played by hand or by using a hand-turned player mechanism fitted onto the side of the case. His system was clearly marked 'Ehrlich's Patents'.

From now onwards, perforated music advanced steadily towards its application in full pneumatic action. The development of the player was to progress in three stages, the divisions between which were seldom clear. The perforated tune sheet initially served to admit and cut off wind to the musical production components directly: in other words, it was a direct valve. Because of this it suffered the same fundamental shortcomings as Dawson's device at the Great Exhibition back in 1851.

The second phase of development came with the interposing of some form of servo mechanism between the tunesheet and the musical components. Usually this was a mechanical keyframe or a set of sprung buttons that were normally held in the 'off' position by the pressure of the music tune sheet.

The third and final phase was the full pneumatic action between sliding valve and musical component. With this, the paper was required to suffer no forces other than those needed to regulate the supply of power to a valves and associated mechanisms which themselves were called upon to do the work of physically causing a sound.

Here is a close-up view of the Racca *Piano Orchestrion* revealing how by removing the drive-belt it could be hand-turned.

Amidst all this progression, the barrel was to have one final fling in the quite extraordinary mechanical/pneumatic push-up piano-player that was dreamed up by Parisian Jean-Baptiste-Napoléon Fourneaux. In two French patents granted to Fourneaux in 1863 and 1871 we find a pneumatic piano player the music for which came from a pinned barrel. This operated pneumatic motors to sound the piano keys. Fourneaux's machine, named the Pianista, was actually built and was widely publicised at the time, actually crossing the Atlantic to be shown at the Philadelphia Exposition of 1876. As a product to put on the market, though, it had one small but very significant drawback: it was considerably larger than the piano it was pushed up in front of!

The potential of the perforated tune sheet had now been established. While a cardboard strip could be made to push small levers up and down, perforated paper was easier to make and to store, but it was impossible to use it to do mechanical work. It could, though, be used as a travelling valve to open and close a small air passage leading via intermediary mechanism to a reed or musical pipe.

By the third quarter of the nineteenth century, there were two distinct methods by which an automatic musical instrument might be controlled using a perforated substance as compared with the traditional barrel. On the one hand perforated paper could be employed to operate a pneumatic valve. On the other, perforated card could be used to move a mechanical intermediary such as a lever.

The earliest use of pneumatic principles in playing music seems to have been the work of a mechanic from Lyons in France, Claude Félix Seytre. His Autophon, patented in 1842, played 'all kinds of melodies by means of perforated cards with square or oblong holes according to the length of the notes to be played'. These holes uncovered openings that were connected by tubing loading from air pressure bellows to small cylinders attached by each key in the keyboard. In each cylinder was a small piston which, when subjected to air pressure, could move a jack to engage with the tail of a hammer striking the string from below. Air pumping was achieved using foot pedals.

It is likely that the first satisfactory method of utilising the power of air as a switch was devised by another Frenchman, Jules Carpentier. Buchner [11] relates that he constructed his first pneumatic instruments for the International Electricity Exhibition in 1880. His 'repeating melograph', first used for the harmonium, punched holes directly in paper strips which were then used to play the music in a specially constructed electrically operated harmonium.

Carpentier produced two more instruments in 1887 – the Melograph and the Melotrope – which he presented before the French Academy. The Melograph recorded music performed on any keyboard instrument whilst it was being played. It did this using a series of electrical conductors leading from contacts beneath the keys of the instrument. As the key was pressed down, current passed to the Melograph which operated along similar lines to a teleprinter. A wooden plaque with a row of flexible metal strips was attached to the instrument in such a way that the strip of metal came beneath each of the keys, forming the contact when the keys were moved.

To 'record' the music, there was a band of paper moved along by an electric motor with a speed-regulating device. Underneath the paper was a perforated cylinder inking-roller which was kept wet with black ink. Above the paper was a row of vertically mounted impression rods that could be actuated by electromagnets. These caused the rods to press down on the paper whenever particular magnets received the current. There were thirty-seven magnets to play thirty-seven keys on the instrument. When these moved, the position of the musical notes was marked on the travelling paper band.

The 'recording' this produced comprised a series of inked lines. The distance between these marks and the edge of the paper indicated the notes to be played, while the lengths of the marks indicated their duration. This was just half of the process for, in order to obtain from this Melographic recording perforated strips for use in suitably equipped mechanical instruments, another roll of paper had to be punched in accordance with the marked paper band. To achieve this, Carpentier invented a hand-driven perforating mechanism equipped with punches. The perforated band this produced might be used to make large numbers of copies in a mechanical perforating machine.

Still there had to be a means of converting these punched strips back into music and to make this possible Carpentier invented a crank-driven mechanism – the Melotrope – which was placed on the keyboard of the instrument to be played. It was in the form of an oblong box and contained thirty-seven mechanisms for the playing of that number of piano keys. Later on this style of piano-player would be termed a 'key-top' player.

At the right-hand end, the perforated tune sheet held down lightly sprung metal fingers. A slot in the music allowed one of these fingers to lift up into a grooved brass pressure roller above it in the manner which Anselme Gavioli was to use on his book-music-playing show organs in later years. The Melotrope's levers were each connected to rocking levers spaced along the length of the box. The wooden plungers which sounded the piano keys were themselves spring-loaded and loosely attached to the rocking levers by a cord which also passed twice around a rotating wooden shaft running the length of the instrument. When a key was raised by the music slot, the rocking lever would cause this cord to be drawn tightly against the rotating shaft. The friction would at once cause the plunger to be pushed downwards on to the piano key. Musical expression was obtained by using the pedals (in the case of a piano), and the volume of sound was controlled by a lever which raised or lowered the key plungers. Both the Melograph and the Melotrope were very popular at the end of the nineteenth century and a large number of pieces of music were 're-corded' in this way.

Carpentier's piano-player used a form of mechanism which I have dubbed the 'kicking-shoe' type. This form of action represented a vast step forward in the development of the automatic piano and its advantages were not equalled until the arrival of pneumatic action. The principal benefit was noticeable in terms of sound volume. With the simple direct linkages used on simple barrel pianos, it was physically impossible to hit the string with any force since the only power available was the lifting of the barrel-key by a barrel-pin. The kicking-shoe action actually needed less initial force to produce an infinitely greater result: the cork-soled shoe was brought into contact with the surface of a revolving cylinder and was immediately and powerfully thrown forward and a connecting hammer struck the piano string hard.

The kicking-shoe method came to be used quite widely by mechanical players for some years. Hupfeld in Germany also used it and it featured in many patents. In terms of practicability, it certainly allowed very thin punched card to initiate a blow of considerable force by inducing shoes or quadrant levers to touch against the surface of a rotating shaft and import movement from them. However, these were fiddly devices to assemble and maintenance posed a great headache, for the check strings which were used to disengage the shoes at the end of each note-strike were prone to breaking and fraying from the momentarily high loads imposed on them.

ELECTRICALLY-DRIVEN KICKING-SHOE ACTION
From an 1895 Patent design this is an application of the mechanical force-enhancing kicking-shoe player system

Piano-players of this period were invariably dependent on purely mechanical action and they played using long and sometimes endless card bands or strips. These offered great advantages over the disc which was limited to how much music could physically be punched into one revolution of a piece of waxed card.

One of the earliest Leipzig makers and distributors was J M Grob, precursor of the Ludwig Hupfeld empire. He was a protagonist of the cardboard disc and his 36-note player was a neat little box affair that stood rather delicately on spindly legs in front of the piano. As the operator turned the handle at the front, the disc slowly turned against a mechanical keyframe operating small wooden fingers protruding from behind. These rested on the piano keys and depressed them according to the demands of the disc.

This type of piano-player was fairly common in the 1880s when several makers brought them to the market. The trade magazine *Musical Opinion* for May 1888 announced one as follows:

> Mr Alfred Lengnick, of Oxford Street, is the sole wholesale agent, for the United Kingdom, of the 'piano player', an attachment which will fit any piano, and by means of which any piece of music may be performed on the pianoforte by putting on a perforated disc and turning the handle of the instrument. It is claimed for this ingenious invention that it has the advantage of not being purely mechanical, time and expression being within control of the player, and with very little practice the crescendo and diminuendo can be exactly rendered. Prices will be, we are informed, forwarded on application.

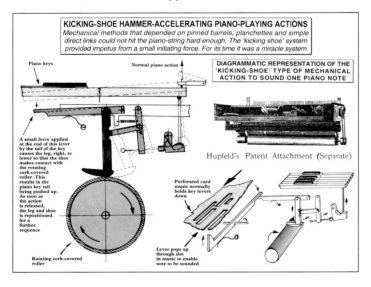

KICKING-SHOE HAMMER-ACCELERATING PIANO-PLAYING ACTIONS
Mechanical methods that depended on pinned barrels, planchettes and simple direct links could not hit the piano-string hard enough. The 'kicking shoe' system provided impetus from a small initiating force. For its time it was a miracle system

Piano keys

Normal piano action

DIAGRAMMATIC REPRESENTATION OF THE 'KICKING-SHOE' TYPE OF MECHANICAL ACTION TO SOUND ONE PIANO NOTE

A small force applied at the end of this lever by the tail of the key causes the leg, right, to lower so that the shoe makes contact with the rotating cork-covered roller. This results in the piano key tail being pushed up. As soon as the action is released, the leg and shoe is repositioned for a further sequence

Hupfeld's Patent Attachment (Separate)

Perforated card music normally holds key levers down

Rotating cork-covered roller

Lever pops up through slot in music to enable note to be sounded

In August 1883, the same publication announced the appointment of a London agent for the invention of a Frenchman, piano-maker Jean Lacape (his name is grossly misspelled in the news item). Lacape's barrel-operated mechanism fitted under the keyboard and appears to have owed some of its detail design to the sewing machine, since a foot treadle was used to rotate a large-diameter flywheel to turn the pinned barrel. The report reads:

> Another mechanical pianoforte! Messrs. Metzler & Co are the agents for Lacafé's *[sic]* clever invention, by which a simple piece of mechanism is adapted to the interior of an upright pianoforte, to play which a special pedal (placed at the side of the ordinary pedals) is put in motion, each stroke of this pedal marking the measure of the air that is being played, and by that means

a more artistic rendering is capable than when a continually revolving handle is used for the purpose. The instrument, possessing a key-board, can be played in the ordinary manner.

Shortly after this, Gavioli introduced a book-playing mechanical piano called the Piano Executant. This was shown at the Barcelona Exhibition of September 1888, and the correspondent of *Musical Opinion* wrote, a little tongue-in-cheek, perhaps, as follows:

> The sole piano forwarded by Messrs Gavioli & Co, Avenue de Taillebourg, Paris, will be found very useful by persons desiring to play the piano, but not knowing how. For, by fixing and turning a handle in the slot projecting from the upper front panel, after laying the long strip of cardboard music, folded as a book, therein, and fixing as directed, the result is music by the yard, or by the hour, churned out as in a regular piano-organ. This is an idea which occurred to the writer many years ago, and the marvel is that so simple an instrument was not produced ten years back. The 'piano executor' will be found valuable.

The writer, who takes the opportunity to stake his claim to having thought of the idea 'many years ago', seems to have been unaware of similar instruments that had been around then for more than forty years. His description of a 'slot projecting from the instrument' suggests that he was no technical man. The Piano Executant is a rare instrument today and I know of only two instruments, one of which was in my own collection for many years and is now in a museum.

One more mechanical action is worthy of mention and this was the 'leaf-system' perfected by South German makers Imhof & Mukle for playing pianos and orchestrions. This comprised a roll of stout manila paper or thin card which was wound onto a large drum and drawn across a mechanical keyframe so as to operate mechanical key action. The card was often up to 100 feet in length and because it travelled slowly it was possible to play a long piece of music with this system.

Imhof produced many fine piano orchestrions which featured complex automaton scenes. Frequently these involved a 'back projection' system where the front of the case, or part of it, was painted as an opal glass screen behind was arranged a travelling transparent belt with figures and objects painted upon it. Behind this would be an electric lamp and when the instrument was switched on a small drive belt from the motor roll would set the scene in motion.

One such model has a waterwheel, a hot-air balloon that apparently crosses and recrosses the vista (suggesting a rather wayward wind direction!), a train that passes over a bridge between two hills, a windmill and a waterfall. This whole effect is achieved in silhouette on the translucent glass painted scene. Imhof pianos, like many other of these very large orchestrion pianos, could be tuned by swinging out the strung back and action: it was hinged at the bottom at the back so that it could be moved down into the horizontal position.

It is to America that one must look for the earliest practical pneumatic-value applications of paper although Germany was not far behind. Probably one of the most misunderstood men in all of mechanical music's history was John McTammany of Worcester, Massachusetts. He was a far-sighted inventor who patented a remarkable series of improvements to the paper-roll system from 1868 onwards. He applied his techniques to the manufacture of organettes but the venture was not a success. Unable to pay the renewal fees on his patents, he had to see each one taken up and successfully exploited by other companies.

McTammany's problem and one which certainly did him a great deal of harm as far as the casual historians have been concerned, is that he did not like to see others taking credit for his own work. Some might say that was a justifiable complaint but when he went into print with a first-rate little book called *The Technical History of the Player [61]*, the world of mechanical music went mad. Poor old McTammany was belittled, castigated and vilified – yet there is no doubt in my mind that it was through his pioneering work that things happened the way they did. He was, for example, the first person to make a simple pneumatic system that used a sliding perforated paper valve, and the first to undertake an on-going programme of development and improvement to it.

McTammany, whose name is almost forgotten today, did much to give us the player organ and organette as well as the player piano yet he was to spend his last years on the outside of the prosperous and profitable industry that he had virtually started. Short-memoried men with fat cigars wouldn't give him the time of day. He died penniless and justifiably bitter in 1915.

In England, Bishop & Down patented a pneumatic system for keyboard playing in 1882, whilst C A Custer of New York contrived what must surely have been the first 'expression' device in 1887. His system graduated the power of touch and operated the piano pedals from 'either barrel or perforated roll'.

Perforated paper now took its place at the forefront of the challenge for the ideal music-programming medium and one of the earliest to exploit this was American Elias Parkman Needham who, from 1877 onwards, presented many improvements in the development of the pneumatic system. It was he who invented the upright player action used in reed organs, which paved the way for the entire later development of paper-controlled music.

Merritt Gally of New York patented in 1881 a pneumatic device for use in playing pianos. In its approach this was some years in advance of its time but, for various reasons, Gally concentrated on perfecting the principles of the small organette rather than those of the pneumatic piano. Gally and, separately, McTammany laid these foundations.

The very first pneumatic self-playing piano is considered to have been the invention of Robert W Pain who, in conjunction with Henry Kuster, built one for Needham & Sons in 1880. This had a 39-note compass. Two years later he constructed an inner player with a range of 46 notes which was for the Mechanical Orguinette Company (later to become the Aeolian Company). It was a time of great progress and Pain was at the forefront of developments when, in 1888, he produced an electrically powered 65-note player.

Perhaps the most attractive style of the Racca *Piano Melodico* was the largest model which was styled like a small grand piano. Besides having a hand-operated 'intensity' lever for soft-to-loud, it had controls for holding off the dampers plus the ability to raise the rear lid to give even more volume to the instrument.

Between the years of 1896 and 1902, the progress and perfection of the external player can largely be attributed to men such as Tremaine, White, McTammany, Gally, Goolman, Doman, Parker, Votey, Kelly, Pain, Brown, Davis, Clark, Hattemer, Winter, Healy, Weser, Salyer, Klugh, Ball, Wuest, Gulbransen and Welin.

The so-called 'American organ', soon to become known almost universally, was developed in the United States [2] and worked on the principle that air was sucked down through the reed, so producing a sound. This differed from the first harmoniums in which air was blown through the reed.

The precursor of the American organ was the organette and in 1881 Moses Harris controlled the mechanical performance of one such device by passing a strip of perforated paper across the air passage to the reeds. He mounted his bellows above these passages. Harris later used the same system on a keyboard reed instrument and also a pipe organ and was thus one of the first to follow Elias Parkman Needham's system. In subsequent years, Wilcox & White and the Aeolian Company were to exploit the pressure or blown reed in their roll-playing organs, as this system produced a louder note with a greater purity of tone that could be voiced almost like a pipe-organ.

The ascendancy of perforated paper as a musical programme medium irrevocably altered the world of mechanical music. The ancient barrel was now relegated to a third-rate position, superseded by perforated paper and punched card. Barrel organs, however, were still to be made for a number of years to come and a wide range of these instruments was included in the 1905 catalogue of Thibouville-Lamy of London and Paris. The barrel piano for street use, as I described in the previous Chapter, was soon to regain its former position in spite of the infiltration by perforated music, while makers such as Pasquale continuing in this line of business until the 1930s.

It was very different in the 1880s, though, and there was a spate of playing systems which, with but few exceptions, left the barrel out cold. It is some of these inventions and ideas that I want to tell you about now because they show a veritable squabble amongst makers first to be different just for the sheer cussedness of being different, and second to be different so as not to tread on somebody's Patent-protected toes.

It all began, of course, not with paper but with cardboard. In Paris, the Gavioli family was renowned for its stupendous dance organs – today we generalise and call them fairground or carousel organs which is not strictly right. Claude Gavioli was also making small portable street organs and an intermediate size that could be pushed around the streets on wheels. He designed and perfected a pneumatic-lever action in which the air valve in a high-pressure windchest was opened by a servo valve in a low-pressure windchest using one of a set of small levers or keys set in a line in a frame – the keyframe. They were operated by slots or holes in the perforated-card tune sheet. This was in 1881.

In Europe it is generally accepted that Gavioli was the first to make serious use of perforated cardboard music in mechanical organs and pianos. The earlier inventions of Dawson *et al* were not really practical and didn't get past prototype stages. Not only did Gavioli think through the whole process but he also thought up the zig-zag folding of the punched cardboard music into a book which could readily be carried and then be fed through the instrument. That his system was successful should be obvious: it is still in use almost one-and-a-quarter centuries later!

PIANISTA THIBOUVILLE.

View of the Pianista placed before the Piano.

This apparatus can be adapted to any piano either of English or foreign make.

View of the Pianista ready to be played.

LATEST IMPROVEMENTS.

Pianista Patented S. G. D. G.

ME THIBOUVILLE-LAMY'S patent Pianista with double pneumatic acti

Claude Gavioli went on to patent a piano player which worked on this same principle in 1884-5. By 1895 Gavioli was using cardboard music to work the keys of all his show organs and, four years later, was using a servo-pneumatic lever-free method that came to be known as the 'keyless' system, in use on some fair organs to this day. This was really an early application of the suction tracker-bar as found in player pianos.

Cardboard music inspired other inventors to think of methods of joining the card into a continuous length. The devices used included metal hinges, cloth strips and wire hinges. Gavioli, a man of intellect who came from a family of clock-makers in Modena, Italy, used a simpler, cheaper and more robust method. He glued up his music strip from a large number of machine-creased, overlapping sheets of card. This produced a hard, durable board which could be punched cleanly with the music apertures, yet at the same time was capable of easy unfolding and refolding in the organ or piano.

Other makers rapidly took up the book-music idea and in London Chiappa applied this music principle in the early 1890s to the street pianos and military band organs he was building. On the continent, Brüder in Germany and all other fair-organ makers gradually changed from the pinned barrel to the perforated-cardboard music form.

Paris was as this time the traditional home of the fair organ and the two top makers in that city were the Gavioli family and the Brothers Limonaire. Both were building book-music instruments and so when, in 1884, the musical-instrument manufacturing and distribution combine of Jérôme Thibouville-Lamy, began work on their Pianista piano-player, it is not surprising to find that they scorned both barrels and paper music in favour of Gavioli-type book music. The Pianista was matched by the production of the Organina, which applied the same principles to organ playing.

Perforated paper had seized the imagination of many inventors, particularly in America where the manufacture of the small portable reed organ known as the organette was booming. Organettes were cheap and easy to make and sold well at a price far less than the cheapest average-quality musical box. Countless different styles were made and many inventors found improvements to patent. Ithaca, New York, was the home of the Autophone Company and this small business made organettes from about 1880 onwards. These mostly played paper rolls or endless paper bands, although Autophone also made the Gem roller organette which, in true barrel organ tradition, played small, wooden rollers bristling with pins. These barrels were pinned spirally and made three revolutions to complete the tune – a system well known in barrel-orchestrion making.

Modell E.

Nussbaum matt und blank oder schwarz. Höhe 138 cm.

Für Akkumulatorenbetrieb (12 Volt) inkl. Geldeinwurf und elektr. Leichtern und zirka 50 Meter Noten, nebst 1 Akkumulator, **spielfertig** . . . . Mk. **1800**

Für Starkstromanschluss (110 Volt Gleichstrom) inkl. Geldeinwurf und zirka 50 Meter Noten, elektr. Leuchtern, **spielfertig** zum Anschluss an vorhandene Leitung . Mk. **1650**

Für Starkstromanschluss (220 Volt Gleichstrom) inkl. Geldeinwurf und zirka 50 Meter Noten, elektr. Leuckern, **spielfertig** zum Anschluss an vorhandene Leitung . Mk. **1700**

Mit Dämpfer-Vorrichtung erhöht sich der Preis um Mk. 50.

As the paper roll evolved, so arose a demand for a method of producing the music both cheaply and speedily. The Auto Music Company in the United States came up with a machine for punching out music in 1881. This made 'stencils' or master rolls from which the music rolls themselves could be punched.

In the following year, two English inventors named Bishop and Down patented a paper-operated piano player. This was followed closely by another invention, this time by one A Wilkinson, who used a calico tune sheet for his piano-player.

During these formative years, methods of perforating the paper were many and varied. In 1883 John Maxfield patented a system of creating the holes in organette rolls using an instrument that was equipped with a number of gas jets. The music roll was burned against a template or pattern to produce the openings. The charred appearance of a 'new' roll of music seems to have had little chance of creating customer appeal. Even worse was to come, though, as by the late 1880s several makers were proposing to sandblast their paper tune sheets against a punched steel pattern.

In shotblasting or punching the paper, loose paper fibres would be created and the suction through the tracker-bar would draw this dust, together with any other particles in the atmosphere, into the instrument, ultimately clogging the tiny valves and exhaust ports and reducing the instrument into silent submission!

But the most common system of roll-making was to use a metal punch to pierce closely-spaced holes or slots in the paper. This overcame all the objections of earlier methods and was the process quickly adopted by the whole music-roll manufacturing industry. It did not, of course, diminish the risk of the odd paper-fibre or atmospheric dust from getting into an instrument that was driven by a process guaranteed to rid an immediate environment of dust – a vacuum!

Realising that excluding dust was more difficult than reducing its effect, two American piano-makers, Frederick Engelhardt and A P Roth, solved this problem in 1901 by splitting the tracker-bar (over which the paper travelled) horizontally and interposing a removable filter that was supposed to trap the dust.

Punched cardboard was not dead and buried yet, though, and as late as 1885 Friedrich Ernst Paul Ehrlich of Leipzig was producing a machine for mechanically playing an ordinary piano. This used a perforated tune sheet combined with an escapement-cocking kicking-shoe mechanism worked by small levers to strike the piano strings with sufficient force. Over the years that followed, Ehrlich made a variety of interesting variations on the theme, but all were basically punched-card players. He used cardboard and zinc discs in his many styles of organette culminating in the successful and widely sold Ariston of 1885 with its punched card disc. This 'software' also

programmed his little Orpheus disc-playing piano of 1887, which was played using Ariston tune-cards.

Ehrlich and fellow mechanical instrument maker Paul Lochmann later manufactured a style of 'long-case' stringed instrument that was a cross between a disc-playing musical box and a piano: they were stringed with an iron frame – and played by a large punched metal disc.

In Italy, cradle of the barrel-operated street piano, Giovanni Racca of Bologna was one of the many makers. In 1886 he contrived a wholly-different piano mechanism that was played using perforated book music. His Piano Melodico was a true *piano e forte* and was to be manufactured in a number of styles and sold all over the world.

Fundamental to the Racca system was a novel tremolo system based on an earlier invention by another Italian by the name of Caldera in about 1875. This had also been taken up in England by London piano-maker Joseph Kirkman and known as the Melopiano. This was a *sostenente* attachment wherein each hammer was attached to an oscillating rail by a flat spring set in motion by a foot pedal and flywheel. The hammers were restrained by checks that were freed when their respective piano keys were depressed, so causing the hammers to strike the strings repeatedly.

In the Racca system, protected with co-patentee Seward, this was achieved in a clever manner in combination with a system of varying the position of the fulcrum to the oscillating bar in order to produce soft playing or loud playing.

Four principal sizes of these attractive machines were produced, the majority of styles being of horizontal layout, the largest of which closely resembling a small baby grand. These were played by punched-card music books, folded Gavioli-style, that held down small spring-tensioned levers. The presence of an opening in the card allowed the lever to rise slightly, drawing a check spring away from the already-vibrating hammer.

Racca and Seward's clever action was wondrously simple and beautifully effective and the Piano Melodico has a distinctive sound that is admired by collectors the world over.

Earlier, in connection with Carpentier and later Ehrlich, I mentioned the 'kicking-shoe' type of action. This comparatively simple system was a clever means of using a very small force to trigger a powerful reaction. Although it probably originated with Carpentier before his 1887 instrument, others applied themselves to its use. Among these were J M Grob, A O Schultze and A V Niemczik of Berlin who in 1886 jointly perfected a kicking-shoe-type player for pianos that could also be

used with organs. Unlike Thibouville-Lamy's instrument of the same period, this was worked by a perforated tune sheet. Levers were moved mechanically by the cardboard disc, allowing segmented arms to wedge cam-fashion on a rotating drum, thereby cocking the piano hammer and striking the string.

It was Grob and, separately, Ehrlich who first applied a variation of the elemental Bartolomeo Cristofori hammer action to the mechanical piano. This was a considerable improvement on the direct-striking-hammer principle inasmuch as the hammer mechanism for one note was progressively cocked by the action (with the ordinary piano, the action is cocked by depressing the piano key), finally bringing the hammer against the string and allowing it to fall back immediately, regardless of whether or not the operating lever is returned to normal position. This made for a prompt action, allowed notes to be sustained by a separate damper connected to the cocking mechanism and also permitted free and easy repetition of the note. Grob's player acted upon thirty-six of the piano's keys.

Ehrlich together with some of his contemporaries adopted an alternative method that used the progressive movement of a lever, pulled by the tune sheet, to cock the hammer and release it. Grob's method, on the other hand, relied on the mechanical fact that a cam can be wedged against a rotating shaft, thereby acquiring a considerable amount of energy for the initial expenditure of a very light force at the opposite end of the cam lever.

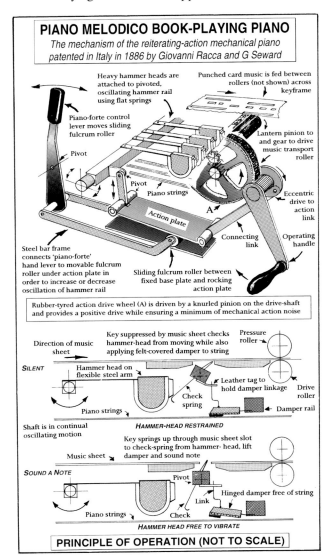

PIANO MELODICO BOOK-PLAYING PIANO

The mechanism of the reiterating-action mechanical piano patented in Italy in 1886 by Giovanni Racca and G Seward

PRINCIPLE OF OPERATION (NOT TO SCALE)

Grob's business later became Hupfeld Musikwerke and so it is no surprise to find that Hupfeld's playing attachment for pianos also used the kicking-shoe action.

A number of very ingenious cardboard-playing domestic pianos were made, particularly those driven by hot-air engines. These emanated from several German manufacturers in Leipzig. The Organista, made about 1890, played, in addition to piano strings, a glockenspiel, a drum and a triangle. Another such instrument, known simply as the Piano-Orchestrion, was a table-like piano and played on strings only. Both these instruments derived their power from a methylated spirits (denatured alcohol) burner powering a hot-air engine located in their lower portions, or could be played by turning a handle.

The first proper pneumatic system to be controlled by a perforated paper roll specifically designed to play an organ was the work of Emil Welte of M Welte & Söhne of Freiburg in Germany. Between 1887 and 1889, Welte took out patents for a paper-roll action to replace the barrels in their large orchestrions and barrel-playing military bands. Welte produced at this same time an air motor for driving the music roll. This was a clever trefoil cam-controlled in-line motor that, in modified and improved form, was to remain a feature of all subsequent Welte mechanical organs and pianos. At the same time he thought up a simple device to allow for the inevitable tendency for a music-roll to speed up as it played due to the increasing diameter of the take-up spool that drew the paper over the tracker-bar. Welte's solution to this was almost childishly simple: he made the spool very large in diameter so that it minimised the effect!

More early refinements were to come, among them that of C A Custer in the United States. In 1887 he designed a keyboard player for a piano in which the power of touch was graduated. At the same time there was provision for operating the soft and sustaining pedals of the piano from the music roll. This was quite probably the first attempt as built-in expression.

Key-top players had begun with the 'church-organist's friend' or 'dumb-organist' which took a pinned wooden barrel and placed it in a box that fitted an organ keyboard with a simple mechanism for playing the keys. This was followed in the 1840s by Debain's Antiphonel, a mechanism that dispensed with the barrel and replaced it with pinned wooden planks. The key-top player was a solution that has appeared at regular intervals throughout the history of the automatic piano, for it has certain charms, namely that it will convert any existing piano into a player. One G P le Dan patented his key-top player for keyboards in 1887. It worked by a series of metal plates with projections which engaged with levers connected to the keys. In this respect it bore a similarity to Debain's player. It isn't certain whether or not le Dan's machine existed but it was to be the last attempt at making a purely mechanical key-top mechanism. All those that were to follow, even into modern times, were either pneumatic or electric.

The taming of electricity was one of the achievements of the Victorian age. While ordinary people justly marvelled at the electric light and the electric motor, inventors were directing their activities in the way of what they termed electro-magnetism and applying movement through solenoid actions. A new form of player action came into being that used the perforated tune sheet.

If the 1880s marked an age where direct current ruled, instruments appeared which must have been a bit alarming to behold for they would have given forth showers of blue sparks as they played. The music-rolls for these were sometimes of thin brass or special paper. Complicated and impractical (in terms of mass-production) systems were dreamed up involving paper coated with a non-conducting substance such as shellac. In place of perforations, some of these had the musical 'notes' arranged on the surface as electrically-conducting portions of the paper where there was no shellac or other insulating material.

Some inventors, no doubt as a result of long and frustrating experiments, sought methods to avoid oxidisation of the electrical contacts. Silver terminals were called for and some even had platinum tips.

Perhaps it was the unreliability of the Victorian electricity supply that prevented the hoped-for mass market from developing for these electro-pianos. Thus these novelties survive only in the Patent archives where inventors allowed their imaginations to exploit these byways of mechanical music.

But electric pianos were manufactured that were an outstanding success. This was guaranteed by the simple fact that they were 'basic' pneumatically-operated instruments whose vacuum supply was created by electric power. They were thus in no way the way-out oddities postulated by odd-ball inventors with their electro-magnetic music-rolls.

By the end of the nineteenth century the disc-playing musical box was perfected, producing its music from tuned steel combs. This same technology was employed to produce a disc-playing piano of small compass. Using metal discs with musical-box-style projections, strings could be hit by hammers or plucked with harpsichord-style plectra. One very successful and popular model was the *Chordephon* made in Leipzig, birthplace of the first disc musical boxes. Initially the Chordephon was hand-turned but by popular demand clockwork variants were quickly introduced. A heavy and decorated cast-iron frame was used, but the device had no case.

These pianos used special storage batteries in the form of wet-cell accumulators in place of the mains power. A drawback was that they were cumbersome and had to be re-charged at regular intervals. For a period these battery-powered automatic pianos enjoyed a good degree of popularity but as mains electricity became more generally available, the heavy and awkward wet-cell batteries were declared redundant.

Electric pianos were ideal in public places and, until the advent of the reproducing piano, never enjoyed a domestic-use market. There was another problem and that centred on people's general lack of understanding of 'the electric fluid'. With its lack of earthing (electrical grounding) it was capable of dispensing electric shocks to those who might incautiously prod where they shouldn't. One can imagine housemaids living in terror of such devices! But although well promoted, electric players were costly to buy and operate.

Like all the systems I have so far told you about, electric pianos had their eccentric element. None, perhaps, more so than the instrument devised by R K Boyle in 1884. His piano had no hammers, the strings being set into vibration by energising

The *Chordephon* was an attractive little instrument that had a good sound. Here is an early example with an under-mounted lever-wound clockwork motor to drive the music disc.

them in conjunction with an electromagnet. And then there was the instrument thought up by A P S Macquisten. His piano played an 'electro-magnetic pattern or Jacquard device', using copper wire feelers to make electrical contact through the perforations in the tune sheet.

It was one of these hybrids that *Musical Opinion's* Leipzig correspondent wrote about on January 22nd 1888:

> Herr R Eisenmann, of Berlin, has brought out a novel kind of piano, with one ordinary hammer action and a second electric action, which can be employed either partially together – that is to say the treble can be played by the electric while the bass is worked by the ordinary hammers, or vice versa – or separately. The electric action produces a marvellous change in the tone of the instrument, which, according to the octave used, sounds like an organ, a violoncello, violin or harp. The electric stream is produced by a small battery of eighteen cells.

This style of sound-production in the piano, while premature in the 1880s, was to recur again in the 1920s and 1930s

With the cover removed to reveal the motor, this 30-note *Chordephon Bijou* played a disc 11¼-inches (28.5cm) in diameter.

with developments such as Millburn, New Jersey, inventor Benjamin Franklin Meissner's electronic piano built in 1930, the Radiano piano, Simon Cooper's 1930 Creatone and so on. The most famous of these hybrid pianos was the Neo-Bechstein designed by Nernst and Vierling and launched in 1933. None of these, however, were 'automatic' in the sense that they were all finger pianos.

Back at the end of the nineteenth century, though, the very association of words 'electric' and 'piano' established interest and created market potential. One of London's established importers of automatic instrument such as the musical box was Henry Klein of 84 Oxford Street. In the summer of 1898, he announced he had taken the agency for the electric piano manufactured by Hupfeld and distributed throughout Europe by H Peters & Son of Leipzig. The instrument sold for the sum of £128 [$515] which made it a very costly instrument.

Hupfeld's electric piano was coin-operated and built around a pneumatic action controlled by a music roll that played the full seven octaves. Operative power came from an electric motor powered by storage batteries that provided enough current 'to play a thousand tunes before the need of re-charging'. At the end of the music-roll, rewinding was automatic. It was therefore a considerable advance on the types of instrument available anywhere else in the world as the time. A slightly cheaper variant was a combined manual and mechanical model that sold for £110 [$440].

The special batteries for these pianos were made in Berlin where no fewer than four firms were engaged in their production expressly for use with mechanical instruments including orchestrion organs. Hupfeld, realising that some people had reserves about electricity in any shape or form and many places did not have an installation – while others had no access to it at all – designed and produced a water motor to drive its instruments between 1890 and 1905.

In the late 1890s, the Krell Piano Company of Cincinnati spent some years in developing an electric piano attachment which, it was claimed, while reasonably priced would be one of the most perfect on the market. Power could come either from the mains or from storage batteries. The inventor was a Mr Simkins who believed that he had devised something to revolutionise the piano attachment industry. The pious belief of its creator was to be proved unfounded and the invention foundered without trace.

In 1911, however, a moderately successful if short-lived electric player was devised. This was the Telektra sold by the Tel-Electric Company of New York. Patented by Timothy B Powers, two models were made both of which played their music from thin perforated brass strip music rolls. With a full electric action, no air or vacuum supply was needed, so any piano could in theory be converted with ease retaining appearance and manual playing facility.

What was unusual about the Tel-Electric system was that it was remotely controllable. The player console was quite separate from the piano and could be placed on a table at some distance from the piano, a power cable passing between the two. By adjusting the variable voltage to each electro-magnetic unit (solenoid), the instrument could be played softly, loudly, or notes be accented at the will of the person seated before the console. Two styles were available, the first being the Tel-Electric with a selling price of $350 [£85] and the other the Telektra at $450 [£112]. This latter version could be played automatically or under the influence of the console.

Another of London's early distributors was William Gerecke, of 8 and 9 Goring Street, Houndsditch. The unfortunate Mr Gerecke (he was declared bankrupt in the early 1900s) advertised as a manufacturer and importer of musical instruments. In 1901 Gerecke introduced the Pneuma, described as a 'self-playing patent apparatus on the Pneumatic Principle – fitted to any New or Old Piano – requires no alteration of the Instrument, which can still be played as a Piano after the apparatus is attached – worked by Storage Battery, or direct from the Lighting Current, or by crank'.

This attachment was made in Berlin by Kuhl & Klatt around 1895 and was promoted as 'the simplest automatically-played piano yet invented'. The Pneuma could be supplied with a piano for £50 [$200] or, alternatively, the mechanism could be installed into any existing piano.

Besides the products of Kuhl & Klatt, electrically-driven pianos were produced by a number of other German manufacturers including Heilbrunn. Heilbrunn & Söhne was founded in Berlin in 1875 and produced several types of electrically-run pianos with 'kicking-shoe' player actions among which was the Virtuola and the Virtuoso. Initially, distribution in Britain was handled by the curiously-named Doremi & Company of 9 Argyll Place off London's Regent Street. The Virtuola was an expression piano (these are described in Chapter 9) and it appeared on the market around the end of 1903; by 1905 it had been superseded by the Virtuoso.

Larger models of the *Chordephon* were soon produced and here, from the Werner Baus collection, is a fine example of the 60-note model that played a disc 19¾-inches in diameter. Note how the makers have capitalised on the disc musical-box style and housed the piano in a smart *jugendstil* styled cabinet. This dates from about 1910.

A private demonstration was given to selected people in the music industry at Doremi's premises on 15 November 15th 1905. The instrument featured was a special music-recording apparatus invented by Heilbrunn and handled by the Heilbrunn Patents Syndicate. No information survives as to how this mechanism operated, but a contemporary report whets our appetite with news that 'impressions that had been made by Scharwanka, Ansorge and other celebrated artists were reproduced'.

Shortly after this event, Doremi faded from the scene and in the following year Sydney C Harper founded the Harper Electric Piano Company in Holloway Road, North London. Later a branch was opened in Paris as 13 Rue Greneta. Harper's business was later reconstructed as a manufacturer of showcards while a new business called the Harper Electric Piano (1910) Company was set up.

The new company continued factoring pianos made in Germany but at the same time declared that it was also manufacturing its own instruments. It embarked on the design of a British electric piano.

The expenditure of a very large sum of money not to mention the time and effort in designing this new instrument failed to reap commercial reward and the outbreak of the First World War curtailed further development. Harpers now abandoned electric instruments and, with the war denying them access to further German-made products, turned its attentions and manufacturing capacity towards making conventional, pneumatic players. The Harper player-piano that followed played 65 noses from 13½-inch-wide perforated paper rolls, most of which were punched out by the Up-To-Date Music Roll Company of Hammersmith.

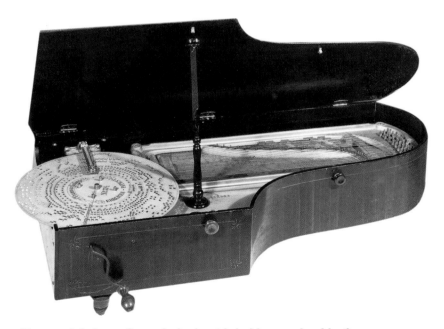

Disc-operated pianos of a much simpler style had been produced by the enterprising Paul Ehrlich of Leipzig as early as 1895. These used the same 24-note punched cardboard music discs as the *Ariston* organette, many hundreds of thousands of which were produced in the closing decade of the nineteenth century. Called the *Orpheus*, this attractive table piano benefited from having access to the vast catalogue of *Ariston* organette music.

The application of electro-magnetic action was to attain its zenith in America where in later years many companies, among them Wurlitzer and the Mills Novelty, made a variety of instruments played electrically from a perforated paper roll.

Mechanical piano-makers grasped the technology of electrically controlled instruments and made maximum use of the opportunities it afforded. This must have delighted men such as Dr Henry John Gauntlett (1806-76) who was organist at Olney in Buckinghamshire because in 1852 he proposed that at some time one organist might be able to play all the instruments in the county thanks to electricity. Eleven years later another organist, the appositely named John Wesley Goundry was granted a British Patent for the playing of organs electromagnetically. His Patent, No 2490 of October 10th 1863, describes many 'improvements' including a solution to Gauntlett's dream, projecting that from one keyboard situated in St Paul's Cathedral every organ in London could be operated by one organist!

Curiously, of all the possibilities that electrical action might have suggested, the one that virtually all inventors overlooked was the potential educational merit of the multiple playing of an instrument as a means of demonstration to students. Not until the very recent introduction of the home computer into everyday life has this been possible and it has brought what the 1980s fondly called 'long-distance learning' within the reach of practically everybody on the globe.

In October 1902, *Musical Opinion* carried the following notice concerning what sounds to have been quite an advanced player made by Ludwig & Company of 970 Southern Boulevard, New York, a company formed in 1889 to make a novel player. Under the heading 'The Ludwig and Co Piano Player', it wrote:

> At St Ermin's Hotel, Westminster, the other day, we were shown this player by the invitation of Mr J H Ludwig of New York. It is a remarkable production, on which thirty-five workmen have been employed for five years; and now we are not sure that the instrument is yet on the British market, for the patents may be offered for sale.
>
> We had the pleasure of hearing much music by means of the player, including 'The Chariot Race' (from 'Ben Hur'), Eilenberg's 'Forest Mill', and a march 'The Coloured Drum Major'. One of the features of the instrument is that the loud pedal is brought into use automatically by means of a music roll; although the performer may use such pedal by touching a stop if desired.
>
> An unique arrangement is that by which (by the addition of six holes in the music roll) the accent to any note required in a treble or bass melody is thoroughly effected. Then, too, the roll is five and a half inches wide – a boon for damp climates.
>
> There are, it is stated, no less than twenty-four new ideas in the construction of the player; and we think that the makers have good 'points', and especially so in this way: the pneumatic tubing to each note is of lead, and even the sides of the sixty-eight tiny

bellows are made of steel, the leather portions being painted aluminium colour. All parts (metal) are produced economically by automatic machinery.

Our space is exhausted; or we should have liked to have written about the firm's piano factory, at which twelve instruments are turned our daily.

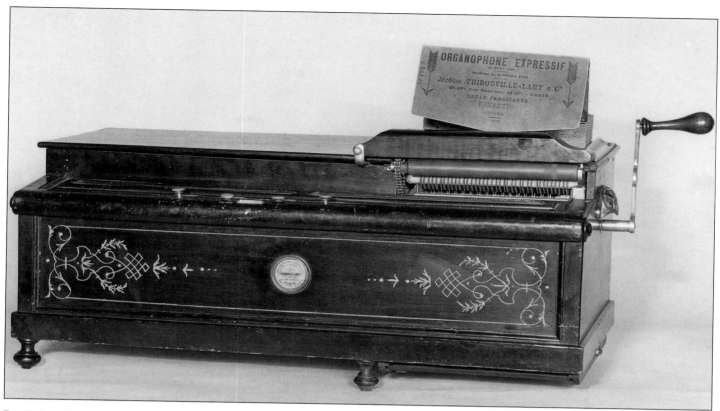

Punched cardboard music folded into a zig-zag book was the invention of fairground organ-maker, Gavioli. Soon this style of musical programme was used for many other instruments. In Paris, Thibouville-Lamy made the 54-note *Organophone Expressif book*-playing reed organ, seen here. This same music, 215mm wide, was also used by Charles Ullmann for his *Piano Executant Artiste*. Curiously, Imhof & Mukle, the makers of Black Forest organs and musical clocks, also used the same width and scale for their 54-note book-playing piano.

The story of Ludwig & Company's meteoric rise is related in Appendix 2. What is intriguing about the report of this device is that it sounds to have been a fairly sophisticated expression piano. Amidst all this progress and development, the ordinary customer faced an all-too familiar quandary. With all this progress and new models being brought out on a regular basis, what was the right time to buy – and what purchase should he make? After all, today's much-vaunted model would be tomorrow's old hat. The same edition of *Musical Opinion* as that quoted above also carried a correspondent's letter. Under the heading 'Mechanical Player and its Music', the writer posed a major question. It ought to have been a warning to the trade, but everybody knew that the question was unanswerable.

Sir, It would be interesting if some of your readers would give their experience of some of the pianoforte mechanical players which have been brought before the public. In looking through your advertising columns I can enumerate some eight different playing actions, and no doubt there are others in existence. In each it is more or less claimed that, while the execution is done mechanically, the expression is entirely in the hands of the operator. One would like to know whether the expression given is sufficient to overcome the mechanical effect which one cannot but think constitutes a drawback to this class of performance. The cost of the paper rolls, whether loaned or purchased, which is hardly alluded to in the various announcements, must be an important item, in addition to the present high prices of most of the players, which prevent very many from entertaining the idea of possessing one. I note that some 'players' do not by any means act on the full compass of the instrument; one, as least, omitting the lower fifteen notes in the bass in addition to some in the treble.

There is no doubt a future before the mechanical player, which appears to have come to stay; though if they get into common use they would seem to discourage the study of the pianoforte as we have always been accustomed to manipulate it. Yours &c, [signed] Observer.

The progress of development in the world of the piano-player and player-piano was a bit chaotic, certainly in the early days. Because people kept quiet about their inventions, the gap between the go-ahead end of the industry and the followers-on was vast. As the trend-setters thought increasingly about expression and other sophistications others were still trying to master the basic properties of spools of paper with holes in.

For an example of a maker tackling a problem from the wrong end, the case of the makers of the Smith Lyraphone, a product from Baltimore, Maryland, is well worth studying. These piano players were unusual by virtue of the fact that the 65-note roll openings in the wooden tracker-bar were of varying size, being small and narrow in the centre and quite long on the outside. This was specifically contrived to allow for mistracking of the paper rolls, yet the inflexibility of the system must have led to its own downfall. The tracker-bar was manufactured by taking two pieces of wood, dividing the note openings with saw kerfs and then gluing in short intercostals. The actual player action was mechanical, being of the kicking-shoe' variety, using a rotating cork-covered roller and levers. The kicking shoes were drawn up into contact with the rotating roller by pneumatic action — an unnecessarily complex arrangement.

The Lyraphone was, of course, an extreme case in which a maker, faced with temperamental, expanding music-rolls, sought not to dry them out or make them narrower, but to increase the risk of mistracking by the simple expedient of expecting the paper to have been wider than normal. Put another way, if you had a new, dry roll straight out of the airing-cupboard it would never play properly!

So the Smith Company failed to tackle the root cause of the difficulty – the poor quality of some paper being used for music rolls. This whole subject is exhaustively discussed in Chapter 11 but here I just want to highlight the root problems of music rolls. Certain physical characteristics of the early papers in use had to be taken into consideration, not the least of which was expansion and contraction in varying moisture conditions. Quite often a roll of paper would swell so much as to wedge itself firmly between the wooden spool ends. Again, the paper would not track properly or wind onto the take-up spool in damp weather.

Adjustable spools had to be invented until the introduction, early last century, of music paper which had a low expansion coefficient. Another problem was fluff, dust and paper fibre from both the surface of the paper roll and also the sometimes ragged edges of the perforations. After a while, the suction at the tracker-bar would dutifully draw any such undesirable debris into the mechanism, upsetting the seatings of the valves and blocking critical-action bleed holes. Filters and dust traps were incorporated until better paper was adopted. The Aeolian Company was the first to fit their piano players with a transparent Celluloid-glazed sliding lid to the spool box assembly just to keep out the dust when the instrument was not in use.

Some paper makers, realising how much paper was being used by the manufacturers of music rolls, bent over backwards to produce special product for this purpose. One of the largest suppliers in Europe was Hoffmann & Engelmann of Neustadt-by-Haardt in Germany. Originally this company supplied its special roll paper to a large number of orchestrion makers but later it was taken over by Hupfeld and so its output was channelled to serving the prodigious roll output of that one major company. This paper-mill always watermarked its music-roll paper at regular intervals along its length with the letters 'H & E' and, further on, the year of manufacture. The production for Hupfeld was always marked with an additional watermark throughout the length of the paper which read, in script, the word *Phonola*.

As the 1890s arrived, the practical simplicity of the basic principles of the paper-controlled pneumatic piano ensured that the quest for a piano-playing system was over. The perforated-paper player piano was to be one of the last contributions in the field of musical instruments of the classic generation. As for the second-generation instruments, they are no longer recognisable as musical instruments. Being nothing more than electronic tone-generators, they rely on the principles of electronics controlled by perforated-paper computer tape, digitally-encoded floppy disc, or programmed computer chip.

Inventors being the way they are, solving a problem does not stop people dreaming up what they imagine to be improvements with the result that there remained the trickle of odd systems for a few years but, seeing that paper music was easy to make, cheap to sell and quite compact, the piano industry at long last united on making pneumatic actions almost overnight.

Many decades of stability would follow in the timeless world of technology. Depression and recession would take its toll of the instrument and today's fad would become tomorrow's antique. Not until the computer came along would inventive Man remember the player-piano and create a 21st century version.

But that's ahead of this story. We are still in the opening years of the 20th century – the Edwardian era when invention and inventor jointly stood for progress. Far from having his first player piano burned by the gathering of irate music teachers, the ideas first thought up by Elias Parkman Needham and John McTammany were warmly welcomed universally. Everyone wanted a self-acting piano and he who made the best and simplest action would be a hero.

With the polished rosewood player pushed up to the piano and a good selection of popular rolls including, perhaps, some virtuoso pieces to impress visitors, every home of the modern Victorian and neo-Edwardian was suddenly complete. All that had gone before was relegated to being old-fashioned and valueless. The sheer convenience and simplicity of the paper roll closed the book on the subject of inventing devices to play the piano. 'Out with the old and in with the new' was the cry: the precursors of the pneumatic piano player were discarded. In but a few short decades, the piano player itself was to suffer the same ignominious end.

In the half-century since the Great Exhibition of 1851, the domestic mechanical piano-player with its cumbersome music programme and operated by a hand-turned crank handle, had given way to the pneumatic player with its simple, cheap, small perforated paper music rolls and operated by foot treadles which acted on exhaust bellows to provide suction which controlled the action. Those antiquated piano-players were still being produced as late as 1909 although the first player-pianos – pianos with interior playing mechanisms – had appeared as early as 1892. By 1901, the player-piano as a complete unit took command of the automatic piano market.

---

1. Dawson produced a descriptive leaflet on his Autophon Improved Organ and this is reproduced in *Barrel Organ [73]*, page 144.
2. In truth, the American organ was a French invention devised by a harmonium-maker in the 1840s that sought to improve the tone by using suction bellows. His idea, however, was not taken up in France until many years after its transatlantic perfection.

A French-made keyboardless mechanical piano that plays 54-note Ullmann-type music. Operated by turning the handle in the front, this piano bears no name.

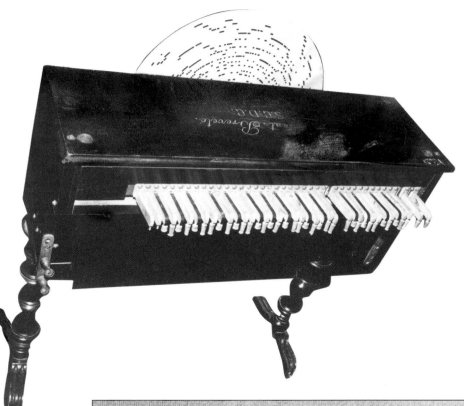

Paul Ehrlich's mechanical piano player operated on 36 of the piano's keys and the musical programme was a 36-note Ariston punched cardboard disc. The machine was lightweight and cheap and enjoyed a brief but profound popularity. Despite its 'improved locking system' to locate it on the keyboard, the lack of precise up-and-down adjustment plus the tendency of the player to wobble from side to side as the handle was turned tended to negate the undoubted cost advantages of a device that had a huge existing catalogue of 'recorded' music available.

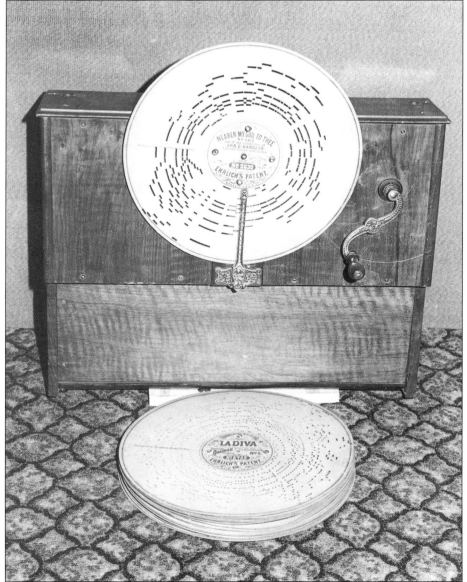

The Leipzig maker J M Grob introduced a more practical disc-driven piano-player in around 1890. Soon taken over by Hupfeld (1892), the Grob cabinet player became known as the *Hupfeld Pianoplaying Apparatus No.10*. This had one big advantage over the earlier Ehrlich device in that the cabinet was built in two telescoping sections that could be adjusted to the height of the keyboard by vertical screw-jacks. The openings for the special jack key can be seen in the top panel at its rear corners.

Hupfeld's development of the Frenchman Carpentier's kicking-shoe action allowed perforated music to be used in a mechanical player. The keyframe only needed lightly-sprung steel fingers that were easily depressed by the thin punched music card, for the only duty they had to perform was to draw a thread link to the 'heel-and-shoe' lever. The force to strike the strings of the piano was applied by a rapidly-rotating roller that caught the shoe and carried it forward so that it could operate a piano hammer action. Here is a piano made in 1902 by the eminent firm of F Geissler of Schutzenstr 13, Zeitz in Prussian Saxony to the South-West of Leipzig. This business, founded in 1878, only ever employed the best and most reliable actions so it speaks well of Hupfeld's player that it was this mechanism factory director Paul Emmerling selected. In this view, the player is seen in its drawer beneath the keyboard.

The Hupfeld action was simple and drew its thin card music-roll from the spindle, left, under the keyframe, right of centre, to the take-up spool, right.

Two views of the kicking-shoe action
that lay at the heart of Hupfeld's
mechanical player. The electrically-
driven roller is rotated by a belt on a
conical pulley. By varying the speed
of the roller, the force with which the
kicking-shoe action operates becomes
adjustable so giving a rather basic
system of piano and forte.

Here is the Hupfeld player ready for action, this time in a 1905 Gebrüder Perzina (Schwerin) piano. To even out the mechanical drag on the music while maintaining it as narrow as possible, the card was drawn through the keyframe by one central sprocket wheel, the holes for which are clearly seen.

The kicking-shoe system was adopted and modified by several makers. The Pianotist Company in London (with its American subsidiary, Adek Manufacturing Company or New York) revised the mechanism and rendered it somewhat neater. Here are two views of it installed in a German-made Steinway upright (the fallboard is marked 'London & Hamburg'). Still electrically-driven, the music is now drawn through the keyframe by the take-up spool and two wooden wheels at curious angles keep the music-roll travelling smoothly from the spindle.

The electric motor and its variable-speed drive can just be seen in this view which also shows the curious rotating tempo knob (right of the keyboard front) and the two central levers for manual adjustment of 'soft' and 'loud' playing.

One novel feature claimed for the Pianotist system was that it could be installed in an existing piano and did not need electricity for operation. Here is a rare survivor of a pedal-operated installation made as late as 1910 by Robert Seidel (Nachf.) & Herman Garn of Wilmersdorf, Berlin. The piano was made for export to Britain where it was retailed by the old-established Liverpool dealers Crane & Sons of 217-227 Scotland Road.

Pianotist music was not cheap to buy. All the rolls appear to have been made in America although the labels all show the London address. The roll numbers seen here extend from No.9 (*Melody in F* by Rubenstein priced at 5s 9d [$1.10]) to No.137 (Overture: *Merry Wives of Windsor* by Nicolai costing 14s 6d [$3.00]); Number 15 at the left is *La Paloma* by Yradier which would set you back all of 4s [$0.80].

After the cardboard music the industry was turning increasingly towards perforated paper that was both cheaper and more compact than the coils of punched card. By the 1910 Leipzig Trade Fair, Hupfeld had introduced his Phonola and DEA pneumatic actions. But Hupfeld's first pneumatic roll-playing pianos were hybrids still operated by turning a wheel. The Clavitist of 1908-09 was a 73-note pneumatic player but still had its entire action under the keyboard. At that time, America was starting to hear more and more of the trade-name Pianola and Hupfeld tried hard to get the industry to adopt the name 'Clavitist' for all players. It was the failure of this that no doubt inspired the brand name that, for Hupfeld, succeeded so well – 'Phonola'.

The Clavitist hand-cranked pneumatic player action was installed in a number of instruments. Here is one by M J H Kessels of Tilburg, North Brabant, Netherlands, that reveals the strong influence of organ-building on the suction bellows driven by reciprocators from the crankshaft, far right. The winding handle is removed along with the bottom board.

In 1884, J M Grob and K A Gutter invented a new portable stringed instrument which they called the Autoharp. This was a small zither-like instrument across the strings of which extended a number of wooden bars mounted in such a way that they could be pressed down like a piano-key. Each carried on their undersides a variety of felt mutes in order that various strings could be silenced. The player strummed the strings with one hand while holding down a sequence of mutes with the other. The result was 'artistic chords' in a variety of keys and all produced without effort. So successful was the Autoharp that soon the principle was taken up by the Leipzig mechanical musical instrument inventors. The roll-playing *Triola* had a simple string-plucking mechanism and the user was encouraged by printed instructions on the music as to which of the six pre-tuned sets of chords to pluck as an accompaniment. Many of these were produced and survive today. The plucking mechanism was a frame of hinged short springs that engaged with the strings as metal control keys sprang up through note-holes in the thick paper roll.

The 17-note *Volks-Klavier* was another paper-roll-controlled automatic zither dating from the closing years of the 19th century. Others of this style included the Symphonion *Koschat* and the *Guitarophone* made by Menzenhauer of Leipzig.

Debain's Antiphonel keyboard-player of 1846 was a key-top unit that converted any keyboard instrument into an automatic. The makers of church barrel-organs had been the first to make such a device: it was called a 'dumb organist' and used a wooden barrel in a box that sat on top of the keyboard and pushed down the keys with felt-tipped plungers. The key-top idea was turned towards pianos with moderate success by a New York company at the very end of the 19th century. The Maestro Company of Eldridge launched a very simple piano-player that revived the key-top principle. At around half the price of the Aeolian Pianola and the Farrand Cecilian, the Maestro cost just $125 (£31.5s). It was a pneumatic instrument playing standard 65-note rolls and played by the simple turning of a handle. A crank propelled parallel rods to operate a double exhauster in the left of the cabinet, the equaliser being in the right-hand side. What the little Maestro lacked in power from its tiny pneumatic motors it ample made up for in ingenuity. Launched in 1899, it was barely up to the job and production had ceased by 1901.

Immediately after the end of the Second World War, the key-top staged a remarkable revival in America with a small flurry of instruments. First, around the 1950s, came the Electrelle, a suction player with full pneumatic action (top) followed soon afterwards by the all-electric Dynavoice electric solenoid-operated player (bottom). Both were full-scale 88-note roll-players.

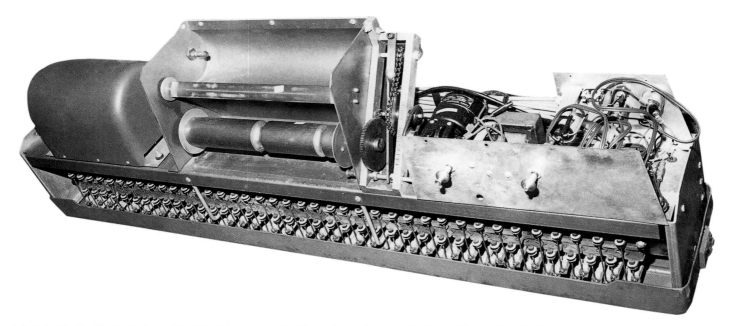

A look inside the Electrelle shows that it is driven by an electric suction unit, housed in the cowling at the left. The powered a small-volume chest with a two-row pneumatic stack that used long, thin motors. Unfortunately, the vacuum unit was very noisy and the device produced a disagreeable whine that combined with its uninteresting amount of power to transport it into an early oblivion. Nobody today even knows who made it!

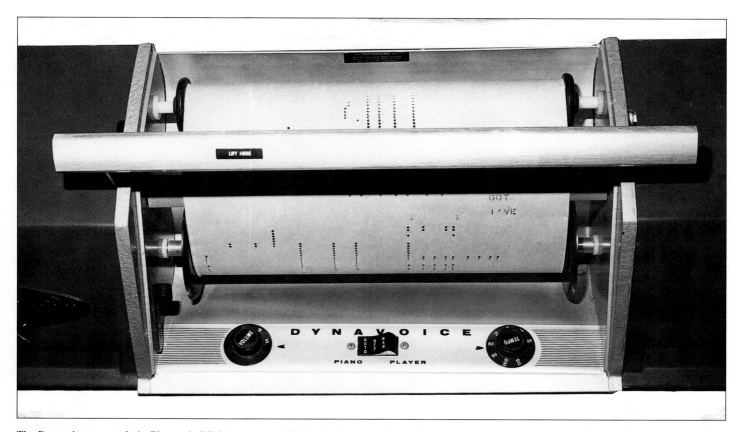

The Dynavoice was made in Plymouth, Michigan, around 1965 with the promotional slogan 'any piano to player piano in 30 seconds'. A rather soulless device in a plastic case, it seems not to have had much success and the business was gone by 1968. This picture shows the lifting handle that swings over the tracker bar, also the simple controls: a central on-off rocker switch, a volume control and a tempo control.

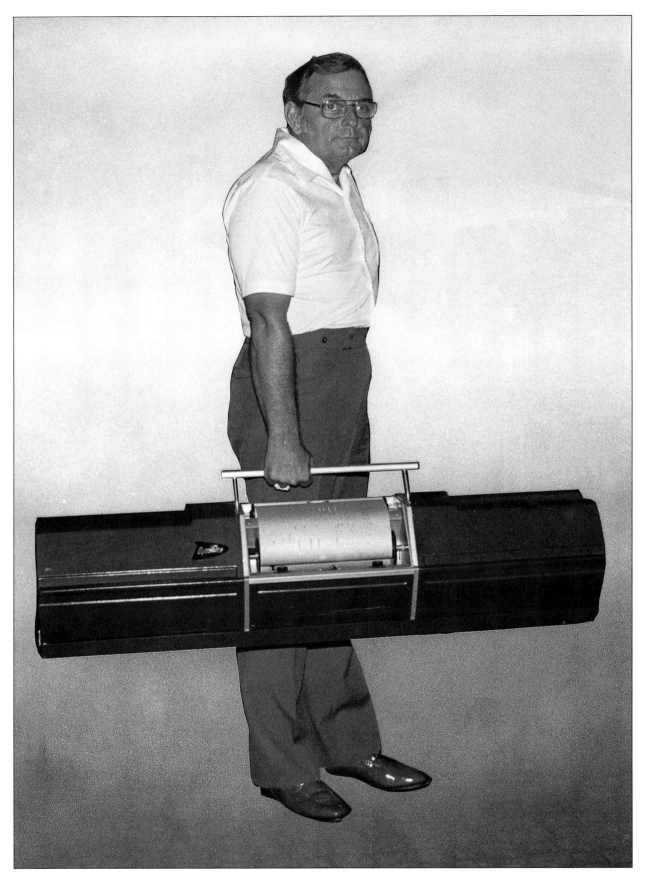

'Have player, will travel!' Museum owner Walt Bellm of Florida, who owns all of the key-tops shown here, shows how the Dynavoice was carried between pianos. A necessary adjunct to these key-tops was the provision of a separate case tray into which the player could be clipped when detached from the piano so as to protect the delicate plungers that protruded from underneath.

Chapter 5
The Technical Evolution
of the Player Piano and its Industry

Thanks to the pioneering work of a number of inventors, among them Pain, Votey and Clark, the pneumatic piano-player became a practical reality in the United States soon after the start of the 1890s. Although to the artist it was more of a crude basic music-player as compared to the sensitive musical interpreter that it would become within the next two decades, it was nevertheless a reliable, albeit fairly rough and ready device. The trouble was that it was unerringly correct, inhuman, was incapable of expression – and sounded mechanical! Nature never being perfect, it was an artistic anathema upon which inventors immediately set to work with a vengeance to improve.

Over the years that followed, under the guise of 'improvement' we find the inevitable battle of the inventors and patentees, each desperately trying to protect his own designs without infringing those already-patented ideas of somebody else. The Patent at this time was viewed as an important arrow in the inventor's quiver. Something that was protected by a Patent (or even an application for one) was revered. Rather in the way that no academic is thought worth his salt until 'he is published', inventors viewed the attribution of a Patent in a similar light. Whether the cost and involvement required in getting a Patent issued was ever worth it or was ever redeemed by unique selling-point sales is unknown. And if you didn't have time to invent something yourself, you bought out the rights to somebody else's work. Aeolian, for instance, bought hundreds of patent rights from inventors all over the place: I have a leather-bound volume in my library from the company's United States Patent Agent prefaced with the message that 'here is a copy of all the Patents we have acquired for you' with the date 1900-1912.

Looking through this litany of inventive prowess, now no more than mute Patents, one is left with nothing but admiration for those old designers who succeeded in inventing improvements to just about every part of the player piano, many of them time and time again. If player-piano makers never made a great deal of money, then there is no doubt that the legal eagles and patent attorneys must have had a field day!

And so the player set out on its uncertain course towards perfection, first in the guise of the cabinet player or push-up piano-player, and then as the interior player or player-piano. Once that hurdle had been overcome, then along came the various expression systems that gave the world first the expression piano and, ultimately, the reproducing piano.

The resource of manufacturers grew steadily and probably peaked for the first time in the 1908-1912 period. The time of the First World War did not stop industrial production of non-War effort goods as it more or less did in the Second World War, but it did put the brake firmly on development. As first the young men were called up for military service and then, progressively, the older, industry had to survive on a rapidly aging work force. Piano-makers, because of their precision woodworking skills, were favoured for the manufacture of aircraft and as materials entered the routine of short supply, piano and player-piano making declined sharply in the period 1916-1918.

The end of the war brought no great celebration in industry for unemployment remained rife and then on top of all that came the great 'flu pandemic which, having begun at the end of 1916, was to circle the globe into 1920 before fading. In its wake it left a million dead – more than the total of lives lost in the Great War. It wasn't surprising, then, that player-pianos were not to the forefront of the public mind in those terrible times.

But once things picked up again, so the inventors got back to work, beavering away at the pneumatic player. It is difficult to say how many manufacturers there were across the world, but there were very many.

Manufacturing came in three forms. First there was the large company that, like Aeolian, made every part in one or more of its factories. Then there was the smaller piano-making business that bought in actions from specialist parts suppliers and fitted them into their own ordinary pianos to convert them into players. And finally there was the player entrepreneur who was not a piano-maker, but bought instruments from various makers, bought in actions and carried out the conversions in his premises, usually completing the process by adding his own name (or a fictitious name) to the finished product.

The type of manufacturer dictated the type of promotion accorded to an instrument. While the first practical production piano-players came from Germany and the United States there was a marked difference between the ways in which the pieces were advertised. In America, resources and promotion were already geared to production of instruments whereas the European players of the time, although probably of better specification, workmanship and performance, were not launched at the market with anything approaching the gusto and financial backing.

The world of gentle, sophisticated advertising found in Germany and London was nothing compared to, say, the Aeolian Company, which produced expensive colour brochures, mounted nation-wide advertising and marketing campaigns – and had the production facilities to cater for the resulting demand. Not that we should look down on the European achievements for, as we shall see, instruments of considerable quality were manufactured in Germany. The products of Ludwig Hupfeld and Emile Welte, for example, were outstanding in their own right. Significantly, England produced no worthwhile contributions until fairly late on in the story although the British market for American and, to a lesser extent, European products was extremely keen.

When Great Britain adopted manufacturing piano-players these were little different technically from the transatlantic imports. Products such as the Malcolm, for example, were good copies of machines such as Farrand with its Cecilian model. With the arrival of the player-piano, two factors were at work. First was the situation where British ingenuity was able to be applied to a new design. Second was the fact that a number of American companies had opened branches in Britain where 'manufacture' was taking place.

It was the perennial problem of reducing Import Tax, so many machines were shipped to Britain as 'knock-down' sets of parts that were locally assembled. While this allowed a degree of licence to be adopted in describing an instrument as 'made in Britain', it sowed the seeds of domestic manufacture.

A clear case in point was Aeolian at Hayes. Initially the company was a 'screwdriver assembly' factory but gradually products were altered and ultimately manufactured entirely. Comparison between Aeolian's American-made instruments with those made in England show that there was a significant deviation from the original. This same trait can be traced in the products of the Regina musical box company which, as an offshoot of Polyphon in Leipzig, began as a kit-assembly plant and went on to design and develop machines that were quite different from the German originals.

Pneumatic actions made in Britain tended to be little different from those tried and tested in mass production in America. Only a handful stand out as being significantly different and whether that difference equates to improvement

was another matter. Two British actions deserve special mention. The first was a normal 88-note action as fitted to the Boyd Pistonola, and the second was a full-scale reproducing action made for Blüthner by the Sir Herbert Marshall Piano Company and called the Carola. The Pistonola was totally original as regards its engineering but its radical method of operation was ultimately its downfall. The Carola was abandoned because it created another standard in a realm where the perceived benefits of being different from everybody else were greatly outweighed by the stark reality that compatibility was the answer to sales success.

Earlier we saw how the English barrel piano saw its early and developmental years in the poorer parts of London, the slums that were to be found in the Farringdon and Clerkenwell areas. If this was home to the 'clattering joannah' of the streets, then the player piano emanated from the sophisticated West End showrooms of plush manufacturers whose names and reputations were already firmly established. Just as Soho was the centre of not just piano-making but also church and chamber barrel-organ building in the early to mid-nineteenth century, so Camden Town in north London became home to the cheaper-to mid-range player pianos made in England. Close to The Regent's Park and Primrose Hill, Camden fostered a clutch of makers just as Hatton Garden became the centre of the gem and jewellery trade, Clerkenwell that of the watch and clockmaker, and Shoreditch the domain of the cabinetmaker. Shops and showrooms ranged from the department stores such as Whiteley's, Harrods, Selfridges, through manufacturers' own showrooms from Bond Street to Oxford Street, to the shops of the many music retailers across the capital. It was the same in New York and in every principal town in the land.

So how did it all begin? More to the point, where did it start? And

The invention of the pneumatic piano-player marked a watershed in the development of the automatic piano. In one move mechanics were forever a thing of the past as the would-be manufacturers suddenly saw where the future lay. Votey's first Pianola of 1896 was a monstrous machine almost as big as the piano it played but very quickly the woodworking skills developed in the reed-organ industry pointed the way to economic production engineering. By the time Votey sold himself and his instrument to Aeolian a neat(ish) cabinet now housed a practical mechanism. Significantly the first batch of Pianolas was manufactured by Farrand, a business well experienced in reed-organ engineering. Here is a specimen from about 1900.

who made the first piano-player? Well, the first thing to dispel is any thought that it was solely an American invention. America was certainly the breeding-ground for resourcefulness and that is where the instrument was perfected, but we cannot prove that America was first. This is because the first piano-player was the outcome of experiments that were carried out independently in three different places – France, Germany and the United States.

In the early days (around the mid-nineteenth century) France was the scene of much pioneering work and a lot of development study. However, France seemed to lose its early interest and world lead in the mechanical piano several years before America picked it up and forged ahead. Both Welte and, later, Hupfeld in Germany designed, built and then produced instruments, but it was in America that the commercial know-how and the necessary brains were available to push an idea rapidly through development stages and into production.

The claim of Germany as the first in the field is not hard to justify when you realise that the largest mechanical music industry in the world was in Saxony centred on Leipzig with Berlin being a close second. The art and craft of mechanical music in the form of the musical box, first capitalised on in the Swiss Jura, was systematically developed in Leipzig where the disc-playing musical box was invented. Subsequently many of the forms of musical automaton that followed were made and sold the world over. Thus Leipzig was in the best possible position to devise a pneumatic action for piano playing.

The ideas conceived wholly in America were the ones that made the largest contribution, if not necessarily the first, in the field of the player piano and thus it is to America that we must go to start our story. The pneumatic piano player, as distinct from the European cabinet-style mechanical machines, appeared in the States in the late 1890s.

In the beginning inventors seemed undecided as to whether suction or pressure was preferable, in other words air at pressure above that of the atmosphere or air below that of the atmosphere, meaning a partial vacuum. Lessons learned from the early reed organ suggested that pressure air was better.

As regards the mechanical operation of a system, very little difference exists between the mechanism that operates at pressure and that which works on vacuum. Yes, of course the principles are quite different, but the components and their motions are very similar. Because the difference in air pressure needed to set a mechanism in motion is very slight, only the fact that suction (partial vacuum) is easier to control meant that vacuum was chosen. However, some later German pneumatic pianos actually worked on pressure using force-bellows in place of exhausters, and requiring air at pressure to be admitted through the music-roll perforations – as in the pressure Orchestrelle reed organ.

Many of the very earliest mechanical pianos that operated by changing the pressure of the air used a positive pressure system that required compressing the air by means of force bellows. In the end, it was the benefits of a system based on vacuum that were seen as more likely to prove successful to the piano player. From then onwards the majority of inventions used air at a reduced pressure.

The principle of the vacuum used in a mechanical musical instrument is generally attributed to the invention of one of the employees of the Mustel company in France. This, though, may not be correct for it seems that the first use of vacuum may have been made by a man from Boston, Massachusetts, by the name of A M Peaseley, who is said to have made a reed organ in 1818 operating this way. This extremely early claim is impossible to corroborate

and was not known to McTammany who wrote at length on all the pioneers of the player instrument.

What is certain is that Jeremiah Carhart, who built an accordion in 1836 and a lap-top organ in 1839, was granted US Patent No.12,837 on December 28th 1846 for a suction bellows. At this time he was working for reed organ makers George A Prince in Buffalo, New York.[1] This important patent was for some reason subsequently declared null and void.[2] However, Carhart joined forced with Elias Parkman Needham in Worcester, Massachusetts, as Carhart & Needham in 1846. Two years later they moved to New York City. Carhart died in 1868 and the business continued under the name of E P Needham & Son. Carhart's suction bellows were applied to the early piano-player of Needham.

In Britain, Alexander Bain of Hampton Wick, Middlesex, was only able to foresee the use of air at pressure (his Patent 11,886 of 1847 refers) and because of this was forced to invent a system of pressure rollers to keep his perforated paper roll in contact with the tracker bar. Meanwhile Carhart's invention actually sucked the paper against the tracker bar, so dispensing with the need for any additional means of maintaining the contact seal.

The Carhart exhaust bellows formed the very cornerstone of the greater majority of player development that took place throughout the world. The method of operating these bellows derived directly from the reed organ in that foot-operated treadles were provided so that pressure with the feet (described as 'in a walking motion, left, right, then left and so on') continuously drew air from within the piano creating a reduced air pressure within. All functions of the piano were then ascribed to 'controlled leaks', the naturally passage of air into the piano (remember that 'Nature abhors a vacuum'!) being caused to perform some controllable function.

As technology improved, Aeolian managed to pack more features into the push-up Pianola. This 1908 model incorporates the movable pointer and tempo scale of the Metrostyle speed indicator with the Themodist note-accenting system. The music roll of the period still only played 65 of the piano keyboard's notes.

Throughout the history of the player there were very many patents covering developments of the bellows action, particularly with regard to the provision of foot treadles for grand pianos and for treadles that could be folded up and concealed out of the way when not in use. Some of the systems invented were ingenious and others verged on the impractical. The wind department (comprising exhausters and suction reservoir) together with its regulation also came in for many little tweaks as makers tried hard to circumvent methods already protected by their rivals.

But there was one aspect of the piano-player and player-piano that was to tax the minds of inventors the world over. It was a feature that demanded two of the things that were hard to regulate with vacuum until the vacuum level itself had been regulated. This was the means for drawing the music-roll across the tracker bar.

The principle requirements were constant speed – regardless of the speed or 'depth' of pedalling (ie vacuum tension), and precise regulation, meaning the operator's ability to control the speed of the roll instantaneously and precisely regardless of the pedalling. The only certain way of attaining this appeared to be to work the roll-drive mechanism by hand like that of the organette and, indeed, some of the early instruments did just that. It was clearly unacceptable. There had to be a reliable method of employing the suction supply already available inside the bellows reservoir.

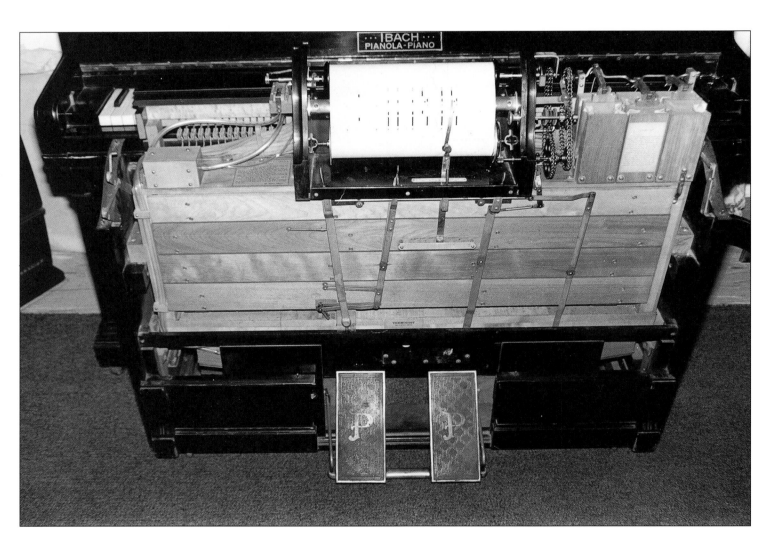

Inside the Pianola cabinet there was very little spare space. Here is a late model Pianola push-up with its case removed showing the four-deck action stack, large roll motor (to the right of the music roll) and control linkages. The Pianola is engaged in playing an Ibach upright piano, itself a Pianola of a later vintage.

Some early instruments transported the roll using a mechanical linkage from the foot treadle by way of a belt, a chain or even bevel gears and shafting. These all suffered from the same very basic defect: the speed of pedalling directly affected the speed of the music. There was another problem. While these systems worked up to a point, they did not make any provision for rewinding the roll at the end of the music, unless one was prepared to pedal the roll back again, nor did such systems respond adequately to anything other than regular pedalling.

If solving the roll-drive was too much of a problem then one could always fall back on clockwork and this method was used by several of the early makers. An early piano-player was the Simplex which employed a large three-spring motor to drive the roll. The Simplex was, of course, a 65-note player and used rolls, which were somewhat narrower than the normal ones. A good proportion of the music for these took the form of accompaniment rolls for vocal songs.

Even a triple-spring clockwork motor was not without its shortcomings and the risk of the mechanism running down during playing provided just another complexity to the business of playing a music-roll. However, Melville Clark made ingenious use of clockwork in his first Apollo 58-note player of 1899. Here the action of treadling turned a crankshaft on a train of gears that rotated the take-up spool, in so doing winding up a clockwork motor through a friction clutch. At the end of the roll, a handle was pulled and the gearing was rearranged so that the roll was quickly respooled under power from the motor.

In spite of the 'innovation' of clockwork, George Howland Davis (son of George H Davis, late founding partner in Hallet & Davis of Boston) chose to fit his piano player of 1901 with a weight-driven rewind. As the roll was played, so was raised a large weight and the potential energy thus stored was used to rewind the music. This was all rather strange since Davis's business, the Electric Self-Playing Piano Company of New Jersey, was set up to produce the Electra piano, an electrically-driven instrument. It seems that failure of the Electra led to a return to more tried and tested methods.

Like Davis, Gilbert Smith of the Smith Lyraphone Company chose clockwork for his 65-note cabinet player called the Lyraphone. In this 1902 instrument, the motor could be used for driving the roll and rewinding it independently of the foot treadles, spring winding being carried out using a suitable handle on the front of the player.

All these machines were nothing more than stop-gap solutions to a problem that really needed somebody having a good grasp of the principles of pneumatics to sort out. That person turned out to be an American named J Morgan who, in 1884, made an 'air engine' that produced rotary motion. This first air motor worked by moving air through a system of bellows and valves to turn a small crankshaft.

Some of these early air motors worked by air pressure instead of suction, a small compression bellows being supplied in conjunction with the foot treadles for this purpose. Another American, George Kelly, thought up the most practical suction drive with his slide-valve motor of 1886. Kelly's motor consisted of a series of sliding plates fitted to a board, each with a matching pneumatic bellows fixed to the other side. Inlet and exhaust ports were cut in the dividing board and each slide was linked with a connecting rod to a crankshaft. Suction applied to the exhaust side of the system would cause each bellows to open and close alternately, the slides regulating the admission of atmospheric air into the vacuum chamber of the motor and serving to turn the crankshaft at a constant speed.

One advantage of this system was that the motor could develop a good deal more torque or power than the earlier pressure motors and was also capable of much smoother action by the provision of four or even five sets of bellows and slides. This had the same effect as a car fitted with a smooth-running multi-cylinder motor as compared with the erratic low-speed behaviour of a single- or twin-cylinder engine.

Real miniaturisation was still a long way off and these early instruments needed to shift a lot of air at low vacuum tension in order to perform both accurately and to maintain a reserve of power. For this reason, the Pianola of the time used no fewer than four decks of pneumatic motors, each of both wide and large proportions. This view from the keyboard side shows how the playing fingers are driven by the various stack motors. Notice the sustaining pedal's mechanical control which could, like the height of the player itself, be adjusted to suit any piano.

The wind motor provided more or less constant speed whiccould be variably controlled by a gate valve. The motor maintained its speed under almost all conditions and speeds of pedalling so long as there was some pressure differential in pedalling so long as there was some pressure differential in the piano system. A flywheel was often provided on the early double-acting three-valve motors to help even out the motion, but the later multi-valved successors usually did not need such an addition.

One of the most compact and sophisticated of all music-roll air motors was that perfected in Freiburg, Germany, by Emil Welte in 1887 and first used to drive orchestrion organ music-rolls. The motor comprised a cone-shaped body carrying along its length three pneumatic bellows arranged at 120-deg. These were linked at their wide ends by connecting rods to a crankshaft which ran, through the centre of the cone and carried at the opposite end a rotating cam which alternately covered and uncovered the entry and exhaust passages to each of the three triangular-shaped bellows. When suction was applied to the exhaust side of the motor, air would be drawn into one of the three bellows, so causing it to turn the crankshaft via its connecting rod and, at the same time, advancing the inlet and exhaust port cam. When a further inlet port was uncovered, the adjacent bellows would begin to inflate, turning the crankshaft and so collapsing the previous bellows, the air from which would be passed down the suction exhaust passage to the inlet side of the main bellows assembly of the whole organ. The continuous application of suction to the exhaust side of the motor kept the system working smoothly, the crankshaft turning with sufficient power to drive the take-up spool. A large flywheel fitted on the end of the crankshaft overcame any tendency to jerkiness. So successsful was the Welte rotary motor that it remained a feature of Welte's instruments right through to the electric reproducing pianos.

It would be a surprise not to find that inventors tried to produce other forms of suction air motor. One of the more unusual of these was the attempt by C W Atkinson to incorporate a motor actually inside the piano roll take-up spool. A feature of Bansall's Universal Piano Player, it was not a resounding success and did not revolutionise the industry.

A perennial problem with spooling paper rolls was that of tracking which means keeping the holes in the paper in line with the holes in the tracker bar. There were two methods of ensuring this: one was to move the spool assembly (both music-roll and take-up spool) sideways as required, and the other was to shift the tracker-bar sideways as required. Of the two, the easier to shift was the spools because all that was needed was to have a system of double-cams to shift each spool chuck, that is both the rewind and the take-up spool. Shifting the tracker-bar, on the other hand, meant resisting the combined resistance of all the rubber tubes attached to the rear of the bar. The preferred method, then, was spool-shifting.

Before that, though, many inventors had a go at controlling the flow of the paper over the tracker-bar. It was some while before it was realised that attempts to constrain the paper from wavering were less likely to be acceptable than finding methods to move either the spools or the tracker bar so that they aligned. Paper constraints merely accelerated wear on the music roll. George B Kelly found that out the hard way with his US Patent number 780,356 of 1904. He guided the music roll in its travels over the tracker board and to the take-up spool by a system of rollers and flanges. While this appeared a good idea, all it really did was to increase the friction and require much more power from the roll-drive motor in order to move the paper. On top of this it must have been an ideal mechanism for pleating the edges of errant rolls.

Maintaining accurate tracking demanded the automatic movement of either the two paper spools or the tracker board itself and the first person to come up with a workable (in theory, at any rate) system was James O'Connor with his patent 789,053. In the first application of his invention he called for the attachment of two pneumatic edge-sensors to be fitted under the sides of the tracker so that they were normally covered

Push-ups developed a style and proportion that was standardised almost throughout the industry. Mass-production at ever-lower cost led to cabinetwork that was more for appearance than skilful durability and in this respect the Pianola was the first domestic article that paved the way for mass-production styles seen also in sewing-machine cabinets and, later, phonograph and wireless cases. Here is an early Pianola playing a grand made by J Bauer of Chicago.

by the music roll. These were connected via a pneumatic valve chest to two small pneumatic motors, one each side of the tracker bar and so placed that they could move the music-roll axis from side to side. In another application of the same system, the shifting was to be carried out electromagnetically.

Although the subsequent invention of Elihu Thomson of Swampscott, Massachusetts, was the subject of infringement claims by O'Connor because it used pneumatics to shift the paper laterally over the tracker, Thomson produced a much neater and more effective tracking system in which one finger running lightly along the edge of the music roll was able to control a pneumatic motor which moved both take-up and music-roll spools either side of an adjustable norm. At about the same time, Theodore P Brown came out with a patent for a manually adjustable music-roll spool position by means of a knurled knob: this moved only the music roll, though.

The Autopiano Company was granted a British Patent number 3310 on February 10th 1909 for a pneumatic music-roll-moving system using balanced pressure (vacuum) ducts in the tracker bar. Two extra holes, one each side, were provided and if the lateral movement of the music roll was enough to uncover one of these, one of a pair of pneumatic motors would be set into motion to shift the spool over.

In the end, two systems were perfected and employed. Besides these two automatic systems, there was the manual form of adjustment either by means of a large knurled brass wheel moving the spools or a screw cam (Angelus action). The pneumatic systems used a variation of the earlier O'Connor system in which two pairs of slightly staggered holes, or a pair of single holes, were covered equally by the travelling roll for equilibrium, or moved back into equilibrium when one was uncovered.

Farrand, having built the first batch of Pianola push-ups for Aeolian, then decided to design and produce its own push-up. The company cleverly produced a very different-looking player that it called the Cecilian. In many respects it was better engineered than the Pianola of the time and was given a very stylish cabinet provided with doors that hid the recessed foot pedals. The Cecilian was a pleasing article of furniture that also made use of metal in its action parts.

The other method was used by Aeolian quite extensively until the middle 1920s and this was a variation of Elihu Thomson's system of using fingers to follow the edges of the paper. Initially, one single finger was used, mounted horizontally inside the spool box so that the left edge of the roll pressed gently against it during playing. Any variation to the left or right caused the inner end of this lever to modify the otherwise balanced air pressure in two small tubes and so shift the roll. This system had obvious limitations and made no allowances for small tears or folds in the roll edge, which, in fact, it helped to extend.

Aeolian then went on to use two fingers as the separate valves of a balanced wind system, one finger on either side of the roll as it passed over the tracker bar. If one of these fingers was depressed, it uncovered the end of a pneumatic tube, so setting the tracking motors in motion. This technique was standard on all the early Aeolian Duo-Art instruments until the mid-1920s and the two fingers served to move both spools relative to the tracker bar. Later instruments reverted to the use of balanced suction via pairs of staggered holes by the roll margins. These were connected to vertically-mounted shifting pneumatics which operated on the tracker bar itself, the spools remaining stationary.

Whichever tracking system was used (and at various times all were in use), there had to be an automatic method of control that was more or less instantly signalled by the music-roll. As it began to shift to one side or the other, appropriate corrective measure had to be commenced quickly before the holes failed to align.

This function was achieved using special holes in the ends of the tracker bar that aligned with the margin of the paper roll. So long as these were both covered by the edge of the paper, tracking was perfect and nothing happened. But if the paper tried to drift sideways, it would expose a hole, allowing air to transfer to a bellows assembly which would gently push the spools over until alignment was once more achieved.

Many player systems employed this method in one form or another. One was the Standard Player Action Company in America. A different version of the same system was used by Aeolian which used delicately balanced fingers that followed the edge of the paper. These covered the ends of small airways that were connected to bellows motors as before. Another type ran the paper between two small brass 'fences' set in the tracker bar which performed similar functions.

A variation of the 'uncovered hole' method was patented in Britain by J J Walker in 1909 and this used special music rolls having a continuous line of central perforations that passed centrally between two holes in the tracker bar. If the roll wandered to one side it would allow air to enter one or other of the holes, so operating valves to the small pneumatic motors or bellows that would gently ease the roll over the opposite way. This system was used by Hupfeld on its early 73-note players. Its big drawback was that the music-rolls had to be specially made, ordinary or 'standard' music being quite useless.

One of the selling points of the piano-player and player-piano was that it was ideal for the family to sing to. This was all very well but as everybody knows there are people who sing and there are those that can sing. The two may not necessarily be the same! To help matters out, the player would have to be able to transpose a music-roll into another key or, preferably, a number of keys. There was nothing new about this and although transposing devices came to be considered as later improvements to the player piano, they were in fact used by Melville Clark in his Apollo push-up of 1899. His 58-note wooden tracker bar could be moved sideways to allow the music to be played in any one of the five keys from Bb to D and the change was made by turning a thumb screw to shift the tracker bar laterally, its lower connections being of flexible rubber tubing. This also served to cater for the irregularities in paper and spool width which, with the early players, varied quite greatly. Melville Clark called this a 'transposing mouthpiece'. Only later did the player piano come to be viewed more as a solo instrument rather than as an accompaniment or backing to a vocalist where transposition was a necessary feature.

The Angelus also featured a transposing device, as much for the correct alignment of rolls as anything else. This was worked by a knurled screw that moved both the take-up spool and the music-roll chuck laterally across the fixed tracker bar.

In later years, with the introduction of quality-controlled paper music and 88-note actions, tracker-bars had to be made of brass to accommodate the closely-spaced nipples for the tubing and the narrow spaces between the openings. These could be shifted through several keys (in the Hupfeld Phonola pianos through no fewer than nine!) by a small transposing lever. Whilst transposition was achieved by moving the tracker bar, some early actions were made in which the music roll and take-up spool were moved instead.

Transposition was a fairly common feature found on push-up players around the early part of the 20th century. It was also a feature of the more popular instruments, push-ups and player-pianos alike, presumably because they appealed more to that class of customer who regularly sang. Better quality instruments and reproducing pianos operated without these novelties and were probably the better for it!

Push-ups were fitted with small wheels to allow them to be easily positioned correctly to the piano keyboard. There was then the matter of levelling the player with the keyboard so that not only were the player fingers exactly in place over the keys but that there was no 'play' or lost motion in the system. This was usually carried out using devices that adjusted the height of the player. The Angelus player, built by the Wilcox & White Company of Meriden, Connecticut, patented on April 8th 1902 a new device to adjust the height of the player to the keyboard. Each note pneumatic of the Angelus after 1902 lifted a pitman that carried a number of notches in its back edge. The keyboard fingers were all carried in a frame that could be moved up and down on guide rails that were provided at each end, so bringing the adjustable fingers into suitable notches on the pitmans. Regulation, although positive, required careful preparation but, once set, would retain its location.

Later models of the Angelus replaced this by two large handles that engaged in a ratchet slot to each side of the front of the case. Turning these adjusted each side of the player to the proper height.

To prevent the players from moving, wheel brakes or wedging devices were provided. This ensured that, in the middle of a fortissimo passage or when the performer was pedalling hard, the player would not roll away or shift its position on the keyboard.

Melville Clark had extended the compass of his Apollo to 65 notes but this still represented only part of the contemporary piano's compass which extended to 88 notes. The arrangement of popular music to the 65-note compass did not necessarily degrade the music but with most so-called classical works or serious pieces of music, in particular those originally composed for a larger compass piano, compression was necessary, normally by 'breaking back' the lowest octave and doubling in the treble to attempt to cover the shortfall.

It was far from an ideal solution to a regrettable situation. From the player action makers' point of view, the only way to increase the compass of the player action was either to increase its depth from three decks of pneumatic motors to four, or to make the component parts smaller. Any change would demand closer machining tolerances in wooden components.

ers. But they remained unmoved and chose to ignore what any fool could have told them, namely that this was the way player actions were going to go. If ever there was an industry blinkered to the key developments taking place around it, then it was the American player industry. The reasons were in part understandable if not exactly excusable. If a sufficient number of the 'old' style of players were on the market, they stood a chance of forcing out of the way the new (and better) upstart. And with the big investments in tools, equipment and machinery at stake it was a gamble thought worthwhile taking. McTammany was later to justify the vested interests succinctly:

> Personally, the writer was opposed to the change at the time, knowing the loss that would be entailed by those who had so recently embarked in the manufacture of the sixty-five note player. And furthermore, many improvements were being developed, and these could be made more cheaply and effectively on the sixty-five than on the eighty-eight player.

In fact, as it turned out, McTammany was wrong. The public, having once been exposed to a player that could sound every note on the keyboard rather than merely a select few, decided they wanted the new instrument. And so his 88-note player proved a great boon for Clark while at the same time bringing almost to ruin those many others who had only recently started making 65-note models. The music-roll makers were equally involved.

The man who did much to spread the message to trade and public alike was Marc A Blumenberg, the enthusiastic musical critic who bought out William E Nickerson's *Musical & Dramatic News* from the Lockwood Press. From this, Blumenberg published a strictly trade magazine called the *Musical Courier Extra* and in this he wrote glowingly of the new Clark player. For the trade, however, it was more of a mortal blow than a shot in the arm, for, as McTammany tells us, many smaller companies had invested great sums of money in perfecting their 65-note and 58-note players and putting them on the market.

Overnight, it seemed, they were obsolete as the trade clamoured for the full-scale player. It was soon realised that huge quantities of 65-note music-rolls were already sold and it would be bad marketing to declare these redundant overnight. And so the transformation created a need for the dual-standard player. Makers sought some interregnum from the inevitable by marketing models with 88-note actions and twin tracker bars with various forms of change-over system so that both 65- and 88-note music rolls could be played. Some used two separate tracker bars, the user swinging or swivelling whichever one he wanted into place. Others used one tracker bar with

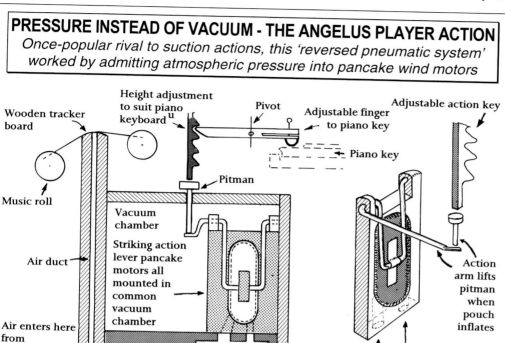

PRESSURE INSTEAD OF VACUUM - THE ANGELUS PLAYER ACTION
Once-popular rival to suction actions, this 'reversed pneumatic system' worked by admitting atmospheric pressure into pancake wind motors

Wooden tracker board

Height adjustment to suit piano keyboard

Pivot

Adjustable finger to piano key

Adjustable action key

Music roll

Pitman

Piano key

Vacuum chamber

Air duct

Striking action lever pancake motors all mounted in common vacuum chamber

Action arm lifts pitman when pouch inflates

Air enters here from atmosphere

Atmospheric pressure

Twin inlets for atmosphere ensure prompt operation of motor and make for a speedy action

Secondary valve

Primary valve

The Angelus operates by admitting atmospheric pressure into each pancake motor, these motors being contained in a common vacuum chamber. The so-called 'inside' pneumatic system, used on both the Angelus piano-players and player-pianos, was also employed in the Angelus player reed organ

Bleed

Pouch chamber

In a masterful bullet-biting act, it was Melville Clark who should have astonished the player world by making the first 88-note player action. His masterly stroke of increasing the compass of the player to a full 88 notes was achieved through smaller, more efficient components aided by the recent adoption of the double-valve action. This meant that the small holes in the tracker-bar were not called upon to control heavy valves in the system, but merely to operate small, lightweight servo primary valves that in turn controlled larger secondaries.

I said the news that Melville Clark had perfected a full-scale player should have astonished the industry because that is what a normal person might expect. In fact it was initially greeted by the industry with surprise, then a sort of smug satisfaction that after all nobody would want to buy such a device, particularly as it would be far more complex and liable to disarrangement. What happened, though, was the reverse and the capabilities of the new player were received by the new musical public with open arms.

One might also be forgiven for assuming that this momentous event would be followed up immediately by other mak-

two rows of openings for the different gauge rolls. All these were endeavours to allow a player owner to make use of both his old 65-note rolls (of which a prodigious number were not just still in use but also being made and sold) and the new, full-scale 88-note ones.

Dual system pianos all carried 88-note actions but had two rows of openings in the tracker bar. One or the other could be selected by moving a large lever that was mounted, usually, in the spool box. To overcome the difference in roll drive methods, the chucks were modified to accept both types of roll, usually by the addition of a loose adaptor for the upper spool that could be fitted to the drive mechanism in moments without needs of tools. Today, with plenty of both 65- and 88-note rolls to be found, possession of one of these dual standard players is greatly desired.

Besides dual-standard players, there was one instrument made which was a triple standard. Hupfeld, which had long produced rolls and instruments for its own 73-note standard, became aware of the fact that the rest of the world was concentrating on 88-note music. In consequence it produced a

Melville Clark's push-up player was called the Apollo and operated 58 notes – the same compass as the early reed-organ keyboard. A very basic player, it first appeared in 1902-03 and incorporated a curious roll-drive connected to the foot pedals by pulleys and belt. While playing, the energy was employed in winding up a clockwork motor which, at the end of the performance, was then engaged to rewind the music roll.

small number of instruments that would play 73-, 65- and 88-note rolls. The tracker bar was normally 73-note but, by pulling it out of the spool box and reversing it, it would play the other two roll sizes. This instrument also had exchangeable gearing for the spool drive so that, as with the Brinsmead Angelus, bottom-to-top rolls could be played as well as the normal top-to-bottom type by moving the take-up spool.

Now forced to change or be left trailing fences behind the front-runners, the industry was empowered to incur the expense of redesign and re-tooling and building the full-scale player piano.

Besides efforts to play the out-moded narrow-compass rolls, there were also ideas about converting the 65-note player to play 88-note rolls and whilst this could be done by exchanging the 65-note pneumatic stack for one with 88 motors it was normally done by fitting an 88-note tracker bar and teeing back the upper and lower notes so that every tracker hole played a piano note – but still only 65 of them! The instruction book describing how to perform this heinous act ran to five editions and was published by *Musical Opinion* and sundries dealer C F Baker.

This was one of the more practical approaches towards this deception. Other ideas were less so. Take the scheme of G F Lyon (granted British Patent No. 25,594 of Nov 18th 1912). He invented a tracker-bar attachment to convert a 65-note player to an 88-note instrument or vice versa by attaching with swing toggle clips on each side an extra tracker bar over the first having the holes re-aligned. This relied on the attachment being a fantastically good airtight fit between the matching faces in order to operate properly.

During these largely experimental early days of the piano-player and player-piano, there were many schools of thought as to how many of the piano's complement of notes should or indeed could be sounded by a mechanical or pneumatic action. Actions were being made which played 58, 65, 70, 73, 82 and 88 notes and this complete lack of standardisation did not foster a progressive industry. It undermined the standardisation of piano-roll inventories and certainly confused player buyers who probably were not sure (or couldn't remember) how many notes their instruments played.

It was not until 1910 that actions and rolls were standardised at 65-note and 88-note. The decision for this was taken at a convention of player manufacturers at Buffalo, New York. This regularising of the piano and roll industry did not affect player organs, which normally used 58-note rolls (the larger two-manual Aeolians used music rolls that were the same width but punched for 116 notes in a tracker bar that had two staggered rows of openings).

The 88-note or full-scale rolls were to become much more popular than the limited scale 65-note rolls. Considered musically, the necessary abbreviation of a musical score to fit into the smaller compass was nothing short of mutilation. From the mechanical standpoint, though, 65-note actions were more reliable. Component parts were slightly larger and because the tracker bar was not so finely pierced it was less prone to clogging with dust and paper fluff. Tracking problems were also of less significance.

I have made numerous references to Wilcox & White's Angelus player as distinct from the many other players around. This was because it was a very different action from anything else that was around. Its most dramatic difference that set the Angelus apart from all other pneumatic player actions was that it made use of flat, pressure-powered pneumatics instead of the usual and generally adopted wedge-shaped suction motors. These diaphragm pneumatics were rectangular and they operated not on vacuum like a wedge motor but on atmospheric pressure used to inflate the diaphragm, so moving the piano hammer action through the action of a cranked-lever linkage.

The Angelus worked very well indeed and was a good and reliable system, if somewhat tricky to service when it went wrong.

An Angelus cabinet player was built with a full-scale 88-note action as late as 1909 but this instrument, a specimen of which is in the author's collection, must be a late example. By this time, the 'inner player' was well on the way to perfection and the market for a push-up had dwindled to almost nothing. It was about this time that Wilcox & White changed their name to the Angelus Piano Company with offices in New York.

Earlier I mentioned tracker bars – the 'mouthpiece' of openings across which the music-roll travels. On the first generation of push-up players this was often referred to as 'the tracker board' and with almost all of the 65-note players and their precursors such as the 58-note early Apollo by Melville Clark, this was made of wood.

The coming of the larger scales called for closer, smaller and more accurate holes and the massive increase in the player market encouraged a gradual adoption throughout the industry of an all-metal tracker bar. Aeolian took out the first patents in 1902 for a tracker bar made of brass tubes, their upper ends flattened into a rectangular shape and cast into a strip of Britannia metal.[3] Connections from the other ends of the tubes to the valve chests could then be made with rubber tubing. Another advantage of the metal tracker was that it allowed simple registration and transposing devices to be applied to it. In later years, metal tracker bars were generally cast in brass since it was actually cheaper to produce

After the radical Angelus, the next unusual instrument to be introduced into England was the Simplex Special Piano Player. This arrived October of 1903 and was a thoroughly novel and possibly unique instrument. Heralded by the press as 'the most radical departure in constructive lines from anything in the piano player field since that type of instrument was first evolved', the Special was a small cabinet standing 42-inches high, 24-inches wide and 16-inches deep. Its uniqueness lay in the fact that as a piano-player it was not placed in front of but next to an ordinary piano.

Provided with its own foot treadles and connected to a pneumatic stack built into the piano by an umbilical cord, this was a short-lived attempt at allowing mechanical or manual playing of a piano without the need to shift around the cumbersome cabinet push-up type of player. None is known to survive and the device was very rapidly superseded by the interior player. Its only rival in style was the Tel-Electric electrically-operated player.

Close-up of the Clark Apollo's roll-rewind motor and mechanism. Centre and in line with the control knob shaft is an unusual centrifugal governor using spring-loaded steel balls on an endless-screw drive. Melville Clark went on the build the world's first full-scale 88-note player in January 1901 and a year later the world's premier 'interior' player-piano. A prolific and important inventor, he amassed more than 250 piano-playing patents between 1897 and his death in 1919.

Actually fitting the player action into the case of the piano itself was the next step forward. Whereas initially actions were bulky and were descended too directly from the cumbersome push-up cabinet player, efforts were rapidly directed to the design and manufacture of purpose-built actions for the so-called 'inner player'.

This was not quite as simple as it may sound for it needed a whole different approach to designing and locating the various component parts. But if putting the action inside the upright was a problem, then that needed to build a player action into a grand piano called for considerably more in the way of alteration and re-design.

Whereas the upright piano provided at least some vacant space inside the case above the keys and in front of the strings, the grand was considerably less accommodating. There just was no suitable space in which to put anything even resembling an ordinary player action. Ever resourceful, here was a problem to be overcome and makers went to it with a vengeance! Some makers placed the entire action beneath the key bed, the best known of these being Ampico. Others divided the action between a top-mounted spool-box and a below-keys pneumatic stack. Aeolian developed a single-valve top stack which was slim enough to fit between the keyboard and the underside of the wrest plank.

Aeolian's Pianola had one serious rival in the world of the piano-player and later player-piano and this was the Angelus developed originally by reed-organ manufactured Wilcox & White of Meriden, Connecticut. The key to the Angelus was the employment of flat pancake or diaphragm pneumatics, cornerstone of an action that was quite different from any other player action on the market. The Angelus push-up had one other unique characteristic: it was also a reed-organ! Playing from 58-note rolls, it could be used as a solo reed organ (with a choice of voices selected using conventional drawstops), a normal piano-player, or an instrument that played both organ and piano in unison. It was called the Angelus Orchestral. The Angelus diaphragm action remained the alternative to the Pianola for many years.

This last method was used by several others but one of the most distinctive variants came from Reginald H Collen, works superintendent at Broadwood Pianos. Collen devised a twin-valve action of extreme compactness in which one valve passed through the stem of the other. This was built as a unit action, each valve block and pneumatic being attached separately to the action board and suction chamber in the same manner as the original Broadwood unit player action patented as number 10,084 of 1903. Collen's new action was patented as number 12,724 of 1913. It was a clever and space-saving approach, but in service it was to prove difficult to regulate.

Innovation in the player industry was never wanting and there was always something new. And almost every week the trade paper *Musical Opinion* announced the launch of a new player. One suspects that after a while those whose business it was to know about such things got a bit blasé. Yet just once in a while something turned up that was really different. Not that that aspect necessarily made it any better, but a point scored for novelty was better than none. Take, for example, the tale of the Pianotist, a remarkable device by any standard and yet, in the end, a catastrophic failure.

The Aeolian Company's cabinet-style Pianola Piano player sold for £65 [$260.00] – quite a considerable sum at the turn of the century. The only British-made player of the time was the Boyd, which sold for £27 10s [$110.00] cash or £32 8s [$130.00] by monthly instalments of 13s 6d [$2.75]. But something appreciably cheaper and, by all accounts, easier to work was about to enter the market. This was a device called the Pianotist.

The New York business of Emile Klaber was already well established as a maker of pianos. Like many American piano-makers, Klaber had eyes on the British market and so his son, Augustus David Klaber, had moved to London where he was in charge of the company's UK operation based at 29 Queen Victoria Street. From here Klaber pianos were distributed in Great Britain. On May 29th 1900 he filed a whole series of Patents for various details of a mechanical piano, including detachable treadles for a player action which could be fitted to a normal piano, a method of driving the tune sheet from the treadles, a pianoforte system for mechanical playing and a device for playing the piano by hand 'when the feet are not available' – no doubt referring to the mechanical piano. Paradoxically, he concluded this flurry of British Patents with one for a tuck-in envelope for printed-paper-rate mail as the normal type of tuck-in envelope was '… often cast to one side remaining unopened'.

Augustus Klaber's endeavours towards the mechanical piano continued and a few months later he formed the Pianotist Company with offices and showrooms at 56 Regent Street, London. His father, Emile, was listed as managing director. The parent organisation was the Adek Manufacturing Company of New York. An elaborate machine was produced for punching out music rolls in May 1901 and in September the firm announced it had perfected a device for 'varying the loudness of automatic piano-players by adjusting the force of hammers on the strings'.

During the summer of 1901, Pianotist undertook an ambitious (by contemporary British standards) advertising campaign to promote their instrument and gave free piano recitals using their player attachment at their Regent Street showrooms. Five styles of the Pianotist were offered, the cheapest of which was priced at twenty guineas [$84.00].

The Pianotist was a mechanical action of the 'kicking shoe' type that played from a roll of thin punched card wound by a handle. Motion for the kicking shoe roller was provided via a single foot pedal worked like a sewing-machine treadle and the whole device fitted under the keyboard of the piano. Presumably it was fitted only to uprights. Despite the Patents taken out for various details of the whole, it was already an obsolescent instrument eclipsed by the burgeoning pneumatic action players. Even so, a long article entitled 'Evolution of the Piano Player' in a 1901 issue of *The Illustrated Sporting and Dramatic News* praised the device, saying that it was considered excellent value for £35 [$140.00]. After singing the praises of the ordinary piano-player at some length, the writer continued:

> Hardly are the words uttered in praise and endorsement of these instruments before a veritable genius arises and condenses the whole operative mechanism into such small space that it can be fitted into *any piano, out of sight,* thus not interfering at any

time with the use of the piano in the ordinary manner. Not content with this unquestionable advantage, the inventor of this instrument has provided what he is pleased to call 'melody stops', whereby 'the otherwise fatal accuracy and equal dynamic force' of all the fingers of a mechanical player may be varied at the will of the performer. The bass notes of a composition may be subdued, and the melody in treble accentuated, or if desired a melody brought out in the bass, while the treble provides merely a whispered accompaniment. This is a great achievement hitherto unknown in mechanical piano-players, and in the opinion of those best qualified to judge, it places this instrument far ahead of any other instrument of its kind. A simple frictional device has been substituted for pneumatics, with a consequent result that only 2 lb pressure is required as against 14 lb necessary to operate the cabinet form of piano-players.

In the opinion of some of the greatest artists and musicians who have seen this invention, it is considered artistically superior to anything of its kind, and such artists and musicians as Adelina Patti (Baroness Caderstrom), Mark Hambourg (the great pianist), Henry J Wood (conductor Queen's Hall orchestra), Wilhelm Ganz, Tito Mattei, Landon Ronald and many others, have not hesitated to put such opinions to paper over their own signatures. From the fact that the *Pianotist* (this is the name of this remarkable instrument) when fitted to a piano in no way interferes with its use, or injures it in any way, it may be reasonably prophesied that the piano of the future will be capable of performing the dual role of 'an old century piano' and a 'new century piano player'. Such manufacturers as Erards, Steinways, Pleyels, &c., &c., are eulogistic in praise of the *Pianotist*, and all those contemplating the purchase of a piano-player would do well to call at the showrooms of the Pianotist Co. Ltd, 56 Regent Street (near Piccadilly Circus), and see and hear this latest invention before finally making their choice.

A strong company has been formed for the manufacture and sale of the *Pianotist*, and as indicative of the success of this instrument it may be stated that a number of prominent people have already availed themselves of an offer made by the Pianotist Company to change their old style instrument for the *Pianotist*, the company making a fair allowance in exchange therefor.

Despite such eulogy, the Pianotist was soon to prove a costly failure and although a number was sold, their mechanisms were intrinsically defective. Soon the company was involved in having to repair examples sold to customers. Having spent a considerable sum in trying to perfect its players, setting up a London operation and now being forced to take them back for re-working, the firm became overstretched and was liquidated. By 1903 it had disappeared.

Nobody knows how many were made and sold and it is today a very scarce instrument. Several have been turned up by diligent collectors but they are not convincing as players.

From failures, let's now look at those serious attempts to improve the player and eradicate one of its principal problems – lack of a means of proper expression. Until that limitation was removed, the player could not honestly be described as anything like a substitute for the human performer.

To begin with there had been mechanical means of making one part of the keyboard sound louder than another. These broad methods had no grounding in musical interpretation and were more novelties than practical means of accenting which means making certain notes stand out from the musical background.

As regards the pneumatic player, though, the possibilities of good note-accenting were at least achievable and the year 1913 proved to be something of a landmark year in development. By that time there were three systems of music-roll note accenting in use. First there was the Themodist type in its various forms which are described in the Chapter on How the Pneumatic Player Works. Then came a system known as the 88-slot (marginal) which had one accent slot for each note on the tracker bar and was the basis of that adopted by Kastner in his Kastonome. This was only used on a limited scale.

Germany was the centre of piano-player development in Europe and the Leipzig company of Hupfeld devised the Phonola push-up which initially used 73-note piano rolls. Here is a Phonola from the early 1900s fitted with the Solodant accenting system. Well-engineered and capable instruments, they were not without fault and, as with so many of these early players, this lay in the layout of the controls. From left to right they comprise a button for 'soft', a lever for bass forte, a lever for treble forte, a switch for 'Solo', a lever for tempo regulation and, more prominent, the hinged, folding palm lever used to work the sustaining pedal.

Finally came the 'Dalian' system which used a double tracker bar with additional note perforations that determined the playing of accents. This was patented (British Patent No.25,790 of November 18th 1911) used in the J H Crowley player piano described in a moment, but was never produced in quantity.

Of the three it was the first that because of its technical supremacy attained international acceptance and a consequently wide adoption.

At the British Music Exhibition held at Olympia in September 1913, a number of manufacturers exhibited player pianos, among them Messrs George Rogers' Rogers Player Piano, William Sames & Company's instruments (which were fitted with either Hupfeld actions or the very successful and cheap Canadian-designed Higel action (with its Solograph theming system), London-made and sold by Heckschers of Camden Town), and the Malcolm player-piano (Malcolm & Company who made both pianos and a player organ), and the Direct Pneumatic Action Company with their Stems player piano fitted with the Arrow action.

The London-made Dalian player piano was also shown. The product of an up-coming piano-maker named John H Crowley of Wedmore Street, Upper Holloway, it was an unusual type of expression piano which, although of excellent potential, was faulted by its requirement of special non-standard music-rolls that had to be made on costly non-standard apparatus. Each note of this full-scale piano was equipped with its own damping pneumatic and regulator. While a common vacuum pressure was used, the strength of the piano hammer blow to the string was variable by the amount of atmospheric air admitted through the tracker bar. This was regulated by the use of music-roll perforations of different widths, loud notes having wider holes than soft ones. A saving grace was that it would also play ordinary 88-note rolls but obviously without expression. Here, in theory at least, was the ideal expression piano, indeed almost a reproducing piano, where every note was characterised by its individual interpretational value. It remained a very costly and consequently impractical player and was never produced in any quantity.

That 1913 Olympia exhibition also served as the showcase for the range of mini-player-pianos made by Barratt & Robinson. These were compact enough to be used in the confined space of a small yacht or boat. The Pedaleon was one of the smallest players ever made. Following early organ-building techniques, the keyboards on some of these pianos were both hinged and sliding, folding up out of the way when not in use to give a piano case little more than ten inches from front to back.

Another London exhibitor was the quality piano-maker John Brinsmead & Sons Ltd. They displayed examples of their Mignon and Aluminium players, the former being of traditional wood construction and the latter a highly durable all-metal action. From Murdoch, Murdoch & Company of 461 and 463 Oxford Street, London, came the Connoisseur Player Piano, the Connoisseur Reed Organ and the Connoisseur Pipe Organ, all being player instruments.

Novelties came in a wide range of degree of unusualness and usefulness. One significant novelty was that of J S Murdoch and J Bennett (granted a British Patent No.20,099 on Sept 6th 1913) who designed an upright player piano in which it was necessary to fold up the normal finger keyboard before automatic playing was possible. This design, subsequently used extensively on very narrow pianos for use on yachts for some while, actually saved on complexity and dispensed with the key and front fall boards.

All the players displayed were equipped with all the usual controls. Each maker strove to give his own distinctive names to these expression levers or buttons and to employ these euphemisms in their advertising. Murdoch's instrument, for example, had the Tempola, Phrasiola, Solotheme, Diminuent, Transposa, Automelle (theme isolator controlled by Themodist-type holes), Autoforte and Autotracker. Armed with that lot, it was always surprising that no enterprising manufacturer ever tried to find a fresh name for the foot pedals. They could have sold more, surely, if they'd called them 'Pedairolas'…

There were very many styles of push-up built, mainly in the United States. One of the more successful was the Simplex invented by Theodore P Brown of Worcester, Massachusetts. A reed-organ maker, Brown was one of the four most significant inventors in the development of the player in America. The Simplex was introduced in 1899 and sold for $225, being introduced later the same year in London at £55.10s. Stylistically it was more elegant than its forebears having much less apparent bulk. Its secret lay in the increased front-to-back depth in which the three-deck pneumatic action was packed with bellows assembly placed conveniently to the front. This allowed the bottom of the instrument to be unencumbered so it could be mounted on legs like a table. The music-roll had to be re-wound by hand after playing, hence the winding crank.

Mentioning curious names for player features brings to mind that one other particular player is deserving of more than passing mention and that was one which arguably was the most revolutionary of them all – the Pistonola.

Early on in the life of the player piano, two young London engineers, H C Coldman and C F Webb, bought one and took it apart to see just what made it work. They were surprised by the seemingly large components and consequently the large amount of air that had to be moved in order to make the mechanism operate. As a consequence of this they came to the conclusion that it ought to be possible to create a much simpler, cheaper and more reliable action if they reduced the volume of air involved. It would necessitate rethinking the entire player action.

The outcome of a long programme of experiment and development was the Pistonola, manufactured by Boyd Limited. This firm had already established a toehold in the self-playing piano market with a 65-note piano player of very angular appearance that sold for £32 8s [$130] together with six rolls of music.

Widely acclaimed as the all-metal player action, in the Pistonola, every player function was conducted by a piston moving in a cylinder. The foot treadles drew air out of a master cylinder using pistons. The master cylinder itself had a spring-loaded piston within it through which vacuum tension could be achieved. Pressure-reducing valves provided both low and high vacuum pressures to operate the roll-drive motor (which was again a piston motor) and the valves.

The valve chest and pneumatics of the ordinary action were replaced by a compact bank of eighty-eight small brass cylinders each no more than half an inch in diameter and each having a small free-moving piston made of compressed graphite with it. Being self-lubricating, the graphite pistons moved readily under the influence of small charges of air pressure or vacuum.

Each piston was connected to its respective piano-action hammer using a cord. When a hole in the music roll opened a hole in the tracker bar, a miniaturised valve mechanism that employed balls rather than pouches and stemmed valves would transfer vacuum to the correct note-action cylinder, the piston would move, setting in motion the hammer action.

Once the tracker bar hole was again covered and closed to atmosphere, the suction would be removed from the piston and it would immediately drop back under its own weight. Compared to the operation of a normal player-piano, appreciably less air had to be shifted to play the Pistonola.

Coldman and Webb were granted a series of Patents on the design, the earliest of which was dated March 10th 1909 and the last being in 1920. The two important Patents were No.14,030 of 1910 which covered the principle of the free piston moving in an enclosed cylinder under vacuum tension, and No.14,580 of 1912 which referred to the valve system that used a small ball to close or open an air path.

One other push-up is deserving of inclusion here and this is both the most attractive and least efficient. James O'Connor invented a 65-note cabinet player that entered production in Baltimore, Maryland, around 1908. This was the Smith Lyraphone and it was housed in a handsome cabinet with side panel legs like a contemporary bureau. Thoughtfully designed and with attractive, symetrically-arranged hand controls, the Lyraphone should have been a winner on all counts. Sadly it wasn't. It used specially-made very wide music rolls that had perforations which were narrowly-spaced in the centre and became wider apart the further outwards they appeared.

Boyd showed their Pistonola to the public at a concert held in Ilford Town Hall on November 26th 1913, the programme including both solo and accompaniment pieces for the player piano. Two models were advertised as available, the first selling for £75 12s 0d [$303.00] and the second, fitted with what Boyd called Modulist and Crescodant manual expression devices, sold at £84 0s 0d [$336.00].

April 1914 saw a public demonstration of the Pistonola at the Corn Exchange in London under the auspices of the London music dealers H Payne & Company. With Stanley Harris at the controls, the Pistonola performed in concert with a tenor, a contralto and a violin.

It was in 1920 that Boyd introduced an improved version that was called the Terpreter. Three versions were available, the Models One and Two, each costing 160 guineas [$672.00], and the Model three at 150 guineas [$630.00]. Neither the Pistonola nor the Terpreter was a cheap instrument.

The Pistonola was an interesting device and when properly adjusted, both the Pistonola and Terpreter were very good players capable of easy and immediate expression from their controls. The action was, nevertheless, prone to malfunctions that were not always easy to trace and rectify. Mr D F Andrews of Boyd Pianos remembers these instruments and relates how some were 'jinx' instruments which were always temperamental. Thus it is perhaps no surprise to find that, by the early 1920s, Boyd was promoting a more conventional player with an imported player action. This was the Boyd Autoplayer, available in a number of different-styled pianos for as little as 108 guineas [$454.00]. One of the controls on the Autoplayer was called the 'Deletor'. The advertising literature wrote of this:

> If a section of the music-roll is not required, this wonderful device will allow the roll to travel in silence at high speed .

There are few Pistonolas in the hands of collectors today, most having been 'converted' either to ordinary finger pianos or scrapped: unlike other less unconventional player actions, the miniscule player action could not be replaced by a standard one.

Many pianos were made both in America and in Europe that had the ability to play several degrees of expression. This meant not just playing soft or loud, but having the ability to isolate phrases and interpret them in a variety of levels of sound.

The call for the accented piano roll, sometimes referred to as 'hand-played', and the instruments upon which to play them remained right up to the thirties. However, the challenge of making a player-piano which could reproduce faithfully the performance of a concert pianist without requiring any dexterity on the part of the owner of the instrument was established very early on. To begin with this goal was viewed as a sort of chimera that might never be attained, yet might possibly be synthesised. In the end, the perfected solution turned out to be a bit of both.

Detail view of the hand controls of the Lyraphone made by the Smith Piano Company. The upper row features strangely-shaped levers at each end, the left one governing tempo, the right operating the piano soft pedal while in the centre in the play and re-roll selector. Beneath these are two up-and-down expression levers, the left working the overall power, and the right the piano sustaining pedal. In the centre is a sliding knob marked 'expression lock'. For any performer accustomed to another player, this one would have posed a formidable challenge as to what lever did what since the controls may have looked good but they were inspirationally illogical.

After a great deal of experimentation, the so-called reproducing piano emerged. It first appeared in Germany, but the generic name that stuck was the one actually patented in America by the Aeolian Company. As with 'pianola', the term 'reproducing piano' came to become the unofficial generic term for all makes of piano which produced a concert rendition of a piece of music from a music-roll that was recorded by a concert pianist whose name would appear on the roll. The evolution of the reproducing piano began fairly early in the history of the player piano.

I have devoted a separate Chapter to reproducing pianos since, while they may be the logical development from expression players, they are very different and, to collectors, rather special.

1. Reed-organ builder Charles C Austin of Concord, New Hampshire, applied this style of operation before 1846.
2. Four years later, in 1850, reed-organ builder Isaac T Packard was granted a patent for a combined force/exhaust bellows.
3. Britannia metal is an alloy of tin, antimony, and a little copper, sometimes with the addition of bismuth (which is expensive by comparison to the other ingredients). There are many recipes for this metal which at one time was used for a wide variety of purposes including casting decorative metalware. Described generically as a fine species of pewter, its colour is silvery white with a bluish tinge. It takes a good polish and a common casting formula was 105 parts tin, two parts copper plus 6 parts antimony.

Turning ordinary pianos into players was the goal of many inventors in the early years. After all, people already had pianos so why should they buy a new one if their existing one could be modified? The problem was that normal pianos seldom had any space inside for a player action. This did not deter people from trying. One of the more outlandish devices was Bansall's Universal Piano-Player introduced in April 1911. The ads claimed that it 'Plays any Existing Piano – without altering appearance or tone'. Such a claim today would result in a Court case for the Universal was anything but discreet. A bellows unit was built into the underside of the piano as usual. A player chest was fitted under the keyboard. The curious bit was the spoolbox. This plugged onto the front of the keyboard, hopefully making an airtight seal on all its 68 tubes – 65 playing notes plus tracking and pedal. The spoolbox also took its main suction through a large wind trunk. Patented in 1910 by R H McHardy (10,352), it was an ingenious notion for the wind motor to drive the music roll was actually underneath the roll at the back of the add-on case. Here the installation is in a stencil piano marked by Luton dealer W T Roberts.

Reverse of the McHardy-patent Universal showing attachment to keyboard front rail.

The 65-note Classic player attachment was patented by G A Smith in 1914 and came in several styles all of which could be incorporated with minimum alteration to the piano case. Each must have been slightly different and depended on the type of piano involved. Key to the neat installation was the folding take-up spool seen here in its stowed position in the top of the spool-frame.

Removing the front fall shows how the spool motor is built in and also how the take-up spool swings down so that a toothed wheel on its right-hand end engages with a pinion from the drive mechanism.

The tracker bar in the Classic had short vertical tubes emerging at right-angles to the tracker holes so that it could be connected from beneath. To get the tubing through to the pneumatic stack under the keyboard, the sides of the keys were cut away to alloy short tubes to pass between. Rubber tubing then united the vertical tubes from the tracker bar to these between-keys connections. The take-up spool is seen folded up for this picture.

Viewed from the side, the extreme slenderness of the Classic can be appreciated as can the need for the foldaway take-up spool.

A very early Steck Pianola in a custom-built Mission-style case. This undated 65-note instrument, thought to have been built around 1910-14, turned up at Tony Morgan's South London workshop some years ago and, although it was initially believed beyond economic restoration, further examination proved just how unusual it really was.

The early Steck Pianola's spoolbox shows the first curious feature – an adaptor secured under a clip above the tracker bar that allows narrower 58-note music rolls to be played. The take-up spool also has adjustable flanges. The early type tempo indicator and basic four-lever hand controls reveal the extreme early period of this inner player action.

All Pianola pianos after about 1914 had the player action stack fitted above the keys. Early examples such as this one had the action beneath, the tubing passing down between the keys.

Certain features of the Pianola remained standard throughout its life such as the manner in which the wind motor suction hose is brought out to a cast iron elbow that is screwed to the case side by an integral support flange. In later models, the entire pneumatic action would be made to fit in the narrow space between the heavy crossbeam under the spoolbox and the tops of the keys.

Hupfeld's Phonola interior player action, like early Aeolian ones, was built under the keyboard. In many ways this was the most convenient place to put it but the downside was the need to get the shortest practical tubing run to the tracker bar – and that meant going between the keys. Notice the extensive use of brass cup-washers to the woodscrews in the player action. Hupfeld went to great lengths to ensure that woodscrews were unable to be over tightened and crush surrounding wood.

As the years passed, actions became smaller and neater. This had two advantages. While taking up less space, there was also less air to be moved and the benefit of this came in power. A superb piano is the Ibach and here is a rare example of an 88-note Ibach Pianola of about 1920.

The Ibach has a Pianola action that is no longer underneath the keys, but fixed into that narrow space above them. The large six-motor roll-drive is seen to the right of the spool box, each seesaw board providing two power inputs.

Transitional model Steck Pianola has early form of underwork where the bellows exhausters are matched by a separate equaliser fitted to the bottom left.

The Brinsmead piano was a quality instrument built to fine standards and possessed of an excellent tone. This maker used the Angelus action for both grand and upright pianos. Here is an example in a case of outstanding beauty comprising finely-matched veneers and beautiful inlay work. It is one of the finest examples known to survive.

This Angelus Brinsmead has the advantage of being able to play three styles of music-roll: the Angelus roll that spools from bottom to top and is 'inside out', and either 65-note or 88-note music rolls. There is a rather unconventional means of changing between music-roll sizes: besides two spool permanent chucks for the different roll ends, there is a lever to reverse the drive for Angelus rolls. The double tracker bar has two widely-spaced rows of holes one of which is covered with a leather apron controlled by a finger wheel selector. Note that the spool drive motor on this player is arranged to the left of the spool-box.

Key to the success of the Angelus system was its pressure-operated diaphragm pneumatics that operated curiously shaped crank-rods to set in motion the piano hammer action.

The Angelus Brinsmead had very individualistic hand controls that involved buttons, levers and a 'rocking tablet'. From left to right these are bass subdue, treble subdue, Melodant on and off (Themodist note-theming system), play and re-roll, metronome (roll speed), sustaining pedal, *ritardando* and *accelerando* rocker (for rapid and momentary changes of tempo not involving the set roll speed).

The Boyd Pistonola was one of the most unusual of the player pianos to emerge. Designed and patented by Coldman and Webb in 1909, the action dispensed entirely with conventional pneumatic motors and replaced every function with piston and cylinder actions. Outwardly it was conventional in appearance.

Removing the case panels showed the secrets of the Boyd Pistonola. Taking up comparatively little space inside the piano, the action was theoretically perfect and demanded the minimum volume of vacuum power. However, in practice it was an action that called for considerable care and attention in service.

The Pistonola's roll drive motor was a small four-piston unit that functioned just like a motorcar engine to drive its crankshaft. Instead of operating directly on the piano hammer action, the pistons were connected by looped cords that engaged in hooks on the piano keys so that the key action was effectively maintained as the source of force to play the piano. Regulation and restoration of this action is not so much complex as rather fiddly: despite its undoubted qualities the sad fact is that it is not an instrument beloved of collectors today.

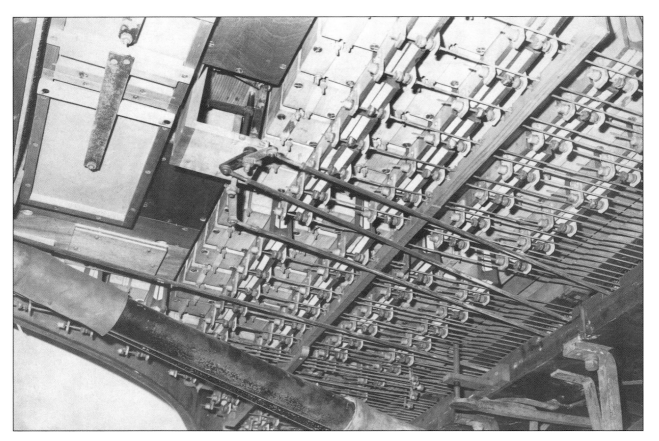

Until the perfection of the compact stack, fitting a player action into a grand piano called for design dexterity. Broadwood created a curious player action that used quite separate, individually-mounted pneumatic motors arranged underneath the piano and operating the piano action using long wire connecting links. Very easy to service, the player was a failure because there was so much mass of mechanism to put into motion and this made proper repetition very difficult to attain. The system, pictured here beneath a 1912 grand, was only used for a short while.

C. R. TAYLOR,

34, COMMERCE ROAD, WOOD GREEN, LONDON, N.22.

Established 1903.   Telephone : Palmers Green 1031.

The practical grand player piano of the 1920s used a narrow-pneumatic three-deck stack place above the keyboard. Here is a standard grand made by C R Taylor of North London showing how the foot pedals are concealed in the piano pedal box.

PLAYER GRAND.

Length 4' 6''   7¼ Octaves.   Schwander Action.   Ivory Keys.

Chapter 6
Perforated Music and
the Wrath of the Copyright-Holders

From the previous Chapter, I mentioned how Welte in Freiburg had shown that an organ could be made to play using perforated paper music and that this quickly lead to the evolution of the player piano in Germany, America and then Britain and France. With the establishment of the reliable and practical player-piano, all that was needed was the music and that was down to the expansion of the output of roll-perforating companies.

But there was a major battle looming over the horizon – a conflict that threatened not just the player piano but also the very existence of mechanical musical instruments all over the world. It all began in those formative years of Leipzig's self-acting piano and organ industry and it centred on the antiquated copyright law in Germany. This effectively prohibited the making of perforated rolls of musical compositions for which copyright existed.

This question of musical copyright was to hamper the development of the player for many years to come, certainly in Europe and to a lesser extent in America. The instrument risked finding itself totally fettered by the non-availability of music. Just as the invention of the motor-car demanded that a man walk in front of it with a red flag, nobody was likely to get anywhere very fast. The simple expedient of putting a tax on rolls, later used almost everywhere, had yet to be thought of.

To go back to the beginning, it was a hurdle that dogged all makers of every type of mechanical musical instrument, not just the piano-player makers. Those who made music-rolls were particularly hard hit because, of course, everybody wanted the latest popular music – and it was these current tunes that the copyright laws assiduously protected.

The first major copyright case had arisen in France as far back as 1865 when Debain became locked in lengthy litigation concerning his Pianista Debain with its music in the form of wooden planchettes.

In Britain, music publishers had long been waging war on those who made illegal copies of music for sale. Almost every publisher fought this conflict but with little in the way of positive outcome. The law said you had not just to find somebody selling copies of your protected music, but had to prove that it was his and that there was intent to defraud. Things had become so bad by 1881 that the publishers banded together and formed themselves into the Music Publishers' Association. Their combined front did little to stem the predicament even though they attracted the services of the best lawyers and mounted numerous prosecutions. The battle lasted a quarter of a century, ignored by a Government that on the one hand was powerless to suppress those crimes and on the other couldn't really care less about the problem. Certainly the music pirates flourished but it is not possible to prove or otherwise that sneaking feeling that by popularising music they may actually have helped the legitimate trade. That thought, a hundred years ago, would have got its thinker lynched!

There is no question that some publishers did suffer from dwindling profits through forged copies of sheet music. In was into this highly-charged atmosphere that perforated music for mechanical instruments arrived. The publishers simply saw it as another way of denying them revenue and so the player-piano and its music was a clear candidate for their vilification.

Legal history, if not legal precedent, was made in the Circuit Court in Boston, Massachusetts, on January 29th 1888. The owners of the rights to a then popular song called *Cradle's Empty, Baby's Gone*, sued John McTammany for reproducing the song on 'perforated sheets'. The judge deliberated and threw out the case on the grounds that the perforated sheets were part of the mechanism and hence 'difficult to regard as sheet music'. Consequently there was no infringement of copyright and he dismissed the appeal.

This outcome came as a terrible shock to the music trade on both sides of the Atlantic, for they believed they had an open and shut case. The British trade magazine *London & Provincial Music Trades Review* commented that it would be a mistake were the British courts to accept the Americans as authorities on the matter. However the British and Americans felt about each other, there was no doubt that the problem was rife in both countries. American publishers were suffering as much as their British counterparts. This may not have been strictly true, though, for Canadian music dealers were known to have been dealing freely in American piratical reprints of British copyrights, suggesting that the British were on the receiving end of a double dose of injustice.

It was not that the copyright business was merely an Anglo-American burden, for, as Welte had experienced, it tended to be global and certainly was rife in Europe. It was in a serious move to remedy this that the Berne Convention was drafted and passed. This gave protection to authors and publishers and established if not exactly a law, then a ruling within which is would be easier to prosecute offenders.

By 1890, most European countries had agreed to the copyright clauses set out in the Berne Convention and the strength of Article XIV of the Convention granted reciprocal rights, subject to specified conditions, to authors in the signatory countries.

Then the French music publishers and editors Marquet took action against musical instrument makers and distributors Thibouville regarding the cardboard book music for his instruments in 1895. Matters were only to get worse as the invention and mass-marketing of the gramophone served only to intensify the rush for litigation against organette makers such as Ehrlich in Leipzig, piano-roll sellers, Aeolian and others.[1]

In the preceding years, increasing numbers of musical copyright cases came before the courts but it was not until eleven years after the original Boston case concerning McTammany that the next big music-roll copyright case struck, this time in Britain. It took place in February 1899 between George Whight and Boosey and concerned music rolls for the Aeolian player organ, forerunner of the Orchestrelle.

This turned out to be a very important case indeed and its ramifications were boundless. London music publishing house Boosey claimed that the rolls were copies, in a different notation, of the music published by them. George Whight as defendant claimed that the rolls were merely part of the machinery for producing sounds. The judge agreed with this point – but then found that because words had been added to the roll indicating 'pace and expression at and with which the said music ought to be played and because the words were taken from Boosey's published sheet-music this was 'flat as a burglary'. Whereupon the court ordered Whight to stop publishing the rolls.

The Music Publishers' Association followed this up with a letter addressed to The Aeolian Organ & Automatic Pianoforte Company (Messrs Whight & Company) advising them that other pieces in their music-roll catalogue were copyright works. Meanwhile there was now an urgent and separate move to extend musical copyright protection to the perforated paper rolls to conform to the Judge's finding.

As one might imagine, the newspapers reported very fully on this case. One outcome was that it drew a curious endorsement for the music-roll from Viscount Knutsford who said that he enjoyed the Aeolian in his bedroom and did not understand how thwarting the production of perforated rolls by extending the copyright protection on printed music to the rolls would aid the composer. 'I should not purchase any of his music [in print] in any case, and I could not read it if I did'.[2] It was furthermore asserted that the publishers' representatives had no desire to halt the sale of 'Aeolians' but wanted only royalties to be paid for the music used.

George Whight appealed, the appeal being heard that December. To everybody's joy (except the music publishers) the verdict was overturned, the Appeal Court asserting that 'the sheet of paper so perforated was not a copy of the sheet of music…' and, furthermore, '…the printed directions… as to time and expression did not constitute an infringement'. The music-roll perforators, their machinery effectively stilled in the production of their earnings' cornerstone of popular music, breathed a sigh of relief – and got their equipment back up to speed.

A curious sequel to this whole business came in 1907 when a copyright-owner took action against the National Phonograph Company in Newark, New Jersey, claiming infringement by making and selling phonograph recordings of his music. The defendants successfully used the arguments of the Boosey *vs.* Whight case.

Copyright became the key issue surrounding the piano-player and player-piano's burgeoning days and it was to present a united front in the Courts of Law that German mechanical musical instrument manufacturers formed themselves into a society early in the 1900s.

Heading this society was Wilhelm Spaethe, whose organ and piano manufactory was situated at Gera, and it was due to repeated pressure brought on the authorities by the society that the Reichstadt finally passed Paragraph XXII of their new copyright law which decreed that copyright need not apply to the playing of music from a tune sheet, but that the tune sheet or music roll must have a copyright or performing-rights tax levied on it at the time of sale. Spaethe had a personal interest in the matter since his firm was one of the largest manufacturers of pneumatic instruments. In a related case, Polyphonmusikwerke in Leipzig, makers of the Polyphon disc musical box, was deprived early on of the rights to make discs of the music of Gilbert and Sullivan because of a dispute over the copyright act prevailing at that period, as applied to their first— and only— disc of their music, which was the Mikado waltz.

In May of 1900 *The Times* in London carried a letter from Henry Reginald Clayton in which he decried the unfair practice of transferring copyrighted music onto perforated rolls. Citing the earlier and prevailing copyright law passed as far back as 1842, Clayton averred that this did not cover the problem. '…in 1842', he wrote, 'automatic melody was a quantité negligeable'. He went on to declare that the German law and its protection of composer and publisher made the distinction between mechanical instruments such as musical boxes, where the law did not apply, and instruments like the Aeolian which were fed the music in re-notated form. He ended with the observation that 'mechanical execution has a deadening effect on the musical sense, checks the progress of art, and should only be turned to as a last resort'.[3] Clayton was, as might be judged, rather biased: he was a barrister, an authority on copyright – and a partner in the music-publishing firm of Novello, Ewer & Company as well as being chairman of the Music Trades Section of the London Chamber of Commerce.

Arthur Boosey, head of the music-publishing house that bore his name, presented a paper at the 1901 music conference in Leipzig entitled 'Appropriation of Copyright Music by Mechanical Instrument Makers' the gist of which was that instruments like the Aeolian were not around at the time of the Berne Convention was adopted and were at that time immune under English copyright law, therefore it was time to modify the Convention.

Between 1900 and 1906 there were countless copyright prosecutions of hawkers selling cheap sheet music culminating in a major shake-up as a result of which Boosey, in something of a volte-face, advised exempting music rolls and gramophone records from copyright lawsuits. It was clearly a battle where the two sides were themselves dividing into factions, a mess only sorted out by the passing of a new Copyright Act of 1906. An outcome of this was that a tax was placed on all copyright music rolls in the form of an adhesive stamp issued by the copyright holder (music publisher) and applied to the paper leader of each copy of a roll by the roll-manufacturer. This then was translated as a royalty payable to the author in the same way as a publisher paid his authors on sales of a book. The stamp was also used on gramophone records, normally stuck on one side of the central title label.

Common sense thus marked a conclusion to a situation that overshadowed the piano-player and player-piano business throughout its formative years. Once sorted out, though, it was as if a major weight had been lifted from the shoulders of the entire industry from makers down to retailers, all of whom had hitherto feared some form of retribution by law.

When you find a piano-roll with a small postage-like stamp stuck on to it, you will know that royalties have been paid on it the first time it was sold. These stamps do not appear on all rolls, though, because the method of collecting royalties changed in later years to one where the roll-producer (and, incidentally, the gramophone-record makers) merely provided a certified statement of sales against which accountants (that other breed of timelessly-wealthy men) could render a statement of monies due. Physically making a musical performance as a piano-roll began with the metrical marking-out of the master-roll from a musical score using pencil, ruler and callipers. Later came the recording piano wherein electrical or pneumatic contacts directly operated a means of marking out the master as the pianist played. Sometimes this was merely an ink trace than then had to be punched but later it was an actual punching machine that the keyboard controlled..

The potential of the music-roll and its recording piano can be demonstrated by a story told some years before the First World War by a well-known American roll manufacturer.

A few specimens of 'Royalty Paid' labels from piano rolls. There were many types, styles, and forms as dictated by the music publishers. Generally their presence is not considered important by piano-roll collectors today.

A famous singer was about to participate in a piano-player promotional recital and, the preceding afternoon, was taken on a conducted tour of the factory. She showed such a great interest in the roll-making department that after a while she was invited to sit at a piano and sing one of her own songs. At the conclusion she was asked if she would sing that particular song in the recital due to begin a few hours later. 'But it isn't even in manuscript,' replied the artiste. 'I haven't had time to write it down and no one could accompany me and I cannot do both satisfactorily.'

She was then told that, although the new song was not written down, she had in fact just cut the master roll by playing upon the recording piano. The song was performed that evening!

The common system of piano-roll recording was straightforward enough. When it came to the reproducing piano, then matters were a little more involved. The celebrated pianist performed upon a grand piano, which, in outward appearance, was no different from an ordinary instrument. However, from the piano ran a heavy electric cable carrying two different sets of wires, one from contacts beneath each piano key and one from positions near where the hammers struck the strings. The cable led out of the recording studio into a soundproof room in which was situated the recording apparatus. Here the wires were attached to electromagnets that operated paper punches in a perforating machine, each punch corresponding with its proper note on the piano. As the pianist played so the punches cut the master roll and made a permanent recording.

That was the process that the makers projected, the inference being that this method of recording secured accuracy of replaying, the length of the perforation being determined by the duration that the recording pianist held down the particular keys. The punches in the machine repeated at the rate of 4,000 cycles per minute, so making possible the accurate recording of the most rapid staccato notes struck by the pianist. The resulting punched hole for the briefest note would be just $\frac{1}{16}$-inch in diameter.

Rhythm of the music was determined by the spacing of the markings or perforations in the master roll as it passed through the recording machine at a constant speed, which was normally eight feet a minute. So long as the rolls made from the master so cut were played back at the same speed, faithful *tempi* would naturally result.

Without doubt this is what the recording engineers' goal was. Whether it was ever achieved seems unlikely for we now know that there was an amount of post-recording editing that took place, some of it being extensive in nature. The big question was to what degree this editing modified the performance.

When the original recording was made, it more than likely contained stray wrong notes which no pianist may entirely avoid when playing passages requiring speed and force. One of the finest pianists of the time noted to his chagrin no fewer than 360 false notes in a single performance! Fortunately, these wrong notes could be detected and corrected under the supervision of the artist himself. Every blemish to the performance could be removed and omitted notes cut into their proper places. Even the touch and rhythm could be improved upon if the artist was dissatisfied with his recording.

It is obvious that, with such revision carefully carried out with the artist, the result was a most polished interpretation. While with a modicum of such 'editing' a fine performance could be produced, too great a dependence on the editor with his correcting pen, sticky paper and hand punch could destroy the very spontaneity which the reproducing system sought to preserve. This explains the statement of Percy Grainger (who studied with Busoni) that his records on Duo-Art represented him not merely as he did play, but as he 'would *like* to play'. Possibly the greatest tribute to the Duo-Art came from Paderewski, who, speaking of the music roll of one of his compositions, said that listening to it gave him the same feeling in his heart as when he played it himself.

The mystique of the automated performance-recording was, sadly, largely mythical, for although the recording pianist finally approved the 'finished' roll, it had probably been through a process that was anything but automatic. Different piano systems used different techniques, of course: on Welte, for instance, a melographic trace was produced for subsequent punching while an engineer was responsible for noting the performer's dynamics. In all cases, a percentage of the performer's performing nuances was manually applied by the 'musical engineers' in the back room after the composer had left his stool and stretched his legs. The size of that percentage seems to have varied enormously and some roll-recordings must have been prepared from perceptive listening rather than the face of infallible technology that was presented to the public.

With the Duo-Art, the touch of the pianist was similarly recorded and reproduced, using the same technique of perforations in the music roll following electrical impulses from contacts within the recording piano. And, as ever, the master roll emerged not so much from the piano as from 'behind the curtain'.

In Chapter 10, I quote some words from recording pianist Harold Bauer which point out the problems of recording performances. That some performers could claim any rights to the originality of certain of their music-roll interpretations seems questionable.

1. See *L'Exploitation Des Oeuvres Musicales par les Instruments de Musique Mécaniques et le Droit de l'Auteur* by Georges Sbriglia (Librarie Nouvelle de Droit et de Jurisprudence, Paris, 1907).
2. Coover *[24]*, p.73
3. Coover, *op.cit*, p.76.

Chapter 7
Sales Peak, Social Influence – and the Decline of the Player

It is more than a hundred years since the first piano-player appeared and almost the same length of time since the first player-piano was developed. Unlike many other old and redundant technologies (for, let's face it, that's really what the automatic piano represents), there has been a sustained interest in it. Museums, exhibitions and collectors around the world preserve these fine instruments for the enjoyment and appreciation of another generation.

But there is another way in which the automatic piano has shown resilience to changing trends. It is still here today in our midst, albeit worked by modern computerised technology, but nevertheless it remains an automatic piano.

Looking back on this rich century-plus, what did the player actually achieve? And was it a help to Man and, perhaps, Music? Or was it all one horrible waste of effort?

I have weighed the evidence carefully and am pleased to find that I can confidently join the 'Ayes' to the right. Yes, the player not just did us all good but it became an integral part of the fabric of both domestic and musical life for pretty well three generations. I don't think there are many other things around the home that can claim a similar consumer appeal – except, perhaps, television.

The importance of the player piano during its life should never be underestimated. While today we may tend to see the gramophone as the first of the modern machines that were to erode its status in the home, that sentiment was not entirely a contemporary one. The player was certainly regarded as of greater interpretational significance than the gramophone by such famous pianists as Leschetizky – who firmly averred his disappointment that it had not arrived on the musical scene a century earlier – and Busoni, who is reputed to have thought it as important an invention as the cinematograph.

By the same token, the player performed a vital role in fostering the growth and development of musical knowledge amongst ordinary people who might otherwise never have had their latent musical interest aroused. This could be proved by an analysis of the type of music-roll that the average Pianola-owner bought. A spokesman for the Perforated Music Company said, in 1913, 'A man buys a player, and the first month he plays rag-time. Then he goes rapidly through the comic opera stage, till he reaches Chaminade and MacDowell. Often he gets no further than that, but an increasing percentage go on to the classics.'

Clearly more people were inclined to take examples of the so-called classical repertoire into their homes when they could 'play' themselves and it has been averred that the reputation of MacDowell in this country was largely due to the influence of the player piano.

There should be no dispute over the claim that during its lifetime the player piano was the most enjoyable mass musical educator the world has ever known. It had vast 'consumer appeal': it was a machine that was exciting to use, to watch and to listen to, and virtually whatever it played made an impression on not just the user but also those around him. And it was sexless – women of all ages were at home with it as were children, the blind – even the deaf, so we are told, could 'hear' the musical vibrations and so enjoy playing it.

The rich era of popular mechanical music really embraced no more than the last decade of the nineteenth century and the first four decades of the twentieth – just fifty years in all. And how the clockwork piano of the café and public house cheered as it pounded out the latest music hall novelty melodies! Here is a French example of this public entertainer.

In the nature of it all, everything sooner or later has to come to an end and in the instance of the player the slippery slope began with the recession, but the rise of cheap and more venturesome attractions such as motoring, the gramophone and wireless ultimately pushed it over the precipice into a period of oblivion. Lifestyle changed dramatically in the 1930s and this played a major part in getting people out and about rather than cooped up with their pianos. Tennis became very popular and replaced bridge as the sport of the middle classes. It was the start of the First Stage of Healthy Living, if you like, and families took to the open air, men took to gardening and family activities centred on walking in the countryside or the escapism so cheaply available at the local Picture House. The cinema could take you to the rest of the world, to experience wondrous sights and styles of living that were far removed from 2a Acacia Gardens in the suburbs of a provincial industrial town.

The peak years had long since gone as the nation prepared for the coronation of the ill-equipped Edward VIII. Those with longer memories going back to the times of another ill-equipped monarch, this time Edward VII, might have remembered, for example, a small news item in *Musical Opinion* for April 1905 regarding the ebullient Edward H Story who had just acquired a newly-bankrupt player business:

A telegram announces the purchase of the Playano Manufacturing Company of Boston by the Story & Clark Piano Company of Chicago. A new piano with interior player, to be known as the Story & Clark player piano, will be put in work at the factory as soon as possible. A player department will be established, whose purpose will be the manufacture of this new interior attachment and also of the cabinet Playano. 'I have read the handwriting on the wall,' says Mr E H Story. 'I am convinced that the player piano has come to stay; so are my associates in the ownership of the company. We feel that the future prospects of the player business are good enough to warrant us in buying a player business outright, and that the Playano Company was the concern to buy.'

Story's words from 1905 were literally from another age – the one of consumer wonderment at the marvel of the automatic piano. Now those same words had a hollow sound as the once-great industry ground to a halt.

Let's remind ourselves of that golden year of 1914 when the player piano was still in the ascendant. It was to be the last summer of tranquillity and, when peace came again, more than a million men would have been slain on the battlefield. Yes, 1914 was the last year of many things.

Besides the music trades journals, the automatic piano had another chronicler in the form of a sixpenny monthly publication for consumers called the *Piano Player Review*. January 1914 saw the publication of its sixteenth number and within its covers was an interesting selection of material penned by its then editor, Ernest Newman. In his editorial he dealt with an attack by the *Yorkshire Observer* on mechanical music. Then he discussed the subject of player-piano classes at competition festivals. Encouraging replies were received from Harry Evans (the then well-known music adjudicator) and from Landon Ronald (later to become Sir Landon Ronald), who was wholly in favour of player-piano classes.

Artistic influences of the time were brought to the forefront in coin-operated clockwork café pianos. Carved and decorated walnut with painted matt glass panels made this handsome Belgian instrument of the 1930s a centrepiece not just of toe-tapping music but of fashion.

If the *Yorkshire Observer* was unimpressed by automatic pianos, then its prestigious Northern counterpart, the *Manchester Guardian,* occupied the counter position. In an outspoken leading article the paper nailed its colours to the mast – it found itself wholly in favour of the innovation. And, no doubt to the Yorkshire paper's dismay, so did the *Sheffield Telegraph* whose editor, J A Rogers, wrote glowingly of the possibilities and opportunities afforded by the instrument.

In 1898 the height of entertainment in the public place would have been this Hupfeld Atlantic piano-orchestrion powered by a descending weight the pulleys for which can be seen at the top of the case. This handsome instrument was sold in Vienna by musical instrument dealer Gustav Stiasny, Kalvarienberggasse 36.

Later that same month a classical song recital was given at Wolverhampton in which every item was accompanied on the player piano. At the same time, player-piano advocate and author Sidney Grew was agitating for barred music rolls – music rolls on which the music notation and bars were printed to aid musical understanding. This was something of a lost cause, a campaign that he waged, largely unsuccessfully, for many years.

Was it the cold draughts of the average London home or an urge to save coal that led people to go out in the evening chill to a player-piano demonstration? Whatever the reason, these events seem to have been popular for in that month Pianola recitals took place in seven large provincial towns, Messrs Boyd gave a player recital in the Town Hall at Ilford, and the Perforated Music Company staged its Riddle-Roll Competition which, like the latter-day bingo clubs, encouraged people to shout as soon as they recognised the mystery roll being played. Naturally the whole idea of a 'riddle-roll' competition was to sell piano rolls, so the more attractive the piece, and the less well-known it was the better. These contests were really a 'hard-sell' promotion that invariably their baffled audiences with new music.

Also that January, *The Times* revealed the fact that the Orchestrelle Company had made a net profit of £171,603 [$686,400]; and the *Financial Times* gave particulars of the failure of another company that had been trying to market a new kind of player piano, with a huge £28,184 [$112,735] deficiency.[1]

In the issue for February we find the popular and eminent conductor Sir Henry Wood (1869-1944) addressing the question of player-piano classes at competition festivals. He wrote:

> Your idea of a class for player-piano performances at musical competition festivals is excellent. It would cause a lot of young people to grind away at the classes — a thing they would never hope to do if left to their own fingers: and it would do more to bring out their interpretive abilities than anything else.

Another one-time player-piano luminary was Ernest Newman. He had written an article for *The English Review* that caused a great stir in the professional world for he held the conviction that the player was of greater importance in teaching music than a concert performance. His words, beginning with 'a defence of the piano-player' and concluding with 'the value of the piano-player', later became the core of his best-seller of 1920, *The Piano-Player and its Music.* Meanwhile *The English Review* was itself a staunch player supporter and it published regular supplements dealing with each make of instrument then being made. As well as those printed words that risked upsetting the establishment, more player piano concerts took place that month in Worcester, Wolverhampton and Dublin.

The issue of *Piano Player Review* for March noted how the piano trade was expressing surprise at the growth of the player piano manufacturers and the increasing sales that resulted. The seeds of unrest were sown and the trade in ordinary pianos appeared to be suffering, at least in the eyes of the retailers. Makers of non-players began murmuring that the *PPR* was doing them no favours. As dissension began to ferment, the player recitals went ahead as ever with concerts given at Tunbridge Wells and Wolverhampton. Again Ernest Newman wrote glowingly about the player piano at competition festivals. Allegedly responding to consumer demand (but more probably realising a market opportunity), on the 26th of that month a London newspaper, *The Globe,* started a weekly player-piano page to appear every Thursday. By the time of the April edition, the alarm of the piano trade hinted at among the March events had been transformed into outright hostility towards the *Player-Piano Review.* The journal came under some sort of trade boycott as it was thought, unjustifiably, that the magazine was being run by a powerful syndicate or company for the exploitation of its own particular make of player piano.

The journal defended itself simply and effectively: there was not a shadow of reason for the fears of the trade. It was at the time running a competition amongst its readers for the best selection of a hundred music rolls. Its treatment of all new players was equal and impartial and it maintained unprejudiced editorial commitment. And to make the point it told of a new piano player system that was under development, its chief claims being sensitiveness and smallness. Part of the player was to be a permanent fixture under the keyboard of the piano, the other part (in cabinet form) was detachable (this was, one imagines, the Universal Piano Player of Messrs Bansall).

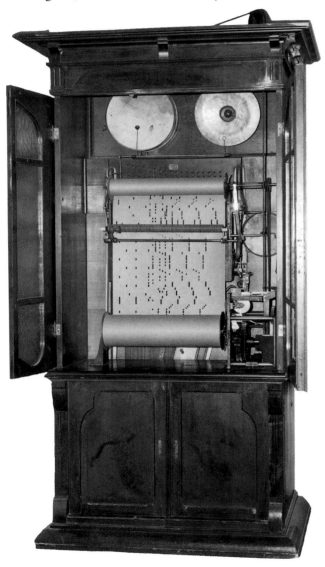

When piano actions were devised that could be operated by rolls of thick paper punched with holes which could push down small steel levers it meant an end to the heavy and cumbersome pinned barrel and allowed greater musical flexibility. The makers of the Polyphon disc musical box in Leipzig produced this piano orchestrion. They named it the *Rossini*.

That month's player recitals, given by various makers, were at Reading, Wolverhampton (yet again), Wells and Grimsby. Dr Smith, principal of the Hull College of Music, ventured to say in an address that 'in the not far distant future the various mechanical piano-players would dominate the musical world to such an extent as to create a slump in piano study'. The *Dundee Advertiser* had an article dealing with the abuse of the player piano— the writer had been on the receiving end of a player-piano fiend next door.

Also happening during April was a great deal of activity in the daily press regarding player-piano matters — encouragingly so. The *Daily Chronicle* came out with a strong article, 'Pianists All: The Printing Press and the Player-Piano', by somebody writing under the soubriquet 'Crotchet'. The *Daily Mail* joined in with 'No More Pianists: the Perfection of the Machine' by 'A Musician', while the *Globe's* subject headings included 'Music for the Player-Piano', 'Treasure Trove', 'The Player-piano from its Educational Aspect', 'A Susceptible Instrument', and so on. A paper called *Civil & Military* printed an interesting article called 'The Player-piano: Variations in Performers'; and five firms were advertising their latest issues of music rolls.

In May, a correspondent in *Musical Opinion* had had a glorious smack at the wickedness in player-piano advertisements. The mechanics' journal *Work* had some articles on 'How to build an Up-to-date Player'. The *Pall Mall Gazette,* under the title 'Music and its Makers: Expression' by 'EE', pointed out how a Pianola can become a bad form of musical self-indulgence 'not far removed from that which consists in eating too many sweets at a time'. To the dismay of parents and music-teachers, W R Hall Caine in the *IOM Weekly Times* advised boys and girls to 'keep away from the piano stool'.

> Girls, I say, leave music to those whose business it is, and crowd not into a profession already crowded and one wherein mechanical arts threaten to outrival the very highest technical skill.

The *Globe* still continued its weekly page for the player piano. One interesting section appeared, 'The Case for Literature', in which the writer protested against 'a sham pretence of enjoyment' that he noticed at piano recitals – and he advocated for player-pianists an honest declaration as to the kinds of music that, fashion apart, really interested them individually. The *New Age* made reference to the piano players – 'A source of misery or delight according to the fitness or otherwise of the performer on it'. 'Crotchet', again, in the *Daily Chronicle,* said: 'It is this scope for personal skill that has made the pneumatically-controlled player-piano so popular.'

By June there was little doubt that the trade journals all seemed prepared for combat. There were exhortations, accusations and general activities surrounding the player piano and its distributors. The *Music Student,* which had arrived at a player-piano page, printed some advice to player-pianists, obviously written by someone who did not possess an instrument. Even so, this paragraph remains good for all time:

> The pianist who, after ten years or more hard labour on the keyboard, imagines he will straightaway obtain full satisfaction from the new mechanical medium is the victim of a grave delusion.

The *Globe* busied itself in preparing some excellent player-pianists' programmes and had an article, 'What it means', that imagined the progress of the player piano in the years ahead. But how different those immediate years ahead proved to be!

Before the heavy guns of the trade could fire any further salvos, the *Piano Player Review* decided to close. Its last issue was July 1914. There was talk that its core advertisers had cancelled and that its financial backers took fright at the way things were going. The truth is lost now but what is certain is that it was an honest publication doing a good job in an industry that was run by bigots. It had reflected technical developments and influenced public opinion in regard to the player piano. Its decline was unwarranted. The main trouble ahead was nothing to do with trade conflict, advertising barriers or petty accusation, but was an event completely beyond the control of the player industry.

On August 4th, Britain declared war on Germany. While initially life was not too badly interrupted, before long the call-up of able-bodied men in all but key industries decimated manufacturing companies such as player-piano makers. Those piano-makers that remained were immediately taken over for aircraft manufacture, it being said that the piano craftsman most easily adapted to the construction of the wooden aircraft of the day.

By the signing of the Armistice on November 11th, 1918, things did not at once pick up to the pre-war level. Post-war Britain and, to a lesser extent, America, were changed worlds facing times that were far removed from 1914. The new age had greater expectations yet a presented a war-weary resolution that brought a sense of reality quite removed from the carefree pre-war days. The reign of George V (the 'Sailor King' as he was known) followed on the anodyne reign of Edward VII who had managed to avoid leaving any impression whatsoever on his people. Indeed, the Victorian era and its trappings had effectively continued up until George's coronation in 1910. The 'gay nineties' thus really ended with the business over the Kaiser's Germany. Now, just four years later, there were the terrible physical and emotional scars of war to be healed. The British people had just 'come of age' and the precious few blessings that many could find were being counted. Having fun, player-piano concerts and singing were patterns that had to be returned to slowly.

But that was not all. I have already mentioned the terrible 'flu epidemic that decimated towns and villages right across the land well into the 1920s. It had begun in the British military camp at Etaples in northern France in December of 1916[2] and from there had travelled the world, killing Germans (who thought we had introduced germ-warfare into the trenches), Americans, Canadians – in fact all races including Ghurkhas.

Besides the 'flu, there was unemployment. Personnel back from war hoped, naturally, to find work. There wasn't any. We put our respected old soldiers on the streets and gave little extra cheer to those many who had lost limbs. For those who had been shell-shocked out of sensibility, medical science didn't think brains could be healed, so committed them to lunatic asylums. As food became scarcer even than during the war, investments and the Stock Market plunged. It was a grim time for everybody and this explains why developments in the world of player-pianos were effectively moribund in the two or three years that followed the end of the war.

It was the end of 1920 before things began to pick up again. People in the trade believed that the hey-days of the player were over but they were to be proved wrong as sales began once more on the ascendant and new peaks were hit in the mid-1920s.

An event took place on September 4th 1926 that would herald the eventual demise of the player. Few recognised it as a threat. On that date the Radio Manufacturers' Association held its first trade show, RadiOlympia, at London's Empire Hall, Olympia. The piano trade watched with a mixture of amusement and disinterest. But amongst the more astute of dealers there was the first inkling of uncertainty for the future. If radio was to become a success and become widely available, it could affect sales of musical instruments, pianos in particular.

Of course, that is just what happened and the 'wireless set' quickly found its way into many homes. For those with the money, the radio receivers were either purchased outright or, because of the then unreliability and expense of replacement valves (tubes), hired from dealers.

The long-established Black Forest orchestrion organ makers Blessing embraced perforated paper music and pneumatic actions in the decade before the First World War. Wolfgang Blessing's Polyvox Model A came in a variety of case styles and comprised 1 51-note piano, 27-note xylophone, 27-note mandoline, 27 flute organ pipes, bass drum, side drum, cymbal, castanets, tambourine and triangle. This example was made around 1920 and has a dark oak case with brass decoration.

In a curious way, trade settled down as the 1920s advanced. It accepted the competition and still managed to thrive. But in America a whole new technology was pioneered in 1928 – the 'talking picture'. This would revolutionise the whole cinema industry and, indeed, the entire social behaviour of generations to come. More immediately, though, it killed off the silent cinema and with it the theatre 'fotoplayer' or player-piano-based musical accompaniment machines.

Few could have imagined just how important the cinema, now with sound film, would become as the 1930s advanced.

But to return to the 1920s, all was going well and player-piano sales were holding up strongly in the face of growing competition for the spare cash of Joe Public in the way of cheap cars, radio and the gramophone. It was about to go pear-shaped again. The Wall Street crash in October 1929 preceded the abandonment of the gold standard in America by four years. Britain abolished the gold standard in September 1931, the value of the English pound rising from $4.86 to $3.49.

In December 1929, *The Music Trade Review* – America's principal music trade journal – celebrated its fiftieth anniversary with a huge gold-covered 90-page issue. It also charted the huge growth of radio in the United States. Manufacturers quickly cleared out factory space to produce the latest products. One headline says it all: *Gulbransen Co Expands Radio Output Thirty Per Cent in November.*

As investments on both sides of the Atlantic dwindled, companies contracted or folded up and the chain reaction was a decline in business confidence that was to experience no glimmer of upturn until well into 1932. There is no doubt whatsoever that the Great Depression did more to kill off the player piano than did any competitive influence from wireless or the gramophone, both of which were to suffer just as severely.[3]

The size of the problem can be judged from the simple fact that in America unemployment hit 13.7 million in 1932 and was to rise to 15 million the following year (it was down to 8 million in 1937). Germany was hit just as hard with 5.6 million out of work and Britain, with an estimated working population of 18.5 million, had 2.8 million on the dole. People who can barely afford food to eat don't buy piano-rolls, let alone player-pianos!

The long-term effect was almost six years of uncertain economy. Remembering that the 1920s had begun with a recession, the outcome was that in the twenty years from 1919 to 1939 the years of economic growth were few and far between – a seven-year period followed by another of five years. It is hard to imagine today the enormous burden of those inter-war years on ordinary business, let alone those involved with what successive Chancellors of the Exchequer like to call 'luxury goods' and you and I might term 'non-essentials'.

Although it was these luxury goods that suffered the hardest and many people were forced to 'downsize' and move into smaller homes where space was at a premium, the player piano did not die without a struggle. It was championed by a number of dedicated player men, not the least being Reginald Reynolds who, having seen his employer Aeolian go to the wall, had the courage to stay in the player business to the bitter end.

At the height of the recession in 1930, *Musical Opinion* published a small booklet called 'Converting a 65-note Player'. This told how a 65-note model could be made to play standard 88-note rolls by the dubious expedient of changing the tracker bar, adjusting the roll drive chucks and T-jointing the upper and lower notes of the 65-note scale to play all the notes of the piano. A simpler method was to tee in all the bass and treble notes of an 88-note stack so that 65-note rolls could appear to play all the notes on the keyboard — in octaves at each end, of course.

Of course it was a brave attempt to revitalise the interest in player pianos but even so this little booklet, which was responsible for modifying and mutilating a number of pianos at this time, proved so successful that during the next six years it ran to four reprints. It was written by Harry Drake, whose player articles were a one-time feature of Musical Opinion. Its legacy is still to be found occasionally today so I always warn people buying a piano to check carefully that a 'full-scale' instrument plays all 88 notes because the presence of an 88-note tracker-bar is no guarantee!

In 1920, seventy percent of the 364,000 pianos manufactured in the United States were players. By 1932 the combined inroads of radio, gramophone and the Depression had made the instrument all but extinct, though rolls could still be bought. In Britain the contemporary player scene was related in *Musical Opinion* for July 1932 by that other bastion of the player piano, Harry Ellingham. He wrote:

> There are unmistakable signs that the player-piano, after sixteen years' partial eclipse, is coming back out of the shade

Many of the larger piano-orchestrions were presented as both status symbols and examples of modernity. This elegant German piano-orchestrion with keyboard was made in 1920 by Gebrüder Weber in Waldkirch.

into clear vision. Wireless, the gramophone and the reproducing piano caused the shadow that covered the true player-piano from view; and how dark has been the shadow can well be gauged by the prominence that the instrument attained up to the time of the Great War and what has happened since.

But none of these things — the war, wireless, the gramophone, the reproducing piano — killed the player-piano. Its ultimate use as the home instrument cannot be doubted. Perhaps the saturation point of listening to wireless and potted music generally is being reached; or it may be that this very element of listening to much music is inducing people to seek personal performance. Whatever may be the cause, no sane survey of the present situation can leave any doubt that the time is here again when the player-piano is emerging from partial obscurity. The demand for the instrument will grow, as people have little inclination and less time to face ordinary piano playing; and it will grow the more rapidly, much more rapidly, in proportion as the instrument is manufactured and presented as a sensitive musical instrument that can with advantage be studied seriously by every untrained lover of good music and taught by professional musicians.

Another man who contributed greatly to resurrecting the player-piano industry in England was energetic and youthful Charles W Bannister, who, in the autumn of 1932, urged the industry to unite and present a common advertising campaign. As an executive of The Pianoforte Manufacturers' Association, Bannister was concerned that piano rolls were still far too expensive and that if there was some way in which demand could be increased then costs might be reduced. He came up with the idea of staging a National Player-Piano week.

The problem of roll cost had not escaped the attention of the roll makers and, indeed, the Muvis piano roll, a standard 88-note introduced in the autumn of 1931 at a price of 2/6d regardless of the type of music, was a conscious effort to re-establish the popularity of the player by offering an extensive catalogue of quality, low-cost rolls that were readily available.

On September 26th 1932, a meeting was held at Pagani's restaurant in London's West End. Piano and player-piano makers, store buyers and dealers all sat down to discuss what could be done to drum up trade which, they believed, had suffered greatly at the hands of the motor car (people were travelling about more for leisure and the car was beginning to assume importance in the range of domestic durable goods) and the increase in the number of people buying their own homes, not to mention that constant claim that wireless and the gramophone must be at the heart of all things bad.

As meeting organiser, Charles Bannister sounded a clarion call to the industry to make the best of the slowly returning prosperity. Why, he told the meeting, he had heard of people who were selling their motor cars because the cost of petrol had just been increased! Bannister proposed that everybody should pull together in staging a week-long event across the country to promote the instrument. He also boldly advocated that the emphasis should be on the player piano and not on brand names. He recalled that before the 1914-18 war opinion had said that the American organ took the place of the harmonium, and the piano superseded the American organ. Now, he urged, was the time for the player piano to oust the ordinary piano!

Bannister's suggestions were greeted with unanimous approval. In truth there wasn't much else that they could have done, sales being so bad. A committee was organised chaired by Plymouth dealer Sidney Moon. It resolved to stage the first Player Piano Week, to canvas makers for support (one immediately pledged £1,500!), to get the British Broadcasting Corporation to broadcast more player-piano concerts, and to try to get Europe's commercial radio station, Radio Paris, to advertise the event on Sundays. The date of the special week was finally fixed as November 21st to the 26th 1932, and the BBC agreed to broadcast a player piano recital by Reginald Reynolds on the National programme on November 24th between 8 and 8.25 in the evening.

The committee, which included Messrs F H Saffell of Triumph-Auto, Findley of Aeolian, E H Aird of Harrods, Pinfold of Godfreys, A H Fawn of the Universal Music Company and Watts of Monington & Weston, proved itself an enthusiastically strong and effective means of promotion and meetings were held up and down the country to spread that enthusiasm.

On October 26th Bannister addressed a meeting of the North-Western Division of the Music Trades Association. Reminded that the very first general radio broadcasts in Britain (in November 1922) were made from Manchester's Trafford Park using a player piano and a gramophone, delegates unanimously agreed to support all moves to re-establish the player piano.

The player-piano week was enough of a success to encourage dealers to hope that the three or four-year old slump, during which time many had been forced to take pianos in part-exchange for new gramophones and wireless sets, was well and truly behind them. Even the Prince of Wales was prompted to respond that 'His Royal Highness, as you know, is intensely interested and keen on the betterment of all industry. He hopes that the steps taken for a national player-piano crusade will prove a great success.' And dealers were reminded of the Cromwellian dictum: 'Don't wait until the iron is hot – strike until you make it hot!' A second player-piano week was promptly scheduled for March 6th–11th 1933.

Playing perforated paper music rolls 32.5 cm (12.3/4-inches) wide, the Weber included organ pipes and a xylophone. Standing 8 feet 4 inches high, it would not fit into today's low-ceilinged homes.

An indication of piano and player-piano sales in the rest of Europe, can be deduced from the published export figures of Germany. They make interesting reading. Where once Britain had been a major importer of German-made musical goods, in particular automatic pianos, the position was now very different. In October 1932, Germany exported 107 automatic pianos to Italy, 90 to Switzerland, 638 to Czechoslovakia, 71 to Sweden and 121 to Austria. Britain took none. In the month of December 1932, Germany exported only eight pianos to Britain – three of them grands and none of them players – yet it sent 67 players to Switzerland, 49 to Italy, 142 to Sweden, 22 to Japan, 12 to Denmark, 225 to Czechoslovakia (which had just begun its own obviously successful player-piano push), and 52 to Austria. Its entire export to the last five countries for that month were made up of players.

Musical Opinion for April 1933 carried notification of the second player week. The editor reported the forthcoming event with enthusiasm. He could, one might say, do little else than write:

> Despite the severe economic depression, unprecedented in the whole history of the world, dealers and the big stores entered enthusiastically into making the second player week a bigger success than the first, the general opinion being that any kind of movement or activity is better than stagnation.

The item went on to describe the support promised by the BBC (it never came), Radio Athlone, Radio Paris and Norway. A quarter of a million circulars were distributed free by committee members by courtesy of the Universal Music Company. The front showed a typical suburban home and the message 'Why is this a Happy Home?' The answer was because it had a player piano 'on which the latest song rolls' could be enjoyed. Large-scale player production, which had helped lower costs to something approaching those of the ordinary piano, plus the availability of deferred terms (hire purchase or 'the instalment plan'), made the player piano universally attractive and promised to put its owner firmly on 'the road back to the personal participation in music'. Deep down inside, the trade and the manufacturers must have known that it was a last gasp, and that the good old days were virtually over.

The British player trade received an unexpected kick in the teeth when, in 1933, import duties on German pianos (not automatic ones) were reduced from $33^{1}/_{3}$-per cent to 20 per cent. The Pianoforte Manufacturers' Association, under its outspoken chairman William Evans, protested that this move could flood the British market with cheap German instruments, so forcing our factories out of business. 'We had nearly two hundred firms producing pianos in this country,' he said. 'As a result of the depression of the last five years the number has already been halved. Another 'bump' from Germany would mean that another fifty would go out.'

He had a valid point, especially as the age of the 'stencil-brand' or imitation quality piano was about to be revitalised. Many of the pianos imported with impressive – but artificially branded – names were of the lesser quality. To the gullible (and

The Operators Piano Company of Chicago introduced a large range of orchestral pianos between its foundation in 1904 and the mid-1930s. Most popular was the Coinola which was blessed with good musical arrangements for its 'O' style music rolls. The Model CO seen here is a rarity today although in its day it was fairly prolific. It was also the second most expensive of a 16-strong catalogue: in 1925 it cost $2,200 (£550).

the world is full of them), the attraction of a nice 'Steinbech' or 'Oberwald' was as irresistible as the promise of a Knighthood to a newspaper-boy.

The experience of the Great Depression, aftermath of the Wall Street Crash, had a sobering effect on ordinary people. It changed attitudes in the same way as there had been major alterations in life-style and outlook following the Great War. This was most noticeable by the manner in which people spent their money. By the summer of 1933, with the economy slowly reviving, there were signs that the days of domestic extravagance that some detected in the latter years of the 'twenties were unlikely to return and while there was a little more cash available in the pockets of the many, it was being spent on other and more important things.

Freedom from worry encouraged escapism and escapism could be bought in two ways. First was the cinema. Second was motoring. The dream of buying a private motor-car for £100 became reality as car-makers entered mass-production and brought down retail prices. And dreams of another sort were to be found in the picture theatre. This was the rich age of the cinema boom and the building of dream-palace cinemas styled in their own very individual version of *art deco* was in full spate.[4]

As for pianos, be they players or otherwise, they were no longer fashionable and the homeowner of the 'thirties dreamed of a radiogram or, perhaps, a refrigerator, not a musical instrument. Evenings around the piano, singing or merely listening, had passed into oblivion as ordinary people began seeking pleasure and relaxation in more active ways. Sports such as tennis, golf and rowing were now embarking on their own boom times.

Still, though, the trade strove to buck the trend. Addressing the Scottish Music Merchants' Association at Pitlochry on June 6th that year, piano maker W H Strohmenger said:

> It is estimated that during the present year the number of pianofortes manufactured in this country [the British Isles] will amount to some seventy per cent less than those manufactured in the peak period, which, when you consider that we have suffered the total loss of the export trade, the forced sale by many private owners, and the enormous shrinkage in all incomes, coupled with the fact that the piano is a luxury, is not a very serious matter. It is very interesting to know that the figures of the last few months would go to show that the recovery is starting, slowly, but still advancing.

Across the Atlantic, the American Society of Composers, Authors and Publishers was expressing concern at what was happening to the music trade and, in particular, to the popular song. It found that the life of a song, measured in terms of how long it was saleable as a printed sheet of music in the store, had been seriously reduced since the introduction of radio. It went so far as to publish a little leaflet called *The Murder of Music* which contained some interesting statistics, some of which I reproduce as follows:

The growth of the Radio Audience, numbers

1925	16,000,000	1929	38,000,000
1926	20,000,000	1930	46,000,000
1927	26,000,000	1931	52,000,000
1928	30,000,000	1932	60,000,000

Total Value Sales of Pianos *(in US$ where £1 = $3.49)*

1925	93,670,000	1929	38,000,000
1927	67,000,000	1931	12,000,000

Total Value Sales of Gramophones (Phonographs) *(in US$)*

1925	22,600,000	1929	31,656,000
1927	46,000,000	1931	4,869,000

Total Value Sales of Radio Sets *(in US$)*

1925	165,000,000	1929	592,068,000
1926	200,000,000	1930	332,198,000
1927	168,750,000	1931	212,040,000
1928	388,000,000	1932	124,860,000

Total Value Sales of Sheet Music *(in US$: compiled from three leading firms)*

1925	2,639,351	1929	2,130,722
1926	3,447,775	1930	1,261,137
1927	2,797,518	1931	861,383
1928	2,790,862	1932	827,154

Employment of Musicians in Motion Picture Theatre Orchestras *numbers*

1925	19,000	1932	3,000

The British player-piano weeks had been something of a success and there seemed no reason why that seemingly successful formula should not be sustained. Anxious to try anything that might boost sales, plans were laid in Britain for a further player-piano week – the second of the year – which would be merged with the Music Trades Association's National Music Week. The event was held from October 9th 1933. During the very first player-piano week around 300 dealers arranged displays of instruments. In the second event, staged the following year, this number increased to 400. Yet more promotion was urged for this third event.

Chicago was a rich centre for automatic-piano construction and another maker there was The Marquette Piano Company on Wallace Street. The brand name Cremona was applied to most of its products. Considered the 'Rolls-Royce' of American mechanical musical instruments, here is the Style G which was available with flute pipes (as here) or violin-toned pipes.

To a certain extent, the campaign brought the hoped-for success, in no small part due to the urgency for a turn of the tide being so great that the campaign involved even more dealers up and down the country. As a result several makers who had ceased making players were inspired to reopen their production lines. And Charles Bannister said again that he was optimistic about the future of the player piano.

The player had one other staunch advocate in the shape of former player-piano expert, Reginald Reynolds. As probably the last link with the Pianola era, Reginald Reynolds[5] has acquired something of a legendary status amongst present-day player enthusiasts, in particular in Britain. Be that as it may, Reynolds was possessed of a rare enthusiasm that shone through in everything he wrote. With the passing of the depression it seemed that the trade had lost faith in the instrument. Reynolds was invited to write about the instrument in the 21st birthday issue of *The Pianomaker, Music & Radio* for June 1934. His words to the trade are worth repeating:

> You say: 'Price counts'. Yes, it does; but the additional cost of the pneumatic action is only a tithe of its actual value to the purchaser. A 'player' piano is worth at least ten ordinary pianos, and viewed from that standpoint is always a good investment.
>
> If you dealers will only have faith in the musical capacity of the instrument and its unique utility for personal performance, you can bring about such a revival of 'player' prosperity, that not only will it benefit you and the manufacturers, but will bring happiness into thousands of homes.

Reginald Reynolds, whose name appears on many of the later Aeolian patents, was an avowed promoter of the instrument, yet however much he eschewed the merits of the player he could not influence public attitudes and market changes. Even as he wrote, the greatest name in player pianos was crumbling. Aeolian in America suffered severe damage by fire and consequently was forced to amalgamate with Ampico, and affairs in Britain had reached a situation from which there was no retreat.

The next National Player Piano Week was fixed for November 5th 1934. The symbolism of selecting Bonfire Night can only have been accidental, for November 5th has throughout keyboard-instrument history been a date dreaded by pianos!

While all this hullabaloo was going on, the Americans trade and retail industry had been earnestly watching events in Britain. They were impressed by the united efforts of the industry towards re-establishing sales. In the early part of 1934, the Chicago *Piano Trade Magazine* discussed the possibility of revival of the instrument in United States, commending to its readers the work of Charles Bannister in motivating British trade. Many American makers, it said, had immediately got out of the business at the onset of the depression, thereby accelerating the decline in the market by cutting off the supply of instruments at source. The outcome had obviously been a market in freefall. That certainly did not happen in Britain where trade confidence tended to be more impervious to the oscillations of the Stock Market.

This same year a controversial yet highly perceptive article appeared on the Continent. Commenting on the early demise of the French player-piano industry in the light of the stoic efforts of the British at resurrecting trade following the Depression, the publication *Musique et Instruments* had some valuable comments to make regarding the reproducing piano:

The player piano, as at first developed, aimed chiefly at facilitating the playing of the piano. To a certain extent it took charge of what may be called the physical part of playing, leaving to the performer the task of phrasing and expression. People were able more easily to become players, but musical qualities were not excluded. On the contrary, these remained, and it was possible to obtain from the instrument all that could possibly be expected. The owner of the player did not become a passive listener, but rather satisfied his musical tastes by musical expression personally applied.

Hupfeld's book-playing piano was aimed at the drawing-room of the discerning private individual rather than for a public place. It could play quite long pieces of music, the only limitation being the size of the zig-zag-folded punched cardboard music book. This was put on the bottom of the cabinet and the leader threaded up under a series of guides and pressure bars to the top. As it played the music would move upwards, over the top, down the back behind the soundboard, and fold up again as a book on the cabinet floor next to where it had all started from. Power for this elegant item of furniture came from a hot-air engine driven by a small spirit burner: this can be seen in the lower left portion of the case. A row of 15 hemispherical bells nested on a common rod can also be played from the music book: these are switchable on and off as required.

The American player makers erred when they changed the instrument into something more automatic. The reproducing piano was introduced, and while a marvel of mechanism, it was inimical to the interests of players. With appropriate rolls, the 'reproducer' could certainly imitate the art of Paderewski and other virtuosi, and this by persons with no knowledge of music whatsoever. The new instrument gained popularity rapidly, but it was short-lived, for there was something psychologically false about the suggestion that the operator was responsible for the result.

The reproducer, entirely automatic, captivated at first those disposed to make little or no effort: it also secured the adherence of some true lovers of music who found in it real opportunities for hearing performances better than they could produce on a foot-blown player. They were satisfied for a time, until indeed they were satiated with the store of rolls at their command, and then they realised that they were no longer making music. They had again been reduced to a state of passive listeners with a stale repertoire: and their taste for the player and its music faded away. These people realised that the radio with its loud speaker offered something more to their taste and in increasing variety.

What this article effectively got over was the notion that the perfection of the reproducing piano had converted good music into background music and aspiring performers on the player-piano into nonentities. In many ways it foretold the way music was to go, being everywhere 'on tap' yet nowhere needing skill or even understanding. Even to this day there is a strong school that eschews the heretical thought that if you want to listen to perfect piano music you buy a compact-disc player, but if you want to make and enjoy music you buy a foot-operated player-piano.

As radio became established in the home – and the annual Radio Show consolidated its place in the calendar – there were those that were far-sighted enough to see leisure time and entertainment in the home as an entity, not as something to treat as a compartmentalised resource. The 1936 RadioOlympia show, manufacturers D E Brasted became the first piano maker to participate at a London radio show – and they did it in style with no fewer than 100 Minipianos on their stand.

In that year, the National Player-Piano Publicity Committee came into action once more, publishing a pamphlet called 'Plea for the Player'. The following February (1937), what was probably the last of the player pianos to be produced in England was revealed at the British Industries Fair by the London makers Barratt & Robinson. This was the Minstrelle Autopiano, which measured a mere 1 ft 5½ inches deep and 3 ft 3 inches high. This used a single-valve action placed under the keyboard. The player controls were accessible with the key fall closed and a transposing tracker bar (which was viewed as vital if the piano were to be used to accompany singing) was fitted.

At this same fair, an exhibitor called Bush Radio displayed models of a strange device called the Bush Televisor Type T5. Selling at 55 guineas [$202] and only usable in the very few square mile area covered by the BBC television station at London's Alexandra Palace, this object caused fresh unease within the piano trade. Will it, they asked one another, affect the piano industry as the invention of wireless did not so many years ago?

How unimportant it all seems now when one looks back to that far-off year. Europe was boiling for war, America and Canada were experiencing the first sit-down strikes in the huge General Motors dispute – and, while Wallace Carothers (1896-1937) was making the first nylon stockings. Meanwhile, Frank Whittle was testing the first jet engine. Humanity was being swept up on a whirl of accelerating technology.

While the world prepared its athletes for the ill-fated 1940 Olympic Games in Tokyo, some fifty seats were booked in advance on the *Hindenburg* airship which was to visit the games. After its 1936 season refit, the giant German dirigible sported a Blüthner piano in its spacious lounge. This special piano, a 5 ft 5 in. grand, weighed only 326 lb instead of the usual 530 lb because of the wide use of duralumin for the frame and all other metal parts (save, of course, the strings). The piano case was covered with light yellow pigskin. It perished along with thirty-six souls at the Lakehurst mast in New Jersey on May 6th 1937.

As late as April 1937, a New York trade paper revealed that there was now a campaign afoot in America to try to revive the player. Several makers were producing new models. And in Britain Charles Bannister's National Player-Piano Publicity Committee was also allegedly detecting a resurgence of interest – again. By this time, though, somebody should have had the gumption to turn off the player-piano's life-support machine. The indications were that each perceived revival was becoming successively smaller. There was no encouraging business-plan and it was time to pull the plug on an industry that wasn't obsolescent so much as obsolete.

The Wurlitzer company of North Tonawanda, New York, advertised with the slogan 'Everything Musical' – and lived up to that claim. Vast numbers of instruments of many varieties were made over the years. Here is a Wurlitzer Model CX piano orchestrion fitted with an automatic roll-changer. Between 1911 and 1930, about 650 were made and sold. The most expensive instrument in the range, the 1920 price was $2,100 (£525).

In the years immediately prior to the 1939-45 war, the progress of radio and the widening interest in television (not to mention improvements in the gramophone industry), the hoped-for last-gasp player revival was not to be. As the world overcame the Depression and its aftermath of mass unemployment, ordinary pianos had picked up sales again, but players were no more. Production had long since tailed off and many makers either went out of business or were absorbed by larger firms.

Inside the Wurlitzer Model CX reveals the extensive instrumentation somewhere beneath which lurks a piano! Curiously the combined suction and pressure wind department is very reminiscent of the design used by Hupfeld in Germany.

The onset of the 1939-45 war marked *finis* to the era. In the short space of about forty years, the pneumatic player piano had evolved from a rather primitive and impractical machine to production mechanism that fitted inside the piano.

As regards accomplishment, in the same period of time it had progressed from being an amusing diversion to something close to perfect performance reproduction. The sad fact was that, like so many great inventions, having gone through the process of evolution it finally emerged as the quintessence of its designed specification only to find that the very conditions that encouraged its development in the first place had changed so much that it was no longer required. Thus in its very prime it became obsolete.

There were certain places where the following for the player-piano has never really waned. In Australia, for example, the instrument is almost as popular now as it ever was, there never having been any marked recession in interest or demand. Indeed, Melbourne's branch of Aeolian, The Orchestrelle Company, was still selling new Duo-Art and other rolls right up to the time of its closure as late as 1976.

There is still a rich trade in restored player-pianos and also in new rolls which are still being produced in quantity in Australia. In both England and America there exists an increasing number of small businesses, often one-man outfits, that will produce new ordinary rolls, or make a copy of an old roll for full-scale or reproducing piano. And the QRS company still survives in the States along with Mastertouch in Australia.

Mentioning Mastertouch, there is an unusual tale to be told about that company. Some years ago, the then proprietors decided to close the business and consequently advertised all the plant and equipment for sale. So great was the response and so positive the regrets that this action was being considered that Mastertouch decided to remain in operation!

The use of computerised techniques in roll-copying has made possible a new generation of music for the enthusiastic player-owner. With the advent of dedicated musical software, the ordinary domestic PC has become one of the sources of new player music.

After the doldrums of the immediate post-war years, and although the 'old-fashioned' pneumatic player-piano is no longer made, interest in player pianos has risen to the point where it is probably an enduring inevitability. As certain of us become more inured to the age of modernity and hanker for things from a past and gentler age, players have become more and more sought-after. Their ownership, once viewed as something of a liability, is now cherished and owners are taking a second look at their pianos and even taking the trouble to learn the proper way to make them perform a roll.

To summarise the history of the player we have charted two periods of peak popularity – the first in the years leading up to 1914, and the second in the years leading up to the Great Depression. After 1929 and the poverty and unemployment that combined with economic uncertainty, the Aeolian empire in America crumbled and the player piano itself, considered invincible by many, lost stature and withered away. While the trade and industry fought to keep it alive, it was a lost cause.

As a product it died in America before 1932, was dead in France by the following year and, in spite of strenuous efforts in Britain as I have already shown, it was a non-seller by 1935. The peak of its popularity lay between 1910 and 1925.

During that time, almost every manufacturer of pianos in America and in Europe fitted player actions to their instruments. There was no question of its being beneath the dignity of the great names amongst makers to build players. Indeed some of the finest instruments bore such gilt-edged names as Steinway, Blüthner, Chickering, Mason & Hamlyn, Broadwood and others. Naturally the better the piano the better the player action fitted and, understandably, it was the practice of these top-class makers to fit reproducing actions such as Hupfeld, Welte, Ampico and Duo-Art.

But now the peak years had long since gone. Edward H Story's words quoted from 1905[6] took on a hollow sound as the industry ground to a halt. As player-pianos fell silent, sadly so did ordinary pianos as fewer and fewer people bothered to learn to play. In Dickensian times almost every home in the land had a piano (what Dickens called 'a Victorian wall-climber') and most people played. It was now very different.

At this point in time, perhaps we should ask a few questions like what good was the player-piano? And what did it do for music?

There is no doubt whatsoever that the piano-player and player-piano became part of the social fabric of their age. Almost everybody knew of their existence and almost everybody thought they were clever. The decline in mass-market music education had already begun but it was still understood that one of the more attractive and appreciated of the social graces was the ability to play the piano. Exactly *how* you played the piano (*i.e.* by foot or finger) probably didn't matter that much so long as you entertained. It thus developed a pseudo-cultural side.

Gebrüder Weber of Waldkirch introduced the Grandezza piano/mandoline/xylophone about 1922. It displayed the characteristic design of the age – almost a hark-bark to Regency – with electric lights having glass-beaded shades suspended in front of blind ovals decorated with carved swags. The music rolls were 32.5 cm (12.3/4-inches) wide.

It was also responsible for educating the increasingly musically-challenged masses about the vast repertoire of music available to them. For the many who could not master the keyboard, it allowed them access to the enjoyment of music through actual 'performance' and brought within the grasp of those with an enquiring, adventurous nature the works of composers to whom they might never otherwise have thought to listen. One composer at least attributed his fame solely to the availability of his music on a piano-roll – Edward Macdowell (1861-1908).

In the days that heralded the 20th century, mechanical piano-playing was a novelty that appealed to the famously-open curiosity of the late Victorian and early Edwardian people. News of a concert played by a robot would almost guarantee a 'full house' as would a circus sideshow starring a bearded woman or a three-legged chicken.

During the decades that followed, curiosity was gradually driven from the mass psyche, first by war and then by an endless stream of scientific and engineering breaks-through that left us more bemused than curious. These days, only talk of an alien from outer space reciting Shakespeare backwards while surrounded by nubile and nude young ladies juggling with live hand-grenades might induce a few people to pay to come and watch. No, we have lost the ability to see things as through the eyes of a child. We've become older, wiser – and colder.

All these aspects conspire to lead us to one of the more curious events that pervaded the closing decades of the last century – the Pianola concerts. Somebody had the brilliant idea that it would be fun to step way back in time and re-enact the events that introduced player-pianos to us right in the beginning by staging a series of paying recitals where the star of the show would be the machine.

One may not fault the concept, yet the reality was generally to act against the reputation of the instrument. It would not have been so bad had these events been staged using a top-quality reproducing piano in its best fettle. Indeed, several recitals were staged using a brand new Estonia reproducing piano fitted with an Ampico action. Also record companies have performed a valuable service by recording the reproducing rolls made by many of the great names of the past. The problem was that these well-meaning events were staged using a push-up piano-player.

While there is nothing intrinsically wrong with that, it remains a primitive device when compared with a reproducing piano. It also depends on the human operator and demands that he be a musician, not merely a lever-fumbler.

Earlier, in the Preface to this book, I suggested that most musicians could not work a player-piano and, conversely, most player-pianists were not musicians, yet there was ample scope for both to live in harmony and for everybody to have pleasure and fun with their own instruments. The problem with London's player concerts was that they offered the public sometimes rather poor piano performances that inspired comments on the lines of 'Well, what do you expect! After all, it's only a Pianola.'

Here's a few extracts from a review of a concert staged in the Purcell Room of the Royal Festival Hall, London, on Tuesday, June 2nd 1981.

> Instead of hearing Chopin's Polonaise which is recognised to be a thundering heroic epic with aristocratic and ceremonial character, requiring great sensitivity and skill on the part of the performer in order to achieve a credible result, the sounds emanating from the Steinway Grand, induced by the Heath-Robinson contraption standing before it, which is an insult to any piano-player ever built, requiring as it does, frenzied pedalling and much perspiration from the operator, were so far removed from anything approaching a musical performance that surely this could not be taken seriously? Neither technically nor musically did [the operator] appear to be in charge, he allowed the machine to run away with him at an incredible speed to the extent that phrasing and modulation became impossible to detect.

The reviewer concluded by observing:

> Frankly these performances were just not good enough for the South Bank and will not do much for attendances at future concerts.

Sadly these events – for there were several of them – were well-intentioned yet I believe caused great harm to the cause of the player-piano. Some recitals, for the record, were very good, especially that which featured unusual music. The reproducing instrument, as I have suggested already, makes a fine concert instrument even on today's platform and before a critical audience. A push-up, however well-adjusted, demands constant practice if it is to attempt adequate playing. It is rather like staging a veteran-car race for an audience accustomed to the speed and excitement of Formula One. No, this was an enthusiasts' idea unwisely allowed the opportunity to misfire.

Such events back in the era of the instrument were excusable as excellent publicity novelties. In 1912, a concert was held at the Queen's Hall in London at which the London Symphony Orchestra conducted by Arthur Nikisch played Grieg's Pianoforte Concerto in A Minor, the solo part being played by Easthope Martin on a player piano. Elena Gerhardt sang several songs to 'pianola' accompaniment at the same concert. The programme was repeated a year later with Camille Chevillard conducting the Lamoureux Orchestra.

But perhaps there never was a 'right' way to promote players! Maybe the instrument was of the sort where the description 'unique' is not sufficient but it had to be subject to qualification in the manner of modern journalese. However unique we wish to consider it, one fact remains clearly in view. While it created a revolution, it was one of such short duration that some people lived right through it.

The seeds of this short-lived revolution were actually there for all to see from the beginning. A revealing assessment of the player in America and those who bought players appeared in an article published in the Chicago *Indicator*. Chicago, it will be remembered, was a major centre of the player industry and thus its local newspaper would have been in a fine position to report on its work. This first-rate assessment, published under the title 'The Piano Player Vogue', was reprinted verbatim in *Musical Opinion* for January 1903:

> The increasing vogue of the piano player is causing widespread comment, not only in musical circles but in the private homes of American citizens who possess no musical education. This vogue is now regarded — and rightly regarded — as one of the most significant phases in the life and advancement of this mechanical age. It is heralded by the enthusiastic as a portent of the dawning of a new epoch, when machinery will still be the motive power of civilisation, but will be applied to uses hitherto deemed sacred from its invading banners. In other words, these persons — dreamers, perhaps, the conservative may call them — regard as now near at hand the day when mechanical inventiveness will invade the precincts of art and will fix its ensign in the very altar of that domain. If this vision is to be realised, the piano player will certainly be the most prominent factor in its accomplishment. The public in general will be pleased, and the piano trade will certainly not lag behind the rest of the world in similar feelings; for it is plain that, when the day of the player arrives, the field of piano enterprise will be greatly enlarged.
>
> The public in general are fonder of music to-day than they were twenty-five years ago. Musical comedy is now the most popular form of stage attraction, and the musical comedy of the day is far in advance of the childish affairs that passed for such in an earlier period. But how to reach, if possible, the causes of the vogue of the piano player as distinguished from the causes of the vogue of music in general?
>
> First, we must recognise the popularity of the piano as an instrument for the home. It has always been great, but never greater than at present; and in view of certain qualities possessed by the piano, which we need not discuss here, it is not likely at any time within the next hundred years to recede from its position. From the piano to the piano player is but a step; a public pleased with one will be pleased with the other.
>
> Another cause of the rise of the player proceeds from our American habits of economising time. Our citizen loves music, but he has no time to spend in studying a complex technique.

Another Weber product was the Unika which offered a single rank of violin-toned wooden organ pipes that could be played in unison with the piano or as a solo effect. These instruments demonstrated both outstanding workmanship and sensitive musical versatility and their tone was superlative. It has to be said that these German-made instruments remain amongst the most musical in the world.

His daughter, perhaps, who would be the proper person to fill this want in his household, is busy working in a store or factory, or goes to high school and must study her Caesar or geometry when she gets home. And then there are many people who have no daughter, or none of the proper age. These matters seem trivial, but they nevertheless have a potent influence.

The third fact is this: With a piano player in your house you can give a friend musical entertainment and discourse with him at the same time. Or if you have nothing to talk about — and this is a contingency that happens with remarkable frequency at social gatherings, especially small ones — you may set your piano at work.

Still another cause lies in the admiration of the public for anything which acts, talks or plays automatically. They wonder at the thing. A wonder is a good thing to subdue and make your own. It pleases you; it will please others. Perhaps it will make them envy you; and what so sweet as envy to the envied? Again, the piano player is a novelty. In all ages novelties have been eagerly sought for, but never has there existed such a craving for them as now. Finally, we must not forget the preparative influences of certain other automatic pleasure making devices that found their way into American households before the general introduction of the piano player. These are principally the music box and the phonograph.

But doubtless, while the present writer has been setting down these reasons, its readers have evolved as many more; and it is remarkable how manifold are the reasons that bring an invention like the piano player into the forefront of public approval.

The player manufacturers themselves were not beyond criticism, however, and a small number were responsible for taking the enthusiasm of the public as an excuse to foist poor-quality instruments on to the market. Another Chicago paper, the *Presto*, wrote on this subject – and again *Musical Opinion* republished the word in October 1905:

Whatever may be the influence of the interior player upon trade (says the Chicago *Presto*) there can be little doubt as to its effect upon the pianos themselves unless the mechanism of the former be reliable and as nearly perfect as anything made by human hands can be. This is a horn of the dilemma that has not been discussed seriously by the trade papers for obvious reasons; but it is nevertheless a point of view that should occupy the careful attention of the piano manufacturers and of the dealers also. When the piano players first appeared as separate instruments collateral or aux-

iliary to the piano, there was no imminent danger to the musical instrument itself; the fame of a musical instrument was not jeopardised by the possible failure of the player. The latter might operate well, and so the combination prove rather a help to the piano's distinction than otherwise; or the player might prove unsatisfactory or troublesome and be set aside as a bad bargain, in which event the dealer had his troubles and in turn the player manufacturer came in for his share of them. But the piano itself took no chances in the final verdict. With the interior player the case is very different. It is easily possible for a piano of great distinction to suffer loss of prestige in a community by the failure or by the fragile character as to durability of a single interior player. The piano is certain to bear the brunt of it, for the distinguished name on the fall board will certainly suffer almost incurable injury if the interior player prove a failure even in partial degree. This makes it a matter of serious consideration from the point of view of all piano manufacturers who have consistently worked for distinction and whose pianos bear names representing a valuable asset in fame or in selling influence. Possibly the interior players are as good, as durable and as perfect in every way as their makers proclaim. Certainly some of them are marvellous creations: but not all of them. Some of them are not at all good specimens, and they are sure to drag down the pianos into which they are placed.

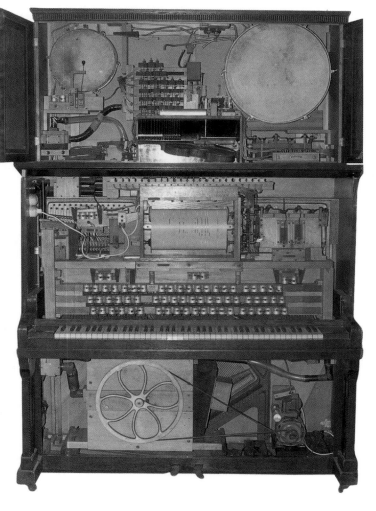

By 1930, musical taste in Europe was changing and the desire for both noise and the visually satisfying gradually began to subsume a culture brought up on fine music and impeccable performance. And so one of the highlights of the Leipzig Spring Fair of 1930 (the showcase exhibition of contemporary technology and industrial progress) was Poppers Violinova. An actual violin was played pneumatically to accompany piano with bass drum and side drum. How different, though, from the elegant Hupfeld instruments that stole the limelight at the Brussels World Exhibition in 1910! Impressive to watch, it was more for the café atmosphere than the salon of two decades earlier. All the same, it was clever. Only this example, though, is known to survive in the Werner Baus Museum.

This is so important a matter that the piano manufacturers cannot consider too carefully the character of the mechanism that is placed in their cases. There seems to be no vital part of the player that is protected securely by patents: this makes it easy to infer that 'they are all alike'. But they are not all alike, and this fact alone should warn piano manufacturers whose products have influence that there is danger in applying the interior players unless there is ample security that the result may not tear down within twelve months the results of the work of a lifetime.

As with so many a new product in a new industry, many manufacturers entered the field. For a variety of reasons, some were less able to survive than others. It became a market where only the fittest would make the grade. Company failures and take-overs were commonplace.

The opportunities for the masses to make music without formal training had begun with the little organette reed organ with its scale of a dozen or so notes. Now the self-playing piano was available in increasing numbers to a public hungry for music of all types. Many new to music derived a genuine and sincere musical appreciation from having a piano initially as a novelty and then finding that they actually liked the increasing repertoire available to them. That excellent barometer of musical progress, *Musical Opinion,* reported in November 1907:

> At the recent Leipzig Fair the chief interest from a musical point of view was the large number of mechanical pianos shown. E Dienst sent one each of his Capella and Perla orchestrions; also an Ariophon mandolin piano. Popper & Co. exhibited orchestrions and electrical pianos. The house of Hupfeld was a prolific exhibitor of orchestrions and of electric instruments. Phillips & Son sent a Tremolant piano orchestrion. Lochmann, amongst other items, a 'string orchestral instrument'. Bruno Geissler, a self playing harmonium.

On the same page was a description of another British-made player – one which made (or tried to make) a feature out of being the cheapest on the market!

> We looked in at the Musicus Piano-Player Co. at Salisbury Road, Highgate, the other day and found the company busy. They manufacture an inexpensive piano, in which is fixed their 'player' mechanism of sixty-five notes. There are several good points in this internal player which were duly explained to the visitor. The treadles are hinged and can be folded in out of the way; the 'player' can be quickly removed for tuning or for replacing a string; the tuner has full opportunity without being encumbered; the music roll is actuated by a three-throw noiseless crank; and there is plenty of room everywhere. A cleverly arranged 'stop' also permits of prompt accentuation; and, finally, it is claimed that 'nothing so cheap has previously been placed on the market'.

Within a few short years this company found itself bankrupt.

The effect of the player on the music world could hardly be described as profound, yet it was responsible for the employment of recording pianists and musically-trained editors. It earned royalties for some composers and increased musical knowledge amongst the masses.

The perfection of the gramophone, the effects of other entertainments such as wireless and, later, television, and perhaps above all else the gradual trend of the family home to become smaller all set the scene for the close of the pneumatic piano era in Britain. War was the catalyst. What remains today is the afterglow of an age of musical achievement that, in its own scale of sphere, was quite as remarkable as anything in the present-day space age.

In the space of fewer than forty years, the player piano had been and gone, leaving in its wake two things: a generation of people who had never needed to learn to play the piano by hand thanks to the player, and several generations for whom musical knowledge and experience had been bought pleasurably at the stools of their player pianos. The gentle educator had achieved more than its promoters could have wished even in their wildest dreams.

The impact of the player had been impressive and important. Just how had it achieved this transformation in so short a period? If we go back to the first decade of this century, we start to see the pattern developing.

The extreme popularity of the piano-player which could convert a normal instrument into a player immediately – and thereby made sound business sense – was such that manufacturers sprang into action in ever-increasing numbers. Every week, another product was unveiled by another company, and the trade papers used headlines such as 'And yet another' and 'Still they come'.

The truly speculative period of the player comprised the decades that bridged the end of the 19th and the beginning of the 20th centuries. Sales of instruments, and market penetration, were very different between the United States and Great Britain. Although some of the figures can only be deduced and are thus merely intelligent guesses and approximations, they show just how attractive the market for pianos would have appeared encouraging companies and inventors to take measures to enter the arena. The difference in market penetration of the piano as an instrument in the homes of the Americans and the British is quite marked.

UNITED STATES

Year	Population	Households	No. of Pianos sold	Market penetration	Total estimate of pianos	Homes with a piano
1890	62,622,250	10,440,000	72,000	0.7%	200,000	3.0%
1900	76,891,220	13,980,000	220,000	1.6%	460,000	3.4%
1905	82,959,221	15,934,000	305,000	1.9%	760,000	4.8%
1910	89,500,000	18,650,000	370,000	2.0%	1.05million	5.6%

UNITED KINGDOM

Year	Population	Households	No. of Pianos sold	Market penetration	Total estimate of pianos	Homes with a piano
1890	34,260,000	6,110,000	50,000	0.8%	170,000	2.8%
1900	38,230,000	7,511,000	71,000	0.9%	205,000	2.8%
1905	40,100,000	8,354,000	75,000	0.9%	270,000	3.2%
1910	42,000,000	8,676,000	78,000	0.9%	335,000	3.9%

I do stress that the figures in these tables are multiply sourced in an endeavour to get as near to the actual as possible. The margin for error is less than 0.1 per cent. The tables reveal that within the space of twenty years the penetration of the piano in the United States increased by some 185 per cent although in that time the number of households only increased by about 78 per cent. In the United Kingdom, however, the same period saw virtually no increase in the penetration of the piano, with manufacture only keeping pace with the increase in the number of households.

The decade that followed saw the massive expansion in player production and, although players in Britain are thought to have represented no more than 30 to 35 per cent of the total output by 1919, in that year 53 per cent of American production was devoted to player pianos – and the peak of production was still four years off.

What this does show is how those makers (and potential makers) so easily interpreted the market conditions as right for certain success. It must have seemed that there was room for everybody, and certainly one more. And even when the first interior player had been introduced to the market – 'the world's first complete piano' – the cabinet-player makers could not see that their market was about to be curtailed.

The Poppers Happy Jazz Band is believed to have been a later conversion of an expression piano by the addition of a separate trapwork case to the top. Because several similar examples are known, it suggests that this was done on a commercial basis, probably as late as the second half of the 20th century.

The majority of pianos on the market were relatively cheap, low-quality models and there were still very many wood-framed pianos that were over fifty years old in regular use. Just how much of that alleged market penetration was devoted to the replacement market rather than fresh business is impossible to say since nobody seemed to understand the subtle but important difference between a replacement-based market and real market expansion.

As an established product that most families aspired to owning, the majority of the public was amenable to buying a new piano and, if that was to be, then it would be one with the player action built inside. This saved space, inconvenience and the continual risk of damage to the fragile wooden fingers of the cabinet player. Even the arrival of Melville Clark's 88-note player did not galvanise the other makers into reading the writing that was becoming ever clearer on the wall.

We have already seen that the result of this inability to read the market correctly was to cost some makers dearly. Many manufacturers were still inventing, patenting and building new push-ups as the buyers in the music stores gleefully were stocking up on 'complete pianos'. All, historically, had never been sweet and rosy, for Theodore P Brown's Aeriol Piano was not a great success on the market. McTammany [61, p.76] gives the reason for the failure as 'prejudice, pure and simple', and adds:

Theodore P Brown was right, the men who looked with indifference and contempt upon his efforts were wrong, and had Brown received the encouragement and co-operation he deserved, he might today [1915] be at the head of the player procession.

And so it was that many good men lost money, many good ideas were lost and many opportunities overlooked. Some may say that there's nothing new in that and it is after all the common scenario not just of a new and developing industry but also the frequently undisciplined progression of any industry at any time in our history. The root cause is clearly not experience or financial advisers – it's something that cannot be changed and it's called 'human nature'.

The outcome was that the history of the player piano was pock-marked with company failures, fortunes lost and, above all, dreams shattered. Along this path of misfortune there were laid low the ideas of some that should have had better fortune, more luck, and a chance to make the market big times. The player inventor was never short of ideas and he continually proved the old adage that there are more ways than one to skin the proverbial cat.

Take the case of Aeolian in Britain. Here was a company that had moved some way to distance itself from its American parent company and was operated largely as an autonomous British business. It still fell victim to the American-originated financial crisis of 1929 but its collapse was through other causes. The British Aeolian empire was to fall victim to its own creation – a new range of expensively-made piano rolls.

With player sales already faltering before the competition created by its rivals for domestic entertainment – the wireless and the gramophone – the company decided to attempt a market boost by introducing a grandiose scheme for a new style of music-roll in 1927 called the Audiographic.

These rolls were printed with an immense amount of information that both prefaced the perforated portion of the roll and ran on throughout its length. It was more of a book with music that told the pianolist everything he could possibly need to know about the music.

Hitherto, attempts at printing information rolls ranging from song-roll words through to Metrostyle markings and the line of dots indicating level of volume, had all suffered from shortcomings because the method of printing could only position these marks approximately on the paper. This margin for error was unacceptable for the new music so Aeolian had designed and built at enormous cost a special printing press that would print expression and phrasing marks to a degree of accuracy never before possible on a piano roll. This printing machine alone set the company back £2,000 [$7,000] and the production cost for each of these special rolls was estimated at £5 [$18] each – an unparalleled price, especially with the impending collapse of the domestic economy.

And when at last, after a lengthy development period during which countless production problems had to be overcome, these rolls were ready for the market, the 1929 economy dampened consumer enthusiasm as certain as a bucket of water on a campfire. A large and expensive advertising programme – just the latest such event in the lavish promotional campaigns undertaken during the company's lifetime – did not bring forth the anticipated fruits. In a short time, the outcome of this profligacy was only as one might have expected. Urgent decisions had to be taken and the expensive production programme was abandoned. With that all the specialist equipment and tooling, which had gone into its realisation, became both redundant and unsaleable.

Few rolls were actually sold and Reginald Reynolds later wrote that in the end they were placed in the lending library where subscribers used to avoid them. The roll library itself was another activity that became an increasingly heavy overhead, for it is doubtful if this far-sighted venture ever paid off. It was, in its time, the largest of its kind in the world.

The enormous loss of capital involved in the Audiographic roll scheme precipitated the company into a major financial crisis and its magnificent premises – the Aeolian Hall in London's Bond Street – had to be put up for auction. When the crash came, Harrods, the large London department store, bought up the remaining assets and took over some of the Aeolian Hall staff. A much smaller Aeolian Company carried on manufacturing at the Hayes factory and when, on November 8th 1932, William Danemann's piano factory in Northampton Street, Islington, was destroyed by fire, Aeolian was able to lease part of its unused Hayes premises to help that business during its rebuild.

By this time Aeolian was no longer a major company in Britain and it contributed a diminishing part to player activities. The final winding up was a lengthy process. How different was this from the situation in Australia where the Orchestrelle Company – Aeolian – remained in business repairing instruments and selling rolls from its Melbourne showroom right up until as late as 1976.

Aeolian was an extreme case where events conspired to initiate downfall. Other smaller makers did not need such convoluted circumstances to bring them to their knees. Merely the collapse of retail sales was enough to cause Banks to call in overdrafts. It was a sad time for many small businesses in many fields.

The Leipzig business founded by Hugo Popper produced a large number of instruments up into the 1930s. The xylophone-equipped Welt pianos of the 1920s included a great variety of case styles, many of which were heavy-looking and inspirationally deficient. However the example seen here and called the Diva, had a satisfyingly chunky appearance heightened by its lights with coloured-bead fringes. For use in a café or restaurant, it could be remotely controlled from a coin-operated wall box, an example of which is seen standing on top of the case.

By the same token, it would be misleading to suggest that the player piano died with or because of the depression of the 'thirties. The benefit of hindsight suggests that it was about ready to go and the external events pushed it over. True, it made a few feeble attempts to regain its former glory as a result of the National Player-Piano Publicity Committee, but it was to all intents and purposes declining by 1929 and moribund after 1937. There was, however, a post-1939-45 war revival and a form of player piano is still being made today but, just like the modern Swiss musical-box industry, the instrument and its numbers represent but a shadow of its former times. From being a consumer product, the player piano is now essentially an enthusiast's one.

In its hey-day, the player represented a truly vast industry that was predominantly spread across the Northern hemisphere. The number of player-piano manufacturers within this great effort is impossible to estimate since almost every maker fitted either his own player action or a recognised action available to him as a kit or unit from a player action maker.

Inside the Popper Diva reveals the sound workmanship associated with German instruments where style and attention to detail were paramount. Note the double inverted seesaw feeders to the wind department.

The educational impact of the instrument on the music-loving public was profound: its subliminal effect in promoting music to others was inestimable. Its uniqueness as a popular musical entertainer was undoubted as, in its peak years, sales boomed both in Britain and America. Pianos with player capabilities went on to ocean liners, troopships – even polar expeditions. They went by their thousands into dance-halls, hospitals and private homes. Interest spread throughout the world and by 1920 Japan had a thriving industry manufacturing *ji-do pianos* (player pianos, literally 'self-moving piano') which cost from 1,400 yen to 3,800 yen for a player grand. Also in full manufacture at this time in Japan were electric coin-freed barrel pianos for cafes.

A measure of this success can be gained from the 1922 *London Trades Directory* within whose pages are listed agents and manufacturers for no fewer than fifty-two different types of instrument, including reproducing pianos. Some of these were inferior pianos but the figures prove the existence of a very considerable demand in Britain. Since the demand here was but a fraction of the American sales, the number of makers in the United States was extremely large and, in the way of things, the precise figure may never be known.

Considerable artistry could be employed in the playing of a music roll and, indeed, a performer who had both flair for musical interpretation and an understanding of the mechanism of his instrument could produce a performance of extremely high quality using the manual expression controls fitted to an ordinary player piano. The logical argument was that, with all the musical notes ready to play and requiring no mental effort, the performer could concentrate all his skills and faculties on the method and style of interpretation. The serious player-piano operator could produce a perfect interpretation from an ordinary roll, given a good piano and the desire to master it and to learn the roll.

Besides the two more obvious elements of the player piano that were responsible for its popularity – entertainment and personal pleasure – it could be used by the serious music lover for the analysis of a piece of music. Even the accomplished pianist could learn much from the music roll that the musical score and his interpretation might otherwise pass over. The Aeolian Company's introduction of 'annotated rolls' was engendered by just this demand. Considerable explanatory text and a wealth of detailed information – including the musical score – was actually printed on the rolls to 'educate whilst playing'.

Indeed, in one interesting experiment to demonstrate the art of the contrapuntal as employed and developed by J S Bach, a piano roll of one of his compositions was reversed so that the high notes became the bass and the low notes the tenor and treble. The result, so it is related, sounded just as melodious as before! The qualifications of the listener on that occasion are unknown.

There was a more serious side to the player piano and this is demonstrated by the activities of the German Honorary Committee for the Promotion of Musical Studies by means of the Duo-Art and Pianola. Savouring strongly of an Aeolian 'quango' or publicity gimmick, this group held its inaugural meeting in Berlin on Wednesday May 18th 1927, and included such musical personalities as Max Bauer, Siegfried Wagner, Bruno Walter and Percy A Scholes. The objectives of the Committee were (a) to further the educational use of Duo-Art and Pianola instruments and music rolls; (b) to comment technically on the music available from the Aeolian catalogue, and (c) to recommend to the company a choice of new compositions to record.

Once very popular and made by the thousand, the Pianolin was the product of the North Tonawanda Musical Instrument Works. Introduced as early as 1906, the coin-operated 44-note electric piano had a violin-toned pipe accompaniment. It dispensed with costly and complicated spoolbox mechanics and played endless music that was allowed to coil up in a hopper. A feature of a number of American instruments, this seemingly alarming state of affairs was proved eminently practical: the paper never tangled and always fed smoothly.

It was at this meeting that Percy Scholes introduced 'The World's Music' series of music-rolls in their various forms. These included the Biographical Roll, the Analytical Roll, the Running Commentary Roll and rolls with explanatory introduction. Aeolian was certainly the most enterprising of the roll makers. With everything looking bright and rosy, nobody could have foretold that within a year or two, Tremaine's empire would be faltering or that the player-piano market was approaching what today we would call 'melt-down'.

Early in the 1930s, more in an attempt to stimulate the dying market following the Wall Street crash than to foster perfection, American dealers organised player-piano proficiency contests for students. Two authoritative books were written by musicologists on the techniques of playing the player piano and the British Broadcasting Company (as it then was) employed a reproducing piano to play not only interval music but also a few scheduled piano music programmes. The instrument had not only become accepted, it was most definitely acceptable.

True as this was, the player piano had a profound sociological effect on the community. As Roehl [91] reflects, it changed the perspectives of youth as a whole generation grew up without the need to learn to play the piano.

Until that time, piano playing was part of home life, part of growing up. Almost everyone could perform to some degree and it was a social grace that, like the ability to dance, play tennis or bridge, stood one in good stead for the rest of one's days. Now there were self-acting instruments and there was no longer any call for tiresome five-finger exercises. All that was wanted was a roll of music. Technical competence had been superseded by rubber tubing, knife-valves and air motors. The delicacy of touch had been replaced by thighs and muscle-power. The *Saturday Evening Post* cartoonist summed up the situation in one sentence. His drawing showed a young girl rather stolidly pumping her way through a roll of music. A woman, in conversation with the child's mother, comments: 'Your daughter's got a great foot for music'.

---

1. This was the failure of the New Trist Player Piano Company Ltd.
2. Initially it was described as 'purulent bronchitis'. By the time it had run its course in 1920, it had killed one million people.
3. The gramophone (phonograph) and the radio receiver eyed each other with deep suspicion like strange cats in the same garden. And both feared the player-piano, which in turn was fearsome of them both. Enterprising makers thought they had the ideal solution to make the best of all worlds by amalgamating the lot into one case. During the late 'teens and the 'twenties a number of players were produced that had gramophones built into them. Most of these heralded from Germany and the United States and were hermaphroditic precursors of the later wireless-pianos – ordinary pianos that incorporated wireless sets in the same cabinet. One, introduced in 1931, was called 'the Wireless Piano' and made in Berlin by one-time player-piano people H Kriebel. Uniting the player piano with a gramophone may be seen as a simple endeavour: in fact the methods suggested were as complex as those laid out in the early days of the player for playing a piano from perforated paper. Powering the gramophone from the piano pedals and the roll motor were tried, springs and electric motors were used and even descending weight mechanisms were patented. Possibly more enterprising if less realistic inventors decided to try to make player piano and gramophone into a mechanism with one programme source by engraving the record track along one edge of the player roll. The advance of the cinematograph inspired applications of optical soundtrack and as late as 1928 one A E Zoppa was granted a British patent for a piano roll with an optically scanned music track down the right-hand edge. If any of these odd devices were ever made, certainly none is known to survive. Yet, strange to relate, the operation of the modern Pianocorder with its compact cassette of magnetic tape bears a passing relationship to this primitive type of endeavour.
4. The picture-palace architecture and décor was an amazing collage of Romanesque, Grecian, art nouveau and art deco together with a certain style that almost subliminally emerged from the great film studios. In 1982 during the course of a series of radio broadcasts tracing the history of music in the cinema, I coined the term Odeonesque to describe this hitherto undefined style. My description clearly met with studied approbation for the word was widely used afterwards, entering circulation in University circles by the following year.
5. Reginald Reynolds was born in London on August 7th 1887 and worked most of his life in the player industry culminating in spending 20 years with Aeolian in London for whom he was to assume the duties of Duo-Art roll recording editor. To him is accorded credit for the first-ever piano-player recital in Britain on March 2nd 1902 when he performed on a Cecilian at Maples department store where he was at that time employed as a piano salesman. Reynolds died on September 10th 1959.
6. Made at the time of the takeover of the Playano Company.

Chapter 8
How the Pneumatic Player Piano Works

A player piano comprises a number of individual parts that function together as a whole. These can be divided into two groups – principal and secondary. The principal sections are (a) the vacuum supply, (b) the pneumatic stack by means of which the piano is played, and (c) the music-roll mechanism.

These components are the 'bare bones' of the instrument. They must interact in specific manners in order to perform a number of different yet related functions that extend from purely mechanical (such as how to rewind the music-roll at the end of the tune) through to individual musical expression (such as the theming of a note or phrase).

What I class as secondary functions are secondary only to the fundamental principals of the primary ones: they are by no means inferior or unimportant. In fact these secondary functions are vital in order to build into the player-piano is very performance capability. These aspects concern how the music roll is driven (unrolled from its spool over the tracker bar to the take-up spool), how it is rewound after playing, how the effects of the piano's soft and sustaining pedals are worked, how notes and musical phrases are accented, and how 'expression' works.

Together with the principal sections already listed, each of these additional functions contributes to making up the complete player piano. If you are going to own and operate a player-piano, then you should understand exactly how it works. Today there are very few player specialists so it is as well that you become familiar with how your instrument operates so that you can carry out those essential 'running adjustments' that may be needed from time to time. In time you will be able to diagnose any faults and then correct them safely without risk of damage to the piano.

Generally speaking, player actions are placed transversely across the front of the instrument above the keyboard. On some players, the action is fitted beneath the key bed. The bellows system on the foot-pedalled piano is always positioned beneath the key bed, this being an obviously convenient position. Connections from the tracker bar, which is most commonly situated at a convenient level in the front fall of the piano case so that the music-roll can be watched, are made to the pouch board by rubber tubing or, in the case of better-made models, by lead tubing. Although a lead-tubed player piano may probably never *need* to be re-tubed, it is so alarmingly heavy as to pose a serious disadvantage to the collector.[1]

The connection between the bellows system and the upper or player action is by large-diameter flexible cotton-reinforced rubber hosing.

I shall avoid going into lengthy details of how the piano itself works for that is outside the scope of this book. The workings of the pianoforte are covered in many good books that you may find in the Public Library's reference section. As for the regulation and adjustment of the piano action, this is covered admirably in a book by Arthur Reblitz [89]. As a starting point, I shall assume that you have a basic knowledge of what happens in an ordinary piano and how, when you press down a key, the effect is

to sound a specific note. Since there is also a difference between the actions in an upright piano and a grand piano, I shall also assume you understand a little of how each operates.

Taking that as our starting-point, and before we move into the realm of automatic pianos and how a pneumatic player action actually operate the piano, we will take a quick look at the piano action and just see which parts have to be set into motion by the pneumatic system. The accompanying illustration of an upright action shows the various parts which combine to make up the mechanics for one key action. You can see how when the pianist depresses a key on the keyboard the action is set in motion, causing the hammer to fly forwards and strike the string.

Two important features to note are the rest rail and the damper rail. Because the hammer is what is called an *escapement* action, no matter how long the pianist holds the key down, the hammer does not stay in contact with the strings but immediately falls back clear of it once it has struck the strings. By holding down the key, all the pianist succeeds in doing is to hold off the damper which is provided to mute the string's vibrations before it may be struck again. In holding off the damper, the string is permitted to vibrate for longer duration than if the pianist were to play the note *staccato*.

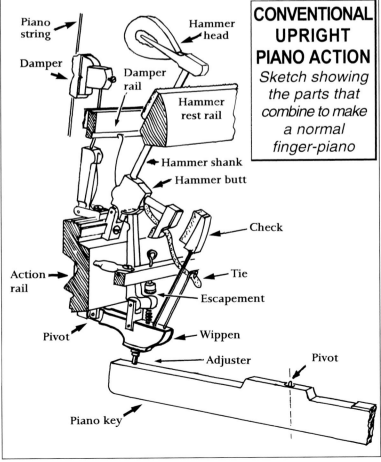

Piano string

Damper

Hammer head

Damper rail

Hammer rest rail

Hammer shank

Hammer butt

Check

Action rail

Tie

Escapement

Wippen

Pivot

Adjuster

Pivot

Piano key

CONVENTIONAL UPRIGHT PIANO ACTION
Sketch showing the parts that combine to make a normal finger-piano

All the dampers can be moved individually in this way, working separately for each note. But all the dampers are freely located upon a rail which itself can be moved away from the string. The action that moves the dampers collectively is called the 'sustaining pedal' – the right one at the lower front of the ordinary piano – which is so often miscalled the 'loud pedal'.

The rest rail is the second of our important features. This is simply the rail against which the individual hammers rest and it can be moved either away from the strings, so allowing the hammer to fly forward a good distance and hit the string hard, or moved closer so that the hammers have only a short distance to travel to do their work and thus hit the strings without great force. This action is controlled by the left-hand pedal at the lower front of the ordinary piano, called the 'soft pedal'. Because moving the rest-rail forward approximately halves the distance that the piano hammer can travel to strike the string it is sometimes referred to as the 'half-blow rail' but this term has a more specific connotation in grand piano actions that also sometimes use a different system which I shall describe later.

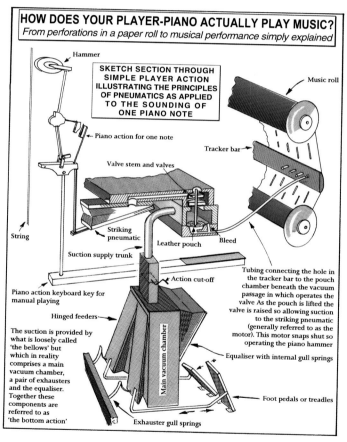

HOW DOES YOUR PLAYER-PIANO ACTUALLY PLAY MUSIC?
From perforations in a paper roll to musical performance simply explained

Hammer

SKETCH SECTION THROUGH SIMPLE PLAYER ACTION ILLUSTRATING THE PRINCIPLES OF PNEUMATICS AS APPLIED TO THE SOUNDING OF ONE PIANO NOTE

Music roll

Piano action for one note

Tracker bar

Valve stem and valves

String

Striking pneumatic

Leather pouch

Bleed

Suction supply trunk

Action cut-off

Piano action keyboard key for manual playing

Tubing connecting the hole in the tracker bar to the pouch chamber beneath the vacuum passage in which operates the valve As the pouch is lifted the valve is raised so allowing suction to the striking pneumatic (generally referred to as the motor). This motor snaps shut so operating the piano hammer

Hinged feeders

The suction is provided by what is loosely called 'the bellows' but which in reality comprises a main vacuum chamber, a pair of exhausters and the equaliser. Together these components are referred to as 'the bottom action'

Main vacuum chamber

Equaliser with internal gull springs

Foot pedals or treadles

Exhauster gull springs

Moving the damper rail from roll perforations, meaning the control of the sustaining pedal was patented by Ernest Martin Skinner of the Aeolian Company on March 21st 1900. Half-blow seems to have been used first in Germany, probably some time about 1904, by Welte and Philipps, although no positive inventor or date can be assigned. A variation of the half-blow technique for upright pianos was patented by Aeolian in November 1907 and consisted of a pneumatic mounted on the side of the piano case (one at each side) which, when they were deflated by being valved to vacuum, drew up bell-crank arms attached to a pivoted rest rail, effectively moving all the hammers closer to the piano strings. This was patented in England on September 10th 1908 (British Patent number 24,522 of 1907).

Next let's be quite clear about the fundamental difference between the piano-player and the player-piano. Both devices do the same thing and have, in general, very similar controls, only the manner in which they convert music roll to musical performance is quite different. The former is an external machine that works a normal piano's *keyboard*; the latter is an internal mechanism that works a player-piano's piano *action*.

For a piano with an 'inner player' (meaning a player-piano as distinct from a piano-player), it is overly complicated to make a machine which will move the keys because the keys are a step beyond the parts we want to move. The key is purely a lever to move the hammer action. The part we have to get at is the hammer action itself.[2] Now there is one part of the hammer action that lends itself admirably to taking both normal keyboard operation and mechanical inducement in its stride and this is the rocking lever that is called the wippen. Everything above the wippen is required to set in motion the sequence of string-hitting while all that is below it is but a means of moving the wippen. This wippen, then, is the starting-point of the chain of sequences that terminate with the striking of a string.

Another aspect of the wippen is that it is so positioned in the piano action that it can be pushed up or pulled up without interfering with any other function of the piano. This means that the installation of a pneumatic action does not interfere with the manual use of the instrument.

In the following sections, then, I shall explain something of how the functions work and for the convenience of both you and me I will break these up into sections as follows:

1. How a player piano uses air in order to operate
2. How suction is created using foot-operated suction bellows
3. How the level of suction is maintained at a constant tension
4. Why every process and function is achieved by a controlled leak
5. The Roll Drive Motor
6. The Spool Box
7. The Speed or Tempo control
8. The Rewind facility
9. How Automatic Tracking works
10. The 'soft' pedal control
11. The sustaining pedal control
12. The Power Governor
13. The Crash Valve
14. Note accenting or Themodising
15. Single Valve and Double Valve Systems
16. The operator and his controls

I have stopped short of dealing with the expression piano in this Chapter for the simple reason that this was the next stage in development before the reproducing piano. In fact, the expression piano was the key to making a successful reproducer, hence these instruments are to be found in the next Chapter.

Before launching into technical explanations, let's make one thing quite clear. The player piano – even the reproducing piano – operates on a very simple principle. While some of the developed applications of this technology often need a bit of thinking about, it is not rocket science and it is well within the ability of the average Pianola-owner to understand his or her instrument. This means you are well-equipped to maintain your player in perfect condition. The only one thing that I do most seriously dissuade amateurs from tackling is *piano-tuning*. This is serious stuff and, despite countless electronic devices on the market and numerous 'helpful' guides, more serious damage can be done through inexperienced tuning than you can imagine – and usually it is damage that cannot be rectified easily or cheaply. I shall have more to say on this in Chapter 18.

Back to understanding your player-piano. Take a little time and trouble to understand it one piece, section or component at a time and you will soon have the confidence to handle any problems that come along. Now let's get on with explaining how the thing works.

1. How a player piano uses air in order to operate

Air is one of the commonest and most versatile fluids on Earth. It has unique characteristics. It is infinitely elastic and makes a superb spring or buffer. Regardless of its pressure, it will always fill a given space at an equal density, expanding to every corner however removed or inaccessible, or compressing to do the same job.

Air exists all around us at a constant pressure of about 14.75 lb/sq.inch. We are totally accustomed to this pressure environment and do not notice it. Just as deep-sea fish are acclimatised to the tremendous water pressures at the bottom of the sea, and, when trawled to surface, expand and actually explode, the human body is also sensitive to changes in air-pressure although fortunately not quite so dramatically as the deep-sea fish! We suffer extreme discomfort if the air pressure around it is greatly varied, especially very rapidly. Airliners have to have pressurised cabins both to provide the crew and passengers not just with enough oxygen to breathe but also sufficient air so that the first symptoms of too low a surrounding pressure – bleeding from the ears, nose and eyes – can be averted. Divers rapidly accustom themselves to the increased pressure on the sea-bed, but on returning to the surface have to be re-acclimatised slowly to normal pressure.

From this you can appreciate not only the importance of air as something that enables us to live, but also that air exerts a pressure. If we can find a way to vary that pressure, then that difference in pressure is an energy source that can be converted into work. This is because in Nature you cannot have two different pressures existing side by side unless one or both are contained. The player-piano uses one contained air pressure inside the instrument, and the normal atmosphere outside it.

We can demonstrate turning a pressure differential into work with a little piece of schoolboy science. If we take a long-necked flask and place a loose-fitting cork in the neck and then draw air out of the flask, the cork will move down the neck of the flask. If we pump air into the flask, the cork will move upwards. It is this desire of air for equality in pressure that causes this to happen. As air is drawn out of our flask, the remaining air is continually expanding to fill the space, becoming rarefied as it does so. The air the other side of the loose-fitting cork, however, is still at 14.75 lb/sq. inch and this pressure pushes the cork down to try to equalise the pressure.

Things that convert energy into work generally suffer from a horrible affliction called friction. If you place a vehicle with four smooth-running wheels on a smooth and level surface, a certain initial effort is needed to start it moving. This is necessary so as to overcome mechanical friction. One man can propel a large coal truck in the railway sidings merely by pushing it, yet it requires three or four men heaving together to set it in motion from a stationary position. Similarly, if you put an object on a sloping surface, it does not immediately rush downwards, but stays put until the slope is increased beyond a certain point. These two examples illustrate the effect of friction and show that there is a time lag before circumstances change to restore equilibrium, and that additional power is needed to initiate the change from immobility to motion.

Fortunately for us, air is not so affected by friction.[3] The moment there is a pressure variation at one point, the entire

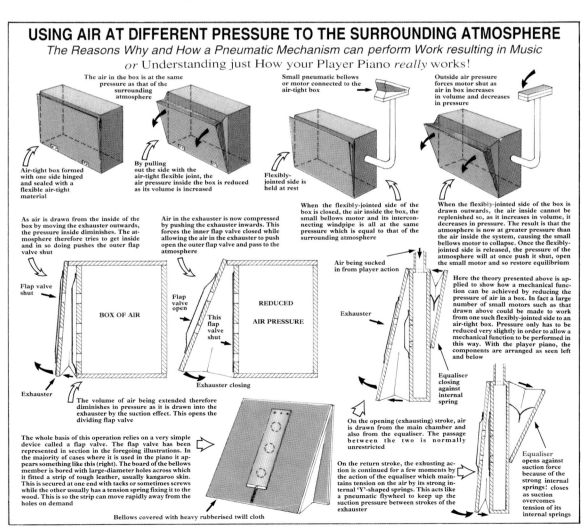

USING AIR AT DIFFERENT PRESSURE TO THE SURROUNDING ATMOSPHERE

The Reasons Why and How a Pneumatic Mechanism can perform Work resulting in Music
or Understanding just How your Player Piano *really* works!

The air in the box is at the same pressure as that of the surrounding atmosphere

Air-tight box formed with one side hinged and sealed with a flexible air-tight material

By pulling out the side with the air-tight flexible joint, the air pressure inside the box is reduced as its volume is increased

Small pneumatic bellows or motor connected to the air-tight box

Flexibly-jointed side is held at rest

Outside air pressure forces motor shut as air in box increases in volume and decreases in pressure

As air is drawn from the inside of the box by moving the exhauster outwards, the pressure inside diminishes. The atmosphere therefore tries to get inside and in so doing pushes the outer flap valve shut

Air in the exhauster is now compressed by pushing the exhauster inwards. This forces the inner flap valve closed while allowing the air in the exhauster to push open the outer flap valve and pass to the atmosphere

When the flexibly-jointed side of the box is closed, the air inside the box, the small bellows motor and its interconnecting windpipe is all at the same pressure which is equal to that of the surrounding atmosphere

When the flexibly-jointed side of the box is drawn outwards, the air inside cannot be replenished so, as it increases in volume, it decreases in pressure. The result is that the atmosphere is now at greater pressure than the air inside the system, causing the small bellows motor to collapse. Once the flexibly-jointed side is released, the pressure of the atmosphere will at once push it shut, open the small motor and so restore equilibrium

Flap valve shut

BOX OF AIR

Flap valve open

This flap valve shut

REDUCED AIR PRESSURE

Air being sucked in from player action

Exhauster

Exhauster

The volume of air being extended therefore diminishes in pressure as it is drawn into the exhauster by the suction effect. This opens the dividing flap valve

Exhauster closing

Here the theory presented above is applied to show how a mechanical function can be achieved by reducing the pressure of air in a box. In fact a large number of small motors such as that drawn above could be made to work from one such flexibly-jointed side to an air-tight box. Pressure only has to be reduced very slightly in order to allow a mechanical function to be performed in this way. With the player piano, the components are arranged as seen left and below

The whole basis of this operation relies on a very simple device called a flap valve. The flap valve has been represented in section in the foregoing illustrations. In the majority of cases where it is used in the piano it appears something like this (right). The board of the bellows member is bored with large-diameter holes across which it fitted a strip of tough leather, usually kangaroo skin. This is secured at one end with tacks or sometimes screws while the other usually has a tension spring fixing it to the wood. This is so the strip can move rapidly away from the holes on demand.

Bellows covered with heavy rubberised twill cloth

Equaliser closing against internal spring

On the opening (exhausting) stroke, air is drawn from the main chamber and also from the equaliser. The passage between the two is normally unrestricted

On the return stroke, the exhausting action is continued for a few moments by the action of the equaliser which maintains tension on the air by its strong internal 'Y'-shaped springs. This acts like a pneumatic flywheel to keep up the suction pressure between strokes of the exhauster

Equaliser opens against suction force because of the strong internal springs: closes as suction overcomes tension of its internal springs

The upper action of an upright player piano removed for restoration. The majority of makes and styles are in many ways similar: this is actually an Aeolian Duo-Art model but besides the added tracker-bar openings (that terminate in a special connector seen on the left side) there is no difference between this and a 65 or 88-note one. The action is built around one centreboard that passes the full width inside the piano case and is screwed down into locating blocks at each end.

The reverse side of the action seen in the previous picture showing a number of broken and disconnected tubes. The roll drive motor is seen to the left of this view, the roll-tracking motors to the right, and the two rows of striking pneumatics at the bottom.

mass of air rapidly sets about adjusting itself either to equal pressure, or to attain a suitable volume to suit the pressure. A mass of air, adequately contained, can be made to do a surprising amount of work, even when the pressure differential from the surrounding air is only a matter of plus or minus a few ounces per square inch.

What about the player piano? Well, in essence a player piano comprises an assortment of small functional devices connected to a chamber in which the air pressure has been reduced to below that of the surrounding atmosphere. Each component or function of the player action is worked by the controlled admittance of air through it and, because the atmospheric pressure is being allowed access to the reduced state of air pressure within, this air can be used to move a valve on its seat or to deflate a bellows to perform mechanical work, or to permit access of other components to the pressure variations taking place.

Expressed in even more simple terms, the player piano is a machine containing a partial vacuum into which air is continually trying to find access through special leaks in the form of controllable valves. In entering the instrument, these leaks can be made to perform a mechanical function.

Incidentally, were you to place a player piano in an atmosphere which is itself a vacuum, or put it on the Moon where the atmospheric pressure is extremely low, then it will not work. Nature abhors a vacuum – and the player piano needs to be able to create a partial vacuum in order to be able to work. *Memo:* Don't send player-piano to Orbiting Space Station. Send phonograph instead…

I know that some people talk glibly about the player working by vacuum but as we have just seen this isn't strictly correct. The word 'vacuum' suggests totality – zero air. Apart from the fact that creating a 100 percent vacuum is almost impossible even in a laboratory, if there were there to be a complete vacuum within the instrument, then the pressure of the normal atmosphere all around would be so great as to implode the player. In a violent and instant attempt to achieve pressure equality between the outside and the inside of the player-piano, it would squeeze up all the tubes, compress the air passages and chests, and render itself incapable of making music all in a split second!

There is just a chance that you could build a player mechanism so robustly that conditions of almost total vacuum might be achieved. The drawback is that it would be impossibly large and enormously heavy. But it would also be quite unnecessary since the conditions whereby the mechanism can and

will play are achieved by the development of merely a *partial* vacuum inside the instrument. The lower the air pressure inside (the greater the vacuum), the quicker will be the response of the instrument and the greater the power exerted by the pneumatic system on the hammers which strike the musical strings but we are still only talking in terms of a few ounces pressure differential. What is more important is the precise control of the processes of pressure reduction within the instrument for it is this that makes possible the artistic rendering of a piece of music.

A high vacuum condition is not required in order to work a player piano. Under ordinary conditions, the instrument will operate perfectly with a pressure difference of just eight ounces per square inch, which is equivalent to less than a four per cent vacuum. Thus only about one-thirtieth of the air inside the instrument must be withdrawn to set in motion the piano action and produce music of about middle strength. An audible sound can actually be achieved using a vacuum of only half this amount. The average player piano is constructed with an air pump capable of operating for short periods of time at a suction of up to two pounds per square inch. This is far in excess of the amount needed under normal circumstances.

Incidentally, we ought to get some definitions right here. Paradoxically, we speak of the 'pressure' of a vacuum when what we really mean is the 'suction' of a vacuum. The pressure referred to here is the amount of pressure which the surrounding atmosphere is induced to offer to the mechanism, by virtue of there existing inside it a reduced state of pressure relative to the outside. Thus a working pressure of two pounds per square inch is the same as a vacuum that produces a rarefaction of the air to two pounds per square inch below that of the normal atmosphere. Some people talk of 'vacuum pressure' but the term 'vacuum tension' is, I think, better since tension implies an acceptable opposite to 'pressure'. So when we talk of tension we mean amount of vacuum, OK?

Although the pressure reduction needed is quite small, the volume of air to be moved is comparatively large and does tend to vary over a wide range according to the parts of the piano action that have to be operated at any one time. A loud, full chord, for example, will require the shifting of more air than, say, a pianissimo passage for a few short notes. The air pump employed is thus a slow-moving low-pressure piece of apparatus. Its operation, in a piano controlled by the performer's feet, must not require excessive physical effort.

2. How suction is created using foot-operated suction bellows

The largest unit in a player piano is that which is used to create suction. Although it is clearly an assembly of a number of quite different parts, it is generally called 'the bellows'. This is a dreadful misnomer since bellows, traditionally, pump air at pressure. But this part of the piano is rife with poor definitions and lax use of English. We talk of 'pedalling' which implies turning a crankshaft by using foot-pedals, yet the piano has no such bellows part. Because the feet do not go round and round as they do on a bicycle pedal, but are rocked to and fro in the motion used by our grandmothers on a spinning-wheel or our mother's treadle sewing-machine, we talk of treadling.

Now although treadling is the most apt word, it is an awful bundle because most people today do not really understand it having never even used a foot-powered sewing-machine let alone a spinning-wheel or a treadle lathe. Even worse, some people talk of a 'foot-pumped' piano, or 'pumped by the feet', neither being accurate, let alone clear since a foot-pump is something to do with a flat tyre and pedalling is either bicycles or, these days, dope.

But if 'bellows' and 'pedalling' are technically incorrect, what words can we use? Well, I've made a 'management decision' as they say when something unpopular is about to be announced. Let's talk of 'exhaust bellows'. As for the other, let's get by as best we can with 'foot pedals' (of the type, perhaps, found in a harp, pipe-organ combinations, kitchen rubbish-bin and the car) and use 'pedalling' in the sure knowledge that we've talked our way around it enough. OK?

Now it's back to a little bit more schoolboy science about bellows, exhausting or otherwise. Earlier I mentioned the business about air always filling a space at the same pressure. Let's demonstrate this. Imagine a box representing a one-foot cube and into this you put a cubic foot of air from the atmosphere – all we have to do is lift the lid and then close it again and we can be certain that the air around us is also in the box. The box is now 'full' of air. If we now make the box airtight and, using a pump, begin to draw the air out of the box, as we reduce its pressure relative to that of the atmosphere, the pressure of the air all over the inside of the box falls to an equal level because air does not pile up, lie in masses of different density or behave in a lumpy way.

Suppose that we now take off one side of our box, and replace it with a loose panel hinged along one edge and joined with an airtight flexible rubber wall between the edges of the side and the rest of the box. If we make a simple non-return valve, such as a leather flap on the inside to cover a small hole, and then blow air into that hole, the increased air pressure inside the box will push out the hinged side. If we now put our non-return valve on the outside of the hole, and suck air out of the box, the hinged side will collapse inwards. Now we can actually see this interesting property of air at work. But how does it work with the player piano?

The air pump in a player piano consists of a chamber having one wall arranged so that it can be moved inwards and outwards by a linkage from a foot-operated pedal. If the chamber is sealed, as the movable side is pulled outwards so the air inside the chamber is rarefied. The air in the chamber is thus at a lower pressure than the outside, free air, because it has been made to fill a larger area than the space it naturally filled at atmospheric pressure. Supposing a pipe from the chamber is led to another, smaller bellows assembly, the air pressure difference in the inside of the chamber will also affect this second bellows which can be used to do work after the fashion of a lever. This represents the rudiments of the player action.

Hitherto, all we have done is to reduce the pressure in our chamber. But as the action of playing is to admit air, and since air continually seeps into the chamber however well we try to seal it, we have to devise a way of repeatedly taking air out of the chamber.

Standard hand controls for the Pianola are, from left, sustaining pedal, bass and accompaniment subdue (two superimposed levers), tempo slide, three-position rewind/silent/normal. This last control can confuse the novice for the 'normal' position means 'play'. The centre position, when properly adjusted, allows the roll to move forward in silence to find, say, a desired point in its length.

In a desire to emulate birds, people in ancient times (as well as some young children today) believed that if you jumped, and then jumped again when you reached the highest point of that first jump, you could just keep on going up and up, jumping and jumping. They did not understand that the action of jumping demanded a reaction to the force – something solid to apply the work of jumping to. You can jump up a flight of steps one step at a time, but where there are no steps you can't keep jumping upwards. It's rather like the strong man who, claiming that he could lift his own weight with ease, stepped into a pair of buckets, pulled upwards on the handles – and couldn't understand why he didn't rise majestically into the air!

Now the player piano poses a problem of similar type. Using the exhausting bellows, we can draw one lot of air out of the chamber, but we have to keep on doing it. If we just move the movable side in and out all we are doing is alternately stretching and compressing a unit mass of air and doing a lot of work to get nowhere. What we need to do is to take one bite out of the air – and then be able to come back for more without replacing the first bite.

We might make this work by separating the movable side from the chamber by another compartment. What we will have in effect is a box to which is connected an extra side fixed over an existing side with a flexible diaphragm or bellows. We can now draw air out of the main chamber, through a hole in the proper side, into the chamber created by moving the extra, hinged side away from the box. But still we must solve the problem of the need to take continual sucks without simply pushing the same volume of air in and out.

The answer lies in the flap valve, surely the simplest and most efficient air valve one could wish for and as useful today as it was when first used two thousand and more years ago – its use was described by the Banu Musa in the seventh century AD and the principle was widely used by the earliest of the medieval organ builders as a key component in their bellows. Rather like a non-return valve, only being fully reversible in the direction of flow that it can control, the flap valve is purely a strip of leather secured at one end over a portion of our movable side which has several holes in it. When the side is pulled outwards, the pressure of air lifts the leather clear of the holes and allows the air to pass through. However, when the side moves the other way, the air pressure presses upon the other side of the leather strip, holding it firmly against the holes and so sealing them.

Since this is an important fundamental of the pneumatic operation of a piano you should understand how it operates before proceeding further. Air pressing on to one side of a movable seal will move that seal to close an opening against atmospheric pressure; air at atmospheric pressure will close the same opening when there is air at a lower pressure on the other side of the seal. The seal can be a leather flap as we have seen here, or it can be a piston, diaphragm, bellows or pouch which the air can move.

I have shown how it is possible to make a device so that we can move a side of an airtight box in and out, systematically reducing the air pressure within by the use of a simple flap

valve. We can work the movable side in and out with a foot treadle or pedal but this is a rather large area to shift. To make the operation easier, we can fit our main chamber with *two* movable sides, each quite separate from the other and small enough to enable it to move easily, so that they will work alternately as the piano operator presses first with one foot and then with the other upon the foot pedals.

Still our pressure-reducing mechanism is short of something. As we pedal, there is a brief moment in each cycle when one of the two movable walls – exhausters as they are called – is at one extreme limit of its position, and the other exhauster is at the other extreme. Under these conditions, the vacuum created inside the chamber will suddenly decrease momentarily. Although this variation is only very brief, it will be quite sufficient to affect the playing performance of the piano. If, for example, this momentary change-over coincided with a rapid passage of music, we would probably lose one or two notes, the music would suddenly change from normal to soft and then back again, and the speed of the music roll, itself driven by an air motor as we shall see later on, might fluctuate.

Hupfeld Phonola controls are very different. Dominating is the pivoted palm or wrist lever than operates the pedal and this, on later instruments such as seen here, can be moved for left or right-hand operation. Left to right: bass subdue button, Solodant theming on-off, treble subdue, tempo control.

This problem can be overcome by the provision of a reserve power of suction – a vacuum accumulator. This is another movable wall to the main chamber, only this one is usually attached on the side opposite the exhausters and it is also a lot larger. It is also freely connected to the vacuum reservoir that is in turn connected to the two foot-powered exhauster.

When it is at rest, this vacuum accumulator is normally held wide open by internal springs pushing outwards on the hinged or movable panel. Now, as we pedal with our feet, air is still drawn out of the main compartment as before, but the difference in pressure now allows the atmosphere to press on the large movable wall and push it in against its internal springs. This makes an air buffer to cater for the moments of lost motion in treadling since it gives an extra quantity of vacuum pressure aided by the internal springs.

In operation, assuming there to be no function of the instrument working, as one pedals so the large movable wall begins to close up against the main compartment until finally it is almost completely shut. If we then stop pedalling with our feet, the large movable wall will gradually open outwards until once more it comes to rest at its widest open position. During all the time it is opening, a working degree of vacuum is being maintained within the compartment. The duty of this portion of the system is to *equalise* the suction pressure (or, if you prefer, vacuum tension) which would otherwise fluctuate with each stroke of the exhausters. For this reason, this device is called the 'equaliser'.

The equaliser therefore serves as a stand-by exhauster that comes into operation when, for the reasons already explained, the foot-operated exhausters are momentarily inoperative. The steadier and more regular the operation of the exhausters, the less work there is for the equaliser to do.

Our bellows system, therefore, comprises a central, main vacuum chamber from which vacuum power can be taken to the playing mechanism, two foot-operated exhausters and the equaliser.

Under certain conditions of playing, it is possible to build up an excess of suction power in the bellows system. If we pedal at a steady rate through a roll of music that contains a pause or a soft passage comprising only a few notes, then we might build up so much suction in the exhausters and equalisers that actual damage might result. This is taken care of by the provision of a spill valve – a device to let in air from the atmosphere when the partial vacuum begins to reach too high a level. The valve is mechanical and is often just a small flap valve somewhere in the system so that, as the equaliser opens to its extreme, a linkage draws back a simple hinged pallet. Those who have church and chamber barrel organs will already be familiar with this sort of simple automatic device that, in the organ, prevents excess pressure bursting the bellows.

In the player piano, the loads imposed on the bellows system during playing are quite considerable. For this reason, the various components of the system are robustly built in hardwood, whilst the equaliser and exhauster panels are made of thick plywood. At a maximum playing pressure of 1½ lb/sq. inch, an exhauster having a surface area of 300 square inches must resist atmospheric pressure equal to a weight of 450 lb, which must be moved by the action of pumping the foot pedals. While in practical terms this is a considerable load to resist, the player performer may be truly thankful for the fact that, as already explained, the air in this connection offers but infinitesimal resistance due to friction, and thus his task is readily accomplished.

The exhausters are provided with either internal or external springs, depending on whether the movable board has to be opened or closed. These steel-strip springs are made of two curved strips of flat steel and joined at one end so that they open out and look like a head-on view of a bird in flight, hence the popular term 'gull-shaped'. Their duty is to prepare the exhausters for another stroke as quickly as possible. The spring

pressure is usually somewhere between 12 and 20 lb. The flexible portions of the bellows are formed in a heavy rubberised twill or duck cloth that is impervious to air.

3. How the level of suction is maintained at a constant tension

In the previous section we saw how the exhausters remove air from the piano and the equaliser serves to maintain a steadying suction reservoir between strokes.

Player pianos, although working generally to the same system, are all different in detail construction. Very noticeable is the wide variation in proportions of the numerous parts of the bellows components. Exhausters and equalisers vary in area and many years ago W B White published an interesting analysis as to why these components do differ so greatly.

We have seen that the equaliser serves as a 'pneumatic flywheel' to the pneumatic system, supplementing the interrupted action of the to-and-fro cycle with a reservoir of power. This is just like the flywheel of a steam-engine, where the mass of a solid flywheel is used to take the crankshaft over the top and bottom dead centre positions. The heavier the flywheel on the engine, the smoother will be its running characteristics. But at the same time it will be slow to accelerate (develop power) and also its power output will be diminished by virtue of the amount of power being absorbed in the task of driving a large mass of flywheel.

American-made Steinway Duo-Art controls differ from those of the Hayes-built UK model. Levers are marked, from the left, pedal, theme graduation (bass and treble), accompaniment graduation, tempo, reroll and play, and motor which controls the on-off power switch to the electric motor.

This can be translated into the interpretation of the duties of the equaliser. Some makers believed that the easier it was for a completely unskilled, insensitive person to play their instrument, the better it was. Others thought it preferable for the player to feel the fluctuations of air pressure beneath his feet. The first type of player action could easily be satisfied by making the equaliser of large proportions. The second type of player demanded that the equaliser be as small as possible. The same effect could be achieved, of course, by varying the size of the exhausters as well.

As it is, the more sensitive a piano is, within certain limitations, the better the instrument is for the serious music lover. Ernest Newman described these variations from the point of view of the listener, and Grew exhorted his pupils to keep one foot always prepared for use to produce a fortissimo passage or to accentuate one note – an almost impossible task with a piano having a large equaliser.

Since the equaliser is such a bone of contention, could it not have been dispensed with? The answer is, unfortunately, no, for, no matter how astute the performer, he would be unable to maintain conditions of anything like constant vacuum pressure with his foot pedals, and his music roll speed would fluctuate considerably. Interestingly enough, this direct-action pedalling was put to good use in the so-called expression stop of the harmonium, and it was also used by both Grenie and Winkel, among others, on pipe organs to vary the timbre of the pipe sound. For the piano, though, it has to be anathema.

I hope that by now you understand the method of driving air out of a chamber to create a partial vacuum. By the same token, you should now have grasped that the act of playing a piano by a pneumatic system admits atmospheric air into the partial vacuum (hence the need for continual effort to maintain that partial vacuum).

4. Why every process and function is achieved by a controlled leak

In the player-piano and earlier piano-player, we have, in effect, two pressures of air to play with. The first is that of the atmosphere in the room around us and the piano. The second is a lower-than-atmospheric pressure that we have created inside the instrument by using the foot pedals. This difference is our power-source – a power that will govern the motion of those functions needed to make musical sounds. It will be continually employed in various ways to make our music. Here's how.

The piano has 88 notes. We have already seen that in the early days of the player only some of these were played from the music roll but, after 1912, makers standardised on 65-note and full-scale or 88-note rolls. It does not matter which of these scales we consider – the mechanism is largely the same.

In order to play, say, an 88-note piano-roll, the action of our piano has 88 separate hammer actions (normally driven by the 88 notes on the keyboard) which are now to be moved by 88 wedge-shaped pneumatic motors. The task is to convert one chamber containing air at reduced pressure into a mechanical system which will move those 88 mechanisms individually or severally as instructed by the pattern of the openings in the music roll needed to correspond to a musical composition. In simple terms, a hole in the paper roll has to result in the sounding of one note of the piano.

We manage to do this with two components. First is the valve chest and pneumatic stack. And second, to control each of the 88 valves and pneumatics in the stack, there is a sliding valve in the form of the perforated paper piano-roll.

Valve chests come in two distinct types – the simple single-valve system and the double valve system that has primary and secondary (sometimes called servo and principal) valves. I shall explain why there were two types of chest action in Section 15 of this Chapter. In the simple, single-valve system, a leather-covered pouch in a baseboard forms the base to a suction chamber. The pouch covers a chamber in the pouch board, which is connected by a thin tube to the tracker bar. This chamber is connected to the vacuum chamber by a tiny open passage called a bleed hole. This at first seems to nullify the whole purpose of having separate chambers and an inflatable pouch. But let's see precisely what happens and how the assembly functions.

Resting lightly on the leather pouch is a stem carrying on it a circular disc that forms a seal on the outside of the suction chamber. When the pouch is inflated, as will happen if a hole in the music roll uncovers the specific passage from tracker-

bar to this particular pouch, the suction in the chamber is communicated to the air contained in an airway above the valve which in turn connects to a pneumatic motor. The air at atmospheric pressure is therefore drawn out of the pneumatic motor so causing it to collapse. By joining the moving part of this pneumatic to the wippen of the piano action, using a push-rod or a wire pull-link, a note can be struck.

The valve stem carrying the valve disc is free to move up and down. It is lightly made and carries a button at its lower end, sitting just a fraction above the pouch, which is made of soft, pliable leather and is glued over the pouch chamber. The main part of the chest through which the valve passes is connected to the partial vacuum produced by the bellows system. The actual sealing disc of the valve is outside this main chamber and in a further compartment that is normally under atmospheric pressure. The valve is thus free to move between the aperture in the main chamber and the aperture connecting the upper compartment with the atmosphere.

Earlier I mentioned that beneath the leather pouch (also sometimes called a 'diaphragm') is a chamber that has an outlet to the music-roll tracker bar. This chamber is linked to the main vacuum supply by a small orifice known as a bleed hole the purpose of which is to quickly equalise the air pressure either side of the pouch after the tracker-bar hole has again been closed.

Roll-drive air motors come in many shapes and forms, the majority employing sliding valves and wire links to drive a crankshaft. The crankshaft is driven by a sequentially collapsing sequence of pneumatic motors, this then operating the valves to repeat the cycle. Early motors were often long and with up to seven motors. The application of the seesaw motor allowed the number to be reduced to three units giving six impulses to the crankshaft. Here is a neat three-unit motor from a push-up player showing how little space it takes up.

Above the main chamber, the further compartment is connected to a pneumatic motor which, by its own weight, remains in the extended or open position under normal conditions. Suction is applied to the main chest, as in normal use, and we assume that the orifice in the tracker bar is also closed off, as by a non-perforated section of the music roll. The valve closes the chamber at the top both by its own weight and also by the difference between atmospheric pressure and the suction of the vacuum pressure. The air beneath the leather pouch is also extracted, as is that in the tube to the tracker bar, through the bleed hole.

The moment a perforation in the music roll opens the end of the tube at the tracker bar, the partial vacuum in the tube and in the chamber beneath the leather pouch is immediately replaced by air at atmospheric pressure. This at once inflates the pouch, pushing up the valve which now makes a seal between the upper compartment and the atmosphere. The suction from the main compartment is thus applied to the air in the pneumatic motor which, exhausted of air, rapidly collapses. This collapsing of the motor is translated into the operation of one of the piano actions, and thus the sounding of a note, by the use of a connection to the wippen.

Earlier I said that there was an open connection between the two sides of the leather pouch called the bleed hole. So why isn't this action negated by the presence of that opening? The answer lies in the size of the hole. It is too small to allow the pressures to equalise when faced with the amount of atmospheric pressure rushing in relative to the amount of suction in the main chamber. The quantity of air in movement is always greater than the capacity of the bleed hole because the opening in the tracker bar is far larger than the bleed.

However, the moment the hole in the end of the tube at the tracker bar is once more sealed, as by the perforation in the music roll coming to an end, the bleed hole serves quickly to reduce the amount of atmospheric air trapped in the pouch chamber and tube. This reduction only has to be fractional before the atmospheric air pressing on the top of the valve has an opportunity to equalise things, and pushes the valve and the pouch down. This seals the aperture in the top of the main chamber and reinflates the collapsed motor, returning the system to equilibrium once more.

Each of the notes to be played in our piano, whether it be 65 or 88, has its own separate valve system and pneumatic motor. These are mounted on to the vacuum compartment beneath which are positioned the individual pouches, each with a separate connection to a different hole in the tracker bar, and above which are placed one valve and one pneumatic motor for each note.

It is clear that the tracker bar is the primary control for the whole mechanism of producing music. Each tracker bar tube ends in a small orifice in a brass bar over which the slid-

An early piano-player roll-drive motor with five motors arranged in a row. Note how the black rubber cloth has worn at the box folds in the motors allowing the white cotton cloth to show through.

ing or travelling valve of the music roll passes. On early instruments playing 65 notes or fewer, the bar was generally made of wood, but with the advent of the full-scale 88-note action it was impossible to arrange the openings (nine to the inch) with sufficient accuracy in wood or to be able to maintain them airtight from each other, so metal was adopted.

Each of the holes in the tracker bar connects with a pouch in the pouch board, the far left one being the extreme bass note of the piano and successively to the extreme treble at the far right. Here I am talking about the number of notes played as, particularly with some of the reproducing pianos described later, the scale was not strictly 'full', several note openings at each end of the tracker being required to perform other duties.

Since the strings of the piano and the hammers that strike them are fairly close together, it would be impossible to mount a workable pneumatic action in one straight line since the pneumatic motors – even the pouches – have a width greater than the distance between two piano keys. To overcome this, it is usual for the valves and pneumatics to be staggered in several rows, usually three, sometimes four.[4]

Letting atmosphere into our player-piano, then, is how it is made to work. It plays by controlling a row of leaks through the tracker-bar that are normally sealed by the paper music-roll. As we shall see, every other function of the player action is worked by similar controlled leaks.

We are now at the stage where we understand, I hope, how the vacuum is achieved and maintained, and how it is applied to sounding the notes under the control of the music-roll.

5. The roll drive motor

Curiously, and despite the importance of the perforated paper piano-roll and also the enormous number of players built with various means of driving the roll, including air motors, the quest for a perfect roll-drive motor was an on-going challenge, the solution not arriving until the closing years of the instrument, when electric drive was perfected.

Because the first pneumatic piano-players were derived from the organette, it is not surprising that the first makers relied upon hand-cranking to transport the music over the keyframe or tracker bar. Next came the clockwork motor with various devices for winding the spring from the action of pedalling, and then came the air engine or vacuum motor. The first to make and market a player with a spring motor was John McTammany who, in 1884, was granted US Patent number 290,697 for such a device. He had also employed an air-operated motor to drive the music rolls on his Taber and Taylor & Farley reed organs.

Melville Clark produced a very practical spring winding mechanism which was wound through a clutch during pedalling and after playing could rewind the roll when a knob was pulled. This was used in the early Clark Apollo players. Meanwhile Theodore P Brown strove to improve Clark's invention for use on his Aeriol player but finally abandoned the task in favour of an air motor

The evolution of the air motor can be traced to McTammany's rotary engine which he described in a caveat filed in September of 1876. He subsequently improved upon the design with what he called his 'intermittent engine' as described in US Patent number 390,386. Next came Lucius T Stanley who, on July 21st 1885, was granted an American patent for a rotary and reciprocating combination engine.

William D Parker now combined with McTammany to produce a very attractive if complicated engine patented in December 1886 (US Patent 355,201). With its external valves, crankshaft and connecting rods it would have done justice to a piece of medieval mechanism. It must also have been very wasteful in its consumption of hard-earned vacuum power.

It was not until the arrival of George B Kelly's air engine, patented in America on February 15th 1887 (number 357,933), that a practical solution appeared. Economic in use, it was smooth and silent in operation while being neat and compact in proportions. Kelly's design was thenceforth adopted throughout almost the entire player industry. The early models had five motors driving a crankshaft; later models with four were widely used and ultimately the double-chamber six-motor model having three large boards was devised by Aeolian.

The music-roll drive works on principles we have already covered and features a number of pneumatics which alternately open and close in sequence. Their sliding motion is passed to a crankshaft using connecting rods. The cycle of each pneumatic is automatically reversed by a sliding valve, one for each pneumatic. In this manner, the rotary motion imparted to the crankshaft is constant, smooth and continuous.

An accompanying illustration shows a cross-section of one pneumatic of the motor and from this can be seen the chamber through which atmospheric air is sucked, and the way this is affected by the sliding valve. To ensure perfectly smooth operation, the air motor works in exactly the same way as a car engine except that

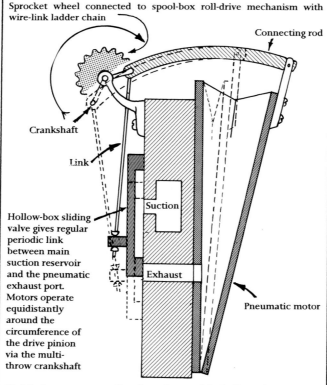

ACHIEVING CONTINUOUS ROTARY MOTION FROM VACUUM PRESSURE
The method by which the music-roll drive air motor of the player-piano operates

Sprocket wheel connected to spool-box roll-drive mechanism with wire-link ladder chain

Connecting rod

Crankshaft

Link

Hollow-box sliding valve gives regular periodic link between main suction reservoir and the pneumatic exhaust port. Motors operate equidistantly around the circumference of the drive pinion via the multi-throw crankshaft

Suction

Exhaust

Pneumatic motor

Sketch shows a cross-section through one of the bellows elements that make up a motor assembly. The unit may have three, four, five or six operating bellows motors. Aeolian and other makers also used a three-element six-motor system, each separate motor forming one of a pair of see-saw rockers on a central board. Adjustment of the sliding valve gave smooth and continuous rotary motion to transport the music-roll

in place of cylinders it uses pneumatics and for fuel it uses the atmosphere in conflict with the reduced pressure within the system. As with a car where a number of cylinders is provided to give smooth motion, the air motor has a number of pneumatics – never less than three, usually four and occasionally five or six.

Just now I mentioned that Kelly's air motor design was used almost universally. One major exception was Welte in Germany. This company was responsible for one of the most attractive and clever wind motors anywhere in the annals of the player. First used on the orchestrion organs which the company made, it became the motive power for the music rolls in all Welte pianos. Welte's trefoil conical motor is described in an earlier Chapter.

The application of electric motors to drive player pianos and keyless pianos did not necessarily dispense with the pneumatic motor-roll drive and even the early Ampico reproducing pianos retained pneumatic drive via a Kelly-type motor.

6. The Spool-Box

The player-piano's musical programme is the perforated paper roll. This paper roll comes wound on to a spool having suitable ends that engage with a free-turning centre at one end, and a chuck drive at the other, both of these being fixtures of the spool box on the piano. The central feature of the spool box is the tracker bar, whose function we have already described.

The roll is placed between the top pair of chucks in the spool box and travels from the top downwards over the tracker-bar to the take-up spool, which is fixed permanently in the box. (On some instruments the roll travels from bottom to top but the principle is just the same). The end of the music roll paper ends in a triangular 'apron' having a loop fixed on it to engage with a hook on the take-up spool.

After the roll of paper has transferred from the music spool to the take-up spool in the process of being played, the paper must be rewound on to the music spool. The end of the paper remains stuck firmly to the music spool, so all that has to be done is to disengage the drive to the take-up spool and move a suitable mechanical linkage, so that the music spool is now driven via the chuck holding one end.

This is nearly always achieved by mechanical means, such as the moving of a free-turning sprocket wheel on a shaft so that it engages with a dog clutch. The spool mechanism is driven by the air motor, described in the previous section. This produces the necessary rotary motion which is applied to the spool-box mechanism through a system of chain wheels and sprockets, gear-wheels and pinions.

7. The speed or tempo control

Earlier we described the air motor, an ingenious piece of mechanism which fulfils its functional requirement under extreme variations of pressure. It is, for example, required to maintain a constant speed from the very gentlest suction up to the maximum suction created for a forte passage of music. It must produce a constant amount of power to keep the music roll moving across the tracker bar, against the suction created between tracker bar and paper by the playing mechanism.

Above all, the performer must be able to control it very precisely to produce instantaneous changes of tempo and smooth *accelerando* and *ritardando*, even to the degree of stopping momentarily and instantly restarting with instant return to a predetermined speed.

An important feature of the air motor is this ability to regulate speed within very precise limits. An easy way to achieve this is to throttle the motor, as one throttles the internal-combustion engine, and regulate the amount of air passing though it. If we allow the motor to draw the maximum amount of atmospheric air into the bellows system, then it will turn quickly. By reducing the amount of air, we can slow down its rotation and adjust the tempo of the music being played from the music roll.

To achieve this a sliding port links the suction side of the motor to the suction of the bellows. This port is wedge-shaped so that, at one extreme of its movement, it presents the maximum-sized opening, whilst at the other it shows a much smaller opening. Control of this sliding port is by a lever or knob, which also operates a pointer along a scale near the music roll so that the player operator can immediately follow any speed direction printed on the music.

The sliding port also has another feature and this is associated with the reroll or rewind mechanism, described in the next section.

This system of regulating the motor speed would be quite perfect were it not for the fact that, as we have already shown, the amount of suction, and thus the amount of potential power for the motor, is varying continually during playing. In fact, so varied is the suction pressure available that were the suction power of the bellows to be connected directly to the roll motor the music-roll drive would fluctuate continuously.

Even by the expedient of the bellows vacuum equaliser, it is not possible to maintain the steadiness of the air motor within the precise limits needed without some other means of regulation for although the equaliser evens out irregularities in suction during playing it cannot cope with quantitative differences such as that resulting from gentle pedalling and rapid pedalling.

With the main vacuum bellows, this equalisation of vacuum tension was achieved using the aptly-named *equaliser* chamber where springs served to keep the pressure constant inside the player action. With the roll-motor, however, the disparity between the small amount of atmosphere being admitted to the main vacuum by the process of its rotation, and the body of that main vacuum is considerable. No simple equaliser could offer the needed precision.

The solution comes from a rather special form of regulating valve called the *tempo governor* which has the ability to monitor the volume of atmosphere entering through the motor (equalling the speed of the motor) and the combined demands made upon it by the main vacuum level on the one hand and the speed (tempo) control on the other.

A special pneumatic bellows or motor is fitted between the roll-drive motor suction and the bellows. Its purpose is to act as an adjustable 'doorway' through which the air motor transfers its atmospheric air on its way to the bellows. Its course through the pneumatic, however, is subject to the control of a novel form of adjustable regulator called a *knife valve*. This is a secondary throttling device, only the operation of this one is quite automatic.

The hinged board of the pneumatic motor controlling this valve is normally held open by an adjustable external tension spring. The air passage into the pneumatic is through a block in one side, across which is arranged a scissors-like gate-valve pivoted on the bottom board of the pneumatic and connected to the movable top board. Precise adjustment of the external tension spring balances the system in order that this regulator motor opens and closes just the vital small amount needed to keep the suction demand constant enough to ensure constant air motor speed. We will find that this form of knife-valve regulator will crop up again in other places in the player-piano action.

In summary, although the operator of the player can control the general amount of air regulating the overall speed of the motor, the rapid pressure fluctuations are smoothed out by this automatic self-acting valve called the tempo governor. When the operator begins to pedal, the amount of suction produced will normally be balanced by the spring force holding the tempo governor open. Supposing now the performer wishes to provide more power to his performance, such as might be required to accentuate a passage, he pedals harder and creates a suction greater than that which the tempo governor spring can resist. The governor closes a little, in so doing allowing the knife to cover part of the inlet hole.

APPLICATION OF THE MOTOR REGULATOR AND TEMPO CONTROL
The components used by Aeolian to regulate the speed of the music roll

Jack-knife valve

Free end of jack-knife valve is retained in a hook attached to the top board of the pneumatic motor

Motor governor pneumatic

Strip steel spring applies closing force to pallet and also to pneumatic motor

Re-roll port, only uncovered when re-roll is selected, applies full suction power to motor to give efficient re-wind of roll

Air from the wind motor enters here

Push-pull control

Sliding port pallet valve

Movement of slide over arrow-shaped airway uncovers progressively larger opening in manifold as control lever is moved to increase tempo meaning speed of playing. Here the sliding pallet is depicted clear of the airway to reveal shape

Top panel removed for clarity: side panel cut away to show interior

Push-pull control from hand controls

To vacuum reservoir (exhaust bellows)

Re-wind port is closed during playing by means of slide   Air from wind motor enters here

Push-pull control rod

Sliding tempo pallet
Flat spring
Flat spring
To suction

Bleed hole to atmosphere uncovered by tempo slide prevents 'creeping' when the tempo is closed to ensure a positive stop. The bleed hole is sealed as tempo is advanced

Tempo port
Rewind port
Jack knife valve port

Tension spring adjuster

The initial effect is to increase the suction power acting on the air motor. If it is not regulated, this will increase the air-motor speed and make the music-roll travel faster. However, as the increased vacuum exceeds the tempo-governor's spring tension, the motor starts to close up, so allowing the knife-valve inside to reduce the aperture through which it must pass to the bellows. The air motor thus continues to run at a constant speed as determined by the operator's normal sliding tempo control.

8. The rewind facility

At the end of a piece of music (or at any other time to suit the will of the player operator), the drive to the take-up spool in the roll box can be disengaged and the music-spool drive engaged, so applying the motor power to rerolling the music.

Do note that air motor always rotates in the same direction and in rewinding the rotational direction of the wind-motor does not change. The apparent reversal of drive is achieved through sliding gears that change the drive while the roll motor carries on as before.

The mechanism of the player action responds to the passage of the music roll uncovering openings in the tracker bar. Now, by drawing the music backwards across the tracker bar during the process of rewinding, it would be perfectly possible for the roll to play. To prevent this happening, the principal airway between bellows and valve chest is cut off during reroll so that there is no suction power in the valve chest.

To speed up rerolling, the sliding port also has a very large rewind opening which immediately applies full power to the motor. This special full-power opening is only brought into operation during the reroll procedure. When the operator moves the reroll control lever to the 'reroll' position, it (a) shuts off the suction power to the valve chest and pneumatic stack, and (b) opens a very large port between motor and bellows so that reroll can be accomplished in the shortest possible time. At the same time, it (c) alters the drive to the roll box, through gearing.

9. How Automatic Tracking works

In order for the music to play perfectly, the paper must 'track' properly as it is drawn over the tracker bar, its holes lining up with the holes in the tracker bar. If the paper is not aligned correctly, the perforations may either miss the tracker-bar openings altogether or partially open two adjacent holes. In either event the effect on the music will be disastrous to the ear.

The control of the run of the paper roll over the tracker bar is called *tracking* and in all but the earliest piano-players, this was carried out automatically. To keep the paper passing across the tracker bar in the proper position, either you move both music spool and take-up spool from side to side, or you move the tracker bar itself from side to side. The amount of lateral shift is only quite small and the shift is accomplished very promptly. As a rule, this promptness of response is adequate to remove any tendency towards over correction.

Both the variations on the principle mentioned here are commonly found in player-pianos although it is more usual to shift the spools. Operation is very simple. Two pneumatic motors are used, normally made back to back with one central fixed board and two hinged sides. The tracker bar is provided with an extra opening at each end, larger than the note holes and square in shape. The connection from one side of the tracker runs to one side of the double motor, and that from the opposite end of the tracker to the other.

Normally the music roll partially covers the holes. If the roll is warped, unfortunately an all too frequent occurrence, then one of the holes becomes covered, fully opening the other. Previously, the air pressure exerted on each side of the motor was equal, but now it is set off balance and so the motor begins to move. A mechanical linkage attached to the moving board of the motor connects to the spoolbox drive mechanism and, through a simple lever, moves the paper spools over until the closed tracking hole is once more opened, restoring the air balance to the motor and bringing the tracking system once more to rest.

To achieve smooth operation without over correction the airways and openings in the motor are comparatively small so that the air shift is slow. This is important for another reason. Sometimes the edge of a music roll may become slightly split. Were the action of the automatic tracking to be very prompt, each of these splits would at once cause the music roll to be shifted. Naturally, where the edge of the roll is very badly damaged or has been folded over (a feature known to Player Piano Group members as 'the Aeolian pleat'), then the principles of automatic tracking are disrupted and the roll may not play properly at all.

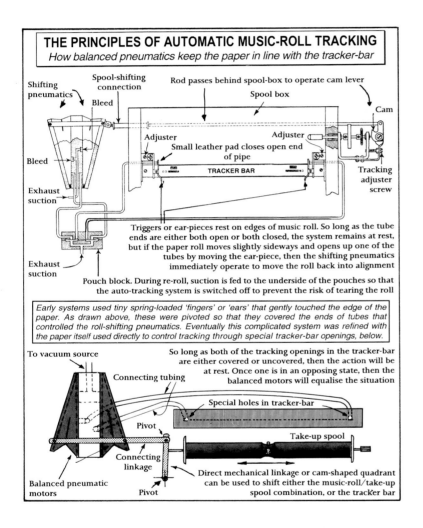

THE PRINCIPLES OF AUTOMATIC MUSIC-ROLL TRACKING
How balanced pneumatics keep the paper in line with the tracker-bar

Shifting pneumatics
Spool-shifting connection
Bleed
Rod passes behind spool-box to operate cam lever
Spool box
Cam
Bleed
Adjuster
Small leather pad closes open end of pipe
Adjuster
TRACKER BAR
Exhaust suction
Tracking adjuster screw
Triggers or ear-pieces rest on edges of music roll. So long as the tube ends are either both open or both closed, the system remains at rest, but if the paper roll moves slightly sideways and opens up one of the tubes by moving the ear-piece, then the shifting pneumatics immediately operate to move the roll back into alignment
Exhaust suction
Pouch block. During re-roll, suction is fed to the underside of the pouches so that the auto-tracking system is switched off to prevent the risk of tearing the roll

Early systems used tiny spring-loaded 'fingers' or 'ears' that gently touched the edge of the paper. As drawn above, these were pivoted so that they covered the ends of tubes that controlled the roll-shifting pneumatics. Eventually this complicated system was refined with the paper itself used directly to control tracking through special tracker-bar openings, below.

To vacuum source
Connecting tubing
So long as both of the tracking openings in the tracker-bar are either covered or uncovered, then the action will be at rest. Once one is in an opposing state, then the balanced motors will equalise the situation
Special holes in tracker-bar
Pivot
Take-up spool
Connecting linkage
Balanced pneumatic motors
Pivot
Direct mechanical linkage or cam-shaped quadrant can be used to shift either the music-roll/take-up spool combination, or the tracker bar

Besides the system already described in which holes are covered or uncovered, there are numerous variations of the principle which was adopted by different makers at various times. I emphasise that all work the same way – balancing two air motors – but how this is done does vary. The means of following the edges of the paper roll as they pass between certain defined limits was first solved by Aeolian which used a single metal feeler which rubbed against (and subsequently wore away!) the left edge of the roll. Any deviation moved the feeler and opened (or closed) the end of a tubular airway.

The earlier modes of the Aeolian Duo-Art used two small feelers which gently touched the edge of the roll during play-

ing. If the roll moved, the feeler would also move but, in so doing, a small pallet at its other end would shut off an atmosphere vent, upsetting the balance of pressures in the double-acting motor. Another method employed small fences at the edge of the music. The roll passed between these two delicately adjusted sprung strips and again any tendency for the paper to wander was converted into adjustment of the roll.

As usual we find that there were many variations on the schemes. Hupfeld, for example, used horizontal see-saw tracker motors. The problem of bringing the roll back into registration was also solved in many ways. Some moved one spool, others both, while yet others moved the tracker bar (as, for example, on the unit-action Broadwood). There were also variations on the Aeolian ear-type tracking system, one of which was a balanced pressure 'thumbnail' valve actually mounted within the width of the tracker bar and between which the paper roll passed. Ampico used this.

The balanced pressure automatic tracking system that uses either one hole or a slightly staggered pair of holes each end of the tracker bar to sense the edge of the music roll was adopted widely. While there was no serious competitor to it, Aeolian realised that in the case of a roll with a tattered edge, a pleated edge or any similar damage, this type of tracking device could actually make tracking much worse. Unable to differentiate between a damaged edge and a genuine shift of the paper, the mechanism would at once attempt to compensate and so throw out the registration of the note perforations with the tracker bar ducts.

One answer might be to use the actual note perforations themselves for tracking rather in the same way that Hupfeld had much earlier tracked from a central row of roll perforations. On January 17th, 1919, Aeolian in London was granted British Patent number 139,257 (in the name of B G Nicholson and Aeolian) for a system which sensed the accurate position of a number of note perforations. Above certain note ducts in the bar were two long and narrow slits so placed that each pair was of slightly less width than the note perforation.

When tracking properly, the note perforation would first open both these slits and then the note-playing tracker duct. All the left-hand slits of the pairs of ducts were connected to one side of a tracker-bar shifting bellows of the familiar type, and all the right-hand slits were connected to the other side of the tracker-shift bellows, both being via a usual type of valve block. What this did, then, was to sense the correct relationship of the music roll to the tracker bar at a number of positions across its width so that, regardless of the width of the roll or the state of its edges, the tracker bar could be moved to align correctly before the note was sounded.

Occasionally, Pianolas are found that incorporate this system but they are scarce and one feels that the high cost of manufacturing the special tracker bar must have made the style overly expensive to build, particularly as many with vested interests in the piano-roll business (and that included Aeolian) would rather encourage owners to discard damaged rolls and buy afresh.

In those pianos where the tracker bar is itself moved, it is made to slide by the selfsame type of mechanism. Whichever system is used, automatic tracking calls for movement of not more that 3/32 of an inch each side of the mean or central position. Usually the distance is far less than this.

Automatic tracking must not be confused with transposition, where the whole roll is allowed to be played in a different key by realigning it with other holes in the tracker bar. This en bloc adjustment is nothing to do with tracking and is usually achieved by moving the tracker bar so that accompaniment for singing can be arranged in a convenient key. It is controlled mechanically by a knob or lever on or in the roll box.

10. The 'soft' pedal control

Part of the pianoforte's ability and charm over most other keyboard instruments is its ability to play softly as well as normal or loud. In a finger piano, this can be achieved either by the touch of the pianist or by the use of the 'soft pedal' on the piano, or a combination of both. The human pianist can achieve a combination of tonal effects largely independent of the pedal control by varying the force with which he strikes individual keys or groups of keys on the keyboard. In this way, he can achieve a whole range of subtle distinctions between a soft accompaniment and an accented melody.

In a player piano, 'softness' is achieved by using the expression control levers so that the piano plays softly, or by using the piano's soft pedal as before.

The operation of the piano's soft pedal moves the hammers closer to the strings so that, not having so far to travel before striking the strings, the sound produced by less force and is therefore quieter than the volume of sound achieved with the pedal in the normal position. This happens because the soft pedal controls the location of the rest rail relative to the strings. By moving the whole rail closer to the strings, the hammer-to-string distance becomes less.

To produce this effect on the player piano is not difficult: in fact it is easily achieved by pneumatic means. Nevertheless, to minimise the 'all-or-nothing' aspect of this effect in making possible a distinction between melody and accompaniment, a preferable solution is to divide the rest rail into two portions, each being free to move independently of the other and each having a separate control. Now this control can be mechanical, by a lever connection, or, more usually, by the employment of a pneumatic motor.

One method of pneumatic control is to provide a button on the control rail which controls a small pallet. The pneumatic that controls the rest rail works on exactly the same principle as the motor used to move the piano action at each string

in normal playing. The difference is that the operating valve, instead of being a travelling one made of paper (the roll) admitting suction to the pedal pneumatic, is a pallet covering the end of the tube open to atmosphere. When the pallet is opened, atmospheric air rushes in, the motor contracts, and the rail is moved.

While the shifting of the rest rail is a feature sometimes found in the upright and occasionally the grand piano, a similar effect is obtainable by varying the amount of suction in each half of the pneumatic chest through a 'power governor'. As we have seen the chest is divided more or less in half, the suction level at the bass end being controllable by either a lever or a button, and the treble similarly under the control of variable suction. This is found on all players and occasionally it is found in conjunction with the overall softening which is achieved through rest-rail movement – the soft pedal. The importance of the power governor will become more apparent in a moment.

The soft pedal effect is achieved on some grand pianos (and is reserved almost exclusively for reproducing models) by the shifting sideways of the entire keyboard by a small amount. This shift moves the keyboard and the complete hammer action so that the hammers instead of striking the full trichord (three strings of each note) only strike two, so producing a softer result. This system, operated on a manual piano by a heavy linkage from the foot pedal, can be artificially produced by the use of a large and powerful keyboard shift pneumatic, often fitted with twin valves to speed its operation.

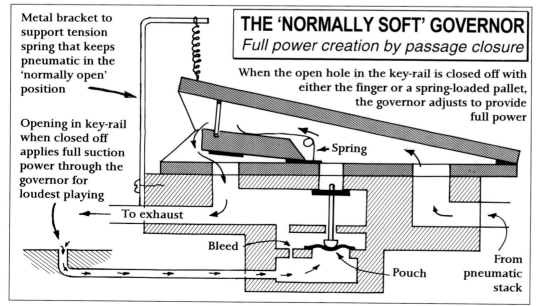

UNGRADUATED PEDAL CONTROL
The 'all-or-nothing' system used in Standard Player Action's popular action

This, the so-called 'Soloist' or 'soft' pneumatic control, is normally open to atmosphere. When the valve is lifted, access to atmosphere is lost and full suction power applied. The motor shuts, moving hammer rest-rail, reducing hammer throw

PNEUMATIC OPEN — Atmosphere is allowed to enter over valve — Exhaust chamber — Bleed — To 'Soft' button

PNEUMATIC CLOSED — Pouch raised to lift valve — Valve — To main suction exhaust — Bleed — To 'Soft' button — Action shifting linkage fitted here

THE 'NORMALLY SOFT' GOVERNOR
Full power creation by passage closure

Metal bracket to support tension spring that keeps pneumatic in the 'normally open' position

Opening in key-rail when closed off applies full suction power through the governor for loudest playing

When the open hole in the key-rail is closed off with either the finger or a spring-loaded pallet, the governor adjusts to provide full power

Spring — To exhaust — Bleed — Pouch — From pneumatic stack

11. The sustaining pedal control

From the ability to play softly, the player piano needs to be able to control the opposite effect – the ability to play at full power. I am avoiding using the misnomer 'loud pedal' but you know what I mean – the means of operating the dampers.

This is the sustaining pedal action and, because all the dampers are moved together throughout the range of notes operated, and because they require considerably more force to move than the rest rail, the operating pneumatic motor is larger than that for the rest rail (soft pedal).

Because the performance of some music often calls for prompt and precise operation of the dampers, it is fairly common for the pneumatic to be governed by two valves. Do not confuse this with the double-valve pneumatic system which I shall describe in a moment. This is still a single-valve system, but the valve is duplicated in the same chamber so as to provide a more positive and rapid suction connection to the motor. Again, the atmosphere end of the control tube can be closed off by a small pallet valve operated by a button on the control rail.

By now you will have noticed that the functions of both the pedal actions of a normal piano can be controlled by pneumatic means and that the method of control is exactly the same as that used to play the piano mechanically. Each pedal-action pneumatic has the same type of control tube leading to atmosphere and governed by a valve, as are the pneumatics in the pneumatic stack. Thus, if we take the ends of the control tubes from their valve pouch chambers to the tracker bar instead of to the control rail, we can operate these functions by punching additional perforations in the music roll instead of having to rely on the player operator to move levers or press the right buttons at the right moment.

HOW PIANO-PEDAL EFFECTS MAY BE WORKED PNEUMATICALLY
Dampers are arranged for operation by hand control or from music-roll hole

High leverage fulcrum lever operates damper lift rod

Tracker bar

Pneumatic motor normally fully open

Button on key-rail for manual control by uncovering tube end

Open to atmosphere

Rotary valve for selecting manual or music-roll control

Exhaust

Pouches

Spring

PNEUMATIC OPEN. The two valves both operate in unison to open an effectively larger area of the windway to the suction port. This quickly vents the motor and ensures speedy pedal movement

Note: Both manual and roll-operated functions are shown in this sketch. However, control is only effected from one or the other at any time, hence the fitting of a rotary switch usually fixed in the run of the control tubing

Manual control pallet open so allowing atmosphere to enter

PNEUMATIC CLOSED. On the Standard Player Action and others, a primary valve is introduced between the control tube and the pouches to obtain increased atmospheric inlet area and thus even more rapid response. The Stradola action actually makes use of a triple valve system here for ultra-prompt pedal movement

Spring

Having found a way of doing these things automatically from the music roll, we find that most player pianos have a device – usually a small lever in the roll box – which disengages these features and brings back into operation the buttons and levers on the control rail. This is usually marked 'Pedal On' and 'Pedal Off'.

12. The Power Governor

Working the soft and sustaining pedals of the normal finger piano by pneumatic means is all very well but the experienced finger pianist will have detected one major shortcoming; there has to be some way to change very rapidly the playing intensity, perhaps only for one note or a chord.

Even the best player performer, operating his foot treadles with the utmost subtlety and understanding, could not achieve this and thus the player piano might soldier on, resigned to being nothing but an obviously mechanical interpreter of music. Happily this is not the case, thanks to the *power governor*. This really comes into its own on grand player pianos. In the grand action there is usually no rest rail and thus it is not possible to move the hammers backwards and forwards relative to the strings. In fact, as noted above, the soft pedal action on the better-class grand shifts the whole action sideways.

While eminently suited to the grand piano, the power governor in various forms can be found in virtually all players. The detail construction and even some aspects of the function may differ slightly, but the purpose is the same.

The power governor consists of a single-valve suction system operated by a pouch connected by a control pipe to a valve (either pallet at the control rail or hole in the tracker bar). All these parts we have already come across in other components.

Inside the pneumatic motor there are two openings. The first is above the valve controlled by the pouch and is arranged so that when the valve is lifted it seals off this port altogether. The second opening is smaller and can be restricted by a pallet valve, hinged to the base of the motor and connected with a link to the top so that, as the motor collapses, so the pallet gradually closes up the port. It is, in effect, another knife-valve. The whole motor is held in the 'normally open' position by an adjustable tension spring.

When the power governor is in use, atmosphere air must pass through the large port (under which is the rising valve) on its way to the bellows. Both this port and the valve are of such a size that, even though the pneumatic is in a state of partial collapse against the spring tension, there will be no reduction in the area of opening. So long as the control button is not touched, the system will be 'freewheeling' and not interfering with the playing in any way.

When the button on the control rail is depressed, it will immediately cause the valve to rise and seal off the large port. The air must now pass through the smaller port, which is controlled by the pallet valve. As the pneumatic collapses, this pallet valve will reduce the size of the port in such a manner that the amount of air passing through this metered opening remains constant.

Remember the tempo governor for the air motor? This is a similar piece of equipment. The operation of the pneumatic is adjusted by the tension of the spring, which offers a resistance to the suction from the bellows. The stronger the spring, the greater the resistance offered and the less it collapses under any given condition of suction in the bellows system. From this we can see that the reduction of playing power can be regulated by the adjustment of the spring. The 'steady state' of the automatic governor can be upset at any time by depression of the button, permitting instantaneous changes from governed to ungoverned pressure and thus from *piano* to *forte* playing.

This device acts almost instantaneously and is prompt enough so that one note or chord in a group can be accented or the dominant note in a bar given the correct emphasis. The power governor, vital to the 'grand' action, is fitted to almost all actions and serves to provide this overriding expression control. Its principle is also the key to 'Themodist' accenting which is described in a moment.

Remember that so long as the control button is depressed, the action can be controlled to play relatively softly. When the button is released, the effect is to provide a forte crash instantaneously, assuming all other aspects of control and the amount of suction in the bellows system to be adequate.

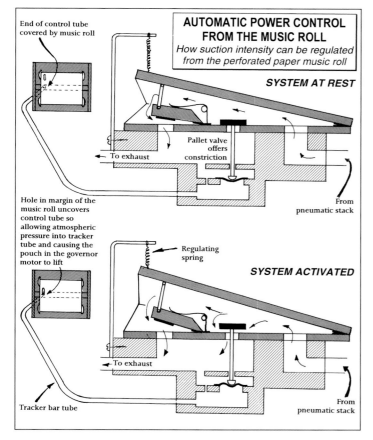

AUTOMATIC POWER CONTROL FROM THE MUSIC ROLL
How suction intensity can be regulated from the perforated paper music roll

End of control tube covered by music roll

SYSTEM AT REST

To exhaust

Pallet valve offers constriction

From pneumatic stack

Hole in margin of the music roll uncovers control tube so allowing atmospheric pressure into tracker tube and causing the pouch in the governor motor to lift

Regulating spring

SYSTEM ACTIVATED

To exhaust

Tracker bar tube

From pneumatic stack

However, it is far easier if, instead of holding down a button for normal playing and releasing it for accented notes, the control is the other way round, the mechanism playing relatively softly at all times, but accents being effected by depressing the button or covering the open end of a normally open nipple. This is indeed the way the power governor is generally made to function so that the playing is at all times relatively soft, no matter how much effort is put into the bellows system. However, if the open end of the control tube is shut off either directly with the finger or indirectly by a button-operated pallet, the operation of the governor will be reversed and the flow of air will be through the main opening inside the pneumatic, allowing an instantaneous response to the vacuum conditions created by the player operator's feet. Among the makers of player who made use of this version of the power governor was Hupfeld, who used it in the Phonola pianos.

Plenty of room for confusion exists over the meaning of the term 'normally soft'. This really means the median of the level of sound being produced; the central path to the left of which is *very* soft and to the right of which is *loud*.

As before, the whole process can be programmed from the music-roll so that we can obtain accented notes automatically. If the theme of a piece of music is to be brought out by its being played slightly louder than surrounding accompaniment notes, the operation of the power governor can be achieved by the use of small marginal perforations leading to a common control tube to the valve pouch. With a divided valve chest, there is a power governor at each end and thus their automatic operation is achieved by there being two sets of controlling music-roll perforations, one at each side of the roll. This is a method of control which forms the fundamental means of 'themodising' as well as the mechanisms within the reproducing piano. The section after next will look at this in detail.

13. The Crash Valve

While looking at accenting devices and before describing Themodising, there is one other device that we should consider alongside the power governor. Although it is not really in the same category, it is also used to create emphasis. This is the *crash valve*, used by a number of makers to enable the player operator to obtain a forte accent by the sudden vigorous use of the player treadles.

Some player enthusiasts prefer not to acknowledge a difference between this and the power regulator, suggesting that they are both the same. True they both perform a similar function but their manner of doing it is quite different.

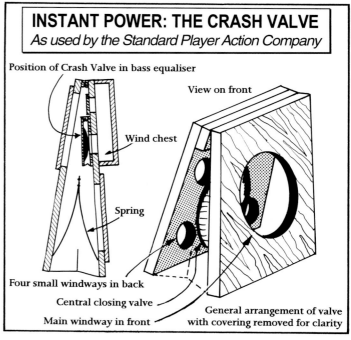

INSTANT POWER: THE CRASH VALVE
As used by the Standard Player Action Company

Position of Crash Valve in bass equaliser

View on front

Wind chest

Spring

Four small windways in back

Central closing valve

Main windway in front

General arrangement of valve with covering removed for clarity

To show what I mean, let's look at the use of the crash valve as applied by the American Standard Player Action Company, an action that features an equaliser for both bass and treble halves of the action. In this mechanism the crash valve is placed over the opening between the bass equaliser and the main suction chest, where it is connected to the upper action. It consists of what appears to be an ordinary pneumatic motor having a large opening in one side and four small openings in the other. Inside is a fixed valve pad, which is connected to the moving wall of the pneumatic itself and is so positioned that, as long as the motor is at rest, air within the crash valve can be exhausted through the large opening, but it can be replaced by air entering through the four small openings on the other side. Under these conditions, the preumatic will not move.

However, if a sudden pressure is applied to the foot treadles, causing the exhausters to work more quickly, the air with in the crash valve us withdrawn at a faster rate than it can be replaced. The upshot is that the pneumatic closes and the valve insside it seals the large opening. The result is the complete isolation of that equaliser. The treble equaliser, having collapsed against its internal V-spring and also a special coil spring provided inside, has become momentarily inoperative and so the situation exists wherin the action has no effective equalisers at all and a sudden forceful push on the treadles operates directly on the channels of the player, without the absorbing and regulating effects of the equalisers. The result is a heavily struck or accented note or series of notes. The moment vigorous footwork is ended, the crash valve opens, the action returns to normal, and the equaliser is released.

14. Note-accenting or Themodising

The human pianist has two hands that normally each play on only half of the keyboard and he can also play loudly or softly by infinitely regulating the force with which he strikes the keys. He can also accentuate certain notes, even certain notes in an *arpeggio* or *appoggiatura,* and change with alacrity from delicate notes to strident ones or to *sostenuto*. All these features, separately and collectively, have to be capable of worthy imitation using the pneumatic system if the player-piano is to be taken seriously.

With mechanical players, the only form of emphasis or accenting that was possible was to soften the bass and allow the treble to play at normal or full volume. With the earliest instruments, this was achieved by a centrally-pivoted bar placed under the keys. When this was central or parallel, then all the notes played at the same intensity. Moving the bar diagonally about its pivot effectively altered the length of the hammer strike from maximum at one end of the scale to minimum at the other. Moving the bar so that it was on the opposite diagonal reversed the effect. It was, you might say, a pretty hit-and-miss effort.

Then came other variations such as divided hammer rest-rails. This made one half of the compass play quietly and the other half at full volume. Again a hit-and-miss effect for in the middle you could have two adjacent notes, one of which would be set to play softly, and the other loud.

When pneumatic player actions came along, the technique was refined greatly by placing a fixed division in the pneumatic stack (the valve-chest) that meant you could individually control the vacuum in each half of the action. By the judicious use of metering valves that controlled the vacuum to each side, you could produce tolerable effects in accenting and sound volume. This control was effected using small levers or, occasionally, buttons positioned on the player control rail. This is the principal employed by all pneumatic players that do not have a specific note-accenting system and it is common to the vast majority of players.

While this system is fine and the skilful performer might use it to a high degree of artistic perfection, it remained difficult to bring out individual notes in a sequence. What was wanted was a way of singling out notes for accent. A number of inventors worked at this goal and there were several successful systems adopted, the commonest being that called the Themodist.

The principal, which is to be found on the majority of quality player pianos, including most European models, comprises a system for accenting individual notes or chords which is a tremendous improvement on the earlier divided hammer rest rail and the variable vacuum tension control. While many will associate the Themodist with the Aeolian Company, it was actually the invention of Hupfeld in Germany and subsequently leased to the American makers of the Pianola. The system was then adopted, under a variety of names by every major piano label in the World. Hupfeld's term was Solodant, while Angelus called it the Melodant and Higel named it Solograph.

A player piano that is equipped with the Themodist can readily be identified by two distinct features. First in the region of the spool box/drive-motor assembly there will be a two-position manual lever marked either 'Themodist on' and 'Themodist off' or, occasionally, the second position will be marked 'normal'. The second distinctive feature is the tracker bar which has two horizontal slots, one at either end, the first immediately left of the opening that corresponds to Note Number 1, and the second immediately to the right of the opening for the last playing note, Number 88.

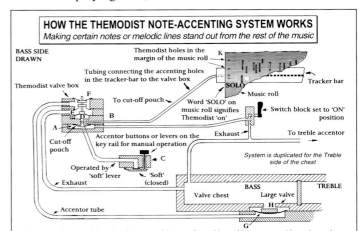

HOW THE THEMODIST NOTE-ACCENTING SYSTEM WORKS
Making certain notes or melodic lines stand out from the rest of the music

Fixed to the bottom of the valve-chest or stack is a small panel into which run two rubber tubes and a large exhaust tube. In this panel is the Themodist accenting valve, 'G'. With the Themodist in the 'on' position, cut-off pouch 'A' is drawn clear of air channels 'B' by exhaust suction. This prepares the system for action signalled by the small accenting perforations in the music-roll margins. The 'soft' levers of the manual expression controls are set to 'on' or 'soft' position, thus closing the small pallets 'C' which shut off open air. The pouch 'D' above channel 'A' is thus deflated by bleed-hole 'E' and valve 'F' is lifted to shut off atmosphere. When a theming hole in the tracker-bar is uncovered, the vacuum in the secondary chamber collapses pouch 'D', dropping valve 'F' and allowing atmosphere into the accentor tube so inflating the large pouch 'G' and closing port 'H'. When a theming perforation in the roll, 'K', admits air down tube 'B', pouch 'D' is lifted. Valve 'F' is raised and 'G' is instantly deflated, opening 'H' to full suction power. This state is shown in the illustration. When the Themodist control is selected to the 'off' position, open air is admitted through the switch block to pouch 'A' which is thus drawn against the channels 'B' by the action of the bleed-hole 'E' and the valves 'F' and 'G' can be operated only by the manual 'soft' levers or buttons. When these manual controls are not in use, they hold pallets 'C' open so that under normal suction power valve 'F' is lifted and pouch 'G' lowered.

A player piano equipped with this form of accenting uses the divided valve chest but does not need a divided hammer rest rail. There is an air-tight baffle inside the pneumatic stack that serves to divide the chest into a bass half and treble half, the 'break' occurring (in an 88-note action) between the 44th note (B) and the 45th (F) in the octave above middle C. This division permits different vacuum levels to exist inside the bass and treble halves of the pneumatic action.

As we have seen, the Themodist action can be selected 'on' or selected 'off' this position sometimes called 'normal'. When the player is used in the 'normal' mode, the vacuum tension available throughout the chest is fully variable under the control of the operator. This control means level or degree of pedalling (overall vacuum tension), and valve-chest levels by use of the usual finger levers.

When the Themodist control is selected 'on', the vacuum tension in the two halves is held at a constant level that approximately equals one-fifth of normal. This is what is known in player-piano terms as 'accompaniment level' and the result is to produce soft-sounding playing. It is achieved by use of a throttle valve positioned in the windway linking the vacuum reservoir and the two halves of the valve chest. Since the valve chest controls the level of vacuum to the pneumatic motors that cause each note to be sounded, the effect is soft playing and regardless of how hard, fast or frequently the operator pedals, the vacuum level within the chest remains constant and diminished.

Themodising will not work unless it is controlled by specially encoded piano-rolls. These rolls are thoughtfully marked as 'Themodist' and by following the instructions printed on the roll the operator has the ability to have certain notes or passages accented automatically.

Notes that have to be accented have a special 'signature' perforation in the roll margins, in the left for a bass note, and in the right for a treble one. In order to maintain the highest accuracy in positioning so as to be able to influence the correct note in, say, an arpeggio, the opening in the paper roll has to be very small – noticeably smaller than the perforation for a musical note. But at the same time sufficient air has to enter the windway in the tracker bar to operate its special valve sys-tem. Remember that the signal comes via a horizontal slot in each end of the tracker bar? Well now we see why it is a slot and not just a normal opening, for the opening in the music-roll paper is doubled with two tiny perforations side by side. Passing over the relatively wide slot in the tracker bar lets enough atmosphere in to work the system. The double perforations, being much smaller than note perforations, admit sufficient control atmosphere at a very precise position. American collectors call these double music-roll holes 'snakebite' perforations. The term is not in wide use in Britain where they are merely described as Themodising perforations. Yes, it is a longer name, but that's the British for you!

So now we have the Themodist selected 'on', valve chest vacuum tension right down to 'accompaniment' level – and along comes a perforation in the music roll that is marked in one of the margins by two small Themodist holes. What happens next?

As soon as the Themodist valve is triggered, it immediately opens a transfer port that bypasses the throttle valve and instantly admits the full vacuum tension from the bellows reservoir to one or the other side of the chest. If any note happens to be about to be struck the instant this full vacuum power is applied, then it will be sounded louder than those notes surrounding it – and the accented note will stand out from the accompaniment.

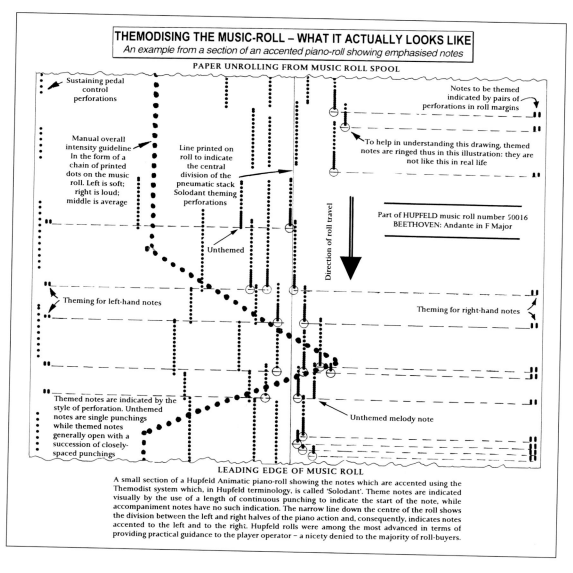

THEMODISING THE MUSIC-ROLL – WHAT IT ACTUALLY LOOKS LIKE
An example from a section of an accented piano-roll showing emphasised notes

PAPER UNROLLING FROM MUSIC ROLL SPOOL

Sustaining pedal control perforations

Notes to be themed indicated by pairs of perforations in roll margins

Manual overall intensity guideline In the form of a chain of printed dots on the music roll. Left is soft; right is loud; middle is average

Line printed on roll to indicate the central division of the pneumatic stack Solodant theming perforations

To help in understanding this drawing, themed notes are ringed thus in this illustration: they are not like this in real life

Part of HUPFELD music roll number 50016
BEETHOVEN: Andante in F Major

Direction of roll travel

Unthemed

Theming for left-hand notes

Theming for right-hand notes

Unthemed melody note

Themed notes are indicated by the style of perforation. Unthemed notes are single punchings while themed notes generally open with a succession of closely-spaced punchings

LEADING EDGE OF MUSIC ROLL

A small section of a Hupfeld Animatic piano-roll showing the notes which are accented using the Themodist system which, in Hupfeld terminology, is called 'Solodant'. Theme notes are indicated visually by the use of a length of continuous punching to indicate the start of the note, while accompaniment notes have no such indication. The narrow line down the centre of the roll shows the division between the left and right halves of the piano action and, consequently, indicates notes accented to the left and to the right. Hupfeld rolls were among the most advanced in terms of providing practical guidance to the player operator – a nicety denied to the majority of roll-buyers.

Fundamental to the operation of the Themodist valve system is that it is extremely rapid with a response time measured in useful small fractions of a second.

So far so good. But the skilled player pianist has a couple of extra tricks up his sleeve. First of all that figure of 'one-fifth full vacuum tension' is an arbitrary figure based on a constant that itself may be anything but. By varying the speed, depth and intensity of his pedalling, the operator can make quite subtle adjustments to the level of vacuum and, but using his Themodist controls in conjunction with his normal bass and treble subduing control levers, he can perform some pianist tricks that Aeolian probably never thought of. On top of these he can superimpose the use of the 'soft' and 'sustaining' pedal effects to achieve an almost infinitely variable colour to his performances. Many of these tricks are discussed in Chapter 16 but a lot of the skill comes from practicing the effect that the controls have.

But even the most skilful player once in a while comes up against an artistic brick wall and such a brick wall exists in this sort of player-piano. When a sequence of notes has to be accented that cross that divide in the valve chest, then getting the accompaniment level absolutely constant between the two halves by using the manual levers, and still being able to accent notes, can be a bit frustrating. It is a problem that the reproducing piano can usually sort out quite easily (but not totally). It remained an insoluble problem to the end of the popular player-piano era, solution only coming with some experimental pianos and modern electronically programmed instruments.

Curiously, one very early instrument almost solved the problem, but it could not be sufficiently refined. That player was the Kastonome which, in theory, treated every note quite individually.

15. Single Valve and Double Valve Systems

Earlier I said that valve chests in player actions were made either as single-valve systems or as double valve systems having primary and secondary (sometimes called servo and principal) valves. The reasons for this are these.

Back at the outset of piano-player and player-piano manufacture it is probably not surprising that makers were faced with immense problems concerning finding suitable materials for their instruments. Many key materials (such as air-tight rubber cloth, for instance) were non-existent.

To build a responsive player, lightness had to be combined with both compactness and the ability to remain airtight. Although the principles of the player action were quickly resolved, very little of the science had been discovered. The outcome of this was that the proportions of various components such as pneumatic motors and valves had to be exaggerated with the end result that they were heavy and tended to be sluggish.

It is understandable that the makers of these instruments chose to err on the side of reliability in making their player pianos, contriving a mechanism in such a manner that it would be dependable.

By far the main drawback was this lack of suitable materials and, to be able to accept a certain amount of air seepage through imperfect rubber cloth, it was necessary to use components of such a size that the mechanism could not be made compact in size. The problem was that it then became 'the law of diminishing returns' for as actions were large, there was more area for air losses. In the early years of the twentieth century, a 65-note player action took up more space and was considerably heavier and less powerful than the 88-note action of the 1920s.

Inevitably, the single-valve action had to move a considerable volume of air which necessitated a lot of vacuum and large valve areas. And this was directly governed by the amount of air that the tracker-bar holes could accept. Even with the comparatively large holes in the 65-note tracker bar which came at six to the inch (as compared with nine to the inch in an 88-note action) the intake of air through one hole was often far short of that necessary to raise the valve quickly enough for all conditions of playing, unless the pump or bellows system was operated at a much higher vacuum pressure than was practical or comfortable for the operator. The action worked well on loud playing but poorly when the music was required to be soft.

Various companies and their designers thought about this and it seems that the twin-valve action came about almost by accident. In organ-building, it was common practice to use a small volume of air to operate one small light valve that it turn acted as a servo to the main or larger valve. This was clearly the thinking behind the first double-valve action which provided a small valve between the tracker tube and the valve which operated the pneumatic motor in the stack. This extra valve would be light enough to lift instantaneously on even a low pressure and it would uncover an air passage large enough to lift the heavier valves which controlled the vacuum supply to the striking motors.

This extra valve was to all intents used as a 'lever' in the system, so that a light force at one end of the system could be made to move a 'heavy' (meaning larger) valve at the other. The tracker-bar hole thus served to move the servo valve to open up a much larger atmospheric-air-pressure inlet to the pouch and attendant valve.

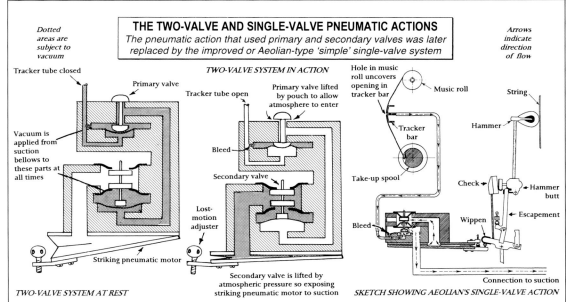

THE TWO-VALVE AND SINGLE-VALVE PNEUMATIC ACTIONS
The pneumatic action that used primary and secondary valves was later replaced by the improved or Aeolian-type 'simple' single-valve system

Dotted areas are subject to vacuum

Arrows indicate direction of flow

Tracker tube closed

Primary valve

Vacuum is applied from suction bellows to these parts at all times

TWO-VALVE SYSTEM IN ACTION

Tracker tube open

Primary valve lifted by pouch to allow atmosphere to enter

Bleed

Secondary valve

Lost-motion adjuster

Striking pneumatic motor

Secondary valve is lifted by atmospheric pressure so exposing striking pneumatic motor to suction

TWO-VALVE SYSTEM AT REST

Hole in music roll uncovers opening in tracker bar

Music roll

String

Tracker bar

Hammer

Take-up spool

Check

Hammer butt

Bleed

Escapement

Wippen

Connection to suction

SKETCH SHOWING AEOLIAN'S SINGLE-VALVE ACTION

The 'double valve' pneumatic system came as the only practical solution to the problems inherent in the player piano and was promptly adopted by all makers. However, in the later years, with the gradual availability of better valve materials and rubber cloth, the raison d'étre for the double-valve system no longer existed whereupon several makers reverted to the undoubtedly simpler and cheaper single-valve system.

On the whole, the majority of player makers believed that the double-valve system, although more complicated to make, was a good insurance policy against any possible malfunctioning of their instruments. Today, with modern materials and an understanding of the dynamics of player mechanisms, we might build a thoroughly reliable and prompt action using single valves.

As far as the player owner is concerned, the pneumatic action, whether of the single-valve type or the double-valve type, is extremely prompt and rapid and will repeat its cycle of operations at least ten times per second under normal conditions.

Now that I have explained how the double valve system operates, let's see what effect it has on the layout of the action. The first thing we find is that with the double-valve system, the valve chest is divided into two portions – the primary and the secondary chambers. It should come as no surprise, then, to find that the valves in the first are termed *primary* valves; those in the other are the *secondary* valves. The way the system works should be self-evident if you have followed my descriptions of pneumatic actions so far. The accompanying illustrations give first a schematic arrangement of the double-valve pneumatic system, and then a section through an actual system. As the pneumatics are normally arranged in three banks, they are drawn thus.

If you look closely you will find there is no vent or bleed hole in the secondary chest. In the single-valve system the bleed provides a vital function and is necessary to reduce the atmospheric pressure in the tracker tube so that the pouch will collapse and close the valve. With the double-valve arrangement, a different arrangement is used, the atmospheric pressure in the secondary channel being allowed to leak into the primary chamber when the primary valve is closed. Remember that the pressure difference has only to be very slight before the valve will close.

16. The operator and his controls

In order to use a player-piano to its best advantage, its numerous features have to be controlled and adjusted before and during playing. For this reason the operator is provided with various simple controls so he can play his roll of music with expression and insert into it his own shades of colour, accentuation, *forte* and *piano* effects.

These controls have to be placed within comfortable reach of the player operator and so it is usual for them to be mounted in a hinged portion of the forward rail of the key bed. In the majority of player pianos, the controls are found mounted in the control rail. These are exposed by hinging down part of (or all of) the key-bed front rail.

First are the soft and sustaining pedal controls which are those primary expressive devices normally to be found fitted to a piano – the two pedals controlling the position of the hammer rest rail and the dampers. In the earlier sections of this Chapter I described how these controls were made to work. Their operating levers or buttons form the cornerstone of the control system. They have to be separate controls because the operator cannot use his feet as might a finger pianist, because he is already employing them in powering the player action by pedalling.

Next to consider are the subduing levers or buttons of which there are two. One looks after the bass end of the instrument, the other the treble and holding them fully over will make the piano play very softly. On some pianos, in particular electric reproducing instruments, there is a special pivoting clip that can be moved so that it holds both levers in the 'soft' position so that the automatic expression devices can work.

Control of the speed of the music-roll is achieved by a lever that is connected to a pointer and a scale in or near the spool-box. There is also a lever having two, sometimes three positions – play and rewind. This operates the mechanical 'gearshift' in the spoolbox to select forward (play) or backward (rewind) while at the same time operating the cut-off valve to the pneumatic stack so prevent playing during rewind.

Some player pianos are provided with an additional control position for this lever called the 'cut-off' or silencer. With this selected, the air motor can still draw the music roll over the tracker bar, but the action will not operate and the roll will travel silently as if on rewind. This is useful if, for some reason, there are portions of a roll which are not required to be heard. All this control does is to operate the slide valve over the large air-transfer port between pneumatic stack and the bellows system. Again, the slide valve cut-off can be made to operate automatically by a perforation in the music roll. Promoted as a sales feature by some makers, it is altogether a singularly pointless control the merits of which I have failed to master in over half a century of player-piano playing.

And so we come to the end of this 'how does it work?' section. All makes of player are slightly different but the principles described here can be found in the greater majority of models. I must add that it would be impossible to write a detailed description to cover the mechanism of every type of player piano. Indeed as the motor car has a wheel at each corner, an engine, gearbox, transmission, steering and brakes, so has the player piano a bellows system, a valve chest, pneumatic stack, tracker bar, basic expression pneumatics, roll drive and controls.

Human nature (and the Patent Infringement laws) being what they are, makers chose to differ in their approach to problems and so every make of action is different in some way or another. However, an understanding of what the player piano is for and what it does and how it works is the key to the ability

When player pianos were manufactured one important adjustment that had to be made was to set the spoolbox components in register with the tracker bar. To achieve this, Aeolian used a special folding iron jig that would fit any type of instrument the company made. Here can be seen an original Aeolian jig in use in an 88-note action. The short chains attach adaptors to allow the jig to fit the spool chucks of both 65 and 88-note spoolboxes. The long vertical slot in the central bar permits visual alignment with the tracker hole.

to tackle work on any make of instrument. There are today few specialists in this field. Many piano tuners try to avoid working on player pianos, primarily because to tune a player piano it is advisable to remove the player action first and this can add several hours to the job as well as risking creating problems for which they have neither training nor experience to confront.[5]

Specialist restorers who do work on players prefer to work on nothing else and they will undertake to rebuild instruments as new. Again, there are dedicated enthusiasts' groups that can help and support the player owner. In America there is AMICA while the British enthusiast has the facility of the Player Piano Group – a unique association of devotees who, among other more practical aspects of pneumatic piano appreciation, have gathered together a rare assortment of player-piano literature and information. Founder of the Group was Frank W Holland, MBE, who established the British Piano Museum – an amazing collection of mechanical musical instruments at Brentford in West London. This means that the player piano enthusiast may never feel 'out on a limb' and, should he find himself in difficulties, there are always fellow enthusiasts who are willing to advise.

In the next Chapter we will look at the developments that lead to the reproducing piano and assess how good were these instruments.

---

1. Lead tube may sometimes oxidise, forming a white of grey powder than can coat the inside of the tubing. The lead may also become crystalline and fracture at bends. At all events, it increases the all-up weight enormously. Where there is the risk of deterioration of any sort, I would recommend that all lead tubing be replaced by rubber on rebuilding the instrument. I shall say more about this in Chapter 13.

2. In some player pianos, the keys move up and down while the player action is operating. This is due to the balanced weight of the pivoted keys following the movement of the wippen rather than driving it and is thus not a direct function of the player. In fact, Aeolian and a few other makers provided a lever beneath the key-bed by the movement of which the keys were locked and could not move. The notion behind this was to minimise the mass set in motion, intentionally or otherwise, by the player action. In an extreme case, if the key were to follow the wippen there might be a minute time-delay between the wippen moving and the key following and this, meeting the fall of the wippen after the note has been sounded, might result in sluggish repetition.

3. This is true at the pressures and speeds that concern us here. At very high speeds, air behaves in quite a different manner: at supersonic speeds it can build up into violent shock-waves. The first investigation into the forces generated both on and by propelling a body through air was undertaken by Alexandre Gustave Eiffel (1832-1923), founder of the world's first aerodynamics laboratory at Auteuil in France. Eiffel's pioneering work was largely forgotten and today most prefer to remember him as the designer of a well-known Parisian tall landmark.

4. In some early and high quality reproducing actions the pneumatics themselves were scaled, those at the bass end being of larger volume (but equal length) to those at the treble.

5. Throughout its history, the player piano and its forerunner the piano player has frightened off piano tuners. Glance at almost any piano trade magazine from the turn of the century to the outbreak of the Second World War and you will be almost certain to find some tuner seeking often very basic advice. In the 1930s in particular, many tuners were frankly afraid of the player and letters to the trade press frequently press home the fact that the majority of these men not only had no experience of the player action, but had no idea as to how it worked, let alone anything approaching basic regulation and servicing. It is thus small wonder that owners of players were actively encouraged from a quite early date to 'convert' their players back to regular pianos. At the first sign of a wheeze or a missing note, many a fine action has been removed and burned. I well remember in my youth courting a beautiful young lady, talented at the violin and a tolerable pianist, whose parents owned a 1930s baby grand – a Steck as I recall – which, at the insistence of a tuner from a highly reputable company, had been deprived of its player action. The felony had been compounded by the affixing to the fallboard of a replacement name transfer bearing the name 'Clementi'. The lady and I went our separate ways, but not as a direct result of the piano.

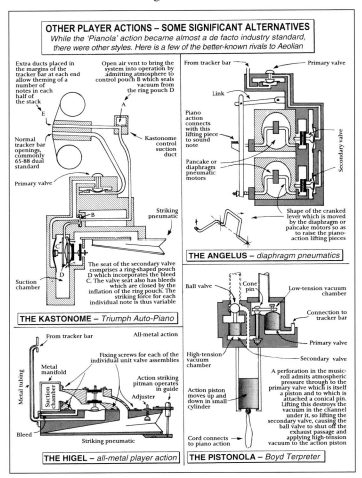

OTHER PLAYER ACTIONS – SOME SIGNIFICANT ALTERNATIVES
While the 'Pianola' action became almost a de facto industry standard, there were other styles. Here is a few of the better-known rivals to Aeolian.

Extra ducts placed in the margins of the tracker bar at each end allow theming of a number of notes in each half of the stack

Open air vent to bring the system into operation by admitting atmosphere to control pouch B which seals vacuum from the ring pouch D

Normal tracker bar openings, commonly 65-88 dual standard

Kastonome control suction duct

Primary valve

Striking pneumatic

The seat of the secondary valve comprises a ring-shaped pouch D which incorporates the bleed C. The valve seat also has bleeds which are closed by the inflation of the ring pouch. The striking force for each individual note is thus variable

Suction chamber

THE KASTONOME – *Triumph Auto-Piano*

From tracker bar   Primary valve

Link

Piano action connects with this lifting piece to sound note

Pancake or diaphragm pneumatic motors

Secondary valve

Shape of the cranked lever which is moved by the diaphragm or pancake motors so as to raise the piano-action lifting pieces

THE ANGELUS – *diaphragm pneumatics*

From tracker bar   All-metal action

Fixing screws for each of the individual unit valve assemblies

Metal manifold

Metal tubing

Suction chamber

Action striking pitman operates in guide

Adjuster

Bleed

Striking pneumatic

THE HIGEL – *all-metal player action*

Ball valve   Cone pin

Low-tension vacuum chamber

Connection to tracker bar

Primary valve

Secondary valve

High-tension vacuum chamber

Action piston moves up and down in small cylinder

A perforation in the music-roll admits atmospheric pressure through to the primary valve which is itself a piston and to which is attached a conical pin. Lifting this destroys the vacuum in the channel under it, so lifting the secondary valve, causing the ball valve to shut off the exhaust passage and applying high-tension vacuum to the action piston

Cord connects to piano action

THE PISTONOLA – *Boyd Terpreter*

The pianos that played both 65 and 88-note rolls have always been sought after, both in the player hey-days and with collectors now. Here is what a typical spoolbox tracker bar looks like with the inner wooden cover removed to expose the tubing. Roll-tracking is achieved on this model by the manual lever seen lower right in front of the take-up spool. In order to play 88-note rolls, a special chuck adaptor has to be slipped over the right-hand spool chuck. This short adaptor has to be kept safe when not in use and in this Aeolian piano it is seen stowed in a suitable recess just above the right end of the tracker bar where it is secured with a swing clip. Look carefully at the end of the take-up spool nearest the camera (left) and you can just make out a knurled wheel which, when turned, moves the flanges of the spool in or out on a screw to allow for any minor variations in width.

The other side of the spool-box reveals the large and sometimes stiff lever that changes the tracker bar openings from 65-note to 88-note. Immediately above that lever is another smaller one for switching the automatic sustaining pedal control on and off. Above the tracker bar is a third lever for switching the Themodist on and off.

Automatic roll-tracking began with systems that used tiny fingers like this to ride along the side of the paper. The finger was balanced so that it normally closed off the end of a tube. A similar arrangement was at the other side of the roll. If the roll wavered, then one finger would no longer seal the tube. The tubes were connected to balanced pneumatics so that one or the other would now shift slightly to re-align the paper by moving the spools or, occasionally, the tracker-bar itself. The fingers were attached to pivots with spring washers so that they could easily be repositioned before playing. Once a music roll edge became torn, this system was very good at shredding the paper.

The balanced pneumatic motors that control the tracking under the influence of the roll-edge fingers, one of which can just be seen at the right. This view also shows the common form of sliding-port pneumatic switch used in players in one form or another where a block of wood with a recess beneath can be slid in a groove to connect or disconnect two windways in the base block.

With the control lever set to the 'play' position, the drive motor directs its power to turning the take-up spool at the bottom. The large wheel at the bottom runs free on the spindle at this stage and the pinion, lower left, is engaging the large wheel (just visible) to the take-up spool.

When set to 're-roll', the pinion at the bottom slides along the shaft to which it is keyed until a pin-type dog-clutch engages with the large wheel that connects by ladder chain to the spool sprocket. Motor power now rewinds the music paper back on to its own spool. The position of the two fixed jockey spools in this action is important to maintain the correct chain tension. Other systems use similar tactics to achieve the same goal.

The tempo indicator on some players carries a pointer such as the one on this Aeolian Duo-Art Pianola. The technique in using the pointer is to set the correct playing speed by the tempo control or to your own individual preference, and then adjust the pointer to follow the tempo line on the music-roll (where provided). Aeolian's Metrostyle rolls demanded almost constant tempo adjustment, so this pointer was essential in order to be able to return to original speed when needed. The pointer has a tension screw on it than can be slackened for adjustment.

The selector levers in a reproducing piano allow one to play either special rolls or normal 88-note ones. This shows the Duo-Art switch in the spoolbox and, next to it, the switch for turning off the automatic pedal control.

Typically the hand controls of a player piano are routed via linking rods and cranks to the action chest. Here in this Pianola we can see one method by which this is achieved. On this action, the lower ends of the levers on the main stack above the keys are secured with spade ends locked with swivelling leaf springs so they can be disconnected easily. Before removing the action, make sure you have disconnected all such levers cranks, wires and so on.

Chapter 9
Expression Pianos and Electric Actions

If the purpose of the player-piano was to simulate the musical sound that could be heard from a manually-played finger-piano, then the next goal was to make it sound more like a human performance. And that quest, unlike the first, was a pretty open-ended assignment because the ultimate goal was to make the instrument play as if a world-class concert (or jazz) pianist was seated before the keyboard. The zenith of the player-piano, then, was to replicate the performance of a concert pianist and that *ne plus ultra* was the reproducing piano, subject of the next Chapter.

On the way to that perfection there were two intermediate forms of the instrument without which the reproducing piano might never have happened. The first was the expression piano, and the second was the electrically-driven action.

It was the discovery of a reliable note-accentuation system that presented the first step on the road to the reproducing piano. As an extension of the basic pneumatic player action it was a sincere attempt to rid the player of the stigma of 'mechanicalism' for while it satisfied some, those with sensibilities more attuned to good musical interpretation quickly found the novelty of the early piano-player irksome. Its problem was that it sounded artificial.

The initial objective was merely to combat those critical brickbats that were thrown at the early instruments: nobody ever imagined that the fidelity of the reproducer might lie ahead. Certainly at the time note-accenting was first achieved, that ultimate goal was as yet undreamed of. The ability to accent a note, and to make it stand out from any others that might be played at the same time, made it possible to pick out the melodic line – the theme – from the accompaniment or counter-melody.

Automatic expression devices first appeared as early as 1901 but these were rudimentary systems. By 1906 player-pianos were available which incorporated seven degrees of expression: these paved the way for the development of the reproducing piano which would faithfully reproduce a named artist's performance on a special instrument equipped with a reproducing action.

At a time when responsible consumer periodicals accurately charted developments in science and the arts, it is to these historically accurate and contemporary reports that one turns for the immediacy of progress. Thus did the *Scientific American* of May 20th 1916 describe the progress of theme emphasis:

> There is positively no element in the player that has been made the subject of so much patient investigation and clever invention as that of theme or solo expression, and, during the past decade, some very ingenious devices have been tried out and placed upon the market with more or less gratifying results.

In the previous Chapter I mentioned some of the earliest attempts at putting expression into the mechanical piano's music and highlighted their crudeness. These merely comprised a means of varying the strength of hammer blow from one end of the keyboard to the other. Although soon after its first use the action was achieved pneumatically, its elemental form was

a rocking, swivelling or otherwise adjustable bar to regulate key depression and force. Credit then to the music-roll arrangers that eventually even this fundamental approach could be used with a degree of musical subtlety.

A good example of this system is presented by the Pianotist, an early mechanical player that used a straight bar for 'expression'. When slid forward at one end under the key bed and pushed backward at the other it effectively altered the degree of key depression or dip. A soft bass and a loud treble or vice versa was the result. The problem was that the stages from the bass to the treble naturally formed a linear progression that was graded evenly from one end of the keyboard to the other. Picking out the theme or accompaniment was, inevitably, an impossible task.

The most impressive attempt at note-theming came with the Kastner Autopiano with its Kastonome action. Here every playing note was given its own theming perforation: when a particular note was to be accented, as the hole passed the tracker bar, a specific accenting hole in either the left or right marginal bank of openings would be uncovered. It was arranged so that only one note opening could be matched by a theming opening at one precise moment. It was a very effective and practical approach, but the player action was overly complicated and difficult to service.

Because the criticism of this swivelling-bar system centred on its creation of a linear effect, then several inventors thought it might work better if the 'all-or-nothing' approach was divided into several steps and tried splitting the bar into shorter lengths. The simplest and earliest attempts at pneumatic expression were already illustrating that a pneumatic solution must be close at hand when Francis Gilbert Webb, described as a music critic of South Kensington, London, devised his cranked, bowed or otherwise bent bar patented in 1904 (No. 4014 of that year). This ensured that the notes at the centre of the keyboard remained more or less unaffected as the bass became softened and the treble strengthened or vice versa.

Expression pianos appeared before the First World War and formed the basis of many of the American combination players right through to the 1930s. By the way, the term 'expression piano' is rather an esoteric term that is understood by player piano people, but not by the masses. For this reason, you won't find an instrument, either new in a contemporary advertisement or second-hand in a newspaper small ad, described thus. And while on about definitions, a combination player is a piano that plays other instruments besides strings such as drum and other percussion, even organ-pipes and sometimes other effects. More on these later on, though.

If the expression piano's principals were created pre-1914, this was, technically, after the first reproducing piano had appeared on the scene in Germany (1904). So what was their purpose? The history was, in fact, two-fold. The earliest of them did inspire progress to the reproducer, while the later examples were developed in spite of the reproducer, being offered as a far cheaper alternative to the full reproducing piano. In this respect they were greatly successful not just because the mechanisms were simpler (cheaper) to make, but because the music rolls were less expensive than the artists' rolls that, besides normal production economics, had to earn back the fee that had been paid to the recording pianist.

The best-known of the expression pianos was the Recordo, an American system that was virtually unknown in Britain. Beginning as a brand name for expression rolls made by the Imperial Music Roll Company, this employed four levels of 'intensity' as well as separate controls for the two-piece hammer rail ('soft' pedal bass and treble), and sustaining pedal. The Recordo system, was used by a number of American player makers and became the most popular of the numerous types of expression piano produced in America.

Unlike all other systems that led up to the performance ability of the reproducing instrument, the Recordo was the product of a music-roll maker, not a piano-builder. It created a unique example of an expression system that could be used across the spectrum of the United States piano-making industry. Because the makers of Recordo rolls didn't offer pianos, the many pianos that would play the rolls were all very different as each set out to create its own way of utilising the expression potential of the special rolls.

Pianos that make use of Recordo-encoded music-rolls are identifiable by the presence of five large rectangular slots in each end of the tracker bar. Music rolls encoded for the Recordo system included the Aria Divina Reproducing Roll; Imperial Automatic Electric; International for Expression Pianos; QRS Recordo, Recordo, Rose Valley Recording Roll, US Auto-Art; Vocalstyle Home Recital Series, Vocalstyle Reproducing; Vocalstyle Reproduco.

Here is a close-up of the tracker bar. The central line of openings is for 88-note rolls: in truth the Kastonome only played 85 of the keyboard's notes. The closely-spaced but slightly offset openings at either end of the centre are for roll-tracking. These work on the principle that if all holes are covered, or all uncovered, then the system is at rest. If one hole is uncovered and its opposite side equal is covered, then the roll must be shifted so as to track properly. The lower row of larger openings in the tracker bar is for playing 65-note rolls. At the bottom far left of the picture can be the spool-box selector lever to switch from 65-notes to full-scale (88-note) rolls.

At its introduction in about 1915, the Recordo intensity openings in the tracker bar could be used in combinations to produce ten or more different levels of expression. After late 1923 these four holes were merely used to produce five intensity or expression levels, each successive level overriding its predecessor rather than supplementing it. A third change of operating principle came in January 1926 when these four openings were utilised in revised combinations to produce up to sixteen levels of expression. In this respect it eschewed the origins of the Aeolian Duo-Art reproducing system.

More importantly from the point of view of the collector, the foregoing highlights that not all Recordo rolls worked the same way and not all Recordo-reading pianos operated on the same principal. This provides an answer to those who have for years complained that some rolls sound in a different way between one type of piano and another, and why some of the rolls are apparently poorly arranged.

Characteristic of these instruments was the absence of the divided valve chest that formed so vital a part of the Themodist and other systems. With the whole pneumatic stack subjected to an even vacuum tension, the available power to produce expression was appreciably less than that in the true reproducing piano. Nevertheless, they were much better than the ordinary player. The down side was that the special Recordo rolls would only work properly on a player action that was made to use the correct version of the roll system.

In the previous Chapter we looked at the Themodist and its acceptance as the 'universal' note-theming or accenting system. Let's retrace our steps a little to how it all began. We have already seen that the first practical attempt at melody emphasis, precursor of theme emphasis, came with the division of the pneumatic stack into two separate compartments, bass and treble. This permitted the vacuum tension in the two halves could be varied independently using hand controls.

Initially the approach was to subdue one half of the action – normally the accompaniment – while allowing the melody (presumably in the treble) to play louder. This musically deficient system was all that was available in the early days. It progressed to the division of the compass of the piano and the pneumatic stack into two halves each of which could be 'graded' using an operator control lever or button. The idea seems to have stemmed from Hupfeld and was first used in their Phonola and Claviola pianos. It was soon adopted by many manufacturers worldwide.

In use and in effect it was little different from the earlier systems employed with barrel pianos, wherein a mechanical link could be pivoted about the keyboard centre, notes to the left sounding progressively weaker and those to the right progressively louder or vice versa. The system clearly had one major drawback for, as with the mechanical subduing control, it was non-selective and every note in the half of the stack played louder or softer than the notes in the other half; the melody and accompaniment notes were invariably given the same degree of accent.

It was, however, the first unsteady steps towards the objective. Inventions came with increasing inevitability as, having identified the problem, every maker wanted to be first with the best system – and every inventor strove to design the ideal system. One idea that was tried was the provision of every note on the piano with two tracker openings, the first for the striking signal and the second to regulate the vacuum tension. The difficulties of manufacturing the tracker bar and punching a roll accurately with perforations of varying widths rendered this impractical for production.

Such a system was patented in America by Robert Willard Pain, described as a manufacturer of 261 West 23rd Street in New York. Pain specified a special tracker bar having two rows of holes that were staggered and described how in order to adjust the vacuum tension for any note whatsoever all that was necessary was to make that particular perforation slightly wider, or twice the width, so that both upper and lower tracker holes were uncovered. He was granted British Patent number 19,527 of 1904 for such a system and Aeolian thought sufficient of this to acquire the patent for their own portfolio. The problems of special and non-standard roll perforating for such a system would have been both uneconomical and a marketing disaster.

All of these ideas, though, represented an industry-wide 'brainstorming session' to come up with the best solution. And it lay close at hand for the system adopted almost universally was eventually invented by James William Crooks of Boston. His system operated using a single special perforation on the left side of the roll and was intended to be used on a player action having just one undivided stack. Crooks' invention enabled certain theme notes to be emphasised regardless of the overall level of the rest of the notes by means of special theming ducts at either end of the tracker bar and special precisely-cut perforations at the sides of the roll to give pneumatic impetus to the required notes. Once again, Aeolian's sleuths spotted the value of the invention – and quickly bought the patent.

The spool-box of the Duo-Art reproducing piano showing the group of four large Duo-Art 'accompaniment' action ports above the end of the normal tracker bar openings. These are matched by four similar ports at the treble end. The openings on this early action are, from the far left, automatic rewind (respools the roll at the end of playing), sustaining pedal, and bass theming (this long, narrow slit is for the two small closely-spaced Themodist punchings in the roll). When non-Duo-Art rolls are played, the full 88-note compass now starts. However, when reproducing rolls are used, the first four and the last four openings are not used for playing notes but for operating the accordion expression motors in various sequences.

Protected in all piano-manufacturing countries, this was the subject of British Patent No. 13,715 of 1900. This design was improved upon by Ernest Martin Skinner of Dorchester in the county of Suffolk, Massachusetts. Again a single stack was controlled by one hole on the left side of the music roll. The British Patent for this was 15,518 also of 1900.

In 1910 Aeolian obtained a Patent for a novel variation on this principle. Covered by British Patent No. 17,884 of that year, this worked in the exact opposite way to the methods hitherto described. Previously, accenting had centred on building up the vacuum tension to enable a note to sound above those around it which had been subdued, and to attain this the themed note had to be cut slightly after the normal or unthemed notes. In Aeolian's experimental system, the reverse applied. The note to be themed was cut in advance of the notes not required and was thus subjected to whatever level of vacuum tension was available.

notes. In theory, this might have opened up opportunities to experiment using varying hammer velocities to work in conjunction with themed music. Like many ideas, the theory was curious but interesting; the reality unreliable and probably unpredictable.

The search, though, was nearing its end and just a few months later Aeolian acquired and patented the system that was to supersede all others. This became known as the Themodist. As explained in the previous Chapter, although the Themodist is always associated with the Aeolian Company, it was actually the invention of Hupfeld in Leipzig, Germany, and the rights subsequently leased to the American makers of the Pianola. It marked a very great improvement on all earlier systems depending on variable vacuum tension control.

The system has already been covered. Its salient advantage was that the positioning of the two controlling holes side by side made certain of functioning even if the roll was slightly off track. At the same time, these relatively tiny holes, although uncovering the tracker bar opening for an instant, succeed in admitting adequate control atmosphere air pressure. This ensures very precise theming capabilities. In that it respected the existing divided stack or valve chest as used by most makers it was an improvement that rendered redundant nothing that all ready existed, for the action was provided with theming holes at both sides of the roll.

The Themodist was the subject of British Patent 20,352 of 1910, and became accepted as the simplest and most dependable accenting system that it was adopted by many other piano-makers (who gave it their own style of name). It helped that it was also accepted by music-roll manufacturers.

Curiously the Hupfeld/Aeolian breakthrough did not mean that theming device invention came to an abrupt end. The matter of Aeolian's sub-licence for the system presented a spur to other makers who tried to seek their own 'North-West Passage'. But in the end it was the gradual standardisation of piano rolls to operate the Themodist system that finally convinced the industry that it had to standardise or face an uncertain uphill struggle. The fact that the Themodist actually worked and worked well was another incentive to accept defeat.

One of the very last of the independents to confront the theming problem in fact looked back to Robert Willard Pain's clever yet impractical 1904 patent for inspiration. This was the work of Paul Brown Klugh of Chicago, who was granted a British Patent number 112,632 in 1916. Klugh's tracker bar had normal openings, but above each opening, and slightly to one side, was a narrow vertical slit.

The normal tracker openings worked in the usual way. Mounted above the hammers in the piano were a set of pneumatic motors, one to each pair of adjacent hammers: since piano music normally does not make use of intervals of a minor second, it was safe to assume that adjacent hammers would seldom be called upon to move together, let alone to require

An electric action with a difference was the Tel-Electric expression piano which played narrow and thin perforated brass music-rolls spooled into a cassette. Here is a Chickering upright revealing the solenoid-controlled playing action under the keyboard. This worked on the keys from beneath, pulling them down with varying degrees of force to give expression. Patented in 1901 by Timothy B Powers, it was widely promoted and around 1910 it cost $350 (£87. 10s). It faded away about 1915 and today is a rare device that only turns up in America occasionally.

To have worked properly, the non-themed notes had to be subdued to a lower level using a sort of 'anti-theme' perforation that subjected the stack to a tension-relieving chamber – a sort of reverse crash valve. In operation, because of the resulting different speeds of the action hammers, this must have brought the theme notes considerably ahead of the subdued theming. These motors controlled an adjustable rest for the hammers, there being no conventional rest rail. The normal location was at a forwards position, but when a note had to be themed, the pneumatic motor was collapsed via its own valve stack, and the hammer rest travelled back from the strings, so allowing the hammer plenty of distance in which to build up velocity.

Like Pain's system, Klugh's patent required roll perforations of two sizes. Normal notes were sounded using normal-sized perforations, but themed notes had to be punched with larger openings so as to open two tracker bar ducts. It operated by regulating the distance through which the hammer travelled to strike the string. Not only was the system very complex, but it was obviously a non-starter on grounds of production costs.

Pain's variable-size roll perforations were the principal behind another potentially brilliant expression system devised in Britain by W H Grimsdale and covered by British Patents granted between 1908 and 1913. Known as the Dalian, this produced accented notes according to the volume of air admitted through the tune-sheet. Grimsdale's first patent (1912 of 1908) proposed an action featuring a series of nested valves that collapsed in sequence like a cascade. The operation relied on a music-roll having the themed or accented notes punched with larger-diameter holes that admitted additional air through 'predictor slots' above each note in the tracker bar.

As with Klugh's version, the problem here would centre on (a) a method of punching a roll having two sizes of openings, (b) the accurate tracking of the roll for the variable holes to be fully functional, and (c) the perfect sequencing of mechanical-pneumatic components - the cascade valves. In operation, the system appears to have worked by suppressing unthemed notes through low-tension vacuum.

Grimsdale's many patents related to special perforating machines and variations on the multiple-valve principal. Piano-maker John H Crowley of Holloway Road, London, built this action and produced a number of pianos that used it but despite heavy promotion in the 1912-14 period, the action seems to have been troublesome from the start and consequently was short-lived. The outbreak of War seems to have killed it off. An American player expert suggested to me some years ago that the Pain/Klugh/Grimsdale principal was taken up by The Cable Company of Chicago and used as the basis for its Solo Carola Inner-Player which used the principal of the 'predictor-slot' above each tracker-bar opening.

Like so many inventions that are radical, the theory may not be faulted, but the reality was clearly another matter. In forty years I have only seen one Dalian action and that drove its owner to distraction! Dalian-encoded music rolls do still turn up occasionally and they play reasonably well on an ordinary 88-note action – without expression.

The Tel-Electric was played from a remote console (called by its maker 'the transmitter') which was joined to the piano by a very thick electric multi-cable. From the comfort of an armchair, the owner could regulate the playing using simple controls in the all-electric spool-box.

If there was one system which had a great deal going for it this was the invention of Maximilian Macarius Kastner, the young German who created the Triumph and Autopiano players. This had the ability to accent any note anywhere in the piano scale while having none of the complexity of Pain's arrangement. Known as the Kastonome, it was an ambitious system that worked very well, at least in theory. It employed an individual accenting pouch for every note, these accenting pouches being connected to a common windway to which atmospheric pressure could be admitted via special additional openings in the tracker-bar sides and controlled by special music rolls featuring marginal holes for the notes to be accented.

The great advantage of the Kastonome system was that it was unnecessary to modify the tension of the vacuum within the whole stack in order to accent one note. All that was needed was to alter the tension in a very small volume of space so as to operate the expression pouch. This created an action that was outstandingly easy to play and responded wonderfully when played with the special Kastonome music rolls. The down side was that it was difficult to maintain in perfect order and over time the gradual deterioration of the highly individualistic Kastonome pouches produced uneven playing and unintentionally accented notes which were virtually impossible to mask.

For all that, it was a very ingenious concept. Each of the additional perforations admitted air at atmospheric pressure to a cut-off pouch that governed the control of suction or atmosphere to a special ring-shaped pouch that formed the seat for the secondary valves. In the same way that one of Aeolian's patents covered the creation of a subdued piano with the accented notes being given 'normal' conditions, as distinct from a normal piano stack under the overall control of subduing controls through which accented notes were produced by increased vacuum tension, the Kastonome worked on the principle of softening all the notes being played with the exception of the notes required to stand out. A correct musical interpretation required the Kastonome control to be switched on and off according to printed instructions on the music roll. Whereas the Themodist might be described as a passive system in that it did not need to be disconnected when not in use and was only operational when the Themodist perforations dictated so, the Kastonome was an active arrangement because it served to subdue the instrument overall.

And here lay what emerged as its principal problem. The design precluded any modification of the underlying playing intensity. When properly adjusted, the accented notes could dominate the music rather than enhance it. Furthermore, when the action was activated, it was dependent on the transfer of precise volumes of air. Moderate dust and dirt could clog the narrow passages in the valve control units. This disturbed the critical balance in the system and, in the worst case, could render a performance so uncontrollable as regards accenting that one would be forced to switch the expression control to 'off'.

It would be wrong to dismiss this important action out of hand because, with care and regular attention, aided by some judicious tweaking of the intensity level, the Kastonome was a very good expression piano. The ultimate problem was really that it was not adopted by other makers so as to make action and roll-production economically worthwhile. It also demanded a great deal of its pouch material in its construction. Overall it was probably ahead of its time.

The Kastonome was invented jointly by Kastner and C Katz in whose names British Patents were taken out for the system as follows: 12,761 May 25th, 1910, and 8723 of April 7th, 1911.

The special Kastonome music rolls, characterised by a central pair of parallel tempo-indicator width lines and a series of small green arrows between them to show speed variations, were the subject of British Patent 26,553 of November 15th, 1910.

Commendable though the system was, Kastner knew that a piano that relied on special music rolls, however good it might be, could never succeed on its own. No other maker used the action so, with the pre-1914 adoption of 88-note pianos with the Themodist accenting system, Kastner dropped the Kastonome. Later (after the war) the company launched their Autopianos with what was called the 'Triumphodist' control – Kastner's own version of the now-universal Themodist system.

The Hupfeld arrangement as eventually improved upon and refined by Aeolian was thus to become the 'industry standard' for theme expression. Much later on when the era of the reproducing piano began, expression and theming came in for further scrutiny and variations on the system were looked at. This was associated with the provision of individual levels of theming.

The principle of Themodist operation has already been described in general terms. Specifically, the theme holes were connected to a regulator pneumatic, the overall level of vacuum tension therein being controlled by a knife valve. The instant a theme hole was uncovered, the regulator moved, opened the knife valve and admitted a higher tension vacuum to the half of the stack in which the note to be themed lay. More than one note could, of course, be themed at one time.

The Te-Electric system. Two models of this unusual action were produced, one playing 65 notes and the other a full-scale 88-note. The rolls were 5-inches wide for the former and 6.3/4-inches wide for the latter. Here is the common 65-note model.

In practice, the faster the speed that the music roll travelled over the tracker bar, the more convincing was the accenting effect. This is a bit of a generalisation, yet it remains true that many of the earlier, slow-travelling rolls (perforated at speeds of 40 and below) were intended to economise on paper and therefore disproportionately greater accuracy was needed to position the theme holes. Usually with this type of roll one found that there was insufficient length of music slot to allow creative theming. This confusing observation will become clearer in a moment.

We have seen that accenting one note calls for increasing the vacuum tension at the moment of exhausting the pneumatic motor to strike a particular string via one of the piano's hammer actions. Although this action takes place almost instantaneously, there is inevitably a very small time lag. It is literally a fraction of a second.

If you have a low-cost roll perforated at, say, 10 feet/minute, this time-lag represents virtually no distance on the paper. On the other hand, if the roll is punched to travel at twice or even three times that speed (meaning that it's twice or three times as long), then that split second now becomes a noticeable fraction of an inch. It is this definable, measurable distance that can now be put to use in a very subtle way.

As an example, imagine a chord of, say, four notes cut into the paper roll so that all the notes start at the same instant and their beginnings are thus represented as a straight line across the paper. If we want just one of these notes to stand out louder than the others, there are two ways to do it. The first is to cut that note with a longer slot in the paper, leaving the other three very short. This means that the unwanted three will damp quickly, leaving the 'accented' note singing out longer because the damper is held off the string. While that system would work very well, it is not actually making one note physically louder and thus more dominant than the others.

Clearly the way to do it is to *theme* the note but if we choose to punch theme holes to line up with the chord, they must affect all four notes and produce for us one loud four-note chord. We are back to where we started.

The solution lies in making use of the fact that the real live pianist seldom if ever will strike four notes evenly all at once. In an exaggerated case, they will sound as an arpeggio, and probably not in the logical order 1 2 3 4, but maybe even 4 1 2 3. This pianistic shortcoming, though, is seldom discernible to the human ear and only really shows up when a pianist is cutting a piano roll and we see that the start of his chord is most certainly not that straight line that perfection led us to imagine.

Back in the early days of piano-roll cutting, the music seldom went anywhere near either a piano or a pianist, but was marked out and punched direct from the score according to the metronome marking. In such instances, all notes and chords were exactly the right length and in precisely the proper position. Because this was not the way a human player performed, the music rolls produced helped give the player piano a bad name for they produced a very mechanical sounding performance, known to musicologists as a *metrical* or *four-square* interpretation.

Great though the human senses are, our ears are one of the least perfect instruments of interpretation, for they tend to allow us to hear a level of perfection that is seldom there. Because of this, it does not matter if, when punching the holes in our music roll, one or more notes are cut marginally late or fractionally early relative to our ideal straight line.

Since the accenting of a note can only take place at the split second when that particular piano action hammer is set into motion, and that once the piano hammer is moving towards the string nothing we can now do can alter its velocity, the technique is to select the note to be accented and cut it with a very slight delay – and then theme that note.

This small act of deception has far greater potential than you may think, for it makes it possible for one note to stand out louder regardless of where the 'soft/loud' controls are held

– up to a level of maximum loudness. It is now a practical proposition to make one note stand out louder in a chord of apparently simultaneously sounding notes, regardless of whether it is the note at one end or in the middle. Used in its developed form in the reproducing piano, this technique of theming individual notes takes precedence over the general level of vacuum in the stack as controlled by the special perforations for controlling the reproducing action.

Remember just now I mentioned roll speed and said that the faster speed provided greater effectiveness? This is so because absolute precision is vital to positioning the theme perforations. This precision becomes a factor of time rather than distance meaning that the faster the paper travels over the tracker bar the greater the distance in front of the note to be accented that the theme holes have to be punched.

Imagine our fast-travelling roll and come back to our four-note chord within which we want note number three to stand out. The effect of making one note louder than the others is only noticeable when the piano is being played at a level of sound below maximum loudness – this is just the same whether the pianist is live or it is you with a paper roll and, if you think about it, is a very obvious statement. So, with the expression levers in use, we come to our four-note chord. As the paper traverses the tracker bar, the perforations for notes 1, 2 and 4 uncover the ducts in the tracker bar and in the usual way set the hammers for those notes on their course to strike the strings. A split second later, our theme duct is uncovered and note 3's perforation uncovers its tracker bar duct. Under high tension, the pneumatic slams the piano hammer at the string at a greater speed than the other three.

Depending on the degree of vacuum tension used for the first set of notes it is now quite possible for all four hammers to strike their strings at one and the same time since three were travelling at a slower rate than the fourth. Hence we can explode the oft-repeated comment from non-aficionados (both concert pianists and laymen alike) that accenting one note in a chord is impossible by player piano.

So far I have mentioned the Kastonome and the Themodist as well as referring to the Triumphodist. But there were several others as well as the numerous names used to describe so-called accenting methods and the rolls from which such effects were produced. In English-speaking countries the most common was the Themodist of Aeolian which, on the roll and box labels, was always indicated by the word Themodist and the presence of a letter 'T' before the roll number. This was found on both the Aeolian rolls produced under the Universal name and the later Meloto when Universal changed its name.

As far as the music rolls were concerned many of those provided with the special twin perforations to operate the Themodist-type of accenting were just marked with the word 'Accented'. Not surprisingly this was a characteristic of the so-called 'hand-played' rolls. In Germany, the word Solodant was used for the same thing.

Besides physically emphasising melody notes in the piano roll (and probably to achieve the kudos of 'added-value' features), Aeolian thought it worth making these notes clearer to recognise in the roll by punching them with a different type of perforation. British Patent number 14,325 dated September 1st, 1904, was granted for a system wherein accompaniment notes are chain-punched while the melody notes have contiguous perforations – individual holes separated by a narrow neck of paper.

Over the years, this procedure was reversed, the accompaniment often had contiguous perforations while the melody line had slotted openings while very long perforations began with a slot followed by contiguous holes. Aeolian's differentiation of types of note perforations stood it in good stead when it came to the Aeolian Pipe Organ with its double-row tracker bar wherein upper manual notes were in single perforations and the lower manual ones were in the form of slots, so that the operator of the instrument could see at a glance where the melody was. For the piano, though, I fail to see an advantage.

Both German and American combination pianos appeared very early on. In Europe the German Kuhl & Klatt type of instrument with its percussion effects brought music into cafes, restaurants and other public places. For such applications, pedalled instruments were obviously undesirable, so electrically-powered suction bellows were devised. Remember that at this time – the late 19th century – electricity was still a little understood commodity and a resource which was restricted to just a few locations. So-called 'mains' power was several decades away and what was so coyly described as 'the electric fluid' had to be provided either by a generating set or, more commonly, a wet-cell accumulator that needed periodic recharging.

A similar situation pertained in the United States where electrically-operated pianos and combination instruments were frequently ahead of the communities they served and demanding accumulator-power. And when the first electric lighting circuits were installed, it was recommended that the user ran his piano off the electric lighting power. Fuses and the proper weight of electric cable were little understood. One wonders how many fires were caused by overloaded lighting circuits!

To begin with, the method of 'pumping' the bellows was to replace the foot-operated pedals by some form of crankshaft that would impart alternate motion to the exhausters. Instead of two exhausters, the crankshaft could more efficiently be employed with three, even four, sometimes five exhausters, the greater the number the smaller in physical size they had to be. But even this was cumbersome until the day somebody realised that converting the human-powered exhaust bellows for electricity was a cumbersome approach and that the real solution lay in designing a specific rotary exhauster that could efficiently operate from an electric motor.

The outcome of this 'logical thinking' process was the rotary pump as exemplified by the pumps commonly used in expression and combination pianos and the later reproducing pianos. These were smaller and more compact than the foot-operated suction bellows.

The combination piano enjoyed an enormous popularity in the United States where makers such as The Operators Piano Company, Peerless, Cremona, North Tonawanda, Nelson-Wiggen, Wurlitzer and Seeburg took the instrument to high levels of perfection. This corresponded to the progress in Europe, where makers such as Welte, Weber, Popper, Philipps, Neue Leipziger Musikwerke A Buff-Hedinger, the Sächsischen Orchestrionfabrik F O Glass, Imhof & Mukle, Hupfeld and others also prospered and perfected their combination pianos.

From these developments came a number of highly specialised and unusual instruments that gained acclaim in their own right. These included the Hupfeld Phonolistz-Violina, a piano combined with three real violins, the Mills Violano-Virtuoso, a special keyboardless expression piano with a real violin, and the family of theatre orchestras collectively known as 'Fotoplayers', technically a brand made by American Photo Player Company.

Within this there was also a subtle change from electrically-driven to electrically-operated systems. The violin-playing instruments serve to illustrate this transition which only lasted for the duration of some of those manufacturers that preferred all-electric rather than pneumatic functioning.

Of the numerous attempts at creating a self-playing violin, only two were of sufficient success that they entered volume production. The first was Hupfeld's Phonolistz-Violina made in Leipzig which, although powered by an electric motor that drove the bellows system, remained entirely a pneumatic instrument. Hupfeld's instrument first appeared about 1907-08 and consisted of an upright expression piano complete with keyboard on top of which was an extension case containing, in the commonest models, three violins, only one string of each being fingered. Later there was a limited production of instruments that played on six violins: no original examples are known to survive but at the end of the 20th century a limited number was hand built in Germany based on surviving illustrations and patent drawings.

The other instrument was the Mills Violano-Virtuoso made in Chicago and an entirely electric instrument. This mechanism, designed by a Swedish émigré Henry K Sandall, was centred on a symmetrically-strung 44-note piano having its lowest notes situated in the centre. This was located in the back of a special decorative cabinet housing also a violin, all four strings of which could be individually fingered and bowed simultaneously. This impressive device entered production around 1910. A later model included two violins. The entire action was solenoid-driven from a direct-current source.

Of the two types of violin-playing piano, collectors in the main accept that the Hupfeld produces a more realistic sound and has a better and larger library of music rolls available. On the other hand, when properly adjusted and regulated, the Mills instruments can give a fair account of themselves. Neither instrument, when not in good order, sounds brilliant!

Hupfeld ceased production of the violin-player on the outbreak of World War I: Mills was still in production until around 1930.

It is unlikely we will ever know how many people attempted to build expression pianos. It would normally be thought that the arrival of the reproducing piano killed off expression piano development. This simply was not so and makers went on to attempt to make a lower-cost player that gave a 'hand-played' performance.

As an example of the businesses that got involved in this field, there is the hitherto unrecorded story of Petters Limited of Yeovil, Somerset. At the outbreak of the First War, many piano-makers turned to aircraft construction because of their woodworking skills. This is a tale of an aircraft-maker turning to piano construction!

The Petter family had already made a name for themselves before the 19th century ended. As iron founders and engineers, they made oil engines and had formed The Yeovil Motor Car & Cycle Company Ltd. Their engines were fitted in early motorcars. Watching for market opportunities, they saw the potential for fitting their motors into the new-fangled aeroplanes and airships. The coming of the First World War brought military contracts and then, because of their experience in wooden pattern-making, an order for aircraft. Robert Bruce, a Lieutenant in the RNVR, joined the company in June of 1915 as manager of the new aircraft department which was located at a site named Westland Aircraft Works. The company prospered and built huge numbers of aeroplanes until, with the signing of the Armistice, there was suddenly no work for the hugely expanded aircraft division of Petters. Quickly the business was forced to diversify into light engineering and the manufacture of milk churns.

Robert Bruce, however, was a talented amateur pianist and had always been fascinated by the player piano. As so many before him and, one must say, since, he believed he could see room for improvement. Seeing a marketing opportunity (how, in those depressed days, one cannot now imagine), he began designing the Westland Player Piano. He hired A D Towner, a man who had gained considerable experience of player action design before the war with C E Lyon, partner and brother of the maker of the Autolyon player. The Lyon players had used off-the-shelf actions, but several Patents had been taken out for the manufacture of their own players. Unfortunately the outbreak of war in 1914 seems to have brought all this to a stop and no Autolyon has been seen fitted with anything besides the early Higel action.

Now Towner set to with Petters Ltd to design a new type of expression piano. Bruce reckoned that he had some advantage over other piano-makers in that his business had its own foundry, pattern-makers and experience. Between January 6th and August 19th 1919, three British Patents were granted for improvements to player pianos. All was not as it should be, though. Neither Bruce nor Westland had any manufacturing experience of pianos, let alone their production and marketing. An ill-considered venture was finally laid to rest when a refusal by the woodworker's Trade Union to allow piece-work in the factory resulted in a strike. No records exist of the number of pianos actually made: reports of 'a small number of pianos' emanating from Yeovil seem not to be substantiated by the Trade. Westland went on to make very successful aircraft and, in recent years, helicopters. That seems to have been a better bet!

The earliest expression pianos were a vital stepping-stone to the next stage in the development of the player-piano – the full reproducing instrument. They became a cheap and often acceptable alternative for the artist-interpretation re-performing piano.

Chapter 10
Reproducing Pianos –
their Evolution and Performance Claims

At the beginning of this book I described how the early musicians, performers and listeners had dreamed of making some device that would preserve extempore keyboard performance so that it could be heard again. The process that came to be known as Melography carefully marked a trace on a moving paper or card strip each time a key was depressed. This form of recording, created at a time long before pneumatic punching methods and before the tape-recorder and computer came on the scene to make it a commonplace occurrence, was as sensational an advance in its day as was placing a man to walk on the Moon in 1969.

If this was the Holy Grail of the keyboard, once achieved it was quickly supplanted by the next great hurdle – making the automatic piano's performance sound less mechanical. In fact, making it sound more like a human, finger-played rendition – although perhaps not exactly a 'warts-and-all' human performance. Every maker of the mechanical piano for the domestic drawing room or concert hall was haunted by the incubus of the mechanical, metronomical lack of feeling in its music. This fear was encouraged in part (and almost wholly sustained) by the always-present street piano that relentlessly ground out melodies beneath our windows.

As we have seen, little by little, the performance improvements re-set the goal-posts yet all this really did was to set people's expectations ever higher. Presented with something described as an improvement, listeners became hypercritical and anticipated more. The real target was, understandably, to interpret music in the convincing style not just of a pianist, but also of a real named artist! And that goal was pursued with equal fervour in Germany and in the United States.

The three key elements to improving the quality of the player-piano's interpretation, meaning making it more like a real human performance, already existed as the 20th century got going. First was the German invention of the note-theming principle. Second was the introduction of automatic playing using electricity as the motive force. And third was the principle of the expression piano.

Attempting to evolve a system that embraced all these facets plus some added performance enhancements was not insurmountable: it merely demanded that the roll of music be provided with some extra perforations to directly operate special action pneumatics. The real difficulty was capturing the nuances of a performance so that not just the accenting was faithfully copied, but also tempo (*rubato* and *accelerandi*), soft and sustaining pedal operation, could all be encoded (a modern word) into a perforated paper roll.

That this was achieved with varying degrees of success marked the fulfilment of the player-makers' dream – a machine that could play not just like a human pianist, but with the performance quirks of a particular *named* concert pianist! As regards variations in tempi, common in normal piano rolls that were printed with instructions to the user as where to slow down, speed up – or even pause, that was easily taken care of by allowing the music roll to run at a constant speed meaning once set at the start of the roll there was no cause to vary it in any way. The remainder of the desired characteristics would

elevate the player-piano and its music to undreamed of heights.

To the player-piano buff, there are three common reproducing systems. This is not quite true, for the list ought to list four, probably five and more likely six – and that's only to consider the big names! If that sounds a head-bender, there's three Welte, two Ampico and one Duo-Art. Other contenders include Hupfeld starting with its Phonoliszt expression piano and continuing with its reproducers in the DEA and Phonola range, Philipps (Frankfurt) with the Ducanola series – and so on. Here's the story in outline.

The pioneering Welte name is associated, confusingly, with three quite different reproducing actions – the 'red' Welte or Welte Mignon of 1904, the Welte-Mignon (Licensee) of about 1915, and the 'green' Welte.

The earliest of these was the original German-made 'red' Welte, so called because of the red paper from which the music roll was punched. This music roll was $12^7/_8$-inches wide punched at not quite eight holes to the inch in pitch.

The Welte-Mignon (Licensee) was the American-designed 'simplified' version introduced only in America shortly after the First World War. This played a standard-width 11¼-inch wide music roll punched at nine holes to the inch pitch. A fea-

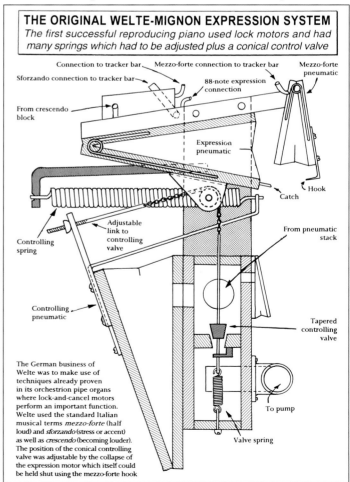

THE ORIGINAL WELTE-MIGNON EXPRESSION SYSTEM
The first successful reproducing piano used lock motors and had many springs which had to be adjusted plus a conical control valve

Connection to tracker bar — Mezzo-forte connection to tracker bar — Mezzo-forte pneumatic

Sforzando connection to tracker bar

88-note expression connection

From crescendo block

Expression pneumatic

Hook

Catch

Adjustable link to controlling valve

From pneumatic stack

Controlling spring

Controlling pneumatic

Tapered controlling valve

The German business of Welte was to make use of techniques already proven in its orchestrion pipe organs where lock-and-cancel motors perform an important function. Welte used the standard Italian musical terms *mezzo-forte* (half loud) and *sforzando* (stress or accent) as well as *crescendo* (becoming louder). The position of the conical controlling valve was adjustable by the collapse of the expression motor which itself could be held shut using the mezzo-forte hook.

To pump

Valve spring

ture of both the 'red' and the Licensee rolls was that both systems employed a system of 'lock-and-cancel' valves, a clear legacy of the organ and orchestrion-organ foundations of the German original. These special valves controlled virtually every operation of the piano and their advantage was that instead of needing a continuous chain of perforations to operate, say, a pedal or an expression volume, only two short perforations were needed – one to initiate the effect and, later, one to cancel it. It made for a simpler and more robust piano-roll having no unnecessary perforations.

The 'green' Welte, on the other hand, was a later development of the original Welte-Mignon that appeared in the mid-1920s. It was evolved by Welte in Germany to overcome some of what was believed to be the shortcomings of the original 'red' rolls. To this end, this action had a totally different expression system operated by a standard-width 11¼-inch music-roll and punched with a hole-pitch of nine to the inch. In place of lock-and-cancel valves it used more conventional contiguous or chain perforations to operate its functions. The action is named after the predominantly green-colour paper used for the music-rolls.

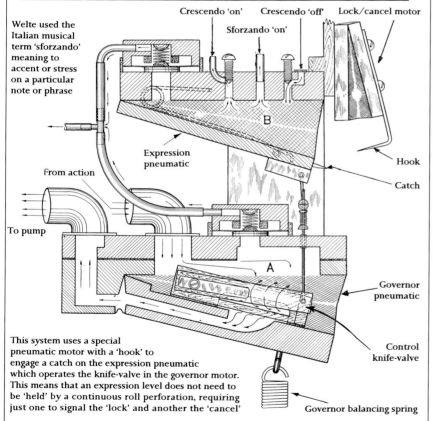

THE WELTE-MIGNON (LICENSEE) EXPRESSION SYSTEM
Although fully re-designed and engineered, this reproducer retained the original 'lock-and-cancel' expression mechanism

Welte used the Italian musical term 'sforzando' meaning to accent or stress on a particular note or phrase

Crescendo 'on'   Crescendo 'off'   Lock/cancel motor
Sforzando 'on'

B

Expression pneumatic

From action

Hook

Catch

To pump

A

Governor pneumatic

Control knife-valve

This system uses a special pneumatic motor with a 'hook' to engage a catch on the expression pneumatic which operates the knife-valve in the governor motor. This means that an expression level does not need to be 'held' by a continuous roll perforation, requiring just one to signal the 'lock' and another the 'cancel'

Governor balancing spring

A significant and important feature of the 'green' Welte is that of all the popular reproducing piano actions (meaning 'the big three') it was the only one to play the entire full-scale 88-note compass while the original 'red' Welte-Mignon and the Licensee played only 80 of the piano's keys – C to G. By comparison, Aeolian's Duo-Art also acted upon 80 notes – C# to

G# – and the Ampico managed slightly better at 83 – B to A.

'Green' Welte pianos are generally scarcer than either the 'red' Welte or the original Welte-Mignon (Licensee).

Both the original 'red' and the Licensee rolls were made to operate at a constant speed of between tempo 80 and 90 whereas the 'green' was pegged to a tempo of 70.

I do not intend to go into exhaustive technical details on how each of these pianos operate and how systems differ. Today there are some first-rate technical manuals on the market for collectors and restorers and these dedicated works specialise in covering the particular type of piano in which you are interested. What I shall do instead is tell you briefly of their history and development and basic operation. Then we will look at how the reproducing piano performs and discuss whether or not it lives up to its reputation.

The first of these very special but, as yet, nameless new-type player-pianos appeared as early as 1904 from the South German factory of Welte. This was an instrument shaped like a sideboard that had no keyboard but was purely a pneumatic reproducer driven by an electric motor that operated a three-element organ-type electric exhaust bellows and actuated via a sticker action. As such it became known as the Keyless Welte and, since it played rolls punched into red paper, it was styled the Keyless 'red' Welte.

This became the first of the breed of reproducing pianos. It was named the Welte Mignon because in Germany at that time – as in England – France, the French, and all things Francophilic-sounding were thought to be the height of good taste and refinement. Giving a German piano a French name was to pander to fashion. Whether meaning delicate, dainty or merely small – all interpretations of the adjective *mignon*, is hard to say! Suffice it to say that when it was launched in America it was described more prosaically as the 'Welte Artistic Player Piano'. Certainly it was petite and, for all its perfection, a good deal smaller and more compact than most American players of its age.

No such Franco-German linguistic niceties surrounded the other main variety of the 'red' Welte – the cabinet player. Rather more than merely a push-up, this was a full reproducer built after the style of the piano-player and would convert any well-adjusted and regulated piano into a reproducer. Styled the Vorsetzer, no more apt name might be found for it: the word *vorsetzer* is a transitive verb meaning 'to set, place or put before' more in the way of a proposition than a mere push-up![1]

The zenith of the Welte-Mignon was the Welte-Mignon *Einbau* reproducing piano. The word *einbau* was used only to differentiate between the complete piano with built-in or interior player mechanism and the Vorsetzer.

Although very early in the history of the reproducing piano, the Welte Mignon possessed a most unusual and highly efficient expression system described in contemporary advertisements as 'the floating crescendo'. Never attempted by other and later makers, this system was constantly variable across the entire sound-volume perspective. There was just one fixed point either side of which the loudness 'floated' and this was the *mezzo-forte*. Control of intensity (loudness) was by a pair of pneumatic power units, one (the *crescendo* unit) operating slowly, and the other (the *sforzando* unit) that operated rapidly. The usual form of expression openings in the music roll governed operation.

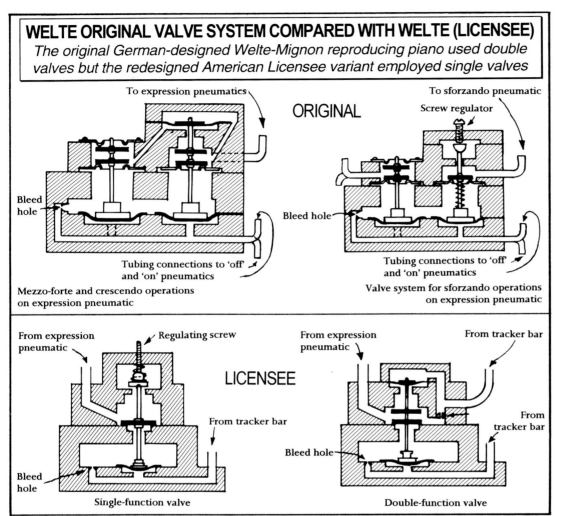

WELTE ORIGINAL VALVE SYSTEM COMPARED WITH WELTE (LICENSEE)
The original German-designed Welte-Mignon reproducing piano used double valves but the redesigned American Licensee variant employed single valves

ORIGINAL

To expression pneumatics

Bleed hole

Tubing connections to 'off' and 'on' pneumatics

Mezzo-forte and crescendo operations on expression pneumatic

To sforzando pneumatic

Screw regulator

Bleed hole

Tubing connections to 'off' and 'on' pneumatics

Valve system for sforzando operations on expression pneumatic

LICENSEE

From expression pneumatic

Regulating screw

From tracker bar

Bleed hole

Single-function valve

From expression pneumatic

From tracker bar

From tracker bar

Bleed hole

Double-function valve

Both treble and bass halves of the piano were under the control of two similar and independent expression units and the method of changing playing volume cleverly used lock-and-cancel valves. These were very economic on their vacuum requirements, one small perforation serving to sequence each valve. Because the lock-and-cancel system was purely binary, each perforation alternately selected or cancelled a valve.

Because there was no 'stage' from which to build changes in volume, any errors in adjustment of the dynamics could mount up until the perceived expression was well out of musical alignment. It was to remedy this that the mezzo-forte unit played a vital part in functioning as a control to re-set the stage at intervals. In practice, the cycling of the three control units at convenient intervals ensures a constant intensity level of sound from which to build crescendos or diminuendos.

After the first Welte-Mignon of 1904, Hupfeld followed two years later with an electric reproducing piano, the first of a large number from this Leipzig maker. The beautifully-made DEA of 1905 played an 85-note compass A to A which was five notes more than the Welte-Mignon in whose shadow it had to exist. This was then followed after the end of the First World War by the Triphonola all-electric reproducer and the pedal-electric version called the Duophonola. This latter version was created to suit those musically-inclined who proclaimed that only by foot-operated reproducing action might the correct expression be induced into an interpretation; a concept that, contrary to some other published sources, began in Germany and from there spread to Britain but never crossed the Atlantic. These two high-quality systems were the first to offer a full-scale 88-note compass A to C.

In the United States, both the American Piano Company and the Aeolian Company were working hard to create a reproducing instrument. For both, the watershed year was 1913 and today it is difficult to determine which was the first to the market. To avoid confusion I shall deal with them alphabetically!

American Piano Company began amassing patents for aspects initially associated with expression pianos and by 1910 was establishing itself in this field. The refinement to reproducing status is thought to have been the work of Chicago-born Charles Fuller Stoddard (1876-1958) whose name was linked with the first Ampico pianos that appeared in 1913.

It is believed that Stoddard built the prototype of his reproducing piano as early as 1907, possibly working on it from 1905. He showed the instrument to Foster of Foster, Armstrong & Co, and Ernest Knabe of William Knabe & Co in 1907. The two men decided to pool their resources and form a new undertaking with Stoddard to exploit his invention. The outcome was the formation of the American Piano Company on June 10th 1908 by the amalgamation of the William Knabe Co, Chickering & Sons, and Foster-Armstrong Co. The new business controlled the manufacture and sale of the following pianos: Chickering (founded in 1823), Knabe (1837), Haines Brothers (1851), Marshall & Wendell (1853), Foster & Co. (1892), Armstrong (1893), Brewster (1895), and J B Cook Company (1900). The combined output of the two founding companies with their various brands was said to be 18,000 pianos per year at the time of amalgamation, so making the syndicate the largest manufacturer of pianos in the world.

The company filed its first Patent in the year of its formation but it was becoming clear that Welte, the first manufacturer in the world to make a reproducing piano, had already covered many aspects of the reproducing action in their own copious portfolio of patents. In 1909 Stoddard made certain revisions to the system and applied for fresh patents in an endeavour to avoid any infringement of the German company.

From the beginning, two names were used at this time – the Stoddard-Ampico and the Ampico-Artigraphic.

The first pianos had no automatic crescendo. Clearly still searching for their identity, in 1911 the company launched its Rhythmodik music-roll catalogue for use on the first reproducers. The following year this became Stoddard-Ampico and on July 15th 1912 the company registered as a trade mark the name 'Ampico'. Stoddard-Ampico now became plain Ampico. Within a year the company had perfected its automatic crescendo system and full-scale commercial production got under way.

By the end of 1919, these two names began to be phased out in favour of a new and novel name – Model A. This action could be fitted into either uprights or, predominantly, grand pianos. These latter installations were carried in a drawer that fitted beneath the keyboard or key-bed. Pulling the drawer forward revealed the spoolbox and controls, none of which was visible when the drawer was closed.

Featuring prominently in the Ampico were features covered by existing Patents that had been granted to the Amphion Company which hadbeen acquired by Ampico together with their Artecho reproducing actions. The Model A action underwent a systematic refinement process but this did not involve altering the roll coding for the expression system. However, finger-controlled expression buttons were ultimately replaced by simpler methods. The Ampico 'step-intensity' valve units, initially complex twin-valve units, were refined as single-valve assemblies and many other similar changes improved the performance and, above all, increased the reliability of the Model A action.

A curious delay interfered with the launch of the product to the public and that was in its advertising. Here Ampico was surprisingly slow off the mark for, on March 1st 1914, Aeolian broke new ground with the first advertisement for a non-German reproducing piano – the Duo-Art. It was some three weeks later before Ampico began its own advertising. From that moment on, however, nothing could hold back the ebullience of Ampico's self-promotion.

Ampico was a thoroughly modern company with an approach to player-piano promotion that considered it merely as another commodity. Consequently the company sought publicity in every way possible. No story was too devious or small to fall short of being 'put out on the wire' to the press. One curious tale appeared in *The Music Trade Review* for February 21st, 1925 that typifies the approach to publicity:

AMPICO MAKES A LONG DISTANCE PLAYING RECORD
Picture Magnate Leaves Instrument Playing in Rush for California and Returns to Find it Still Operating

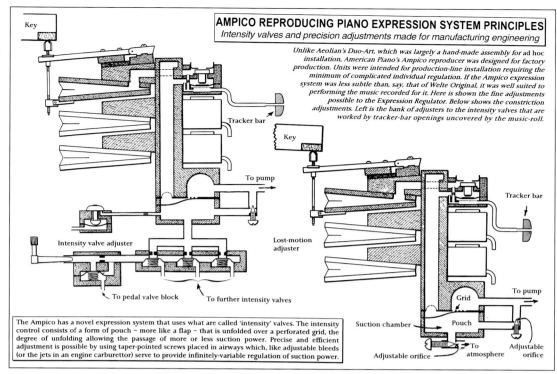

AMPICO REPRODUCING PIANO EXPRESSION SYSTEM PRINCIPLES
Intensity valves and precision adjustments made for manufacturing engineering

Unlike Aeolian's Duo-Art, which was largely a hand-made assembly for ad hoc installation, American Piano's Ampico reproducer was designed for factory production. Units were intended for production-line installation requiring the minimum of complicated individual regulation. If the Ampico expression system was less subtle than, say, that of Welte Original, it was well suited to performing the music recorded for it. Here is shown the fine adjustments possible to the Expression Regulator. Below shows the constriction adjustments. Left is the bank of adjusters to the intensity valves that are worked by tracker-bar openings uncovered by the music-roll.

Key · Tracker bar · Key · To pump · Intensity valve adjuster · Lost-motion adjuster · To pedal valve block · To further intensity valves · Tracker bar · To pump · Grid · Suction chamber · Pouch · Adjustable orifice · To atmosphere · Adjustable orifice

The Ampico has a novel expression system that uses what are called 'intensity' valves. The intensity control consists of a form of pouch – more like a flap – that is unfolded over a perforated grid, the degree of unfolding allowing the passage of more or less suction power. Precise and efficient adjustment is possible by using taper-pointed screws placed in airways which, like adjustable bleeds (or the jets in an engine carburettor) serve to provide infinitely-variable regulation of suction power.

John Kunsky, the moving picture magnate of Detroit, gave a farewell dinner on the night of his leaving for California. He and his friends were enjoying his Ampico and during the playing of the 'Ave Maria' it was discovered that they had just time to make their train. They hurried from the house, leaving the Ampico still playing, believing, as usual, it would stop automatically. Unfortunately, however, the 'repeat' device was on and when they returned from California, a month later, the roll was still playing and had played continuously during their absence as no one had been in the apartment during that time. Both instrument and motor had been doing duty for a solid month. Calculations show that the 'Ave Maria' was repeated 8,640 times.

Other 'stunts' were equally curious and it is a measure of either shortage of news material or contemporary excitement about such matters that Ampico (and, it has to be said, Aeolian with their Duo-Art in due course) were seldom out of the press. The paid advertisements, though, were the most revealing when one probes into styles of paid promotion (*see* Appendix 1).

Towards 1929, a much-vaunted 'new Ampico' was introduced that completely revised and re-engineered the earlier system. Quickly this became known simply as the Model B. Its most distinctive feature was that the spoolbox would accommodate large-diameter music rolls that would play for up to half an hour. The large-diameter take-up spool gave the revamped drawer installation a very different appearance.

The Model B Ampico was only ever installed in grand pianos and featured a reproducing mechanism radically redesigned from the earlier Model A. It was more prompt and thus more accurate and, despite a thoroughly re-engineered expression system, was actually simpler in operation. Responsibility for the re-design was Clarence B Hickman who worked on the project from 1925 until it was ready for production in 1928. The theory of 'backwards compatibility' seems to have been forefront in his mind for, although the expression system is so different, the Model B rolls were encoded in such a manner that they would also play on a Model A. The earlier Model A rolls, however, while capable of being played on a Model B, resulted in a somewhat lack-lustre performance.

Seeing it as a first-rate opportunity to make money, the Ampico's makers made quite a speciality of producing special-order, customised pianos in cases and styles to suit the décor of their more wealthy customers' homes. These unique instruments, known to Americans as 'one of a kind' pianos, were so prolific that it has been estimated that they made up between five and seven per cent of the entire output of Ampico pianos and represented between ten and twelve percent of the company's profits!

All good things, though, come to an end and the rich days of the buyers of Model B Ampicos were cut short by the Great Depression of 1929. Ampico continued to make a very few small and special instruments (one was the spinet-style 'Baby Ampico' of 1937-38; another was the extraordinary Ampichron, an electrically-driven timer that marked the passing hours by turning the piano into a chiming and musical clock), but the hey-days were never to return.

Next to be looked at is the Aeolian Duo-Art, first seen in America also in 1913 and, fairly quickly, exported to Britain where it underwent changes associated with large-scale production at the Aeolian UK factory at Hayes, Middlesex, to the west of London.

First demonstrated in New York in the autumn of 1913, the Duo-Art was fitted into an American-built Steinway grand and was immediately accepted pretty well on equal terms to the rival Ampico. Unlike the Ampico, however, apart from the changes between UK-built and US-built actions, the Duo-Art system remained largely unchanged until production ceased around 1936.

and perfected – well, there are no names that we can record. For them posterity has left nothing more than a name and an action.

This paucity of material in print relating to the technical development of the Duo-Art is hard to understand. Nobody, it seems, ever thought to chronicle the development of this popular instrument. By contrast, the Ampico is marked by an almost embarrassment of historical writings, the most recent of which are the Hickman Diaries edited by Richard J Howe which form a marvellous, if tantalisingly incoherent, addition to our knowledge of the technical history of the Ampico system. Yet there is no such counterpart for the Aeolian system.

The origins of the Duo-Art, as best we can piece together from the fragmented details that are common knowledge, all began when in 1898 Aeolian first placed onto the market Edwin Scott Votey's push-up pneumatic piano-player, the Pianola.

Within a few years, the process of continual improvement brought to this instrument an ingenious device for accenting selected notes – the theme notes of a musical score. It was on March 21st, 1900, that Ernest M Skinner was granted the first of two Patents for the note-accenting system that would become known as the Themodist. It was an extension of the principle patented by James William Crooks of Boston and initially employed an undivided chest and a single control perforation.

I have already commented a good deal on the Themodist (*see* previous Chapters) but one interesting feature of his Patent is worth highlighting and this concerns the possibility of accenting just one note in a simultaneous chord. In practical terms, this has always been thought impossible with the normal reproducing piano and yet it was precisely that which Skinner proclaimed in his Patent.

On the second page of the text accompanying his Patent, he writes:

The higher air-tension operating the accented notes moves the piano hammers so much more quickly than the notes which are not accented that it results in a simultaneous or practically simultaneous attack on the strings. It is true that the high tension is also acting upon the keys first struck; but they have progressed so far that the effect of the high pressure is lost on them.

This is a most interesting assumption since it flies in the face of the subsequent exhaustive experiments that appear to suggest otherwise. Indeed, Aeolian in Britain went to extraordinary lengths shortly before the outbreak of the 1939-45 war to try to achieve this. Their research engineer Gordon Iles actually solved this by using a special tracker bar having two parallel rows of apertures and connected to a 'double' Duo-Art action. Unfortunately, success came too late since the market was virtually non-existent. Furthermore the solution would have been prohibitively expensive to manufacture. Iles called this IST which stood for *isolated simultaneous theme*. I shall relate this story in a moment but first let's make

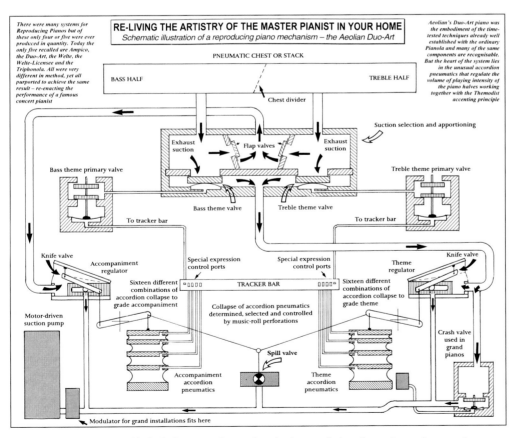

There were many systems for Reproducing Pianos but of these only four or five were ever produced in quantity. Today the only five recalled are Ampico, the Duo-Art, the Welte, the Welte-Licensee and the Triphonola. All were very different in method, yet all purported to achieve the same result – re-enacting the performance of a famous concert pianist

RE-LIVING THE ARTISTRY OF THE MASTER PIANIST IN YOUR HOME
Schematic illustration of a reproducing piano mechanism – the Aeolian Duo-Art

Aeolian's Duo-Art piano was the embodiment of the time-tested techniques already well established with the ordinary Pianola and many of the same components are recognisable. But the heart of the system lies in the unusual accordion pneumatics that regulate the volume of playing intensity of the piano halves working together with the Themodist accenting principle

PNEUMATIC CHEST OR STACK

BASS HALF — TREBLE HALF

Chest divider

Exhaust suction — Flap valves — Exhaust suction

Suction selection and apportioning

Bass theme primary valve — Treble theme primary valve

Bass theme valve — Treble theme valve

To tracker bar — To tracker bar

Knife valve — Knife valve

Accompaniment regulator — Theme regulator

Special expression control ports — Special expression control ports

Sixteen different combinations of accordion collapse to grade accompaniment — TRACKER BAR — Sixteen different combinations of accordion collapse to grade theme

Motor-driven suction pump

Collapse of accordion pneumatics determined, selected and controlled by music-roll perforations

Crash valve used in grand pianos

Spill valve

Accompaniment accordion pneumatics — Theme accordion pneumatics

▸ Modulator for grand installations fits here

Curiously very little is known about the design and development of this system. What is clear is that Aeolian bought a large number of relevant patents and their engineers into its organisation. As for those that designed, engineered, tested

it clear that without doubt, this is a characteristic that cannot be replicated by either the Ampico or the Welte systems.

Curiously it was nine years after the Welte-Mignon and thirteen years after Skinner's Themodist patents before the first Duo-Art reproducing piano appeared. And, while the Ampico history seems better documented, one gets the feeling that you are being told what the company and its personnel wanted us to know.

The simple fact is that early invention of the Ampico and Duo-Art actions was suggestive of some form of collaborative operation. While Ampico went in for its intensity valves and rolling curtain expression regulators, Aeolian used expression accordion bellows in the Duo-Art to form a variable expression suction control. Yet there is some slight but tantalising evidence to suggest that the inventor of the Ampico system, Charles Stoddard, might also have been behind these. Was it a system that Stoddard devised for the Ampico yet somehow scrapped in favour of another expression system? It seems that we may never know for certain.

There seems little doubt that, despite the hiatus over making its wares known to the public, Ampico definitely preceded Duo-Art.

The first Duo-Arts used a double-valve chest after the ordinary player piano actions, but soon changed to single-valve chests which remained throughout the major part of the system's existence.

Early Duo-Art installations in upright pianos used a specially-designed four-exhauster suction bellows driven by a crankshaft and electric motor, all mounted beneath the keyboard in the area normally occupied by foot-operated bellows. This large and cumbersome installation is known to some collectors as the 'steamboat' pump. While this may be a bit unfair to steamboats, it is certainly descriptive of the engineering involved.

At the same time, grand installations used a separate, cabinet-housed suction pump that could be placed either in the piano-stool or at some convenient or even remote location. Generally made to stand next to the piano, these could be housed in a basement room and connected to the instrument by a large air trunking.

These separate pumps were to remain an optional feature of Duo-Art grands for many years and they had the particular advantage of being both inconspicuous and silent in operation.

More usual, though, was the Aeolian box pump, a fully-enclosed four-lobe suction generator powered by an electric motor and connected to it via a conventional 'V'-sectioned rubber belt. This was similar to the box pump used by Ampico in its grands.

In the full reproducer, each half of the Duo-Art action is controlled by a pair of expression regulator assemblies. Aeolian describes these two as theme and accompaniment regulators. Each is possible of adjustment to one of sixteen degrees of expression ranging from very soft to moderately loud. The relationship between the theme and accompaniment halves can be exchanged one for the other if required, and themed notes, produced with the Themodist system.

While the Ampico takes its origins from a scale of intensity steps or degrees that are governed by a crescendo mechanism with expression provided by the sudden activation of intensity steps and the speed of crescendo, the Duo-Art builds its performance entirely around the Themodist principle. This simple feature represents the one fundamental difference between the two systems.

Electrically driven upright and grand Duo-Art pianos were all full reproducers. Some foot-operated non-electric examples were also produced in limited numbers and these were only part-reproducers, relying on the skill of the operator to fill in where the automatic expression left off. These are not to be confused with the aptly-termed 'Pedal-Electric' grand installations. These are full reproducing installations that may be operated in the normal way using the electric motor, or by foot. When under foot operation, it is seldom possible to produce the desired vacuum tension at all times, and so the reproduction is not quite so authentic as when in the automatic mode, *i.e.* electrically-driven.

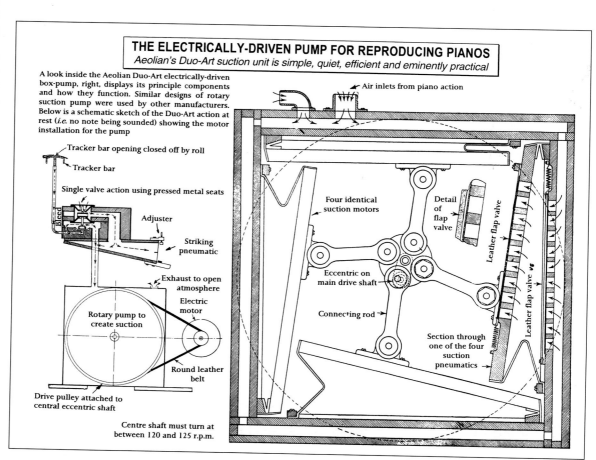

THE ELECTRICALLY-DRIVEN PUMP FOR REPRODUCING PIANOS
Aeolian's Duo-Art suction unit is simple, quiet, efficient and eminently practical

A look inside the Aeolian Duo-Art electrically-driven box-pump, right, displays its principle components and how they function. Similar designs of rotary suction pump were used by other manufacturers. Below is a schematic sketch of the Duo-Art action at rest (*i.e.* no note being sounded) showing the motor installation for the pump

Tracker bar opening closed off by roll

Tracker bar

Single valve action using pressed metal seats

Bleed

Adjuster

Striking pneumatic

Exhaust to open atmosphere

Electric motor

Rotary pump to create suction

Round leather belt

Drive pulley attached to central eccentric shaft

Centre shaft must turn at between 120 and 125 r.p.m.

Air inlets from piano action

Four identical suction motors

Detail of flap valve

Leather flap valve

Eccentric on main drive shaft

Connecting rod

Section through one of the four suction pneumatics

Leather flap valve

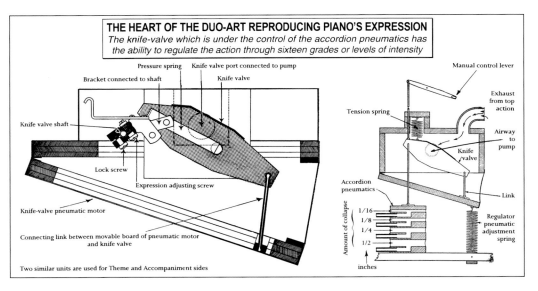

THE HEART OF THE DUO-ART REPRODUCING PIANO'S EXPRESSION
The knife-valve which is under the control of the accordion pneumatics has the ability to regulate the action through sixteen grades or levels of intensity

Pressure spring · Knife valve port connected to pump
Bracket connected to shaft · Knife valve
Knife valve shaft
Lock screw
Expression adjusting screw
Knife-valve pneumatic motor
Connecting link between movable board of pneumatic motor and knife valve
Two similar units are used for Theme and Accompaniment sides

Manual control lever
Exhaust from top action
Tension spring
Airway to pump
Knife valve
Accordion pneumatics
Link
Amount of collapse
1/16
1/8
1/4
1/2
inches
Regulator pneumatic adjustment spring

the valve chest with all the action pneumatics, which was situated beneath the keybed, with the tracker bar tubes and this was achieved by passing the tubing straight down through shaped keys that allowed clearance slots between. Convenient though this was, certainly as regards the length of rubber tubing used in the action, it made normal piano servicing rather difficult. In later installations, the practice was adopted of dividing the bundle of tubing and taking half over and down the bass side, the other over the treble side. Cumbersome though this at first seems, it had certain very positive advantages over those that took their tubing the short route down through the keybed. First it allowed relatively simple removal of either or both top and bottom actions, and second it made possible the easy withdrawal of the keyboard for adjustment.

British-made Duo-Art grands from about 1926 onwards had the entire action mounted on top of the strings, a clever and very narrow chest being fitted beneath the spool-box.

I described the installation as *almost* always on top of the keyboard because after the 1930s Depression many things changed. On July 31st 1932 it was announced that Aeolian and its arch rival American Piano Company were about to merge into a new corporation to be known as Aeolian American. This was to have far-reaching consequences for both companies and, as we shall see, both reproducing systems.

After the merger, there was a period of retrenchment while the market settled itself to a new level following the Wall Street Crash and depression years, and then, in the spring of 1934, design work on a completely revised reproducing system began. Although there is no published evidence to support this, my interpretation of the events that followed the merger is that further development of the Ampico action was abandoned. For some years existing action parts were built into pianos such as the late 1930s Baby Ampico.

However, all new design work was channelled into the Duo-Art. This policy change may have been in recognition of the fact that the Duo-Art system had greater potential as a faithful musical interpreter than the Ampico.

To reproducing piano fanatics this will appear as a red rag to a bull, yet from the musical standpoint, there is no question in my mind that of the two the Duo-Art system possessed greater potential. It remains a moot point whether that potential was adequately exploited.

The late Harvey Roehl was a long-standing collector of reproducing pianos. Furthermore he was a good amateur pianist and musician so I believe we should hear his comments on this horny subject, despite the fact that they were quite the opposite of my own.

> My opinion is that all [makes of reproducing piano] are capable of doing a magnificent job of reproducing human artistry, and I have no preference, one over the other.
>
> The difference comes in the coding of the rolls. About three out of ten Welte rolls are coded sufficiently well to give good pianistic renditions of the artist; perhaps seven out of ten Duo-Arts, and maybe nine-and-a-half out of ten Ampicos.

Pedal-only Duo-Art pianos were always referred to by long-standing, experienced player-men and tuners as 'half Duo-Arts' because there is only one set of expression accordions and these are used to regulate the accompaniment power. In my opinion these are little more than sophisticated expression pianos rather than reproducers. As in the full Duo-Art, the effect relies on the Themodist to create expression, in this instance to a greater extent. The problem of restricted pedal-powered suction remains a limitation: an example that I owned and restored some years ago proved that it was extremely difficult to achieve a roll-performance approaching the fidelity of a full Duo-Art. The theme power is dependent on the skill and foot-power of the operator.

While these instruments are simpler and cheaper in construction they remain a poor alternative to the full Duo-Art, especially the Pedal-Electric. Fortunately, perhaps, they are few and far between – although that fact alone makes them curiously desirable!

During the 1920's Aeolian seems to have made a very small number of Duo-Art push-ups – a sort of Aeolian *vorsetzer*. None appears to have officially entered the company's product catalogue and, in fact, there are no records of such an instrument in the Aeolian archives. However, at least two examples are known, one being in the collection of the late Akio Morita, founder of the Sony Corporation. These sophisticated instruments must have been hand-built at enormous cost. In the past forty or so years, two other Duo-Art cabinet players have been designed and built by enterprising enthusiasts, the best-known being that of Gordon Iles for Gerald Stonehill in London which has an entirely original expression system to play original music rolls. More on this in a moment.

As with the Ampico, Aeolian went in for custom-styled casework. At one time there seemed so many different cabinet styles that we are left thinking that choice and decision were probably the hardest part of the purchasing process. Besides an extensive range of off-the-shelf designs, the company matched its rival when it came to unique design and manufacturing capability, both as regards carving and exotic painting. Like Ampico, these customised specials were very costly and amounted to a considerable proportion of company turnover and profit. No accurate estimates survive, however.

Duo-Art installations, both upright and grand, were almost always above the keyboard with the spoolbox positioned behind the key fall. In the grand, this necessitated connecting

I suspect, but cannot now confirm, that here Harvey may have been considering lighter, perhaps even popular music-rolls for without doubt Ampico excelled at this genre. Much as I respected Harvey and still respect his beliefs, I can only think that perhaps he never heard enough well-adjusted 'red' Welte pianos playing good rolls.

By the late summer of 1935 Aeolian American Corporation announced its fully-revamped Duo-Art system. Different in almost all respects from the earlier system, this was contained in an Ampico Model B type under-keyboard drawer and in the player action much use was made of metal components. Most noticeable, though, was the substitution of fan-shaped expression bellows in place of the parallel-action accordion-type expression bellows of old. Shaped like the feeders of a mediaeval pipe-organ, these marked an acceptance of that which organ-builders had known for centuries, namely that fan-shaped bellows were more efficient than see-saw or parallel feeders or reservoirs. This is because there is considerably less inertia in moving such a bellows because of the 'positive fulcrum' effect.

The revised Duo-Art came to the market far too late. Most of the trade journals took no notice of it, stores shunned it, consumers turned their back on it. It was swansong and failure rolled into one. Like so many inventions the path to perfection was cut short by the obsolescence of the very concept. The perfect mangle was pipped to the post by the arrival of the first washing machine and spin-dryer!

One other diversion remains to be described while we are looking at the Duo-Art. The Aeolian Company also made reproducing pipe organs. These were unusual hybrid instruments in their own rite for they were designed in built along unconventional lines. Voiced along the contemporary lines of American church and chamber organs, Aeolian organs were not rich in diapason tone and the greater majority of the pipework was of metal. Many of the reed stops that organ-builder's created were normally labial pipes (pipes with normal mouths and lip forms) voiced to impersonate soft woodwind effects, or given beating reeds that spoke under pressure into chambers of varying shapes that acted as resonators. Aeolian found it could produce a fair replication of these voices by using ordinary metal pipes and placing a free-reed (in simple terms a harmonium-type reed) in the foot so that the pipe became a resonator and the normal voicing of the pipe-mouth was redundant.

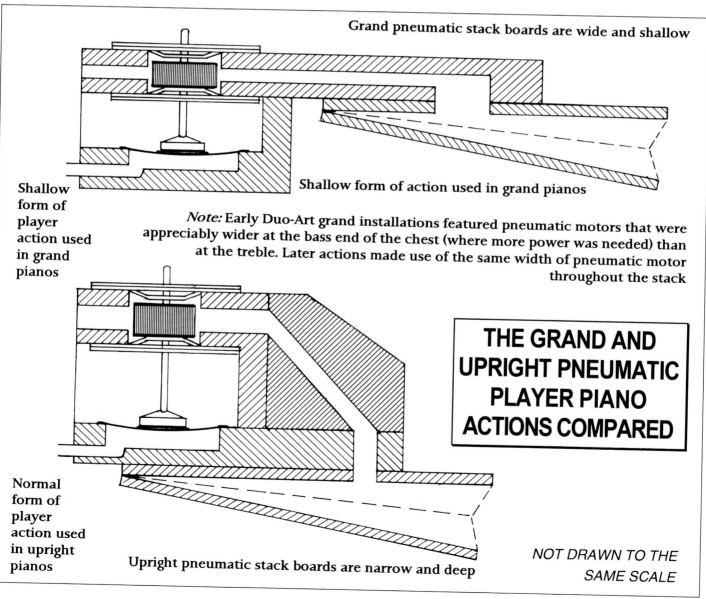

Grand pneumatic stack boards are wide and shallow

Shallow form of player action used in grand pianos

Shallow form of action used in grand pianos

Note: Early Duo-Art grand installations featured pneumatic motors that were appreciably wider at the bass end of the chest (where more power was needed) than at the treble. Later actions made use of the same width of pneumatic motor throughout the stack

Normal form of player action used in upright pianos

Upright pneumatic stack boards are narrow and deep

THE GRAND AND UPRIGHT PNEUMATIC PLAYER PIANO ACTIONS COMPARED

NOT DRAWN TO THE SAME SCALE

While traditional organ experts thought this pretty dreadful, the effect, one has to admit, was not just good but more than adequate for the domestic or residence pipe organ market. Aeolian's pipe organs were both extremely expensive and very popular with the *nouveau riche* of rapidly-developing America. The reproducing pipe organ gave forth a human-like interpretation of an actual recorded performance via a special music-roll that not just performed the musical notes but controlled the operation of the stops or organ voices, and what Aeolian grandly termed 'shades' but the rest of the world understood as swell-shutters.

Early in 1927, Aeolian pulled off something of a coup in the American residence-organ market[2] when it devised a detached player console for the Duo-Art Pipe-Organ. This was a separate cabinet that housed the roll-playing mechanism and its controls as well as the complicated system of electrical relays and switches needed to control the actual organ. Called the Concertola this could be mounted at some distance from the actual organ to produce the ultimate "Aaah!" factor from guests and unsuspecting visitors.

The first reproducing piano to be made looked very little like a piano of any kind. In fact it had no keyboard so could not be played other than by music-roll. The product of an age when ostentatious presentations were anathema, hiding the piano was an earlier form of the practice of the 1960s of hiding the TV set in a desk or cupboard. This model of the keyless Welte-Mignon, in panelled cabinet, was made in 1908 could double as a sideboard. Within is a top-quality Feurich piano and the piece was sold in Paris by Steinway.

In the summer of 1928, the Concertola was being promoted for the Duo-Art piano as well as the pipe-organ. Naturally a different application of the same idea, the piano-playing Concertola was connected to the Duo-Art piano by an electric cable and in many ways reminded one of the old Tel-Electric system of seventeen years earlier. There were three models of the Concertola, all considered today to be extremely rare. The first was capable of playing one roll. The second contained a multiple roll-changer of the style developed by Hupfeld and Welte for their instruments early in the 20th century. This could take up to ten standard Duo-Art rolls and play them sequentially. The third type would also play the longer Duo-Art rolls (Aeolian's answer to Ampico's 'jumbo' Model B rolls) that would play for between twenty and thirty minutes.

The Concertola was a cunning and well-engineered contraption comprising a Ferris-wheel-like autochanger that carried the music rolls and could play them one after the other. It worked in the same way as Hupfeld's system for orchestrions. Welte pipe organs had a similar system but compared to Duo-Art was something of a Heath Robinson device that employed an endless-chain roll-changing system.

In all cases, the control of the Concertola was again remote from a small rectangular box that could be placed on a convenient table and connected to the Concertola with its own cable. This box contained the controls for operating the Concertola and, in the case of the multi-roll-changer types, could be used to sequence or repeat any of the rolls in a customer-specified order.

This device was a 'last fling' for Aeolian as the 1929 Wall Street Crash heralded the three-year Depression within which Aeolian and Ampico were to merge. Because these separate cabinets were independent of the pianos that they controlled, they were readily lost or discarded and of the two or three hundred that are thought to have been made and sold, fewer than a score are known today.

Earlier I mentioned the work of Gordon Iles in Britain. First we have to go right back to the early days when the reproducing piano was merely a twinkle in its inventors' eyes. This means taking a fresh look at the principle of note-theming that ended up as the Themodist for, despite what Skinner claimed in his Patent, the reproducing piano was to have one short-coming.

Themodist or not, it was verging on the impossible to 'theme' or accent any note that was played with an instant group such as a chord or very rapid arpeggio. Pain had attempted it, somewhat arbitrarily, back in the early years of the 20th century, and Kastner had gone a long way towards this with the hugely over-engineered Kastonome. However both these systems had the disadvantage that they were not 'passive' systems (in other words select on and forget), but were instead fully interactive. In the intervening years since their introduction, player actions and music had together come along considerably. And now, with the availability of the Aeolian-created theming action pattern rapidly becoming adopted world-wide, whatever new system created had to be fully compatible with normal Themodist and Duo-Art rolls.

So important was this challenge that without doubt the first maker to succeed in this quest would reap a rich reward in the market. There were several other systems that came close to the idea. The most interesting of these, yet equally the most impractical if only on the grounds of economy, was that patented in London as early as 1909 by Arthur Ronald Trist of the Trist Piano Player Company.

Trist had begun in business with a push-up player and an under-capitalised company (Trist Piano Player Co) which quickly was forced into liquidation. He immediately set up a new firm and spent much time and money attempting to perfect what would have been an isolated theme system. It is unlikely that he ever actually produced any pianos with his invention: as with many inventors up and down the years, he seems to have been a perpetual improver rather than the designer of a product that could be manufactured for sale.

He did profess the conviction that neither pneumatics nor electricity offered sufficient advantage on their own, but by employing a combination of the two, then isolated theming was attainable. Between 1909 and 1912 he took out Patents for at least five electro-pneumatic devices – and these were developed from an even earlier Trist patent of 1906. The basis of his system lay in a three-ply laminated music roll made of thin metal sandwiched between paper. Note-theming was achieved in the accepted pneumatic way by marginal perforations which passed right through the roll. However, this was only part of the process for accenting: note *sensing* was achieved by electric tracker brushes and the music rolls contained 'partial' perforations which only exposed the metal foil, while the full perforations operated the pneumatic chest.

One major advantage of the Trist system (which no doubt would have been of a certain attraction) was that it was possible to control up to three instruments at once from one spool box and music roll. These did not even have to be pianos and might be any keyboard instrument, even a reed or pipe organ. But it was a complex piece of equipment that was called upon to sense notes as well as determine the notes. It also required an electricity supply (which, as we have seen, was not always an easy thing to find at that period) as well as somebody to pedal the pneumatic action. The high cost of making a saleable player on this system more or less killed it off. Trist seems to have abandoned both player pianos and the music industry after this and went on to perfect a three-colour printing process.

It was at this point that Gordon Iles came into the picture. And he was to succeed where others had failed, only to be beaten by the financial collapse of Aeolian in London. Iles was born in 1908, he studied music at Cambridge under Dr Cyril Bradley Rootham (born 1865; died 1938), where he had charge of the University's Duo-Art, a Weber Model 12 pedal-electric grand. Rootham, a composer in his own right, used the instrument more as an ordinary piano than as a reproducer and, although he had contributed to the Aeolian 'World's Music' series, he did not have an especially good opinion of it and was never slow to point out the occasional lack of what later became termed *isolated simultaneous theme* or IST for short. He conceded that it was extremely good in the case of certain recordings, but not all.

Iles himself was a pianist of above average ability and he was also aware of the Duo-Art's shortcomings. Fortunately he had the time to study the problem in some depth. He also was in a doubly fortunate position through a happy coincidence. His father, John Henry Iles, had at one time been a journalist and became president of the London Press Club. Britain being a nation where even otherwise intelligent people regard their sport with almost Divine reverence, his prowess as a one-time County cricketer was remembered by many, in particular that he had played for Gloucestershire with the legendary W G Grace. This achievement brought him to the notice of the managing director of Aeolian in London, G F Reed, and as a result they became not only firm friends but Iles Senior became public relations and advertising adviser to Reed.

As part of the job he was expected to know the Aeolian product inside out and as a consequence the Iles home had just about every model of the Pianola from the 65-note cabinet push-up to the most sophisticated electric Duo-Art grand. Gordon, with or without his father's knowledge or approval, made it his business to strip all of them down to their smallest part so that he soon became thoroughly acquainted with the art and practice of pneumatic action.

Welte-Mignon keyboardless pianos came in several case styles. This one, a restrained *jugendstil* approach with strong hints of the Romano-Greco, is one of the more common forms of this highly collectable reproducing piano.

Giving a man like Iles the raw materials for technical and artistic development was akin to the child in the chocolate-factory adage. Very soon he had succeeded in creating a prototype Duo-Art action of his own that was considered to be 'remarkably fine'. This was in 1926. Both Iles Senior and Reed were much impressed and the suggestion was made from his father that Gordon should tackle the problem of IST. It should be emphasised that all that followed was an entirely British development that was quite separate from the American parent company Aeolian. By this time, the UK division had long been operating as a separate organisation in any case.

Presented with this challenge, Iles agreed to solve it – and was immediately sent a special top-line Weber Duo-Art that he installed in his workshop at his home. Here research and experiment in IST began in real earnest and Aeolian's chief technical superintendent at Hayes in Middlesex, Harry W Palmer, was instructed to manufacture all the prototype components that Gordon Iles designed and send them without delay to the Iles home at Broadstairs in Kent.

The whole operation was to be conducted in the greatest possible secrecy since the company policy was that the public should be made to believe that the Duo-Art with its Themodist constituted the ultimate in perfection and left nothing further to desire. Any suggestion of IST would undermine this propaganda and affect sales of the existing instruments.

After working for less than two years, Iles announced he had completed his IST Duo-Art. Those who heard the IST in operation immediately became aware of the very definite improvement in reproduction that it gave.

Gordon Iles' achievement could not have come at a worse moment for the Hayes-based company for it coincided with the height of the development work on creating 'The World's Music', a special educational music-roll label. Aeolian was spending vast sums of money on special-purpose equipment to manufacture the decidedly non-standard rolls, one feature of which was the long text-printed leader to each roll.

It was also a watershed time for Aeolian in Britain for it had also redesigned the basic piano-playing valve stack and been granted a Patent (number 323,005 dated September 17th 1928) in the names of C F Cook and H W Palmer for an action that featured hingeless, square striking pneumatics as distinct from the usual wedge-shaped 'motors'.[3]

Organising a revolution is all very well, but launching three wholly-new approaches at the same time was both very costly and extremely risky. As it turned out, it was suicidal for just one of these new developments – the educational music-roll launch – proved sufficient to force the company into penury. The Wall Street Crash and the Great Depression administered the *coup de grace* and the financial collapse of the company was a matter of course. IST was abandoned.

The Aeolian-Iles IST system centred on the use of a special twin valve chest[4] employed in conjunction with a tracker bar having a double row of holes, the two rows being very close together. The top row included Themodist ports but were fixed with a minimum (extremely soft) level of accompaniment. The lower row of ducts were accompaniment only and were under the influence of the usual variable Duo-Art level as set by the music-roll accompaniment perforations.[5] This bottom row was not provided with Themodist ducts.

The Leipzig manufacturer Hupfeld also developed a reproducing piano which was known as the Hupfeld *DEA*. It was introduced a year after the Welte-Mignon and is said to have been the inspiration behind Emil Welte realising that the market really needed a piano that had a keyboard as well as a reproducing action. The *DEA* was a one of a family of player pianos, one of which was to make the first *Phonoliszt-Violina*, pictured elsewhere in these pages. Using a 106-hole tracker bar, the music rolls were a massive 15.15/16-inches in width and played from bottom to top as seen here in this rather poor photograph from Lithuania.

This special tracker bar was made in an ingenious way. Some of the early pre-Duo-Art tracker bars had comparatively narrow note slots and so two of these were cut lengthwise and the portions with slots joined together to form a single bar in which the two rows of holes were together very little wider than the single row in a standard bar.

In use, if a themed note was provided with a theme perforation, as normally found in a roll, and set back by a fraction of an inch corresponding to the space between the two rows of holes in the double tracker bar, then the themed note or notes arrived at the first row at the same time as the forward-cut accompaniment notes. These, not being provided with Themodist perforations, would either not have sounded at all when they passed the first row or at most would barely have played due to the low level setting of that valve stack.

The result of this was that themed notes could be played simultaneously with accompaniment notes. In this way it was only necessary to arrange rolls to play at a tempo setting of no more than 100 and sometimes even less in order to provide full IST without losing maximum repetition. An extra – and economically important – advantage was that the rolls would also play satisfactorily when used on standard Duo-Art instruments although without, of course, the 1ST effect.

The opposite also applied and ordinary Duo-Art rolls would also play in the normal way on a special IST instrument. The 'stop' slot position between the treble Themodist and soft pedal slots in the tracker bar was used, in the case of an IST piano, to bring the mechanism into operation, otherwise the lower row of holes only functioned. One or two patents were taken out but were allowed to lapse when the Aeolian Company folded.

Following the contraction of the Aeolian Company after the Great Depression, IST was of no further interest to what was left of the business. It was only built into one piano as a commercial venture and this was undertaken entirely as a private venture. Iles Senior had been responsible for the building of the Dreamland Super Cinema at Margate in about 1936 and Gordon Iles co-operated with the John Compton Organ Company in designing the organ. Part of the installation was an IST Duo-Art on the stage which could also be played with expressive touch from the organ console. This unique piano and installation was destroyed by enemy action during the war.

Aeolian had earlier experimented with another method of achieving IST which used a standard tracker bar but had the disadvantage that it required the use of special rolls which could not be used on standard instruments. In this system, each slot in the tracker bar had three functions which, as before, were brought into action through a perforation aligning with the 'stop' position. These three functions for each note-playing hole were: [1] to sound a note; [2] to cancel the playing power of the adjacent tracker note-playing hole; [3] to theme exclusively the note corresponding to the slot on the left.

In this design the system made the logical, but not exclusive, assumption that in normal music intervals of a minor second (two piano keys side by side played at the same instant) are seldom encountered. Accordingly it used the normal tracker hole next to the one being played for theming by first signalling a cancel to its normal playing function, and then causing it to react to the opening of the note channel to its left. Were the minor second actually to occur, then the theming of one of the notes would be impossible by this method, although imaginative Themodist cutting could no doubt be used to some advantage.

Hupfeld's *DEA* appeared in 1905 and, like the Welte, was a superbly-built and incorporated all-metal tubing. The tracker bar displays the characteristic 'trademark' feature of this reproducing action – three additional expression holes forming a second row of openings in the centre. The *DEA* provided six levels or intensities of expression for each half of the keyboard.

In use, if a note to be themed had a single pip perforation next to it on the left, it would be themed without the production of what might appear to result as a discord. As you might expect, the operation of this IST system was achieved in conjunction with a special twin valve chest of similar design to that employed in the Iles twin-bar system described above. To make it work, though, it needed the addition of a rather complex bank of cancel membranes.

Although this system proved completely reliable, it had obvious limitations and was restricted for its full effect to using special rolls which could not be used on any other playing mechanism.

It is believed that one example of an experimental type of Aeolian IST player survives. Built as a *vorsetzer* and formerly in the private collection of the late Akio Morita of the Sony Corporation in Japan, this plays special rolls that are wider than usual and which incorporate a number of non-standard features. The tracker bar, for example, has two special theming holes above the blocks of four expression-controlling holes at each end. There are also several additional tracker-bar ports outside these.

And thus ended the quest for pneumatically-themed notes. Like so many inventions, it reached perfection at a time when nobody wanted it. The demand is there again today, only now the answer is wholly electronic.

Gordon Iles was a man of immense talent and his work in player-piano pneumatics was to have immense importance during the war years when he built on the experience gained in America where the Link Piano Company had devised a synthetic flying trainer – the Link Trainer – using player-piano technology. Iles developed the so-called Silloth Trainer for training bomber pilots. This was built like a modern flying simulator and could replicate the flying aspects of an actual aircraft type.[6] In the years that followed the ending of the 1939-45 war, he established the Artona Music Roll Company at Ramsgate and at the same time built the remarkable Duo-Art Robot, a unique *vorsetzer* mentioned earlier that was the brainchild of Gerald Stonehill.

Hupfeld's most successful reproducing pianos were based on the *Phonola* range of players that followed the *DEA*. Here is a Blüthner *Solophonola* fitted with *Tri-Phonola* reproducing action. This early example is actually a pedal-operated instrument as distinct from the more usual electric power-source. The tracker bar had 98 openings to accommodate the 11.1/4-inch wide rolls which offered full-scale 88-note coverage, the remaining holes being used for expression.

So far in this Chapter, the evolution of the reproducing piano from the normal player-piano by way of the expression piano and the system of note-accenting has accepted without question the fidelity of the reproducing system. This is based wholly on the premise that a reproducing piano-roll which is signed by a renowned pianist will enable the owner of a reproducing piano to hear an 'exact' live replication of that renowned pianist's piano-playing on his own instrument. It is now time to investigate and re-evaluate these claims.

First, though, I must point out that the term 'reproducing piano', now used as a generic term for this form of player-piano, was actually invented by Aeolian for its Duo-Art. Ampico called theirs a 're-enacting piano' while the Welte-Mignon Corporation of New York chose 'reperforming piano'. It was a simple process of confusing the customer and did nobody much good.

All the makers of reproducing pianos made claims for their instruments which were sometimes extravagant,[7] while standards of advertising were often downright objectionable, particularly in America, where Ampico engaged in a demeaning public denigration of its rival, the Duo-Art. How the two companies fared when the exigencies of commercial interest and the depression brought the two systems under one and the same roof has never been related.

The *Tri-Phonola* action took up every inch of available space in the area above the keyboard as this view shows. The roll-drive motor lies flat to the lower right of the spoolbox with the horizontal inverted see-saw motors for the automatic roll-tracking above. *Phonola* hand-controls comprising a healthy mixture of push-keys and levers were always rather complicated, although they were simplified in later models by having a useful palm-operated sustaining pedal lever to replace the finger key seen far right of the control fallboard here. The only finger to work the 'loud' pedal on this piano was the little one!

But one of the attributes that all the makers made a great feature of was the ability to perform absolutely faithfully in the manner of the original roll – in other words to play exactly the way the original artist played. Thanks to skilful and masterly editing by persons whose knowledge of both music and the pneumatics of their piano systems was second to none, this was a goal more often than not achieved. Indeed, the recording artist was encouraged to sign the master roll to say that it had his approval: he was unlikely to sign out a roll that did not do justice to his playing.[8]

This was in general satisfactory with the proviso that certain types of music were difficult if not impossible to reproduce pneumatically. Towards the end of the era, for example, there were some Ampico rolls that must be rated as interpretational failures not just on the basis of their having been badly played but because the system could not cope with the demands made upon it.

From material that has come to light over the years it is possible to have a better idea as to how the process of 'recording' was undertaken both in general and by specific makers. In simple terms, the pianist was hired to give a piano performance that was converted into a master roll, whereupon the recording pianist was asked to listen to a performance from that master roll and then to sign it as a faithful interpretation of his playing.

This procedure seems always to have been applied and always to have worked. What has never really been looked at was what happened to the master roll between its being 'cut' and the playback for artistic approval. We now know that the answer was 'quite a lot' and, in some instances, 'a very great deal'.

In all the pictures of the Welte recording studio – and Welte made a fortunate practice of photographing every performing artist with the senior Welte team – there is a curious tall cabinet near to the piano. Looking not unlike an ancient telephone switchboard, it has two large rotating knobs on the front. All through the performance, an engineer sat at this device watching the pianist closely and manipulating the knobs.

In New York, Ampico made two 'recordings', one indicating the movements of the keyboard and the other those of the pedals. At one point they also made a phonograph recording at the same time as the master roll, the reason being that there was a tendency with some roll-editors to impose more of their own characteristics onto the performance than was acceptable and the sound recording was a reminder as to how it should sound.

It is clear that often-extensive work went on between the 'cut' and the playback. Highly skilled editors sought out and corrected wrong notes: one performance by a renowned concert artist amassed a total of 360 incorrect notes while it used to be said that the audience at a concert by Cortot would travel miles to hear his wrong notes!

The matter of performance authenticity has been argued over for years. Half of the problem is that the makers never said anything about editing but let it be thought that the artist

had sat at the recording piano, made a master roll – and then that roll had been copied for sale to the public. The inference was thus not just how good the technique was, but how good the piano and its system was.

The first reproducing piano-player to be put into production was the Welte-Mignon *Vorsetzer* which entered the market around 1904. It became an immediate sensation with its ability to recreate an artists' performance on any piano. It played the wide red-paper music rolls and thus is generally known to collectors as the 'red' Welte player. While others made reproducing pianos, few had the quality of Welte which built on its extensive organ-manufacturing craftsmanship. The *Vorsetzer* style of 'red' Welte remained in production well into the 1920s by which time the era of the ordinary 'push-up' piano-player had long passed. Designed by Emil Welte and Karl Bokisch, the heart of the Welte reproducing action was the ability to employ variable suction pressures to vary piano expression. Curiously the Welte firm was able to claim the concept as a Patent as a result of which every other maker of reproducing piano actions had to pay a royalty: both Aeolian and Ampico paid a royalty of $2.50 on every instrument they made. In this picture the *Vorsetzer* is positioned for playing a normal grand piano.

Musicians and collectors have argued over this horny problem for many years without getting anywhere really. To me, the authority of the recording and the system is whether the artist really did approve of it. Since I can find no instance of an artist denouncing a roll, then the assumption has to be that the play-back roll was at least almost as good as the original performance. I suggest that it doesn't really matter how this result was achieved so long as it was achieved. If it took sixteen people and a thousand cups of coffee doesn't enter into it.

What is quite clear is that some rolls required a great deal of editing to achieve that goal and also that many top artists were not all that accurate as pianists! Perhaps, in the fidelity of the hand-played recording artist, they ought to have left a few wrong notes in – except that as we all know even by the second time of hearing the nerves cannot stand it! As with modern recording techniques, everything wrong or extraneous had to be edited out.[9]

And so the manufacturers blatantly sought their endorsements from those that would provide. I would not suggest that 'inducements to provide' were offered but you can make up your own mind regarding items such as that widely used in Welte's advertisements. This quotes Professor Arthur Nikisch who apparently said:

> In my opinion the Welte Mignon reproducing apparatus is an epoch-making invention. The artist's performance recorded in the apparatus is right in every respect, not only concerning the pure technical virtuosity but also the musical, poetical element. It is so frankly natural that one really thinks the artist is there in person and that one hears him play. The value of this invention is not only in the teaching influence on the one learning but also in a quite marvellous way for those who wish to sit down comfortably to an hour of artistically enjoyment and only wish to listen to an accomplished artist.

Many years ago I wrote that thanks to the reproducing piano it was possible today to gain some fair impression of how a pianist of the past used to play. It also enabled us today to hear what was considered (at the time the particular roll was made) to be an acceptable interpretation of a piece of music. A large number of the pianists that recorded on piano roll never made gramophone records and those that did were confronted by the technical limitations of the acoustic recording studio.[10]

Now, though, should I reconsider those sentiments? I think not for in the final analysis if the original pianist approved the performance, then that should be sufficient guarantee for all time. The precise path to that objective is really of no concern to us, merely that the objective was actually reached.

Where our fidelity concept breaks down, though, is outside and beyond the recording on the music roll and lies fairly and squarely in our own piano! Every reproducing piano cannot but be set up in a slightly different way and it is this that can alter our playback of a seventy or eighty-year-old recording. And this is something for which, no matter how hard we try and with the finest attention to detail in the world, we cannot be entirely certain. This, then, is the weakness in the concept of the reproducing piano.

---

1. To get an idea of both the subtlety and suitability of this fine word, be reminded of the construction using the irregular intransitive verb *dürfen* 'to permit' or 'allow' as in *darf ich Ihnen etwas vorsetzen?* (May I offer you anything?)

2. There were other makers of similar instruments, among them Estey (also better known as a reed-organ builder) and Skinner.

3. The use of parallel striking pneumatics had been included in a British Patent number 4804 dated February 26th 1909 in the name of C Katz and M M Kastner.

4. Aeolian had used the twin chest as the basis of a rudimentary, non-automatic theming system as early as 1916 when, on November 28th of that year, it was granted British Patent number 111,349 for variable-tension striking pneumatics under the control of a tune sheet or from special buttons provided for the purpose in the key-slip.

5. The double-row tracker bar used in conjunction with two valve chests, one at a high vacuum tension and the other at low, the whole combined with accenting ducts, had been the subject of British Patent number 7698 dated March 26th 1914, in the name of D Kennedy.

6. See the article 'How the Duo-Art Won the War', in *The Music Box,* 1975, Volume 7, *pp.*131-133.

7. Although one should bear in mind the large number of testimonials from, apparently, top-quality pianists back in the days of the piano player who claimed that the instrument gave them the satisfaction which only a live player could hitherto provide. Testimonials, one is inclined to think, were bought at a high price.

8. Clarence B Hickman, interviewed in the book *The Ampico* (Robert J Howe) paints a slightly different view although his comment, made by a then old man forty or fifty years or so after the event, might be taken *cum grano salis*: '[the master roll] was… put on the piano… and [the editors] would make such corrections as they thought it needed. Then when they had it in the form that they thought was good, they would invite the artist to come and listen to it. Well, he would make changes, too, and they just sat there with a sticker [*sic*] tape the, plugged up the holes and punched them according to the way he said it should be. And what usually happened was, that the poor artist got sick and tired of having to wait and make all these corrections, and so finally he'd just approve it even though it wasn't like his own recording.'

9. An insight into the editing process is to be found in an interview with Clarence B Hickman contained in *The Ampico* by Richard J Howe (pp.61 *et seq*). It has to be said that this book dispenses amazing flashes of historical information, yet neither the interviewer nor the editor demonstrated either the wisdom or insight to follow up the many tantalising leads that it presents. Remember it was the philosopher Plato (*c.*427-347*BC*) who asserted that 'you have to follow the conversation whithersoever it may flit.'

10. An insight into just why player-piano rolls and, later, reproducing rolls may be able to give us a better idea of musical interpretations of these early days than the surviving phonograph and gramophone recordings can be deduced from the following extract from a letter which Busoni wrote to his wife in November 1919:

> "My suffering over the toil of making gramophone records came to an end yesterday, after playing for 3½ hours! I feel rather better today, but it is over. Since the first day, I have been as depressed as if I were expecting to have an operation. To do it is stupid and a strain. Here is an example of what happens. They want the Faust Waltz (which lasts a good ten minutes) *but it was only to take four minutes!* That meant quickly cutting, patching and improvising, so that there should still be some sense in it; watching the pedal (because it sounds bad); thinking of certain notes which had to be stronger or weaker in order to please this devilish machine; not letting oneself go for fear of inaccuracies and being conscious the whole time that every note was going to be there for eternity; how can there be any question of inspiration, freedom, swing or poetry? Enough that yesterday for nine pieces of 4 minutes each (half an hour in all) I worked for three and a half hours! Two of the pieces I played four or five times. Having to think so quickly at the same time was a severe effort. In the end, I felt the effects in my arms; after that, I had to sit for a photograph, and sign the discs. — At last it was finished!"

In a later letter, just before he gave his last public concert in 1922 at the age of fifty-six, he wrote from his London hotel to his English manager:

> "The conditions are most unfavourable. The room, the piano, the chair not inviting. I have to start like a racehorse and to end before four minutes have elapsed. I have to manage the touch and the pedal differently from how I do it usually."
>
> "What, in heavens name! can be the result of it? Not my own playing, take it for granted!"

Busoni was admittedly an unconventional performer whose personality and creative imagination frequently coloured his interpretations so much that, as Claudio Arrau once said, 'very often the composer was almost totally lost'. I cannot comment on that but nevertheless his words on the techniques and demands of the recording studio remain valid and forcibly demonstrate the enormous value of the reproducing piano and its music and, to a lesser extent, the ordinary player piano.

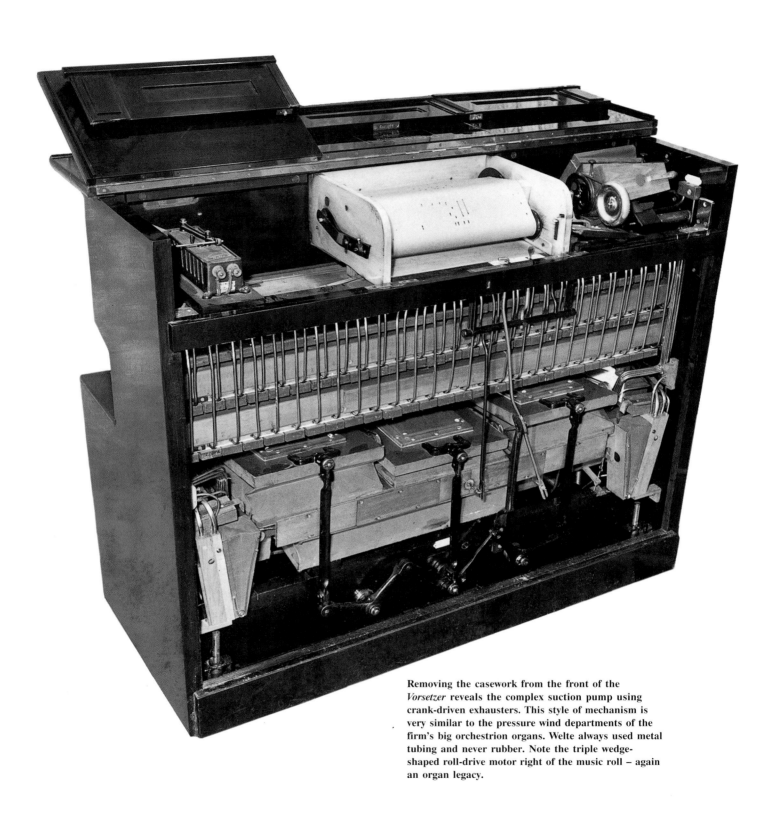

Removing the casework from the front of the *Vorsetzer* reveals the complex suction pump using crank-driven exhausters. This style of mechanism is very similar to the pressure wind departments of the firm's big orchestrion organs. Welte always used metal tubing and never rubber. Note the triple wedge-shaped roll-drive motor right of the music roll – again an organ legacy.

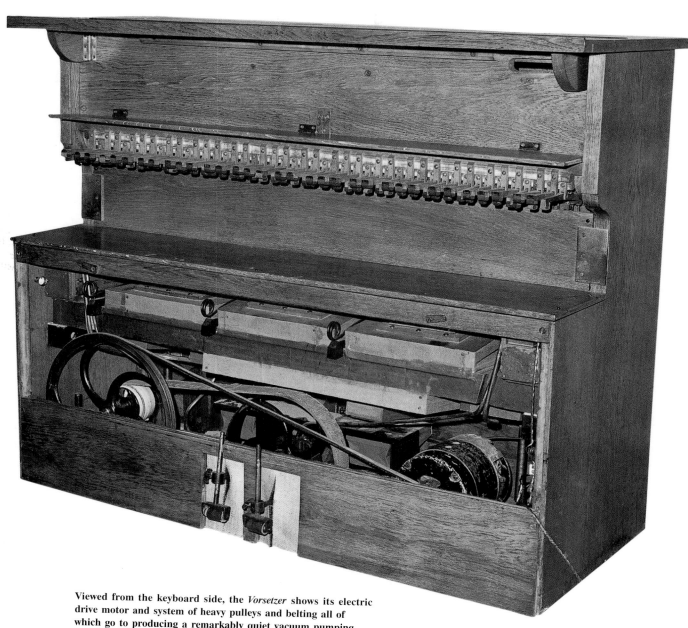

Viewed from the keyboard side, the *Vorsetzer* shows its electric drive motor and system of heavy pulleys and belting all of which go to producing a remarkably quiet vacuum pumping system. The keyboard fingers can also be seen: each is adjustable to take up lost motion.

Welte offered the *Vorsetzer* in a variety of case styles to suit the needs of various markets. Here is a particularly elegant one in use playing an American Chickering grand.

The Welte-Mignon with its special rolls outlived the switch to the narrower rolls and remained in vogue well into the 1920s. Here is a 1922 installation in a Steinway. This view clearly shows the unusual Welte roll-drive motor and, immediately in front of it, the heavy flywheel that was found necessary to give smooth running at all speeds.

The 'red' Welte action was built into a number of quality pianos of the time. Here is an early installation in a Steinway grand pictured in the magnificent surroundings of the now-defunct West Cornwall Museum of Mechanical Music near Penzance.

A rare style of Steinway-Welte was the so-called Vertical Grand – *Vertigrand* for short. Standing well over six feet high, this veteran dates from about 1910. The piano fallboard bears the legend 'New York and Hamburg' which confirms it as a German-made model.

A view into the back of the Steinway-Welte *Vertigrand* explains why the piano is so tall – the entire pump work is placed in top of the normal piano. Looking a little like something from a Victorian factory, the exhausters are driven through speed-reducing pulleys, belting and cranks by the electric motor, right. Just right of the central vertical case-panel board can be seen the main eccentric to which connecting rods are pivoted to work the two cast iron crank levers that actually do the work.

In the United States, development of the Welte-Mignon (Licensee) action allowed a much wider market to the company. Here is an installation in a grand piano made by J Bauer & Company of Chicago. The under-keyboard pull-out drawer was an American invention most likely first used by Ampico.

Looking into the drawer of the Welte-Mignon (Licensee) the simplicity of the controls leads some collectors to confuse this action with that of the similar-looking Ampico Model A.

Before the invention of Aeolian's rotary pump in its familiar square box, British-built Duo-Art reproducing pianos featured what some collectors call 'steam-boat pumps'. Like the Welte, Aeolian used three exhausters driven by a multiple belt-and-pulley system from an electric motor. To the left (bass) end of the keyboard next to the exhausters can be seen the expression accordion pneumatics. A characteristic of Hayes-built Duo-Art actions is the large round 'Temponamic' control used to wind up full power during playing. It also doubles as a speed control, sliding from side to side.

The Duo-Art reproducing piano came in a style that was only known in Britain – the pedal-electric model. Here is a Steinway that can be played either entirely automatically by electric pump, or pedalled like an ordinary player-piano. Here the piano is set up for foot-playing. The foot pedals fold up into a box that also mounts the normal piano pedals.

An American Steinway Duo-Art shows the very different hand controls that were used as compared to those seen in the earlier English Duo-Art pictures. The switch farthest right is for the motor.

An operator's view of a British Duo-Art installation in a Steinway grand showing the dual-purpose Temponamic knob right of lower centre. This regulates tempo as well as hand-controlling/overriding the playing intensity. The tempo indicator in the spoolbox has a pointer that is seen here swung to the right-hand side out of the way.

One of the many case styles offered to the American market was this Louis XVI design in walnut.

Another case style, also described as Louis XVI, was this offered in walnut or mahogany. These opulent cases were expensive and it is uncertain how many were actually sold.

For the man who wanted Colonial best in his piano-case, then he need look no further than Aeolian's Design No.3030 described as 'early Sheraton'. This costly casework was of: 'finely figured East Indian satinwood with pale mahogany banding and solids'. Harewood was used for the groundwork of the music-desk and the legs and the decoration was of oak leaves of rosewood 'with acorns in boxwood and pearwood'. The design obviously owed as much to late Adam as early Sheraton.

The Ampico Model A action was installed in many instruments. Invented by Charles Stoddard and others it remained in production well into the 1920s. Here is a Marshall & Wendell piano.

A very light case distinguishes this fine German-made
Grotrian-Steinweg fitted with an Ampico Model A reproducing action. The piano dates from 1927.

A 1931 Marshall & Wendell with Ampico Model B action. In all
these instruments, the drawer could be closed during playing so
that there was no visible indication to the observer. The events
of the Wall Street Crash followed by the world recession that
heralded the 1930s really put paid to further development of the
reproducing piano. As much as anything else, because the
financial crisis came so soon after the Model B Ampico was
introduced, these instruments are far rarer than the earlier
style.

Improvements to the Ampico action lead to the introduction of the
Ampico Model B. As seen here in the drawer mechanism of this William
Knabe piano, it presented a rather neater appearance.

The founder of the great Sony Corporation in Japan was the late Akio Morita. Aside from running his electronics business, Morita was a devotee of the reproducing piano having been exposed to them while living in New York. As a result, his home in Tokyo was rich in both pianos and rolls while through his recording business he experimented in making compact discs of his collection. He acquired and regularly used a unique instrument, seen here – a hand-built Duo-Art 'vorsetzer' of which he was justly very proud.

London player-piano connoisseur Gerald Stonehill in London designed this special Duo-Art 'vorsetzer' some years ago for the purpose of playing his extensive collection of Duo-Art music rolls. Built for him by former Aeolian man, the late Gordon Iles of Ramsgate, the machine has been extensively employed in roll-recording by several record companies. It is pictured here playing gooseberry to a pedal-electric Duo-Art grand.

Chapter 11
The Music Roll, Piano Repertoire and Presentation

Within the section on pneumatic players there has been much talk of music-rolls – the programme for the player-piano in all its developed forms from basic push-up piano-player through to the reproducing piano. While the duties of the music-roll and how it is driven has already been dealt with in the earlier Chapters, the history and development of the roll itself is worth highlighting. The principle of using paper-as-a-valve is as old as the pneumatic player itself but the development of the paper roll, how it is made, used and preserved is such an involved and lengthy topic that I thought it best to devote one specific Chapter to the subject. This means that most that you need to know about the music-roll is in this section. Repairs to music-rolls form an attachment to Chapter 13, while how to handle and use a music roll is to be found in Chapter 15.

To make this Chapter easier to navigate your way through, I have divided it into eight distinct sections. They are:
1. History of the Music Roll
2. Music Roll Scales
3. Music roll paper
4. How music rolls were made
5. The price of music rolls
6. Repertoire, Artists and Reproducing Rolls
7. The availability of Music Rolls – Libraries
8. The types of music rolls

A possible ninth aspect – collecting music rolls – is discussed elsewhere for the simple reason that, unlike the above list of subjects, collecting is rather more esoteric than something to be pigeonholed with an emphasis on practicality.

1. History of the Music Roll

At first glance the notion of a lengthy chapter about spools of paper with holes in doesn't sound much like fun reading. The truth is that it's much more than just that. There's music rolls and music rolls, some good, some bad, but almost all different. And some may actually harm your player-piano. In fact, it is one of those subjects that could easily fill a whole book. I shall merely outline the history and refer the serious meticulist in matters historical to other books.

Briefly, with the coming of the small self-playing reed-organ or organette, the musical programme was cut into strips of thick paper which, when passed over the tracker bar which allowed air to the correct sequence of reeds in order to produce music. The tracker-bar, then, was rather like a mouth-organ and the perforated paper served as a sliding valve. The big advantage over all other systems that had started with the pinned cylinder and progressed through punched cardboard or thin metal, was convenience and, as far as the music was concerned, a massive reduction in bulk. By the time the pneumatic player action for the piano was developed, punched paper music-rolls were fully established.

Actually making the holes in the music roll involved another long series of inventions for systems that were anything but perfect. These began, not unnaturally, with the organette makers. As described in Chapter 4, one proposal suggested that a master tune sheet be made in metal and then used as a template in a sand-blasting plant, the sand perforating the paper where the master left it unprotected. Another was to burn the holes against a gas jet, again using a metal master mask. Both these systems suffered similar disadvantages. First they were time-consuming and fiddly, able to make only one roll at a time. Second they could not to produce a clean edge to the perforations. Sand-blasting produced an irregular, fibrous paper rag while burning generated a charred paper ash residue which, in the case of a suction instrument, would be drawn in to interfere with the valves and bleeds.

Mechanical punching was the only really practical solution but it was not a simple matter to build a machine that would make a perfect, truthful copy from a master roll each time. Eventually the arrival of accurate and rapid hole-punching machinery meant that up to sixteen rolls could be produced at once and the holes were cleanly cut without loose fibres. A whole new industry sprang up designing and building roll-punching machinery and of those built the most versatile and therefore most popular with the roll-manufacturers was the Acme which was fast and precise. At the other end of the scale was the Leabarjan home perforating machine designed for the enthusiast who wanted to experiment cutting his own rolls. Here precision lay totally in the hands of the operator and the home-made rolls could be very good indeed.

The most sophisticated equipment was that used for punching the special rolls for reproducing pianos and these machines were invariably designed, engineered and built by the companies that manufactured the pianos themselves. Hence makers such as Aeolian, Welte and Duo-Art used machines that were individual to their own systems.

Now there are other widths for piano-rolls, in particular the 73-note Hupfeld type but since these instruments are quite rare, I shall not dwell on them specifically. In any case, the competent restorer should be able to tackle anything if he follows the general guidelines in this book. Likewise there are rolls with different compasses that play various numbers of the notes of the piano. And to make life difficult for the restorer, some makers (Hupfeld in particular) would put the expression perforations (soft, sustaining and accenting) in the middle of the roll rather than at the edges.

The Orchestrelle player reed organ plays special 58-rolls that are $10\frac{1}{8}$-inches wide perforated at six holes to the inch. The roll drive system is the same at the 65-note player-piano with a metal spade drive end. The large two-manual Solo-Orchestrelles play rolls that are exactly the same width and style, only they are made of much finer-quality paper and have twice the number of perforated tracks – 116 to be precise. The roll apron or leader is also of glazed and printed linen instead of paper.

Rolls for the Wilcox & White Symphony are punched the same pitch as those for the Orchestrelle but the paper is slightly wider at $10\frac{1}{4}$-inches. A major difference, though, is that the roll travels from bottom to top when laying and if you need to adjust a Symphony roll for playing on the Orchestrelle, then it has to be completely unspoiled, turned over and re-attached to the spool before being rewound – a task best carried out with a hand-operated music-roll rewinding machine that you can make from the parts of an old spool-box, a baseboard and a handle.

There are also special rolls that relate to particular instruments such as some expression pianos and piano orchestrions both German and American. For details of these I commend the works of Reblitz [89, 90] and Bowers [6].

I think it is unnecessary to say that 65-note rolls do not play on 88-note pianos or vice-versa, but if I don't and some idiot tries it I could be cursed for not having told them!

As explained earlier and also in the next section, music rolls settled down to a three-size availability – 58-note Orchestrelle, 65-note and 88-note piano rolls. All were perforated, the majority with round holes, a few with oval holes and fewer still with square holes. But all had holes. Even the early one with slotted perforations could, with application of poetic licence, be described as having holes. Only one maker that I have found ever attempted to replace that standard with a wholly-new one that would have risked destabilising the whole roll-making industry and confusing those already with piano-rolls. This was the German maker William Spaethe who, in 1924, patented a new type of narrow music-roll in which the perforations were described as being 'narrow transverse rectangular slots' arranged at different angles, some horizontal, others pitched at various angles. It was all part of a scheme for an expression piano. Despite the patent, thankfully Herr Spaethe must have seen sense, for no herringbone-punched piano-rolls appear to exist.

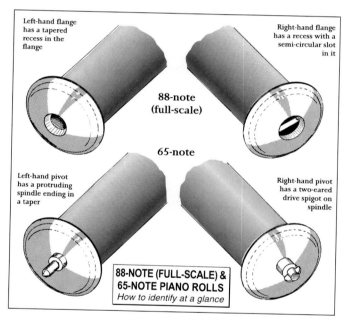

I mentioned just now that the White & Wilcox Symphony music roll travels from bottom to top and this exposes another puzzle for collectors – why? In fact if you compare player actions from the two centers of early player invention you make an interesting discovery, namely that almost all of the German-designed and built instruments played their rolls from bottom to top, while almost all of the American ones played from top to bottom. This is, as you might expect, a generalization for there are exceptions in both groups. But the reasons why are not hard to imagine.

When German engineers first contemplated the pneumatic piano, they tackled the job from a historical experience of mechanical musical instruments that, at that time, went back more than 200 years. Furthermore they were essentially musically-trained inventors.

In the barrel organ and orchestrion, as built by Welte, Imhof and the forerunners of the Hupfeld company, the barrel rotated towards the front or clockwise when viewed from the left side. Ordinary musical notation, however, travels from left to right. The convenience of engineering a lever to be lifted by a pin from behind gave us the universal standard for mechanical organ barrel direction. The pneumatic piano, however, had no precedent. Admittedly there were reed organettes but these were not built by piano-makers.

My belief is that the logical direction was thought to be for the perforations representing the musical notes to pass from bottom to top as a simple transition from the left-to-right staff notation. This was the direction adopted by the original red-rolled Welte and all the Hupfeld instruments starting with the DEA player onwards.

In America, however, the first use of the perforated paper roll began with the organette that was made by reed-organ makers as chronicled so adequately by McTammany [61]. These played their music rolls from left to right. The first player reed organs were developed directly from the organette, Aeolian's 46-note instruments being no more than enlarged organettes. To adapt the roll-playing mechanism for these, it was rotated through 90 degrees in the horizontal plane so that the roll played from the rear to the front.

The development of the player-piano (first via the piano-player) saw this mechanism tilted forwards through 90 degrees in the vertical plane. And that became the accepted style from that point forward driven by the two opposite halves of the industry – the piano-makers and the music-roll makers.

At some point (I estimate it to have been between 1907 and 1910 based on the few dated rolls of that period that I have found), the sheer volume of instruments and music-rolls made to what we might call the American system inspired German makers to change their spool direction. It must have been a move urged upon them by other European territories where American makers had already established a marketing toehold.

By the time of the German volume production of 65 and 88-note piano-rolls, all were on the American system. Welte, though, had a unique product in that no other make of roll but its own would play on its reproducing pianos, so that company retained its original roll direction as did several of the other piano-orchestrion makers that had 'unique' actions.

A large proportion of the cheaper piano-rolls were produced nowhere near a piano or even a pianist, but were drawn out on paper masters by skilled musical technicians who could both read music and work a pencil. These were known as *metronomic* rolls because there were cut to the metronome beats, all notes in a chord starting in a straight line across the paper, and so on. They were boring to listen to. And because the paper was encouraged to travel at a constant speed according to the tempo mark on the roll leader, the result was not really very musical.

Of course, the skilled player could play about with the speed control and vary the tempo of the music, linger longer on a note, speed up through a phrase and so on. This was known as 'putting some expression' into it. Then Aeolian had a bright idea! Why not print a line on the music roll showing recommended variations from the pre-set tempo which the player could follow! And, to make the job easier, fix a nice brass pointer on an extension to the tempo lever so that the player could pit his (or her) wits at following the wavy line on the paper!

And so was born Metrostyle. Hailed as a latter-day miracle advance in technology, the red wavy line probably earned Aeolian a fortune for Metrostyle, patented before 1908, was promoted as a significant feature. Together with a wavy line of dots of a different colour to indicate playing intensity (from double *pianissimo* to double *forte* or very soft to extremely loud), Aeolian made the best rolls. Combined, then, with the note-accenting of the Themodist, their rolls were the best outside Germany.

Naturally other makers soon found ways to copy most of the principles but the Metrostyle remained Aeolian's dubious jewel in the crown – dubious because it was very difficult to get the wavy line printed on the paper roll in exactly the right place, particularly under production conditions. Many were the subsequent attempts at the accurate printing of information on piano-rolls. Even so, the person who concentrated hard enough to follow the Metrostyle markings accurately probably wasn't able to concentrate on the music he was playing.

2. Music Roll Scales

The two most common types of player-piano action are operated using music rolls having paper 11¼ inches wide perforated for either 65 notes at six holes per inch, or 88 notes (so-called 'full-scale') at nine holes per inch. It is important to observe that the width of the paper in both rolls is the same.

The compass of the full-scale 88-note player piano was from Contra-A to c^7 whilst the range of the 65-note instrument ran from A to $c\#^6$. The perforations for the full-scale roll were spaced at nine to the inch while the 65-note roll is perforated at six to the inch.

While the paper in both rolls is the same width, the method of driving the spools is different and this is why 65-note rolls are actually wider in total and require longer boxes. The common 88-note rolls are driven by a moulded-in recess with a driving 'dog' in it while the 65 note roll has a protruding metal spade-end drive connecting in a slotted chuck in the spool-box.

The common Duo-Art and Ampico reproducing piano rolls are all made to the standard 11¼-inch width but are perforated to operate functions in a different sequence. This means that the catalogues of Hupfeld Animatic T/Triphonola rolls (11⅝-inch wide), Duo-Art rolls and Ampico rolls are all different and cannot play properly on an instrument of another system. This is because the expression holes that control the different systems are all in the wrong place. Nobody thought to simplify things by designating the same function to a hole in all systems: that would have taken away the marketing edge in having special music rolls that would only work on that particular type of piano.

The enterprising piano-owner may wish to try out rolls that are not intended for his instrument. In this case you can apply a piece of sellotape over the ends of your tracker-bar so that music-roll expression notes do not appear as false notes. Never try to tape up the holes in the paper: only apply tape to your tracker bar – and remember to take it off afterwards! And never under any circumstances attempt to repair paper, roll-boxes or apron tabs with sellotape: it is most damaging to use anything other than paper and thin liquid brown glue. Much more on this in later Chapters.

3. Music roll paper

If you think about it for a moment, paper is a pretty poor choice for making music rolls. Fairly low down in the table of durable engineering materials, paper is readily torn, has a low resistance to wear and tear and is extremely susceptible to changes in humidity. On top of that, over a period of time some of the early acid-rich papers undergo chemical change and can become brittle to the point of shattering. And if it is badly stored, many old types of paper attract fungus, rot and insect attack.

It was these known characteristics that faced the first makers of perforated paper rolls. The act of punching holes or slits in the paper further weakened it. In damp weather and in the unheated environment of the Victorian home, the robustness and stability of the roll was poor.

No, given the choice today's engineer would select just about anything except paper! But in the early days of the pneumatically-controlled player mechanism there was no alternative – no stable thin plastic sheet or untearable paper substitute. It was paper or nothing.

For these reasons the earliest makers of music-rolls suffered a constant quest for suitable paper. Makers of organettes which played paper music were not really concerned because the width of their music rolls was small (usually around 5½-inches) and

WIDTHS AND CHARACTERISTICS OF COMMON TYPES OF MUSIC-ROLL		
Instrument	*Paper Width*	*Type of Spool Drive*
Aeolian Orchestrelle	10⅛ inches	Projecting pivot on left end of spool, projecting pivot with drive lugs on right end of spool
Aeolian Pipe Organ	10⅛ inches	As above (Reproducing organ rolls are 15¼″ wide)
Wilcox & White Symphony	10¼ inches	As above but roll is wound in reverse on spool
Piano, 65-note	11¼ inches	Projecting pivot on left end of spool, projecting pivot with drive lugs on right end of spool
Piano, 88-note, Full-Scale	11¼ inches	Recessed hole in left end of spool, recessed hole with drive slot in right end of spool
Piano, Hupfeld Phonola range	11⅝ inches	Projecting pivot on left end of spool, projecting pivot with drive lugs on right end of spool
Piano, Welte-Mignon (original red paper rolls)	13½ inches	As above

NOTE: The *Orchestrelle* and *Symphony* rolls are for player reed organs. *Symphony* rolls also fit the *Angelus* reed organ/cabinet-style piano-player combination. Both of these instruments play 58-note rolls. The *Aeolian Pipe Organ* plays 116-note music rolls of the same width as the 58-note *Orchestrelle* rolls. The method of driving the music spool on rewinding, perfected by Aeolian, was adopted almost universally. The only variation is the 65-note rolls as described above.

the holes in the tracker bar were large. This meant that if the paper swelled with dampness, the small compass of notes that the organette played would not really be affected. Organette tracker-bars had large openings: the paper could be half a hole out of alignment without any musical degradation.

But once the player piano came along, there were fresh problems. The wider the paper became, the greater the variation in width that dampness could produce. For both convenience in buying, selling and domestic storage, the piano-roll needed to be as narrow as possible. But this had to be balanced with the number of notes that could be played. Initially this was 46, 58 or 65 which called for that number of rows of holes to be punched in the paper. There had to be sufficient overall width so that adjacent holes would not readily tear. The next thing was that to accommodate that number of openings in the paper the holes in the tracker bar had to be as small as possible.

This was, of course, something of a double-edged sword because the smaller the tracker-bar openings, the less the paper had to swell for the rows of holes in the paper to get out of alignment with the tracker bar. It's called mis-tracking and produces discordant music.

In the burgeoning days and despite high-quality paper-making being a long-established craft, player-piano music-roll makers were in something of a cleft stick. Hand-made paper only came in sheets, and rolls of paper only came in what was called web form – a style that was developed to produce the coarse paper for newspaper-printing. Calendered brown wrapping paper was available as early as 1872 but this was thin and tore too readily.

This dubious quality of available paper was a problem that confronted every manufacturer. The search was for a paper that was thin yet smooth, stable enough not to expand and contract excessively under changes in humidity, and available by roll in large quantities. Furthermore, it had to be capable of being perforated easily and cleanly by a metal punch without leaving paper dust or 'fluff'.

Virtually all papers of the period were highly hygroscopic which means that they readily absorbed moisture from the atmosphere. Accordingly music rolls made from this sort of paper commonly swelled with changes in humidity. Under excessive conditions the music roll could swell so much that it would not unwind from its spool. Even worse, if it could be persuaded to unwind, it would then tear its edges as it was wound onto the take-up spool. The music roll with split, torn and folded edges

One of the largest piano-roll makers in London was the Perforated Music Roll Company in City Road. The firm's large premises occupied a huge factory and warehouse but in March of 1918 fire swept through the entire building in a £4,000 ($16,000) blaze that also destroyed the adjacent premises of the Imperial Cork Manufacturing Company. The following day workers arrived to find their livelihoods had gone up in smoke. Here two men survey the remains of the upstairs storeroom: tens of thousands of burned piano-rolls lie at their feet. Although rehoused in another building the uninsured business never recovered and was gone in a couple of years.

rapidly became worse until it reached the point where its condition began to affect the playing. Tears would become larger, notes would sound unintentionally or not play at all. And if the piano happened to have an automatic tracking device on its tracker-bar, the repeated variations in width due to the tears and folded-back bits would make the paper move fairly rapidly from side to side making things even worse. Now wrong notes would start to sound, other notes wouldn't sound at all, and so that particular roll was for the bin – or, as I shall explain later, a candidate for extensive repair.

It is important to note here a lesson that poor-quality paper taught player owners, and that was that if a music roll becomes damaged, repeated playing will only make it infinitely worse and very quickly, too. In other words, once damage has started, it will accelerate with every play. At the first sign of damage, today's player owner will stop, take out the roll, wind it on by hand and put it on one side for repair.

But to return to the end of the 19th century and the early part of the 20th, until better paper came along, there had to be a way of coping with a roll of paper the width of which could vary so the first change, more in the way of damage-limitation rather than offering a solution to the problem, was to provide the spool with an adjustable flange that could be pushed in or pulled out to accommodate the variable width of the paper.

Aeolian was probably the first piano-maker to offer a simple answer in the form of a loose flange which could be slid along the wooden roll core. The German maker Welte had been using a similar system for orchestrion paper rolls since the turn of the century. In their application, they produced beautifully engineered spools that had a telescoping end.

Reproducing piano rolls were suitably ornate as much as anything else to justify the extra cost above normal rolls for remember the recording artist had to be paid a handsome fee for his services. For this reason the roll leaders or aprons frequently contained up to five feet of information as well as a portrait of the pianist with his endorsement over his signature, and, where available, a picture of the composer. Here is a roll recorded by Busoni in Aeolian's lavish 'The World's Music' series.

This stop-gap solution was easy to apply and so within a short space of time the majority of roll-manufacturers took up the adjustable-width spool by devising various methods of moving one of the flanges. At the same time, improvements in automatic roll-tracking systems allowed some extra tolerance in paper width so allowing increased latitude in spool-making. The flanges now did not have to be so close-fitting to the paper width.

But the rolls themselves were made in such a way that deterioration was an almost inevitable result of removing the new roll from its box. And it was all due to the manner in which the rolls were perforated.

Sustained (long) notes were cut as a long slot in the paper. These long cuts were a constant source of trouble. The edges of the slot could catch in the roll and tear or, even worse, the paper would waver and close up. If a heavy and sustained chord was punched so that a lot of long slits were close together, the paper between, being supported only at its ends, could drift to one side. This was known as 'ribboning' and the effect was to silence the note and sound the one next to it. It was unpleasant to say the least. Attempts to reduce the effect began by breaking up the length of these long-note perforations by leaving a narrow cross web of paper at intervals of an inch or two. So long at these webs were no wider than the opening in the tracker bar, they had no audible effect on the note, the damper not having time to travel towards the string before it was pulled off again.

This particular problem had only occurred when 58-note and 65-note rolls were cut. For organettes, the heavier paper was less affected and so it was not an issue. But if matters were already marginal with the 65-note rolls (as well as the 58-note Orchestrelle rolls), then it was about to become infinitely worse with the introduction of the 88-note player action and its much smaller, closer-together tracks of perforations. Perforations in paper make it easy to tear the paper, a feature much cherished by toilet-paper makers and dispensers of postage stamps, yet not one high on the list of desirables in the world of piano-roll punchers.

These problems were largely overcome in 1914 when all but the very cheapest roll-manufacturers adopted the use of what they called the 'contiguous' perforation. In this perforating improvement, instead of square or rectangular punches being slightly overlapped to produce a slot, long notes were now punched as a row of closely-spaced yet separate perforations. In general these were circular in shape but some of the earlier square openings remained, their spacing being adjusted so that the unsupported slit of paper was as short as possible. The new perforations specified a variable gap between perforations that varied according to the speed at which the paper was propelled across the tracker bar. They were arranged to be close enough to prevent the primary valves from fluttering, yet far enough apart to reduce any tendency to roll tearing.

Contiguous perforating was first adopted in Britain by the roll-making factories of Broadwood Pianos and the Perforated Music Company. The system was refined (or perhaps 'fine-tuned' is a better term) so that notes began with a short slot (so as to ensure a positive start to the note in cases where the pouch/bleed relationship was marginal) and were then continued with contiguous punchings. This feature was closely tied to themodising melody notes and the slot allowed sufficient roll-time for the two small themodising signal perforations in the roll margins to operate.

Right from the earliest times of paper rolls for playing organettes, there had been various attempts at strengthening the edges of the paper strip. It was soon discovered that whatever resolution was tried, the physical properties of the paper so treated across its width were changed. If the paper was made stiffer or thicker at the edges, the outcome was to cockle the paper in the centre so that it lifted off the tracker bar allowing unwanted notes to sound. Also, a roll with stiffened edges spooled unevenly and loosely so that any distortion through dampness was amplified.

While these problems were well understood in the 1890s, German maker Hupfeld actually experimented with reinforcing the edges of the music-rolls for its Duophonola piano. This was done by painting a band of special varnish down each side of the roll. Although only 3/8-inch wide and very thinly applied, it proved a mixed blessing since, although it certainly reduced the chances of edge damage, it had the effect of making the rolls spool up loosely. As already pointed out, loosely spooled music rolls were even more susceptible to attracting moisture. This distorted the paper, made it track badly, and started the problem over again. Hupfeld's experiment took place in the 1920s and was soon discontinued.

Now Hupfeld was a classic example of a music-roll maker built onto a highly-successful mass-producer of quality instruments. The company's prodigious demands for quality paper for its perforating machinery was exceeding the quantity available from the suppliers – a mill called Hoffmann & Engelmann of Neustadt-by-Haardt which was providing music-roll paper to a number of German instrument makers. The matter was resolved by the simple expedient of buying the paper mill and so acquiring the entire paper production for its own roll-perforating plant. In the heyday of Hupfeld music-roll manufacture, the company employed 2,000 workers in its five factories and used fifty million metres of music-roll paper every year – rather more than needed to encircle the earth at the equator! A by-product was almost half a ton of paper holes (punchings) per week, these being used as fuel for the steam-engine that drove the perforators.

Making piano-rolls could be tackled in three ways. First was the laborious process of taking a musical score, a pencil and a long roll of paper. Because these rolls were marked out and then punched strictly to the 'measure' or metronome they were styled as 'metrically cut' and tended to sound rather wooden because they were strictly to tempo. These comprised very many of the early rolls and virtually all of the Orchestrelle player-organ music-rolls. The second way was to play the music on a piano to which some form of electro-mechanical recording system was attached so that pressing down a key marked a point – or a line – on a roll of paper. These were better and, often called 'hand-played', featured a degree of expression. The third sort was the reproducing piano by means of which a pianist's nuances of playing could be encoded in the paper so that when the roll was played back on a similar instrument the result was a 'real' performance by the named recording artist. Here in the New York studios of Ampico a pianist is 'recording' a piano roll.

Other companies that used vast quantities of special roll-making paper included the Stuttgart firm of Philipps (which used paper from W Adolf Beck in Karlsruhe) and the Freiburg factory of Welte, which latter discovered a particularly fine quality red paper that was calendared on both sides and which punched cleanly. This paper, made in Dresden by the Sächische Papierrollen-Fabrik Jakob David, was used for both orchestrion rolls and Welte-Mignon piano rolls right up to the outbreak of the 1914-18 war.

The quality of the paper became increasingly important as instruments developed and made more demands on their musical programmes. For a start, any variation in the suction on the music roll as it cross the tracker bar could produce a variation in speed, so friction had to be kept to a minimum which meant that the smoother the paper the better. It also had to punch cleanly with leaving paper fragments or fibres that could be sucked into the tracker bar and ultimately affecting either the movement of the valves or, just as bad, blocking the bleed holes. Paper travelling across a brass tracker-bar is extremely abrasive – just look how polished your tracker is: that's all done by paper. But if the paper is too abrasive, it can actually wear away the corners of the brass bar and start affecting the tracking of the paper.

Low-cost roll-makers still tended to use any paper they could find and it soon became apparent that if you played cheap rolls on your piano you could actually cause if not exactly damage, then maladjustment. Pleas from makers such as 'Use only so-and-so's music rolls: other makes may damage your piano' thus carried some credibility and were not entirely wistful attempts at sales hype.

There was one more trick that cheap roll-makers had up their sleeves and that was slow speed! You could compress a long piece of music onto a short length of roll paper if you slowed down the speed at which it travelled across the tracker bar. Now this was all very well but it meant that any speed adjustments called for but minute variations of the player-piano controls. And that was often beyond the ability of the pianolists. Reproducing piano rolls all play at a constant speed and travel relatively rapidly across the tracker bar. This allows plenty of leeway for expression.

Manually-played rolls need the same sort of characteristics if they are to be played sensitively. What this demonstrates is that even today the cheap, low-cost *short* music-roll can be a waste of money. I will stick my neck out and say that there are some of these rolls that you will never be able to play properly. I know that there are many that I can't play because the notes are punched too close together on too short a length of paper.

Britain's last major roll-maker was Artona run by one-time Aeolian man Gordon Iles. Here he is seen setting out the layers of paper to create a punching run. Up to a dozen rolls (thicknesses of paper) could be punched at once.

Music rolls made for export to tropical countries faced special problems and there were tales of the paper degrading from temperature, humidity and fungal growth. As late as 1922 a company called Hydroloid Ltd (*Exportingenieure für Papier und Zellstofftechnik, Gessellschaft*) was granted a British Patent (No.203,567) for special tropicalised music-roll paper which was:

> …treated preferably before perforation with a sizing material squeezed between pressure rolls, and hardened by alum or other hardening material mixed with the size or applied subsequently. After hardening, the paper may be softened and rendered tough, like leather, by treatment with glycerine, &c. A coating of varnish may afterwards be applied to prevent the glycerine from absorbing moisture. For music rolls intended for tropical countries, the paper may be treated finally with molten or emulsified wax or the like.

And then, perhaps, dusted with gravel? It does sound a bit like roofing-felt but does suggest that tropical degradation was a real problem. I have never found any rolls made of this paper. Mind you, I might not have recognised them as music rolls!

4. How music rolls were made

The section on music-roll history highlighted the evolution of the machine-punched music-roll. These machines operated from a master roll that operated rather like the ancient system of the Jacquard loom. The master roll controlled a mechanical reading system that operated the actual paper punches either through pneumatic or, later, electro-magnetic action, the latter being much quicker.

Systems for converting manuscript music into punched paper were numerous. Before the advent of the recording piano, music was laid out laboriously on a long, wide sheet of thick paper that was marked with a grid [see Ord-Hume 72]. The note position together with its length was then marked with a pencil until the whole melody was noted on the piece. This was now checked over before being punched by hand. This master roll was then attached to the perforating machine that punched the actual roll. The thick master card served exactly the same task as the pattern card in a Jacquard loom. Music rolls made in this manner tended to sound very mechanical because there was no expression by way of pianistic artistry. For this reason, they are often known as 'metronomic', 'metrically-cut' or 'four-square cut' rolls and are accorded little interest by the serious pianolist.

The next improvement came with the recording piano that took the ancient quest of Melography (recording extempory keyboard playing so that it could be repeated) roaring into the age of the player piano. Here a special piano was connected directly to the roll-perforator. As the pianist played the music, an additional action, either pneumatic or electro-magnetic, transferred the keyboard action to paper punches that cut a hole in the master roll each time a key was depressed. Because no pianist is every *absolutely* accurate in his fingering, the master roll could then be edited to remove wrong notes (tape them over) and hand-punch in missing ones. This master was now ready for copying, the production punching machine turning out up to sixteen copies at a time.

Gordon Iles is seen hand-punching corrections into a master roll. This set of pictures dates from the late 1960s.

Each copy was then inspected, usually by women hand-spooling them through on a smooth table. If the roll had to be printed with words (song roll), a tempo line (invented by the Aeolian Company in 1901) or expression line or other instructions, this was now done on a form of rotary press where the printing (text or other marks) was arranged on a long endless band. The start of the roll was aligned with a mark on the band and, as the paper and band travelled together, the printing would transfer to the paper. The process was, in effect, a form of offset lithography – without the stone part.

The end of the roll was now glued to the spool core and the paper wound on. At the start of the roll, the specially-printed thick paper apron, often decorated and with a tapered fore end, was then pasted on, the title label affixed, and a roll-end tab with short length of chord and an eyelet stuck on to keep the roll from unspooling. It was then ready for boxing and dispatch.

Cheaper rolls dispensed with the extra work and cost of the separate apron and merely cut the fore end of the roll to a suitable 'V' shape and stuck the roll title label to that. The roll-end tab was then applied directly to the paper end. Under conditions of normal use, this tab would usually tear off quite quickly. And, to save money, they would dispense with the securing cord and eyelet, substituting a rubber band that, over time, went hard and brittle and marked the paper.

Making the spools onto which the music-rolls were fixed and rolled up marked yet another associated industry. To begin with they were almost always of softwood with the flanges made either of hardwood or metal. In 1913, the invention of the Bakelite (Leo Hendrik Baekeland's mouldable synthetic resin created by the mixture of phenols and formaldehyde) marked the introduction of the first plastic spool ends but these proved unacceptably brittle and if you dropped the roll on the floor, even in its protective cardboard box, the spool end could completely shatter. Many other materials were tried but improved mouldable synthetics, developed after 1920, gave us the first reasonably durable spool flanges.

Talking about music rolls mention should be made of one rather odd scheme that worked yet failed because it was too clever. This was the Golden Tube music rolls for both 65- and 88-note music. First advertised in 1912 as the Suprema Golden Tube Piano Player Roll, the invention was patented in Britain by A Dow and J Bennett on July 26th 1910 (UK Patent number 17,757) with improvements on June 10th 1913 (patent number 13,371 in the names of A Dow and J Allwood). The system was quite clever in that it actually did away altogether with the spool, the roll being sold in a cardboard tube and then slid on to a special fluted spool core provided with a detachable end. With this device, the piano owner bought just one spool with which to play all his Golden Tube rolls. The patents were the property of Murdoch, Murdoch & Company of Hatton Gardens, London.

The failure of the innovation lay in the fact that it created a fresh music-roll standard and, for the owner, would have meant re-cutting all the music on all the rolls onto Golden Tube cores. In more recent times, owners of vinyl records faced a similar dilemma when Compact Disc records were introduced, only in this instance the many advantages overrode the disadvantages. Golden Tubes were actually killed off by the outbreak of the First World War when declining player-piano sales conspired with material shortages.

neat cloth-weave pattern and the screw top offered good roll storage although the roll was not ventilated and in theory could suffer attrition through humidity.

Orchestrion rolls were very costly. This was because the instruments themselves were hugely expensive and thus the market was restricted to those with both space and wealth. And to store these expensive musical repertoires special cabinets were made for storing the canisters. In the instance of the player-piano, it was a mass-market instrument and the smaller piano-rolls were much cheaper to buy. In fact, for most of the player-piano era, the market for the music was predominantly price-sensitive. A tin, no matter how nicely decorated and presented, was just too expensive. Piano-rolls, then, came in cardboard boxes. But if that sounds a simple solution, then it was to prove anything but!

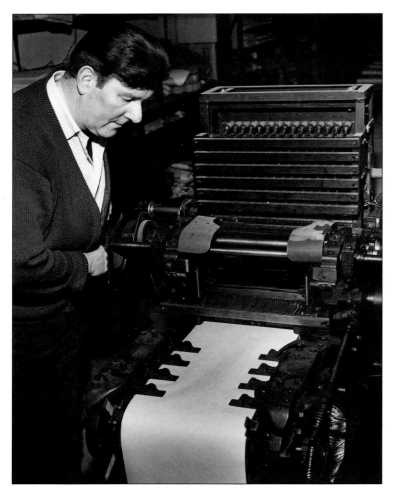

The sandwich of a dozen rolls of paper passes through the punching heads of the Artona machine. The multiple clamps that hold each section of paper prevent the sandwich from fanning and producing variations in punchings between top and bottom layer.

Initially the box was made to carry 65-note rolls and it was found that the protruding metal ends of the roll quickly damaged the ends of the box. To avoid this, a small trunnion-like block of wood with a slot in it was glued into each end of the box so that the two metal ends of the spool were located in the recesses suspending the whole roll clear of the box top, bottom, sides and ends.

There were large numbers of patents covering the design and embellishment of the boxes, how they were made and folded and how they were opened. Because of the shape of the rolls, the boxes tended to be very square in cross-section and, since the lids were often tight-fitting, they were not easy to open. One way of overcoming this was to provide a narrow strap along the bottom of the box into which the hand could be inserted to provide sufficient resistance against the fingers of the other hand pulling up on the lid.

Boxes with hinged, 'flip-top' ends were used by one maker; others hinged the box lid along its length to make it even easier to open. The best boxes were made of that quality of cardboard known in the industry as straw-board and which is quite yellow in colour and is also very thick. The box parts were fully cut, joined with interior fillets, glued up with a white lining-paper, and the exterior covered with a neatly-folded outer sheet glued on. This could be printed with the maker's or agent's name. And finally a neatly printed label was applied to the end of the lid, often to both ends so that whichever way round the roll was replaced on the shelf the title could be rear.

Such labour-intensive boxes were clearly doomed to be short-lived as the market called for ever-cheaper music-rolls, so they were eventually superseded by folded-lid boxes by the end of the player-piano era. Even so, the top-quality rolls always came in the expensive, assembled box.

One of the largest makers of music-rolls in England was the Perforated Music Company. With showrooms at 94 Regent Street and a library at 81 Beak Street, off Regent Street, their head office and factory was 197-199 City Road. Their trade mark was 'Imperial' and in 1910 they advertised as manufacturing rolls for many instruments, including Pianola, Orchestrelle, Symphony, Amphion, Broadwood, Apollo, Angelus, Hardman, Forte, Metzler, Simplex, Humana, Aristo, Neola, Humanola, Aeriola, Pianotist, Kimball, Chase & Baker, Sterling, Triumph, Rex, Imperial, Electrelle, Cecilian, and Autopiano. All their rolls were made at City Road and, by 1914, their premises were extended with the acquisition of the adjacent buildings, numbers 201 and 203. In March 1918 a calamitous fire gutted the entire factory, destroying all the plant and equipment as well as hundreds of thousands of rolls and their masters. The business was re-established on a much smaller scale at 6 Bride Street, London EC, where it continued for a few years until the general slump in the music-roll trade in the late twenties and early thirties.

5. The price of music rolls

The cost of music rolls was generally governed by two factors – first the quality of the roll itself and second, in the case of the reproducing piano's rolls, the artist who had recorded it. Performers were not generally paid a very high sum although a handful of the topmost players demanded – and got – considerable sums to cut rolls for the bigger companies. Of the very many manufacturers of rolls that got on the music-roll bandwagon, it has to be said that quite a large number turned out poor-quality rolls often poorly punched in cheap paper.

Some manufacturers manufactured own-brand rolls for other firms and, while some of these represented 'small' firms, the quality of their branded rolls usually matched the major output of the producer especially since they used the same paper. The list of makers and brands in Appendix 4 should help the identification of makers and their quality.

Manufacturers organised the sale of rolls through published catalogues that were usually up-dated every year and refreshed with monthly leaflets showing the latest releases. These catalogues form an invaluable source of reference not just on roll availability and price but also on contemporary musical taste. Here are examples of some prices from a century ago.

The music rolls made by the Kastner company under the name Kastonome were priced in no fewer than fifteen groups which were not indicated by any prefix or suffix to the roll number. The price of rolls was 2s 6d [$0.50], 4s, 4s 6d, 5s [$1.00], 5s 6d, and so on in sixpenny steps up to the most expensive at 10s 6d [$2.10].

In addition to making rolls for its special Kastner-action players, the firm also produced ordinary music rolls for both ordinary 65- and 88-note instruments and a supplement marked No. 30 and dated November 1912 lists 65-note rolls all in the 7700 series and 88-note versions all in the 83000 series. Prices are apparently reduced from catalogue prices – 8s rolls at 6s; 7s rolls at 5s 3d, and so on.

An undated Kastner Triumph catalogue of 65-note rolls runs to 430 pages and starts with roll number 1001 (Bartlett's *Polka de Concert* for 6s) and, with the exception of some random gaps towards the end of each thousand numbers, runs to 7702 and then jumps to what may well have been a new series started at 9012 continuing to 10791 (arias from Handel's *Messiah* for 8s). There is then a major jump to 60217 (a potpourri of music from Mozart's *Zauberflöte* arranged, Lord preserve us, for four hands and exchanged for the sum of 8s). Again there are some quite major random gaps leading up to the final title in the catalogue, roll number 77239 - Elgar's *Sonata*, opus 28, fourth movement for 7s. This sonata was presented complete on four consecutively numbered rolls and the immediately preceding roll listed is 76935, the *Automobil* [sic] *March* from *The Dollar Princess,* premiered in 1909. Almost all the final rolls were what would be grouped as 'classical', including music by 'Tschaikowsky', Weber, Wagner, Schubert and so on.

Prices of the Kastner Triumph 65-note rolls were listed at 2s 6d, 3s 6d, 4s, 5s, 6s, 7s, and 8s. Indicating that the catalogue dates from the period when the full-scale piano was making its presence known, the catalogue in my library bears a rubber stamp reading: 'Catalogue prices subject to discount of 3d in the Shilling 6/- Nett being the most expensive roll'.

The master roll is being 'read' by a pneumatic head that controls the actual punching machine.

The American label Farrand published its Cecilian-brand rolls from as little as 2s 6d [$0.50] up to a maximum of 8s, the price steps being 2s 6d [$0.50], 3s 6d, 5s [$1.00], 6s, 7s and 8s. The European maker Kastner made special rolls for the Kastonone Autopiano and Autogrand in the years that led up to the outbreak of the First World War. All Kastonome rolls carried the prefix K and the first roll, K1, was Liszt's *Rhapsodie Hongroise, No. 2*. This was priced at l0s 6d [$2.15]. The last roll in this catalogue was K2933, Mendelssohn's *Songs Without Words*, No. 2, priced at 6s 6d. However, there appears to be a gap between K2639 and the final just two numbers in the K2900 series.

Aeolian's first catalogues were published in New York. At the turn of the century it is no surprise to find that these were all devoted to ordinary 65-note rolls for the Pianola and its predecessor, the Aeriola. These American catalogues were also used in London with the price bands overstuck with a label showing comparable prices in shillings and pence. By April of 1903, The Aeolian Company was advertising that 'there are 9,106 different pieces of music at present available to owners of the Pianola. And new ones are added to this number at the rate of over two hundred a month.' The Pianola at this time cost all of $250 [£62 10s].

The Orchestrelle Company in London – Aeolian's British distributor – issued its 'Catalogue of Music for the Pianola and Pianola-Piano' for June 1910 with a notice on the title page advising to its library subscribers as follows:

NOTICE TO LIBRARY SUBSCRIBERS

All rolls in this catalogue are available to subscribers to our Music Roll Library under Class A. Only rolls in the Pianola column are available under Class B.

The catalogue, still containing only 65-note music rolls, is arranged in three columns headed 'Pianola', 'Metrostyle' and 'Themodist'. Not all titles were available under all three columns, which meant that the enthusiastic roll collector occasionally had to compromise. The roll numbering system gives little clue as to the type of roll except in the case of the Themodist rolls. Plain numbers, sometimes but not always with a suffix L or Y are used for Pianola and Metrostyle rolls, but all Themodised rolls bear the suffix T. Where the Metrostyle number already has a letter prefix, the letter T preceded the existing prefix. As an example, Verdi's *Aida* in transcription by Rosellen appears as a Pianola roll number 62931 costing 8s, as a Metrostyle roll number 73781 costing 10s [$2.00], and as a Themodised roll number T73781 also priced at 10s. However, Cecile Chaminade's *Air de Ballet* appears as Pianola roll number 8683 costing 2s 6d [$0.50], as a Metrostyle roll number Y8683 for 5s [$1.00], and a Themodised roll, also 5s, number TY8683. Dubourg's *Valse Chaloufre* comes as a Pianola roll on L2848, as a Metrostyle roll number L12294, and as a Themodist roll number TL15239.

Also available were so-called 'autograph interpretation' rolls either with a plain number or the prefix L. These featured interpretational markings either by the composer or by a named performer (for example, Wanda Landowska annotated roll number 69581, Muzio Clementi's *Sonata*, opus 26 No. 2 in F sharp minor).

Some evidence of system appears in the Aeolian numbering system when the numerical catalogue is consulted. Roll number 1, we find, is Glazounov's *Serenade Espagnole*, opus 20 No. 2 in A for cello and pianoforte - an accompaniment roll. Many of these low-numbered rolls were of music for small group or duet and occasionally we find duet music arranged for two Pianolas (the Mozart *Sonata in D*, opus 53, for example, appears on six rolls, two for each of the three movements and marked 'first piano' and 'second piano': numbers are 69a, 69b and so on to 71b).

The extent of Aeolian's musical output is clearly demonstrated by the reversion to number 1 again after the last of the first series numbers in this catalogue - number 77409 being a medley of popular German songs and obviously dating from before the time when War directed that German music was not popular with the British market. But, after all, this was well after the date of catalogue issue - 1910. However, at this point or thereabouts, the system reverted to 1 again, this time prefixed with the letter L. Roll L1 was Barnby's *The Soft Southern Breeze* in B flat. The last in this catalogue, numbered L3 172, is the two-step from the 1909 musical *The Dollar Princess*.

The numerical arrangement of autograph interpretations shows that the numbering system was not substantially different and that number allocations came from the main list; that is to say, numbers in this list (which are, by the way, all Metrostyle rolls) do not appear in the earlier, cumulative list. To begin with, though, the same numbers were used: and these were the ones with a double letter prefix. For example, the *Bagatelle*, Opus 63 Number 1 in D Major by Moszkowski was available as a Pianola roll on 1079 and as a Metrostyle roll on Y1079. However, the 'Autograph Interpretation' with markings by the composer himself was available as YA1079. Fairly early on (after 36 numbers in this catalogue), the system reverted to 'ordinary' numerical, complicated only by the non-conformity of the numbers. Homer N Bartlett's *Ballade*, not available on Pianola, was on Metrostyle as 72131 and on Themodist as T72 131. However, Bartlett's own interpretation was on 63251. Moszkowski's *Pièce Rustique*, Opus 36 No. 8 could be had on Pianola 9382, Metrostyle 70461 or Autograph 63271.

As with the main numerical listing, Aeolian began to run out of numbers and after the 79000s reverted to an L-prefixed series of five numbers. The first roll was L14000, Elinescu's *Scena Pastorala Romana*. Many of the boxes for these autograph rolls bore labels on their lid tops reading 'Interpretation Indicated by...' followed by the name of the composer or annotator.

Tucked away at the back of this 1910 catalogue is a small section headed 'Foreign & Special Music' with the warning that 'music listed under this heading will not be placed in the circulating library'. Then there is an explanatory note saying that 'the rolls listed under this heading have been manufactured to meet the requirements of foreign and special trade. As these rolls are not of general interest they are neither carried in our ordinary stock nor included in the Library, but copies can be purchased on giving a few days' notice.' The first of these rolls is *Annie Laurie*, surely one of the best-known and most popular folk tunes. Perhaps the decision to segregate this one came from a non-Scots-loving American. Prices in this catalogue run from 2s 6d to 10s [$.50 to $2.00].

The first full-compass player that could make use of all 88 notes of the piano was invented by Melville Clark around 1902 but it was not until 1908 that the full-scale player began to make inroads on the market. In fact the acceptance of all the different specifications inspired Melville Clark to introduce a player mechanism that would cater with all five of the roll compasses in use in America in the first decade of the century – 58, 65, 70, 82 and 88! He advertised it as 'five players in one'. After 1908, though, makers began to concentrate on just three roll compasses – 58 notes (for player reed organs like the Orchestrelle), and both 65 and 88 notes for the piano.

In effect, then, the 65-note player was obsolescent by 1910. By the end of the First World War, it was quite obsolete although there was of course a very great number of instruments still in the prime of their lives and giving good service in many homes the world over. Writing was nevertheless on walls and so in June 1920 Aeolian issued its last catalogue of 65-note music. Instead of the rolls being individually priced, they were coded A, B and C, so reducing to just three the different price brackets.

This was, certainly as far as the full-scale or 88-note roll catalogues were concerned, a very useful change because any price variation only required the insertion of a revised code price sticker in the catalogue front. With this change, there was also a radical revision of the roll-numbering system, for the price code now became part of the roll number as a suffix. For example, Mozart's *Adagio Favori* was a Themodist roll price-coded A (the cheapest and in this case costing just 5s), so the number on the roll was T72763A, this final letter being somewhat smaller than the type size used for the prefix letter and numbers. Rolls with the suffix B were priced at 7s 6d and those with the letter C cost 10s. A roll of one of my own grandfather's compositions, *Soldiers of the Entente*, a military quick march, was numbered T16425B. But to revert to the 1920 final 65-note roll catalogue, the Foreword comments:

> Owing to the fact that this Company and the other principal makers of Piano Players have for some time discontinued the manufacture of instruments of 65-note scale, the demand for 65-note music has decreased to such an extent that, in order to maintain a satisfactory output of 65-note rolls, and to provide adequately for those customers who still have 65-note instruments, it is necessary that we should concentrate on the manufacture of one class of 65-note roll only.
>
> Therefore, *all* 65-note music is issued in standard form, i.e. without the Metrostyle line, but with Themodist perforations (with few exceptions).

An example of one of the few exceptions was Weber's *Grande Polonaise*, Opus 21 in E flat major, which, although a C-class roll - the most expensive - was simply numbered 1341C, indicating clearly that it was un-Themodised. A quantity of L-prefixed numbers still survived. The highest-numbered roll in this catalogue was T104822A, Irving Berlin's fox-trot *My Bird of Paradise.*

In July 1924, Aeolian in London issued a matching catalogue of full-scale music. This followed the same general lines as the pioneering 65-note catalogue, only prices were coded into six sections: A = 6s, B = 6s 6d, C = 1 is (these all being Metrostyle-Themodist), and D = 7s 6d [$1.50], E = 10s [$2.00], F = 12s 6d [$2.50] (these all being full-scale hand-played). Aeolian song rolls had their own price of 6s 6d. The Foreword warned that hand-played rolls and song rolls are not available from the circulating library.

The main bulk of this catalogue is devoted to the Themodist-Metrostyle roll but it also includes 76 vocal accompaniment rolls that were Themodist only, and 60 instrumental accompaniment rolls, again Themodist only.

Ballads and light songs plus what were called 'vocal dances' were issued as song rolls, with an introduction advising that:

> Aeolian Song Rolls are issued in the most popular key bringing them within easy reach of most voices but as the compass is stated in most cases it should be noted when selecting titles.

This point does not arise, of course, for those whose instruments are fitted with the Aeolian Transposing Device, which, lying completely out of sight behind the tracker bar enables the player to raise or lower the key by moving a small lever.

Full particulars of this apparatus which may be fitted at a moderate cost, will be sent on application.

Each of the song titles that followed included the key and the numbers had no suffixes, for example *Asleep in the Deep*, key D - D to B (H W Petrie) 26111. Some of the rolls were available with words in French and English, Italian and English, solely in French and solely in Spanish. These vocal dances were intended to be sung and danced to.

A small additional section was included under the heading 'Illustrated Music Rolls' which consisted of music, words and pictures. Totalling five and numbered consecutively from 26199 to 26203 inclusive, the first four were nursery rhymes while the fifth and last was called 'Children's Popular Songs and Games'. This gave the owner *London Bridge* and *Jolly is the Miller.*

Hand-played rolls all had three-figure numbers plus the prefix A. Chopin's *Andante Spianato and Polonaise*, Opus 22, played by Alfred Cortot, therefore carried the number A609F, indicating that it was one of the most expensive rolls at 12s 6d. The Foreword to this section reads:

> Hand-Played rolls differ from the ordinary roll in that whereas the latter is cut in strict time, the former are produced by a pianist whose actual playing with all its slight variations from strict tempo, is transmitted to the cutting machine. Even in the hands of a not very expert player they are extremely pleasing to listen to while those who study their instrument and give attention to arriving at artistic renditions, will find them interesting and enjoyable to play, as they do not interfere in any way with perfect personal control.

This rather clumsy explanation seems a poor attempt at convincing player owners to part with more money for the undoubted (in most cases) merits of the hand-played roll.

On both sides of the Atlantic the relatively high cost of music rolls was now the major limiting factor in the popularity of the player piano and its music. The installation of extensive machinery for the mass production of music rolls brought about a dramatic reduction in roll prices. These are shown in the July 1928 London catalogue where the rolls were arranged in the same manner as before only this time rolls in price brackets A and D cost 4s, B and E cost 5s 6d, and C and F cost 6s 6d. Aeolian song rolls were also down at 4s 6d, while 65-note rolls were reduced. A rolls were 3s from 5s; B were 4s 6d from 7s 6d, and C were 5s 6d from 10s [$2.00].

By this time, the growth in interest in dance music necessitated the issue of a separate catalogue for the 'vocal dance' category. The number of song rolls had also increased and consequently required a larger section in the catalogue. An addition to the 'Illustrated' music rolls series bringing the total to six was *John Peel*, numbered 26430. Hand-played rolls had also multiplied from 4½ pages to more than 11½ pages with a few in the four-figure numbers.

The last complete roll catalogue which Aeolian issued in Britain was in July 1932. From then onwards, until the company closed in around 1938, only monthly supplements were published.

Back in 1913, the introduction of the Duo-Art necessitated a catalogue of special reproducing rolls. These were frequently listed alongside Pianola rolls. As before, the last complete catalogue came out in July 1932. All Duo-Art and AudioGraphic Duo-Art rolls had a small letter suffix which again was a price code. The suffix A indicated the minimum price of 5s 6d for ordinary Duo-Art, and 6s for AudioGraphic Duo-Art; B was 6s 6d (7s); C was 7s (7s 6d); D was 7s 6d (8s); E was 8s (8s 6d); F was 9s (9s 6d); and G was 10s (10s 6d). An example of the 10s [$2.00] roll was Bach's two-part inventions numbers 1, 6 and 8 played by Bauer (roll No 6392 G). All Biographical Duo-Art rolls were in this class-G price band.

All AudioGraphic roll numbers, whether for Duo-Art or straight Pianola, had the prefix D, and hand-played rolls (naturally not applicable to the Duo-Art) carried the prefix either D or A, then the number and the usual price code letter. Song rolls all had five-figure numbers with neither prefix nor price code suffix and were all one price – 4s 6d for 88-note, and 3s for 65-note.

The pedal-electric Duo-Art piano was an English market model that is virtually unknown in America. Also made only for sale in the United Kingdom is the pedal Duo-Art, a sort of half-and-half instrument produced only in upright format, which was fully Duo-Art in the treble but had only one set of expression accordions. Because the theme holes in the accompaniment were not read by the tracker bar in these instruments, special rolls with a boost to the accompaniment were cut for these foot-operated Duo-Arts in England. These rolls are generally unsuitable for use on the fully electric and the pedal-electric models. All London-made rolls carry the figure '0' as the first digit of the number, and in the December 1922 monthly supplement Maurice Ravel's *Miroirs* played by the composer on roll number 082 cost all of 20s.

Among the many types of roll that Aeolian issued in Britain were accompaniment rolls divided between vocal and instrumental, the AudioGraphic which came as annotated, analytical, running comment, biographical, children's rolls, playtime series (words, music and pictures), and school songs. Then there were hand-played, song rolls (words and music), illustrated song rolls (words, music and pictures), special song roll (only one issued - *Songs for the Camp Fireside* - which presumably required a player piano to be taken along with the tent and the sleeping bags!), accompaniment rolls (with words) which were intended for use with gramophone records, and so on. On some of the biographical rolls, the first 8 feet of paper was provided for reading prior to the appearance of any music at all!

One of these types of programme roll introduced by Aeolian was the so-called 'World's Music' educational series first introduced about 1925-6. These were printed with particular emphasis on the presentation of extra-perforal information in the way of woodcuts on the apron to depict the composers, plus other illustrations printed throughout the extensive biographical prologue. The rolls, issued with yellow box labels, were the brainchild of Percy Scholes, who was responsible for a major programme of expanding the scope of the piano roll for Aeolian. The rolls were, of course, more expensive and, when the financial crisis heralded by the 1929-30 Wall Street crash came to pass, Aeolian was forced to abandon the scheme.

In September of 1924, the Aeolian Company in London introduced its own little magazine called *The Duo-Art and 'Pianolo'-piano Monthly*. This 12-page bulletin of new rolls and cameos on musicians and their music is today rare, although it ran for about thirteen years. Prior to this, the company published a monthly pocket-sized booklet of new releases, the first issue being in 1908.

Occasionally the task of the music-roll editor was not all that different from that of the original pianist as he strove to correct the extensive and varied mistakes of some recording artists. Wrong notes were an ever-present and understandable feature of the master roll which a careful comparison with the score could aid in removing. But sometimes it was more than that. Ignace Paderewski's Duo-Art recordings were a good case in point. Although a brilliant and talented performer, Paderewski's almost complete lack of formal musical training had left him with some serious technical faults. This came to ahead in his piano rolls when it was found that his hands did not play together. The job of trying to sort out his piano rolls was beyond the capabilities of the editor, so Rudoph Ganz was given the task of trying to make some sense out of them. In fairness it should be pointed out that Paderewski never wanted to be considered a virtuoso pianist, but would have preferred to have been remembered as a composer.

Making piano rolls had its lighter side. Duo-Art recording pianist Robert Armbruster (born in Philadelphia in 1896) was at one time in charge of operatic, semi-classical and salon music, and one day a roll appeared labelled *Loof Lirpa*. None of the team was able to identify it, but apparently there was some general agreement that it sounded like a Brahms intermezzo. Finally it was realised that the title was 'April Fool' spelled backwards - and that the 'unknown Brahms' was actually a roll of 'Peas Porridge Hot' spooled backwards. A technician who had been on the receiving end of numerous studio pranks had been 'getting his own back'.

The hey-days of the great Aeolian empire were, nevertheless, short-lived as the company underwent a spate of serious problems in the United States. The depression of the early 1930s was bad enough, but then the company sustained a serious fire at its factory, and largely as a result of this in 1932 it merged with the American Piano Company at East Rochester. But even worse the company decided it was no longer economically viable to pay recording artists fat fees for a performance – and the fidelity of performance was discarded. All the great claims made for the Duo-Art system were now cast to the four winds and, in a retrograde step of monumental proportions, from about 1934 onwards the rolls were not made on a recording piano but were marked out on special master stencil paper, the marks for notes and expression being made with blue and red pencil.

The music-roll had thus come the full circle as the company reverted to hand-cutting of masters as it was in the 'dark ages' of metrically-cut rolls. In 1941, all production of rolls ceased and the plant went over to war production. The flagging popularity of the player piano did not encourage the company to maintain any of its old plant and so machinery and equipment was unceremoniously scrapped.

Aeolian in Britain was to last a little longer than its American parent and it strove manfully into the 1930s thanks to series such as the *Daily Express* Piano Playing Competitions for which it made a special series of Duo-Art rolls of the test pieces.

Eventually, and despite the efforts of the player piano industry to give sales the kiss of life, stark reality stared everybody in the face, Aeolian included. When, in September 1939, Britain and Nazi Germany found themselves cast into the melting-pot of World War Two, the demise of the player-piano seemed somehow of little consequence.

So far we have only been looking at Aeolian. Of course, there were others and Britain and the United States sported many different roll-makers all of whom produced catalogues and all of whom marketed their rolls at competitive prices.

One popular high-quality brand was the Animatic manufactured by Hupfeld and these, in my opinion, represent probably the finest of all the 88-note full-scale rolls ever made outside those for the reproducing piano. Properly interpreted, these excellent hand-played-type rolls can be as good as if not better than many a Duo-Art or Ampico roll. The word Animatic, says the catalogue 'is a play on the word "anima" (soul)'.

Animatic rolls were sold in London by Blüthner & Company Ltd at its showrooms at 17-23 Wigmore Street. The earliest catalogue in my library bears a pencilled date of May 1927 and contains 144 pages. Animatic rolls could, of course, be used with any make of 88-note piano. The full title was 'Animatic Artists' Roll', and they were the nearest things to a reproducing type of performance. Each roll bore the name of the recording artist. These rolls were coded with Roman numerals for pricing so that rolls catalogued with the suffix 'I' cost 5s 6d, those with 'II' cost 8s, and those 'III' were 11s. They were therefore a lot more expensive than the three categories of hand-played Pianola roll which sold at 4s, 5s 6d and 6s 6d.

A few rolls had letter prefixes. Those with an 'A' before the number were intended as accompaniment rolls, and those with an 'O' indicated that the roll was not hand-played but was, presumably, metrically cut.

All the rolls in this catalogue have five-digit numbers in the 50000 series and no fewer than 149 separate recording artists' names are listed. Some of the rolls are issued in more than one part, in which case there are small suffix letters, as for example in the case of J S Bach's Organ Toccata and Fugue arranged by Stradel and played by Anton Rihden. The three movements provide parts 1, 2, and 3 and are numbered 59355A, B and C, each being a Code III roll selling at the maximum price of 11s.

Ampico reproducing piano rolls came in such a variety of classifications and styles that a detailed analysis of them would take up a volume of its own: in fact it has done so in Elaine Obenchain's monumental *Catalog [68]*. I shall therefore confine myself to a few abbreviated historical pointers.

Before Ampico, rolls were issued on the Rhythmodik label. The product of the American Piano Company, Rhythmodik was a straight 88-note roll with a numerical numbering system which Obenchain considers probably began with the figures '10'. Following the numerical title-identification digits was an

extra digit that denoted the size or playing length of the roll. Known size numbers range from 2 (the smallest) up to 9 (very large). Preceding the numerical group was a letter used to denote the price code of the roll, 'A' being the cheapest.

Originally Ampico rolls were called Stoddard-Ampico and the coding of these was the reverse of their Rhythmodik counterparts so that the size digit came first, then the reversed number of the roll itself, and finally the price code letter. The last-known Stoddard-Ampico roll is 20721A, *Omar Khayyam*.

Next came Ampico-Artigraphic, and finally just Ampico. Between April 1921 and February 1922, the manufacturer began to use a dated number system but this was abandoned due to what must have been mounting confusion at all levels. Rolls so numbered included classical, popular and ballad series.

Roll-playing musical instruments for use in public places posed a serious problem for potential operators in that the rolls had to be changed repeatedly. The German makers Hupfeld were the first to think of an automatic roll-changing system. Others followed and automatic instruments became less burdensome to operate. Here is an eight-roll changer mechanism on a piano-orchestrion. The revolver mechanism indexes one roll at a time, draws its leader to the take-up spool, plays it, and then rewinds it automatically while the revolver system brings another roll into register for automatic playing. This could be set to play continuously. Note just right of centre the glass vial mercury switch. These were common in the days of the early direct-current electrically-operated mechanisms.

The standard numbering system was introduced as early as 1916 and apart from the brief interlude described above it remained in use up to the demise of Ampico in 1941. The classical series ran from 50004 to 71903; the popular series ran from 200002 to 216673; and ballad from 11 to 3171.

A 'Jumbo' series, introduced in November 1929, was the equivalent of the long-playing piano roll. Packed in 4-inch wide boxes, the roll numbers all began with the numbers 10 and all terminated with the number 5. These rolls played for an average of 20 minutes and some up to 30 minutes. Numbers ran from 100005 to 101065. There was also a 'descriptive story' series beginning with the figure 9 with numbers running from 90003 to 90143, the last digit referring to size. These rolls had words printed on them but, unlike song rolls, they were intended for reading rather than singing. They were introduced briefly in 1925, a maximum of fifteen titles being prepared.

Ampico also introduced a vocal accompaniment series. First seen in mid-1924, these were virtually discontinued in June 1927 although a final one appeared in 1929. Numbers ran from 30001 to 30751. But it was a violin accompaniment series that proved to be the shortest lasting, beginning effectively in mid-1925 and ceasing a year later. Only four rolls appeared, numbered 40003, 40013, 40023 and 40031. All bore the suffix letter G. There was also a short run of 'unnumbered' rolls. These were demonstration or free-gift rolls and no numbers appeared on the box. However, by playing the roll through, the number would be found stamped on the end of the roll. The unusual Christmas *Greetings* Ampico rolls of 1925-8 are featured in this list which runs from 4760 to 7133 and comprises a mere nine rolls.

Of the catalogues Ampico issued, the earliest full specimen I have is dated July 1916, and is 'for the Ampico Artigraphic and Stoddard-Ampico Player Pianos'. This has a mere 72 pages, and rolls are priced from 75 cents for *Aloha Oe* (Hawaiian Song), on 28911A played by Andrei Kmita, to $3.50 for Leopold Godowsky playing Chopin's *Polonaise, Opus 53*, on 6566M.

Price code letters on these rolls were A = 75 cents [3/9d]; B = $1 [5s]; C = $1.25 [6/3d]; D = $1.50 [7/6d]; E = $1.75 [8/6d]; F= $2 [10/-]; G= $2.25 [11/3d]; H= $2.50 [12/6d]; J = $2.25 [11/3d] (same as G); K= $3 [15/-]; M = . $3.50 [17/6d]; N = $3.25 [16/3d].

The July 1920 catalogue displays the same confusing pricing suffixes, but once more they are different. Starting this time at 0 = $1; E = $1.25; F = $1.50; G = $1.75; H = $2; J = $2.25; K = $2.50; L = $2.75; M = $3; N = $3.25; P = $3.50.

The vast 351-page 1925 catalogue, superbly printed with illustrations, short biographies of many of the composers and artists, and notes on the music, reveals that the same Hawaiian song, played by the same pianist and now renumbered 570520, carried a price of $1, while the Godowsky Chopin was just $2. Indeed, this catalogue reveals that there were only five price steps indicated by the code letters, namely: D = $1; E = $1.25; F = $1.50; G = $1.75; and H = $2.

After 1930, the price structure remained in five degrees, but the price code letter no longer formed part of the roll number.

The other name in the 'big three' of reproducing pianos was that of Welte. Not only were Welte reproducing pianos very expensive, but their rolls were extremely pricey. The Welte (Licensee) catalogue of rolls, published in England at London's Steinway Hall in October 1922, listed 3,755 titles of which the most expensive was Fanny Bloomfield-Zeisler's performance of Beethoven's *Sonata*, Op. 111, in C minor (second movement), which cost all of £3 19s. Song rolls and accompaniment rolls were generally cheaper and short pieces of music could be had for as little as 10s 6d [$2.10].

By 1926, however, Welte perfected new paper-perforating machinery and, in the face of competition from other manu-facturers whose rolls not only sold for less but showed every sign of moving lower still, they were forced into revising their charges.

Writing in the foreword to the 1927 London catalogue, one-time well-known organist Wallace J Madge commented: 'With the publication of this New Catalogue, our pink Number List of January 1st, 1926, (containing new reduced prices), and our Interim List of Welte Music Rolls of October 1926, become unnecessary, and can be thrown away, as both the new reduced prices for rolls and the Interim List are embodied in this Catalogue.'

Fanny Bloomfield-Zeisler's Opus 111 of Beethoven now cost 24/- [$4.90] per movement, and the Welte price structure ranged from 10/- [$2.00] in one-shilling increments up to the maximum of 24/-. Even so, it was expensive for the music lover to build up a repertoire of Welte music rolls.

The methods by which Welte rolls were recorded are shrouded in mystery. In an article contained in the journal of *the British Institute of Recorded Sound,* John Farmer states that, unlike Aeolian and Ampico, Welte always insisted that their recording system was fully automatic and did not ask for the services of the pianist in the later stages of preparation of the master roll. It seems that the recording piano had a trough of mercury beneath the keyboard. Each key had a light carbon prong suspended from its lower side which dipped into the mercury when that note was played. This was said to have enabled the recording of the exact force and duration of the note. This does, however, seem unlikely, but the late Richard Simonton, who befriended Edwin Welte during his later years, told John Farmer that the carbon prongs were in fact suspended from the key by a fine coil spring and consequently the depth of penetration of the carbon rod in the mercury would have varied with the force with which the key was depressed. From this, it would follow that the resistance to the flow of current would vary slightly with this depth of penetration and if this could be traced against each note a fairly good idea of the pianist's dynamics would be obtained. But, as John Farmer rightly asserts, the techniques of electrical measurement with the limited knowledge available at that time makes even this explanation a little unlikely. Undoubtedly this is not as reliable a recording system as one which directly measured hammer velocity and Farmer suggests that this maybe one reason why some of the passages in Welte rolls tend to sound a little rough.

The De Luxe Reproducing Roll Company was a branch of the Auto-Pneumatic Action Company which produced the Welte-Mignon (Licensee) reproducing action for sale to independent piano manufacturers. Roehl relates:

> In the late 1920s, Welte (Licensee) rolls were grouped into four price steps, each indicated by the prefix letter to the four-figure roll number, for example C-7690, *Peer Gynt Suite* played by Richard Singer. Cheapest rolls were those with the letter Y prefix. These were $1.25. Those preceded by the letter B were $1.50, X were $1.75, and C were $2.00 [10s].

It behoved the makers of reproducing rolls to have a cavalcade of prestigious names of not just pianists but musicians on tap (meaning pay-role). Like letterhead politics and their attendant retired Army majors beneath the names of a few redundant elderly Knights, this was obviously advantageous to the major roll companies. Aeolian had the services of Leeds-born Percy Alfred Scholes (1877-1958) who advised on rolls, promoted the Pianola and Duo-Art and wrote several books for the company. Ampico had at its command Philadelphia-born Sigmund Spaeth (1885-1965). Both these musical polymaths lived into their eighties but, while Scholes is not known to have made a piano roll, Spaeth did record two - a parody of the tune *Yankee Doodle,* and a whimsical medley called *Songs you forgot to remember.* Spaeth served with Ampico between 1920 to 1927 as education musical director. Subsequently, he became renowned for his American radio series as 'The Tune Detective', on which for some seven years he invited listeners to tax him with music to which he would almost always find the title. In England, Percy Scholes left a more erudite monument in the form of the *Oxford Companion to Music,* a reference work now in its 11th edition.

Although generally speaking the German companies were content to let the names of their recording artists speak for themselves as regards carrying a message to the public, Welte in England could hardly stand by and see its two big rivals move into an area of associated musical literacy which it couldn't match, and so Wallace J Madge, FRCO, was hired to 'edit' the roll catalogues.

6. Repertoire, Artists and Reproducing Rolls

A reproducing piano was not likely to sell unless the music it played could be identified with a known artist or artiste the reputation of which was both widespread and admired. As a consequence the three big names in the business – Welte-Mignon, Ampico and Duo-Art – set about getting pianists under contract so that they might record for that label alone. It was a 'dry-run' for the record industry that followed and worked just the same way.

First off was Welte-Mignon who signed up:

Béla Bartók *(1881-1945)*
Claude Debussy (1862-1918)
Gabriel Fauré *(1845-1924)*
Alexander Glazounov *(1865-1936)*
Rugggiero Leoncavallo *(1858-1919)*
Theodor Leschetitzky *(1830-1915)*
Darias Milhaud *(1892-1975)*
Raoul Pugno *(1852-1914)*
Ottorino Respighi *(1879-1936)*

Next come the Aeolian Company which signed up exclusively:

Claudio Arrau *(1903-1991)*
Cécile Chaminade (1857-1944)
Georges Enesco *(1881-1955)*
George Gershwin *(1898-1937)*
Percy Grainger *(1882-1961)*
Myra Hess *(1898-1966)*
José Iturbi *(1895-1980)* [also recorded for Ampico]
Sergei Prokefiev *(1891-1955)*
Igor Stravinsky *(1882-1971)*

By far the largest catalogue of recording artists was held by Ampico and among these were the following artists that the company recorded exclusively:

Rudolph Friml *(1879-1972)*
Fritz Kreisler *(1875-1962)*
Mischa Levitzki *(1898-1941)*
Benno Moiseiwitsch *(1890-1963)*
Mieczyslaw Munz *(1900-1976)*
Leo Ornstein *(1892-2002)*
Sergei Rachmaninoff *(1873-1943)*
Moriz Rosenthal *(1862-1946)*
Sigismund Stojowski *(1869-1946)*

In the way of things, not all contracts were cast-iron and 'arrangements' could be made to borrow or transfer performers. The result was that there were numerous artists who re-corded for more than one system and others whose rolls made for one system were 'reprocessed' to suit another. Occasionally the original recording system is unknown. If we number the systems as Welte = 1; Hupfeld DEA = 2; Duo-Art = 3; Ampico = 4; and Angelus Artrio = 5; then the list with systems is as follows:

Eugen d'Albert *(1861-1932)* Recorded for Hupfeld; issued on 1, 2, 3, 4.
Wilhelm Bachaus *(1884-1969)* Recorded for Hupfeld; issued on 2, 3, 4.
Harold Bauer *(1878-1951)* Recorded for Hupfeld & Duo-Art; issued on 2, 3, 4, 5.
Ferruccio Busoni *(1866-1924)* Recorded for Hupfeld; issued on 1, 2, 3, 4.
Teresa Carreño *(1853-1917)* Issued on 1, 2, 3, 4.
Alfred Cortot *(1877-1962)* Recorded for Hupfeld; issued on 2, 3, 4.
Ernö von Dohnányi *(1877-1960)* Issued on 1, 4.
Arthur Friedheim *(1859-1932)* Recorded for Hupfeld; issued en 1,2,3,4.
Ossip Gabrilowitsch *(1878-1936)* Issued on 1,2,3,4,5.
Rudolph Ganz *(1877-1972)* Recorded for Hupfeld; issued on 1, 2, 3, 4.
Walter Gieseking *(1895-1956)* Recorded for Hupfeld; issued on 1, 4.
Leopold Godowsky *(1870-1938)* Issued on 3, 4, 5.
Enrique Granados *(1867-19l6)* Issued on 1, 3.
Edvard Grieg *(1843-1907)* Recorded for Hupfeld; issued on 1, 2, 4.
Mark Hambourg *(1879-1960)* Issued on 1, 2, 3, 4.
Josef Hofmann *(1876-1957)* Issued on 1, 2, 3, 4.
Vladimir Horowitz *(1904-1989)* Issued on 1, 3.
Frederic Lamond *(1868-1948)* Recorded for Hupfeld; issued on 1, 2, 3, 4.
Wanda Landowska *(1877-1959)* Recorded for Hupfeld; issued on 1, 2, 3, 4.
Ethel Leginska *(1890-1970)* Issued on 3, 4, 5.
Josof Lhévinne *(1874-1944)* Issued on 1, 4.
Pietro Mascagni *(1863-1945)* Recorded for Hupfeld; issued on 1, 2, 4.
Herma Menth *(1890?-1968)* Issued on 3, 5.
Yolanda Mero *(1887-1963)* Issued on 1, 3, 4, 5.
Elley Ney *(1882-1968)* Issued on 1, 3, 4.
Guiomar Novaes *(1896-1979)* Issued on 1, 3.
Vladimir de Pachmann *(1848-1933)* Issued on 1, 3.
Ignace Paderewski *(1860-1941)* Recorded for Duo-Art; issued on 1, 3.
Maurice Ravel *(1875-1937)* Issued on 1, 3.
Artur Rubenstein *(1886-1982)* Issued on 3, 4.
Camille Saint-Saëns *(1835-1921)* Recorded for Hupfeld; issued on 1, 2, 3, 4.
Wassily Sapellnikoff *(1868-1941)* Recorded for Hupfeld; issued on 1, 2, 4.
Xaver Scharwenka *(1850-1924)* Recorded for Hupfeld; issued on 1, 2, 3, 4.
Ernest Schelling *(1876-1939)* Issued on 1, 3.
Elie Schmitz *(1889-1949)* Issued on 3, 4.
Artur Schnabel *(1882-1951)* Issued on 1, 4.
Alexandra Scriabin *(1872-1915)* Recorded for Hupfeld; issued on 1, 2, 4.
Richard Strauss *(1864-1949)* Issued on 1, 4.

How were these 'conversions' made – especially since we know that rolls made on one system cannot readily be used on another? Well, many of the conversions were carried out by editor-technicians who adjusted the expression marks for one reproducing system to those of another. With skill and a detail understanding of the two systems concerned, the results were usually very good indeed. Having said that, though, just once in a while you find a conversion that has not really worked and you can hear that something is not quite right.

Besides the 'big three' (which we know to have been five!) there were several other transfers: a few of the early Welte-Mignon recordings were transferred to the Artecho/Apollo, Artrio, Recordo and other systems. Transfers were also made from Duo-Art to Ampico, Ampico to Artecho, Hupfeld to Ampico and Duo-Art to Artrio.

7. The availability of Music Rolls – Libraries

Libraries are said to date back to 1,700 BC and a public library was set up at Athens by the unfortunately-named Pisistratus about 540 BC. Modern Europe has had libraries in the 14th century while the United States really had little outside university libraries until the founding of the Astor Free Public Library in New York, a magnificent gift from John Jacob Astor worth (in 1839) £80,000 [about $4.25m today).

Lending libraries were to enjoy a boost in the early part of the 19th century; they were an established fact in all areas by the time of the 1851 Great Exhibition. Even working-class people had access to books – something that Napoleon would not have tolerated! But if libraries existed for books, and in the last half of the 20th century would stretch to include long-play records, video tapes and compact discs, then it was no wonder that somewhere in between these should lie the first public music-roll lending libraries.

And so it came about that the Public Library of Kansas City, Missouri, became probably the first such institution to introduce such a facility for its members. It was all due to a benefactor who, in 1914, presented some 500 music rolls for the benefit of the community. As far as I can determine this is a unique instance of a public music-roll library in the United States. Player-piano manufacturers occasionally ran their own lending libraries for the benefit of their clients, but they were few and far between and there range of activities was limited to metropolitan areas only.

The specialist libraries for music rolls were strictly managed by the makers of the instruments and were considered as part of the cost of sales. It was, of course, good business for, with the relatively high cost of some rolls, the opportunity to borrow those rolls for a token rental charge ought to encourage both player sales and inspire the owner to buy a favourite music-roll.

Above all, the library was a way of maintaining the owner's interest in his instrument. Indeed, so popular were the libraries that even after roll production costs had been cut by the introduction of mass-production machinery, it remained an important part of many a companys' business.

Other than a few isolated examples in America, the United States was too large and diffuse an area for the successful and economic operation of a system similar to that found in Britain. By sharp contrast, the proliferation of music-roll lending libraries seem to have been a feature peculiar to the British where the lending libraries were an early and successful innovation.

The first library I can trace seems to be that set up by Aeolian based at Aeolian Hall, New Bond Street, London. Originally known as The Orchestrelle Company's Music Circulating Library, all of the library's rolls bore special labels on the boxes and a rubber stamp on the roll apron identifying them as library property. This lending library stocked both 65- and 88-note rolls and also, later, reproducing rolls for the Duo-Art.

Aeolian's roll library was probably the first of its type anywhere in the world. Subscribers were charged four guineas (£4.20 [$7.00]) for a one-year subscription, or three guineas (£3.15 [$5.30]) for six months. For this they were then entitled to borrow rolls of their choice from the current company catalogue. Subscribers who lived in the London area could take out a dozen rolls of music every two weeks while those described as country subscribers were allowed two dozen rolls once every four weeks. In all instances, subscribers had to pay the cost of carriage which itself might just have presented an additional limiting factor on roll-borrowing. By comparison, those in the London postal area were offered the benefit of free delivery and collection.

After Aeolian, other companies soon followed suit and set up their own libraries. Steinway began a library and approval service for Welte-Mignon rolls from Steinway Hall, while Ampico did the same from its Regent Street showrooms. The larger retailers, being established specialists in selling players, also created libraries only these were not necessarily tied just to one roll brand. They were, if you like, 'free houses' and two of the largest were those created by the Knightsbridge (London) department store Harrods and also Selfridges in Oxford Street.

Although ideal in concept, in practice these libraries were not all that they were cracked up to be. It did not take long for the problems to show up and soon they became a cause of some dissatisfaction among subscribers. A most telling article appeared in *The Piano-maker* for April 1919. This is a fine cameo on the methods of running a business at the end of the First World War. In fact it is so significant that it is worth quoting in full:

> For sheer ineptitude, unnecessary expenses, inefficiency, waste, extravagance, general muddle and universal dissatisfaction, there is probably nothing to compare, in any section of the pianoforte trade, with the present rotten methods employed in the running of the music rolls libraries. A couple of decades ago this vital point, in connection with the development of the player and player-piano, loomed darkly in the future; to-day the whole question is nothing less than a gross scandal and, in important respects, a fraud on the public. Take any town, even the largest, a town of enormous potentialities for the player-piano industry, like, say, Birmingham; what do we find? A dozen firms of repute, of whom perhaps eight are in the front rank. Each professes to run its own library—or rather *dual* library, for both 65 *and* 88 note rolls have to be stocked. Thus we get at least eight firms running, and running most atrociously, sixteen libraries.
>
> This means, in sequence, sixteen assistants at least sixteen rooms for storage, sixteen ledgers, and so to do; problems, every day and everywhere, innumerable as to collection and delivery of rolls. Changes innumerable from one library to another by dissatisfied customers, who find out in turn each library a ghastly failure. No responsible management, incompetent buying, apologies galore without any improved service, often 40 per cent of rolls delivered faulty. The proprietors, in turn, find the library business an unmitigated nuisance, an expense, and *inter alia,* owing to want of centralisation, music dealers can rarely get an assistant to remain long in the library department. Chances of promotion and increased pay being practically negligible.
>
> Now, the key to the problem is, undoubtedly, centralisation. Turn all the libraries, for example, in Birmingham, into one; take ample premises— capable of expansion that is - in some central position, not by any means necessarily in a main street. Secure a staff sufficiently large to deal with the rolls on a good, well planned system. Run on a sufficiently comprehensive scale, it

should be possible to finance a good first-class man as manager at, say, £400 per annum; assistants under him in charge of the receiving room, to test all rolls returned as they come in, and before being re-placed on the racks; a staff to advise customers, a checking hand, with other details considered on their merits.

Take buying: dozens of libraries are actually being run to-day by girl assistants, whose sympathies are either entirely musical comedy or ragtime. It is simply an insult to ask any cultured musician to join such libraries, classics being really unobtainable. On the other hand, dealers have everywhere sold very expensive player-pianos, well-knowing that their own library is a delusion and a snare; thousands of rolls their own customers would care for (and ask for) possibly lying idle on the shelves of a competitor. Another dealer will take a remarkably good profit on a sale, and leave his *unsuccessful* competitor (the irony of it!) to incur the risk and loss in connection with running the library.

One can to-day assert, with confidence, that the player-piano industry stinks in the nostrils of large numbers of wealthy people in all directions; very largely through avoidable mismanagement of the library question. In no town is delivery guaranteed: whereas, given centralisation a suitable collecting and distributing van would serve each district in turn, the fact and dates would be advertised, and the stigma removed from dealers of bungling this important detail in connection with the advance of their business.

A certain firm may advertise 25,000 rolls in its library; but half are 65 note, which leaves 12,500. Of these about 10 per cent at least are faulty (some libraries have as much as 25 per cent faulty rolls) and two-thirds of the residue are out on loan, and even this is a favourable estimate. And, those joining, have to either fetch rolls themselves or wait weeks until the piano van is going "somewhere near" (ye gods!). By parcel post carriages become a serious item.

To sum up: so long as dealers in *every* town regard the library question, individually and collectively, as a d—d nuisance (this is their attitude) no improvement is likely to be made.

On the other hand, subscribers, with scarcely an exception, would willingly double their rates of pay *if only* a first-class library were at their disposal, with guaranteed free and prompt collection in their respective districts. The present writer has for years discussed this part, of finance, with large numbers of grievously dissatisfied customers, and can speak with some authority.

Of course, centralisation still leaves difficulties to be surmounted. Take the public book free libraries: with only one book returned weekly, perhaps. The indexes, cross indexes, dockets, cards, etc; how much more complicated things are in the music rolls library, with very often 36 rolls returned at a time, and reasonable precautions required not to send, in return, perhaps a dozen rolls the customer sent back a few weeks ago!

It would have to be made clear that no touting or canvassing (for exchanging player-pianos) was a stipulation on the part of the staff. With this fact staring subscribers in the face, both in the prospectus, and via framed notices on the walls, no dealer would have any fear of unfair dealing, and would automatically recommend each and every purchaser of a player-piano to the library. In fact, there should be no other library but this one to send customers to. Run on a big scale, with a big catalogue, competent management, well organised, success would never be in doubt. Towns at least fifty miles round Birmingham, for example, could and would be served, and probably further a-field as well. P.P.

One feels that PP, whoever he (or she) was, must have had a pretty rotten experience in hiring rolls for his piano. Apart from suggesting, twice, that he lives in Birmingham, he does manage to give us a fair idea of the problems that beset the otherwise enterprising dealer. Some of the situations he suggests still sound awfully familiar to most of us today!

But back to the history of the libraries. Many of them were the last bastions of the player-piano era in Britain, continuing through to the outbreak of the Second World War in 1939. One library survived into the immediate post-war years while a new business, the Music Roll Exchange, was to remain in business selling off ex-library rolls, some actually brand new, into the mid-1950s. It was here that I bought a complete set of rolls of Beethoven sonatas for £2 ($3.35) in 1950. They were all new and unused, still largely sealed and not even opened!

The lending libraries for rolls were 'of their time' and probably could not have survived the demise of the industry. In their favour one has to accept that they did an enormous amount of good in a small sector of the market by enabling the enthusiastic player-pianist to try out music with which he may not have been familiar before committing himself to a purchase.

8. The types of music rolls

It being realised that successful player-piano marketing actually began with ensuring that the customer knew how to work the thing (meaning get music from it hopefully without brute force), Aeolian thoughtfully produced what it called an 'Instructional Roll'. This was a normal-looking roll but it contained pedalling and accent exercises that served as short demonstrations as to a suggested way of playing the instrument. It also served to highlight if the piano was not adjusted properly. Various other makers followed with their own styles of Practise Roll and these are even today quite useful pieces to have in your collection for they bear printed instructions as to their proper use.

Do not confuse these practice rolls with two other types of roll. First and foremost is the Test Roll, which is specially perforated so that each note from the lowest bass to the highest treble, is tested for repetition and damper adjustment. Some test-rolls also include very short extracts from pieces of music chosen to demonstrate clearly features that have just been tested. Usually these are limited to just one or two familiar phrases.

The second type of music roll that might be confused with the Practice Roll is the 'trailer' roll that Aeolian gave to its dealers once a month. This played fairly long extracts of new releases and were provided so that the salesman could demonstrate the latest music to his shop customers. Trailer rolls are scarce to find because at the end of the month they were usually discarded. Even so, they only have a novelty value because a succession of short extracts from a series of melodies makes for limited entertainment.

Early on, the practice of marking instructions on rolls was adopted. Tempo lines, Themodist indications and accents were all features of music-rolls by the end of the first decade of the twentieth century. Along with the 'pedal line' or expression line (which indicated whether a section was to be played *pianissimo* or *fortissimo* and also gave advance warnings of such changes as *crescendo, diminuendo,* pause, tempo changes and so on), the instructions were printed on a rotary stencilling machine which pressed a suitably marked stencil band on to the paper roll as it was passed under it. A similar system was used by the advanced makers of music rolls who printed their tempo lines in different colours (often red or green) and other marks in more colours.

At the time when the player-piano arrived in the Victorian home, it was a time when many people sang and possessed a repertoire of popular songs. The makers of instruments soon cottoned on to the simple fact that it would be a good idea to produce rolls on which the words were printed. This would allow several people to gather around the pianolist and, reading over his shoulder, sing along to the music. So was born the so-called Song Roll. The invention was a mixed blessing since in the hands of the less scrupulous it could be turned into a valuable piece of commercial advertising or even political propaganda.

In America during the 1920s a particular kind of song roll appeared having words that were not quite suitable for the vicar's tea-party. These had lyrics of a vulgar or ribald nature more suited to the Rugby Club than the family parlour. Like all things that are rather left of the thin blue line, there turned out to be a demand for these sing-along centrefold substitutes and the dealer who wanted to make a fast buck had no qualms about stocking them. Mind you, the content of a vulgar song a hundred years ago would today probably pass as no more than saucy for Tom Lehrer's lyrics were just as blue. As Harvey Roehl relates *(Player Piano Treasury,* page 154) the thought of 'filthy piano rolls' as a latter-day variant of 'filthy pictures' must sound amusing to a 21st century reader.

Nevertheless, the 1920s represented a strict time when morals, family values and regular worship formed the mainstay of life. The very existence of this sort of piano-roll became a highly contentious subject and many a righteous dealer expressed his disgust eloquently in the local papers. This sort of protest, I am sure, acted as good publicity for the dealer and increased his legitimate trade through his demonstration of good community values. Such pious and pure thoughts held sway at that time and if the dealers were going to be vocal about filthy song-rolls, then the Q-R-S roll company recognised a good publicity opportunity themselves. They openly sided against the peddlers of dirty piano rolls and initiated a crusade against them. As I suspect they hoped, this received wide coverage in the trade press in response to a mass of letters from dealers who had been offended. One wrote:

> We think it's demoralising and vicious. How do you feel about it? We are enclosing a few excerpts of a new song, just published. Suggestive songs for grown-ups are bad enough, but when it comes to corrupting the minds of children we draw the line. We don't want profits from such a source.

From the furore created by these rolls we might conclude that they must have been really filthy. So far, in fifty-odd years of collecting piano rolls I have never come across anything more suggestive than *I Know a Lovely Garden* in E flat by Guy d'Hardelot on Aeolian 26119! And then, during the 1960s, a friend in America proudly produced an obviously cheap-cut, poorly boxed roll with a title that I cannot quite remember but it was something to do with a young lady who enjoyed some popularity amongst her men friends. Gleefully, my friend played it to me – and sang the words. Yes, they were rude but not as offensive as some of the stories and jokes in common circulation. Well, times have certainly changed! As collectors' items at least, their rarity must make them worth having.

As well as the song roll, there was also the Accompaniment Roll. The idea behind this was to offer a piano accompa-

Many have been the attempts at home-made roll-punching. Indeed the post-war revival of roll-making was spear-headed by an urge to make music from perforated paper. Here the Author is punching a roll using a machine designed and built by Tony Morgan.

niment to another solo instrument. Rather like the interesting 'Music Minus One' series of tapes produced to provide backing to the amateur performer (and enterprising street musician), this allowed not just singers but other soloists a chance to play in duet, trio and sometimes quartet. Accompaniment rolls are rare to find today since they are not in themselves musical entities.

So much for the popular rolls. What else made up the catalogue? The answer is everything from popular music through to the classic and opera, operetta, military marches, national songs, hymns – everything. It was a rich repertoire for the collector.

One make of 65-note roll that turns up regularly is the Angelus which was made for use on the Angelus player. At first sight, these look fine – until you try to put them into your piano's spool-box. Unless the piano is an Angelus, of course, the first thing you notice is that the spade ended drive pivot for the spool-box chuck is on the left side instead of the right-hand end of the spool. To play an Angelus roll on a normal 65-note player, carefully unspool the roll onto a clean floor in a series of overlapping loops so that the paper does not crease, crinkle or tear. When you get to the end, tear the paper off the spool, turn the now-empty spool end for end so that the spade ended drive pivot is now on the right-hand side, place a line of office paper adhesive (not the wet glue but the stuff that comes as a semi-dry stick) along the spool core and refix the paper roll end and wind the paper back on the spool. Do not alter the position of the paper! All you need to do is remove and turn over the spool as described. You will note that instructions or words on the roll must now be read through the paper and that they are backwards. This is correct.

The nadir of the player piano began with the First World War, picked up once the post-war depression ended, and then enjoyed average success until the time of the Wall Street Crash. But all types of piano have their ups and downs. The Enquiry Department of that illustrious glossy magazine *The Connoisseur* offered a Basingstoke (Hampshire) reader some disheartening news in response to a question in its issue for February 1912.

Pianos such as the one you describe are almost unsalable at the present time, but a dealer might give you 30/- to two gns [$6 to $9.00] for the case, as pianos of this kind are frequently transferred [*sic*] into desks.

Fortunately we then discover that the reader was describing a square or table piano and not a player, although today a good early 'square' is worth a great deal.

But if pianos have had their bad times, so have music-rolls. During the privations of the war years when many people were short of fuel and some resorted to burning furniture to keep warm, piano-rolls were seen as good fuel for they tended to burn slowly. Frank Holland used to relate how after the Aeolian Company's British factory at Hayes, Middlesex, was shut up prior to being sold off, he visited the place on December 31st 1952. 'As I walked in,' he told me, 'I saw a chap about to throw the *last* Duo-Art roll on the Tortoise stove for heating. I yelled out "Stop! May I have it?" He threw it to me, I caught it and I still have it! *Minute Waltz*!'

If that tale marks the low-point, then take heart, for the music-roll business is booming again. As owners of classic player-pianos increased and instruments were restored rather than scrapped or converted to 'ordinary' pianos, the demand for perforated paper music rolls has expanded. In America the Q-R-S company has never stopped roll-making. While its monthly production may have dropped well below its output in the peak times – in the 1920s it sold as many as 10m rolls per

year - it has held on to its niche in the business. After World War Two sales declined to an all-time low of under 200,000 rolls per year, yet now, with virtually all other mainstream roll-producers having disappeared, it has returned to being a major producer for an albeit smaller marketplace. Today it makes rolls of both traditional and new popular music. There is also a large manufacturer in Australia plus an increasing number of small businesses making specialised, high-quality rolls, both re-cuts of old music rolls as well as newly-arranged music.

Throughout its history, the peculiar technical and performing advantages of the player piano have encouraged a number of composers to write for the instrument. Opportunities to exploit a freedom from the limitations of the human player and his mere eight fingers and two thumbs have allowed extended and even simultaneous use of every keyboard register as well as the playing of chords in excess of 10 notes while repetition and 'stretch' could be almost limitless. Although Camille Saint-Saëns wrote for Aeolian's 116-note Pipe-Organ (*Fantasie pour Orgue Aeolian*), neither he nor Cecille Chaminade (who composed for the same instrument) truly took advantage of the possibilities open to them.

More recent composers have not ignored the capabilities of the player-piano either. Igor Stravinsky used the player piano for an early version of *Les Noces* while others including Casella (1883-1947), Goossens (1893-1962), Paul Hindemith (1895-1963), Herbert Howells (1892-1983), and Gian Francesco Malipiero (1882-1973) experimented with its abilities. Unlike Saint-Saëns and Chaminade, though, there has been an increasing understanding of just what can be done with a player-piano. Perhaps nowhere is this more noticeable than in the more recent contributions by Conlon Nancarrow (1912-1997) whose challenging music is both technically clever and inspirational in its musical freedom.

In concluding this rather long Chapter on music rolls, I would like to mention one feature of the finger piano that had an interesting impact on the player piano and, particularly, certain types of music roll.

If you look at some ordinary pianos, especially quality American instruments from the late 1890s, you will see that they have a third pedal at the bottom of the case front between the 'soft' and sustaining pedals. This third pedal is sometimes referred to as the 'sostenente' pedal, more properly *sostenuto*. The purpose is to operate a mechanism that holds the dampers off the strings of the notes after they have been played. In other words, it is a selective sustaining pedal. The effect is to allow strings to continue vibrating after the finger of the pianist has left the key. In a normal piano action, of course, the moment the finger is raised the damper drops back to mute the string that has just been sounded.

There is nothing really new about this effect and its benefits were understood at the end of the 18th century when inventors were trying all sorts of ruses to alter in some way the sound of the piano. So-called sostenuto pianos were once all the rage. At a time when all pianos had wooden frames and were lightly strung, this was an important feature in the interpretation of some sorts of music. As pianos adopted iron frames – plates as they are called in America – and heavier stringing was used, the sostenuto was less important overall and it was generally done away with. But the ability to 'hold down' a note – of no immediate consequence on a percussion instrument like a piano – began to find a new favour with some musicians. No doubt inspired by the harmonium stop developed by the best French makers and called *prolonguement*, (this was invented by Louis Pierre Alexandre Martin from Sourdun, a senior worker at Jacob Alexandre's reed-organ factory between 1841 and 1845.) somebody noticed that not only would a string continue to vibrate, but that it could produce a faint tapestry of harmonics as it responded to other strings that were vibrating at the same time.

Of course, most people could not really hear the difference on an ordinary piano played in an ordinary manner. The concert pianist, however, enjoyed the effect it made possible. So did the piano salesman.

American makers of quality grands, predominantly, but not exclusively Chickering, reintroduced the middle pedal in a big way. As far as most were concerned, though, it was a novelty, a marketing tool – a 'gizmo'. If your piano had only two pedals and somebody else's had three, well, the rest is human nature!

Sostenuto was, however, *there* to stay, if not exactly *here* to stay!

Consider now the player piano. It controls its dampers in two ways, first by a pneumatic motor that operates the sustaining pedal (to hold off all the damper at once), and by the length of the musical note for, so long as the tracker bar hole is 'open' (a long slot in the paper), then the damper is 'off' that particular note's strings. It was this relatively simple fact that impressed an Aeolian inventor named George Swift when he realised the blindingly simple fact that sostenuto could be put into the music-roll without having to bother about a 'third-pedal' piano control.

Now George Swift's patent was not directly intended to answer the sostenuto question, for it was largely concerned with a matter that Engramelle [29] and Dom Bedos [3] had faced a century and a half earlier. This was a simple mechanical fact about all music, namely that notes that are expressed as divisions of a length actually have to be shorter than that division if they are to be heard individually. Without getting into musical notation, for I promised I would avoid that, if a full note has a value of one, and a half-note a value of half, if you play two half-notes on the same key or string, then they equal the time space of one – and you will only hear one long note! Naturally with a piano this is less noticeable than on an instrument that is naturally sustaining like a pipe or reed organ.

The essence of music is, curiously, not so much the notes as the spaces, or silences, between the notes. Now come back to the half-note analogy. If both notes are true halves, only one will be heard when they are played in quick succession. What we actually want to achieve is 'sound-silence-sound-silence' so we can hear two notes. Suddenly our half-note has actually become a lot shorter. There's nothing magical about this: it's mere simple acoustics and for the live pianist he does not give it a second thought. 'Tap-tap' on the key – and out come two notes in the musical time of one!

It is only when you get into the realms of mechanical music that the impossibility of a half-note actually being a half of a particular measurement in distance, time or sound really matters. The half must be less – probably no more than $^3/_8$ or even ¼!

Barrel-organ makers both explored and exploited this lacuna of conventional musical notation. The barrel piano was not sensitive to this at all since it had no 'long' notes or barrel bridge-pins to bother about. But the pneumatic player was different. Here the length of the note could be accurately cut as a longish 'dash'-shaped slot in the paper. Of course, if the same note was repeated rapidly we were back to the old 'two halves don't equal one whole' limitation – and the slots were cut shorter than their true metrical length.

Music-roll cutters had a small ace up their sleeves, though. This lay in the piano's sustaining pedal and two or more repeating notes could be struck quickly and while the string was still vibrating from the first hammer-blow by applying the sustaining pedal to keep the dampers away from the strings. The two notes were still distinct, but their duration (really meaning their division) was blurred.

Once sustaining pedals could be controlled from the music-roll, this effect was widely used for musical nuance and, using a term from the arcane world of true pianism, it was the antithesis of 'flutter-pedalling' which is where the pianist can obtain some delightfully curious tonal effects by the rapid and specific operation of the soft-pedal.

Now back to George Swift. I suspect that like many people of his era not only could he play the piano but he could play it quite well. In fact, he lets slip in the long text of his Patent that his job is arranging music for the Aeolian Grand, forerunner of the Orchestrelle player reed organ. I can imagine that while listening to some player-piano interpretations he found himself just a little disenchanted with the sound he heard. If the sostenuto pedal was little more than a fashion-fad on the ordinary piano, what it could do was quite important when you came to playing a music roll – Swift calls it 'a sheet'.

Swift realised that lengthening some notes (called *legato* by the finger-pianists) was the cornerstone of making a normally 'flat' mechanical interpretation take on at least some of the aspirations of a hand-played music-roll. He said as much so in his Patent which was granted in December 1906. In fact he was clever enough to appreciate just why written-down, conventional musical notation is really so imprecise. He wrote:

> In carrying out the present invention, where the musical score indicates staccato, the shortest perforation of the entire perforated roll may be employed. For legato… the perforations are not to terminate one where the next commences…but are to be prolonged, and therefore overlapped considerably, by a small increment of length just as though a blurred or dissonant effect were to be expected. I know of no musical notation which would correspond with or indicate any such overlapping of the musical tones themselves, and as the effect produced by a sheet so perforated simulates the most perfect legato-playing without any blurring or dissonance it is not conceivable that it really occurs to any appreciable extent in the music produced. The amount of such prolongation, overlap, or increment may be… more than the entire length of a sixteenth-note without increment. The increment may be a fixed amount. Thus the perforation for such a short note may be doubled in length, so that, for example, the first one of three such notes shall not terminate till the third commences. Such increment or prolongation when applied to a whole note is by itself hardly noticeable to the eye [*surely he means ear. AO-H*]. I have not, therefore, discovered that the increment or overlap is in any way affected by the length of the musical note, whether a sixteenth, quarter, or whole note, nor yet by the number of notes in a given measure, whether thirty two thirty-second notes or but a single whole note. The increment or prolongation may be represented by a constant length, such as one-eighth of an inch for all portions of the melody or harmony to which it is desired to apply it at a given tempo or speed of the mechanism, and since my said discovery it is at once demonstrable in the following manner that such increment or prolongation should to obtain the best results vary in respect to the tempo of the movement being rendered, though the reason why was for a long time not clear to me.

The full impact of this discovery – one may hardly call it an 'invention' – was not to come for several years. And, strangely, not from Aeolian, but from its rival, the American Piano Company. Its first quality music-rolls, hand-played and later to become the Ampico, were issued under the Rythmodik label. Now the New Jersey-based Rythmodik Music Corporation was affiliated to the American Piano Company and it produced very cleverly-edited music rolls. With a bit of experience in looking at music notation written as rows of holes in paper you begin to see the difference and why the makers had as their slogan 'it's all in the roll!'

The secret of the early Rythmodik music rolls and their quite marked difference to music rolls of other manufacture was really rather simple. As a 'hand-played' recording, two innovations were applied. First was the improvement in that the music paper travelled at a constant speed so that any variations in tempo or phrasing put in by the 'recording' artist were faithfully reproduced simply by leaving the tempo control well alone.

A basic feature already used by Welte and Hupfeld in Germany, Rythmodik seems to have been the first American maker to apply it to their rolls. The second difference was that the rolls were meticulously cut to indicate legato with sostenuto punching. Again a first to combine the features that formed the cornerstone of the later reproducing piano. Credit, though, goes to the man whose curiosity exploited the feature for the first time – George Swift.

There's always something new to be learned from a collection of piano-rolls, not just in the way they are made but in the way they are adjusted to give the best performance. This is why metrically-cut rolls were not just pretty awful on the senses, but actually harmed the instrument's reputation.

It would be nice to think of the player as a substitute for a live performer – after all that is the message player-piano salesmen have shouted at the market since the first mechanical players back in the 1880s. In truth, it is only a mechanism with all the imperfections that separate a machine from a living being. But the real beauty of the player is that, given a good music roll that is sensitively arranged and punched, the human interface can, with practice, provide just that edge which will make a performance that much more realistic.

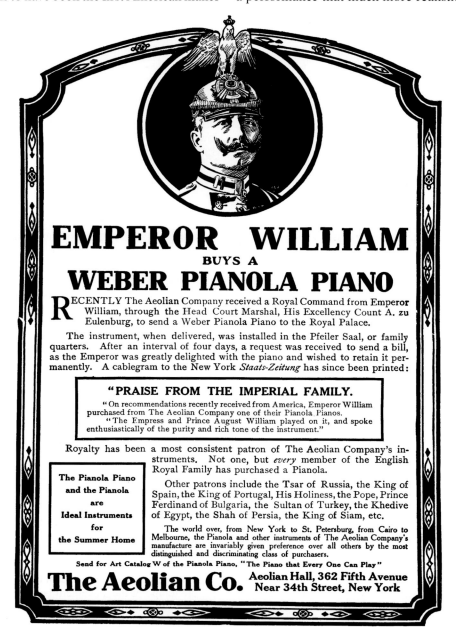

Chapter 12
The Player-Piano in the 21ˢᵗ Century: High-points and Weaknesses

I began this book by describing briefly the history mechanical musical instruments. It is not all past history, though, and it is reassuring to be able to record that there is still an industry of sorts out there. Unlike the old times, though, it has polarised into two widely separated sectors. First there is the production of cheap curios and trinkets. Second there is a cottage industry representing the needs of serious collectors and producing high-quality components, accessories and services.

After World War II a considerable effort was mounted to revive the Swiss musical-box industry. A number of makers set up manufacture concentrating on small, mass-produced items for the novelty and tourist markets. Key to low-cost production was up-to-date methods of manufacture generally attained at the cost of high quality. The musical repertoire of these items comprised merely popular or traditional melodies and the arrangements were very simple and unchallenging.

The majority of these small firms either went out of business or were amalgamated. The surviving business of Reuge is now the largest and has embraced modern technology and manufacturing processes whilst at the same time producing some very high-quality limited-edition musical boxes for the collectors' and investors' market.

Since the 1950s, Japan has created a musical-box industry and the largest maker, Sankyo Seiki, operates a fully automated factory at Suwa, Nagano, capable of turning out 100 million pieces a year ranging from simple 12-note mechanisms up to those having combs of 50 teeth. There is also a number of small firms making both new musical boxes and high-quality arrangements of music for playing on traditional disc machines.

In Britain and America, several businesses provide both new discs and replicas of old discs for musical boxes. One British firm has an inventory of equipment to make 100 different brands and sizes of disc and makes highest-quality discs using computer-controlled equipment to ensure unprecedented accuracy.

Manufacture of new street organs, particularly in the Low Countries, reflects the sustained interest in this form of music and some fine instruments made in the traditional manner have appeared during the closing decades of the 20ᵗʰ century.

The barrel organ, in particular the small street variety, has also experienced a strong revival during this period. The barrel, however, has given way to alternative technologies. First is the use of perforated paper rolls so allowing much longer pieces of music to be provided. Second is the application of solid-state music memory to produce a composite instrument which,

while still possessing a fully-mechanical organ action with bellows and pipes, plays from an electronic memory bank which can offer up to 100 tunes on one changeable plug-in Electronically-Programmable Read-Only Memory (EPROM) module.

This resurgence of interest in mechanical music also saw an attempt, in the 1950-60 period, to revive the player-piano and American makers launched small, so-called 'spinet' models for the modern home which played ordinary 88-note music rolls. Also produced were several styles of electrically-operated key-top player to mount onto an ordinary piano keyboard. Largely because, due to their ultra-compact size, these could not produce enough suction power, these were not successful.

Digital control of pianos, initially from specially encoded cassette tapes, then from a digitally encoded disc, and now increasingly from solid-state circuitry, has also given the instrument a new lease of life. The first of these, the Superscope Marantz *Pianocorder*, was launched in America in 1978. This offered live recording (Melographic recording) and playback and at least one Pianocorder action was successfully installed in a modern harpsichord. The principle employed electronically-operated solenoids to set in motion the keyboard action.

The post-war revival of player pianos encouraged some makers to put new and modern models back into production. Among these was Aeolian in America which confusingly revived the name 'Duo-Art' but spelled it 'Duo Art' – and applied it to normal 88-note pedal-operated mini-pianos. These were masterpieces of post-modernist confusion as regards style. This one, complete with cabriole legs, was simply called 'Pianola' and appeared in 1958.

Solid-state electronics and advanced computer technology have helped create a new market for the self-playing piano in hotels and restaurants. Several Japanese companies have introduced instruments that will play a pre-recorded programme from floppy diskette and one installation in particular, the Yamaha concert grand, can perform to the very best of reproducing-piano capability. Such instruments cannot, however, be classified as 'mechanical'.

Over the years, there have been numerous attempts at making a playable copy of an old, rare or otherwise valuable piano-roll. What may at first sight seem a simple, if laborious, task is, in fact, one of the most complex if an accurate copy is to emerge at the end. Many have tried to make automatic copying machines but the majority of those in the past have hit fairly elemental, yet complex problems that have defeated most of the early technologies. Expressed in simple terms, the problem involves the automatic and reliable location of a hole to be copied since the automatic systems that many tried all managed to extend perforations and render the copy musically blurred, occasionally unintelligible.

Those that persisted succeeded one way or another and, short of using original perforating machinery and original masters, roll-copying was nevertheless accepted as a laborious and largely hit-and-miss undertaking that really demanded the creation of a new master roll.

Sophisticated electronic circuitry seemed to offer the solution but it wasn't until the age of the computer that precise copying became possible. Even so, everybody who makes or copies rolls today can be expected to have made a huge investment not just in the technology but also in hand-made equipment and machinery. Putting holes in paper, dismissed by many as being of least consequence, costs money. Putting them in accurately is a high-price involvement.

Modern technology has ensured that the player piano has entered the modern age with a new life and an infinite repertoire. In 1986, the Viennese piano-makers Bösendorfer produced a form of reproducing piano which, said the company, could reproduce every nuance of a performance. Optical sensors scanned the keys, hammers and pedals 800 times a second and the information produced was fed into a computer which then processed the data, interpreted it and could then store it either on magnetic tape or a floppy disc which could then be played back on the piano as an authentic performance.

Bösendorfer was not the first to introduce solid-state electronics and computer technology to the modern piano. The first disc-controlled computer player-piano appeared a few years earlier with instruments such as the Yamaha Disklavier, a grand piano with computer disc drive.

This is not intended to be a book on computer skills, nor do I pretend to be more than a raw amateur with computers, but it would be an oversight not to give you a brief description of how electronics and the computer is applied to the piano.

Another curious exercise in design was the Pianola Masterpiece model complete with country-style spindle legs.

Just now I mentioned the Bösendorfer and Yamaha instruments. In this type of automatic piano, the pneumatic action is replaced by a series of solenoid that operate the piano action. In computer language, the music is translated into a series of 'on' and 'off' operations, each of which can be calibrated independently with an individual dynamic intensity. This sequence of electronic events is then 'read' by a sequencer which is a register into which events are read against a time-base. This function operates to an international standard that is called Musical Instrument Digital Interface or MIDI for short.

Curiously this is a very basic system but like so many things simple it actually works very well. It is simple because it is strictly binary in operation and that is exactly how a piano-roll/tracker bar system works. Because MIDI incorporates a simple time-base and the ability to read sequence files against this, MIDI is absolutely ideal for reading, storing and translating the movement of piano keys. It is, in fact, the ideal performance-recording tool.

However, I feel bound to point out that these instruments are in no way equal, let alone superior to pneumatic reproducing pianos. While I have seen claims made for them that they are 'the new reproducing piano', this they most definitely are not. They are, at best, equal to a mid-range expression piano of around 1910 meaning that there is no accurate equivalent to Themodising, nor is there sufficient breadth of difference between 'soft' and 'loud' playing intensity. To the listener, they are bland producers of good-quality background music of the type heard in restaurants and hotel foyers the world over. And nobody has yet been able to estimate how long these electronic actions will last: built to a price (I avoided saying *down* to a price), the solenoids used in some instruments of this genre seem prone to wear. A more knowledgeable friend, invited by me to comment on the component parts of a well-known action of this type seemed unimpressed by the quality of the parts, suggesting that 'they'll be going noisy in a few years'.

Not, it should be added, that there's anything new about solenoids: the method of operating a switch or mechanical lever using an electrical device such as this was understood in the 19th century and Aeolian's Concertola piano-roll-player, and Duo-Art Pipe Organ detached consoles used solenoids. They have also been used in the organ-building industry since before the time of Robert Hope-Jones. Solenoids used in the modern pipe-organs are visibly different from those in the modern piano and have been proven to operate perfectly in some instances for almost sixty years.

This brings into sharp focus the act of a collector I know in the southern states of America who, faced with rebuilding his Model B Ampico, elected to throw away all the original parts and build in a MIDI-driven player action. This is not the action of a responsible collector who has the prime responsibility of preserving the surviving instruments from the past for the enjoyment of future generations. Now had this man installed his modern action into an ordinary finger-piano, then everybody would have smiled benignly on him. As it is he is now doomed forever to ride the stormy skies cursed with a leaky push-up and one popular song-roll.

Some collectors and computer-enthusiasts have set themselves the task of attempting to devise reproducing-piano coding that might enable an accurate electronic version of a reproducing roll. To the best of my knowledge no such quest has met with unreserved success, nor has the further goal of converting a coded roll from one reproducing system to another.

Meanwhile there is a formidable number of collectors who devoutly believe that the computer and its very infallibility offers a guarantee of perpetuity and that it should be possible to 'scan' paper piano-rolls and convert a stack of old rolls into a couple of compact discs. Regrettably nobody has successfully tested the durability (in archival terms) of computerised documents of any sort.[1] And because a piano-roll of any sort contains infinitely more information than a binary-coded MIDI-file may ever contain (here I refer to the information on paper quality, paper markings and watermarks, spool styles, spool labels, box styles, box labels and so on and so on) I see no point in making such copies since we have already had to accept that their performance will always be below that of a well-regulated player-piano with a decent paper roll.

Styled the Duo Art Early American, this Aeolian creation of 1966 was built as the Hardman Duo.

Is there a place for the MIDI-operated piano? Yes, of course there is. It forms a different and quite separate form of automatic piano that is ideally suited to those no doubt many applications where a real player-piano with its paper rolls would be an encumbrance, an eyesore or counter to the décor. Yes, MIDI-pianos are here to stay, but to compare one of these with a real player-piano or, even worse, a reproducing piano is to state that cats and dogs are the same because they both have a leg at each corner and a thing that wags at the back.

Personally I am full of admiration for the computer wizards amongst us who are pushing forwards the boundaries of automatic piano technology. My proviso is that, unless there is some really dramatic change in performance that lies just around the corner, and unless a computer disc becomes as permanent an archive as a piano-roll, then the computer wizard and the player-piano enthusiast should happily ride side by side but never attempt to harm one-another's instruments! Just suppose we offered to convert a PC to read a piano-roll in place of a floppy disc: I'll bet there'd be uproar if it were even suggested!

A curious device produced in California towards the end of the last century was a thing called the Power Roll and the claim was that it could turn your own player-piano into a musical instrument without need for perforated paper. In other words, you could play your player without using music rolls. Designed to look like a contemporary piece of early 20th century piano hardware rather than like a computer, this would operate an ordinary player-piano electronically by employing a solenoid-controlled air valve to replace the duties of the paper roll. To this end it was located over the tracker bar using the spool-box chucks just as a normal roll would be fixed. A small cable connected the Power Roll to either a computer or a CD-reader. When powered up, this clever box of tricks 'worked' the tracker bar just like a music-roll, opening and closing the holes to atmosphere electronically. All you had to do was provide the necessary vacuum by pedalling. The musical programme offered on CD was a library of 450 Ampico roll recordings transcribed to disc. Of course, you were left to put in the expression yourself by hand, but it was nevertheless a cheap and satisfactory solution to the problem of storing bulky piano rolls. As an alternative, for the electric reproducing piano, MIDI-encoded reproducing interpretations were also said to be available from the makers, Broadmoor Research Corporation.

Perhaps the most extraordinary development in this sphere has come about through the perseverance of retired university professor Sid O'Connell who has managed the unique feat of effectively reversing time when expressed as a sequence of operations. He has successfully taken an early gramophone record of piano music and translated it from acoustic recording to pneumatic piano-roll. Where a popular jazz pianist of the past, who never made piano-rolls but made records, his interpretational style and presentation can now be made into a piano-roll that has all the fidelity of a 'hand-played' roll of the past. A development of this is the reading of a piano-roll, converting it into a stream of binary data and then re-recording by computer, the piano-roll now capable of replication as a compact disc.

Without doubt, the survival of the player-piano into the 21st century owes its *raison d'être* to the world of collectors. But it also received another boost to its popularity for the greatest revolution has come about through technology that was unheard of even twenty years ago. The translation of piano-rolls into MIDI files that can be exchanged across the internet, the creation of new musical recordings that can be played on a player-piano without the aegis of a piano-roll and methods of creating and reducing scores for the computer-controlled piano represent thoroughly exciting new challenges and opportunities.

Septagonal spindles identified this, Aeolian's 'Mediterranean' model, also from 1966.

From music of the past which, I venture to suggest, is a 'known quantity', I feel bound to dwell on the changes in music that have taken place since the last commercially-cut piano-roll was offered on the market. I want to tell you the 'dark secret' of the player which, in simple terms, is that it is hopeless with some of today's music. I'll explain what I mean.

A great deal of today's music reflects what is called 'modern taste'. While this may call into question the meaning of the word taste and raise doubts as to whether taste dictates trends, or trends develop into taste, there seems no doubt that what we tend to describe as modern music is derived from a basis that is quite different from that upon which music was established in the past.

If the definition of musical creativity is itself a matter of conjecture, the person who listens to much of the output of today's composers finds himself left contemplating sounds that seem to reflect the disturbed minds that are the product of an age where the sanctity of the family unit, the unity of worship, established social values and the cornerstones of honesty and integrity are all aspects subsumed by the violent culture of the TV age, drug culture and movie violence. Like some modern art, it seems the product of deranged mind and a stomach exposed to an excess of mature cheese partaken of with the wrong wine.

Budding composers today seem mostly to produce 'works' that are derived from inadequate musical ideas where the deficiencies in melodic line are, hopefully, both masked and dignified by an abundance of percussion. Unresolved chords, discord and intervals of the minor second proliferate in a manner that would convince an old-school music teacher of his total failure to communicate to his student the poetry of rhythm, beauty and the delight of the Muse.

At the other end of the composing range, thematic repetition is so often thought an acceptable substitute for creative composition and conceptual development. In the 1930s, novice pianists were taught how to 'vamp' a tune by merely providing a succession of chords. This was as close to being a proper piano-player as some people ever got, yet it is the more remarkable that one popular modern pianist today has a tremendous following yet he merely produces a repetitive sequence of vamping chords. No amount of *leidenschaften* can conceal bereft inspiration!

The player-piano has found itself a tool for much modern music over the past two decades. Some of this has been interesting and reveals that the composer understands how to exploit the capabilities of the automatic piano. Other works merely confirm that inspiration is a lost cause.

Player pianos have, however, attracted the attention of those fringe artists who see things in a different way to most of us. As long ago as the 1950s, somebody photographed the waves of the sea, somehow transferred the image to a piano-roll – and went ecstatic over the result. Others have staged, purely in the interests of their art, we are told, player-piano races where the same roll is put on two or more instruments and played together for some reason that escapes me. The performing of music-rolls upside down and backwards, occasionally done as a joke ever since piano-rolls began, is now done seriously in the hope that it will create a new composition from an old composer which is reminiscent of the belief that a million monkeys let loose on a million typewriters must one day create a Shakespeare play.

Less stylistically disturbing to the eye, the Aeolian Musette player of 1967 came with a light-coloured case finished in unmatched wood veneer in the Scandinavian style – hence the attribution 'Danish'.

Drawing with a pencil around a body (presumably young, female, nubile and nude) has reputedly inspired a music-roll while making an endless loop of perforated music and threading it through two facing player-pianos was seriously considered (by one new-age musician) to offer certain unspecified musical advantages. However one attempts to view such matters, this type of nonsense devalues the player-piano, music and our very sensibilities. All of this is really rather childish but if it gives people pleasure then it is probably wrong to be too critical. My words to anybody contemplating his (or her) own version of such rubbish is just to pause a moment and ask yourself how your contribution to musical history will be viewed in, say, fifty years time.

During the closing decades of the 20th century, the player piano underwent an accelerating resurgence of interest, not just amongst collectors like you and me, but with composers and people who, years earlier, would probably not have given the instrument a second thought.

The work of Conlan Nancarrow (*b.* 1912; *d.*1997) in creating a variety of interesting pieces for player piano probably did more for the reputation of Conlan Nancarrow than for the player piano, but was nevertheless something of a watershed in the history of the player. Nancarrow's use of the player was inspired and totally novel. Unlike composers before him who had written for the idiom, he approached his subject methodically – in fact almost mechanically – with a list of all the things that the player could do whereupon he sat down and employed every one of them extending from instantaneous chords that embraced vast clusters of notes to high-speed glissandi that encompassed every note of the keyboard upwards and downwards in a vast sweep of sound. Other than the curiosity that was the underlying motivation for his *Composition for Two Player Pianos* (largely unplayable because of the problems of sustained accurate synchronisation), he revelled in the freedom from pianistic limitation and wrote music that could not be played adequately by a human performer (although some tried forsaking care and tempi to the four winds). No, Nancarrow's music was about the player piano and only the player could perform it as the composer wished.

Other composers have also used the player in recent years, either, like Nancarrow, as an original compositional basis, or as one subsequently adopted. The music of Gyögy Ligeti (*b.* 1923) falls neatly into both these categories. But it is in exploring Ligeti's very complex musical structures that we discover the player-piano's greatest weaknesses.

Now right at the start of this book I promised not to talk in musical gobbledegook and to constrain myself to the sort of musical notation represented by holes in paper. Here, though, to explain my point adequately, I have to make a brief foray into the dark realms of musicology and its jargon-speak. Bear with me a minute: I shall not wander too far away from our subject and I think you will understand what I'm getting at.

The musical example that I wish to cite comes from one of Ligeti's books entitled *Etudes for Piano*, very modern pieces that have become known to pianists because of their extreme difficulty and to pianolists because there is a sense of implied importance in trying to perform them with the feet or, come to that, automatically by electric piano.

One particular piece, classified as No. 14a, carries a revealing title that translates as 'Infinite Column' which, when listening to this music, is revealing. It is a supremely difficult piece (for me, at any rate), mainly in that the pianist's two hands perform with different dynamics that change from left to right continually. This music is a vast acoustic pyramid of sound from which notes appear to tumble apparently willy-nilly with the sound version of a mudslide.

Now there is actually a player-piano recording that has been issued of this piece. It has been released on CD. That it is played at almost exactly twice the intended speed (indicated by Ligeti's own metronome mark on the printed score) is only the start of the problem that, in my opinion, demonstrates very clearly where the player-piano fails.

When punched as a music-roll, the effect of this complex score becomes awesomely gruesome, for the person pedalling the player is faced with an absence of thematic material around which he might weave some semblance of expression. Bereft of the musical clues that make a manual performance, he pedals on regardless through great sweeps of notes, tumbling parallel thirds and cascades of chords that make neither sense to him nor, unfortunately, to any of his listeners. Furthermore the pattern of perforations in the music roll that practised pianolist may learn to recognise as what passes for a theme cannot, in this case, be discerned.

In written-down musical notation of this complex piece, however, something rather magical takes place. It's still the same sweeps, tumbles and cascades but the skilled performer who all the while he is playing is scanning the bars ahead of his hands can detect a thematic structure the presence of which is totally denied to the pianolist. It is rather like driving a car through a series of obstructions in that the eyes, looking ahead, can spot a clear path a view of which is denied to the passenger who only watches where the car is at a particular point in time. The manual pianist 'speed-reads' ahead and intuitively recognises the multiple themes and the interweaving countermelodies.

While the pianolist is unable to see these visual clues to what lies ahead, the finger pianist not only has the opportunity to consider his phrasing in advance of the instant of playing, but also can add interpretation and emphasis (not quite the same as accenting) to the best of his skills.

Where does this leave the automatic piano? I'm afraid the answer is well behind. Admittedly I am taking just one composer's music and merely one folio of pieces, yet it is important that we consider these for they represent a clear example of the player-piano's limitations. The gap between the manual performance and the one by the pianolist becomes for once a veritable chasm for here we have a salutary demonstration that mathematical accuracy just is not sufficient in some musical interpretation for it renders unintelligible that which has a supreme subtlety.

The rhythm of these pieces has to be felt in both the fingers and the soul, not merely counted out as a distance on a piece of paper.

You will probably already be ready with a comment as to why these so-difficult pieces of music are not recorded on reproducing piano rolls and the answer is that, other than hand-editing, there is no foolproof performance-recording equipment for piano rolls today, only computer-controlled systems. Yes, certainly expression can be put in the laborious way by hand-punching, but one questions whether it can be accurately interpreted today: the modern roll-music-arranger is by definition an amateur whereas once it was a full-time profession with all the skills that accompanied it.

The music of Conlan Nancarrow, on the other hand, has painstakingly been encoded for Ampico through the initiative of Dr Jürgen Hocker in Germany. Dr Hocker, an authority on the music of Nancarrow, whom he knew well, has given numerous performances of these pieces via his special rolls.

Nancarrow possessed a curious fascination for the abilities of the player-piano and he experimented freely with the instrument in some novel ways. In one piece, he wanted to exploit the relationship between the left hand and the right hand as regards speed of interpretation. This piece begins with the right hand portion playing very fast against a very slow left hand. Gradually the speed of the right hand slows as the left hand goes faster. At a mid-way point in the music, both are playing at the same speed, but gradually the relationship is reversed until the left hand is playing very fast and the right hand very slowly.

To create this unique piece of music, Nancarrow realised that mathematical precision was the solid route to success, so he made two identical sets of cardboard templates for marking out the bars on the piano-roll. These began very wide at one end and narrowed to very slim at the other by even intervals. The two sets of templates were then laid onto the piano roll, the widest one matched with the slimmest one, until the end of the sets of templates was reached where the slimmest was against the widest. These then gave the effective bar widths for each half of the piano keyboard. Musically the result is challenging and almost impossible to play by hand.

Unlike Ligeti, for whom the player was a musical accessory, Nancarrow saw it as a golden opportunity to conduct experiments that were generally beyond human capability. It can be argued that Nancarrow's music may be as philosophically designed as the interpreted waves of the sea, yet it has the virtue of being interesting, inspired and an on-going promotion for the automatic piano.

What this tells us is that, as with everything else in this life, the player-piano has some limitations and the further we explore the realms of those limitations the more we expose its interpretational weaknesses. This does not detract from its rich abilities in the broad musical sphere, only point out the edges of a performance 'envelope' beyond which we explore at our peril. It is clear to the collector who has a musical background that the Ampico is directed more towards the corpus of popular classics, light and salon music and, later in its life, popular music at which it excelled. The Duo-Art, although theoretically a more clumsy action, was better suited to playing classical music but also excelled in the broader repertoire. The original 'red' Welte, however, was theoretically a cumbersome action yet was a supreme interpreter of the finest music in the classical repertoire.

That class of music styled 'modern' by its very nature is taxing to the performer and also to the listener who is frequently called upon to 'work very hard' to understand the music. In the vast majority of 'old' music the listener had the easiest job and his senses were enticed rather than challenged. In my opinion this probably marks the boundary of that which is possible on the player-piano and that which is not. It is an argument that will be debated long and hard by die-hard factions in the realm of player collectors and alluded to, possibly cynically, by generations of musicologists for whom, remember, the player is the veritable cuckoo in the nest.

But the often self-consciously serious world of modern music also has a lunatic fringe that extends to no music at all, where, like the Emperor's new clothes, people go ecstatic over the interpretational nuances of absolutely nothing! Here the work of John Cage and his three-movement *'Four minutes, Thirty-three seconds'* stands supreme for it can be performed expertly by anyone merely by sitting in front of a silent piano, arms folded, for just that length of time. During one of the Purcell Room player-piano recitals in London this piece was 'performed' on a player-piano earning from *The Times* reviewer Max Harrison the shrewd comment: 'Last night's world premiere of this composition on piano rolls (one roll for each movement) was the only time the limitations of this method of recording were not readily apparent.'

In this section I have highlighted what I believe to be the areas in which the player cannot adequately cope. I believe that our understanding of the instrument must be as unbiased as possible and to overlook its warts is unrealistic. At the same time, just because your expensive high-performance luxury sports car cannot be driven above 20 miles-an-hour over a ploughed meadow should not detract from your enjoyment of it!

1. There are plenty of systems for storing office documents on disc. These have to be kept for seven, maybe ten years. Piano rolls have already survived, in some cases, nearly 125 years.

It was back to cabriole legs and an uncharacteristic heaviness for Aeolian's Duo Art French Provincial style model. What Aeolian missed out on all these was a basic fact that people who wanted a piano – and a player to boot – did not want to have to pedal the thing. What was wanted was an electric pump to take the sweat out of the music-roll.

Another Aeolian Musette player was the 'Italian Provincial' with square tapered inlaid legs. This was by far the most attractive of a rather mixed bunch of case styles that Aeolian believed would capture the imagination of the 'sixties public.

In the 1980s, QRS the music-roll makers thought up a novel marketing aid for their music-rolls – a player piano! In a total reversal of the whole history of the automatic piano (where the maker of the piano has eventually found himself drawn into making the music for the thing), here was a roll-maker deciding to go into players! Of course, they did not actually make the pianos themselves but that didn't matter: it was a player with the name QRS on it! Quite different from Aeolian's attempt at wooing a wrongly-identified style-conscious end of the market, QRS went for practicality and simplicity – and an electric pump! While full-compass, the player was compact with conventional but very attractive style.

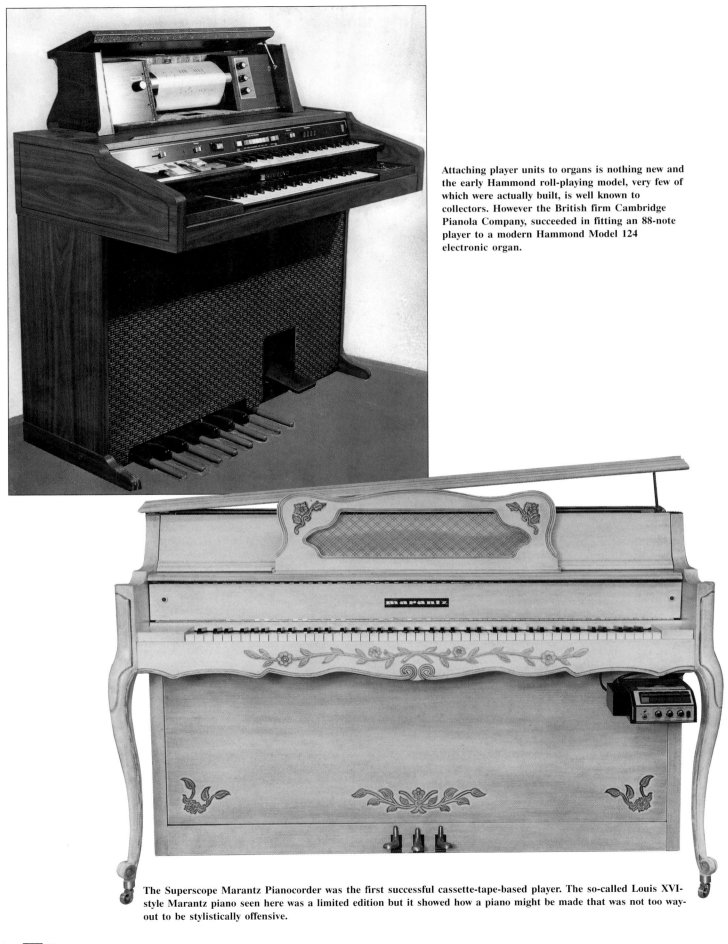

Attaching player units to organs is nothing new and the early Hammond roll-playing model, very few of which were actually built, is well known to collectors. However the British firm Cambridge Pianola Company, succeeded in fitting an 88-note player to a modern Hammond Model 124 electronic organ.

The Superscope Marantz Pianocorder was the first successful cassette-tape-based player. The so-called Louis XVI-style Marantz piano seen here was a limited edition but it showed how a piano might be made that was not too way-out to be stylistically offensive.

The Marantz player system allowed one either to play back specially pre-recorded data cassettes or to record your own performances again as data tapes. This pioneering player system inspired a number of installations by amateurs but the consensus of opinion was that it was a tricky job for the ordinary enthusiast to get right. One man who made a huge success of his installation was William Edgerton of Darien in Connecticut who succeeded in converting a brand new harpsichord made in Boston by Eric Herz. The player unit, seen on the chair at the right, is connected via a conventional electric cable.

The revolution in player systems that began with the tape cassette, extended through Compact Cassette to Compact Disc, and then moved into the realms of solid-state computer technology and Random Access Modules, now brings musical capability of a quality and accessibility never even dreamed of by the pneumatic and electrical engineers of the early 1900s. Here, in December 1982, the author is seen being suitably overwhelmed at the sight of a cassette containing some hours of music for the then-latest Technics synthesised pianos. Great as these are, there is somehow something missing – like watching the perforated paper unfold before your eyes.

Chapter 13
Looking after Automatic Pianos and Music Rolls: Tools and Skills Needed

After all the foregoing, you have a pretty good idea how the player-piano works. Living with one (or more) of them means that you have to minister to its occasional needs, be they mechanical or pneumatic. As you now see, they are not so mysterious once you understand how they are made and what each function does. Back in Chapter 8 I explained that every action of the player piano was through a controlled leak. Now this means that a leak in the right place is vital. That it is controlled is even more vital. But if there are any other leaks in your instrument – and I mean any at all other than those we have already talked about – then your piano will not play!

The player-piano is totally dependent on working the way it was originally intended and if your bellows are leaky, your tracker-bar tubing broken or your wind-motor bellows motors perished, then comparatively enormous quantities of atmosphere are entering the hallowed vacuum area within and totally swamping the action. In automobile terms, you lose compression and the more you lose the less power you have until the car stops completely.

Lesson One in Maintenance: Suspect leaks if the piano will not play properly or if its performance suddenly drops. Seek for leaks with the zest of a truffle-hunter for the rewards shall be great! Ignore a leak (or a potential leak) at your peril. Things can only get much, much worse! And ten minutes spent on a repair now will be better than a month when the thing has gone completely kaput! Learn that the words 'that will be good enough!' are totally fallacious! Also know that your instrument has a cunning trick up its sleeve: it will always go wrong and give trouble when you are demonstrating it before friends. The more important (or qualified) the audience, the more it will develop tantrums. The moral is simple! Beat it at its own game by not allowing it the slightest opportunity of going wrong!

If something stops happening very quickly (*ie* it worked OK this morning, now it won't), then suspect something fundamental and simple like a hose has come off somewhere. If something stops happening very slowly over a period of time, the gradual deterioration probably indicates something more serious such as perished bellows motors or a build-up of dirt and dust in the motor. All these things are quickly sorted out once you know your player piano thoroughly.

There is a very competent book on restoration that I heartily recommend if you are faced with the rebuilding of a derelict instrument (*see* Reblitz *[89]*). Another recent book that will guide you through some of the necessary work and your understanding of the processes of restoring mechanical musical instruments is *Restoring Musical Boxes & Musical Clocks [83]*. Despite its title, I think you will find it useful in that it describes and shows you how to undertake many of the general processes of repair and restoration. Besides showing principles and methods of working with rubber cloth and leather,

it also offers advice on cabinet work, in particular details such as the Spreckle joint for timber, and wooden panel stitching, processes that are associated with, and recommended in, professional-quality case-repair. Fundamentally, this book outlines restoration procedures that apply to just about any form of mechanical musical instrument. It also describes in some detail the subject of tuning and musical temperament.

This maze of rubber tubing is the rear view of a 65/88-note player. This instrument was fully restored less than twenty years ago using grey rubber tubing. This stuff, unlike red or black rubber, has a great deal of filler in it besides the natural rubber and this causes premature hardening. If you look closely you can see that almost every one of the tubes in the upper portion is fractured at the nipple.

While I leave the minutiae of rebuilding to these other books, I want to dwell on the sort of running repairs that will keep your player sweet. At the same time I want to comment at length on materials because there are substances around today that were never even heard of in the time of original manufacture.

First a gentle word of warning! You can restore your player-piano in your lounge or living room, but I wouldn't recommend it, particularly if you have a house-proud partner. While a proper workshop may be the ideal, not everybody has such a facility but perhaps you have a spare room in which to work. You will need a space that is ideally at normal house temperature and free from damp and cold.

Now to the subject of tools for the job. Other than the normal complement of hand tools, you should have on hand the following: screwdrivers – one long with 1/4-inch wide blade; one long 'watchmaker's'-type, 1/8-inch wide blade; one very short stubby, 3/16-inch blade; an assortment of small electrical-type screwdrivers: one surgical scalpel: one pair of long-handled tweezers (surgical forceps are ideal): one small magnet (for lifting dropped screws out of inaccessible places): one pair snipe-nosed pliers: one pair round-nosed pliers: one pair of sidecutters: one pair of endcutters: one bradawl (for feeling for hidden holes): one roll of masking tape (for closing up tracker bar and securing loose pieces during disassembly): sundry dental probes are also useful for getting into awkward places.

Very useful additions to this range are a rechargeable electric screwdriver such as the Black & Decker, and a small electric drill. There are often so many screws used in a windchest that a power driver makes sense and can save you blisters. Use power drivers only for *removing* screws, never for replacing and tightening because they can often provide so much torque that they will strip the thread in their holes.

Sundries which you will need comprise an assortment of pieces of felt offcuts in various thicknesses and qualities, and a few square feet of bushing felt in thicknesses from 1mm to 3mm. You will also need some small cardboard boxes or plastic boxes in which to store screws and small parts as you remove them. You may also like to have some white self-adhesive labels to mark parts for identification. And try to get some transparent polythene dust-sheets – dust-sheets because you should cover up dismantled parts to keep them clean and transparent because then people can see what's underneath and will not be tempted to think it's an armchair and sit down.

Finally, in these introductory notes, do not fall into the trap of trying to take the easy way out and replacing a defective gasket with glue, or gluing pieces together either side of the same gasket. This destroys all possibility of ever being able to make a simple running repair should it be necessary, and you will be cursed by future restorers. One of my own instruments had suffered at the hands of a 'gluer-upper' at sometime in its past life. It took long hours of unnecessary work to put this right.

There are many ways of starting an argument and one sure-fire way is to get two player-piano experts together and get them going on the subject of materials. I guarantee you'll have hours of enjoyment and a ferocious debate. The main reason is that there are two schools of thought about practically everything. And both have their ardent supporters.

Many of the airway connections in a player of any sort are completed by tubing. In the earliest days this was occasionally of lead but with the increasing availability of good quality rubber tubing and its convenience of use rapidly replaced metal.

Today there's a variety of synthetic substances on the market to replace rubber. Modern plastics are very light in weight, are much more supple under a wider range of conditions than rubber, and are easily available. However, they are not without their disadvantages. To me, the biggest is that they are simply not original to an instrument.

My work in museum-standard conservation and restoration has to conform to strict guidelines when it comes to replacing materials and this extends to using the same materials as when the instrument was built.

In close-up the rubber has lost its elasticity and become brittle. The tube to the left has been pulled off its nipple and yet is still bears the shape and form of the nipple having set rock hard around it. Notice also the huge quantity of dirt in the ends of the metal tubes. All this has to be cleaned out before re-tubing.

'Absolute nonsense!' cries the man from the other side of the table. 'Do you think that if Aeolian had access to polyvinyl tubing they wouldn't have used it? What do you say to that, then, eh!'

Yes, I reply, but the point is that they *didn't* have that material so they used rubber and this means that a restoration to original condition must use the same materials.

'But I don't *care* about original materials!' screams the man defiantly. 'It's *my* piano, I *paid* for it and I'll do *what I dam' well like* with it!'

OK, so it's a case of 'no argument'. And don't think that this is a totally invented encounter: I've had dozens and dozens of them across the years. Sometimes they are good, honest chaps who just feel that modern materials, *because* they are modern, must be better. I can't always fault that argument. Others are the maverick ones who saw bits off their instruments to install computer playback loudspeakers and solenoids.

They are the destructive ones for whom I feel sorry. Like the collector I visited in America several years ago. He possessed a wonderful collection of instruments and proudly showed me how all of them could be controlled remotely by a computer keyboard and pre-recorded computer discs. In another life I am sure he was the sort of chap who scrapped the organ-barrels of a street organ and fitted a then-new book-playing system in its place!

No, spare me the wanton destructors! I don't wish to have any part in the movement that courts modernisation over and above conservation and preservation. It is conservation and preservation that are the divine cornerstones of true restoration and the motivating force behind the genuine collector.

It was told to me by an informed collector in Connecticut many years ago that Aeolian had a special policy on tubing. That maker was determined to put into its player actions the finest materials money could buy at the time. While other manufacturers were paying less than a half-cent a foot for their tracker-bar tubing, Aeolian was having their tubing specially made at a cost of a cent and a half per foot. This attitude certainly paid off in the long term, for many Aeolian pianos continued to work well on the original rubber materials for at least half a century. And that could hardly be said of any other brand of player action.

The problem that player-piano collectors and restorers inherited after the 1939-45 war was that the rubber industry had changed and many of the one-time staple-diet production lines had been discontinued as the pattern of product demand gradually changed. The simple truth was that rubber manufacturers no longer knew how to produce the better grades of rubber. Besides, they were too involved with other and more profitable lines (one being synthetic rubbers and plastics) to bother about what was now a very small line to service a cottage industry.

So what about rubber versus plastic tubing? In truth, I don't suppose it matters a lot because it is not a permanent alteration and plastic can be replaced later if needed. Personally, I am a rubber man. I've always preferred rubber and always used rubber. You are safe with rubber. It is a natural substance, it ages predictably and its side effects are predictable. You won't get into trouble by using rubber. But plastic! Let me tell you a little story.

In the 1970s my late friend, the American publisher and piano expert Harvey Roehl, recounted a salutary tale of something that had happened to him in the mid-1960s. It concerned a local physician friend to whom Harvey recommended the services of a well-qualified piano technician to rebuild the reproducing mechanism of her magnificent Steinway XR Duo-Art which was housed in a specially-carved walnut case. In due course, the job was completed and the instrument performed well.

This was the age of clear plastic tubing that many restorers used on both sides of the Atlantic. Ten years later, Harvey got the message that the D-A was no longer giving of its best so he went over to take a look. Plastic tubing had been used throughout the instrument. What was different was that now this tubing was exuding what looked for all the world like black crankcase oil, even to the extent of dripping it onto the Oriental rug underneath!

While Harvey couldn't imagine what this was all about, he nevertheless lost no time in removing all of the tubing. One of his colleagues at the college where he taught for many years was an outstanding organic chemist, so he was asked to investigate. Some time later the report came that a careful analysis, using sophisticated laboratory equipment as well as a chemist's general knowledge, confirmed that the oily mess was merely a special chemical used in compounding the product. Exposure to atmosphere had gradually released it and turned in black!

For some complicated chemical reason, plastics such as that formulation used in making the raw tubing must have in them an ingredient that insures that the material stays flexible. This is called a 'plasticiser' and under certain conditions it will leave the parent material and collect on the surface. This particular piano had been in a normal living room, so one may only assume that the vacuum inside the lines prompted the condition.

Another American collector was so shocked to hear of this that he wrote: 'I was using clear plastic tubing regularly until about three or four years ago. I then noticed pianos previously done had turned 'oily' after about three to five years, including some tubing in my stockpile at home. In view of this I stopped using clear tubing, as I didn't want this to happen again. I might add this tubing was purchased from several reputable piano supply houses. Almost all of the clear tubing I ever purchased did this after a while and as a result I have since been using neoprene tubing only.'

Two types of plastic tubing exist, Neoprene and, in the United States, Tygon. But these have odd and sometimes unpredictable characteristics one of which is a curious intolerance of paint! A number of American collectors reported that Tygon would not stay on a nipple if that nipple had first been painted. Some chemical reaction between the plasticiser in the paint and that in the plastic was taking place.

Much of this plastics problem has come about because modern rubber tubing may not be to the same quality as the old stuff, some of which has long-since rotted away while other examples are as fresh and pliable today as when put on in the early 1900s. American collectors had to use a grey-coloured rubber at one time which hardened, pre-set on nipples and deteriorated within a decade or so. Another collector/restorer Stateside wrote to me about this, saying: 'In the 1950s I had an experience with some grey tubing which is still being sold to unsuspecting people in the same poor quality that was offered 20 years ago. The similarity with the old original tubing ends with the colour. It lasted only a year before hardening on the nipples and dropping off. I concluded that it would be a waste of time to do a fine restoration job using materials that were so worthless.' Warning! Grey or brown rubber tubing indicates a high percentage of filler indicating cheap quality and poor durability.

In Britain there's a choice between red or black rubber tubing, each having slightly different characteristics.

In America, the move to plastic was spurred by the one-time poor quality of the rubber tubing available. One widespread theory was that it was increasing pollution that was affecting latex-based products. The popular plastic substitute called Tygon was made in two qualities, one for use in food dispensers, and another for chemicals and suchlike. It soon became apparent that the food quality tube showed fewer tendencies towards plasticiser migration.

Equally vociferous in defending their corners are those of the neoprene brigade. They will tell you that neoprene has excellent aging qualities. It does not harden or deteriorate with any great rapidity – unless it is stretched or kinked. However, any disturbance from the original form creates a stress that can lead to breaking, splitting and cracking. If neoprene tubing is stored it might last for years. However, this is not the normal use of the material.

Several varieties of neoprene exist starting from a fairly stiff or hard type that is created with a few additives. This is the one most commonly selected for player use.

Durrell Armstrong of The Player Piano Company in Wichita wrote that:

> …a mixture of about half neoprene and half gum rubber is the most serviceable. Both have qualities that depend on one another for stability. The gun rubber has the elasticity to stretch without breakdown and the neoprene has the good aging quality. Pure gum rubber has a life of about five years. I am speaking of the amber-coloured surgical tubing. There are many other varieties of gum rubber combinations with varying purpose, cost, and degrees of stretchability.

Armstrong has been selling what he described as 'soft' neoprene tubing – a half-and-half mix – for many years for the tubing of tracker bars and says that, although it will not have full recovery after removing from the nipple and replacing it, is durable and is far better off than plastic tubing of equal age.

Virtually all plastic tubing, however, suffers from one inherent defect in that over time it becomes less supple and can lose its original shape meaning cross-section. Any plastic other than neoprene sets up a chemical reaction with brass. It will create a slime that can be of a blue-green colour, this aiding the tubing to fall off in hot weather when the plastic is more supple. This is because you cannot guarantee the stability of the catalyst used in its manufacture: that used in most vinyls is historically unstable.

All tubing, both rubber and plastic, develops 'set' when stretched on to a nipple. That of a plastic tube can become rigid, inflexible and, as we have seen, wet-lubricated through chemical reaction. Rubber tubing, on the other had, does not always go hard and unless disturbed, the 'set' will not loosen on the nipple. If rubber tubing has to be stretched excessively to fit a nipple, then the weak spot created by the 'waist' will perish quickest and first which is why rubber tubes often break off just short of the nipple leaving the nipple piece intact and in place.

Neoprene tubing shrinks both in size and length during that part of its manufacturing process known as curing. The amount by which shrinkage occurs varies but it is about twelve percent – that's the equivalent of more than one foot in ten! This is why the bore or inner diameter varies so much with tubing of this type. When used on tracker bars, some of the tubing will be loose while other lengths will be tight. The variation is most noticeable on the small bore tubing where tight fit is most critical.

Some of the cheaper, poorer grades of rubber tubing have a high mineral content in the form of fillers used to make the basic rubber content go further. Rubber that contains no fillers is generally brick red in colour. Black rubber tube contains some fillers, while grey rubber, as we have just seen, contains an enormous quantity of fillers, often easily visible on the surface which is dull in texture. This grey tubing deteriorates in a peculiar manner: it hardens quickly and goes brittle. Like uncooked macaroni, it shatters and sections break off if it is bent. In America, cheap rubber tubing has much larger tolerances concerning dimensions than high quality tubing, so the bore may be variable. Fitting this to, say, a tracker bar nipple could therefore mean that the stuff falls straight off.

So that, very briefly, is the argument concerning rubber *vs.* synthetics. I have tried to express both sides fairly. The choice is really up to you but I have made my own position clear – it's rubber for me every time – red rubber!

I mentioned just now the lead tubing that many early actions used. This was particularly so with some of the earliest push-ups. Apart from the obvious fact that a lead-tubed action is going to be very heavy, the quality of the lead varied greatly. Some of it is as good today as it was when first soldered on. Other times the lead has corroded both inside and out and become embrittled which means that it has developed a crystalline structure than renders it fragile, especially where it passes through wood. Where possible, cut a sample tube with a fine saw (don't use nippers: this will close up the tube ends and give you more work) and look inside for any white or grey powder. This is the indication of lead-corrosion and means you should replace it all otherwise it will clog the valve seats and the bleeds. If the tubing is clean, then rejoin your cut tube with a short rubber sleeve and leave alone.

Heavy hoses, such as those used to direct vacuum from the reservoir into the valve chest or pneumatic stack, are always of large-diameter and originally were made of cloth-wrapped (twill-sealed) rubber of the style used in car radiators of the old style. You may be lucky to obtain short lengths of this self-same material from a car servicing specialist shop, but alternatively thick-walled red rubber tubing can be used as a good substitute. The bore of this hose is almost always $5/8$-inch. Some player actions also use $11/16$-inch bore rubber hose. Do check exactly what you need for your particular instrument before you go a-hunting and spending hard-earned cash.

Fitting rubber tube onto nipples is a job that can be remarkably sore on the fingers. Some restorers recommend using water as a lubricant to help the rubber onto the metal while others swear by soft soap. I have tried both methods and find fault with each. Naturally you must never use anything containing oil or grease since this would quickly rot the rubber. Vaseline comes into this category. However, chemists and drug-stores sell tubes of what is called surgical lubricating jelly that is rubber-friendly. This is ideal. Spread a little on the tip of your forefinger, rub with the thumb and then run along all the tracker bar nipples in one pass, rubbing your jelly-covered fingers on each one. You will now find that the rubber slips on very easily as far as you need without progressively tearing the skin from your fingernails. Do not try to lubricate the end of the rubber tubing instead since this will not be as effective. Furthermore there is the chance you will create a meniscus of lubricant inside the tube that will transfer onto the nipple and might set as a cap when dry.

Surgical lubricant has one other advantage. When it dries, which it does by evaporation, it forms a very slight bond between the rubber and the nipple. It is *very* slight, but it is a reassuring additional security.

From player-piano tubing to player-piano cloths. All the bellows and motors in these instruments were covered in rubberised cloth: some very early push-ups had leather and, occasionally, cardboard with leather-strip hinge reinforcements.

Rubberised cloth, occasionally given its inventor's name as Mackintosh (named after Charles Macintosh, *b.*1760; *d.*1843, and spelled without the 'k') cloth, has been around since James Sym's invention of the amalgamation of cotton and rubber in 1823. The material, as specified, has a smooth texture and is completely airtight. Unfortunately, the material that is usually found is rough-textured and full of pinholes! The original cloth as used by Aeolian in America was specially made for the company to a very high standard. Some of it remains serviceable a century later.

The main use for this material was in the manufacture of observation balloons where its suitability depended on its resistance to the passage of gas. The base of cotton cloth was rendered impervious by a coating of uncured latex rubber: a thicker grade of cloth was made either by using a tougher substrate (such as linen) or by laminating two thicknesses of cotton cloth together with the rubber coating between. As balloons were gradually phased out of use there was a decline in this prime use that resulted in the quality of the product deteriorating greatly. Without tight Government-inspired specifications to adhere to, less attention was paid to its manufacture. The outcome was poor-quality rubber cloth that was not totally impervious to air. It is thus reassuring to note that the original Aeolian specification has been resurrected and new cloth is available today that is as good as the original.

Natural rubber deteriorates with time through two main causes – sunlight and the acid in polluted air, in particular that generated as a by-product of gaslight. Unfortunately both have been common in most homes since earliest times, although the march of electric lighting in our homes has just about eradicated that problem. It is also gravely affected by contact with oils (both mineral and vegetable) and their derivatives, as well as all forms of grease.

Keeping sunlight or direct rays of the sun from those parts of an instrument covered in rubber cloth is fairly straightforward, but it remains a consideration as does the potential problem of tobacco smoke and coal-dust.

Rubber cloth on the pneumatic motors of a player action is exposed to repeated folding along pre-determined crease lines and, with time, the rubber coating becomes dried out and changes from being pliable and airtight to being friable and powdery. In extreme cases it will separate from the cloth as black dust, leaving the white cotton showing through. With motors in anything like this condition there is no alternative but to recover them: you cannot 'patch up' or effectively 're-seal' the cloth.

As with rubber tubing, people have long sought a substitute. The arrival on the scene of plastics seemed to offer a suitable alternative. Polythene sheet was eyed for a while until it was realized that sticking it to wood was almost as impractical as sticking it to itself as necessary in making an air-tight lap joint. Polythene was a non-starter.

Early in the 1960s there came what everybody thought was the long-awaited breakthrough! It originated not from the player piano people but from organ-builders in America who were accustomed to using large quantities of thin brown leather (zephyr skin) which was widely used on small bellows motors.[1]

The quest for a substitute had taken a turn for the urgent because the leather then available to them had gradually declined in quality and it was also deteriorating rapidly in urban areas due to air pollution. Organ-builders had tried oiling the leather with silicone preparations that were thought to aid preservation, but in the end this proved to be worse than no treatment at all; under certain humidity conditions mould was forming on the silicone-treated leather resulting in very rapid breakdown.

Organ-builders never use rubber cloth because they cannot be convinced of its durability. However, the new plastic materials held out hopes of a better if not cheaper alternative to the declining stocks of suitable-quality leather. They experimented first with a polyurethane coated nylon cloth called Numalon. This produced encouraging results and inspired exploration of other polyurethane materials. The organ-building industry received joyously the eventual news that a replacement for brown leather had been found. It was a strong, flexible film only two thousandths of an inch thick which couldn't be broken by flexing and apparently would not deteriorate from atmospheric pollutants. It had the characteristics and texture of semi-transparent latex sheeting. And there was a special adhesive which stuck the material to both timber and to itself.

As a material for making pouches it was seemingly ideal; instead of using thin brown zephyr skin leather and gluing on each of 88 piano circular pouches individually, you simply glued a wide strip of it flat on the pouch block and then easily heat-formed over each pouch-board recess into the desired pouch shape. After a year of testing, Polyurethane came through with flying colours.

The first people to make use of this were the makers and restorers of church and cathedral organs. In a short while, the majority of American organ builders had converted to Polyurethane. Many hundreds of pneumatic motors and pouches were covered in this attractive substitute to rubber cloth. It was so much thinner that an action covered with this material was not just perfect but could be more prompt in response.

Player piano restorers quickly got to hear of the material and across the world the demand for the new stuff accelerated to a clamour. Many piano actions were restored using Polyurethane.

It all seemed too good to be true. Reality would prove that it was. The first problem struck a major New York City pipe organ builder (Austin Organ Co) who was horrified to find that a chest that he had re-covered with a 1964 brand of polyurethane film decayed and became unusable some nine years later. Speaking to the manufacturer of the material in question, the pipe-organ builder was told that this kind of failure was not unique. Apparently in some cases, the polyurethane films had disintegrated within two to three years. Even more disturbing was the fact that it didn't take unusually high levels of air pollution to cause such damage.

A litany of problems was suddenly unleashed on the musical-instrument building and repair industry, not to say those player-piano enthusiasts who had eagerly grasped Perflex with open arms. It was also found that even when using the recommended adhesives with the best polyurethane films there was substantial creep of the material; the film would move sideways relative to the surface it was supposed to be adhered to. In other instances, the use of pressure in a pneumatic device would actually begin to peel the film away from its adhesive, since none of the adhesives used on polyurethane films, traditionally described as PVC glues, actually achieved a true chemical bond being by nature more of a contact cement.

But perhaps the worst scenario concerned those pouch boards that had been covered by strips of polyurethane and then had the pouches dished afterwards using a heat source and a forming tool. The problem now concerned the phenomenon of plastic 'memory.' The film would retain its pouched configuration until it was exposed to a subsequent heat source, such as a close-by electric lamp. This heat source would then cause the film to 'remember' its original flat shape, with the result that the dished pouches would slowly disappear. The loss of pouch action that then occurred resulted in the malfunctioning of the instrument. For a player-piano it was just as catastrophic.

But there were those prepared to stick with it and solve its problems. An answer that seems to have met with success is to vacuum-form individual circular pouches. In dispensing with the element of heat, these pouches do not suffer from the 'memory' problems and one company in America makes sets of piano pouches in this manner. These have the unquestionable benefit of being chemically inert and having no equal in performance as to sensitivity, air tightness, and resistance to changes of humidity and temperature.

Now I have tried polyurethane film and pouches and have not personally felt easy over the use of such radically different materials. At the time, American restorers claimed that their hands were forced by the lack of suitable high-quality thin leather, citing that the tanning quality of leather has declined over the last several decades. In Europe that is not the case and extremely high-quality skins are readily available. Admittedly they are expensive, but they are original, natural substances and they are very easy to use. These days properly tanned zephyr skin is available and for me this would always be both my preference and my first choice.

Again, there are two schools of thought over these plastics and I am sure that it's a sure-fire way to start a fight going amongst player-piano fanatics to so much as mention the subject. From the safe distance of an author's chair I shall continue to recommend real, original materials as being safe, predictable, reliable and if it was good enough for our ancestors, then it's good enough for you and me!

I might add that over the past fifty years I have always maintained a perfectly open mind concerning new materials and techniques, certainly as regards anything outside conservation work. In this time I have experimented with some weird and wonderful substances and processes as part of my policy of giving everything a go if it sounds feasible. There has to be more reason for my having gone the full circle aside from just sheer pig-headedness!

Another question I am frequently asked concerns quantities of materials needed to rebuild the average player. It does vary from instrument to instrument but as a rule a complete rebuild will involve about 2½-square yards of thin rubberised cloth (this is generally known as 'pneumatic cloth'), and 1½-square yards of thicker bellows cloth (usually – originally – two-ply twill cloth). You will need a small supply of off-cuts of sheepskin and thin piano felt. The average tracker-bar assembly will use between 175 and 210 linear feet of rubber tubing depending whether it is a 65-note or an 88-note action. For sundry hoses the average player uses five feet of $5/_8$-inch bore twill-covered hose, and three feet of $11/_{16}$-inch bore rubber hose.

At this point in this discussion on materials, I want to talk about glue. Arguments over adhesives make those of rubber tubing and cloth pale into insignificance! It's a tough world tackling restoration work!

As far as player restoration is concerned, there are only two types of glue – natural or animal glue (which includes Pearl, Seccotine and fish glue varieties), and synthetic which embraces PVA and other resin formulations. Now each has a place with the restorer and each has the opportunity to play a part in the process. First and foremost, one requirement is paramount and that is that the glue joint can be undone for a later restoration. Joints made with so-called 'permanent-bond' glues, 'super-glues' and water-tight glues cannot be undone without damaging one or both surfaces. Never be tempted to use these adhesives: the 'Bad Place' is filled with so-called restorers who made glue joins that could never be taken apart and their penance is to sit out for all time on a damp rock to which they are irrevocably secured with an 'instant glue' while they watch pretty girls and wonderful player-pianos parade past for ever.

Synthetic glues have the great benefit of being easy to use and quick-drying. They also tend to contaminate base wooden surfaces making a return to natural adhesives at a later restoration that much harder.

Natural glues are slower to use and, in the case of hard, sheet glue (traditional horse glue) and Pearl pelleted glue, need careful preparation in a double glue-boiler, and careful application so that the joint does not cool too quickly.

To summarise the glue situation, hot brown glue is always preferable but in some instances it is awkward to use and when used over large surfaces, such a degree of special pre-treatment is needed (heating the surfaces to which the hot glue is applied to limit premature cooling) that it cannot be guaranteed to produce a perfect bond. The best form of brown glue is that which is a patent variety that maintains liquidity at room temperature by virtue of simple additives in manufacture. So called fish glue comes into this class as does Seccotine and its family of adhesives.

Properly used in selected applications, PVA glue almost always gives a good bond and, being soluble in water, it can be washed off at a later date if required.

Again the choice is up to you although I would be the first to add that any type of PVA glue is neither original nor advised for conservation use or repairs.

Back to the mail-bag and the next topic of questions concerns pouches and whether or not they have to be sealed. Pouches, traditionally, have been made of fine brown leather known as zephyr skin. They are dished after application by being stretched using a shaped hand mandrel. They are never made of rubber cloth[2] nor are they made of white sheepskin. They are secured to the pouchboard with brown glue sometimes called hide-glue, fish-glue or Seccotine which are all processed glues that may be applied and use cold.

All thin leathers are porous to a varying degree and this porosity is generally controlled by adjusting the bore of the bleed holes so that the pouch functions adequately. I have said earlier that every function of the player piano is by controlled leak and a pouch is no exception except that the main control is the size of the bleed hole. This would have been adjusted individually to each pouch depending on the degree of porosity of each individual pouch. It was usually an accepted problem since the leakage was normally very slight. However, some original manufacturers preferred a treatment in manufacture to limit or otherwise reduce this natural porosity. Substances used to seal the pouch had to conform to simple rules: they had to remain 'dry' after application and must not act hygroscopically (attract moisture) afterwards, and they had to allow the pouch leather to remain supple at all times and under the anticipated range of temperature and humidity conditions to which the instrument might be subjected in its life.

One very good substance was the simplest – French chalk. Rubbed into the finished leather surface, the minute particles of powder effectively closed off the tiny natural pores of the leather. A second substance used by some makers was the white of an egg. A tiny dab of this mucous on a cloth was wiped into the surface of the leather and when it dried it became invisible while performing as intended. In the mid-1930s the last generation of players were all treated with dilute rubber cement: this was reduced to the consistency of water and painted onto the leather.

All these treatments worked, although few today would use dilute rubber solution[3] on the grounds of availability. For some reason, today's restorers all seem to look to more complex modern substances to do this job. What's wrong with a chicken's egg, I ask! Or some powdered French chalk from the pharmacy? No, a lot of people have tried a lot of other substances ranging from something called 'mink oil' (which may be OK for a squeaking mink but which I wouldn't risk anywhere near a pouch on a piano) to Neatsfoot oil, silicone oils and greases.

I am sure that everybody now knows that anything with silicone in it is to be avoided at all costs since silicone tends to migrate into everything around it. If you must go for a modern synthetic sealant, then use white PVA glue mixed one part glue to eight parts water and rub this in with the finger. It's not original, but unlike silicones and greases, oils and potions, it's harmless and will stay where you put it.

Now to the repair and restoration of music-rolls and first a most important word of warning concerning transparent sticky tape. This ubiquitous material has its uses in doing up parcels and packages but please *NEVER* use it to repair damaged paper. And *NEVER* use it to stick, join, repair or cover paper of any kind. This is because it discolours with age, indelibly turning the paper brown as the adhesive permeates the paper and becomes impossible to remove. *This kind of tape spoils paper forever.*

Originally there was a gummed semi-transparent tape called 'music-tape' that was ideal for repairing torn paper. You moistened the glue surface (licked it) and stuck it down. It was readily soaked off when no longer needed and because the glue was fine and water-soluble did not spoil the paper. There is today a quite expensive professional paper repair film that is very thin with an inert conservation-quality contact adhesive. Tapes such as these are fine but *NEVER* use the ordinary adhesive tape you buy at the stationer's store. Also avoid any of the self-adhesive papers or labels because this type of 'dry' or contact glue may 'creep' from around the edge and cause adhesion where it is not wanted.

Keeping your piano-rolls in good condition will make them last longer and ensure that they play to the best of their ability. First off, then, is to buy yourself a packet of spare or replacement roll end tags so that when, as does happen all-too frequently, the tag by which you hook the roll to the take-up spool breaks or comes away from the roll apron, you can make an immediate repair. Often people who should know better have a tendency to stick the apron to the take-up spool with sticky tape or, just as bad, to push the metal link of the take-up spool through the roll paper. Neither of these practices is acceptable in the home of the conscientious player-pianist.

The forepart of the music-roll – the portion that is trimmed to a triangular shape at the point of which the tag is attached – is called the apron and, as its name suggests, it is there to protect the rest of the roll. It is the part that takes all the handling when you are putting a roll into the piano and taking it out again. It gets dirty and, in some cases, torn. With cheaper types of music roll, the apron is formed out of the ordinary roll paper while in better-quality rolls it is made of a stiffer paper that is glued to the edge of the roll proper.

Today, collectors' societies on both sides of the Atlantic produce replacement aprons in a variety of styles to replicate damaged originals. The same goes for box and roll labels that have become dirty, torn or are missing altogether.

Replacement roll boxes are also available but always, wherever possible, try to repair the original boxes simply because even the best of the newly-made boxes are not a patch on the old ones when it comes to quality and durability. Repairing a box means understanding how it was made in the first place. The modern box-making method is 'crease and fold' which does not give you nice sharp corners. The earliest boxes were all made of separate pieces of card carefully edge glued with reinforcement strips and then a paper cover. Occasionally there was even a glued paper liner, the whole being assembled on a former so that the box was perfect in dimensions and adequate in size.

Although this is all a bit fiddly, it is neither impossible to restore one of these boxes, nor is it impossible to make a new one. The limit is your own wish and skill. I have made replica 'original' boxes in batches of six at a time and, because they have to be left to dry in stages, find that I can easily turn out a batch in an evening, finishing them off the following one. All it takes is accuracy with a sharp modelling knife, some good thick card and a lot of patience. More than patience, though, is the will to succeed! Boxes made this way are just so much better than the ones commercially made and they are actually far cheaper in the long run.

Now to the actual paper roll. Three forms of physical damage are common. First is the tear which may start from a long perforation or be caused through negligent handling. Second is the pleated edge where a narrow margin of the paper is folded over for some length of the roll. This effectively makes the roll slightly narrower than it should be and plays havoc with automatic tracking systems. In fact, auto tracking will systematically make a pleated roll worse as it continually shifts back and forth to try to align the paper. Third is the roll that is warped through dampness or having been left half unrolled on a piano for some time. It is amazing how many people do this: they play part of a roll and then leave it *in situ* for an indefinite period. This is bad practice.

There is a very useful piece of equipment that you can make if you have more than the occasional music roll to repair and this is a re-spooling or editing table. It is best made out of old redundant player piano spool-box parts but you can use your own ingenuity as you please. The accompanying sketch shows the principle. With a device like this you can safely unroll a length of roll across the flat centre of the table where you can examine it and work on it in comfort. You will need to arrange some form of tension-brake on the take-up spool for on rewind there are times when it is very useful to be able to put tension into the roll-winding.

The secret of repairing tear is to make sure the paper is completely flat before attempting any patching: use a heated iron to get the creases out and, if you have a steam iron, a gently steaming before ironing will make a perfect job of it. All patches want to be of thin paper and should be as short as possible to prevent cockling as the glue dries. Use a thin brown office-type mucilage and carefully roll the patch on using a small squeegee roller. If the patch extends over some of the perforations do not worry as these can be re-punched later when the paper is perfectly dry.

Pleated edges require careful treatment if they are to lay absolutely flat and here the first task is to open them out. If you use something with a sharp edge it will cut the paper. The best tool for this is an artist's pallet knife that has a fine edge as distinct from a cutting edge. With practice you can run this along in the fold of the pleat turning the paper back as you go.

If you merely iron the pleat flat there's a pretty good chance that it will simply pleat again when it is rolled up. I have a technique that works although I have heard some collectors disagree with me. It is to use a household starch spray that you can buy in an aerosol canister. The technique is to spray the edge of the paper with starch and then iron it absolutely flat using a medium heat. This straightens out and slightly stiffens the paper edge while adding a tiny amount of reinforcing 'body' to it.

Edge tears in the paper are best patched with thin white paper. Do not cut the pieces you use with scissors or a knife, but tear them to produce not just a ragged edge but also a feather edge. With practice you can tear little pieces of paper

so that the edges are feathered. This makes a better bond when you glue them to the roll and also ensures that the paper is not thickened too much. For an average edge tear, the paper patch should be no more than 3/8-inch (about 9mm) wide and ought to extend about the same distance into the roll from the end of the tear.

The golden rule is to use very small patches and lots of them rather than to use long strips otherwise the roll will cockle and become unplayable. And by using water-soluble office paste, at some stage in the future they can easily be removed.

Once the patches are quite dry, those perforations that have been covered up in the repair process may be re-punched. To do this, buy a pin-punch from the hardware store that has a tip about 3/32-inch (1.5mm) in diameter and hone it absolutely flat so that the edges are quite sharp. Either do this on a grindstone (rotating the punch all the while to ensure a completely flat, sharp end) or on a fine carborundum oil-stone.

Obtain a flat piece of lead about 1/8-inch (2mm) thick and a couple of inches square and place this under the piece of the music roll where you have to punch the hole. If the original hole is still in the roll under the patch, find it accurately with a hand-torch and mark the exact centre with a pencil. Now place the punch firmly on the paper with the lead beneath – and give a short sharp tap with a hammer. This will make a perfectly clean hole in the paper. The piece of lead can be used over and over again and finally turned over to use the other side.

Now for the warped roll. Rolls become warped (meaning that they flow from side to side when passed over the tracker bar because they have changed from being parallel strips of paper) through damp. Incidentally a damp roll, if wound onto a spool, may well jam against the sides of the spool flanges and cause pleating.

There are all sorts of ways of curing warped rolls, some of which are extreme, others far less so. Let's look at the easiest. If you have your roll-editing table, then slowly spool the roll from one end to the other a few times. The very action of getting dry air to the paper is often enough to cure a minor to moderate waver. If you haven't a roll-editing table, then try spooling back and forward in your player-piano's spoolbox. Sometimes the mere act of playing a roll once or twice can solve a minor problem.

During the Great Storm that struck Southern England in 1987, falling trees destroyed a number of player-pianos in a collection near where I then lived. At the same time, a collection of valuable piano-rolls, exposed to the elements, was saturated. Determined to try to salvage what I could for the owner, I spoke to several other collectors who had faced similar problems in the past. The suggested solution from a friend in Connecticut seemed radical and yet it worked.

The secret was to run the paper over a smooth surface containing a heating element. I used an infra-red glass-sealed element from an electric fire and arranged at right-angles to the paper path on the editing table. Over this was a curved polished metal cover; in actual fact it was a section of a towel-rail mounted between metal supports. When switched on, this metal surface quickly got very hot, in fact too hot to touch. Quickly unspooling and then respooling the damp paper roll allowing it to pass speedily over this heating element dried out the paper without cockling and to everybody's amazement, not the least my own, the rolls once more played perfectly! The secret was not to pause the paper on the hot metal lest it scorch or contract too much, but to move it firmly and briskly at a constant speed.

Warning! If you make anything at all like this using an electric element, make certain you have an assistant with you at all times to switch the power off at the end of each pass otherwise you will *burn the paper!* An alternative heat source might be hot water, steam or even a hot-air gun plugged into the end of the towel-rail. And whatever you do, don't touch things that are hot. Not, of course, that you will but these days if you don't tell people the obvious some may burn themselves and get nasty! And while about it, be advised that sawing your fingers off ruins your chances of ever playing the piano properly! There; that's enough of the 'health and safety' warnings!

So much for the running repairs to your player-piano. By this stage you know almost all there is to concern you about the thing and its music. Well, not quite because you still have to learn how to play it and then how to look after it on a long-term basis. If it feels as burdensome as having to look after a

neurotic dog, then you might just be right. Mind you, you don't have the vet's fees to worry about.

---

1. Finest-quality leather maintained in reasonable conditions can last a long time. The bellows leather in English church and chamber barrel-organs is often as good after 200 years as the day it was first applied. A few years ago, while restoring a 150-year-old German residence organ, I was amazed to find that the original zephyr skin used for the action motors was as good as original. After exhaustive tests on samples, I decided that it was not worth replacing since it was so good.
2. Some very cheaply-made American player actions did in fact use rubber-cloth pouches and these invariably were fitted with smaller-than-usual bleed holes. One maker who used this type of action, which also had 'non-detachable' glued-on pneumatics, at one time was Gulbransen.
3. At one time restorers used rubber solution diluted with Evostik solvent.

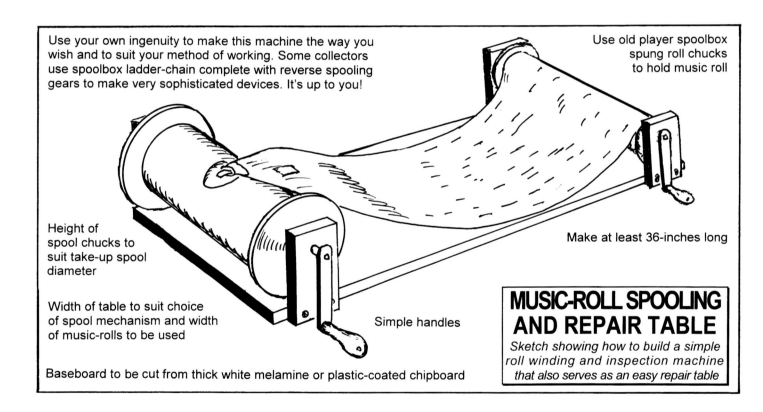

Use your own ingenuity to make this machine the way you wish and to suit your method of working. Some collectors use spoolbox ladder-chain complete with reverse spooling gears to make very sophisticated devices. It's up to you!

Use old player spoolbox spung roll chucks to hold music roll

Height of spool chucks to suit take-up spool diameter

Width of table to suit choice of spool mechanism and width of music-rolls to be used

Make at least 36-inches long

Simple handles

Baseboard to be cut from thick white melamine or plastic-coated chipboard

MUSIC-ROLL SPOOLING AND REPAIR TABLE
Sketch showing how to build a simple roll winding and inspection machine that also serves as an easy repair table

Chapter 14
Conserving the Barrel
Piano and Adjusting its Music

By their very nature, barrel pianos are disarmingly simple machines. Purely mechanical in action (although there were a few interim barrel orchestrions built that had mechano-pneumatic actions), there is little that could be described as 'mechanism'. Unfortunately, this does not mean that there's nothing to go wrong and as any barrel-piano restorer will be happy to tell you, there's a lot to watch out for and some critical adjustments that must be made if the instrument is to sound its best.

Unlike the pneumatic player and the reproducing piano, there is currently no information in print that describe the restoration process for these instruments so this Chapter will be filled with rather more practical content than for the pneumatic player. Even so, some of this detail will be of use to you in handling other strung-back instruments and automatic pianos.

Although it was made in a number of sizes from the tiny Hicks-style portable through to the cart-mounted street and cafe clockwork varieties, the barrel piano retains essentially the same principles of playing. This means that the restoration of one size can be used as a guide to the restoration of other and larger types.

As with all mechanisms, whether simple or complex, a thorough understanding of the way the instrument operates is essential if overhaul and restoration is to be successful. Before tackling the job, then, have a good look at the illustrations in this chapter and follow the way the mechanism actually operates. Of prime concern is the relative position of the barrel to the keyframe; this is the main factor to observe if proper playing of the piano is to be achieved. As with any barrel instrument, this set-up is crucial: fullest particulars can be found in Ord-Hume [83]. Once you have grasped this, repair and regulation are largely a matter of applied common sense.

There are three types of barrel piano that you may find. First is the small and very simple Hicks-type of portable piano, hand-operated and capable of being dismantled on the kitchen table. Then there is the large, hand-turned street barrel piano of comparable size and proportion to the conventional domestic pianoforte. The third type is the clockwork cafe or public-house type of piano. A variation of this is the piano-orchestrion, sometimes of piano proportions but more usually in tall, vertical format and always characterised by the addition of a percussion department comprising instruments such as drum (occasionally bass and side drums), tubular bells, glockenspiel or xylophone, triangle, cymbal, castanets and tambourine. These various types are shown in the accompanying illustration.

In general, piano-orchestrions have iron or part-iron frames, all others are of wood. As ever, there are occasional exceptions!

When you restore an instrument, particularly something like the early portables that are very old and increasingly rare, remember that your aim should be to conserve and preserve. Resist the temptation to try to improve on the original in any way. And, as a matter of good museum practice, keep a record of the work you do, write it or type it out on a piece of paper with your name, address and date and conceal it somewhere in the instrument for the benefit of a later owner or restorer. With large instruments, you can easily seal this document in an en-velope and pin it to one of the posts behind the soundboard. If new parts have to be made, always try to preserve the old pieces that you are replacing. Later generations may learn something from the original which is not apparent to you today.

To make easier to find your way through this Chapter, I have divided it into ten distinct sections. They are:
1. Portable street barrel piano
2. Large barrel-playing street piano
3. Dismantling and cleaning
4. Case repair and refinishing
5. Restoring the barrel and its drive cog
6. The keyframe
7. The soundboard and bridge
8. The wrest plank or pin-block and re-stringing
9. Assembly, adjustment and playing
10. Clockwork barrel pianos

To start with let's look at the little portable street barrel piano of the type associated with the Bristol family of makers, Hicks. This instrument is small enough to be able to work on easily and if we can understand how this operates and become familiar with its parts and principles, we are half way along the road to tackling the larger pianos.

1. Portable street barrel piano

Begin by making a close examination to find out what work must be done to bring it back to good playing condition, then see what parts, if any, must be made. At the same time check what work needs to be done to the case to restore its appearance. Since most of these very early portable pianos can be classified as rarities and antiques, don't forget your documentation which can include photographs if you wish.

These instruments are almost always dirty and damaged so the first task is to take it apart for cleaning. The first part to be removed is the barrel followed by the keyframe. Start by making certain that the keyframe is pushed forward from the barrel piano by turning the tune-change cam on the outside of the case to move the keyframe forward on its pivots.

The system of tune-changing used by these small barrel pianos is almost identical to that employed by the English church and chamber barrel-organ change method employing the notch-plate and knife.

The barrel access door on the right-hand side of the case is usually secured either by a wire which passes down through the case side (seen when the front panel and barrel lid are removed) or by a turn-button on the inside of the door. This door has two little locating studs protruding from its flat bottom edge which engage in holes in the case side level with the floor of the piano. This door provides the end bearing for the barrel, so its security is vital and if these studs are missing or if the holes into which they fit are oversize you will have to replace the studs using sawn-off short wire nails or by inserting a new strip of wood into the case into which you can drill fresh locating holes.

Lift out the door and expose the end of the barrel at its spindle. Usually this is supported in a wooden cradle to facilitate sliding in and out, but sometimes the cradle is missing. Its absence does not affect the working of the instrument, although it is a good idea to make up a simple cradle so that, when the door is removed, the barrel does not drop down on the pins at that end.

Hold the protruding spindle with the right hand, raise the tune-selecting knife on the other end of the case with the left hand, and draw the barrel out slowly, watching that the pins do not foul the case round the doorway. Remove all loose dust and dirt with a brush. Because barrels are made of softwood, they may have attracted the attention of woodworm. More often than not this can be cured and all made well again. At this stage it is a good plan to treat any infestation with a proprietary worm-killer. Because this produces gases that may be injurious to health, apply the fluid in a well-ventilated room. Use the fluid liberally and let it soak well into any infected parts, particularly the barrel ends and the drive cog. Because several applications may be needed to do this job properly and since it is advisable to allow a day or so between each treatment, the sooner you apply the first treatment the better. Store the barrel away from your workplace to avoid breathing the fumes.

Remove the crank handle by turning it anticlockwise while holding the worm-shaft against rotation. Originally, these handles were threaded on to the end of the worm-shaft as far as a protruding stop so that they could be removed easily without the handle having become 'thread-bound'. Sometimes this protruding dog is missing and you may have to apply a little force to unscrew the handle. Take off the bearing block which supports the inside end of the worm-shaft. This is fixed with two screws from the outside of the left of the case. When the block is free, a little juggling is often necessary to free both it and the worm-shaft from the case, the worm-shaft having to be moved back a little to free it from its bearing in the case front.

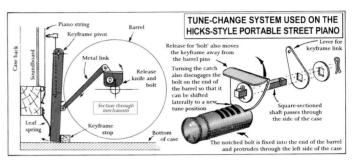

THE TUNE-CHANGE SYSTEM USED ON THE HICKS-STYLE PORTABLE STREET PIANO

Disconnect the tune-selecting knife, the keyframe linkage and the cam and put them aside for cleaning. All the brass parts, including the handle and worm-shaft, can be treated with any suitable metal polish. Stubborn dirt stains – common enough on these parts – can be removed with a brass wire brush or the application of a piece of fine, worn emery-cloth (or wet-and-dry abrasive paper) lubricated with metal polish.

You now have the empty piano case complete with the stringed portion or 'strung back'. If the strings are all present and in fairly good condition, there is no need to remove them unless the wrest plank is badly split or the wrest-pins loose. The wrest-pins should all protrude from the wrest-plank at the same angle – a little above the horizontal. If any are bent downwards, it is a good indication that the pins have become loose in worn, oversize holes, or that the wrest-plank itself is split. Clean the wire strings with soft wire wool to bring up the bright metal beneath surface rust.

Most of these small portable pianos employed a strung back having, usually, twenty-three notes, sometimes twenty-six. On most instruments the tuning scale was marked above each pin, there normally being three strings to each note over the tenor and treble parts of the scale, the bass notes having two or just one string. Only the bass notes use 'wrapped' strings: these have copper wire coiled round them to increase their mass without increasing their length so allowing them to vibrate at a low frequency and sufficient tension.

If the instrument needs a complete rebuild, continue to strip the instrument but do bear in mind that, if it is basically sound at this point, there is no need to proceed further and you can continue with replacing any broken or missing strings, tuning and then reassembly.

Next check over the soundboard, tapping it with your knuckle to see that it reverberates and does not rattle or sound dead. Cracks and splits, as well as dry joints, must be made good and ideally all repairs should be carried out from the back. This means removing the complete soundboard by carefully prising off the small wooden moulding around its boundaries and then easing the whole board out. In some early pianos, though, it was firmly glued into place and cannot be taken out.

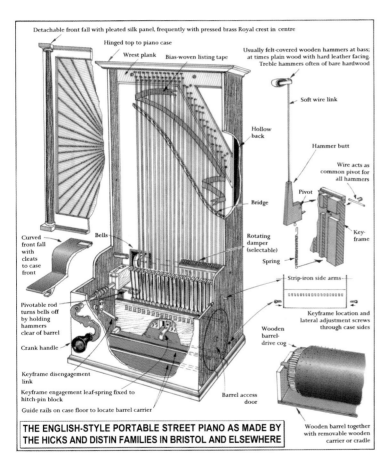

THE ENGLISH-STYLE PORTABLE STREET PIANO AS MADE BY THE HICKS AND DISTIN FAMILIES IN BRISTOL AND ELSEWHERE

Now for the keyframe. This is pivoted on two pins, one either side of the case, and attached by a linkage to the simple tune-change cam lever. Unscrew this first, and then insert a flat-bladed screwdriver between the inside of the case and one of the metal keyframe pivot arms. Slightly twist the screwdriver until the arm comes free from the pivot on one side. Rotate the whole keyframe so that the free end is pivoted towards the strings so that the other pivot arm can be disengaged from the pin in the side of the case. You can now lift out the complete assembly of keyframe and hammers and put it to one side.

If the back of the piano is cased and veneered, as in early ones, you can only work from the front, raking out narrow cracks and forcing in hot brown glue and thin strips of softwood filling. If you can get to the back of the board, glue a patch of short-grained wood veneer about ½-inch or ¾-inch wide over the split. Wipe surplus glue from the front face of the soundboard with a damp cloth and leave to set. Do not nail or tack this veneer strip, but press it with weights or wedges of scrap wood to exert setting pressure. See that in packing to apply setting pressure you do not distort or dish the soundboard or damage the bridge.

As in full-size pianos, the strings are not all of the same thickness: usually at least three different gauges of wire are used, the thinnest for the highest notes. Again, the bass notes are wrapped strings, so these have to be considered separately. If possible, measure the gauge of the wires before removing them, or at any rate keep specimen strings and mark which groups of notes used the same gauge of wire. There are some more points to make on wire later on.

To remove a string, slacken off the wrest-pin first, unhook the string from its lower peg (hitch-pin) at the bottom of the strung back, and then uncoil it from the wrest-pin (tuning pin). It is not advisable to remove the actual wrest-pin unless it is so loose that it can be pulled out with the fingers. This is because the pin was originally a very tight fit in the board and its unnecessary removal will make it looser on replacement. Again, if the pins have been taken out for cleaning (they are often rusty), do not clean the portion that enters into the wood.

If the pins are very loose the piano will not stay in tune, since the tension of each string will exert a torque greater than the frictional resistance offered by its wrest-pin in the wrest-plank. Resistance can often be improved by removing the pin and thoroughly rubbing the shank with powdered rosin. If the wrest-plank holes are slightly oversize and the pins still turn, then you must carefully redrill them very slightly larger, making sure that the drill goes in at the proper angle. Fit new oversize pins which you can get from the piano sundries supplier. Should the new pins be a little too long, you need to drill the holes sufficiently deep so that the string hole on the new pin lines up with those in the other pins. If the wrest-plank holes are very badly oversize, ream them out to a clean, circular shape and plug them with a hardwood peg well glued in. Trim this off flush with the plank when dry and drill slightly undersize to take the pin. At all times after removing wrest-pins coat them with powdered resin before replacing. Never be tempted to hammer home a new or old wrest-pin: the shanks are finely threaded and so they should be screwed home with the tuning key.

The keyframe of the portable piano of the Hicks and Distin type is a single board that provides both a mounting and a pivot for the hammers. Each hammer has a spring which is long and thin and formed of brass wire. These become brittle with age and break. Generations of 'repairers' have replaced them with rubber bands which have lasted a short while until the rubber has perished. After upwards of two hundred years those springs that have not broken have become stretched or 'tired' and, since it is important that all hammer springs have as close to the same tension as possible, it is a good idea to replace the lot. If, however, the original springs are all present but have become weak, either shorten them if they will take such treatment without breaking or make new ones.

New springs are easy to make. Save the best of the original ones to use as a pattern not necessarily for length but for style and detail of the hook ends.

Start by preparing a mandrel of 16 swg (standard wire gauge) piano wire which you can obtain from a model-supplies store. It must be absolutely straight and about four inches long. one, a model-makers' lathe and set it to its slowest-possible speed.

A well-used Spanish-made street piano comes into the workshop. The first thing is that the case is so old that it has come adrift at the left front edge and been reinforced with hardware brackets. The line of the hammers tells that it has had a long, hard life. In this particular instance the whole case was dismantled saving and repairing those few decorative parts which could be re-used. A new case was then made from solid elm and the position of all fixings transferred very accurately from the original to the new timber. Never attempt to make a case from multiply or other man-made board: only ever use solid timber – 'tree' wood!

Use thin brass or phosphor bronze wire (called '00' in music wire gauge or 008-inch in diameter) and fix one end to the chuck close to the end of the mandrel. Wear stout leather or gardening gloves to hold the wire during winding otherwise it may cut through your fingers. The process of spring-making is very quick and consists of holding the thin wire firmly against the mandrel with the thumb while supporting the rear side of the mandrel with the forefinger. Set the chuck into slow motion and wind on the music wire to make a tight, even-coiled spring of sufficient length (about ½-inch less than the overall length between hammer and lower hook). Stop the chuck, slide the new spring off the mandrel and snip the ends to about ¼-inch long. Form the loop ends using watchmakers' round-nosed pliers. The hammer end it is fixed with a thread loop. If the loop is broken, make a new one of button-thread poked through with a needle and knotted into place.

See that the hammers move freely in their slots in the frame. Unless they have become loose and have developed a lot of side-play, it is best not to remove them. If they must be separated, this is done by withdrawing the hinge wire after you have disconnected and removed all of the springs.

If the hammers are stiff in their slots, pump powdered graphite into the gaps on each side to lubricate. Never use oil or grease only dry graphite lubricant – oil and grease attract dust and dirt. The ideal graphite to use is of the type sold by locksmiths to lubricate door locks and it usually comes in a puff-container. It is marketed in Britain under several brand names, one of which is Foliac.

If the hammer heads are leather-covered, check that the leather is properly attached – it frequently comes away at the top and bottom of the hammer. Should the leather be grooved by the piano strings through prolonged use, then you may be able to tease it with a fine wire brush.

On larger instruments that use felt-covered hammers similar to those on a pianoforte, you can 'needle' the felt or re-shape the hammers with a file as described later on. If the leather facings are very hard, as is quite usual on the older instruments, it is better to replace all the leathers using skin of matching quality and thickness. Remember that the harder the surface of the skin, the more strident the tone: the softer the skin, the mellower the sound produced. Usually you will find that a thin chrome leather or fully stretched skin makes a good replacement.

The heavy hammers of the large street piano can be revitalized using a piece of thin kangaroo skin of the type used for making bellows flap-valves in the pneumatic player piano. Never re-cover just one or two hammers: do them all otherwise the tone will be uneven.

See that the keyframe hinge-pivot support arms are not loose and at the same time check that the strip steel spring in the bottom of the case which pushes the frame out from the back is in good order. Renew the strip of thick and fairly hard felt against which all the hammers rest. The old stuff often goes rock hard and lets the hammers lie badly. Replace with a good piano felt. Also renew the pads on the blocks in the case bottom against which the keyframe rests when backed away from the barrel.

A frequent point of wear and damage is at the hammer tails. These are made of hardened steel and are consequently very brittle. If they are out of alignment you may be able to bend them slightly but more often this results in them breaking. Once a hammer tail is broken off flush with the wooden hammer butt, there is usually insufficient of the stump protruding for you to grasp with the pliers to draw it out.

To replace broken hammer cut away a little wood all around the broken pin using a modelling knife or scalpel until enough of the metal is exposed to enable you to get a grip on the stump with fine pliers or even the side cutters. First heat the stump with a soldering iron to loosen it in the wood then gently ease out the root of the pin, twisting it a little as it comes to free it from the wood. Make your replacement from hard steel stock (the broken shank of an old drill, for example) or from thick piano wire, which you can grind up to square section on a small grindstone. Do not let the hardened wire get too hot in this process, otherwise you will destroy the hardness and temper.

Alternatively, you can use an ordinary 2-inch wire nail, again grinding it up to the proper cross-section on the grind-stone or with a flat file. Now harden it by heating it to blood red, quenching it in water, polishing it on fine emery, reheating to a light straw colour and then quickly quenching in oil. Because wire nails are made of low-carbon steel, this will leave the new pin slightly more flexible to allow for any gentle bending necessary in realignment while at the same time being sufficiently hard on the surface.

Now fill the hole in the wooden hammer butt with synthetic resin glue such as Araldite and press in the new pin. See that it lines up exactly with all the others along the keyframe and that it is spaced equally with all the others. Leave the glue to set for the proper length of time, and then file up the point to the correct shape.

Careless use and bad tuning often results in a split wrest-plank or pin-board. This one is beyond economic repair and must be replaced with a new one made from well-seasoned beech or elm. Note the poor stringing practice demonstrated at top right.

Finally, check the alignment (side to side) and protrusion of all the hammer pins by lining up with a straightedge and a rule. This must be even because if there is any variation that particular hammer will strike its strings at a different force or intensity. Time spent aligning these hammer tails is vital to the performance of the finished piano. Finally refit the hammer frame, reconnect the linkage which allows the frame to be moved in and out while changing the tune, and see that it is properly pressed by the case spring.

This procedure is identical to that used on the much larger street piano.

The early portable pianos were often finely made so it is worth spending time and taking trouble to restore them to their original beauty. Badly damaged case parts can be replaced almost invisibly using the techniques of wood-stitching for bad splits, and 'spreckle' joints to hide cross-grain splits. These are all processes described in Ord-Hume [83] so details need not be repeated here.

Complete any final treatment of the exterior of the case that you think necessary. French polish or natural beeswax-based polish should be used rather than paint or varnish. The pleated silk commonly found in these instruments will probably long-since have perished and probably been replaced with cloth or even wood. The original silk was fan-pleated on an inner frame and radiated from a central point often covered with a medallion or the Royal Coat of Arms pressed in brass. If you haven't the skill to replace the fan pleating, then use a simple vertical pleated design. Since the sound of the piano passes through this, do not back the silk with any rigid panelling: the inner front frame will be sufficient to support it.

Refit the brasswork to the case (tune-change knife and so on), and refit the crank-handle and worm-drive shaft, firmly screwing its block to the case. See to it that the sprung, adjustable bearing piece for the inside bearing of the worm-shaft is working properly – this is intended to diminish wear and tear on the barrel cog by keeping the worm in firm contact with it.

Put the barrel back into the piano, seeing that it is located properly in the bearing provided for the brass pivots at each side. The right-hand bearing is in the barrel access door. If these bearings are loose or sloppy, then the instrument will not work properly and you should have new ones made to fit into the woodwork. There should be about 1/64-inch maximum side play in the bearings – some play is not only unavoidable but actually desirable otherwise the access door cannot be angled into its location when supporting the barrel bearing.

Check two things at this point – first that the keyframe does in fact clear the barrel pins when in the proper position, and second that the keyframe is parallel to the barrel and not leaning closer to one end than the other. If the former applies, you must adjust the linkage and probably make a new connecting link of slightly different size. If the latter is the case, then there are two small wooden blocks in the case bottom against which the keyframe is encouraged to rest by its spring. One or both of these may be missing, or they may need replacing. This is easy – they are only small pieces of ½-inch square lumber. Face each one with a leather or piano-felt pad.

With the tune-selector knife engaged in the first slot in the barrel stud, see that the hammer tails are in line with the pins. Play the instrument and see that it performs a recognisable tune and is not in fact playing part of two tunes at once. On some instruments, there is a small screw through the side of the case with which the keyframe can be moved laterally just sufficient to bring the hammer tails into register with the barrel pins. Where this is not fitted, you must pack one or the other of the keyframe pivots with a thin washer to move the frame over a little.

It is quite likely that the instrument will sound very tinny and devoid of resonance. This is because the hammers, instead of just striking the strings and springing back clear of them, are remaining in contact after striking, so muting the strings. Earlier I mentioned the importance of having all the hammer springs of the same strength so that the hammers all offered the same resistance to the barrel pins on the hammer tails. Now you must ensure that the hammers, when at rest, are not touching the strings. As the hammer heads are fixed to stiff wires which pierce the hammer block, all you have to do is to bend the hammers to achieve a nominal clearance of about 1/16-inch. When bending the hammers, bend the wire by holding the end of the wire close to the hammer block and do not, for example, take hold of the hammer head and try to use it to lever the wire. This will split the head and can crack the block. Bend only the wire.

At this point the piano will begin to produce acceptable music. Bear in mind that the hammer tails must lie in a straight line parallel to the axis of the barrel both in plan and elevation, that the pins must be straight in the barrel and that the hammer tails must all be firm in their blocks.

The last job on the mechanism is to damp off the 'dead' portion of the music strings above the bridge. This is done by threading cotton tape through the strings as shown in the illustration. Use $^5/_8$-inch or ¾-inch wide cotton bias binding in red or crimson to match the original. The tape is easily threaded between the strings with a wire hook. The fish-mouth ends serve both for decoration and to prevent fraying. The proper name for this tape is 'listing' and without it no barrel piano will play clearly.

Your portable barrel piano should now play perfectly. Where a damper is fitted, it is usually nothing more complicated than a round wooden rod traversing the strings just above the hammers and carrying in a slot along its length a strip of felt. The rod, protruding through the case side, has a knob by which it can be turned to press the felt strip on to the strings. You may have to replace tattered or moth-eaten felt here. Some pianos were also equipped with two small bells of indeterminate pitch which were secured on a bracket let into a cut-out in the soundboard and struck by the two hammers at the extreme left. There was usually a method of disconnecting these during playing – generally a knob on the left outside of the case which rotated a U-shaped wire against the hammer connecting wires, so pushing them clear of the barrel pins which controlled them.

2. Large barrel-playing street piano

So far we have been looking at the portable barrel piano. Once you are familiar with the action of the little piano and the principles of its overhaul and repair, it is but a small step to the much larger street barrel pianos, cafe or clockwork pianos and piano orchestrions. All work to achieve the same result – the striking of strings by hammers controlled from pins on a barrel. There are notable differences and some important points to watch, particularly with the popular street piano usually seen on a handcart, but the point is that we have already dealt with much of it in miniature!

The case comprises a solidly-built heavy-section timber framing for the back, with a spruce or clear pine soundboard carrying the bridge (with some pianos more than one bridge). The top cross-member of the piano frame is fronted by the wrest-plank (pin-block) that carries the wrest-pins (tuning pins) for the strings. The bottom of the piano locates the hitch-pin block to which the other ends of the strings are attached. They are hooked onto sprags (short iron pins) driven in the timber.

The tune barrel, usually and originally mounted on a wooden cradle to make it easier to slide in and out without damaging the pinning, is slid into the case through a circular removable door in the right-hand side panel. With hand-cranked pianos, the left end of the barrel carries a broad wooden gear-wheel engaging in a brass worm-shaft fixed in the case at the left side of the front and rotated by a handle. Later pianos had a more durable cast gear ring screwed to the end of the barrel. Pianos driven by a clockwork motor – automatics, as Pasquale and others preferred to call them – had, in place of the wooden or cast-iron gear, a thin iron gear-wheel to mesh with a broad pinion on the spring motor. This was usually fixed below the barrel at the left side of the case.

Tune-changing (most barrels were pinned for eight or ten tunes) uses a progressive snail cam, which was fixed to the left end of the case, to shift the barrel 'odd numbers' one way and then back on 'even numbers'. The steel axis of the barrel rested against the 'staircase' faces of this cam so that as it was turned, the axis was moved along an increment sufficient to bring another tune's set of pins in alignment with the hammers.

Although the instrument is much bigger than the small portable piano, the distances between the rows of pins for the tunes are quite small meaning that it is easier to get out of adjustment and play out of register.

Control of this snail cam is by a handle on the outside of the case. To avoid damaging the hammer-tail pins and the barrel pins, when you turn the snail cam handle this also rotates a cam lever that automatically moves the keyframe away from the barrel pins. In this way it is possible to change the tune at any time – even in the middle of a melody – without risk of damage to the instrument.

I said just now that the barrel shifted 'odds up' and 'evens down'. This is because the large wooden barrel is quite heavy and the return (lateral shift) is aided by a large leaf-spring contained in the barrel access-door on the right of the case. Now the distance from the first tune position to the last is about than an inch. To have the barrel jumping back that distance on its powerful pressure spring would make a loud bang and risk damage to the piano. For that reason, on an eight-tune barrel, the changes would be 1,3,5,7,8,6,4,2, and then back to 1 again. This makes for smooth and silent action. Naturally this sequen-

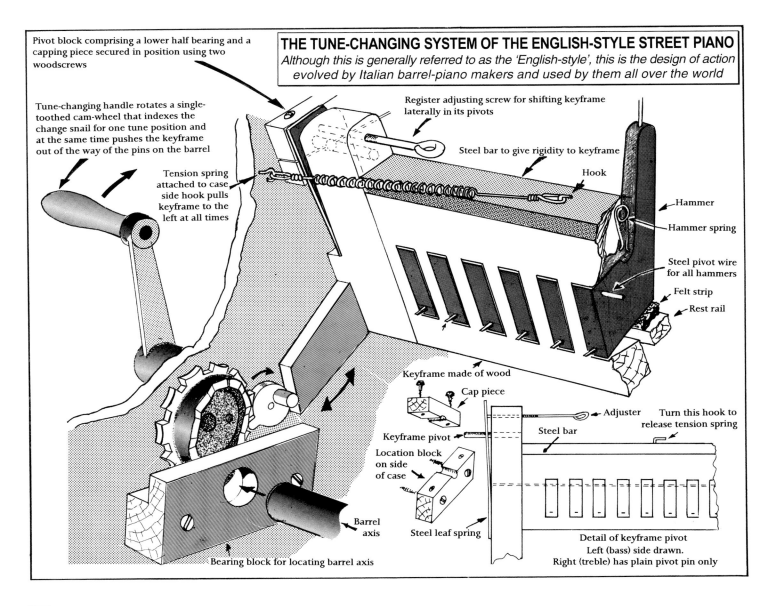

Pivot block comprising a lower half bearing and a capping piece secured in position using two woodscrews

THE TUNE-CHANGING SYSTEM OF THE ENGLISH-STYLE STREET PIANO
Although this is generally referred to as the 'English-style', this is the design of action evolved by Italian barrel-piano makers and used by them all over the world

Tune-changing handle rotates a single-toothed cam-wheel that indexes the change snail for one tune position and at the same time pushes the keyframe out of the way of the pins on the barrel

Register adjusting screw for shifting keyframe laterally in its pivots

Tension spring attached to case side hook pulls keyframe to the left at all times

Steel bar to give rigidity to keyframe

Hook

Hammer

Hammer spring

Steel pivot wire for all hammers

Felt strip

Rest rail

Keyframe made of wood

Cap piece

Keyframe pivot

Location block on side of case

Adjuster

Turn this hook to release tension spring

Steel bar

Steel leaf spring

Barrel axis

Bearing block for locating barrel axis

Detail of keyframe pivot
Left (bass) side drawn.
Right (treble) has plain pivot pin only

tial change is merely of mechanical convenience and the tunes on the tune list are numbered in the order they would normally be played, namely one through eight to conform to the turning of the tune-change handle.

3. Dismantling and cleaning

To dismantle the instrument, first remove the upper case fall (lift the top lid to locate and undo the catches at each side), then the barrel fall. To avoid risk of damage to the key-tails and the barrel pins, next take out the keyframe. This is held in position by three springs, two large wire pressure ones that hold the keyframe in contact with the tune-change cam, and a tension spring that connects the left end of the frame to the left side of the case.

Start with the pressure springs at each side. These stout wire uprights usually have their top ends bent over to form a handle and they are fixed to the case as shown in the drawing. Hold the spring by the handle, push it forward, move it towards the centre of the piano to disengage the screwhead locating its upper portion, let it back and then jigger it off the large centre pivot-screw which passes through its two or three centre coils. They are clearly handed left and right so you cannot easily replace them the incorrect way.

Now take off the tension spring. This is looped around a stout wire lug threaded into the iron capping of the keyframe. Hold this lug firmly in the pliers and rotate it anti-clockwise for 180 degrees so that it is in line with the loop of the spring. Put a wad of cloth over the spring and hold the coiled part firmly while springing the loop from the lug with a screwdriver. It is then easily unhooked from the case side.

Unscrew the two small wooden capping pieces from the keyframe pivots. The frame is now free to be lifted out. However, it is comparatively heavy, awkward and a tight fit in the case and, whilst with experience you can do this single-handed, it is better to have someone to help. Check that the hammers do not jam between the strings as you get it free and, most important, avoid the hammer tails: not only do they have a habit of catching in your clothing, they may also be very sharp if the piano has had a lot of use.

To remove the barrel, first turn the tune-change handle until the barrel has shifted to its closest position to the left side of the case, then open the circular door in the right side of the case. This is doweled into the case at the bottom and is locked in the proper position by one or sometimes two stout, wooden turn-buttons on the inside. The door also carries a stiff leaf-spring to hold the barrel firmly against the change cams at the other end of the case, and locates the right-hand barrel axis bearing.

The barrel would originally have been located in a wooden carrier or cradle but over the years this may have been lost or discarded. Place some thick cloth or sacking on the floor onto which you can lay the barrel. Drawing out the barrel is best achieved with an extra person to guide the far end of the barrel while you gently lift and pull from the right end. Watch that you do not lift the barrel so much that the pins catch on the access door surround. Now lay it out of the way on the floor.

Those pianos fitted with tremolo mechanisms are a little more complicated to strip but it is all largely a matter of common sense and simple engineering usually involving bevel gearing and rather a lot of ancient black grease.

If the strings are all present but lightly rusted, you can largely restore the tone by giving them a stiff brushing with a wire brush. If this does not bring up the shiny metal it means that the wire is pitted – a sign of bad rusting. Strings in this condition tend to sound 'dead', particularly in the extreme treble register. The only solution is restringing.

Large barrel pianos are strung in a different way from the smaller ones, and tend more to follow the style of the conventional piano. Better made instruments have strings which end only at the wrest-pin, the other end forming a U-turn round the bottom peg and then coming back up to the wrest-plank again. This means that one broken string requires the replacement of the adjacent strings also, since it is one continuous piece of wire. These pianos also feature a continuous pressure bar or agraffe which holds all the strings down firmly before the wrest-pins and ensures contact with the first bridge. The illustration shows these points.

Bass strings – the wrapped ones – are formed of single strands only with eye ends on the bottom pegs. Again badly corroded or broken ones must be replaced. Always use the old one, where present, as a pattern for the string-maker to copy and if part of the string is broken, measure what should be there and give him an accurately dimensioned sketch.

Clear away any broken strings and give the inside of the case a thorough clean. Where the harp or strung back is not in bad condition, you can, as before, proceed immediately with reassembly. Pay particular attention to the soundboard and the bridge, also look to the rear of the piano and check for loose soundboard braces.

4. Case repair and refinishing

Street pianos have often had a pretty tough life and quite often the cases are in poor condition with knocks, splits, possibly evidence of earlier crude repairs, and with a paint or polish finish that is well past its prime.

Where the winding handle fits into the case, oil-sodden wood is almost always present. Make good any really bad pieces of timber by dovetailing in fresh wood or 'stitching' in a patch. Many of these street pianos were varnished and imitation-grained and most received so many coats of paint and varnish during their lives that a covering of paint almost 1/16-inch thick is not uncommon. A few were done up very attractively with enamels and decorative lining with wheeled barrows to match but these are the exception rather than the rule.

With the larger instruments, there was nothing special about the wood used, so do not enthusiastically scrape down to bare wood and expect to find anything more exotic than fairly clean knotty pine. One of the best modern treatments I have seen on a street piano is one which probably demands far more work than any other – thorough sanding to a dead smooth surface followed by a black mirror finish like a normal piano. Since the casework is usually well knocked about, chipped and split, such a labour of love is seldom justifiable and the best and simplest finish is probably to strip down to the bare wood, apply a dark stain and then several coats of copal varnish. When the final coat has hardened properly, rub it all over with fine wire wool to produce a slightly matt surface. This will enable you to rub in a final coat of household wax polish which will give the casework an attractive finish without the garish gloss of a varnish finish.

An alternative finish is to apply an undercoat of paint and then put on a brush-grained finish using scumble, finishing off with copal varnish.

Many years ago I came across a few very early (mid-19th century) pianos that had come from the Canon Wintle sale had extraordinarily beautiful cases that cannot have supported long life in the harsh conditions of Victorian street musicians. These were decoratively veneered and panelled with architectural detailing – really exercises in stylistic fantasy unsuited to their environment.

5. Restoring the barrel and its drive cog

Frequently the teeth of the wooden cog on the barrel end become damaged and worn. This is caused by friction (insufficient lubrication of the drive worm), insufficient downwards pressure on the worm shaft so allowing the worm to lift and chew the tops off the teeth without properly engaging them, or just pure and simple overuse. The more common cause, though, is woodworm.

Where worm has infested the barrel, the cog-teeth will have been weakened so much that they crumble to dust. If the cog is extensively damaged, then the only solution is to carve up a new one from a beech log whose centre becomes the barrel axis. Make certain that the new cog is precisely the same diameter as the old one. If you cannot make a new one yourself, a cabinetmaker should be able to oblige but he will want the barrel as a guide. Show him the delicate pins and then wrap the body of the barrel in foam plastic packing to protect them.

Where the cogs are only partly worn, you can make a new insert yourself, spiling off the profile for the new piece from part of the existing cog. Where one or two teeth only are damaged, you can cut in a new tooth by notching the cog and gluing in a strip of straight-grained ash or beech, carving it to shape when set. The illustration shows these steps clearly.

Now for the barrel. We must may particular attention to the state of its pinning. More often than not the surface is covered with paper through which the pins have been hammered. Brush all loose dust off the surface with a stiff hand-brush.

The important thing to ascertain is that the barrel remains cylindrical when turned on its axis. There is not a great deal you can do with a barrel that is severely oval (more than 1/8-inch). Contraction of the barrel staves may have created splits in the carcase surface. So long as these are only very narrow and only a few inches long, it is best to ignore them. Longer ones should be filled with thin glue. More serious are splits visible in the ends that might indicate that the staves or carcase planks are coming away. Small splits near the ends can be glued and closed up with large G-clamps. Special techniques are used for splits nearer the centre: here you must make up long screw-type hose-fastening clips (like very large Jubillee clips) and use thin straps to pass between the barrel pinning.

If the barrel is fitted into a carrier, see that it is not loose or broken and make good any slack joints. The carrier should slide easily in the rails provided for it in the bottom of the case. See that the tune-changing stud is tightly fixed to the barrel but *do not turn it* as this will alter the precise registration of the tunes.

Any badly bent barrel pins should now be straightened with fine, flat pliers. The pins were almost always made of thick, fairly soft wire, so there is little danger of their breaking off.

A common fault with old, well-used barrels is that the pins become loose through, most probably, misuse. It is occasionally possible to replace a loose pin with a longer one that will be better supported through extending into virgin wood. This is not always the case and you will have to resort to sealing in very loose pins using a quick-setting synthetic resin glue. First make absolutely certain that the pin it in the correct position, both in line with others in its particular track, and from side to side (longitudinally). Use a plastic or wooden probe to put a little adhesive around the base of the pin.

By the way, the protrusion of the pins from the barrel surface is important. Any pins that stick out further will (a) play late, and (b) sound louder *BUT* there is an exception to this rule! For rapidly-repeated notes, it is usual for the hammer not to be drawn back as far as for a normal note. This is really an aid to repetition and in this instance the pins for repeated notes are often 'shorter' (meaning they protrude less) than the others. Be aware of this and don't attempt to pull them up to size: if you do the musical effect will be lost.

6. The keyframe

As in the smaller instrument, the case sides, as well as forming part of the enclosure, also locate the action parts, simple that they are. A wooden block positioned on each inside face of the side holds the keyframe on a pivot, so that the entire frame can be rotated towards or away from the strings. This keyframe carries the hammer tails which are usually formed in two parts lapped and glued together from close-grained ash or beech. A flat-sectioned iron pin is provided in the lower part of this sail to engage wish the barrel pins. From the top of the hammer tail projects a stiff wire that carries the actual hammer head, usually of wood wrapped with felt, sometimes with a sheepskin overwrap. Some makers used plain wood hammers, occasionally leather faced, particularly in the treble register where a much more percussive sound was required to enable the note to sing out above the more resonant and louder bass strings.

Each hammer is pivoted on a continuous wire hinge and fitted with a safety-pin-type spring beneath to keep is firmly engaged with a felt strip-covered fixed rest-rail when the hammer was not in use striking the string.

The keyframe position is controlled by a cam on the outside left of the case and maintained by special springs. Turning the cam pushes the keyframe away from the barrel, so moving the tails of the hammers away from the barrel pins. This is so that, when the barrel is shifted, there is no fear of hammer tails and barrel pins making contact and becoming broken or bent. The keyframe must be moved to this 'free' position before shifting the barrel and if it does not move – due, say, to the linkage being loose, missing or broken – then you must push the frame back against its spring with a long screwdriver and hold it there while the barrel is withdrawn from the other side of the case.

Although much heavier in construction, the principles are the same as with the smaller piano detailed above.

If a street piano has suffered long-term exposure to dampness, the hammers in the keyframe may either be very tight and difficult to move in the keyframe, or so loose and rattling that the barrel pins push the hammers sideways rather than allowing them to be drawn back and strike the piano strings. Both problems can be rectified with the keyframe on the bench.

Start by disconnecting all the hairpin hammer-springs using a special tool which you can make as shown in the illustration.

Provided that the keyframe is dry, tight hammers can be freed by rubbing graphite in powder form on the hammer butts. Loose hammers can be packed out by sticking small pieces of gummed brown paper on the butt flanks and then rubbing in graphite. Much of the trouble in a well-worn piano stems from the actual hammer axis being worn. This is a long strip of wire which is threaded through all the hammers in the keyframe so that they can pivot on it.

Begin by disengaging all the hammer springs. These are rather like large safety pins and are disengaged using a special tool. The springs can be removed completely, if necessary, with a pair of long-nosed pliers. Any missing or broken ones must be replaced using thick piano wire obtainable from model engineers' shops.

Carefully clamp the keyframe in the bench vice, number the hammers from one end to the other (and don't forget to number the keyframe to show which end is 'Number One'!), and unbend the ends of the pivot wire which is usually of brass. Grasp one end in the jaws of a good solid pair of pliers and twist and pull to withdraw the whole length of wire. Often some considerable force is needed to do this because, over a long period of use, the friction of the hammers wears away at the contact area of the wire, virtually turning it into a sort of multi-throw crankshaft. In very severe cases you may be forced to sacrifice one or more hammers by breaking them out so that you can cut through the wire hinge and pull out from each end.

Once the hinge is withdrawn you can examine the hammer butts. Where they are loose you will invariably find that their flanks have become rounded. Sand the flanks flat again using fine paper resting on a sheet of glass to provide a flat surface to rub against. The small amount of wood you remove can be made up by one or two layers of brown sticky paper stuck on. In severe cases you may need to glue on a face of veneer which can then be sanded down to the correct width. Once the hammer butt is the right width so that it is once more a reasonably tight fit in its slot in the keyframe, lightly dampen each side of the butt by breathing on it and then rub powdered graphite into the flanks.

If you had to break a hammer butt to remove the hinge, now is the time either to make a new one out of clear maple or to glue up the old one which may have broken along the grain. If the two mating faces are complete and clean, repair is straightforward. Use two long thin brass screws, preferably round-headed and 1½-inches in length by 3/32-inch shank diameter. Make a bench fixture to hold the top half of the hammer butt firmly in place and drill two 1/16-inch diameter holes from the underside. The holes should be the same depth as the length of the screws. Now drill both holes 3/32-inch in diameter for a depth of not quite an inch. The screws will thus hold the wood without expanding it and risking binding the hammer in its slot in the keyframe. Apply a little glue to the mating wood faces – not so much that it will be forced out in excess to cement the hammer butt into the keyframe. Work the two parts together a little to exclude air bubbles and then screw up tightly. Wipe excess glue off the flanks and put a thin strip of plastic sheet between the hammer butt and keyframe slot on both sides so that they will not stick while drying out.

Measure the diameter (gauge) of the old wire hinge. It is usually about 18 swg. Obtain a length of 16 swg piano wire from a model shop: it is sold in straight lengths of about three feet. Using a grindstone or carborundum stone, form two cutting edges on one end just as if you were sharpening a drill. Put the other end of the wire in the chuck of the electric drill and very gently drill through the pivot points using the piano wire cutter to ream and polish the bore. If the wire is not long enough, work through with a length from each end. Finally cut off the last inch or so of the piano wire to include the cutter you have just used and put this short piece in the drill. Now ream through each hammer butt one at a time. The new pivot hinge will be a piece of 16 swg brass wire (or whatever the gauge of the piano wire reamer was) which must be pointed on one end and then gently pushed into the pivot hole, engaging the hammers one at a time.

Where hammer tails are bent out of alignment, they can usually be eased back into position by gently bending them with a pair of heavy pliers. Remember, though, that these tails are extremely hard and brittle. Broken tails are replaced exactly as described in the section on portable pianos.

The wire extensions that fit into the top of the shank or butt and carry the actual hammer heads are made of soft iron wire and are usually rusty. Clean these with wire wool and straighten them up by tapping them with a hammer on a flat surface while rotating them axially. Finish them with black enamel and set them aside to dry. Do not under any circumstance get paint on the wood of the hammer shank or on to the hammer-head.

Occasionally these hammer wires break off or come loose at the butt. Where they have come loose, remove the wire and fill the hole with Araldite two-part synthetic resin adhesive. Push the wire into the hole and wipe off the excess adhesive before it sets. Where the wire has broken off, try to free the stub end in the manner described earlier for hammer tails using a soldering iron and pliers. The other end of the wire is usually threaded into the hammer head. Make a new wire from soft iron or mild steel. Cut a sufficient length and hammer a flat portion onto both ends. Remember that the wire should fit about 1½-inches deep into the hammer shank or butt. Glue the new wire and make certain both butt and hammer head are in the right plane, at the right angle, the correct length – and are not twisted.

The hammer heads usually have felt covers like normal piano hammers, or are formed with hard felt with a leather cover wrapped around the outside. The style varies from maker to maker and most used plain wooden hammers of hardwood for the treble hammers or where a tremolo effect was fitted. However, the bass and tenor hammers were invariably felted.

Sometimes the felt has sprung free from the wooden part of the hammer head. Glue it back into position and hold it tightly until set using a large spring paper-clip. Where the part of the hammer which touches the musical strings is compressed or deeply ribbed, carefully dress the felt back into shape using a new flat file or medium grade sandpaper. Work round the hammer head in one direction only – towards the striking face – from the top and then from the bottom.

Replace the hammer springs using the tool shown in the illustration.

Draw back all the hammers and see that each one requires approximately the same force and offers the same resistance. Any slow or sluggish hammers will affect the playing of the piano and, where they are stiff through friction in the frame rather than because of flaccid springs, you should liberally apply powdered graphite to the hammer flanks. Remember, never use oil or grease and certainly not any silicone compound.

Between the hammers and the keyframe there is a strip of felt upon which the hammers sit when at rest. If this felt is hardened or moth-eaten, the hammers will not sit evenly at rest and, more important, the hammer tails may scrape the tune barrel. To examine the felt, hold all the hammers forward with a strip of stiff wood. Tease up the felt with a wire brush if it can be re-used, otherwise strip it off and replace it with a length of 3/16-inch thick hard piano felt available from a piano sundries dealer.

As before, if the piano is to play properly, the hammer tails must be perfectly in line and must all protrude by exactly the same amount. If their ends are rounded through constant use over a long period, the tendency will be for the barrel pins to push them sideways, so wearing away the hammer butts and the pivot wire. Hone these points absolutely dead in line laterally and as regards protrusion. Use a carborundum stone but take great care not to slice your fingers should the stone slip.

Finally, look over the keyframe for other damage or defects. The extension lever on the left side which engages with the tune-changing mechanism must be a good tight fit; it is screwed to the main keyframe member.

7. The soundboard and bridge

If you have removed the strings, brush out all the accumulation of dust and dirt from inside the instrument. You may choose to scrub the inside of the case with a little water and detergent, but do not over wet the wood or allow it to soak up too much moisture. Do not wet-wash the soundboard, which is of thin spruce or clear pine. Wiping it with a damp cloth moistened with a little washing-up detergent should be sufficient to restore its brilliance. You can rub down the soundboard with fine sandpaper and wire wool prior to re-varnishing if needed. Stains are best removed by scraping with a single-edged razor-blade in the direction of the grain before sanding.

Where the strings remain serviceable and do not need re-placement, the soundboard can still be brushed free of loose dust using a dry long-haired paint-brush. More stubborn dirt can be cleaned by carefully poking small pieces of cloth along the soundboard surface under the strings.

Just as with the smaller piano, pay particular attention to see that it is not split and that the diagonal bracings which are glued to its back (the sound-bars) are all secure and not loose at the ends or in the middle. Like the diaphragm in a loud-speaker, the sound of the piano is amplified and projected by the process of putting energy into the board which in turn vibrates and transmits it. Any splits severely reduce this ability and will diminish the volume of sound produced, make parts of the scale sound 'dead' and, in bad cases, cause a disagreeable vibration or buzzing sound.

Loose sound-bars will cause an annoying rattling sound and can often be detected by tapping the soundboard all over with a padded hammer and listening to it reverberating. If the wrest-plank, detailed in a moment, has come away from its attachments and has tipped forward, then the top edge of the soundboard may be bowed or crushed and you will have to remove the soundboard and re-glue the beading piece by means of which it is secured to the case.

It is important that the soundboard must 'float' within the case by a certain amount and for this reason it is only attached rigidly at the sides and top, its other portions being no more than located. Many pianos have been altered during their lives and hence the soundboard and bridges may show signs of modification. If you can see where bridge positions have been changed or parts (invariably at the bottom end) removed or repositioned, do not try to bring the piano back to its pre-modification condition as it will no longer play properly. The soundboard alterations will have resulted in changes to the tuning scale that will have influenced the way the music is pinned to the barrel. Clean off the surface of the soundboard and give it a coat of copal varnish or, if you prefer, rub it well down and give one or two coats of clear polyurethane varnish.

As ever, examine very closely for cracks and splits. In the case of bad splits, proceed as described earlier but force in shaped strips of well-glued softwood. When set, remove surplus wood and glue with the bevelled edge of a broad wood chisel.

Occasionally the soundboard is badly bowed. Usually there is not much you can do about that and, so long as the bow does not touch the strings and still allows the strings to press down on the bridge with a reasonable force then it is better to leave it alone. If bowing is excessive, remove the sound-bars from the back, straighten them or, if badly warped, remake them, and refit. Should that not be possible, make a new soundboard from top-quality boat-builder's clear pine or Sitka spruce. Follow the grain direction, dimensions and, particularly, the thickness of the original.

Incidentally, *always* check the sound-bars or ribs on the back of the soundboard for security.

Examine the bridge (or bridges if there is more than one) very carefully for security, cracks and missing bridge pins. It must be firmly glued and screwed to the soundboard and the pins which align each string must be all present. Missing or broken ones can be replaced by headless panel pins but these must be inserted at the proper angle. Do not try to bend them to the proper angle after driving them in straight – that will split the bridge.

Before replacing the strings, if you have removed them, re-varnish the soundboard. Use only an oil-based copal varnish available from quality woodwork stores and artists' sundries suppliers. Do not use any other form of varnish, particularly anything that seals the wood so it cannot 'breathe'. Never ever use any synthetic varnishes such as polyurethane or silicone substances: these will spoil the appearance of the instrument and will shorten its life. Timber, remember, needs to breathe and silicone synthetics prevent this happening.

8. The wrest plank or pin-block and re-stringing

Street pianos were exposed to all kinds of weather meaning not just rain, damp fog, frost, snow and roasting hot sun but also rapid changes in temperature and humidity. The most highly stressed part of the instrument was the strung back itself and temperature and humidity variations caused the total force of the string pull to vary. At the time this was generally described as 'going out of tune', the effects may remain today in the form of a cracked or split wrest-plank. A plank in this condition will neither be stiff enough to resist the string pull nor will it hold its wrest-pins tightly in place. It must be repaired or, in some cases, replaced.

Examine the wrest-plank for splits, in particular around the pin holes. Any signs of splitting means that the plank has failed and the wrest-pins will be working loose. This is bad news on a street piano where it is necessary to tune them very frequently because each move of the pin will worsen the situation. If they are slightly loose, you can buy a little time by rubbing powdered resin on them. If the holes in the block are greatly oversize and distorted so allowing the pins to pull downwards under the tension of the strings, you should bore out the holes, glue in a hardwood dowel plug and re-bore them marginally undersize but in exactly the original position.

Splits come in two sorts: the facing of the wrest-plank is a veneer about 1/16-inch thick and this sometimes cracks. This is not very serious although it often looks worse than it is. You can fill up these cracks with hot brown glue. Much more serious, however, are deep splits where the pins have acted as wedges to split open the plank along its grain.

Occasionally you will find that the total string tension has pulled the wrest-plank from its supports at either side and from the posts at the back, so tipping it forward. Again this has to be remedied.

The plank – pin-block in America – is made of well seasoned hardwood, usually beech and sometimes maple or ash, with a front face of vertical-grained hardwood, such as oak, and the whole covered with a horizontal-grained veneer occasionally of a wood such as bird's-eye maple. The cross-section is not rectangular but trapezoidal, the greater thickness being along its lower edge.

Despite its thickness, because there are between two and five or more lines of wrest-pins closely spaced along its length (the greatest number over the treble register), there is a tendency for the plank to split. As the plank is surprisingly deep and thick this indicates the terrific load imposed by the strings.

Where it has developed lateral cracks it is sometimes possible to close these together using clamps and long coach bolts. To do this you must first remove all the strings and wrest-pins. The back of the piano originally had a detachable frame of thin wood covered in cloth: this may have been lost in the distant past. This conceals the heavy wooden posts that support the wrest-plank. Look carefully round the points of contact between plank and these posts for looseness or opened joints. You may find it necessary to remove the soundboard to gain better access to the wrest-plank. Where cracks show evidence of such separation, rake them as wide as you can without worsening the damage, force in synthetic resin glue (I use Croid, but be cautious as many of these glues can give you dermatitis) and clamp up tightly using very large G-clamps or sash-cramps.

If you have to remove the plank completely, once it is in this partially-unglued state this is fairly easily done but take care that you do not cause any further damage to the piano. Again to do this you must first remove the soundboard.

Use a broad chisel and a heavy hammer to separate the glued joints between plank and posts and the shaped pieces of heavy hardwood packing between the posts. Try to remove the wrest-plank in one piece but, if you cut it, measure several distances across it before cutting and make marks so that the precise length of the plank can be re-established when the two pieces are lined up together after removal.

Choose well-seasoned beech for the replacement plank and keep it indoors in a warm room for three months or so before you start to work with it. I once had the experience of replanking two pianos with wood that I considered to be adequately dry. Both pianos worked loose again within months, so take time over sorting out and drying the wood. See that the fresh timber is not warped, bent, twisted or otherwise distorted either in length or width.

Taking the old plank as a pattern, stretch over it a wide sheet of thick tracing paper and tape it to the plank edges with parcel tape. Using a solid wax marking crayon (the thing which used to be used by shoemakers and was called heel-ball[1]), rub all over the paper on the plank as if you were making a brass rubbing. This will transfer the position of all the wrest-pin holes and other marks on the old plank as well as the exact profile of the plank itself – its edges. This is important since some planks may taper and others have cut-outs in them for percussion instruments such as nested bells. The reason for using a wide piece of tracing paper is so that the paper itself cannot distort excessively and produce errors when it comes to applying the paper pattern to the new plank.

With the new piece of wood lying flat on the bench, do not at once cut it to final dimensions, but leave it oversize on all faces and edges except thickness until you have fitted the cladding and the veneer. I use a 5 or 6 millimetre planking of ash or oak. Usually ash is easier to obtain planed to precise thicknesses, so you may prefer this for this job. Although width is not critical, try to get your planks as wide as possible – about 6 inches if you can. Cut them into oversize lengths that are the width of the wrest-plank, and lay them across the face. Compare the general layout of the plank to the rubbing of the old one and try to avoid getting the joints in the cladding where you will later on be drilling for pins. Ideal alignment may well be impossible: just aim for the best. Now mark the pieces of ash in pencil with a number and a mark to show which is the top of the outermost face. Gather them all together and plane up the edges so that they are quite square.

Liberally coat the face of the wrest-plank with proprietary synthetic resin glue and begin reassembling the ash planks to it, making sure that you properly glue the butt joints between each piece. When all the pieces are in position, press them together end to end with bench wedges and wipe surplus glue from the upper surface with a damp cloth. Lay a sheet of thin plastic over the whole and now place a length of smooth, flat timber on top. Clamp this sandwich together at closely spaced intervals and then leave the whole thing to dry for at least a week.

When dry, unclamp the sandwich, remove the clamping wood and the plastic sheet and thoroughly sand the surface of the ash cross-planking using a power sander of the orbital type. Take your new piece of veneer and glue this into place. You can either use one of the patent dry 'glue-films' for this (in which case you iron on the veneer using a hot smoothing iron), or you can use synthetic resin glue spread very evenly on to the plank. Roll the veneer into position on the glued surface and smooth it initially with the palm of the hand. Now take a squeegee roller and roll all over the veneer exerting pressure to force out air bubbles and surplus glue. Once again clamp up the whole thing and leave it to dry.

Take the newly laminated wrest-plank complete with clamps and clamping boards and put it somewhere dry and warm for as long as you can – a few weeks in a domestic airing cupboard would be ideal.

During the time this is taking place, you can always work on the case of the piano, stripping off the old finish with a proprietary paint-stripper and then rubbing down the bare wood prior to refinishing it either in black paint or whatever you choose.

Once the plank is set, sand the veneer face and apply one coat of copal varnish. When dry, give it an even, thin coat of artist's spray-on adhesive. This is used in drawing and art offices for mounting artwork and in Britain goes under the trade name Spray Mount. Now carefully position and roll on the tracing paper rubbing of the old plank. Do not use any conventional 'wet' glue or paste as this will make the paper expand and destroy the accuracy of your work. Cut off surplus paper overhanging the edges of the wood and now cut the plank to the drawings, ideally using a power saw to cut through paper pattern and timber. Work accurately and, if the edge of the original plank was chamfered, reproduce this chamfer most accurately.

To bore the wrest-pin holes, you must use a drill mounted in a stand, as this will enable you to set the correct angle for the holes so that all the pins can be tilted at the same precise inclination. Set the drill stop on the drill press so that each hole is the right depth. Do not bore the hole longer (deeper) than is necessary.

The drill should be slightly less in diameter than that of the wrest-pins you will be using – about 7 to 10 thousandths of an inch smaller. Use a new, sharp drill: once a drill has been resharpened, unless it has been done on a proper engineer's drill-sharpening machine, it may well no longer be accurate enough to drill a hole of the correct diameter.

Once all the holes are drilled, check against both the rubbing and the original that you have not missed any detail. Now peel off the paper pattern and wash off any traces of the adhesive with white spirit. Slightly counterbore all the wrest-pin holes with a 120-degree rose bit held in a carpenter's brace.

Before fitting the new plank into the piano, prepare everything first during a 'dry run' so that when you come to gluing up you have everything to hand – the right clamps set to the correct gap, the proper wooden packing and clamping pieces and the right tools. Mix up your glue and, to protect your hands from the adhesive, wear either thin latex or plastic disposable gloves.

This is the point where you can spoil all your good work through carelessness, so take great pains to see that the new plank is properly seated and well glued into position. The back posts and their intercostal blocks must all be firmly fixed one to another as well as to the plank.

Leave the glued-up piano for at least two days to dry before attempting to unclamp. Remove surplus glue and generally clean up round the new work. Now the original, old plank had the tuning scale impressed into the wood with metal punches and for a really professional job you should buy a set of ¼-inch metal letter punches and copy the markings of the old plank onto the new. The method is to take, for example, the C punch, make sure that you position it against the right set of wrest-pin holes, and give it a tap with the hammer. Just how hard you hit it will be determined by practice on a scrap piece of wood. For sharps it was fairly common with some makers to use the letter 'X' so that C, C sharp, D, D sharp, E would appear as C, X, D, X, E and so on. Once you have marked all the string-tuning instructions, take a clean piece of cotton rag and put a tiny quantity of black enamel paint on it. Roll the cloth into a ball and rub it over each letter you have stamped into the varnished wood. The black paint will fill or stain the bruised wood in the letter, making it easier to read. Finally, give the whole plank a second coat of copal varnish, taking care to see that it does not trickle into the wrest-pin holes.

Once a hole is drilled into wood, it gradually starts to close up a little as the wood fibres recover. Take a hand reamer the same finish size as the original drill and clear out each wrest-pin hole, taking care not to enlarge it above its intended diameter.

Next examine the hitch-pins at the bottom of the piano below the soundboard and to which the lower ends of the strings are attached. The treble end of the piano also has a diagonal hitch-pin block and this should be checked for splits, cracks and looseness in exactly the same way as the wrest-plank. Any repair work follows the same pattern. However, partially loose hitch-pins can be fixed securely and a partially split hitch-pin block made good by facing it with a 16 gauge steel plate.

First remove all the hitch pins and any really loose ones should have their holes bored out and plugged with hardwood dowelling. Smooth the outer surface of the wood. Make your steel plate so that there is a 2-inch wide lower flange which can fit under the hitch-pin block and be securely screwed into place. The positions of the actual hitch-pins are transferred to the metal and drilled through at an angle as before. New hitch-pins can be made by cutting about 1¼-inches off the pointed end of a 4-inch wire nail and using these points hammered well into the timber through the steel plate so that about 3/8-inch protrudes.

Not all pianos need this level of rebuilding, even if the pins are slightly loose. Where no splits in the wrest-plank are obvious, but the pins tend to be only a little loose, a special preparation available from piano-tuners' and sundries stockists will tighten them up. To apply this, lay the case down so that the wrest-plank is horizontal and then paint the special liquid round the loose pins, leaving it overnight to soak in and do its job.

If you are going to restring the piano and have removed or replaced the wrest-pins, remember that when you screw them into the wrest-plank (pin-block) they must all have the same degree of protrusion. When up to pitch, the coil taking the tension of each string must be the very bottom one on the pin closest to the plank. This means that before starting stringing, the hole in the pin should be about ¼ to 5/16-inch above the surface of the plank. Don't put the pins in just yet, though.

Once all this is done and the soundboard replaced, you can prepare for restringing. If you plan on doing more than one piano, or if you want to make a particularly neat job of your piano, I strongly recommend buying a piano-wire looping tool. This makes forming the eye end on the very stiff piano wire a simple task and gives your work that professional touch.

Without overstepping the limits of justifiable restoration, you can decidedly alter the tone and performance by restringing with slightly thinner wire. The effect is to brighten the sound and often to accentuate the treble and tenor registers – these last frequently being 'woolly'. It is entirely up to you what you do here, but I have been agreeably surprised at the improved tone achieved by restringing a 23-note Hicks piano with strings two gauges thinner throughout (for 36-gauge wire I used 38-gauge). The tension on the piano frame is also lessened by stringing thinner. Needless to say, you should not try to use thinner wire for the wrapped bass strings as these are best left as intended. A major reason for restringing with a slightly thinner wire is to reduce the strain on an elderly piano frame. There are other things which you can do, legitimately, to amend tonality and these will be discussed further on.

Wrapped bass strings are readily obtainable and, since it is not possible to cut down regular pianoforte strings because of the resultant loosening of the winding, do not be tempted to re-make the wrapped bass strings yourself. This is a skilled job for a professional string-maker who can wind on exactly the correct thickness of copper wire. Send the old strings as a pattern or if there are strings missing, give him the dimension based on that of original strings to either side.

For ordinary unwrapped strings, buy your new music wire from a piano sundries house in half-pound coils for the bass strings, and 4-ounce coils for the treble. The treble wires being shorter, you will not use so much wire as you will for the full-length bass strings.

Stringing is a job which gives you sore fingers. Begin with the longest unwrapped string and hook it on to its proper peg at the bottom of the harp.[2] Lead the wire straight up to the wrest-pin hole – make sure that you line up with the correct one – and cut the wire exactly 1⅞-inches longer so that you have that much wire protruding above the pin.

Place the new wrest-pins in their holes as you go – this will allow you more room to manoeuvre than if you put them all in first. Start the pin by tapping it in gently with a hammer until the wire hole is about ¾-inch from the wood surface. Cut the new wire two inches longer than the hitch-pin to wrest-pin distance with the wire located on the hitch-pin, form a right-angle bend in the last ⅞-inch of the wire, push this into the wrest-pin wire hole and, using the tuning hammer, wind the pin in, coiling the wire round and down the pin as you go. See that the angled end does not slip out of the wrest-pin.

The amount of overlength on the wire gives you about three and a half turns on the pin. There should be between three turns and four but they should all be the same. See that the coils lie side by side and do not overlap each other. The bottom coil should be about 1 millimetre from the surface of the wrest-plank. If it is more than this, slacken off a little and tap the pin again with the hammer. Do not at this stage attempt to bring the new strings up to any tuned pitch.

Before applying the last half turn of tension, thread the lower end of the wire around its proper bridge pins and that the wire is pressed down to the bridge surface at these pins.

This serves to stop off the length of string which is capable of producing the desired note for given tension. Bring each string just tight and no more until all the wires are in place. Proceed with all the strings in this manner, lining each one properly in place on the wrest-plank and also its bridge pins.

Now bring the piano roughly up to tune so that the strings can stretch. Do this working from the middle outwards in both directions and do it roughly: this is called 'chipping up' and is purely a means of applying tension to the newly strung back to give it a chance to settle down. 'Rolling' the strings with the end of a cross-pane hammer will help evening out the stretch: press the hammer in contact with the wires and rub then up and down briskly a few times above and below the bridge.

The last job is to weave the listing tape through the 'dead' part of the strings as with the smaller piano. For the large instrument, it needs to be a heavy bias linen tape.

Finally comes proper tuning, and for a newly-restrung piano this will take several days – sometimes a week – to do properly, for the strings must be given time to stretch and the piano harp-frame allowed to accommodate itself to the tension. The combined load on the wrest-plank when all the strings are tensioned is quite considerable and it is perfectly normal for the plank to warp a little. Excessive deformation now or at any time in its previous career will result in splitting or tearing away from the supports.

The technique of tuning these street pianos has always been somewhat arbitrary. They were never expected to produce concert-pitch music, nor were they intended to be tuned to a set pitch. The fact that the notes may be lettered to the scale is an indication of preferred pitch. It is an unfortunate fact of life that with some street pianos, especially the older ones that may have warped frames, bringing them up to the correct pitch may actually hasten their destruction. Old pianos that may be suffering from 'tired' glue in their frames may not be able to take the strain of modern correct pitch and either the plank will split or, even worse, the plank may start to tip forwards about its lower edge.

These structural defects can be cured by the process of intelligent restoration but even so, unless you intend the piano to be played in consort with another instrument, it is not a bad idea to tune it anything up to a full tone flat. For each semitone lower than normal pitch, the strain on the frame of something like the typical 46-note street piano can be reduced by the weight of the average man.[3]

I don't intend to provide a treatise on piano tuning for there are many handbooks on the subject. For a guide to the aspects of tuning, see Ord-Hume *[83]* which explains the principles involved. It is very difficult to get the street piano to sound perfectly in tune, mainly because the wooden frame does tend to distort a tiny amount with changes in temperature and humidity while the wrest pins may not remain as secure as those in an iron-framed

piano. Nevertheless, the careful amateur should be able to tune his street piano so that it ends up sounding reasonably tuneful.

Do remember the main tenet of piano tuning, and that is that the tuning lever has to be treated gently when 'pulling up' a string. The higher up the scale you go, the greater the tension of the strings relative to their length and gauge and also the less you must turn the lever to adjust them. Also, because the string is in two parts (the part between the wrest-pin and the bridge and that between the bridge and the hitch-pin), it is necessary to overtighten the string a semitone and then bring it down to the correct pitch to help to even out the tension in the two halves. Even so, a barrel piano needs frequent adjustment until it will hold its tune for a reasonable length of time and this is because the bridge pins effectively break the string into two lengths and even with rolling it takes a while for both halves to assume the same tension.

Before leaving the subject of tuning, I caution that the barrel piano, with its wooden frame, will generally not hold its tune for long. I expect to have to tune my own instruments at least once a week, particularly if they are in regular use since the act of hammering a string helps to stretch the string and loosen the wrest-pins a fraction. Once the piano is in reasonable tune, though, it is usually just a question of a little polishing up of the pitch here and there – a task that need take no more than fifteen minutes.

9. Assembly, adjustment and playing

Before beginning reassembly, check over the tune-changing mechanism and see that it works properly. It should be lubricated with a good graphite grease. If the bearing for the changing handle is worn so that the handle is sloppy, take off the handle, remove the shaft and make a new bearing.

Fully-restored barrel piano-orchestrion fitted with a new keyframe. It is vital to ensure all the key points are not just evenly-spaced but are in the correct line from end to end of the barrel, and also at an equal height.

Replace the keyframe on the half-trunnions in the case sides, screw back the trunnion bearing capping pieces, replace the two stout wire springs which press the frame against the changing mechanism and reconnect the tension spring which pulls the frame up against the left side. Hook this over the lug on the keyframe and turn the lug back clockwise to hold it securely. Turn the tune-changing handle to see that the mechanism works properly and then set it so that the keyframe is held out in the between-tune position so the barrel can be replaced.

Gently slide the barrel back into the instrument, taking care not to catch the pins on the access door or on the hammer tails. At the end of its travel, see that the arbor is located properly on the changing cam and that the drive-worm is correctly engaged in the barrel cog. The end of the barrel may need to be lifted slightly to get it into the proper position.

See that the stout leaf-spring in the access door which pushes the barrel against the change mechanism is free and able to do its job. A light film of graphite grease is applied with the finger to the working face of this through the hole on the inside. Note that this end bearing of the barrel is adjustable on the access door, for the wooden block, screwed inside the door to support the barrel arbor, can be loosened and moved a fraction up and down and from side to side. Unless playing the piano shows that the barrel is in the wrong position, it is extremely unwise to upset the setting of this bearing, so leave it well alone.

Refit the door and lock it with the turn-buttons. Reconnect the special wire spring which presses down on to the rear bearing of the winding handle. This must be a very stiff fit as if it is loose (or absent) the crank-handle worm-drive will not press down onto the cog teeth hard enough and will rapidly wear away the teeth.

Let back the keyframe with the change lever. The fore-and-aft position of the keyframe is vital. If the hammer tails are too close to the barrel, besides risking scoring the barrel surface, rapidly repeated notes will not sound distinctly as there will be insufficient space or time for the hammer to fly to the strings before the tail catches on the next barrel pin. If the hammer tails are too far away, the sound will be weak and sporadic. Adjustment for this is by the two vertical, eye-ended adjusters, one each end of the keyframe. Make sure that the keyframe is parallel with the face of the barrel – a visual check, looking down behind the barrel, will verify this.

At rest the hammer tails must be no closer than $^3/_{32}$-inch from the barrel surface. Turn the adjusting screws equally until this is achieved. The hammer heads must not be in contact with the strings otherwise they will 'block' them, so preventing them from vibrating. Just as important, nor must they be more than $^3/_{32}$-inch away from them when at rest. Coarse adjustment is made by regulating the thickness of the hard felt rest-rail strip on which the hammer butts rest. Fine adjustment is made by carefully bending the wire part of the hammer shank.

Some barrel pianos have extra features such as mandoline or tremolo mechanism, moving picture displays and suchlike. This particular street instrument has an automatic damper controlled by special bridges at the worm end of the barrel that work a special key connected to a lever assembly that moves a felt-covered damper rail up and down while playing. Extras like these need special attention to ensure smoothness and effectiveness of operation.

Now play the piano again. At the end-of-tune position, stop and check that when the hammers are at rest they are just short of the strings, otherwise, as before, the strings will be muted. They are easily bent into the right position.

The tunes must now be put into register, so wind the tune-change handle until the barrel is at its farthest-left position. This should mean that the farthest-right pins are now in the playing position – play the piano and check. If they are not, then the keyframe must be moved laterally, using the horizontal, eye-ended adjuster at the left end of it. This must only be done at the end-of-tune position otherwise pins and tails will be broken. Once the last tune on the right of the barrel has been accurately registered, turn the tune-changer until the barrel is at its farthest to the right, so bringing the last set of pins on the left end of the barrel under the hammer-tails. Play this one and make any necessary adjustments to the lateral position of the keyframe. Note that quite frequently you must strike a practical medium between all the tunes on the barrel so that they all play with more or less equal success.

It will probably be necessary to polish up the tuning at this point. It is advisable with these instruments to 'stretch' the octaves a shade in the extreme treble; this means tuning the top four or five notes a fraction sharp. Because these top strings are so short, they tend to sound percussive and their often-indeterminate pitch can be helped by this marginal sharpening.

10. Clockwork barrel pianos

First let it be understood that 'clockwork' means a mechanism of wheels and pinions driven either by the energy stored in a descending weight or from a wound-up spring. 'Clockwork' does not immediately imply 'clockwork motor' meaning spring-powered.

Many barrel pianos and barrel piano-orchestrions were weight-driven. In these, a very heavy driving weight, usually of iron, rarely of lead, is wound up into the top of the case using a hand winch and ratchet. As it descends it powers the mechanism to turn the barrel. These weights are extremely heavy. Be warned: *NEVER* move an instrument with the weight wound up into the top as it may be top-heavy and fall over. Wherever possible, run the instrument right down and then remove the weight before shifting. As much as anything else it will be lighter!

Originally, the line for the weight was of gut. With time this can wear and break, allowing the weight to fall free. I once had to repair an instrument where the weight, fully wound, had broken away in the middle of the night. It had destroyed the bottom of the case – and then gone straight through an expensive parquet hall floor into the basement of the house. The repair bill was enormous. I always recommend replacing the line with flexible woven stranded wire rope that is tested to twice the load needed. Do not use synthetic fibre rope such as nylon or the material you buy from chandlers for yacht-rigging: this stretches far too much under constant load.

Coin-freed automatic pianos are always 'clockwork', sometimes by weight, sometimes by spring-powered clockwork. These latter use are large spring-driven motors. Both are played by the insertion of a coin that is dropped down a chute into a counter-balanced coin tray the pivoting of which frees a stop-start sprag from the motor governor. At the end of the tune (they frequently play twice for one coin), the coin is tipped out and the balanced tray allowed to rise up and re-engage the motor governor stop sprag.

The motors were most commonly wound directly from a handle on the outside of the case. Occasionally chain-driven winding handles would be used in instances where the motor was mounted too low in the case for practical direct hand-winding.

Since the inventions and improvements of Antonelli and others, the majority of street and clockwork barrel piano makers employed the same basic mechanisms. This means that the works of the 'automatic' piano (one driven by a clockwork motor and probably coin-operated) are basically the same, with the exception that there is no crank-handle to play the instrument and an additional handle is provided to wind the clockwork.

Be warned that the springs used in clockwork pianos are very powerful indeed and any unskilled attempt at dismantling the motor can result in the release of a coil of steel of such power that it could cause serious injury. If the spring is broken, and unless you are a competent engineer, I do not advise you to try to repair it yourself. It is safer to give it to some small engineering workshop to put right. Usually, when a spring does break, it fails at either the inside end (the piece which hooks on to the winding arbor) or the outer end where it is looped and riveted round one of the assembly posts of the motor cage.

The motor will need cleaning if the piano has been used in a public place and this can usually be done without taking it from the instrument. Do not try to dismantle the gear train and the endless screw carrying the governor. If you tamper with this, any power left in the motor will immediately be released and the least that can happen is stripped gears and a broken spring. If it is necessary for some reason to dismantle the governor, then let the motor run right down against its Geneva stopwork and only remove the governor when there is no longer any force in the motor to turn it. Lubricate the motor with grease.

Be warned that even with no power on, and the motor apparently fully exhausted, there is still fearsome energy stored in the heavy-gauge strip steel coil of spring. Do not dismantle the motor cage or frame unless you know precisely what you are tackling: these springs can kill.

Coin-operated automatics are in no way complex devices. The number of revolutions and the instruction to start or stop the mechanism come entirely from the motor unit and not from the barrel or any part of it, so it is important that the barrel be inserted in exactly the right position. If this is not done, the music will stop and start in the middle of the tune. Examination of the barrel will show one point on its periphery where there is a clear line along it, devoid of pins. This is the start/stop position and usually you will see also small prick marks or ink dashes to mark the alignment of the hammer tails at the start of the first tune position.

Positioning the barrel is thus very important. Instead of being rotated by a wide, coarse-threaded wooden cog, the barrel carries on its left end a large diameter but comparatively narrow iron gear-wheel that meshes with a wide pinion carried in the top of the clockwork motor. Here I am referring to the more common type of automatic with the motor fixed at the left end under the barrel; other types will be similar in general arrangement, although slightly different in detail.

First see exactly where the stop/start position on the barrel is and gently slide the barrel into the case. You will need to lift up the left end of it to seat it on the drive pinion and at this point see that, when the keyframe is lowered into the playing position, the hammer tails will fall more or less exactly into the centre of the 'no-man's-land' of the barrel. If it does not, then index the barrel one tooth at a time until this is reached – you can easily do this by repositioning the barrel (with the keyframe held clear, of course).

The final check on this positioning is to locate the barrel completely – that is, with the door closed to support the right-hand barrel arbor – and play the instrument. The music should stop exactly at the end-of-tune position with none of the hammers partly lifted.

If the piano plays too slowly or too fast, then you can regulate the speed by the adjustment of the collar which prevents the centrifugal governor from flying out too far. To make the music play faster, you must allow the governor to fly out farther, so the collar is moved farther down the endless screw carrying the governor. To make the music slower, you must restrict the fly of the governor by moving the collar farther up the shaft.

When it comes to piano orchestrions and other varieties of the barrel-operated piano, the principles described here will form a basis of the skills needed to tackle the job. Watch for controls such as automatic dampers for *piano* and *forte* playing, special keys to bring on effects, and the careful adjustment of percussion linkages to achieve optimum results in playing. All tend to be individual in design to the many various makers, so my words can be no more than general.

In conclusion, here is a list of some of the things which can go wrong with barrel pianos, both hand-turned and clockwork, and how to put them right. In this computer age it's called troubleshooting.

a] Piano will not play, although barrel is turning.

Keyframe held off so that the hammer tails are not engaging. Cause might be dirt, stiffness, or the breakage of the springs which press the keyframe against the tune-changing trip lever.

b] Barrel will not turn, or turns sporadically when handle is turned to play.

This means that the drive-worm on the handle shaft is slipping and can be due to badly worn barrel cog teeth or to the breakage of the spring-loaded inner bearing (on small pianos), allowing the drive-shaft to ride up.

c] Clockwork piano plays jerkily.

Spring not wound enough (or the Geneva stopwork is wrongly positioned so that the motor cannot be wound enough, or the spring has been shortened/replaced by one too weak). Might also be that the keyframe is too closely engaged with the barrel, so putting a very great load on both the barrel pins and the hammer tails.

d] Music barrel shows fresh scoring from hammer tails.

Keyframe too close to barrel or the hammer-rest felt has become hard and compressed, so allowing the odd hammer to come too far back. Rectification is to adjust the positioning of the keyframe or remove it altogether and refelt the rest-rail. This used to be adjusted by many piano hirers by packing between the compressed felt and the keyframe with scraps of card. This certainly worked but is hardly a repair!

e] Instrument plays discordantly.

Keyframe not in register with barrel pins or the hammer tails are bent, so picking up pins from the next tune. Check the hammer tails carefully for vertical and lateral alignment. Note that all the tails must also be exactly the same length otherwise some notes will sound late due to the hammer being held back longer by the barrel pins. The barrel pins must also be straight. Check the barrel arbor leaf spring in the barrel access door and see that it is moving the barrel properly.

f] Instrument plays nine tunes perfectly and the last (or first) tune unmelodiously.

This means that the keyframe is registered one complete tune out of position and you must take the barrel back to the first tune position, check the registration, then repeat the checks at the last tune position. This is a very common fault with pianos where a previous repairer has failed to appreciate what he has done wrong – or omitted to do.

g] Clockwork piano plays with excessive mechanical noise.

Badly worn gears in motor-drive or, most likely, the stop/start detent is not disengaging fully from the governor sprag, causing a rapid 'tick' as the piano plays. Adjustment is to regulate the coin-tray arm or bend the governor sprag slightly.

h] Repetitive notes do not sound – hammers stop short of strings.

This means that the keyframe is too close to the barrel. Adjust the two vertical, eye-ended adjusters. Note that, on tremolo arrangements, every note has its own individual hammer adjustment.

i] Music sounds dead, particularly in the treble.

This may be due to very rusted strings which are now useless and must be replaced, or due to the fact that the hammers are striking the strings too close to the bridge. It is practice for the hammer to strike the strings at a distance between one-seventh and one-eighth of their length (this is the 'speaking length' between the bridges, of course), to produce the best and purest tone. Demonstrate this on a string near the centre of the piano by plucking the string at various positions along its length. Barrel-piano makers were not so fussy about this fact, but a dead string usually means that you must make the hammer hit the string a little farther out from its end. Try resetting the hammer by bending the wire slightly whilst maintaining the correct clearance between the hammer and the string when at rest – about 1/16-inch.

j] Music sounds dead and tinny in places.

Check the hammer clearance. If the hammers are actually touching the strings when at rest, the string is muted or 'blocked' and cannot sing out. Bring all hammers to within 3/32-inch of the strings.

If you have followed all these points, and appreciate how the barrel piano works, then you can confidently tackle similar barrel-operated percussion instruments. One golden rule, and this applies to all mechanisms. It is better to spend time thinking about the job carefully before starting work than to dash ahead and risk irrevocable damage by over enthusiasm and lack of understanding.

---

1. Heel-ball is a polishing mixture used by shoemakers and consists of a solidified mass of hard wax and lamp-black.
2. The term 'harp' here is used to refer to the strung portion of the piano, which, in full-sized instruments, is also referred to as the 'strung back'.
3. This is, I know, an imprecise figure and the exact strain on a piano-frame is hard to determine, but my calculations suggest that this is a fair approximation. At least it gives you an indication of the total forces that a piano frame has to contend with.

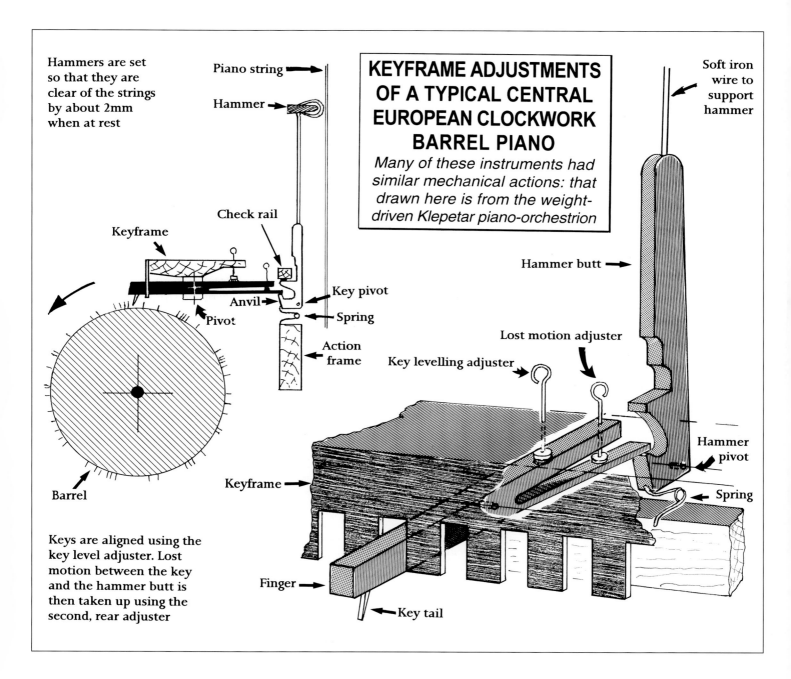

Hammers are set so that they are clear of the strings by about 2mm when at rest

Piano string

Hammer

KEYFRAME ADJUSTMENTS OF A TYPICAL CENTRAL EUROPEAN CLOCKWORK BARREL PIANO

Many of these instruments had similar mechanical actions: that drawn here is from the weight-driven Klepetar piano-orchestrion

Soft iron wire to support hammer

Check rail

Keyframe

Hammer butt

Key pivot

Anvil

Lost motion adjuster

Pivot

Spring

Key levelling adjuster

Action frame

Barrel

Keyframe

Hammer pivot

Spring

Keys are aligned using the key level adjuster. Lost motion between the key and the hammer butt is then taken up using the second, rear adjuster

Finger

Key tail

Chapter 15
How to Play the Player Piano Artistically

Who needs instructions on how to play a player-piano? After all, it's automatic, isn't it? You put your feet on the pedals and away you go! Well, as with most things in life, the answer's both 'yes' and 'no'. It looks simple enough and it is easy to play, but what I really want to try to get across is how you can get the very best out of your instrument. You'll note that this Chapter is called 'How to play the player piano artistically'. The 'artistically' bit is really the important part but long before you approach that stage, there is the unavoidable first hurdle of actually *how* to operate the machine. It's a bit like driving a car. Sure, it goes by itself without having to be pushed, but you still have to learn to drive before you can go in for Formula 1 racing.

To convince you that the machine is deserving of a bit more than just a cursory tramping of the feet, there's a little story that I have told before in an earlier book but it is well worth bringing back to life for it is a salutary lesson for us all.

Back in the days when Britain's Player Piano Group founder Frank Holland still lived in the aged and disintegrating Victorian church that was home to the British Piano Museum by the Thames at Brentford to the West of London, he telephoned me one evening to say that a very talented lady collector/player-piano-player was visiting the Museum that evening and Frank was staging an exclusive party for a few fellow enthusiasts to hear her play. An evening at Frank's unconventional home-cum-museum was not to be turned down lightly and so I duly arrived at the Church door and rang the bell. Inside was Frank, several museum helpers and a small band of fellow guests and amidst these was the lady we had all come to hear play her own favourite piano-roll. The main attraction from her point of view appeared to be that Frank had in his Museum a Pianola exactly the same as hers at home!

Note the scenario! The lady was skilled at operating her own instrument at home and playing her favourite music roll. Now she was going to play the music she know so well on a piano that, while identical to her own, was a different instrument. And she was about to do this before an assembled gathering of receptive admirers in the main hall of the British Piano Museum.

The dear lady sat down and off she went, her sensitive feet pedalling the way she had pedalled many hundreds of times before upon similar pedals, her fingers setting the controls to positions she knew instinctively. Almost immediately it was pretty obvious that she was in trouble. The instrument she was trying to play would not respond in the manner in which she expected it to, she could not create the accents, her tempo changes were not right: in fact, she sounded like a raw amateur who had never so much as sat at a player before! As this piano reacted in quite a different manner to her own, all that were present felt her acute embarrassment. She gallantly pedalled her way to the end – and we all politely applauded her performance. She did not look happy.

The lesson had been a painful but nevertheless important one. You see, every player piano is very slightly different. Originally, probably, when they left the factory they were all similar, but over years of use (and mis-use) and one or more re-

builds, too many variables in the system have been moved, adjusted, mis-adjusted and altered. This does not mean that a restored player piano is rubbish: it merely means that you cannot – must not – expect two instruments, *however identical they may appear*, to perform in exactly the same way.

When you sit down at a strange player, be aware that this individuality exists and that the really experienced player instinctively knows that he must adjust to the piano, not the other way around. You must play it for half an hour or more to get the true feel of it. This is no admission of failure or shortcoming. Even driving a different car takes a while to adjust. In the world of music, a solo violinist may occasionally suffer the misfortune of a broken string while in mid-performance. Customary concert tradition will usually mean that the First Violinist (the leader of the orchestra) will at once hand the soloist his own instrument to enable the performance to continue – and quickly replace the maestro's busted gut. Audiences like this: it shows a strong *camaraderie* on the platform. What generally surprises them, however, is that the grateful soloist suddenly sounds like a first-year pupil and sometimes plays quite badly on his borrowed fiddle. The reason is that fiddles all play in a different way – very slightly, admittedly, but enough to be noticeable. And when a visiting organist finds a nice church organ he hasn't played before, he would be very foolish to launch straight into his party-piece without first spending up to an hour quietly trying out the way the organ works and trying out its various registers. Nothing is worse than confusing your stops because you momentarily forget that it's not your usual mount, and drawing the Tuba Mirabilis instead of the Harmonic Flute. That sort of performance certainly gets you remembered but for not quite the right reason!

All this shows that the player-pianist can be forgiven if he or she is persuaded to try out a 'foreign' player and makes the proverbial pig's-ear of it. The wise player-pianist, though, might quietly try out the instrument first – and then play a piece of popular music that is not so demanding as to touch and nuance as, for instance, a Chopin etude or one of Beethoven's thrilling piano sonatas.

At this point I shall blow the gaff on one of the arcane secrets that player-piano owners have kept to themselves under pain of having their tracker-bar holes sealed up with Super-glue. There *is* no right way to play a player-piano! Mind you, there is a vast number of *wrong* ways to work the instrument. So long as we both understand that, let's look at trying to get the best out of our instruments.

Back in February 1904, *Musical Opinion* reported on a Pianola concert at the inauguration of London's new home of players. Whoever was the actual reporter, he proved to be a highly perceptive individual. It is, initially, difficult to determine upon which side of the fence he sits. Is he pro-Pianola – or as anti as anti can be? Read his words and take note – for he turns out to be something of a shining light amidst those critics, both ancient and modern, for whom mechanical music is an abomination.

> I wonder what will be the future of the mechanical piano player. The other day I attended the opening of the Aeolian Hall,

and in the program of the concert the Pianola took a large part, both as soloist and as accompanist to songs and violin pieces. The instrument was skilfully manipulated by a Mr Schulz, who managed the wind supply [he really means vacuum, but confusion has always reigned – *A O-H*] with an evenness, which the amateur could hardly hope to equal without long practice. That the machine player is capable of expression is evident enough; but it was clear to me that only a musician who knows the music by heart can ever hope to get the best results out of the Pianola. And what applies to the Pianola no doubt equally applies to other instruments of the same type. I shudder to think of the travesty of classical music which these mechanical players might be guilty of in the hands of a manipulator who had no knowledge of music. Expression would doubtless degenerate into a meaningless contrast of pianissimo with fortissimo and of quick tempo with slow – a contrast, however, by no means confined to mechanical players.

Of course, one misses the different tone colour which a skilled pianist can obtain from the piano with his fingers; but I believe that this can be imitated to a great extent by a careful graduating of the force of the wind supply. The merits of the instrument, on the other hand, are obvious. Its performance is certainly correct with a correctness which is almost uncanny. No pianist ever plays a composition with such note perfection. And then – this opens a very wide field for speculation – it places the lover of music in the position of a conductor of an orchestra, who can hear his ideas realised by his players without playing himself. For those who do not trust their own ideas of a composition, the rolls are marked by well known pianists, whose indications can be faithfully followed by the manipulator when once he has acquired a certain amount of skill. After all, music does not exist for the sake of the concert virtuosi…

And yet, although this technical; perfection is not to be attained by the ordinary amateur, there is all the same a knowledge of what constitutes executive art, in which the tyro may often gave finer ideal than the professional, who more often than not has taken up the art of piano playing because he possesses some physical aptitude rather than because he has a mind singularly open to musical impressions. For that reason we are compelled to wonder why many artists who have gained such technical mastery over their instruments exhibit such a misunderstanding of the music that they play. Many an amateur pianist who is baffled by the difficulty of executing rapid passages of arpeggios, and who never hopes to be able to play runs with the evenness which he knows quite well they require, is nevertheless a better judge of how a composition should be played than the professional pianist to whom these matters present no kind of obstacle. The Pianola enables this common type of amateur to realise his ideals. It opens the door for him to a limitless field of artistic enjoyment. The necessity of possessing a knowledge of music prevents the use of the Pianola becoming a mechanical means of degenerating a taste for music, which might happen is just as good results could be obtained by those ignorant of the art as by those who have knowledge of it. And there can be no doubt that the close knowledge of the great masterpieces of art which these mechanical players must give to those who use them will have an influence for good.

Well, whoever the unnamed correspondent really was, he managed to hit just about every single nail firmly on the head! He managed to determine that some (not all) professional pianists could play so well that they cannot hear the music (absolutely true) while many Pianola-players who cannot themselves play the music can hear it and know how it should be played. He also suggests something that you and I already know – that there are actually music-lovers out there who *(a)* can't read music, and *(b)* can't play an instrument! Heavens above! cry out the old-school musicologists who avidly believe that music, like nuclear science, is not for ordinary folk who haven't studied very hard to earn the right to listen to the stuff.

Now, contemporary with the production of player pianos, several authors sat down and attempted to write instructions on how the thing should be played. As far as I am concerned, these writers broke the first rule of any instruction book in that, like most of today's manuals for computer software, they made the assumption that the reader knew more than he did. Player-pianists presumably purchased their players because they were not perfect performers themselves. We already assume that to the owner of a player the ordinary printed notation of music (crotchets, quavers, clefs and staves) is an unsolved riddle. Then why illustrate elementary manuals with screeds of printed musical extracts? That really is going to inspire the player owner to take up golf!

The musical notation of the player piano is a long strip of paper with holes in it and the instruction manual that forgets that is well out onto the thin ice in mid-pond. The musical device that is the most important to the player-pianist is his ear for, after a while, he develops a pretty good idea as to how he wants to hear the music sound. The rest is practice and experiment until that elusive sound or other effect he wants to experience or create is heard for real.

Sydney Grew, long-revered pundit on player-piano matters, in his 1922 book *The Art of the Player-Piano* offered rather negative advice in the form of a throw-away comment when he wrote: 'I find that it takes about three years to make a good player-pianist of a man or woman of average musical intelligence.' Oh dear! I bet that turned off many an anticipant player-pianist! Far better had he said that the player-pianist who spends time practising will gradually play better and better until he achieves perfection – or as near to perfection as he wants to go.

Let's get another aspect clear immediately. There is no mystery about operating a player-piano and to pretend that there is distorts the reality. Working a complex machine, using a computer – all these things require a degree of training that is pleasurable in varying degrees. Playing a player-piano has to be in this category. If it isn't then we're wasting each other's time.

The first thing to face is how to sit at a player piano. The height and angle of the stool really do matter for the correct playing position will be less fatiguing. Certainly if you have never pedalled a player before, or if it is some while since last you confronted your player, then you will be fatigued quite rapidly by playing. Just as with cycling or gardening, too long a first session will give you aches and pains. The player-pianist will suffer sore ankles and tender calf muscles while an unpadded stool can produce sore thighs and buttocks while playing havoc with other muscles you'd rather not think about.

The proper player-piano stool has a slightly sloping seat that enables you to sit just a little bit higher than you might normally sit to play by hand. The slight slope also allows your legs to move without being bruised by continually striking the fore edge of the seat. The key to easy playing is to sit comfortably and slightly further back from the keyboard than for hand-playing in such a way that you can easily reach and operate the hand controls on the front slip rail while at the same time placing both feet evenly on the pedals so that the heel is more or less on the pivot-point or hinge-point of each. Let's emphasize here that the pedals I am talking about are the exhauster treadles, not the normal soft and sustaining pedals of the piano itself.

Some people, when they pedal a player, hang on to the edge of the keyboard like grim death and, from the rear, look like a Tour de France competitor, shoulders swinging from side to side, knees going up and down and the whole scene displaying obvious expenditure of huge effort. The only thing missing is the gaudy go-faster Lycra suit and Jason's helmet. This is *not* the way to play! By all means relax into the music and swing your shoulders and body with the music if you wish, but don't do it because you *have* to.

It is pretty bad form to play an instrument as if you are fighting the mechanism in order to get the better of it. If you are relaxed at the piano you will extract a better sound from it. Remember the piano is neither horse nor bicycle. A tricky taskmistress, yes, but little more. The secret of success lies very firmly with the pedalling and how you are sitting.

Practice using merely the joint of the heel to pivot the foot forwards and backwards so that the pedal moves easily. All the movement wants to stem from your ankle. It's a good idea, until the movement comes naturally, to place a large book or even a tea-tray on your lap so as to ensure that your knees really do not go up and down. All the movement needs to be nowhere else but in the foot. And when, later on and after a lot of practice, you want to accent a note or a chord, you will do it merely by giving a quicker dab at the pedal with the ball of the foot.

Sometimes you just cannot get the feel for the pedals. The cause is then the height and the position of the stool. Try moving the stool to a different distance from the piano and adjust the height a little. The worst possible scenario is to be too low.

Unlikely though it may sound, some years ago a very well-known and respected British piano collector who had recently added a player to his collection, begged me to go and 'sort it out' because it simply wouldn't work. I explained it was a difficult 150-mile round trip for me but he was insistent and agreed to pay all expenses. I duly went along to his magnificent collection, sat at his newly-acquired player and found that it worked quite well. I then asked him to show me how he had been trying to operate it. He had his stool set too low…

The act of playing means moving the foot pedals up and down, pivoted about their heel positions. Your practice will start with the even, equal pedalling, first one foot then the other. Gradually as you gain in experience you will learn to adjust the whole rhythm of your pedalling to suit the needs of the piano and the music. You will learn to 'feel' the degree of vacuum in the reservoir and also learn to make minute adjustments to the rate and depth of pedalling, eventually how to pause completely for certain effects. More on that later, though.

Of course playing a player piano is more than simply treadling away and there are various hand controls by which the music had been adjusted. There is a tempo lever, various devices for accenting or subduing all or part of the keyboard, the control for raising and lowering all the dampers on the strings (the sustaining pedal) and a system for rewinding. While all types and makes of player have controls for these functions, their presentation is individual to that maker. As an example, the tempo-adjuster on the Pianola is a sliding lever, but the Angelus achieves the same function by use of a rocking tablet on the key slip. Over the years some controls may actually have been changed by previous restorers.

How an instrument is set up, meaning the adjustment of the controls, is naturally an individual thing and this explains why one may be able to play one's own instrument perfectly yet may have difficulty in playing another.

Now I suggest that apart from setting the tempo of the music roll, and rewinding it at the end, you abandon all hand controls until you have mastered the use of the feet. The reason for this is that the feet are astonishingly sensitive and the bellows of a well-adjusted and restored player-piano can give all the expression you need, at least to begin with, by modulating the use of the feet. In fact I have successfully trained novice pianolists by making them sit on their hands while playing merely with their feet. On some pianos this is easier to do than on others but I can assure you that not only is it perfectly possible but it is the best test of a player owner's understanding of his own instrument. Certainly a highly-skilled pianolist will have no problem in producing an acceptable performance from his instrument while seated thus upon his hands.

To refresh our memories over how the controls actually work, remember that the foot pedals perform two distinct functions. First they operate the exhausters to provide the power for all the playing functions. Generally speaking, the greater the suction the louder the instrument can sound (assuming all other controls left alone). Conversely, the less the suction the quieter the piano may sound, the same conditions regarding the other controls applying. Second they operate the music-roll drive motor that means the mechanism that draws the music roll over the tracker bar. There is one difference, though, and that is that in a properly-regulated instrument the degree of suction, meaning the intensity of pedalling, should not affect the speed of the music. Naturally there is a point of minimum suction beneath which the music roll will slow, but in general, however hard you pedal, the music will not go faster, and however gently you pedal – within reason – the music should not slow. This is because the music-roll motor has a tempo control that is governed by a form of regulator.

When you begin playing for the first time, set the tempo control to the speed indicated on the music-roll and then leave well alone. As you become much more experienced you will wish to make continual minor adjustments to the speed of the music to suit you personal whim and this is where the use of the finely-adjusted tempo lever comes into its own. On a Metrostyle roll, for instance, the suggested speed of the music is indicated by a line that you are advised to follow with the point of the tempo lever in the spool box: this calls for continual adjustment.

My words about varying speed (*tempi*) do not, of course, apply to the reproducing piano and its special music rolls: these are cut at a constant speed as are so-called hand-played rolls. Not that this should deter you from making adjustments to suit your personal taste. It is, after all, your piano!

The next feature to experiment with is the accenting devices. There are two basic types of accenting the first of which concerns use of the two subduing levers that control the bass and the treble half of the keyboard (in truth the pneumatic stack rather than the actual keyboard). The second type is the so-called 'solo' or Themodist type of control. Themodist being the name adopted by Aeolian, other makers called their variants on the system by different names such as Melodant, Solodant, Themola and suchlike. There were some accenting systems that operated on a different principle such as the Kastner Kastonome which, while still operated by the piano roll, achieves its result by a different route.

The essence of expression is the creation of notes of differing intensity. Get it clear in your mind just what accenting means and how it is achieved. If an instrument is playing at maximum volume (strength, if you like), then there can be no way of making any note anywhere stand out over the others.

The softer the playing of surrounding notes, the more pronounced any note that is accented will sound. Taken to its ridiculous extreme, with the subduing levers at fully subdued, the only notes that will sound will be the accented ones!

For the first example of how this is done, we will imagine a player that has no 'automatic' accenting system such as the Themodist, but merely has the subduing levers that adjust the degree or tension of the vacuum in each and of the valve chest.

The accenting itself is achieved in two ways. With the subduing levers in the mid-way position so that the piano plays softly, a quick and extra dab on one foot pedal will be enough to make a note or a chord sound louder than the surrounding texture. Try it for yourself. You will find that it is impossible to have any effect on the note if you attempt the accent when the note perforations are actually over the tracker bar and the note is already 'open'. If you make the accent too much before the note opens the tracker hole, then the affect will largely be lost. This is why, with Themodist-type perforations, they are always arranged slightly ahead of the note or notes that they are to 'themodise'.

The knack, then, is to accent the note just a fraction before it plays. That distance is measured in *time*, not the length of paper-roll. If you experiment, then you will find for yourself just the right position.

Depending on the level of suction in the two halves of the chest (as governed by the position of the subduing levers), the degree of emphasis possible on a note is that gained by momentarily releasing the subduing lever. This means bringing the lever fully to the right for a split second or two. This can further be modified by use of the toes of one foot to add an additional accent.

It all sounds dreadfully complicated yet with practice you will discover your own methods and in doing so gain a lot more experience of how your instrument works. By the way, it doesn't matter which foot you accent with: practice using them alternately until you are comfortable with the procedure.

With the automatic accenting systems, a different sequence comes into play. Control of the Themodist is normally by a lever in the spoolbox which activates the themodising openings in the tracker-bar and the normal operation of the subduing controls is altered. The Angelus type of action, for instance, has buttons that are pushed down with the fingers to subdue: under 'solo' control these buttons become automatically fully depressed and play no part in the performance. With the Themodist on the Pianola, the levers should be held fully to the left (on the Duo-Art pedal-electric models a special metal clip is used for this purpose: few survive since, being a 'loose item', most have got lost over the years). With these levers held over, it is now impossible to make any significant difference in volume by using your foot, but the intensity of the Themodised notes as indicated by the music-roll will now be directly affected by your footwork. It is for this reason that some music-rolls are printed with instructions when to turn on the 'solo' (Themodist) and when to return to 'normal'. If you ignore these instructions some strange effects can be achieved, so it's best not to ignore the instructions!

Don't worry if at first you don't understand any of this. Experimentation is free and cannot damage the piano or the music-roll. And if you do it in private, you cannot harm your reputation, either!

So far I have said nothing about the sustaining lever. This single control is probably the least understood control of the whole player mechanism. Properly used it can put so much colour into an interpretation. Improperly used it can convert a performance into a jangling blur of sound. In your ordinary piano, the sustaining pedal (please don't call it the 'loud' pedal – there is no such thing) controls the dampers that are fitted to the individual hammer action for all the strings that are provided with dampers – normally everything up to the last octave or so at the treble end. Their purpose is to 'dampen' or dull the sound of the big, heavy strings that make up the ordinary modern piano so that they do not harmonically blur the other notes.

To explain what this means, if you strike the key of your piano to play one of the lowest notes on the keyboard, and hold the key down, you will hear that the note rolls on and on and takes some while to fade away. Try this on other notes up the keyboard. The higher you go, the shorter the duration of the note. This is why the extreme high notes do not need dampers because their sound dies away almost immediately.

Now try another note at the bass end only this time let go of the note immediately it sounds. The note quickly dies back. The reason for this is that each piano hammer controls a felt damper or pad that presses on the string. With the note held down, the pad is held away from the string, so letting it vibrate. Releasing the note brings the pad down onto the vibrating string and quickly stills it to silence.

Now besides being controlled by each individual hammer, these damper felts can be raised or lowered altogether because they are arranged to pass through a guide rail that can be moved, usually (in the case of the ordinary piano) by the pianist's right foot

To raise the damper rail, the ordinary pianist will press down with this right foot. Surprisingly, this one action requires more force than does the operation of any other component in a piano action. And when it comes to operating the damper rail automatically under the control of the music-roll, the need for extra force has to be met by a demand for more suction and a noticeably bigger pneumatic motor.

Operating the sustaining pedal by pneumatic, automatic means incurs a momentary drain on suction. Because the sustaining pedal has to move rapidly and because it must carry quite a load, the pneumatic to control it is usually quite large and has a large vacuum opening. The result is that this sudden call on suction power can occasionally be felt on the foot pedals especially during the playing of quiet passages. On some piano actions this is much more noticeable than others and the effect can be that one or two notes coincident with this drain may actually not sound. You may choose not to use the automatic sustaining-pedal control, but to use the passage of the sustaining pedal perforations in the music roll as a guide to moving the finger lever.

While most player-pianists have their own views on this, and I have been drawn into heated arguments by some, I claim that this is a defect that doesn't matter. With practice, you get to know that changing gear while driving up a steep hill means that momentarily you may lose speed but you learn to compensate for it before the need to cascade down through the gearbox. The experienced player-pianist develops a similar knack that compensates for any power loss through the sustaining pedal.

The use of the sustaining pedal is one of the hardest aspects of playing the piano that a pianist must learn. Its misuse results in musical murder. When I teach students, I always tell them to keep their feet clear of the piano's pedals until they have mastered the bit with the hands. Once the finger dexterity becomes second nature, then we can begin to address what to do with the sustaining pedal.

For the player-pianist, the first task is to forget the popular name for this thing – the loud pedal. If you want to play loudly then use your feet more vigorously, use your subduing levers sparingly, and accent with your toes. The sustaining pedal not only encourages the notes that are played while the dampers are free from the strings, but it encourages other notes that you have not played to sing slightly in acoustic sympathy. This is most effective over the lower and middle keyboard registers. Because of this feature, the sustaining pedal is effective over the whole range of musical intensity from very soft to loud, although the acoustic harmony effect tends to diminish the louder the overall level of piano sound and is replaced by a growling blur that is no doubt beloved by electric guitarists with a distortion pedal, but is fairly bad practice for the player-pianist.

So far I have said nothing about the other pedal on the piano – the soft pedal. This is a method of playing the instrument quietly and there are two types found on modern pianos. The commonest is the one invariably used on upright pianos and this consists of a rail that moves the entire hammer action closer to the strings when the pedal is depressed. This means that the hammer has less distance to travel towards the strings and so there is less energy in the hammer blow meaning a quieter sound is produced.

The second type of 'soft-pedal' action is generally only employed on better-quality grand pianos and consists in shifting the entire keyboard and hammer actions to the right by about a quarter of an inch (5mm) so that the hammers only strike some of the strings. Remember that the bass notes of a piano are each represented by two heavy metal strings; the middle registers by three and the treble by four (these numbers have varied between makers and over the years but the principle remains). By shifting the piano action sideways, the bass hammers only strike one string, the middle registers just two and the treble also just two. Result? Softer sound. In reproducing pianos, this keyboard shift is fully automatic while in manual actions it is more usual to lift the rest rail under the hammers of an up-striking action (meaning one that is under the strings – the commonest type) similar to the upright player's principle.

Earlier I said that the feet were the most expressive part of a player-pianist's anatomy. It always amuses me to watch some player-piano operators at work and to see how they continually make minor adjustments to their instrument with fingers tweaking levers, buttons being pushed, and a general air of hard work being transmitted. The reason they do this is because since the music is 'automatic', they want to be perceived to be having an influence on it. Had they the arms and hands of Siva I am sure that each would be fully employed!

I am not saying that all adjustment to tempi, subduing or accenting, working the sustaining pedal and so on is fatuous showmanship, but that a good deal of it is! Back to sitting on your hands – experiment and practice getting almost every effect you want merely with the feet and using the toes for accents. The valves and the slides on a trombone are actually not necessary, but they make playing it a lot easier.

A word on footwork. Pedalling strictly left-right-left, pedalling in time with the music, pedalling to a metronome, the clock or anything else is simply dreadful. How can you be sensitive to the music or make any accenting if your feet and moving mechanically! If I have to suggest the most common fault with pianolists, then it all lies in the pedalling. I have already mentioned knees that go up and down, feet that move like those of troops on a route-march and some of the other pitfalls of the novice pedaller. Now I want to talk about rhythm.

Rhythm is what *music* has, not feet. Do not pedal with the regularity of an automaton, but pedal easily and steadily, feeling the demands of the mechanism through your soles. Pedal deeply but when the music suggests, pedal lightly and gently. Make the stroke length variable and do everything you can to disassociate your rhythm with that of the music. Keep the toes ready for an accent and learn to be able to put that accent in with either foot at *any* stage of the pedal stroke.

With pedalling there are some very interesting effects to be gained. One of which I am very fond is the *un*-accent. The term is my own: you won't find it in any training manual. Like everything else it calls for musical awareness and dexterity. For me, the Chopin Nocturnes call for this procedure because there are frequent *cantabile* sections that contain softened chords. While you can fully subdue on these in the usual way, my method of un-accenting can produce a truly delightful and sudden pianissimo that I cannot achieve in any other way. The technique is to approach the notes, chord or cadence that you wish to soften in a passage and then in the same manner as one might accent the passage, I make a short and precise hesitation in pedalling. This momentary reduction in available suction can produce the most exquisitely softened passage. You can also vary the harmonic content by applying the sustaining pedal at the same moment. It calls for practice, but do try it. For the listener it can prove quite magical.

As an aside, one of my own instruments is a large Aeolian Steck 65-88-note Pianola built with a massive and extremely heavy Gotha frame. This is very easy to play and I often demonstrate this by using just one foot on one treadle. Because it is such an easy piano, I can do almost everything by way of expression merely using one foot. This may be an exceptional instrument, but I tell you this to show that your feet really are a player-pianist's best fingers!

The music roll is your performance and if the roll becomes damaged, the music will be affected. It is therefore a good idea to look after your rolls very carefully. They may be up to a hundred years old and may be a little delicate. Or they may be quite recent re-cuts bought new within living memory. It doesn't matter which, however, for both can be badly damaged by improper handing. Here is a quick guide to looking after your music.

First storage. Try not to store rolls upright (vertically) but preferable lay the boxes flat. A special shelf or roll-cabinet is the idea storage medium, but do not stack the boxes more than two or three deep otherwise pulling one out will result in an expensive cascade to the floor and damaged boxes.

When you have chosen a roll to play, cultivate a procedure so that you ensure the roll is returned to the right box. There is nothing more frustrating than finding the wrong rolls in a box. I make a point of placing the box and its lid side by side on the piano lid while I am playing a roll so that afterwards there is no question as to which box it has come from – more on this in Chapter 18.

Use the same technique if you are playing more than one roll. To make life easy, if you are giving a recital, say, to some friends and have six rolls to play, open each box, lift the roll so that it is at an angle in the box and sloping towards you. After you have played the first roll and rewound it, put it into its box and pick up the next in sequence and so on.

A jumble of rolls is not a good idea. It looks untidy and you will not be able to find the particular ones you want. Sometimes, when you buy a second-hand piano roll, it comes without its box, with the wrong box or with a damaged box. In both Britain and America, newly made replacement boxes for piano rolls can be bought through the various collectors' associations. If the rolls or their boxes do not have the right label, fix a new one – replacement labels from the major roll brands are also available today. If you have to resort to making one yourself, try to avoid writing one up: do it on your word-processor – merely because it will look neater.

Now to playing music-rolls. Take the roll out of its box, hold it loosely in an upright position so that the driven end of the spool (the end with the slotted recess if it is an 88-note one, or the one with the spade-shaped spigot if it is a 65-note) is lowermost and tap it gently a few times on a hard surface to knock up the paper to one side. Now check that the 'Reroll-Play' control on the piano is set to the 'reroll' position – it should have been left that way after the previous roll was removed and put back into its box. Do not touch the foot pedals. Hold the roll tightly so that the paper does not 'cone' or otherwise loosen and in such a way that the direction of unrolling is from the top side towards you.

Insert the left end into the left side spool-box chuck. With one or more fingers on the outside of the right-hand spool flange, gently push the roll to the left. You will feel the left chuck move inwards against its compression spring. Insert the right-hand end of the roll into the right-hand spool drive-chuck. Turn the roll by hand until it clicks into place. Make certain the spool is securely located in its pivots before letting go of it. Now take the tag fixed to the pointed or tapered end of the apron and pull it down to the lower take-up spool – the one that stays fixed in the spool-box. Turn this spool until you can fasten the roll onto the securing hook. Wind the take-up spool by hand for one turn to see that the paper is not wider than the gap between the spool sides. If the paper has swollen and is a tight fit, this may tear the edges so move the spool flanges apart: there is usually an adjustment screw (on better makes of instrument) that allows you to move the flanges in and out by a small amount. Once you have done this, you are ready to play.

Set the control to 'play', set the tempo control to the desired number and start to pedal.

After the end of the roll, stop pedalling and move the tempo control lever to 'zero'. This stops the paper moving without suddenly releasing the tension on the drive chuck. Failure to do this at the end of the roll will damage the roll as the drive motor attempts to pull the gummed end of the roll off the spool to which it is secured. Now select 'reroll' and slowly but steadily pedal as the roll rewinds. Do not hesitate or vary the speed of pedalling during rewind otherwise the roll will wind loosely and be prone to distortion with humidity changes. Many player actions have a small leather brake-pad which works on the drive of the take-up spool so that the rewind is maintained under slight tension. This usually doesn't work very well, so gently place a finger on the edge of one flange during rewind. This will ensure proper tension on the paper during rewind.

Never leave a roll in the spoolbox, never leave a half-played roll either. Always respool, remove the roll, loop the securing string round the roll and onto its tag, grasp the roll firmly in the hand, move briskly left and ease it out from the right-hand side before replacing it in its box and putting the lid back on.

Yes I know it's a bit of a rigmarole and yes I know I've overstated the obvious, but if I don't and somebody damages a roll they'll be able to turn round and say 'Ord-Hume didn't warn us about that!'

Now at last you can practise playing your player-piano!

Learn to experiment. Try anything and everything to achieve the sound you want. Unless you want to become a mediocre performer, practice. Master your own techniques because your instrument, if it is even only in average adjustment, is capable of producing such superb effects. With a good restoration and fine adjustment, you have at your command the finest mechanical musical interpreter you could wish for. If you don't learn how to get the best from it you are being unfair to your instrument, not to mention yourself.

Chapter 16
Roll-Playing Reed Organs: The Aeolian Orchestrelle

The great success of the domestic piano's rival – the reed organ (variously known as pump-organ, parlor organ [US] and by the generic term *American organ*) – gave it an established image in the home. It is not surprising, therefore, that the first paper-roll-playing keyboard instrument was not the piano but the reed organ. Curiously, as time would tell, it would never equal the player-piano in popularity.

While they were to be made in Germany, France and North America, it was in the last-mentioned that the instrument flourished and the era of ordinary reed organs was a rich soil into which player technology landed. There were approximately 245 makers of instruments in America and Canada and leading maker Estey Organ Company stated in early 1800 that 500 people were employed in the industry producing more than 60 organs a day or one organ every ten working minutes.

When first the roll-playing mechanism was introduced to the reed organ early in 1880 it was the leading reed organ maker W W Kimball of Chicago that grasped the nettle with both hands. In this instrument the seminal patents of Frederick W Hedgeland regarding player mechanisms were to be employed for the first time. This was in 1892 and the company's first commercial player was on the market by 1897. Kimball, though, was not the first and the number of brands that reached the market in the last two decades of the 19th century was quite staggering.

Of all these, it was Aeolian's Orchestrelle that won the popularity stakes, was sold widely in Europe, Britain and America and, consequently, is today the most common form of perforated-paper-roll-operated player organ to survive. Of those numerous other brands or makes, a one-time close runner was the Wilcox & White Symphony. American maker of quality reed organs Estey made player instruments of this type, so did Mustel in France, Schiedmeyer in Germany and Bell in Canada. In terms of tone and musicality, the first choice must be the Mustel followed by the Schiedmeyer with the Orchestrelle in a fairly close third place. The big difference was that both the French and German contenders were horrendously expensive and, in the case of the Schiedmeyer, rather heavy in styling and ugly! They are also very rare, surviving numbers being few indeed. Orchestrelles, on the other hand, are fairly common. Here I might recommend use of the book *Harmonium [80]* which describes in great detail the reed organ, its elements and its construction.

The sound of this instrument is produced by 'free reeds' – thin and flexible metal blades that are individually fixed by one end into a metal frame. The passage of air through the frame and around and past the reed causes the reed to move back and forth very rapidly in the tight-fitting opening. It is this very rapid vibration that produces the musical sound and one reed is used for each pitched note of the scale.

The first player reed organ of any sort was the small organette which was played using perforated metal or card discs, or zig-zag folded perforated cardboard books of music similar to that used on the majority of fairground organs. These date in general from the 1870s although the principle was demonstrated, without too much success, by an experimental organ shown at the Great Exhibition in London in 1851. By the mid-1880s, the instrument had reached a high degree of perfection and market acceptance throughout America, Germany and Great Britain. Organettes proliferated and their large numbers brought cheap music to many who could not afford music of any other sort, least of all the much more expensive Swiss-style musical box and the piano-player.

The reed organ itself had gained public acceptance in both America and France from a much earlier date. The French and German inventors produced the small pressure-blown harmonium (which was generally known in America by the generic term 'melodeon' or, occasionally, 'melodium'). It was, however, the French who discovered that if instead of *blowing* the reeds by admitting wind at pressure to them, finer tones could be produced by *sucking* air through to reed by using a suction bellows.

Like so many good ideas, though, the French did not capitalise on this invention and it was not until much later that the self-same discovery was made in America. Organs that sucked their reeds instead of blowing them were dubbed *American organs*. This terminology was a little unfortunate for it was picked up all over the world and the genus 'American organ' was manufactured in many parts of the globe including France, Germany, Great Britain and just about everywhere else that had a musical instrument-making industry. This tended to backfire at a later stage where a certain preference for British-made or European-made instruments existed. 'American' organs did not necessarily *come* from America!

In 1914, right at the start of the First War, Popper & Company of Leipzig announced their elegant Estrella instrument that would play both 'hand-played' artists' music rolls as well as 58-note Orchestrelle music. Another Leipzig company, Adolf Buff-Hedinger, launched its Premier-Auto-Harmonium around the same time, while makers Hofberg produced a player-harmonium in 1925, but it was the Schiedmayer Scheola series of player reed organs that represented the pinnacle of the genre. With 8½ rows of reeds representing 10½ different registers or stops, this was tonally an extraordinary organ. The range comprised models with names such as the Palestrina, Parsifal and Amforias, these were very expensive instruments.

Significantly, British-made contenders were few and far between, perhaps the best-known being the Maxfield organ. This was patented in 1896 and models cost up to £25 [$100]. The instrument was the product of one of London's numerous manufacturers of reed organs, harmoniums and piano-players. It used music rolls which were narrow by comparison with others - a mere 5½-inches wide - and was altogether a small instrument having only 31 of its 61-note keyboard notes playable from the roll.

Another was the Phoneon introduced in the early summer of 1898 by Malcolm & Co and retailed in London by Murdoch & Co. of 91, Farringdon Road. *Musical Opinion* said, in May that year:

> The instrument is a large American organ, playable either by the manual or by the use of perforated rolls.
>
> However, we think even a good performer would prefer to use the automatic arrangement, and thus devote his time to the

marks of expression, &c. Phrasing he need not attend to, as the use of the perforated rolls arranges this matter.

Music can be started at will; for directly the player touches the pedals a wind motor is set in motion, this apparatus in turn revolving the perforated tunes. Messrs. Malcolm & Co. have been working at their invention for a long time and have succeeded in placing the retail price of the instrument at 36gs. (£37.16/-) [$151].

The Phoneon we saw was over 6ft. high and contained two full sets, many stops (including one with which to arrange the 'tempo', and two swells...

Another short-lived competitor in the London market for self-playing reed organs was the Wallis Auto-Organ advertised for sale in 1898 at a price of £60, $240). Another attracted the attention of this same musical trade digest for March 1901:

The Bell Organ and Piano Co. (the London branch is on the Holborn Viaduct) are controlling the Bellolian, the invention of Mr. Charles Warren, whose name is prominent in London patent annals, and who for years has made a study of pneumatics as applied to organs. We are informed that the instrument is attachable to any reed organ, and my means of the invention the keys are worked automatically as the perforated music unfolds. The most striking feature of the invention is claimed to be its simplicity; thus whilst the idea is an improvement on other arrangements of the kind, the cost of construction is much less. Mr. Warren intends to reside in Guelph in order to superintend its manufacture.

There were several other makes and makers, including the Orpheus introduced in Britain during 1902 by the Clark Apollo Company, and the Olympia, described as 'an American organ with self-playing mechanism', but products of these companies are seldom encountered today. This is a pity because the later models which tried so unsuccessfully to capture the market dominated by American products and those of Aeolian in particular were, generally, of a superior quality. It was the old story, though, for these models came in too late at a time when the demand was no longer expanding but had begun to contract.

I alluded earlier to the Mustel Concertal produced in Paris by the famed Mustel company. This was one of the finest of all player reed organs and judged so for a number of reasons. First it featured a tonal basis which was far more colourfully and artistically established than that of the single-manual Orchestrelles. Secondly the keyboard was truly divided between left-hand and right-hand stops (unlike the Orchestrelle which is purely divided in half with two draw stops to operate on each full rank of reeds). And thirdly, was the highly-developed Mustel system of control using locking knee swells almost as *sforzando* pedals, and combining the *prolonguement* stop for bass notes and the foundation setting of the organ into two small treadle cheeks which could be operated by the twist of the foot while pedalling. It was also extremely expensive: in 1900 a Mustel Orgue Céleste with two manuals and eight rows of reeds, double expression, percussion métaphone and prolonguement cost (in London) 500 guineas (£525, $2,100.00; today £32,222, $7,800.00). Significantly, so good was the Mustel that it was taken as the basis of the Shiedmeyer Scheola, a high-quality German contender for the market and, as might be expected, equally unsuccessful in reaching big time sales.

Another maker was Estey which produced a range of very high-quality reed organs. This company made fullest use possible of the tonal opportunities of reeds and resonating chambers in its instruments: one model, the Phonorium, was expressly for use in church and halls. But all this is away from the story

that developed from the first attempts to incorporate the technology of the simple little organette into a keyboard reed organ.

There is some evidence to suggest that the very first free-reed instrument to be fitted with a perforated-card-playing pneumatic action was an Estey instrument modified by John McTammany in 1876. This was the culmination of experiments which began with a mechanism devised by him in about 1868 for the automatic playing of organs. He was granted a patent filed on September 7, 1876.

The first serious attempts to produce such an instrument were undoubtedly the work of McTammany who, in 1880, was modifying the Taber reed organ to take his player action. During the following year, he similarly modified organs made by Taylor & Farley. By 1882, both these companies were defunct and McTammany became associated with the Munroe Organ Reed Co as a result of which that company's large reed organ called the Orchestrone was offered with McTammany player action in 1885-6.

In Worcester, Massachusetts, the reed organ makers Mason & Risch were in production with a reed organ that they called the Vocalion. Introduced shortly before 1890, the Vocalion was characterised by its tones which were produced by voicing its reeds in a special way and placing each one in a specially-shaped chamber or 'qualifying tube' after the manner discussed by Helmholtz in his studies and researches into sound. In 1890, Mason & Risch changed its name to The Vocalion Organ Company. The rights to this name were eventually sold to Aeolian in 1903.

The story of the Aeolian Company has already been related from the player-piano aspect. As for reed organs, though, it was William Barnes Tremaine who took on the rights to manufacturing the product of two inventors, Englishman Newman R Marshman of New York City (who worked for reed-organ makers Mason & Hamlin) and Mason J Mathews of Boston, Massachusetts. In 1878 they had devised a small paper-roll-playing reed instrument which they called the *orguinette*. To begin with this was made by the Munroe Organ Reed Co but Tremaine acquired the business and upon which the whole empire of Aeolian was established. Tremaine set up the Mechanical Orguinette Company to make and market a product that was to sell in thousands. Later on, the *Celestina* was also introduced with considerable success. This was an enlarged variant of the first *orguinette*.

It was against this background that, in 1883, the first Aeolian organ appeared. It was built for the firm by the Munroe Organ Reed Co (more on this company in a moment) and the basic style was known as the 1050. It played 46-note music rolls. This inauspicious beginning was plagued with troubles stemming not just from production problems, but a combination of marketing inexperience and under-capitalisation.

Both the Orguinette and the Celestina relied on two associated products for the production of their music – the perforated paper rolls (which were made by the Boston-based Automatic Music Paper Company), and the actual organ reeds, produced by the Munroe Organ Reed Co, established in Worcester, Massachusetts, in 1860.

The Aeolian Organ Company was founded in 1887 and located at Garwood, a sparsely-populated area of New Jersey. The firm built homes locally for its employees creating what was called the township of Aeolian. With the Aeolian organ in production, albeit as a sourced product, Tremaine played a masterful stroke. In 1888, he acquired all the patents and stock in trade of the Automatic Music Paper Company. He now formed the Aeolian Organ & Music Company to manufacture automatic organs and music rolls. Four years later, he completed the integration of the new company by purchasing all the patents owned by the Munroe Organ Reed Co. He now controlled all the prerequisites of success. This coincided with the introduction of the first player-piano, the 65-note Aeriol of 1895.

Tremaine's son, Harry Barnes, born in Brooklyn 1866, became Aeolian Company president in 1898. Remember it was he who triumphed was to defeat the prophets of doom and launch the Pianola piano-player. In 1903, he brought into the business all the piano and organ plants that had been supplying Aeolian with components. Among these was the Vocalion Organ Company, makers of the built-up sets of reeds, called tone-ranks, for the player organs. Some of these were made to Vocalion patents by the A B Chase Company which had been formed in 1875 to build reed organs and was itself later to be controlled by Aeolian. Aeolian now advertised that it operated manufacturing plants in Aeolian, Meriden and Worcester. Its prestigious offices were then at Aeolian Buildings, 362, Fifth Avenue, and 34th Street, New York City.

But to return to the 1890s, these were the years of success for Aeolian and the company introduced an improved style of the player reed organ. This was the Model 1500, again using a 46-note roll and for the first time a C-compass instrument (at this time the greater majority of American-made reed organs of all types were based on the F compass although Estey had made a model for sale on the European market in the 1870s that extended from C to C).

Aeolian's range was extensive, varying in physical size and the number of ranks of reeds contained. These models ranged from the small $75 Princess Aeolian, the Style 1250 at $300 [£75], and the Style 1450 at $350 [£87.50], through to the large 58-note Model S Aeolian Grand with an almost piano-size case at $750 [£187.50]. This used the system of reed boxes and resonant sound-cavities that had been invented by the Vocalion Organ Company, a business that Aeolian had recently purchased a controlling interest in. By 1897, the company was also selling a luxury variant called the Aeolian Orchestrelle – the very first Orchestrelle model – at a staggering $1,500 [£375]; today worth $22,275 [£24,132]. The Orchestrelle was certainly pitched as a top-end, luxury market artefact. This had a 58-note compass extending from C to A

With the short space of a year or so, the 58-note Orchestrelle was, along with the Aeolian Grand, the undoubted leader in the field of self-playing large-compass reed organs.

By the turn of the century, Aeolian decided to unify their brand names and so the name 'Grand' which was used for the harmonium-type blown Aeolian 58-note organ was replaced by the name 'Orchestrelle' and from hence forth both blown harmonium-type instruments and sucked American-organ-type models shared the same name.

In the capital, though, one of the earliest importers of automatic musical instruments was George Whight. He opened his business in 1886 at 143, Holborn Bars and between 1893 and 1896 he traded alone as a musical instrument manufacturer and importer at 225, Regent Street. George Whight stocked the first Aeolian player organs in the late 1890s. In *Musical Opinion* for 1st September, 1888, we read:

>   Messrs. G. Whight & Co., of Holborn Bars, have secured the sole agency for the Wilcox & White organs.

The following month, Whight was advertising 'The Victolian Organ - plays Music of every description without the performer being a musician'. This cost 17 guineas ($71). Here Whight gave his address as 225 Regent Street and described himself as 'sole importers of the Victolian and Aeolian'. Which manufacturer produced the Victolian might have remained conjectural had it not been for sight of an American advertisement where the identical instrument is described as the Aeolian *Princess*. An unusual feature of the Princess/Victolian concerns the arrangement of the music roll: it was horizontal. Because of this, collectors had always thought that it was a Wilcox & White product, in particular as in a later notice, also in *Musical Opinion*, for 1st November that year, Whight wrote:

>   Wilcox and White genuine American Organs Are Unsurpassed in Quality of Tone, Rapidity of Action, Ease of Operation, Elegance of Design, Durability, and General Excellence…

At this particular time, Wilcox & White of Meriden, Connecticut, built only ordinary manually-played instruments. This company was a true pioneer in many ways and was later to use the same action principles that it used in the Symphony in its refreshingly different Angelus player-pianos.

The first Wilcox & White 'Symphony' player organ appeared late in the 1880s and was to remain in production until the very early years of this century. Even though it was a well-made instrument, it never gained the popularity of its Aeolian rival. An unusual mutant of the Angelus action was the Angelus Symphony - a piano-player which incorporated several ranks of reeds. With this instrument, the operator could perform either reed organ or piano, or both together just by selecting the stops on the player. These were at one time very popular and there are still a few to be found although it assumes that the tuning of the organ will match the pitch of the piano.

To return to George Whight's London business, this prospered and soon he was handling Aeolian organs having, one assumes, dropped the earlier Wilcox & White agency. By December of 1889, he was advertising the self-playing Tonsyreno, 'This Unique and Wonderful Instrument renders any and every description of Music in the most Charming and Orchestral style, rivalling the most skilled Musicians'. Capable of being played by hand or by perforated paper roll, this 46-note organ retailed 'from 41 Guineas'.

In 1899, the newly-founded Orchestrelle Company, British subsidiary of the Aeolian Company in New York, bought out George Whight's business. The new management was naturally totally dedicated to Aeolian products and the takeover was masterminded by H B Tremaine. He became president of the new concern and the sales manager was a Mr O Sundstrom. While the change was taking place, Mr A J Mason, a senior New York executive, came over to London. The main thrust of the business at this time was to be the new Pianola piano-player but Orchestrelles were also promoted at prices ranging from 70 gns (£73.10s; [$295.00]; £4,720 [$4,370.00]) to 600 gns (£630; [$2,520.00]; £40,430 [$9,355.00]).

Later on, the business was renamed The Aeolian Company Ltd. Initially, The Orchestrelle Company ran the premises at 225, Regent Street with the old Whight wholesale warehouse at 51, Farringdon Road. Until the end of 1908, there were assembly facilities for imported kits of parts and, later, the manufacture of pianos at Elm Street and Britannia Street off the Grays Inn Road. The Orchestrelle Co moved into 135/137 Bond Street, better known as the Aeolian Hall and established a large construction and assembly factory at Silverdale Road, Hayes in Middlesex.

George Whight had traded well and, on his death in 1906, he was found to be worth nearly £40,000 ($455,200) – a considerable sum of money in those far-off days. He lived at 13, Wood Lane in Highgate, North London.

There were thus quite a few makes of pneumatic player organ on the British and American markets, but in terms of popularity and hence numbers made, the outright leader had to be the Aeolian Orchestrelle. It was produced in the United States and, for the UK market, was shipped over as sets of knocked-down components that were then assembled at Aeolian's British factory at Hayes in Middlesex.

The Aeolian Grand had a reed chest rather like a contemporary harmonium or parlor organ. It was a single-cavity chest mounted vertically and which contained ranks of reeds closed off with mutes at the front and a double air-admission pallet at the rear or inside of the box. Tonally this was as effective as the different ranks in a harmonium but, as in the harmonium, the system was not very brilliant in acoustic terms.

Roll-playing reed organs represented a byway of the rich domestic reed organ market. Most of the organ builders had origins in the piano business and the two aspects of musical instrument making were closely allied. An early instrument was the Wilcox & White 58-note Symphony. This played five octaves on the F-F keyboard compass that was standard in America at the time but which restricted sales in Europe. Produced in a variety of case styles, the Symphony did not have the tonal range or capabilities of the Aeolian Orchestrelle yet enjoyed considerable popularity in its day.

A leading tonal inventor of the time was a Scot named Baillie-Hamilton who had emigrated to America where he founded The Vocalion Company making reed organs to his special patent. The story of this can be found in *Harmonium [80]*. Baillie-Hamilton's demonstration of what could be done with a free reed and an acoustic chamber led to a tie-up between Vocalion and Aeolian as regards the manufacture of tone-ranks. These were designed using principles invented and patented by one M S Wright and the greater majority of Orchestrelle tone ranks bear a white paper label proclaiming Vocalion as their manufacturer with the legend: 'The M S Wright / Pneumatic System / Patent No 509506 / Nov 28th 1893.'

The workings of tone-ranks will be discussed in the following Chapter.

Orchestrelles appeared in at least 16 styles and sizes between the close of the last century and about 1920. They were all extremely expensive when compared to any other make or brand of automatic instrument and it was this that gave them a high degree of exclusivity. The style of advertising was both lavish and extensive, dwelling mostly on the more up-market, exclusive publications.

It was around 1903 that Aeolian introduced the first 'Solo Orchestrelle' into Britain. This instrument, while having only one keyboard like any other Orchestrelle, allowed a two-manual playing capability in that it was possible to play the melody on one set of stops while the counter melody or accompaniment was played on another. To permit this very sophisticated feature, the self-playing part of the organ was in effect two instruments, each controlled by different openings in the tracker bar. This duplicity increased the number of openings from 58 to 116 alternately assigned to different halves of the organ. To make the instrument play, special 116-note music rolls were used and the tracker bar featured two staggered rows of small holes. A special three-position selector lever allowed the operator to isolate the upper row of perforations from the lower, so allowing a separate stop registration for each row and allow two-manual musical interpretation. Alternatively, the two rows of openings could be pneumatically connected in reverse (to reverse the stop setting) or, for the third position, united so that normal 58-note rolls could be used.

The mechanics of the Solo Orchestrelle were employed in a number of styles from thence onwards, the Model F being both the largest and the first. By around 1909, the company was producing models such as the more compact XY and XW with two-manual player layout.

It seems that although production of music rolls for both the 58-note and 116-note Orchestrelles continued at least as late as October 1921 (the latest catalogue I have seen), production of reed organs was discontinued around the time of World War 1.

The technique of the Orchestrelle was used as early as 1900 in the operation of a pipe organ as distinct from the free-reed Orchestrelle and Aeolians made a large number of residence Player Pipe Organs. These would also play both 58 and 116-note rolls and, in fact, all the 116-note rolls are labelled 'Aeolian Pipe Organ' although they are perfectly suitable for the solo-equipped reed-playing Orchestrelle.

The first of these instruments to be seen in Britain was described thus by the London musical magazine *Musical Opinion* for February of 1904 – although the correspondent does not seem too certain of his ground and has some shaky ideas about how electric motors operate:

There is now on view at the Orchestrelle Co.'rooms a handsome large two manual pipe organ (built by this firm at Garwood, New Jersey), playable by means of perforated paper rolls. Special '116 note' music - on which there are two separate rows of holes - is used, the topmost series of which causes the swell organ to play, whilst the bottom set of perforations acts on the great organ. An electric pneumatic action is used. On one keyboard a solo can be performed, an accompaniment being possible by the paper rolls acting on the other manual; or the possible by the paper rolls acting on the other manual; or the positions concerning the melody and accompaniment may be reversed. In an adjoining room there is erected an echo organ, the music from which is obtained from the key-board of the two-manual instrument. An electric motor is utilized for blowing, the current from which passes through chloride into three separate accumulators. Of course, if an automatic rendition be not desired, the organ can be played in the ordinary manner. Certainly, all interested in the 'king of instruments' should visit Aeolian Hall, New Bond Street.

By 1905, Aeolian in America was advertising the Aeolienne, a keyboardless console for playing pipe-organ rolls. This was not the same as the Aeolian pipe organ's remote console. All Aeolian's pipe organs, incidentally, were made at their New Jersey plant.

Although the Aeolian Pipe Organ is obviously related to the Orchestrelle and although both play the same rolls (with the exception of the Duo-Art Pipe Organ with its 17-inch wide reproducing music rolls), the actions are quite different and so, other than acknowledging its existence here and through the pages of contemporary advertisements, I shall here say no more.

There were several exclusive models made, especially as regards case design and I have seen a British-cased Orchestrelle in a fully-styled Jacobean oak case. Another, found in North America by Bill Edgerton in 1979, was most unusual in being a reed organ that played from Aeolian Duo-Art pipe-organ music-rolls. Instead of normal pull-push draw-stops it had rocking tablets like a much later electric organ. Most curious feature was that the keyboard folded up flush with the case like that of a ship's piano to reduce the depth of the case when not in use. The foot treadles were also fully-recessed into the case bottom. Special cases were made and I think the reason why Aeolian was amenable to the customised instrument was that they could charge a great deal for it. Orchestrelles were extremely expensive.

An interesting and late development came just before the 1939-45 war by which time Aeolian had long since merged with the Skinner Organ Company in America. In January of 1938, the Hammond Corporation, already earning a reputation for its electronic organs, manufactured a small batch of pneumatically-sensed roll-playing models. Known as the Home Model B-A or Aeolian-Hammond player organ, the player units were manufactured in Boston, Massachusetts, by the Aeolian-Skinner Company. The music rolls looked like normal Aeolian pipe organ rolls and were the same width but in fact had 120 tracker openings spaced at 12 to the inch.

The Orchestrelle Company prospered and in 1912 became The Orchestrelle Co. Ltd. formed to acquire the whole of the capital of the various Orchestrelle Companies in various parts of the world. At the beginning of 1914 this new company submitted its first annual report that showed a net profit of £34,000. It paid a 5% dividend on its ordinary shares. The consolidated accounts revealed a profit of £79,000 – an increase of £12,300 – and a total accumulated surplus of $162,000 pushed the company into a position as a very attractive investment proposition. A contemporary writer commented: 'These figures as a satisfactory index of the way in which the player-piano trade has been developing lately'. War, just around the corner, was about to alter all that. The final name change came as 1917 drew to a close. From October forward, The Orchestrelle Company Limited would be known as The Aeolian Company, Ltd. The management remained unaltered.

But to return to the subject in hand, an extended discussion on the history of the various makes of player organ such as Welte, Walcker and others including, of course, Aeolian, along with some specifications from a number of pipe organs fitted with roll-playing actions, is to be found in my book *Barrel Organ [73]*. This includes details of the behemoth among player organs, the enormous Austin Quadruplex with its 240-hole tracker bar and 21½-inch wide music rolls, the Phoneon, Welte Philharmonic and so on. Additionally, the book *Harmonium [80]* explains how the various parts of the ordinary reed organ operate.

An amusing tale concerns one tiny part of the Orchestrelle that is common to all large reed organs – the *tremolo* stop. This is a long, narrow-chord rotating wooden and cardboard fan set in motion immediately in front of one rank of reeds. The result may vary from a bleat to a warble: some (and I am one of them) do not always think that it sounds musical and the late Bruce Angrave dubbed it 'the waffle stop'. Inexperienced players of Orchestrelles use this indiscriminately while better players use it rarely and then only for brief musical effect.

The quest for the ideal reed organ tremolo dominated the life of an American inventor named La Fayette Louis who, before 1864, had schemed out half a dozen systems ending with a crank-driven mechanism that raised and lowered a swell-type shutter over the reed box. Louis tried hard to sell his ideas into the trade but the manufacturers could all see what was wrong with it while he couldn't. Then in that year of 1864, American-organ maker Riley W Carpenter sat fanning himself in church one warm Sunday and noticed how the fan, close to his ear, altered the sound of the organ. Metaphorically shouting 'Eureka!' he went home, made a rotating fan in his own parlor organ, wound a string around the handle and got his daughter to revolve it while he played. Refined, properly drawn out and, by 1965, patented, Riley was a happy Carpenter and tried to license other makers in Boston and New York but was unsuccessful so he sold half of his rights to a manufacturer named Hitchcock of New York. Then he negotiated a licence with Estey, receiving $2 (10s) royalty on each fan put into an organ. Later he sold the remaining interest in his patent to Saxe & Robertson, Estey's New York agents. The following year Mason & Hamlin were licensed by Hitchcock on the same terms.

A tale in the *New York Tribune* told how an Estey organ was being played at the New York State Fair when, as the fan tremolo was brought into play, a burly Yank was reduced to tears, exclaiming 'They can't beat that in heaven!' The tremolo was certainly flavour of the month and soon every maker clamoured to use the thing until no organ was thought complete unless it had its little cardboard fan that made its four-foot stop warble like a jay.

There was a problem, though. Carpenter and Hitchcock still owned the patent and the bandwagon-rushing makers had omitted that little nicety of applying for a licence. Top of the pile of culprits was none other than Aeolian who's head, Tremaine, was summoned to Court. He argued, rightly, that the Louis patent pre-dated that of Carpenter, but Law, being an ass the world over, disagreed. It went to the Supreme Court where the verdict was sustained.

It was around this point that things went from comedy to farce. While parlor organ makers Burdett in Chicago and Shoninger of Woodbridge, Connecticut, took out licences, Tremaine came up with a master stroke and combined his tremolo with its little air-motor built onto it: hitherto it had been belt-driven from a separate motor. Re-enter La Fayette Louis who now applied for a patent for a combination of the motor shown in one of his previous patents when used with a tremolo – and tried to sell it, patent pending, to Mason & Hamlin, drawing up a contract to sell the invention to them, just in case his patent application was unsuccessful. The upshot was as predicted: he did not get his patent and, despite numerous attempts to bend history and market devices of a similar nature, he failed. To help him on his way to secure fame, he then allowed Estey a free licence, but that did nothing for his cause. Mr Louis was forgotten, his inventions overlooked, and Riley Carpenter's sweaty brow may now be blamed for that warbling thing within the chest of your Orchestrelle!

The task here, though, is to see how to take the Aeolian Orchestrelle apart, give it a new lease of life – and then play it.

The London business of Malcolm & Company introduced its Phoneon player organ in the early summer of 1898. It was retailed by Murdoch & Company and sold for 36gns ($152). In conformity with almost all European keyboard instruments, the compass was 61-notes C to C of which only 31 could be performed from the music-roll.

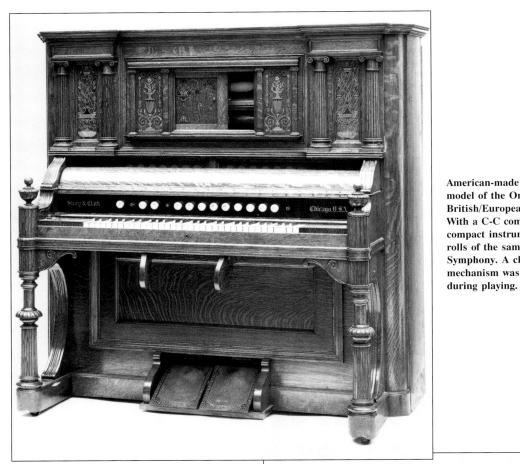

American-made Story & Clark included this model of the Orpheus expressly for the British/European markets.
With a C-C compass of 61-notes, this quite compact instrument played 58-note music rolls of the same type as the Angelus Symphony. A clockwork roll-rewind mechanism was automatically wound up during playing.

Forerunner of the Aeolian Grand, the F-F compass Tonsyreno that played 46-note music rolls. Introduced into Britain in the summer of 1889 was the first Aeolian reed organ to have a keyboard: the earlier Syreno was merely a roll-playing organette. Despite the 12 stop knobs, this was merely a two and a half rank reed organ fitted with the usual mutes and a knee swell (seen beneath the keyboard).

All Aeolian's large player organs were built to the C-C compass with a view towards the world market. The smallest was the Grand, a suction instrument that played 58-note rolls. Case styles were always extremely ornate and decorative. Later suction models would confusingly also be called Orchestrelles.

Most popular of the pressure Orchestrelle models was this, the Model V, the 'V' meaning simple that and not indicating a Roman five. Two knee swells offered a progressive full-organ (left) and a Venetian swell (right).

There were two sizes of tone-rank used by Aeolian, the second being about ten percent larger all round than the standard. There is no record that is known as to why this should be, but those instruments built with the larger and longer ranks were slightly wider and had a somewhat different tone. Here is one of the large-rank specimens, a two-manual roll-player (116-note/58-note action) in a handsome mahogany case with gold silked panels.

The Model F Orchestrelle is the largest of the 58-note models. This one, housed in a magnificent oak case, was once the property of the Author while an identical example was in the collection of the late Bruce Angrave. The voicing of the tone-ranks was particularly beautiful.

Aeolian in Britain offered to install Orchestrelles in any situation and even to make cases that would match the décor of the room. Many so-called 'library' cases are known but one of the more unusual is this one in Jacobean Oak made to match the austere settings of some now-forgotten West Country baronial mansion. It is hard to find this sort of case attractive, especially when we see how magnificent some of the cases actually were.

The finest player reed organs were made by Estey in America and Mustel in Paris. When the German piano-makers J & P Schiedmayer of Stuttgart wanted to introduce a player reed organ, they imported the heart of the instrument from Mustel. The outcome was the astonishing Scheola which, with its astonishing range of voices, is one of the most impressive player instruments the Author has ever performed on. This one is owned by Werner Baus of Kaufungen, Germany.

Welte made much larger player organs that were suitable for large houses or chapels. Harrods department store in West London was at one time a Welte distributor and it had this fine Philharmonic Organ on show in its music division where it was regularly demonstrated both by hand and by roll. Dismantled and returned to Germany shortly before the outbreak of War, it did not survive: had it remained in Harrods it might still be in existence today.

From roll-playing reed organs to full-scale reproducing pipe-organs was, at the time, a mere short step. Welte installed what was effectively a 'red' Welte action into a pipe organ to create this Philharmonic Reproducing Pipe Organ which has two manuals, a 27-note radiating pedal board and, for the benefit of those to whom such things matter, a total of 471 pipes shared between ten ranks. Still driven by its original quarter-horsepower 50-volt DC motor with separate music-roll rewind motor, this handsome instrument is part of the collection of the British Piano Museum.

Aeolian also made reproducing pipe organs in America and this is the console of one it its grandest built for R P Butchart of the Butchart Gardens, British Columbia. Serial number 1477, this is a Duo-Art Pipe Organ playing special 176-note music rolls. To allow for variations in the enormous width of these rolls – they are 15.3/16-inches across – the tracker bar is manufactured in seven sections that can be minutely adjusted for total overall width while playing.

Orchestrelle promotions all centred on the refinement of the instrument and the benefits over the piano. Here, from the magazine *The Illustrated London News* of February 1909 is just such a promotion.

THE ÆOLIAN ORCHESTRELLE

The instrument which allows you to play in your own home all the music played by the orchestra.

THE Æolian Orchestrelle combines, in one instrument which anyone can play, the tones of the many instruments which form the orchestra. The voices of the Æolian Orchestrelle are clear and faithful tonal counterparts of the instruments they represent, and so you are enabled to play orchestral compositions with full and appropriate tone-colour.

In addition there is the Solo effect. This allows you to play a solo on any instrument you may select and accompany it with whatever other instruments you may consider requisite. When you elect to play, say, one of Wagner's works on the Orchestrelle, you play that composition with its full tone-colouring : you are not getting the comparatively weak and colourless effect of an adaptation to a single-toned instrument such as the piano.

You are invited to call at Æolian Hall for a practical demonstration of the Æolian Orchestrelle. Full particulars will be sent to anyone who writes for Catalogue " **4.**"

The Orchestrelle Company,
ÆOLIAN HALL,
135-6-7, NEW BOND STREET, LONDON, W.

Chapter 17
Restoring and Playing the Aeolian Orchestrelle

Throughout the ever-growing corpus of literature on mechanical musical instruments one may search in vain for anything on the matter of Orchestrelle-servicing. Other than my own 'service manual' produced for private circulation almost 35 years ago, plus a few articles in the Player Piano Group Bulletin, the written word is absent! Not that there's any shortage of Orchestrelle enthusiasts nor even of instruments. More to the point, Orchestrelles are considered by many people to be 'difficult', 'very complicated' and 'almost impossible' to repair. Now I felt just that way when I tackled my first one forty years ago. While it's different to the piano, it's not all that strange to us. And if, as most of us have at some time in our lives, had a go at a harmonium, then we are well on the way to making a success of restoring 'one of the tall ones' as a Scandinavian collector liked to call his Model Y.

Unlike Aeolian's reproducing-pianos, which were cased at Hayes, Middlesex, the greater majority of Orchestrelles have American-made cases. The exceptions are those that were expensively tailor-made for wealthy customers: one instrument has been seen in a very austere Jacobean oak case with iron strap hinges! Nobody knows how many instruments were built in the various styles and designs. What is certain is that many different case styles existed for the various forms and that the models themselves underwent an almost continuous process of design improvement and refinement.

In its most obvious form, the stop controls, for example, progressed from being a wholly mechanical linkage of levers and wire pull-downs to an all-pneumatic system where rubber tubing connected stop-board bleed valves to valve units on the side chests. The former was a direct transfer of the current systems used in the genus American organ or, as it is called in the United States, the 'parlor organ'.

But there were other alterations, some so subtle that only the person who has seen and rebuilt many instruments may detect them. The spoolbox and its drive mechanism came in for several small but significant changes, while the long motor regulator bellows at the back went from being all cloth-covered to the cheaper form of cardboard with leather hinges.

The tone ranks themselves were made in two different lengths: some of the larger instruments, in particular the Model F, came in two widths, one being a good 12 inches wider, yet these differences (which greatly improved the sound) were not necessarily delineated in the catalogues. Two Model F instruments apparently in identical case styles, for example, are known to me. One, in the Birmingham Museum, is of the wider type while my own example is narrower. The only obvious exterior indication is in the width of the carved outer bays of the upper casework.

All instruments appear to have a four-figure serial number stamped at the top of the treble-end backboard. In Britain the majority of instruments seen have had numbers in the 8000-series although other numbers exist from 2000 to 6000. One model has a serial number in the 1700 series.

These instruments are simply magnificently made. Apart from the sheer awe of detail design in them which inspires in one a sense of wonder at how somebody could have designed and built such a complex piece of wooden machinery, the quality of workmanship and materials used in their construction is superb. Such deterioration as has taken place over the years is often due to no more than plain and simple *anno domini*. Wear and tear has, generally, been well resisted. Even the rubber cloth of bellows is in most instances in a far better state of preservation than that of player pianos made 30 years later.

Orchestrelles' worst enemy is damp storage conditions: the old oil-rubbed varnish case finishes were always susceptible to crazing and cracking. Whatever finish Aeolian used on their cases, it seems to have fared better than most. Damp will swell close-tolerance moving parts and call for slow, long-term re-acclimatisation to avoid warping.

Restorers of these pieces soon begin to understand the philosophy of the original builders. Indeed, if you learn to think like the Aeolian craftsmen, then you will find your job that much easier. Screws for securing parts, particularly the parts of the case, were frequently hidden in places where one might least expect to find them! And screws in inaccessible places inevitably make one wonder whether the workers who made these instruments were normal human beings...

All in all, the owner of an Aeolian Orchestrelle has custody of an outstanding piece of musical equipment. Its restoration is a massive task even if only because it is an assembly of so many different pieces. Its rewards, though, are inestimable.

Principles of restoration as laid down in Ord-Hume *[83]* and of reed organs *[80]* will act as your guide and not be repeated here.

As before, to help find your way through this Chapter I have divided it into sections:
1. How it Works - the 58-note and 116-note Systems
2. How to Dismantle the Instrument
3. The Wind Department
4. The Keyboard and Primary Valve System
5. The Secondary Valve System
6. The 58/116/Grand Changeover System
7. Tone Ranks, Backboards, Side Chests and Stops
8. The Keyboard Action and Spoolbox
9. The Roll-Motor and Speed Regulator
10. Reassembly and Regulation
11. Fault-finding and Trouble-shooting
12. The Aeolian Grand
13. How to Play and Enjoy the Orchestrelle
14. The Solo Orchestrelle and its special roll markings
15. Notes on the Music Rolls

1. How it Works - the 58-note and 116-note Systems

There are three principle types of Aeolian roll-playing organ – the suction model 58-note instruments, originally called Aeolian Grand, and the pressure model 58-note and 116-note Orchestrelles. Confusingly, suction Grands were later also styled as Orchestrelles. They are, though, easy to identify because pressure Orchestrelles have multiple backboards securing individual tone-ranks while the suction instrument has a plain back to the reed chest and is more like a harmonium tipped up on its fore-edge. The 116-note models were referred to as Solo Orchestrelles.

In the suction model, air is exhausted continually from the inside of the organ by means of large exhausters similar to those of the player piano. Because, however, the volume of air at atmospheric pressure which is admitted to the inside of the organ during playing, particularly when playing a sustained chord on full organ with all the stops drawn, is very large, the player-organ has exhausters and a suction reservoir or equaliser which is of considerably larger proportions than those to which we are accustomed to finding in a piano. Whereas the piano has two exhausters and an equaliser of about the same size, the player-organ has two exhausters and a vacuum storage reservoir, which is generally as big as can be accommodated inside the lower part of the instrument.

There is another point to be remembered and that is that the pneumatic system that forms part of the automatic playing of the organ is also a vital part of the organ when it is used for manual playing. There is thus still need to treadle when playing by hand so that there is air pressure differential inside the instrument to allow the reeds to speak. From this we can readily see that there must be some form of shut-off or by-pass valve, which cuts out the keyboard for automatic playing, yet may readily bring it back into function whilst at the same time shutting off the mechanical part of the action – that is essentially the tracker-bar and roll-winding air motor.

The suction models use piano-type action pull-down motors to control the movement of double-jointed pallet valves contained inside the case back. Removing the back of the upper organ will reveal these long vertical wooden pallets with their action levers connected to wires that bass down through the lower edge of the chest and connect to the wedge-shaped air motors. Restoration of these instruments is virtually the same as the American Organ or harmonium (for detailed servicing of these instruments see Ord-Hume [80]).

In order for Aeolian organs to operate they are dependent upon there being two ways in which a particular note can be sounded. First is the keyboard by use of which a note will speak (provided that at least one register or stop is drawn first). Second is the use of a perforated paper music roll passing over the tracker bar. Both these actions are separate and one is disengaged whenever the other is in use. This means that, unlike the player piano, you cannot accompany the music roll performance by the addition of a hand-played interpretation. This feature exists with the Aeolian Pipe Organ, but not the Orchestrelle.

The majority of 'voices' of the instrument come from individual long boxes of reeds, one for each note, than span from side to side of the instrument from left to right (bass to treble end) between two vertical wind trunks, one at each side. These are called tone-ranks and will number up to nine in total. Those voices that do not have their own tone-ranks are produced by sets of wooden strips lined with felt and moved in such a way as to modify the sound of an existing stop. They are called 'mutes' and, like the proper voices of the tone-ranks, they are controlled by stop-knobs on a board mounted above the rear of the keyboard keys.

Each tone rank is divided into two unequal halves across its length corresponding to the break at the 21st note from the bass end. The purpose and advantages of this break are described in Section 7. The most immediate effect of this is that to play the whole tone rank from the lowest note to the highest means that *two* stops must be drawn – one controlling the lower notes and the other the upper notes. Each of the portions of the tone rank can thus be controlled individually by selecting one or both of the two corresponding stop knobs. This will become much clearer when you read the section on how to play your Orchestrelle. When a stop is drawn (this means 'selected') a pallet inside the vertical wind trunk corresponding to the side selected (*ie* bass or treble) is opened, so allowing pressure to pass into the length of the tone rank up to but not beyond the divider.

In this condition, a rank of reeds (a stop) is 'live' and will sound whatever notes are indicated from the music-roll or, when under 'manual' control, the keyboard.

For this to happen, though, a separate system must be used to send a signal to every one of the tone-ranks note by note. This is provided by the secondary valve chest, which, like the tone-ranks, is connected between the two side wind chests. Unlike the tone ranks that have selecting pallet valves, this chest is fed with pressure power at all times. This enables every tone-rank that is selected (already open to pressure) to be able to sound whatever notes are signalled from this secondary valve chest.

The Aeolian Orchestrelle requires no fewer than three different air pressures in order to operate. These are [a] ordinary atmospheric pressure, [b] medium pressure for sounding the reeds, and [c] high pressure for operating certain of the control valve functions. The first of these pressures is naturally catered for by the atmosphere, but the other two have to be created artificially by the expedient of bellows. And, thanks to the provision of a small set of additional bellows actually inside the main bellows, the two different wind pressures are produced from one bellows assembly.

2. How to Dismantle the Instrument

Stripping the Aeolian Orchestrelle is a bit of a daunting task requiring care and attention to detail plus a lot of room! An ordinary Model V, when dismantled, and allowing for space in which to work, will practically fill a living room when ren-

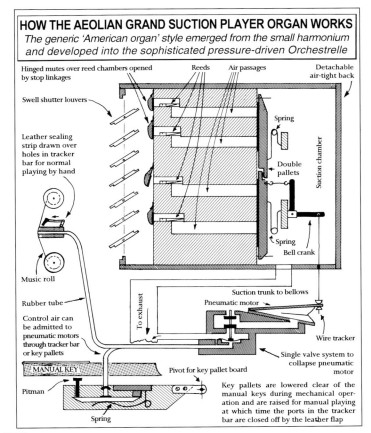

HOW THE AEOLIAN GRAND SUCTION PLAYER ORGAN WORKS
The generic 'American organ' style emerged from the small harmonium and developed into the sophisticated pressure-driven Orchestrelle

Hinged mutes over reed chambers opened by stop linkages

Reeds

Air passages

Detachable air-tight back

Swell shutter louvers

Spring

Leather sealing strip drawn over holes in tracker bar for normal playing by hand

Double pallets

Suction chamber

Music roll

Spring
Bell crank

Rubber tube

Control air can be admitted to pneumatic motors through tracker bar or key pallets

To exhaust

Suction trunk to bellows

Pneumatic motor

Wire tracker

Single valve system to collapse pneumatic motor

MANUAL KEY

Pivot for key pallet board

Pitman

Spring

Key pallets are lowered clear of the manual keys during mechanical operation and are raised for manual playing at which time the ports in the tracker bar are closed off by the leather flap

dered into its component parts. In fact, there is some truth in the assertion that the sum of its component parts is infinitely greater than the whole!

Orchestrelle-builders were masters at putting screws in places which, to the mere mortal, are highly unlikely, extremely difficult to find and impossible to get at. Always be aware of this for visible screws are invariably the easy ones while the hidden ones are there somewhere to tax your ingenuity.

Never replace an old screw with one of those modern star-headed Philips-type screws: the shank thickness and screw pitch is quite different from that of a normal woodscrew. And avoid Archimedean-type or 'Yankee' pump screwdrivers. Although there are many, many screws to tackle, these time-saving 'drivers can so easily result in stripped threads and damage to the surrounding woodwork.

One special screwdriver you will have to make. Buy a really hefty screwdriver with a 3/8-inch wide blade – and cut the handle off it at a distance of about half way down the shank. Now find a length of steel tubing (gas tubing is ideal) about 30-inches long into each end of which you can force the two halves of your screwdriver. Braze or pin them into place so that you now have a jumbo 'driver almost three feet long. This is needed for getting at otherwise impossible case screws.

Have a good bright flashlight or torch with you and a mains-powered inspection lamp. Acquire an assortment of cardboard or plastic boxes into which you can put screws and small pieces as you remove them. And a wax crayon or Chinagraph pencil so that you can identify each box as to the precise location on the instrument of its contents.

Because Orchestrelles get very dusty and dirty with the years, keep a good suction cleaner on hand, a handful of paintbrushes of various sizes for dusting (some restorers recommend old brushes for the purpose: for the extra cost involved, I would always recommend using new ones which have softer, more pliable bristles and can thus do things which many a used brush cannot do), an ample supply of clean, soft cloth dusters, and a bowl in which a weak mixture of warm water and washing up liquid may be mixed for wiping down dirty parts.

If you are the cautious type and are tackling, hesitantly, your first rebuild, equip yourself with plenty of means of identifying parts such as self-adhesive labels, felt-tip pens (to write on the labels, not the wood), chalk, thin string, tie-on labels and thick rubber bands.

And keep a notebook and pencil close at hand for drawing or listing items as well as making helpful notes for your own use. The careful restorer treading on uncertain ground and not wishing to take chances may also wish to set up a camera and flash-gun with remote control with which to record difficult operations as they take place.

A few surgical or dental-type tools are useful. Locking forceps, oblique stitch scissors, long-handled grabs, dental probes and, very important, an inspection mirror, are all worth their weight in ivory to the true Orchestrelle man.

For the major tasks of dismantling and re-assembly, an extra pair of hands is vital. As you can't grow these, prepare a friend or two for the challenge of a lifetime and work carefully together. It is very easy to do irreparable damage to an Orchestrelle by, for example, not supporting parts properly during removal or replacement of screws.

Plastic bags of various sizes come in useful for storing components: seal them with masking tape and write an identification on them with a felt-tipped marker. Large sheets of transparent plastic will be invaluable for use as dust-sheets and for wrapping up component parts as they are cleaned and serviced. Avoid conventional dust-sheets: you cannot see what's under them and an incautious dust-sheet removal can do damage to delicate parts. For safety, always go for the transparent cover.

Stripping the Orchestrelle begins with taking off all the easy bits and stacking them as far away from the instrument as is convenient. You won't want later on to be carrying tone-ranks to the only vacant corner of the room by picking your way over case parts put in piles around the organ. No, stack from the distant parts of the room inwards. It makes sense. Don't stack against the door, though...

This fine specimen of a Model V Orchestrelle belongs to a private collection in North Carolina. The dismantling process begins by lifting off the entire pediment of the case: it is merely located on top of the sides and front. This can be followed by the removal of the proscenium front (which is secured by turn buttons), the entire upper front frame and the side panels at the case assembly join which is level with the keyboard.

The top of the instrument is hinged at the back and this is freed by knocking out the hinge-pins and taping them to somewhere safe so they don't get lost. One person at each side can now lift off the complete lid. Within the centre of this lid is attached a fragile wooden frame covered with wire-woven mesh to let the sound out. This mesh will be black with age and probably torn from where things (music rolls and cats) have stood on top of the organ. Remove the frame and make good any damaged cross-members, then re-cover it with a plain fine-weave cloth. Follow the original style for securing the cloth. You can use ordinary office staples for this job, so long as they are on the underside and so don't show on refitting the frame into the case lid.

The lower back of the instrument has a screwed-on frame of more durable construction and this, too, is covered with mesh which will probably be equally dirty and more than likely in worse condition than the lid fabric. Remove this frame. The upper portion of the organ case comprises the tone-rank backboards and presents to you a mass of woodscrews. Leave these well alone for the moment: we will deal with them specifically in another section.

Standing at the keyboard, first close the hinged keyboard fall, then reach up and over the top edge of the front panel – the one fitted immediately above the narrow, full-width panel which has the spool-box access door in it – and you should find two turn-buttons, the swivelling of which will free the whole front so allowing you to lift it out.

To remove the narrow lower panel, look inside to see what sort of attachments it has. Some of these have simple turn-buttons, others have woodscrews into the slots of which have been brazed half-washers to convert them into finger screws. Once these are removed, actually taking this panel out requires care because it may foul the lower edge of the spool box. On several styles, the panel does not lift up to be slid out of the case, but is physically pulled forward off the side supports. Look carefully to see how it is secured before pulling, pushing or twisting.

The whole lower front of the case from the level of the keyboard downwards is created in one piece with the two side panels to form a large and heavy 'U'-shaped assembly. Because this also locates the two foot pedals for the pressure pumps, the webbing strap (which very frequently breaks or becomes frayed in use) must first be removed from the underside of each pedal board or alternatively from the top of each compressor. This is an awkward job and you may decided it is easier to cut the webbing and replace it later.

Remove the flat wooden cover-board that protects the key springs underneath the keyboard, then locate and remove the two angled screws that secure the flat cheeks. Each side of the keyboard is fixed to the case trusses (these are the two thick case parts each side of the keyboard) by screws. Once these are removed you will find there is a little up and down 'play' in the key-bed proving that it is no longer attached to the case front.

The attachment screws for the front are only accessible from inside the case where they were originally positioned by, apparently, intelligent and very strong mice. Getting at them is where your extremely long screwdriver is needed to reach down to their heads. Note a curious situation when you remove this 'U'-shaped piece. You now have doubled the floor-area required by your dismantled Orchestrelle! And this is only the start!

Proceed in a like manner to remove all the case panels. Be warned that the instrument is braced with metal supports to the lower part of the case and removal of this leaves the whole instrument both top-heavy and unstable. Clamp on wooden supports to avoid the risk of falling: you might be trapped underneath it!

The upper front of the organ is closed in with shaped thin wooden side extensions across which span the venetian swell shutters with their control push-pull rod. Unscrew these and carefully remove the shutter frames: in small models this is one frame but larger instruments have two frames that are butted together and their shutters united by a central wooden link lever. Be aware that as well as being secured with round-headed wood screws provided with steel clamping washers, these frames were originally located with small dowel pins as well as screws. These often get broken but they are important and if missing or broken ought to be replaced.

The rocking lever (above right-hand keyboard cheek) that links them to the knee-swell. Because the horizontal tone-ranks containing the reeds are all different sizes and widths (but constant in thickness top to bottom) the upperwork is slightly angled because the bass end protrudes more than the treble. The vertical supply trunk or side chest can be seen at the far right: a similar one feeds the left side and the tone-ranks extend between the two. Also visible here is the added frame that supports the stop-selection linkage. While larger, pneumatic actions use small pouch motors for this function, this instrument has rocking wooden trunnion levers connected to the above-keyboard stop knobs by levers and wire pull-downs.

You will now find the 'bare bones' of the instrument consists of a 'table' upon which is built the whole upper organ including keyboard. Beneath the table is a very large air pressure reservoir fed by two compression feeders. To each side of the instrument are vertical wind conveyances between which the secondary valve chest lies at the bottom followed by the horizontal tone-ranks fixed separately one above the other. Linking the whole tone-rank-valve assembly together are the backboards.

The larger 116-note 'two-manual' models divide their stack of tone-ranks half way up. This means that each of the backboards is in two halves (upper and lower) and each side chest is also in two pieces – more on these in Section 6.

3. The Wind Department

Generally the outer covering of the bellows, which is of thick rubberised cloth, is found to be sound but look carefully for signs of wear at the folds and corners. For the heavy-duty reservoir Aeolian applied the organ-builders' technique of 'flattening the corners' with a small square kilter piece or trinkle of stiffening that serves to avoid the otherwise sharp, pointed fold in the cloth.

The parts that do wear, though, are the leather flap-valves in the feeders and inside the reservoir where a secondary bellows provides air at a higher pressure for the valve system. Fortunately, Aeolian thought of that one, too, and the flats of both bellows and exhausters are provided with detachable inspection panels to give good access to the insides of the otherwise closed components.

These access panels have gaskets that are of thick porous paper which when compressed makes an airtight seal. Try not to damage these but if you do, strip the damaged one off completely and replace using thick blotting paper or thin white sheepskin.

To allow air to pass into the bellows for compression leather flap valves are provided. These were originally of kangaroo skin which is a thick brown skin that is roughened on both surfaces. Because this leather has to be very thick and therefore has limited stretch, the flap-valve strips are normally tacked on at one end and held tight over the windways with springs.

If the strips are in any way distorted or other than absolutely flat, then they must be replaced. An organ-builders' supplier will stock kangaroo skin or its nearest equivalent.

Examine all the valves for condition and freedom of operation, and check all the bellows cloth for porous patches. Small areas on folds that are showing signs of wear can be re-proofed by brushing on a dilute mixture of white PVA glue.

4. The Keyboard and Primary Valve System

All keys should be removed and the pins upon which they are mounted and pivot must be free of all corrosion. Polish them and if necessary lubricate the openings in the underside of the keys into which they fit using a very small puff of dry graphite powder.

See that the keyframe is tight and undamaged and examine the small wooden push-rods (the pitmans) to see they move freely. Remove them and rub graphite powder into any that are tight.

The pallets in the keybox that access the primary valves are all held down with wire springs: see that none of these are broken and that they are all exerting the same closing force. This box is connected to the *high-pressure* wind supply. As with all windboxes closed with a screwed-down lid, check the woodwork for splits and cracks, and see the gasket is serviceable.

The primary valves in the Orchestrelle must only travel a very short distance in order to fulfil their function. This distance is 3/64-inch and is best set using a thin piece of wood veneer as a gauge.

5. The Secondary Valve System

When a signal from either the keyboard or the music-roll triggers the primary valve it admits high pressure air to the pouch-board that controls the secondary valve assembly that spans the bottom of the tone-ranks and lies along the lowermost edge of the backboards. This arranges the valves in two staggered rows in the same horizontal plane.

The operation of these valves is by the same pressure system that controls the tone ranks and allows the reeds to speak. This is referred to as *low-pressure* air but as we already know this is air at positive pressure (above atmospheric pressure as distinct from vacuum). The drawing explains how the system works.

The secondary valves in the Orchestrelle must travel a greater distance than the primary valves because they have to close off a relatively large windway in the low-pressure system, so they are set to $3/32$-of an inch. This is measured with the lowermost button resting on the fibre disc in the centre of the pouch and with the lower disc of the valve resting over the lower opening. To adjust the setting of these valves, both upper and lower valve discs are threaded on to their wire stems and by rotating them the clearances may be set accurately. This is done by holding the valve wire stem in a pair of thin-nosed pliers and turning the valve clockwise (to slacken) or anti-clockwise (to increase) the gap.

6. The 58/116/Grand Changeover Unit

A feature of the 116-note Solo Orchestrelle as distinct from the ordinary 58-note models is the ability to reverse the manual settings, changing Manual II to Manual I and vice-versa. It is also possible to unite both rows of tracker-bar holes so that ordinary 58-note music rolls can be played. This mutation is achieved by a simple pneumatic system controlled by a mechanical lever.

The switching is arranged by bringing each action windway to a flat (meaning unrecessed) pouchboard which is bored to bring the airway in and to take it out again. These are called 'airway sealing pouches'. Because there is pressure in the air supply, the pouch is held away from the ends of both airways, so allowing a continuous wind supply. This same arrangement is repeated for the tubing for each manual and a similar valve arrangement is provided to reverse the two manuals. This is depicted in the accompanying illustration.

Each of these lines of pouches is contained in an air-tight wooden box that is normally vented to atmosphere. However, when it is required that the manuals be reversed, air at pressure is admitted to this box, so closing all the pouches and preventing the normal passage of air signals to the respective pouches controlling the secondary valves. In achieving this, however, the pneumatic signals are diverted through a bypass that is 'T'-jointed into the airways. The signals from 'Manual I' now go direct to 'Manual II' and vice-versa.

To combine the signals from both rows of tracker bar holes so that 58-note rolls may be played, a further set of airway sealing pouches is provided with its own air-tight cover box. These again operate diversionary airways so allowing the signals to combine in a 58-note performance.

Do look carefully at the drawings as these will make understanding the system far quicker than words.

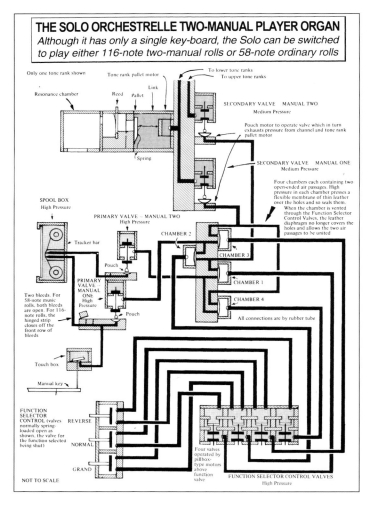

Only one tone rank shown

Tone rank pallet motor

To lower tone ranks
To upper tone ranks

Resonance chamber

Reed
Pallet
Link

Spring

SECONDARY VALVE   MANUAL TWO
Medium Pressure

Pouch motor to operate valve which in turn exhausts pressure from channel and tone rank pallet motor

SECONDARY VALVE   MANUAL ONE
Medium Pressure

Four chambers each containing two open-ended air passages. High pressure in each chamber presses a flexible membrane of thin leather over the holes and so seals them. When the chamber is vented through the Function Selector Control Valves, the leather diaphragm no longer covers the holes and allows the two air passages to be united

SPOOL BOX
High Pressure

PRIMARY VALVE – MANUAL TWO
High Pressure

CHAMBER 2

CHAMBER 3

Tracker bar

Pouch

CHAMBER 1

PRIMARY VALVE – MANUAL ONE
High Pressure

CHAMBER 4

Two bleeds. For 58-note music rolls, both bleeds are open. For 116-note rolls, the hinged strip closes off the front row of bleeds

Pouch

All connections are by rubber tube

Touch box

Manual key

FUNCTION SELECTOR CONTROL (valves normally spring-loaded open as shown, the valve for the function selected being shut)

REVERSE

NORMAL

GRAND

NOT TO SCALE

Four valves operated by pillbox-type motors above function valve

FUNCTION SELECTOR CONTROL VALVES
High Pressure

7. Tone Ranks, Backboards, Side Chests and Stops

The Orchestrelle reeds are mounted in boxes called 'tone ranks', one for each stop or register. The tone ranks of the instrument comprise the long shaped and tapered chests which each contain one set of reeds and which are mounted across the instrument from left to right (bass to treble end) between the two vertical wind trunks at each side.

Of constant thickness, their width varies from widest (greatest projection forwards) at the bass end to narrowest at the treble. Some are gracefully bellied or curved. This is because the large reeds of the lower notes require larger resonating cavities (called Helmholtz chambers) in which to speak than do those of the higher treble register. The shape of the cavity also modifies the individual timbre of sound, each tone rank producing a different 'voice'. There are some with various shapes of wooden mute, either in the form of wooden boxes affixed across the fronts of all the reed cells, or in the form of hinged thick wooden strips. These also serve to modify the sound made by the reed.

On the tone ranks, some of the treble reeds - usually about the top dozen or so - have tiny holes pierced from the front into the reed chambers. When these particular reeds are sounded, part of the wind supply is vented through these bleeds because the top note reeds, being very small, are more easily overblown. These tiny openings avoid that in normal use. Do not attempt to open out these holes. Make sure that they are clear and not blocked and take care not to enlarge.

Each tone rank is divided into two unequal halves across its length (tonal scale) corresponding to the break at the 21st

note from the bass end. The effect of this is that to play the whole tone rank from the lowest note to the highest means that two stops must be drawn - one covering the lower 21 notes and the other controlling the upper 37 notes. This means that each of the two unequal portions of the tone rank can be controlled individually by selecting one or both of the two corresponding stop knobs. How and why this is beneficial will become much clearer when you read Section 13 entitled *How to Play your Orchestrelle*.

Each pair of stops on the Aeolian Orchestrelle, to the left and right of the stop-rail centre above the keys, controls one or the other, or both portions of one row of reeds in the tone rank and there are 58 reeds (notes) in each.

When a stop is drawn (meaning selected by pulling out the stop-knob) a pallet inside the vertical wind trunk corresponding to the side selected (*ie* bass or treble) is opened, so allowing pressure to pass into the length of the tone rank up to but not beyond the divider.

Some of the reeds are visible from the front, others are hidden away deep inside their cells. However they are mounted, all are provided with identical pouches and spring-loaded pallets in order to sound. Because these pneumatic components are fitted inside the tone ranks and isolated from sun and most atmospheric pollutants they generally do not deteriorate meaning they do not need replacement. I have only ever come across two that needed replacing and this was easily done using 'perfection' skin and using the adjacent pouch as pattern and style guide.

Each tone-rank is located between the side windways or chests and attached to the heavy-looking backboards of the organ. Now be warned that these thick and solid looking boards are anything but as robust as they appear because they are themselves multiple wind conveyances. Each board carries a number of passages, top to bottom, that unite a passage connected to the secondary valve chamber at the bottom to every tone-rank chamber for that same particular note in the scale. The boards are a series of hollow passageways bored through on the inside with alternate rows of piercings to each tone-rank chamber. The large number of screws visible from the back of the organ represents carefully-positioned staggered rows that hold and support the tone-ranks, clamping them back to form an airtight seal against the correct airways. A simple seal of very porous thick paper (actually it is just like heavy-duty blotting-paper) closes the gap between the two and forms a compression seal.

Most Orchestrelle owners will say that the tone-ranks are not physically screwed to the side-chests, the seal being a square pouch of soft leather that actually inflates to create a closure. This may not always be so and I have seen three models where each tone-rank is screwed to the side windways. Make certain of this by unscrewing the outer covers boards of the side chests to reveal the windway closure pallets – and look for screws!

Removing tone ranks means disconnecting them from the backboards. There are two staggered rows of long round-headed woodscrews with steel washers and, on many models, fitted with small spring washers between head and plain washer. These are not locking washers (as some have suggested) but provided to take up any slack generated by expansion and contraction. Take out all the screws from the bottom row of fixings so as to leave the tone-ranks hanging by the top row. With the aid of one or, preferably, two assistants, steady the tone rank at each end from the front while taking out the other screws, starting at the middle and working out one at a time until finally only one screw at each end is holding it – then take those out. This avoids any tendency to twist the heavy tone-ranks and tear the wood around the screws.

Lay the tone rank flat if possible, otherwise stand it up against a wall, bass (wide) end lowermost.

Opening up a tone rank can only be done when it is removed from the instrument. Remove the fixing screws securing the upper face of the reed box. The actual form this process takes differs from rank to rank. After all the woodscrews are taken out, do not forget to unscrew the long threaded wire which holds down the centre of this top panel against the divider between the upper (treble) and lower (bass) portions of the rank at the 21st note position. This can be a problem to relocate in its hole on re-assembly and the only solution is careful probing with the threaded end to seek out the hole in the nut plate. You must hold the rod upright - and have patience.

Generally it is not necessary to remove any of the reeds unless they are dumb or have defective speech. As the reeds are blown, normally clean air from inside the organ is passed out through them during playing and this helps prevent dust entering the reed passages and clogging them. The deep setting of many of them combined the added protection of the mutes (where fitted to some ranks) and swell shutters plus the casework all help to keep them clean. If they have got dirty, though, withdraw them using a proper reed extractor and wash each one individually in industrial alcohol or methylated spirits (denatured alcohol). Hold each one up to the light and check there is no visible obstruction to their vibration.

Many of the reeds are extremely fragile – the piccolo reeds, for example, are both delicate and tiny needing only the gentlest cleaning with an artist's camel-hair or sable brush. Let the reeds dry before replacing and save yourself time and trouble by only removing the reeds one at a time and then laying them out in the right order. Do be careful brushing reeds as some are tissue-paper-thin and the tongues are all-too easily snapped off or bent.

Never scrape a reed tongue with anything hard or metallic since this will risk removing metal and altering the pitch of the reed.

The body of the tone rank can be wiped down with a lightly-moistened clean cloth with a touch of liquid detergent on it, and then wiped off with a soft cloth dampened with clean water. Don't get water inside the tone-rank: this will create ten times more work. Finally, when all is dry, apply a coating of shellac-based varnish. Remember never to use any synthetic varnish such as polyurethane.

Some ranks have their own felt-edged shutters or mutes. See that these are free from moth or moth-damage. Even if you are renewing these felts, still check for moth first because if you find moth damage there could be eggs around which need the use of a vacuum cleaner to remove. Should you find moth in one felt, you must assume that it is everywhere else and not only remove and replace all the felt, but use the vacuum cleaner at every stage. Missed eggs hatch, producing more moth grubs that will devour your handiwork. Remove moth and felt with the cleaner and a soft brush followed by a damp cloth wipe.

To sound a note in a tone-rank, first air is fed at pressure to the particular rank through the vertical side chests. The rank is now 'activated'. To sound a note, either from the keyboard or from the music-roll on the tracker bar, air inflates a pouchin the secondary valve assembly at the bottom of the backboards. This vents air from a particular channel in the backboard, so allowing the particular pallet in the tone-rank to draw back and allow the air pressure in the tone-rank to pass out through a corresponding reed to produce sound.

Removal of the swell shutters and the baseboard to the swell box displays the tone ranks and reveals their different individual shades or mutes as well as design variations in order to produce different voices. These tone ranks are attached to and cantilevered from the backboard 'honeycomb' windways. They are also very heavy. When dismantling always label the order in which they are assembled.

The seal between tone-rank, valve chest and backboard is made with a small white fibre washer placed round each airhole to form a sealing. These must not be damaged in any way: if any are, then remove every trace of the original and replace with a ring of new thick white blotting paper located on the board surface only using a very mild office paste: the purpose is purely to locate them and they are held in place by pressure of being squeezed when the tone-ranks are replaced. Replacement gaskets must be of the correct thickness otherwise the note concerned will cipher (sound continuously).

Each backboard carries along the lower edge of its inner face a pair of small wooden locating dowels which engage in matching holes in the organ table. These are important as if they are broken off accidentally and their absence is not detected, they may result in holding the boards away from the valve chest, so causing a leak.

Furthermore, if too many are broken off, the entire organ could be assembled out of alignment. In those models where the tone ranks are not located through the insides of the side chests by woodscrews, the position of the tone ranks and therefore the relative position of all of them are dictated by the accurate initial positioning of the backboards.

So long as the outer backboards have their dowels, the absence of a few on the centre panels will not be critical, but if these dowels are missing from too many places, you must replace them. Drill out the broken parts and glue in a replacement dowel peg into the backboard only. It should protrude from the surface of the backboard by no more than one-quarter of an inch.

Two-tier models of the Orchestrelle – the Solo Orchestrelle – such as the Model F and the Model Y, are provided with an assembly joint half way up the back. This joint lies in the same plane as the joints in the vertical side chests and is provided so that the tall instrument can be conveyed in halves through a normal doorway. A perforated leather gasket runs between the two halves of each backboard. If the bottom halves have missing dowels, you may find a nasty gap between upper and lower parts on reassembly.

Sometimes, however, a previous restorer has not been so particular and so if a gap does exist, make up a very soft seal of thick, unstretched sheepskin, perforate to match the holes and glue it to the tops of the lower boards when they are in place. After the glue has set, cut through the new seal to coincide with the width of each backboard. This allows you to remove an individual backboard to get at the valves if necessary without tearing the gasket as would happen if it were to be in one continuous piece across all the boards.

Fortunately I have never come across a de-laminated backboard although this is always a possibility if a dismantled instrument has been badly stored in a damp atmosphere. The compression exerted by the screws would normally be expected to resist separation in an assembled instrument.

Were the boards to leak, though, it would obviously have a material effect on the instrument's performance, the opening of one valve probably venting several adjacent passages instead of one, and so causing several notes to sound together in a discord.

If this is suspected, remove the boards, strip off any leather edge gaskets and tone-rank gaskets, warm the wood by standing it in a warm place, and then run diluted hot brown glue through each channel, taking care to see that it does not settle and harden to obstruct windways. Pour a large quantity of the glue, diluted to the consistency of very thin syrup or lubricating oil, through each passage, one at a time, letting it drain out the other end. After the last of the liquid has drained away, clamp the board rigidly between large pieces of smooth wood to that (a) it won't distort in drying or set warped, and (b) any gaps can now be closed up in glue.

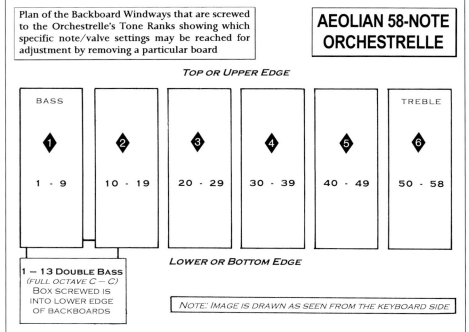

Plan of the Backboard Windways that are screwed to the Orchestrelle's Tone Ranks showing which specific note/valve settings may be reached for adjustment by removing a particular board

AEOLIAN 58-NOTE ORCHESTRELLE

TOP OR UPPER EDGE

BASS

TREBLE

◆1   ◆2   ◆3   ◆4   ◆5   ◆6

1 - 9   10 - 19   20 - 29   30 - 39   40 - 49   50 - 58

LOWER OR BOTTOM EDGE

1 – 13 DOUBLE BASS (FULL OCTAVE C – C) BOX SCREWED IS INTO LOWER EDGE OF BACKBOARDS

NOTE: IMAGE IS DRAWN AS SEEN FROM THE KEYBOARD SIDE

Before replacing backboards, blow through each passage. Ideally connect your suction cleaner the other way round and use the hose to direct the stream of air through each and every opening to clear any particles of dust, old paint or dried glue.

If you have to store backboards for some while before reassembly, then store them flat in a dry room away from heat, moisture and draught to avoid any possibility of warping.

Should you need to remove a backboard to make adjustments to the valves, it is relatively easy to take off just one board, taking care to ease it out from between its fellows without damaging the timber. Do watch, though, to check that on replacing it none of the soft, blotting-paper washers between the holes in the inner face of the backboard and the holes in the tone ranks are missing or crumpled: if this is so, then air will leak and you will have a note which speaks all the while.

The stop system is developed from that of the harmonium or genus American Organ. Early examples have mechanical linkages that draw back a lever which rotates a steel rod mounted in felt-lined bearings. A crank at the far end aligns with a pallet operating lever in the vertical side chest. This mechanism has often developed a lot of rattle or looseness over the years caused by the compression and hardening of the felt-lined bearings. Remove each steel rod one at a time, clean it, paint it with black enamel paint, renew the felt-lined bearings, put the rod back and reconnect to the stop knob and the side chest pallet pull-down.

Later and larger instruments had a pneumatic stop-change system that had the great advantage of being totally quiet, requiring hardly any force to operate, and having fewer moving parts. The stop knob served to rotate a small tablet that closed off a small windway in the bed of the stop table. A rubber tube connected this windway to a valve block on the outside of the vertical side chest or windway. Activating the pouch with air raised the valve and vented the air pressure in a square-shaped pneumatic motor attached to the tone-rank access pallet, so opening it.

8. The Keyboard Action and Spoolbox

The keys of the keyboard are mounted in a wooden frame so that they are free to rock up and down. Beneath these keys lie a series of long wooden levers that are centrally pivoted so that they rock like an inverted seesaw. They are so arranged that when a keyboard key is depressed, a short wooden push-rod called a pitman pushes down and transfers movement to one of these levers rocking it so that its other end rises beyond the length of the keyboard key. To keep these levers in the normal or 'up' position, a series of harmonium-type key springs is mounted under the keyboard, one to each lever. These keep the levers up and, by pushing all the pitman rods up, keep the keys in the 'silent' position. The drawing shows this function.

Mounted over the inner ends of the keyboard levers is a long wooden box containing pallets that control the airflow to each secondary valve block by the lowermost edge of the backboards. These pallets are lifted by a further set of pitman rods made of thin, light, wood. The diagram shows the method by which a note is sounded manually and via the tracker bar.

The spoolbox on the pressure Orchestrelle is enclosed in a box with a sliding glass door. With the glass closed, the pressure of air during playing forces the door out against its seals to make an almost air-tight enclosure. Opening this enclosure is achieved by locating and rotating a number of sickle-shaped hooks. These sickle hooks are used in many places on the instrument, particularly for positioning the flanges of airways.

When all are undone, the spoolbox can be opened along its seal and the outer portion removed. The bare spoolbox is provided with a wooden extension board to its left the purpose of which is to complete the air-tight box by allowing interior space for the sliding door. This extension is screwed into the side of the spoolbox from behind. Before taking it off, disconnect the air pressure feed pipe from behind the board. Note that many of these pipes are made of tubes of glued and rolled paper and may be fragile. Should they be replaced with more durable rubber hoses? I think not. They are easily repaired and, if the worst comes to the worst, you can make new ones using a broom-handle of the right diameter as a mandrel.

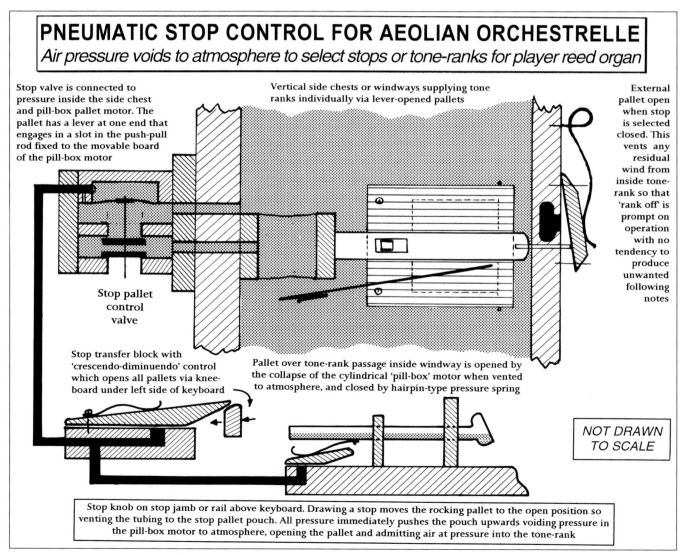

PNEUMATIC STOP CONTROL FOR AEOLIAN ORCHESTRELLE
Air pressure voids to atmosphere to select stops or tone-ranks for player reed organ

Stop valve is connected to pressure inside the side chest and pill-box pallet motor. The pallet has a lever at one end that engages in a slot in the push-pull rod fixed to the movable board of the pill-box motor

Vertical side chests or windways supplying tone ranks individually via lever-opened pallets

External pallet open when stop is selected closed. This vents any residual wind from inside tone-rank so that 'rank off' is prompt on operation with no tendency to produce unwanted following notes

Stop pallet control valve

Stop transfer block with 'crescendo-diminuendo' control which opens all pallets via knee-board under left side of keyboard

Pallet over tone-rank passage inside windway is opened by the collapse of the cylindrical 'pill-box' motor when vented to atmosphere, and closed by hairpin-type pressure spring

NOT DRAWN TO SCALE

Stop knob on stop jamb or rail above keyboard. Drawing a stop moves the rocking pallet to the open position so venting the tubing to the stop pallet pouch. All pressure immediately pushes the pouch upwards voiding pressure in the pill-box motor to atmosphere, opening the pallet and admitting air at pressure into the tone-rank

The pressure Orchestrelle requires a leather-faced sealing strip to be positioned over the tracker holes during rewind and manual playing. Early instruments used a reddish-coloured leather that deteriorates into powder all too readily with age. If the sealing strip has gone hard, is cracked or split, or missing altogether, then create a new one from soft bellows leather sewn into a loose cylinder around the polished and plated steel frame provided for it.

The roll drive mechanism with its chucks and gearing is very similar to that on the player piano and is attended to in the same way. A control found on 116-note instruments is a tracking key that protrudes through the front of the airtight box at the right lower side. This allows adjustments to be made as necessary to the roll alignment during playing.

9. The Roll-Motor and Speed Regulator

To drive the music roll the familiar type of multi-wedge motor driving a crankshaft and sliding valves is to be found. Unlike the piano, though, that in the Orchestrelle is enclosed in a box to which air pressure is admitted. Instead of vacuum and atmosphere, these work on atmosphere and pressure. However, regulation of the speed of the motor is a version of the piano's familiar speed-regulating knife-valve only again this works under pressure. The regulator is a long, slender vertical bellows motor at the rear of the instrument at the treble end. Regulation is by a tension-spring adjustment.

Cleaning and servicing the drive motor also calls for checking the overly-long drive chains that connect with the spoolbox assembly via rather long layshafts that rotate in felt-lined bearings. Wear and play in these bearings will almost certainly affect the ease and steady speed of playing, so take pains to eliminate all such signs of age.

10. Reassembly and Regulation

Putting the Orchestrelle back together is a job where the occasional help of two other pairs of hands is invaluable.

The sequence of building up from the main 'table' begins with the keyboard and primary valve chest together with its windways. Next the long block that mounts all the secondary valves is positioned and screwed from the ends through the side chests. At intervals it is mechanically tied to the table with metal 'L'-shaped brackets.

Next comes the building up of the sequence of tone-ranks so first fit into position the first and the last backboard so that the tome-ranks can be located and screwed loosely into place. Now begin building up the tone ranks from the bottom one which fits immediately above the secondary valve chest.

A very good seal is provided between the tone rank ends and the side chests using a partially inflatable square seal with a windway hole in the middle. Because it is only glued to the side chests around its extreme edges, when air is admitted to the side chests this seal bellies out slightly under wind pressure so making an air-tight seal.

However, if you attempt to slide the tone-ranks in between the side chests the chances are that you will catch this leather seal and tear it. I use two thin sheets of film transparency (old overhead projection sheets or pages of litho film are ideal) that are positioned over the seal at each side. Push the tone rank into position so that it slides over the film at each end. Find and locate the top row of fixing screw holes in the first and last backboard and loosely put in the woodscrews. When the rank is properly aligned, replace all the upper row of screws in the first and last backboards and do them up reasonably tight. Finally pull out the film sheets over the seals at each end.

Repeat the process for the remainder of the tone-ranks until all are in place. If you are rebuilding a tall instrument with extended backboards, you must complete positioning and tightening up all the lower ranks before starting on the top ones by fitting the side chest extensions first.

Check for any broken woodscrews or split timber: remove broken screws either by heating with a soldering iron and then twisting out with fine-nosed pliers or, if that fails, drill them out using first a narrow-bore drill and increasing the size until the whole screw is free. Plug the now-oversize hole with a glued-in softwood dowel and, when dry, redrill for a fresh screw.

With all the tone-ranks in position, put into place the remaining backboards noting that the last one may be a tight fit due to all having expanded slightly. Make certain the backboards align top and bottom and now complete the top lines of tone-rank screws. Don't forget the plain metal washers (sometimes there are coiled spring washers as well) and do not overtighten these otherwise you will crush the timber and strip the threads.

With all top screws in, now position the bottom rows and repeat the tightening process.

Connect motor and governor, spoolbox and all connections. Now set up the pouch and valve-assembly clearances. This is done with the secondary valve assembly closure strip unscrewed so that the inside of the chamber can be seen from the rear of the organ.

When the pouch is in normal, deflated state, the valve button should just be resting very lightly in the red fibre disc in its centre. In this position, the lower valve disc, viewed through the back, should be resting evenly in the bottom of the chamber, and the upper valve $3/_{32}$-inch from the inside of the upper board. In other words the valve must travel $3/_{32}$-inch when the pouch inflates in order to cause the instrument to speak. This compares with the keybox primary valve settings of exactly half that amount – $3/_{32}$-inch.

Proceed with all parts except swell shutters and case components. Now the instrument can be tested for manual playing and checking for leaks. Note that it is easier to make the instrument play manually than it is to achieve perfect response from the music-roll where adjustments generally have to be more precise. Ideally use a 58-note test-roll for this operation. Mark on the keys with a soft pencil (not a felt-marker unless it is guaranteed capable of being washed off) those notes that do not repeat, do not play or which play all the time.

Corrections to these faults are set out in the next section.

Replace all the remaining interior parts such as swell-shutters and linkages, connect up the mechanical or pneumatic linkages between the stop knobs and the stop pallets in the side chests and now refit the case. If this needs repair or refinishing, then do this before refitting. Lastly replace the top of the organ case and its central panel through which the sound passes out.

11. Fault-Finding and Trouble-Shooting

With a good grounding in pneumatics and player piano work, problems with an Orchestrelle are readily solved. Here is a list of twenty-six common running defects and their remedies. *a] When played manually, one or more of the notes sound continuously.*

This can be due to one of three causes. First a key sticking in the down position because the keyboard bat pin (the forward location for the key) is bent or rusted, creating friction. This is cured by removing the key, checking the felt bushing in the slot underneath the front of the key into which the bat-pin slips, examining the bat pin itself, cleaning it and, if necessary, applying a few drops of glycerine to it.

Second is that the pallet beneath the keyboard which operates for manual playing has a loose or broken spring. This is easily cured by making and fitting a new spring formed out of piano wire. Usually if one spring is broken or 'tired', others may be in equally poor condition. Replace all 58.

Third is a pneumatic leak through a broken or damaged tube from the tracker bar to the primary valve, a misadjusted secondary valve possibly not seating through dirt or a foreign body forced into the seal's surface, or the leather faced sealing strip over the tracker bar is not covering the openings properly.

b] When played from the music roll, some notes do not sound, even when they are sustained.

This means there is either a blockage in the tracker bar hole or its rubber tube, or the valve clearance is incorrect. Alternatively there may be a perforated pouch.

The tracker bar holes should be sucked out one at a time using a tracker pump. Identify exactly which tracker bar hole corresponds with the defective note or notes. Use a rubber tube to blow carefully into the correct hole and check that the pouch is moving freely and not leaking. If it is leaking, replace it or seal with diluted rubber solution. Check the valve is moving freely and see that the valve discs are in the proper position: occasionally a valve disc may strip its thread on the wire rod and then move into such a position that it cannot do its job. If this is so, a small drop of glue on top of the defective disc will resecure it.

c] When played from the music roll, one or more notes are slow to speak and will not repeat.

This means that the bleed holes are too large or the valve clearance too great. Check the latter and retry before tackling the bleed holes. The traditional way of sticking sticky paper over the bleed hole and re-piercing it with a needle can be used: better to renew the bleed disc entirely and start from scratch with a new hole. Remember to start small and gradually increase until the correct size is found.

d] When played from the roll, some notes are prompt in speech but will not repeat staccato, producing one long note instead of a number of short ones.

The exact opposite of the previous problem and indicates that the valve clearance is too little or the bleed holes too small.

e] When one note speaks, an adjacent one 'whimpers'.

This means that some of the air from one windway in the backboard is getting through to another and can be due to the backboard not being tightly screwed to the tone-ranks, dirt trapped between backboard and tone ranks so preventing it from being tightened properly, or the small blotting paper washer between tone-rank hole and backboard being torn, folded or missing. See section on backboards to find which to remove to remedy the particular note.

f] Organ will not play at all from the music roll.

This means that the keyboard manual-playing stop-knob is disconnected from the keyboard manual-pallet rail underneath, so leaving open both the mechanical playing airways in the tracker-bar and also the key pallets.

g] When played manually, certain notes suddenly begin to screech.

This means that a pallet is not closing in a stop. A common fault with suction operated organs, this affects only Aeolian Grand models. Rectify by locating the reed, removing the controlling pallet at the back of the vertical chest and

either re-leather the sealing face, or tease up the nap of the existing skin using a fine wire-brush.

h] When pedalling, the air motor to drive the music roll is sluggish, erratic or inoperative.

Assuming the drive chain and sprockets to be accurately aligned and free of movement, this may be due to damp affecting the sliding seals of the motor, a loose airway, or the control valve being disconnected.

i] When pedalling a pressure instrument, the instrument is very easy to pump but the sound is erratic with a wavering tendency and the bellows storage reservoir relief valve can be heard open most of the time.

One of the tension springs that keep the reservoir normally closed is broken or loose.

j] On pressure models, the rewind for the roll is very slow and requires heavy treadling.

This is due to the shut-off valve, which cuts air pressure from the roll-box, not closing properly. With the roll-box open, the rewind will speed up, but air is still being wasted. If you can hear and feel air at pressure coming from the windway into the roll-box during rewind, remove the cover of the spoolbox and check the operation of the valve when the 're-wind' stop knob is drawn. If it does not close fully, then adjust the linkage until it closes and makes a proper seal.

k] The organ plays on rewind.

The fault lies in the control slide pallet and play/rewind pallet in the control box. The positions of the pallets relative to the positions of the controls have been altered so that the wind supply is still being admitted to the playing portion of the organ while the action has been set into the rewind position. Adjust accordingly so that as rewind is selected, the motor governor port is open at full power but the pallet controlling air to the player action is properly closed.

l] The organ plays at an irregular tempo, slows down on heavy chords, runs fast when only playing a few notes and generally seems impossible to regulate using the tempo control.

Suspect the setting of the motor governor bellows. Wind in the leather nut by a turn or two at a time. If this has no effect, then it is probable that the pallet inside is leaking and take the necessary action to repair.

m] A reed suddenly produces a muffled, flat tone.

Either a piece of dirt has got onto the reed, or it has fractured through age. Draw out the reed with a reed hook (remember always to use this tool with infinite care and engage it only in the recess in the reed plate, otherwise the reed tongue may be damaged), and examine it. Holding the reed up to the light should reveal a thin clear passage round both sides of the tongue and also at the tip. Dirt will block this view. See earlier for details on reed cleaning. If after this treatment the reed still sounds flat, then it may be fractured. Some cracks are impossible to see, even when viewed closely with a strong glass. A cracked reed cannot be repaired: it must be replaced with a new one. Most large piano sundries houses also carry reeds and, if they cannot match it with an entirely new reed, they can fit a new tongue and re-voice the old one for you if you send them also the reed an octave above and an octave below the damaged one. Remember, each set of reeds in the Orchestrelle is different, so you cannot use any reed just because the pitch is the same. The reeds will be a different shape to produce a differing timbre.

n] A reed suddenly starts to buzz and generally sound like a demented wasp when played.

This means the reed tongue has become loose in the reed plate. This is very rare since almost all Orchestrelle reeds are double-riveted, but it was a common occurrence with the early reed organs and can happen with later instruments. With great care, re-rivet the tongue by clenching the rivets with a hammer and centre-punch. Ensure the vital clearance all round the reed tongue so that it can vibrate.

o] Squeaking foot pedals.

Lightly oil the bearings.

p] Swell shutters close with a bang.

Renew the felt buffer strips round their edges.

q] Roll drive motor has plenty of power but spoolbox action sluggish.

Dismantle components and wash in solvent to remove hard old oil/grease. Re-assemble and lubricate with oil. Check drive chain tension, adjusting jockey pulley tension as necessary.

r] Instrument is very hard to pedal.

Indicative of major leaks in numerous places. Do not attempt 'running repairs' as it needs a total overhaul.

s] Instrument lacks power and volume.

See [r] above.

t] Instrument has not been serviced for its lifetime and doesn't work at all.

See [s] above.

u] Massive losses of pressure during playing

Assuming that the instrument is normally airtight and working well, it may be that, although all joints are tight and the action appears responsive during re-roll, the bellows action becomes loose during playing, requiring excessive speed of pedalling to play – and then without promptness.

This needs careful diagnosis. The trouble invariably lies with the secondary valves either because they are too great in diameter following renewal, or because they are improperly centred and adjusted. This means the valve can 'float' in the open position evacuating the air pressure from the whole row of secondary valves through the defective valve or valves. It only requires one or two faulty valves to destroy the pressure differential. Rectify by checking:

1) valve condition, diameter, seating, levelling, centring.

2) valve setting in both normal (lowest) and open (highest) position. If the pouch lift is insufficient to raise the valve against its upper seat, the system will leak.

3) pouch operation and freedom of movement; if insufficient, check bleeds in the primary valve bank (remember, there are no bleeds in the secondary valves).

Valves must be light, smooth in operation, have parallel faces properly gapped and secured, and must be neither too large in diameter nor too small.

Pouches must be light, airtight, prompt and unrestricted. The fibre disc in the centre of each pouch must not be missing.

v] Bellows resistance during rewind, notes play

The main valve to the motor/spoolbox wind supply is defective. Selecting 'rewind' must shut off the wind supply to the spool box either by mechanical pallet (easy to check) or by pneumatic value (check by pulling down the protruding valve stem on the valve stem block). The slide in the motor valve box (to the right of the keyboard and attached to the inner face of the treble end vertical wind chest) may be restricted in motion, or its face may be dirty or pitted, or its guides may have become detached or broken, or its operating wire to the wooden or metal trunnion lever may have become distorted or adjusted to the wrong length with the leather nuts.

w] Instrument slows down during heavy pedalling, speeds up during passages of soft pedalling or low wind demand.

Adjust the tension of the motor regulator spring and the setting of the inner pallet inside the motor regulator bellows. May be caused by slack springs allowing the governor to close up too readily. Have someone pedal while watching closely the movement of the regulator. If it closes up quickly, take off the gull springs and open then wider by bending carefully. In case of broken springs, your piano supplies house can supply replacement gull springs. Do not replace with a coil spring: the rate (meaning its characteristics) of the spring is quite different.

If the springs are OK, adjust the closure of the pallet inside the governor bellows by adjusting the leather nut on the screw-threaded steel wire protruding through the centre of the governor movable board. Usually the problem is that the pallet closes too soon, so turn the leather button clockwise one turn at a time and try again until the optimum setting is obtained.

x] Note ciphers (plays all the while)

If the same note ciphers in all ranks when those ranks are selected, then check for dirt lodged under the primary valve holding the air supply open to the secondary valve pouch. Check for dirt under the secondary valve so preventing the valve from dropping back with pouch and allowing one channel of the backboards to be vented continually.

If one note ciphers in just one tone-rank, suspect a perforated tone-rank motor, defective spring or pallet inside the tone-rank. If it is a treble note in a rank of small reeds (*ie* flute or oboe reeds), check that the reed chamber bleed hole (situated under the front of the reed chambers over the treble end) is clear. Probe this carefully – incautious prodding can damage the reed.

Check individual tubing, particularly the short lengths of tube inside the spool box which pass from the tracker bar nipples to the back of the spool box nipples. These tubes are only a few inches long and are often overlooked in servicing

If the model is a suction Grand type (*ie* spoolbox is open as in a player piano and with a leather flap which comes down over the tracker-bar openings, check that the leather is properly seated. Another problem with the Grand is that the keyboard pallet springs may break, become slack or misalign, so allowing atmospheric pressure in through the keyboard end of the tubing for one keyboard note.

y] Note fails to sound on all tone ranks

If one note is silent, this is probably due to a defective secondary valve either through not being lifted sufficiently or through incorrect setting. Check tracker bar hole. Check primary valve for operation. Check if reed has broken or is prevented from vibrating through dirt.

If one note on only one rank fails to speak, always first suspect the reed. Draw it out and check that it is not broken, cracked or being jammed by a particle of dirt.

If one note on one rank sounds very flat (*ie* its pitch drops and remains incorrect), this means that the reed has cracked. Replace with a new reed.

z] If keyboard action is erratic and not prompt

Provided operation of the instrument from the tracker bar is correct and assuming the mechanical or pneumatic control to the key touch-box is operative (*ie* wind is admitted to the pallet box controlled by the key tails), the fault lies solely within the keyboard and touch-box area.

Check for freedom of key pitmans which should all offer positive but gentle resistance from the inner pallets. Failure to do so means a broken pallet spring holding a valve open (note sounding all the while). Alternatively, the special and delicate one-way flap valves in the touch-box may be curled and so not sealing properly. Check the keyboard springs that hold the individual keys up. If there are massive failures, suspect the whole relative position of the keys to the touch box for if they are too high, all the notes will be open the play. Adjust individual pallets and levers to produce a slight clearance (*ie* 0.01-inch).

Final Observation:

The Orchestrelle makes plenty of pressure wind to play the organ. However, as with the supply of vacuum in a player-piano, fundamental problems can accumulate to reduce the supply below operating level. For this reason if you have a number of keyboard notes all ciphering, then it creates a massive loss of power. As with any mechanical organ (the barrel organ in particular), check each note individually and carefully, in this way reducing the power loss until the very last cipher is removed.

12. The Aeolian Grand

The Grand is descended directly from the genus 'American Organ' or 'parlor organ'. It is a suction instrument built along the principles of the harmonium. Like its fellow suction instrument the player-piano, the Grand has an 'open'-type roll drive motor. Like a harmonium, all the reeds are arranged in a single pan that is mounted vertically at the back of the instrument. Piano-type wedge-shaped pneumatic motors actuate wire pull-downs to open large pallets in the reed pan while the speaking of stops is controlled by mutes or closures mounted over the front of the reed chambers.

Reed-organ and harmonium restoration is covered in depth in Ord-Hume *[80]*.

13. How to Play and Enjoy the Orchestrelle

Although the Orchestrelle is one of the most satisfying of all mechanical musical instruments upon which to play, and while many survive both in Europe and in the United States, few owners understand how to get the very best out of them. In this section I want to explain the secrets of expressive and sympathetic playing in easy, non-technical language. While the instructions refer to the 58-note model, the comments and advice apply equally well not just to all Orchestrelles but also to other player organs such as the Wilcox & White Symphony, Estey, Phoneon and lesser specimens.

There can be fewer sounds less impressive or more devoid of musical expression than those that emanate from an Aeolian Orchestrelle played by somebody who has no knowledge of the instrument or awareness of its capabilities. So often I have seen instruments with the left-hand knee board – the full-organ or 'tonal' swell – tied over to a case column with a piece of string so that the organ is playing everything it has got all the while. About just as bad is to see an instrument with its right knee board – the swell shutter control – also tied over.

This overlooks the strong probability that in playing the organ at 'full organ' or maximum power all the time so every single reed in all tone ranks is sounding a note, the power of the organ, far from being increased, is actually being diminished since it is spread over so many resources. Far greater expression comes from playing quietly on perhaps just one stop.

The Orchestrelle is not just a reed organ. It is an orchestral instrument inasmuch as that it comprises a collection of different voices – some loud, some soft, some mellow, and some which are fluty, nasal or brassy. It is the subtle interplay of the Orchestrelle's voices that gives it its extreme beauty and flexibility as a musical interpreter.

Now much of the subtlety of playing comes quite naturally to a person who can claim to be a talented finger performer. But most of us who own mechanical instruments may not have that extra ability which enables the more fortunate ones to read music. We may be unable to understand so much as a note of written music, let alone understand the nuances of performance. There again, playing even a reed organ properly takes a greater degree of skill than may at first be apparent.

After rebuilding your instrument, it is a bit pointless if you cannot then spare the time extra to learn the right way to make it produce the sort of breathtaking performance that can draw gasps and applause from your listeners. To get the best out of your Orchestrelle and your music rolls, you must learn, practice and experience for yourself until you become adept at the use of all tone controls which include, besides stops, the subtleties of pedalling, correct and precise tempo variations, and the use of the two knee swells.

Do not adopt a 'rule of thumb' reaction to loudness markings on the music roll. 'PP', 'FF' and all the shades between do not necessarily mean that you have to play up to full organ with all the stops out, nor that the swell shutters should be open or closed. The position of the swell shutters depends for any particular effect on the stops that you are playing on.

As an example, if one considered the Trumpet stop to be one of the loudest, if not the loudest, in the treble, you may find an interesting effect by playing a passage on the quieter French Horn stop with the swell shutters fully open, then for the next musical passage, change to the Trumpet – and at the same time close the swell shutters, so producing a sound which is actually quieter. But this is advanced stuff, so let's begin by learning a bit more about the stops, their names and how they divide.

The basis is a sound pitch that is quantified as 'eight feet', invariably written '8 ft' and indicating that the tone is 8 ft pitch. This is the sound produced by an open organ pipe eight feet in length. Middle C on such a pipe will coincide with middle C on the Orchestrelle when you have drawn an 8 ft or 'foundation' stop. A piano has the same basis and middle C on both instruments will have the same pitch.

The majority of Orchestrelle stops comprise registers of 8 ft pitch. On larger models there is an extra rank of much smaller reeds that produce the bright 2 ft tone called Piccolo. Between the two lies the Flute stop at 4 ft. If you play one note on an 8 ft stop, then draw a 4 ft stop with it, two tones will sound that are one octave apart. If you play the same note and also draw a 2 ft stop, three notes will sound, each one an octave above the first. The immediate effect will be to make the note sound 'bright'. If you experiment with the same note playing but now close the 4 ft stop, you will hear two notes that are spaced two octaves apart and sound 'very bright'.

The keyboard of the Orchestrelle plays 58 notes which matches the number of notes on the ordinary 58-note Orchestrelle music roll, but there is a division at the 21st note from the bass – this is G sharp. From this break upward, starting with the A, the stops in the treble will sound: from this break downward, the stops in the bass will sound. Note that the break comes well to the left of the centre of the keyboard, so do not get confused over which stops play which portion.

The bottom 13 notes of the keyboard as far as C two keyboard octaves below middle C can be extended an octave lower by the addition of a 16ft bass or sub-bass register, but more of this one later.

If you draw an 8 ft stop in the treble and a matching 8 ft stop in the bass – this means one on the right-hand side of the middle of the keyboard and one on the left-hand side, then you can play a complete scale of the same tonality from top to bottom. Now push in these stops and draw a 4 ft in the top (treble) and a 4 ft in the lower (bass) and once again you will find you can play a complete scale of the same tonality from top to bottom. The difference is that it is played one whole octave higher than the scale played on the 8 ft stop and middle C has effectively moved one octave up the keyboard.

There is a number of combinations of stop names on Orchestrelles and there are numerous variations which means that a comprehensive listing is rather pointless. However, there are several recognisable tone colours which, although they may be called by different names, are characteristic of the instrument. Here is a typical set, divided between treble and bass and starting from the softest stops which happen always to be in the centre:

Bass Treble Tone

Muted Strings / Muted Strings *8 ft*
Aeolian Harp / Aeolian Harp *8 ft*
Viola / Violin *8 ft*
Gemshorn / French Horn *8 ft*
Horn / Euphone *8 ft*
Bassoon / Oboe *8 ft*
Flute / Flute *4 ft*
Cornopean / Trumpet *8 ft*
Contra Bass *16 ft* *[stand-alone bass octave]*
Double Bass *16 ft* *[stand-alone bass octave]*

On some larger models, you will also find:

Flute Diapason / Doppel Flute *8 ft*
Piccolo / Piccolo *2 ft*

In your first attempts to learn to play the Orchestrelle, I suggest that you follow closely the steps I shall set out below. This will give you a painless demonstration of what can be done and inspire you quickly to invent and develop your own special techniques.

1] Select a fairly short music roll preferably of a piece of music that you both know and like. This should not be a fast, complicated piece but, ideally, a hymn, serenade or waltz.

2] Leave both knee swells well alone and avoid the temptation to so much as touch them until you are proficient enough to be able to play a roll using all the other accessories provided by the original makers to enable you to give a good account of both the roll and yourself. And a good performer can get by without using either knee board, considering both as nothing more than a bonus to his playing. While this is correct, I will show you how to integrate your playing with these knee boards – but not just for the moment.

3] Sit comfortably on a proper organ stool – note that the usual piano stool is not suitable and a sloping-topped organ seat will make you feel much more at ease. You must sit at the proper height so that when your feet are on the pedal boards, your thighs are straight or pointing slightly downwards.

4] Learn and then practice the right way to pedal. To start with, cultivate slow, regular and full pedal strokes – left, right, left – using the ball of the foot to push down the pedal. Keep your heels near the front or hinge-line of the pedal boards. Don't rock from side to side on your seat as you pedal – imagine there's a pile of books on your head! If you do want to sway about in the saddle, make sure that it is to the musical inspiration and not as an adjunct to – or a result of – pedalling. More on pedalling later.

5] Find out and remember which stops on your instrument are the soft-speaking ones, and also those that are loud. Set the instrument to 'Manual' and put your finger on a key – any key will do – and listen to the sounds produced by each stop individually. Note that the texture of the sound sometimes varies across the keyboard and that some stops sound best over certain parts of the keyboard. Try various combinations of stops and see how the tonal colours can be changed, augmented and subdued by the management of the stops.

6] Draw out the tempo and re-roll stops (where the tempo control is a sliding lever, put it over to the left which is the slowest or stationary position). Place your selected music roll in the spool box, rotate the bottom spool by hand until the paper fully covers the tracker bar. In the case of pressure models, now close the sliding glass spoolbox door. Push back in both the tempo and re-roll controls (in the case of the slide tempo control, you can leave this alone at this point).

7] Start to pedal to bring up the air pressure in the reservoir. With the Aeolian Grand, of course, you will be bringing up vacuum. Feel with your feet the gentle increasing resistance as the reservoir fills and the sound of the spill valve operating will tell you when things are ready.

8] Draw two stops only, one each side of the centre, such as *Muted Strings*.

9] Move the 'tempo' lever or knob so starting the roll moving. Few tempo readings on these instruments seem to be correct, so adjust the speed to get the speed which you feel to be correct.

10] As the roll plays, correct the speed as you wish and watch the pattern of perforations in the music roll as it travels over the tracker bar and listen to the notes played.

You will soon learn to associate the notes of music that you hear with the position of the holes in the music roll. Note how music consists of phrases which are either successive or are interwoven together in the form of melody and counter-melody. The implied pause between phrases is the only place where you should ever consider changing stops – never ever in the middle of a note and seldom if ever in the middle of a phrase, but we will return to this in a moment.

As with a music roll on a player piano, you cannot hope to be able to give a good performance until you have practised the roll and decided on your own performance as to choice of stop registration (the ranks of reeds you will wish to use for various parts of the music), and just where you will make these changes.

Practice using the same stop settings until you get to know the music well. But don't be afraid to vary the registration as often as you wish until you have produced a result that pleases you. I will tell you much more about the matter of stop selection – termed 'registration' – further on.

Once you have become reasonably proficient at operating the hand controls of the Orchestrelle and have a fair idea how the instrument sounds in various stop combinations, you can now start to experiment with the swell shutters – incidentally, in Aeolian terminology they are called 'shades' but you can forget that for now. With these closed, the whole organ is, in effect, operating in a box and so the sound is subdued. If you move your right knee to the right, so pushing the knee-board over, the shutters will open and the organ will sound progressively louder as you open up the swell.

Notice the effect these shutters have on different stop combinations. Notice you can play a soft horn-toned stop with the shutters closed, then exchange the horn for muted strings and open the shutters fully – and get almost the same volume of tone. This is a basic and important secret to effective playing and is a question of balancing all the many variables of stop combinations with swell-shutter positions to produce either a constant level of sound, or a varying one.

Learn to balance the volume of sound produced by judicious use of the swell and various combinations of stops. Fully open for *Muted Strings*, half open for *French Horn*, and closed for *Trumpet* – and you should achieve the effect of constant volume.

Now so far I have said nothing about the left knee-board. This is also a form of swell, but it works in a different way altogether. This opens up every stop so that you can play 'full organ'. Naturally, rather like the multiple electric socket adaptor which lets you plug in so many electrical appliances to one wall-socket that you blow the fuse, the full organ swell is the easiest control to misuse.

From an earlier Section, you will recall that there are also two types of full organ. One, the commonest, is the cranked lever which presses against all the stop controls at each side of the keyboard at once, so putting everything on. The other is a much more delicate device called by Aeolian the 'tonal' system which is a true *crescendo-diminuendo* control. A feature found on all Orchestrelles with pneumatic stop control, the operation of the pedal progressively opens the stops from the softest through to the loudest by opening pallets on a simple control box.

The tonal type of swell action allows voices to be added one at a time and in a specific sequence, so that you can build up the full organ sound gradually just by the gentle and gradual moving of the knee board.

Whichever type of swell your organ has, it can be used in several ways. First it can be used for those short *tutti* passages where full organ is really needed. And second, it allows you a breathing space in which to change your stop settings. Remember, when this 'tonal' or left-knee swell is applied, it overrides the stop knob positions on the stop rail above the keyboard. This means that with the left knee-board in use you can open or close stops at will without affecting the full-organ sound you are producing with the tonal swell. Let me give you an example of both these types of use.

There are many pieces of music where the melody is played on a solo voice, probably with the swell shutters fairly wide open to enable it to sing out. At intervals, a full orchestral *tutti* or chord may be interspersed. If you try to open the right-knee swell fully for this, the effect will be minimal: if you try to execute a very smart movement of the stops, you will need great skill (and probably ten fingers on all five hands) to get the right effect. What you can do, though, is to keep your melody stop(s) drawn, and introduce full organ briefly by a quick outward movement of the left knee swell.

The second use is more subtle. Let us take, say, the opening of a Rossini overture where full orchestral chords announce a theme played by a solo voice. The double forte opening bars just cannot be selected and cancelled in the time allowed, so here you start the music roll with only the solo melody stops drawn – and start playing with the left-knee control fully open. After the introductory full orchestra parts, you close the tonal swell and allow the solo passage which follows to be played on the solo stops you have already set.

Again, during the music you may build up gradually to a greater volume of crescendo followed by a solo part. Here you build up in the usual way by adding stops. At the double forte

(FF) mark on the music roll, you put on full organ with the left-knee swell so overriding the stop selection. This gives you time in which to close all the stops more or less at leisure while still playing full organ, and select your solo voices to follow. These are then introduced by the simple expedient of closing the tonal swell.

There are other combinations of these effects which incorporate the normal right-knee swell shutters. Here you can swell up on full organ, or, by starting with the swell shutters fully open, you can swell down, *ie* diminish the volume at full organ.

Except when using the pneumatically-operated tonal swell, which is sequential in its selection and setting of the stops, all movements of the full-organ or left-knee swell should be swift, otherwise you may get some strange noises like bagpipes starting up as the wind is admitted to each fresh register in the middle of a succession of notes. With the pneumatic swell, however, the opening can be as slow or as fast as you like.

In concluding my remarks about the knee swells, you should cultivate the ability to pedal the organ bellows normally while sitting more or less still on the stool. It is wrong and uncomfortable, not the least tiring as well, to pedal as if you are a sprint cyclist taking a steep hill. As with the player-piano, proper pedalling technique will enable you to operate the knee swells evenly, precisely and with steady accuracy however hard or soft you are pedalling.

If you find it physically impossible to co-ordinate up and down with the feet and knees wide apart (perhaps if you are a lady and wearing a tight skirt or perhaps have suffered a strict up-bringing), then as a last resort you can control the knee boards with your hands. The disadvantage here is that while operating knee swells by hand, there is nothing else that you can do like changing stops unless you have an incredibly long and preferably hooked nose. Better you cast reserve to the four winds and practice the speedy parting of the knees.

No, real Orchestrelle-players have very mobile thighs and are not averse to waggling the knees from side to side with joyous abandon.

So far, other than to mention that there are two types of tempo control found on Aeolian Orchestrelles, I have said very little about tempi. Now is the time to put that to right.

The two tempo control systems used both work the tempo governor in exactly the same way. One is a simple stop-knob that moves in and out, its position generally being indicated according to a scale and pointer. The other is a lever that moves from left to right across a scale. Neither, as already inferred, is absolutely accurate in terms of the legend printed on the scale. Both, however, can be adjusted to be extremely precise as a means of controlling the speed of the music. Neither should be relied upon!

Proper use of the Tempo control is important during roll-playing. It is not sufficient to set a tempo and leave it at that: more often than not, the music roll will call for speed variations during playing, or your own sensitivity towards the music you are playing may dictate that you will wish to make corrections to the tempo as you go along.

First of all – speed. The musical term shown on the roll apron or leader and indicating 'slow' is *Largo*: that for 'fast' is *Presto*. Between these two opposites lie several steps and it will pay you to learn their proper sequence so that, for example, if you have to change from *Allegretto* to *Andante* you will instantly know whether you must play faster than you are now, or slower.

The steps, from slowest to fastest, are as follows:

Largo
Larghetto
Adagio
Andantino
Andante
Moderato
Allegro Moderato
Allegretto
Allegro
Presto

There are other intermediate terms but these are seldom to be found on Orchestrelle music rolls. What is not so easy to quantify is just what these terms mean, for there is no standard tempo indication for them. This is one reason why it is helpful – sometimes – to adopt the initial tempo setting or number printed on the roll apron. It is, though, not always an accurate indication.

The actual speeds indicated by the two extremes are largely a matter of taste and depend on the way in which the roll itself is cut. *Largo* might be between 20 and 30 on the indicator scale; *Presto* from 100 to 120. But it doesn't really matter for you yourself will know the speed at which the music should be played. Intuition like this is not hard to acquire and again is the reward for practice. Use tempo markings as *relative indications* – and don't be a slave to them!

During playing, the music roll will sometimes show speed variations. For example a symbol rather like a crescent moon with a dot inside it means 'hold' or pause on that particular note, chord or silence. How long you pause is a matter of choice and individuality, but the important thing is not to slow down as the mark approaches, but to stop the roll very quickly and accurately with the mark over the tracker bar. Immediately after the mark, you must return to the proper speed and again the acceleration must be as near to instantaneous as possible and, above all, precise.

Sometimes you will see the abbreviation *rit* placed against a perforation or phrase, and this is short for *ritardando* which means that you must gradually slow down until the next command appears. This will usually be *Tempo* which means the same speed as you were before the *rit* symbol – and this again means back to the original speed. Here's how to do it precisely.

If your instrument has a speed control knob, place the knuckle of the forefinger against the stop rail and move the knob using the thumb and the second (longest) finger. This means that your fingers will slide against each other and it will be easy to revert to the original tempo when the mark on the roll comes into position over the tracker bar. Similar techniques can be used with the lever control type, the basic technique being to establish a fixed point with the knuckles or other fingers so that the control can be brought back to that point. And that way you can ignore the numbered scale!

Earlier I said that the Orchestrelle was a set of individual voices. In fact, think of it either as a choir or as an instrumental group, and remember that each choir and instrumental group has soloists: it is the solo voices that have the greatest character and often the greatest effect. Next to them, small groups of individual voices have subtle tonal shades. If you don't like the 'choir' analogy, think of the artist carefully mixing his paints to produce delicate shades.

Practice the building-up of tones, but do it first without using the swell. The tonal sequence will run something like this:

Muted Strings
Aeolian Harp
Violin
French Horn
Gemshorn
Trumpet
Flute

Notice that in this list I have placed the trumpet before the flute, yet the trumpet *(8 ft)* is the louder instrument and the effect of the flute *(4 ft)* is to enhance the trumpet sound with a sound an octave higher.

You will also see that I have omitted the oboe. This is because its use will inspire a whole new tonal path. Adding the oboe to the list above will not really help much. A suitable oboe tonal build-up might better be:

Muted Strings
French Horn
Oboe
Flute

and two interesting small groups of solo voices are:

French Horn
Oboe

and:

Muted Strings
Oboe
(with optional addition of Flute)

Another one to try is Oboe and Trumpet and listen how the oboe colours the trumpet when the latter is used as a prime solo instrument.

So far I have said very little about the accompaniment stops to the left, bass end of the keyboard. Essentially the same rules apply. However, it is mistake to follow the very common practice amongst insensitive Orchestrelle players of 'matching the accompaniment stops to the melody' and pulling out similar ones each side. It is often better to have an accompaniment that is somewhat 'thinner' than the melody. For the reason, don't overload the left-hand stop selection – but do watch out for those pieces of music that take a solo theme and run it from the bass end through to the treble: unless you have the ranks selected through from one end to the other, you will get a nasty audible 'step' in the middle where, for example, you may change from one tonality to another in mid-flight! This is where experience and knowing your music roll comes in handy.

Where and when should stop changes be made? On the majority of Orchestrelle rolls, this is left entirely to the performer and his own appreciation of the music. After you have played your chosen practice roll through a few times, you will detect where there are thematic changes or where one phrase ends and another begins. These are in effect musical 'sentences' or phrases that stand out and are separated by the unwritten, implied punctuation of good music. It is at these points that you can consider altering registration – this means making stop changes. With a lot of practice, you can 'read' these points in the patterns of perforations in the music roll.

No rule-book says that you *have* to keep altering your choice of stops. Remember the old barrel-organist's tale about the player who had had the same stops drawn for forty years and saw no reason for change to his habit! Stop-changes highlight these musical phrases and make your performance colourful and individual.

Cultivate the ability to make crisp and positive stop changes: a stop closed slowly, or opened uncertainly can produce some unexpected noises which are jarring to the ear. Building crescendo passages using individual voices and without using the full organ left-knee swell needs skill in knowing the effect of each stop combination over that particular area of the keyboard. Normally extra voices should only be added between phrases and the build-up should be from the softest-voiced ranks up to the Trumpet stop, this being the loudest. Trying to build up on a loud voice seldom works and usually serves only to thicken the music, like adding starch to porridge.

The exception to this rule is the higher-pitched stop such as Flute *4 ft* of Piccolo *2 ft*. As an example, build up a crescendo from French Horn through to Trumpet, missing out the Flute. This is the sort of climax to a work that usually terminates in massive chords or arpeggios. Now add the Flute and the treble will immediately brighten and stand out, the effect being heightened if you can soon afterwards add the Piccolo, although this in itself is a relatively soft stop.

Another possible exception is the Oboe to Trumpet combination where the Trumpet is playing as a solo with the swell shutters other than fully open. To this can be added the Oboe to produce a nasal twang to the tone, rather like the Nazard in pipe-organ terminology.

In involved, 'busy' musical strands, it is often necessary to suppress the bass so that the melody will stand out. I refer here, of course, to 58-note music rolls. If you have, say, French Horn, Flute and Trumpet in the treble, it will probably be inadvisable to match these in the lower half of the keyboard, so, besides the *16 ft* tones, use only one or at the most two prominent bass voices. Sometimes the *4 ft* Flute can be of advantage in the bass to heighten a thick bottom-end sound.

The art of good Orchestrelle playing is to cultivate the ability to build up to a *crescendo* in a piece of music from one solo stop by the subtle addition of extra tones in such a manner that the listener cannot immediately detect where the additions are made yet is able to notice the change in overall effect. This may at first appear to negate the statement that it is the solo voices that have character. The difference is that here I am referring to the gradual modification of a tone by the addition of more voices to create a musical effect – a *tonal climax*.

Just as important is the smooth *decrescendo* – taking away the extra voices starting from full organ and gradually easing back to just a solo voice. The ability to do this, and to know just where and when and which voices to adjust, is the mark of a skilled player who has practised his music roll very carefully.

Remember that there is only one thing worse than changing from Aeolian Harp to Trumpet in the middle of a *pianissimo* passage – and that is to do it in the middle of a chord!

So far I have spoken about adding voices to reach a *crescendo*, and then taking them away for a diminuendo. There is another subtle effect to be learned – and that is adding voices up to full organ while achieving a *diminuendo* effect at the same time. This apparently impossible objective is most effec-

tive for some orchestral-type pieces of music. The technique is very simple, but requires practice. It consists of balancing the increasing volume of sound from additional voices by gradually closing the right-hand knee-board controlling the swell shutters. Along with this comes softer and softer pedalling.

Pedalling is another skill to be practised. At the beginning of this section I spoke about even, regular pedalling. Now you should start varying the amount of wind you produce by pedalling. Learn to make wind on demand – pump just enough wind to make the instrument sound and no more. Pedal not so soft as to make the roll motor stop, or to lose individual notes – this is an old lesson learned by player-pianists and barrel-organists.

Those who are really adept at operating a player piano will appreciate the extreme shades of musical effect which can be achieved without touching the hand controls, just by using the feet in a gentle and subtle way. The player-pianist knows how to accent a chord with a quick dab of the foot at the right moment. If really expert he also knows and can achieve the opposite effect which is to approach a chord and at the very split second before the chord sounds forth he momentarily stops pedalling to obtain a deliciously soft chord or terminal of a cadence.

Although by comparison with the player piano, the Orchestrelle with its great reservoir of air is not such a subtly-built monster, also a reed requires the passage of air through it otherwise it just will not sound, much may still be done with the pedal footwork.

Talking about footwork, I strongly urge anyone who pedals anything, be it piano, harmonium or Orchestrelle, to avoid the almost universal habit of regular, even pedalling. I know that all the old *How to Play the ****ola* manuals advocated steady pedalling but it is the very worst thing to do. Of course, when you start to pedal an instrument for the first time, you must do just that but, as you get the upper hand of the thing, break the habit. One can become unconsciously attuned to the tempo of the music and the beats in the bar become related to thrusts on the pedals. When you want to work up to a *crescendo* or accent, your studied rhythm restricts you. It also upsets the tempo of the music.

Right, I can hear somebody saying that an organ needs blowing at a steady pressure or it sounds horrible. Pipe organs, I'll agree, will overblow and produce nasty noises if under- or over-blown. This was a characteristic encouraged by Grenie of Bordeaux in 1810 when he built his *Orgue-Expressif*. The Dutch builder Winkel appears to have worked along similar lines. However, the reed organ has much greater latitude in its blowing. The volume of sound can be modified appreciably by how you blow it (although some ranks such as the tiny reeds in Flute and Piccolo stops are prone to overblow unless you are careful), and to a certain extent it is possible to accent on the Orchestrelle in the same manner as in the player-piano. The effect is not so instantaneous, though, because there is a much larger volume of operating air to be acted upon than in the piano whose vacuum is capable of relatively large modifications at short notice.

Once you have learned how to control your Orchestrelle and move on to exploring its musical abilities, practise pedalling in no recognisable rhythm. An irregular number of short strokes with one foot, steady long ones with the other; allow the organ to breathe gently during easy passages where you are playing just a few notes on one stop, and then 'get up steam' for the major passages.

This is what is so drastically wrong with fitting a blower to an Orchestrelle or player reed organ of any kind – it takes away the ability to blow the organ to suit demand and mood and all the music comes out the same: an acoustic version of a sausage machine.

Of course, there are conditions when a blower may be resorted to. If you, as the Orchestrelle owner, don't really *like* music, or if you are very, very old and feeble with a weak heart, poor hearing and a tendency to heartburn, then by all means have a blower fitted, but only in such a way that when the next owner comes along, hopefully in the not too-distant future, he can throw the thing away and return the instrument to its proper musical state.

Scott Joplin annotated all his piano rags with the message 'Do not play fast: ragtime must never be played fast.' Let me suggest an equally pertinent remark to the Orchestrelle player. 'Do not play the Orchestrelle too fast, and do not play with more voices than are absolutely necessary. Play softly – then you will find that people will listen to you!'

Now to that which is probably the most misused of all effects on the player reed-organ. This is the *Vox Humana*. Many people think that the *Vox Humana* is as vital to a performance as is the music roll itself, and accordingly keep it drawn throughout their entire performance. This just is not so. Personally, I dislike this mechanical adjunct to the reed organ in all its shapes and sizes, but this is just my way of looking at the thing.

The *Vox Humana*, once misnamed by a lady who was possessed of limited intellect but astute interpretation as the 'Nux Vomica', is a device for which, like weed killer or tomato sauce, there is a right time and place. There is a right and a wrong way to use it, so let's see what can be done to justify its existence.

On the Orchestrelle as in most other reed organs, the *Vox Humana* consists of a pneumatic paddle-motor driving a long, longitudinally-pivoted blade of thin wood or cardboard (in cheap organs) which is mounted in front of the treble end of one tone-rank, usually the Flute or French Horn. Because it is situated inside the swell shutters, once it is set in motion by drawing the appropriate stop, its effect can be heard across most of the treble register stops and is more noticeable on some rather than others. Which these actually are you can determine for yourself but it is normally the Flute register.

The effect is to turn a perfectly good, stable reed sound into a sort of rapidly-fluctuating 'wah-wah-wah' which, with some kinds of music, can produce tears in the eyes of the sensitive and induce an urgent desire to be sick in others. It is an effect beloved of Holywood (which always uses very cheap reed organs to produce the sound effects in cathedrals for some unknown reason) and the winsome blondes who once sewed samplers by the Sunday fireside and read pulp-book romances.

A properly set-up *Vox Humana* operates promptly the moment its stop is drawn, rotates at a steady pace, and stops immediately the draw-stop knob is pushed in. Its rotation ceases not just because the wind supply has been cut off, but because a small mechanical brake connected to the stop control linkage is brought to bear on the rotating shaft, at the same time opening a valve to vent the inside of the paddle motor of all wind.

The *Vox Humana* used during rapid music which comprises a lot of short notes, does nothing advantageous for the music. In fact you can seldom detect its influence. Where there are long melody notes, however, the effect may be quite pleasing when used in moderation. One dramatic effect can be achieved during the playing of slow pieces of music where the high melody notes stand apart from the rest of the notes. The piece should be played using something like Flute and French

Horn plus *Vox Humana*. At a suitable point and during the sounding of a long, sustained note, the *Vox Humana* is closed, so producing the effect of hardening the sound being produced. Try this immediately before a *crescendo* starts to build and the result can be extra dramatic.

If you want bathos in terms of musical performance, play all your hymn rolls and romantic songs on Muted Strings, Aeolian Harp and *Vox Humana*. I find this a good way to empty the house of unwanted musical guests...

If you seek to play a music roll to absolute perfection, then practice it. And, as a final dodge, if invited to play for an audience, be it a gathering of friends or otherwise, only select those rolls that you know! With lots of Orchestrelle experience, you might just be able to get by with a performance of a new roll, particularly if it is a piece of light music such as a waltz or a popular selection where you can 'read' the messages in the roll perforations, but more than likely your audience will become uneasy, talk among themselves, and finally shuffle away, leaving you pedalling your heart out and wishing you had never bothered to start.

And there's another lesson! *Never* abandon playing a roll in the middle: that is an admission of defeat...

Practice. *Practice*. Now go and practice *some more!* Just because the notes are all there already doesn't mean that you can convert the holes in the paper into good music automatically!

Finally, learn to read the pattern of perforations in the roll, if not exactly in terms of the correct notes, then at least as to style and rhythm and what's likely to happen next. Practice very carefully your phrasing of pieces, learn the subtleties of pedalling (and don't stand for the nonsense spouted forth by player-piano buffs that the Orchestrelle isn't sensitive to pedalling and nor can it be). Cultivate an absolute knowledge of what tonal effects your instrument can produce. And learn to 'hear' the sound you want to achieve before you start.

The essence of good playing is practice and also experimentation. Remember the mnemonic **HELP** – Hear, Experiment, Learn, Practice – otherwise you may be beyond aid! Try operating any instrument without practice and you will be in trouble. The Orchestrelle is no different.

14. The Solo Orchestrelle and its special roll markings

The twin-manual or 116-note music rolls used on the Solo Orchestrelle carry upon them various legends other than those of a direct musical kind. These music rolls are also made to play on the Aeolian Pipe Organ. Although no production Orchestrelle ever had more than one manual (keyboard), these rolls could play on two distinct sets of stops or registers so as to give a 'two-manual' rendition. This was done by having two sets of perforations superimposed in the paper roll. In other words, the first hole is for the lower row of tracker-bar openings, the second for the upper one, the third for the lower, the fourth for the upper and so on across the width of the music roll. This means that certain openings play on one manual, others on the second.

Generally speaking, the upper manual perforations are easily visible because they are of a different design. These comprise a short 'dash' followed by a series of small circular punches for as long as the note is intended to play. The lower manual cuttings are all in the form of long dashes.

Occasionally, the performer is instructed to reverse the stop settings from one row of holes to the other. Rather than do this by quickly operating the stop knobs, there is a neat pneumatic changeover system whereby the stop settings are kept the same but the action of the two rows of perforations is reversed from the tracker bar. The action of this control is described in Section 6 above.

All this is summarised by the following notes that relate to the operation of the Aeolian Solo Orchestrelle and refer to the printed instructions found on the music roll.

NORMAL Top Manual roll perforations all speak on Manual II. Lower Manual roll perforations all speak on Manual I.

REVERSE Top Manual roll perforations all speak on Manual I. Lower Manual roll perforations all speak on Manual II.

GRAND Both Manuals play together on the lower row of perforations only.

Stops marked in **blue** are usually for the upper row of holes while those marked in **red** are usually for the lower row of holes.

UNISON or **TONAL** means full power, *ie* all stops sounding by the use of the left knee control.

MELODY is usually cut for top row of openings in the tracker bar.

The disposition of the stops is as follows:

Manual I:
> *Strings:-* Dolce Violin, Violin
> *Woodwind:-* French Horn, English Horn, Piccolo
> *Reed:-* Pizzicato

Manual II:
> *Strings:-* Muted Strings, Aeolian Harp
> *Woodwind:-* Orchestral Flute
> *Reed:-* Oboe, Clarionet [also loud strings]

Pedal: Contra Bass.

15. Notes on the Music Rolls

It is the mark of a poor sportsman and a vandal to write on the music roll. He who puts clues as to where to change stops on his roll is obviously trying to run before he can walk. He's also spoiling the roll for the next guy who may want to play it in a different way.

Don't write on your rolls.

If you *must* write on them, use a very soft pencil... It is easier for the next owner to rub out.

A partially dismantled Model F reveals the horizontal join between the upper section tone ranks and the lower one. One tone rank has been removed immediately above the separation.

Two-manual or Solo Orchestrelles have their drawstops separated into 'Manual 1' and 'Manual 2' groups. This picture also shows the selector lever for playing 58-note 'Grand' rolls or 116-note 'Solo' rolls: there are two positions for this setting – 'normal' and 'reverse', the latter switching the settings for the manual selections. At the back of the lever is the simple six-tube selector with its button-end valves. Beneath this lever is the tempo control that regulates power to the wind motor.

Aeolian roll-playing pipe organs were always extremely expensive. The makers prided themselves in the fact that they earned their profits from charging very high prices for their instruments. Even so, many of their ranks of metal pipes were, in truth, no more than reed resonators and this accounts for the wide tonal difference between, say, a Welte Philharmonic reproducing pipe organ and an Aeolian. The latter generally lacked the important diapason foundation tone and, with a preponderance of 8-ft stops, was rated as acoustically bland. Nevertheless the instruments enjoyed popularity both in America and Britain where their high price was, to a certain type of buyer, a recommendation in itself. Here, from a Californian collection, is the console of a genuine two-manual model playing either 58-note or 116-note rolls. In the contemporary American style of design, Aeolian persevered with the perfectly straight, non-radiating pedal board – a feature that lost them some sales in Britain where serious organists demanded the Royal College of Organists' specification for concave and radiating foot boards.

Many would say that Aeolian's finest achievement was the company's range of roll-playing Pipe Organs. Here is the smallest model supplied showing the diminutive console. Known as the 'Stock Model' in the 1920s this cost £2,500 ($10,000). This specimen originally belonged to Douglas Berryman in Cornwall.

At the very top of the Aeolian Pipe Organ catalogue was the Reproducing instrument which, like the Duo-Art piano, could be played entirely without human intervention, stop-selection and swell-shutter operation all being under the control of the perforated paper roll. Heart of the Duo-Art pipe organ was the player mechanism, often supplied as a separate electro-pneumatic unit attached to the organ itself by a heavy cable. This luxurious instrument could play 58 note rolls, 116-note pipe organ rolls or the special 176-note Duo-Art rolls. Here is a close-up view of one of these detached consoles showing the infinitely-variable seven-section tracker bar to cater for the needs of roll-tracking so wide a paper roll. This player was formerly in the long-defunct West Cornwall Museum of Mechanical Music.

Chapter 18
Living with the Self-Playing Piano - Care and Maintenance

Over the preceding Chapters I hope I have managed to show you that the player piano is a very simple device while at the same time representing an impressive assemblage of delicate parts. The sad fact is that they are all waiting for the slightest opportunity to go wrong! It's life! Join two pieces of wood together and sooner or later they fall apart. Players are the same. And the real reason why is that the modern home is a veritable incubator of potential disasters for such sensitive instruments. Old pianos and antique furniture survive on borrowed time in the average family home of today. And the reason is not too hard to find: it's the environment, central heating and air-conditioning. Our homes today are styled to accommodate Modern Man with his (or her) heightened sensitivity to heat, cold, draughts and all the other things that our forefathers cheerfully accepted as being part of normal life.

This is reflected in the design of our homes with large windows, blank walls, polished floors, synthetic carpets and drapes, furniture covered (and stuffed) with inert synthetic material and the absence of an open fireplace.

Let me explain how all this can upset your player piano – in fact *any* piano as well as your best antique furniture.

Furniture and pianos are made of real wood which means that its stability is to a great extent controlled by the atmospheric conditions around it. In the homes that abounded at the time these pieces were first made, houses were finished and furnished in equally natural materials. Wood-panelled walls, panelled ceilings, heavy curtains and drapes of natural fibres and furniture upholstered in natural materials all served to act as a natural reservoir of humidity. In very hot weather, changes in humidity within the house were very slow because of the sheer bulk of natural material that contributed to the overall humidity. The furnishings and the décor created a natural reservoir.

Because of this, severe temperature changes in summer or winter presented little problem to furniture since the sharp 'spikes' of change were evened out into gentle curves as humidity flowed slowly from furnishings or back into them.

At the same time, the Victorian or early American home was always well-ventilated. Open fireplaces ensured that the air in a room was changed at least five times an hour: the average for a British home as late as 1930 was estimated to be seven times an hour.

These conditions were absolutely perfect for the stability and conservation of furniture and pianos. While excessive damp in wintertime could pose a threat, especially if combined with a porous or stone floor, the general level of the environment was amenable.

Modern homes are very different. The wide use of man-made materials in construction and decorating a room dispense almost entirely with the humidity reservoir facility. Central heating looks after constancy of temperature while at the same time vastly increasing the troughs and peaks of humidity. The lack of an open fireplace restricts the movement of air. And furnishings upholstered in inert man-made materials deprive the room of any moisture 'bank' facilities. Result? All the moisture demands created by the environment have to be met by those items in the room made of natural materials – antique furniture and your long-suffering piano!

Now it's not all bad news. All of these negatives can be addressed by intelligent thinking and a sympathetic approach to the needs of your player piano. All you have to remember is that pianos (and furniture) do not respond well to sharp changes in their environment and that humidity change is far more damaging than temperature change. Humidity change is one of the conditions that is most rapidly accelerated by both central heating and by air-conditioning.

In simple terms, looking after a player is a matter of common sense. In an ideal world, the room would be maintained at a constant temperature and, just as important, constant humidity. Obviously this is not on unless you live in a museum. You can go so far as to keep to the constant temperature bit and all will be well until you have a dozen people round for a party whereupon the humidity will suddenly go through the roof!

One beneficial point is the size of a player piano. It is a relatively large quantity of wood that consequently changes its moisture content very slowly and can cope quite well with short-duration but rapid changes in temperature and humidity. Longer periods of variation can do considerable damage. For example, putting your piano in an unheated garage while you redecorate the music room can quite quickly put a piano out of action.

Even moving a piano from the shop or showroom where you bought it to your home (or moving between two houses) can change the instrument.

As a golden rule, if you move a piano in this manner or buy a new piano that arrives on the back of a truck, put it in its room, remove all the removable case panels, in particular the front fall and music stand, open the key fall – and then leave the instrument for a week. Let in breathe! In the case of a grand, opening the lid and holding it at full stick (where you have a choice of stick height) together with the key fall open will do the trick.

If you try to play the instrument during this time, it will probably sound and play badly. Do not be discouraged: it takes time to get accustomed to its new surroundings. With an electric reproducing piano it is not a bad idea to set it to replay and let it play an old roll over and over again for an hour or two. This will get room-temperature air and adjust to the surrounding humidity through the mechanism and help in the acclimatising process.

Where to put your piano? As we have seen, the killer for all pianos and good furniture is central heating. My own music room is kept ventilated but unheated unless I have visitors when a fan heater is placed in the middle of the room for a while. The chances are that you will have to keep the piano in a centrally-heated room. Provided you are intelligent about it, then it is not the end of the world. Never put a piano (or any other furniture, come to that) closer than two feet from a radiator or six feet from a direct heat source (fan-heater or open fire).

Some collectors make a point of having plenty of flowers, even indoor plants, in their music-rooms. Besides brightening up the place, these are Nature's ideal moisture reservoirs and watering the plants regularly re-humidifies a dry atmosphere.

There are, though, other menaces in your home! Insects can be a nuisance, yet house-spiders are tolerated because they keep your home free of other and less-peace-loving insects. Dust can be a menace in the house, too. The problem is that the player-piano will help keep your house free of dust and dirt. And there lies the really big problem – a player-piano, being a suction-powered instrument, is like a giant vacuum cleaner with a fine propensity for gathering cigarette ash, chimney soot, dried mud from your shoes – and whatever other small particles of foreign matter may be in the room. And where does it go? Straight into the valve system with its delicately-adjusted bleeds and finely-set gaps.

Of course one has to be realistic about such matters. Players were meant to live in homes that were a good deal dirtier and dustier than the homes of today. And players were robustly made to cope with the detritus of living in an age far less hygienic than ours when vacuum cleaners were both rare and inefficient.

The main difference was that they needed – and received – regular attention. Twice a year, or sometimes more frequently, the piano-tuner called, cleaned the action and set it back to tip-top condition. Any degradation in performance was unnoticeable. What happens today, though, is very different. The average player-piano is lucky if it ever sees a piano-tuner, let alone receives the sought-after attention. No, the truth is that player pianos live in a less forgiving environment today and what the modern home lacks in good old-fashioned dirt is made up for by systematic (if unintentional) neglect.

Now before you go off convinced that you would rather look after a Labrador with an attitude problem than have to live with a player-piano, let me admit to exaggerating just a little. My embellishment to the truth is merely to point out that pianos, like plants, need a little attention and a bit of thought before they will burst forth into bloom (or should I say tune?) and reward you with their best.

Several times in this book I have mentioned tuning and issued dire warnings about leaving piano-tuning to the professionals. I now want to tell you why and to emphasise just how much unwitting damage you can do to your piano in trying to tackle this final job yourself if you are not properly trained.

This is the great age of 'do-it-yourself' with everybody in the land spending more and more of their leisure time house and garden building. City businessmen show Churchillian aspirations and go bricklaying in their spare time. Many people undertake high-quality cabinet-making as a hobby while others confidently tackle household plumbing, plastering and other similar tasks that once were the province of none but the hired professional.

There are, nevertheless, several professions into which the thoughtful amateur has yet to make inroads. One is brain-surgery – and the other is piano-tuning.

The problem is that it all seems so easy! Every music-store sells electronic tuning aids that show precisely how to tune an instrument to extreme precision and there are even several books on how to go about tuning. Now all this is fine for guitars, banjos and even musical clocks and pipe organs. You can't do too much damage to these things if once you have grasped the principles. But pianos are very different.

Most pianos have 88 notes, the bass (lowest) one represented by one or two really heavy-gauge steel strings that are copper bound. As you progress up the scale, the strings get thinner and, if they are copper-bound (as all of the lower oc-

tave strings are) the binding gets thinner, too. Then the strings change to ever-thinner plain wires, first as three separate strands to a single note and then to four and sometimes five until you reach the extreme treble (highest) note. The strings vary in length from quite long to extremely short but, regardless of their length, type or number-per-note, they all exert tension on the piano frame.

Early pianos had wooden frames and the tension of the strings eventually caused the frame to distort, sometimes crack or actually fracture. And the tuning pins to tension each wire gradually became looser and looser until they could not hold the string tension. At this point the piano was either scrapped or expensively rebuilt. That is one reason why there are very few early wood-framed pianos surviving outside museums and piano-collections.

Later pianos made use of a cast-iron frame or plate that reinforced the piano and resisted the string tension. Adding truth to the adage about giving somebody an inch and they'll take a mile, this encouraged piano-makers to increase the string tension even more. That allowed thicker, heavier strings. The piano sounded louder because the stringing was heavier and to sound it the hammers became larger – and so on and so on. Result? The tension on the frame went up like a rocket.

Now there have been many calculations as to the total stress on a piano frame measured in pounds, tons, kilograms and just about every other unit of measurement you can think of. The problem is that no two seem to agree and estimates of the tension vary wildly. It also depends how you calculate it for the total tension is a very complex calculation. Somebody not so long ago calculated that there was total of 42 tons of tension in the frame of a modern grand piano. Now I don't know whether that is right or wrong: from previous experience I suspect it's just a guess. The point is the total tension doesn't really matter. What does matter is that it is one heck of a lot!

Piano-tuning directly modifies string tension meaning the tension in the piano-frame. If that tension is incorrectly or unevenly applied it can distort the piano frame. There is also the manner in which the tuning pins are turned with the tuner's tuning-key (called, incongruously, a tuning hammer). The pins have to be turned with great caution to ensure that, under the tension of the string wraparound, they are gently rotated and not bent. Strings then have to be tensioned so that both halves of the string (the part that sounds and the part that is the 'dead' side of the soundboard bridge) are at exactly the same tension. All this before we get to the niceties of counting the frequencies and listening for a 'beat'.

All this is really serious stuff and comes from many years of training. Careless tuning can damage the piano and loosen the tuning pins. It can also spoil the strings, not to mention distorting the bridge and consequently cracking the actual soundboard. Take my word for it that you are far better off paying a professional to tune your piano than attempting it yourself unless you have adequate training and practice.

I am sorry to labour this point, but I have seen too many instruments spoiled by the well-intentioned efforts of amateurs and I am doing you a favour if I can convince you of the seriousness of the matter. Better a small sum to a professional tuner than a huge sum to have to dismantle the piano to replace a major part of the body through folly.

So you have your piano in a carefully-ventilated stable environment. All is well! Or is it? How can you do more harm after that! The answer is all-too easily – and one sure-fire way to spoil any antique, be it table or piano, is the enthusiastic housewife or home help. A few months ago, an acquaintance of mine hired a new housekeeper who had all the right back-ground and references. During her first day she caused an es-timated £2,500-worth of damage. That's about $4,000. How? By polishing.

Good furniture is always wax-polished. Many pianos were at one time given a varnish finish, others were French-polished. The treatment for these is always a preservative wax applied periodically and shone with a lint-free duster. This wax polish is the finest preservative it is possible to have. It is natural, it is flexible and it is eternally attractive.

So when the new housekeeper sprayed an aerosol polish containing silicon she destroyed the patina on the instrument which was the result of many years of careful treatment.

Silicon-based polishes form an artificial coating on sur-faces that cannot readily be removed. It bonds with a waxed surface and cannot be removed without stripping off the en-tire polished surface. If you value your player-piano or any other furniture come to that, avoid at all costs all aerosol pol-ishes whether described as silicone-based or otherwise. Only ever used quality furniture polish, preferably beeswax-based.

For precisely the same reason, replacement of traditional polished or varnished finishes by polyurethane-based paint-on varnishes ought to be a capital offence. These varnishes look awful because they put a false wet-look gloss on materials that should be waxed. Above all, because they are synthetic and related to plastics, timber coated in this material cannot breathe and so will be prone to warping, shrinkage and crack-ing.

If the problems of the player-piano in the home seem rather intimidating, then surely the apparently rich and pro-fessional world of museums can be depended upon to possess and show off the very finest and best-kept instruments in the world. Not a bit of it! Many of the so-called museum collec-tions are depressing demonstrations of high-level curatorial ineptitude to which the public is generally encouraged to con-tribute by way of an admission fee.

Across the world, museums abound that aspire to display collections of mechanical musical instruments. Several are of the highest quality and standing and maintain their instruments to perfection. One of the leaders in this category is the Na-tional Museum in Utrecht, a State-run enterprise that has both excellent State-funded management and a World-class policy as regards restoration, conservation and display. The pianos in this collection, for instance, are professionally maintained at the highest possible condition and play to perfection. Fur-thermore they are demonstrated by professionally trained and knowledgeable guides.

It would be nice to find this really rather simple policy the norm in the world of museums. Sadly this is very far from the case. One South German museum that is on the tourist itiner-ary and is thus responsible for 'entertaining' a truly vast num-ber of visitors every year insists on demonstrating some of the worst-maintained instruments it has been my misfortune to hear. This museum, visited by tourists who come from far and wide, ought to be one of the best in Europe. Its founder-direc-tor is both a leading German expert in mechanical music and a man who thoroughly understands pneumatic instruments. But visitors are treated to a tiny fragment of music that is itself fragmented from a couple of reproducing grands that are in such a poor playing condition that the impression visitors take away with them is of how very poor these old-timer pianos re-ally were.

Another museum, this time in America, displays delicate pneumatic instruments in a large warehouse-type building that

has no environmental control. Not surprisingly the instruments have suffered terribly. Tour guides who clearly have but mini-mal training and no knowledge of the instruments give brief demonstrations of once-superb top-quality reproducing pianos that simply do not play properly. Again, the visitor impression is that the old instruments were rubbish in their time and are rubbish today. Some of the tour guides adopt a patronising attitude to the instruments as if to endorse the dreadful per-formance with an implied 'Well, what do you expect from such an ancient instrument!' This completely overlooks the fact that at one time they represented the pinnacle of pianistic perfor-mance, an objective perfectly capable of being re-attained to-day.

At a private collection in America's East Coast area, the owner welcomes visitors with a performance on a piano that is a travesty of its true capability while an Aeolian Orchestrelle, with all its stops fully drawn and the swell pulled over, wheezes ineptly through an American patriotic song that, while just recognisable to an English visitor with a musical ear, clearly baffled some of the American visitors when I chanced by there.

At the British Piano Museum, now called The Musical Museum, the late and greatly-missed Frank Holland's philoso-phy was that everything had to be in tip-top condition. Re-membered for being a rather unforgiving host, Frank would not tolerate anybody making a sound during the playing of a roll on any of his pianos. He was particularly insistent that young children either be excluded or their parents held responsible for the slightest noise emanating from their siblings. If all that sounds pretty dreadful, it was merely one of Frank's idiosyn-crasies for he was, besides being extremely knowledgeable in many fields, one of the kindest and best friends one might have. And his instruments were always faultless because he was his own severest critic.

Earlier I mentioned the State-funded Nationaal Museum van Speelklok tot Pierement (National Museum From Musi-cal Clock to Street Organ) in Utrecht. Besides the fact that all of the instruments are maintained to the highest degree of per-fection, when a music-roll is performed it is allowed to play in full in the exact manner that was originally intended.

Barrel pianos fall into the same regime. So many people who demonstrate these devices simply turn the handle while displaying an inane grin on their faces. Usually they only play a fraction of a tune and they do it without feeling. If the piano happens to be in tune, then it's a rare bonus. This sort of dem-onstration simply is not good enough to honour the reputa-tion of mechanical instruments.

These examples show some of the display and exhibition variations around the world. My advice is that if you visit a collection or museum (especially if you have had to pay to get in) and the instruments are defective or incorrectly demon-strated, then wade in and say so! Automatic pianos are worth far more respect than many give them.

If you do not know how to keep your instruments in tip-top condition, there are plenty of knowledgeable people around through the membership of the various mechanical musical instrument societies around the world who will assist you.

Let me tell you a little story that's nothing to do with pi-anos. In fact, it's about a fair-organ. Some few years ago I had staying in my home an outspoken young Dutchman who was very knowledgeable about mechanical instruments and, above all, had a brilliant ear for musical pitch. Possessed of a fine command of the English language but possibly lacking in that element of tact that is endemic in the Britons of a certain type and style, he was always free with his views – whether or not they were invited. And so it came about that one Saturday morning when we were out walking and talking we both became aware of the sound of a distant fairground-organ. Yes, the travelling fair had arrived on the village green. We hastened into the mêlée of showmen, steam engines and modern rides with their raucous amplified pop music following our ears for the instrument we had initially heard. Finally we stood before a pleasingly-cased Gavioli showman's organ playing at full belt some suitably Edwardian popular ballad. The organ was well painted but, to put no finer point on it, sounded a little rough at the edges. My friend marched up to the large gentleman wearing the boiler suit, cloth cap and coloured choker who was tending it.

"Good morning, Sir," he began with the sort of overt good humour that prefaces worse – much worse – to follow. "What a splendid organ! When last was it tuned?"

"This marnin'!" came the rather *unrefined* response offered with the directness of somebody about to add 'and what's it to you?'

"Good heavens!" said my young friend to whom both tact and fear are quite foreign. "But can't you hear – it sounds so dreadful! Who did it for you?"

"I done it meself!" came the truculent if ungrammatical rejoinder. He slowly put down his oily rag and turned towards us. I grabbed an available close-by arm and hurried my friend into the anonymity offered by the crowd before the offended Gaviman could disentangle himself from his show front and give chase.

I am not sure what the moral of that story is other than to suggest that maybe you should always fear the best in your friends and visitors – and beware the directness of a comment. Some can hurt or annoy. Just make sure you don't earn it!

Which brings me nicely to dealing with other people's pianos. There's a great temptation to be critical of another's instrument: it's called human nature. That's not to counter that occasionally it takes a third party to recognise something that the owner, through living with his instrument, has not noticed. Do remember, though, that the things never done in real life are to criticise another man's driving ability, his golf-swing or his wife. And never tell a man what you think of his piano or his choice of music *unless he specifically asks you for an opinion!*

Even casual comments can be incautiously barbed. It may well sound better after it's been properly adjusted and with a better music-roll on it – but avoid saying so, directly at least! That way you preserve friendships and noses. Always offer to help, but never do so unless the owner takes up your offer. I mean it is thought rather bad form for the host to leave the room for a moment only to find, on his return, that you've already taken the case apart and are gleefully re-setting the adjustment that he spent hours on only this morning.

When visiting a friend with a reproducing piano, always take note of how the other guests behave! A gathering of piano enthusiasts is a gathering to be seen – and there lies the pun! Usually it is an atmosphere of supreme reverence and no conversation, You enter a room where there is a piano playing – but at first you see nobody, for they are all lying on their backs under the piano watching the parts moving about!

Years ago I played a cruel jape on a good friend that I rather regretted afterwards. It was a simple instance of a juvenile practical joke that went a bit too far. I was invited to dinner in North London by the owner of a very fine Duo-Art grand where I joined a small gathering of admirers in his music room. Several eminent British pianolists, among them self-confessed experts, made up the group. In my trouser pocket I had concealed a perfectly ordinary player-piano brass elbow from one end of which protruded a two-inch long piece of rubber tubing. While everybody was looking upwards, I surreptitiously dropped this on the carpet between the up-turned knees and retired to watch the result.

As soon as somebody noticed it, a shriek went up and the piano was promptly switched off in mid-arpeggio. Then the experts got going trying to decide *[a]* what it was and *[b]* where it was from. Very quickly, each had identified it 'positively' and produced his individual definite answer to both questions. I should have mentioned earlier that there were six of them.

Within minutes, screwdrivers were produced, pliers were urgently called for and produced and, to my horror, the under action was quickly reduced to component pieces laid out on the Axminster. Too late to confess, too embarrassed to comment, I had to watch this painful process unfold. Curiously – and here is the value of experts – somewhere was found for the little brass elbow and its short length of tube, and the action was carefully reassembled.

The story is not quite over yet, for at the end of a very long evening's work, the consensus of opinion, again from the experts, was that it actually sounded much better and the extraneous bit of stuff I had introduced to the party made 'all the difference'. I could never have owned up to the ruse and nor can I ever tell anybody that it was I who was responsible for the whole sad event! I trust you not to give me away…

Lastly, let me pass on a tip. Almost everybody I know has got at least two wrongly-boxed rolls. Sometime, in a hurry, a roll has got into the wrong box and its original box later used as a 'temporary' box for another. Of course, the two boxes and their rolls will never again come together to be correctly sorted out. Then it will happen again and the mis-boxed roll tally moves up to four – and so on and so on. The awful truth is that we've all done it – even I!

To avoid this happening to you, adopt some simple 'roll discipline' with your piano. When you are playing a roll, put the box with its lid on top of the piano where it can be seen. One additionally advantage of this is that you will always know the title of the piece you are playing. The main one, of course, is that it should be easy to put the right roll back into the box.

The late Frank Holland was fanatical about observing this. But, he had more rolls to get confused over than most of us.

Appendix 1
How They Sold Player Pianos:
The Old Adverts of the Day

Producing player pianos was one thing: getting the public to buy them was another. At the end of the 19th Century this was done in the manner now familiar to us today – by shop display, demonstration and advertising. At that time, though, this type of product promotion was very new. Advertising in particular was restrained and generally aimed at the middle and upper class end of an undeniably class-conscious market. However, because many of the instruments that were offered for sale were of American origin, American methods of promotion were quickly introduced into Britain. This style of advertising was frequently viewed with a mixture of horror and trepidation in an era where advertising 'copy' was a curious, even coy, mixture of blatant lies and restrained British under-statement.

There were other ways of promotion and one quickly introduced to Britain by Aeolian was that of product endorsement. In truth it was not an entirely new approach and for years statesmen and nobility had been attributing their health and wealth to various pills, potions, things in bottles and suchlike. The merits of the spa resorts and the seaside, reclining armchairs, bath chairs and hernia trusses were mere extensions of these claims.

As for player pianos, here was something very different! The business of product endorsement, still practised to this day by product-vendors that hire pop stars, film idols and sportsmen, probably savours of 'last resort' tactics to the thinking man. Nowhere was this better epitomised than with the player piano and, before it, the piano-player. Makers did their utmost to cajole leading pianists and conductors to allow themselves to be photographed with their particular instrument, or quoted in the form of an endorsement. Somehow this was particularly transparent and the thought of a top concert performer sitting down and pedalling his way through a music roll was, to the reader of but average intelligence, ludicrous. It clearly did not escape one particular correspondent to *Musical Opinion* who, in January 1902, wrote:

> I am quite at a loss to explain how it comes to pass that distinguished pianists possess these instruments, and should be glad to know whether in each instance current coin of the realm had been paid for the clever machine. I should have thought that a Pianola would be about as useful to a performer as a pair of nutcrackers to an ape!

Oh dear! The industry had been rumbled! But there were more benefits to the player piano, if not necessarily for the pianist, then for the listener. It is related how one of the top concert performers, having cut a reproducing roll, discovered to his chagrin that he had struck no fewer than 360 wrong notes in his performance. It was possible to 'adjust' the master roll to remove these to the undoubted relief of the recording artist and the pleasure of the customers that bought the roll. After all, who could tolerate a performance of anything that was redolent with wrong notes: even one wrong note would grate the sensibilities!

Pianists, whether or not they endorsed player pianos, were sometimes victims of their own success. Put another way, the hype was occasionally greater than the reality. Camille Saint-Saëns (1835-1921) reputedly commented that he had 'heard piano salesmen get a better tone from an instrument than [some] professional pianists'. What price, then, perfection? Not a lot, it seems. Very recently (2003) a commercial CD recording of an international pianist was released that had one particular keyboard note so badly adjusted that the sound died instantly regardless of the pedal. Incredible though it may seem, neither pianist nor recording engineers chose to notice. But you and I will forever hear that maladjusted action.

We have seen how these highly sophisticated reproducing pianos and their actions were expensive and followed a number of attempts over the years at achieving partial expression from music rolls by simpler methods. We have also seen how electric 'expression' pianos with up to half a dozen steps in 'expression' were popular in the 1920-30 period. These offered what might be called ungraduated pedalling as compared with the Duo-Art, which provided no fewer than sixteen different 'shades' of dynamic intensity to cover all extremes of *fortissimo* and *pianissimo* and to produce finely graded crescendos and diminuendos.

The Aeolian Company used the Duo-Art action in its pianos, both grand and upright. In the course of its advertising campaign, Aeolian promoted a series of concerts at Aeolian Hall, New York, at which the New York Symphony Orchestra performed piano concertos with the piano solo part being supplied by a Duo-Art playing a roll. The artist who had originally recorded them always signed these rolls, and it was widely publicised that the soloist at one such concert – Harold Bauer – would be in Chicago at the time of his New York 'performance'. The incentive to witness the great man performing in person was thus replaced by curiosity at watching a machine!

At a London concert, a performance of a Liszt rhapsody was shared between the pianist Cortot playing 'live' and a previously recorded music roll by Cortot. The effect, we are told, was so dovetailed that music critic Ernest Newman said: 'With one's eyes closed, it was impossible to tell which was which.'

The player makers' enthusiasm knew no bounds and their 'ad' copy reflected this. While American adverts tended to suggest that house visitors were generally spoiled grown-up brats 'who expected so much' (which begs the question 'why invite them in the first place?'), the British equivalent was to suggest that a winsome blonde pedalling her way through a music roll was certain to get her man, while the pipe-smoking well-dressed man could woo the woman of his choice with his pedal dexterity.

The Great War altered the emphasis and here we were regaled with images of gallant soldiers going 'over the top' while back home unhappy loved ones wistfully worked their knees up and down through patriotic songs. Not until the carefree 'twenties did we find the pleasures of the dance-floor, the tennis-court and the country club as backgrounds for players, although this time they were usually fully-automatic reproducers.

The styles of promotion are thus every bit a reflection on contemporary social standards, moral climate and both economic and political climate. Some carried strong messages; others were banal and urbane, yet all are part of the player's history.

On the following pages is a representative selection of these advertisements, both trade and consumer, and predominantly from Great Britain but with a comparative eye on events in the United States. In total I have selected some 54 notices from 1901 through to 1929, and each projecting a facet of sales promotion. Many refer to Aeolian for it is by watching in one maker the gradual changes in promotion methods over the years that we begin to appreciate changing taste and fashion. Wherever possible, each is fully annotated as to source and date, and carries a commentary.

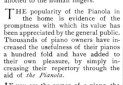
Aeolian in New York manages to get Pianist Josef Hofman to accept a Pianola! Possibly the earliest examples of this sort of endorsement. *The Literary Digest, March 1901.*

Aeolian was not the only US maker to have set up shop in Britain. Melville Clark also had a toehold in the British market for the Apollo which was cheaper than the Pianola. Here the advertising copy is of an explanatory nature, quoting endorsements from Pachmann and Emil Bach. *The Royal Magazine, 1901.*

What Aeolian in New York could do, The Orchestrelle Company in London could match! Paderewski, approaching the peak of his popularity, now decided that he, too, needed a Pianola as, apparently, had Sauer and Rosenthal before him. *Chambers Magazine, May 1st, 1901.*

The World=Famed
ANGELUS PIANO-PLAYER

As purchased by ROYALTY and the World's Greatest Musicians.

THE MOST PERFECT AND ARTISTIC IN TOUCH AND EXPRESSION.

CAN BE OBTAINED AS

Piano-Player Only

OR WITH

Orchestral Organ Combined.

With the ANGELUS you can produce the following effects:—

PIANO PLAYING ALONE   PIANO WITH VOICE
ORCHESTRAL ORGAN ALONE   PIANO WITH VIOLIN OR FLUTE
PIANO WITH FULL ORCHESTRAL ORGAN COMBINED

TESTIMONIAL from
Madame
CLARA BUTT :—

" I think ' The Angelus' splendid! Apart from the pleasure it gives one, I am sure it is instructive in every sense of the word.
" I have heard all the other inventions of this kind, but the ANGELUS is far and away the BEST."

Full Illustrated Catalogue
Post Free.

J. HERBERT MARSHALL,
REGENT HOUSE,
233b, Regent Street, London, W.

Aeolian's only major rival for the British market was the Angelus for which J Herbert Marshall was the enthusiastic but not very creative agent. Marshall promoted the product heavily and extensively but seldom varied his presentation: in later years the copy was small and repetitive. *The Royal Magazine, 1901.*

APOLLO PIANO
☙ PLAYER.

THE LATEST TESTIMONIAL!
MADAME ADELINA PATTI writes :

CRAIG-Y-NOS CASTLE, *May 31st, 1902.*

"The Apollo Piano Player I have purchased from you is marvellous, I cannot find words to express my admiration for this most wonderful invention. I have seen others, but yours is the one I consider perfect, both for Piano and Voice. The transposing device is most ingenious, and I congratulate you on this greatest of all musical inventions."

ADELINA PATTI,
BARONESS CEDERSTRÖM.

*"THE APOLLO" is the most perfect and simplest Piano Player in the World.
No Lessons Required.*

£52 nett.

The only Piano Player that transposes any Composition to suit the Voice or Instrument into ANY KEY.

WRITE FOR OUR ILLUSTRATED CATALOGUE "Y."

119, REGENT STREET, LONDON, W.

Now it was the turn of the Apollo to link up with a very popular performer of the time, this time the great singer Adelina Patti. It was a clever move to associate a singer rather than a pianist with a piano-player for surely the vocalist is more likely to have a use for such a contrivance. The subtlety was most likely lost on the readership though. *The Illustrated London News (Coronation Souvenir), June 1902.*

A Pianola for Christmas

THE PIANOLA MASTERS ANY PIANO—ANYONE CAN MASTER THE PIANOLA.

Every musical composition contains an idea just as every story embodies a plot. Reading is practically a universal accomplishment, and to understand and appreciate the plot of a story is therefore a simple matter. It would be equally easy to grasp the idea in a musical composition were one able to play, but unfortunately comparatively few can play the piano by hand. The difficulty lies in the acquisition of technique or key-striking. By the purchase of a Pianola this difficulty is eliminated ; the Pianola possesses unlimited technique – the technique of the world's music. Further, the Pianola provides in a simple manner for playing with expression. Three little levers control the whole keyboard of the piano, and with them the person playing exercises full command over *tempo*, accent, and all effects of light and shade. A Pianola makes for brightness in the home. Especially is this so at Christmas time, for at dances, parties, and other social functions its value can scarcely be estimated.

The Pianola may be had on the Hire System. It costs £65.

The Orchestrelle Company,
225 Regent St., London, W.

City Showrooms : 67, 69, 71 Farringdon Road, E.C.
AGENTS IN ALL PRINCIPAL TOWNS.

We shall be glad if you will call, or write for our special catalogue. When writing please ask for "Connoisseur" Catalogue

The whole piano-player industry was shocked by a bold and pioneering move by Aeolian that Christmas. The Orchestrelle Company took a full-page advert in colour! The contemporary three-colour printing process was used to render an artist's painting into vibrant colour with blue border and black text. The stakes had been raised again! *The Connoisseur, December 1902.*

He plays best who plays The Cecilian.

THE CECILIAN
The Perfect Piano Player.

THE CECILIAN
is the Premier Piano Player of the Day.
Childlike Simplicity.
Exquisite Delicacy.
Infinite Capacity.
Tremendous Technique
A Mechanical Triumph
An Artistic Ideal.

THE CECILIAN
Free Daily Recitals
in our Spacious Salon
44, Gt. Marlborough St.
3.30 to 4.30.
Special Recitals.
Wednesdays.
With Soloist.
Admission by Visiting Card.

WE are now established in magnificent Premises at 44, Great Marlborough St., London, W., where we carry an exceedingly Large Stock of the Cecilian Piano Players and Cecilian Music, operating the Circulating Library direct with purchasers of Cecilians in all parts of the United Kingdom, and supplying Music at very short notice, through our numerous Agents, who are thus saved the trouble and expense of carrying a stock of Music Rolls.

FARRAND ORGAN CO.
44, GREAT MARLBOROUGH STREET, LONDON, W.

Send for Descriptive Booklets.

That same month, Farrand moved into its new premises off London's Regent Street and took a full-page advert in the trade's leading paper. *Musical Opinion, December 1902.*

Growth of Appreciation.

An Instance

A CAREFUL investigation of the Pianola invariably leads to surprise and delight. The more you see and hear the instrument the better you enjoy and appreciate it. This is invariably the rule, and the more musical a person is the more appreciative he becomes.

Josef Hofmann, the famous pianist, when he first saw the Pianola, said of it :

"I anticipate much pleasure from learning to play this exceedingly ingenious device which reproduces with such astonishing accuracy the masterworks of music."

A month later, April 18, he wrote :

"I find that your instrument offers facilities for expression that will enable an intelligent player to give a very close imitation of hand playing. I have been surprised to discover to what an extent one can, with a little practice, control the dynamic effects."

Hofmann also says in the same letter :

"In all the essentials of artistic piano playing, the Pianola is the best instrument of this type."

The Pianola does not injure the piano in any way. Its felt-covered fingers rest upon the piano-keys and strike the notes in their proper relation one to another as indicated on the music-sheet. With its aid any member of your household may play upon the piano even if he or she literally does not know one note from another—not only one or two selections, but every piece of music ever written for the piano-forte. Grand and light operas, Liszt's Rhapsodies, Sousa's marches and the latest popular airs are practically " at your fingers' ends." You have all the pleasure of hand-playing because you control the expression, which is the soul of music. Estimate for yourself the profit and pleasure the Pianola would bring you in a single year.

We are demonstrating the possibilities of this remarkable instrument to all who call at our exhibition rooms. We are always glad to show the instrument to anyone sufficiently interested to visit us. You need not feel the usual hesitancy about going to see a thing you do not expect to purchase. as we have rooms especially set apart for displaying the Pianola, and employ a large staff of men whose sole duty it is to play the instrument and explain it to visitors.

The marked popularity of the Pianola in the home leads to the belief that an examination of this instrument is to the interest of everyone.

The Pianola *can be bought by monthly instalments if desired.* Price £65.

Send for Catalogue G.G.

THE ORCHESTRELLE COMPANY,
225 REGENT STREET, LONDON, W.

The Connoisseur

The Metrostyle Pianola.
The only Piano-player indicating interpretation as well as providing correct technique.

NOTE.—The word 'Pianola' stands for the name of one instrument, and not for piano-players in general.

THE first aim of a piano-player is to enable anyone to play the piano so far as key-striking is concerned. The object and attainment of the Pianola are much higher. It provides for rendering music with expression, so that the result is musical and artistic, and such as entitles the instrument to rank as a musical invention of the highest importance.

Every roll of music prepared for the Metrostyle Pianola has been played over by some musician of repute — Paderewski, Bauer, Carreno, Moszkowski, Strauss, Chaminade, to mention a few well-known names.

A red line which the interpreter marks on the music-roll indicates his idea of its rendition, and the person who owns a Metrostyle Pianola can faithfully reproduce the artist's playing. It may be that you have not heard a great pianist play ; but if you obtain a Metrostyle Pianola you can play as he plays, and in your own home. It is not binding on you to follow the Metrostyle marking absolutely. It may be used in whole or in part, or disregarded altogether. and you are free to give your own interpretation : but the value of the Metrostyle Pianola is that for the first time in the history of music it is possible to put on permanent record the playing of great musicians for anyone to reproduce now or at any future time.

The Metrostyle Pianola may be seen by anyone who calls at Aeolian Hall. When writing for particulars, please specify Catalogue AA.

THE ORCHESTRELLE COMPANY,
Aeolian Hall, 135-6-7, New Bond Street, London, W.

Time passed by and the industry copywriters never seemed to tire of the task of re-inventing their wheel. Advertising 'copy' at this time tended to be wordy and rather patronising. *The Illustrated Sporting & Dramatic News, April 1904.*

The ANGELUS DIAPHRAGM PNEUMATIC and the HUMAN FINGER

The Diaphragm Pneumatic when in action or "striking" is filled with buoyant air. which gives a resilient touch, just like the human finger. Note the absence of creases or corners, which insures greater durability.

DIAPHRAGM PNEUMATIC INFLATED FOR STRIKING

The Bellows Pneumatic is worked by an exhaust; that is, when it strikes a note the air is entirely withdrawn from it, which causes it to collapse with a hard staccato touch, in no way resembling the pliancy and flexibility of the human finger.

BELLOWS PNEUMATIC WITH AIR EXHAUSTED FOR STRIKING

THE Diaphragm Pneumatic is the only means ever devised to give the real human touch. When in action it is an air inflated cushion, with the same firm but resilient and buoyant touch that characterizes the human fingers. All other pneumatics are collapsed when in action, withdrawing from them the buoyancy of the air, resulting in a hard, mechanical touch. The

Diaphragm Pneumatic

is an exclusive feature of the

ANGELUS

and together with the famous Phrasing Lever (patented) and the wonderful Melodant (patented) have made the ANGELUS pre-eminently *the* artistic piano-player.

KNABE-ANGELUS	EMERSON-ANGELUS	LINDEMAN & SONS-ANGELUS	ANGELUS PIANO
The Peerless Knabe Piano and the Angelus.	The sweet-toned Emerson Piano and the Angelus.	The original and celebrated Lindeman Piano and the Angelus.	An excellent piano made expressly for the Angelus.

THE WILCOX & WHITE CO.,   **MERIDEN, CONN.**

Pioneers in the Piano-Player Industry

ANGELUS HALL   REGENT ST.   LONDON

In America, some makers preferred to blind their readers with science. In this notice from an unidentified American magazine of about 1904, the Wilcox & White Company has chosen to tell its potential customers all about diaphragm pneumatics filled with 'buoyant air'. But did it sell pianos?

Aeolian in the shape of London's Orchestrelle Company continued to spend heavily on promotion and took expensive space in all the leading magazines, often paying premium price for 'special position' status. By now the Pianola had gained a new selling point – Metrostyle. *The Connoisseur, September 1904.*

THE SIMPLEX PIANO PLAYER

The New Way

is the easiest to manipulate of all the piano players, and gives greater control and range of expression than any other instrument of the kind. That is our statement to you, and it is supported by what Mascagni, Madame Calvé, and other leading musicians have said in praise of the SIMPLEX. But we do not wish you to be guided by our opinion or the opinion of musical experts, however famous. We say to you,

TRY FOR YOURSELF.

Sit down to the SIMPLEX, and sit down to the other piano-players, and ascertain by actual trial which offers you the greatest advantages. With the SIMPLEX PIANO-PLAYER anybody, whether ignorant of or expert at music, can play anything.

Price £52 net.

Easy Terms of Payment can be arranged. Illustrated Catalogue No. 15 Post Free on application.

WHOLESALE DEPOT: The Simplex Piano-Player Co.
15, Colonial Buildings, Hatton Garden, London, E.C.

WEST END DEPOT: 15a, Hanover Square, W.

CITY DEPOT: 104 & 105, Bishopsgate Street Within.

And 84 BRANCH DEPOTS.

The Old Way

The ease with which a machine might be worked was always best got across by portraying a young woman confidently working it. This was a recurring theme as depicted in this unidentified advert from a British consumer periodical of about 1904.

Psychology was another powerful weapon in the advertisement-writers' quiver. Especially when it came to promoting not a piano-player, but one of the earliest player-pianos. Here the American reader is told outright that the Cecilian appeals to everyone, and that means you! *Harper's Magazine, November 1905.*

In the United States, a curious and oblique approach was used to induce sales. What purported to be 'Paris society' or, as in this case, 'London society' was promoted as a reason why, if the American hostess wanted to be well-thought-of, she should do as they (apparently) did in the fashionable mansions of London – and buy a Pianola piano-player! *Munsey's Magazine, June 1905.*

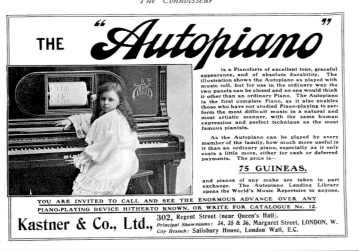

THE "*Autopiano*"

is a Pianoforte of excellent tone, graceful appearance, and of absolute durability. The illustration shows the Autopiano as played with music roll, but for use in the ordinary way the two panels can be closed and no one would think it other than an ordinary Piano. The Autopiano is the first complete Piano, as it also enables those who have not studied Piano-playing to perform the most difficult music in a natural and most artistic manner, with the same human expression and perfect technique as the most famous pianists.

As the Autopiano can be played by every member of the family, how much more useful is it than an ordinary piano, especially as it only costs a little more, either for cash or deferred payments. The price is—

75 GUINEAS,

and pianos of any make are taken in part exchange. The Autopiano Lending Library opens the World's Music Repertoire to anyone.

YOU ARE INVITED TO CALL AND SEE THE ENORMOUS ADVANCE OVER ANY PIANO-PLAYING DEVICE HITHERTO KNOWN, OR WRITE FOR CATALOGUE No. 12.

Kastner & Co., Ltd., 302, Regent Street (near Queen's Hall).
Principal Showrooms: 34, 35 & 36, Margaret Street, LONDON, W.
City Branch: Salisbury House, London Wall, E.C.

Kastner, although also advertising a complete player-piano, manages staid and rather boring words ending with an invitation to visit the company and see the enormous advances that the text has barely described. *The Connoisseur, December 1905.*

You may not be able to read music—but you *can* play it

Not so very long ago there was but one way to master the piano, and a very laborious way it was. Scales and exercises, exercises and scales, year in and year out—that was the only way that one could obtain musical proficiency. The Pianola Piano has changed all that. With the Pianola Piano you start to-day where the scales and exercises ended—as a proficient pianist. You get straight to the real pleasures of music—the expression of your thoughts and emotions.

The Pianola Piano

READS THE MUSIC—YOU INTERPRET IT

The music-roll takes the place of the sheet music, the delicate mechanism of the Pianola Piano is the brain that reads the notes, and the fingers that play them. The rest is left to you, and by the wonderfully susceptible devices of the Pianola Piano you are enabled to interpret the music in your own way equally as much as if your hands were touching the keys. Note by note the music is wholly under your control.

The word "Pianola" is a trade mark, and therefore if you would have the only piano-playing instrument recognised by the great musical authorities, and possessing the exclusive devices which have made it famous, you must choose no instrument that does not bear the word "Pianola."

The Pianola Piano is a combination of the Pianola with the famous Steinway, Weber, or Steck Pianos

Call at Æolian Hall, or write for Catalogue "X"

THE **Orchestrelle Co.** AEOLIAN HALL 135-6-7 New Bond Street, London, W.

AD. XIX

A change in the British promotion of the Pianola player-piano is noticeable around this time. An inference at educational merits is contained in a well-written advert that suggests both ease of use and personal control. *The Connoisseur, c.1907.*

Insure Against Dull Evenings

BY SECURING A

PIANOLA PIANO.

SOON, very soon now, we shall be in the dark days of winter. Perhaps you have recollections of how long and dreary the evenings can be ; perhaps you have experienced days which seemed to be "all evening."

Owners of Pianola Pianos do not find that time hangs heavily on their hands ; they can fill their homes with melody ; they are always able to find enjoyment absorbed in a merry whirl of light and catchy airs or seriously studying the master works that have been written for the piano.

Why do you not do likewise ? Why not make music this winter's recreation ?

If you already own a piano why not exchange it for a Pianola Piano, receiving for it its full value ?

The Pianola Piano, as its name implies, is a high-grade piano embodying the Pianola with its unique devices, the Metrostyle and Themodist, and so can be played by hand or music rolls. The piano part may be either the Weber or Steck piano, both instruments of the very highest grade.

The Metrostyle is a guide and instructor in unfamiliar compositions, as it admits of the reproduction of interpretations specially provided by famous musicians. The Themodist accents the notes of the melody and prevents the theme being overpowered by the accompaniment.

The Pianola Piano can be obtained either for Cash or Deferred Payments. You are invited to call at Æolian Hall for a practical demonstration. Full particulars are given in Catalogue "T."

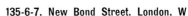

THE ORCHESTRELLE COMPANY,

ÆOLIAN HALL,

135-6-7, New Bond Street, London, W

Seasonal changes were another boost to sales. References to the dark days of winter and dull, dreary evenings were to present just the right climate for suggesting that the reader needed a Pianola to prevent 'time hanging heavily'. Here the man of the house leans nonchalantly in the doorway as the apple of his eye somehow manages to sort out her feet under a voluminous (not to mention hazardous) skirt. *The Sphere, October 10th, 1908.*

2 [SUPPLEMENT.]   THE SKETCH.   SEPT. 2, 1908.

Piano-playing is no longer the privilege of the gifted few— it is within the ability of all.

BY reason of the Pianola, the Metrostyle and the Themodist, the Pianola Piano places everyone on an equality in the producing of music—allows everyone to play according to their own desires. Were the Pianola Piano not equipped with the Metrostyle and Themodist it would be difficult for the non-musician to play an unfamiliar composition artistically. He would have full control over the music, but he would not know how to use that control. The Metrostyle directs his control and enables him to give an artistic rendering. When he has learnt, by using the Metrostyle, the intricacies of rhythm and tempo he can dispense with its use and play the piece in accordance with his own ideas of interpretation.

The Themodist is the only satisfactory means of accenting melody notes, of giving to each note its true musical value.

You can exchange your present piano for the Pianola Piano, receiving its full value. Full particulars of the Pianola Piano are given in Catalogue "N."

THE ORCHESTRELLE COMPANY,

ÆOLIAN HALL,

135-6-7, New Bond Street, London, W.

The outright benefits of the Pianola were now presented in a compelling, direct manner. Still, though, we find piano-playing the province of the woman who, when she is not pedalling the Pianola, is twirling ridiculously long necklaces! *The Sketch, September 2nd, 1908.*

As if to suggest that might just be a shortage around the corner, more psychology went into suggesting that you dare not risk having to face the New Year without a Pianola! *The Illustrated Sporting & Dramatic News, January 1909.*

IX.

Some sound home truths expressed in well-honed (for the time) text but ending with a firm bash at its rivals and their 'so called Player-Pianos'. Once again the man of the house prefers to listen to his companion play rather than take any active part in the proceedings. Incidentally, this is the first Aeolian (London) advert to be signed by the agency artist Howard Somersett. *The Connoisseur, April 1910.*

A sure-fire way to antagonise your readers today might well be to ask them if some pretty well-known character was unknown to them. But miraculously The Orchestrelle Company got away with asking some condescending questions. *The Connoisseur, c.1909.*

Two More Royal Patrons For The Pianola

The Queen of Italy

The King of the Belgians

Other Royal Patrons:

Her Late Majesty, Victoria, Queen of England
Her Majesty, Alexandra, Queen of England
H. I. M. Dowager Empress of Russia
H. M. Queen of Spain
H. M. Queen of Norway
H. I. M. The German Emperor
H. M. The Austrian Emperor
His Late Majesty, Carlos, King of Portugal
H. I. M. The Tsar of Russia
H. M. King of Spain
H. M. Tsar of Bulgaria
H. M. Shah of Persia
H. M. King of Siam
H. M. Khan of Baloochistan
H. R. H., George, Prince of Wales
H. R. H., Henry, Prince of Prussia
H. I. and R. H. Archduke of Austria
H. R. H. Duchess of Argyll
H. R. H. Princess of Battenburg
H. R. H. Duchess of Fife
H. R. H., Victoria Mary, Princess of Wales
H. R. H. Princess of Schleswig-Holstein
H. R. H. Princess of Hohenlohe-Langenburg
H. R. H. Princess of Hesse
H. R. H. Duke of Connaught

THE manager of the Aeolian Company's Paris branch writes: "In addition to the names of distinguished patrons in Italy, our Turin agent has recently received an order to exchange the ———— Piano-player, in the possession of Queen Helena of Italy, for a Themodist PIANOLA, which I believe is the only piano-playing instrument at present in the possession of the Royal Italian Family. This is of course not counting the Duchess d'Aosta and the Queen Dowager, who purchased instruments from us some time ago."

The manager of the Aeolian Company's London branch writes: "The new King of the Belgians purchased a PIANOLA when he was Prince of Flanders. To make your list of Royal patrons correct, the name of the Prince of Flanders should be omitted and the King of the Belgians added."

Royalty is in a position to know and secure the best article of its kind in every department of manufacture. It occasionally happens, however, as in the case of Queen Helena of Italy, and the late King Carlos of Portugal, that some other make of Piano-player is originally selected. *But it is especially significant that as the Royal owner acquires familiarity with instruments of this type, the Pianola is eventually substituted.*

THE AEOLIAN COMPANY

AEOLIAN HALL,   362 Fifth Avenue,   NEW YORK

The Connoisseur

Portrait specially drawn for the Orchestrelle Co. by Joseph Simpson, R.B.A

Saint-Saëns endorses the Pianola

"I must congratulate you on your wonderful invention, the Metrostyle. It will always be of exceeding interest both to the composer as well as to the public. To the former it provides a permanent record of his own compositions, and it enables anyone to play these compositions in the way the composer intended."   C. SAINT-SAËNS

THE Metrostyle is found only in the Pianola, and the Pianola can be had combined with the world-famous Steinway, Weber, and Steck Pianos. The complete instrument—the Pianola Piano—is the Piano of to-day.

With a Pianola Piano in your home the whole world of music is yours to explore at will. No other instrument can or does offer you so many facilities for the study and enjoyment of music. It is only by the purchase of a Pianola Piano that you can enjoy the full fascination of playing *all* the music you would like to. As the Pianola is of such interest to men like Saint-Saëns, Paderewski, Richter, Strauss, and the many others whose opinions we have lately published, is it not of the greatest importance to *you* to spend a few minutes at Æolian Hall investigating the Pianola Piano? And yet you have apparently omitted so far to find out of what intense interest the Pianola Piano *must* be to you. On the Piano which is already in your home you can at best play but little. Why not see about exchanging that piano for one on which you can play everything?

You can obtain the Pianola Piano either for cash or by deferred payments. Call at Æolian Hall for a practical demonstration of this wonderful instrument, or write to us for the full particulars and terms of purchase, which are given in Catalogue "A.A."

  THE ORCHESTRELLE CO.,
ÆOLIAN HALL,
135-6-7, New Bond Street, LONDON, W.
And at PARIS : BERLIN : NEW YORK : MELBOURNE : SYDNEY, etc.

XI.

And 1912 brought back to the forefront a fresh round of unlikely endorsements. Here the illustrious Charles Camille Saint-Saëns apparently bounds to laud the advantages of the Metrostyle. *The Connoisseur, January 1912.*

In America, the readers were clearly tiring of being told which great pianist had just bought himself another Pianola. They expected better than that – and Aeolian gave it to them – Royalty, no less! Again there seems to be some licence as to whether or not the kings and queens listed actually paid money for their Pianolas. Top of the list, for example, is Queen Victoria. Can you imagine our aged Monarch, still in her protracted mourning for her beloved Albert forty years back, and approaching the end of her long life (she died in 1901) buying a Pianola, let alone using it! *Country Life in America, 1910.*

The man who founded the London Promenade Concerts, no less, was next in line for patting Aeolian's back. Incidentally, Aeolian commissioned the artist Joseph Simpson to create these black and white likenesses of the celebrities: the originals used to hang in London's Aeolian Hall. *The Connoisseur, March 1912.*

The Connoisseur

Sir Henry J. Wood endorses the PIANOLA

"I have heard your Pianola to-day for the first time, and I am intensely interested and astonished at its marvellous performances. It is musical and artistic, and when used in connection with the Metrostyle simply stands alone and cannot be classed with any other instrument played by auto-means.
(Sir) "HENRY J. WOOD."

THE Pianola Piano removes all the manipulative difficulties of piano playing and guides you as surely as if the great composers themselves were prompting you, but still leaves you free to interpret music in your own way. The music-roll plays the notes—faultlessly. The expression, the feeling, the tempo, the modulations are yours.

Your interpretation is personal, and distinctive; your feelings have full sway over the melody, and in this the Pianola Piano is peculiar. Those remarkable devices, the Metrostyle and Themodist, which give you so complete a mastery over the music, can never be duplicated by any other piano-playing instrument. The Pianola Piano is a combination of the wonderful Pianola with the world-famous Steinway, Weber, or Steck Piano.

Portrait specially drawn for the Orchestrelle Co. by Joseph Simpson, R.B.A.

THE METROSTYLE bestows upon you the gift of musical understanding. Shows you how the great composers or their most gifted exponents would interpret the melody you are playing. The world's leading musicians have declared that they would give no serious consideration to any piano-player without this device.

THE THEMODIST brings out the complete melody of the simplest ballad or the most complicated composition. It accents, note by note, the actual melody and subdues all other parts, whether above or below. The Themodist gives you an absolute governable touch. It is an exclusive feature of the Pianola Piano.

Call at Æolian Hall and hear the Pianola Piano play your favourite melodies, or write for Catalogue "A.A."

 **THE ORCHESTRELLE CO.,**
ÆOLIAN HALL,
135-6-7, New Bond Street, London, W.
And at PARIS, BERLIN, NEW YORK, MELBOURNE, SYDNEY, etc.

The name Pianola is not, as many think, a name for any and all piano-playing devices. It is a Registered Trade Mark, applicable only to the instruments made by the Orchestrelle Co.

XIII.

Humperdinck Endorses the PIANOLA ::

❝ "The Metrostyle Pianola which I have just heard has filled me with admiration and wonder. Although I have heard instruments play the piano before, I had no idea it was possible to play with the taste and expression of an artiste, and the Metrostyle, it seems to me, is almost as valuable as the instrument itself. Your success with the Metrostyle Pianola should be very great."

(Signed) E. HUMPERDINCK

Specially drawn for the Orchestrelle Company by Joseph Simpson, R.B.A.

THE critical perception of the famous composer of "The Miracle," "Die Königskinder," and "Hansel and Gretel," is captivated by the artistic charms of the Pianola. It has filled him with "admiration and wonder."

❝ How much greater the pleasure and wonder of the untaught musician who, although ignorant of every law of music, finds himself able to sympathetically interpret the works of the great composers. Yet that is the power the Pianola bestows.

❝ With a Pianola Piano the difficulties that have stood between you and the enjoyment of music exist no longer. You actually become the versatile musician you have so often longed to be. You play brilliantly, no "stumbles" or hesitation mar your performance. Although the Pianola Piano plays the right notes for you, the interpretation is wholly yours; and if the love of music is strong within you, your rendition may be as sympathetic as that of the composer himself. This wonderful response to the player's will is found only in the Pianola Piano with the Metrostyle and Themodist.

THE METROSTYLE

The Metrostyle is the feature of the Pianola Piano that first won for it the unstinted praise of the most famous musicians. The Metrostyle enables the novice to play the most complicated music with all the colour and feeling of a finished musician. It is the only practical expression guide ever invented.

THE THEMODIST

The Themodist brings out the melody clearly above the accompaniment. This device gives notes their true value that the composer meant to be sounded delicately, and prevents them from obscuring the melody a common defect in other piano-playing instruments. The Themodist gives an absolutely governable touch.

❝ *The Pianola Piano is a combination of the only perfect piano-player : the Pianola—with the best in pianos—the famous Steinway, Weber, or Steck Piano. Call at Æolian Hall and play it for yourself, or write for Catalogue "A A"*

THE ORCHESTRELLE CO.,
ÆOLIAN HALL,
135-6-7, New Bond Street, London, W.
And at PARIS, BERLIN, NEW YORK, MELBOURNE, SYDNEY, etc.

XXL

Humperdinck was the next master to be courted and won over by Aeolian. He believes the Metrostyle to be the most tasteful thing he has come across. *The Connoisseur, April 1912.*

An artistic triumph for the Pianola

Played at Queen's Hall with the London Symphony Orchestra, conducted by Herr Arthur Nikisch,

the Pianola recently vindicated once and for all the unique position which it holds in the artistic world. On this occasion the Pianola was used to play the well-known Greig Concerto in A Minor and the Liszt Hungarian Fantasie. The Pianola was also used to accompany the celebrated vocalist, Miss Elena Gerhardt, in songs by Strauss and Wolf. Immense enthusiasm was aroused amongst the public and press by this concert, but none greater than that of Herr Arthur Nikisch himself, who wrote after the performance : "Save for the fact that the instrument supplies the performer with absolutely perfect technique, the Pianola should never again be referred to as a mechanical instrument."

Call at Æolian Hall and play the Pianola Piano, or write for Catalogue "AA".

THE ORCHESTRELLE Co. Ltd.
ÆOLIAN HALL
135-6-7, New Bond Street, London, W.

A I   XVII

KRANICH · & · BACH
Ultra-Quality PIANOS and PLAYER PIANOS

The Kranich & Bach makes its appeal to people whose musical tastes are above the average—people who appreciate real tonal beauty—people whose business intelligence teaches them that cheapness of price means disappointing weakness of construction, transitory tonal qualities and false economy —people who know that only in the substantial, artistic construction of the Kranich & Bach, can they get the permanent worth which they seek.

Obtainable anywhere—write for catalog

KRANICH & BACH, 235 E. 23d St., New York

Player Grand Piano—supreme in artistic playing possibilities—the only player grand piano without evidence of self-playing mechanism when played manually.

$1,250
(f.o.b. N.Y.)

In America Kranich & Bach secured sales by oblique humiliation. Its pianos, they said, appealed to those people 'whose musical tastes are above the average'. No aspiring player-piano owner would want to be identified by others in his social circle as a person who preferred an *inferior* player piano! One interesting aspect of this well-presented photographic advert is that while the player is still a female, her two men are looking on attentively and clearly focussed on her music. *Arts & Decorations, September 1912.*

That great concert venue London's Queen's Hall, destroyed during the blitz yet still desperately missed by many a serious music-lover, was the venue of a curious public concert under the baton of Arthur Nikisch. The soloist wasn't even a player-piano: it was a piano-player! And The Orchestrelle Company made the very most of it! *The Connoisseur, August 1912.*

The Orchestrelle Company had a new policy now – Keep it Simple! Take one feature of the Pianola and concentrate on what it does. *The London Magazine, October 1912.*

Back to teaching, this time let the master performer teach you how to play. Paderewski once more gets roped in to promote the Metrostyle. *The Connoisseur, May 1913.*

The coming of the electric piano revolutionised the American home. Now the woman could be portrayed as the one relaxing in an armchair while the piano did all the work. The text explained how you could now listen to the finest artists in the world in your own home. Compelling stuff from this unidentified by c.1912 copy.

How Mme. Bloomfield-Zeisler played a jest on some friends

Mme. Bloomfield Zeisler, the eminent pianiste, while playing to some friends suddenly rose and left the piano. Her playing, however, continued to the bewilderment of the company.

Mme. Zeisler laughingly confessed that a player attachment on a second grand piano in the studio had been started at a given signal. Mme. Zeisler was acting a part, while the player produced the music. Several guests, however, still objected that the technique and interpretation were Mme. Zeisler's own, whereupon she further explained that the instrument was the Welte-Mignon Autograph Player, which actually rendered her own playing and so exactly that the most delicate musical judgment could detect no difference.

The WELTE-MIGNON AUTOGRAPH · PIANO

brings to your home the personal interpretations of the world's greatest masters of the piano. Seated comfortably in your easy chair you can hear the marvellous technique, the brilliance, the living soul of Paderewski, of Hofmann, of de Pachmann, of Grieg, of Busoni, of all the masters of the pianoforte

M. WELTE & SONS, Inc.
273 FIFTH AVE.   NEW YORK CITY

Welte Mignons built in following styles: Welte Piano, with keyboard; Welte Piano without keyboard; and Welte Attachment to grand pianos.

Suddenly, the player-piano – this time a reproducing one – takes a back seat and, no longer centre-stage, the subject of this advert is a stylish trio more or less ignoring the Welte-Mignon in the background. *Country Life in America, c.1913.*

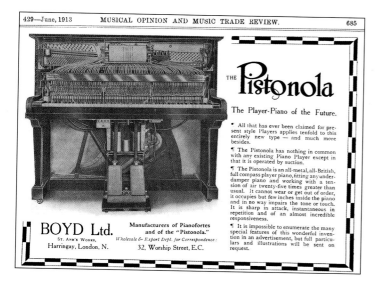

429—June, 1913   MUSICAL OPINION AND MUSIC TRADE REVIEW.   685

THE Pistonola

The Player-Piano of the Future.

¶ All that has ever been claimed for present style Players applies tenfold to this entirely new type — and much more besides.

¶ The Pistonola has nothing in common with any existing Piano Player except in that it is operated by suction.

¶ The Pistonola is an all-metal, all-British, full compass player piano, fitting any under-damper piano and working with a tension of air twenty-five times greater than usual. It cannot wear or get out of order, it occupies but few inches inside the piano and in no way impairs the tone or touch. It is sharp in attack, instantaneous in repetition and of an almost incredible responsiveness.

¶ It is impossible to enumerate the many special features of this wonderful invention in an advertisement, but full particulars and illustrations will be sent on request.

BOYD Ltd.
ST. ANN'S WORKS,
Harringay, London, N.

Manufacturers of Pianofortes and of the "Pistonola."
Wholesale & Export Dept. for Correspondence :
32, Worship Street, E.C.

In London, the extraordinary Pistonola took the player world by storm just before the First World War. No fragile wood, no leather pouches and no rubber cloth – just carbon pistons sliding in metal cylinders! Was this the way ahead? The industry held its breath. *Musical Opinion, June 1913.*

The Pianola Piano
is the choice of kings.

The manufacturers of the Pianola Piano have been favoured by Appointments to practically every reigning house in Europe.

In just the same way that the leading musicians of every nation have recognised the technical and artistic value of the Pianola Piano and have accorded it their praise and support, so the rulers of nations, first in all matters of culture and good taste, have given the Pianola Piano a prominent place in their households and bestowed their highest honours upon its makers.

Whilst the Pianola Piano is to be found in the homes of kings, its pleasures may be enjoyed by all, for it is sold at prices so low and on terms so easy that any home can own one.

Learn to-day how easy it is to purchase a Pianola Piano by giving your present piano in part exchange, and make your home, in the matter of musical resources, the equal of a king's palace.

The Pianola Piano is the famous STEINWAY, WEBER, or STECK PIANO with a genuine Pianola contained within its case. It is illustrated and described in Catalogue "A.A."

The ORCHESTRELLE Co.
ÆOLIAN HALL
135-6-7 NEW BOND STREET, LONDON, W.

It was several years since Aeolian had banged the Royalty drum in America. Now The Orchestrelle Company in London picked up on it, only here it decided not to print the tedious list of kings and queens that had been sent – er, sorry! Had *bought* – Pianolas. *The Connoisseur, June 1913.*

The Connoisseur

The highest development of the Piano and the Pianola
in one instrument.

The grand piano is the piano in the highest stage of its development. It is the invariable choice of concert pianists, and every person of deep musical feeling aspires to have one.

The Grand Pianola Piano
(Steinway, Weber, or Steck)

represents the successful union, in one complete instrument, of the grand piano and the genuine Pianola. By its means those who have no technical knowledge of music can play every musical work of importance ever composed, and command in its performance the beautiful quality and rich volume of tone which only a grand piano can give.

In appearance this instrument retains all the artistic lines of the ordinary grand piano, and offers the musician exactly the usual facilities for hand playing.

The grand pianos in which the genuine Pianola is incorporated are the famous Steinway, Weber, and Steck, all of which stand in the front rank of modern pianos.

Call and Play the Grand Pianola Piano at Aeolian Hall, or write for Catalogue "A.A."

The ORCHESTRELLE Company
ÆOLIAN HALL
135-6-7 NEW BOND STREET, LONDON, W.

The same publication, the following month, this time with a player who appears to have dressed the part so that he can pedal a grand before a party of the revelling classes. The peak of London Aeolian promotion was being approached in terms of presentational quality and perfection. *The Connoisseur, July 1913.*

MADAME CHAMINADE AND THE PIANOLA AT ÆOLIAN HALL.

But a few months ago the Pianola was heard with the London Symphony Orchestra, conducted by Herr Arthur Nikisch, at the Queen's Hall, London, and the praise on this occasion established for all time the supremacy of this instrument.

Further proof that the artistic capabilities of the Pianola places it far above all other piano playing instruments was given recently at Aeolian Hall, when Madame Chaminade, the eminent French composer, played in compositions for two pianos, the other part being played by means of the Pianola.

None but an instrument capable of the most subtle nuances of expression and of exactly reproducing the varying touch of the human hand could have scored a triumph in such close contrast to the hand-playing of a brilliant pianist performing in works of her own composition.

No one contemplating the purchase of a piano-playing instrument should have any but the one recognised by the great musicians of the day the genuine Pianola Piano which combines the Pianola and its exclusive devices with the famous Steinway, Weber or Steck Pianos.

Call at Aeolian Hall and play the Pianola Piano, or write for Catalogue "A.A."

THE ORCHESTRELLE COMPANY,
ÆOLIAN HALL,
135-6-7, New Bond Street, LONDON, W.

A hark-back to that Queen's Hall performance on push-up as an Aeolian Hall recital takes place in which the then 52-year-old and ever-popular Cécile Chaminade played a sort of mechanical *quatre-mains* with a Pianola push-up. *The Connoisseur, August 1913.*

MELVILLE CLARK

APOLLO
Player Piano
Quality—Quality—Quality

That's what Apollo salesmen *talk*—that's what the instrument *delivers*—that's what the purchaser *gets.* The man who buys on price alone doesn't want the Apollo. Folks who are looking for the highest quality obtainable in music won't have anything else.

You never even heard of a pianist who couldn't accent or omit the melody, yet the Apollo is the only player piano that accents the melody or any single note of it or omits it altogether playing only the accompaniment. The Apollo plays by a direct down touch on the piano key—just like a human being. No other player piano does *this.* These are but two of the six great features which make the Solo-Apollo the musical marvel of the age.

And now, in addition to the regular Apollos, we offer the Apollo Automatic which does *by itself* all that the finest pianist in the world can do manually. We will be glad to prove our statements if you will give us the opportunity.

These 2 Books Gratis
Write for them! They tell the whole story!

MELVILLE CLARK PIANO COMPANY
EXECUTIVE OFFICES: 403 FINE ARTS BLDG.; CHICAGO
NEW YORK SHOW ROOMS: 33rd STREET & FIFTH AVENUE
SAN FRANCISCO SHOW ROOMS: 233 POST STREET

Kindly mention Everybody's Magazine in writing to advertisers or visiting your dealer.

While the large names fought a costly battle in the specialist upper-crust periodicals, other makers could only aspire to the more popular press. In America Melville Clark chose a two-colour presentation for a rather attractive *art nouveau* Christmas promotion. *Everybody's Magazine, December 1913.*

The entertainment of guests

is a problem which exercises the minds of all hosts and hostesses at this season of the year. To provide a diversion of general interest—one that appeals alike to both sexes and all ages—is not easy. There is but one source of entertainment that never fails to do this, and which can never be exhausted—the Pianola Piano.

THE PIANOLA PIANO
makes social gatherings successful.

The human element which enters so largely into a performance on the Pianola Piano sustains the interest of the listeners ; indeed, if you employed a famous pianist you could not give your guests more pleasure. The temperament of each player is transmitted to the music through the intensely susceptible expression devices of the Pianola Piano.

No other piano-playing instrument can provide playing of such an artistic and personal character and yet at the same time enable one to exactly carry out the composer's intentions.

The Pianola Piano is a combination of the famous STEINWAY, WEBER, STECK, and STROUD Piano with the genuine Pianola. All models may be purchased upon easy terms, and may be seen at Æolian Hall. If you cannot call, please write for Catalogue "AA."

THE ORCHESTRELLE COMPANY,
ÆOLIAN HALL,
135-6-7, New Bond Street, LONDON, W.

Tetchy house-guests became the theme for Pianola's Christmas promotion as now it was implied that the instrument could make social gatherings successful. This time, the whole roomful of people appears captivated by the hostess's skill with the rubbers. *The Connoisseur, December 1913.*

Little could anybody know but it was to be the last peace-time Christmas for a long time as The Orchestrelle Company chose the nation's popular humorist and satirical weekly to start its seasonal campaign. *Punch, December 3rd, 1913.*

At last we see a man on the Pianola stool while the woman of the house looks suitably diffuse and quizzically at events unfolding in front of the instrument. Here the 'copy' appeals to the parents to remind them that if they want their children to grow up to appreciate good music, then they must grow up with a Pianola. *The Connoisseur, February 1914.*

A wholly new departure was the proclamation of craftsmanship displayed in the New Year promotion by Aeolian in London. Here we are told not about ease of playing, about Metrostyles or anything, but we are reassured that the Pianola is made by men who know what they are about. The inference is that all other players must be built by bricklayers or imbeciles. *The Connoisseur, January 1914.*

Meanwhile, Aeolian's arch rival in London was still the business founded by Sir Herbert Marshall. He was so keen on the Angelus that he bought all rights to the name and the instrument for British manufacture and he certainly poured money into the business. His advertisements, though, betrayed the clear fact that he used no agency to write his 'copy', nor used a proper publicist. All the ads were clearly 'home-grown' and more or less identical. Usually restricted to a quarter-page space, this one is a whole half-page! *The Connoisseur, April 1914.*

Courting to the strains of a Pianola marked a change in emphasis that summer. Apart from the fact that the pedal-box doors appear closed and excluding the possibility that it is a pedal-electric grand, this girl is playing music but her mind clearly isn't on the job. The suave chap in the morning suit with his hand in his pocket and knees bent, seems rather uncomfortable as he looks into her eyes... *The Connoisseur, June 1914.*

The Orchestrelle Company seems to have changed its tack very suddenly that year. Perhaps it changed ad agencies, who knows! There was now a far more mature approach heavy on artistic presentation. The subject of this one – memories – was to prove prophetic in the months ahead. *The Connoisseur, April 1914.*

It is now 1915 and the world has changed for good. Artist John A Harris portrays a powerful message as the man, back from the Front, injured, bandaged and wrapped in a blanket, pleads 'Talk of anything but the war'. Here the Pianola has changed to become an instrument of soothing and comfort. *Unidentified, c.1915.*

Meanwhile, in the United States, the ravages of the European war were a long, long way away as Kranich & Bach promote a special handsome-looking upright player to mark its Golden Anniversary. The piano was a good one at $700 [£175]. *The Etude, 1915.*

The new catalogue of Pianola music offered the opportunity to buy the latest music for your instrument. We are reminded that this is a wartime advertisement by the message to 'help the Red Cross fund'. *The Strand Magazine, July 1915.*

"The Marseillaise"
is the greatest war-song ever written.

Written by a soldier for soldiers, its inspiring words and martial strains have cheered French soldiers into battle for over a hundred years. To play it is a fit tribute to our gallant Allies, who, side by side with our own indomitable Army, are fighting the greatest fight that has ever been fought for liberty and honour.

If you owned a "Pianola" Piano you could render "The Marseillaise" with all the fire and vigour that has made it famous, even though you possess no musical knowledge.

The "Pianola" Piano
enables you to play the National Anthems of the Allied Nations as well as all the marching tunes of our "Tommies."

You could not choose a better time at which to buy a "Pianola" Piano: the gloom of the dimly lighted streets, the anxieties through which we are passing, would be forgotten in the pleasure that awaited you in your own home.

The "Pianola" Piano (Weber Model) is made in our factory in England, and is not—and never has been—a German instrument. This and the famous Steck and Farrand models are all offered on **SPECIAL WAR TERMS.**

Write for the Illustrated Catalogue "H" and the particulars of the liberal allowance we make on ordinary pianos if given in part exchange for a "Pianola" Piano.

THE ORCHESTRELLE CO.,
Æolian Hall,
135-6-7, NEW BOND STREET, LONDON. W.

Back in Britain, the only way to buck up the spirits was to sing patriotic songs – either our own or those of the countries overrun by the enemy. We fought hard in France and so we adopted the French national tune *The Marseillaise* as 'the greatest war-song ever written'. Whether it was or not didn't really matter. *Unidentified 1916.*

The family with soldiers away at battle, bereavement and a longing for peace. All these were things to which the Pianola might just be able to bring solace. Once again the woman plays the instrument and the soldiers and airmen are back from battle. Or is it all an illusion? We are left wondering. A whole clutch of advertisements of this period dwelled on the emotions of longing, of separation and of hope. *Unidentified 1916.*

This is the Instrument that changed my ideas of Player Pianos

THE idea of the Player Piano attracted me because I thought I should find what I had long sought—the power to play as I felt I wanted to play.

In my enthusiasm I examined Player after Player, and great was my disappointment. . . . With nearly all the instruments I tried, I could play up to a certain standard—good enough for many people, perhaps. But I was critical.

I did not want only to *have* music. I wanted to share the musician's joy in *producing*. Was it a vain wish?

I had almost resigned myself to that belief when I discovered the TriumphAuto.

Here was an instrument which it was easy to see was different from every other Player. It was sensitive, *it seemed to understand me*. As I timidly moved the control levers, and sought to put my own interpretation into a little thing of Chaminade's—a thrill went through me. . . . Here it was, the instrument I had dreamed about—the Player which could give me the power I had long sought—the power to play and share the joy of the artist who produces.

The word "Autopiano" is not registerable as a trade mark. We have therefore adopted the registered word "TriumphAuto," which stands as a protection to the public against imitation of the original Kastner instrument. The Triumph-Auto is the same instrument as the Kastner, but produced by a British firm in a British factory, by British workers.

TriumphAuto

PLAYER PIANO

"It makes musicians of us all."

We invite you to our showrooms to enjoy a demonstration—you will be under no obligation, and you can test your own powers of expression on the TriumphAuto—or write for descriptive Catalogue "K."

TRIUMPHAUTO LTD.

Manufacturers of the Kastner Auto Player

191, REGENT STREET, LONDON, W.1

Once War was over, the country experienced two more debilitations in quick succession. One was the great influenza epidemic that took as many victims as the entire war dead, and then was the economic recession of 1919-1920. It took hard work and a brave face to see much of a future ahead but the newly-reorganised Kastner business saw the chance to make that future – with a big black-and-white advert in a coloured feature! *The Connoisseur Christmas Supplement, December 1920.*

Now daddy plays

POOR daddy used to say he was a stranger to his own children, but that was before he got the TriumphAuto. All fond of music, none of us played well, and our strumming and vamping got on daddy's nerves, so we visited friends for musical evenings. Daddy didn't come—usually too tired after the business day. Then he got the TriumphAuto. Now things are different; he's quite a new daddy; we never dreamed he had so much music in him. You see, the TriumphAuto is *different* from an ordinary player-piano. Daddy can play anything—classical masterpieces, song accompaniments and dances—*but it's daddy playing*; it's all his own expression and touch. Now we're usually at home, and friends foregather for *our* musical evenings.

The TriumphAuto is built in several styles of Grand, Baby Grand, and Cottage Models, with beautifully finished cases, in a variety of good woods.

You should send for the free illustrated book, which explains the unique controls—the Triumphodist, the Temponore, and other features, which make good music a possible art for you—or call at the Triumph-Auto Showrooms and test this instrument yourself.

Payment Terms arranged to suit you

TRIUMPHAUTO Ltd., 191, Regent Street, London, W.1

TriumphAuto

"It makes musicians of us all"

December, 1923.—No. cclxviii   XVIII

TriumphAuto briefly entered to sophisticated player-piano clique and took space along with the best in the better magazines. Here the thrust is that 'poor daddy' was a stranger to his own children until he bought one of the company's products whereupon 'he's quite a new daddy'. *The Connoisseur, December 1923.*

The 'Duo-Art' plays to you.

THE 'DUO-ART'

The Greatest Piano in the World

THE pleasure of listening to music, and the supreme joy of creating music; these are the paramount reasons for the piano in the home. The 'Duo-Art' provides both of these as no other piano can provide them. By the aid of 'Duo-Art' music Rolls made by world-famous artists, the 'Duo-Art' plays for you the most inspiring pianoforte music, reproducing exactly all the artistry and individuality of the pianist's original performance. It enables you to hear Paderewski, Hofmann, Bauer, Grainger, De Pachmann and scores of other great artists as well as the best players of dance and popular music, in the comfort of your own home and as often as you desire.

The 'Duo-Art' is also a piano of fine tone, responsive action and great durability, either one of the world's three most famous pianos, the Steinway, Weber or Steck.

In addition to its keyboard for regular hand playing, the 'Duo-Art' is fitted with exclusive 'Pianola' action and devices which enable even those who do not know a note of music to play dances, popular songs, or the greatest classical selections, with the utmost perfection and expression.

THE 'DUO-ART' IS OBTAINABLE BY A LIBERAL EXCHANGE AND CONVENIENT PAYMENT SYSTEM WHICH MAKES ITS PURCHASE SIMPLE AND A SOUND INVESTMENT.

You are cordially invited to call at Aeolian Hall at any time to hear the great masters' interpretations upon the 'Duo-Art' Piano.

If unable to call, write for Catalogue G. 2.

The AEOLIAN Co. LTD.,

Aeolian Hall,

NEW BOND STREET, W.1.

The 'Duo-Art' A 'Pianola' piano, the finest player piano in the World.

The 'Duo-Art' A piano of unsurpassed musical beauty for hand playing.

The emphasis of the market changed significantly during the first half of the 1920s. So did patterns of readership. By now the magazine *Punch* enjoyed the sort of sale that even today a publisher would only dream of. And the readership profile included the rising Middle Classes that Aeolian now had to turn to for its sales. *Punch, September 10th, 1924.*

Paderewski

The 'DUO-ART' 'PIANOLA' PIANO

IF Paderewski came into your home to play your piano it would be an event you would never forget. In spirit he *can* be with you, for his glorious art and his wonderful technique are available to everyone who owns the greatest and most complete of modern instruments— the 'Duo-Art' Piano.

Over 150 great pianists have recorded the world's best music, classic, popular and dance which the 'Duo-Art' will play to you, mirroring perfectly the artist's original performance.

Great pianists play to you— you also become a finished performer

The wonderful 'Duo-Art Pianola' Piano is not only a marvellous Reproducing Piano; it is, also, a perfect piano for hand-playing, either the Steinway, Weber, or Steck, and in addition it is the gift of music to you, yourself. The 'Duo-Art' endows you from the moment it enters your home with a technique comparable only to that of the great masters. It gives you, through the medium of the simple and flexible 'Pianola' controls, the power of perfect self-expression. It opens to you and all your family the whole world of music—classic, operatic, popular, dance—you can play it all exactly as you feel that you want to play it.

Call at Aeolian Hall and hear the 'Duo-Art,' or write for catalogue G 2 and convenient payments, and piano exchange terms.

INVISIBLE FINGERS

THE AEOLIAN COMPANY, LTD.
AEOLIAN HALL, 131-137, NEW BOND STREET, LONDON, W.1

"The 'Duo-Art' for surpasses all others in musical value and in repertoire."
I. J. Paderewski.

After all those years, Paderewski retained his image as a popular pianist, despite a sojourn as his country's first-ever prime minister. Aeolian had no second thoughts in apparently getting the maestro to endorse the Duo-Art. *Punch Almanac Number, November 3rd, 1924.*

Once more Aeolian turned to the theme of memories with advertising that went overboard with sentiment. 'Somewhere in music there's a sympathetic chord for every memory...' Ghostly females enfolded in vast gowns shimmer to the sound of the Duo-Art. Really! *Punch, January 27th, 1926.*

MEMORIES

A perfume borne on the passing air, a fragment of an old song—of such are the unseen fingers that turn back the pages of the book of memory. Hoarded treasures that are ours and ours alone. Who hath not the means to awaken old and cherished memories is poor indeed.

The 'DUO-ART' 'PIANOLA' PIANO

Somewhere in music there's a sympathetic chord for every memory; the joys, the sorrows, the very thoughts of mankind throughout the ages have been translated by the immortals into music, the most beautiful language of the universe.

Seated at your 'Duo-Art' 'Pianola' Piano all this wealth of music is yours; you are a finished pianist with a repertoire many times greater than that of a virtuoso—great classics, delightful salon pieces, popular airs, sparkling dances or song accompaniments—your 'Duo-Art' is so delicately responsive to your touch and mood that you can play them all with absolute personal expression.

If you desire to listen to music, the 'Duo-Art,' through the medium of its new self-governed pneumatic action and specially prepared music rolls, will play for you the actual interpretations of the leading pianists, with all the charm, spirit and individuality of the original renditions.

In addition to these features the 'Duo-Art' is an exquisite piano for hand playing, either the magnificent Steinway, the beautiful Weber or the rich-toned popular Steck.

THE 'DUO-ART' IS EASY TO OBTAIN.

We invite you to call at Aeolian Hall to hear your favourite artist interpreted by this wonderful instrument. A substantial reduction in price, very advantageous piano exchange values, and convenient payments can make purchase easy.

New List D.G.2 of REDUCED PRICES FREE ON REQUEST

THE AEOLIAN COMPANY, LTD.
Aeolian Hall, NEW BOND STREET, W.1.

No matter how diversified the day's interest, at eventide the 'Duo-Art' brings perfect enjoyment—music beautiful and inspiring beyond words.

An evening of joy with
The 'DUO-ART' 'PIANOLA' PIANO
STEINWAY, WEBER OR STECK PIANO

DINNER is over, the flickering firelight peoples the room with strange shadows, and your mood turns towards music. Now is the time when you will most appreciate the beauties of the 'Duo-Art.'

Now the dreamy loveliness of a Chopin Nocturne, played by Pachmann, will most appeal to you, the fire of the incomparable Paderewski thrill with the glory of his genius, and in turn Cortot, Bauer, Busoni, and a host of other world-famous pianists will come to entertain you—to cheer and inspire you with the best that music holds.

The majority of the concert pianists of international fame now record their interpretations only for the "Duo-Art" Pianola Piano, and only this instrument plays their authentic recordings, autographed as genuine.

And later when lights go up.

Switch on the light, and in merry mood the "Duo-Art" is ready for you, the gayest and most popular music imaginable. One dance after another—each more fascinating than the last, played with the sparkle and rhythm that make time and feet fly in unison.

The "Duo-Art" makes each one a great pianist.

Tired of dancing? Then let each in turn play his fancy; a popular number, a classic, or a song accompaniment for singing. The "Duo-Art" is a "Pianola" which enables everyone to play any kind of music, with perfect control and expression.

To those who have the ability to play by hand the "Duo-Art" is a still greater joy—for it is either one or only the three classics of the Pianoforte World, the famous Steinway, the beautiful Weber, or the rich-toned Steck.

You are cordially invited to visit Aeolian Hall to inspect and play the Upright and Grand Models of the "Duo-Art." Prices are moderate, convenient payment terms are available, and a liberal allowance will be made on your present instrument.

Catalogue DF will be sent on request.

THE AEOLIAN CO., LIMITED,
Aeolian Hall, NEW BOND STREET, LONDON, W.1.

As the 1920s progressed, the player piano market was approaching a denouement that would begin with the Wall Street Crash and grind to a slow and painful halt by the mid-1930s. For now, though, the Duo-Art was not so much a musical interpreter as a piano that could sooth and entertain the couple relaxing by their fireside. Aside from the wartime ads, this series was one of the memorable and clever of Aeolian's London promotional campaigns. *Punch's Almanac, November 2nd, 1925.*

We'll leave TriumphAuto to sum up the achievement of the player piano. Just a few months later it would be October and the Wall Street Crash the effects of which would not just kill the automatic piano in America but would spark the recession in Britain that coloured the early 1930s.

ACHIEVEMENT!

THOSE who are fond of music but cannot play a note on an ordinary piano, can achieve their desire and indulge their musical inclinations to the full with a Triumph Autopiano.

The latest numbers from Musical Comedies, up-to-date Dance Music, or the Masterpieces of the great composers can be played with perfect expression and time.

To those who are fond of singing, the Triumph Autopiano gives endless pleasure. With the Triumph Song Rolls the words are easily read whilst playing, and the latest transposing device enables one to sing in the Key to suit the voice. The time and expression levers are so simple to operate that anyone can be a perfect accompanist.

Why not exchange your silent piano for a

Triumph Autopiano

which anyone can play?

Visit our Showrooms for a demonstration and inspect the large selection of Upright and Baby Grand Triumph Autopianos always on view, or if unable to call, write for Catalogue "T."

Payments by monthly instalments can be arranged and any ordinary piano taken in part exchange. | *There is a Circulating Library Service of over 20,000 Music and Song Rolls to choose from.*

TRIUMPHAUTO, LTD.,
TRIUMPH HOUSE (Opposite Galeries Lafayette)
187-191, REGENT STREET, LONDON, W.1.

Appendix 2
List of Makers, Main Agents &
Inventors of Self-Playing pianos

The purpose of providing a list of makers is to enable the owner of a piano who is curious to learn something of its maker and to be able to find out some of the history of his instrument. To many there is a fascination about the men behind the pianos, who they were and where and when they worked. Armed with this, the owner should be able to identify his instrument with others from the same manufacture. That, at least, is the theory.

In practice, it's not such a simple task because makers tended to be itinerant and, having established one center of manufacture, often moved to set up another. Italian barrel piano makers, as we have already seen, built instruments all over the northern hemisphere – and in the main they were all the same as regards design and construction. Often precise identification has to depend on more than just a name. With luck the maker may have left an address label or printed tune-sheet. Other times we have to resort to trying to identify the music played as a guide to maker, date and venue.

But there were so very many makers in all parts of the world that no matter how hard we try, there is the nagging doubt that we can but scratch the surface.

The earliest mechanical stringed instruments that can be identified today are from the workshops of Bidermann, Langenbucher, and Runggel in the sixteenth and seventeenth centuries. After that it comes as a disturbing surprise to find that the eighteenth century turns up little if anything in the way of positively identifiable makers.

String-playing musical clocks and the street piano appeared in the 18th century, string clocks around the middle and the piano at the latter quarter. Barrel pianos began for the home and migrated to public places and the great outdoors.

Street pianos or barrel pianos heralded from distant centres such as Italy, Spain, France and Germany. The Italians who sought their fortunes in foreign countries went to London, Barcelona, Nice, Paris, Belgium, New York - in fact they travelled far and wide. These makers, along with those who made similar instruments but who were of British origin such as the Hicks and Distins of Bristol and London, I have listed as fully as possible.

Perforated music, both in the form of cardboard and paper, played such a valuable part in the development of the self-acting piano that I have listed those who played an important part in its evolution and early application.

Pneumatically played pianofortes emanated from France, Germany and the United States, but by far the greatest contribution and the largest volume of player-piano production heralded from America. A number of later British piano manufacturers fitted imported American-made actions, particularly those produced by the Standard Player Action Company, and by the Canadian Otto Higel Company. Significantly, although British-made actions were devised and built, they were soon almost all ousted by American ones. Many British companies who sought to develop new actions did not succeed in terms of volume sales.

It is thus not only pointless but also quite impossible to list every maker of these later instruments, or to describe every particular modification employed by various builders. I have therefore chosen to deal only with the makers of player and reproducing pianos who contributed something of importance to history, and have also tried to list most of the makers of player pianos, since these were part of the formative period of the vast industry that was to follow.

Throughout this listing, to avoid repetition in the case of the city of New York in New York State, where the city is specifically referred to the name of the state is omitted (for example Fifth Avenue, New York, USA). However, this only applies in that instance and hence Syracuse, for example, is still expanded as New York (the state), USA.

The changes in the names of countries that have taken place over the past century should also be borne in mind. Austro-Hungary was replaced in Germany by Czechoslovakia, and Russia in Europe became the Union of Soviet Socialist Republics in 1923 with the consequent change of the names of many towns and cities, for example St Petersburg was known as Leningrad before it returned to its original name. The maps of today do not always show the names common in former times. Because of this, geographical data should be verified against the status of the date of the entry.

In conclusion, a listing of makers tends, on the face of it, to be about as entertaining as an evening spent reading the 'phone book. I have, I hope, overcome this problem by providing a brief synopsis of the activities associated with the various names, where applicable, usually offering additional data to those given in the preceding chapters. The enthusiast is therefore recommended to include this chapter in his reading, rather than to bypass it as an occasional reference section.

A.P.I. (Autopiani-Pianoforte Italia), 20 corsa Lecce (17), Turin, Italy. Maker of player pianos listed in 1930 directories

Accentiola-Adalbert Piano Company. Player piano introduced in 1914 by Adalbert Piano Company. The outbreak of the First World War seems to have put an immediate stop on this. No examples seen. *See* **Adalbert Piano** Company.

Ackotist Player-Piano Company, Fall River, Massachusetts. Established in 1906. Inventors of the Pianotist kicking shoe player action based on the Hupfeld system. Two closely-related companies were the **Pianotist Co** in America and the **Ackerman Player Piano Co** of New York. *See also under* **Pianotist Company.** The **Adek Manufacturing Company** was also under the control of the same operation headed by Edwin D Ackerman.

Adalbert Piano Company, 44 Commerce Road, Wood Green, London, N. Advertised in 1914 as makers of the Accentiola player piano. Previously known as **Accentiola-Adalbert Piano Company.**

Adams, George. Published in 1747 his *Adams' Micrographia Illustrated* in which is described, in a catalogue, as '...a particularly new and curious Machine, containing a Movement which plays either an organ or Harpsichord (or both if desired) in a masterly manner'. The precise details of his device are today unknown.

Aeolian Company, The, Aeolian Buildings (subsequently Aeolian Hall), 362 Fifth Avenue and 34th Street, New York, and, later, 29 West 42nd Street. This was the giant piano and organ-manufacturing enterprise created by William Burton Tremaine (1940-1907) in 1887-1888 out of the Automatic Music Paper Company of Boston. It was initially known as the Aeolian Organ & Music Company making automatic organs. In 1892 Tremaine acquired all the patents of the Monroe Organ Reed Company of Worcester and in 1895 introduced the Aeriol self-playing piano. In 1903 he organised the Aeolian, Weber Piano & Pianola Company capitalised at $10,000,000 controlling the following subsidiary companies: The Aeolian Co, the Orchestrelle Co (London), The Choralion Co (Berlin), The Aeolian Co (Paris), The Pianola Co Proprietary Ltd (Melbourne and Sydney), Weber Piano Co, George Steck & Co, Wheelock Piano Co, Stuyvesant Piano Co, Chilton Piano Co, Technola Piano Co, Votey Organ Co, Vocalian Organ Co, Stroud Piano Co, and the Universal Music Co (piano-roll makers). These companies employed between them some 5,000 people world-wide and besides extensive piano factories in America included the Munck factory at Gotha in Germany (later to become the Steck plant), and Weber at Hayes in Middlesex, England. The total capital under Tremaine's control was $15.5m, which was more than the capital invested in the entire piano and organ industry in America in 1890. Aeolian finally amalgamated with its rival American Piano Corporation *[qv]* in September 1932 and remains in business to this day. Makers and owners of the Pianola invented by Edwin Scott Votey *[qv]*. *See also under* Tremaine, *also under* Weber, *also* Kohler Industries.

Aeolian Company, The, Salle Aeolian, 32, Avenue de l'Opéra, Paris. Aeolian Company's Paris headquarters for player and reproducing pianos, Orchestrelles and music-rolls.

Aeolian Company, The, Aeolian Hall, 135-6-7, New Bond Street, London, W. London offices of the American parent. Player and reproducing pianos as well as music-rolls and Orchestrelles. Unlike the other national branches, however, Aeolian in England became a self-sufficient operation with its own manufacturing plant at Hayes, Middlesex. Here, initially, 'knock-down' items from the Aeolian Garwood factory in New Jersey were assembled but largely through the factory expansion and re-equipment attendant with First World War aircraft production, the operation became increasingly independent. Its dilatory approach to paying Aeolian New York a share of its profits was in part responsible for the financial deprivations of its parent. British Aeolian survived up to the outbreak of the First World War but was not wound up until some years after the end of the war. The products of Aeolian New York and Aeolian Hayes began to differ as early as 1914 and by the early 1920s the variation between British-made Duo-Art actions and those in America was marked. The only instrument not to show great deviation from original design was the Orchestrelle with the exception of case styles, there being numerous instances where 'custom-built' cases were made in England. The mechanism including tone-ranks and all detail components was all American-made and Hayes-assembled to the end.

Aeolian Company, The, Calle Nicholás Mario Rivero, II, Madrid, Spain. The Madrid offices of the American parent. Player and reproducing pianos as well as music-rolls and Orchestrelles.

Albareda, Pablo, 36 S Pedro, Villafranca del Panadés, Spain. Set up his business in 1887 as an agent and hirer for street pianos. By 1909 his address was 125 Plaza de la Estacion.

D'Alessandro, Mich, Casalincontrada, Chieta, Italy. Barrel-piano maker listed in directories for 1930.

Allevi, Francesco, Corso Carlo Alberto, Porta Milano, Vercelli, Italy. A maker of street barrel pianos who flourished in the early part of this century. Disappeared by 1914.

Allison Pianos Ltd, 65 Chalk Farm Road, London, NW1. Established in 1840 by Arthur Allison, the business was first located in Wardour Street, Soho. A separate company, Ralph Allison & Sons Ltd, seems to have united in 1906 or 1907 and the business moved to North London, the premises first being the Apollo Works, Leighton Road, Kentish Town, also Charlton King's Road, NW. By 1926, the business was at Prebend Street, Camden Town, close to the railway station. Produced pianos of the cheaper to mid-quality range. Made a number of players in which was in-

stalled the Kastner or Kastenome player action. In 1929 the business and name was bought by piano makers Chappell & Company which also bought Clementi's old business – the firm of Collard & Collard. By 1934 Allison had developed a range of player uprights and grands under the name Allisonola.

Alminana, Enriqué, 109 Marques del Dueco, Barcelona, Spain. Barrel pinner and piano maker who was associated with the business of **Casali** *[qv]* around 1920.

Alvarez, Jose Belmez, Córdoba, Spain. Maker of street pianos, *fl.*1903.

Ambridge & Son, Henry, Fountayne Road, Broad Lane, Tottenham, North London. Established as piano-makers in 1890. Makers of the Paragon piano player, *fl.*1909.

Amelio, Giacomo, Mondovi, Cuneo, Italy. Maker of barrel pianos, *fl.*1930.

Amelotti, Vve, 5 chemin de Madeleine, Nice, France. An Italian by birth, Amelotti made coin-freed cafe pianos and large barrel-playing mechanical jazz bands. A specimen of the latter by this early twentieth-century maker has a 39-note wooden-framed, overstrung piano, side drum with four sticks, bass drum coupled with cymbal (one stick), eight tubular metal bells, two temple blocks. The distributor for northern France was S Rolleau of Nantes, whose name sometimes appears as well as that of Amelotti. By 1920 the business of Castaud Robuschi *[qv]* was described as 'successor to Amelotti'.

American Photo Player Company, 62 West 45th Street, New York; 64 E Jackson Boulevard, Chicago, Illinois; 109 Golden Gate Avenue, San Francisco, California. Operated a factory at Berkeley, California. Business founded around 1908 to make piano-orchestrions for accompanying silent movies. It named its products 'Fotoplayers'. The last was manufactured around 1925 although models were still being sold from stock as late as 1928. Following financial problems in 1922, the business was restructured and, by 1925, the operators were the Robert Morton Organ Company of Van Nuys, California.

American Piano Company, Knabe Building, 437 Fifth Avenue, corner 39th Street, New York City, USA. Incorporated on June 10th 1908 by the amalgamation of the William Knabe Co, Chickering & Sons, and Foster-Armstrong Company The new business controlled the manufacture and sale of the following pianos: Chickering (founded in 1823), Knabe (1837), Haines Brothers (1851), Marshall & Wendell (1853), Foster & Company (1892), Armstrong (1893), Brewster (1895), and J B Cook Co (1900). The combined output of the two founding companies with their various brands was said to be 18,000 pianos per year at the time of amalgamation, so making the syndicate the largest piano manufacturer in the world. In 1924, the company acquired Mason & Hamlin and later also several other companies including Franklin, Gabler, Holmes & Co, Laffarge, and J & C Fischer. The company moved almost immediately into the design and manufacture of players and in 1914 introduced an electric piano player called the American Electrelle which could be incorporated into any existing grand or upright. This was claimed to have been 'the perfected result of years of work and experiment by the best mechanical skill' and to have cost half a million dollars to perfect. In 1915, the company acquired the interests in the Flexotone-Electrelle which was a combination pneumatic and electric piano player. This was described as a kicking-shoe-type of mechanical action using a tracker bar to which was mounted a set of silver-coated fingers. When an opening in the music-roll was presented, these fingers made contact with a set of silver-plated buttons to complete an electric circuit. Curiously, the openings in the tracker bar also admitted air which ensured that the fingers made contact. Once contact was made, electro-magnets caused the cork-covered shoes to contact a continuously-revolving roller. This action applied a sudden force to the piano hammer action to sound a note. A form of expression was provided by a four-section hinged rest-rail each portion of which could be moved to lengthen or shorten the stroke of the piano-action hammer from the rest. This highly-complicated and superlatively redundant action was dropped in favour of the Ampico reproducing piano whereupon American Piano Co formed an operating organisation called **Ampico Corporation** *[qv]*. The company had worked towards designed a reproducing piano and its initial model was marketed under the name Artigraphic with music rolls to match. This was in 1911. By 1912 the Artigraphic name was replaced with that of Stoddard-Ampico: trade-mark records show the first use of the name Ampico on July 15th, 1912. Three years or so later, the roll-name changed again from Stoddard-Ampico to Ampico Artigraphic.In 1932 the company amalgamated with **Aeolian** *[qv]* as Aeolian-American, so also acquiring the brands of Steck, Stroud, Weber, Wheelock and others. During the summer of 1929, American Piano Company discontinued making reproducing pianos, production having effectively ceased before the Wall Street Crash. With the company's stock suddenly valueless, a receiver-in-equity was appointed on December 18th that year. Reorganisation was the result of rationalization and the creation of a new firm – American Piano Corporation – on June 6th 1930. Ultimately, following a merger with rivals Aeolian the business became the Aeolian-American Corporation. *See references under* **Maestro**.

American Piano Player Company, 828-840 South 26th Street, Louisville, Kentucky, USA. Founded by George S Williams in 1909, this company carried a capital stock of $25,000 [£6,250] (according to Q David Bowers) and purchased a 100,000 sq.ft factory from the American Tobacco Company to produce a player piano with the mechanism, including spoolbox, mounted under the keyboard. Bowers relates that most of the parts appear to have been made by Wurlitzer. The action of the mechanism was not, however, adequately perfected and involved the company in costly after-sales repairs. As a result of this, the business became over-extended and was declared bankrupt on December 1st 1910. Only one instrument is known to survive.

American Player Action Company, 2595 Third Avenue, New York City, USA. Also sometime at 437 Fifth Avenue. Makers of 'improved' player actions which featured the benefit of having all adjustments carried out from the front. *Fl.*1920.

American Player Piano Company, 15-19 Canal Place, New York City, USA. Makers of a player piano called, rather patriotically, the American Player Piano, *c.*1910.

Amphion Piano Player Company, Elbridge, New York, USA. Founded by Lewis B Doman in 1896 to manufacture the Amphion piano-player and Maestro keytop player. Doman was born in England in 1868 and emigrated with his parents at the age of seven, settling in Elbridge. In 1909 the company moved to larger premises in Syracuse (*see next item*). Doman remained with the company under the subsequent management of the American Piano Company and went on to develop a reproducing player for pipe organs. Doman died in 1935. *See also under* **Maestro**.

Amphion Company, Syracuse, New York, USA. Originally the Amphion Piano Player Co *[qv]*, specialists in the manufacture of high-quality player-piano actions. Introduced the Artecho reproducing action as well as its own Dynachord 'Art Expression Player'. Was eventually acquired by American Piano Company (the makers of Ampico) and Amphion technology appeared in all the early and Model A Ampico reproducing instruments. Amphion was also a co-owner, with Wurlitzer, of the Apollo Piano Company. Amphion's Artecho reproducing action was also known as the Celco under which name it was installed in Emerson, Lindeman and A B Chase instruments. Advertised 'the new Amphion Accessible Action' with demountable valve and striking pneumatic units. *See also under* **Maestro**, *also* **Chase, A B**.

Ampico Corporation, 27 West 57th Street, New York City, USA. Established in 1915 by the American Piano Company (hence the name: AMerican PIano COrp). Makers of the Ampico reproducing piano action as initially invented by Charles Fuller Stoddard. President was George G Foster and, besides Stoddard, the research and development department included the youthful and talented Dr Clarence N Hickman (1889-1981) and John

Anderson from Chickering. The development work was formerly located at 38th Street, but moved into the new Chickering building in 57th Street. The system was the outcome of a long-drawn-out experimental period during which time many changes were made, a problem when early music-rolls are played on later systems. Between 1913 and 1920, for example, the expression system was redesigned six times and the crescendo speed was changed in 1920. Until 1918 the player action was built by the Standard Pneumatic Action Co but after that date the Amphion action was substituted. A feature of the early instrument, the so-called upside-down valve-block, were reversed in 1924 and, in 1922, lead tubing was used in place of rubber. These early models, categorized first as the Stoddard-Ampico (until around 1917), then (retrospectively) Ampico A, were superceded by a whole new action more closely allied to the Artecho system than the original Ampico. This was the Ampico B. In 1925, following in the 1924 foot-steps of Aeolian and its Duo-Art, Ampico reduced the size of its striking pneumatic.In is the concensus of opinion amongst collectors that the Model B was not as good at its job as the Model A. During 1925 and 1926, Hickman developed a machine for recording dynamics of the piano using the spark chronograph technique. In 1932, the company merged with Aeolian into Aeolian-American Corporation. A London company was formed in the early years; this was Ampico Limited, 233 Regent House, London W1, and the company survives today, its business being connected with aluminium windows and the building trade.

Andersson, Anders Gustaf and Jones Wilhelm. The brothers Andersson lived in the village of Näshult near Vetlanda, Sweden. They designed and produced an improved version of the **Nilsson** *[qv]* Pianoharpa which they patented in Sweden as number 2239 of 13 August 1889. Shallower than the original instrument, each barrel played twelve melodies tunes and there was a choice of any three from a total of 12 different barrels offered to the customer.

Anelli (soc. An), 3 p. Castello, Cremona, Italy. The old-established family of musical-instrument makers began with Pietro Anelli in 1836. By 1909 the business was at Corsa Umberto I.2 as distributors and repairers of musical instruments. By 1926 the business had become a 'societie anonyme' and was described as makers of mechanical pianos, autopianos &c.Producers of player pianos, *fl.*1930.

Angelus Piano Company – *see under* **Wilcox & White.**

Antonelli, Domenico, 59 Great Ancoats Street and 2/4 Blossom Street, Manchester, England. Described as 'Manufacturer of Piano-Organs', Antonelli produced clockwork barrel pianos and in November 1901 was granted a British patent for a coin-feed, clockwork barrel piano, incorporating a method of removing the barrel for changing without disturbing the rest of the mechanism.

Antoniazzi, Andrew. An Italian emigrant who established the B.A.B. Organ Company *[qv]* in Manhattan, having spent six years with Maserati *[qv]*. He was a maker of street barrel pianos.

Apollo Company Ltd, The, 119, Regent Street, London, W. Makers of the Apollo piano-player and player-piano. This company presented one of its piano-players to Pope Leo XIII who took delivery of it at the Vatican. Makers of the Clark-Apollo music-rolls. *See also* **Clark-Apollo.**

Apollo Musikwerke Max Espenhain & Company, Dorotheenstrasse 27, Leipzig-Gohlis. In 1895 Gustav Max Espenhain was one of the three founders of a business called Kalliope-Musikwerke A-G based as Dorotheenstrasse 20 in Gohlis, a Leipzig suburb. They manufactured the Kalliope disc-playing musical box. In 1898 the business was re-structured and Espenhain moved from musical boxes to pneumatic pianos forming the Apollo Musikwerke that year for the manufacture of pneumatic-action orchestrions and piano-orchestrions. The company was closed by 1909.

Apruzzese, Andrew, Carrera de S Francisco (El Grande) 7, Madrid 5, Spain. An Italian who went to Spain in 1883, Apruzzese settled in Salamanca where he made street barrel pianos or 'organillos'.

In 1906 the firm bearing his name moved to Madrid where it still exists today under Antonio Apruzzese, who was born in 1906 and is the last surviving member of the family, and is the only barrel-piano restorer left in Madrid.

Aristos Player-Piano Company, 5 Urswick Road, Hackney Station, London, NE. In 1920 advertised as makers of the Aristos player but not seen again. This was the address of **Bansall & Son** *[qv]* and appears to have been a very short-lived subsidiary since Bansall continued as makers of finger pianos into the Second World War.

Arno, Antonio, 17, San Jeronimo, Barcelona, Spain. Street-piano hirer, *fl*.1909.

Arosio, Emilio, Corso Roma 39, Lodi, Milan, Italy. Established in 1893 as maker of barrel pianos and musical instrument dealer, *fl*.1909.

Arrigoni & Company, John, 158 Great College Street, London NW. 'Also at Baden Baden, Steam Works, Bruder & Sons, Waldkirch'. Advertised in 1892 as barrel piano and street organ maker. His association with Bruder, a maker of street pipe organs, suggests that he was an agent and probably not a manufacturer of these. By 1896, he had been absorbed by Cocchi, Bacigalupo & Graffigna at the same address and his position with the firm was that of manager. However, two years later, the firm reverted to J N Arrigoni & Company at the same address. By 1912 Arrigoni was at 62 Halliford Street, Islington, advertising as a mechanical-piano maker. A cabinet-maker by trade, he had come from Italy and began by doing street organ and piano repairs. He was still in business in 1922, as witnessed by his signature inside a street organ with that date.

Artola Player Company, 506 Republic Building, Chicago, Illinois, USA. Makers of a pneumatic player action for pianos called the Artola. This action was used in particular in the Artonian player-piano made in Elgin, Illinois, by the **E P Johnson Piano Company**.

Arvati, Claudio, Via Pescheria 6, Mantua, Italy. Listed in 1909 as a maker of harmonicas and dealer in musical instruments, by 1930 was described as a maker of barrel pianos.

Assereto, Antonio, Via Modre di Dio 5r, Genoa, Italy. Agent for barrel pianos, *fl*.1909.

Atkinson, C W – *see under* **Bansall & Sons**.

Aubry, Emile, 200 rue Lafayette, Paris, France. An engineer who, with Gabriel Boreau, invented the Violiniste pneumatic violin-player combined with a piano in 1926.

Auto Pneumatic Action Company, 653 West 51st Street, New York, USA. Founded in 1900 by Charles Kohler in order to cater for the demand for a reliable player action. With John C Campbell, Kohler had operated piano-makers Kohler & Campbell, founded in 1894. Kohler died in 1908 and his family formed an administrative company called Kohler Industries, Auto Pneumatic Action Company were manufacturers of the Welte-Mignon (Licensee) reproducing player-piano action, which played standard-width white paper rolls, as distinct from the original or 'red Welte' which was made in Germany and played 13½-inch-wide music rolls of red paper. The formation in 1910 of the Standard Pneumatic Action Company *[qv]* with its address in the same block, suggests a tie-up: both actions were similar in both appearance and engineering. Both companies seem to have been associated in one degree or another with Kohler Industries (the original Welte-Mignon (Licensee) patents were in their name) which was a victim of the Wall Street Crash, collapsing in 1930. Auto Pneumatic, which had manufactured all the early Ampico actions for American Piano Corporation until that company's acquisition of Amphion *[qv]*, was acquired by Aeolian at this point. *See also under* **Kohler Industries** *in Appendix 2.*

Autona Company, 23 Court Street, Boston, Massachusetts, USA. Patented an 'inner player' player piano in June 1899, which featured the music roll attached to a hinged spools frame under the keyboard. It is not known if this was ever built or produced, but it certainly was several years ahead of the successful inner player actions.

Auto-Grand Piano Company, The, New Castle, Indiana, USA. Established in 1904 by Albert Krell for the manufacture of the Auto-Grand piano player. *See also under* **Krell**.

Automatic Musical Company, Binghamton, New York, USA. Founded *c*.1900 by two brothers named Harris, this undertaking produced a number of electric pianos as well as being involved with two violin-playing machines, both called Royal Violista and designed by Professor Wauters. About 1910, the company entered financial problems and a committee of creditors was formed to operate the concern. This was headed by Edwin A Link who was with the Schaff Piano Company from which the Harrises bought their pianos for conversion. Link saw the potential of the company, left Schaff, and refinanced the business. Now called the Link Piano Company, production restarted in 1913 and in 1916 the business became incorporated. Production was around 300 coin-operated pianos and 12 or more theatre organs a year. The premises were at 183-185 Water Street and there was an office at 532 Republic Buildings in Chicago. Link used basic pianos supplied by Haddorff Piano Company of Rockford, Illinois. The business ceased in the late 1920s. *See also* **Link Piano Company, Inc.**

Automatic Musical & Device Company, 22 Fifth Street, San Francisco, California, USA. Believed to be a dealer in electric pianos but may also have been involved in conversion and/or manufacture, *fl*.1909.

Automatic Musical Instrument Company, 27 Penton Street, London N. Business set up in 1884 to market the Miranda Pianista, a push-up player originally invented by Thibouville-Lamy, Paris. The Miranda, premiered at the Furniture Exhibition at the Agricultural Hall, Islington, London, was to be factored by musical instrument agent, dealer and representative Ellis Parr who was the co-patentee of the Symphonion musical box which played discs. Construction of the Miranda was to be undertaken in Germany by Haake, the German piano makers in Hanover whose pianos Parr already distributed in London. Parr first advertised the Miranda Pianista in July 1885 from his premises at 99 Oxford Street. Immediately Jérôme Thibouville-Lamy of Charterhouse Street in London wrote to the trade press advising that the Miranda was covered by his patents and was no more than an early example of his design that had now been superseded. No more was heard of the Miranda and the AMIC and its holding company, Automatic Music Company of 3 Copthall Buildings, London EC, quietly faded away.

Automatic Piano Player Actions Ltd, 50a Hammond Street, Southall, Middlesex. A firm run by one Palmer and listed in 1934 directories.

Automatic Player-Piano Company, 5 Urswick Road, Hackney Station, London, NE. Business listed in 1934 directories. Nothing further known.

Autopiano Company, 12th Avenue, 51st and 52nd Streets, New York City, USA. Makers of the Autopiano player piano, also the Triumph and Pianista cabinet piano players. Established in 1903 by R W Lawrence, made only player pianos. Described as being one of the first concerns to market a successful player piano, the first being shipped in 1904. Its premises were also said to form the largest player-piano factory in the world. One model of its player was equipped with the Welte-Mignon action. The Company was described in 1920 as having $1m capital stock, fully paid up. In 1915, made one of the earliest electrically pumped player pianos.

Auto Pneumatic Action Company, 651-653 West 51st Street, New York City, USA. Founded in 1900 by Charles Kohler who formed his team with, among others, Thomas Danquard who had secured a patent in 1904 for what he called the 'flexible finger' by means of which the wippen of the piano action was attached directly to the player mechanism. By the early 1900s it had become the largest produced of player-pianos in the United States. It was to produce of the Welte-Mignon (Licensee) action. President was W C Heaton whose company developed the Licensee, a foot-operated (*ie* non-electric) version of the German Welte-Mignon launched by the company at the end of 1926.

B.A.B. Organ Company, 336 Water Street, Manhattan, USA. Founded in 1912 by an Italian, Andrew Antoniazzi, who had been with street-piano maker Maserati for six years. Antoniazzi was joined in partnership by Borna and the firm began by making street pianos. Later on, Dominic Brugnolotti, formerly with Molinari, joined, and the firm converted a number of cardboard-playing organs to a new system of their own using double-track paper rolls. Later still, they took over the former Molinari factory in Brooklyn and built organs. Fried *[35]* relates that Brugnolotti and Borna died, and Antoniazzi sold the remains of the business to former Senator Charles Bovey of Virginia City.

Bacchetta, Camillo, 4 via Lodi, Crema, Cremona, Italy. Maker of clockwork barrel pianos, *Fl.*1930.

Bacigalupi, Peter, 1261 Market Street, Nr Hotel Whitcomb, San Francisco, California, USA. Descended from the street-organ-building family of Bacigalupo, this branch of the family altered the name to Bacigalupi. Peter held the San Francisco distribution rights for a number of American mechanical pianos, including Wurlitzer, Cremona and North Tonawanda.

Bacigalupo, Giovanni, 79 Schönhauser Allee, Berlin N, Germany. Giovanni Bacigalupo was born in London in 1889 and initially worked with the street piano and organ-makers **John Cocchi** *[qv]*. He then went to Germany settling in Berlin where he began in business on his own in 1900. Here he produced six different types of small, portable street organ. In addition he made street barrel pianos. As Bacigalupo-Söhne at 74a Schönhauser Allee described as street-organ repairer right up until the time of his death on July 10th 1978.

Baga, Constantine, 5a Bakers Row, London EC. Very little is known of this barrel-piano maker who was in business around 1890 to 1892. Name is also noted as a repairer.

Bailleul, L, 23 place de Rihour, Lille, France. Maker of mechanical pianos, *fl.*1909.

Baldwin Piano Company, 267 Wabash Avenue, Chicago, Illinois, USA. Dwight H Baldwin (1822-1899) was a music teacher who subsidized his income by selling pianos for the Cincinnati firm of Decker Brothers. Baldwin had employed as an assistant Lucien Wulsin, Louisiana-born in 1845. So useful was this young man that he entered into partnership with his employer in 1873 as D H Baldwin & Company. Largely through Wulsin's hard work, the business of piano-manufacture began in earnest. After the death of Baldwin Wulsin's son Clarence took command of the company and with George W Armstrong quickly established the Baldwin name as a top-class piano brand. Entered the world of player pianos and, in 1920, advertised the Manualo as 'the player piano that is all but human'. When shown at the 1914 London Exposition, this won the Grand Prize. Later produced the Modello at the beginning of 1928.

Bansall & Sons, Albert Works, Clarence Road, Hackney, London NE. Founded in 1883, Bansall was a maker of the cheaper quality of pianos. Produced the Universal Piano Player patented in 1910 by R H McHardy (Pat No.10,352). This novel detachable player fitted against the front edge of the keyboard and when not in use was small enough to fit inside the piano stool. Dual standard 65/88 note rolls could be played. The player action (bellows and chest) remained fitted into the piano. The premises were destroyed in a £13,000 ($52,000) fire in July 1917 but the business reformed in new premises at 5 Urswick Road, Hackney Station, London, NE where it also made the Aristos player piano for which a separate but short-lived company was set up as the **Aristos Player-Piano Company.**

Barratt & Robinson, 288-310 York Way, Kings Cross, London N7. Founded in 1877, this piano maker was set up by the brother of Tom Barratt who built up the famous soap business of A & F Pears, and James Robinson who was also a pioneer of amateur photography. The company became one of the foremost late Victorian piano-makers. It manufactured a number of small pianos (the Corona) and players for use in boats and yachts, one model being the Pedaleon player shown by them at Olympia in 1913. In 1917 the business was sold to Frederick Saffell who had just emerged from the aftermath of Kastner and Triumph-Auto. Saffell kept Barrett & Robinson going and expanded the business selling instruments through furniture outlets. During the 1930s, Barratt & Robinson resurrected the Triumph-Auto Ltd name through Saffell. His lasting contribution to the name was the design, in 1935, of the remarkable Ministrelle miniature piano 'for the home that has no room for an ordinary piano'. This allowed the business the distinction of making what was probably the last player piano in England as late as 1937 – the Minstrelle Autopiano – a very small instrument indeed. Barrett & Robinson's strength was that it made every part of a piano in its own factories at a time when it was common practice to buy in parts, especially the action.

Bastida, Ramon, 21 Pizarro, Valencia, Spain. Makers of street-barrel-pianos, *fl.*1909.

Bates & Son, Theodore Charles, 6 Ludgate Hill, London. Organ builder who also made a large number of quality barrel organs for use in churches and the home. During the second half of the nineteenth century, T C Bates also made barrel pianos powered by weight-driven clockwork which were either solely mechanical or of the barrel-and-finger variety for normal playing as well as automatic performance. The business of Bates underwent several changes of address and style as noted in Ord-Hume *[73]* but instruments have been dated between 1833 and 1847.

Battaglia, Mercurio, Ragusa Inferiore, Syracuse, Italy. Barrel-piano maker *fl.*1930. Also made street organs.

Baylis & Son, John, 60 Great Saffron Hill, London. Originally as John Baylis at this address. Maker of portable street pianos. Also some time at 6, Chapel Street, Pentonville (address noted on instrument). *Fl.c.*1840. Described on their trade label as being a 'Manufacturer of Barrel Organs', they also advised that they could provide 'Old Barrels re-set to Modern Music'. This label was embellished with an engraving of a Hicks-style portable street piano. No precise dates have so far been traced for this company.

Beale & Company, Rundle Street, Sydney, Australia. The name Bealehas a long association with Anglo-Irish music: it was the musicologist Frederick Beale who, in 1840, first coined the word 'recital' to describe Liszt's 'recitals on the pianoforte'. Other Beales were in the music trade in Ireland and London as early as the 1780s, possibly as publishers (although not listed in Kidson). Octavius Charles Beale was born in Ireland and when, at the age of just four years, his parents joined the exodus abroad, he found himself in Tasmania, then called Van Diemen's Land, in 1854. Although later to return to Ireland for his education, the young Beale worked in Melbourne and later New Zealand (where he represented the piano-action company of 1810-established Henry Brooks & Co, later to become Herrburger, Brooks Ltd, makers of Schwander and Brooks actions and Shenstone keys) until, in 1879, he began in business under his own name as importers of sewing machines and pianos. Both were expensive commodities after shipping from Germany, centre of manufacture for the former and a leading provider of the latter. Beale was urged to undertake local manufacture and, with the backing of several of his trade outlets, he opened a small factory in Trafalgar Street, Annandale (New South Wales) in 1893. Beale recognised one major problem with the European piano in Australia and that was that it was very difficult to keep in tune due to the low humidity and high temperature of the climate. Beale replaced conventional tuning pins with a tapered peg in the iron frame. Unusually this only passed through the frame, tuning being accomplished by loosening a setscrew from the back. The tapered peg in its machined hole in the frame held the tuning in all temperatures. Beale, whose work revolutionised the design and manufacture of the so-called tropicalised piano, took out world patents for this between 1902 and 1904. The Annandale factory expanded to become the largest in the colonies and was also one of the best equipped. Around 1910 Beale moved into player pianos, the earliest – an 88-note instrument – being fitted with his own player action. However by the start of World War One Beale players were equipped with the Canadian-built Higel player. By 1922 Beale was using Louis B Doman's Amphion action imported from the United States. This was the move that took Beale into the world of reproducing pianos and shortly afterwards the Beale-Ampico was introduced. Only one of the later Ampico Model B instruments was built and this is at present in a private collection in Australia. Beale was killed in a road accident in December 1930. Throughout his life he never lost contact with Britain and made many return visits to London being admitted a Freeman in 1918 following his high office in the Livery Company of Musicians. The Beale business continued into recent times: when post-war conditions threatened closure of the UK corporate British Piano Actions in 1950, a consortium of piano makers and suppliers from around the world was set up by Alfred Knight (London). This comprised Paling (Australia), Heintzmann (Canada), Pratt, Read (USA), Bothner Polliack Group (South Africa), and Beale. The business finally closed in 1975. In its heyday it had branches in Armidale, Grafton, Maitland and Newcastle (New South Wales) with its main premises at 482 and 484 George Street, Sydney. The firm also had branches at Rundle Street, Adelaide, and Brisbane Street, Launceston, Tasmania. Australia's leading piano and player maker, Beale's contribution to the development of the instrument is significant. A widely compassionate man with active interests in the humanities, Octavius Charles Beale was also a notable authority on Australian timbers – an offshoot from his quest for piano-building woods.

Becacria, Luigi, Cassine, Alessandria, Italy. Church organ builder who also made barrel pianos, *fl.*1930.

Bechstein-Welte Company Ltd, 65 South Molton Street, London W1. The London address of Welte *[qv]* and that of the make of piano which specialised in the Welte installation, *fl.*1926.

Beckx-de La Fai, Spoorstraat C.14, Tegelen (Limburg), The Netherlands. Established by Petrus Johannes Beckx (1859-1929) in 1889 as an importer and distributor of piano-orchestrions. Subse-quently advertised as a manufacturer of orchestrions. Made 'Perfecta' music rolls for roll-playing piano-orchestrions.

Bedos de Celles, François. Born 1709, died 1779. A Benedictine of St Maur, Dom Bedos de Celles was both an organ builder and a writer on music and he published his monumental three-volume work *L'Art du Facteur d'Orgues* ('The Organ-builder's Art') between 1766 and 1778. Still a classic reference work, it contained an expansion of the teachings of **Engramelle** *[qv]* and devoted considerable space and many superb engravings to the craft of mechanical organ making and the arrangement of music for barrel pinning. His work on barrel pricking has been translated into English (*for a modern summary see* Ord-Hume *[72]*).

Behr Brothers & Company, 11th Avenue and 29th Street, New York, USA. Henry Behr was born in Hamburg in1848. His father was a hardware dealer who had a thriving export trade with America and had opened up a New York company in 1846. This was so successful that the Behr famile emigrated to New York in 1849. After serving his adopted country with honours, Henry started out on the road as a glue-salesman in which work he mixed with and earned the respect of the piano trade. When, in 1875, a major client was declared bankrupt, Behr saw an opportunity and bought the business. The following year he and his brother Edward formed Behr Brothers which in 1881 became Behr Brothers & Company. Henry's son William J, was born in Brooklyn in 1872 and was admitted to partnership in 1899. Produced fine instruments and devised significant improvements to pianos. In 1899 introduced its first piano player.

Bellotti, Ditta, Via Savonarola 17-19, Alessandria, Italy. Established in 1868 as maker of barrel pianos. Exhibited two instruments at the Turin National Exhibition of 1884. Also had premises at Via Alessandria 3, Acqui. By 1930, business was at 27 Via Savonarola making pneumatic pianos.

Bendel, Carl, Saulgau, Wurttemberg, Germany. Founded in 1892 for the manufacture of piano orchestrions, handling and distribution of mechanical musical instruments and phonographs. Manufactured book-playing pianos operated automatically by hot-air engines as well as clockwork models; *fl.*1909.

Beretto, Giuseppe, Via Cardano 46, Pavia, Italy. Agent and hirer of street pianos, *fl.*1909.

Bergel, Josef, Topferg 9, also Altestr 11, Rumburg, Bohemia. Maker of barrel pianos and piano orchestrions, *fl.*1903.

Berliner Orchestrion-Fabrik Franz Hanke & Co, GmbH, 39 Chausseestrasse 88, Berlin N, Germany. Established in 1900 as makers of piano-orchestrions and electric pianos.

Bermejo, Victor, 50 Ave Maria, Madrid, Spain. Maker of street pianos, *fl.*1903.

Bernasconi, Giuseppe e Figlio, Via Galliari 6, Treviglio, Bergamo, Italy. Founded in 1904 as a maker of barrel pianos and handler of musical instruments. By 1930 the business was at 10 via San Gallo in Treviglio and advertised as makers of barrel pianos and both clockwork and electric instruments. Probably related to:

Bernasconi, Silvio, Treviglio, Bergamo, Italy. Maker of street organs, *fl.*1930.

Berry-Wood Piano Player Company, 20th and Wyandotte Streets, and Southwest Boulevard and 20th Streets, Kansas City, Missouri, USA. Also offices and factory at 348-50 Canal Place, New York City as well as a very successful branch in San Francisco. Berry-Wood played a prominent part in the American coin-operated automatic piano industry prior to the First World War. While little is known of the men behind the business, the style and quality of their instruments is respected by collectors today. All Berry-Wood instruments were based on the piano and all had keyboards unlike the products of some of their rivals and successors. The first product came in the opening months of 1907 with the Auto Electric Piano Player for use in public places such as bars. This was a coin-freed electrically-played piano having the curious feature of an endless-roll-playing mechanism attached to the back of the instrument. Provided with a heavily-made four-posted frame, this was installed between the two central posts and carried a large bin into which the endless loop of paper could fold. Immensely popular, it achieved its popularity through many counts, not the least of which was that the customers in the bar could not interfere with the mechanism, only insert more money! Four years later came the first orchestrion comprising piano with an extensive additional instrumentation said to equate to a ten-piece orchestra. A feature believed unique was the provision of a special drum-beater that allowed what was called 'drumming on the rim' whereby the edge of the drum might be struck as well as the skin. By 1913, Berry-Wood announced its move into the world of silent-picture movie theatre instruments – the so-called photoplayer. These, though, do not seem to have materialized for none is known, nor were there any catalogue illustrations. However, the aftermath of the First World War saw hard times for this one-time hugely successful business. In 1919 it closed down and, without the valued after-sales support of the manufacturer, many commercial users discarded their instruments. Although the number of instruments quickly declined, new music was still being punched for them until at least 1925.

Berthold & Company, Julius, Klingenthal, Saxony, Germany. Makers of roll-perforating machinery for making piano rolls, *fl.*1910.

Bertoldi & Company, E, 810-812 Laconia Street, Philadelphia, Pennsylvania, USA. Maker of street pianos, probably at work *c.*1930-40. One instrument seen, a 22-note straight + 26-note tremolo piano playing, among others, *Me and my Shadow*, *Charmaine*, and *Ain't she Sweet*.

Berutti, Luigi, 180 bis strada Casale, Turin, Italy. Maker of player pianos, barrel pianos and electric pianos, *fl.*1930.

Behning Piano Company, 1945 Park Avenue, New York City, USA. Henry Behning (*b.* Bridgeport, Connecticut, 1859) and his brother Gustav (*b.* New York, 1868) were the sons of Hanover-born Henry Behning (1832-1905) who had learned the trade of piano-making in Germany, emigrating to America in 1856. Here he founded his own piano firm in 1861 as Henry Behning & Son. The business was one of the earliest to take up the manufacture of automatic pianos, introducing its first player around 1903. Behning held some two dozen patents on the early refinement of the instrument and was to produce good-quality player-pianos.

Bianchi, B, Gambolo, Pavia, Italy. Barrel-piano maker, *fl.*1930.

Bidermann, Samuel, Augsburg, Germany. One of the fathers of the 'Augsburg school' of musical instrument craftsmen, Samuel Bidermann (1540-1622) was renowned for the making of musical automata of the highest quality, specializing in small clockwork-driven mechanical spinets with keyboards, barrels and clockwork motors. A skilled maker of musical automata who also used water to power some of his pieces. At least three of his clockwork spinets are still in existence.

Bidermann, Samuel, Jnr. The son of the aforementioned, Samuel Jnr (1600-1647) followed exactly in the footsteps of his father: in fact the work of the two is hard to separate. Maker of musical automata including a sewing basket with an organ mechanism constructed prior to 1625. Also at work with clockwork spinets. *See also under* **Langenbucher.**

Bidermann, B. Probably related to the family of Samuel Bidermann, he made mechanical spinets which played from barrels during the 1740s.

Biso & Campodonico, Piazza Verdi 23, Spezia, Genoa, Italy. Founded by Biso and Giuseppe Campodonico for the manufacture of pianos, harmoniums and barrel pianos and the distribution of other musical instruments, *fl.*1909.

Blessing, Wolfgang, Unterkirnach, Germany. The Blessing family was famed for the manufacture of orchestrion organs through the work of Martin Blessing (1774-1847), Jacob Blessing (1799-1879), and Wolfgang Blessing with other members of the family until the main business closed during the 1920s. Repair work was carried on right up into the 1950s. It was around 1910 that Blessing introduced the Beethophon reproducing piano, a short-lived entry into this market. This played special hand-played rolls but never entered volume production: it was discontinued by 1914.

Blüthner & Company, Ltd, 7, 9, 11 and 13 Wigmore Street, Cavendish Square, London W1. The ancient business of this piano-maker began with the birth of Julius Blüthner in 1824 at Falkenhain, Saxony. He made his first grand piano in 1853 in Leipzig and from that point went from strength to strength. It was the opening of the London showroom in 1896 that brought this fine instrument to the British market under the leadership of founder-directors W M Y Maxwell and W J Whelpdale. After Whelpdale died in 1913, the business was run by his son Arthur. The first player pianos appeared in about 1905. Fitted Hupfeld actions into reproducing pianos up until the time of the First World War when German goods were no longer available Blüthner now developed its own action which it called the Carola. This was manufactured at Acton by the Sir Herbert Marshall Piano Company. Although a wholly-British company by this time, the company suffered at the hands of patriots during the First World War: on one occasion a brick was cast through the showroom window. The firm felt obliged to advertise that 'Blüthner & Company Limited is an English Company, registered in 1896, and there are no Foreign Shareholders, all Shareholders are British-Born Subjects'. Within a few years of the end of the war, though, the company was back to fitting Hupfeld reproducing actions at which time the company advertised its instruments under the name Blüthner-Hupfeld as 'the player-piano for the connoisseur'. Solophonola and Triphonola grands were very high-quality instruments. Blüthner pianos are famed for their patented 'aliquot scaling' by which a fourth string is provided in the treble to enhance the tone. The British company, while independently operated, remained closely connected with its German originator. Julius Blüthner died in 1910, the business continuing in the hands of his sons Robert and Bruno. The Blüthner name became synonymous with highest quality instruments.

Boccarena, Giuseppe, Rieti, Perugia, Italy. Barrel organ and piano maker, *fl.*1930.

Bockisch, Karl. Born in 1878 the son of a family of Alsace vintners, Karl Bockisch was brought up in Anaheim, California, which was a community founded by German immigrant farmers. The family was unable to make a success of its new home and so finally returned to Germany where Karl married the daughter of Emil Welte. By 1900, Bockisch had become so closely involved with the family business that he had virtually assumed control as manager and decision maker for the Welte Company. It was he who first conceived the idea of the reproducing player piano which, despite his protest, became known as the Welte-Mignon. Hugo Popper of Leipzig became a close friend of Bockisch (*see*

Bowers [6]) and during the first decade of this century they maintained close business ties with collaboration extending to the co-production of orchestrions. The Mignon was introduced in 1905. Popper died in 1910 after which time sales of the Mignon in Germany and America, hitherto largely due to Popper's endeavours, reverted to Welte and Popper's company promoted its own reproducing piano, the Stella. But it was Popper who organised most of the recording contracts with artists to make rolls for the Mignon. Bockisch died in 1952.

Bona, Erneste, & Antoniazzi, Andrew, 338 Water Street, New York City, USA. Erneste Bona was an accomplished musician. Andrew Antoniazzi was a talented street-piano builder and also a barrel-arranger who started in business in 1912. The two were described on their trade card as 'Manufacturers of Cylinder Pianos & Organs'. With Brugnolotti were subsequently to be founders of the **B.A.B. Organ Company** *[qv]*.

Bonafede, Giuseppe, 15 via Ricasoli, Rome, Italy. Barrel pianos, *fl.*1930.

Bonini, Umberto, 4 via Alboino, Pavia, Italy. Maker of barrel pianos, *fl.*1930.

Borella, Juan, 14 Comandante Cirujeda with a branch at 8 Tabernillas, Madrid, Spain. Established in 1860 as makers of street barrel pianos. Still in business 1909.

Borno, Fratelli, Ragusa Inferiore, Syracuse, Italy. Barrel piano maker, *fl.*1930, also made street organs.

Bouffier, Milan, Italy. Reported to have exhibited a barrel piano at the National Exhibition held in Turin in the summer of 1884. No further details.

Bourquin, Éduard Jacques, 10 rue des Petites Ecuries, Paris, France. Bourquin was a Swiss engineer who was making mechanical barrel pianos in Paris and musical boxes from about 1885 onwards. In 1922, he applied the so-called revolver barrel-change mechanism to a mechanical piano. Each of the multiple barrels played one tune or selection and, as the barrel played, it rotated on a spiral, so allowing long musical pieces to be performed on a number of revolutions. At the conclusion of one barrel's music, the revolver mechanism would automatically index another barrel into playing position and so on, allowing a lengthy repertoire to be performed more or less without interruption.

Boyd Pianos Ltd, 19 Holborn, London EC1. With a factory at St Ann's Works, Warwick Gardens, Harringay, London N4. Old-established piano-makers owned by the Samuel family who also owned the distributors Barnett, Samuel (originally founded in 1832 as musical instrument wholesalers and importers Samuel Barnett & Sons, Ltd) and also the Decca gramophone company. Became Boyd Limited shortly before the First World War. Later had showrooms in New Bond Street, London W. The early days of the company are rather obscure. Manufactured the Boyd piano player - the only British cabinet-style or push-up player - which was a 65-note instrument and sold for £27 10s [$105] with six rolls of music, *c.*1908. This was followed by the production of an unusual player-piano *c.*1914 which was called the Pistonola. This all-metal action was designed by two university students, H C Coldman and C F Webb, and employed, as its name implied, pneumatic cylinders and pistons for all the functions of the instrument. Even the foot treadles were coupled to reciprocating pistons in cylinders and the air reservoir was a further cylinder. The subject of a number of patents, the system made for a neat and compact mechanism, but it was said to have been difficult to regulate properly. After the end of the First World War, the action was drastically revised and called the Terpreter and described as 'the highest achievement in player-pianos'. Boyds also fitted conventional player actions into their upright pianos. The Boyd Autoplayer was made in several sizes, among them what was called the world's smallest player piano - the Model Six. Full-scale action, accenting device and all controls were packed into a piano just 3ft 9in. high, 4ft 9in. wide and 2ft 1inch from front to back (*but see under* Barratt & Robinson). The Terpreter was the developed form of the Pistonola and models 1, 2 and 3 were priced at 160 guineas (£163.00 [$650.00]) for the Models One

and Two, and 150 guineas (£152 10s [$605.00]) (Model Three). Boyd suffered an uphill struggle with their players. The Pistonola action had been far from trouble-free and dealers were hesitant to take on the Terpreter although it was a different, more conventional and reliable player action. In 1928, Boyd merged with its neighbouring Harringay piano-maker Brasted Brothers. By the early 1930s, the company was offering special deals to anybody who would buy an instrument. One, carefully noted in manuscript on a four-page brochure headed 'Special Supplement detailing Three Important Offers', says '64 guineas cash. £5 deposit & £3 a month. Cash in 6 months at 5% interest extended over 3 years'. *See also under* **Brasted** of London.

Braida, Giovanni, Cuneo, Italy. Barrel-piano maker, *fl.*1930.

Brasted Brothers, H F & R A, Hermitage Road, Finsbury Park, London. Founded by Harry Brasted in 1870, the original factory was in Clapton's old tram terminus – 46a, De Beauvoir Road, Haggerston Station. After World War One the business was run by his three sons Percy, Harry jnr, and Bert. In 1919 Brasted built new works in Finsbury Park and in 1925 bought the 100-year-old Eavestaff company from W E Eavestaff and produced a quality piano under that name. In 1928, Brasted merged with a Boyd Ltd and Barnett, Samuel, also of Harringay, to form the Associated Piano Company. It also opened a new factory at Prince George Road, Stoke Newington, London, to coincide with expansion just before the Wall Street Crash. In 1934 Brasted bought the rights to the miniature ordinary piano made by Lundholm of Stockholm and produced it in London as the Minipiano – one of the marketing successes of the late 1930s. These were also the first-ever pianos to be manufactured in bright-painted colours. Percy Brasted took the instrument to the United States where it was licence-buiult by **Hardman Peck**.

Brasted, S.A, 532, chaussée de Waterloo, Brussels, Belgium. The Ancient Établissement Brasted (Société Anonyme) is thought to have no connection with the London business of the same name. The business was established around 1921 and made both pianos and player-pianos some of which were fitted with the Kastner Autopiano action. By 1926 instruments were built that were fitted with the patented player action devised and built in Leipzig by piano-action-makers Paul Strauch of 8 Hebelstr (W.33).

Braun, Franz, Hutbergasse 8, Rumburg, Bohemia. Established in 1895 as makers of barrel pianos.

Brewer-Pryor Piano Manufacturing Co, Binghamton, New York, USA. Makers of automatic pianos and also harps. Showrooms and shop at 728 Main Street, Buffalo, New York.

Brinsmead & Sons, Ltd, John, 18, 20, 22 Wigmore Street, London, W. John Brinsmead (1814-1908) was born in Devon and went to London at the age of twenty-one working as a journeyman in pianoforte case-making. Through frugal living, he had saved enough capital to start out on his own in 1836 and, initially with his brother Henry (d.1880), began making pianos on the top floor of 35 Windmill Street off Tottenham Court Road. Moves to larger premises came in 1841 and 1863 and John Brinsmead was granted a number of patents for various improvements to the piano. A factory was opened in Grafton Road, NW. After his death, the business was continued by his eldest son Thomas under whose curious misguidance the business, at one time holders of The Royal Warrant, rapidly declined. In January 1920 the business was declared bankrupt and the unsold piano stock was found to be very sub-standard. Bought by Cramer for just £4,000 [$16,000], and restyled John Brinsmead (1921) Ltd, the firm was to see good times again. Made a range of quality player pianos fitted with the Angelus diaphragm player action.

British Automatic Piano Syndicate Ltd, Established at the end of 1901 with £5,000 [$20,000] capital in £1 shares. No further details.

British Player Action Company Ltd, Stour Road, London E3. Makers of the Arcadian player action and Arcadian player upright piano. Advertised in 1930 as 'the latest development and ideal in its responsiveness . Also had premises at 17 Crouch Hill, Finsbury Park, London N4. The company appears to have been formed in 1928 but did not survive after 1930.

Broadmoor Research Corporation, 1709 First Street, Unit C, San Fernando, California 91340, USA. As the 20th century drew to its close, this company unveiled a curious device named The Power Roll by the use of which a player piano might make music without the aegis of ordinary perforated paper music rolls. Located over the tracker bar using the spool-box chucks just as a normal roll would be fixed, this controlled the tracker bar in the same manner as a music-roll, opening and closing the holes to atmosphere electronically. All the user had to do was provide the necessary vacuum by pedalling. The musical programme offered on Compact Disc was a library of 450 Ampico rolls into which the pianolist could insert his own interpretation. As an alternative, for the electric reproducing piano, MIDI-encoded reproducing interpretations were also said to be available from the makers. The device was invented by Larry Broadmoor.

Broadwood & Sons Ltd, John, Conduit Street, London W. The oldest firm of keyboard instrument makers in existence, Scottish-born John Broadwood (1732-1812) started his own business in 1773. Famed pianoforte makers that produced the Broadwood unit player action known by the name of its inventor as the Welin system. Later introduced player pianos fitted with the Duola action. In October of 1924 introduced pianos fitted with the Artrio reproducing action supplied by Sir Herbert Marshall & Sons. With the start of the Depression that followed the Wall Street Crash, Broadwood suffered severely and by May of 1931 was offering for discount sale Broadwood pianos very cheaply – obviously a close-out sale. Artrio Angelus Electric 'was £300 [$1,200], now 69gns [$300]'; Amphion Broadwood Electric 'was £298, now 69gns'; and an unpriced Amphion Broadwood Pedal Electric.Non-electric (foot-operated) instruments listed were Artrio Broadwood Angelus 'was £252, now 62gns'; Broadwood Angelus 'was £240, now 59gns'; Amphion Broadwood 'was £186, now 59gns'; and the Broadwood Duola 'was £115 [$460], now 59gns [$245]'. A distant arm of the Broadwood family also operated a business as Broadwood White & Co at Helmsley Piano Works, London Fields, London, NE. This business also produced players, fl.1915.

Brown, Theodore P, 7 May Street, Worcester, Massachusetts, USA. Maker of reed organs who invented a piano with interior playing mechanism under patents granted on April 7th, June 15th,

and December 7th and 14th 1897. Went on to make cabinet players under the name Simplex which sold for $225 [£54.00] in 1899.

Bruder Loos, 97-8 Seestadtl, Bohemia. Established in 1847 as makers of orchestrion pianos and mechanical organs.

Brugger & Furtwengler, Staraja Basmannaja, Haus Raichinstein, Moscow, Russia. Established in 1832 as manufacturers of organs and mechanical musical instruments. Were making barrel organs and orchestrion organs in 1903 as well as acting as agents for piano orchestrions and barrel pianos.

Brun, J M, 23-27, Cours Victor Hugo, Saint-Etienne (Loire), France. Makers of cylinder piano orchestrions and cafe pianos under the name Le Brunophone, also coin-freed electric piano orchestrions provided with lighting effects; fl.1920.

Brusasco, Vitt, Via San Chaira 54, Turin, Italy. Barrel piano agent, fl.1909.

Brusco, Bartolomé, 34 Cadena, Barcelona, Spain. Barrel-piano maker, fl.1903.

Brusco, Juan, 15 Rosal, Barcelona, Spain. Barrel-piano maker, fl.1903-9.

Bruttapasta, Cesare, 15 via Montoro, Rome, Italy. Maker of street barrel pianos with manufacturing premises at 98 via Flaminia, fl.1930.

Buff-Hedinger, A – see **Neue Leipziger Musikwerke Adolf Buff-Hedinger.**

Bush & Gerts Piano Company, Clark Street and Chicago Avenue, Chicago, Illinois, USA. William L Bush was born in Chicago in 1861. He was to go down in American piano history when, on January 4th 1912 he succeeded in promoting to Congress a Bill to eradicate the growing practice of 'stencil pianos' that bore either no maker's name whatsoever, or a fictitious one. Subsequently he funded the National League for the Maker's Name'. John Gerts was born in 1845 in Westphalia, Germany. In 1870 he went to Chicago and studied piano-making, beginning his own business in 1882. Meeting up with the brothers William H and Walter L Bush (see next entry) the three created a partnership named W H Bush & Company in 1884 having a $20,000 start-up capital. In 1890 this was re-named Bush & Gerts Piano Company with $400,000 capital. A brochure published in 1910 and devoted to describing how to play the Bush & Gerts Player Piano, tells us that Bush & Gerts made its first grand in 1887 and its first concert grand in 1904 as a result of which it established a 'complete and separate' grand piano department manufacturing 'four different and distinct scales'. John Gerts died in 1913.

Bush & Lane Piano Company, State and Adams Street, Chicago, Illinois, also Holland, Michigan, USA. Walter Lane was born in Berkshire, England in 1868 and emigrated to Toronto, Canada, in 1885. Soon afterwards he secured work with piano-makers A B Chase in Ohio where he studied his trade for four years. After meeting the brothers William H and William L Bush, he formedpartnership with them in 1901 as the Victor Piano and Organ Co of Chicago. In 1904 this was changed to the Bush & Lane Company. The capital stock vale in 1906 was $112,500 and by 1913 it was worth $300,000. Produced player pianos fitted with the Cecilian player action. This business clearly ran concurrently with that of **Bush & Gerts** [qv].

Buzzi, Agostino, Mondovi, Cuneo, Italy. Barrel piano maker, fl.1930. Also made barrel-and-finger pianos.

Cable Company, The, 240 Wabash Avenue, Chicago, Illinois, USA. Established in 1880 by Herman D Cable as piano makers. Took over the piano-manufacturing interests of Conover Brothers in 1892. Famed maker of player pianos one of which, the Euphona Home Electric, could either be pedalled or operated electrically. Popular instrument was the Carola Inner Player of around 1906-7, and the Solo-Carola. The man behind the design of Cable's players was Paul B Klugh (born Detroit, 1878 of Dutch origin) who was one of the most inventive player-designers in America at the time and was to be granted a number of patents. He had worked (1902-04) with William B Tremaine's Aeolian Organ & Music Co on self-playing organs. By 1913 he was vice-president of Cable.

Cadini et Cie, 13 Rue Assalit, Nice, France. A maker of barrel pianos, *fl.*1903.

Calame, Roberto V, Calle Uruguay 183, Salto Oriental, Uruguay. Est 1907 as importers of musical instruments including 'Phonolas and Angelus'.

Calmont & Company Ltd, S, 83 New Oxford Street, London W. Nothing is known of this business other than that it retailed the Musetta piano player (manufactured by Buff-Hedinger of Leipzig), *c.*1907. By the following year, the **Harper Electric Piano Co** was distributing this instrument. Calmont and Harper shared the same workshop address.

Calvo, Ignacio, 13 Caravaca, Madrid, Spain. Barrel-piano maker, hirer and repairer, *fl.*1909.

Campodominico, Giuseppe, Via Genova, Spezia, Lugria, Italy. Agent for street pianos *c.*1903.

Campora, Fratelli, Vico Orti San Andrea 32, Genoa, Italy. A maker of barrel organs and barrel pianos for street use, *fl.*1903.

Canova, Joseph Piana, 16 Sekforde Street, Clerkenwell, London EC. Patented a tremolo action for barrel pianos on 24 September 1902. He was probably a technician/mechanic working for one of the manufacturers, since his name is not recorded as a maker. Clerkenwell was an area that provided workshops for a number of Italian immigrants.

Canova, Vincent, and **Hartley, Henry** - *see under* **Hartley.**

Capdeville, V, Société du 'Pianiste Executant', 19 passage Ménil-Montant, Paris, France. A maker of mechanical pianos, *fl.*1903, who may have been in association with Ullmann *[qv]* through the mechanical piano-player Pianiste Executant.

Capra & Company, Alexander, 11 & 13 Hatton Yard, Hatton Wall, London EC. Founded by Alessandro Capra sometime before 1887 when, as Capra & Company, he was manufacturing barrel pianos at 20 Warner Street, Clerkenwell. By 1890 he was trading from the Hatton Yard address but the firm had ceased business by 1894, probably when Capra went into partnership with G B Rissone *[qv]*.

Capra, Rissone & Company, 30 Warner Street, Clerkenwell, London EC. Manufacturers of street barrel pianos that advertised in 1886. Alexander Capra was originally in business on his own until taking Rissone as a partner. Rissone subsequently took over the business in his own name (*see* **Rissone**).

Capra, Rissone & Detoma, 30 Great Warner Street, Clerkenwell, London EC. A British Patent number 4725 dated 16 November 1880 was granted to A Capra, J B Rissone and S Detoma for an improvement to a barrel piano action whereby the instrument could be played manually or mechanically via a pinned barrel. Of normal upright piano format, the barrel mechanism fitted under the keyboard in a suitably wide and deep belly with a winding handle at the right. Known as the 'Per Omnes Pianoforte', the inventors advertised in 1881: 'The attention of the Profession and Trade is called to the above Patented Pianoforte, which can be played either by the ordinary Key-board, or by a handle, thus supplying an Instrument suitable alike for the Tutored and Untutored. Any tune can be played on these splendid instruments. The "Per Omnes" arrangement can be attached to any Piano as at a small cost. Barrel Pianos supplied with all the Latest Improvements. Stock always on hand. Great attention paid to Pianos for Export. List and Designs on application.' Clockwork pianos by this maker are frequently found with Keith Prowse motors incorporated. This is the only reference so far traced to Capra, Rissone & Detoma although Rissone *[qv]* seems to have remained in business for some while under his own name. One imagines the Per Omnes turned out not to be… Receiving order made against Rissone on September 28th 1905. **Pasquale** *[qv]* was later at this address.

Carchena, Angel, 4 & 6 Cabestreras, Madrid, Spain. Maker of street pianos, *fl.*1903.

Carinzio, L, Via Ricatti, Treviso, Italy. Barrel piano agent and repairer, *fl.*1909.

Carpentier, Jules. Born in Paris in 1851, Carpentier became a student at the Polytechnique and studied for a career as a precision-instrument constructor. However, he became fascinated by the science of electricity and in particular telegraphy. His early work as a railway engineer was transcended by his electrical inventions and he exhibited electrically operated musical mechanisms at the International Electricity Exhibition held in Paris in 1880, among his inventions was a recording harmonium or Melograph by the use of which musical notes could be marked for punching into long strips of paper that could later be played back on a key-top piano-playing attachment which he called the Melotrope. He claimed the invention of both instruments although the principle had been used earlier by others. Even so, he did show the first pneumatic instrument of piano form in 1887 in France, in which year he placed it before the French Academy. In 1903 he was selling the Melograph and Melotrope at 16-20 rue Delambre. Carpentier was also involved in the making of the first phonograph designed by Charles Cros, which preceded the invention of Thomas Edison by some months.

Casali, Luis, 38 Amalia and 10 Flores, Barcelona, Spain. An Italian who settled in Barcelona during the 1880s and began manufacturing barrel pianos. His partners were Pombia (who owned the business and was responsible for the manufacture of the instruments) and Subiranda (who scored and arranged music for the barrels). Ultimately, Pombia left the business and probably returned to Italy (*see* Pombia), whereupon Casali described himself as 'successor to Pombia' on his letterheads. The business was variously at Torres Amati 1 and at Poniente 88. Gold medals for Luis Casali instruments were awarded in Spain and Brussels in 1886 and 1895 and the business was still functioning in 1909. Makers of some very good and high-quality barrel pianos.

Caus, Salomon de. A French engineer who, whilst in the service of the Elector Palatine in about 1600, described in his book *Les Raisons des Forces Mouvantes* the method of pinning music to a barrel and illustrated his words with six bars from a madrigal by Alessandro Striggio.

Cazorla, Luis, 14 Agula, Madrid, Spain. Barrel-piano maker and hirer, *fl.*1909.

Cazzullo, Alberto, 24 R vico Dragone, Genoa, Italy. Maker and repairer of barrel pianos, *fl.*1930.

Cesa, Carlo, Casa Bergonzolli, Novara, Italy. A maker of barrel pianos and organs for street use, *fl.*1903.

Chancellor & Son, Lower Sackville Street, Dublin, Eire. Advertised as 'photographers, jewellers, watch & clock manufacturers, opticians &c', this firm was distributor of the German Piano Orchestrion driven by a hot-air motor.

Chase Company, The A B, 8-12 E 34th Street, New York City, USA. Also at Eastern Warerooms, 86, Fifth Avenue, Norwalk, Ohio. The A B Chase Company was founded in 1875 making reed organs but by 1885 had begun building pianos at Norwalk, Ohio. Founder A B Chase died in 1877, the reins being picked up by Ohio-born Calvin Whitney (1846-1905). The firm's first player piano was the Artistano grand designed by William F Cooper. This was an attachment that could be fitted to the front edge of the keyboard of either upright or grand instruments and was available in 65-note, 88-note or 65/88-note combinations. By 1909 Chase was producing the Duplex player-piano.

Chase & Baker, Jewett Avenue and Belt Line, Buffalo, *also* 10 E.34th Street, New York, USA. Established by George A Baker in 1900 for the manufacture of player pianos and music rolls. New York branch at 10 East 34th Street, and one in Chicago at 209 State Street. A prolific and important industry in the early days of piano players and player pianos. New York salesroom: 236 Fifth Avenue. German office at Pickhuben 4, Freihafen, Hamburg.

Chase & Baker Piano Player Company Ltd, 45-47, Wigmore Street, London W. British distributors of Chase & Baker player pianos, piano players and music rolls, the piano players under the name Pianosona, *c.*1909. The majority of these US company London offices did not survice the First World War: those that did in the main became wholly British-owned companies.

Chiappa Ltd, 6 Little Bath Street, Holborn, London (now renamed 31 Eyre Street Hill, Clerkenwell Road, London EC1). Fair-organ makers and repairers who are still in business. Founded in 1864 by an Italian, Giuseppe (Joseph) Chiappa, at an address near Farringdon Road. He subsequently went to America and started a barrel-piano and fair-organ manufactory in New York. However, he soon returned to London to organise a factory at the present location as Joseph Chiappa & Son. He made street pianos (until about 1925), street organs, street harmoniums, skating rink bands, clockwork pianos and cafr pianos. These last played an improved form of Jacquard card-music as well as being available with barrels. He was a pioneer in the manufacture of cardboard music for street pianos. Also pinned barrels for Imhof & Mukle orchestrions and mechanical pianos at one time. Giuseppe's son, Lodovico, subsequently took over the firm and his son, Victor, ran the company until his death in 1978. The firm still exists producing punched-card music for fair organs and restoring instruments. The northern branch of the London firm was set up in the 1880s as Chiappa & Sons, 5 Jersey Street, Ancoats, Manchester.

Chiappa & Fersani, 6 Little Bath Street, London EC. Giuseppe Chiappa went into partnership with Fersani, manufacturing street barrel pianos, and in 1878 they jointly patented a street piano with cornet accompaniment, the instrument being both piano and organ.

Chiappo, Felice, Turin, Italy. Maker of barrel pianos who exhibited three instruments at the National Exhibition held in Turin in the summer of 1884.

Chicago Player Action Company, Rockford, Illinois, USA. Makers of player actions. No dates.

Chickering & Sons, 263, Wabash Avenue, Chicago, Illinois, USA. Jonas Chickering (1798-1853) began making pianos in Boston in about 1823 and, with various partners, did quite well until 1852 when fire totally destroyed his factory in a $250,000 [£11,200] blaze. Rebuilt on a larger scale, Chickering's business prospered once more. Jonas Chickering is remembered as 'the father of the American piano'. On his death two years later, his three sons took command under the style of Chickering Brothers. The final change came in 1892 with the esatablishment by Clifford C, Fred Wilby, and Wallace Wiley Chickering of Chickering & Sons. Makers of high-class pianos incorporating a number of clever inventions and improvements, particularly in stringing. Produced best-quality reproducing grands fitted with the Ampico action that are considered to be the equal in quality to Steinway.

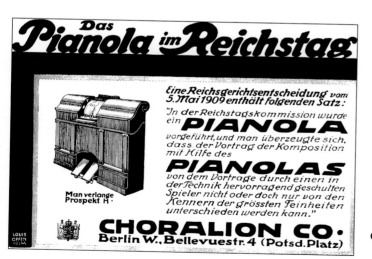

Choralion Company mbH, Bergstr 34, Berlin N 4, Germany. Showrooms at Bellevue-Str 4. Founded by Aeolian Company and managed by Frank W Hessin. The Germany headquarters for the Pianola player-pianos, Duo-Art reproducers and

Orchestrelles. See also **Generalagentur der Choralian Company Frank W Hessin.**

Christman Piano Company, 567-601 East 137th Street, New York City, USA. Established in 1885. Made a series of player uprights and grands using an action that fitted on the front of the keyboard.

Cicopero, Francesco, Corso Buenos Aires 66r, Genoa, Italy. Barrel-piano maker and hirer, *fl*.1909.

Clark, Melville. With little doubt, Melville Clark was the most influential person in the developmental history of the player piano. Its invention and perfection was due in no small measure to his inventive mind. Born in Oneida County, New York State, he began as an apprentice to a piano tuner and then went to California where he began a factory for the production of high-grade reed organs. He sold out in 1877 and finally went to Chicago where he began making reed organs under the name of Clark & Rich. In 1884 he joined with Hampton L Story (born Vermont, 1835; famed maker of pianos and reed organs) and his son Edward H Story in the making of reed organs under the name of Story & Clark. Melville Clark was the inventor of many important improvements in connection with the reed organ. The business grew so much that branches and workshops were set up in London and Berlin. The former was started in 1892 with Charles H Wagener at its head. In 1900, Clark severed his connections with what was now called the Story & Clark Piano & Organ Company after what Dolge refers to as '16 years of zealous activity', and started the Melville Clark Piano Company with a capital of $500,000, erecting new factory premises at De Kalb, Illinois. From then on, Clark's inventive prowess dominated the world of the piano player and the player piano for almost two decades. A correspondent writing in the Chicago *Indicator* early in 1912 said: 'It is getting to be such a common thing to expect the granting of a patent to Melville Clark of Chicago every week or so, that one is disappointed if a week rolls by without such an event happening.' Indeed, over 250 patents were granted to Clark, his first being number 576,032 of 1897. He staggered the piano-player world by bringing out the world's first full-scale or 88-note player in January 1901, the first 88-note interior player in 1902, the first full-scale grand piano, and the transposing device that was used under licence by very many makers. Clark called his player the Apollo, scorning the use of an air motor and applying spring motor roll rewind right up until a very late date. He also invented the Apollophone, an upright Apollo with a phonograph built into the left side of the front fall. He established a piano roll factory at De Kalb –Q-R-S - which was operated for many years by his brother, Ernest G Clark. Melville Clark died in 1919. Although his exact dates are unknown, he is thought to have been about seventy-two years of age. Also at some time he was operating the **Melville Clark Piano Company** at 17 Van Buren Street, Chicago.

Clark Pneumatic Action Company, 518 Prairie Street, Milwaukee, Wisconsin, USA. Produced a device called the Auto-Namic, which was claimed to be 'the reproducing device which turns aplayer piano into a reproducing piano at a very small cost. The Auto-Namic is a perfect action control for automatic player pianos. Installed with any [brand of] player action...A New Basic Principle is applied in Auto-Namic – It is the only "single unit" reproducing device in the world.' The piece of equipment, a hand-sized pneumatic assembly, apparently offered sixteen 'tensions' from a single pneumatic and was piped direct from the tracker bar without any valves. Nothing further known.

Clark-Apollo Company, 67 Berners Street and 119 Regent Street, London. Established in the summer of 1901 with £12,000 [$48,000] capital to exploit the Apollo piano player in England. The directors were John Beare, Jacques Ullmann (of the Paris firm of Ch & J Ullmann), Henry Kaim (of F Kaim & Sohn, the German piano manufacturers), E Rink (of Ullmann's London office) and C H Wagener (of the Melville-Clark Company). Also produced a range of music-rolls under the name Clark-Apollo. *See also under* **Apollo Company.**

Claviola Player Action. *See* **Klinker &** Company.

Clementi, Collard & Company, 26 Cheapside, London. Musical-instrument makers. Muzio Clementi, acclaimed keyboard performer and composer, was formerly a partner with the firm of barrel-organ and piano makers, Longman & Broderip, and on the dissolution of that firm he set up in business on his own. Finally, he took into partnership John Collard and in about 1820 the partnership produced the Self-Acting Pianoforte barrel piano.

Clough & Warren Company, 213 Woodward Avenue, Detroit, Michigan, USA. Established in 1850. Makers of reed organs who also produced player pianos and player actions for both organs and pianos. Operated by the brothers George P and Joseph A Warren in 1909.

Cocchi, Giuseppe, 8-9 Farringdon Road Buildings, London EC. Maker of barrel pianos in 1880. Later became:

Cocchi, Bacigalupo & Graffigna, 158 Great College Street, London NW. Describing themselves as 'Successors of John Arrigoni & Co', these three Italians were street-organ and piano makers who founded their London business in 1896. **John Arrigoni** *[qv]* was manager for the firm but by 1898 the firm had reverted to the title of **J N Arrigoni & Company** at this address while Cocchi, Bacigalupo and Graffigna went to Berlin to establish a new business (*see next entry*). The son of Giuseppe Cocchi, **John Cocchi** *[qv]* remained in business in London.

Cocchi, Bacigalupo & Graffigna, Schönhauser Allee 78, Berlin N, Germany. After their London barrel-piano business failed, the three Italian craftsmen returned to the Continent, setting up business in Berlin about 1898 as makers of street pianos, barrel organs, orchestrions and 'hand organs'.

Cocchi, John, Lychenerstrasse 2-3, Berlin N, Germany. Maker of barrel organs and piano orchestrions who was functioning in 1903. Possibly the same as:

Cocchi & Son, John, 2 Childs Mews, Dirleton Place, West Ham, London E15. Described as 'manufacturers of Mechanical Organs and Pianos', they specialised in the repair of these instruments and were at this address until at least 1935.

John Cocchi & Son,

Manufacturers of

Mechanical Organs & Pianos.

Terms· STRICTLY CASH,

◆

2. CHILDS MEWS' DIRLETON PLACE,

WEST HAM, E.15

Cohen & Company, Ltd, Philip, 14-15 Little Camden Street, London NW. Established in 1893, Philip Cohen was a piano-maker and an agent for instruments produced in Berlin through Ferdinand Manthey, an old-established agency for many small Berlin brands. Around 1910 introduced a piano-player called the Playetta. The business survived the 1914-18 war but closed sometime between 1920 and 1924.

Coldman, C H - *see under* **Webb, C F.**

Coll y Carriga, 117G Mayor and 6 Peracamps, Barcelona, Spain, Barrel-piano maker, *fl.*1909.

Collard Moutrie Ltd, 50-52 Southampton Row, Holborn, London. Was agent for the Ehrlich 'Virtuos' piano player (*see also* **Fabrik Leipziger Musikwerke**).

Colombo, Giovanni, Sobborgo S. Andrea, Novara, Italy. A maker of street barrel organs and pianos, *fl.*1903.

Colonia Player Piano Company, 72 Wells Street, Berners Street, London W. Makers of the Colonia player piano.

Conservatory Player Action Company, 32 East Monroe Street, Chicago, USA. Sole licensees and manufacturers of the Harcourt Moto-Playo Bench which was a piano stool containing mechanical player-piano pedalling feet. 'Solves the Problem of the Home Piano Electrically-Played' (not much in the way of being a very helpful description).

Continental Musikwerke Hofmann & Czerny, XIII/4, Linzerstrasse 176-80, Vienna, Austria. Founded in 1902 by Julius Carl Hofmann for the manufacture of the 'Continental' barrel-operated piano orchestrions which were handled for them by H Peters of Leipzig, the major distribution house that esported all over Europe and elsewhere.

Coppleston & Company Ltd, 94 Regent Street, London W. Distributors of the Ideal Mignon player action and the Sterling and Mendel players. Also at 85 Newman Street, Oxford Street. This business appears in 1908-13 directories, but not in that of 1914.

Godone, Gasparo, Turin, Italy. Maker of portable street pianos of the style associated in England with Hicks. A most attractive tall and slender example was sold by auction at the Galerie de Chartres, France, in May 2003. This was marked with a diamond-shaped label bearing Gordone's name and address expressed in the pittoresque style of the early 19th century as *Contrade de Doragrossa, Dirimpetto alla Trinita, in forno della Corte, Porta No.7, 1.ᵉ Piano* '[in] the district of Doragrossa; facing to the Trinity; at the bottom of the courtyard; door no 7, first [ground] floor'. This six-tune 23-note instrument was provided with a movable felt damper that could be interposed between strings and hammers by turning an external knob. The absence of any signs of external accoutrements leads French mechanical musical instrument specialist Philippe Rouillé to assume it was only ever used as an indoor instrument. A similar barrel piano by the same maker survives in the Marino Marini Museum at Ravenna, Italy.

Corvino, Enrico, Via S. Carco 26, and Strada Trinita Maggiore 27, Naples, Italy. A maker of street barrel pianos, *fl.*1903. By 1909 was at Via San Sabastiano 29.

Costa, Jean, 50 rue du Roveray, Eux Viven, Geneva, Switzerland. Repairer of street barrel organs and barrel pianos, *fl.*1903.

Costa, Bartolomeo, Via S Maurizio 25, Turin, Italy. Maker of street pianos, *fl.*1903-9.

Courteuil, M de. A Frenchman who, in 1852, was granted a patent for a perforated strip of cardboard to replace the planchette type of piano keyboard player invented by Alexander Debain.

Crassely & Rähse, Neustadt 14, Löbau, Saxony, Germany. Founded by Ferdinand Rähse in 1881 for the manufacture of pianos. By 1909 was advertising electropneumatic instruments. Maker of a piano orchestrion which played perforated-paper music rolls. Housed in an ornate cabinet reminiscent of the style used for the larger Polyphon musical boxes, the instrument sold for 950 marks complete with twelve rolls of music in 1903.

Criado, Alejandro, 57 Embajadores, Madrid, Spain. Barrel-piano maker, repairer and hirer, *fl.*1909.

Croubois, A, 48 rue des Juifs, Granville, France. Established in 1920. Makers of good-class clockwork orchestral barrel pianos for use in cafes. One seen is marked 'Pianos Automatiques Croubois' and has 51 notes in a semi-iron frame with drum, triangle and two castanets. The date of this instrument is *c.*1923.

Crowley, John H, Wedmore Street, Upper Holloway, London N. Established as a piano-maker in 1912, John Crowley advertised as manufacturing uprights, grands and players. He was closely associated with W H Grimsdale who patented a series of improvements to player technology. Crowley, who described his business as 'authorised representative of Grimsdale's Patents, Limited', built the Dalian-system player piano, an advanced but complicated and expensive expression instrument for which Grimsdale held a number of patents issued between 1908 and 1913. This, like the idea of Klugh (*see under* **Cable** and **Pain**) required a music-roll with two sizes of perforation. A number of instruments appeared before the First World War. Under the slogan of 'The Piano of Quality', the business expanded and by 1920 was located on a two-acre factory site, Quality Works, Rookery Road, Watford, Hertfordshire. Crowley's meteoric rise to success continued and the business became John H Crowley & Company by 1925. However, the sharp downturn in sales during the 1929-31 financial recession put the firm out of business. Crowley pianos, despite their undoubted early popularity, are rare today: the Dalian player is even rarer.

Crowshaw, London. A barrel-organ manufacturer *c.*1790, who produced an instrument (still extant in the Moss collection) which incorporated a 12-note dulcimer in addition to organ pipes and normal percussion accompaniment. The dulcimer was operated from the pins on the organ barrel, using keys on the same keyframe as those of the organ proper. No other example of the work of this maker is known.

Cuconato, Antonio, Via Torino 11, Turin, Italy. Barrel-piano maker, *c.*1903. By 1930 was making clockwork pianos at 12 via San Ottavio, Turin.

Cuevas, de Jose, 8 Tabermillas, Madrid, Spain. Barrel-piano maker and hirer, *fl.*1909.

Czech, Karl: Kröna 81. Brünn, Austria. Manufacturer of Stephanie orchestrions, including piano-orchestrions, *fl.*1909. *See also* **Stefanie-Werke-Filiale, Möldner & Skreta.**

Dachs, Juan, 41 Rosal, Barcelona, Spain. Barrel-piano maker, *fl.*1903.

Dale Electronics, Inc, Yankton, South Dakota 57078, USA. The Dale Lectronic was a modern key-top player developed in the 1960s using a vacuum to read the paper music roll and pouches to translate the signals into electric signals to solenoids which depressed the keys of the piano. The system was adopted for building into new pianos by **Wurlitzer.**

Davenport-Treacy Piano Company, 518-526 West 55th Street, New York, USA. Daniel Francis Treacy (1846-?) joined the piano-frame (plate) making business of Davenport & Oothout at Stamford, Connecticut, in 1872. Two years later he bought out Oothout and became half-owner. The demand for cast-iron piano frames (plates) was such that additional foundries were opened Boston, Massachusetts. In addition Treacy began making pianos and player-pianos in New York at 1907 Park Avenue. In 1912 he formed the Carter Piano Company and, in addition to instruments with the Davenport-Treacy name, produced the Carter piano and player piano. These were all fitted with bought-in player actions including some, if not all, from the Standard Player Action works. Makers of the Auto de Luxe player piano.

Davis, Joseph, 11 Catherine Street, Strand, London (1819-28); also at Blackfriars Road in 1829 and at 20 Southampton Street, Strand, London (1844-8). Makers of barrel organs who also advertised 'Self-performing piano harp'. It is uncertain just what this device was.

Dawkins & Company, Thomas, 205-7 City Road, London EC. The Dawkins musical instrument factoring business was founded in 1870. Distributor of the Orpheus player piano. A barrel piano bearing this name, measuring 38 inches by 18 inches, was sold in London by auction at Christie's South Kensington in 1967. It would appear that Dawkins was agent for a manufacturer of Hicks-style pianos. The business was a well-known musical-instrument importer.

Dawson, Charles, Hardinge Street, Islington, Middlesex. In 1848 he produced a mechanical organ worked by perforated cardboard of the Jacquard type in place of the usual barrels. It was not a success, since he used the perforations in the card to effect directly the admission of wind to the pipes, and the gradual opening and closing of the airways that resulted produced a disagreeable wavering at the beginning and end of each note. This organ was shown at the Great Exhibition of 1851.

De Roy, Eugene, 20, Longue-Rue Pothoek, Anvers, Belgium. Maker of pneumatic player pianos and piano rolls under the name 'The Symphonia', *fl.*1930.

Debain, Alexandre François. Born in Paris, 1809, he trained as a cabinet-maker. In 1825 after completing his apprenticeship he worked in several piano factories, ultimately becoming foreman. In 1834 he began his own factory in Paris, invented several musical instruments and devoted a great deal of time and effort to perfecting and ultimately producing his Antiphonel keytop player for piano or organ, which used pegged planchettes for the music. The Antiphonel was also built into pianos and combined instruments. The Paris address was 15 rue Vivienne and initially sales in London were handled by Novello & Company, 44 Dean Street, Soho. Prices ranged from 55 to 90 guineas [$228 - $378]. The British Patent for the Antiphonel was number 11,359 of August 29th 1846. Debain died on December 3rd 1877 and his business was absorbed into that of Rodolphe as Maison Rodolphe Fils & Debain réunies, at 15 rue de Chaligny, the factory being at Nogent-sur-Seine. Ultimately this business was taken over by the old established harmonium builders, Christophe & Étienne (variously described as founded in 1861 and 1832) as Christophe H & Étienne, Rodolphe Fils, A. Debain, Cottino (Anciens Etabl réunis). The Piano Mécanique version of the Antiphonel was a finely engineered instrument. During the 1880s a London office was opened as Debain & Company at 41 Rathbone Place. This advertised 'pianos-mécaniques' and 'pianos-orgues'.

DeKleist, Eugene, Düsseldorf, Germany. Born Eugene Von Kleist in 1867, he worked for Limonaire Brothers, makers of fair and band organs, as their representative in Belgium and, later, in London. He was then requested, as a mechanical-organ expert, to establish the North Tonawanda Barrel Organ Factory in North Tonawanda, New York, USA. The business was financed by the Tonawanda Carousel Factory and deKleist became its manager. They built their first organ in 1891. DeKleist ultimately separated his company from the North Tonawanda parent company and, in 1903, the barrel-organ factory became the deKleist Musical Instrument Company. Wurlitzer commissioned them to make a coin-freed electric piano and deKleist developed a ten-tune barrel piano featuring pneumatic action which he called the Tonophone. Wurlitzer finally absorbed the firm in 1908.

Delmastro & Cia, Giuseppe, Corsa Vitt Emanuele 24, Turin, Italy. A maker of clockwork barrel pianos for use in cafes and public places, *fl.*1903. By 1909 was at Via dei Fiori 25.

Denis, Carlo, Via Giovenone 5, Vercelli, Italy. Barrel-organ and piano maker, *c.*1903. By 1909, the name was Giorgio Denis at the same address but described as a barrel-piano hirer.

Deponti (Ditta), Carlo, Via Della Rocca 1, angolo Via Maria Vittoria, Turin, Italy. Literally 'The House/Firm of Carlo Deponti'. Famous maker of pianos who also made fine-quality barrel pianos. Exhibited three barrel pianos at the National Exhibition held in Turin in the summer of 1884. By 1903 as this same address the business was listed as Carolina Deponti described as a barrel-piano maker.

Detroit Music Company, 288 Woodward Avenue, Detroit, Michigan, USA. Makers of player actions listed in 1909. It was managed by M A van Wagoner who also operated a musical instrument retail outlet under his own name in Lapeer.

De Vecchi, Emilio, S. Michele, Verona, Italy. Clockwork barrel piano-maker. One model, the 'Orchestrina Jazz Band', came with art nouveau case, glass front, mandolin, drum, tambourine, cymbals and castanets and was intended to form a substitute for a dance-hall band.

Dicran, Z, Constantinople, Turkey. Maker of portable street pianos, *fl.*1904.

Dienst, E, Langestrasse 39-40, Leipzig-Göhlis, Germany. The factory was at Eisenacherstrasse 39/40 in Göhlis. Established in 1871 and run by founder August Eduard and Johannes Dienst, and Hermann Gansauge. He was a pioneer manufacturer in a city that was to be synonymous with the mechanical music industry in Germany. The 1900 advertisements promoted this fact, proclaiming *Erste Leipziger Accordion und Musikwerke-Fabrik* – 'First Leipzig accordeon and mechanical musical instrument factory'. Dienst made orchestrion organs, orchestrion pianos, played by barrel and pneumatic actions. Used the instrument family names of Pneuma as did the Berlin maker Kuhl & Klatt), and

Mezon. Bowers *[6]* relates that the pneumatic mechanisms of the roll-playing Dienst instruments were licensed under the Hupfeld patents. There is also a strong visual similarity between the early electric pianos made around 1900 by Dienst, Hupfeld, Kuhl & Klatt, Heilbronn and others of the period. August Dienst died in 1912 at the age of 69.

Direct Pneumatic Action Company Ltd, 8a Dorset Street, Baker Street, London W. Makers of the Direct Arrow action. Also sole British agent for the imported Standard Pneumatic actions. They produced the Stems player piano fitted with the Arrow action *c.*1911 and shown at Olympia in 1913. *See also:* **Kastner & Company Ltd.**

Distin Henry, 2 Church Lane, Temple Street, Bristol. Maker of barrel pianos who marked some of his instruments 'Henry Distin (from the late Joseph Hicks)'. He was also a piano tuner and is shown in Bristol Poll-Books of 1845 and 1852 as a 'Barrel Pianoforte Mkr.' Joseph Hicks is known to have died in 1847. Maker of portable Hicks-style street barrel pianos.

Dodds, Ernest H. A London-based inventor who, soon after 1914, devised a new type of valve for exhausting the motors of the player action of a piano. This made use of an L-shaped hinged valve flap. Piano-makers Blüthner were so impressed with its possibilities by virtue of its simplicity that the company enthusiastically took up the manufacture. Dodds's first British Patent was not granted until May 21st 1919 (number 153,928). He was granted a patent for improvements to it on August 12th 1920 (number 171465). This valve was used in the Blüthner Carola action which also made use of a metal bleed hole with screw adjustment. Dodds was granted a later patent in conjunction with Blüthner for an adjustable take-up spool (number 199,933 of June 12th 1922).

Dogliani, Pier Nicola, Via Caraglio, Angolo via Ospizi, Cuneo, Italy. Piano manufacturer who also made barrel pianos, *fl.*1930.

Dolge, Alfred. Dolgeville (Brockett's Bridge), New York, USA. There is only one good reason for including detail of this man in a list of piano-makers. He himself was not a manufacturer but his contribution to the American piano and its industry was immeasurable. By Dolge's efforts in perfecting high-quality piano felt, almost every American piano maker was to benefit. He made and covered hammers to the highest quality. Born in Chemnitz, Saxony, in 1848, he came to America to bring industry and a new style of industrial humanity to his employees. His expansion of a small village community into an industrial settlement known as Dolgeville began in 1881 and his many business activities expanded. A mixture of economic downturn and over-enthusiasm brought downfall on May 5th 1898 with the appointment of liquidators. Dolge moved to California and eventually began afresh in a much smaller way. His lasting contribution to history, though, lies in his two books (*see* Bibliography) on the crucial years of the American piano and player-piano industry. In his 73rd year, Dolge died in Milan on January 5th 1922.

Doll & Sons, Jacob, 117-24 Cyprus Avenue, New York City, USA. Jacob Doll was born in Rohrbach, Southern Germany, in 1849 and traveled to America alone at the age of 14 determined to make a career in 'the new world'. Having apprenticed himself to various firms around New York, he established himself as a piano manufacturer in 1884, Doll formed a business called the Electrova Company specialising in coin-freed pianos. These instruments appear to have been manufactured by others and factored by Doll. By 1909 he operated a number of factories in the area offering other makers piano frets, complete piano cases, a string-making service, &c. He produced the Pianette piano and a range of player pianos. Jacob Doll died in 1911 leaving his sons Otto, George, Frederick and Charles to continue the business making coin-operated electric pianos.

Donadini & Pohl, Cesare, Landsberger Allee 18, Berlin N, Germany. Established in 1880. A maker of barrel pianos who patented in 1865 a combined manual and barrel piano. This was exhibited at the Melbourne Musical Industries Exhibition in April 1888. Was still in business in 1909.

Dorchin, Armand, 40 Rosal, Barcelona, Spain. Barrel-piano maker, *fl.*1903.

Douillet, A, 59 rue de l'Ourcq, Paris. Makers of player pianos with 65- and 88-note compass. Successor to the business of A Gehrling, founded in 1842. Special hinged player action enabled it to be pulled outwards and over the top of the case to facilitate tuning and adjustment.

Duchácek, Ladislaus, Patackygasse 114, Turnau, Bohemia. A maker of musical automata and mechanical stringed instruments, *fl.*1903.

Dusart-Boutemy, H, 135 rue de Valenciennes, Raismes, France. Makers of mechanical pianos and orchestrions, established in 1897, *fl.*1920.

Duval, Rena, 42 rue de la Vega, Paris, France. Specialist in the restoration and repair of mechanical pianos, *fl.*1920.

Duwaer & Naessens, Kalverstraat 26, Amsterdam, Holland. Proprietors: Ludwig Hupfeld, A-G. Distributors of Hupfeld products established in 1903 and managed by W Naessens. Also at Kneuterdyk 20, Hague. Distributors of orchestrions and electric pianos. A major Dutch distributor for automatic musical instruments.

Dynavoice, Inc, Plymouth, Michigan, USA. Electrically-operated portable key-top piano-player advertised as 'any piano to player piano in 30 seconds'. *Fl.*1965. Out of business by 1968.

East Anglian Automatic Piano Company - *see under* **Wintle, Canon A O.**

Eckhardt, J C, Pragstrasse 72-4, Kannstatt, Germany. Manufacturer of musical Christmas-tree stands who appears also to have handled barrel pianos and organs, *fl.*1903. Was formerly in Stuttgart.

Ehrlich, Friedrich Ernst Paul, Breitenfeldstrasse 31, Leipzig-Göhlis, Germany. Paul Ehrlich (1849-1929) was a leading inventive genius in the burgeoning days of mechanical music in Germany at the closing decades of the 19th century. His influence cannot be overstated. A prolific innovator in the field of mechanical musical instruments, particularly organettes, he made disc-playing musical boxes, small reed organs and pianos which played from perforated cardboard or paper music. He manufactured the small 24-note Orpheus disc-playing miniature grand piano which played the same punched cardboard discs as the Ariston organette, and also the Automat piano player in the late 1880s. This also played from cardboard discs. Some models also used metal discs made of punched zinc. Two distinct models of the Automat were built; one was a push-up style resembling that made by **Grob** *[qv]* and the second was of similar format but was clamped on top of the piano keyboard. Ehrlich's business was the **Fabrik Leipziger Musikwerke** *[qv]*. In 1904, this became the **Neue Leipziger Musikwerke A Buff-Hedinger** *[qv]*, at the same time that Ehrlich started a new business with his brother Emil (see **Ehrlich's Musikwerke Emil Ehrlich**).

Ehrlich's Musikwerke Emil Ehrlich, Magdeburger Strasse 13, Leipzig-Göhlis, Germany. Established in 1903. Manufactured the Orphobella player piano and a hand-cranked machine called 'Ehrlich's Instrument'.

Eich, Pierre, 5 rue du Roitelet, Ghent, Belgium. Maker of barrel organs, orchestrions and electric pianos. Also acted as agent. Instruments made by Eich included Solophone and the Piano-Jazz. Eich bought in pianos from quality German factories, including Forster. The factory closed in 1939.

Eisert. See **Erste Reichenberger Orchestrion-Fabrik L Eisert.**

Electric Self-Playing Piano Company, New Jersey, USA. Full address unknown. Company formed in 1897 to manufacture the Electra piano. Designed by George Howland Davis (son of George H Davis, late founding partner in Hallet & Davis of Boston), the instrument failed to materialise and the company seems not to have produced anything. Davis went on to use the same name for an electric roll-perforating system in 1906.

Electrelle Company, 30 King Street, Manchester, England. Makers of the Electrelle piano player.

Elias, Jaime, Palma de Majorca, Baleares, Spain. Modern maker of miniature street barrel pianos *(manubriet)* complete with dogcart.

Emerson Piano Company, 560 Harrison Avenue, Boston, Massachusetts, USA. Founded in 1849 by William P Emerson who died in 1871 leaving the business to one William Moore who sold it to P H Powers, O A Kimball and J Gramer in 1879. They set up the Emerson Piano Company with Patrick H Powers as president. Piano manufacturers who introduced the Accompano electric player upright. Became part of United Piano Corporation set up in April 1922.

Engelhardt Piano Company, St Johnsville, New York, USA. German-born Frederick Engelhardt came to New York with his parents at the age of ten and eventually worked at the Dolgeville piano factories before going to Steinway & Sons for seven years. In January, 1889, he formed a partnership with A P Roth and set up as Roth & Engelhardt, piano-action makers. In 1898 they put there first player piano on the market. This was known as the Peerless followed by the Harmonist and thence on to the range of coin-freed automatic player pianos operated by endless music rolls for which the name is mostly remembered today. Roth retired at the start of 1908 and Englehardt was joined by his sons Alfred Dolge and Walter Ludwig to form the business of F Engelhardt & Sons. It then became a subsidiary of the Peerless Piano Player Company, a business created to build the Peerless

Orchestrion. This was an 88-note piano with a re-wind music drawer that held music rolls playing up to fifteen melodies. A rank of 32 wooden pipes (either wiolin or flute voicing) plus drums, triangle, crash cymbal. Castanets and solo mandolin. *See also* **Roth & Englehardt.**

Engramelle, Marie Dominique Joseph. Engramelle (1727-1781) was a French cleric, student of the arts and sciences, engraver, and builder of mechanical musical instruments. As a monk serving for as time as prior of the Augustine monastery of la Reine Marguérite he suffered persecution during the years after the Revolution. After hearing an Italian musician performing keyboard sonatas at Nancy, Engramelle thought up a machine which would preserve such performances and repeat them at will on the keyboard. His subsequent analysis of music which could be re-performed mechanically resulted in two fundamental observations: a form of shorthand for indicating exactly all forms of musical ornamentation, and the establishment of the principles of mechanical music in the form of converting music to pins and staples on a barrel. Although the craft was already well-established, it was not until Engramelle published his study *La Tonotechnie, ou l'art de noter les cylindres* ('Tonotechnique, or the art of placing the notes on cylinders') in 1775 that the procedure was properly defined. Although Engramelle's process 'for geometrically dividing the notes' was greeted with mixed opinion by the musical world, the description of his invention of the numbered dial (*cadran*) and its application in 'notating' the cylinders of mechanical musical instruments represented an important step forward in his own time and constitutes an invaluable source of information today on French and late baroque performing practices. While Engramelle's numbered dials and their use was cumbersome, the principle was viable and the only improvement in the intervening two-and-a-quarter centuries had been the replacement of the dial and pointer with the dividing head or worm-wheel. Engramelle's work was subsequently revised and expanded by François Bédos de Celles. It was he who first set out the importance of the *silent* portion of a sound which established the whole character of a series of notes. Engramelle's work was subsequently expanded in the work of **Bedos de Celles** *[qv]*. The system of noting the barrels of street pianos and even of the metrical punching of music rolls was entirely based on Engramelle's writings.

Erard. *See under* **Odeola.**

Erhardt & Company Ltd, C, 36 Southwark Bridge Road, London SE. Established before 1900 as a supplier of piano and organ sundries, distributors of American organs, and player pianos. Handled the Gehrling player piano actions.

Erste Prager Musikwere & Orchestrionfabrik Diego Fuchs, Wenzelsplatz 13, Prague, Austro-Hungary. Established in 1903. Makers of barrel piano orchestrions.

Erste Reichenberger Orchestrion-Fabrik L Eisert, Breite Gasse 29/31, Reichenberg, Austro-Hungary. Founded in 1905 by Frau Lina Eisert and Gustav Eisert for the manufacture of orchestrions and electrically-driven keyboard instruments

Estey Organ Company, Birge Street, Brattleboro, Vermont, USA. Jacob Estey (1814-1900) began his career as a plumber working thus until 1855. During part of this time, an area of a building he owned was rented out to a melodeon builder, Edwin B Carpenter, whom he was later to join in a partnership. This ultimately led to the formation of the Estey reed-organ business founded by Jacob Estey and Julius J Estey. Became prolific and inventive makers of high-quality American organs with branches in Atlanta (Georgia) and Boston (Massachusetts). In 1872 it was incorporated as the Estey Organ Company. Subsequently formed the Estey Piano Corporation in Bluffton, Indiana, with premises at 237 North Union Street. In February 1917, *Musical Opinion* recorded that: 'The Estey Organ factory… has recently seen the completion of its 400,000th organ… The organ was en route for New York, and the entire journey of 196 miles was made by motor lorry.' The business prospered even in the face of declining interest in the reed organ, and managed to survive into the 1950s, the last reed organ being made in the mid'fifties. In 1961, the business finally became Estey Electronics, Inc.During its existence, it made around half a million reed organs and around 3,500 pipe organs under the guidance of five generations of the Estey family. The London agency was originally Hodge & Essex of 42 Holborn Viaduct (qv) who exhibited Estey organs at the International Exhibition, Crystal Palace, in April 1884. During the early part of the 1920s the company built a number of player pianos. Its most successful roll-playing instruments, however, were its player reed organs and residence pipe organs, few of which appear to have been produced.

Établissements 'Oreste', 41 Boulevard de Riquier, Nice, France. Manufacturers of player pianos and piano-orchestrions, *fl.*1930.

Etzold & Popitz, Querstrasse 4-6, Leipzig, Germany. Founded in 1864 at Katharinenstrasse31. Managed by David Popitz, Otto Dannenbaum, Hermann Neukamm, and Wholesalers and distributors of the barrel piano-orchestrion 'Eldorado' with mandoline, xylophone, &c, and the pneumatic orchestrion 'Serenata'. Advertised (in 1909) an electric piano with violin', about which no details are known. Also distributors for Polyphon, Symphonion, Kalliope and Lochmann Original musical boxes and disc-played stringed automata. Appear not to have been makers but this company's name appears on many instruments.

Fabrica Italiani Pianoforti F.I.P, 55 Via Moretts, Turin, Italy. Makers of player pianos, *fl.*1930.

Fabrik Leipziger Musikwerke, Leipzig-Göhlis, Germany. Founded in 1877 by the brothers Friedrich Ernst Paul and Emil Ehrlich, for the manufacture of mechanical musical instruments. This firm produced the Virtuos pneumatic piano player *c.*1903.

Fabrik Mechanischer Zithern 'Chordephon' Claus & Company, Waldstrasse 20, Leipzig, Germany. Run by Hans E C Felix and Armin Kreckler, this firm was founded in 1895 for the manufacture of the Chordephon, a mechanical zither which was played using a perforated metal disc. Examples were made that were both hand-cranked and powered by a clockwork spring motor. It was in production in 1903.

Faccini, A, Ernest Street, Stepney, London E. In business as hirer of street pianos, *fl.*1930. Described as 'proprietor and dealer in Mandolin & Piano Organs'.

Falcone, Vedova, 5 via Arsenale, Pinerolo, Turin, Italy. Barrel-piano maker, *fl.*1930.

Fantosca, Pasquale, Avellino, Italy. Street-organ and piano maker, *fl.*1930.

Farrand Organ Company, 1256 12th Street, Detroit, Michigan, USA. Originated by a number of organ-builders as the Detroit Organ Company in 1881. It operated as a co-operative but did not succeed. In 1883 it was acquired by C J Whitney, a prominent music dealer, and Edwin Scott Votey, a practical organ man, and incorporated as the Whitney Organ Company. In the same year the business was joined by W R Farrand who became financial manager while Votey was in charge of manufacturing. In 1887 Whitney retired and the business became the Farrand & Votey Company turning the following year to church-organ manufacture. The inventions and improvements evolved by Votey were numerous. He then designed and built the first piano-player which he called the Pianola. In 1897 he joined the Aeolian Company having bought the organ and piano-player interests of Farrand & Votey. Aeolian ordered 1,000 Pianola players which were then built in Farrand's Detroit factory where production continued until Aeolian opened its new factory at Garwood, New Jersey, in 1900. At this point the Farrand business was reformed as The Farrand Organ Company specializing in reed organs. It also designed and produced a new piano-player which it called the Cecilian. It was consciously different to the Pianola and employed a very individual 65-note music roll 13¼-inches wide with a curious feature aimed at curing the problems of paper expansion: the holes were closer together at the center and became wider spaced towards the edges. The Cecilian sold for $250 [£62.0.0] in 1901. An associate company, the Farrand Piano Company at 12th Street and Grand Trunk Ry, was given over to the making

of player actions and complete player pianos which were described as 'the perfect piano player'. Their advertising is remembered for its eye-catching advertisements asserting '6 points of superiority' showing a cabinet-style push-up in the open palm of a hand – displaying six fingers. The company remained closely allied to Aeolian until 1915 when it filed for bankruptcy. Farrand's London business, Farrand Organ Company, was set up in 1899 with premises in Denman Street, Bermondsey, moving to 44 Great Marlborough Street in 1902, closing shortly after the outbreak of the First World War. Manager was William David Wood.

Fasch, José, 9 Meliodia, Barcelona, Spain. Barrel-street-piano agent and hirer in business in 1903.

Fassano, Constanzo, Largo Tarsia 21-2, Naples, Italy. Street-barrel-piano maker and hirer, *fl.*1909.

Feilitzsch et Cie, Hans von, 104 rue de Laeken, Brussels, Belgium. Agent for barrel organs, barrel pianos and electric pianos, *fl.*1903.

Feiss Brothers, 240 Chapel Street, Prahan, Melbourne, Australia. Established in 1886. Agents for Imhof & Mukle's Black Forest orchestrions and mechanical pianos in 1888.

Fernandez, Roman, 14 Flor Baja, Madrid, Spain. Maker of street pianos, *fl.*1903.

Ferrari, Angel, 4 S Pedro, Villafranca del Panadés, Spain. Agent and hirer for street pianos, *fl.*1903.

Ferrari, Fratelli, Via Savonarola 24, Alessandria, Italy. Barrel-piano agent, *fl.*1909.

Ferraro, Angelo, 6 via Losanna, Milan, Italy. Maker of barrel pianos, *fl.*1930.

Foucher, George, Manufacturer of pianos and organs, 'patent barrel organ, new mechanical pianoforte performing by hand and handle' in 1881.

Foucher, Gasparini, 17-19 rue de la Vega, Paris. Maker of barrel organs and pianos for street use, *fl.*1903.

Fourneaux, Napoléon. Born in Paris 1830, Napoléon Fourneaux created the first-ever pneumatic piano-player. The son of Napoléon Snr (1808-1846), an innovator of free-reed instruments, the younger Napoléon devised a mechanical piano-player called the Pianista which he patented in 1863. While mechanical in action, this is the first known pneumatic player, the playing mechanism being controlled by a pinned barrel turned by a handle. A barrel-organ-type sticker/key action controlled the passage of air to small pneumatic motors, one for each key of the piano. Each pneumatic, which received its operationg air supply from a compression bellows, depressed a finger on the piano keys. The instrument, which stood somewhat larger than the pianoforte it was designed to play upon, was exhibited in America at the Philadelphia Exposition of 1878.

Francioli, Antonio, Intra, Novara, Italy. Barrel-piano maker, *fl.*1930.

Francone, Giuseppe, Via Gioberti 27, Turin, Italy. Piano and barrel-piano agent, *fl.*1909.

Francone, Vincenzo (Vedova), Via San Dalmazzo 16, Turin, Italy. Maker of barrel pianos, *fl.*1909.

Frankfurter Musikwerke-Fabrik J D Philipps & Söhne, Solmstr. 9, Frankfurt, Germany. Established in 1877 by Johann Daniel Philipps who, at the age of 23, built a barrel-played orchestrion for a Frankfurt hotel and dance-hall. Weight-driven clockwork instruments were initially the company's speciality. By 1909 the company was run by August and Oswald Phillips and in 1911 the company was re-formed as simply the **Frankfurter Musikwerke-Fabrik** with its factory in Bockenheim. Barrel-operated instruments were retained in the company catalogues as late as 1909 although the first roll-playing pneumatic orchestrions had first appeared in 1896. Produced a large variety of player pianos and piano-based instruments such as the Pianella series the several dozen styles of which extended from small upright pianos with mandolin attachment up to piano-orchestrions in excess of 12 feet in height and including many ranks of pipes. These instruments included the Silvia, Iris, Caecilia, Ideal and Harmonia some of which were electrically-driven. Produced music rolls under the trade-name Philag promoted as being narrower than those of its rival piano-orchestrion manufacturers and therefore less susceptible to mis-tracking problems caused by damp. Perfected, in 1912, a motor for winding two tune sheets at once and, in 1916, a special roll-tracking device. Also at Berlin, Essen and Leipzig. *See also under* **Philipps & Söhne, J D.**

Frati, Chairo, 5 Farringdon Road, London EC. Believed to be a son of the founder of the famous Berlin firm of orchestrion organ makers, Chiaro Frati advertised as a maker of barrel pianos in 1876. He subsequently removed to 19 Great Bath Street, Farringdon Road, London EC.

Frati & Cie, 10 place Daumesnil, Paris 12e, France. Branch of the Berlin maker of orchestrion pianos and electric pianos.

Frati & Company, Kastanienallee 32, Berlin N37, Germany. Founded by Anselmo Frati in 1875 and financed by Giovanni Bacigalupo (1847-1914). Both were barrel-organ builders from Genoa in Italy. Frati had learned his trade with Gavioli in Paris and subsequently worked in London. The business, which the two men jointly owned, prospered until the closing years of the last century when failing health and mental illness caused Frati to return to Italy. The business was continued under various titles by Bacigalupo and his subsequent partners, John Cocchi and Graffigna, until finally it was managed by Heinrich Schmithals. Electric pianos under the name Fratinola were produced in much later years until, with its market failing (the company still made barrel-playing instruments at a time when everybody else was producing paper-roll-playing machines), it was bought out by the **Frankfurter Musikwerke-Fabrik J D Philipps** *[qv]*. Frati himself had died in the early 1890s. At the International Exhibition held in April 1884 at the Crystal Palace, Sydenham, London, Frati was awarded 'special mention' for barrel pianos.

Freiburger Musikapparate-Bauanstalt, GmbH, Haslacherstrasse 145, Freiburg-im-Bresgau, Germany. Manufacturer of upright and grand reproducing pianos under the name Evola. Little is known about this business other than the survival of some advertising literature in The Library of Mechanical Music & Horology archives. Paul de Wit, in *Zeitschrift für Instrumentebau* (September 15th, 1929) announces the firm as a late entry for the catalogue of the Leipzig Autumn Fair, commenting: 'Great credit is due to the reproduction piano Evola… Mr Nikolaus Eschmann, director of this new enterprise, has two decades experience in the industry…' There is an almost certain link to the close-by business of M. Welte & Söhne in that the electric player mechanism depicted features the Welte trefoil roll drive motor and rotary exhaust pump. The business advertised 'complete instruments with simplest accessibility and operation' also the 'supply of individual components'. Highlighting its own music-roll factory, it promotes 'rolls made for nearly all systems', 'Specialist in Evola 98-note rolls for the Welte instruments [and] 88-note standard rolls for electric pianos'. The firm possibly foundered in the Depression: nothing further is known.

French & Sons, 1st Avenue and 18th Street, New Castle, Indiana, USA. The Jesse French Piano & Organ Company was founded in 1875 by Jesse French whose father had emigrated from England in 1820. His aunt, incidentally, was one of the pioneers that petitioned Parliament for woman's suffrage. Advertised 'artistic pianos and players' in 1902, the year in which the firm became incorporated. In the following year acquired the **Krell Piano Company** *[qv]* and became the Krell-French Piano Company. Soon afterwards, upon the retirement of Krell, the company became The Jesse French & Sons Piano Company. It is unlikely that French made his own player actions: the one example recorded was fitted with a Standard Player Action.

Fuchs, Diego. See **Erste Prager Musikwere & Orchestrionfabrik Diego Fuchs.**

Fusco, Giuseppe, p. Pola, Treviso, Italy. Maker of barrel pianos, *fl.*1930.

Fusella, Giuseppe, Via S Dominico 34, Turin, Italy. Barrel-piano maker, *fl.*1903-9.

Fuzelli, Joseph, 379 Great Ormond Street, London W. Maker of street barrel organs and barrel pianos.

Gall, Johann, Arnau, Bohemia. A maker of street barrel organs and pianos. No other details.

Ganter, Karl, Furtwangen, Bad Schwarzwald, Germany. A specialist in the making of weight-driven clockwork units supplied to many makers of piano and pipe orchestrions, *fl.*1903.

Garcia, Doroteo, 4 S Cayetano, Madrid, Spain. Barrel-piano and barrel-organ maker, repairer and hirer, *fl.*1909.

Garcia, Pedro, 30 Abades, Madrid, Spain. Barrel-piano and barrel-organ maker, repairer and hirer, *fl.*1909.

Gargallo, Tomás, 178 Conde del Asalto, Barcelona, Spain. Specialised in pinning music for street pianos, *fl.*1903. By 1909 was at 154 Conde del Asalto.

Garisch & Co (A & G), 28 viale Vittorio Veneto, Milan, Italy. Distributor of pianos, player pianos and music rolls, *fl.*1930.

Garolachi, Vincente, 6 Sombreria, Madrid, Spain. Barrel-piano maker, *fl.*1903.

Gasparini *(Successor to Foucher-Gasparini),* 17 and 19, rue de la Véga, Paris. Makers of clockwork barrel pianos for cafés and also of book-playing organs, *fl.*1920.

Gast & Company. See under **Pianoforte Fabrik 'Euterpe'.**

Gattino, Onor, Via Madama Cristina 105, Turin, Italy. Agent for barrel pianos, *fl.*1909.

Gavioli & Company, 5 Jersey Street, Great Ancoats, Manchester, and 2 bis avenue de Taillebourg (place de la Nation), Paris, France. Makers of mechanical organs and pianos c.1888. In 1885 they were at 55 Blossom Street, Ancoats, Manchester.

Gavioli & Company, L, 5 Little Saffron Hill, London EC.Street-organ maker who also advertised mechanical pianos in 1870. By 1880 was at 1 & 2 Farringdon Road, London EC.

Gavioli et Cie, Société. Founded in Paris at 2 avenue de Taillebourg by Ludovic Gavioli, an Italian, with his sons Claude and Anselme;the Gaviolis can truthfully be said to have been the fathers of the fairor showman's organ. Their inventions both in the tonality and mechanics of these instruments, along with the practical improvements in perforated music, were to influence all that came after them. The cardboard-music playing piano was one direct result of their associated work. Ludovic Gavioli was a native of San Geminiano and came to Paris at the end of 1852. He was a meticulous organ-builder who made very fine secular organs, although he did build one for Queen Isabella II of Spain which played hymns. Ordinary barrel organs represented a steady business but the firm was to find its wealth and success in fair organs and, during the late 1850s, the family concern was joined by Prosper Yver, a financier. After the war of 1870, the Gavioli factory was moved to Alsace in eastern France. There followed a period of decline in business and in 1901 the firm lost its foreman, Charles Marenghi, who was their principal expert. Marenghi established his own successful firm in the same line of business. Earlier, in 1892, Gavioli had introduced 'book music' and the book-playing organ which used perforated-cardboard music folded zigzag fashion to form a thick 'book' of music. This was fed through a pneumatic system named the 'mechanical-pneumatic Touch Key', Gavioli's term for the key frame with its projecting key tips. Gavioli was also responsible for the invention of the portable street organ, many interestingly voiced organ pipes, organs that used two wind pressures from one air source, primary and secondary pneumatic systems for fair organs, and a 'keyless' tracker box along with automatic stop selectors and cancellers. Most of the famous names amongst Italian/French fair organs and their makers served their apprenticeships with Gavioli. In the irony of things, many of these names continued in business long after Gavioli, among them Marenghi and also Chiappa. Limonaire Brothers took over the remains of the Gavioli concern and continued to supply perforated music until they themselves went out of business in 1918. Gavioli built the 'Guitharmony' - a barrel-operated guitar with string-plucking mechanism.

Gazza, Giovanni, 71 Roosevelt Street, Manhattan, New York, USA. Took over the barrel-piano and organ business of G Mina of 2 First Street, Manhattan, on his death. The business did not prosper and was closed by 1902.

Gehrling & Cie, 59 rue de l'Ourcq, Paris 19, France. Charles Gehrling established his piano and organ sundries house in 1842 with Albert Douillet. Specialised in piano actions but early in the 1900s introduced the Gehrling Piano-Player followed by the Gehrling Interior-Player. This was handled in London by Erhardt & Company Ltd of 36 Southwark Bridge Road, London SE which advertised in 1908.

Generalagentur der Choralian Company Frank W Hessin, Unter den Linden 71, Berlin NW. Established in 1901 as the German company representing the Aeolian Company and handling the Pianola and Orchestrelle instruments. Became known as the **Choralian Company mbH** and by 1909 was at Bergstrasse 34, Berlin 4.

Gérard & Cie: 4/6 Rue des Fabriques, Brussels, Belgium. Distributor of automatic musical instruments, mechanical pianos and orchestrions. Handled Popper products from Leipzig and branded as its own. Specialised in electric pianos. Also had branch showrooms in Ghent at 23 rue du Hainaut, and Anvers at 28 rue des Fortifications (opened in 1912). Introduced a 'piano à Clavier' which was like a normal upright but had a clockwork-operated barrel mechanism mounted on top of the top lid, also a 'piano electrique' that was probably made by **Kuhl & Klatt** in Berlin. Other electric pianos included xylophone and mandoline attachments. Handled products from Hupfeld and Weber.

Getto, Francesco, Via Marsale 5, Ivrea, Italy. 'Pianoforte e Organi a Cilindro.' Maker of barrel pianos similar in style to the portable Hicks pattern, but strung much lighter to produce a most pleasing bright tone. Also made barrel organs; *fl.*1930.

Giacchetti, Giuseppe, Cigliano, Italy. Maker of barrel organs and pianos, who exhibited two barrel pianos at the National Exhibition held in Turin in the summer of 1884. Was still in business in 1903.

Giannini, Giacomo, Corso Vitt. Emanuele 132, Ban, Italy. Agent for barrel pianos who also hired and carried out repairs, *fl.*1909.

Gilardenghi, J, 12 rue du Fort, Marseilles, France. Barrel-piano agent and hirer, *fl.*1909.

Gillone, Gaudenzio, Via del Ponte, Casale Monferrato, Alessandria, Italy. Maker of barrel pianos, *fl.*1930. Specialised in instruments for indoor use in dance-halls. Marini notes, regarding one instrument, that it is of extremely high mechanical quality adding that 'every note has its [own] damper' and that it has three drums. The musical; arrangements are described as 'refined'.

Gilone, Giuseppe, Casale, Italy. Exhibited two barrel pianos at the National Exhibition held in Turin in the summer of 1884.

Giuliano, Vittorio, Via Monteoliveto 61, Naples, Italy. Barrel-piano agent and hirer, *fl.*1909.

Giummarra, Gaudenzio, Ragusa Inferiore, Syracuse, Italy. Maker of barrel organs and pianos, *fl.*1930.

Gössel, Josef & Adolf, VI, Gumpendorfer Str. 81 and I, Teinfaltstr. 9, Vienna, Austro-Hungary. Makers of barrel piano-orchestrions established in 1854.

Gray, Robert and William. The surviving trade label announces '4 New Road, near the end of Portland Road (London). Maker of Barrel Organs, Harpsichords and Pianos.' Probably built barrel pianos or spinets c.1800, but no instruments have so far been discovered.

Grelli, Giuseppe, 3 via Tornasacco, Ascoli Piceno, Italy. Barrel-piano maker, *fl.*1930.

Gribble Music Company, 919 Grand Avenue, Kansas City, Missouri, USA. Introduced c.1955 a modern device called Magic Fingers which could convert an existing piano into a player, or could be built into a new instrument. It was not a key-top player, but fitted under the keyboard in a drawer. It was engineered by the Midwest Research Institute but rather quickly disappeared largely through the fact that it was not portable (like a key-top) but had to be installed.

Griseri, Fratelli, Via San Sabastiano, Centallo, Italy. Maker of barrel pianos, *fl.*1909.

Griseri & Varetto, 14 Warner Street, London EC. Producers of street pianos c.1880.

Grob, J M, Leipzig-Eutritzsch, Germany. Founded in 1872 by J M Grob, A O Schultze and A V Niemczik for the manufacture of mechanical musical instruments. Patented a means of playing a piano or organ using a perforated tune sheet in 1886. This employed cam-shaped levers which, when raised through the holes in the music, wedged against a rotating drum and so impelled the piano hammer - this was what became known as the 'kicking-shoe' type of action. In 1888, Grob patented a tremolo or staccato action for barrel-operated pianos using a revolving cranked shaft engaging the barrel keyframe key. Also perfected a system of continuously beating hammers and associated check action similar to that used by **Racca** [qv] of Bologna. Made a disc-operated piano player which operated on 36 notes of the piano. Grob first began making instruments in 1883, having in the previous year secured the sole rights for the Ehrlich Ariston organette. His first patents date back to 1884. Grob died in October 1891 and the following year the business was taken over by **Hupfeld** [qv], the name being changed to Hupfeld Musikwerke.

Hupfeld henceforth claimed the date of foundation of his business as 1872 - that of Grob. Grob is best remembered for his work in pioneering the disc-operated mechanical piano player, a device with which both he and Ehrlich were closely associated and which subsequently Nyström in Sweden used for playing a reed organ.

Gröndahl's Flygel- & Pianolager, Karl Johangade 17, Christiana (the old name of Oslo), Norway. Founded in 1904 by Andreass Backer Grondahl as distributor of player pianos, piano players and electric pianos.

Güell, Pablo, 13 Rosal, Barcelona, Spain. Barrel-piano seller and hirer, *fl.*1909.

Guérin et Cie, Charles, 3-7 Boulevard des Vignes, Marseilles, France. Makers of barrel pianos under the brand name Massilia; *fl.*1920. By the 1928 directory the business was styled Ch Guérin, Deychamp & Cie as manufacturers of automatic pianos with interchangeable cylinders. A choice of electric or clockwork motors was offered.

Guilbaud Frères, les Etabts, Labaule, 2 rue Charles Baudelaire, Paris, France. This business were among the first to manufacture clockwork barrel pianos which featured overstrung, partly iron frames. Also made piano-orchestrions. A label on one 48-note cafe piano states: 'Mfg. Pianos Automatiques en France & Belgium'.

Gulbransen, Dickenson Company, 3242 West Chicago Avenue, Chicago, Illinois, USA. Established in 1906. Makers of the Gulbransen player piano. In 1909 the company was at 37 Union Park Street. Swedish-born Axel G Gulbransen evolved what was to become the famous trademark of an upright piano being 'pedalled' by a crawling baby with the words 'Easy to Play'. Later used the peculiar slogan 'The Registering Piano' describing as 'through the pedals you *register* your touch…' Produced a large number of player-pianos and also actions for others to use. Gulbransen pianos were tonally exceptionally good, well-scaled and with minimal variation across the scale (most pianos have a mid-to-treble tonal weakness). The early Guldransen actions, however, were extraordinarily cheaply produced. Apart from being fully-glued together, the pneumatic motor boards were of very poor quality timber that was so waney that attempts to chisel them off the action board for repair invariably meant that the wood split. Harvey Roehl told the author that this was because the actions were made for just $15 (£3.15/-) and retailed to the trade at 100 percent mark-up. He also said that if a stack was found to be defective, it was replaced without demur – and the old one used to keep the factory furnace going. These glued stacks gave way to better-made, screwed stacks during 1926. In 1923, the so-called 'White House' model cost $700 [£175]; the 'Country Seat' model $600 [£150], the 'Surburban' model $495 [£125]; and the 'Community' model just $420 [£105]. A good Gulbransen player-piano works very well, but overhauling one is a major undertaking – not impossible, but time-consuming. Later Gulbransen player actions were screwed together and, while more expensive to build, were very much easier to service.

Günzel & Rosenberger, 7 Victoria Avenue, Bishopsgate Without, London EC. Distributor of the Berlin-made Spaethe piano/organ player known as the Pianist.

Haake Söhne, Rudolf, Karlsruhe I.B, Furtwangen, Germany. Also at Mannheim. Makers of hot-air engines for mechanical musical instruments, including piano orchestrions. These little motors, set in motion by a spirit burner, developed one-sixtieth of a horse-power and were priced at 38 marks each. These details were advertised in 1897.

Haddorff Piano Company, Rockford, Illinois, USA. Charles A Haddorff was born at Norkköping, Sweden, in 1864 and became a cabinet maker as well as an accomplished amateur pianist. After studying the art of piano-building he emigrated to America in 1892 and in 1902 started his business with the goal of making the finest piano possible. His forte was in the creation of the piano scale, a task requiring the finest scientific understanding of the production and distribution of sound. He devised a highly-specified tonal design that he named the 'Homo Vibrating Sound

Board' and was the instigator of many patents for new inventions. The tonally-innovative Haddorff piano was once a greatly-cherished instrument. Introduced the 'Clarendon' player piano in 1909.

EVERYBODY'S MAGAZINE

RICH TONE

STRIKE any note on the Haddorff, and you will notice that it is unusually rich and powerful. Sound a chord, and you will perceive an unlooked for luxuriance in the harmony. Then play any melody, softly or brilliantly, and you will realize that the Haddorff yields a remarkable wealth of music.

HADDORFF PIANO
The Piano with the "Homo"-Vibrating Sounding Board.

The sounding board has hitherto been the Cinderella of the piano—much of its wonderful musical richness hidden. But now with the Haddorff Piano the sounding board has come into its own. This is the only piano with the "Homo"-Vibrating Sounding Board, which makes possible a tone of fullest richness—the "Homo"-tone.

We cannot describe a tone in words; but we can and do say in all earnestness that you are missing something excellent until you hear the Haddorff.

There is probably a Haddorff dealer or owner in your community, and it will be an easy matter for you to hear the instrument. Let us give you a letter of introduction which you can use if you wish. Also let us send you our interesting booklet, "The Homo-tone."

Grands, Uprights and Player Pianos, All Excellently Made.

HADDORFF PIANO CO.
312 Evans St.   Rockford, Illinois

The advertisements in Everybody's Magazine are indexed. Turn to page 4.

Hall, R, 19b Wilbury Grove, Hove 3, Sussex, England. Advertised as a 'piano organ specialist.' A restorer of barrel pianos who also repinned barrels. An instrument by Pasquale of 5 Phoenix Place, London, repinned and restored by Hall, is in the Lancaster House collection in London. It plays the popular American tune *Davy Crockett.*

Hallet & Davis Piano Company, 146 Boylston Street, Boston, Massachusetts, USA. Established in 1839 by Russell Hallett and George H Davis producing quality pianos. In 1905 the firm became a division of the Conway Musical Industries and distributed Conway and Lexington pianos. Made the Virtuola upright player and the Solo-Virtuola expression piano. This played rolls having 75 playing notes and 21 expression openings. Later a fine range of reproducing grand pianos using the Angelus name which earlier had been used for its pedal player pianos. Owned the Simplex Player Action Company.

Hanke & Co, Franz. *See* **Berliner Orchestrion Fabrik Frank Hanke & Co, GmbH.**

Hardman Peck & Company, Fifth Avenue and 19th Street, New York, USA. Leopold Peck (1842-1904) was born in Austria. He went to America and teamed up with piano-maker John Hardman. Hardman's father Hugh was born in Liverpool, England, in 1815 and went to America to begin making pianos in 1840. John Hardman became a partner in about 1874 and in 1880 Peck bought an interest in the business. Peck's business acumen and scientific approach to piano-building advanced the company dramatically. Developed a piano player which was said to have cost the company $400,000 [£100,000] to bring to perfection in 1905 the year in which the firm became incorporated. London agents were Hardman & Goetze Agencies (which also handled the

German Goetze pianos) of 98 Leonard Street, City Road, London EC. Hardman also produced the Autotone player piano featuring the 'Accentor' control. The company had a branch at 524 Fulton Street, Brooklyn. The Hardman piano player, said in 1905 to have been the smallest on the market, cost £29 [$115] (Eclipse model); £39 [$155] (Standard model), and £44 [$175] for the Perfecta model. The cases were available in a choice of woods.

Harper Electric Piano Company, 258-262 Holloway Road, London N, and 83 New Oxford Street, London W (premises shared with **S Calmont,** *[qv]*). Established in 1906 by Sidney C Harper as distributors of the Premier piano and player. By 1908 was advertising as agents for the Musetta piano-player and player-piano. Reformed as:

Harper Electric Piano (1910) Company Ltd, 258-262 Holloway Road, London N. Makers of electric self-acting pianos, who exhibited such instruments in 1911 at the Coronation Exhibition (Shepherd's Bush), at the Earls Court Exhibition and also the Festival of Empire at the Crystal Palace. At the Music Trades Exhibition of the same year (August) at the Agricultural Hall they showed one model fitted with xylophone and mandolin attachment which could be turned on or off at will. This was intended for use in cafes, restaurants and hotels. The firm remained in business through the 1930s although, judging by the rarity of their instruments today, their production must have been small. Most of their music rolls appear to have been made by the **Up-To-Date Music Roll Company** *[qv]* and were 13 $^5/_{16}$-inch wide.

Hartley, Henry, and **Canova, Vincent,** 39 Corporation Street, Birmingham. In January 1910, they jointly patented a roll-rewinding system for use with music-roll playing street pianos or organs. At the completion of one paper roll this clever but simple device indexed another music roll into position for playing whilst an independent mechanism rewound the other regardless of the length of either roll. This pre-empted similar systems for pneumatically-controlled domestic instruments. The two men also made other ingenious devices including an expression system for a pneumatically-played street piano (British Patents No.189 and 220 of January 1910 refer).

Hasbrouck Piano Company, 539 West 21st Street, New York City, USA. Makers of a player piano called the Tone-ola, *c.*1910.

Haupt, A E, Ausere Weberstr. 69, Zittau, Saxony. Established in 1846. Piano orchestrion maker specialising in instruments driven by weights or motor or hand. *Fl.*1909.

Hays & Company, Alfred, 82 Cornhill, London EC. One-time musical-instrument dealers, this firm exists today as a theatre-ticket agency. Their name and former address (above) appears on a small portable barrel piano in a rosewood case similar to the Hicks style and appearing to date from the second half of the nineteenth century. It is likely that, as with barrel pianos bearing the name Keith Prowse, Alfred Hays did not actually manufacture these instruments. Also sometime at 74 Cornhill, EC3, and 26 Old Bond Street (*c.*1923).

Hedke, Wilhelm, Neu-Lichtenberg, Friedrichstr. 27, Berlin, Germany, Founded in 1890 as piano makers. Produced the 'Artist' piano player and, in 1908, the Ideal player piano.

Hegeler & Ehrlers, Blumenstrasse 56-7; Brüderstrasse 20a; and Heiligengeiststrasse 31-2, Oldenburg i Grossherzogt, Germany. Established in 1895 as makers of pianos. Managed by Hermann Hegeler and Heinrich Ehlers, this company introduced in 1908 an upright piano with a violin which played in unison with the two upper octaves of the piano keyboard by means of trackers. The violin, played by belt-driven rotating bow wheels, was mounted on top of the piano and inside the case, where it was hidden from view. Called the Geigenpiano, it seems to have been a short-lived device. This business also had branches in Bremen and Bremerhaven.

Heilbrunn Söhne, K, Keibel-Strasse 39, Berlin NO 43, Germany. Established in 1875 by W Heilbrunn and S Blüth. Makers of electrically-driven mechanical instruments including the Virtuos player piano. Used the 'kicking-shoe' form of action.

Hicks, Geo[rge]: 14, Charles Street, St. James, Bristol, England. 'Organ builder and manufacturer of cylinder pianos' reads the label on a portable street piano by this maker. A further example in the Jere Ryder collection has a date, possibly that of a repair, of August 1842. Name also seen on other portable street pianos. He may be the same as:

Hicks, George, Brooklyn, Long Island, USA. Probably immigrant, in business between 1848 and 1864. Two small barrel pianos seen labelled 'George Hicks, Hand Organs and Cylinder Pianos'.

Hicks, John, Cobourg Street, Clerkenwell, London EC. A barrel-organ maker *c.*1850, related to the Bristol family of Hicks, organ and piano makers, who made the first street barrel piano in England about 1805. Sometime also at Chapel Street, Edgware Road, London. The ramifications of the Hicks family are difficult to unravel but various members made many barrel pianos, mainly of the portable, street type, in the first half of the nineteenth century. With the common misuse of the term 'barrel organ' - even contemporarily - John Hicks may indeed have been a maker of barrel pianos. A testimony that he repinned barrels is contained in Vol III of Mayhew, *London Labour and London Poor.*

Hicks, Joseph, 13 Penton Street, Pentonville, London N. Maker of barrel organs and cylinder pianos *[sic]*, whose name appears on a particularly fine 41-key piano in a rosewood case with two barrels bearing the watermark date 1846. This piano is 5 feet 9½ inches high, 39 inches wide and 21 inches deep. He died in 1847.

Hicks, Joseph, Bristol, England. *Fl.*1816-47. Whether related to, or indeed the same as, Joseph Hicks above is uncertain: a problem seems to lie in the numerous members of the family, their frequent use of family Christian names, and their extensive travels. An early pianoforte has been seen with a label reading 'Henry Distin (from the late Joseph Hicks), Barrel Pianoforte maker, No 2, Church Lane, Temple Street, Bristol'. Bristol directories, examined by Langwill, list Joseph Hicks as a musical-instrument maker, who was made Freeeman of Bristol on October 12th 1812, at the following addresses: 11 Griffin Lane and Trenchard Street (1816-29); Trenchard Street (1830); 3 St Augustine's Place (1831); 16 Lower Park Row (1832-41); 17 Lower Maudlin Street (1842-4); 17 Montague Street (1845-7). *See under* **Henry Distin.**

Higel Company, Inc, Otto, 680 King Street, Toronto, Canada. Otto Higel was born in Germany where he trained as a piano-maker. He emigrated to the United States in the 1870s, eventually settling in Toronto where he opened up in business as a piano action-maker, supplying to the Canadian and eventually US piano trade. With the coming of the player-piano and, particularly, the 'inner' action, Higel quickly saw a market for a build-in unit that would enable a piano technician to convert an ordinary piano into a player with a separate bottom action and a top player action. By 1908 Higel had designed a novel low-cost player action that used metal components for the valve casings. The Higel metal player action was first patented by Otto Higel and G C Heintzman (British Patent No. 21,946 of 1909), improved upon under Patent No 14,572 of June 17th 1914 under the name of W E Evans, and finally developed as the two-valve

Metalnola by Higel under British Patent No. 100,286 of May 15th 1916. With demand for a low-cost reliable action in Britain as well as North America, Higel formed a British subsidiary, Higel Ltd, 149 Albion Road, Stoke Newington, London, N16, in 1909. As well as supplying all piano sundries for the trade, it was here that 'knock-down' action kits shipped over from Canada were assembled. The high cost of duplicate moulds for the cast alloy components (made in aluminium and mazak) meant that all metal parts were Canadian-made but increasingly other parts were made at the company factories. The company assertion that the actions were 'manufactured in Britain' was thus only partly true. However, in October 1913 the company announced in the trade press the opening of a factory 'for the manufacture and sale of the Higel-Player [sic] Action'. When the Metanola was introduced it was hailed as 'the player action of the future' with 'unique construction of valve castings… made in one piece of non-corrosive metal… the vertical valve assures positive seating under all conditions… accurate… dependable… efficient'. The Metanola action was nevertheless an expensive product and the principal output was the more-conventional wooden action. The Higel actions were also available in the United States (through the company's division at Corner Bronx Boulevard and Nereld Avenue, New York City), and Berlin, Germany. [Detail from Ted Rivers, Toronto]. The Higel was widely used in British-made pianos but, while reliable, achieved a largely unjust reputation as being hard to repair. Higel also operated as an organ, piano and player sundries supply house for the technician and published a regular pocket-sized catalogue from Toronto.

Hillier Piano & Organ Company, 288 York Road, Cattle Market, London N. Founded in 1855, the Hillier business made the cheaper class of mainly upright pianos. By 1909 the business was run by E S Hillier. In 1908 introduced the Hillier player piano. None has been seen. The company did not survive the war years.

Hoch, Hermann, Kaiserstrasse 313, Solingen, Germany. Founded in 1876. Trade supplier of electric pianos, musicwork and orchestrions.

Hofmann, Julius Carl, 111 Hietzingerkai, Vienna, Austria. Barrel-piano maker, who perfected a *piano e forte* (soft and loud) effect for his instruments in 1905. *Also as:*

Hofmann & Czerny, XVIII/2, Sandleitnerg 79, Vienna, Austria. Founded in 1902 for the manufacture of piano orchestrions 'for public places and private houses'. The instruments were made under the Continental brand name as **Continental Musikwerke Hofmann & Czerny**. Promoted, in 1909, a piano-orchestrion equipped with keyboard to allow a performer to play along with the mechanical performance. Also acted as general distributors of the instruments from **H Peters & Co** of Leipzig.

Holland, W, 39, Lamb's Conduit Street, London, EC. A Hicks-style portable street piano has been seen bearing this maker's label reading; 'W Holland, Musical Instrument Maker and Music Seller [address] near the Foundling. Instruments tuned and let on hire'. The Foundling Hospital once formed a main feature of this East End street. No direct records have come to light on this late 18th/ early 19th century maker. Humphreys & Smith ('Music Publishing in the British Isles') list Henry Holland, organ-builder, and James Holland, music publisher and bookseller, as contemporary, while Rosamond Harding [43] shows only an 'H Holland' at Bedford Row. Directories have failed to elucidate further. Assuming that W Holland made the barrel-piano seen (as distinct from being a factor), he appears as a competent builder.

Hopkinson Ltd, J & J, 44 Fitzroy Road, London NW. An old-established piano-maker, John Hopkinson began business in Leeds in 1835, coming to London in 1846. He is accredited with the invention of a fast-repeating piano action that was shown at London's Great Exhibition in 1851. The business of father John and son James operated from many addresses in London (Rosamond Harding [39] lists no fewer than 25 between 1849 and 1900). Later established in London's Soho, the firm is thought to have been the first to introduce the Boudoir grand in London. After the First World War the Hopkinson business was run by George Hermitage: he died in November 1923 and the name and business was acquired by George Rogers & Company. Advertised in 1908 was the Hopkinson Player and, later, the electrically-powered 65-note Electrelle the development of which put the business into bankruptcy followed by restructuring in July 1913.

Horvilleur, H, & Presberg, Georges, 32 rue des Archives, Paris, France. Clockwork barrel pianos with interchangeable cylinders. Established in 1893 at 7 rue du Temple. *Fl.*1920.

Hromádka, August, Josefstadt-Sterngasse, Temesvár, Hungary. A maker of barrel pianos, *fl.*1903. By 1909, August had disappeared but another maker of similar name – this time **Norbert Hromádka** – was working in the same trade at Elisabethstadt, Hunyadistrasse 50. This is possibly a father-son succession.

Hündersen, A, Dornbush 4, Hamburg. Agent for barrel pianos, *fl.*1903.

Hunt & Bradish, Warren, Ohio, USA. Patented a small pianoforte controlled by a perforated paper roll, *c.*1880.

Hupfeld A-G, Ludwig, Apelstrasse 4, Leipzig, Germany. Ludwig Hupfeld (1864-1949) formed his business in 1872. His partner was Otto Tetzner (1869-?). The Hupfeld business took over the business of J M Grob [*qv*] on July 1st 1892 and in 1904 became 'Aktiengesellschaft'. It became a renowned manufacturer of mechanical musical instruments producing barrel piano orchestrions under the name 'Atlantic'. In 1892, it pioneered a pneumatic action for the playing of pianos using perforated paper music producing electric pianos under the name Phonola. It introduced first a 72-note cabinet-style piano player called the Phonola and later Dea, Phonoliszt, Konzert-Phonoliszt, and Konzert-Clavitist. The range of player pianos included the Solophonola, Duophonola and Triphonola player pianos, the last two being reproducing instruments. Also made the Dea which was a pneumatically played violin attached to a piano, and the Dea-Violina and later Phonoliszt-Violina which was a piano surmounted by three violins all played pneumatically and driven by an electric motor. The last instrument was launched in 1910 and became a sensation of the Leipzig annual musical industries trade fair. Hupfeld's association with Blüthner Pianos in London led to their sharing the same premises (7-13 Wigmore Street) in the 1920s. Prior to this, their London agent had been a Mr M Sinclair, who established the Solophonola Company at 16-17 Orchard Street. By the mid-1920s, the Hupfeld London address and showrooms were at 28-30 Wigmore Street where it displayed the Phonoliszt-Violina, an instrument similar to the earlier Dea-Violina but based on their very fine all-metal player piano, the Phono-Liszt. In 1916 the company was granted a German patent for a multiple roll-changing mechanism that could be fitted to pneumatic orchestrions. This could take up to a dozen music rolls and play them sequentially and automatically. Hupfeld's Leipzig factory with its six floors and large wings was the largest in Europe devoted to mechanical musical instruments. In November 1926, Hupfeld amalgamated with **Zimmermann** [*qv*], becoming Hupfeld-Gebr Zimmermann and changing its address to Petersstrasse 4, Postschliessfach 215, Leipzig Cl, between 1926 and 1928. All Hupfeld music rolls, including those made under their registered trade mark 'Animatic', were made on special paper bearing the watermark 'Phonola' and the year of manufacture - a unique feature indeed. Hupfelds excelled in the production of the all-metal player action in later years, dispensing with wood, rubber tubing and cloth. The Hupfeld reproducing actions were widely used in Blüthner pianos. The firm is thought to have remained in existence until the outbreak of the 1939-45 war. The Vienna address was VI Mariahilferstrasse 9. Wholesale distribution of Hupfeld products was through several leading agents including H Peters & Company of Leipzig, Henry Klein in London and Guldman & Company (*est* 1896) of 7, Sugar Lane, Withy Green, Manchester, who also handled Racca cardboard-playing pianos.

Ibach & Sohn, Rudolf, Neuer Weg 40/42, Winkelstr 5/7, and Alter Markt 4, Barmen, Germany, with a branch at Mittelstr 25, Schwelm (Westfalia). Johannes Adolf Ibach (1766-1848) opened his first workshop at Beyenburg near Düsseldorf in 1794. Carl Rudolf Ibach (1804-1863) expanded the business and the business entered the 20th century as Rudolf Ibach Sohn. Remembered as the moving force behind the return to the importance of piano-case decoration and design, Rudolf II embraced the reproducing piano era and was one of the earliest manufacturers to fit the Welte-Mignon red-paper-roll system to his best instruments. While considered by some to have sustained an old-fashioned appearance to their pianos, the Ibach piano is remembered as a first-class instrument to rival the best in the world.

Icart, Antonio, 23 San Agustin, Tarragona, Spain. Established in 1875 as a maker of street pianos and also a hirer of these instruments, *fl.*1903.

Imhof & Mukle. Founded at Vöhrenbach in the Black Forest in 1845, the Imhof family is associated with high-quality barrel-operated pipe-organs and orchestrion organs. Instruments of the highest possible quality emerged from their workshops and, with a rich export trade, the family sought overseas representation. The upshot was the formation, in 1870, of Imhof & Mukle at 46 Oxford Street, London. In 1883 it moved to larger and new premises at 110 New Oxford Street. The business was also sometime at 547 Oxford Street and additionally had a 'manufactory' at 9 Sandiland Street, Holborn, London, in 1880. Daniel Imhof took out British Patents in 1866 for improvements in the machinery of chimes and the striking of drums and other instruments of percussion by self-acting organs'. A very handsome drawing-room barrel piano has survived complete with two barrels, each of which bear a pre-pinning barrel label stating 'Imhof & Mukle'. The music dates from c.1846. With the coming of the 1920s, the firm stocked player pianos and had its own music-roll company (Mukle & Davis's Muvis rolls made by the **Up-to-Date Music Roll Co** with its eponymous brand name Muvis).

Imperial Organ & Piano Company Ltd, 45 King's Road, Camden Town, London NW1. Piano and organ manufacturers who also made a combined piano and organ as well as player pianos c.1930.

Industria Nazionale Autopiani e Pianoforti (I N A P), 3 via Biella, Turin, Italy. Makers of player pianos, *fl.*1930. Operated by Giuseppe Cavana.

Jacob, L, Kugl Hofl, Stuttgart, Germany. A manufacturer of disc-playing piano orchestrions c.1895-1900.

Jacquard, Joseph Marie, Lyons, France. Joseph Marie Jacquard (1752-1834) was a silk-weaver and straw-hat maker who perfected a loom that could weave patterns automatically. Developed between 1801 and 1808, it made use of cardboard strips, suitably perforated, to control the weaving functions in the cloth-weaving loom. His invention was intended as a means to the production of woven patterned carpets and was to become the Jacquard Loom. Because it was thought likely to cause unemployment amongst the loom workers he was faced with a barrage of hostility but his loom's advantages were eventually accepted and by 1812 there were 11,000 is use in France. The system of punched holes used to operate a mechanical, electrical or pneumatic function that he developed was to be used half a century later for making the music programme for an organ, so replacing the bulky wooden barrel. Several inventors were responsible for this stage, among them Claude Félix Seytre who used perforated card to play a musical instrument in 1842. Not until the 1880s, however, was punched card successfully used in production piano-players. From there it was but a logical step to the perforated paper music-roll. The name of Jacquard therefore goes down in history as the man who paved the way to the piano-roll.

Janisch, Franz, Neubaugasse 47, Vienna VII, Austria. Franz Janisch succeeded the business of his father Josef as manufacturer of orchestrions, barrel organs and other music wares as well as acting as a distributor of other mechanical musical instruments. He is known to have been at work 1900-1910. His name appears on a large piano orchestrion in the Walt Bellm collection, Sarosota, Florida.

Jebavy, Franz, Reichsstrasse 118, Trautenau, Bohemia. Maker of piano orchestrions and barrel organs, *fl.*1903.

Jenkinson Player Action Company, Inc, 912-14 Elm Street, Cincinnati, USA. In 1913 advertised 'turn your straight pianos into players' using prefabricated components.

Johnson Piano Company, E P, 34 N Grove Avenue, Elgin, Illinois, USA. Factory in Ottawa, Illinois. Makers of the Artonian player-piano. *Fl.*1930.

Jones, Thomas Linforth, 53a Franciscan Road, Tooting, London. An engineer who devised and patented in 1905 a method of operating a coin-freed clockwork barrel piano in a public place from remotely situated coin boxes. The slot boxes could be situated anywhere in the building and the release of the piano's clockwork was through 'electro-magnetic contacts'. He was later to improve upon his system in collaboration with G Phillips.

Jorio, D, Modane (Savoy), France. Maker of barrel pianos, *fl.*1909.

Jorio, Amedeo & Fratelli, Giuliano di Roma, Rome, Italy. Street-organ and piano maker, *fl.*1930.

Kamenik, Joseph, Prague, Czechoslovakia. A maker of street barrel organs and pianos who was the last maker to follow his trade in that city, c.1926.

Kaps, Ernst, Semininarstr 20, Dresden, Germany. Established in 1858, the Kaps business was one of Germany's oldest piano-makers. Operated by Konsul Ernst Eugen Kaps and William Ernst Kaps, by the turn of the century this large business manufactured a range of self-playing pianos and other instruments, automata, phonographs, &c. The London agent was Philip Cohen, 224 Brixton Road, London SW.

Karn & Company Ltd, D W, 3 Newman Street, London W. The D W Karn Company was set up at Woodstock, Canada, in 1865 to manufacture the 'Karn-Organ' harmonium-style reed organ. Later moved into player systems for pianos and manufactured the Pianauto piano-player. The business established two branches, one in Ottawa and, as early as 1867, this one in London. Listed in 1909 it appears to have closed by 1912.

Kästner, Maximilian Macarius. Born in Germany in 1876, Kastner was the inventor of the Triumph piano player, the Auto Piano player piano, and the Kastonome expression piano. Interned as an alien during the First World War, he returned to player pianos after the war only to lose his life in an accident in 1924.

Kästner-Autopiano Akt-Ges, 6 Wittenbergerstrasse, Leipzig, Germany. Also registered as Kastner & Company Pianos-Apparate Akt-Ges. Makers of player pianos and actions. This business patented a system of unit valves for the player in 1929 in which each pneumatic and motor was fashioned in metal and could be removed and replaced in a few moments. This dispensed with the wooden action components and wooden valve chest. Also produced music rolls. The company also had a controlling interest in the Rachals and Lipp piano factories. The London offices were at 196 Great Portland Street (*see below*).

Kastner & Company, Ltd, 34-6 Margaret Street, Oxford Circus, London W. Maximilian Kastner established his business in London in 1903, later expanding it with premises in Germany (see above) and Amsterdam. He manufactured the Kastner-Autopiano expression instrument, later called the Triumph, as well as the Kasto player action to fit in existing pianos. Manufacturer of piano rolls who made a large quantity of both 65- and 88-note rolls. Other addresses recorded for Kastner in London before the First World War included 196 Great Portland Street, 191 Regent Street and 62 Conduit Street. The original Kastner actions were German-built in Leipzig and the Kastner Triumph piano-players were much cheaper than the Pianola of Aeolian. The peak of Kastner's London business followed the patenting of the British-made Kastonome in 1911 and 1912 but with the outbreak of the First World War both material and labour were in short supply. Having a German-sounding name was also a bad marketing move but worse was to come: under the Trading with the Enemy Act (1916), the business was forcibly wound up in December 1916, a receiver being appointed to the Auto-Piano Company. There was considerable resistance to the application of the Act in this instance with the directors of this British company raising strong objection. This was on account of the fact that the company had been manufacturing pianos and players in England since 1912 and fitting them into both British and German pianos. Its Kastonome player was a complex assembly which had a separate theme hole for each note in the tracker bar. Unique is the appearance of the Kastner tracker-bar for it has a matrix of holes at each end – 9x4 at the bass end, and 6x9 at the treble. The playing compass was 85 notes. The company also made ordinary player actions in Britain that it marketed through its associate company, the Direct Action Company, under the name Arrow. In spite of this strong connection, the Act was enforced and the company wound up. The associate company became the **Direct Pneumatic Action Company** *[qv]* and on June 11th 1917 a new company was registered - Triumph Auto Pianos Ltd *[qv]* - with a capital of £20,000 [$80,000] to carry on the business. One of the directors was Frederick H Saffell of Teignmouth Road, Brondesbury in north London. Saffell started work for Kastners in 1907 and remained with the business until the last war. He was also associated with the running of piano makers Barratt & Robinson up to the time of his death in 1975. Triumph-Auto Pianos Ltd was to survive until 1929 when it was liquidated, only to be reborn as Triumph Auto Pianos (1930) Ltd with a £150,000 [$600,000] capitalisation. It was later amalgamated with Barratt & Robinson. The complexity of the original Kastner action with its double pneumatic valve seats was ultimately replaced by a more conventional type of player action in which the so-called Triumphodist control was operated by the normal Themodist-type roll perforations. One of the late player products was the Maestrel piano. The Kastonome action was not fitted after 1914. The Kastner Autopiano action was fitted into a number of pianos including Allison, Lipp and Rachals, both these last-mentioned being Kastner subsidiaries. Maximilian Kastner was interned during the war in North London's Alexander Palace military prison but after the end of hostilities he was released and began to rebuild his shattered business. Sadly he was denied success, being knocked down and killed in a motor accident in 1924.

Keith, Prowse & Company. 159 New Bond Street, London W. Founded by R W Keith, the company first appeared at 131 Cheapside between 1829 and 1832, and then at 42 Cheapside between 1832 and 1846 in which year Keith died. William Prowse, a partner, continued on his own between about 1846 and 1865 when H Bryan Jones joined Prowse and the title reverted to Keith, Prowse & Company. The business was the manufacture and sale of musical instruments and the publishing of music. The company had its own piano factory making both ordinary instruments and barrel pianos, one of which was a clockwork-driven model for use in public houses and suchlike. This was called the Pennyano, had a compasss of 48 notes and played 10 tunes. Many other barrel pianos of the coin-freed variety bear this name, sometimes carved on the front barrel fall, but it is thought that many of these were not made by the company but commissioned Irom other, better known clockwork-piano makers. During the First World War, Keith, Prowse made new music for German piano orchestrions and orchestrion organs. By 1939 the business had many branches across London where it retailed gramophone records and operated as music publishers and sellers, as well as instrument dealers. It also sold theatre tickets and, having survived the 1939-45 war, concentrated increasingly on this business and that of travel, tourism and corporate hospitality at sporting events until its financial collapse (with debts of an estimated £7m [$12.6m]) on September 9th 1991 and subsequent closure.

Kelly, George Bradford, Jamaica Plain, Suffolk County, Boston, Massachusetts, USA. A builder of reed organs and an early pioneer in self-playing reed instruments, Kelly invented a wind-operated music-roll motor in 1886. This was the subject of US Patent number 357,933 dated 15 February 1887. This made use of sliding valves and closing ports to pneumatic motors. This type of motor was at once adopted and, upon expiration of the patent, was used widely throughout the world with but slight variations. He was a prolific inventor and was finally acquired by Aeolian and in his subsequent patents gave his address as 362 Fifth Avenue, New York - that of his employers.

Kibbey & Company, H C, 209 State Street, Chicago. In 1909 were described as makers of automatic pianos.

Kimball & Company, W W, Wabash Avenue & Jackson Boulevard, Chicago, Illinois, USA. Founded in 1857 by William Wallace Kimball (1828-1904). Continued by his son, Curtis N Kimball (1862-1936) who oversaw the introduction of the Kimball player-piano action in 1906. A maker of consistently good instruments that saw service on the US concert platform, the Kimball company expanded into theatre, concert and residence organs, some with player actions. In 1932, the firm bought the Welte-Tripp Organ Corporation of South Beach, NY, together with its music-roll libraries, recording devices, patents, good-will and machinery. However (as recorded by Van Allen Bradley in his book *Music for the Millions*, 1957) it soon had a white elephant on its hands thanks to the Depression which, combined with the rise of the phonograph, dealt the American player piano and player organ industries a deathblow.

Kintzing, Peter, Neuwied, Germany. A maker of musical clocks who moved to Paris and *c.*1780, in collaboration with the master cabinet-maker Roentgen, created a musical automation comprising the figure of a young girl with articulated arms, hands and fingers who played upon a stringed instrument. Peter Kinzing (sometimes 'Kintzing') is remembered for his development of the compound musical clock combining the stringed back of a harfenuhr with a pipe organ. A number of these compound clocks still exist, a famous one being the so-called Marie Antoinette clock at Nemours Mansion, Wilmington, Delaware, the twin of which is in the Conservatoire des Arts et Mètiers in Paris. The collaboration of Kinzing with Roentgen led to the establishment of a school of compound musical clock making at Neuwied where a small number of makers created and signed very similar instruments all featuring the dulcimer/organ combination. All date from the period around 1780-1795 and represent the pinnacle of the genre.

Klein & Company, Henry, 84 Oxford Street, London W. Agents for mechanical music work, particularly Polyphon musical boxes and Amorette organettes. Also was agent for Peter's electric pianos made in Leipzig. In 1901, one example of these sold for £128 [$510].

Kleinschmidt & Company, Adolf, Herderstr. 4, Braunschweig, Germany. Established in 1902 as makers of piano orchestrions operated by descending weights.

Klepetár, Hynek, 11 Zelèzna ui, Prague, Czechoslovakia. Maker of electric pianos and piano orchestrions, *fl.*1930. Possibly successor to:

Klepetár, Ignaz, Eisengasse 11 and Gensengasse 24, Prague, Czechoslovakia. Warehouse and depot for electric pianos and piano orchestrions, *fl.*1909.

Klepetár, J, Prague. Maker of weight-operated barrel piano orchestrions, early twentieth century. One example seen featured a 37-key iron-framed piano with drum, triangle and cymbal.

Klingmann & Company, G, Wiener Str. 46, Berlin SO 36, Germany. Business founded in 1869 and run by Bruno and Hermann Klingmann. Makers of 65- and 88-note player pianos under the name Lyrist.

Klinker & Company, 15/17 Fore Street, London, EC, also at 30 Wigmore Street. Described as agents and distributors of piano players and player pianos, Klinker advertised in June 1904 that it held the 'sole agency' for the Claviola Player Action. Whether this was just an action or a push-up piano-player is uncertain although by the price it suggests that it the latter. Described as having a compass of 72 notes and having all-brass tubing. Price was 50 gns [$210]. The company was a distributor for Hupfeld so this was probably one of their early products. The 72-note compass is curious, though, for Hupfeld was, at this time, mainly 73-note. The Claviola player piano was made in America by **Ludwig & Company**: there seems an uncorroborated connection.

Knabe & Company, William, Fifth Avenue, Corner 39th Street, New York City, USA. Valentin Wilhelm Knabe (1803-1864) was a Prussian born in Kreuzburg who emigrated to Baltimore in 1833 and eventually was to found, in 1837, the business that was to become one of America's most distinguished piano makers. Later joined with his sons Ernest (1837-1894) and William II (1841-1889) to form Knabe & Company. It was Ernest who developed the grand and upright piano stringing scales that were to give their pianos their particularly-admired characteristics. Knabe expanded with factories at Baltimore and Maryland. Initially made player pianos fitted with the Angelus action. In 1908, together with makers Chickering and Mason & Hamlin were the first to be absorbed into the American Piano Company. From then on the Knabe name became associated with top-quality Ampico-action reproducing instruments. After the bankruptcy and subsequent reorganization of the American Piano Company, Knabe became part of the Aeolian Corporation in 1932.

Koenigsberg et Cie, 28 rue Camusel, Brussels, Belgium. Makers of parts for electric player pianos, established in 1900.

Kohler & Campbell, 50th Street and 11th Avenue, New York City, USA. Founded in 1896 by John Calvin Campbell (1864-1908) and Charles Kohler (1868-1913). Both were residents of Newark and both studied 'scientific' piano design and construction. Producers of the Pianista pneumatic push-up cabinet-style piano player. The company slogan was 'Knows no technical difficulties'; *c.*1899. With the sky-rocketting popularity of players, the business opened a second division devoted entirely to the making of 'interior' player actions for player-piano makers. Produced several designs of action at different prices including the Autopiano and the Standard.

Kohler Industries, New York City, USA. Manufacturers of the Welte-Mignon (Licensee) action for reproducing pianos. They also controlled the Auto Pneumatic Action Co; the Standard Pneumatic Action Co; DeLuxe Player Roll Corporation (subsidiary of Auto Pneumatic Action Co); Republic Player Roll Corporation (subsidiary of The Autopiano Co), and a number of piano makers, sundries concerns and associated makers. In 1927, Kohler Industries bought the Simplex Player Action Company, the primary competitor of Standard Pneumatic Action Company. The Welte-Mignon (Licensee) action was installed in over a hundred different American pianos and their slogan was 'The Master's Fingers on your Piano'. Kohler Industries was liquidated on September 16th, 1930. The goodwill and assets of Auto Pneumatic, Standard Pneumatic and Simplex Player was acquired by Aeolian.

Kotykiewicz, Theofil, Strassengasse 18, Vienna, Austria. Peter Titz began his musical instrument business in 1852 making reed organs. After his death the business was taken over by Teofil Kotykiewicz, jnr. Invented the Kromarograph recording harmonium *c.*1900. An example of this curious device survives in the Deutsches Museum, Munich.

Kowatz, M, Bahnhofstr. 25, Beuthen Ober-Schlesien, Germany. Established in 1893 as makers of piano orchestrions and agents for other mechanical musical instruments.

Kranich & Bach, 235-237 East 23rd Street, New York City, USA. Helmuth Kranich was born in 1833 in Gross-Breitenbach, in the German province of Thuringia. Jacques Bach was born in the same year at Lorentzen, Alsace. Both emigrated to the United States where they met as members of a seventeen-strong group of piano-makers who had the Utopian goal of forming a co-op-

erative. In April 1864 they formed the New York Pianoforte Company. Two years later, after endless squabbling amongst the 'members', it was clear that the group could not survive as an entity. In July 1866 six of the founders left, amongst them Helmuth Kranich and Jacques Bach, and formed the firm of Kranich & Bach Company. Neither of the founders was destined for long life, Bach dying in 1894 and Kranich in 1902. In May 1890, however, the firm was changed into a corporation under the directorship of Frederick and Alvin Kranich and Louis P Bach. The business made high-quality pianos and were responsible for several inventions well-received in their time. One was the so-called 'Isotonic' pedal which dispensed with the shifting-keyboard system of 'unacorda' playing in grand pianos. The company made good player pianos that are respected by collectors today. Ultimately became part of the **Aeolian Corporation.**

Krell Auto-Grand Piano Company, Connersville, Indiana, USA. Makers of the Krell Auto-Grand upright piano as well as the Auto-Player and the Pian-Auto. *See also under* **Auto-Grand Piano Co.**

Krell Piano Company, Richmond and Harriet Street, also 118, 4th Street, W, Cincinnati, (with a branch at Portsmouth) Ohio, USA. Albert Krell was born in Cincinnati in 1859 and became one of the pioneer developers of the player piano in America. In 1899 he showed an electric piano in New York that was played by magnets beneath the piano keys and powered by a number of wet-cell batteries. Produced the Royal piano and player-piano. The Krell interior player had a unit pneumatic action, similar to that used in Britain by Broadwood in its first player grands as well as Link and a very few others. These large individual units were arranged under the keyboard in four rows and each unit could be easily and readily removed for examination. Combined with the **French Piano Company** *[qv]* as the Krell-French Piano Company in 1903. The following year Krell formed the **Auto-Grand Piano Company** at New Castle and, later. Connerville, Indiana. Albert Krell resigned in 1905.

Kriebel, H, 28, Rheinsberger Str 59, Berlin N.28, Germany. The business of Herman Kriebel was established in 1863 and later became one of the many minor makers of player-piano in Berlin. By the early part of the 20th century, founder Herman had died leaving the business in charge of his widow, Anna, and son Herman Jnr. The business survived the First World War and is remembered for its introduction, in 1931, of 'The Wireless Piano', a normal upright incorporating an all-mains wireless receiving-set in the left upper panel, and an electric gramophone in the opposite panel while a loudspeaker was placed centrally in the front. This was detachable and could be placed elsewhere if desired. Another version, for use in public places, included an electrically-driven player mechanism so offering a complete entertainment system. While Germany was not as affected by the Great Depression as Britain and America, its export sales were and within a very short space of time both The Wireless Piano and its makers were gone.

Kuhl & Klatt, Wusterhausener Str 17 and Runge-Strasse No 18, Südost-Passage, Berlin SO 16, Germany. Martin Hesse and Paul Klatt described themselves as manufacturers of pneumatic self-acting musical instruments, but it appears that they were also agents. The business, established in 1899, was renowned for electric pianos, in particular those equipped with accumulators for providing power. These were marketed under the name Pneuma and a similar device was available for church organs under the name Pneumatist. The Vorsteller was the name of Kuhl & Klatt's player action.

Labrador, Battasar, 127 Toledo, Madrid, Spain. Barrel-piano and organ hirer and repairer, *fl.*1909.

Lacape et Cie, Jean, Paris. Set up in business making pianos in 1857. In 1882, patented a treadle-driven mechanical piano, playing either from a barrel or mechanically from a tune sheet. Won a bronze medal for barrel pianos at the Brussels Exposition in 1883.

Lafleur & Son, J R, 15 Green Street, Leicester Square, London WC. Established in 1780. Producers of street pianos in 1880. Later at 147 Wardour Street as music publishers and importers of woodwind, string and brass instruments,

Lakin & Company, R J, 67 Besley Street, Streatham, London SW16. Established at this address in 1934, Lakin came originally from Bristol. He advertised as maker of 'mechanical organs' but it is not known for certain whether or not he did actually make barrel organs or barrel pianos. It is known that he sold both music and mechanical street pianos and organs. He also did repairs until ceasing business in 1943.

Langenbucher. A family of renowned makers of musical automata that lived in Augsburg, Germany in the l6th and early 17th century. There appears to have been two strains to the family, one headed by Achilles Langenbucher (Augsburg Freeman 1611, died *c.*1650) and Veit Langenbucher (born about 1587; died *c.*1631). Small clocks with automata, clockwork spinets and automated scenes were produced by these names. An extraordinary insight into the relationship between Balthasar Langenbucher (son of Veit) and the other famous Augsburg automata-makers appears in *Die Welt als Uhr* (edited by Klaus Maurice and Otto Mayr) in a paper by Eva Groiss. An English-language version of this appears as 'The Bidermann-Langenbucher Lawsuit' in *Music & Automata*, Vol 1, pp 10-12.

Lauberger & Gloss, Trostgasse 108/110/121, Vienna X, Austria. Established in 1900 as a maker of pianofortes and piano actions and run by Anton Lauberger, Peter Proskowec and Theodor Gloss. In 1912 was advertising as specialists in 'Konzert-Pianino, Pneuma and other instruments', which appears to suggest that they were agents for Berlin- and Leipzig-made instruments. Described as 'Grösste u Leistengsfähigste Pianofabriken der Österr Unger-Monarchie. En-gros-Export'.

Leabarjan Manufacturing Company, 521 Hanover Street, Hamilton, Ontario, Canada. Founded in 1911 to market a small table-top music-roll perforating machine for the amateur to punch his own music rolls. It was designed by John C Lease. With the assistance of Carl Bartels and the finance of a man named Franz Janzen, the choice of company (and product) name was derived from the first three letters of each name - Leabarjan. A thoroughly practical if slow-to-use machine, it required dedication to make more than a short and simple musical arrangement since it was limited in matters of speed. The total number sold is believed to be fewer than 1,000 and the business closed in 1928.

Leidi, Allessandro, Via S Lazzaro 9 (Via Osia), Bergamo, Italy. Barrel piano maker, agent, hirer, *fl.*1907.

Leipziger Orchestrionwerke Paul Lösche, Blumenstr. 10-14, Leipzig-Göhlis, Germany. Founded on October 2nd, 1902, by Paul Lösche. Manufactured a wide range of electric pianos and piano-orchestrions. A major maker, Lösche marketed his products primarily in Germany, Belgium and England. Among these instruments were two models of Art-Playing pianos that played hand-played music rolls performed by stated artists. The business closed around 1930.

Liebetanz & Richter, Grabschenerstrasse 85, Breslau, Germany. Established in 1902 and managed by Karl Krause, made piano orchestrions. By 1909 the firm had shifted to Grabschenerstrasse

Liebmann, Ernst Erich, Hainstrasse 10, Gera, Reuss, Germany. Established in 1871 as a harmonium builder who also made a self-playing device for harmoniums called the Liebmannista covered by German Patent number 283302. Also made the Kalliston organette.

Limonaire Frères, 166 Avenue Daumesnil, Paris, France. The old-established business of Limonaire Brothers, set up in 1840 for the making of street organs, dance organs and organs for public places, turned to the manufacture of barrel pianos early in the 20th century and, after the end of the First World War, launched a range of piano-orchestrions and player-pianos. The company speciality was its 'electric orchestras' playing perforated paper music rolls. Clockwork barrel pianos were made until around 1923.

Lindner Sohn, Julius P, Heilgeiststrasse 86, Stralsund, Germany. Piano makers founded in 1825. By 1908 were manufacturing electro-pneumatic player pianos.

Link Piano Company, Inc, 183-5 Water Street, Binghamton, New York, and 532 Republic Building, Chicago, USA. Founded in 1916 by Edwin A Link, formerly of the Schaff Piano Company of Huntington, Indiana, out of the remains of the Automatic Musical Company *[qv]* which had entered financial difficulty as early as 1910. This had been one of the earliest makers of coin-operated pianos in the States and sold the Encore Banjo and the Hiawatha Self-Playing Xylophone. Now bankrupt, Link was appointed chairman of the creditors' committee. He realised the opportunity to re-form the company and so founded the Link Piano Company. This was to turn out about 300 coin-operated instruments a year. Incorporated in 1916, Edwin A Link's son, Ed Link, later took over many of the firm's patents and applied them to the manufacture of the famous pneumatically operated Link Trainer still in use with many flying schools. The Link company's primary contribution was as makers of coin-operated pianos and instruments with orchestral effects as well as pipe organs and piano orchestrions.

Lipp & Sohn, Richard, Weigenburgerstrasse 32, and Schillerstrasse 12, Stuttgart, Germany. Founded in 1831. By 1900 the business was run by Paul Beisbarth and Karl Fischer. Manufactured player pianos including the Duca-Lipp electrically operated reproducing piano. Introduced in the spring of 1910, this cost £300 [$1,200]. None is known to survive. The London showrooms were at 56 Berners Street, off Oxford Street, Mr Fritz Willeringhaus being manager. Lipp became a wholly-owned subsidiary of **Kastner** after World War One. Built the Lippola player fitted with the Kastonome player action. Later built pianos with Higel (Canadian) actions.

Lissi Gaetano, Piazza Alessandro, Como, Italy. Barrel piano maker and handler, *fl.*1909.

Llinares, Vicente, 11 Peu de la Crue, Barcelona, Spain. Manufacturer of small street pianos including modern miniature instruments playing 23 notes on metal rods and known as 'Impuesto de Lujo a Metálico'. Known to be in business in 1930, the firm's trademark 'Faventia' appears on instruments at least until the 1990s.

Lochmann, Paul. *See* **Original-Musikwerke Paul Lochmann, GmbH.**

Longman, John, 131, Cheapside, London. A maker of church and chamber barrel organs, *fl.*1801-22. Patented a keyboardless barrel-playing upright organ driven by weight-operated clockwork. Several examples survive, the most ornate of which is to be found in the Nationaal Museum van Speelklok tot Pierement (former Cyril de Vere Green Collection) and in The Morris Museum, New Jersey (former Murtogh Guinness Collection).

Lorenz, Wenzel, Schillerstrasse 176, Trautenau, Bohemia. Established in 1892. Maker of weight-driven piano orchestrions, *fl.*1909.

Lösche, Paul. *See* **Leipziger Orchestrionwerke Paul Lösche.**

Luche, C, 70, rue des Tournelles, Paris, France. Maker of clockwork and electric café pianos under the trademark 'Pianos ELCÉ'. *Fl.*1930.

Ludwig & Company, 970 Southern Boulevard, New York City, USA. John Ludwig, born in New York in 1858, was the son of an émigré piano-maker from Hamburg, Germany. Charles A Ericsson was a Swede, born in 1859 in Gothenburg who moved to New York with his parents in 1866. He trained in piano-making and then, with Ludwig, formed a partnership with him in 1889 (some sources give 1888). The business enjoyed a rapid rise in reputation established by the award of a prize medal at the 1901 Pan-American Exposition held in Buffalo, NY (and remembered more for the assassination of President McKinley than for its exhibits), for 'The Ludwig Piano and The Claviola Piano Player'. In 1902 the business was formally established as Ludwig & Company. It took over piano-makers Perry Brothers, built factories and, unusually, opened a series of retail outlets. A subsidiary business known as The Claviola Company was set up before 1910 to concentrate on player pianos. In 1933 the business was acquired by **Ricca & Son** of 604 E 132nd Street and 884 E 134th Street, New York City. Ricca was founded in 1891. John Ludwig is known to have retired in 1911 and the Ludwig retail outlets to have continued well into the 1930s in Philadelphia, Pittsfield and Scranton. In 1952, the Ludwig name was acquired from Hugo F Ricca by Atlas Piano Company of Chicago which maker discontinued the name the following year.

Lüneburg & Company Musikwerke GmbH, Altona on the Elbe, Germany. Founded in 1908, the office and works were at Rothestrasse 64. The products included the Chitarrone electric expression piano, and orchestrions Bellisore and Annalies.

Machineki & Söhne, F, XVII/3, Ortliebgasse 5, Vienna, Austro-Hungary. Established in 1882 as makers of mechanical musical instruments. Built a barrel-playing piano orchestrion called the International.

McTammany, John. Few people have been subjected to such universal lack of acclaim as John McTammany (1845-1915). He remains probably one of the most underrated inventors in the history of the player piano. History has not treated him well because, having been cheated of his early inventions and patented ideas, he chose to try to defend himself. In so doing, he dragged the names of others into the legal limelight and thus acquired the unwarranted image of a busybody and troublemaker. Posthistory has done him no favours either for, in having limited resources, he could no longer pursue his rightful rewards through the medium that, in America at least, is indispensable – the Courts of Law. Even to this day – almost a century after the events – there are those that still deride his claims. The facts are that McTammany was the real pioneer of the use of the sliding paper valve as applied to the playing of a reed instrument and he made the first player reed organs at Cambridge, Massachusetts, that played perforated paper music. Inventor with a number of patents to his credit, his earliest auto-playing organ dates from around 1864 although it was not to be patented until 1876. Although his claim to be the inventor of the player piano stems solely from his reed organ system, it is true to say that applied pneumatics owe much to his pioneering work. Born in Glasgow June 26th, 1845, John McTammany moved to America in 1857 to join his father who had emigrated in 1847. While others successfully clawed their way up through the fortunes of life, McTammany led a hard life and was never comfortably off. Possessed of insufficient funds to renew his patents, he had to watch helplessly as they were exploited by others. He died penniless on March 26th 1915 in the military hospital, Stamford, Connecticut, and was given a public funeral with music provided on a grand player piano. He left behind the manuscript of a strange and highly personal, perhaps biased book called *The Technical History of the Player*. Published soon after his death and prefaced with a valedictory foreword by William Geppert, editor of *The Musical Courier Extra*, the author subtitled himself 'the inventor of the Player Piano', a credit that the publishers saw fit to preserve. Although written in somewhat embittered vein, this book has been the misjudged and misunderstood testament to his life and claims and survives today as a most unusual yet invaluable reference work

Maestro Company, The, Box 10, Eldridge, New York, USA. Produced the Maestro cabinet piano-player *c.*1899 at $125 [£31 8s] - half the price of the rivals Pianola and the Cecilian. A utility player which stood on four spindly legs. Also made key-top player of the same namewhich was operated by turning a handle. This was sold for $40.00 [£10.00] around 1900. The Maestro was the first pneumatic keytop player establishing a genus that recurred at intervals over the next sixty years or so. It was designed by British-born Lewis B Doman (1868-1935), inventor and player innovator who later played a major part in the invention of the Ampico action. In 1907, Maestro moved to Syracuse, New York and changed its name to The Amphion Piano Player Company *[qv]* at the same address. Doman became chief engineer to offshoot The Amphion Player Action Company. It was this company that manufactured the Ampico mechanism in Syracuse until the late 1920s when manufacture was shifted to East Rochester, New York.

Malcolm & Company, John, Erskine Road, Regent's Park, London NW. The piano-making business of John Malcolm was established before the First World War and was incorporated with **John G Murdoch & Company Ltd** *[qv]* as a subsidiary. Makers of the Malcolm piano player. By the time of the 1930s Depression John Malcolm & Son was one of the three leading manufacturers of piano actions in the country. This followed a 1928 take-over bid that led to a consortium management buy-out spearheaded by James Murdoch.

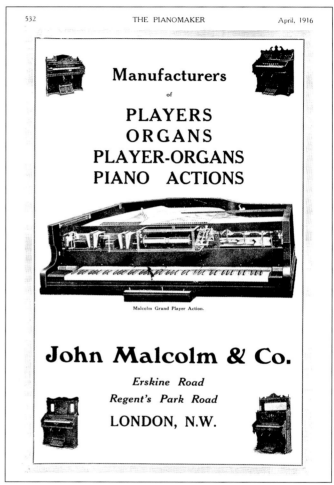

Mannheimer Musikwerke Maria Schmid, S.6, Nr 3, Mannheim, Germany. Established in 1908 and managed by Emil Schmid, maker of both piano- and pipe-orchestrions, as well as gramophones. Handled various makes of mechanical musical instruments.

Manufacture Français de Piano Automatiques, à Buisson-Rond, près Chambéryt (Savoie), France. Manufacturer of electric pianos with barrels. Advertised (in 1928) all types of automatic piano, jazz-band pianos and piano-orchestrions, all with interchangeable cylinders.

Maraschi, Francesco, Corso via Cene, Porta Novara 11 and Via Principe Amedeo 17, Vigevano, Pavia, Italy. Founded 1898. Agent and hirer of barrel pianos.

Marazzi, Ach, 50 Vico del Governo Vecchio, Rome, Italy. Street organ maker, *fl.*1930.

Mariani, Louis & Antonio, 133 Nueva, Figueras, Gerona, Spain. Street-piano agents, *fl.*1903. By 1909 Louis was still operating from this address but Antonio was at 15 Nueva, presumably on his own, also trading as an agent.

Marks & Harnett, 4 & 5 Rosoman Mews, London EC1. Advertised as manufacturers of 'piano-organs' from 1918 to 1919. No other information available.

Maroni, Giorgio, Varese, Como, Italy. Barrel-organ and piano maker, *fl.* 1930.

Marquette Piano Company, 415-17 15th Street, Chicago, Illinois, USA. Established in 1905. Makers of electric player pianos, orchestrions and photoplayers under the name Cremona. J P Seeburg *[qv]* originally worked for the company before setting up in business for himself *c.* 1907. In the early 1920s, when Marquette was not as successful as the Seeburg company, Cremona-labelled instruments were made using some Seeburg parts. One style of Cremona - the Style 3 - was made for Regina Music Box Company of Rahway who sold it as the Reginapiano. Some time after 1909 the company moved to 2421-39 Wallace Street in Chicago. Products are highly prized by collectors today.

Marromarco, Vincenzo, Piazza Arcivescovado 69, Bari, Italy. Street-piano and organ agent and hirer, *fl.* 1909.

Marshall Piano Company, 1508-1514, Dayton Street, Chicago, Illinois, USA. Controlled by J P Seeburg, the Marshall player piano was 'built to meet the requirements of the great majority of player purchasers'. *Fl.* 1920.

Marshall & Sons, Sir J Herbert, Angelus Hall, Regent House, 233 Regent Street, London W. Makers of the Artistyle player-piano music rolls. These provided printed accenting instructions to the melody notes so enabling the performer to interpret the music in a recommended way by reading the roll as he played it. Marshall also made player pianos and extended the music-roll side to include the Angelus Artistyle and the Artist Song Rolls labels. Later a separate company was formed called **The Artistyle Music Roll Company** with premises at 204-6 Great Portland Street, London W1. Marshall also extensively handled the Angelus diaphragm player action made by **Wilcox & White Company,** Meriden, USA, which was first applied to cabinet piano-players but was later supplied as an action for fitting in pianos by Brinsmead, Winkelmann, Emerson and Knabe. Supplied the Artrio reproducing action to other British makers. Also manufactured a reproducing action called the Carola which was made for Blüthner in its factory at Acton, Middlesex. The company also manufactured its own player pianos and at one time the Angelus was a close rival to the Pianola. Sir Herbert Marshall & Son was a family musical-instrument business started in Leicester at Belvoir Street in the 1860s and later at 34 Granby Street. In 1878 the business also opened in London. Run by two brothers, Herbert and Ernest: Herbert 'Bertie' Marshall was knighted by King Edward VII in 1902. When a Wilcox & White salesman introduced the Angelus to Ernest Marshall he was captivated with it and saw a great future for it in Britain. He bought the UK rights to the Angelus trade-mark. Initially Angelus actions were installed in ordinary pianos in a factory in Chalk Farm but when his timber supplier, George Rose, emigrated to Australia he allowed his name to be used for the new 'complete' piano. This was the Marshall & Rose Angelus. With the surprisingly close co-operation of Bechstein, Grotrian Steinweg and Blüthners, the scaling of the Marshall & Rose scale and tone was perfected. Eventually this instrument would be supplied to Blüthner in Germany to complete their own range. By the 1920s, Ernest Marshall became sceptical about reproducing pianos believing the era to be over. However, pressure from Ampico led him to adopt this reproducer and launch the Marshall & Rose Ampico. This marked the end (with an amusing twist) to a long and expensive feud between the Sir Herbert Marshall business and The Aeolian Company which had spent vast sums of money in advertising trying to queer the pitch of Marshall and the Angelus – largely without success (*see* Appendix 1). However, the end really was close and Ampico sent over 2,000 actions but only a few hundred were sold. Ampico then pulled out leaving Marshall with a warehouse of brand new actions. Marshall teamed up with cinema-organ makers Compton, and devised a method of connecting an Ampico grand piano to the organ for center-stage remote playing. The first installation (at the opening of the Empire Theatre Leicester Square with Reginald Foorte on the organ) brought

the house down when 'the phantom piano' (painted metallic blue) suddenly began to play. After that, Ernest Marshall sold every one of the Ampicos in stock. However, the deal was done at financial stretch and with the Depression at hand, two creditors in the music trade (one later established as a fraudster) forced the business into liquidation. Ernest Marshall bought the trading names from the liquidator and formed the Marshall Piano Company to look after the player side of the business and the roll library most of which (some 65,000 music rolls) had been sold to Harrods by the liquidator. The original company still exists as part of the group established in 1939 by Whelpdale, Maxwell and Codd with a factory in Clapham, London.

Marshall & Wendell Piano Company, Albany, New York, USA. Between 1830 and 1840, Albany became an early centre of American piano-making and a clutch of makers set up their workshops there. One of the early businesses was the partnership of Marshall, James & Traver, a short-lived enterprise which, in 1836, became Marshall & Wendell. This firm was thus one of the oldest of the established piano makers in America and quickly gained a reputation for high-quality instruments later winning exhibition awards for quality and tone. In 1900 the company moved its factory and offices to East Rochester and upon the formation of The American Piano Company in 1908 became part of that combine. It opened showrooms at 439 Fifth Avenue, New York where its instruments, including players, were held in highest esteem. Ampico reproducing actions were fitted in many grands by this maker. While upright Ampico installations were few and far between, the majority were in Marshall & Wendell instruments and known as the Style 5GE. The company was renowned for the beauty of its artistic case styles, both upright and grand.

Marteletti, Giuseppe, Vicola Giovanni Lanza, Casa propria, Casale Monferrato, Italy. Established in 1860 to manufacture barrel pianos and organs. By 1909 was producing very attractive clockwork instruments. Also operated a depôt in Alba.

Marteletti, Fratelli, 31 via Giovanni Lanza, Casale Monferrato, Alessandria, Italy. Maker of barrel pianos, *fl.* 1930.

Martinez, Antonio, 19 Mesoneros Romanos, Madrid, Spain. Barrel-piano dealer and hirer, *fl.* 1909.

Martinez, Fermin, 17 Brava Murillo, Madrid, Spain. Barrel-piano dealer and hirer, *fl.* 1909.

Maryland Automatic Banjo Company, 323 Calvert Street, N. Baltimore, Maryland. Maker of automatic banjos. *fl.* 1909. Probably a short-lived venture as no subsequent reference is known.

Maserati, Caesar, 92 New Chambers Street, New York, USA. An Italian organ maker who also built street barrel pianos mounted on carts, which he sold and hired out. He was in business in 1906 and his colleague, **Antoniazzi** *[qv]*, was later to establish the **B.A.B. Organ Company** *[qv]*. *See also* **Tomasso, Emilio.**

Massa, Antonio, Via Nizza 23 and Via Goito 15, Turin, Italy. The brothers Antonio and Giacomo Massa were makers of street barrel pianos and also had a large business hiring them out, *fl.*1909.

Maxfield & Sons, Ltd, 324-6 Liverpool Road, London N. Makers of the Maxfield piano player and also piano rolls.

Mazza, F, 112 via Consolazione, Rome, Italy. Maker of barrel pianos, *fl.*1930. *See* **Monetta.**

Mechanical Orguinette Company. Formed to manufacture Mason J Matthews' 'Orguinette' table reed organ which played perforated paper rolls. The firm then made the Aeolian player reed organ at which time it was amalgamated into the kernel of the Aeolian Company *[qv].*

Melnik Orchestrionfabrik, Albert, Reichsstrasse 61, Trautenau, Bohemia, Austria. Established in 1903 as maker of piano orchestrions, among which was the Delphin. In 1909 advertised: 'Best known and cheapest cylinder-musikworks with weight drawing up. Piano-orchestrions, specialities in mandolin and xylophone-works... Unexcelled durability and musical beauty...'

Mélodia Company, 39, rue La Boétie, Paris, France. Makers of a reproducing piano called the Mélodia. Action uncertain but may be a Duo-Art offspring. Premises were close to those of Gaveau, makers of a grand Duo-Art. *Fl.*1932.

Melville Clark Piano Company, Steinway Hall, 409 Steinway Building, Chicago, USA. Born in Oneida County, New York, Melville Clark (1850-1918), a member of the Storey & Clark Company of Chicago, took out patents for his Apollo piano player in 1899. The first Apollo played 58 notes and used a clockwork motor rewind system for the music roll. This cabinet-style player stood 36 inches high, was 41 inches long and 12 inches wide. Introduced in 1900, it also featured a transposing tracker bar - one of the first. Melville Clark was probably the first to make a piano with the player mechanism inside the case, *c.*1901. In 1902, he was the first to make a full-scale 88-note player action and was also the first to fit a player action into a grand piano (1904). In 1909, the Clark company was producing a player action to cater for five different sizes of rolls -58, 65, 70, 82 and 88 notes.

Menzel, Wilhelm, Warschauer Strasse 58, Berlin O, Germany. Established in 1890 as maker of pianos. Produced a patented pneumatic player action and also a range of player pianos.

Merlin, John Joseph.. Born at Huys near Liege in 1735, Merlin spent six years in Paris before coming to England in 1760 where he lived in the suite of the Spanish ambassador, Count de Guentes, in Soho Square. A talented musical instrument maker and inventor, he took out a patent in 1774 for a 'compound harpsichord' which was a combined harpsichord and piano with a downstriking action. In this year he was living in Little Queen Ann Street, St Marylebone and describing himself as a Mathematical Instrument Maker. Preserved in the Deutsches Museum, Munich, is a five-octave compound harpsichord inscribed: 'Josephus Merlin, Privilegiarius Novi Fortepiano Nr. 80, Londini, 1780'. Unusual is the fact that this mechanism is fitted with a copying-machine driven by a clockwork motor which notes the music being played as pencil marks on a long endless band of paper. Merlin went on to establish and operate a museum of novelties in Princes Street, Hanover Square. He invented an invalid chair (probably the first such device) and also the roller skate. Busby relates in his *Concert Room Anecdotes* (II, 137), how Merlin attended a ball at Carlisle House and traversed the room on his skates while playing the violin, an escapade which came to an abrupt end when he collided with a very valuable mirror which he smashed along with his fiddle while causing himself severe wounds. He died in 1804.

Migliavacca, Ettore, 3 via S Teodoro, Pavia, Italy. A maker of clockwork barrel pianos who also operated a factory at 16 via Casa del Popolo. *Fl.*1930.

Miglietti, Giovanni, Via Morosini 11, Turin, Italy. Founded in 1905 as makers of components and other parts for barrel pianos.

Mina, Giovanni, 2 First Street, Manhattan, New York, USA. An Italian who emigrated to America in 1880 and set up in business making barrel pianos and barrel organs and pinning carousel organ barrels. On his death, the business was taken over by **G Gazza** *[qv]* and moved to 71 Roosevelt Street nearby, but the business did not prosper and soon closed.

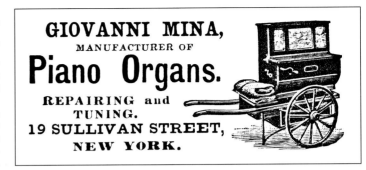
Minicucci del Manzo & Company, Torre del Greco, Naples, Italy. Agent and distributor for Racca's Piano-Melodicos and other mechanical instruments, *fl.*1909.

Miolis, Lino, 12 via Ormea, Turin, Italy. Maker of barrel organs and pianos, *fl.*1930.

Miralles, Antonio, 16 Amazonas, Madrid, Spain. Barrel-piano agent, dealer and hirer, *fl.*1909.

Modern Interaction Player Manufacturers, 23 South Street, Clair Street, Toledo, Ohio, USA. In 1920s advertised: 'Our specialty is Electrical Attachments for Foot-Pedal Player-Pianos . . . Automatic Speed Control Rewinders and Metal Pumps.' A short-lived enterprise of which no further details are known.

Mojon, Manger & Company, Bartletts Buildings, London EC.Well-known makers of large-size musical boxes, some with dancing dolls and orchestral effects. Also made coin-freed cylinder musical boxes and, later, mechanical harmoniums and pianos. Their factory, which produced watches and clocks as well as musical boxes, was at Chaux-de-Fonds, Geneva, and they had a branch warehouse at Oxford Terrace, Coventry. Their pianos were most probably manufactured for them in this country and branded. John Manger is described, in a patent application of 1886 relating to musical boxes, as being a 'Musical Box Importer'.

Mola, Cav Giuseppe, via Nizza 82, Turin, Italy. Founded in 1862 as makers of pianos, harmoniums and church organs who also made barrel pianos, *fl.*1909.

Möldner & Skreta. *See under* **Stefanie-Werke-Filiale.**

Molinari & Sons, G., 112 32nd Street, Brooklyn, New York, USA. The Molinari family were Italian imigrants who brought Italian street piano and organ technology to America. Produced many small barrel organs and barrel pianos for street use. The factory was started during the Civil War and for sixty years the family sustained the business, Joseph Molinari running a shop at 153 Elizabeth Street, Manhattan, where, it was advertised, all kinds of mechanical musical instruments could be purchased.

Moller, H P, Copenhagen. Makers of street barrel pianos of the smaller, portable type. A surviving specimen is in the shape of a lyre or guitar and is said to date from *c.*1850.

Mondini, Vedova Luigi, Corso Vitt Emanuele 40, Cremona, Italy. A maker of barrel pianos, *fl.*1903.

Monetta, Riccardo, 112 via della Consolazione, Rome, Italy. Maker of barrel pianos and barrel organs, *fl.*1909. Shared premises with **Mazza** *[qv].*

Montanini, Antonio, 9 corsa Milano, Novara, Italy. Maker of clockwork barrel pianos, *fl.*1930.

Montanini-Castaldi & Pomelia, Borgo San Agabia 83, Novara, Italy. Makers of barrel organs and barrel pianos who advertised their speciality as mandolin-pianos, *fl.*1909.

Mortier, Judocus, Ghent, Belgium. A maker of extremely fine compound music clocks who flourished in the 1780 period. His style, associating a pipe organ with a dulcimer, follows that of the Neuwied school of Peter Kinzing. In fact the similarity is quite remarkable even as far as the detail design of component parts and their relationships. Nevertheless, while a contemporary of Kintzing, Mortier cannot be found to have an association with the Kinzing instruments other than the belief that he must have seen one in order to make such a similar work himself. The clockmaking Mortier family was very small and localised: the Ghent registers list only Ludovicus and his two brothers, Judocus and Johannes. All three were members of the Guild of Clockmakers registered in 1773, 1782 and 1790 respectively. Two examples only of their musical clocks are known to exist: one in the collection of the late Murtogh Guinness in New York and the other in my own collection. Both mechanisms are essentially identical, that of the Guinness example housed in mainly conventional longcase clock case, whereas my example stands almost fourteen feet high in a richly-made and decorated cabinet after the style of Roentgen. There seems no connection between the clockmaking Mortiers of the 18th century and the dance-organ making Mortiers of the late 19th century.

Motor Player Corporation, 536 Lake Shore Drive, Chicago, Illinois, USA. Makers of the Electora vacuum pump for player pianos which 'eliminated foot pumping' when installed in a player. Patented on October 28th 1919, US Patent No.1,320,224. A mere seven inches in diameter and ten inches in height. Marketing began in February 1919. The device could also be housed in a piano bench where it was out of sight if not entirely out of earshot. In this form it was known as the Moto-Playo Bench and during the 1920s it achieved modest sales in the US.

Müller, Emil, Friedhofstr. 40-2, Werdau, Saxony, Germany. Established in 1887 as harmonium manufacturers. Produced a harmonium player called the Harmonista.

Muller, P A, Pau, France. Built a mechanical musical-performance recorder c.1907 and an electric piano-roll cutting machine, c.1910.

Murdoch & Company Ltd, John G, 91 & 93 Farringdon Road, London EC.During 1903 extensively advertised the Malcolm cabinet-style piano-player priced at 50 gns [$198.00] if bought on Hire Purchase, or £42 [$165] if bought for cash. The instrument was made in Erskine Road, Regents Park, by **John Malcolm & Co Ltd.** Piano-action and player-piano makers **John Malcolm & Sons** was a wholly-owned subsidiary. In the 1920s the last Murdoch family member, James Murdoch, ran the business. Later was distributor of the Minerva piano players. Murdoch had the distinction of being the only piano factory during the First World War to be destroyed following one of the air-raids: on December 18th 1917 a Zeppelin dropped a bomb that started a vast fire.

Murdoch, Murdoch & Company, 461 & 463 Oxford Street, London. Musical instrument manufacturers and retailers. Operated a piano factory in Lewisham. Agents for the Phoneon cabinet-style piano player first shown in Glasgow at the Musical Trades Exhibition in 1901. In 1913 exhibited the Connoisseur player piano at the British Music Exhibition, Olympia. There was also the Connoisseur Reed Organ and Pipe Organ, both being player organs. It is believed that all Connoisseur products were imports of American origin. Murdochs also made the Golden Tube series of music rolls.

Musicus Player Piano Company, 2 Salisbury Road, Highgate Hill, London N. Makers of the Musicus piano player c.1909. By 1920 was advertising the Auteola player-piano.

Musola Company, 2443 Massachusetts Avenue, Cambridgeport, Massachusetts, USA. Makers of player actions and the Musola player c.1908.

Mustel & Cie, 46 rue de Douai, Paris 9e. Factory at 48 rue Pernety, Paris 14e. Established 1853. See **Mustel, Charles Victor.**

Mustel, Charles Victor. Born at Le Havre in 1815, Victor Mustel began his career as a musical-instrument manufacturer with reed-organ makers Alexandre. In 1853 he set up in business on his own, making harmoniums and pianos, including mechanical instruments. Until the early 1920s, the address was 46 rue de Douai, Paris 9e, with a factory at 14 rue Marie-Anne Colombier, Bagnolet (Seine). His two sons, Charles (1840-1893) and Auguste (1844-1919), succeeded him on his death in January 1890. Mustel made extremely fine reed organs on the American organ principle and also marketed the Welte Mignon keyboardless reproducing piano under the name Mustel Maestro. The London showrooms were at 80 Wigmore Street. The Paris showroom moved to 16 Avenue de Wagram, where it remains to this day as a showroom for electric organs and hi-fi products. Victor Mustel's grandson, Alphonse Mustel, managed the business for some years and was awarded the distinction of Chevalier de la Legion d'Honneur in 1906.

Musumeci, Mario, via Opificio 4-10, Catania, Sicily, Italy. Founded in 1898 as manufacturer of barrel pianos and an agent for hiring, fl.1930.

Nallino Frères, 36, rue Bonaparte, Nice, France. In 1909, Florent Nallino and his brother Joseph were working separately in adjacent premises in the rue de la Villefranche making and hiring street organs. By 1930 it was possibly a second generation of Nallino brothers who were building clockwork pianos. However, the firm claimed its origins as 1872.

National Piano Company, Boston, Massachusetts, USA. Makers of 'the most up-to-date player in the world' - the Air-O-Player, which was 'the first perfected metal action'. This was in 1913 and it was installed in Briggs, Merrill and in Norris & Hyde instruments.

Needham, Elias Parkman. In 1846, Jeremiah Carhart (inventor of the suction bellows for reed organs) and E P Needham formed a company to manufacture reed organs. Initially this was at 172 Fulton Street in New York, later moving to a new six-storey building at 99 East 23rd Street. The business became Needham & Sons and later Needham Piano & Organ Company with a factory at Washington, New Jersey, and headquarters at 96 Fifth Avenue, New York. Accused by **John McTammany** [qv] of pirating many of his ideas, Needham took out many patents including one for the invention of the upright action used in reed organs and which formed the basis of most organettes and player pianos, wherein a sheet of perforated paper passes over the reed opening. He owned altogether 15 patents that he later sold to the **Mechanical Orguinette Company** [qv]. He made the Needham Paragon piano player.

Nelson-Wiggen Piano Company, 1731-45 Belmont Avenue, Chicago, Illinois, USA. Established c.1920 for the manufacture of coin-operated electric pianos, the majority of which were of the keyboardless variety with names such as Danc-O-Grand, Harp-O-Grand, and Pian-O-Grand. Used player rolls made by **Clark Orchestra Roll Company** [qv]. The company produced quality instruments up to the time of the Depression and their pianos are today considered to be amongst the best in terms of build-quality and musicality.

Neue Leipziger Musikwerke Adolf Buff-Hedinger, Möckersche Str 29-33 and Herlossohnstrasse 14, Leipzig-Göhlis, Germany. This company was formed in 1904 to take over the **Ehrlich** business which made disc-playing organettes under several names, the most popular of which was the Ariston, and disc-operated piano-players. Several different types of player action and piano player were introduced, including the Premier pneumatic action, the Premier player piano, piano orchestrions, both barrel and pneumatic, the Primavolta electric piano, the Xylophon-Klavier, and the Toccaphon. One instrument, renamed the Musetta for the UK market, was retailed in 1907 by the London firm of **S Calmont & Co Ltd.**

New Trist Player Piano Ltd. See **Trist Piano Player Ltd.**

Newcombe Piano Company Ltd, 121 Bellwoods Avenue, Toronto. Makers of player actions fl.1909. A short-lived business that was reputedly absorbed into that of **Otto Higel.**

Niagara Frontier Musical Instrument Manufacturing Company, Tonawanda, New York. Makers of self-acting stringed instruments, fl.1909.

Niagara Musical Instrument Company, North Tonawanda, USA. Produced instruments similar to those made by the North Tonawanda Musical Instrument Works factory, which included coin-freed barrel pianos.

Nilsson, I F, Öster Korsberga, Lemnhult, Saxhult, Sweden. Sometime about 1884-5, Nilsson invented an instrument which he named a 'pianoharpa'. A table-like cabinet contained a simple pinned barrel and piano action having a compass of 18 notes. It was subsequently improved upon by the brothers **Anders Gustaf** and **Jones Wilhelm Andersson.** *[qv].*

Nixon, C E. An American doctor and amateur illusionist who built an interesting modern android, in the form of the reclining figure of the goddess Isis playing a zither. The full-size automaton comprorised a large cabinet apparently filled with fake mechanism upon which the figure lay with a stringed zither. When set in motion the fingers of the android appeared actually to perform upon the strings. The truth was rather less remarkable for, like the famed Turk of von Kempelen's chess-playing 'automaton', the fake mechanism concealed a human performer. A clever curio, it survives in a leading private collection.

North Tonawanda Musical Instrument Works, North Tonawanda, New York, USA. Founded in 1893 by **Eugene DeKleist** *[qv]* as the North Tonawanda Barrel Organ Factory and incorporated in 1906 with premises at Payne Avenue, North Tonawanda, this business produced a range of band organs selling from $250 [£62] to $3,000 [£750]. These had pneumatic action and were played by endless-paper music. The firm also made coin-freed instruments including the Pianolin and the Mando Piano Orchestrina. Besides its own instruments, it produced the Tonophone barrel piano for Wurlitzer. It was ultimately taken over by the Remington Rand Company, although it continued as a fair-organ manufactory until the mid-1920s.

Nyström, Johann Petter, Karlstad, Norway. Nyström built a number of attractive reed organs in the 'parlor organ' style under the name 'Nyström's Reform-orgel' which could be played by means of an Ariston-like cardboard disc. These were covered by certain patents. During the period 1906-9, several patents were issued in the name of C W Nyström of the Nyström company for music recorders (melographs), including one which could be used as a key-top player for piano or organ. This model, subject of British Patent number 21,594 of September 30th 1911, was electromagnetic.

Odeola, 11 rue du 4-Septembre, Paris 2e (factory at 6 rue Marc Séguin, Paris 18e), France. Makers of player pianos and piano rolls. Subsidiary of the ancient firm of musical instrument makers Erard, formerly Blondel & Cie and originating in 1779.

Operators' Piano Company, The, 715 North Kedzie Avenue, Chicago, Illinois, USA. Little is known of the founders of this once-famous and key maker of mechanical musical instruments other that the fact that its president was Louis M Severson. Makers of coin-operated pianos with percussion and orchestral effects under the name Coinola, and the Reproduco, a player pipe organ and piano for accompanying silent movies. The factory was at 16 South Peoria, Chicago. Founded (according to Bowers) about 1904 (yet in no directory before 1908), the company flourished until the mid-1930s. By the early 1920s it listed its office and factory at 1911-13 Clybourn Avenue, Chicago. The company also produced the Multitone series of pianos for Welte, and the Empress Electric for the Chicago store Lyon & Healy.

Orchestrelle Company Ltd, The, 225 Regent Street, London W. Formed early in the 1900s, this was a British-owned, American-financed subsidiary of the American Aeolian Company. It was created to take over the operation of George Whight, Aeolian's London distributor, who was approaching retirement. Orchestrelle was later known as The Aeolian Compny Ltd. By 1904, The Orchestrelle Company was at the Aeolian Hall, 135-6-7 New Bond Street, London W, and was distributing the Pianola piano player and the Pianola player piano as well as the Aeolian Orchestrelle player organs. The instruments were manufactured in America, shipped to England and assembled at the Aeolian factory at Hayes, Middlesex. Increasingly more manufacture was carried out on pianos at Hayes. *See* **Aeolian Company.** The company had agents in Edinburgh (Methven, Simpson & Company) and Glasgow (Marr, Wood & Company). Early in 1930 the firm was dissolved, the assets being taken over by Harrods. The first address of the Orchestrelle Company was in Elm Street, off the Gray's Inn Road, London WC. The firm produced a large number of music rolls including the Metrostyle (which referred to the metronome or speed line printed on the roll) and Themodist (accented rolls), as well as music rolls for the Orchestrelle and the Aeolian Reproducing Pipe Organ. In 1909 advertised the Gregorian player organ. Received the Royal Warrant for 1916 [on the List of the Lord Chamberlain.]

The excellence of the Pianola Piano extends to the smallest details

The Pianola Piano has exclusive expression devices which lift it far above any other piano-playing instrument—the fact is one upon which the greatest musicians are agreed. But, forget for a moment that these devices exist, and still the Pianola Piano ranks before all others.

This is the reason—there is vastly more in the construction of a piano-playing instrument than the mere assembling of parts—the perfect piano-player can only result from knowledge gained in the manufacture of the complete instrument by one firm.

THE PIANOLA PIANO

owes its pre-eminence to perfect construction

As manufacturers of The Pianola Piano, we are pioneers of the industry—the instrument we manufacture to-day has necessarily reached a higher degree of constructional development than any other—experience has taught us the exact adjustments, the perfecting of | delicate mechanism, the choice of material necessary to obtain the perfect result. The pianos employed—the **Steinway, Weber,** and **Steck**—are each of them examples of the highest attainment of the piano-maker's art.

Do not think that every piano-playing instrument is a Pianola, or is constructed like a Pianola. The word is a trade-mark, and applies only to one specific instrument.

Call at Æolian Hall and learn why The Pianola Piano is the most perfectly constructed piano-playing instrument, or write for Catalogue M.

THE ORCHESTRELLE COMPANY,

ÆOLIAN HALL,

135-6-7, NEW BOND ST., LONDON, W.

Orchestrionfabrik Albert Melnik, Trautenau, Bohemia, Austria. Founded in 1903 for the manufacture of barrel-operated piano orchestrions worked by descending weights and marketed under the name Delphin.

Original-Musikwerke Paul Lochmann GmbH, Querstrasse 17, Leipzig, Germany. Factory at Am Bahnhof, Zeulenroda. Established in 1900 by Paul Lochmann of Symphonion disc musical box fame and Ernst Lüder. Produced piano orchestrions played by pinned barrel and later by cardboard roll and all bearing the trade name 'Original'.

Orozco, Carrillo Primo, 97 Bravo Murillo, Madrid, Spain. Barrel-piano agent, dealer and hirer, *fl.* 1909.

Orsenigo, Giovanni, via Umberto 1 and Vicolo dell'Arco 27, Casale Monferrato, Italy. Maker of barrel organs and barrel pianos, *fl.* 1909-30. Marini comments that Orsenigo united manufacturers into an organisation to voice their common grievances. As president of this body he staged a meeting in Turin to protest against the Acts that prohibited Saturday music and dancing during the days of the Fascist regime. Marini adds that it was in the dance-halls that barrel pianos were mainly the music-providers and there gained their status and popularity.

Ottina & Pellandi, via Solferino 5, Casa Propria, Novara, Italy. Established in 1884 for the manufacture of mechanical pianos, barrel organs and street instruments. Also were leading exporters. Marini asserts that this manufacturer was the first in Italy to adopt the spring motor (1902). They were also responsible for many other innovations, not the least was the application of the Italian style of Art Nouveau to their piano cases. Probably continued as:

Ottina, Fratelli, 30 via Dante Alighieri, Novara, Milan, Italy. Maker of barrel pianos, *fl.*1930.

Otto Manufacturing Company, 107 Franklin Street, New York City, USA. Founded in 1875 by Frederick Gustav Otto as F G Otto Company for the manufacture of surgical instruments and wet-cell electric batteries. With his three sons Albert, Edmund and Gustav, Otto's business thrived and at one time it employed sixty workers in a factory at 48 Sherman Avenue. In due course, this was extended into the adjacent premises, 50 Sherman Avenue. The business went on to manufacture a unique design of musical box (the Capital 'cuff' box) devised by Ferdinand Schaub. In 1904, patents were granted to Schaub and in 1906 a newly-formed subsidiary, The Otto Manufacturing Company, was set up to design and manufacture a disc-playing clockwork piano. This, the Pianette, played 39-notes from interchangeable punched steel discs 21-inches in diameter. Although retailed in Chicago by the Lyon & Healy department store, few have survived: the Pianette remains an extremely rare instrument today. A store full of derelict Pianettes was discovered at the former Otto premises by the late Hughes Ryder of New Jersey and some thirty-five years on these are now in the process of restoration.

Paci, Giovanni, Ascoli Piceno, Italy. Maker of barrel pianos, *fl.*1930.

Packard Company, Fort Wayne, Indiana, USA. Founded by Isaac T Packard in 1871 as the Packard Organ Company, a manufacturer of reed organs. He was joined by piano-maker Albert Sweetser Bond and the business was re-styled as the Packard Company to reflect the manufacture of pianos as well as organs. Maker of player pianos, including models fitted with the Welte (Licensee) reproducing action.

Padula, Paolo, Grassano, Potenza, Italy. Church-organ and barrel-piano maker, *fl.*1930.

Pain, Robert Willard, 261 West 23rd Street, New York City, USA. A manufacturing organ builder who at various times had premises at 157 East 32nd Street and 362 Fifth Avenue, New York. Probably the first to construct a pneumatic self-playing piano in America. In conjunction with Henry Kuster, he built a 39-note instrument for Needham & Sons in 1880. In 1882 he produced for the **Mechanical Orguinette Company** (which later became **Aeolian**) an inside player with 46-note compass, and in 1888 he made a 65-note electric player. One of the earliest to experiment with creating an expression action he was granted British Patent number 19,527 of 1904 for a pneumatic piano having a special tracker bar with two rows of holes that were staggered. He described how in order to adjust the vacuum tension for any note whatsoever all that was necessary was to make that particular perforation slightly wider, or twice the width, so that both upper and lower tracker holes were uncovered. Although it would have required specially-made and therefore uneconomical music rolls, Aeolian thought sufficient of the patent to acquire it for their portfolio.

Palma, Fortun, 11 piazza Colombo, Genoa, Italy. Agent for automatic pianos and the Pianola, *fl.*1930.

Palop, Pedro, 99 S Vicente, Valencia, Spain. Barrel-piano and harmonium maker, *fl.*1909.

Pape, Jean-Henri. Originally Johann Heinrich Pape, he came to Paris from his home country, Germany, in 1811 and worked for Pleyel as a piano maker. He also at some time worked in London. He introduced no fewer than 137 inventions, among them the first use of cross-stringing in Paris in 1839. In 1851 he made a clock-

work barrel and finger piano. Between 1844 and 1848, he was in business at 106 New Bond Street, London. Prior to this, c.1839, he was at 21 Little Newport Street, Leicester Square, and New Bond Street, and in 1846 an address at 75 Grosvenor Square was additional to the one in New Bond Street.

Parker, C W, Abilene, Kansas, USA. Established in 1892 and described as a maker of barrel pianos and organs, by 1909 the business was advertised as distributing military band organs for merry-go-rounds and so forth.

Parker, William D, Meriden, Connecticut, USA. Initially Parker was employed by G W Ingalls & Company of 25 Hermon Street, Worcester, Massachusetts, the company which made the first organettes for John McTammany. He was then with the Taber Organ Company in that town until finally he joined Wilcox & White Co where he was responsible for much of the design for the Angelus player action, in particular its vertical diaphragm pneumatic motors. Inventor of many improvements to the pneumatic control of musical instruments which led to the successful piano player, player organ and player piano. He and **Needham** *[qv]* laid the foundations for all pneumatic actions for such instruments.

Parr, Ellis. *See under* **Automatic Musical Instrument Company.**

Pasquale & Company Ltd, 73 Basinghall Street, Clerkenwell, and also 9 Phoenix Place, London. This address proves to be that of Guy Fermor Denys, an accountant, suggesting that when the firm became a limited liability company, this was merely its registered address. Certainly there are many other addresses associated with the Pasquale activities. Founded by Gregori Pasquale c.1894 to make barrel pianos. Post Office directories show Gregori Pasquale & Company, 'piano organ manufacturers', at 5 Phoenix Place between 1894 and 1895, then as Pasquale & Company (1896-1901); Pasquale & Co Ltd (1902-1917). Devised a means of putting the springs of automatics into the ends of the barrels themselves. A good maker of bright pianos. Partners were Charles Romano of 6 Victoria Dwellings, Clerkenwell Road, and Amato Pasquale of 5 Phoenix Place, Calthorpe Street, Gray's Inn Road. Between 1909 and 31st May 1917 business was at 9 Phoenix Place; from then to 1941 was at 12 Poole's Buildings, Mount Pleasant (but Rates Books show Pasquale at this address in October 1906). On February 1st 1907, the business was taken over by Andrea and Germaro Ciniglio who continued to trade as Pasquale & Company Ltd. (Later history researched by A G Bird.)

Pastore, Frederico, Spalto Marengo 4, Alessandria, Italy. Barrel-piano maker, *fl.*1903.

Peerless Piano Player Company, 2 East 47th Street, New York City, USA. A business formed by **Roth & Engelhardt** *[qv]* for the manufacture of a range of piano-based mechanical instruments. Operated branches at Windsor Arcade, Fifth Avenue, New York; St Johnsville, New York; 274 Wabash Avenue, Chicago. Produced the Peerless Orchestrion, an 88-note piano with a fifteen-roll automatic player mechanism. Makers of ordinary player pianos as well as coin-operated pianos with percussion and orchestral effects; also photoplayers.

Perotti, Cav Carlo, via Ormea e Galliari 41, Turin, Italy. Established in 1870. Perotti was a large maker of barrel pianos and organs, cafe pianos, clockwork pianos, &c, *fl.*1903. That he was an important maker is indicated by the fact that the address shown was that of his showroom and shop, while he operated a workshop at via Canova e Marocchetti.

Pesaresi, Luigi, 30 Warner Street, Clerkenwell, London EC. Founder of the firm of Pesaresi & Son, manufacturer of barrel pianos. Later as:

Pesaresi & Son, 30 Warner Street, Clerkenwell, London EC. A small maker of street pianos, mostly 40- and 44-note tremolo clockwork and hand-cranked models, who first set up business in 1898.

Pesaresi, Son & Spinelli, 8 & 9 Early Mews, Arlington Road, London, NW1. **Loretto Spinelli,** formerly a partner of **Rossi** *[qv]* and latterly working on his own, joined Luigi Pesaresi and his son in 1930 making and hiring street pianos. In the early hours of November 12th 1935, the factory premises were almost entirely destroyed by fire. The business then moved to 12 Field Place, St John Street, Clerkenwell, London EC1, where it advertised 'piano-hire' before finally going out of business in 1941. Their names appear on many barrel pianos. A transfer (decal) on the front of a 44-note hand piano formerly in the collection of the late Mr Taylor of Albany Farm, Forest Road, Newport, Isle of Wight, read: *Pesaresi, Son & Spinelli, Patentees & Makers of "Symphonia" autos. 12, Field Place, St John Street, Clerkenwell, EC1. TERminus 3993."*

Philipps & Söhne, J D, Frankfurter Musikwerke Fabrik Akt-Ges, Frankfurt a-M, Germany. Johann Daniel Philipps had begun making mechanical instruments when he was a mere 23, when he made a barrel orchestrion for a dance hall at Frankfurt. In 1877 he teamed up with one Ketterer with a branch factory in Vöhrenbach in the Black Forest. Nine years later the business changed its name from Philipps & Ketterer to the Frankfurter Musikwerke-Fabrik J D Philipps & Sohn of Bockenheim, Frankfurt. The two sons were August and Oswald, who later took over control of the business. Music rolls and, later, piano orchestrions used the trade mark Philag - a simple eponymous contraction of the name. Initially the company made barrel pianos and orchestrions and their resemblance to Welte is interesting. Although the company continued to list barrel orchestrions in its catalogue until as late as 1909, the first Philipps paper-roll-playing instrument was introduced in 1896, again closely following the progress of Welte. By the early years of the century, Philipps had become a major manufacturer of orchestrions, many of them incorporating pianos. The company also introduced some special narrow music rolls for the later series of these which were only about 23 cm in width. The company introduced a practical multi-roll revolver-system - believed to be the first in the world - as early as 1903 and this was covered by German patents in 1905. The style and construction of these revolver mechanisms is still considered to be the best of all the types tried. The Duca series of reproducing pianos was introduced about 1921. The fact that Philipps was only ever granted a few patents for player pianos in the United Kingdom, and none of these was for action parts, supports in some measure the belief I have that the similarity between Welte and Philipps reproducing actions is due to the fact that they share a common design for which no doubt Philipps paid Welte a licence fee. In 1923, Philipps acquired the German company **Frati & Company** [qv] of Berlin. Frati was making an electric piano called the Fratinola and the Fratihymnia. Philipps also acquired in 1925 the Wilhelm Arnold piano factory at Aschaffenburg, which had been founded in 1886. Highly respected as makers of first-class instruments, the business of Philipps was thriving through the 1920s, but as the decade ended so did the era of the piano orchestrion and by 1930 the business closed.

Piacenza, Cipr, 8 via Belfiore, Cremona, Italy. Barrel-piano maker, *fl.*1930.

Pianista, 64 rue Lafayette, Paris. Company formed to exploit Fourneaux's Pianista piano player.

Pianex Company, The, 29, 31 and 33 Station Buildings, Haggerston, London NE. Makers of the Pianex piano player, *c.*1908. No further details.

Piano, Jules, 30 rue Arson and rue Beaumont, Nice, France. Successor to Tadini & Cie, maker of barrel organs and barrel pianos. At this address *c.*1908; later at Rouleaux d'Armand Nallino, Nice, where he specialised in large coin-freed instruments which incorporated percussion effects for use in cafes.

Pianofortefabrik 'Euterpe' Albert Gast & Company, Frankfurter Allee 117a, Berlin, Germany. Piano makers established in 1886 and makers of the Gast's Klavierspielapparate player piano and action. By the turn of the century was producing the Euterpe cabinet piano-player.

Pianotist Company Ltd, 56 Regent Street, London, W. Founded in 1901 by Emile Klaber of the Klaber piano manufactory in America, the parent company was involved with an empire of piano companies all run by entrepreneur Edwin D Ackerman (*see under* **Ackotist**). Initially at 94 Regent Street from which address the company announced its first product – the Rex push-up piano-player which retailed at 25 gns [$105]. A London factory was set up at Clipstone Street and there was developed and marketed an under-keyboard playing attachment called the Pianotist which played wide, thick paper rolls similar to the early Hupfeld player system. The operation of the Pianotist was virtually the same as that of the Hupfeld, both being of the mechanical 'kicking shoe' variety. However, there was one significant difference in that the music-roll was reversed and turned through a rightangle in order to play. As the thick punched paper unspoiled it was folded under a roller arranged at 45 deg. to the inside of the instrument, taken over the keys in the keyframe and finally on to a take-up spool placed at rightangles to the music-roll. Later versions dispensed with this reverse-turn and took the paper horizontally from one side to the other over a central tracker or keyframe. The system was technically inferior and few instruments have survived in complete condition. On July 16th 1907, the Official Receiver liquidated the business after revealing that the accounts showed a deficiency of over £31,000 [$124,000] while the assets were valued at just over £1,000 [$4,000] - and they were covered by mortgage debentures. The failure of the company was attributed to the large cash expenditure accompanying efforts to perfect the piano-player, and in repairing defective examples under guarantees given at the time of sale to the public. Early Pianotists were played like the Hupfeld by turning a handle but later variants used foot treadles purely as a means of rotating the kicking-shoe roller and the music transport system. Their premature marketing and largely untested designs were the prime causes for the failure of the company.

Pietro, Volonté, Como, Italy. An early Italian maker of portable street pianos, fl.1810, that are similar in style to the Bristol Hicks ones yet without the quality or finesse. Curiously they are described, by Marini, as 'for indoor use'.

Pilcher, William, Stockbridge Terrace, Pimlico, London. Maker of barrel pianos. In business from *c.*1820 until he retired in 1862. Sometime at 23 Upper Belgrave Square, Pimlico. Also made barrel organs and harmoniums.

Pittaluga e Figlia, 17 via Gioffredo Mameli, Sampierdarena, Genoa, Italy. Maker of player pianos and electrically operated pianos, *fl.*1930.

Pizano, Roque, 8 Cirés, Barcelona, Spain. Street-piano agent and hirer, *c.*1903-9.

Playano Manufacturing Company, 12 Osborne Street, Cambridge, Massachusetts, USA. Established before 1902 at this address making the Playano piano player. The business was purchased by **Story & Clark** [qv] in 1905. This was Story's first move into player pianos and the take-over preceded the establishment of a player department at the Chicago factory. Announcing that the Playano interior player as well as the cabinet player would soon be introduced, Edward H Story said: 'I am convinced that the player piano has come to stay; so are my associates in the ownership of the company. We feel that the future prospects of the player business are good enough to warrant us in buying a player business outright, and that the Playano Company was the concern to buy.'

Playola Piano Company, 209 State Street, Chicago, Illinois, USA. Makers of player pianos, *fl.*1908.

Pleyel Wolf Lyon & Cie, 22-24 rue Rochechouart, Paris 9e, France. Founded in 1807, Pleyel was an early and highly respected Parisian piano maker with a factory at St Denis, Seine. Later as Pleyel Lyon et Cie, then Pleyel et Cie. The company also made the Pleyella player piano and music rolls. The London branch was Pleyel Wolf Lyon & Company at 79-80 Baker Street, where the Pleyella and Pleyel music rolls were handled.

Poggio, G, 1 via Lodi, Alessandria, Italy. Maker of barrel pianos, *fl.*1930.

Polizzi, Damiano e Figli, Caltanissetta, Italy. Barrel-piano maker, *fl.*1930.

Polyphon Musikwerke, A-G, Wahren, Leipzig, Germany. The company more usually remembered for its disc-playing musical-boxes produced in 1898 a disc-playing piano called the Polyphon Concerto. Using the expertise perfected in the manufacture of the disc musical box, Paul Riessner developed the Concerto which played piano strings, drums and bells from a 32-inch diameter metal disc. The Polyphon piano orchestrion was sold at a branch located at Burgstrasse 2, Berlin C. This was managed by George Preuss and established as offshoot of the Leipzig company. *See also under* **Regina Music Box Company.**

Pombia, Pietro, Borgo San Agabia 37, Novara, Italy. Barrel-organ and piano maker, *fl.*1903-9. May have been related to the Pombia of **Luis Casali** *[qv]* connection.

Pomella, P, 25 corso Milano, Novara, Italy. Barrel-piano maker, *fl.*1930.

Poole Piano Company, 5 & 7 Appleton Street, Boston, Massachusetts, USA. Founded by William H Poole (1864-?) in 1893. Produced a number of piano players.

Popper & Company, Reichstrasse 33-35, Leipzig 1, Germany. Founded in 1891 by Hugo Popper (1857-1910) for the making of pianos and the distribution of orchestrions. Agents for mechanical musical instruments made in Leipzig and also the German distributors for **Racca** *[qv]*. Makers for a wide range of mechanical pianos, instruments with orchestral effects and so on. Also produced a reproducing piano called the Stella. Branches at rue Nationale 93, Antwerp; Junkernstrasse 4, Breslau, and Bahnhofstrasse 83, Essen.

Porta, Francesco, Biella, Novara, Italy. Agent for barrel street instruments, *fl.*1903.

Porta, Salvatore di Ros, Piazza Delle Guardie, Catania, Sicily. Barrel pianos, *c.*1903.

Porto & Figli, Rosario, via Maddem 141a, Catania, Sicily, Italy. Established in 1860. Makers of musical instruments including barrel organs and barrel pianos, *fl.*1909.

Potthoff, Ludwig, and Golf, Hilmar, Berlin, Germany. In 1884 Potthoff and Golf perfected a barrel/keyboard piano that could be played either by hand or by hand-cranked barrel. The piano comprised a normal action and the barrel was placed under the keyboard, transmitting playing movement through a series of levers and cams to a secondary set of key levers mounted above the normal manual set of keys, thereby setting the complete piano action into motion.

Poyser, T H, 39, Hermitage Road, Harringay, London, N. During the time of the First World War, offered a player attachment that was claimed to fit inside an ordinary piano. Available in both 65 and 88-note versions, Poyser's so-called 'Classic' attachment, for which British Patent No.2852 of 1914 had been awarded in the name of G A Smith, comprised a fairly normal bottom action, and a very slender spool assembly that fitted inside the top door of the piano case. Not particularly successful and only two have been seen.

Pozzi, Eredi di Francesco, Treviglio, Bergamo, Italy. Barrel-piano maker, *fl.*1930.

Pozzi, Fratelli Ditta, 6 via Trieste, Mantua, Italy. Barrel-piano maker, *fl.*1930.

Pozzi & Fratelli, Francesco, Viccolo Zanda, Treviglio, Italy. Maker of barrel pianos and barrel organs, *fl.*1903-30.

Pozzi & Varesi, via Carloni 7, Como, Italy. Barrel-piano maker, *fl.*1909.

Pozzouli, Vincenze, 45 Warner Street, Clerkenwell, London EC. A maker of barrel pianos who patented, in 1906, a street piano producing a mandolin tone by using four bridges, the first being mandolin, the second piano, the third a second mandolin and the fourth a bass piano. He used hammers fitted with hardwood heads.

Prado, Edouardo, 10 Torrijos, Madrid, Spain. Maker of street pianos also operating as hirer, *fl.*1903.

Prado, Thomas, 8 Salitre, Madrid, Spain. Maker of street pianos, *fl.*1903.

Pratt, Read Player Action Company, Deep River, Connecticut, USA.

Described as 'a subsidiary of Pratt, Read & Company, ivory cutters, key and action makers, and suppliers to the piano trade since 1806'. Manufactured what it called 'an electric bottom unit' which replaced the foot-operated exhausters of an ordinary player by an electric reproducing action. The company's player actions, fitted into the Pratt Read piano, included a five-key transposing tracker bar, the whole bar being slid left or right under the music roll. The company's first inner player was, like many others of the time, a single-valve action. During the early 1920s the company introduced an upright reproducing player action called the Model P which played the QRS Recordo, US Auto-Art, Melodee 'Expression', Vocalstyle 'Reproduco' and, according to the brochure, 'other expression rolls'. This all-electric reproducer was followed by the Model PC Combination Reproducing Action which 'can be used in three ways – as a straight piano, a regular foot-expression piano, and as an electric-reproducer'. Very little is known about the Pratt Read action other than that which survives in the company's own promotional literature: it is thought to have been produced only for a limited time. London office at 21, Mincing Lane. Parent company Pratt, Read was the largest piano-action maker in the World.

Price & Teeple, 206 Wabash Avenue, Chicago. Makers of player pianos including the Symphonola and the Carleton Electric Player Style X for use in public places.

Priori, A, 15 via degli Umbri, Rome, Italy. Barrel piano maker, *fl.*1930.

Prosperio, Giuseppe, M Monti 40, Como, Italy. Barrel-piano maker who also made and sold organs, *fl.*1909.

Protze & Company, GmbH, Josef, Nr 839 Georgswalde, Bohemia, Austro-Hungary. Founded in 1905 as factor and distributor for piano orchestrions.

Prowse, Keith. *See* **Keith, Prowse.**

Prowse, William. A barrel piano in the Guinness Collection, New York, bears the label: 'Patent William Prowse, late Keith, Prowse & Company, manufacturer, 48, Cheapside, London'. *See also* **Keith, Prowse.**

Puglisi, Giuseppe, Catania, Sicily. Established in 1820 as a maker of barrel pianos, Puglisi was the only maker of these instruments in Sicily. He also made or handled other automatic instruments, *fl.*1903.

Pusteria, Frederico, Varese, Como, Italy. Barrel-piano maker, *fl.*1930.

Pyrophon-Musikwerke Ernst Berger, Tauchaerstrasse 9, Leipzig 25, Germany. Established *c.*1905 as makers of electro-pneumatic pianos and orchestrions. No instruments known.

Quaglia, & Company, Battista, via Mondovi, Cuneo, Italy. Barrel-piano maker, *fl.*1930.

Racca, Giovanni, via Milazzo 18, Bologna, Italy. Maker of barrel pianos, who produced some unusual grand-format pianos playing barrels and, later, diminutive models that played from folded cardboard book-music. He patented an unusual reiterating-hammer system for his bookmusic piano in conjunction with G Seward in 1886 and the trade name for his instruments was 'Piani Melodici'. Four models were produced, ranging from four to six octaves, fully chromatic, and these mostly played serious music from beautifully arranged scores. These were true pianofortes, having both sustaining and soft controls. He also made a piano orchestrion called the Verdi. His products were distributed in Germany by **Popper** *[qv]* and in France by **Stransky Frères** *[qv]*. In England, Racca pianos were distributed in Britain through wholsesale agents Guldman & Company (*est* 1896) of 7, Sugar Lane, Withy Green, Manchester, who also handled Hupfeld electric pianos.

Rachals & Company, M F, Glockengiesserwall 18, Hamburg, Germany. Piano makers founded in 1832. In 1910 manufactured the Triumphola piano player and, later, the Triumphola-Piano player piano. Company operated by Adolf F Rachals. After 1920 became a subsidiary of the **Kastner** business.

Ragone, Michele, Cava dei Terreni, Salerno, Italy. Maker of church organs who also manufactured barrel pianos, *fl.*1930.

Ramos, Manuel, 16 Dupl Palma, Madrid, Spain. Maker and agent for street pianos in business in 1903.

Rampone, Alfredo, 17 via Mazzini, Omegna, Novara, Italy. Barrel-piano maker, *fl.* 1930.

Rasero, F Illi, Corsa Alfieri, Asti, Italy, Maker of barrel pianos, *fl.* 1930.

Ratti, Fratelli, Fabbrica Durini, Como, Italy. Barrel-piano maker, *fl.* 1909-30.

Regina Company, The, Rahway, New Jersey, USA. Established in 1892 initially as a division of the **Polyphon-Musikwerke** *[qv]* in Leipzig. Makers of disc-playing musical boxes who produced, in about 1900, a very large mechanical disc-playing piano called the Automatic Regina Concerto. This weighed 950 Ib, stood 8 feet 2 inches high, 45 inches wide and 27 inches deep. In addition to the piano, the 32-inch diameter steel disc played bells, cymbal and snare and bass drum. With its quadruple spring motor, this enormous machine changed its discs from a storage rack of ten contained in the base, in the same way that the Regina and Polyphon musical boxes changed their discs. The Regina was developed from the single-play, 32-inch disc size Polyphon produced in Leipzig. Both instruments were from the brains of Gustave Brachhausen and Paul Riessner. Also produced the Sublima Piano Junior which was a piano played using '…a large roll of heavy and very durable paper, the power being furnished either by Spring Motor or Electric Motor as desired'.

Restagno, Cav Vincenzo, 90 corsa Vittorio Emanuele, Turin, Italy. Maker of player pianos with factory at 5 via Romagnosi. *fl.* 1930.

Rialto Player Piano Company, 15, Castle Street East, London, W. Offered a player action that could be attached to an existing piano shortly before the First World War. The initial British Patent for a retractable roll-playing mechanism that fitted beneath a piano keyboard was the work of one E F Day (Pat No 17,644 of 1911 [unfulfilled]). The final version was the design of P Schlottki (Pat No 7,415 of 1913 assigned to Rialto Player Piano Company. The Rialto fitted to the front of the keyboard and a pneumatic action, with foot treadles, was installed in the usual position in the bottom of the case. Only one example has been seen by the author. Not a successful device.

 THE **RIALTO ACTIONS** for every existing Piano are rapidly gaining ground.

RIALTO ACTIONS have already been installed in hundreds of different styles of Pianos.

A HIGH CLASS PLAYER at a MODERATE Price.

RIALTO PLAYER PIANO CO. 15, Castle Street East, London, W.

Showing Rialto Player when in use.  Showing Rialto Player when not in use.

Ricca & Son, 881-903 Southern Boulevard and 884-904 East 134th Street, New York City, USA. Luigi Ricca was born in Naples in 1853 and came to New York in 1886 where he joined the German Conservatory of Music faculty and taught guitar and mandolin playing. Dissatisfied with the quality of the available instruments he began, in 1890, making these instruments to his own design. His venture was successful and in 1898 he began manufacturing pianos. This work expanded with a new factory in 1903 and, with the introduction of electric and player pianos, the business made a speciality of these. Luigi Ricca headed his company with sons H F Ricca and E I Ricca. In 1933 acquired **Ludwig & Co.**

Ricca & Company, C, 12/13 Poole Buildings, Clerkenwell, London. This seems to be the first London address of **Carlo Ricca** *[qv]* which he occupied until April 1st 1906 when the building was burned out. The premises were refurbished and occupied that November by **Pasquale & Co Ltd.**

Ricca, Charles, 21 Merlin's Place, Wilmington Square, London WC. Also known as Carlo Ricci. Manufacturer of 'piano organs', established in 1914. *By 1917 as:*

Ricci & Son, Carlo, 37 Claremont Mews, Clerkenwell, London EC. Barrel-piano makers who ceased trading in 1925.

Riemer, Bernhard, Chrastava, Northern Bohemia. Bernhard Riemer made barrel organs that featured a separate drive for the barrel and the bellows so permitting music to be played at any speed desired without losing wind. In 1896 his three sons, Robert, Julius and Jindrich, took over the company and made barrel organs of fine tone and attractive appearance. Then barrel pianos were produced and, after 1903, pianos played by perforated music. Their products were exported to France, Belgium, Germany, Switzerland and Russia. They also made and patented an invention called Automaton, which made mandolin music to the accompaniment of lighting effects and which was driven by an electric motor. This was allegedly a great success and sold well. The company won a gold medal for automatic musical instruments at an exhibition at Usti on the Elbe. They also made some fine orchestrions at Chrastava and, later, sold radio sets and ordinary pianos.

Rigoni e Figli, Ditta, via Inferiore, Treviso, Italy. Maker of clock-work pianos, *fl.* 1930.

Rissone & Company, J B, Poole's Buildings, Mount Pleasant, London WC. Maker of barrel pianos established under this title in 1902. Formerly in partnership as **Rose, Coop & Rissone** *[qv]* and as:

Rissoni & Company, Giovanni, 30 Warner Street, Clerkenwell, London EC. Formerly with Capra, Rissone took over the Capra business and continued at the same address from 1887, manufacturing street barrel pianos.

Robazza, Benedetto, via Cavour 143, Rome, Italy. Agent and hirer of barrel pianos and organs, *fl.* 1909.

Robino, Simon, 59 Oldham Road, Manchester, England. Described as a musical-instrument maker, he took out a patent in 1906 for producing a tremolo effect on a barrel piano. In his system, bell-cranks pulled the hammer down against a rotating star wheel, to impart the beating motion (British Patent number 14,977, of July 2nd 1906).

Robuschi, Castaud et Cie, 5 Chemin de la Madeleine, Nice, France. By 1920 this firm was advertising as successor to **Vve Amelotti** *[qv]* as makers of automatic pianos with interchangeable cylinders. Makers of mandolin and piccolo pianos.

Rodrigues, Antonio, 2 S Cayetano, Madrid, Spain. Hirer of street pianos, *fl.* 1903.

Rognoni, Ercole, 8 via Conchetta, Milan, Italy. Street-organ and piano maker, *fl.* 1930.

Rolfe, William, 112 Cheapside, London. A music seller and publisher who also made pianofortes in 1796. In 1806, the business became William Rolfe & Sons and, in 1813, additional premises were to be found at 28 London Wall. In 1850, the business moved to 61 Cheapside, and from 28 to 31-32 London Wall. It seems that there were three subsequent addresses until 1890, after which date the name disappears. With Samuel Davis, William Rolfe patented improvements to barrel-operated pianofortes. On August 11th 1829, Thomas Hall Rolfe was granted British Patent number 5831 for such improvements, one of which was for a method of pinning barrels so as to play 'piano' or 'forte'. This name is associated with high-quality domestic barrel-and-finger instruments.

Rolleau, S, Nantes, France. Distributor of mechanical pianos and mechanical jazz bands. *See* **Amelotti, Vve.**

Romano & Bouffeaux, 21b-23 rue du Pont-de-l'Avenue, Laeken, Brussels, Belgium. Maker of automatic pianos. Was listed in 1909 directories and later became:

Romano-Bilotti, S, 23 rue du Pont-de-l'Avenue, Laeken, Brussels, Belgium. Listed in directories *c.* 1930 as maker of automatic pianos. Several have been seen bearing the legend 'Romano-Laeken'. A Charles Romano was a partner in the business of **Gregori Pasquale & Company** *[qv]* in the closing years of the last century.

Rose, Coop & Rissone Ltd, 135 Regent Street, London W (1902) and 71 Mount Pleasant, Clerkenwell, London EC (1905). Manufacturers of barrel pianos, who subsequently took out patents covering an action operated pneumatically from cardboard music.In 1906 the firm was making piano players. John Rose was described as 'mechanic' and Thomas Coop as 'musician' and the secretary of the company was Reginald Albert Goodman. *See also* Rissone.

Rosener, F, Schönhauser Allee 157, Berlin N, Germany. A maker of barrel pianos who exhibited at the Melbourne Musical Industries Exhibition in April 1888.

Rossi, Italy. Rossi returned to Italy from London where he had worked with **Pasquale** *[qv]* and also **Spinelli** *[qv]* and, *c.*1920 onwards, produced an attractive range of clockwork barrel-playing cafe pianos which incorporated percussion effects. Probably same as:

Rossi, N, via S. Marria 11, Turin, Italy. Maker of barrel pianos, *fl.*1903.

Rossi, G, Peppena e Figlio, Lugano, Switzerland. Makers of clockwork café pianos, *fl.*1930.

Rossi, Pasquale & Company, 49 Warner Street, London EC. Barrel-piano makers *c.*1896. This short-lived partnership ended when Pasquale set up on his own the following year and **Spinelli** took his place with Rossi.

Rossi & Fils, 385 rue du Progrès, Brussels (Schaerbeek), Belgium. The Belgian branch of this firm of barrel-piano makers. They received gold medals for barrel pianos at exhibitions in 1906 and 1907. Then from 1909 as **Rossi & Tullio** at the same address. Maker of mechanical pianos.

Rossi & Spinelli, P C, 49 Warner Street, London EC. Makers of barrel pianos from 1897. Later as Rossi & Spinelli, 22 Baker's Row, Warner Street, London EC.Barrel-piano makers established at this address in 1915 and remaining until 1919, when Rossi returned to Italy. Spinelli was in business on his own until he united with **Pesaresi** *[qv]*. The various partnerships all made both wooden and iron-frame barrel pianos.

Roth & Engelhardt, Windsor Arcade, Fifth Avenue, New York, USA. Frederick Engelhardt was, like so many successful American piano-company founders, a German who emigrated to the States with his parents when he was ten years old. After a career which included serving as a cavalryman in the US Army he joined Steinway & Son spending seven years in charge of their action department In January 1889 he teamed up with A P Roth and founded his own company. In 1898 the first piano-player was introduced. This was called the Peerless which was soon followed by the Harmonist, both cabinet player and player-piano. Roth retired at the beginning of 1908 and Engelhardt brought in his two sons, Walter Ludwig (1884-?) and Alfred Dolge Engelhardt (1881-?) and changed the name of the business to F Englehardt & Sons, later to the Engelhardt Piano Company. Later owned and operated by the Peerless Piano Player Company of 2 East 47th Street, New York (founded in 1889). Later produced the coin-operated automatic player pianos operated by endless perforated tune sheets for use in public places.

Röttig, Josef, Rumburger Str 612, Georgswalde, Bohemia, Austro-Hungary. Sole agent for piano orchestrions by **Franz Simch** *[qv]*, *fl.*1909.

Roura, Agustin, 20 Arco del Teatro, Barcelona, Spain. Street-piano agent and hirer, *c* 1903-9.

Rovira, José, 9 Monserrate, Barcelona, Spain. Barrel-piano maker, *fl.*1909.

Sächsische Revolver-Orchestrion-Fabrik F O Glass, Markneukirchenstr 160 M, Klingenthal, Germany. Manufacturers of a 'revolver'-type barrel orchestrion in 1903 and also an attractive, large piano orchestrion. These keyboardless instruments, described as 'pneumatic orchestrions', carried model names such as Valsonora and Eldorado.

Salengo, Luigi, Pinerolo, Turin, Italy. Maker of street pianos, *fl.*1903.

Salvoni, Pindaro, Cortona, Arezzo, Italy. A maker of barrel pianos, *fl.*1903.

Sanchez, Antonio, 30 Abades, Madrid, Spain. Hirer of street pianos, *fl.*1903.

Sanches, Maria, 15 Alinendro, Madrid, Spain. Barrel piano and organ dealer, and hirer, *fl.*1909.

Sandell, Henry Konrad. Born in Sweden in 1878, Sandell went to Chicago, at the age of ten. When he was twenty-one, he took out his first patents for a coin-operated automatic violin, played electromagnetically. He joined the Mills Novelty Company of Chicago in 1904 and for the next twenty years concentrated on the automatic violin, producing the first practical instrument in 1906 called the Violano. By 1912, he coupled his Violano to a 44-note piano and so was born the Violano-Virtuoso, which was designated one of the eight greatest inventions of the decade by the US Patent Office. Roehl *[84]* suggests that the Violano-Virtuoso must first have appeared in 1909. Sandell went on to develop instruments with two and three violins and then the Violano Orchestra - a separate cabinet containing percussion instruments which could be coupled to the Violano. The instrument was operated by a perforated paper roll. Next he devised the Melody Violin, which was not roll-operated but could be played like a piano from a keyboard. Sandell, who accumulated something like 300 patents for violin-playing mechanisms during his lifetime, died on 29 January 1948 at the age of seventy. A deeply religious man, he refuted claims made on his behalf that he was a genius, claiming dedication to an ideal as being his motivating force.

Sarraceni, Benedetto, Angri, Salerno, Italy. Maker of barrel pianos, *fl.*1930.

Sassi, P, via Vescovado 7, Alessandria, Italy. Street-piano builder and hirer, *fl.*1909.

Sasso, Giovanni, Piazzetta del Carmini 3-4, Vercelli, Novara, Italy. Barrel-piano maker and hirer, *fl.*1909-30.

Sawin, Mich Domnikowskaja, Haus Tscheswiakoff, Moscow, Russia. Maker of orchestrion organs as well as church organs. He also handled piano orchestrions, *fl.*1903.

Scavarda, Ditta, 8 via Ottolenghi, Asti, Italy. Maker of barrel pianos, *fl.*1930.

Schaff Brothers Company. Chicago, Illinois, and Huntington, Indiana, USA. Founded in Huntington in 1868. Chicago branch run by John A Schaff at 118 Michigan Street. In 1907 opened a branch in New York at 411 E 91st Street supplying player pianos also piano strings. Schaff Brothers advertised 'high grade pianos and player-pianos'.

Schaub, Ferdinand. *See under* **Otto Manufacturing Company.**

Schmidt, Johann Gerhard Gottfried, Köpenick, Berlin, Germany. Improved on the system devised by **Potthoff & Golf** for playing a piano both manually and by a barrel mechanism and, in 1887, took out patents for a barrel action of great simplicity, wherein the barrel mechanism was called upon only to move the piano hammer when playing mechanically, instead of the complete hammer action.

Schröder, Auguste, Ackerstrasse 68a, Berlin N, Germany. A maker of mechanical pianos and organs, *fl.*1903.

Schübbe & Company, Uferstrasse 5, Berlin N, Germany. Founded in 1894 by Friederich Schübbe and Wilhelm Schnürpel. Claimed to be the oldest established firm of piano-orchestrion builders as well as the largest in Berlin; they produced an instrument resembling, in appearance and specification, the American 'photoplayer' style of effects piano.

Schulz Company, M, 373 Milwaukee Avenue, Chicago, Illinois, USA. Mathias Schulz was born in Warburg, Germany, in 1842 to a newly-widowed mother. A hard childhood led him to hanker for the opportunities of the 'new world' for which he chose London as a stepping stone. Here he worked in a piano factory for two years, saving money for a passage to America. He sailed in 1868 and made his home in Chicago where he founded a cabin-making business. Married with a son, Otto, Mathais's company grew rapidly and by 1889 and now with Otto as vice-president, the business of M Schulz Company, claiming foundation in 1869, concentrated on pianos and reed organs. But Mathais neglected his health for business and died in 1899 aged just 57. Otto Schulz took up the reins and opened up a branch in Minneapolis, Minnesota. He then drove the business into the era of the player-piano with a novel and ingenious single-valve action that incorporated a great deal of clever and original thinking. The Schulz Reproducing Grand was a quality instrument available with either the Welte-Mignon action or the Aria Divina. A factory was operated at 716 S First Avenue, Minneapolis, Minnesota. Some contemporary references, as well as recent ones (*see* Bowers *[6]*) misspell the name as 'Schultz'.

Schwesinger Piano Player Company, 81 Park Place East, Detroit, Michigan, USA. Makers of player pianos, *fl.*1909.

Scialanti, Alessandro, Piazza Principessa Margherita 161, Rome, Italy. A maker of fair organs, *c.*1910, who also made barrel-operated street pianos. By 1930 was at 175 via Cavour making barrel pianos.

Seeburg Piano Company, J P, Seeburg Building, 419 W Erie Street, Chicago, Illinois, USA. Justus Percival Sjoberg was born in Gothenberg, Sweden, in 1871 and came to America at the age of sixteen. Apprenticed to the Smith & Barnes piano factory in Chicago. After a spell with several other piano makers he changed his name to Seeburg and, in 1907, opened the J P Seeburg Piano Company at 704 Republic Buildings where he specialized in coin-freed electric pianos and, later, orchestrions. Became one of the most significant manufacturers of this type of instrument and was quick to enter the market for specialist photoplayers.

Seifert Musikwerke-Fabrik, Gebrüder, Domstr. 56, Cologne, Germany. Founded in 1908 by Gotthard and Eduard Seifert as makers of electric pianos and orchestrions.

Seybold, René, 1 route de l'Hôpital, Neudorf, Strasbourg, France. Manufactured player piano called Gabriella. In 1923 began making orchestrions. Later opened a factory at Bischwieler and secured licence from Höhner of Trossingen to make music rolls for the Magic-Organa self-playing accordion and to incorporate accordions in piano orchestrions. Produced a large variety of piano and percussion-based accordion-accompaniment instruments and perfected a 42-note player action from an 8-inch wide roll. Manufacturer of cinema organs and music rolls. René Seybold died aged 82 in 1972.

Seytre, Claude Félix, Lyons, France. In 1842 patented a Jacquard-type perforated card system for playing music and made an instrument named the Autophone.

Sharp, Thomas, Manchester, England. Thomas Sharp appears to have been in business for less than a decade making Hicks-style portable street pianos. Local directories show the first entry as 1850-51, 'T Sharp, Piano-forte Manufacturer, Chapel Street, Salford'. The 1852 entry shows the address as 6 Hall Street and in 1855 he is listed as being at 50 Great Ducie Street, Strangeways. There is no entry for him in 1858. One piano has been seen bearing the label: 'T Sharp. Piano-forte Maker, 48 Great Ducie St, Manchester'. This is on a well-preserved instrument in the Queen Victoria Museum and Art Gallery, Launceston, Tasmania.

Simch, Franz, Rumburger Str. 458, Georgswalde, Bohemia, Austro-Hungary. Founded in 1902 as an importer of piano orchestrions. *See also* **Rottig, Josef.**

Simoni, Gaetano, Bologna, Italy. Maker of barrel pianos established in 1889 and renowned for making instruments with a most unusual and beautiful 'voice' together with mechanical perfection yet in the end let down by rather poor musical arrangements.

Simmons, William, London. Granted British Patent number 4030 dated May 14th 1816. This referred to a barrel piano or harpsichord having interchangeable pegs on the barrel to enable new music to be set at will. No further details available.

Simplex Piano Player Company, Boston, Massachusetts, USA. Business formed by Theodore B Brown *[qv]* and originally (c.1904) at 10 Blackstone Street, Worcester, Massachusetts. Later relocated to Boston and owned and operated by **Hallet & Davis Company,** also of Boston, to produce piano players. Also as the Simplex Player Action Company at the same location. In 1927, the business was bought by **Kohler Industries** *[qv]* as it was seen to be the primary competitor of **Standard Pneumatic Action Company,** a business formed by Kohler.

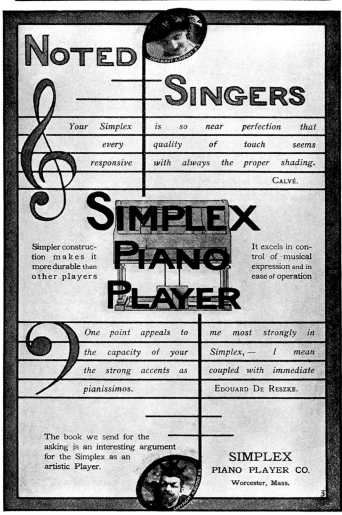
Simplex Player Piano Company, 244 Tottenham Court Road, London. Originally part of the American **Simplex Piano Player Company** but operated more of less autonomously as a British business managed by F S Heiden-Heimer. A factory was set up at 113 Cottenham Road, North London. Maker of the Airmatic piano player, *c.*1909.

Smeetz, P, 10 place du Concordat, Curghem, Brussels. Agent for orchestrions, barrel organs and barrel pianos, *c.*1903.

Smidt & Company, Ed, Georgstrasse 48, Hanover, Germany. Maker of piano orchestrions, in business in 1903. Not in 1909 directory.

Smith, Barnes & Strohber Company, 471 Clybourn Avenue, Chicago, Illinois, USA. Later at 1875 Clybourn Avenue. Makers of the Chicago Electric-brand coin-operated pianos which appear to have been built using parts from other instruments or may have been bought in complete. Similar to instruments made by the **Operators' Piano Company** [qv].

Smith Lyraphone Company, 210 Charles Street North, Baltimore, Maryland, USA. Originally the Smith Piano Company formed by Gilbert Smith, the firm manufactured the Lyraphone 65-note cabinet player invented by James O'Connor, which featured a tracker board with holes of increasing width either side of the centre. By 1909, the business had adopted the heading title and was located at Hanover in Pennsylvania. A Lyraphone is preserved in the Walt Bellm collection, Sarasota, Florida.

Société des Pianos Pneumatiques Français, La, 47 rue de Rome, Paris. Makers of the Monola player piano, a full-scale instrument advertised c.1928-30.

Societa Italiana per gli Organo a Cilindro, via Torniolli 285, Milan, Italy. This name, associated with street barrel organs and pianos c.1903, is probably that of an agent or distributor rather than a maker or repairer.

Solavaggione, Ditta G, 9 via S Dalmazzo, Turin, Italy. Maker of barrel organs, barrel pianos and clockwork pianos, fl.1930.

Solé, José, 18, 21 &23 Arco del Teatro, Barcelona, Spain. Street-piano agent and hirer, fl.1903-9.

Soler Soler, Vincente, 9, Mayor y 1 paseo del Obelisco, Castellon, Spain. Maker of mechanical pianos, fl.1930.

Spadari e Figli, Mich, Affile, Rome, Italy. Maker of cylinder pianos, c.1930.

Spadaro, Fratelli, via Baraccha, Reggio Calabria, Italy. Barrel-piano maker, fl.1930.

Spaethe, Wilhelm, Bismarckstr. 11, Gera, Reuss, Germany. Piano maker founded in 1859. Factory in Langenberg. Makers of the Pianist player piano and piano player. Spaethe made player pianos and organs and was also president of the mechanical musical-instrument makers' society, formed in Leipzig to fight the restrictions of the old German musical copyright laws governing music rolls. Opened a London office at 7 Victoria Avenue, Bishopsgate Street Without.

Speranza, Fratelli, Vico 2, Montesanto, Italy. A maker of barrel pianos, fl.1903.

Spiegel & Sohn, L, Musikwerke-Industrie, Kaiser-Wilhelm-Str18, Ludwigshafen, Germany. Founded in 1862, Spiegel was an agent, repairer and retailer of mechanical musical instruments including disc musical boxes, electric pianos and orchestrions. By 1909, the Ludwigshafen address was managed by Fritz Karl Spiegel. Other addresses at E.2, Nr 1, Mannheim (est 1903); Bahnhofstr 4, Pforzheim (est 1908), and an office under the name Schweizer-Musikwerke-Central J Spiegel & Sohn at Freie Str 103, Basle, in Switzerland (established in 1908).

Spinelli, Loreto, 49 Warner Street, London EC.Barrel-piano maker who was variously associated with **Pesaresi** [qv] and **Rossi** [qv]. By 1926 his address was 40 Hollingsworth Street, Barnsbury, London N1, and he advertised as 'maker of automatic pianos'. He manufactured barrel pianos until 1930, by which time he had united with Pesaresi.

Standard Pneumatic Action Company, 638-52 West 52nd Street, New York City, USA. Founded in 1910, this company appears to have been associated with the Auto Pneumatic Action Company [qv] with whose action it shared many similarities. The Standard player action, mass-produced by this company, was installed in a large number of American-built player pianos as well as roll mechanisms for photoplayers by makers such as Wurlitzer and American Photo Player Company. First president of the company was A W Johnston. The business advertised that on October 9th 1916 it shipped its 100,000th Standard player action six years to the day after the shipment of the very first. *See also:*

Standard Player Action Company, 638 West 52nd Street, New York City. President W. A. Mennie. Associate company of above. Produced a journal called *The Standard Player Monthly* which contained information about the company, its products, people and personalities. This journal ran from 1916 to the end of 1921.

During the first year of publication, the magazine reveals that the company was making 9,000 pneumatics a day and making one complete player action every four minutes. The company had its own leather tannery employing 30 men on making pouch leather, a vast timber department incorporating the very latest kiln-drying plant, and a wood-machining department where multiple operations could be carried out at a single pass: one such machine could bore 32 holes in a pouch board at once. By the summer of 1921 the company was promoting the fact that no fewer than 102 makes of player piano now fitted Standard Player Actions. *See also under* **Kohler Industries** *in Appendix 2.*

Stangalini, Angelo, via Gal. Ferreris 16, Vercelli, Italy. Maker of miniature barrel pianos, fl.1903.

Stangalini, Giuseppe, Milan, Italy. Exhibited two barrel pianos at the National Exhibition held in Turin in the summer of 1884.

Starr Piano Company, Richmond, Indiana, USA. Established in 1872. In 1869 James S and Benjamin (?-1903) Starr came across a piano and melodeon factory at Ripley, Ohio, run by an Alsation named Trayser. The Starrs acquired an interest in the business and when Trayser retired in 1878, Milo J Chase took over the business changing the name to the Chase Piano Company. Six years later the Starr brothers took over and re-named the business the Starr Piano Company. By 1909 the company was primarily engaged in player-piano production and particularly player-action manufacture. It advertised as having branches in Los Angeles, Indianapolis, Detroit, Cincinatti, Cleveland, Dayton and Toledo. The principal factory was at 138 Pennsylvania Street, Indianapolis. Produced pianos under the names Starr, the Richmond, the Trayser and the Remington player piano.

Steck. The New York piano-making business of George Steck & Company was founded in 1857. Steck was born as Hesse Kassel in Germany in 1829 and went to America in 1853 where he started his business four years later with the intention of only making top-quality pianos. He is credited with having popularized the upright piano in the United States (as distinct from the grand and table pianos of the time) through the perfection of tone and stringing scales. George Steck retired as president of his company in 1887. The business was then run successfully under the control of George Nembach from Saxe-Coburg who had been with the company since 1865. In 1903, with the expansion of W B Tremaine's Aeolian conglomerate [qv], the Steck business was absorbed to expand the Aeolian portfolio of quality piano brands. When Aeolian sought a wider German distribution, the business of Ernst Munck of Gotha was selected through the Choralian Company, Aeolian's subsidiary in Berlin. This was in 1903, a year after Munck Snr had died. Within two years, the Munck business, operated then by Ernst's son, Ernest J Munck, was sold to Aeolian for the purpose of manufacturing instruments for Europe. It was decided that the name 'Munck' was not ideal so the business was re-named 'Steck' even though the younger Munck remained as director. From this curious union came the renowned Gotha-framed range of Steck upright pianos which were only distributed in Europe – arguably the largest and heaviest instruments of their type. The business was known as Steck-Piano Gesellschaft, mbH, (formerly E Munck), Oststrasse 51, Gotha.

Steenbekken, Felix. Maker of mechanical pianos c.1890-1900. An instrument in a private collection in France has drum, cymbals, castanets and xylophone accompaniment. No address or localtion traced.

Stefanie-Werke-Filiale, Möldner & Skreta, Trautenau, Bohemia: Makers of Stefanie 'piano-orchester' advertised in 1904. *See also* **Czech, Karl.**

Steinway & Sons, 107-111 E 14th Street, New York City, USA. Henry Engelhardt Steinweg was born at Wolfshagen, Germany, in 1797. Self-taught, he made his first piano in 1825 and exhibited pianos of his own make at the 1839 Brunswick Trade Fair. Business prospered and his three sons Theodore, Charles, and Heinrich joined the firm. The political upheaval of the late 1840s virtually paralysed German industry. The time was right to leave and, while

Steinweg survived in Germany, Heinrich left for America with four of his sons and his three daughters changing the end of his name along the way to the more acceptable Steinway. After many vicissitudes and family tragedies, Steinway pianos were established successfully in America and, in 1877, a European sales office was opened in London at 15 and 17 Lower Seymour Street – this was Steinway Hall. Steinway received its first Royal Warrant in 1890. Mounting competition from Germany, however, posed not only a threat to the British piano industry, but also to imports. Rival quality piano makers Bechstein and Blüthner both opened London showrooms. The German headquarters and factory was in Hamburg at St Pauli 6, Schanzenstr 20/24 with other premises at Ludwigstr 11-14, and Kampstr 8/10 with a retail outlet at Jungfernstieg 34. This European arm also prospered eventually, making Steinway pianos for the British market. It created the curious situation where pianos bearing the same name hailed from two factories, one in Germany and one in America. Both were then, as today, ranked top of their league, yet when, some years ago, the BBC ordered six new Steinway grands and six US-made instruments arrived, they were rejected in favour of German-made ones claiming that the sound and touch were different. Steinway never made player pianos but supplied instruments to Aeolian to be fitted as necessary and then sold as Steinway instruments. Aeolian negotiated to fit Duo-Art reproducing actions in Steinways and these were converted by Aeolian in both New York and Hayes, Middlesex. Both installations were quite different, the US-made Duo-Art being different in detail from the British examples. Steinway's rigid contract structure with Aeolian is said, in the end, to have contributed to Aeolian's American company failure following the Wall Street Crash.

Sterling Company, Derby, Connecticut, USA. Established in 1860 as the Birmingham Organ Company. In 1871 Charles A Sterling took over the business and, two years alter, set up the Sterling Organ Company. Piano manufacture began in 1885. Soon afterwards J R Mason joined the business and through his direction the firm moved into piano-players. Produced the Sterling player piano action, *fl*.1909.

Sternberg-Armin ès Testvere, Budapest, Hungary. This firm was a general agent and distributor for the Piano Melodici. The name has been seen deeply engraved on the hinged front fall of a 30-note instrument. *See also* **Racca.**

Stuer, Wilhelm, Warschauerstrasse 18, Berlin O, Germany. Established in 1894. Maker of piano-orchestrions. By 1909 was at Memeler Str 14, Berlin O, 34.

Stichel, Ferdinand, Sophienstr. 43, Leipzig, Germany. Established in 1877 as piano maker. Produced the Claviola piano player.

Stingl, Gustav, VII, Mariahilferstr. 17, Vienna, Austro-Hungary. Described as the largest piano-orchestrion maker in Austro-Hun-

gary, Stingl was granted both Austrian and German patents for improvements to barrel piano-orchestrions.

Štoček, Hynek, Trautenau, Bohemia (Austria). Made an electrically driven keyless piano with percussion accompaniment, *c.*1920.

Stoddard, Charles Fuller. Born in Chicago on December 26th 1876, son of a furniture dealer, Stoddard developed an early interest and ability in pneumatic control. Around 1910, he decided that the player piano could be improved upon and so he gave up his $8,000 [£2,000] a year job with American Pneumatic Service Company of Boston to concentrate on the project. Within 18 months, he had developed a system which could re-create piano dynamics and expression by automatic pneumatic means. Although piano makers who were invited to hear his system remained unimpressed, George G Foster, head of the **American Piano Company** *[qv]*, was sufficiently interested to buy both it and the services of the inventor. After the crash of the stock market in 1929 and the resultant slump, Stoddard moved into the restaurant business and opened what was probably the world's first 'automatic' catering business in New York where food was scientifically prepared, the numbers of guests accurately recorded and the progress of individual diners' dishes displayed by lights from kitchen to waitress. He went on to distinguish himself in this new field until he suffered a stroke in 1956, a second stroke causing his death on 29 April 1958 at his New York apartment in Riverside Drive. Stoddard was a man of great genius, entirely self-taught, to whom is owed the entire success of the Ampico system which, although subsequently improved from the Stoddard-Ampico of the late 'teens in conjunction with Clarence Nichols Hickman, was the first reproducing action which could be mass-produced without losing quality.

Story & Clark Company, 315-17 South Wabash Avenue, Chicago, Illinois, USA. Considered a major mid-west keyboard instrument manufacturer, the business was founded in 1884 by Hampton L Story (1835-*c.*1901) who was a dealer in reed organs, and Melville Clark (1850-1918), a prominent organ builder. The manufacture of pianos began in 1895 and the firm prospered moving, in 1901, to a new factory in Grand Haven, Michigan. The acquisition of the Playano Manufacturing Company in 1905 marked the company's move into mechanical pianos and this began with the Playano cabinet piano-player. Later moved into player-pianos and produced a range of mid-priced instruments that featured the Repro-Phraso accenting device. Also made a 'miniature' full-scale upright only 50 inches high.

Stransky Frères, 20 rue de Paradis, Paris, France. Main agent for **Racca** *[qv]* mechanical pianos and other similar instruments, including the Autopianiste mechanical player, *fl*.1903.

Stransky, Vienna, Austria. This name is associated with **Hupfeld** *[qv]* and in particular with the Phonoliszt-Violina. May have been an agent or distributor, *c*.1911. There was, *c*.1930, an Anton Stransky in Graslitz working as a maker and exporter of stringed musical instruments at 63 Rathausgasse.

Stridente, via Antonio 22, Naples, Italy. Name seen on barrel piano; not in 1903-1909 directories.

Strixione, Ferruccio, 60 via del Fico, Genoa, Italy. Barrel-piano maker, *fl*.1930.

Strohmenger & Sons, J, 86, Brompton Road, London, SW, also 105 High Holborn, WC. Factory at 167-171 and 206, Goswell Road, London, EC. Founded by John Strohmenger in 1830, the business was once a major and successful London piano-producer turning to player pianos very early on: the first interior player was marketed shortly after 1907. In 1929, when many companies were suffering greatly in the Depression, Strohmenger was bought by piano makers Chappell and effectively ceased.

Stults & Bauer, 738 Broadway, Brooklyn, New York, USA. Established in 1880 as piano makers. In 1909 advertised as makers of player piano actions. The company finally moved to 338-40 East 31st Street, New York City.

Stycha, J, Prague, Austro-Hungary. Produced a barrel-operated piano orchestrion *c*.1890.

Superscope Marantz Corporation, California, USA. Founded by John S Tushinsky (1910-1988). Introduced the Pianocorder, a solenoid-driven electrically-operated piano-playing system that was played using digitally-encoded music on a 45-minute tape-cassette, c.1977. UK agents were Kemble Pianos Ltd of Bletchley, who priced it at £1,495 ($2,700) in 1980. Three models were made – a reproducing piano, a *vorsetzer*, and a kit for the piano-technician to install in any piano. Never achieving sales success to the level Tushinsky projected, it was finally sold to Yamaha Corporation of America. One installation (by William Edgerton of Darien, Connecticut) noted in a modern harpsichord.

Symanski & Söhne, Chlodna 34, Warsaw, Poland. A manufacturer of street and fair organs who also built barrel pianos.

Symphonion-Fabrik A-G, Schkeuditzer Str 13-17b, Leipzig-Göhlis, Germany. Established in 1889. While primarily remembered as pioneering makers of disc-playing musical-boxes, this business also produced other types of automatic musical instruments. In 1908 introduced an electric piano called the Symphoniola.

Tadini, Emile, Nice, France. Maker of well-engineered and artistic clockwork café pianos c.1920. No longer in business by 1930.

Tagliabue, Giuseppe, via Sambuco 15, Milan, Italy. A maker of 'barrel keyboard instruments, *fl.* 1903.

Taylor & Company, C R. Established in 1903 at 26 Runton Street, Elthorne Road, Holloway, London N, after the 1914-18 war the business moved to large premises at 34 Commerce Road, Wood Green, London N22. Made cheap uprights and grands and from around 1929-34 period produced players using the British-built Higel action of Canadian design. On 21 February 1936 the factory was severely damaged by fire and, already hit by the economic depression, the business did not resume.

Taylor, Samuel, Bristol, England. A cylinder piano in the F F Hill collection bears a label reading: 'Samuel Taylor, Musical Instrument Maker, No 26, Host Street, next to Colston's School, St Augustine's Place, Bristol. Manufacturers of Barrel Organs and Cylinder Pianofortes. NB Country Orders punctually attended to'. *Mathew's Directory* for 1854 and 1855 lists S Taylor at 27 St Augustine's Place and describes him as an organ and pianoforte maker. In the Bristol rate books for 1855-7 he is listed under Host Street but without a number.

Taylor, Thomas, Sheffield, England. A cylinder piano with this name and inscribed 'Maker, No 79' (no doubt the serial number of the instrument) and also bearing on the pleated silk front the Royal Arms in brass, exists in the F G Turner & Son collection at Horsham. It is likely that this maker was related to the Bristol family but this has not been corroborated. Another is in the J F Young collection, Lincolnshire.

Taylor, William, Bristol, England. A cylinder piano formerly in the collection of the late Gerry Planus bears a label reading: 'William Taylor, 57, Broad Quay, Bristol. Manufacturer of Cylinder or Handle Piano-Fortes and Organs. Extra cylinders set to Piano-Fortes, Organs and Musical Clocks - Old Ones re-set. Harps and Piano-Fortes Tuned and Repaired'. A barrel organ of the same outward appearance and case design was recently rebuilt by the author. *Mathew's Directory* for 1837 lists William Taylor as a musical-instrument maker of 69 Stokes Croft, at which address he remained until 1840. In the 1841 Directory he is listed as 'musical instrument maker and nautical stationer' at 57 Broad Quay where he lived until his death at the early age of 39. He was buried on 10 December 1847. His home was continued in the name of Ruth Taylor but her precise relationship is unknown.

Taylor, W F, Bristol, England. A cylinder piano dated 1848 in the F F Hill collection bears a label reading 'W F Taylor, Musical Instrument Maker, No. 57, Broad Quay, Bristol'. The classified Bristol trades directory lists W F Taylor at this address as a musical-instrument maker. He was contemporary with S Taylor but is also listed elsewhere in the same directory as a music teacher. Whether W F is the same as William or was brother or father to the latter is not certain. The Taylors, like the Hicks, were clearly a large family, it seems, with various members in the profession of music in one aspect or another. All Taylor-named cylinder pianos closely resemble the Hicks pattern and it could be conjectured that the Taylors, like Distin, may at some time have worked under Hicks.

Tel-Electric Company, Pittsfield, Massachusetts, USA. Formed in 1905 to produce an electrically operated expression piano playing system called the Telektra. Patented by Timothy B Powers in September 1901, the Telektra comprised a bank of solenoids attached beneath the piano key bed and connected by a cable to the remote console called by the makers 'the transmitter'. This detached spool box console played using a punched brass music roll and incorporated a series of function controls that could be operated remotely from the owner's arm-chair. A thick electric cable attached this console to the piano. The action was very simple, being entirely electro-magnetically controlled, the tips of metal fingers making contact with a 'tracker bar' through perforations in the tune sheet. Originally the music rolls were made of thick, semi-waxed paper but later the music was provided in the form of a metal cassette from which was drawn a long strip of perforated brass strip. Two models were made, the Tel-Electric with a 5-inch wide roll, and the Telektra with one 6¾-inches wide. The former played 65 of the piano's notes using 73 holes to include expression and accent, while the latter was a full-scale 88-note player. By 1911 the company had offices and showrooms at 299 Fifth Avenue, New York City. The instrument enjoyed reasonable success and many thousands were sold until around 1915 or so.

Tenoudji, André, 20 rue de Paradis, Paris, with factory at 3 rue Lafitte. Makers and repairers of player pianos and cylinder pianos, *fl.* 1920.

Testé, Joseph-Antoine, Nantes, France. A mid-nineteenth-century instrument maker, who invented a musical instrument that he called the Cartonium. This had forty-two free metal reeds and played music from perforated Jacquard-type cards. Patented in 1861, it incorporated a mechanism that could also punch the cardboard for the instrument to play.

Thibouville-Lamy, Jérôme, 68, 68bis & 70 rue Réaumur, Paris, France, and 10 Charterhouse Street, Holborn Circus, London. Old established musical-instrument manufacturers, who were makers and distributors of musical boxes of the cylinder-playing type from about 1865 onwards and, later, were agents for makes other than their own. In 1884 they advertised two devices. One was the Pianista described as an apparatus which can be placed before any piano or organ to perform songs, dances, operatic and sacred music mechanically with the greatest exactitude of expression by means of perforated cardboards'. This instrument, of the push-up player style, played book music by turning a handle. Felt-covered fingers played the piano keys pneumatically, there being a bellows system operated by foot treadles. This device, although superseded by paper-roll music, was still being advertised in 190S. At the same time was offered the Organina Thibouville which 'possesses the tone of a harmonium' and won two gold medals at the International Exhibition of 1885. This again played perforated 'cardboards'. The firm also manufactured barrel organs for street use and, in 1890, they produced reed organs playing Gavioli's design of book music which they called the Organophone Expressif, and another smaller device called the Coelophone. The business had an American office at 15 Great Jones Street, New York City.

Thièble, Léon, Ruyaulcourt (Seine-et-Oise), France. Early 20th century maker of piano-player action named the Autopianiste, *fl.*1909.

Thim, Johann, Trautenau, Bohemia, Austro-Hungary. Maker of piano orchestrions, *fl.*1905.

Thompson-U'nette Piano Company, 2652 West Lake Street, Chicago, Illinois, USA. Maker of the U'nette player-grand advertised as 'Music with you in it'. A division of the Thompson Piano Company of 268 Wabash Avenue.

Tinel, A, 14 Marché aux Oeufs, Antwerp, Belgium. Agent for electric pianos and orchestrions.

Tomasso & Son, A, 17 Colne Road, Winchmore Hill, London N21. Clockwork and street barrel-piano manufacturers in business repairing and hiring out street pianos at 4a The Broadway, Palmers Green, London N14. In 1936 the firm was at 18½ Douglas Place, Clerkenwell, London EC, from where it advertised as repairers of 'automatics' (clockwork barrel pianos). Victor Tomasso died in 1968 and the business was dissolved.

Tomasso, Emilio, 69 Cherry Street, New York City, USA. Barrel-piano manufacturer who advertised himself on his instruments as 'successor to Cesare Maserati & Co, Mechanical Organ Manufacturer'. *See also* **Maserati, Caesar.**

Tomasso. Ernesto, 1 St Mary's Lane, Quarry Hill, Leeds, Yorkshire. Barrel-piano maker related to Antonio Tomasso who, with his brother Benedetto, took out patents in 1908 for a tremolo device employing a rotating shaft having four concave flutings.

Tomasso & Phillipo, 5a Baker's Row, Clerkenwell, London EC.Luigi Vincenzo Tomasso was born in 1862 at Cassino and was brought to England in 1867 with his sister, Niccolina (aged seven), and brother, Antonio (aged three). He immediately was forced to contribute to the family income and became a street musician at the age of just eight years. Fortunately, like many Italian children of even humble background, he was an accomplished performer on the concertina. From 1876 until 1882, he was apprenticed to **Chiappa** making barrel organs and pianos at their Clerkenwell factory. In 1882 he started his own factory making these instruments at Baker's Row. His brother Antonio worked for him. In 1883 he married Domenica Capaldi and, in 1889 at the age of twenty-seven, he started a factory at 1 St Mary's Lane, Leeds 9, Yorkshire. The Clerkenwell factory was continued by Antonio. There was also a somewhat short-lived factory at Pea Street, Glasgow (1892-3). Luigi's family had continued to expand and there were now five sons, all of whom worked in the trade. Although clockwork pianos were made in large numbers, they also produced hand-operated street pianos on carts, and these may frequently be found with a tremolo arrangement on the treble strings as well as travelling picture fronts. Later, electric player pianos were built. The shadowey figure of **Phillipo** remains just that but it has been suggested that he had put some money into the business and was thus not an active partner. Luigi Vincenzo Tomasso died on Good Friday, 1944, at the age of eighty-two, and all the pianos which had been hired out were then sold by auction excepting one which still remains with the family.

Tonk & Brother, Inc, William, 259 Wabash Avenue, Chicago, Illinois, USA. The Tonk family held extensive interests in the musical instrument business in Chicago in the early years of the 20th century. Max Tonk headed the Tonk Manufacturing Company, set up in 1873 to make organ and piano stools and benches. Tonk Brothers Company imported musical instruments as well as undertaking some manufacture. But it was William Tonk & Brother, Inc, founded in 1893, who imported pianos and mechanical instruments. In 1881 they opened a new company in New York City (452/456 10th Avenue) and stocked player pianos. No evidence of their actual manufacture exists so these may just be imports despite contemporary advertisements that suggests they were Tonk-manufactured, and an oblique statement in Dolge *[22]* giving them as makers.

Tremaine, William Burton. William Burton Tremaine (1840-1907) was one of the largest and most significant entrepreneurs in the history of the player piano for without his foresight and leadership the instrument in America might have lagged behind the rest of the world. He entered the piano business (*relates Dolge [22]*) in 1868, organising the Mechanical Orguinette Company in 1876 to market Mason J Matthews' paper-playing reed organ or Orguinette. In 1883 he acquired the Aeolian Organ Company and in 1888 the patents and stock in trade of the Automatic Music Paper Company of Boston, Mass. He then established the Aeolian Organ and Music Co making automatic organs and music rolls. In 1892 he purchased all the patents of the Munroe Organ Reed Company of Worcester, Mass, and in 1885 introduced the Aeriol self-playing piano. He was succeeded as president of the Aeolian Company in 1899 by his son, Henry 'Harry' Barnes Tremaine, who was also president of the Weber Piano Company. The groundwork of the Tremaines did a great deal to foster the player-piano industry and the ascension of the Aeolian Company, which went from strength to strength, was due entirely to the foresight of William Burton Tremaine at a time when there was neither encouragement nor demand for such instruments. He appreciated the power of money, buying not only the patents he needed to put his company in the forefront but also the best brains, such as Kelly, Pain, Votey and others. *See also* **Aeolian Company**.

Trevisan, A, 183 borgo Aselo, Castelfranco Veneto, Treviso, Italy. Maker of automatic pianos and cylinder pianos, *fl.*1930.

Trist Piano Player Ltd, Gresham Street, London EC. Arthur Ronald Trist invented a system of playing a piano or organ using an electro-pneumatic player action in which special music rolls, made of layers of different substances, could be perforated in part to expose electrically conductive layers beneath. He referred to these as 'the conducting sheet' and 'the non-conducting sheet'. When 'read' by a metal contact finger, a solenoid was energised, so opening the airway controlling a fairly conventional twin-valve (or triple-valve) system. Trist patented his music roll system (British Patent No.709 of 1906) and subsequently a number of different types of player action. Trist Piano Player Ltd was formed in 1908 to exploit his patents. Trist's inventions were as remarkable as they were numerous and he patented (number 535 of 1909) a note-accenting system that used double valves controlled by electro-magnetic fingers acting through holes in the music roll. The factory was at St Albans in Hertfordshire. This company carried on until September 1911 when a voluntary winding-up was agreed to although apparently the company was not technically insolvent. The liquidator contacted **Maximilian Macarious Kastner** *[qv]* and as a result a new company was formed, called the New Trist Player Piano Ltd, on December 11th 1911, with Kastner as managing director. Meanwhile Chase & Baker had filed a claim against the company for £1,000 in connection with music rolls made and supplied to the old business. Besides Kastner, the other directors were the Right Hon Earl of Plymouth (who resigned on June 13th 1913), Sir Ernest Clarke (who resigned on March, 5th 1913), Count Alexis de Toper and A R Trist. There was an agreement with Kastner's own company, Kastner & Co Ltd, under which Kastner & Co had the rights to sell Trist products. The ramifications of Trist came to a head at the end of 1913 when the creditors' meeting was held following a net loss in the year ended December 12th 1912 of £706. The factory ceased working in March 1914 through lack of working capital and persistent disagreements among the directors. Trist himself attributed the failure to the inability of the directors to agree about methods of conducting business. The relations between Kastner and the other directors became so strained that harmonious working was impossible. Although no products of the Trist business are known to survive – indeed there is little evidence that it ever produced anything – the story of this small business is typical of several which were founded on one man and his inventions. What makes this one the more interesting is that Kastner should have been involved with it. A brilliant designer, like many inventors Trist appears to have had little interest in production.

Triumph-Auto Pianos Ltd, Triumph House, 185-191 Regent Street, London, W1. Founded out of the business of **Kastner & Company Ltd** and The **Auto-Piano Company** which were compulsorily wound up in December 1916 under the Trading with the Enemy Act (1916). There was considerable resistance to the application of the Act in the instance of the Auto-Piano Company for it was a British company comprised entirely of UK directors. On top of that, the company had been manufacturing pianos and players in England since 1912 and fitting them into both British and German pianos. In spite of strong objections, the Act was enforced and the company wound up. New companies were quickly formed to continue the trade, one being the **Direct Pneumatic Action Co** *[qv]* and on 11 June 1917 Triumph Auto Pianos Ltd was registered with a capital of £20,000 [$80,000]. It advertised under the name TriumphAuto Ltd. On December 2nd 1930, a new company was registered – Triumph Auto Pianos (1930) Ltd – with a capital of £150,000 [$600,000] to acquire the assets of the old firm. In 1931 the Triumph Autopiano was priced at just £66 (the Empire) with models costing up to £248 (the Autogrand). *See also* **Kastner & Company Ltd.**

Turconi, Joseph, Galata, rue Camondo 11, Constantinople, Turkey. Maker of street pianos who was in business in 1903. Exhibited a barrel piano at the National Exhibition, Turin, held in the summer of 1884.

Ucci, Gino, corsa Vittorio Emanuele, Castellamare Adriatico, Penne, Italy. Maker of barrel pianos. 'Successor to Chieti', *fl.*1930.

Ullmann, Charles & Jacques, Paris, Ste Croix and London. Described as makers of musical boxes and also the Piano Executant Artiste, a 54-note book-playing mechanical piano. Believed more likely to have been distributors. Charles Ullmann also founded the Société du Zonophone and was a part-owner of the Fonotipia record company. By 1930 business was styled L'Industrie Musicale 'Ancien Etablissement Ch-J Ullmann' at 11 rue du Faubourg-Poissonnière.

Unger, Johann Friedrich. Einbeck, Germany. An inventor, *fl.*1745, who invented mechanisms for recording pieces of music for mechanical instruments using a keyboard and pens on a paper strip (melography) in 1752.

United States Novelty Company, 121, 11th Street West, Kansas City, Missouri, USA. Advertised as makers of automatic pianos, *fl.*1909.

Universal Piano Company, 190-192 Southern Boulevard, New York City, USA. Manufacturers a player-pianos (advertised as 'straight 88-note'). Part of the Aeolian Piano conglomerate. Also makers of music rolls.

Valente, Anthony, 42 Thompson Street, Oldham Road, Manchester. In 1885 he advertised himself as 'mechanical organ maker' although whether this was barrel organ or barrel piano ('piano-organ') is unknown.

Van der Does, C F, Lange Houtstraat 9, s'Gravenhage (The Hague), The Netherlands. Established in 1840 main agents for pianos and organs. In the 1930s handled a player-piano called The Mignonola.

Van Roy, Pierre Paul, Aalst, Belgium. Maker of large clockwork barrel pianos, *fl.*1920-30. There was another barrel-piano maker of this name (P Vanroy) said to have worked in Hamburg in the 1920s who built large orchestrion-type instruments with percussion effects. It is now thought these were one and the same man.

Varetto Brothers, 17 Milton Street, Lower Broughton, Manchester. Described as organ builders and repairers, they were agents for Chiappa music books and fair organs. They also specialised in the repair of street and fair organs, pianos, etc. A German-built street organ has been seen bearing the above address and the date August 1931. The business of Varetto Brothers was finally bought out by Chiappa.

Varetto, Peter, 87 Oldham Road, Manchester. Described as a mechanical-organ maker in 1885, he was also a repairer of street pianos.

Varetto, Pietro, 14 Warner Street, London EC. A maker of barrel pianos who advertised as such in the London Directory for 1881. Most probably connected with, if not the same as, the 'Pietro' (Peter) Varetto later in Manchester.

Vassalo, Vincento, 1 via Michele Angelo, Turin, Italy. Maker of street barrel organs and pianos, *fl.*1930.

Vela, Benito, Pueblo Español, Barcelona, Spain. Makers of modern miniature barrel pianos, which are more novelties than practical street instruments. These are mounted on detachable dogcarts with shafts and the whole is gaily painted. Termed *pianos a Manubrio*, these have iron frames and are well made using modern materials and methods such as nylon bushes and moulded parts. They have 32 notes, two clapper blocks and a triangle.

Velazquez, Isabelo, Los Molinos 5, Bajoiqda, Madrid 20, Spain. Repinner of street piano barrels, *fl.*1930.

Verbeeck & Son, J, 85 Barnsbury Road, London N1, and 79 Copenhagen Street, London N1. Advertised as makers of mechanical organs, Verbeeck was an organ builder by trade. He sold book music for both fair organs and book-playing pianos between the years 1924 and 1942, when he ceased trading.

Verbeeck, Pierre, 109 Duinstraat, Antwerp, Belgium. Fair, band and street organ maker. At the outbreak of the 1914-18 war he came to England as a refugee and opened a fair-organ factory in Blrmsngham, selling also book music for both fair organs and book-playing pianos. He advertised as a maker of mechanical organs. In 1924, he moved to 85 Barnsbury Road, London (*see* **Verbeeck & Son**), finally selling out to Chiappa in 1942. He died about 1954.

Viazanni, Clerkenwell, London EC.An Italian who used to do maintenance and repair work on organs and, in particular, Imhof & Mukle orchestrions. He is likely to have been associated with the repair of barrel pianos as well.

Vickers Ltd. *See under* **Wearham, J.**

Victoria-Musikwerke Tismar & Burr, Anklamerstrasse 32, Berlin N. Founded by Berthold Tismar and Willy Burr, this firm produced an electromagnetic piano orchestrion in the early part of the 20th century.

Vietti, Pietro, via Madama Cristina 18, Turin, Italy. Maker of barrel pianos, in business in 1903. By 1909 was listed at via Ormea 12, Turin.

Villa, Luigi, 18 Granville Square, Farringdon Road, London EC.Manufacturer of automatic barrel pianos, who patented in 1903 a method of displaying advertisements in the front fall of a street piano. The front fall had a glass central window behind which was an endless band that passed around vertically-mounted rollers either side of the piano front. A system of levers and linkages converted the continuous rotary movement of the barrel into an intermittent motion to display signs in the window.

Da Vinci, Leonardo. Italy. The greatest figure of the Italian Renaissance, Leonardo (1452-1519) was a prodigious inventor who remained unfettered by either doctrine or convention. Whether his designs represented things he built, or merely thought out from his active brain and reasoning remains unknown. The many hundreds of pages of his sketch-books show an almost alarming variety of ideas. One of these was for a mechanical spinet 'with drum' (meaning, most probably, a pinned barrel). This is reputed to have been 'made'.

Viore. Michele, Pinerolo, Turin, Italy. Maker of fair organs and street pianos, *c.*1903.

Vittore, Vicola Consolata 3, Turin, Italy. Maker of barrel pianos, *fl.*1903.

Vogliazzo, Palmino, 8 via Quintino Sella, Asti, Italy. Barrel-piano maker, *fl.*1930.

Vose & Sons Piano Company, 158-60 Boylston Street, Boston, Massachusetts, USA. James Whiting Vose, born in 1818, made his first piano in 1851 having learned his trade in the various Boston factories. With the introduction to partnership with his three sons the business was incorporated in 1889, all the stock owned by the Vose family. Although the company claimed to have been established in 1851, this is not totally correct and research now suggests that 1853 is a more likely date. By 1910 the firm had introduced the Vose Piano Player and, later, a player piano.

Vosgien, Luigi, Fuori Porta Milano, Strada per Pernate 121, Milan, Italy. One of the first Italian makers of large barrel pianos suitable for open-air use and dance-halls. Marini attributes him to Novara and says that his instruments possess exceptional qualities of manufacture and 'uncommon shape'. One instrument in the form of a grand piano with a large barrel where the keyboard fall would normally be. Advertised as 'successor to I Colombo', was maker of street barrel pianos, *fl.*1903.

Votey, Edwin Scott, Summit Union County, New Jersey, USA. Edwin Scott Votey (1857-1931) was a practical organ builder, with experience of both reed and pipe instruments. He took over the Detroit Organ Company and, later, with the partnership of Farrand formed the Farrand & Votey Organ Company which later also made pianos and players. Votey is credited with being among the first to make a practical pneumatic piano player although Theodore P Brown was granted patents for an 'inner player' in 1897. Votey's invention was the first Pianola push-up and he applied for a patent on January 25th 1897, a patent being granted on May 22nd 1900. The rights to his instrument were acquired by Aeolian along with the services of its creator. It was Votey who subsequently lengthened the forepart of the grand piano case to allow the player mechanism to be placed inside instead of being a mere external attachment. This important development was subsequently adopted by other makers: most importantly the trade in innovation, thought long to be merely East to West, was now reversed – and Votey's grand piano case modification was taken up by Hupfeld in Leipzig.

Wallis, Joseph, 133 & 135 Euston Road, London NW. A maker of mechanical pianos who, in 1876, was classified in the London Trade Directory as a maker of 'street and saloon' pianos. Produced a cheap pneumatic player prosaically named 'The Wallis'. The business had a factory at 50, Isledon Road, Finsbury Park, North London, but after this was burned down in the early 1920s, new premises were taken at 53b, Carysfort Road, N.16.

Warnies, Leon, Amsterdam, Holland. In 1875 he started renting out street organs and pianos which he repaired and maintained. He died in 1902 but his widow continued the business until competition from the phonograph forced closure.

Wauters, (Professor), Binghamton, New York, USA. Worked for the Automatic Musical Company of Binghamton, which produced self-playing banjos and xylophones playing paper rolls. The firm ultimately became the **Link Piano Company** making coin-operated paper-roll-playing, keyless café pianos. Professor Wauters produced a self-playing violin for the company in 1907. Pneumatically operated, the instrument took seven years to develop and played special 65-note music rolls.

Wearham, J. After the First World War, armaments and aircraft makers Vickers Ltd, like every other manaufacturer that had been caught up in war-time production and expansion, suddenly found itself with no work. Companies finding themselves in a similar position had turned to sewing machines, motor-cars, furniture and caravans. Vickers decided to explore the self-acting piano business. One of its design team was Jack Wearham who identified a niche market for the company – a player attachment that could convert any ordinary instrument into a roll-player. In exploring the potential, Wearham came up with a novel and unique approach – a hand-pumped key-top player. The outcome was British Patent No 186,680 (June 29th 1921) issued in the names of Vickers Ltd and J Wearham. The essence of this instrument was that it could be 'folded, collapsed, or divided into sections, in order to reduce its length for packing into a poprtable case'. It was played using a hand-pumped exhauster while the pneumatic motors directly depressed the piano keys via a rubber button on the ends of their lower boards. The following month a further Patent was granted (No 189,175 of July 22nd 1921) an again in the name of Vickers Ltd and Wearham. In this revised design, the hand-operated exhausters were provided with an automatic 'shifting centre' so that movement of the feeders was gradually and automatically reduced as the tension in the reservoir increased. The feeders, in which the 'player' inserted his hand under a strap rather like the retaining strap of a concertina, were positioned either side of the tracker bar/music roll assembly. Tempo and volume (accenting) were adjusted by levers on the feeder boards. Meanwhile changing market conditions made Vickers reconsider the piano-player market as a result of which the company dropped both the project and Jack Wearham. He, however, continued the project as a spare-time activity. Eight years later, at London's Bishopsgate Institute, Wearham laid on a demonstration of his latest version. *The Gramophone* for March 1930 reported on the event, saying that 'one of its greatest assets is that it is portable; it weighs very little more than the average portable wireless set'. In its latest form, the player folded in half and was transported in a specially-designed case. While the demonstration concerned standard 88-note music rolls, the point was made that 'it is practicable to produce an instrument for use with rolls of about half the present width'. Commenting that the instrument 'revealed a particularly human touch', the magazine went on to say that 'There was a noticeable absence of mechanical effect and the effect was both brilliant and convincing'. The inventor thought that with mass-production, the price could be as little as £20 [$80] and as soon as the necessary financial support was guaranteed, a manufacturing company would be formed. The timing was bad: the Wall Street Crash heralded a hiatus in the British economy and Jack Wearham and his key-top player were never heard of again.

Webb, C F. Collaborator with H C Coldman in the design and development of the Boyd Pistonola player piano. *See under* **Boyd.**

Weber Gebrüder, GmbH, 3 Bismarckstrasse, Waldkirch-im-Breisgau, Baden, Germany. Founded in 1880. Makers of orchestrion organs, who also produced mechanical pianos and piano orchestrions such as the Unika, the Grandezza and the Brabo, which were basically roll-playing pianos with mandolin, xylophone, string-toned organ pipes and timpani accompaniment. Very fine and high quality instruments were produced along with their music rolls many of which were arranged by Gustav Bruder. The heydays of the company were in the second half of the 1920s when there was a great demand for this type of instrument from restaurants, cafes and dance-halls.

Weber Piano Company, The, 362, 5th Avenue, New York City, USA. Founded in 1852 by Albert Weber (1828-1879) who was born in Bavaria and went to America at the age of sixteen. Largely self-educated and a good musician, his first workshop was on White Street, New York, but soon moved to West Broadway. Despite being burned out two years later, he set up an even bigger factory on the corner of Broome and Crosby Streets. Quickly he perfected a high-quality piano that speedily established the Weber name alongside other top US makers such as Chickering. His death at the early age of 50 placed the firm in the hands of his son Albert Jnr (1858-?) who, in establishing a branch of the business in Chicago (1880), claimed to be the first New York piano-maker to open a division in that city. Albert Jnr was the originator of the term 'baby grand'. On the ascendent at this time was William E Wheelock (1852-?) who was volume-producing a high-quality piano. Needing to expand production to meet demand, Wheelock bought first the Stuyvesant Piano Company and then, in 1892, the Weber business. William E Wheelock became president of the Weber Piano Co in 1903 in which year Harry B Tremaine (son of the founder of the 1888 business Aeolian Organ & Music Company, and its president since 1898) formed the Aeolian, Weber Piano & Pianola Company. Capitalised at $10,000,000 [£2,500,000], this embraced the Aeolian Co, The Orchestrelle Co (London), The Choralion Company (Berlin), The Aeolian Company (Paris), The Pianola Company Proprietary Ltd (Melbourne and Sydney), the Weber Piano Company, George Steck & Company, Wheelock Piano Company, Stuyvesant Piano Company, Chilton Piano Company, Technola Piano Company, Votey Organ Company, Vocalian Organ Company, and the Universal Music Company. Weber pianos attained very high status and in 1904 the company received royal warrant of appointment as piano-manufacturers to the Court of Spain from Alfonso XIII. *See under* **Aeolian**.

Wegener, J, Leipzig, Germany. Built mechanical virginal in 1619 which played three tunes on a barrel and had moving figures. The instrument is now preserved in the Paris Conservatoire.

Weigel, C H, Reichstrasse 30-31, Leipzig 10, Germany. Makers of mechanical musical instruments, who were also agents for Symphonion and Adler disc musical boxes, piano orchestrions and electric orchestrion pianos.

Weisser, Ambrosius, Unterkirnach, Baden, Germany. Formerly the firm of Hubert Blessing established in 1849, this firm made orchestrion organs and also, at the beginning of this century, piano orchestrions, among them being the Germania.

Welte Artistic Player Piano Company, 18 East 17th Street, New York City, USA. When the Welte reproducing piano began to be marketed in the United States around 1907, this was the name of the company established for the purpose. Advertisements read: 'The Welte Artistic Player-piano - in Europe the Mignon. Gives the Absolutely True Reproduction of the Individual Play *[sic]* of the World's Most Famous Pianists'. Later at 273 Fifth Avenue, New York. Established by:

Welte, Edwin. Born in 1876, the grandson of Michael Welte who in 1832 founded the famed firm of orchestrion builders at Freiburg in the Black Forest, Germany. His father was **Emil Welte** who founded the American arm of the company in 1865. Edwin and his brother-in-law, **Karl Bockisch,** perfected the Mignon reproducing piano which first appeared in 1904 and was marketed the following year.

Welte, Emil. Eldest son of Michael Welte, Snr, he took out the first patents for 'the use of paper music rolls in connection with a pneumatic action' in 1887. This was to replace the expensive and cumbersome organ barrel with its accompanying paraphernalia and limited repertoire. His work opened up the way to the player piano. Left Germany for America in 1865 and opened a shop on East 14th Street, New York City, opposite Steinway Hall. This was known as M Welte & Sons Inc. Later a studio was opened at 557 Fifth Avenue. This showroom remained open until the start of the First World War, when it was compulsorily sold by the Alien Properties Custodian.

Welte-Mignon Corporation, 297-307 East 133rd Street, New York City, USA. Founded as M Welte & Sons at 49 W 30th Street, New York, to handle organs and orchestrions made in Freiburg, Baden, Germany, it also handled the Welte Mignon reproducing piano. During the First World War, this was taken over under the American Alien Properties Act and sold off. It was subsequently reformed as The Welte Artistic Player Piano Company at 398 Fifth Avenue, New York City. This company, established in the 1920s, copyrighted in 1924 the title 'reperforming piano' as a description for the 'Welte-Built Welte-Mignon'. This played the original wide red-paper rolls. Meanwhile another and separate derivative, the **Auto Pneumatic Action Company** *[qv]*, had designed a modified Welte-system reproducing piano action called the Welte-Mignon (Licensee). Both were early victims of the Wall Street Crash, Welte-Mignon Corporation going into receivership early in 1929 having spent several months trying to seek a re-finance package. The Auto Pneumatic Action Company, or Welte-Mignon (Licensee) had become part of the **Kohler & Campbell** player-piano-making group (founded in 1894) whereupon it was closed down during the summer of 1930. Aeolian, already in a depressed market, saw a possible benefit in offering two reproducing pianos, in particular as the Licensee had a small but steady and specialized following. The company accordingly completed some Welte instruments and continued roll-making for a short while until in May 1932 the roll-producing side was sold to Q-R-S and the Welte pianos and their reproducing system abandoned.

Welte & Söhne, M, Lehener Str. 9, Freiburg-im-Breisgau, Germany. Founded by Michael Welte (1807-80) at Vöhrenbach and established in Freiburg in 1833, the business became world-famous for its orchestrion organs and later for the invention of the Welte-Mignon reproducing piano which was largely the work of **Karl Bockisch** *[qv]*. The perforated-paper-roll pneumatic system was then applied to Welte's orchestrion organs and the Welte Philharmonic Autograph Organ – a full reproducing-action pipe organ. The firm of Welte produced a wide assortment of mechanical musical instruments incorporating pneumatic action and paper music rolls, including a 'motion picture and cabaret midget orchestra', Brass Band Orchestrion and Concert Orchestrion. Later, offices were opened at 273 Fifth Avenue, New York, USA. Subsequently reformed as the **Welte-Mignon Corporation** *[qv]*. *See also under* **Freiburger Musikapparate-Bauanstalt, GmbH,** and brand-name **Evola.**

Weydig Piano Corporation, 133rd Street and Brown Place, New York City, USA. In the latter days of the player-piano era in the United States, this company, established in 1880, produced an upright player called the Radi-O-Player which was a combined player piano and radio. The venture was a failure and the company dissolved in 1926.

Wiedemann, Hugo, van Woustraat 114, Amsterdam, Holland. Founded in 1900 for the distribution of electric pianos and piano orchestrions. Agent for Frati & Company. Branches in Antwerp, Amsterdam and Ghent.

Wilcox & White Company, Meriden, Connecticut, USA. Founded in 1876 by Horace C Wilcox, a silver-plate manufacturer, and Henry Kirk White, an organ builder from Brattleboro, Vermont. Wilcox provided the financial backing. White had been building organs for forty-eight years and his three sons joined him in making instruments (James, Edward and Howard). The company's first automatic instrument was the Symphony roll-playing organ, introduced about 1888. In 1891, one of the company employees, William D Parker *[qv]*, took out a patent on a roll-operated player piano but there are some doubts as to whether it was ever produced. Six years later, Edward H White and Parker invented the Angelus piano player, produced from 1898 until at least 1906. Several versions were made, including one with a reed organ built in: this was called the Angelus Orchestral and played from 58-note Angelus rolls and later 65-note ones. The Angelus was different from all other players in that it operated by means of flat action motors or 'diaphragm pouches'. These were pressure-operated. James White's son Frank C (born 1870) invented the Angelus Artrio reproducing piano in 1915. The company produced music rolls under the name Voltem, having for some years contracted to the Mel-O-Dee roll factory of Aeolian which was situated across the street from the Wilcox & White factory. Its extensive promotion for the Angelus advertised that 'the Artistyle, the Melodant, and the Phrasing Lever, known to musicians as 'The Three Wonders of the Angelus', are exclusive features of the Knabe-Angelus, Emerson-Angelus and Angelus Piano'. At this time, Wilcox & White had a London address at Regent House, Regent Street – the home of its long-term agent, Sir Herbert Marshall Piano Company. By this time a separate piano-manufactory had been established in New York as the Angelus Piano Company. But Wilcox & White's days were numbered and the company went bankrupt in 1921. What remained was taken over by the F G Smith Piano Company, with the plant and machinery going to the Conway Company, owners of the Hallet & Davis Piano Company. Simplex redesigned the Angelus action, which was then marketed under the name Super Simplex. (Information largely researched by Alan R Pier.) Manufactured the Artistyle 65-note piano roll. Subsequently changed over to 88-note rolls under the name Artistyle also Regent, the brand name used for dance and ballad-song rolls with words. Handled in Britain by The Marshall Piano Company Ltd. of Orchard Street, Oxford Street in the 1930s and, after the Second World War, at Troy Court, 216 High Street, London, W8. Henry Kirk White died on January 13th 1907.

Wildbredt, Ernst, Grosse Frankfurterstrasse 44, Berlin N, Germany. Manufacturers of electrically operated pneumatic-action pianos and piano orchestrions as well as ordinary player pianos. Made instruments with flute and percussion effects. Patented automatic roll rewinding, *fl.*1910.

Wintle, Algernon O, *(Canon),* The Old Rectory, Lawshall, Nr Bury St Edmunds, Suffolk, England. During the agricultural depression following the First World War, Canon Wintle provided employment for many ex-servicemen in the repair and renovation of barrel pianos. No new pianos were actually made, it is thought, but many very old ones were restored, tuned and provided with newly repinned barrels. Working in a workshop in the grounds of Lawshall Church, Wintle made a speciality of converting former clockwork public-house pianos into hand-operated street instruments which were then sold or hired out to charitable organisations. The name of the original maker of the piano was almost always obliterated and the name of Wintle's company marked in place. The barrels were all stamped before pinning with an oval, blue rubber stamp. Canon Wintle, who confessed that he 'couldn't read a note of music', made many new programmes for barrels, his own confessed masterpiece being the setting of Mozart's *Eine Kleine Nachtmusik* on a barrel. He was largely self-taught and acquired a healthy mastery of his craft. His trade mark in musical arrangement was what he fondly termed his 'bang in the bass' which was an accompaniment feature when, to emphasise the music, he would arrange to have some six or eight adjacent hammers all strike their strings at one and the same time to produce a bang. Wintle died in 1959 and the business closed. Most of his remaining stock was sold and much of his paperwork and records were destroyed by his family, who had shared neither his ideals nor interests. Some 130-odd pianos and many crates of spares were examined by the author in 1973 prior to their sale to the then West Cornwall Museum of Mechanical Music.Among the copious spares was ample evidence that Wintle had been planning to produce a number of new, small street pianos of about 30 keys. A quantity of cast aluminium key frames and their casting pattern were found along with some small barrels. Plans to complete the restoration of many of these instruments were set back when most of the very early pianos along with many of the case parts were destroyed by an arson attack on a warehouse in Penzance.

Wright Piano Company, Queen Street, Camden Town, London NW. In 1906 introduced a piano player and a player piano under the name Regal. No further details.

Wright & Holmes Brothers, Forest Street, Rochdale Road, Manchester. Describing themselves as 'mechanical organ builders and repairers', this firm flourished between the two wars and a fairground barrel organ has been seen with a repinned barrel bearing the date 1929, written before the barrel paper was pinned. They probably serviced street barrel pianos as well.

Wurlitzer Manufacturing Company, The Rudolph, North Tonawanda, New York, USA. The Wurlitzer family – one might describe it as a dynasty – began with the Markneukirchen violin maker Hans Adam Wurlitzer (1732-1795). His son, Franz Rudolph of Schoneck, followed in his father's footsteps and made musical instruments, particularly brass. He emigrated to America in 1853 at the age of twenty-two and opened a factory in Cincinatti in 1861 to manufacture military band instruments. He then undertook selling coin-freed Regina disc-playing musical boxes. Around this time he was joined in business by his three sons, Howard E (born 1871), Rudolph H (born 1873) and Farny R (born 1883). They began by making military band organs in 1907-9. Moving to North Tonawanda, the first factory opened in 1908, doubled in size the following year and again in 1911, expanding yet further until it covered some 60 acres of ground. Produced many player pianos including a number of expression pianos and also grands fitted with the Apollo reproducing action. Wurlitzer commissioned the first coin-freed electric player piano - a 10-tune barrel instrument - from deKleist, which firm he subsequently bought up in 1908 (*see* **North Tonawanda Musical In-**

strument Works). He made extensive use of electric, electro-magnetic and pneumatic action, paper-roll-actuated, for a wide variety of mechanical instruments. These extended from the popular 44-note Peerless electric piano, a range of piano-orchestrions and dance organs. Warehouses were maintained in Cincinatti, Chicago and New York as well as a large factory at North Tonawanda, New York, where the business still exists.

Xuciá, Pablo, 26 calle Laforja, Barcelona, Spain. Maker of street pianos and portable street organs, *fl.*1930.

Yamaha. Japanese piano-maker that, in the 1970s began experiment-ing with electronically-controlled pianos operated by computer software. The outcome was the Disklavier player-piano which played musical programmes using 3.5-inch floppy discs and Yamaha's digital technology. Produced a synthetic piano called the Clavinova.

Yote Manufacturing Company, The, Four Oaks, Sutton Coldfield, Warwickshire, England. A business set up by W J Riley who be-gan making player-piano tracker-bars in 1906. The business ex-panded to embrace improved spoolbox running gear (designed by Riley to British Patent 23,079 of 1909), a method of transpos-ing involving music-roll shifting (subject of another Patent), and other parts all devised and many patented by him. Yote compo-nents such as pedal sets, spools, unions and elbows, adjustable wires and valve seats were supplied to many British player-pi-ano-makers. Yote also advertised that it would make compo-nents to special designs as required. The Yote business, a sig-nificant force in the development of the early player, cannot be traced after the 1930-31 economic recession, the probability be-ing that it closed during this time. The name occasionally ap-pears on components found in actions. A rare provincial busi-ness for its time.

Zanoni, Giacinto, Canneto Sull'oglio, Mantua, Italy. A church-or-gan builder who also made barrel pianos, *fl.*1930.

Zari, Fratelli, 13 via Carducci, Milan, Italy. Maker of player pianos, *fl.*1930.

Zimmermann, Gebrüder. The piano-making business of Zimmermann, properly entitled the **Leipziger Pianofortefabrik Gebrüder Zimmermann A-G**, was founded at Stötteritzer Weg, Molkau-Leipzig in 1885. Founder Max Zimmermann learned his trade at the factory of Steinway in New York and in 1884 with his brother Richard first set up to make pianos. The following year the business became a limited liability company. In 1926, Zimmermann's business absorbed that of **Ludwig Hupfeld** *[qv]* and remains in existence today as **Hupfeld-Zimmermann**. Max Zimmermann died in Dresden on 31 May 1937.

Zimmermann, Jules Heinrich, Leipzig, Germany. Manufacturer of the Fortuna disc-playing musical boxes, small portable barrel or-gans and street pianos. Exhibited an electric piano at the Crystal Palace in 1900.

Zordan, Ditta, Cogollo del Cengio, Vicenza, Italy. Maker of church organs who also made barrel pianos, *fl.*1930.

Zyob, A. Said by Chapuis *[17]* to have built a book-playing piano in 1842. No further details or references have been traced.

Appendix 3
List of Automatic Piano Brand Names

The name on an instrument can be a good clue to the identification of its maker. It is not foolproof, neither is it infallible and you need to know that a large number of manufacturers of instruments, particularly those in Germany, sold their products via an agent or distributor. These agents generally fitted their own nameplates to the machines that they factored. Some large distributors actually commissioned instruments to be produced under their own name, so clouding the issue further. Generally speaking, though, it is usually possible to find out the original maker either by tracing the serial number or by attributing the brand name.

The nefarious matter of 'stencil-makes', rife in the industry that produced ordinary pianos at the turn of the century, also affected, to a lesser degree, player pianos, especially those made for the larger retailing companies. British department stores and piano specialists such as Harrods, Dale Forty, Selfridges, Army & Navy Stores and Gamages all contracted for pianos to be supplied by various makers with their names on the fallboard. It has to be said that this type of business was in general undertaken by the producers of cheaper player pianos as distinct from the major names such as Broadwood and Steinway. But, as in Germany and America, people did not shun from getting as close to an established and respected name as they could.

Called 'passing off', names that have been seen include 'Broadmead' (clearly cashing in on Brinsmead and Broadwood), 'Steinwech' and 'Steinbach' (for Steinway), while the number of player with names ending in 'ola' was rife. The name used by Aeolian was seen almost as a generic term for the player even at the time of manufacture, so other makers tried desperately to get as close to 'pianola' as they could. But the company that managed to get closest was Pianora in America. Today they would probably not have been able to get away with that, but laws of 'passing off' were still to be clarified and proven a century ago.

In this Appendix, I have listed those brand names that I can identify for stringed instruments of the piano type. Because this book also deals with roll-playing player organs, I have included these as well for your convenience. In the space available, only the briefest details are to be found here – sufficient to meet the needs of this Appendix. For more details of the specific manufacturer, you should first consult Appendix 2 which gives some details of the makers shown here. Those seeking yet more information should refer to the works shown in the Bibliography.

A word on dates. The actual dates of a manufacturer, where known, are found in Appendix Two. In this listing any dates shown relate to the proven use of that name. Where a date is provided, the *floruit (fl.)* date shown means that the name was in use around such-and-such a year. Where the date is uncertain, the word *circa [c.]* is given before the year.

This list cannot attempt to be comprehensive but it is a reliable conspectus of perhaps ninety percent of the brand names and is the result of my observations over half a century. Neither of us should be surprised if more names turn up! I have, for instance, listed only a few of the more popular player

pianos. Nevertheless, it should be a reasonable guide. I have also, in the main, avoided eponymous names in the belief that the maker must automatically be known.

Ackotist. Player piano mechanism fitted in Pianora player pianos by the Pianora Company, 133 West 24th Street, New York, USA, *fl.*1909.

Accentiola-Adalbert. Player piano introduced in 1914 by Adalbert Piano Company. The outbreak of the First World War seems to have put an immediate stop on this. No examples seen. *See* **Adalbert Piano Co** in Appendix 2.

Accompano. Electric player upright introduced by the Emerson Piano Company of Boston, Massachusetts.

Aeola. Early electric cabinet-style piano-player, maker uncertain, *c.*1908.

Aeolian. Piano players and player pianos made by the Aeolian Corporation, New York, London, &c. Name also used by the company for player reed organs, residence pipe organs and music-rolls. In London and *c.*1898, can be associated with the name of Geo Whight who handled Aeolian products in the early days.

Aeolion Musik Automat. Not a piano of any kind, but a 'flute orchestrion' made by Hupfeld in Leipzig producing. Claimed to have a 'deep sonorous organ like tone *[sic]* produced by 100 organ pipes playing music using perforated paper music.

Aeriol. The first self-playing piano introduced by Aeolian in 1895 and quickly replaced by the Pianola. The Aeriol name was also used for piano rolls for a short while, replaced by rolls marked Aeolian Piano.

Aida. A barrel-operated mechanical piano driven by a descending weight. Manufactured by Hugo Popper, Leipzig, early 20th century. Popper made many mechanical pianos and piano-orchestrions, some with and others without keyboards for manual playing.

Airmatic. Piano-player apparatus offered in London by the Simplex Piano-Player Company of 244 Tottenham Court Road, London, and advertised in 1908.

Air-O-Player. 'The most up-to-date player in the world'…'the first perfected metal action'. Made in 1913 by National Piano Company of Boston, Massachusetts.

Allan Reproducing. Australian agent's label seen on Welte De Luxe Electric rolls.

Allisonola. Player pianos made in London by Allison Pianos.

American Player Piano. Player piano made by company of same name.

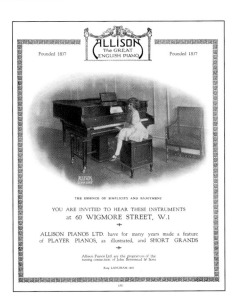

Founded 1837   ALLISON The GREAT ENGLISH PIANO   Founded 1837

THE ESSENCE OF SIMPLICITY AND ENJOYMENT

YOU ARE INVITED TO HEAR THESE INSTRUMENTS
at 60 WIGMORE STREET, W.1

ALLISON PIANOS LTD. have for many years made a feature
of PLAYER PIANOS, as illustrated, and SHORT GRANDS

Allison Pianos Ltd. are the proprietors of the
tuning connection of John Brinsmead & Sons

Reg. LANGHAM 1415

Amphion. Player piano made in Elbridge, USA, by the Amphion Piano Player Company.

Ampico. Famed reproducing piano action made by the American Piano Corporation of New York and used in a number of instruments.

Angelus. Piano-players and player-pianos made by Wilcox & White Company, Meriden, USA and handled in Britain by Sir Herbert Marshall, London. *Also:* Reproducing piano made by Hallett & Davis Piano Company, New York.

Animochord. Barrel-operated piano-orchestrion. Described in advertisement as 'the first real string orchestrion' with violin, viola and cello (these being imitated by organ-pipes) with the accompaniment of a Feurich piano. Made in Leipzig by Popper c.1907.

Annalies. Electric piano-orchestrion made in Altona by Lüneberg & Company.

Antiphonel. A fully-mechanical key-top player made by Alexander Debain of Paris for pianos, harmoniums and organs; *fl.*1862 and operated by wooden planchettes. Later produced as a complete piano with finger action and separate mechanical action, and as a mechanical-only keyboardless instrument. *See also* **Piano Mécanique.**

Apollo, Apollo-Grand, Apoloette, Apollo-Phone. Names of player pianos made in the USA by Melville Clark Piano Company. One monstrosity was the Melville Clark Apollo-Phone introduced in

1924. This was an upright player-piano with a phonograph or gramophone record-player built into the upper left side of the case next to the spool box. In addition to operating in two different media (a gramophone and a piano-player), it was also possible to operate the two in some semblance of synchrony: Q-R-S produced a limited number of special rolls that were labeled 'To accompany Victor Recording No.— as sung by Enrico Caruso' or similar artist. These instruments and their piano-rolls are today extremely rare. *Also:* Piano-player and player-piano made by The Apollo Company, London. *Also:* Piano-orchestrion made by the Apollo Musikwerke Max Espenhain & Company of Leipzig, *fl.*1903.

Apollonion. A concert organ made by an instrument-maker named Roeller of Hesse-Darmstadt which had 'two rows of keys which might be played as a pianoforte and as a chamber organ, combined at the same time with a musical automaton'. Early nineteenth century. Nothing further known.

Arcadian. Electrically-operated roll-playing piano orchestrion made by Peerless of Chicago around 1925. *Also:* Player action and player piano made in London by British Player Action Company.

Arcophon. Barrel-operated piano-orchestrion. Described in advertisement as 'the first 'string piano' with hand-playing'. Made in Leipzig by Popper c.1907.

Aristos. Player piano made in England by Bansall & Sons, London.

Arrow. Stems player piano made in London by Direct Pneumatic Action Company.

Artecho (Art-Echo). Reproducing piano action made by Amphion Company as American Piano Company. Associated with and similar to the Celco.

Artigraphic. An 88-note foot-operated player piano made by American Piano Company for the purpose of playing Ampico reproducing rolls without expression. The tracker bar, which has its extreme end holes suitably blanked off, transposes the roll into five keys. The niche for this player appears both curious and singularly pointless.

Artist. Player piano made by Bell Piano & Organ Company of Guelph, Ontario, and London. *Also:* Piano player made in Berlin by Wilhelm Hedke.

Artistano. Player piano made in New York by Chase Company.

Artola. Player piano action made by Artola Player Co, Illinois.

Artonian. Player piano made by E P Johnson, Elgin, Illinois.

Artrio. Reproducing action by Broadwood & Son, London.

Atlantic. Barrel-operated piano-orchestrions made in Leipzig by Hupfeld.

Auroro. Barrel-operated piano-orchestrion. Made in Leipzig by Popper c.1913.

Austria. Piano orchestrion made in Leipzig by Popper.

Auteola. Piano-player/player-piano by Musicus Ltd and advertised in 1920.

Auto Electric Piano Player. Instrument made in Kansas City by Berry-Wood.

Auto-Grand. Upright player piano made by Krell Piano Company of Cincinnati.

Auto-Manual. Player piano made by the Bacon Piano Company of New York, *fl.*1909.

Auto-Namic. Device introduced by Clark Pneumatic Action Company, Milwaukee, that claimed could convert any player piano into a reproducing piano at a very small cost.

Auto-Orchestra. Pneumatic piano orchestrion, coin-operated and electrically driven, made by Berry-Wood Piano Player Company of Kansas, c.1910.

Auto-Organ. London-made player reed organ made in 1900 by Auto-Organ Company London agents: Wallis Ltd. Nothing further known of this clearly short-lived enterprise.

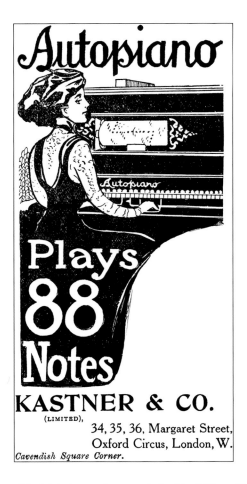

Auto-Player. Upright player piano made by Krell Piano Company of Cincinnati.

Autoforde. Player piano made in New York by Hardman, Peck & Company.

Autogrand. Player piano made by Kastner in London.

Autoharmonicon. Self-acting pianoforte shown at the Great Room, Spring Garden, London, early nineteenth century. It has been suggested that this may be an instrument by Merlin but there is no evidence.

Autolectra. Electrically-operated player piano made in New York by the Auto-Electric Piano Company, fl.1909.

Autoleon. Low-cost player piano made by Triumph Auto Piano and sold for £84.

Autolian. London-made player piano sold by Munt Brothers Limited, of Clapham Junction and advertised in 1908.

Autolyon. Player piano made c.1910 by L G Lyon, 116 Camberwell Road, London, SE. Did not make player action but believed to have fitted either Simplex or Higel. During 1911 and 1912, C E Lyon and A D Towner were granted two British Patents for a player mechanism. Towner subsequently was designer and co-patentee with Petters Ltd (Westland Aircraft Works) in their short-lived player-piano manufacturing venture in 1919-1920.

Automat. Piano player made by Ehrlich in Leipzig.

Automatic Regina Concerto. Large disc-playing piano-orchestrion made in New Jersey by Regina Music Box Company.

Auto-Namic. Player piano action made by Clark Pneumatic Action Company of Milwaukee.

Autopiano. Player piano made in New York by the Autopiano Company and in London by Kastner.

Autopianiste. Mechanical pianos made by Thièble at Ruyaulcourt, France, and distributed by Stransky Frères, fl.1909.

Autoplayer. Player-piano made in London by Boyd Ltd.

Autotone. Player piano made by Hardman, Peck & Co of New York, fl.1909. *Also* upright player piano by Chappell's of 50 New Bond Street, London, W, fl.1911.

Autotype. Player piano made by Bush & Lane using the Unitype action comprising a single deck of pneumatics, each only ½-inch in width

Badenia. Orchestrions made in Vöhrenbach by Imhof & Mukle, fl.1909.

Banjorchestra. Electric, coin-freed orchestrion made in New York by Engelhardt Piano Company.

Beethophen. Reproducing piano made in Unterkirnach by Wolfgang Blessing.

Bellisore. Piano-orchestrions made in Altona-Ottensen (Hamburg) by Lüneburg & Company.

Bellolian. Player attachment for reed organs made in 1901 by Bell Organ & Piano Company, London (subsidiary of US company).

Bianca. Barrel-operated piano-orchestrion made in Leipzig by Popper, fl.1909.

Bohemian Harmonicon. Orchestrion made in Bohemia and sold by Harris, Heeley & Company of High Holborn (London) and Birmingham, mid-nineteenth century.

Boyd. Piano player cabinet-style made in London by Boyd Pianos.

Brabo. Large piano orchestrion featuring violin-toned organ pipes, xylophone and mandoline, the whole operated by perforated paper roll. Also fitted with a normal keyboard for manual playing. Made in Waldkirch by Weber after the First World War.

Braumuller. Player pianos made c.1909 by the Braumuller Piano Company of New York.

Bravissimo. Orchestrions made by Popper in Leipzig, fl.1909.

Brisgovia. Piano orchestrion made by Welte of Freiburg, fl.1909.

Brunophone, Le. Coin-freed electric piano by Brun in France.

Cabaret. Electrically-operated roll-playing piano orchestrion made by Peerless around 1925.

Caecilia. Piano orchestrion made by Frankfurter Musikwerke-Fabrik J D Philipps & Söhne,

Calame. Player piano made by Robert V Calame of Salto Oriental, Uruguay, fl.1909.

Capella. Orchestrions made in Leipzig by Dienst, c.1909.

Capitol Jazz Concert Orchestra. *Same as* **Mando-Orchestra** *[qv]*.

Capitol Symphony Orchestra. Coin-freed piano-orchestrion made by the North Tonawanda Musical Instrument Works, New York.

Carleton Electric Player. Electric player piano made by Price & Teeple in Chicago.

Carmen. Mandolin orchestrions made in Leipzig by Popper, c.1909.

Carmina. Piano orchestrion made by Popper, Leipzig.

Carola, Solo-Carola. Player pianos and reproducing pianos made by Blüthner & Sons.

Cartonium. Mechanical free-reed instrument patented 1861 by Joseph Antoine Testé of Nantes, France and played by perforated cardboard.

Cecilian. Player pianos made in USA by the Farrand Organ Company of Detroit.

Celco. Reproducing player pianos by United Piano Company which combined the interests of the Lindeman Piano, A B Chase of Norwalk and Emerson whose initials made up C(hase), E(merson), L(indeman); Co(mpany). Also associated with and similar to the **Art-Echo** of American Piano Company. _Also:_ Reproducing piano action made by Amphion Company.

Celestino. Automatic zither made in Altona, (Hamburg) by Luneburg, _fl._ 1909.

Chitarrone. Electric expression piano made in Altona by Lüneberg & Company.

Chopin. Orchestrions made in Freiburg by Welte & Sohne, _fl._ 1909.

Choralion. Pneumatic player piano made in Berlin by Goetze.

Chordaulodion. Orchestrion built by Kaufmann in Dresden, 1815.

Chordephon. Mechanical zither played by disc made in Leipzig by Fabrik Mechanische Zithern 'Chordephon', _fl._ 1909. About 1910, this company was acquired by Weissbach, makers of the Komet disc-operated comb-playing musical box.

Circe. Orchestrion made in Leipzig by Popper, _fl._ 1909.

Citoplex. Automatic roll-changing mechanism invented by Hupfeld to allow selection or continuous playing from Hupfeld electric player pianos. Six or eight rolls mounted in 'carousel' frame: as one roll is played, the next is prepared and is put into play while the previous one is re-rolled.

Clarabella. Piano orchestrion made by Popper, Leipzig.

Clarendon. Player pianos made by Haddorff Piano Company of Rockford, Illinois.

Classic. A short-lived pneumatic player action made in London by T H Poyser very soon after the end of the 1914-18 war and still being promoted in 1920. Advertised as a 65 or 88-note player, it fitted inside the top door of an ordinary piano case. Only two have been seen and the action is very basic.

Clavimonium. Combined piano and reed organ made for early silent cinema use by Hupfeld, Leipzig. Played using perforated rolls.

Clavinova. Modern Japanese-made electronic piano-player made by Yamaha. _See also_ **Disklavier.**

Claviola. New York-made player pianos by the Claviola Company (medal awarded 1901 Pan-American Exposition) and sold in London under Klinker & Co, _c._ 1909. This appears to have been an offshoot of Ludwig & Company. _Also:_ Player piano by F Stichel of Sophienstr 43, Leipzig and Zwenkau.

Clementi. A name used for automatic musical instruments made in Hamburg by Gotz & Company, _c._ 1909.

Coinola. Coin-freed electric pianos made by the Operators' Piano Company, Chicago.

Colonia. Player piano by Colonia Player Piano Company of London, 1909.

Columbia. Player piano distributed in London _c._ 1909 by Malcolm & Company of Erskine Road, Regent's Park.

Commandant. Piano orchestra made by Imhof & Mukle, Vöhrenbach.

Con Amore. A roll-operated piano-orchestrion driven by a descending weight. Manufactured by Hugo Popper, Leipzig, early 20th C.

Concertal Mustel. Range of large reed organs costing from 240 to 400 guineas ($1005.00–$1680.00). Made by Mustel of Paris and capable of manual or paper-roll playing.

Concerto. Large disc-playing piano-orchestrion made by Polyphon Musikwerke in Leipzig.

Connoisseur. Player pianos, player reed organs and player pipe organs made in USA and distributed in UK by Murdoch, Murdoch & Company, London.

Continental. Piano-orchestrions made by Hofmann & Czerny of Vienna and sold by Peters of Leipzig, _fl._ 1909.

Corona. An expression piano (semi-reproducing) made by Frankfurter Musikwerke-Fabrik, _fl._ 1909. Also mechanical musical instruments made by Sachs Musikinstrumente-Manufactur Schuster & Company of Markneukirchen, _fl._ 1909.

Corrector. Piano orchestrion made by Imhof & Mukle, Vöhrenbach.

Cottage Orchestrion. Welte & Söhne of Freiburg, _fl._ 1909.

Cremona. Early American electric pianos, piano-orchestrions and photoplayers made in Chicago by Marquette Piano Company.

Cylindrichord. A mechanically-operated stringed instrument made before 1852 by the organ builder John Courcell of London.

Cymbalophon. Automatic musical instrument made in Leipzig by Wilhelm Dietrich, _fl._ 1909.

Daimonion. Clockwork piano made _c._ 1903 by Fabrik Leipziger Musikwerke (Ehrlich).

Danc-O-Grand. Keyboardless electric pianos by Nelson-Wiggen of Chicago.

Danubia. Orchestrion made by Popper of Leipzig, _fl._ 1909.

Dea. Pneumatic roll-playing player piano, also early reproducing piano, made in Leipzig by Hupfeld.

Dea-Violina. Piano-violins player made in Leipzig by Hupfeld.

Delila. Piano orchestrion made by Popper, Leipzig.

Delphin. Piano-orchestrion made in Trautenau, Austria, by Albert Melnik, _fl._ 1909; _also_ player-piano made in Tilbourg, The Netherlands, by makers M J H Kessels, holders of the Dutch Royal Warrant.

Desdemona. Barrel-operated piano-orchestrion together with full percussion effects made by the Sächsischen Orchestrionfabrik F O Glass of Klingenthal. Described as producing 'very loud mu sic', several styles of case, at least one with an illuminated painted scene in the façade. Produced around 1910.

Diadem. Orchestrions made in Leipzig by Popper, *fl.*1909.

Diaphon. Self-playing reed organ, probably by Kimball of USA, sold by Felvus Henn in Glasgow, *fl.*1899.

Dinorah. Orchestrion made in Vöhrenbach by Imhof & Mukle, *fl.*1909.

Disklavier. Modern 'solid-state' electronic piano-player made in Japan by Yamaha. *See also* **Clavinova**.

Donar. Military band orchestrion made by Welte, Freiburg.

Duca. Expression player piano made in Frankfurt by Frankfurter Musikwerke J D Philipps & Söhne, *fl.*1909.

Ducanola. Player piano/reproducing piano, J D Philipps & Söhne. Dutch agent was D Goldschmeding, Keizersgracht 305, Amsterdam.

Duo-Art. Reproducing piano system made by The Aeolian Company, New York.

Duola. Pneumatic player-piano action made by John Broadwood in London.

Duophonola. Pedal-electric reproducing piano made by Hupfeld in Leipzig.

Duplex. Musical automata produced *c.*1902 by Metall-Industrie Schönebeck A-G, Schönebeck, Saxony, Germany. *Also:* Player piano made by Chase Company, New York. *Also:* Player piano made in London by H Rayner of 46 Rathbone Place, *c.*1912.

Dynavoice. Electrically-operated key-top player made in Plymouth, Michigan, for a short while. Gone by 1968.

Eldorado. Barrel piano-orchestrions made in Leipzig by Sachsische Orchestrion-Fabrik F O Glass and distributed by Etzold & Popitz, *fl.*1909.

Electra. Electric player piano made in New Jersey by Electric Self-Playing Piano Company.

Electrelle, *also* **Flextone Electrelle.** Electric player piano made by American Piano Company. In 1909, UK manufacture of the player action began in Manchester by Electrelle Company. *Also:* Player piano made in London by J & J Hopkinson.

Electrolin. A 44-note electric piano made in US, similar to Pianolin, maker unknown.

Electrova. Electrically-operated, coin-freed pianos made by Jacob Doll & Sons of New York, *fl.*1905-20.

Eldorado. Barrel piano orchestrion by Etzold & Popitz of Leipzig. *Also:* Barrel-operated piano-orchestrion by the Sächsischen Orchestrionfabrik F O Glass of Klingenthal.

Elite. Orchestrion made by Gebruder Weber, Waldkirch.

Empire. Orchestrion made by Dienst of Leipzig, *fl.*1909. *Also:* Player piano made in London by Triumph-Auto Pianos.

Empress Electric Piano. Electric pianos made by the Operators' Piano Company, Chicago, for Lyon & Healy's store.

Erato. Orchestrions made by Gebrüder Weber of Waldkirch, *fl.*1909.

Erika. Keyless piano playing endless music rolls made *C.*1927 by Weber of Berlin.

Eroica. Orchestrions made in Leipzig by Popper, *fl.*1909.

Euphonia Home Electric. Player piano by The Cable Company, Chicago.

Euterpe. Piano orchestrion with drum, cymbals and castagnettes and the addition of a pipe organ and harp. Played from perforated music roll. Made by Weber of Waldkirch. *Also:* Cabinet piano-player produced by Pianoforte-Fabrik 'Euterpe' Albert Gast & Company of Berlin at the turn of the century.

Excelsior. Piano-orchestrion made in Zittau, Germany, by A E Haupt, *fl.*1903.

Excelsior Orchestrion. Barrel piano made by Peters, Leipzig. Hand-cranked.

Expressionola. Expression piano designed by R S Howard and built by the Howard-Stowers Company Inc, New York, and introduced towards the end of 1928.

Faventia. Modern street pianos by Vincente Llinares, Barcelona, Spain.

Favourite. Piano-orchestrion by Popper, Leipzig, hand-cranked, *fl.*1909.

Felix. Orchestrion by Popper, Leipzig, *fl.*1909.

Flexstone Electrelle. *See* American Piano Company.

Flexotone-Electrelle. *See* **Electrelle**.

Fotoplayer. Early cinema music player made in 1920S by American Photo Player Company of New York.

Fratihymnia. Piano-orchestrion made in Berlin by Frati. In 1923, company was bought by J D Philipps & Söhne but continued business under Frati name.

Fratinola. Electric pianos made in Berlin by Frati, *fl.*1902.

Frederick. Player piano made by Frederick Piano Company of New York, *fl.*1909.

Friburgia. Piano-orchestrion made in Freiburg by Welte & Sohne, *fl.*1909.

Gasonella. Automatic piano made by Fuchs of Prague, *fl.*1909.

Gehrling. The Gehrling Piano-Player and the Gehrling Interior-Player were made in Paris by Gehrling & Cie and distributed in England by Erhardt & Company Ltd, 36 Southwark Bridge Road, London SE.

Geigenpiano. Player piano & violin combination made in Germany by Hegeler & Ehrlers.

Gérard. Name of French distributor for player pianos and Popper piano-orchestrions. Label invariably obscures original maker's name.

Germania. Piano-orchestrion made by Weisser of Unterkirnach, *fl.*1909.

Gladiator. A roll-operated piano-orchestrion driven by an electric motor. Manufactured by Hugo Popper, Leipzig, around 1920.

Gladiator, Le. Book-playing mandolin sostenuto piano similar to Piano Melodico *[qv]* made in Paris by Ch & J Ullman to Racca's patents.

Goliath. Piano-orchestrion made by Popper, Leipzig.

Grandezza. Piano orchestrion made by Weber, Waldkirch.

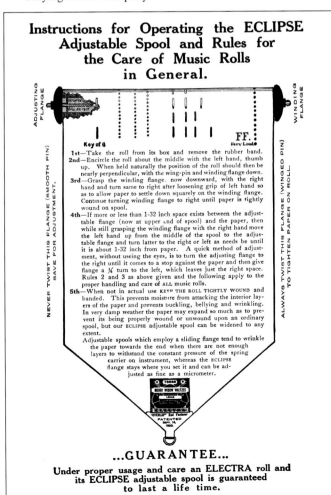

Instructions for Operating the ECLIPSE Adjustable Spool and Rules for the Care of Music Rolls in General.

ADJUSTING FLANGE

WINDING FLANGE

NEVER TWIST THIS FLANGE (SMOOTH PIN) SAVE FOR ADJUSTMENT.

ALWAYS TWIST THIS FLANGE (WINGED PIN) TO TIGHTEN PAPER ON ROLL.

Key of G

FF.
Very Loud

1st—Take the roll from its box and remove the rubber band.

2nd—Encircle the roll about the middle with the left hand, thumb up. When held naturally the position of the roll should then be nearly perpendicular, with the wing-pin and winding flange down.

3rd—Grasp the winding flange. now downward, with the right hand and turn same to right after loosening grip of left hand so as to allow paper to settle down squarely on the winding flange. Continue turning winding flange to right until paper is tightly wound on spool.

4th—If more or less than 1-32 inch space exists between the adjustable flange (now at upper end of spool) and the paper, then while still grasping the winding flange with the right hand move the left hand up from the middle of the spool to the adjustable flange and turn latter to the right or left as needs be until it is about 1-32 inch from paper. A quick method of adjustment, without useing the eyes, is to turn the adjusting flange to the right until it comes to a stop against the paper and then give flange a ¼ turn to the left, which leaves just the right space. Rules 2 and 3 as above given and the following apply to the proper handling and care of ALL music rolls.

5th—When not in actual use KEEP THE ROLL TIGHTLY WOUND and banded. This prevents moisture from attacking the interior layers of the paper and prevents buckling, bellying and wrinkling. In very damp weather the paper may expand so much as to prevent its being properly wound or unwound upon an ordinary spool, but our ECLIPSE adjustable spool can be widened to any extent.

Adjustable spools which employ a sliding flange tend to wrinkle the paper towards the end when there are not enough layers to withstand the constant pressure of the spring carrier on instrument, whereas the ECLIPSE flange stays where you set it and can be adjusted as fine as a micrometer.

MERRY WIDOW WALTZES

"OVERLAP" 2nd Featured
PATENTED
SEPT. 18, 1906.

...GUARANTEE...
Under proper usage and care an ELECTRA roll and its ECLIPSE adjustable spool is guaranteed to last a life time.

Graziella. Electric piano with xylophone and mandoline plus violin-toned organ pipes. Made by Weber of Waldkirch, *fl.* 1909

Gregorian. Player piano marketed in London by the Orchestrelle Company, *fl.* 1909.

Guitharmony. Mechanical guitar operated by pinned barrel made in Paris by Gavioli, *c.* 1900.

Harmonia. Piano orchestrion made by Frankfurter Musikwerke-Fabrik J D Philipps & Söhne,

Harmonist. Player piano made by Engelhardt Piano Company, New York

Harpeco. Expression piano made by Peters & Company of Leipzig, *fl.* 1909.

Harper. Electric player pianos made by Harper Electric-Piano Company Ltd, Holloway Road, London.

Harp-O-Grand. Keyboardless electric pianos by Nelson-Wiggen of Chicago.

Harald. Piano-orchestrion made by the Waldkircher Orchestionfabrik, *fl.* 1909.

Helios, Helios-Pepita. Orchestrions made by Hupfeld in Leipzig, *fl.* 1909.

Herold. Orchestrions made by Imhof & Mukle in Vöhrenbach, *fl.* 1909.

Higel. Pneumatic player pianos and actions made in Toronto by Higel Company. For the UK market, Higel teamed up with piano-makers Lipp & Sohn of Stuttgart and introduced the Higel-Lipp upright.

Hillier. London-made player piano made by Hillier Piano & Organ Company.

Hopkinson Player. Player piano made in London by J & J Hopkinson.

Humana. Player pianos advertised in 1908 by Marshall of 233, Regent Street, London.

Humanola. Push-up piano-player sold by Metzler & Company Ltd of 40-43 Marlborough Street, Regent Street, London W. Retailed at £25.00 [$100].

Humor. Orchestrions made by Popper of Leipzig, *fl.* 1909.

Ibachiola. Player piano produced by Rudolph Ibach. Said to have retailed at an astonishing £2,500 ($10,000).

Ideal. Early American cinema music player made by North Tonawanda Musical Instrument Works, New York. *Also:* Piano orchestrion made by Frankfurter Musikwerke-Fabrik J D Philipps & Söhne. *Also:* Player piano made in Berlin by Wilhelm Hedke.

Ideal-Mignon. The name of a small player action introduced in 1910 by Coppleston & Company Ltd of 94 Regent Street, London, and made to sell at 45-50 gns [$190 - $210]. Coppleston was also agent for the Detroit-made Sterling player piano (*fl.* 1908-1912) and the Mendel (*fl.* 1908). No connection with Welte (Welte-Mignon).

Iduna. Orchestrion by Popper of Leipzig, *fl.* 1909.

Imperial. 44-note electric piano made in US, similar to Pianolin, maker unknown.

Imperiola. Player piano made under the name of Obernmeier by Wilhelm Menzel at 34 Warschauer Str 58, Berlin, Germany, and distributed in England in the years immediately before the First World War by London agents S Warschauer of 52a Bow Lane, Cheapside. The coincidence of name/address is curious yet correct.

International. Barrel-operated piano orchestrion made in Vienna by Machineki & Söhne.

Irene. Orchestrion made in Vienna by Hofmann & Czerny, *fl.* 1909.

Iris. Piano orchestrion made by Frankfurter Musikwerke-Fabrik J D Philipps & Söhne,

Irmgard. Orchestrion made in Vienna by Hofmann & Czerny, *fl.* 1909.

Isola. Orchestrion made in Waldkirch by Gebrüder Weber, *fl.* 1909.

Italia. Barrel-operated piano-orchestrion. Made in Leipzig by Popper *c.* 1913.

Juno. Orchestrion made by Fuchs of Prague, *fl.* 1909.

Kasto. Player actions made by Kastner.

Kastonome. Expression piano made by Kastner.

Kimball. Pneumatically-operated foot-pedalled 88-note player piano made by W W Kimball of Chicago

Kino-Pan. Keyboardless electric piano for theatre use made in Leipzig by Hupfeld.

Kino-Violina. Similar to **Phonoliszt-Violina** but with the violins in a separate case for use in theatres.

Klara. Orchestrion made in Vienna by Hofmann & Czerny, *fl.* 1909.

Klavier-Automaten. Piano player made by Fabrik Leipziger Musikwerke and operated by a cardboard disc, *fl.* 1903.

Kleng-Duplex. Player piano advertised by piano-makers Bertram Ison of Brewery Street, Caledonian Road, London, *c.* 1912.

Konzertist, Welte-Mignon Konzertist. A roll-operated electric expression piano with real violin accompaniment introduced at the Leipzig Spring Fair of 1930 by Popper of Leipzig.

KosMos. Player piano made by Lehmann & Company of Berlin, *fl.* 1909.

Krone. Coin-operated automaton made by Berliner Musik-Industrie A Pietschmann & Company, *fl.*1903.

Liliput. Piano orchestrions and other mechanical instruments made by Ernst Holzweissig Nachfolger, Leipzig, *fl.*1909.

Lippola. Player piano made by Lipp & Sohn and fitted with the Kastonome player action.

Lochmann Original. This name was used on mechanical musical instruments made by Original-Musikwerke Paul Lochmann, Zeulenroda and Leipzig, and applied to both disc-playing comb-playing musical boxes and also mechanical pianos with percussion accompaniment. *Fl.*1909.

Lohengrin. Orchestrion made by Imhof & Mukle, Vöhrenbach.

Lola. Barrel-operated piano-orchestrion incorporating mandoline, xylophone, castagnettes, drum and cymbal and driven by a descending weight. Made in Leipzig by Popper, *c.*1909.

Lord. Piano orchestrion made by Imhof & Mukle, Vöhrenbach.

Loreley. Orchestrion made by Popper of Leipzig, *fl.*1909.

Louis. A roll-operated piano-orchestrion driven by an electric motor. Manufactured by Hugo Popper, Leipzig, around 1920.

Lucia. Piano orchestrion made by Imhof & Mukle, Vöhrenbach, *fl.*1909.

Lucretia. Orchestrion organ made by Imhof & Mukle, Vöhrenbach, *fl.*1909.

Ludwig. Piano-player made by Ludwig & Company/Claviola Company, New York, *c.*1908.

Luna. Orchestrion made by Popper of Leipzig, early twentieth century.

Lusitania. Orchestrion organ made by Dienst of Leipzig, early twentieth century.

Lux. Orchestrion made by Ernst Holzweissig Nachfolger, Leipzig, *fl.*1909.

Lyraphone. Cabinet piano-player made in Baltimore by the Smith Lyraphone Company.

Lyrist. Ordinary 65- and 88-note players and an expression piano made in Berlin by Klingmann & Company, *fl.*1909.

Maesto. Large piano orchestrion with full percussion and organ played from perforated music roll. Made by Weber of Waldkirch.

Maestro. Key-top piano-player made by Amphion Piano Player Company.

Maestro-Pianoforte. Keyless reproducing piano, same as Welte-Mignon, made in Paris to Welte patents by Mustel and sold in London by Metzler & Co, Ltd, 40-43 Gt Marlborough Street, *fl.*1906.

Magic Fingers. Key-top piano-player made around 1950-60 in Kansas City by Gribble Music Company.

Majestic Junior. A 44-note endless roll electric piano made by The Lyon & Healy Piano Company.

Malcolm. London-made player piano by John Malcolm & Company and sold by Murdoch, *fl.*1908.

Mando Piano Orchestrina. Coin-operated piano made early twentieth century by North Tonawanda Musical Instrument Works, New York.

Mando-Orchestra. Coin-freed piano orchestrion made by North Tonawanda Musical Instrument Works, New York.

Mandolin Quartette/Sextette. Piano orchestrions made by Wurlitzer, New York.

Mandolina. Electric orchestrions made by Hupfeld of Leipzig, *fl.*1909.

Mandolinata. Orchestrion made by Sächsische Orchestrion-Fabrik F O Glass and distributed from Leipzig by Etzold & Popitz, *fl.*1909.

Manualo. Player piano by Baldwin of Chicago.

Mars. Mandolin orchestrion distributed in Leipzig by Holzweissig Nachfolger, *fl.*1909.

Massilia. Barrel pianos by Charles Guérin of Marseilles.

Matador. Piano orchestrion made by Popper, Leipzig.

Maxfield. Player piano made in London by Maxfield & Sons, *fl.*1908.

Mauretania. Orchestrion made by Dienst of Leipzig, *fl.*1909.

Melodant. Player piano made by Marshall in London.

Mélodia. Player pianos by Mélodia Company in Paris.

Melograph. Music recording machine for automatic instruments made by J Carpentier of Paris also a similar device with the same name by Baron Pilar von Pilchau, Petersburg. Both *fl.*1909.

Melotrope. Instrument for fitting to a keyboard and playing music prepared on the **Melograph** *[qv]* made by Jules Carpentier, Paris, *fl.*1909.

Mendel. Player piano distributed by Coppleston of London. *See also* Ideal-Mignon, Sterling, *and* Mendel.

Metanola. Player piano action by Higel of Toronto. Pianos fitted with this action bear this name on fallboard.

Mignon. Reproducing piano action made in Germany and New York by Welte of Freiburg, Germany, *fl.*1909.

Mignonola. Player piano handled in the 1930s by C F van der Does of s'Gravenhage (The Hague).

Mimosa. Orchestrion made in Leipzig by Popper, *fl.*1909.

Minerva. Piano-player sold in London by John G Murdoch & Co Ltd.

Ministrelle Autopiano. Very small player piano made in London by Barratt & Robinson.

Miranda-Pianista. Early name for Pianista *[qv]*.

Modello. Player piano introduced *c.*1928 by Baldwin.

Monola. Player piano made in Paris by La Société des Pianos Pneumatiques Française.

Multitone. Series of electric pianos made by the Operators' Piano Company, Chicago, for Welte.

Musetta. Player piano made by Neue Leipziger Musikwerke and distributed in London by S Calmont (in 1907) and then Harper Electric Piano Company Ltd, both of 258-262 Holloway Road, *fl.*1908.

Mustel Maestro. Welte Mignon keyboardless reproducing piano branded for French market by Mustel of Paris.

Musicus. London-made piano-player made by Musicus Piano Player Company.

Nero. Orchestrion made in Leipzig by Popper, *fl.*1909.

Newa. Orchestrion made in Leipzig by Popper, *fl.*1909.

Nordstern. Mechanical musical instrument made in Aurich, East Friesland, Germany, by Kittel, *fl.*1909.

Norma. Orchestrion made in Leipzig-Göhlis by Dienst, *fl.*1909.

Oberon. Orchestrion made in Leipzig by Popper, *fl.*1909.

Odeola. Player pianos made in Paris by Érard.

Ohio. Piano-orchestrion made by Popper, Leipzig.

Olympio. Self-playing organ made *c.*1909 by Farrand Organ Company in USA.

Orchestral Automaton. Mechanical musical instrument made by Leipziger Musikwerke Phoenix (Schmidt & Company).

Orchestrelle. Player reed organ made by the Aeolian Company of New York and London.

Orchestrina. Coin-freed piano orchestrion made by North Tonawanda Musical Instrument Works, New York.

Orchestrion. Instrument built in Dresden by Kaufmann in 1851.

Orchestrophone. Self-playing organ (reed) known as Green's Patent Orchestrophone sold in London by Cullum & Best

Organista. Keytop-player attachment made by Thibouville-Lamy of Paris, *fl.*1909.

Organola. Self-playing attachment for pipe organs made by Walcker of Ludwigsburg, Germany, *fl.*1909.

Organophone. Self-playing reed organ made by Thibouville-Lamy of Paris, *fl.*1909.

Original. Disc-playing musical boxes and piano-orchestrions made by Original-Musikwerke Paul Lochmann in Leipzig, *fl.*1909.

Original Konzert-Piano. Disc-playing piano orchestrion made by Original-Musikwerke Paul Lochmann, Zeulenroda and Leipzig, *fl.*1909.

Orpheus. Self-playing organ made by Story & Clark and F Kaim & Söhne, *fl.*1900. Later called **Orphic**.

Orpheus. Small piano played by perforated card discs made by Ehrlich in Leipzig.

Orpheusharmonicon. Orchestrion built in 1814 by Leonard Maelzel.

Orphic. *See* **Orpheus** (self-playing organ).

Orphobella. Keyboard playing attachment made in Leipzig by Ehrlich's Musikwerke, *fl.*1909.

Otero. Piano orchestrion with mandoline, xylophone, drum, cymbals and castagnettes and played from perforated music roll. Made by Weber of Waldkirch and incorporated a Feurich piano.

Othello. Barrel-operated piano-orches-trion driven by a descending weight or electric motor. Manufactured by Hugo Popper, Leipzig, *c.*1913.

Paganini. Piano-orchestrion made by Philipps of Leipzig.

Pan. Orchestrion made by Hupfeld in Leipzig.

Paragon. Player pianos and player organs made *c.*1909 by Needham Piano & Organ Co, USA. *Also:* Piano player made in London by Ambridge & Son of Fountayne Road, Broad Lane, Tottenham..

Patriarch. Orchestrion made by Imhof & Mukle, Vöhrenbach.

Pedaleon. Very small player piano made in 1913 by Barratt & Robinson.

Peerless. Push-up piano-player, player pianos and piano-orchestrions made in St Johnsville, USA, by Peerless Piano Player Company, a division of Roth & Engelhardt & Sons

Pennyano. Coin-freed clockwork barrel piano made by Keith, Prowse Ltd, *c.*1895-1918.

Per Omnes Pianoforte. Barrel mechanism for operating pianos made by Capra, Rissone & Detoma, London.

Perfecta. Player piano made in London by Morton Brothers & Company of 20 Highbury Place.

Petrophon. Automatic musical instrument made in Leipzig by Peters & Company, *fl.*1909.

Phadra II. A barrel-operated mechanical piano driven by a descending weight. Manufactured by Hugo Popper, Leipzig, early 20th Century. Popper made many mechanical pianos and piano-orchestrions, some without keyboards for manual playing. Main distributors for Popper was Holzweissig Nachfolger whose name label frequently obscures that of the manufacturer.

Philharmonic Autograph Organ. Reproducing pipe organ made by Welte of Freiburg.

Phoneon. 61-note pneumatic-action player reed organ made in 1898 by Malcolm & Company, 91 Farringdon Road, London, EC, and selling for 36 guineas [$150].

Phonobella. Player piano made in Leipzig by Hupfeld.

Phonola. Player piano made in Leipzig by Hupfeld.

Phonolett. Orchestrion made in Leipzig by Hupfeld.

Phonoliszt. Player piano made in Leipzig by Hupfeld. Also **Phonoliszt-Violina** piano combined with three violins all pneumatically-operated.

Photo Orchestra. Electrically-operated roll-playing piano orchestrion made by Peerless around 1925.

Pialo. Player piano made by Singer Piano Company of Chicago, *fl.*1909.

Pianauto. Player piano made in Canada by Karn & Company and sold by them in London from 3, Newman Street.

Pian-Auto. Upright player piano made by Krell Piano Company of Cincinnati.

Pianella. Piano-orchestrion made in Frankfurt by Frankfurter Musikwerke, *fl.*1909. *Also:* Piano-orchestrions made by Philipps, Leipzig.

Pianetta. Player piano made ID 1910 by the London Piano & Organ Company, 14 Holmes Road, Kentish Town.

Pianette. Same as **Regina Sublima** *[qv]*. Name used by Lyon & Healy, Chicago. *Also:* Player pianos made in New York by Jacob Doll & Sons. *Also:* Disc-playing piano made in New Jersey by F G Otto Manufacturing Company.

Pianex. Piano player made in London by The Pianex Company.

Piani Melodici. Mechanical pianos by Racca of Bologna. *See* English name form **Piano Melodico.**

Pianino. Mechanical piano made in USA by Wurlitzer, *fl.*1909.

Pianist. Piano player made in Gera by W Spaethe, *fl.*1909. Distributed in London by Günzel & Rosenberger, 7 Victoria Avenue, Bishopsgate Without.

Pianista. Initially called Miranda-Pianista. A piano player operated by perforated rolled cardboard 10¼-inches wide and made in Paris by Thibouville-Lamy, *fl.*1909. *Also:* Cabinet piano player by Autopiano Company of New York. *Also:* Very early mechanical piano-player made in Paris by Napoléon Fourneaux. *Also:* Cabinet piano player by Kohler & Campbell of New York.

Piano-Jazz. Barrel piano-orchestrion made in Belgium by Pierre Eich.

Piano Mécanique. Mechanical piano player made by Debain in Paris.

Piano Melodico. Mechanical piano operated by perforated cardboard music made by Racca of Bologna and also by Spaethe in Gera, *fl.*1909. *See also* **Gladiator, Le.**

Piano-Accordion-Jazz. Mid-twentieth century cafe instrument made by Seybold of Strasburg-Meinau.

Pianocorder. Electronically operated player piano action controlled by tape-cassettes and introduced by Superscope Marantz Corporation in California towards the end of the 1970s. Solenoid-driven hammer actions. Sole UK distributors were Kemble Piano Group of Bletchley, Buckinghamshire.

Pian-O-Grand. Keyboardless electric pianos by Nelson-Wiggen of Chicago.

Pianola. Name given by Aeolian to its piano-players and player-pianos. Very early on this registered trade name became an unofficial generic term for roll-playing piano-players and player-pianos with the result that other makers sought hard for names that sounded like 'pianola' in order to exploit the market following of Aeolian.

Pianolin. Coin-operated musical automaton made by North Tonawanda Musical Instrument Company, New York, *fl.*1900.

Piano-Melodico. Mechanical-action book-playing pianofortes made by Giovanni Racca in Italy.

Pianon. Player piano made by Welte of Freiburg, *fl.*1909.

Pianophon. Player piano made by Asmus of Berlin, *fl.*1909.

Pianophone. Orchestrion organ made in Berlin by Cocchi, Bacigalupo & Graffigna, *fl.*1902.

Pianora. Player pianos made by the Pianora Company, 133 West 24th Street, New York, USA, *fl.*1909. Blatant trade-off on registered trade-name 'Pianola'. Player mechanism was called the Ackotist.

Pianosona. Player piano made by Chase & Baker.

Pianotist. Piano player attachment made by Pianotist Company in Leipzig, *fl.*1909, and by Klaber in New York.

Pianovo. Barrel-operated piano-orchestrion, German-made, *c.*1910. Maker unknown.

Piccolo. A barrel-operated mechanical piano driven by a descending weight. Manufactured by Hugo Popper, Leipzig, early 20th C. Popper made many mechanical pianos and piano-orchestrions, some with and others without keyboards for manual playing.

Pistonola. Player-piano made in London by Boyd Ltd.

Playano. Piano player made in Cambridge, Mass, by the Playano Manufacturing Company, itself part of Story & Clark who first used the name.

Playetta. Player piano made in London by Philip Cohen & Company Ltd.

Playola. Expression piano made in Chicago by Playola Piano Company, *fl.*1909.

Pleyella. Player piano made in Paris by Pleyel Wolf Lyon & Company.

Pneuma, Pneumatist. Player organs and player pianos made by Kuhl & Klatt in Berlin, *fl.*1909.

Pneuma. Self-playing attachment for pianos operated electrically and made by Kuhl & Klatt of Berlin. Marketed by Wm Gerecke in London, *fl.*1900. In 1895, dealers Hampton & Sons of Pall Mall advertised the Pneuma as 'the simplest automatically-played piano yet invented'.

Posauto. Roll-playing single-manual pipe organs made *c.*1910 by the original Positive Organ Company of London.

Power Roll, The. Modern electronically-operated system for playing a pneumatic player piano without using a music roll. Device fits over tracker bar of instrument. Made by Broadmoor Research in California.

Pratt Read. Pneumatic player piano actions made in Connecticut by Pratt Read.

Premier. Player pianos and piano-orchestrions made *c.*1909 by Neue Leipziger Musikwerke A Buff-Hedinger and distributed in London by Harper Electric Piano Company.

Primavolta. Electric player piano made *c.*1909 by Neue Leipziger Musikwerke A Buff-Hedinger.

Protector. Orchestrion made in Leipzig by Popper, *fl.*1909.

Protos. Orchestrion made in Leipzig by Popper, *fl.*1909.

Psycho. A large 'electric orchestra' made in 1874 by Neville Maskeline with the collaboration of the American, J A Clarke, and used at the Egyptian Hall during Maskeline's magic displays. The instrument was not truly mechanical, being controlled by an operator from a keyboard.

Puck. Orchestrion made in Leipzig by Popper, *fl.*1909.

Radi-O-Player. Upright player piano incorporating a radio receiver made in New York by Weydig Piano Corporation.

Ramona. Piano-orchestrion playing 88-note or special piano rolls made 1923 by Albert Imhof.

Recital. Player for organs made in Epinal (Vosges), France by Didier & Cie, *fl.*1909.

Reclame. Piano-orchestrion made in Vöhrenbach by Imhof & Mukle.

Recordo. Expression pianos made by a variety of manufacturers to a common specification. Music rolls played include the following makes: Aria Divina Reproducing; Gulbransen Reproducing Roll; Imperial Automatic Electric; International for Expression Pianos; Mastertouch Expression Roll; Melodee Expression; Pianostyle for Expression Pianos; Q-R-S Recordo; Recordo; Rose Valley Recording Roll; Symphonola; US Auto-Art; Vocalstyle Home Recital series; Vocalstyle Reproducing; Vocalstyle Reproduco. The first company to make Recordo rolls was The Imperial Roll Company around 1916 under the name Imperial Automatic Electric.

Regal. 44-note electric piano made in New York City by Ricca & Sons. *Also:* Player piano introduced in London in 1906 by Wright Piano Company.

Regent. Orchestrion made in Leipzig by Popper, *fl.*1909.

Regina. Barrel-operated piano-orchestrion driven by a descending weight. Manufactured by Hugo Popper, Leipzig, *c.*1913. No connection with the American-made disc musical box of similar name.

Regina Sublima. Mandolin-action perforated card roll-playing piano made by Regina Music Box Company of New Jersey, USA.

Reginapiano. Electric piano made by Regina Music Box Company, New Jersey, USA.

Registering Piano, The. Descriptive name applied by Gulbransen to their player pianos.

Remington. Player piano made in Indiana by Starr Piano Company.

Reproduco. Pipe organ photoplayer made by Operators Piano Company, Chicago.

Resotone Grand. Pneumatically played glockenspiel comprising 46 flat metal bars struck by felt-covered hammers. Plays 9¾-inch wide endless paper rolls. Made *c.*1900-1910 by Resotone Grand Company of New York.

Rex. Piano-orchestrion made in Leipzig by Popper, *fl.*1909. *Also:* Cabinet-style push-up piano-player made by the Pianotist Company, London.

Rialto. Attachable piano-playing action made by Rialto Player Piano Company of London.

Richmond. Player piano made in Indiana by Starr Piano Company.

Roland. A roll-operated mandolin piano-orchestrion driven by electric motor. Manufactured by Hugo Popper, Leipzig, early 20th C.

Rossini. Piano-orchestrion played by perforated cardboard and made by Polyphon, *fl.*1909.

Salon Orchestra. A roll-operated electrically-driven piano-orchestrion made for use in dancehalls and restaurants. Manufactured by Hugo Popper, Leipzig, circa 1920.

Selecta. Orchestrion made *c.*1920 by Lösche in Berlin.

Serenata. Pneumatic-action orchestrion distributed by Etzold & Popitz of Leipzig, *fl.*1909.

Sextrola. Coin-freed electric piano orchestrion made by North Tonawanda Musical Instrument Works, New York.

Si-La-Fa. Orchestrion made in Leipzig by Popper, *fl.*1909.

Silvia. Piano orchestrion made by Frankfurter Musikwerke-Fabrik J D Philipps & Söhne,

Simson. Orchestrion made by Popper of Leipzig, *fl.*1909.

Slavia. Piano-orchestrion made in Prague by Fuchs, *fl.*1909.

Solea. Large piano orchestrion with full percussion played from perforated music roll and illuminated pictorial scene in the front of the case. Made by Weber of Waldkirch around 1909.

Soleil. Orchestrion organ made in Berlin by Cocchi, Bacigalupo & Graffigna, *fl.*1902.

Solophone. Barrel piano-orchestrion made in Belgium by Pierre Eich.

Solophonola. Player piano made by Hupfeld in Leipzig.

Solotist. Musical automaton made in Berlin and sold by Choralion Company (Aeolian), *fl.*1909.

Solo-Virtuola. Expression piano by Hallet & Davis of Boston.

Sonora. Orchestrion made by Dienst of Leipzig, *fl.*1909.

Starr. Player piano made in Indiana by Starr Piano Company.

Stella. Reproducing piano also a piano-orchestrion made in Leipzig by Popper, *fl.*1909.

Stella. Name of a pneumatically-played 65-note push-up piano-player marketed in 1910. The instrument had a hand-rewind system like the early Simplex and Pianotist players.

Stellamont. Orchestrion made in Leipzig by Dienst, *fl.*1909.

Stems. Player piano made by Direct Pneumatic Action Co Ltd, 3, 4, 5 Kendrick Place, 8a Dorset Street, Baker Street, London, W.

Stefanie. 'Piano-orchester' advertised in 1904 and made by Stefanie-Werke-Filiale of Trautenau, Bohemia.

Sterling. Player piano made in Detroit by The Sterling Company and distributed in Britain *c.*1912 by Coppleston & Company of 94, Regent Street, London.

Strauss. Orchestrion made in Waldkirch by the Waldkircher Orchestrionfabrik, *fl.*1909.

Styria. Large piano orchestrion with full percussion and organ played from perforated music roll. Also fitted with a normal keyboard for manual playing. Made by Weber of Waldkirch.

Sublima, Sublime Piano Junior. Electric or clockwork pianos made in New Jersey by Regina Music Box Company.

Symphonia. Clockwork barrel pianos made in London by Pesaresi, Son & Spinelli.

Symphoniola. Player piano produced in Leipzig-Göhlis by Symphonionfabrik A-G, *fl.*1909.

Symphonista. Electric piano also known as the Corona Xylophone. Seven models available from £125 [$500] to £215 [$860]. Probably made by Popper; sold in London by New Polyphon Supply Company, 2 Newman Street, in 1908.

Symphonola. Player piano made by Price & Teeple in Chicago.

Symphony. Self-playing reed organ made by Wilcox & White of Meriden, Conn., USA.

Sympletta. Piano-player apparatus offered in London by the Simplex Piano-Player Company of 244 Tottenham Court Road, London, and advertised in 1908. Rather basic piano player made in England by Simplex *c.*1910.

Tarantella. Mechanical musical instruments made by Ernst Holzweissig Nachfolger of Leipzig, *fl.*1909.

Telektra, Tel-Electric. Electrically-controlled player piano operated from remote console. Made by Tel-Electric, New York City.

Tell. Violin-piano-orchestrion made by Imhof & Mukle, Vöhrenbach.

Terpretor. Player-piano made in London by Boyd Ltd.

Titania. Mandolin-orchestrion made in Leipzig by Popper, *fl.*1909. Name also used by Lösche.

Toccaphon. Xylophone piano made *c.*1909 by Neue Leipziger Musikwerke A Buff-Hedinger.

Tone-ola. Player piano made in New York by Hasbrouck Piano Company.

Tonika. Orchestrion made in Leipzig by Popper, *fl.*1909.

Tonograph. Mechanical music recorder invented in 1899 by Robert A Galley, son of the US organette inventor.

Tonophone. Electrical barrel piano with pneumatic action made early twentieth century for Wurlitzer by North Tonawanda Musical Instrument Works, New York. Designed by Eugene de Kleist.

Tonsyreno. Roll-playing reed organ manufactured by Aeolian as a prelude to the Orchestrelle *[qv]*. Distributed in London *c.*1889 by Geo Whight whose label is always displayed.

Traviata. Orchestrion by Dienst of Leipzig, *fl.*1909.

Trayser. Player piano made in Indiana by Starr Piano Company.

Tremolo. Orchestrion made in Leipzig by Symphonion-Fabrik, A-G, *fl.*1909.

Tribut. Orchestrion made in Vöhrenbach by Imhof & Mukle, *fl.*1909.

Trio. Electrically-operated roll-playing piano orchestrion made by Peerless around 1925.

Triola. Mechanical zither played by perforated paper roll. Made by Polyphon Musikwerke in Leipzig, *fl.*1919.

Triphonola. Reproducing piano made by Hupfeld in Leipzig.

Triumph. A barrel-operated mechanical piano driven by a descending weight. Manufactured by Hugo Popper, Leipzig, early 20th Century. Popper made many mechanical pianos and piano-orchestrions, some with and others without keyboards for manual playing. *Also:* Cabinet piano player by Autopiano Company of New York.

Triumphator. Orchestrion made in Leipzig by Popper, *fl.*1909.

Triumphola. A. Player piano made by Rachals & Company in Hamburg, also Kastner in London, *fl.*1909.

Trompeter von Sackingen. Piano-orchestrion made by Imhof & Mukle in Vöhrenbach, *fl.*1909.

Tzigana. Mechanical musical instrument made by Ernst Holzweissig Nachfolger, Leipzig, *fl.*1909.

U'nette. Player pianos by Thompson-U'nette piano company of Chicago.

Unika. Piano-orchestrion made by Weber, of Waldkirch.

Universal. Orchestrion made by Hupfeld in Leipzig, *fl.*1909.

Universal Piano Player. Player piano action made in England by Bansall & Sons, London.

Universum. Mechanical musical instruments made in Frankfurt by Seip, *fl.*1909.

Valsonora. Barrel-operated piano-orchestrions under this name were introduced by the Sächsischen Orchestrionfabrik F O Glass of Klingenthal between 1899 and 1912. Models O, OO, XIV and XVIII have been seen in old advertisements, mostly featuring a 24-note piano, 8-note mandolin, 8-note xylophone, triangle, side drum and cymbal. A bass drum was available at extra cost. A wide variety of case styles was available, some with illuminated-image façades and automaton scenes.

Venezia. Piano orchestrion with mandoline, drum and cymbals played from perforated music roll. Made in Waldkirch by Weber.

Verdi. Automatic book-playing piano made by Racca of Bologna, *fl.*1909. *Also:* Orchestrion made in Leipzig by Popper, *fl.*1909.

Verophon. Mechanical musical instrument made by Richter & Cie of Rudolstadt, *fl.*1909.

Victolian. Self-playing reed organ manufactured by Aeolian and distributed in London by George Whight *fl.*1900.

Virtuola, Solo-Virtuola. Player piano and expression piano introduced in 1911 by Hallet & Davis of Boston who owned the Simplex Player Action Company.

Virtuos. Piano player by Fabrik Leipziger Musikwerke.

Violano. Piano-orchestrion made by Weber, Waldkirch.

Violano-Virtuoso. Self-playing violin with piano made by Mills Novelty Company, Chicago, in 1908.

Violetta. Orchestrion made by Popper of Leipzig, *fl.*1909.

Violin Orchestra. Piano-orchestrion made by Philipps of Leipzig.

Violina-Phonoliszt. Combined player piano and violins made in Leipzig by Hupfeld, *fl.*1909.

Violiniste. A pneumatic violin-player combined with piano made by Emile Aubry and Gabriel Boreau in Paris in 1926.

Violinovo. Electric expression piano with real violin accompaniment introduced at the Leipzig Spring Fair of 1930 by Popper of Leipzig. Extensively advertised over 1930 and 1931, only one example is known today.

Virtuos. A 73-note expression piano made in Berlin by K Heilbrunn Söhne, *fl.*1909.

Virtuola, Solo-Virtuola. Player piano and expression piano introduced in 1911 by Hallet & Davis who owned the Simplex Player Action Company.

Vision. Orchestrion made in Leipzig by Popper, *fl.*1909.

Vocalion. Player piano made by the Aeolian Company in New York, *fl.*1909. *Also:* Self-playing organ made by the Vocalion Organ Company, Worcester, Mass, USA, *fl.*1909.

Volksklavier. A mechanical zither-type instrument made *c.*1890 in Germany.

Vorsetzer. A 'push-up' piano player made by Welte. Fully electric and reproducing from special music rolls. More of a descriptive transitive verb than a proper model name.

Walkure. Orchestrion made by Imhof & Mukle, Vöhrenbach, *fl.*1909.

Wallis. Cheaper brand of player piano made by Joseph Wallis & Son Ltd of 50, Isledon Road, Finsbury Park, North London (showrooms 133-135 Euston Road).

Wearham. Experimental key-top player made in Britain by Vickers Ltd.

Weiner Schrammel. Orchestrion made in Leipzig by Popper, *fl.*1909.

Welt-Piano-Stella. Orchestrion made in Leipzig by Popper, *fl.*1909.

Welte. Player pianos made by Welte & Sohne, Freiburg.

Welte-Mignon. Reproducing piano made in Freiburg and New York. Branded for French market by Mustel of Paris as the **Mustel Maestro.**

Welte-Mignon (Licensee). Reproducing piano and action developed by Kohler & Campbell of New York.

Wireless Piano. Upright piano, sometimes also an electrically-driven player piano, incorporating an all-mains radio and electric gramophone introduced in 1931 by Kriebel of Berlin.

Wisteria. Electrically-operated roll-playing piano orchestrion made by Peerless around 1925.

Xilonella. Orchestrion made in Vienna by Fuchs, *fl.*1909.

Xylophon. Piano-orchestrion made in Frankfurt by Frankfurter Musikwerke, *fl.*1909.

Xylophon-Klavier. Electric piano made *c.*1909 by Neue Leipziger Musikwerke A Buff-Hedinger.

Zamba. Piano-orchestrion made in Leipzig by Dienst, *fl.*1909.

Appendix 4
Music Roll Makers and their Brand Names

The music roll is the heart of the player-piano. Without it, the piano is merely a silent piece of furniture. But besides providing the musical programme, the rolls themselves have a fascination to collectors. Some form thematic collections of music on different roll labels; others collect only one brand of roll. If the appeal of roll types lies at the heart of the automatic piano collector, then so does information regarding the rolls and who made them, where and when. The problem is that the name on the roll can sometimes indicate the type of piano for which it was made and occasionally the make of the roll may be mistaken for that of the piano itself.

Over the years I have received hundreds of letters on this subject, so here is an attempt to consolidate as much of the data as possible. I published the first list in the specialist magazine *Music & Automata* in 1987: since then the list has expanded considerably. Nobody can ever be sure how many roll-makers there were. Some have left no information at all, just a few tantalizing roll names. At least some were dedicated or branded production by the large factories for a particular store that wanted its own name on rolls it sold. Many of these cannot readily be traced today, so this list contains some unknowns. Perhaps you can supply some missing detail!

In some ways, history is repeating itself. Between 1920 and 1930 a large number of small business sprang up to produce piano-rolls. Some were destined to be short-lived, others were forced out of business by the 1929-1932 Depression. Since the 1960s there has been an increasing number of people taking an interest in roll-making. In the main this has been restricted to roll-copying ('re-cuts') but an increasing proportion of new music is being made available. The advent of technology, which has brought the science of music-arranging for rolls almost into the realm of the computer game, has produced a flood of new rolls. Sophisticated roll-punching machines, many of them the work of amateur craftsmen, have revolutionized roll quality.

There is a difference, though, between making your own roll and setting up a production line as witnessed by the rapid turnover of businesses. Once a huge investment is made in equipment, human nature spurs one on to generate return. And many who have enjoyed making rolls as a hobby suddenly realize that, like the girl who works in a chocolate factory, they never want to see another piano-roll again!

This quirk is evident in these listings of businesses and their trade names. In size these organization ranged from the giants like Universal, Perforated Music and Q-R-S to extremely small undertakings such as the Medcraft operation in a small house in suburban Harrow Weald, Middlesex. The Medcrafts, incidentally, were pioneering makers in the British post-Pianola era roll making.

The first part of this Appendix lists brand names of music rolls and refers them, where possible, to their makers. The second part gives a list of known roll-manufacturers. Both are displayed alphabetically. These data have been prepared with the assistance of several people in particular J B Roth, Elmhurst, New York; Michael Broadway; Bill Edgerton, Connecticut; the late Harvey Roehl, Vestel; Tony Morgan; Dr Antonio Latanza and Dr Jan Jaap Haspels. Special thanks to those others that have allowed me to trawl their roll-collections, and also The Guildhall Library, London, for access to their surely unique London postal and business directories collections.

Music rolls were produced by an equally large number of manufacturers throughout the world and once again any attempt at listing in entirety is realistically impossible. It is only to be expected that, with the huge quantity of player pianos being turned out, both the largest number and concentration of roll makers was in the United States and at one time or another more than fifty companies were engaged in the business of manufacturing rolls. England also possessed quite a few, including subsidiary companies of both American and continental European makers.

The Names of Rolls

Abbate Special
Accen[t]ist
Accentuated – Made by Aeolian/Universal
Ace
Acme - *See* **Atlas Player Roll Co.**
Acme - *See* **Republic.**
A.C.M.C.
Accentor Made by Hardman & Peck.
Aeolian [*and subsidiaries*] - Made by Aeolian/Universal

Aeolian, Aeolian Grand. 58-note music rolls for the Aeolian player reed organ and Orchestrelle.

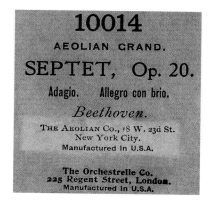

Aeolian Song Roll
Accentuated (English Themodist)
Broadwood, John
Autograph
Duo-Art
    Audiographic
88-Note Universal
Mel-O-Dee
Meloto (England)
Metro-Art (decoded Duo-Art with Themodist)
Metrostyle
Pianola
Pianola Audiographic
Pianolist's Library
Themodist Metrostyle
Triumph (England)
Uni-Record
Uni-Solo
Universal

Aeriol. First name used by Aeolian in 1895 for piano rolls, replaced by the Pianola.

Angelus Melodant Artistyle - *See* **Wilcox & White.**

Angelus Artistyle

Agovino
Alector - *See* **Paramount**.
Altoona (Pennsylvania)
    Master
    Superba
    Victory
Amati.
Ambassador. Makers of Ambassador label rolls by Autoplayer Piano Company.

Artist Song Roll
Artrio
Animatic. Player rolls made by Hupfeld.

American. Made by the Capitol Roll & Record Company - *See also* **Columbia-Capitol.**
American Piano Company - Made by American Piano Co, *also* Marshall Piano Co, London

Ampico
Ampico Artigraphic
Ampico-Stoddard
A.P.C. (American Piano Control)
Rythmodik (green)
    (red label record)
    (Solo-Elle)
Lauter
Solostyle "Melody Marked"

Animatic T. Reproducing roll made by Hupfeld for Triphonola pianos. Renamed Tri-Phonola.
Anton Mervar - *See* **Original.**
Antpusaico
A.P.C. Music rolls marked American Piano Control with the name of American Piano Company.

Apollo. F.I.R.S. Milano. Black plastic ends, contiguous perforations, fine box, coarse orange-coloured paper. Gold boxes label, attractive apron, 88-note.

Apollo. Music rolls for the Apollo Concert Grand. Paper width 15.1/8-inches. *See under* **Artecho**, *also under* **Clark**.

Apollo X - *See* **Clark**.

A-R - *See* **Atlas Player Roll Co.**

Aria Divina Reproducing Roll. Reproducing rolls made by Imperial Music Roll Company. *See also* **Q.R.S.** [Recordo coded]

Arista-Venus

Aristo
　　　Temponome – special music rolls made for Kastner.

Aristokrat-Autokrat

ArMaN. Popular music piano rolls made in Belgium by Atelier Musical.

Armonic. Good-quality Spanish-made piano-rolls in the main devoted to popular music; label marked "Pedal-88 note **t** CANT". All boxes for rolls have a common height (depth) for ease of storage. Trade-mark of name radiating from rising sun's rays.

Arranged - *See* **Q.R.S.**

Art Music Production Tommasello & Co. Music Rolls made in New York by Pianostyle.

Artcraft. Modern music rolls including Duo-Art recuts made in Maine, USA by Playrite.

Artecho. Reproducing piano action made by American Piano Company. Later re-named Apollo. Rolls by Q-R-S.

Artempo - *See* **Bennett & White**. Blue label on box top showing a grand piano coupled to a roll-perforating machine. Legend "Artempo Hand-Played".

Artisong

Artistone

Artist Song Roll. Music rolls punched by Imperial for Aeolian.

Artistouch. Special pipe organ rolls produced by the Clark Company of Chicago.

Artistyle - 65-note piano rolls by Wilcox & White for the Angelus player-piano. Grey printed apron with orange-red adhesive label. Handled by Herbert Marshall & Sons, London. Subsequently changed over to 88-note rolls under the name Artistyle also Regent. Associated in Britain with Sir Herbert Marshall & Sons.

Artigraphic – *See* **American Piano Company**.

ARTo. Music rolls made in Orange, New Jersey, by Standard Music Roll Co with singing 'staff-note' on right side. Four similarly-named variants: ARTo Standard Instrumental; ARTo Word Rolls; ARTo Popular Rolls; SingA Word Rolls. Also **Arto Roll** ['Artists Own Roll'] 'The Artist's own Hand-Playing Cut in the Roll'. Slogan: '88 full score arrangement 88'. Trade mark ARTo [*qv*].

Artona. Music rolls manufactured by Artona Music Rolls Ltd of Ramsgate, Kent.

Artrio. Reproducing piano-rolls made for the Angelus Artrio action. *See* **Wilcox & White.**

Atlas Player Roll Co
Acme
A-R
Atlas
Bamberger
Broadway (later made by Q.R.S; used Imperial numbers)
Eclipse
Emkay (meaning Max Kortlander)
Harmony
Herman's (meaning Herman Kortlander)
Landay (later made by Q.R.S; used Imperial numbers)
Metro
Ray-Dio
Regent
Ritz
Simplex
Supreme
Wissner
Globe

Audiographic. Introduced by Aeolian in 1929 - *See* **Aeolian Duo-Art.**

Audiographic Music rolls launched at the beginning of 1928 for Duo-Art and ordinary 88-note player piano. Part of the series 'The World's Music'.

Aurora. 88-note rolls made by Gorli, Milan, Italy. Green surfaced paper apron printed in gold. Slightly green paper, contigious perforations.

Austin Quadruplex; Premier Quadruplex. Music rolls for the Premier Quadruplex Player pipe organ made in America by Austin Organ Co.

Auto Art - Expression piano rolls made by US. *See* **United stateS.**

Auto De Luxe Welte-Mignon. Music rolls made by Auto Pneumatic Action Company, New York.

Auto Inscribed - *See* **National.**

Autochord - *See* **Imperial.**

Autograph - *See* **Aeolian.**

Autograph – Hand-played music rolls by Q.R.S.

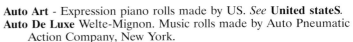

Autograph Hand Played - Hand-played music rolls by Q.R.S.

Autografo - *See* **Pasquale Music Roll.**

Automatic Electric [Recordo coded] - Made by Imperial Player Roll Co

Autoplayer (Standard, Accentuated, word-rolls) sold by British Autoplayer Co in London. Made by Aeolian/Universal

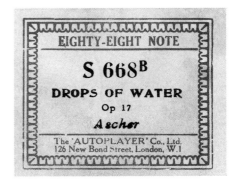

Avitabile Brothers. Italian music rolls made and sold in New York by music dealer. Maker unknown.

Bamberger- *See* **Atlas Player Roll Co.**

Batik - 88-note with unusual red-brown apron with bold slash brand name across in silver. Markes 'Made in Germany'. One roll num bered 21/1 *Tutankhamen-Shimmy* by Jara Benes clearly dates from after Howard Carter's discovery of the Egyptian tomb in November 1922. The world went 'King Tut' mad 1923-25.

Bennett & White Inc
> Artempo Hand-Played

Baker & Co, C C (Chase & Baker)
> Selected

BEst Music rolls made by Juan Battista Blancafort of Barcelona, Spain.

Biondo Special - *See* **Connorized**.

Bluebird Series - *See* **Q.R.S.**

BluesTone. Modern recuts of jazz and reproducing piano rolls by BluesTone Music Rolls, Illinois, USA.

Boston Store - *See* **Imperial**.

Brilliante - *See* **Columbia-Capitol**.

Broadwood, John – Music rolls made by Aeolian/Universal for Broadwood's players pianos

Broadwood [player-piano makers] (Standard, Accentuated) – Made by Aeolian/Univeral

Broadway. Music rolls made in Australia by Anglo-American Player Roll Co, later absorbed by Mastertouch.

Cable-Nelson

Capitol. Made by the Capitol Roll & Record Company - *See* **Columbia-Capitol**.

Capitol Roll & Record Co. - *See also* **Columbia**.

Columbia (*c*.1920-24) Capitol
> Cecile
> Challenge
> Stark
> Sterling
> Supertone (made for Sears & Roebuck);
> Synchronized Caruso

Cecile. Made by the Capitol Roll & Record Company - *See* **Columbia-Capitol**.

Cecilian. Music rolls made by The Farrand Company

Celebrity Hand-Played Roll.

Challenge. Made by the Capitol Roll & Record Company - *See* **Columbia-Capitol**.

Chase & Baker - *See* **Baker & Co.**

Cigna, F[ratelli]. Fabrica Rulli Musicale, Biella, Italy 88-note straight

Clano Special
Clark
      Apollo (reproducing)
      Apollo X (88-note)
CMC – *see* Capitol Roll & Record Co
Collection Francis Salabert. Music rolls marked L'EMP and made in France.

Colley's Patents - *See this name under Manufacturers' listing*

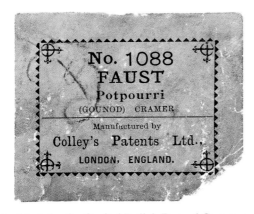

Columbia. Made by the Capitol Roll & Record Company *c.*1920-24 - *See also* **Columbia-Capitol.**
      Brilliante
      Cecile
      Challenge
      Orpheum
      Red Seal
      Stark
      Silver Jubilee (made for a Boston store)
      Sterling
      Supertone
      Synchronized
Concert Edition - *See* **Connorized.**
Concert Series [1] - *See* **International.**
Concert Series [2] - *See* **Q.R.S.**
Connazional. Made by Connorized Music Co. *See* **American 'Automusic' Company.**
      Concert Edition
      88-Note
      Fireside Series
      Uke Roll
      Biondo Special
      N.B.S.
      F. Pennino
      Editore E. Rossi
      Italian Book Co, NY.
      L'Insuperabile

Connorized. Made by Connorized Music Co. *See* **American 'Automusic' Company**

C.R.S.   Rollos 88 Notas [Spain]

Dahlmont. Music rolls made in Australia by Anglo-American Player Roll Company for Melbourne department store.

Dalian - *See* **Imperial.**
De Luxe (A.M.R. Co)
De Luxe - *See* **Welte-Mignon.**
DeLuxe. Music rolls together with Unisolo brand produced in Philadelphia, Pennsylvania, by unknown maker that operated in 1916.
Dea. Early reproducing piano roll made by Hupfeld
Diamond. Music rolls made in America by The Imperial Player Roll Company.
Diana Madrid. Quality 88-note rolls made in Barcelona, Spain. Very decorative lithographed box with name 'DIANA' right across the top. The apron is equally decorative, the whole executed in shades of brown.

Dominant
      Triumph
Donat Langelier, I. - *See* **Vocalstyle.**
Dualano. Music rolls made for and sold by Dale, Forty & Co Ltd, 65-note.
Duca (Ducartist) Künstlerrollen. High quality reproducing piano rolls made by Philipps in Leipzig.
Duo (QRS-Imperial)

Duo-Art - *See* **Aeolian.** Later Duo-Art Organ rolls made by Aeolian-Skinner.

Duo-Art (reproducing) - *See* **Universal.**
Duophonola - *See* **Hupfeld.**

Echo. Music rolls made in England in the early 1920s by Siggitson & Perkins of London.

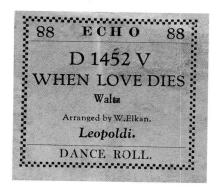

Eclipse - *See* **Atlas Player Roll Co.**
Edition Musicale Perforee, L' (L.E.M.P.). Paris-made music rolls
Editore E. Rossi - *See* **Connorized.**
    8.T.8. (read as 'eighty-eight).
    88-Note - *See* **Connorized.**
    88-Note Universal - *See* **Aeolian.**

Electra – Made by the Standard Music Roll Co, NYC.

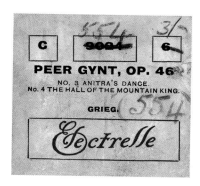

Electrova
Emblem - *See* **United stateS**
Emkay - *See* **Atlas Player Roll Co.**
Empeco. Made in Leipzig by Concordia-Notenrollenfabrik. Full-scale hand-played piano rolls; also 88-note rolls for 'Jazzband-Instrumente' also made in Leipzig.

Empire Music Roll. Music rolls made in England in the early 1920s. No maker identified.
ERA. Piano rolls made in Madrid by Rollos ERA, S.A.

E.T. Paull's Original Orchestrated Piano Rolls.

Editions Francis Salabert. Piano rolls made in France: *see* Edition Musicale Perforee, L' (L.E.M.P.).

E.M.P.A. Sold by the European Music Publishers' Association.

Evola. Standard and 'artist's' rolls made by Freiburger Musikapparate-Bauanstalt, GmbH, Freiburg-in-Bresgau.

Euterpe. Dutch-made piano rolls

Excello - *See* Herbert.

Excelsior. Music rolls made by G Bacigalupo in Berlin for electric pianos.

Fairview - *See* Imperial.

Famous

Famous Marches - *See* Music Note.

Favorita

Filmusic
>   Picturoll
>   P-O-P

Fireside Series - *See* Connorized.

F.I.R.S.- *See* Apollo, Milan

F.I.R.ST. (Fabbrica Italiana Rulli Sonori Traforati) Vocalist

Front Porch. Modern music rolls made by BlueStone Music Rolls at Grayslake, Illinois

Full Scale 88 Note - *See* Standard.

Gamage. Rolls branded by London department store and same as Omnia.

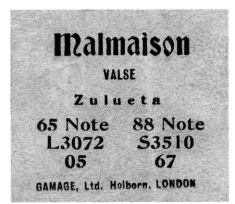

Ged's Player-Piano & Music Roll Co

Giacini Special

Giudice Special - *See* Verdi.

G.K. Music rolls made in Spain. Maker unknown.

Globe - *See* Atlas Player Roll Co.

Gloria
>   R.G.S.

Golden Age. New rolls by Wenker, Phil, of California.

Golden Tube, Suprema - *See* Murdoch, Murdoch & Co.

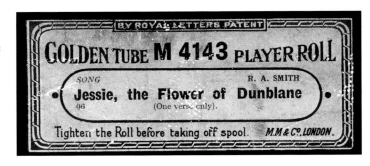

Grausso

Green. 'Welte Green' is a collector's term for the reproducing piano rolls made by Welte-Mignon in America that are punched in green paper. - *See also* Welte-Mignon

Griffith

Gulbransen. Music rolls made in USA by Gulbransen Music Roll Corp.
>   Recordo

Hand Played - *See* National.

Hand Played – Rolls made by Universal for Aeolian

Hand Played. Music rolls made for The Hand Played Music Roll Co, *c.*1928-30.

Harmel

Harmonic

Harmony - *See* Atlas Player Roll Co.

Harrods (Standard, Accentuated) – Rolls made by Universal for London department store.

Heisigenrollen. Modern piano rolls of modern keyboard music made in Germany.

Herbert
>   Excello

Herbert Marshall, Sir (Artist Song Roll, Artistyle, Regent Song, Regent Dance) - *See* Universal.

Herman's - *See* **Atlas Player Roll Co.**

Higel

Solodant 188-note self-apron roll with blue-bordered label

Hit - *See* **Imperial.**

Hitz - *See* **Staffnote.**

Hollandia – made in Amsterdam by Hollandia-Rollen.

Hollywood. 88-note rolls, plain apron with adhesive label. Ragtime and jazz titles. Issued post-war but appears to have ceased trading c.1970s. Punched by QRS, published by Hollywood Player Roll Co.

Humana - *See* **Standard.**

Hupfeld Animatic – Made by Hupfeld & Co, Leipzig

Duophonola
Dea
Phonola
Triphonola

Ideal. Made in New York City by Plaza Music Co.

Ideal - *See* **Rose Valley.**

Ideal (Spain)

Imperial. Hand-played rolls by Imperial Player Roll Co. Unlike normal rolls, these were called 'records'.

Autochord
Automatic Electric [Recordo coded]
Boston Store
Dalian (for Crowley players)
Diamond
Fairview
Hit
Linenised (British)
Lyric
Marionette (Recordo)

Recordo
Red Star
Rialto
Rothchild
Solo Carola
Symphony
Welte Special

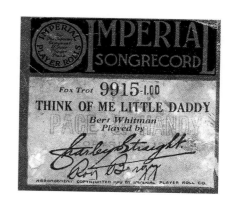

Imperial Linenised. Rolls made by the Perforated Music Co, London.

Inst-ar-Roll

International Made by International, Brooklyn, New York. Name and this address on roll tag. Self apron with printed label reading 'International' and duplicating that on the roll box]. Box is covered with black fabric-grained paper bearing repeated scroll cartouches with the brand name. 88-notes. Concert Series

Expression Piano [Recordo coded]
Majestic
Melotone
Pennant
Sublime

Italian Book Co., New York - *See* **Connorized.**

Italian Music Roll. Rolls made in New York by Artista

Italianstyle. Music rolls made by Paramount, New York, USA

I.X.L. Music rolls made by the short-lived I.X.L Company of Philadelphia.

Jazz Rags. Popular rolls introduced in 1916 by Imperial Player Roll Company.

JazzMaster. Modern piano rolls of piano jazz made in Britain during the 1980s.

JazzMan. Modern label for jazz and ragtime piano music.

Jewel - *See Plaza Music*

Juelg

Kastonome. Made by Kastner, London.

Kegg Organ Builders. Modern re-cut 176-note rolls for the Duo-Art Reproducing Pipe Organ by Kegg of Ohio.

Keynote - *See Musicnote Roll Company.*

Keystone. Present-day recuts of Ampico and Duo-Art music made in Pennsylvania by Keystone Music Roll Co.

Kilgen. Special music rolls made by Kilgen Organ Co of St Louis for Kilgen Dual Control pipe organ only.

Kimball

Kimball Electramatic - *See* **Q.R.S.**

Klavier. Modern rolls, especially reproducing piano re-cuts, made by Mr and Mrs Powell in California.

Klean Kut

Landay- Piano rolls for Landay Brothers made by Q-R-S.

Lauter - *See* **American Piano Co.**

Le Due Sicilie. Italian song rolls made in New York. Maker unknown.

Leabarjan. Generally home-made piano rolls made on a home-perforating machine marketed by the Leabarjan Mfg Co Hamilton, Ontario. It is believed the company may also have produced piano rolls at some time: several 'special' rolls have been found that bear signs of factory production rather than amateur effort.

L'EMP Music rolls made in Paris by L'Edition Musicale Perforée

Linenized - *See* **Imperial.**

L'Insuperable - *See* **Connorized.**

Little Gem

Little Wonder

Lyric - *See* **Imperial.**

Madrid (Spanish)
 Oriental

Majestic - *See* **International.**

Majestic - *See* **Pianostyle.**

Malcolm Libraries Ltd Name seen on music rolls manufactured by Malcolm in London.

Marionette. Recordo encoded music rolls. - *See* **Imperial.**

Marvel

Master - Made by Altoona Music Roll Co.

Master Record - *See* **National.**

Mastertouch. Music rolls made in Australia by Mastertouch.

Medcraft. Quality reproducing roll re-cuts made in England by Harry & Sylvia Medcraft.

Mel-O-Art

MelOdee Expression Roll. Recordo coded, made by Mel-O-dee.

MelOdee. Quality 88-note jazz roll recuts made *c.*1960 by Givens-Gourley, Inc.

Mel-O-Dee - *See* **Aeolian.**

Melographic. Music rolls made by The Melographic Roll Co, NY.

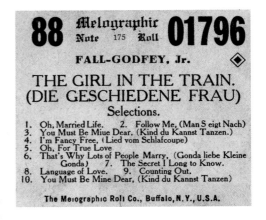

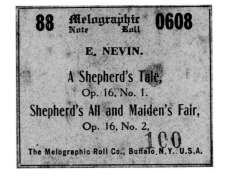

Meloto. Rolls introduced in January 1925 by Aeolian's Universal Music Co Ltd subsidiary. Early rolls were marked The Meloto Co Ltd.

Meloto (in Standard, Dance and word-rolls for singing to) - *See* **Universal.**

Melotone - *See* **International.**

Mendelssohn. Made in Boston, Massachusetts, by Mendelssohn Music Co.

Metro - *See* **Atlas Player Roll Co.**

Metro-Art – Piano rolls made by Aeolian/Universal

Metronamic - *See* **Universal**.

Metrostyle - *See* **Aeolian.**

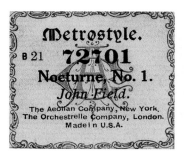 

Metrostyle - *See* **Universal.**

Mignon

MM & Co –Music rolls by Malcolm, London.

Mongillo Special ['Copyrighted 1918'] Made in New York by Antonio Mongillo

Monarch. Music rolls made in Australia by Anglo-American Player Roll Co.

Mono - *See* **Rose Valley.**

Musical Specialties

Music Box

Music Note

    Famous Marches

    Keynote

Muvis. Made by Mukle & Davis Ltd (The Up-To-Date Music Roll Co). Wholesaler: G F Baker & Co Ltd, London.

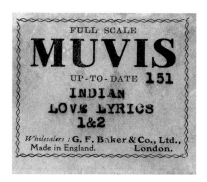

National Music Roll Made by National Music Roll Co, New York.

    Auto Inscribed

    Hand Played

    Master

    Peerless Rolls

National Automatic Music

N.B.S. - *See* **Connorized.**

New-Phono. Music rolls made in Barcelona, Spain, by **New-Phono.**

Niagara Music Co. 198, Terrace Street, Buffalo, New Jersey.

Octave [Oktave] Organ Rolls (88-note piano-type rolls for all 88-note players). Provided with organ registration instructions. Cut by Play-Rite and also on yellow paper by QRS of Buffalo for Mike L Walter, 488 Fredericka Street, North Tonawanda, New York, 14120. High quality 1980s production concentrating on serious, classical titles from the organ world.

Omnia. Piano rolls made in London by Perforated Music. Same label as rolls made for Gamage's Store.

Onix (Equador)

Orient

Oriental - *See* **Madrid.**

Original

> Anton Mervar

Original-Künstler-Notenrolle – Handgespielte. Music rolls made by Blohut, Meissner & Co of Leipzig.

Orpheum - *See* **Columbia-Capitol.**

Orpheus. Music rolls made in Britain and sold under the name of The Roll Music Co Ltd.

Otto Higel Made in Canada by **Higel.**

Pagano

Palazzolo

P.A.M.P.A. (Perfuracion Argentina Musical Para Autopiano, Argentina)

Paramount

> Alector (Greece)

Parex. Music rolls made in London by David Mundell.

Pasquale Music Roll

> Autografo

Passaro, Frank - *See* **Schettino.**

Peerless Rolls - *See* **National.**

Pennant - *See* **International.**

Pennino, F. Rolls made by **Connorized** for music dealer Francesco Pennino in Brooklyn. Believed the same as Russo's Music Roll, also labeled as Brooklyn-based.

P.E.P. - *See* **United stateS.**

Perfecta (Standard, Accentuated) – Music rolls made by Aeolian subsidiary **Universal** for sale in France under the Perfecta label. Perfecta was run by René Savoye from 5 Avenue de l'Opera, Paris, with a factory at 51 Avenue Gallieni, Bagnolet (Seine).

Perfecta Muziekrol. Piano-orchestrion rolls made by Beckx-de la Fai of Tegelen, The Netherlands.

Perfection. Music rolls made in Orange, New Jersey, by Standard Music Roll Co Also made for Murdoch, Murdoch & Co.

Perforetur. Modern music roll label produced in East Sussex by Perforetur Music Rolls (Michael Boyd)

Phantom Player. Made by Universal and relabeled for Phantom Players Ltd of London. Glazed red linen apron.

Philag. Well-made music rolls made in Bayern, Germany, by Philipps A-G Piano-u Orgelwerke, roll-making subsidiary of the main J D Philipps company in Frankfurt am Main.

Phoneon – Player reed organ rolls made for Malcolm & Co.

Phonola - *See* **Hupfeld.**

Phonoliszt-Violina. Music rolls for the combined piano and violins made by Hupfeld.

Pianist. Music rolls produced for William Spaethe, Berlin & Gera.

Pianola - *See* **Aeolian.**

Pianola Audiographic - *See* **Aeolian.**
Pianolist's Library - *See* **Aeolian.**
Pianostyle (88-note, plain apron with adhesive label. Made in Brooklyn, NY.)
    Expression Piano [Recordo coded]
    Hand Played
    Majestic

Pianostyle. Music rolls made in London by David Mundell.

Picturoll - *See* **Filmusic.**

Play-a-Roll - *See* **Standard.**

Play-Rite. Piano rolls made by the Play-Rite Music Rolls in California.

Playtime. New 58-note organ, 65 and 88-note piano rolls made in England by Laguna.

Playrite - *See* **Staffnote.**

Plaza Music
    Ideal
    Jewel
    Winner

Powell. Ampico and Duo-Art re-cuts made in California by Klavier Music Rolls. *See also* **Klavier.**

P-O-P - *See* **Filmusic.**

Precision. Made in California, USA, by Precision Music Rolls. Current specialist in recut Ampico reproducing rolls.

Premier - *See* **Rose Valley.**

Princesa. Music rolls made in Barcelona, Spain, by Moya Hermanos.

Purple - *See* **Welte-Mignon.**

Q.R.S. – Made by the Q.R.S Company
    Aria Divina Reproducing
    Arranged
    Artecho
    Autograph
    Autograph Hand Played
    Automatic
    Bluebird Series
    Concert Series [decoded Artecho]
    Kimball Electramatic
    Recordo]Recordo coded]
    Red Star (green and white label, red star central top), Dating from 1923.
    Rythmodik
    Solo Elle
    Story Roll (large blue label; QRS-copyrighted 1918; roll with brief introductory text & running story)
    Temposet
    Tempographic

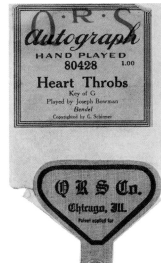

RagMaster. Modern piano rolls of piano jazz made in Britain during the 1980s by The Piano Roll Co.

Ray-Dio - *See* **Atlas Player Roll Co.**

Recordo - *See* **Gulbransen** [Recordo coded].

Recordo - *See* **Imperial** [Recordo coded].

Recordo - Five-level expression rolls made by **Q.R.S.**

Recordo - *See* **Vocalstyle** [Recordo coded].

Recordo - *See* **Wurlitzer** [Recordo coded].

Red. 'Welte Red' is a collector's term for the original, wide-paper reproducing piano rolls made by Welte in Germany. They are punched in red paper. - *See also* **Welte-Mignon.**

Red Label Hand Played - *See* **Wurlitzer.**

Red Seal - *See* **Columbia-Capitol**.

Red Star - *See* **Imperial.**

Regal. Music rolls made in Australia by Anglo-American Player Roll Co.

Regent. This was the brand name used for dance and ballad-song rolls with words made by Wilcox & White as a second brand to its main Artistyle label. Regent Dance and Regent Song rolls were subsequently produced in England by Aeolian/Universal and Handled by The Marshall Piano Company Ltd of Orchard Street, Oxford Street.

Regent Dance. Rolls made by the Universal Music Co for the Artistyle Company of Sir Herbert Marshall Ltd.

Regent Song - *See* **Regent.**

Republic
     Acme

R.G.S. - *See* **Gloria.**

Rialto - *See* **Imperial.**

Ritz - *See* **Atlas Player Roll Co.**

Rolla Artis. Name used by Wurlitzer, associated with Paul Zacharias, probably made by Josef Blohut in Leipzig.

Rollo Mexico (Mexican)

Rollos Nacionales (Mexican)

Rose Valley. Made by Rose Valley Music Co of Philadelphia, USA.
     Ideal
     Mono
     Premier

Recording Roll [Recordo coded]
     Unico (Italian)

Rolla Artis

Rothchild - *See Imperial*

Royal

Rushworth & Dreaper. Brand of piano rolls made for department store by Aeolian/Imperial.

Russo's Music Roll. Rolls made in New York by Connorized for Brooklyn-based music dealer. Believed the same as Francesco Pennino

Rythmodik - *See* **American Piano Co.**

Rythmodik - *See* **Q.R.S.**

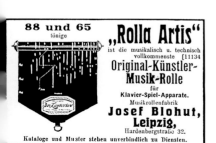

S.M. Full-scale hand-played music-rolls made by **Felix Schüller of** Leipzig from 1930 onwards. These are believed to include 'hand-played' renderings created from Welte-Mignon reproducing rolls without the Mignon expression codings. Welte themselves never made ordinary 88-note rolls.

S & P. Music rolls made in London by Siggitson & Perkins Company.

Savoia

Schettino. Made in New York by Schettino Music Roll Co. 'Copyrighted by Schettino'. Pressed brass-coloured roll ends. Low serial numbers, looks Italian. Sold by 'Frank Passaro, 2091 First Ave. bet: 107th and 108th streets, New York.' Numbers seen: 'Lettera a Mamma' [110]; 'Telefonando' [115]; 'Maria Roas' [123]; 'Voce e Mamma' [124] suggesting but a small catalogue.

Selected - *See* **Baker & Co.**
Serenata
Serenate
Sherman-Clay (custom accompaniment rolls) Sherman Clay & Co
Simplex - *See* **Atlas Player Roll Co.**

Singa - *See* **Standard.**

Sir Herbert Marshall. Rolls made for this player-piano maker by Aeolian/Universal.

Solo Carola. Hand-played by Imperial Player Roll Co. Unlike normal rolls, these were called 'records'.

Solo Elle. Hand-Played music rolls marked SOLO*ELLE* and made by Q.R.S.

Solodant - 88-note made by Otto Higel, Canada

Solostyle - *See* **American Piano Co.**
Southport. Modern hand-played music rolls made by Malcolm Robinson, Southport, England.
Splendor
Staffnote. Made by Billings Player Roll Company, Milwaukee.

Hitz
Playrite

Standard

Arto (Artist's Own)
Electra
Full Scale 88 Note
Humana
Perfection
Play-a-Roll
Singa
Voco

Starck (made by Imperial)

Stark Made by the Capitol Roll & Record Company - *See* **Columbia-Capitol.**
Starr
Sterling. Made by the Capitol Roll & Record Company - *See* **Columbia-Capitol.**
Story Roll - *See* **Q.R.S.**
Sublime Quality early range of operatic rolls with words. Roll lettered and priced in Italian. Self apron with borderless white label with bold brand name in red. Sold at $1.50. - *See* **International.**

Superba - Made by Altoona Music Roll Co.
Superrolls

Supertone Made for Sears & Roebuck by Capitol Roll & Record Company - *See* **Columbia-Capitol**

Supertone - *See* **United stateS.**
Suprema Golden Tube - *See* **Murdoch, Murdoch & Co.**
Supreme - *See* **Atlas Player Roll Co.**
Symphony - *See* **Imperial.**

Symphonia. Music rolls made in Anvers, Belgium, by Eug De Roy.
Synchronized. Made by the Capitol Roll & Record Company - *See* **Columbia-Capitol.**

Tempographic - *See* **Q.R.S.**
Tempola. Modern player-piano rolls newly-made by Tempola Music Rolls, Missouri, USA.
Temponome. Special version of American Piano Company Rythmodik roll made for Kastner. Followed the early style of the American original roll in that it produced a 'third-pedal' interpretation, long perforations allowing notes to sing out in sympathetic vibration. *See* **Aristo.**

Temposet - *See* **Q.R.S.**
Tesio Special
Themodist – Piano rolls made by Aeolian/Universal and bearing Themodist markings.

Themodist Metrostyle - Piano rolls made by Aeolian/Universal and bearing Themodist and Metrostyle markings.

Themostyle
Trionfol. Made in France
Triphonola - Reproducing roll made by Hupfeld for Triphonola pianos. Originally Animatic T.

Triumph - Piano rolls made by Aeolian/Universal.
Triumph. Music rolls made by Kastner.
Triumph (Standard, Word Roll) - Piano rolls made by Aeolian/Universal.
Triumph - *See* **Dominant.**

Uke Roll - *See* **Connorized.**
Unico - *See* **Rose Valley.**
Uni-Record - *See* **Aeolian.**
Uni-Record - *See* **Universal.**

Uni-Solo. - *See* **Aeolian.**
Unisolo. Music rolls together with DeLuxe brand produced in Philadelphia, Pennsylvania, by unknown maker that operated in 1916.
United stateS [U.S]. Music rolls made in Chicago by United States Music Company. Roll boxes blind stamped 'The Roll of Honor'.
    Auto Art [Recordo coded]
    Emblem
    P.E.P.
    Supertone
Universal. Wide range of music rolls including Accentuated, hand-played, song roll, standard, and Uni-Record. Company owned by Aeolian. Manufactured very wide range of rolls for a number

of different instruments (including the Aeolian Orchestrelle), outlets and labels. Rolls made include the following branded products:

    Aeolian Grand (for the Orchestrelle 58-note player organ)
    Aeolian Piano
    Aeolian Song Roll
    Audiographic (for Duo-Art and ordinary 88-note player piano)
    Duo-Art (reproducing)
    Hand Played
    Meloto (in Standard, Dance and word-rolls for singing to)
    Metro-Art
    Metronamic
    Metrostyle
    Themodist
    Uni-Record
    Autoplayer (Standard, Accentuated, word-rolls)
    Broadwood [player-piano makers] (Standard, Accentuated)
    Harrods [department store] (Standard, Accentuated)
    Sir Herbert Marshall (Artist Song Roll, Artistyle, Regent Song, Regent Dance)
    Perfecta (Standard, Accentuated)
    Triumph (Standard, Word Roll)
    Universal (Accentuated, Handplayed, Song Roll, Standard, Uni-Record).

Upright and Grand. Piano rolls by Eric D Bernhoft of San Francisco.

U.S. - *See* **United stateS.**

U.T.D.

Venus. Italian song rolls made in New York for the Venus Music Company of Brooklyn. Maker unknown.

Verdi. Giudice Special

Veri's Victor. Piano rolls made by Dellazoppa & Morixe, Montevideo, Uruguay.

Victoria/Victoria Popular. Music rolls made in Barcelona, Spain by Juan Battista Blancafort.

Victoria. Music rolls made in Milan, Italy, by Schöne & Bocchese.

Victoria-BEst Spanish-made piano rolls handled in Britain by Kastner.

Victory – Made by Altoona Music Roll Co.

Virtuolo Solo Roll. For Hallet & Davis Piano Co's Solo-Virtuolo expression piano. Boxes are in dark purple with bright red labels. Punched by Aeolian.

Virtuoso

Vocalist - *See* **F.I.R.S.T**

Vocalstyle

    Home Recital Series [Recordo coded]
    J. Donat Langelier Recordo [Recordo coded]
    Reproducing [Recordo coded]
    Reproduco [Recordo coded]

Voco - *See* **Standard.**

Voltem. Hand-played music rolls made by **Wilcox & White**. 'The Music Roll De Luxe'. 'Reg. U.S. Pat. *Off.*'

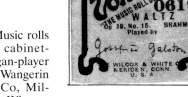

Wangerin. Music rolls for the cabinet-style organ-player built by Wangerin Organ Co, Milwaukee, Wisconsin, which were in the main for use in funeral parlours where a regular organist was not available. Not for pianos.

Weile Special - *See* **Imperial.**

Welte-Mignon. De Luxe Reproducing Roll Corp, NY.

  De Luxe

    Licensee. New York-made rolls for American-designed Welte-Mignon (Licensee) action.

    Green. German-made rolls for Freiburg-designed Welte-Mignon revised action.

    Purple Seal. New York-made rolls for American-designed Welte-Mignon (Licensee) action.

    Red. Original wide rolls for 'red' Welte actions made in both Freiburg and New York

Whiteleys. Branded music rolls made by Perforated Music in London.

Wilcox & White. Music rolls made by Wilcox & White of Meriden, Connecticut, USA. *See* Voltem.

  Angelus Melodant Artistyle

  Artrio

Willert, Chas. L.

Winner. Made in New York City by Plaza Music Co.

Wissner - *See* **Atlas Player Roll Co.**

Wurlitzer. Music rolls made in Cincinnati, Ohio, by The Rudolph Wurlitzer Manufacturing Company.

  Recordo (Treasure Chest of Music)

  Red Label Hand Played

  Rolla Artis - *See also* Josef Blohut in makers' listing

Yamaha Music Rolls. Piano rolls made in the early 1920s by Nippon Gakki, Hamamatsu, Japan. Trade-mark is three tuning-forks crossed to form a six-pointed 'star' with the central fork handle at the top.

The Makers

A B Consumers Music Co, Station C, Buffalo, New York, USA. Makers of piano-rolls.

Ackotist Player Piano Company, Fall River, Massachusetts, USA. Makers of piano-playing actions. Also made piano rolls for the Ackotist system. *Fl.*1907.

Aeolian Company, The, Aeolian Hall, 689 Fifth Avenue, New York, USA. Makers of the Duo-Art and other music rolls. In January 1915 Aeolian began issuing regular Duo-Art Bulletins to deal exclusively with these music-rolls which, at that time, were being published at about ten a month. The last one produced came out in September 1927. Within the first of these little magazines is the telling remark that 'a comprehensive catalogue of 100 rolls has preceded this Bulletin.' In the autumn of 1925, launched the 'Authors' Roll' which included on the apron the printed words of the song complete with descriptive text. During the 1930s, Aeolian experienced a serious fire after which the business was combined with the American Piano Company. In the course of manufacturing economies brought about by the amalgamation, very late Duo-Art rolls were actually printed with Ampico labels. Curiously, after the effective demise of the parent company, the British subsidiary, long-since an autonomous operation, survived much longer. Aeolian Company Ltd was based at Hayes with its London headquarters at the Aeolian Hall, New Bond Street. Music rolls were manufactured by Universal Music Company [qv], a business controlled by Aeolian. It survived World War II and was finally wound up in the 1950s.

Aeolian Company, The, 24 avenue del Conde de Peñalver, Madrid, Spain. Manufacturer of music rolls, listed in 1930 directories.

Aeolian Company, The, 66 rue La Boëtie, Paris, France. Manufacturer of music rolls listed in 1930 directories. This address is immediately adjacent to the premises of L'Édition Musicale Perforée [qv].

A K OK Music Roll Manufacturing Company, 322 E 70th St, New York City, USA. Manufacturers of music rolls listed in 1930 directories.

Altoona Music Roll Company, Altoona and Lansdale, Pennsylvania, USA. Founded in 1919. Makers of 'Victory' instrumental, 'Superba' and 'Master' word rolls. Distributed by Victory Music Stores Co, Victory Building, 35th Street at 7th Avenue, New York, 1035 Chestnut Street, Philadelphia, Pennsylvania, and 1603 Pitkin Avenue, Brooklyn, New York.

American 'Automusic' Company, 53 Broadway, New York City, USA. Made music rolls for the Encore Automatic Banjo, *fl.*1900-1903. Managed by a man called Andrews, superintendent of the factory was a Mr Conrou. President was a Mr O'Connor. Became the Connorized Roll Company [qv].

American Piano Company, 437 Fifth Avenue, New York City, USA. Manufacturers of pianos and also the Ampico reproducing piano. Makers of Rythmodik Record Music Rolls. In May of 1911, the company announced plans to produce hand-played rolls under a licensing agreement with Hupfeld Ltd and by that September American Piano was producing its own rolls of this style. These were to be called 'Regular Artigraphic' for use on any normal 88-note player, and 'Special Artigraphic' only to be used on the Artigraphic Player. This player piano was to become the Ampico and its special rolls were renamed Rythmodik. Registration for this trademark was January 5th 1912, the first advertisements for the rolls coming a month or two later. At the middle of 1912, the Rythmodik music roll catalogue listed some 150 rolls played by top pianists of the era such as Busoni, Bauer, Grieg and Brockway. By 1914 this total had risen to 600. The rolls made use of extensions to perforations that allowed what the makers called 'singing tones' and this development was the subject of a 1911 patent. In May of 1918, American Piano Co absorbed the business and closed it down, selling the remaining roll stock to Q-R-S. It then went on to produce the Ampico rolls on former Rythmodik machinery. All Ampico music rolls produced between 1912 and the end of 1920 appear to have counterparts with Rythmodik labels. According to Richard Howe, though, the converse is not true: less than 40 percent of the recordings first issued as Rythmodik music rolls were also issued for the Ampico. One series of rolls prominently marked with the initials APC and transcribed as American Piano Control. *See also under* Rythmodik Music Corporation.

Amphion Player Piano Company, 437 Fifth Avenue, New York, New York City, USA. Maker of music rolls listed in 1930 directories.

Ampico Corporation, 27 West 57th Street, New York City, USA. American Piano Corporation division. Maker of music rolls listed in 1930 directories.

Anglo-American Player Roll Company, Solway Buildings, 112, Johnson Street, Fitzroy, Victoria, Australia. Established in 1921 by Lennard Earl Max Luscombe (b.1894; d.1957). Manufactured player-piano rolls under the label Broadway and the slogan 'For better musical arrangements'. Also used roll names Monarch and Regal. Luscombe, described as a child-prodigy, became conductor and arranger for the Majestic Theatre Orchestra in Melbourne when he was only 18 years old. After visiting the United States and touring many of the major music-roll manufacturers, he realized his vocation and decided to bring music-roll making into Australia. He almost certainly made the first piano-rolls in Australia initially using brown wrapping paper, the music laid out by hand and cut with a penknife. Later he imported roll-making machinery from America including an electric punching machine that was described as state of the art. After Luscombe's death the business was continued by his partner, Charles Urquart, who had joined the firm in 1924. In 1958, Urquart sold the business to the son of rival Australian roll-maker Mastertouch's founder, George H Horton, and the inventory was transferred to Sydney.

Apollo Company Ltd, The, 233 Tottenham Court Road, London, W. Makers of music rolls for the Clark-Apollo. *Fl.*1906-1910.

Artcraft Music Rolls, PO Box 295, Wiscasset, ME 04578, USA. Makers of new piano rolls, *c.*1995. As well as recuts there are also interpretations of more modern composers' music. Duo-Art recuts have, in some instances, been given revised dynamic markings which in general have tended to diminish their value as authentic recordings. This address is also that of *The Pianola Quarterly* the editor of which is L Douglas Henderson.

Artista. *Name seen but no further details.*

Artistyle Music Roll Library, 18a Orchard Street, Oxford Street, London, W1. *See under* The Marshall Piano Company, Ltd.

Artona Music Rolls Ltd, 14 Vale Square, Ramsgate, Kent. Described as successors to the Universal Music Company Ltd. Artona music rolls were produced by Gordon Iles, formerly of the Aeolian Company where he worked as inventor, designer, theoretician, etc. Iles ran the business cutting rolls on an old Aeolian roll puncher which he modified to suit his own needs. Production began soon after the Second World War and ceased shortly before Iles's death in about 1978. Artona rolls were straight 88-note and there were also copies of Duo-Arts, including the test roll. Not generally considered a high-quality roll.

Atelier Musical, 63 Chausée de Waterloo, St Servais B-5002, Belgium. Makers of new rolls of popular music under the label ArMaN.

Atlas Player Roll Company, General Office and Factory: 35-37 Fifth Street, Newark, New Jersey, USA. Also branch at 219 South Tenth Street, Philadelphia, Pennsylvania, AND 246 Stuart Street, Boston, Massachusetts. Makers of Atlas Player Piano Rolls and A-R Player Rolls. *Music Trade Review* for October 24th 1925 reported that 'all of its popular word rolls, commencing

with November releases, will contain a new open square cut'. Atlas sales manager J C Fonner asserted that 'the new open cut roll induces additional power through the pneumatics in sluggish player-pianos and makes them act instantly'. The square holes, apparently, allowed instantaneous and full opening of the tracker-bar openings. By 1929 Atlas was also exclusive distributor for Vocalion records manufactured by the Brunswick-Balke-Collender Co. Still active in 1930s.

Autoplayer Piano Company, 120, Albert Street, Slough, Berkshire, England. Enterprise founded in the 1980s by Paul Young and Stephen Brown. Makers of Ambassador label rolls cut on perforating machinery based on equipment originally belonging to Artona at Ramsgate. Young was killed by a piano he was delivering in his van when it broke loose in a road accident in December 1988. Company continued under the name of Apollo. *See also under* British Autoplayer.

Auto Pneumatic Action Company, 653 W 51st Street, New York City, USA. Maker of music rolls for the Welte-Mignon (Licensee) under brand name Auto De Luxe Welte-Mignon. The company was formed around 1920 at 619-629 West 50th Street. Its president in 1924 was William J Keeley: by 1928 it had moved as above and the president was W C Heaton. The foot-operated Welte-Mignon (Licensee) piano was launched by the company at the end of 1926. *See also under* Kohler Industries *in Appendix 2.*

Automatic Music Roll Company, 1510 Dayton Street, Chicago, USA. Owned by Seeburg. Founded *c.*1920 at the time Q.R.S ceased making Seeburg rolls. Company did not, however, punch its own rolls these were done for it by the Clark Orchestra Roll Company. Automatic ceased business in the late 1920s according to Bowers, yet was still listed in 1930 directories. *See also:*

Auto Pneumatic Action Company, P.O. Box 3194 Seattle, Washington, 98114, USA. Music rolls copying business set up by Frank Adams in 1970s to specialize in reproducing roll re-cuts. Business operated for about 10 years.

Automusic Perforating Company, 53 Broadway, New York, USA. Makers of music rolls. James O'Connor was president.

Bacigalupo, G, Finnländische Strasse 13, Berlin N.113, Germany. Maker of Excelsior music rolls for electric player pianos. Traded under the name of under 'Excelsior' –Notenrollenfabrik, *fl.*1925. By 1930 was listed at 71a Schönhauser Allee (also 79), Berlin. Also made street, show and dance-organs.

Baker & Company, Ltd, G F, Xaltona House, Leeke Street Corner, King's Cross Road, London WC1. Established 1897, this sundries house advertised in January 1932 that they had been appointed wholesale distributors for Meloto and Universal Player Rolls. The company already distributed Muvis rolls made by the Up-to-Date Music Roll Co. These full-scale rolls classified as dance, popular and classic, sold at 2s 6d each with a tester at the same price. Meloto and Universals were classified at this time as dance, song and classic at 3s, 4s 6d and 5s 6d each. Baker's infor mation leaflet on converting a 65-note piano to play 88-note rolls ran into a fourth reprint as late as the early part of 1936. At that last stage the company reported that its sales of Muvis and Universal rolls were holding up well. This company's name appears prominently on the roll boxes and might be mistaken for that of a maker.

Beck, W Adolf, Hirschstr 52, Karlsruhe, Baden, Germany. Supplier of paper and cardboard for both music rolls and orchestrion music. In 1909, advertised as also a producer of music rolls.

Beckx-de la Fai, Spoorstraat C.14, Tegelen (Limburg), The Netherlands. Importer and distributor of piano-orchestrions. Maker of 'Perfecta' music rolls for roll-playing piano-orchestrions.

Bennett & White, Inc, 67-71 Goble Street, Newark, New Jersey, USA. Began business in 1913. Advertised in 1920 as makers of the Artempo Word Roll. The slogan was 'Music as actually played'.

Benrath & Frank, Duren-Mariaweiler, Germany. Manufacturer of paper and board for perforated music roll manufacturing.

Bernhoft, Eric D, PO Box 421101, San Francisco 94142, USA. Modern player rolls under the label 'Upright and Grand'.

Billings Player Roll Company, Milwaukee, Wisconsin, USA. Established in 1921 and founded by Fred C Billings, a prominent figure in the player industry. Makers of 'Staffnote' music rolls.

Blancafort, Juan Battista, Rambla de Cataluna 7, La Garriga, Barcelona, Spain. Founded in 1905, Blancafort was to become Spain's largest manufacturer of piano rolls, both 65- and 88-note, turning out large quantities for export throughout Europe. Produced rolls under the Victoria brand name. Curiously the address was also that of Augustin Guarro *[qv]*, described as a music-roll manufacturer and associated with the Victoria-brand rolls. Supplied rolls for distribution in London by Kastner Autopiano which issued an English-language catalogue in March of 1925. Although the company advertised music by the classical composers, from the theatre, and from modern dance, almost all the Victoria-brand rolls that have been seen were of popular Spanish music. Production was divided into two main categories – metrically-cut rolls selling at six Pesetas, and Cantor (hand-played) rolls at seven Pesetas. Still in business in 1930. Rolls characterized by having oval perforations. During the early 1920s introduced a second brand using a similarly-themed roll label using the name of 'Best'. These were all 88-note

Blohut, Meissner & Co, Moltkestr. 80, H, Leipzig, Germany. Established in 1907 by Josef Blohut, Hugo Meissner and Felix Schüller to manufacture music rolls made under the label Original-Künstler-Notenrolle and usually marked Handgespielte. Produced a large number of rolls for distribution in England and having markings and titles in English. The business appeared to flourish but seems not to have survived the First World War. By 1930, Josef Blohut was listed at 11 Naumburger Str, Leipzig, where he was manufacturing music rolls in a small way.

BluesTone Music Rolls, 485 Gatewood Lane, Grayslake, Illinois 60030, USA. Modern makers (1988) of piano rolls specializing in jazz and ragtime recuts but also Duo-Art, Welte Licensee and Ampico rolls. Labelled Front Porch. Operated by Rob DeLand.

Bol, Joseph, 61 rue d'Angleterre, Brusselles, Belgium. Advertised as makers of piano rolls *c.*1930.

Braiterman-Fedder-Company, Mel-O-Art Division, Brafco Building, 414-416 E Pratt Street, Baltimore, Maryland, USA. Makers of the Mel-O-Art Player Roll. Still listed in 1930 directories.

British Autopiano Company: Makers of Maestrel. No further details. Uncertain as to whether this was a piano or music roll name.

British Autoplayer Company, Ltd, The, 126 New Bond Street, London W1.

British Autoplayer Company, 126 New Bond Street, London, W. Produced 65-note music rolls until the mid-1920s.Retailer of music rolls that appear to have been produced by Universal: the labels are almost identical as is the label paper. *Fl.*1928.

Broadmoor Research Corporation, 1709 First Street, Unit C, San Fernando, California 91340, USA. Makers of a device called The Power Roll that claimed to convert any player-piano into an electronically-operated roll-free performer so that the instrument might be played without music-rolls. Fitting into the existing spool-box, the Power Roll had a CD-based library of 450 Ampico rolls or could be fitted with a MIDI interface.

Broadwood, John, Conduit Street, London, W. Founded in 1723, the house of Broadwood is famed an a piano-maker. Once it began making player pianos, it also branded its 'own' music rolls. Furthermore the company operated its own roll library. All rolls were produced by Aeolian and re-labelled. Broadwood seems to have discontinued its own roll branding before the outbreak of the First World War.

Capitol Roll & Record Company, 721 North Kedzie Avenue, Chicago, USA. Shared premises with the Operators Piano Company and was a subsidiary of Operators who made the Coinola and Reproduco instruments. Began life pre-1924 as the Columbia Music Roll Company at 22 South Peoria Street, Chicago. In 1924, was re-named and re-located as the Capitol Roll and Record Co. Ceased trading *c.*1934. Trademark was the letters CMC in a circular motif. Produced rolls under labels Columbia (*c.*1920-24), American, Capitol, Cecile, Challenge, Stark, Sterling; Supertone (made for Sears & Roebuck); and Synchronized.

Chase Company, A B, 86 Fifth Avenue, Norwalk, Ohio, USA. Founded by A B Chase in 1875. After his death just two years later, the business was run by Calvin Whitney who was among the first to take up the player piano. Makers of Duplex player action followed soon afterwards by the Artistano. In the 1920s, the Chase business was amalgamated into the United Piano Corporation set up by Chase at its Norwalk premises. Produced the Celco.

Chase & Baker Company: Buffalo, New York, USA. Makers of the Chase & Baker 'lint paper' music rolls 'for Standard (65 note) Piano Players' [1907]. Branch of the Chase & Baker Company of 209 State Street, Chicago, Illinois, USA. Makers of piano players and music rolls, *fl.*1909. London branch as:

Chase & Baker Piano Player Company Ltd: 45/47 Wigmore Street, London, W Manufacturers and suppliers of music rolls.

Choralion Company, mbH: Bergstrasse 34, Berlin N.4, Germany. Also at Bellevuestrasse 4, Berlin W.9. German branch of Aeolian Company *[qv]*. The business seems to have got its rolls from London, relabelling product from The Orchestrelle Company. It is also believed that some rolls were made by the German branch of Editions Musicales Perforees being in most cases the semi-handplayed EMP ('S.M.') arrangements although carrying the British Themodist number. Choralion may have added their own Metrostyle line to suit.

Cigna, Fratelli, Biella (Novara), Italy. The Cigna Brothers were musical instrument distributors who also marketed their own branded nicely-turned-out 88-note piano rolls during the late 1920s and early 1930s spoiled only by rather poor punching in a coarse straw paper. Rolls marked Cigna.

Clark Collector's Classics, 163, Main Street, Thomaston, Maine 04861, USA. Modern operation making quality re-cuts of 1920s dance-music.

Clark Orchestra Roll Company, 131 Second Street, De Kalb, Illinois, USA. Founded in 1920 by Ernest G Clark who was at that time in charge of the coin-operated roll division of the Q.R.S company. Ernest Clark was the brother of Melville Clark, player piano pioneer and original founder of the Q-R-S company. Made all rolls for Nelson-Wiggen Piano Company. During 1930s the business made pipe-organ player rolls for an action that controlled an instrument having 65 stops (registers). These, provided with a green label, were marked 'Standard Pipe Organ Recordings'. Also made a roll named 'Artistouch' for a cinema organ. Clark remained in business until the early 1940s when the machinery was acquired by Roesler-Hunholz in Milwaukee, Wisconsin. For some reason, the new owners never collected their purchase and the machinery, together with all the master rolls, was eventually scrapped. *See* Automatic Music Roll Company.

Colley's Patents, Limited, 3-12 Marine Street, London, SE. Manufacturers of piano rolls in business *c.*1908. On April 15th that year, the business advertised rolls at prices between 1/- and 4/- [$0.20 - $0.80] with the notice: 'These rolls are manufactured by us under our own Patents, and are British Manufacture throughout... We have a large number of 'top sheet rolls' the music of which is correct, but the perforations are not so clearly cut at the perfect Rolls, the price of these are 6d to 2s' $0.10 - $0.40].

Columbia Music Roll Company, 22 South Peoria Street, Chicago, Illinois, USA. Makers of the Columbia Music Roll which advertised as being 'The only truly synchronized word roll having the words printed exactly opposite their corresponding notes'. Company began c.1920 to supply rolls for the instruments of the Operators' Piano Company of which it was a subsidiary. In 1924 became the Capitol Roll and Record Company [qv]. A short-lived undertaking.

Columbus Music Roll Manufacturing Company Inc, New York City, USA. Maker of music rolls listed in 1930 directories.

Concordia-Notenrollenfabrik Grieshaber & Co, AG: Leipzig-Gohlis. Germany. In 1927 manufactured the Empeco roll and the 88-note rolls for the 'Jazzband-Instrumente' made by Schubert Fabrik für selbstspielende Musikinstrumente Chemnitz. In 1921, Concordia began production of Empeco rolls which, until 1919, had been made by a firm called Pude. Another maker of these rolls was Michael, Preuss [qv].

Connorized Music Company, 144th Street and Austin Place, New York City, USA. Piano roll manufacturers, listed in directories 1908-15, but probably operating until much later. By 1926 was known as Connorized Player Roll Company, 817-21 East 144th Street, New York City. At this time was advertising the 'Uke' Word Roll which 'enables anyone without knowledge of music to instantly play ukelele and banjo' using a piano roll with ukelele fingering pictographs on the left-hand side and words to the right. Price 75 cents each.

Connorized Player Roll Co, 817-21 East 144th Street, New York City, USA. Piano-roll manufacturers. In 1911 introduced a 'Special Concert Edition' of rolls comprising 'musically artistic arrangements for musically cultured people'. By 1913 they had launched 'The Connorized Concert Phrased Roll', a hand-played roll said to have 'won favour among musically cultured people for artistic superiority'. Roehl comments that by 1925 the company was reaching out for markets and claimed to have the largest selection of Italian songs and dances issued by any player roll company. Their catalogues of Polish, Bohemian, Lithuanian, Slavische, Hungarian, Jewish, Spanish and other national music was claimed by them to be the most complete on the market. In an endeavour to maintain the popular end of the market the company came up with an unusual combination roll called the 'Uke' Word Roll. This special type of piano roll incorporated not only words but also printed fingering to enable a person to accompany the music on a ukelele or banjo. These cost 75 cents each and, in a novel marketing move, people could apply for a free sample roll to try out.

Dale, Forty & Company Ltd, 80-83 New Street, Birmingham, with branches at 24 Promenade Villas, Cheltenham; High Street and Castle Arcade, Cardiff; 118 The Parade, Leamington; Market Place, Cirencester, Gloucestershire; 14 King Street, Stroud, Gloucestershire; King Edward's Road, Swansea; and Queen's Arcade, Wolverhampton. Dale, Forty was once a very large chain of instrument retailers founded in Cheltenham in the year 1800. One of the earliest of the dedicated stores, it expanded into the other locations shown above before 1909. By 1925, there was a London showrooms and head office at 106 Great Portland Street. It introduced the Dualano Music Roll, initially 65-note and possibly later 88-note rolls. The label referred to the name as 'registered' and described them as 'artist-read, tested and approved'. The label continued, saying 'obtainable only from the Sole Proprietors'. Whether they actually manufactured rolls is uncertain, but the rolls appear to have been made by the Perforated Music Roll Company and have the same slate-blue aprons with the title printed in the central circular cartouche.

Dastot, P, 19 rue Francois-Bonvin, Paris, France. Manufacturer of music rolls listed in 1930 directories.

De Luxe Reproducing Roll Corporation, 12th Avenue & 51st Street, New York City, USA. Originally at 653 West 51st Street. Subsidiary of the Auto Pneumatic Action Company, producers of the Welte-Mignon (Licensee) reproducing piano action whose New York City premises it shared. Still listed in 1930 directory. Welte-Mignon (Licensee) rolls were standard width music-rolls converted from the original wide red-paper rolls. Used the name DeLuxe.

Dellazoppa & Morixe, Plaza Independencia, 733, Montevideo, Uruguay, South America. Enrique Dellazoppa was in business prior to 1908 as a musical instrument and gramophone dealer. Music rolls bearing the label 'Rollo Victor' were marketed sometime in the 1920s bearing the legend: *Gran Premio y Medalla de Oro en la Exposition del Centenario de Durazno. Fabricado per la casa de musica.* The rolls may thus have been made in Spain and branded.

Deo Roll Company: *See reference under* Link Piano Company.

De Roy, Eugene, 20, Longue-Rue Pothoek, Anvers, Belgium. Manufacturer of piano rolls under the name 'The Symphonia'. Fl.1920-1939.

L'editions Musicales Perforees - *See reference under* Choralion and S&M. *Also:*

Edition Musicale Perforée, L', 64 rue La Boëtie, Paris, France. 'Editions Salabert, Francis-Day, etc'. Manufacturer of good quality piano rolls. Advertisement in 1930 directory carried the statement that 4,500 titles were [then] available. This address was immediately next door to that of the Aeolian Company in Paris.

Editorial Euterpe, PO Box 3144, Valparaiso, Chile. Listed as makers of piano rolls in 1930 directory.

Eerste Hollandsche Muziekrollen Fabriek, Keizersgracht 263, Amsterdam, The Netherlands. One of the centres for music-roll production in Europe was the Low Countries and soon after the First World War a man named L Rosenberg started a business which he called De Eerste Hollandsche Muzeikrollen Fabriek' ('The First Dutch Music-roll Factory'). All the rolls seen have been 88-note. The initials EHMF not only identified the rolls but also formed the trademark. Fl.1922-1932.

Eilers Music Company, 514, Market Street, San Francisco, California. Established in 1889 and became a major music and instrument outlet with branches in Eureka, Oakland, San José and Stockton. Major distributor of band organs, pianos, piano orchestrions, automatic violins and theatre organs. Offered branded music rolls but not believed to have manufactured. Heavily hit by Prohibition in 1920, sold its entire music-roll stock to Peter Bacigalupi of 1261 Market Street (nr Hotel Whitcomb), San Francisco. A Nevada area salesman for Eilers played a prominent part in establishing the theatre Fotoplayer business [6; p.369].

España Musical (S.A), calle Pizarro, Zaragoza, Spain. Manufacturer of music rolls, listed in 1930 directories.

Euterpe Muziekrollen Fabriek: 263 Prinsengracht, Amsterdam, Holland. Formed c.1920 by A Stober for the production of rolls for Philipps Pianella pianos and piano-orchestrions. Still operating in 1929. The Amsterdam-based musical instrument distributors Duwaer & Naessens (distributors for Hupfeld and Welte instruments) was the main agent until 1930 when the business was amalgamated with that of Kettner's Pianohandel of 9 Choorstraat, Utrecht, when the name was changed to Kettner & Duwaer.

'Excelsior'-Notenrollenfabrik *see under* **Bacigalupo, G.**

Farrand Organ Company, 1256 12th Street, Detroit, Michigan, USA. Founded in 1884 to make the Olympia organ. Moved into piano-players by the end of the 19th century with the Cecilian player action, later incorporated into player-pianos. The company also made its own piano rolls under the Cecilian name: they were not cheap, the most expensive retailed at $3.00 [15s] while the piano-player was priced at $250 [£62.00]. Cecilian music rolls are 13" wide and are stamped with the legend 'Music Sheet Patd Nov 13th 1900'. Farrand was the first roll-maker to support its pin-ended rolls on wooden blocks in the cardboard roll-box. Cecilian player actions were also supplied to other piano makers. By 1909 the company had opened a special factory purely for the manufacture of this action: also in Detroit this was simple called The Farrand Company and it was situated at 12th Street and Grand Trunk Railway. Sometime after 1908 Cecilian standardized their music-roll widths to 11¼-inches.

Farrand Organ Co, 44 Great Marlborough Street, London, W. Manufacturers and suppliers of Cecilian music rolls. British arm of US company founded in 1899.

Filmusic Company, 6701-15 Santa Monica Boulevard, Hollywood, California, USA. Also some time at Los Angeles. Makers of 88-note rolls under the 'Filmusic Picturoll' and 'Pop' labels, scored specially for the American Photo Player Co 'Fotoplayer' instruments.

F.I.R.S. Milan, Italy. Makers of Apollo music rolls distinguished by being punched in orange paper with a calendered off-white apron. Rolls and boxes with complex, ornate labels comprising a label printed with the title overlaid with a separate window label in maroon with the name and border in gold. Despite the similarity with the next name no link has yet been established.

F.I.R.S.T. (S.A.), 3 via del Teatro, Cremona, Italy. Manufacturers of music rolls, listed in 1930 directories.

Fischer A-G, A E, Postfach 2, 30 Katharinenstr, Bremen, Germany. Manufacturer of music rolls, listed in 1930 directories.

Fluess, Louis, 65 rue de la Hache, Borgerhout-Anvers, Belgium. Listed as makers of piano rolls in 1930 directory. Made rolls for Philippe Pianella pianos.

Freiburger Musikapparate-Bauanstalt, GmbH, Haslacherstrasse 145, Freiburg-in-Bresgau, Germany. Manufacturer of standard and 'artist's' [reproducing piano] rolls under the name Evola.

Givens-Gourley, Inc, Wexford, Pennsylvania, USA. In the early 1960s Larry Givens and John Gourley started in business as manufacturers of player piano rolls using the brand name MelOdee. Specialised in jazz roll recuts.

Globe Company, The, 154 North 11th Street, Philadelphia, Pennsylvania, USA. Founded in 1919 with the intention of making high quality rolls. Makers of Globe music rolls which were said to use 'highest quality of paper'. Became part of the Standard Music Roll Company of Orange, New Jersey, which company then applied the name Globe to its line of cheaper music rolls.

Gorli, Milan, Italy. Makers of Aurora 88-note rolls. Attractive aprons printed 'Rulli sonore – 88 Note'.

Grieshaber, Josef, 3 Blumenthalstr, Leipzig, Germany. Listed under this name as music roll manufacturer in 1930 directory. *See also under* Concordia-Notenrollenfabrik.

Guarro, Augustin, 7 Rambler Cataluña, Barcelona, Spain. Founded in 1860. Piano manufacturer with factory premises at 12 calle Aurora. A manufacturer of music-rolls, both 65- and 88-note. Curiously the address is also that of Blancafort, maker of Victoria-brand music-rolls.

Gulbransen Music Roll Corporation, 3232 W. Chicago Avenue, Chicago, Illinois, USA. Incorporated 1926 to make 'new improved music rolls true to hand playing minus mechanical effects'. New York City address was 599 Eleventh Avenue.

Gulbransen, Dickinson, Company, 37 Union Park Street, Chicago, Illinois, USA. Makers of piano players and player pianos who also manufactured and supplied their own music rolls.

Hand Played Music Roll Company Ltd, The, 1, Hanover Yard, Hanover Street, London. Specialist makers of piano rolls founded in the 1920s and remaining in business until at least 1935.

Heisig, Wolfgang. Grimmaer Str. 16, D-04703 Leisnig, Germany. Modern maker of rolls who began hand-cutting music in 1989. Has catalogue comprising avant-garde classical piano music including Nancarrow and Ligeti.

Herbert Co, The, Newark, New Jersey, USA. Manufacturers of 'square-cut' music rolls which apparently were piano solo arrangements of orchestral music.

Higel, Ltd, 149 Albion Road, Stoke Newington, London. British division of the Otto Higel Company of Toronto, piano makers, player-piano action makers and manufacturers of music rolls. Listed in 1930 directory.

Himpsl, Frank, 8-3 Deptford Court, New Jersey 07728, USA. Maker of modern piano rolls since 1970 on JazzMan label which includes JazzMan Archive and Phantom Fingers. In combination with jazz roll artist John Farrell.

Hoffmann & Engelmann, Neustadt a.d. Haardt, Germany. Paper-manufacturers who specialized in high-quality paper for music rolls. The 'H &E' watermark appears on Hupfeld music rolls for pianos and orchestrions.

Hollandia Kunstspel-Muziekrollenfabriek, Lijnbaansgracht 56, Amsterdam, Holland. Formed c.1924 for the manufacture of piano rolls. Enterprise set up by a player-piano enthusiast named August H Jansen. Specialised in 'artistically-played' and hand-played music rolls. Rolls have plain box labels marked HOLLANDIA-ROLLEN and some bear a simple rubber stamp giving name and address of the business.

Hollywood Player Piano Roll Company, 8416 Beckford Avenue, Northridge, California, 91324, USA. Modem brand name punched by QRS for company which, related Frank Holland, ceased trading c.1970. Made Duo-Art and other multi-tune orchestrion rolls as well as range of ragtime and jazz piano rolls marked Vintage.

Horton & Co Ltd, G H - *see under* **Mastertouch Piano Roll Company**

Hubert, Jos, 210 Mallinckrodtstr, Dortmund, Germany. Manufacturer of music rolls, listed in 1930 directories.

Hupfeld A-G, Ludwig: Apelstrasse 4, Leipzig, Germany. Established in 1872. Manufacturers of very large quantities of music rolls for its own instruments. In August 1926, Hupfeld merged with Zimmermann: Made last pneumatic instrument in 1932. Last roll catalogue published 1934. Still in operation today under the name V.E.B. Union Piano Co. Reproducing rolls for DEA and Triphonola pianos, the latter also being marked Animatic-T. Quality paper rolls with coarse green paper aprons printed in magenta 'Künstler-Rolle – Artists' Roll (-) Rouleau d'Artiste – Rollo de Artista. Originally the title of the music was printed as part of this apron design but as demand for titles fluctuated, these aprons would be re-labelled with an adhesive sticker. Often part of the original title remains visible. Hupfeld rolls are of excellent quality.

I.X.L. Company, Philadelphia, Pennsylvania, USA. Manufacturers of piano rolls. According to Harvey Roehl, did not produce in large quantities. Initials intended to indicate the legend 'I excel'.

Ideal Music Roll Company, 55th Street & Hunter Avenue, Philadelphia, Pennsylvania, USA. Makers of piano rolls. *See* **Rose Valley.** It appears that the two names must have been contemporary since in 1929 Rose Valley advertised under that name, yet in the 1930 directory, which presumably went to press in 1929, the company is listed under both Ideal and Rose Valley.

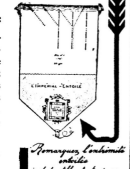

Imperial Linenised. These rolls were made in London by Perforated Music Company and were characterized by having glazed linen aprons. Produced 65-note song rolls between 1910-1918 and after a major factory fire in March 1918 made rolls having paper leaders in standard form for a short time. *See under* **Perforated Music Company, Ltd.**

Imperial Music Company, 27 & 29, Queen Victoria Street, London, EC. *Fl.1905. Musical Opinion,* May 1905, says: 'At 27, Queen Victoria Street, E.C., the Imperial Music Co. supply music for all piano players'. Were they makers, wholesaler/distributors, importers or what? In 1917 advertised 'Songrecords' Solo Carola Records, Imperial hand-played, Diamond, and Automatic Electric Player rolls. Possible connection with the later Imperial Music Roll Company (*see below*).

Imperial Music Roll Company, 57 East Jackson Boulevard, Chicago, Illinois, USA. Believed the same as the Imperial Player Roll Company which was formed by the Cable Company of Chicago in 1915. One of its officers was Thomas E Kavanaugh who, according to the late Harvey Roehl, subsequently became general manager of the National Music Roll Manufacturers Association which was based in Chicago. This organisation was controlled by Cable which, again according to Roehl, explains why, in addition to the regular lines of Imperial Hand Played Records and Imperial 'Songrecords', it was the sole licensed manufacturer of Solo Carola Record Rolls. Manufacturer of music rolls operating by at least 1916 (probably mid-1915) which produced the first Recordo expression-coded music rolls, initially under the name 'Imperial Automatic Electric'. In that same year introduced the 'Jazz Rags' label. The slogan accompanying these rolls was 'Hear the moaning saxophone and tango banjo reproduced realistically on the player piano'. Imperiola was the name given to a range of artists' impression music rolls and the name was also applied to a player-piano although whether or not this was associated with the music-roll company is uncertain. Also traded under the name Imperial Player Roll Company at this address. There may also be a connection between this firm and the much earlier firm previously detailed: the name 'Imperial' is perhaps more likely to have British origins than American.

Imperial Player Roll Company – *see* Imperial Music Roll Company.

Individual Player Roll Company, 63 Storms Avenue, Jersey City, New Jersey, USA. A specialist, small company set up by a man named Anthony Galasso with the intention of 'recording player rolls for song writers, composers, and dealers'. Advertised that 'we will record your own song or composition for player piano rolls under your own special label'. Still listed in 1930 directories.

International Automatic Music Company, 65 W, 67th Street, New York City, USA. Retailers of music rolls listed in 1909 directories. Possibly manufacturers?

International Player Roll Co, 66 Water Street, Brooklyn, New York City, *and* 125 N 9th Street, Philadelphia, Pennsylvania, USA. Established in 1919. Advertised word rolls for expression pianos. Also some time at 30 Main Street, Brooklyn. Listed at Water Street address in 1930 directory. Ultimately became part of QRS Company *[qv]*.

International Roll Company, USA. Manufacturer's name on 'Sublime' roll label. No address but could be one of the numerous Italian-operated labels that sprang up around 1925-30.

Italian Book Company, 145-47 Mulberry Street, New York City, USA. Manufacturers of music rolls listed in 1930 directories and seen on music roll labels.

Kastner & Co, Ltd, 34, 35 & 36 Margaret Street, Cavendish Square, London, W. Manufacturers of piano rolls for the Kastonome 88-note player piano and later for ordinary players.

Kegg Pipe Organ Builders, 11366 Cleveland Avenue, NW, Uniontown, Ohio 44685, USA. Company began making recut rolls for the Aeolian Duo-Art reproducing pipe-organ in 1998. These 15¼-inch wide rolls are punched at 12 holes to the inch in two staggered rows making 176 notes in total.

Keystone Music Roll Company, PO Box 650, Bethlehem, Pennsylvania 18016, USA. Formed in 1986 by the acquisition of Klavier in California. Re-located to Pennsylvania, the business began production in 1987 specialising in high-quality recuts of Ampico and Duo-Art rolls punched mainly on original machinery. Also punches Hot Piano Classics' rolls *[qv]*. Run by Richard Groman and Robert Taylor. *See also* Klavier Music Rolls.

Kibby Manufacturing Company, Marine Building, 136 West Lake Street, Chicago, USA. Makers of the 'Klean-Kut' 25-cent 88-note music rolls.

Kilgen Organ Company, George, St Louis, Mo, USA. Makers of quality pipe organs. Around 1932 introduced the Kilgen Dual Control pipe organ player which used music rolls the same size as standard piano rolls (11¼-inches wide and punched at 9 to the inch) with 100 perforations in total. Punched in a greenish dry waxed paper, these do not play on a piano because the special organ control perforations are situated at various positions around the center of the tracker bar. The rolls and their boxes have orange labels with the brand name and design printed but with the roll title and number typewritten. Thought to have been produced by the Clark Company of Chicago and believed similar to Clark's Artistouch pipe organ rolls.

Kimball Co, The W W: 308 5. Wabash Avenue, Chicago, Illinois, USA. Maker of music rolls listed in 1930 directory.

Klavier Music Rolls, 5652 Willowcrest Avenue, North Hollywood, California, 91601, USA. In 1974 address changed to 10515 Burbank Boulevard, North Hollywood, California. Modern maker of music rolls operated by Harold Powell and his wife Mildred. Produced music rolls under the name Klavier, as well as 77-note, Ampico and Duo-Art re-cuts. In 1987 became Keystone Music Roll Co.

Krauss, Paul, 19 Wissmannstr, Leipzig-Neuschonefeld, Germany. Manufacturer of spools for music rolls, fl.1930.

Laguna Rolls, Lagoon Road, Pagham, Bognor Regis, Sussex, PO21 4TH, England. Small privately-owned firm operated by Steve Cox to produce piano rolls under the name Playtime. Specialised in hand-played jazz and Duo-Art recuts. At the end of 1998 the business was sold to a new owner, Nigel Perry and moved to 36, The Square, Earls Barton, Northampton, NN6 0NA. By 2003 it was reported to have closed.

Lambert-Bronze, M, rue Clenenceau, Ans, Belgium. Listed as makers of piano rolls in 1930 directory.

Leabarjan Manufacturing Company, Hamilton, Ontario, Canada. Makers of a clever and simple hand-operated home-perforating machine that enabled enthusiasts to make their own piano rolls. It is believed the company may also have produced piano rolls at some time. Characterised by square-shaped punchings.

Leipziger Pianoforte-u. Phonolafabriken Hupfeld-Gebrüder Zimmermann A-G, 4 Petersstrasse, Leipzig, Germany. Successors to Hupfeld [qv] which manufactured rolls for many years. After the merger with piano-makers Zimmermann, it continued producing music rolls under this name.

Lind. Music rolls. According to Bowers was only a sales organisation which pasted its own labels on Clark rolls and sold them under the Lind name.

Lindenberg Piano Company, Columbus, Ohio, USA. Very little is known of this company other than that it designed, patented and produced a device called Adapto that could be built into an ordinary piano to convert it into a player. Said to require no extra space in the piano case, the Adapto comprised a pneumatic stack that fitted directly under the keys and 'plays on the keys with the Human Touch', a slimline bellows and pedal system to fit in the case bottom and a basic spool box and roll motor with attendant tubing for mounting in the top of the case front. The product was advertised for but a short while around 1921.

Link Piano Company, Inc, 183 Water Street, Binghampton, New York, USA. Music rolls made expressly for their own player pianos and other automatic musical instruments. Was formed out of the Automatic Musical Company. When Link ceased manufacture, one of its arrangers, G Raymond Deyo continued manufacture for some while using the brand name DEO and perforating machines which produced holes slightly larger than the originals. Still listed in 1930 directory.

Lirón Gordo y González, 12-14, calle Sevilla, Madrid, Spain. Described as 'successors to Salvi', advertised as maker of mechanical pianos and music rolls in 1930 directory. Also handled gramophones and sheet music.

Lyragraph Music Roll Company, 19 Gainsborough Gardens, Golders Green, London, NW. Advertised 'Lyragraph' music rolls in *Musical Opinion* for February 1914, page 420. 'Having only been on the market a few months, but their excellent musical arrangement, high class finish, most durable paper and low price has obtained us extensive orders from a great number of piano dealers and manufacturers. Ask for catalogue and terms'.

Lyric Piano Company, 632 Race Street, Cincinnati, Ohio, USA. In 1918 advertised The Lyric Special, a common 88-note player piano, for $325 (£81.5/-) while also offering used players at $175, $200 and $250. The instrument was also available on hire purchase at $2.00 a week.

Maldonado, Manuel, Jr. Tepic, Nay, Mexico. Manufacturers of music rolls, listed in 1930 directories.

Malone's Music Company. See under Play-Rite Music Rolls, Inc.

Marshall & Sons Ltd, Sir Herbert, Angelus Hall, Regent House, 233 Regent Street, London W. Makers of Angelus, Artistyle, and Angelus Artistyle music rolls. As agents for the Ampico reproducing piano in Britain, distributed Ampico piano rolls. Later as The Marshall Piano Co. Ltd, (at 18 Orchard Street, Oxford Street, London Wl), operators of the Artistyle Circulating Music Roll Library at 18a, Orchard Street (in the 1930s) and (post Second World War) at Troy Court, 216 High Street, London, W.8. Published catalogue of 'Artistyle Music Rolls for all Standard 88-Note Full Scale Player Pianos'. Also known as the Artistyle Music Roll Library. Manufactured Artistyle and Regent rolls, the latter being dance and ballad-song rolls with words. Ar tistyle rolls, described as 'hand-played', were manufactured both in Britain and America by 1925. Remained selling rolls well into 1941 and, until 1954, was selling Ampico rolls (for which it held the franchise) from its Troy Court premises at 2/6d [$0.51c] each.

Marshall Piano Company Ltd, The – see under Marshall & Sons, Ltd, Herbert.

Mastertouch Piano Roll Company, Petersham, Sydney, New South Wales, Australia. Chicago-born, George Harry Horton went to Australia as an associate of the Pianola Company, an Aeolian subsidiary. Here he was a partner in the Sydney distributor E F Wilkes & Co Ltd run by Ted Wilkes which subsequently secured the agency to market Gulbransen player-pianos. Faced with the difficulty of obtaining piano-rolls, Horton set up the firm of G H Horton & Co Ltd in 1919 and established the Mastertouch label

setting up a large factory in City Road. Horton designed a novel pneumatic carbon-ribboned recording machine that made possible a reliable reproduction of an artist's performance. In 1957, Horton acquired the Broadway roll-label from founder Len Luscombe (*see under* The Anglo-American Player Roll Company) who made the first piano rolls in Australia. The Mastertouch company, based then in Canterbury, New South Wales, took over the Q-R-S label in Australia. It produced mostly 88-note piano-rolls packed in thin card boxes with broad black and white diagonal stripes. Still in operation today owned and operated (1975) by Barclay Wright who joined the business in 1956.

Maxfield & Sons Ltd, 324/326 Liverpool Road, London, N. Manufacturers of piano-player mechanisms and also makers of the Maxfield music roll, *fl.*1909.

Medcraft, Brookslee, Brookshill Drive, Harrow Weald, Middlesex, England. Sylvia and Harry Medcraft set up their own music-roll business at their private home during the early 1970s using perforating machinery that they designed and built themselves. Made high-quality copies of Duo-Art rolls. Their scientific approach to their work advanced roll-copying technology while their skills at making their own equipment were second to none. Made made improvements to both player-piano actions (one was a well-engineered variable-speed drive motor for piano-rolls) and perforating equipment. A unique undertaking whose activity ended on the death of Harry in 1990 aged 84 years, and, later, Sylvia.

Mel-O-Art Player Roll Manufacturing Company Inc, 414-416, East Pratt Street, Baltimore, Maryland, USA. Music roll manufacturers, *fl.*1928, that specialised in old-time and blues melodies. A division of Braiterman Fedder Company, Brafco Building, Baltimore.

Mel-O-Dee Music Co Inc: 5th Avenue & 54th Street, New York City, USA, also in Chicago. A subsidiary of the Aeolian Company [qv]. Factory at Meriden, Connecticut, devoted to the manufacture of music rolls. Was originally called Universal. In 1923 claimed to be the largest piano-roll manufactory in the world. Described as makers of 'The World's Finest Music Roll'. In 1922 advertised that its music rolls had contigious perforations to resist tearing, were printed with song-roll words as distinct from being merely stenciled, and had metal spool ends. Still listed in 1930 directories.

Melographic Roll Company, The, 25 Jewett Avenue, Buffalo, NY, USA. Manufacturers of Melographic rolls featuring a special lint-free pale green paper that was said to offer increased stability and resistance to 'extreme' atmospheric changes. Published separate catalogues for 65- and 88-note rolls.

Meloto Company Ltd, The. Hayes, Middlesex. An Aeolian company, subsidiary of The Universal Music Co Ltd. Name only appears to have been used for a short while (1925-c.1929) before reverting to the Universal name.

Mendelssohn Music Company, 171 Tremont Street, Boston, Massachusetts, USA. Makers of the Mendelssohn Perforated Music piano rolls. Seems to have been a short-lived enterprise first appearing in 1928 but out of existence two years later.

Michael, Preuss & Co, GmbH, 12 Warschauer Strasse, Berlin. Manufacturer of Empeco-type music rolls marked 'Einheitsrolle für Jazzband-Instrumente 88-er Teiling'.

Mills Novelty Company, 4100-4118 Fullerton Avenue, Chicago, Illinois, USA. Manufactured music rolls for its own instruments, starting c.1912.

Mongillo, Antonio, 131 1-2 Mulberry Street, New York City, USA. Music publishers, musical instruments, sheet music, strings, library, &c. Listed in 1909 directories as retailers of music rolls. Retailers of the 'Mongillo Special' music roll advertised on labels as 'Copyrighted in 1918'.

Morancho, F, 67 Urgel, Barcelona, Spain. Manufacturer of music rolls, listed in 1930 directories.

Moya Hermanos, S. En C, 476 Cortes, Barcelona, Spain. Manufacturer of music rolls, listed in 1930 directories.

Moya Hermanos (S and C), 476 Cortes, Barcelona, Spain. The brothers S and C Hermanos are listed in 1930 directories as being manufacturers of music-rolls. Manufactured music rolls with the brand name Princesa.

Mukle & Davis: 4 Leysfield Road, Shepherds Bush, London, W12. F G Mukle (son of Leopold Mukle accredited with the introduction of the orchestrion into Britain) and a man named Davis traded originally as Up-To-Date Music Rolls Limited *[qv]* and, *c.*1926, were at Wescombe Works, King Street, Hammersmith. Later as Up-To-Date Piano Roll Co. In 1929, Mukle and Davis introduced a new piano roll which they called the 'Muvis' retailing at 2/6d. Sole distributors were G F Baker of Xaltona House, Leeke Street Corner, King's Cross Road.

Mundell, David, High Road, Chadwell Heath, Essex. Manufacturer of piano rolls under the names Pianostyle and Parex. *Fl.*1929-30 when Parex 88-note music rolls were priced at 2/6d each with song rolls, complete with words, at 3/9d. Curiously poor rolls that lead one to suspect that the maker was neither musical nor tried out the rolls he issued to verify musical continuity.

Murdoch, Murdoch & Company, Hatton House, Hatton Garden, London, BC. Also at 463 Oxford Street. Inventors, patentees and makers of Suprema Golden Tube Music Rolls, first advertised in 1912. Later retailed Perfection-brand rolls with an apron tag printed 'Manufactured for Murdoch, Murdoch & Co, London, Patent Applied for'.

Music Roll Company, The, 92 Great Portland Street, London W.1. This address was valid in 1908 but by 1919 the business was located at 78 Great Portland Street, with 'factory and wholesale department: 5, Ogle Street, London W'. This location was described, in an advertisement for April, 1919, as 'late Lumsden & Co'. The same notice referred to the business as 'piano player and player piano dealers & experts' adding that it had 100,000 music rolls for sale or on hire from its library. The Manchester agents were Vernon W A Cook of 373 & 362 Chester Road. By the time of the 1930 directory, the address was 78 Great Portland Street.

Musicnote Roll Company, 106-108 River Street, Dixon, Illinois, USA. Division of the Englehardt-Seybold Company with factories at St Johnsville, New York. Besides making rolls for the Peerless automatic pianos, Roehl states that their regular output of 88-note rolls were under three brands – Master Records, Auto-Inscribed, and Hand-Played. Also made rolls for orchestrions as well as photoplayers. Makers of the Keynote song roll.

National Music Roll Company, 26 William Street, St Johnsville, New York, USA. Subsidiary of National Electric Piano Company and a division of the Englehardt-Seybold Company. Music rolls: Master-Record, Hand Played, and Auto Inscribed. In addition it made all the rolls for the Peerless automatic pianos, photo-orchestras and orchestrions. Listed in 1930 directory as National Electric Piano & Roll Co.

New-Phono, 35 & 37, Ancha, Barcelona, Spain. Said to have been founded in 1834. Described as a manufacturer of music rolls in 1930 directories. Rolls have blue-green paper aprons. Also edited music and made phonographs.

Niagara Music Company, 198 Terrace Street, Buffalo, New York, USA. Music roll manufacturers, *fl.*1909.

Nippon Gakki, Seizo Kabushikikaisha, Hamamatsu, Japan. Between 1921 and 1932, this company is reported to have made about 80 player pianos for which music was provided under the Yamaha Music Rolls label. The music so far found comprises Japanese traditional music arranged for piano. Where the rolls were punched is unknown. (Information from Vernon Brown).

Octave Organ Rolls: 488 Fredericks Street, North Tonawanda, New York 14120, USA. Makers of a limited edition of quality 88-note rolls suitable for piano but intended for 88-note player organ. All musical performances from the classical repertoire and recorded mostly on the Q-R-S recording piano by organist Lee Teply. Rolls are cut by Play-Rite in California for the owner of Octave, Mike Walter. *See also* Walter, Mike L.

Orfeo, S.A, Rambla de Cataluña 97, Barcelona, Spain. Makers of Orfeo music rolls, *fl.*1927.

Orpheus Music Rolls. *See* Roll Music Company.

Paramount Music Roll Mfg Co, 145-147 Mulberry Street, New York, New York, USA. Listed as piano roll manufacturers in 1930 directories and described as 'makers of Italian Style' music rolls.

Perfecta, 5, avenue de l'Opéra, Paris, France. René Savoye, director. Music-roll makers advertising 'exclusively French music rolls' and 'for all pneumatic instruments'. This business succeeded the ancient firm of Henri Zacconi *[qv]* and operated a factory at Bagnolet, Seine. Brand names Perfecta and Le Cantola. *Fl.*1920. Became a subsidiary of Universal.

Perforated Music Company, Ltd, Great Eastern Street, London, EC. Very large and early manufacturer of piano rolls in the main produced and branded for other organizations, piano makers, retailers, department stores and suchlike. *Musical Opinion* for May, 1905, carries the following note: 'The business of the Perforated Music Co, Great Eastern Street, EC, has increased so much lately that additional premises have been taken in the City Road. These manufacturers claim that they are able to supply the latest compositions long in advance of their American competitors; and that their agents include this new music in their libraries'. The new address was 197/199 (sometime 197-203) City Road, with sale and showrooms also at 94 Regent Street and 81 Beak Street, London, W (advertised from this address in August 1909). Makers of Imperial Linenised music rolls. Distinguished by their green cloth leader, the spools have pressed metal flanges. Described as 'Indestructible rolls', the cloth apron featured a hook and securing string. 'No more troublesome rubber bands,' proclaimed the advertisement, 'but instead, a neat little cord attached to our new LINENIZED FRONT'. Company also made the Omnia roll as well as branding rolls for Whiteleys department store, Bayswater, London. Produced 65-note song rolls 1910-1918. In March 1918, a huge fire destroyed the premises and all the machinery together with the entire library of master-rolls. The business was quickly re-established at 6 Bride Street, London EC and continued, in a much smaller way, until 1924 by which time it had declined even further. During these obviously difficult times, the rolls were produced with paper leaders in standard form. With one perforating machine and a staff reduced to five, the business was reduced to a minor operator bereft of its master rolls and unable to supply its customers. As a consequence the business was liquidated that year.

Perforation Musicale, La, 22 rue Delambre, Paris, France. Manufacturer of music rolls listed in 1930 directories.

Perfuracion Argentina Musical Pawn Autopiano, Argentina. Makers of P.A.M.P.A. music rolls.

Perforetur Music Rolls, Michael Boyd, Unit 3, Mercatoria Business Centre, 100, Norman Road, St Leonards on Sea, East Sussex, TN38 0EJ. Makers of Perforetur music rolls. Re-cuts of classical music and some Duo-Art and Ampico reproducing rolls,

Peschke & Company, C, S.14, Kommandantenstr. 50, Berlin, Germany. Proprietor shown as M Rosenfeld. Makers of piano rolls *fl.* 1909.

Phantom Player Ltd, 22, Soho Square, London, W. The Phantom Player was an electrically-driven key-top piano-player that appeared briefly during the 1930s revival of this form of instrument. To provide a selling catalogue, a list of 100 piano-rolls was packed into the box with the device. Although clearly identified with a colourful label, Phantom never made their own rolls, but branded Aeolian rolls made by Imperial. Because so very few instruments appear to have been put onto the market (in half a century I have found two!), I suspect rolls were only ever bought to fill a specific order, so we could be talking about a 'roll-production' of extremely small numbers.

Philipps A-G Piano-u Orgelwerke, Aschaffenburg, Bayern, Germany. Branch of main J D Philipps company in Frankfurt am Main. Produced high-quality music rolls under the name Philag. In 1923, J D Philipps bought the Frati mechanical organ business which it continued under the Frati name. Introduced a reproducing roll labeled with an open monogram reading PH & S followed by the words 'Philipps Reproduktions-Klaviere'.

Piano Roll Co, The, 62 Hanover Gardens, Hainault, Ilford, Essex. Makers of Jazzmaster piano rolls. Formed in 1976 by John Farrell, John Sirett and George Huggett. Later at Tanglewood Cottage, 56 Monkhams Lane, Woodford Wells, Essex, IG8 0NR (1989). In production until around 1992.

Pianostyle Music Company, Inc, 83 33rd Street, Brooklyn, New York, USA. Founded in 1913 and remained in business throughout the period of popularity of the player piano. Described by Harvey Roehl as one of the best-known names in the trade. With a staff of 100 people made rolls not only for the domestic trade, but also had a considerable export trade to South America and Europe. Still in business under this name in 1930. Eventually became part of Q.R.S. Not to be confused with the very similar English Pianostyle label and in Essex by **David Mundell** *[qv].*

Play-Rite Music Rolls, Inc, 1612 East 14th Street, Oakland, California 94606, USA. Founded in 1963 by John Malone, a machine engineer, as a family business under the name Malone's Music Company at P.O Box 1025, Turlock, California. Devoted efforts to the making of style A, G and O coin-freed electric piano rolls as well as music rolls for carousel organs. Moved on to re-cut Ampico, Duo-Art and Welte-Mignon (Licensee) reproducing rolls. During 1975, Malone's experience in machinery automation inspired him to adopt the computerization of the music-roll perforation operation. At this point the business was joined by a fellow enthusiast and businessman, Elwood L Hansen (who would handle finance and marketing) and California roll collector Robert Kolsters. The name of the business was now changed to Play-Rite Music Rolls, Inc with John Malone as general manager and a second manufacturing facility set up near the original plant in Turlock. After three years of painstaking work, the new business was ready to launch what it described as the ultimate in 88-note music rolls – the Play-Rite Live Performance Series. By 1980 the Play-Rite catalogue listed both Ampico and Welte Licensee re-cuts but also some newly-recorded rolls for both systems. By the 1960s was owned by Ray Siou who manufactured Duo-Art and multitune orchestrion rolls. Makers of Octave Organ Rolls. *(see also under* Walter, Mike L.)

Plaza Music Company, 10 West 20th Street, New York City, USA. Produced 'Winner' and 'Ideal' music rolls, the former described as 'the only perfect 10-cent roll on the market'. Trade mark was a triangular pennant with the name 'Winner'. The 'Ideal' at 25 cents had a trademark in the shape of a horizontal diamond with the word IDEAL across it. There seem to have been two similar brand names and labels.

Pleyel, S.A, 252 Faubourg St-Honore, Paris, France. Manufacturer of pianos and other musical instruments, also produced music rolls under the label Pleyela with an address at 20 Avenue de l'Opéra in Paris. *Fl.* 1925-32. Later rolls showed the Faubourg St-Honore address.

Poch, Juan, 7 Condesa de Orleans, Sarriá, Barcelona, Spain. Manufacturer of music rolls, listed in 1930 directories.

Popper & Co, Reichsstr 33/35, Leipzig, Germany. Established by Hugo Popper in 1891 as a maker of automatic pianos including the Welt-Piano Stella, Electric pianos, piano-orchestrions and suchlike. Popper made many varieties of these instruments, both with and without keyboards for manual playing. Produced variety of music rolls for them.

Precision Music Rolls, 1043 Eastside Road, El Cajon, California 92020, USA. Present-day piano-roll producer run by David L Saul. Specialist in Ampico recuts.

Q-R-S Music Technology Company, 26 East Jackson Boulevard, Chicago, Illinois, USA. One of the oldest makers of perforated music in the United States yet one which, curiously, has forgotten much of its origins. Along with this, nobody can recall what the initials ever stood for although many have come up with *bon mots* starting with something like 'Quality Roll Service' although somebody also suggested that the rolls were 'Quite Really Something'. Even uncertainty surrounds how to present the company initials and it has been used as Q-R-S, QRS, and Q.R.S. Its beginnings can be traced to the Melville Clark Piano Company of Chicago of which it was founded as QRS Music Rolls, a subsidiary. Later it was Story and Clark Pianos and described as a QRS subsidiary. The business had premises at De Kalb, Illinois, as early as *c.*1900. The De Kalb factory for the manufacture of perforated paper music is listed in the 1909 International directory where it states 'also in Chicago'. Soon afterwards it listed premises in both New York City and San Francisco. The company was re-structured in 1920 by which time it had become by far the largest concern of its type in the world. In 1926, president was T M Pletcher who organised purchase of the United States Music Co, described as 'one of the best known makers of music rolls in the country', for about half a million dollars. The company's December 1932 Bulletin revealed that from that month forward Q-R-S would assume all responsibilities for the manufacture and distribution of Welte Licensee music rolls. The Q-R-S business underwent numerous changes of ownership across the years. The business made piano rolls for many different companies, labels and systems including Aria Divina reproducing piano and Recordo expression pianos. In 1930 directory it was listed as the Q-R-S De Vry Corporation as 333 North Michigan Avenue, Chicago, Illinois. During this time the name was also applied to wireless-set valves as Q-R-S Red Top Radio Tubes, launched in 1925, along with phonographs (gramophones) and records, as well as motion picture camera projectors. One once-affiliated business, Q-R-S Neon Signs, still exists today as a separate entity in California. This was the zenith of the Q-R-S company's music-roll business and so great was the demand for rolls that the firm operated branch factories in Chicago, Boston, Cincinnati, Detroit, New York, Pittsburg, St Louis and San Francisco (475 Brannan Street). while Q-R-S Canadian Corporation were at Toronto and Montreal. European factories were set up in Utrecht, The Netherlands, and Sydney, Australia. Then came the stock-market crash in 1929-30 whereupon Max Kortlander, a staff roll-recording artist for Q.R.S during the 1920s, acquired the company. He re-named it the Imperial Industrial Corporation and moved the firm to the Bronx, New York. The name Q.R.S, however, stuck with the product and by the 1960s it was a small operation with about eighteen staff. Kortlander died suddenly on October 11th, 1961, aged 71. His brother Herman and his widow Gertrude operated the company for a few years until April of 1966 when Ramsi P Tick, former manager of the Buffalo Philharmonic Orchestra, stepped in and formed a new company called Q.R.S. Music Rolls, Inc, which took over the assets and interests of the Imperial Industrial Corporation. He moved the business from the decaying surroundings of the Bronx to his hometown, Buffalo, where he was born on November 12th, 1924. Survives into the 21st century and is today at 1026 Niagara Street, Buffalo, New York, 14213. From the hey-days of the 1920s when the company turned out ten million piano rolls a year and could absorb any of its rivals that it wished, it is now a small business turning out around half a million rolls per year.

Q-R-S Canadian Corporation, Ltd: 259 Spadina Avenue, Toronto, Canada. Listed as makers of piano rolls in 1930 directory. The Canadian-made music rolls were clearly distinguished by a large maple leaf on the box label as well as the legend 'The Only Made in Canada Music Roll Co.' *See* main entry for Q-R-S above.

Racca, Giovanni, 7 via Zamboni, Bologna, Italy. Manufacturers of the punched cardboard-playing Piano-Melodico who subsequently moved into the manufacture of perforated paper piano rolls, listed in 1930 directories.

Recordo Player Roll Company, 57, East Jackson Street, Chicago, Illinois, USA. Founded in1922 from the Imperial Music Roll Company *[qv]*, whose address it shared, to manufacture Recordo expression piano rolls. Secretary of company was George W Eddy. Was finally absorbed by Q-R-S *[qv]*.

Reitzammer, Johann, Hirschelgasse 26, Nurnberg, Germany. Founded in 1908 for the manufacture of piano and organ music rolls.

Republic Player Roll Corporation, 645-651 West 51st Street, New York City, USA. Makers of Republic hand-played music rolls. Paul B Klugh, president. The company closed in 1922.

Rex Music Rolls, *see* Rialto Player Piano Co.

Rialto Player Piano Co, Ltd, 15 Castle Street East, London, W. Makers of the Rex Music Roll. Notice in *Musical Opinion* for May, 1913 *[p.606]* 'REX MUSIC ROLLS. Who Manufactures or who can Supply them? Reply to… &c' – surely a novel publicity stunt that was, for its time, a clever way to attract attention.

Riessner, Br, Schmiedeberg Bz, Halle, Germany. Manufacturer of music rolls, listed in 1930 directories.

Robinson, Malcolm, Southport, England. Modern hand-played music rolls made on the Southport label.

Roesler-Hunholz, Inc, 258-260 Scott Street, Milwaukee, Wisconsin, USA. Maker of music rolls listed in 1930 directory. Their main operation was the manufacture of reproducing player mechanisms for pipe organs.

Rogge, Emil, Pankstr 22, Berlin, N20, Germany. Manufacturer of piano rolls for electric pianos, *fl.*1909.

Roll Music Company Ltd, The 1 & 3 Sun Street, Finsbury Square, London EC. Makers of Orpheus music rolls proclaiming 'British manufacture'. All seen are 65-note. Brown glazed paper apron beraring line drawing of Orpheus and his lyre.

Rollos Era S.A: 5 Alvarado, Madrid, Spain. Manufacturer of music rolls, brand name ERA. *Fl.*1928-32.

Rollos Mexico. Music-roll makers *fl.*1970 in Mexico City.

Rose Valley Music Company, 55th Street and Hunter Avenue, Philadelphia, Pennsylvania, USA. Also sometime as The Rose Valley Co at Media, Pennsylvania. Makers of Ideal music rolls. Trade mark was a horizontal diamond with the word 'IDEAL' over. In 1929 advertised Ideal Word Rolls as 'the quality roll' at 75 cents.

Royal Music Roll Company, Main Street and Hertel Avenue, Buffalo, New York, USA. Music roll manufacturers. Trade mark on label is a lyre.

Rythmodik Music Corporation, Belleville, New Jersey, USA. Founded in 1917. Affiliated to the American Piano Company of 437 Fifth Avenue, New York. Makers of Rythmodik Record Music Rolls for 88-note players with the slogan 'Its all in the roll'. The secret of the early Rythmodik music rolls and their quite marked difference to music rolls of other manufacture was really rather simple. As a 'hand-played' recording, the music paper traveled at a constant speed so that any variations in tempo or phrasing put in by the 'recording' artist was faithfully reproduced simply by leaving the tempo control well alone. A basic feature already used by Welte and Hupfeld in Germany, Rythmodik seems to have been the first American maker to apply it to their rolls. In November 1920 Rythmodik announced it was to cease manufacture of music rolls and discontinue offering Rythmodik rolls for sale. It added that American Piano Company was to devote its entire music-roll activities to the manufacture and development of special rolls for the Ampico Reproducing Piano. American Piano Co absorbed the Rythmodik production facilities marking the end of the Rythmodik Music Corporation, while the entire finished stock of Rythmodik rolls was disposed of to Q-R-S. *See also under* American Piano Company.

S.M. Semi-hand-played music rolls made by **Felix Schüller.** *See also under* Choralion.

Sachsische Papierrollen-Fabrik Jakob David, Wettiner Str 34, Berlin N, Germany, Supplier of paper for music rolls who, by 1909, was also producing music rolls.

Salvyer, H M, 460 Abingdon Avenue, Bloomfield, New Jersey, USA. Described in 1930 directory as a 'master [music roll] maker & perforating' operation.

Schettino Music Roll Company, New York, USA . Makers of Italian music rolls in America. Retailed by Frank Passaro, 2091 First Avenue between 107th and 108th streets, NY.

Schöne & Bocchese, 13p. Aspromonte, Milano, Italy. Manufacturers of music rolls, listed in 1930 directories. Produced rolls brand name Victoria.

Schüller, Felix, Leipzig 15, Germany. Introduced S.-M brand hand-played music rolls around 1920 and exhibited that year at the Leipzig Fair. Both 65- and 88-note rolls were offered as well as player actions. High quality rolls. By 1930 the business was listed in directories as Felix Schüller A-G, 22 Sedanstr, Leipzig.

S.E.C.I.M, 30 bis, rue Cauchy, Paris, France. Manufacturer of perforated music rolls for the Violinista listed as such in 1930 directories.

Seybold, Rene, 1 route de l'Hôpital, Strasbourg-Neudorf, France. Manufacturer of music rolls listed in 1930 directories.

S & P Music Roll Company, Ltd, 27 Lots Road, Chelsea, London, SW.10. Company set up at the end of 1924 by G E Perkins and one Siggitson. It proved to be a short-lived enterprise set up by the side of the Thames by the Power Station for the purpose of making low-cost piano rolls. The company's own music rolls, branded S & P, were launched through direct sales to retailers in the Hammersmith and Chelsea area. It also produced rolls under other names, none of which has yet been positively attributed with the probable exception of Echo. All rolls seen carry serial numbers in the 6000 series which might indicate that this number was the company's starting-point. The business existed until about 1926 after which no reference to it can be traced through Post Office directories. The whole area was heavily bombed during WWII and the premises are no longer traceable.

Skinner Organ Company, 677 5th Avenue, New York City, USA. Listed in 1930 directory as a maker of music rolls for pipe organs.

Smith & Son Ltd, James, 72-76 Lord Street, Liverpool, Lancashire. This business, established in 1829 as music-sellers, became a major musical-instrument distributor and advertised as *The North of England 'Pianola', 'Duo-Art' – and Audiographic Music Roll Library.* Although not a manufacturer, James Smith's labels and decorative printed aprons appear on many rolls from the 1920s. Brick-red box-lid labels featured on the rolls this well-known business sold. Most seem to have been produced for them by Imperial.

Southport Roll Company, 39, Sydner Road, London, N16 7UF. Operated by Malcolm Robinson. Maker of new hand-played popular music, also re-cuts. *Fl.*2000.

Soc An Brevetti Barbieri per Applicazioni Elettro-Musicali, 26 via S Vincenzo, Milan, Italy. Manufacturers of music rolls, listed in 1930 directories. All rolls seen (about ten examples) have been of high-quality and, curiously, all marked as not being for public sale. All have typewritten box labels and hand-written roll titles.

Staffnote Player Roll Co, 1721 Fond du Lac Avenue, Milwaukee, Wisconsin, USA. Manufacturers of music rolls listed in 1930 directories.

Standard Music Roll Company, Factory and Main Office 29-35 Central Avenue, Orange, New Jersey, USA. Salesrooms at 225 Fifth Avenue, New York City. Makers of ARTo and VOCo Word music rolls advertised with the legend: 'They teach you to sing' and featuring a 'Note Patented Word Music Staff' which was the printing of the words down the right-hand edge of the roll across a five-rule 'staff'. The company advertised that, at $1.00 [5s], 'they cost less than inferior rolls'. Also made Perfection Hand Played Rolls. From the beginning, this maker paid attention to the appearance of its roll-boxes, realizing that part of the acceptance of the player-piano and its music in the home was an ability to blend with the surroundings. It advertised that 'all ARTo rolls are contained in beautiful sepia art boxes, suitable for use in any drawing room'. Also manufactured 'Electra' music rolls which featured the 'Eclipse' adjustable spool and was promoted heavily in 1914. Amongst curious claims made for this roll was 'An improvement in the musical effects of all rapidly repeated passages and short notes, resulting from an actual 15% gain of time registration between the smallest perforations and the tracker apertures. There is a gain in this respect of 16% over standard 65-note rolls… All paper trouble is minimized as a result of reducing our paper length 15%, viz: (1) the long perforations when shortened give no trouble through 'buckling'; (2) the paper guides better as the reduced speed… (3) there is 15% less paper to shrink, expand, tear, wrinkle, etc.' Thus curiously described in what appear contradictory terms, this roll was the product of a series of patents taken out by an electrical engineer named G Howlett Davis who proposed a whole system from recording to perforating all controlled by electric current. In May 1917 advertised the 'SingA' word rolls. Also said to be 'Member of the National Association of Music Roll Manufacturers of America' with branches as 1437 Broadway, New York City, 431 William Street, Buffalo, New York, and 1129 Chestnut Street, Philadel-

phia, Pennsylvania. Later product was the Standard Play-A-Roll. *See also under* Kohler Industries *in Appendix 2.*

Symphonia, The (Eugene de Roy), 20 Longue rue Pothoek, Anvers, Belgium. Described in 1930 directories as manufacturers of music rolls for pianos and orchestrions.

Tempola Music Rolls, 341 State Highway P, New Madrid, Missouri 63869, USA. Small present-day maker of piano rolls operated by Andrew Taylor.

Triumph Auto Ltd, 185 Regents Street, London W. Listed as makers of piano rolls in 1930 directory, roll-manufactory at Johnson Street, Westminster, London, SW.

U.M.E.C.A, Sco. An, 14 Doctor Santero, Madrid, Spain. Manufacturer of music rolls, listed in 1930 directories.

United Piano Corporation, Norwalk, Ohio, USA.

Union Player Music Company, Jamestown, New York, USA. Roll manufacturers who claimed so produce 'the only perfect music roll'. Claimed to do away with all player troubles, the spool had automatic adjustable flanges that opened when playing and then closed and locked when re-rolling.

United States Music Company, 2934-2938 West Lake Street, Chicago, and 122 Fifth Avenue, New York City, USA. Established in 1906. Roll manufacturer which started in business making orchestrion rolls. Before 1913 the firm had discontinued this line and made ordinary piano rolls on spools made of rubber. 'Originators of Rubber Spools, patented November 5th and 26th, 1912'. Makers of the 'US' piano rolls described as 'The Best Player Music Rolls', the trademark being 'The Emblem of Music Roll Perfection'. President was Arthur A Friestedt, vice-president and sales manager was George L. Ames. Output in excess of 2,000,000 rolls/year. By 1913 the trademark was a large letter Q with the legend 'Quality Perforated Music Rolls'. By 1922, had additional premises at 122 Fifth Avenue, New York. In a clever promotion (1922) it offered exchanges on old player rolls, crediting at 33 cents per roll. In November 1926, Q.R.S bought the US company for half a million dollars, and the following January added Imperial to its clutch of companies and brand names.

Universal Music Company, The, 29 West 42nd St, New York, and 425 South Wabash Avenue, Chicago, USA. Canadian branch at 10½ Shuter Street, Toronto. In 1909 was listed in directories as being as Meriden, Connecticut. Makers of Universal and Uni-Record music rolls. In 1916 advertised as 'The Oldest and Largest Music Roll Company in the World'. Subsidiary of Aeolian Corporation which, ca. 1920, changed name to Mel-O-Dee *[qv].*

Universal Music Company: Hayes, Middlesex, England. British subsidiary of the American organization, itself a subsidiary of Aeolian. Makers of music rolls for The Aeolian Co. Ltd and The Orchestrelle Company. Among the names of rolls issued were: Aeolian Grand (for she Orchestrelle 58-note player organ), Aeolian Song Roll, Audiographic (for Duo Art and ordinary 88-note player piano), Duo-Art (reproducing), Hand Played, Meloto (in Standard, Dance and word-rolls for singing to, introduced around 1925), Metro-Art, Metronamic, Metrostyle, Themodiss, Ausoplayer (Standard, Accentuated, word-rolls), Broadwood (Standard, Accentuated), Harrods (Standard, Accentuated), Sir Herbert Marshall (Artist Song Roll, Artistyle, Regent Song, Regent Dance), Perfecta (Standard, Accentuated), Triumph (Standard, Word Roll), Universal (Accentuated, Handplayed, Song Roll, Standard, Uni-Record). The late Frank Holland maintained that all music-rolls sold in England were made by Universal, which is not correct although a large number were branded by them. At the end of the war, the company restarted production but the days of the player had passed – as had, for the immediate time being, the availability of good music-roll manufacturing paper. The poor quality of the 1946 roll-production had to be seen to be believed. In November the decision was taken to close the business and it officially went into liquidation on November 28th. The machinery and stock-in-trade was subsequently purchased by Gordon Iles of Artona Music Rolls Ltd *[qv].*

Universal Music-Roll Co, 100 Norman Road, St Leonards on Sea, East Sussex. Newly-made rolls under the label Perforetur, Duo-Art and standard full-scale, *fl.*1995. Later under ownership of Michael Boyd at 18 Cinque Ports Street, Rye, East Sussex, TN31 7AD.

Up-To-Date Music Roll Co, 4 Leysfield Road, Shepherds Bush, London, W12. Company formed by the brothers S and P Mukle who were the grandsons of Leopold Mukle, orchestrion-organ maker of Albany Street, London, N. Made Muvis piano rolls, *fl.*1932. *See also under* Mukle & Davis.

Victor Music Roll Co, 2830 West Lake Street, Chicago, Illinois, USA. Maker of music rolls listed in 1930 directory.

Vocalstyle Music Company, The, 412-26 East Sixth Street, Cincinnati, Ohio, USA. Makers of the Vocalstyle music roll and 'Vocalstyle complete song rolls'. Claimed to have produced the very first song roll with words printed on the paper, producing this as early as 1908. Brands included Home Minstrel Series, Children's Game Series, Nursery Rhymes, Slumber Songs for Children Series, Vodvil-style Rolls, and Riley Recitation Rolls. In 1930 directory it listed as the Vocalstyle Music Co, Inc, at 1107 West Jackson Street, Cincinnati, Ohio. Eventually became part of Q.R.S. Two trade-mark-branded types, the first, showing a banjo-plucking, check-trousered minstrel, called 'Home Minstrel Rolls', and the second, branded by an elegant couple in evening dress dancing, as simply 'Vocalstyle rolls'. Also produced Vocalstyle 'Reproduco' expression piano rolls. The business closed in February 1927 and the stock and inventory was acquired by Q.R.S who apparently destroyed almost all the Vocalstyle masters and sold the machiunery

Voigt, Adolf Ernst, 9 Konigsberger Str, Berlin, Germany. Manufacturer of music rolls, listed in 1930 directories.

Walter, Mike L, 488 Fredericks Street, North Tonawanda, New York 14120, USA. Owner of the Octave Organ Rolls business. These are 88-note piano-roll-type hand-played interpretations of classical organ works and printed with a guide to registration. The box label originally spelled the name as Oktave but this was later altered so the present form. A high-quality product made from Mike Walter's own master rolls and punched by Play-Rite of California. A small and highly specialised brand. First began *c.*1985. *See also* Octave Organ Rolls.

Welte, Freiburg, Germany. Makers of the Welte-Mignon reproducing piano and its wide red-paper music rolls. The US market proved the most involved for the company, in particular with the introduction of American-made products using the Welte name. After the introduction of the Welte-Mignon (Licensee) standard-width rolls, Welte launched its own standard-width music-rolls bearing the name Original Welte-Mignon. Towards the mid-1920s, Welte in Germany introduced a wholly-new reproducing system that used standard-width music-rolls but was coded in a different manner from any of the foregoing Welte-named systems. This is known, to collectors, as the 'green-paper Welte-Mignon'. The US operation was M Welte & Sons, Inc, 273 Fifth Avenue, New York City.

Welte-Mignon Corporation, 704, St Ann's Avenue, Bronx, New York. The American company set up to develop the Welte Mignon (Licensee) system and to produce music rolls for it.

Wenker, Phil, 2805 Arlington Avenue, Riverside, California, USA. Modern maker of music rolls under the Golden Age label. Mostly piano jazz and re-cuts.

Wilcox & White, Meriden, Connecticut, USA. Makers of Voltem hand-played rolls. These had the sub-title 'The Music Roll De Luxe' and she message that the roll was 'registered at the US Patent Office'. The rolls have a brown and red label stuck onto the self-apron above which is a printed photograph of the artist. A light blue leather-finished fabric tag bears the rubber-stamp message 'Patented Sept 13, 1904 No. 770103'. A printed notice on the roll reads: 'This music sheet and record is covered by and made under United States Letters Patent dated December 4th, 1900; October 31st, 1905; and February 6th, 1912, and is sold by The Wilcox & White Company…' Makers of the Angelus player action and the Angelus Artrio reproducer.

Willrath, E & B Barnlck, 28 Ferdinandstr, Berlin-Lichterfelde-Ost, Germany. Manufacturer of music rolls, listed in 1930 directories.

Wurlitzer Manufacturing Company, The Rudolph, 121 East 4th Street, Cincinnati, Ohio, USA. Branch of main company based in North Tonawanda, New York, USA. Manufactured music rolls for its own instruments in very large quantities. Brand names includes Autograph Reproducing Piano, Caliola; Concert PianOrchestra (these used the J D Philipps' Pianella Caecilia scale for instruments made in Frankfurt by Philipps); Automatic Harp; Mandolin PianOrchestra; Mandolin Quartette, Military Band Organ; MO (mortuary organ); Organette, Paganni Violin Piano (again Philipps scale); Pianino, Rolla Artis; Solo Violin Piano, Theatre Organ; as well as 65 and 88-note straight piano rolls.

Zacconi, Henri, 59 rue Orfila, Paris 20, France. Manufacturer of music rolls, maker and repairer of all types of mechanical musical instument, *fl.*1909. Business later taken over by Perfecta *[qv]*.

Zacharias, Paul, Weststrasse 26, Leipzig, Germany. Founded in 1885, Zacharias was a piano sundries supplier and retailers' agent who also handled music rolls. His name has been linked to the manufacture of Original Künstler Musik-Rolle Rolla Artis but this cannot be confirmed. By 1930 the business was listed at 31 Inselstr, Leipzig.

Appendix 5
What's it Worth? Valuation & Price Guide

It is inevitable that any attempt at suggesting a value to an automatic piano is fraught with problems even if only because such a valuation is dependent on so many variables. There are fluctuations in the market, bad days in salerooms, short-lived bouts of marketing euphoria and, in the end, no steady-state platform of either sales or values. The variables include international economies and the fluidity of the market as a whole. At a specific level, it is a simple question of supply and demand. As an author, this section of this book is the one for which I have the least confidence for, unlike National Debts and gold, the value of any antique goes up and down like a fiddler's elbow. Any valuation is thus potentially short-lived and runs the real likelihood of being out of date before it ever appears in print!

Investors and collectors understand that the value of these goods may vary from day to day and that the real value is whatever you may get for it (or sell it for) on any particular day.

As if that were not enough to deter the would-be estimator, there's another and rather fundamental question: what do we mean by 'value'? It is not generally appreciated that there are at least four valuations that can be applied to any object, a mechanical piano included. These are:

(a) *valuation for probate (requiring a legally-acceptable worth of asset);*

(b) *valuation for insurance (entailing a replacement cost);*

(c) *an average retail price (which can be by private sale or through the trade);*

(d) *a likely price at auction (which is an estimate of a net value less any commission).*

In addition to these there are three other criteria that are even less tangible. First is the musical performance; second the mechanical significance of the instrument; and third is the stylistic importance of the whole. These last three are more likely to be the concern of the museum collection.

This basic fact of multiple-choice valuation is invariably overlooked by those who seek to earn a living by publishing so-called 'price-guides'. These are the ones who foist incomplete information onto an unsuspecting readership. At best, these publications are poor barometers of the market and should thus be avoided like the plague for they offer such scant information on the merchandise they purport to price as to make their ownership an irrelevance. The shrewd person will at once understand that 'like--for-like' identification is imperative and these guides, despite their high-sounding names, fall so far short of providing that depth of information that they are quite worthless. True valuation means more than compiling a list of attained sale prices.

Regardless of all this, prices may only be a loose guide since if somebody really wants to buy a piece, then the price may become but a secondary consideration. If two or more people at auction have their sights set on such a piece, then estimates can appear dramatically inadequate as the potential buyers push the price upwards: I have seen an unrestored reproducing piano with a worth of £2,000 sell for more than three times that figure just because a number of people were after it.

There is no short, simple, straightforward, ideal or correct solution! What I have decided to do is to take key examples from the illustrations in this book and apply to them an average retail sale price. This price is that which you might expect to be an average price (10 per cent either way) and is my own estimation based on my experience in the field and on current sale prices both at home and abroad.

Criteria used in Valuation

In all instances, the valuations given are intended to apply to examples that are similar in every respect to the illustrations to which they relate. It is also considered that condition is comparable. Items in poor condition are worth appreciably less: a player piano given a value of £1,000 may only be worth a fraction of that figure if it is in unrestored or derelict condition, while a heavily-modified piano with non-original parts may actually prove unsaleable!

Again, the availability of music for the instrument is an important consideration. While a 'green' Welte in good order but with only two music rolls may sound highly attractive, you will still have to spend a lot of money buying the odd second-hand or re-cut rolls before you have a decent library of music for it.

With a repertoire of rare or unusual rolls, an instrument may be worth appreciably more than a similar specimen with a few rolls of popular music. Similarly, an instrument of historical, mechanical or developmental importance will attract an appropriately higher valuation. At the same time, a reproducing piano with no rolls is worth less than one with a 'reasonable' repertoire which may, for example, be any number between 12 and 200 depending on the scarcity of the roll-format. A scarce or unusual-compass piano, such as a 73-note Hupfeld, will be of little value if the chances of getting music for it are such that they have to be measured in units of blood-out-of-a-stone.

A case in an exotic wood may be worth more as well: player-pianos were sometimes made in richly ornamented mahogany, oak and walnut cases, each worth a very different price.

Condition

Instruments have been valued as in perfect restored condition. Unrestored, incomplete or damaged examples are invariably worth considerably less than the lowest estimates suggested. Commonly-found items, such as ordinary player-pianos, may be no more than 10 percent of the notional value if not working: rarer pieces retain more of their value even when unrestored: perhaps losing no more than 40 percent of notional value. In all cases, though, professional restoration is costly; your own work is time-consuming. This is the single most important aspect to consider when assessing value-for-money.

How to use this Guide

The first number shown is the page number within the text. There then follows a brief description of the item and then a valuation in £ Sterling and US dollars.

Where dollar prices are shown these do not represent a straight £/$ conversion but will reflect the rarity and frequency of that item in America or Britain. For example, the Welte (Licensee) is far more common in America than in Britain and so the retail value is somewhat different. It will also reflect the current market situation for types of automatic pianos on either side of the Atlantic.

Of the instruments illustrated in these pages the majority is valued here with the exception of those pieces for which a market value cannot be determined on the grounds of (a) rarity, or (b) uniqueness. If an instrument is to all intents and purposes 'unknown' in one or the other country, no value is shown.

In all cases it is assumed that the instrument is in restored condition and is accompanied with a suitable and reasonably-sized repertoire of music. The rarity of an instrument is given precedence over artistic merit in the case of early pieces: artistic criteria govern the price structure of later instruments.

Music Roll values

46-note rolls are scarce: in good playing condition they may be worth £3-£4: *$8-$10* each.

58-note rolls are less scarce: in good playing condition reckon on £2-£3: *$6-$10* each.

65-note rolls are common: in good playing condition reckon on £0.50-£1.50: *$1-$2* each.

73-note rolls are scarce: in good playing condition they may be worth £8-£10: *$15-$20* each.

88-note rolls are common: in good playing condition reckon on £0.50-£1.50: *$1-$2* each.

Angelus (Symphony) rolls are scarce: in good condition reckon on £3-£5: *$6-$10* each.

Duo-Art rolls are scarce: in good playing condition reckon on £4-£6: *$10-$15* each.

Ampico Model A rolls are scarce: in good playing condition reckon on £8-£10: *$10-$15* each.

Ampico Model B rolls are scarce: in good playing condition reckon on £8-£12: *$12-$20* each.

Welte 'red' rolls are scarce: in good playing condition reckon on £10-£15: *$25-$30* each.

Welte Licensee rolls are scarce: in good playing condition reckon on £10-£12: *$25-$30* each.

Recordo rolls, all types, are scarce: in good condition reckon on £ - -£ - : *$45-$70* each.

Multi-tune **Coinola 'O'** rolls are scarce: in good condition reckon on £- -£ - : *$75-$100* each.

Phonliszt-Violina rolls are scarce: in good condition reckon on £30-£50: *$100-$150* each.

Mills Violano rolls are scarce: in good condition reckon on £16-£20: *$50-$100* each.

Aeolian Pipe Organ rolls are scarce: in good condition reckon on £10-£15: *$25-$30* each.

Aeolian Duo-Art Organ rolls are scarce: in good condition reckon on £16-£20: *$35-$50* each.

Damage to a roll by way of tears or even pleats drastically affects its value and the percentage of depreciation incurred depends on the rarity of the roll itself: a 65-note roll that is torn will be worthless; but a 'red' Welte will preserve a percentage of its value despite a small tear. In almost all instances of 'scarce' rolls, modern re-cuts are available today. In the greater majority of cases, these new rolls are more valuable than the originals because in general they are produced in only limited editions (maybe only 20 copies) and are of better-quality paper.

As with instruments, the rarity of the music – and market demands – plays a part in roll-valuation. A popular or rare musical work will incur a price premium and this will also be affected by demand. At present, 'ragtime' music rolls (piano rags, the compositions of Joplin and suchlike) incur a large premium because they are in demand by player-piano collectors.

What's it Worth?

<u>Page</u> 10. Early street piano on donkey-cart in good or restorable condition: £500-£1,500: *$900-$2,500*.

11. Late street piano on reproduction hand-cart in good or restorable condition: £800-£1,500: *$900-$2,000*.

13. Pedal-electric Steinway Duo-Art grand, fully-restored: £8,000-£10,000.

16. Blüthner Triphonola grand, fully restored: £10,000-£12,000: *$20,000-$26,000*.

17. Longman clockwork piano, fully restored: £15,000-£20,000: *$30,000-$40,000*.

18. Portable street piano with moving figures, restored: £21,000-£23,000: *$24,000-$30,000*.

19. Antiphonel piano, fully restored: £26,500-£30,500: *$30,000-$34,000*.

20. Piano orchestrion weight-driven, restored: £10,000-£12,000: *$8,000-$10,000*.

22. Piano orchestrion weight-driven, restored: £21,500-£30,000: *$20,000-$30,000*.

24. Café clockwork piano, restored: £12,000-£14,500: *$12,000-$15,000*.

27. Racca piano, largest model, restored: £5,000-£6,000: *$7,000-$10,000*.

28. Welte-Mignon upright, restored: £7,500-£10,000: *$28,000-$35,000*.

32. Hupfeld Triphonola with detached pump, restored: £12,000-£14,000: *$22,000-$30,000*.

33. Small street piano, reiterating action, restored: £900-£1,300: *$1,500-$2,500*.

34. 88-note Higel upright player, restored: £1,000-£1,500: *$2,000-$2,500*.

38. Hupfeld Phonliszt Model A, restored: £100,000-£145,000: *$180,000-$240,000*.

40. Hupfeld Phonolizst Model B, restored: £125,000-£175,000: *$220,000-$300,000*.

42. Fotoplayer, twin-roll with two side-chests, restored: £180,000-£200,00: *$220,000-$300,000*.

43. Whitlock Model B automatic harp, restored: *$24,000-$35,000*.

44. Regina Sublima Piano, restored: *$5,000 - $7,000*.

45. Kuhl & Klatt xylophone piano: £10,000-£12,000: *$18,000-$22,000*.

46. F G Otto Pianette, restored: *$15,000 - $20,000*.

49. Eich Solophone, restored: £10,000-£12,000: *$18,000-$22,000*.

52. Mills Violano-Virtuoso, restored: £14,000-£20,000: *$30,000-$40,000*.

53. Weber Grandezza, restored: £12,000-£14,000: *$18,000-$22,000*.

54. Seybold Piano-Accordeon-Jazz, restored: £14,000-£20,000: *$25,000-$35,000*.

55. Fotoplayer, twin-roll with two side chests, restored: £180,000-£200,00: *$200,000-$250,000*.

57. Aeolian Duo-Art in decorated case, restored: £10,000-£12,000: *$18,000-$22,000*.

59. Long-case dulcimer clock with matching side chests, restored: £80,000-£120,000: *$200,000-$250,000*.

64. Bidermann/Langenbucher compound musical table clock: £180,000-£200,000: *$200,000-$250,000*.

72. Debain planchette piano, restored: £2,500-£3,000: *$6,000-$8,000*.

74. Debain planchette/finger Piano Mécanique, restored: £8,000-£10,000: *$9,000-$12,000*.

75. Imhof & Mukle twin-barrel domestic piano, restored: £2,500-£3,000: *$4,000-$5,000.*

81. Hicks-style portable street piano, restored: £1,500-£2,000; *$1,800-$2,500.*

93. Danish portable piano, restored: £1,200-£1,500: *$1,200-$2,000.*

96. Hicks drawing-room piano, restored: £1,500-£2,000: *$3,000-$3,500.*

104. Street piano on hand-cart, restored: £800-£1,500: *$900-$2,000.*

105. Spanish street piano on original hand-cart, restored: £2,500-£3,000: *$4,000-$5,000.*

106. EAPPC-rebuilt street piano, no cart, restored: £1,500-£2,000: *$3,000-$3,500.*

108. Clockwork-piano for bar, French, restored: £2,500-£3,000: *$4,500-$6,000.*

110. Café clockwork piano, French, restored: £5,000-£8,500: *$6,000-$9,500.*

111. Clockwork-piano, public-house, Keith Prowse, restored: £3,000-£3,500: *$4,500-$5,500.*

114. Swiss-made café-piano, 1930s, restored: £1,500-£2,000: *$3,000-$3,500.*

115. French-made café piano, Crubois, restored: £2,500-£3,000: *$4,000-$5,000.*

117. Nilsson Pianoharpa table piano, restored: £800-£1,500: *$1,000-$1,800.*

120. Racca Piano Orchestrion with hot-air engine, restored: £3,000-£3,500: *$4,000-$5,000.*

125. Racca piano, largest model, decorated, restored: £5,000-£6,000: *$7,000-$10,000.*

129. Chordephon disc-playing string instrument, restored: £3,000-£3,250.

131. Chordephon upright 60-note disc-playing string instrument, restored: £5,000-6,500; *$25,000 - $35,000.*

132. Ehrlich Orpheus disc-playing table piano, restored: £2,500-£3,000.

133. Gavioli Organophone Expressif reed organ, restored: £2,500-£3,000: *$8,000-$10,000.*

136. Ehrlich disc-operated mechanical piano-player, restored: £500-£1,000; *$800-$1,200.*

137. Hupfeld 'kicking-shoe' mechanical player piano, restored £1,500-£2,000: *$3,000-$3,500.*

140. Steinway Pianotist mechanical player piano, restored £1,000-£1,500: *$1,200-$1,800.*

143. Hupfeld Clavitist hand-operated pneumatic player, restored: £1,500-£2,000: *$3,000-$3,500.*

145. Triola mechanical zither, restored: £1,000-£1,500: *$1,200-$1,800.*

145. Volks-Klavier 17-note automatic zither, restored: £800-£1,500: *$1,000-$1,800.*

146. Maestro key-top piano-player, restored: £500-£1,500: *$1,000-$2,000.*

146. Dynavoice electric key-top piano-player, restored: £500-£800: *$500-$1,000.*

150. Early model Pianola Metrostyle/Themodist piano-player, restored: £200-£800: *$500-$1,000.*

155. Farrand Cecilian piano-player, restored: £300-£800: *$600-$1,100.*

158. Melville Clark Apollo piano-player, restored: £150-£200: *$200-$250.*

160. Wilcox & Wehite Angelus organ/piano-player, restored: £800-£1,500: *$1,000-$1,800.*

162. Simplex piano-player, restored: £250-£300: *$250-$300.*

163. Smith Lyraphone piano-player, restored: £400-£500: *$800-$1,000.*

165. Bansall's piano-player, complete, with piano attached: £150-£200.

166. Poyser's Classic piano-player, complete, with piano attached: £100-£150.

170. Early Steck Pianola in Mission-style case, restored: £500-£800: *$500-$1,000.*

174. Hupfeld interior player/expression piano, restored: £1,000-£1,500: *$1,500-$1,800.*

175. Ibach upright Pianola of 1920, restored: £1,500-£2,000: *$3,000-$3,500.*

177. Brinsmead Angelus upright, restored: £1,400-£1,750: *$2,500-$3,000.*

181. Boyd Pistonola, restored and working: £800-£1,500: *$1,000-$1,800.*

184. Broadwood grand with Broadwood unit player action, restored: £1,000-£1,500: *$1,500-$1,800.*

190. Belgian café piano in carved & mirrored case, restored: £1,500-£2,000: *$3,000-$3,500.*

191. Hupfeld Atlantic weight-driven piano-orchestrion, restored: £1,500-£2,000: *$3,000-$3,500.*

192. Polyphon Rossini roll-playing piano-orchestrion, restored: £3,000-£3,500: *$4,000-$5,000.*

193. Blessing Polyvox piano-orchestra, restored: £10,000-£12,000: *$18,000-$25,000.*

194. Gebrüder Weber Brabo keyboard piano-orchestrion, restored: £9,000-£12,000: *$14,500-$20,000.*

196. Operators' Piano Co Coinola Model CO, restored: *$25,000-$35,000.*

197. Marquette Cremona Style G piano-orchestrion, restored: *$14,500-$20,000.*

198. Hupfeld book-playing piano, longcase model, restored: £8,000-£10,000: *$10,000-$12,500.*

199. Wurlitzer Model CX piano-orchestrion, restored: *$15,500-$25,000.*

201. Gebrüder Weber Grandezza keyboard piano-orchestrion, restored: £11,500-£16,250: *$16,500-$21,000.*

202. Gebrüder Weber Unika keyboard piano-orchestrion, restored: £10,000-£12,500: *$14,500-$18,000.*

203. Poppers Violinova expression piano-orchestrion and violin, restored: £18,500-£25,000: *$18,500-$20,000.*

206. Popper Diva roll-playing café piano-orchestrion, restored: £8,000-£10,000: *$10,000-$12,500.*

208. North Tonawanda 44-note Pianolin electric piano, restored: *$14,000 - $18,000.*

257. Welte-Mignon keyboardless reproducing piano, restored: £9,500-£12,250: *$18,000-$25,000.*

258. Hupfeld Dea reproducing piano, restored: £3,000-£3,500: *$4,000-$5,000.*

260. Blüthner Solophonola reproducing piano, restored: £10,000-£12,000: *$18,000-$22,000.*

264. Welte-Mignon *Vorsetzer* reproducing piano-player, restored: £10,000-£12,000: *$18,000-$22,000.*

266. Steinway Welte-Mignon grand reproducing piano, restored: £10,000-£12,000: *$18,000-$22,000.*

268. Steinway Welte-Mignon Vertigrand reproducing piano, restored: £12,000-£14,000: *$20,000-$25,000.*

269. Welte-Mignon (Licensee) grand, restored: £12,500-£15,000: *$12,500-$16,000.*

271. Aeolian UK Duo-Art upright, early triple pump, restored: £6,000-£7,500: *$14,000-$16,000.*

272. Pedal-electric Steinway Duo-Art grand, fully-restored: £8,000-£10,000: *$18,000-$20,000.*

275. Marshall & Wendell Ampico Model A grand, restored: £8,000-£9,000: *$7,900-$12,000.*

276. Grotrian-Steinweg Ampico Model A, restored: £12,000-£14,000: *$20,000-$25,000.*

276. Marshall & Wendell Ampico Model B grand, restored: £9,500-£12,250: *$15,000-$20,000.*

301. Modern (1950s) electric Pianola, 'spinet' style, restored: £500-£800: *$800-$1,200.*

307. Modern (1950s) Aeolian 'Musette' player, restored: £650-£950: *$1,200-$2,200.*

345. Wilcox & White Symphony player reed organ, restored: £1,000-£1,500: *$2,500-$4,000.*

346. Malcolm Phoneon player reed organ, restored: £1,000-£1,500.

348. Story & Clark Orpheus player reed organ, restored: £650-£900: *$1,200-$2,000.*

348. Aeolian Grand, F-F compass 46-note player reed organ, restored: £550-£800: *$1,200-$2,200.*

349. Aeolian Grand, C-C compass 58-note player reed organ, restored: £1,000-£1,500: *$2,000-$3,500.*

349. Aeolian Orchestrelle Model V player reed organ, restored: £1,500-£2,000: *$8,000-$12,000.*

350. Aeolian Orchestrelle 116-note player reed organ, restored: £2,800-£4,000: *$10,000-$14,000.*

351. Orchestrelle Model F 116-note player reed organ, restored: £4,800-£5,500: *$20,000-$30,000.*

352. Scheidmeyer Scheola 2-manual player reed organ, restored: £10,000-£12,000: *$25,000-$35,000.*

352. Aeolian Duo-Art Pipe Organ, medium-sized model, restored: £15,000-£20,000: *$30,000-$35,000.*

353. Welte Philharmonic Reproducing Pipe Organ, restored: £16,000-£22,000: *$45,000-$65,000.*

Support Organisations
For Player-Piano Enthusiasts

Player-piano collectors and hobbyists are well-served around the world by collectors' societies and groups that can offer help and support. The literature available through these organisations is of immense benefit. All of these societies are of international status and have world-wide membership. Here is a list of them in alphabetical order of their home countries:

AUSTRALIA

Australian Collectors of Mechanical Musical Instruments (ACMMI). *Secretary:* Ian Savins, 19 Waipori Street, St Ives, New South Wales 2075, Australia. Formed in 1971, this is a small group centred on Sydney that holds regular meetings every two months to meet the needs of collectors of mechanical musical instruments. It publishes a regular Bulletin and encourages the setting up of groups in all of the Australian States. In English.

FRANCE

Association des amis des instruments et de la Musique Mécanique (AAIMM). *Secretary:* Michel Gollet, 113, rue du Mont-Cenis, 75018 Paris, France. The original French society for collectors of all mechanical instruments, founded in 1975. Publishers of high-quality quarterly magazine *Musique Mécaniques Vivantes*, A4 size (ISSN 1156 – 3125), on mechanical music some of which is related to player pianos. In French.

Perforons la Musique. *Secretary:* Lorraine Aressy, 27 Rue Labat de Savignac, F31500 Toulouse, France. Devoted to the instruments that play perforated music including pianos. In French.

GERMANY

Gesellschaft für Selbstspielende Musikinstrumente e.V. (GSM) *Secretary:* Ralf Smolne, Emmastrasse 56, D-45130 Essen, Germany. Publishes four times a year a large and very high quality quarterly magazine (*Das Mechanische Musikinstrument*), A4 size (ISSN 0721-6092), on mechanical music, a good deal of which is devoted to piano-related items. For the depth and thoroughness of their members' research this collectors' association has for long led the field in authoritative mechanical music literature and research. In German.

GREAT BRITAIN

The Player Piano Group (PPG). *Secretary:* Tony Austin, 93 Evelyn Avenue, Ruislip, Middlesex HA4 8AH, Great Britain. This group, which has concert pianist Peter Katin as president and Sir Charles Mackerras as patron, was founded in 1959 by the late Frank Holland. It produces a quarterly magazine (*Bulletin*), A5 size (*no* ISSN reference) which is well illustrated and contains plenty of articles of interest as well as reports of members and their activities. In English. There are several affiliated regional groups centred in Lancashire, Gloucestershire, Warwickshire and Middlesex.

The Musical Box Society of Great Britain (MBSOGB). *Secretary:* Alan Wyatt, P.O. Box No. 299, Waterbeach, Cambridge, CB4 8DT, Great Britain. Second oldest mechanical musical instrument society, it was founded in 1962. Publishes four times a year a high quality quarterly magazine (*The Music Box*), A4 size (ISSN 0027-4275), on mechanical music, some of which is devoted to piano-related items. In English.

THE NETHERLANDS

Nederlandse Pianola Vereniging. *Secretary:* Jo Jongen, Oude Vischmarkt 15, 5301 CZ Zaltbommel, The Netherlands. This small but enthusiastic group produces a first-rate quarterly magazine (*Pianolabulletin*), A5 size (ISSN:1568-2943) which is fully illustrated and is always packed with news and information. In Dutch.

Kring van Draaiorgelvrienden (KvD). *Secretary:* J van Oost, Naaldwijkseweg 262, 2691 PW s'Gravenzande, The Netherlands. Founded in 1954 to preserve Dutch street-organs, this organisation now has members all over the world and while devoting its major activities to organs, orchestrions and organ-building, is devoted to all mechanical musical instruments. Publishes four times a year a large and very high quality quarterly magazine (*Het Pierement*), A4 size (ISSN 01 68 98 94), on instrument history and restoration, predominantly mechanical organs. In Dutch.

UNITED STATES
OF AMERICA

American Musical Instrument Collectors Association (AMICA). *Secretary:* Robin Pratt, 630 East Monroe Street, Sandusky, Ohio 44870-3708, United States of America. One of the longest-established player-piano collectors' groups. Publishes a regular A4-sized magazine containing much of interest to the collector of reproducing pianos as well as ordinary player pianos. In English.

Musical Box Society International (MBSI). *Administrator:* MBSI, PO Box 551083, Indianapolis, Indiana 46205-5583, United States of America. One of the oldest collectors' groups devoted to mechanical musical instrument hobbyists in the world. Publishes three times a year *Mechanical Music* A4-sized magazine (USISSN 11045-795x) which is fully illustrated and contains information on musical boxes and all forms of mechanical music including player pianos. Much of interest to the collector of reproducing pianos as well as ordinary player pianos. In English.

Bibliography

1. Adlung, J: *Musica mechanica organoedi*. Berlin, 1768, *facs.ed:* 1931.
2. Bassermann-Jordan, Ernst von: *Uhren*. Braunschweg, 1976.
3. Bedos de Celles, Dom François: *L'Art de Facteur d'Orgues*. Paris, 1778.
4. Bekker, L J de: *Stokes' Cyclopaedia of Music and Musicians*, Chambers, Edinburgh, 1911.
5. Billings, Robert, *and* Billings, Ginny; *The Billings Rollography (Q-R-S, Recordo & Solo Carola rolls)*. Pub by authors, Velmont, California, 1990.
6. Bowers, Q David: *Encyclopedia of Automatic Musical Instruments*. Vestal Press, New York, 1972.
7. Bradley, Van Allen: *Music for the Millions*. Henry Regnery, Chicago, Illinois, USA, 1957.
8. Brauers, Jan: *Von der Äolsharfe zum Digitalspieler*. München, 1984.
9. British Patent Office, *Musical Instruments, 1870-1920*, Abridgement Class 88, HMSO, London.
10. Buchner, Alexandre [*ed Philippe Rouillé*]: *Les instruments de musique mécanique*. Paris, 1992.
11. Buchner, Alexandre: *Hudebni automaty*. Prague, 1959, Eng. trans. as *Mechanical musical instruments,* London, 1959.
12. Calboli, Raniero Paulucci di: *Les Musiciens nomads d'Italie*, Dureaux de la Revue, Paris, 1903.
13. Calboli, Raniero Paulucci di: *Lacrime dell'emigrazione,* Forli, Italy, 1905.
14. Calboli, Raniero Paulucci di: *I Girovaghi Italiani*, S Lapi, Castello, 1893.
15. Caus, Salomon de: *Les raisons des forces mouvantes*. Frankfurt am Main, 1615, 2nd ed: 1624.
16. Chapuis, Alfred, & Gélis, Edouard: *Le monde des Automates*. Société Anonyme des Impressions Blondel la Rougery, Paris, 1928.
17. Chapuis, Alfred: *Automates, machines automatiques et méchanisme*. Lausanne, 1928.
18. Chapuis, Alfred: *Histoire de la boîte à musique et de la musique mécanique*. Lausanne, 1955.
19. Chapuis, Alfred; & Droz, Edmund: *Les automates*. Editions Griffon, Neuchâtel, 1950.
20. Chapuis: *Automates, machines automatiques et méchanisme*. Lausanne, 1928.
21. Cleland, T M: *The Ampico*. American Piano Corporation, New York, 1922.
22. Clinkscale, Martha Novak: *Makers of the Piano 1700-1820*. [Volume 1] Oxford University Press, Oxford, 1993.
23. Clinkscale, Martha Novak: *Makers of the Piano 1820-1860 Volume 2*. Oxford University Press, Oxford, 1999.
24. Coover, James [*edit*]: *Music Publishing Copyright & Piracy in Victorian England*. Mansell, London, 1985
25. Dolge, Alfred: *Pianos & Their Makers,* Covina Publishing Co, 26. Covina, California, 1911, facs.ed: Dover Publications, New York, 1972.
26. Dolge, Alfred: *Men Who Made Piano History* (original title: *Pianos & Their Makers, Volume II*), Covina Publishing Co, Covina, California, 1876, facs.ed: Vestal Press, Vestal, New York, 1980.
27. E(arl), S G: *How To Repair the Player Piano*, Musical Opinion, London, 1920.
28. Ehrlich, C: *The Piano, a history*. London, 1976.
29. Engramelle, M D J: *La tonotechnie ou l'art de noter les cylinders*. Paris, 1775, facs.ed: Minkoff, Geneva, 1971.
30. Faust, Oliver C: *Technical Treatise on the Construction, Repairing & Tuning of the Organ*, Boston, 1949.
31. Fluctibus, Robert de (R Fludd): *De naturae simia* . Oppenheim, 1618.
32. Fox, Joseph: *Mechanical Music in the American Home* [article], "Music & Automata", Vol 1, No. 3, London, 1984.
33. Fox, Joseph: *The Aeolian Orchestrelle* [article], 'Music & Automata', Volume 1, No. 4, London, 1984.
34. Franz, Eleanor: *Dolge*. Herkimer Historical Society, New York, 1980.
35. Fried, Freederick: *A Pictorial History of the Carousel*. A S Barnes, New York, 1964.
36. Gellerman, Robert F: *The American Reed Organ*, Vestal Press, Vestal, New York, 1973.
37. Givens, Larry: *Rebuilding the Player Piano*, Vestal Press, Vestal, New York, 1963.
38. Givens, Larry: *Re-enacting the artist: a story of the Ampico Reproducing Piano*, Vestel Press, New York, 1970.
39. *Great Industries of the United States*, [var. authors], Burr & Hyde, Connecticut, USA, 1872.
40. Groiss, Eva: 'The Bidermann-Langenbucher Lawsuit' [article] in Maurice, K, & Mayr, O: *Die Welt als Uhr: Deutches Uhren und Automaten 1550-1650*. Deutscher Kunstverlag, Munich, 1980, English trans as *The Clockwork Universe: German Clocks & Automata 1550-1650*. Neale Watson, New York, 1980. Abst. as *The Bidermann-Langenbucher Lawsuit* [article] in 'Music & Automata' Vol 1 No 1 pp.10-12. Music & Automata Publications, London, 1980.
41. Groves, Sir Charles [*edit*]: *Dictionary of Music*, London, 1st ed, 1879-82. Also: Sadie, Stanley [*ed*]: *The New Grove Dictionary of Music*, Macmillan, London, 2001.
42. Haine, Malou: *Les facteurs d'instruments de musique à Paris au 19me siècle*. Editions de l'Universite de Bruxelles, Belgium, 1985.
43. Harding, Rosamond E. M: *The Piano-Forte. Its History Traced to the Great Exhibition of 1851*. Cambridge University Press, Cambridge, 1933. *Reprint*: New York: Da Capo Press, 1973: rev. 2nd ed: Gresham Books, Old Woking, Surrey, 1978.
44. Haspels, Jan Jaap Leonard: *Automatic musical instruments, their mechanics and their music, 1580-1820*. University of Utrecht, Utrecht, The Netherlands, 1987.
45. Haspels, J J L: *Musical Automata*. Utrecht, The Netherlands, 1994.
46. Hoffmann E T A: *Die Automate*. Berlin, 1819.
47. Howe, Richard J: *The Ampico reproducing piano*, Musical Box Society International, Houston, Texas, 1987.
48. Hupfeld: *Dea-Violina*. Leipzig, Germany, 1909.
49. Jüttemann, Herbert: *Mechanische Mussikinstrumente*, Verlag Bochinski, Frankfurt, 1988.
50. Jüttemann, Herbert: *Schwarzwälder Flötenuhren*. Waldkircher Verlag, Waldkirch, 1991.
51. Kidson, Frank: *British Music Publishers, Printers & Engravers*. W E Hill, London, 1900.
52. Kircher, Athanasius: *Musurgia Universalis*. Rome, 1650, facs.ed: 1970.

53. Kircher, Athanasius: *Phonurgia nova*. Campidonae, 1673, facs.ed: 1966.

54. Kitner, Mike, & Reblitz, Arthur A: *The Mills Violano-Virtuoso…* Vestel Press, Vestel, New York, 1984.

55. Komlós, Katalin: *Fortepianos and their Music*. Clarendon Press, Oxford, 1995.

56. Kowar, Helmut: *Mechanische Musik: Eine Bibliographie*. Vom Pasqualihaus, Vienna, 1996.

57. Langwill, Lyndesey G; & Boston, Noel: *Church and Chamber Barrel Organs*. Edinburgh, 1967, rev 2nd ed: 1970.

58. Langwill, Lyndesey G: *An Index of Musical Wind Instrument Makers*, Langwill, Edinburgh, 1980.

59. Lindwall, B: *The Andersson Pianoharpa*, 'The Music Box', [article] Vol. 8, pp.330-334, London, 1978.

60. McTammany, John: *The History of the Player*, New York, 1913.

61. McTammany, John: *The Technical History of the Player*, New York, 1915, facs.ed: Vestel, 1971.

62. Marcuse, Sibyl: *A Comprehensive Dictionary*, Country Life, London, 1966.

63. Marcuse, Sibyl: *A Survey of Musical Instruments*, David & Charles, Devon, 1975.

64. Marini, Marino: *Guida Introduttiva agli Strumenti Musicali Meccanici*. Collezione Marino Marini, Ravenna, 1973.

65. Michel, N E: *Michel's Piano Atlas*, California, 1969.

66. Michel, N E: *Michel's Organ Atlas*, California, 1970.

67. Michel, N E: *Historical Pianos*, California, 1970.

68. Obenchain, Elaine: *The Complete Catalog of Ampico Reproducing Piano Rolls*. William H Edgerton. Connecticut, 1977.

69. Ord-Hume, Arthur W J G: *Orchestrelle Servicing Manual*, priv circ'd, London, 1970.

70. Ord-Hume, Arthur W J G: *Player Piano - The History of the Mechanical Piano & How to Repair It*, Allen & Unwin, London, 1970.

71. Ord-Hume, Arthur W J G: *Clockwork Music - An Illustrated History of Mechanical Musical Instruments….*, Allen & Unwin, London, 1973.

72. Ord-Hume, Arthur W J G: *The Mechanics of Mechanical Music*, Ord-Hume, London, 1973.

73. Ord-Hume, Arthur W J G: *Barrel Organ, A History of the Mechanical Organ & How to Restore It*, Allen & Unwin, London, 1975.

74. Ord-Hume, Arthur W J G: *Musical Box*, Allen & Unwin, London, 1980.

75. Ord-Hume, Arthur W J G: *Defining a musical clock*, [article] 'The Music Box', Vol. 9, No 8, Christmas, 1980, pp-350-355. Revsd 2nd ed under same title in 'Antiquarian Horology', (Bulletin of the Antiquarian Horological Society), Vol. 13, No 4, June 1982, pp.340-358.

76. Ord-Hume, Arthur W J G: *Joseph Haydn & the Mechanical Organ*, Cardiff University Press, Wales, 1982.

77. Ord-Hume, Arthur W J G: *Restoring Pianolas and Other Self-Playing Pianos*, Allen & Unwin, London, 1983.

78. Ord-Hume, Arthur W J G: *Cogs and Crochets: A view of mechanical music*, [article] 'Early Music', Vol. 11 No. 2, April 1983.

79. Ord-Hume, Arthur W J G: *Pianola: The History of the Self-Playing Piano*, Allen & Unwin, London, 1984.

80. Ord-Hume, Arthur W J G: *Harmonium; The History of the Reed Organ and its makers*, David & Charles, Newton Abbot, 1986.

81. Ord-Hume, Arthur W J G: *The Musical Box; A Guide for Collectors*, Schiffer, Pennsylvania, 1996.

82. Ord-Hume, Arthur W J G: *The Musical Clock*, Mayfield, Ashbourne, Derby, 1996.

83. Ord-Hume, Arthur W J G: *Restoring Musical Boxes & Musical Clocks*, Mayfield, Ashbourne, Derby, 1997.

84. Palmieri, Robert [ed]: *Encyclopedia of Keyboard Instruments*. Garland, New York, 1994. 2 rev ed. New York, 2003.

85. Pierce, Robert: *Pierce Piano Atlas*, (revision of [56]), Long Beach, California, 1965.

86. Petrak, Albert: *Complete Classical Duo-Art Catalogue*. Petrak, Maryland, 1963.

87. Pratt, Waldo Selden [edit]: *The New Encyclopedia of Music & Musicians*, Macmillan, New York, 1945.

88. Protz, Albert: *Mechanische musikinstrumente*. Bährenreiter, Kassel, 1939.

89. Reblitz, Arthur A: *Player Piano Servicing & Rebuilding*, Vestel Press, Vestel, New York, 1985.

90. Reblitz, Arthur A, and Bowers, Q David: *Treasures of Mechanical Music*. Vestal, New York, 1981.

91. Roehl, Harvey: *Player Piano Treasury*. Vestal Press, Vestal, New York, 1961; 2nd rev. ed: 1973.

92. Roell, Craig H: *The Piano in America, 1890-1940*. University of North Carolina, North Carolina, 1989.

93. Rose, Malcolm, and Law, David: *A Handbook of Historical Stringing Practice for Keyboard Instruments*. Lewes, East Sussex, Rose, 1995.

94. Sachs, Curt: *Real-Lexikon der Musikinstrumente*, Berlin, 1913, revsd 2nd ed: Dover Publications, New York, 1964.

95. Saul, David L: *Rebuilder's Illustrated Guide to the Model B Ampico*. Vestel, New York, 1982.

96. Sbriglia, Georges: *L'Exploitation Des Oeuvres Musicales par les Instruments de Musique Méchaniques et le Droit de l'Auteur*. Librarie Nouvelle de Droit et de Jurisprudence, Paris, 1907.

97. Schott, Gaspar: *Magica universalis naturae et artis*, Bamberg, 1674.

98. Schott, Gaspar: *Technica curiosa*, Nuremberg, 1664.

99. Simon, Ernst: *Mechanische Musikinstrumente früherer Zeiten und ihre Musik*. Breitkopf & Härtel, Wiesbaden, 1966; rep. Wiesbaden, 1980.

100. Smith, Charles Davis: *Aeolian Duo-Art Reproducing Rolls – A Complete Catalogue*. C D Smith, Monrovia, California, 1987.

101. Smith, Charles Davis: *The Welte-Mignon: Its Music & Musicians*. Amica International, USA, 1992.

102. Spaeth, Sigmund, and Howard, John Tasker: *The Ampico in Music Study*. American Piano Corporation, New York, 1925.

103. Spillane, Daniel: *History of the American Pianoforte*, Spillane, New York, 1890, 2ed. De Capo, New York, 1969.

104. Stephenson, H W: *In Search of Hofmann or The Technology of the Reproducing Piano*. Pub by the author, Ramsey, Isle of Man, 1992.

105. Suidman, Peter, Speetjens, Frits, and Mathot, Gustave: *Pianola's*. Nederlandse Pianola Vereniging, The Netherlands, 1981.

106. Tushinsky, J S: *The Pianocorder Story*, Chatsworth, California, 1978.

107. Vaucanson, J: *An Account of the mechanism of an automaton*. London, 1742, facs. 1973 in Ord-Hume [55] above.

108. Vaucanson, J: *Le mécanisme du fluteur automate*, Paris, 1738, facs. Musical Box Society of Great Britain, London, 1970.

109. Volpe, C: *Italia Moderna*, Sansoni, Italy, 1972.

110. Wainright, David: *The Piano Makers*. Hutchinson, London, 1975.

111. Wilde, D: *The Piano Roll*, The Liszt Society Journal, Vol. 5, 1980.

112. Zucchi, John: *The Little Slaves of the Harp: Italian Child Street Musicians in 19thC Paris*. McGill-Queen's University Press, Montreal, 1992.

Periodicals:

'Pianolabulletin', journal of the Nederlandse Pianola Vereniging (initially as 'Piano Bulletin') 1981-current.

'Player Piano Bulletin', journal of the Player Piano Group, London. 1959-current.

'Player-Piano Supplement', *The Gramophone*, London, February 1924-March 1925 (*all published*).

'Bulletin', journal of AMICA (Automatic Musical Instrument Collectors' Association), California, USA, 1963- current.

'London & Provincial Music Trades Review' [*periodical*], London, 1877-1916.

'Music & Automata' *[journal],* London and Guildford, Vol. 1, No.1 (1982) – Vol. 4, No.16 (1992).

'Music Box, The' [*journal*], Musical Box Society of Great Britain, London, 1962-79.

'Musical Opinion & Music Trade Review' [*periodical*], London, 1877-1938.

'Das Mechanische Musikinstrument', journal of the Gesellschaft für Selbstspielende Musikinstrumente.

'Het Pierement', journal of the Kring van Draaiorgelvrienden.

Transient sources:

Much store is set by some on the Internet as being a universal 'chat-room' and source of all knowledge. Those who pursue these outlets maintain them as invaluable assets. While it is true that this is today's ideal method of communication and information, it should not be overlooked that it is a transient, volatile source. Future generations, seeking the written word from the 21st century, may be dismayed to find that of the myriads of words, ideas and opinions people created all have just disappeared into thin air, leaving as substantial an influence as the beat of a butterfly's wings! *Caveat actor et emptor!*

Index

This Index provides cross-referenced access to all names, subjects and concepts. An exception concerns those names contained in Appendices 2, 3 and 4 which are themselves alphabetically presented: These are excluded. An exception is made in the case of embedded or subsidiary items in these Appendices. For example, **Blüthner & Company** on *page 405* will not be found since it is self-indexing, but within this entry references to *(a)* Julius Blüthner's first grand piano; *(b)* W J Whelpdale; *(c)* the Carola player action; *(d)* Sir Herbert Marshall Piano Company, are incorporated in this index. Throughout page numbers in **BOLD (black)** typeface refer to pages containing a photographic illustration.